The Sociology Project

Jeff Manza
Richard Arum
Lynne Haney
Jeff Goodwin
Colin Jerolmack
Ann Morning
Kathleen Gerson
Eric Klinenberg
Caroline Persell
Paula England
Gerald Marwell
Florencia Torche
Ruth Horowitz
Guillermina Jasso
Harvey Molotch
Thomas Ertman
Jennifer Jennings
Lawrence Wu
Troy Duster
Steven Lukes
Patrick Sharkey
Vivek Chibber
Kirsten Kramar

Pearson

Editorial Director: Claudine O'Donnell
Acquisitions Editor: Keriann McGoogan
Marketing Manager: Christine Cozens
Program Manager: Madhu Ranadive
Project Manager: Kimberley Blakey
Developmental Editor: Lise Dupont
Media Developer: Tiffany Palmer
Production Services: Aptara
Permissions Project Manager: Kathryn O'Handley
Photo Permissions Research: Integra Publishing Services, Inc.
Text Permissions Research: Integra Publishing Services, Inc.
Art Director: Alex Li
Interior Designer: Aptara
Cover Designer: Anthony Leung
Cover Image: Joson/Getty Images
Vice-President, Cross Media and Publishing Services: Gary Bennett

Pearson Canada Inc., 26 Prince Andrew Place, Don Mills, Ontario M3C 2T8.

[ISBN 0133768910/9780133768916]
1 17

Library and Archives Canada Cataloguing in Publication

Manza, Jeff, author
The sociology project/Jeff Manza [and twenty-two others].

Includes bibliographical references and index.
ISBN 978-0-13-376891-6 (PDF)

1. Sociology. I. Title.

HM585.M35 2016 301 C2016-907845-0

ISBN 13: 978-0-13-376891-6
ISBN 10: 0-13-376891-0

Brief Contents

Contents

Preface

In *The Structure of Scientific Revolutions*, his famous study of the history of science, Thomas Kuhn argued that introductory textbooks are inevitably the most backward part of any scientific field. He suggested that because they seek to appeal to the lowest common denominator to maximize their audience, they reproduce out-of-date ideas and findings far removed from the cutting edge of knowledge. Even worse, Kuhn argued, these texts reinforce popular, but out-of-date, dogmas that stand in the way of progress. Worst of all, they provide beginning students an entirely misleading view of the discipline. When it comes to sociology textbooks, Kuhn's claim is reinforced because of the simple fact that sociology is such a wide-ranging discipline, with many rich subfields with their own bodies of scholarship and knowledge. No one author (or small team of authors), however well-meaning and determined, can possibly attain mastery of the whole discipline and adequately convey that knowledge to students.

We created this introductory text in the hopes of overcoming the problem Kuhn so famously identified. Our aim is nothing less than to reinvent the way we write introductory sociology texts. We envision an entirely new kind of introduction to the discipline, one that draws on the collective wisdom of a large, successful sociology department and its faculty to bring to our students and readers the real excitement of each of the main subfields of sociology. Rather than reproducing what is said in existing textbooks, as so often happens, the chapters in this book are freshly authored by one or more faculty members from the New York University Sociology Department who write and teach in the area. In this way, we seek to bring together the best of sociology as a discipline to meet the challenge of reaching our students.

At the centre of this book is a set of tools for learning how to ask hard questions about the world around us. These tools are what we call, following C. Wright Mills (1959), the "sociological imagination." In every chapter, we draw upon contemporary research findings, those of our colleagues and in some cases our own, to puzzle through how individuals are shaped by the contexts in which they live and act. We treat social norms, organizations, institutions, and global dynamics as a linked set of puzzles to explore. Rather than simply giving answers, we identify the kinds of questions that sociological researchers ask and introduce some ways of thinking about how to answer those questions. We do not suggest that all of the answers are at hand, but we show how and in what ways sociologists and other social scientists struggle to answer them. If nothing else, we hope that our readers will take away from this book a new determination to question things.

We have entitled our text *The Sociology Project*, both to reflect our commitment to a collective agenda of our field as an evolving project and, as we offer a book that is available in both print and in a fully digital format, because we want to signal to our readers our intention to continue to develop the book in future editions as sociology itself evolves. New findings, theories, and ideas are constantly being developed. Our book will continue to evolve as research develops in new directions, and we look forward to revising our ideas and questions as the evidence suggests we should. But perhaps most importantly, we think of *The Sociology Project* as a dialogue with our readers—including both our students and our colleagues around the country. We invite you to engage and challenge us where we come up short, tell us what we are doing wrong, and share ideas you have for the presentation of sociology as a field.

Jeff Manza for the NYU Sociology Department
New York City
October 2014

This Canadian edition supplements the research done by faculty from the New York University Sociology Department using Canadian data and research to explore their sociological questions in the Canadian context. Following the existing structure of the book, I adapted the U.S. edition to illustrate significant similarities and/or differences among Canada, the U.S., and other countries throughout each chapter. Often the similarities were pronounced, other times they were subtle. Using Canadian data and research to explore the big questions asked by the U.S. experts in the field, we can observe how the differences between Canada and the United States are often connected to different cultural histories or social policies adopted by our governments and other institutions to address particular issues such as health, poverty, income inequality, same-sex marriage, taxes, parental leave, daycare, education, immigration policy, or crime control. Throughout the chapters, students can learn about the impact of social norms, organizations, and institutions unique to Canada and reflect upon how these sociological differences may have either a positive or negative impact on individuals' quality of life in both countries and others around the world.

Kirsten Kramar
Calgary, AB
May 2016

Features of the Canadian Edition

- New learning architecture aligns core content with learning objectives and assessment to help better track, measure, and report on student performance.
- Updated research and data throughout, including new research on economic inequality, crime and deviance, immigration policy, same-sex marriage, health and aging, and work.
- Chapter 2 covers sociological theory, going beyond standard coverage of classical social theory to present contemporary innovations and a new generation of social theory and theorists.
- Chapter 9 asks why Canada and the United States, both very wealthy countries, continue to have high rates of poverty and income inequality.
- Chapter 10, devoted to race, ethnicity, and immigration, examines distinct eras of immigration policy in Canada, including post-9/11 security developments. It also examines the relationships among First Nations, Metis, Inuit, and Aboriginal peoples and non-Aboriginal peoples in Canada.
- Chapter 16, about health and medicine, explores the social context of health and illness and provides a sociological perspective on the differences in health outcomes across different countries, including Canada.

The Sociology Project in REVEL™

- Images, videos, and interactive data visualizations are deeply integrated with core content.
- Integrated writing opportunities prompt students to engage their sociological imaginations and think critically about the research and theory presented to them.
- Assessment opportunities following every Big Question section and at the end of the chapter help students measure their understanding of key concepts before moving on.

REVEL™

Educational technology designed for the way today's students read, think, and learn.

When students are engaged deeply, they learn more effectively and perform better in their courses. This simple fact inspired the creation of REVEL: an immersive learning experience designed for the way today's students read, think, and learn. Built in collaboration with educators and students nationwide, REVEL is the newest, fully digital way to deliver respected Pearson content.

REVEL enlivens course content with media interactives and assessments—integrated directly within the authors' narrative—that provide opportunities for students to read about and practice course material in tandem. This immersive educational technology boosts student engagement, which leads to better understanding of concepts and improved performance throughout the course.

Learn more about REVEL

http://www.pearsonhighered.com/revel/

Supplements

The following instructor supplements are available for download from a password-protected section of Pearson Canada's online catalogue (www.pearsoncanada.ca/highered). Navigate to your book's catalogue page to view a list of those supplements that are available. See your local Pearson Canada sales representative for details and access.

Instructor's Manual.

PowerPoint Presentations.

Computerized Test Bank. Pearson's computerized test banks allow instructors to filter and select questions to create quizzes, tests, or homework. Instructors can revise questions or add their own, and may be able to choose print or online options. These questions are also available in Microsoft Word format.

Learning Solutions Managers. Pearson's Learning Solutions Managers work with faculty and campus course designers to ensure that Pearson technology products, assessment tools, and online course materials are tailored to meet your specific needs. This highly qualified team is dedicated to helping schools take full advantage of a wide range of educational resources, by assisting in the integration of a variety of instructional materials and media formats. Your local Pearson Canada sales representative can provide you with more details on this service program.

Pearson Custom Library. For enrollments of at least 25 students, you can create your own textbook by choosing the chapters that best suit your own course needs. To begin building your custom text, visit **www.pearsoncustomlibrary.com**. You may also work with a dedicated Pearson Custom editor to create your ideal text—publishing your own original content or mixing and matching Pearson content. Contact your local Pearson Canada sales representative to get started.

Acknowledgments

I would like to thank the extraordinary team at Pearson Canada for their dedication to this very important project. In particular, I want to thank Lise Dupont, Senior Development Editor, with whom I worked closely for keeping volumes of material organized and on track. I am extremely grateful for Lise's careful attention to detail and good humour that carried the project along to completion. I am also grateful to Matthew Christian (Director of Digital Solutions), Claudine O'Donnell (Editorial Director), and Madhu Ranadive (Program Manager) who championed the idea of a Canadian edition of this unique sociology textbook. I would also like to thank the other members of the Pearson Canada team who contributed to this project, including Kimberley Blakey (Project Manager), Sadika Rehman, and Kathryn O'Handley (Project Manager, Permissions).

As drafts of the Canadian Edition began to appear, we received help and guidance from a panel of external reviewers compiled by Pearson Canada. Every chapter benefitted from their feedback, and we thank them all for their help, including those whose names do not appear in the alphabetical list below:

Seema Ahluwalia, Kwantlen Polytechnic University

Lauren Barr, University of Western Ontario

Darlene Balandin, University of Western Ontario

Patricia Corcoran, George Brown College

Stephen Decator, St. Clair College of Applied Arts and Technology

Deborah Davidson, York University

Richard Element, John Abbott College

Tara Gauld, Confederation College

Wendi Hadd, John Abbott College

Kristen Hopewell, University of British Columbia, Okanagan

Chantelle Marlor, University of the Fraser Valley

Barry McClinchey, University of Waterloo

Greg Nepean, University of Guelph-Humber

Penny Poole, Fanshawe College

Alice Propper, York University

Peter Ove, Camosun College Lansdowne

Dana Sawchuk, Wilfrid Laurier University

Michael Seredycz, MacEwan University

Luba Serge, John Abbott College

Alison M Thomas, Douglas College

Jen Wrye, North Island College

My Sociological Imagination

At the centre of this book is a set of tools for learning how to ask hard questions about the world around us. These tools are what we call, following C. Wright Mills, the "sociological imagination." Below are some stories about how some of the authors who contributed to this book developed their sociological imaginations, beginning with a personal story from the Canadian author that addresses the question "Why learn to think sociologically?"

Kirsten Kramar

In my role as a professor of sociology, I am often asked the question "Why study Sociology?" I explain that learning to view the world through a sociological lens allows students of the discipline to develop what C. Wright Mills in 1959 called a "quality of mind" known as the "sociological imagination" (Mills, 2000, p. 13). Developing a sociological imagination is achieved by critically evaluating aspects of society to which we have all been exposed and linking these to our own personal experiences. Learning to see the world using a sociological imagination can be quite difficult because sociologists examine phenomena with which we are familiar, but do so in a different way. At the outset of my classes students will often describe sociology as just "common sense." But they soon come to learn that this notion is inaccurate. Instead, it is more accurate to say that developing a sociological imagination involves asking questions that help us to understand how and why the "common sense" we learn in a variety of institutional settings, such as our families, schools, or churches, comes into *being* as "common sense" and shapes our individual experiences. In other words, having the quality of mind known as a sociological imagination allows us to understand how certain ideas are taken for granted and become popular and dominant in different social contexts. In this way, we can start to see how these seemingly neutral "common sense" ideas and practices are the product of dominant power relations that shape our own individual lives. Learning to think sociologically offers students of the discipline the opportunity to develop a cognitive ability and to apply that ability to answer a wide range of questions about the impact society has on us as individuals and to offer alternative ideas for transformative social change. It allows us to see through the facades of social structures and understand how these structures can shape our lives in positive and negative ways that are not of our own making. This is what Mills refers to as "the promise" of sociology (p. 19). Its unique approach to studying the social world transports us from our own private orbits by showing us how and why our own personal troubles are public issues, shaped and re-shaped by the society in which we live.

Richard Arum (Chapters 1, 8, 9)

Although I grew up in the suburbs of New York, I had an unusual background as my father was a sports promoter, and cultural icons and civil rights heroes such as Muhammad Ali spent time in our home. This early personal exposure shaped who I was and the choices I made as an adult. In the years following, I received a teaching certificate from Harvard University and subsequently worked as a teacher in a segregated public high school in Oakland, California. In that institutional setting, in order to make sense of the dysfunction of the school as an organization as well as the impact that the school was having on the lives of the students, I increasingly was drawn to asking sociological questions of the world. To move beyond simply asking these questions, I enrolled at the University of California–Berkeley with the goal of developing sociological tools and skills to better understand the problems around schooling in America. For me, developing a sociological imagination was an attempt to develop a set of analytical competencies to participate actively in policy discussions that could substantively improve the outcomes of youth.

Vivek Chibber (Chapter 20)

I came to sociology largely by accident. When I graduated from college, I knew I wanted to go to graduate school to study the political economy of capitalism—how it works, where it comes from, and why people put up with it. But issues like these were rapidly receding from the research agenda of most disciplines. I had no particular interest in sociology. But as it happened, there was a good group of people at the University of Wisconsin sociology department who focused on just this subject. So I decided to do my PhD there, mainly because I thought I would get what I wanted—and become a sociologist in the process. My research interests are still largely the same, though with a focus on the developing world.

Troy Duster (Chapter 16)

The first 16 years of my life were spent in a low-income, racially segregated neighbourhood on Chicago's South Side. It was a period in the United States in which racial segregation was taken for granted at barber shops, bowling alleys, swimming pools, and many public accommodations—even in the urban North. Frank Wong, the son of a Chinese restaurant owner in the area, was the only student in my high school who was not African American. Then, at age 17, I crossed town to attend Northwestern University, where I was one of only seven African Americans on a campus of over 7,000 whites. Anthropologists call it "culture shock" when the deep assumptions about what is normal are disrupted by new circumstances, whether by travel to a foreign country or by being thrust into an unfamiliar social world where previously held assumptions have little or no relevance. For me, sociology provided a handle on my situation, a way to understand why and how people explain away their privilege as if it were an individual accomplishment. I watched with the astonishment of the outsider how people from wealthy families concluded unreflectively that the way the world was ordered was natural and right. Of course, many poor people also see the way the world is organized as normal, so that was no surprise. But it was the attempt to explain the "why" that caught my attention, intrigued and stoked my intellectual curiosity, and brought me into sociology.

Paula England (Chapter 11)

My mother didn't have enough money to go to university and never considered a career after she married at age 19 and became a stay-at-home mom to four children. Later, when I was grown, she claimed she was lucky to be able to stay at home with her kids. But she also talked about feeling underappreciated by my dad. Gender inequalities often made her feel "less than." Dad had the education, not her, and she often felt that principals, doctors, and community leaders didn't respect "just a housewife," even though she saw importance in what she was doing. I became fascinated by sociology, seeing it as a way to understand social causes of human suffering. I wondered how much my mother's suffering would have been lessened had the gender regime been different. My early research focused on why some occupations are filled mostly with men and others mostly with women, why women earn less than men, and why mothers earn less than women without children. These topics interested me because I wanted to understand the social forces that hold women back. Later, I began to study the increasing trend toward young couples having unplanned pregnancies followed by births outside of marriage. Currently, I'm conducting a study of relationships and sex among college students, trying to understand how the sexual revolution intersects with the gender revolution.

Thomas Ertman (Chapter 2)

As an undergraduate I was passionate about both history and philosophy, but as graduation drew nearer, I wasn't sure how these interests could be reconciled. It was a history professor who suggested I might consider studying sociology because the field encompasses both social theory and historical sociology. I took his advice and quickly discovered that there is hardly an area of life, past or present, to which the sociological imagination cannot fruitfully apply itself. I myself have written and taught on the emergence of the state in the West; democracy and dictatorship in nineteenth- and twentieth-century Europe; the development of opera and ballet as art forms; and music, literature, and painting in France and Germany. The common thread that unites this research has been the inspiration I have derived from the classical social theorists, especially Max Weber. Although he died nearly a century ago, his writings remain as relevant as ever to our world.

Kathleen Gerson (Chapter 12)

My sociological imagination began when I realized I was part of—yet stood apart from—the world around me. Born in the deep South, I grew up in a community where traditional homes and worldviews were the norm. Yet my own family was headed by a single mother strongly committed to social justice. As I developed a sense of being both an insider and an outsider, I learned to see the world from several vantage points at once. A move to San Francisco during adolescence deepened my questioning of what others took for granted. By the time I reached college, these experiences had attuned me to the power of social contexts. Sociology offered a place to address the big issues facing contemporary societies. With that aim in mind, my research focuses on gender, work, and family life, with an eye to understanding the new work and family pathways emerging in the United States and other postindustrial societies. Although I rely on a range of methods, I specialize in qualitative interviewing. My goal is to uncover how personal biographies intersect with social institutions to bring about social change. I have written books and articles that offer innovative frameworks for explaining the revolution in gender, work, and family patterns, and my current research focuses on the new worlds of work and care, where occupational paths and personal relationships are increasingly uncertain.

Jeff Goodwin (Chapter 17)

I grew up at a time when the U.S. government was trying hard to destroy domestic social movements, especially the Black Power and the anti–Vietnam War movements, as well as revolutions overseas, particularly in Cuba, Vietnam, and Chile. I remember vividly the killing of students at Kent State University who were protesting the invasion of Cambodia, something that was pretty scary for a young kid. I was also scared and anxious when my older brother was drafted into the military, but fortunately he was not sent to Vietnam. All this made me interested in why people protest and rebel, sometimes violently, and why governments sometimes use violence against their opponents. I came to understand how the sociological imagination that C. Wright Mills described—the capacity, that is, to see how seemingly personal grievances are in fact linked to social structures and shared with others—is a prerequisite of political protest. While I was studying rebels in college and graduate school at Harvard, I also joined the ranks of movements that were trying to stop the U.S. government from supporting brutal armies in Central America and the racist government in South Africa. I have been studying social movements (and occasionally participating in them) and revolutions ever since.

Lynne Haney (Chapters 1, 2, 3)

Sometimes I think I was born with a sociological imagination—although that would be thoroughly unsociological of me to say. I grew up in the California Bay Area in the 1970s, when the feminist, civil rights, and gay rights movements were at their peak—and all kinds of identities and relationships were being questioned. As a result, thinking sociologically seemed to be in the air; everyone was asking the big questions about why the world was the way it was. But then the context changed and morphed into the 1980s of Ronald Reagan and social conservatism (as well as bad hair and bad fashion). And much of the social and cultural questioning I grew up with began to wane as more rigid and limiting assumptions about the world and our places within it became acceptable. This shift left me wondering how people come to accept or reject received wisdom: Was it just a matter of who had the power and resources to impress their version of reality on others? Or was there some way to discern fact from fiction, myth from reality? It was around this time that I discovered social science research. As a young college student, sociology appealed to me because it seemed to offer the empirical tools to resolve many political and social conflicts. It offered the possibility that not everything was relative, a matter of opinion, or open to ideological debate. In this way, although I've had a sociological imagination for a long time, it was not until I learned to conduct social research that I could use my imagination productively—as a way of teaching myself and others how to learn from and be surprised by the social world.

Ruth Horowitz (Chapter 15)

As I reflect on my experiences as a teenager living abroad, first in Buenos Aires, Argentina, then in a small French village, and later in a tiny Mexican village, I can understand why I became a sociologist. In Buenos Aires I saw heavy gates around large homes clearly meant to keep strangers out, but the walls around the poor neighbourhoods appeared designed to keep people in. Why, I wondered, did the walls have different meanings, and why were the poor treated differently? The French teens seemed different than me. Was it because they were French and I American, they lived in a small town and I was from Boston, or their parents owned a butcher shop or worked in factories and my father was a professor, I wondered? As an undergraduate I decided to become a sociologist and researcher when I tried to analyze what I had seen in the Mexican village where I lived and found we had violated many social norms. I saw that research would help my understanding, and more research was necessary to truly understand the lives of others. With new experiences as a public member on medical licensing and disciplinary boards, my research evolved from the study of urban ethnic communities, gangs, and teen mothers to the regulation of physicians.

Guillermina Jasso (Chapter 10)

I was born half a mile from the border with Mexico in the old Mercy Hospital that faced Jarvis Plaza in Laredo, Texas. But I did not know that my parents were "immigrants." In the Texas textbooks, *immigrants* were Southern and Eastern Europeans who lived in crowded tenements and had bad habits. Every year Martin High School, the only public high school, graduated a class of securely anti-immigrant students, the vast majority of whose parents or grandparents had come from Mexico. No one had told these Shakespeare-quoting, Bach-playing, Rodgers and Hammerstein–whistling, Lerner and Loewe–dancing boys and girls that we, too, threatened the American way of life.

I grew up passionate to understand the way the world works. In time I got a PhD and began studying fairness, theoretically with probability distributions, empirically with vignettes. One day in 1977 I got a call from the Commissioner of the Immigration and Naturalization Service. Would I join his staff and advise him on the social science underlying immigration issues? "But I don't know anything about immigration," I said. "You know more than you think you know," he said quietly, "and you can learn the rest."

And that is how I started studying immigration, and how I learned that my parents were immigrants and that I was born in the fabled second generation.

Jennifer Jennings (Chapter 15)

I grew up in suburban New Jersey and, after graduating from college, taught high school English and social studies in urban public high schools. My students were overwhelmingly poor, and I recognized that many of their problems succeeding in school stemmed from health issues they faced on a day-to-day basis. Though my research in graduate school initially focused on education, the insight I had as a teacher led me back to studying health and education disparities. My current work in this area focuses on the effects of one's state of birth on his or her mortality and morbidity as an adult, as well as how systems that measure hospitals based on their patients' outcomes affect the quality of care that patients receive.

Colin Jerolmack (Chapter 18)

As a beginning graduate student interested in city life, I spent a lot of time wandering around the streets of New York's Greenwich Village. I was particularly drawn to neighbourhood parks that were undergoing renovations because the process of deciding how to redesign the parks afforded a window into how community members used, imagined, and complained about their public spaces. I was surprised to learn that many civic associations and park users complained about pigeons, whose feces made park benches unusable and posed a potential disease threat. However, in observing public behaviour I saw that pigeon feeding was a popular activity among park visitors. I realized that urban wildlife impacted how people interpreted and experienced their public spaces, for better and for worse. Over time, I became fascinated by the ways that the natural environment shapes city life, and I came to see that people's responses to urban wildlife revealed how they draw boundaries between environment and society. Because of the humble pigeon, I developed a passion for environmental sociology without even leaving the metropolis.

Eric Klinenberg (Chapter 6)

I grew up in the centre of Chicago, and my interest in the sociology of culture and cities grew out of my experiences there. I lived in a bohemian but rapidly gentrifying neighborhood called Old Town, a place that was long famous for its vibrant street life and for its blues clubs, jazz bars, cafés, and counterculture scenes. Chicago is a segregated city, and Old Town is wedged between two of the city's most affluent areas, the Gold Coast and Lincoln Park, and Cabrini Green, a housing project (recently demolished) where most of the residents were African American and poor. I was always puzzled by this arrangement, and trying to understand it as a child was the beginning of my sociology career.

My research examines cities, culture, climate, and communications. My first book, *Heat Wave: A Social Autopsy of Disaster in Chicago*, explores two questions: Why did so many people die during a short heat spell in 1995? And why was this disastrous event so easy to deny, overlook, and forget? My second book, *Fighting for Air: The Battle to Control America's Media*, examines how media consolidation has affected newspapers, radio stations, television news, and the Internet, and tracks the emergence of the global media reform movement. My latest book, *Going Solo: The Extraordinary Rise and Surprising Appeal of Living Alone*, analyzes the incredible social experiment in solo living that began in the 1950s and is now ubiquitous in developed nations throughout the world.

Steven Lukes (Chapters 2 and 7)

My first book was about the life and ideas of Emile Durkheim, one of the founders of the sociological tradition, whose classic works raise large questions about how to understand what *social* means and why the explanations typical of economics and psychology, at the level of individuals and their interactions, will always be inadequate. They also leave other questions unaddressed: They largely neglect power relations, class, and other social conflicts within societies. My subsequent work has addressed both sets of questions, with books on individualism, on power, and on Marxism. I started to think sociologically about morals when still an undergraduate student: Where our moral judgements come from, if not from our social context, and why they should apply beyond it, are questions I continue to pursue. Reading Durkheim's great book on religion led me to ask to what extent our religious, scientific, and even logical thought is socially shaped.

Jeff Manza (Chapters 1, 2, 5, 7, 8, 9, 16)

Growing up in the college town of Berkeley, California, my family was neither elite (my parents worked for the local university, but not as professors) nor unprivileged. I experienced the differences between these worlds, and in particular the inequalities they represented, as an endlessly fascinating puzzle. I was also always interested in politics and occasionally participated in political protests and movements. My intellectual interest in sociology began to develop while I was an undergraduate student because it provided a way of connecting my emerging concerns about inequality and injustice with a set of theories and ways of studying how those inequalities persist. Since then, I have been exploring how social inequalities influence political life. More recently I have become interested in how public opinion does or does not shape government policies and how and when public attitudes can be manipulated or misused by political elites. I hope that my work can contribute, in some small way, to making American democracy more representative and egalitarian than it currently is.

Gerald Marwell (Chapter 13)

My mother said I was always an "oppositional" child. I grew up in a religious home and went to parochial school, but I never understood what these old stories had to do with me or my world. And I was angry that my friends were out playing ball while I was stuck listening to old men telling me to sit still. I went to MIT to become an engineer, but I discovered interests in economics and psychology instead. I disagreed with the oversimplified psychology that underlies economics and hoped that sociology, the most general of the social sciences, might let me pursue both of my interests. And I fell in love: with all of sociology, and all of social science. Where else can you spend your life thinking about the human condition and get paid for it? Most of my work has been on offering alternatives to economic theories of "collective action," or cooperation, particularly in social movements. Religion is not so different from social movements, in that it requires commitment and faith. So, in my late sixties I finally took up the question that has puzzled me my entire life: Why are so many people religious? Why is religion so important in the world?

Harvey Molotch (Chapter 4)

I came to sociology through a college professor of philosophy who thought that a book by a sociologist, C. Wright Mills, called *The Sociological* Imagination (1959), contained profound social and ethical lessons. I read Mills and absorbed the idea that meaningful community cannot happen when some people have so little power compared to others. The solution, as Mills advocates, is for people to link up with others to see their problems as common ones, caused by the same types of external forces. Particularly in regard to cities (which became a focus of my own research), I learned how business groups, mostly based in real estate, dominate urban agendas and promote projects regardless of their social and environmental impacts; "growth machines," I called them. I came to wonder why so many people went along even when the results were so counter to their own interests. I've always been interested in physical things, like buildings and sewer lines, and more recently in the apparatus used in security, like at airport gates. This combines my interest in cities and their stuff with my abiding fascination with ordinary goods of daily life—toasters and toilets, for example.

Ann Morning (Chapter 10)

My sociological imagination developed from my experiences growing up with people from many different cultural backgrounds. I was raised in Harlem, the famous African American neighbourhood in New York City. But even though my home community was very ethnically homogeneous at the time (it isn't anymore), I was exposed every day to people from all over the globe because I studied at the United Nations International School. The contrast between those two worlds really got me curious about how social environments shape our thinking. As a sociologist today, my research focuses precisely on how people from different social backgrounds think differently about some of the things that seem most natural or objective to us, like racial identities or scientific knowledge. My research connecting these areas was recently published in my first book, *The Nature of Race: How Scientists Think and Teach about Human Difference* (Morning, 2011).

Caroline H. Persell (Chapter 14)

While I was in graduate school at Columbia University, James Coleman and others published a major study showing that schools made little difference in the achievement of students because the variations within individual schools was almost as great as the variations between schools. This rocked the scholarly world and got me thinking about whether it captured all the colours in the educational spectrum. In my visits to many inner-city schools, I had seen students and teachers with lots of energy, ambition, and intelligence working hard to do the best they could in the underresourced conditions they were in. At the same time, I knew that other types of schools, like private boarding schools, were not included in the Coleman study, and wondered how education differed for students at such schools. A question of enduring interest to sociologists is how social and economic advantages are transferred from one generation to the next in a society that purports to frown on inherited privilege. Peter Cookson and I addressed this question by studying elite boarding schools in the United States and England, and found out that they perpetuate intergenerational inequality not just with money but through a range of school practices.

Florencia Torche (Chapter 9)

I grew up in Chile, one of the most unequal countries in the world. Growing up, I could "breathe" inequality not only in the economic disparities between the poor and the rich but also in the wide gaps between cities and the countryside, the economic segregation of schools and neighbourhoods, and the way people of different classes related to each other—when they did—as if they were citizens of different worlds. As a child, I took inequality for granted. As a college student, I gained the tools to understand that high inequality is not "natural." Rather, it exists and persists because of specific policies and institutions—and it can also be changed through policies and institutions. My research became a way to systematically understand how inequality is reproduced across generations—that is, how advantages and disadvantages are transmitted from parents to children, and the role that education and marriage can have. Many of my studies use cross-country comparisons to examine how institutions shape inequality. My most recent research elucidates how the context individuals live in shape their life chances early in life—as early as in the prenatal period.

Lawrence L. Wu (Chapter 19)

I was born in New York City but mostly grew up in Los Angeles, in the northwest corner of the San Fernando Valley in a city called Chatsworth. As a sociologist, my areas of specialization are in social demography, particularly in the social demography of the family, meaning that I have written on fertility (and especially nonmarital fertility), cohabitation, marriage, and divorce. Many social demographers use big data sets in their research, and I am no different, so I'm more than a bit of a numbers geek. What fascinates me the most as a social scientist is the fact that so much of our social world has changed so very quickly and what this means, in turn, for each of us as individuals living in an ever-changing world. This also means that as a numbers geek, one of my other areas of specialization is in statistical methods for studying change, both change historically and change as people's lives unfold from birth through adolescence and into adulthood.

Chapter 1

The Sociological Imagination

by Jeff Manza, Lynne Haney, and Richard Arum

Manoocher Deghati, File/AP Images

Facebook is controversial in some parts of the world for its ability to allow people of different beliefs to find each other. Why are social media so powerful?

Learning Objectives

1.1.1 Discuss how a sociological imagination helps to challenge stereotypes.

1.1.2 Explain the process for forming sociological questions.

1.1.3 Identify the types of questions that sociologists are particularly well equipped to explore.

1.1.4 Discuss the wide range of topics and areas of life that sociologists study.

1.2.1 Analyze how families and communities shape the social development of children.

1.2.2 Explain how our identities impact our opportunities in life.

1.2.3 Discuss how the schools and organizations we participate in shape our lives and identities.

1.2.4 Analyze the ways in which the social and economic context we are born into shapes the opportunities available to us.

1.2.5 Explain the distinction between social interaction and social structure.

1.3.1 Discuss the origins of sociology as a discipline.

1.3.2 Explain the roles of industrialization and urbanization in the development of sociology.

1.3.3 Compare and contrast sociology with the other social sciences.

1.3.4 Identify some of the spin-off fields that originally started in sociology.

Who are we? When asked to describe ourselves, we tend to think in terms of our individuality: our likes and dislikes, our interests and skills, our experiences, our friends and partners. But there is a lot more to each of us than that. What about the time and place in which we live? It wouldn't really be appropriate to answer the question by saying, "I am a person living in North America in the twenty-first century," but clearly who we are is at least partly the result of where and when we were born and live out our lives. In fact, we are all products of multiple contexts, such as the families we grew up in, the neighbourhoods and communities we lived in, the schools we attended, the jobs and work experiences we've had, the groups and organizations we belong to, and so forth. Yes, we are individuals, with our own desires, tastes, talents, and dreams. But we are also *social* beings, connected to other people in a wide variety of different ways. What it means to be human is in large part defined by the simple fact that we are constantly interacting with others.

The social nature of our lives has become increasingly clear in recent years. In 2004, a Harvard undergraduate named Mark Zuckerberg created a website originally intended for students at Harvard to make social connections with each other. The idea caught on like wildfire, and the social networking site Facebook was born. Facebook is now a worldwide phenomenon with hundreds of millions of registered users. It allows individuals to link to and communicate with "friends" (actual or virtual friends) and create or join communities of users. Through these networks, individuals become linked together. Facebook's founders probably didn't realize that in developing the initial idea for the program, they drew upon some very basic sociological ideas about how **social networks** (the ties between people, groups, and organizations) work. Facebook and its many spin-offs draw from a basic sociological insight: Human beings are not simply individuals with a few close friends and family members who otherwise only randomly bump into strangers in the course of their daily lives. Rather, we all are part of normally hidden social networks, in which we know people who know other people we don't know but who have much in common with us (such as common interests, backgrounds, and areas of expertise). Facebook and other social networking programs (LinkedIn, a social networking site aimed at connecting people together through their jobs, is another good example) use an algorithm that makes these normally hidden connections between people suddenly visible.

Facebook's success in connecting networks of like-minded people has been sufficiently powerful that some governments and citizens around the world have attempted to curtail its use out of fear that it can help people create and spread antigovernment ideas or mobilize groups of citizens to protest in the streets. In the last couple of years, for example, Facebook has been blocked in countries such as China, Syria, Pakistan, and Iran. In other, less threatening but important ways, Facebook appears to change the nature of relationships, making it much easier to develop new contacts as well as to keep in touch with old friendships even after people geographically drift apart.

The entire social networking phenomena, of which Facebook is but one example, highlights some of the ways in which learning sociological ideas can help us better understand the social worlds around us. Social networks and social media highlight a feature common to all societies: Our existence is always connected to our relationships to others. Hidden in our individual biographies is a story about **society**, a large group of people who live in the same area and participate in a common culture. **Sociology**—the study of societies and the social worlds that individuals inhabit within them—faces the specific challenge of trying to uncover and analyze the patterns that lie beneath the surface of these social worlds for individual lives. Sociology is not the study of individuals, but rather the study of how we live together. To put it another way, sociology is the study not of human beings, but of what it means to be human.

The example of Facebook and other digital technologies that have emerged over the past 20 years or so exemplifies another key point: Societies are always evolving and changing, and in the process, these changes raise new puzzles and challenges for understanding the human experience. Sociologists are asking hard questions about how social changes like the rise of social media are changing how individuals and societies relate to one another: How has new technology changed the form, content, and character of friendships and groups? How has online dating changed the nature of intimate relationships? How has technology changed the way work is organized, how employment is found, and what kinds of jobs are likely to be available in the future? New technologies are helping governments to spy on their citizens much more intensively than before; what does this mean for democratic rights? And not just governments are acting in this way: Universities and employers are increasingly reading social media produced by prospective students or job applicants to evaluate them beyond traditional means. Today, our "digital footprint" forms a part of who we are in a way that would have been completely unimaginable a couple of decades ago. All of these developments concern the relationship between individuals and their social worlds—a subject at the heart of sociology.

The Big Questions

Each chapter identifies a set of questions that have defined the research and teaching puzzles of that topic. These questions organize each chapter and provide a lens for exploring sociological thinking about the topics covered. In starting from questions, not answers, and puzzling together in the search for answers, you will learn to think sociologically. In this first chapter, we will explore the following questions:

1. **What is the sociological imagination, and why is it worth acquiring?** In this section, we introduce the concept of the sociological imagination and explore how it helps us learn to ask hard questions.
2. **What are social contexts, and why do they matter?** Sociology is fundamentally concerned with how we are influenced by society. All of us are situated in an array of social contexts. How do these influence us and our behavior?
3. **Where did sociology come from, and how is it different from other social sciences?** Here we examine the context in which sociology began to develop and explore the question of how sociology "fits" into, and relates to, the other social sciences.

1.1 What Is the Sociological Imagination, and Why Is It Worth Acquiring?

Andy/Fotolia

The Sociological Imagination

Since the inception of sociology, researchers in the discipline have puzzled over how we are connected to each other and the broader societies in which we live. A **sociological imagination** is the capacity to think systematically about how things we experience as *personal* problems—for example, debt from student loans, competing demands from divorced parents, or an inability to form a rewarding romantic relationship—are really *social* issues that are widely shared by others living in a similar time and social location as us.

The sociologist C. Wright Mills (1916–1962), who coined the term in 1959, wrote that "the sociological imagination enables us to grasp history and biography and the relations between the two within society" (Mills, 1959, p. 6). To understand the world around us, and to begin to think in a deep way about how it works and how we might improve it, is to recognize the extent to which our individual lives are strongly shaped by where, when, and to whom we were born, and the range of experiences we have had as a child, as an adolescent, and later as an adult. At each stage, we are both individuals and members of a social world. Our opportunities and potentials are always influenced by the inequalities and injustices we encounter, but understanding these requires that we think about them sociologically. In short, the sociological imagination helps us to ask hard questions and seek answers about the social worlds we inhabit. Used wisely, it will also provide tools to navigate those worlds more effectively in pursuit of the goals we have for ourselves.

The sociologist C. Wright Mills coined the phrase "the sociological imagination."

Yaroslava Mills

Looking Through a Sociological Lens

1.1.1 Discuss how a sociological imagination helps to challenge stereotypes.

A sociological imagination challenges some very basic impulses all of us have. To simplify a complex world, we often take for granted that things around us are somehow inevitable or natural. If we have grown up in a social context where marriage is defined as a lifelong commitment between a man and a woman, we might be quick to conclude that such an arrangement was the way that intimate relationships were simply meant to be. But if we look at different societies and over time, we will soon see that marriage is only sometimes a lifetime commitment between a man and a woman. In other contexts, as well as our own society, intimate relationships may be between two men, or two women, or among varying romantic partners. A sociological imagination helps us to understand that a diversity of intimate relationships is possible and to question our assumptions about a particular form of marriage being natural as opposed to social in origin.

In a similar fashion, we are also often quick to identify differences across groups of people—men and women, rich and poor, whites and other races, people of different religions—as inherent characteristics of the members of these groups. But this assumption—that "group" characteristics apply to all members of the group or to any one individual—is incorrect. Making faulty generalizations about individuals based on what we think we know about the groups they are members of is what is known as a **stereotype**. For instance, some people (and evidently many employers) think that older individuals are not as good workers as younger people. It *is* true that at some point, if we live long enough, we will become too old to perform jobs that we may have done for many years. But that does not mean that a specific person is incapable of doing a job because of age, no matter how old he or she is.

A sociological imagination challenges stereotypes by raising questions about where they come from, what they are based on, who stands to benefit from them, and why they are harmful. Sociology gives us tools to understand and think critically and creatively about everyday assumptions (such as stereotyped thinking) that others make. It shows us that the things we often take for granted are a lot more complicated than they appear. Making the world more complicated is a challenge, but possessed of a sociological imagination, we are able to be more active and effective participants in everything we do.

Dennis MacDonald / Alamy Stock Photo

Some assume that overweight people have caused their own obesity by overeating and under-exercising. But sociologists studying obesity in America have pointed to social factors that contribute to many North Americans gaining weight. These factors include increasingly sedentary lifestyles centred on office jobs and leisure activities (such as watching TV or sitting in front of computers), the rise of the fast food industry, the increasing proportion of processed foods in the North American diet, suburbanization, and reliance on the automobile to get around instead of walking.

Engaging Our Sociological Imaginations: From Personal Puzzles to Sociological Questions

1.1.2 Explain the process for forming sociological questions.

Everyone possesses some elements of a sociological imagination. Whenever we try to make sense of something in the social worlds around us, we are beginning to think sociologically. But just observing the world around us in a more critical way does not fully engage our sociological imaginations. A sociological imagination instead requires that we start to ask deeper and more meaningful questions about the everyday world around us. It does not allow us to settle for simple answers in understanding human beings and the societies they inhabit. *It is our ability to ask hard questions, instead of just accepting easily available answers (or stereotypes), that is the hallmark of a good sociological imagination.*

Where do sociological questions come from? Most professional sociologists, including many of the authors of *The Sociological Project*, have had experiences in their lives, before they began doing sociological research, that ignited their sociological imaginations. For some it was triggered by a particular event, while for others it may have developed more slowly—a combination of things that inspired them to seek to develop this way of thinking. The short author biographies that appear at the beginning of this book give you some idea of the range of these moments. But you don't have to be a professional sociologist to develop your sociological imagination or ask sociological questions! One situation that often triggers our sociological imagination occurs when we see that some kind of widely shared assumption we have long taken for granted is incorrect. That can literally happen at any moment, but when it does, and as we start to question previously held ideas in a new way, we are taking the first step toward developing a sociological imagination.

Of course, we can also actively engage our sociological imaginations rather than waiting for some surprising puzzles to emerge. One way is to think critically about "common sense." Commonsense ideas are often very useful. Innumerable pearls of wisdom are found in commonsense *aphorisms*, which are short phrases stating a truth or opinion. Examples of aphorisms include "look before you leap," "a rising tide lifts all boats," and "birds of a feather flock together." We've all heard some of these phrases, and in many cases it is valuable to follow the wisdom they suggest. Standing at a busy intersection, we *should* look carefully before walking out in front of traffic. It is usually easier to make friends with someone when you have common interests. In such cases, common sense provides a useful guide to being human.

But if we look closely, we quickly notice there is a problem. Almost every commonsense aphorism makes sense only in some contexts but not others (Watts, 2011). In fact, most commonsense aphorisms have an equally attractive but entirely opposite aphorism. For example, compare "look before you leap" to "he who hesitates is lost"! In some situations, it is important to seize opportunities before they disappear, while in other cases care and due diligence are recommended. So which is correct? They cannot both be right all of the time. The answer is that it depends on the context. The minute we recognize this, we are beginning to think like a sociologist. We have to know *which* commonsense rule to apply in which social context if we are to be competent at being human.

Once we learn not to take stereotypes and commonsense knowledge for granted, we can begin to ask questions. And once we learn to start questioning things, we are on the road to developing a sociological imagination. But what are these questions? Reading this text will open up many issues and questions to investigate (see "The Big Questions" on page 3). But for now, here are a few examples. Think about eating at a restaurant or school cafeteria. If you look around, you probably will notice that there are relatively few, if any, groups that include both whites and persons of colour. Or visit a bunch of churches: you will rarely find large numbers of whites and persons of colour worshipping together. Why is it that, long after the Charter of Rights and Freedoms ended legal discrimination, women earn less pay than men for the same work, and same-sex couples were denied the right to marriage for decades? These questions are explored in the chapters that follow. Thinking about questions like these and others, we begin to notice that common sense and stereotypes are not helpful and that deeper understanding requires us to question our assumptions.

Asking questions about things we have previously taken for granted is an exciting and creative activity, but it also may upset people around us. Challenging family members at the dinner table about their own stereotypes may lead to puzzled looks or even strong words. Most people do not enjoy being challenged in this way. Similarly, large corporations or other organizations also may not like it when their workers or members start to ask questions rather than simply doing (or believing) what they are told. School authorities often do not like it when students, parents, or outside observers raise questions about the character and quality of student learning or teaching in the school. Governments in particular do not like it when their citizens begin to interrogate topics officials would prefer to keep secret, such as covert surveillance operations or corruption.

Sociological Questions: A Detailed Example

1.1.3 Identify the types of questions that sociologists are particularly well equipped to explore.

To get a better sense of how sociologists use questions to craft research projects, let's consider in more detail a current research project undertaken by Richard Arum, one of the authors of this chapter, which examines a topic of interest to many of the readers of this text. Arum had taught at several universities in the United States and was puzzled by what he perceived to be the relatively modest amount of learning that was actually going on at these universities. We usually take for granted that colleges and universities are places where teaching and learning are prioritized, but Arum began to question this premise. To investigate whether (and why) there is a lot less learning going on in higher education than is typically assumed, he and a collaborator have been carrying out a project following more than 2,000 young adults as they progressed through 24 diverse colleges and universities in the United States and then as they left university to work, live with friends, move in with romantic partners, or return to live with their parents (Arum & Roksa, 2011, 2014). The students in the study had quite different experiences and fared very differently in terms of learning outcomes. Some of these students were in educational settings where they were exposed to challenging coursework and successfully moved into well-paying jobs immediately following graduation. Yet many more students did not enjoy such fates. In fact, two years out of university, 24 percent of graduates in the study were back living at home with their parents or relatives.

Student debt in Canada is much lower than in the United States. According to the Project on Student Debt, in 2009, graduating U.S. seniors with student loans owed an average of $24,000 (Robinson, 2011). In 2012, Statistics Canada conducted a survey of financial stability and found that the median student loan debt in Canada is $10,000 (Statistics Canada, 2014). According to a report by the Canadian Federation of Students, those who take loans from the federal student loan program (Canada Student Loans Program) graduated with an average debt of $28,495. This figure does not account for provincial loans, lines of credit, or credit card debt. Nor does the figure include the cost of borrowing. The average borrower will pay over $10,000 in interest over 10 years while paying off the debt. The outstanding student debt owed to the federal loan program is estimated to be $16 billion (Burley & Awad, 2015). See Figure 1.1 to find out more about the rising cost of tuition in Canada.

Richard Arum and Josipa Roksa, in their project tracking the education and employment experiences of American university students, found that students' experiences varied widely. Consider two of the students tracked in Arum's U.S. project: Maria and Robert. Maria attended a highly selective, residential liberal arts university in a small Midwestern town in the United States. She had come to university with a high SAT score and three high school Advanced Placement course credits. In university, she quickly decided on becoming a social science major after taking a small freshman seminar with a sociologist who did her research on urban youth culture. Maria spent a semester of her junior year abroad in Europe, and during her semesters at university she reported that she met frequently with her instructors outside of class to discuss her work and that faculty at the school had high expectations for students like her. She also reported that her classmates—many of whom she had come to know well, as the university had integrated her academic program with her residential dorm—were equally encouraging of her focus on academic work. On average, she estimated

Figure 1.1 The Rise of Student Debt in Canada

SOURCE: From "Infographic: An Education in Inflation 2014," by the Canadian Centre for Policy Alternatives, September 10, 2014, retrieved from https://www.policyalternatives.ca/publications/facts-infographics/infographic-education-inflation-2014.

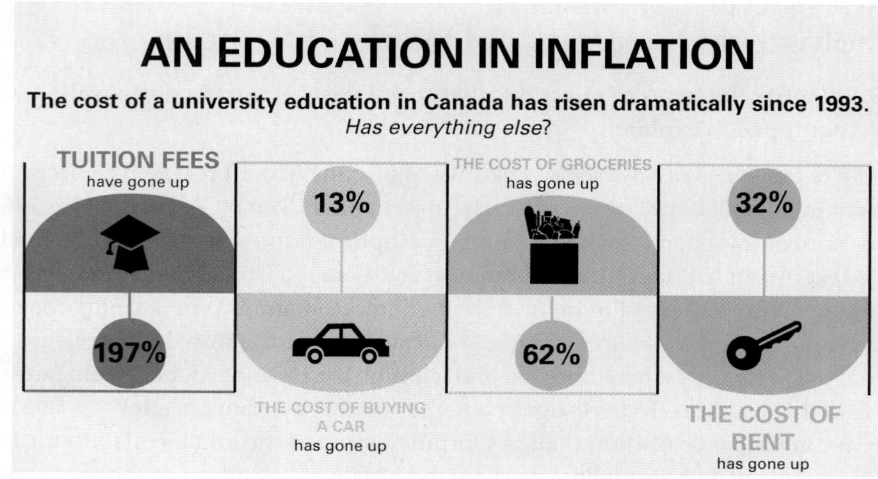

devoting 20 hours per week preparing for classes, many of which had significant reading and writing requirements. When her performance on tasks that required critical thinking, complex reasoning, and written communication was measured, her scores moved up dramatically from freshman to senior year. Two years out of university, she was living with a friend she had met in university and was working at a job where she made slightly more than $38,000 per year. Although she had assumed a great deal of student debt, she was on a path to adult success. See Figure 1.2 to learn how typical Maria's post-university employment was.

Contrast Maria's university experiences with Robert's. Robert attended a high school that was predominantly nonwhite, and then he enrolled in a nonselective, large public university in his state known as something of a "party school." Like many of his classmates, he entered university without any Advanced Placement coursework completed and did not score particularly well on the SAT. In university, he reported rarely meeting with his instructors outside of class. When asked about whether faculty

Figure 1.2 Employment Status of Recent U.S. College and University Graduates

What kinds of jobs are recent college and university graduates getting? Fifty-six percent are working in fields that require a degree, but 22 percent are working in fields that do not, apparently taking jobs for which they are overqualified. And the bad news is that another 22 percent are out of work altogether.

SOURCE: Data from John J. Heldrich Center for Workforce Development at Rutgers, 2011.

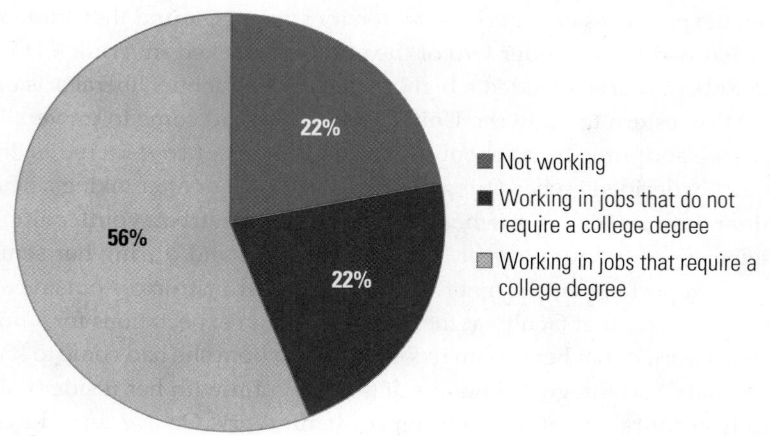

had high expectations for students like him, he reported that they largely did not. He muddled through coursework with passing grades but did not find his coursework either interesting or challenging; he found himself increasingly focused on socializing with his friends and earning spending money to support activities outside of school. Like many of his peers, he only studied about eight hours per week; when he did prepare for his classes, he often found himself doing so with his friends, who ended up frequently distracting him from really focusing on his work. During his senior year, when we tested his performance on the same tasks that Maria completed, we found no improvement in his performance even after he had attended university for four years. He was not alone. Arum and Roksa found that slightly more than a third of students in their study demonstrated no meaningful improvement on a test of general skills (Arum & Roksa, 2011). And Robert was not rewarded in the labour market when he graduated in 2009. Two years after graduation, he was about $30,000 in debt for a university degree, unemployed, and living back at home with his parents. About the only things he had in common with Maria were a heavy debt load and a degree.

How can we understand why these two students had such different educational experiences and ended up on such different paths? There are many ways in which the ideas and research of sociologists give us the tools to understand how Maria's and Robert's lives are unfolding the way they are. The most obvious commonsense answer is simply that Maria has just worked harder than Robert. And there appears to be some truth in that. But that is not likely the entire story. A sociological view of student experiences in post-secondary education poses a range of questions about how individuals (like Maria and Robert) and institutions interact in complex ways. Some of the questions sociologists might ask include the following: How did Maria's background improve her educational experience, and how did Robert's handicap him? Why is Robert (and others like him) able to spend less time on his studies now than students did a generation ago, but still earn passing grades? Why are certain post-secondary institutions more focused on academic learning than others? Why do some schools become known as party schools, and what are the consequences for students attending those schools? How has the nature of campus life changed in the past few decades? Are students more or less likely to join organizations or to interact with each other collectively during their university years than at other points in their life? As the ratio of male to female students on university campuses changes, how have dating and courtship patterns altered? And is the United States alone in these changes in higher education, or are there global shifts underway to change the meaning and experience of university across national borders?

As these examples all suggest, sociological questions are concerned with a broad canvas of the modern world. Sociological questions range widely from the basic units of human life—such as individuals' relationships with others—to the groups and organizations we are a part of, all the way up to a now rapidly changing global economy that is impacting all of our social relationships.

As we move through the book, we will be introducing big questions concerning many of the most important topics sociologists are currently examining. But our first big point is this: Learning how to ask the important questions, and to think hard about how to probe for answers, is the heart of the sociological imagination.

The Endless Reach of the Sociological Imagination

1.1.4 Discuss the wide range of topics and areas of life that sociologists study.

There are very few areas of life that cannot be studied sociologically. Consider a few of the different areas that some of the sociologists involved with *The Sociology Project* have examined in their own research:

- Harvey Molotch wrote a book about the sociology of the toilet and another book about how other common household products are invented.

- Colin Jerolmack wrote a book about the relationship between humans and pigeons across the world.
- Eric Klinenberg wrote a book on why so many people died in certain neighbourhoods in Chicago during a heat wave in 1995.
- Kathleen Gerson wrote a book about the conflicting relationship expectations of young men and women in the twenty-first century.
- Jeff Goodwin wrote a book about how and why revolutions occurred in some places, but not others.
- Steven Lukes wrote a book on how sociological ideas can better inform complex moral debates.

The fact that the sociological imagination can be employed to explore many aspects of the human condition does not mean, however, that anything goes. In each of these cases, sociologists draw upon a particular way of asking questions and a particular set of theories about where to start looking for answers. Sociologists also deploy a common set of systematic tools for studying those questions. But there is one unifying theme. All of the questions sociologists ask build off a common starting point: How and in what ways do social contexts matter? We explore this in more detail in the next section.

1.2 What Are Social Contexts, and Why Do They Matter?

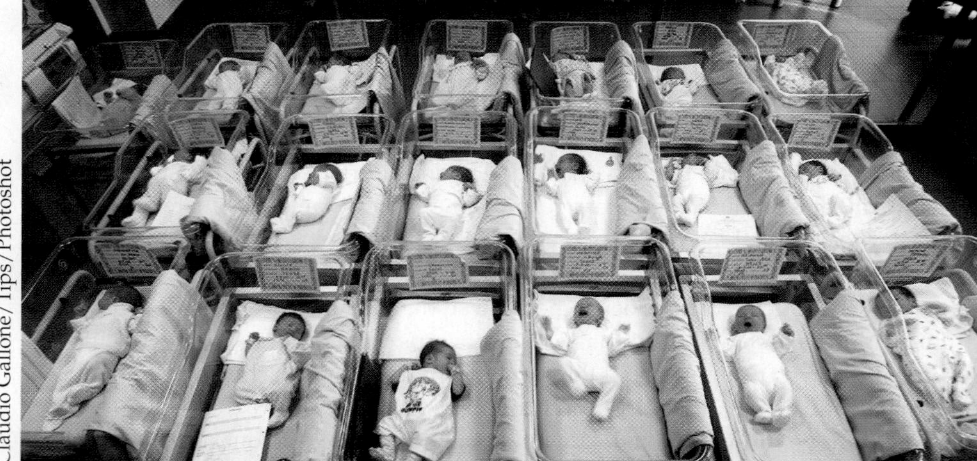

Claudio Gallone/Tips/Photoshot

Social Contexts: From Individuals to Societies

Sociology is fundamentally concerned with how individuals participate in, and are influenced by, the society in which they live. The stories of post-secondary students Maria and Robert provide one example. We refer to this influence of society on individuals as the **social context**. What is this context? What do we mean when we refer to it?

One way of thinking about the diverse kinds of contexts individuals face is through the following thought experiment. Imagine being in the maternity ward of a large hospital, looking at a group of newborn babies. They are all helpless and adorable, with a full life ahead of them. In a perfect world, they would all have an equal opportunity to develop their many talents and abilities and succeed in life. In fact, we might look at those cute little creatures and think to ourselves, "Any one of these babies could one day be running a country." But we also know that the odds of such an outcome vary widely. Why?

At its core, the sociological imagination is the idea that individual lives unfold in contexts—in this case, social environments, including economic and cultural conditions, in which each of these infants will grow up and live. And those contexts are going to be very different for some babies than others. We don't know, looking at the babies in the cribs, which ones will have strong family support and encouragement growing up, be able to attend good schools, or find good employment opportunities as an adult. To be sure, if we did know something about the contexts each of these infants will grow up in, we would be able to make much better-educated guesses about their prospects in life. So what are these contexts? We can immediately identify a variety of factors that are going to influence each baby's life:

- the child's immediate family (past and present), most importantly the parents' education level, wealth, and income;
- the neighbourhood and community the child will grow up in (and will live in as an adult);
- the education the child will get (including the quality of the schools he or she will attend);
- the types of organizations (churches, clubs, or groups) the child will join or have access to; and
- the type of employment the child will find.

There are also other, broader contexts that each of these babies is born into that are important to keep in mind:

- the country the child is born into (a rich country, a poor country, or a rapidly developing country) and
- the period of history in which he or she is born.

Each cute little baby will, in fact, enter a social world that will have a huge impact on where he or she ends up. Let's review some of these different contexts in more detail.

Families and Communities

1.2.1 Analyze how families and communities shape the social development of children.

We are born into families, and generations of sociological research have stressed the importance of families and family situations as a key to understanding how individuals develop. Our families shape who we are in a variety of ways: by giving us racial, ethnic, and religious identities; by teaching us the basic rules of society and how to behave in society or in particular social settings; by exposing us to certain networks of people; by the financial resources that our parents can invest in our education and development, as well as the emotional and cognitive capacities they have developed in us through lifelong interactions; and (possibly) by the extent to which they are willing and able to help out later in life as we become adults and perhaps even attempt to raise a new generation of children of our own (such as helping us to buy cars or houses or to pay for weddings).

This brings a second important context into view: the neighbourhood and community in which we grow up. Living in a safe neighbourhood with good schools, surrounded by families who encourage their children to do well and to be ambitious and confident, creates a different set of pathways from that experienced by a child living in an impoverished, high-crime neighbourhood with poor schools. The latter environment can have many negative consequences, including not just obvious things like the continual risk of being a criminal victim and the lack of people who can provide positive social networks, but also more subtle things like increased stress levels that will reduce sleep and school performance.

For instance, in his groundbreaking recent research, New York University sociologist Pat Sharkey has discovered a link between neighbourhood violence and children's school performance (Sharkey, 2010). He discovered that in the week following a homicide in their neighbourhood, children in Chicago scored significantly lower on reading and vocabulary tests than they had in the week prior to the homicide. Among other things, Sharkey's research teaches us how violence can be absorbed by and transmitted through neighbourhood contexts—and how children, who are perhaps the most vulnerable to such exposure, experience its effects at school as well as home. Aside from our interest in reducing violent crime, Sharkey's work suggests we need to also think about the consequences of neighbourhood violence on innocent children.

Identities and Groups

1.2.2 Explain how our identities impact our opportunities in life.

Our **identities**—the conceptions we and others have about who we are and what groups or categories we are members of—provide another important type of social context in which individual lives unfold. We are born with certain physical attributes—most notably the colour of our skin and our sex (although one or both may be ambiguous) and possibly a disability or an unusual physical characteristic (such as our height or weight). Our family and society immediately imposes upon us other identities, such as giving us a religion and a national or ethnic identity, before we are old enough to play any role in choosing them ourselves. As we move through life, we may be able to change some of these identities, and we often pick up new ones. However we acquire our identities and the groups that those identities place us in, they are important factors in predicting where we end up in life, the kinds of opportunities we have, and how the rest of the world views us. Some identities may be benign or neutral, and some may be positive or beneficial. But some may be harmful. For example, in virtually all societies that have ever been studied, men have more status and power than women; having the identity of "male" or "man" has historically conferred important benefits. Similarly, around the world today, members of dominant racial and ethnic groups have more opportunities and collect more rewards than members of other groups.

The sociological imagination forces us to take context into account when thinking about any particular unemployed or poor person.

Amble Design/Shutterstock

Schools and Organizations

1.2.3 Discuss how the schools and organizations we participate in shape our lives and identities.

From the families we are raised in to the neighbourhoods where we grow up, to the identities we have or adopt, the social contexts of individual lives then flow outward to the schools we attend and the organizations we join. Education is such an important element of our development that it is hardly surprising that the quality and types of schools we attend will have a huge impact on our lives. We will revisit the importance of education throughout this book. But other, less obvious organizational connections we forge are important as well: the churches, synagogues, or mosques we attend; the unions or professional associations we join as adults; the clubs and political groups in which we choose to participate. All of these are contexts where we may gain important types of experience and insights, and/or find opportunities. The doors to special opportunities that may (or may not) open for us down the road hinge partly on what kinds of groups we place ourselves in and what kinds of contacts we forge in those diverse contexts.

Social and Historical Contexts

1.2.4 Analyze the ways in which the social and economic context we are born into shapes the opportunities available to us.

C. Wright Mills emphasized that the sociological imagination connects individual biographies to history (Mills, 1959). What exactly does that mean? For one thing, the social, economic, and historical contexts we are born into matter enormously for what we likely can achieve and do. For example, an African American male born in the South in 1900 (during the era of Jim Crow, in which laws and opportunities in the South were explicitly designed to privilege whites) faced a very different environment and very different opportunities from the same man born today, simply by virtue of the time and place he was born. A child growing up in a working-class family in Detroit in the 1940s (when the automobile industry was booming and the city was home to a large number of well-paying working-class jobs) had a different set of economic opportunities than the same child growing up in contemporary Detroit (where in recent years the area has been hard hit by a devastating decline in manufacturing jobs, and unemployment among people without post-secondary degrees is very high). Women entering adulthood in the 1950s faced a different set of choices and cultural expectations from women entering adulthood since the gender revolution of the 1970s, when occupations and opportunities historically closed to women opened up and the ideal (if not always the reality) of egalitarian marriage developed. All of these contexts are influenced by a global environment. We live in an era when events in regions and countries around the world deeply influence our lives—and vice versa. In particular, many types of jobs once done in North America are now performed by workers in other countries. As jobs, ideas, and technology move around the globe at an unprecedented pace, it is increasingly clear that we are connected to people and places far away.

Consider the issues of unemployment and poverty. What causes people to be poor? If we use our sociological imagination to think about an unemployed person not as simply an individual but as part of society, we consider poverty not an individual problem but a social one. Doing so allows us to reframe the question so we no longer just ask why this person is in this situation, but why so many individuals are in this situation. To do this, the sociological imagination asks us to take account of context. Where is this happening? Which industries or regions are particularly hard hit by unemployment in the current economic context?

The sociological imagination forces us to take context into account when thinking about any particular unemployed or poor person.

Jim West/Alamy Stock Photo

Sociology as the Study of Social Contexts

1.2.5 Explain the distinction between social interaction and social structure.

Having explored the critical idea of social context, we can now define more fully and clearly what we mean by *sociology:* Sociology is the study of the diverse contexts within which individuals' lives unfold and the social world is created. The social worlds humans create have two key components: social interaction and social structure. **Social interaction** refers to the way people act together, including how they modify and alter their behaviour in response to the presence of others. Social interaction is governed by a set of **norms**, which are the basic rules of society that help us know what is and is not appropriate to do in any situation. The violation of norms of behaviour will cause us all kinds of problems. As we interact with others, we engage in a process of working within those rules and norms to try to present a pleasing version of ourselves to others. Examples include our Facebook and professional website profiles, our business cards, and the different ways we characterize ourselves in social settings when we meet new people or introduce ourselves to a group. For example, the authors of this chapter are sometimes sociologists, sometimes professors, sometimes parents, sometimes politically active citizens, and sometimes various other things, depending on the situation. In choosing among these identities, we are engaging with the social world. We always occupy the same body, but who exactly we are (or how we characterize ourselves) depends on our social contexts.

The importance of the "social" part of social interaction becomes most clear to us when we violate societal rules of acceptable behaviour (or when we imagine the social sanctions that would follow if we did violate the rules). Consider this example: What would happen if a student in a university classroom were to suddenly stand up on her or his desk and shout profanities at the instructor or fellow students? Even if any of us might occasionally feel like doing this, there are powerful constraints that discourage such action. Without anyone saying anything, we understand that if we did this, our classmates might shun us; the instructor might reprimand us or, perhaps, call campus security to escort us out of the class. So even when we are annoyed or frustrated or bored in our classes, or in similar situations like being in seemingly endless meetings or standing in long lines, we generally know to keep our true feelings to ourselves.

But even if you think there is no chance of any significant consequences, you still know when a behaviour is wrong. How? Sociologists argue that we censor ourselves because of our concern for the social consequences of our action. We learn and absorb societal norms from our interactions with important others (such as parents, friends, teachers, ministers, or mentors). Knowing the rules, or norms, of any situation is important for avoiding embarrassment and acting appropriately in different contexts, because most of the time we want to "fit in" wherever we find ourselves.

Meeting other people involves a complicated set of social norms that can vary depending on cultural practices, the type of situation, and other factors. Handshaking is one way people commonly greet each other; however, there are different kinds of possible handshakes. We take social cues to know which handshake is appropriate.

Stephen Coburn/Shutterstock

Where do these norms and rules that govern social interaction come from, and why do they persist over time? Part of the reason is simply that people just do what is expected and in the process reinforce and reproduce those rules (or, sometimes, subtly begin to change them). But there is more to it than that. Sociologists use the concept of **social structure** to describe the many diverse ways in which the rules and norms of everyday life become enduring patterns that shape and govern social interactions. Social structure, in a sense, lies in the background of every social interaction. Social structure is a messy but important concept, one we explore in more detail throughout the book. It includes everything from enduring customs and traditions to formal laws and regulations that governments establish.

We can identify two critical components of social structure. First, every society has a complex set of roles and **social hierarchies**, a set of important and enduring social positions that often grant some individuals and groups higher status and more power than others. Whatever role or position we occupy in any interaction—student, child, parent, leader of a group, member of a group, and so on—our actions, and indeed our range of options for action, are impacted by the rules and powers that are associated with that role. For example, the child is supposed to defer to the parent, the worker to the business owner, and the patient to the doctor.

The second aspect of social structure is comprised of the norms and **institutions** of society. *Institutions* refers to longstanding and important practices (like marriage, families, education, and economic markets), as well as the organizations that regulate those practices (such as the government, the legal system, the military, schools, and religious groups). Institutions are a difficult but vital concept that we will encounter throughout the book. The concept includes a wide range of different types and forms of societal organization, but what institutions have in common is that they provide the framework for interaction to occur and frequently organize existing norms into enduring patterns of behaviour. For example, consider what a simple contract or agreement between two people entails. Each person makes a commitment to the other (such as "I will pay you a certain amount of money each month to mow my lawn"). Even a simple contract like this includes a lot of institutional elements. There are longstanding societal norms about contracts: We are expected to live up to the terms that we agreed to (are we "a man [or woman] of our word"?). Fortunately, most of the time people do what they promise. But what happens when someone fails to live up to the agreement, even after a polite reminder? In the background of this seemingly simple contract lies a legal system and government policies that help to enforce a contract if someone fails to do what he or she promised. Let's say that I've paid you in advance to mow my lawn, but that for whatever reason you fail to mow it. In modern societies like Canada, I don't have to threaten violence or hire a thug to beat you up to get my money back. Instead, I can turn to institutions—such as the legal system—to get my money back. I can invoke laws that require you to live up to your end of the contract or return my money, laws that go back centuries and give me some assurance that if you fail to do what you promised, I will have some recourse to recover my losses (without resorting to violence). Indeed, the very existence of these laws provides powerful incentives for you to live up to your end of our agreement. And this is only a simple contract; imagine contracts involving two large corporations and billions of dollars! It is precisely because institutions are in place that contracts large and small can be entered into with confidence.

These two aspects of social structure—roles/hierarchies and norms/institutions—provide essential frameworks for almost everything we do in our daily lives. Most importantly, they inform each other—through our social interactions, we reinforce norms and institutions, and those norms and institutions shape and guide our interactions with others. In spite of their importance, however, social structures are rarely obvious to us. Because they lie in the background of our experience, we may not notice that they are there until we start to study them and try to become conscious of their existence. In many cases, social structures become visible when they limit our freedom in some way. Sometimes the rules, customs, laws, and regulations of society can prevent us from doing something we might do if we were completely free of all social structures. For example, if there were no laws or norms against cheating, it is certain that there would be vastly more of it than there is today (and *even* with a wide variety of restrictions, many people cheat in various ways anyway).

1.3 Where Did Sociology Come From, and How Is It Different From Other Social Sciences?

Dominic Harris/Alamy Stock Photo

The Sociology of the Social Sciences

We can apply the sociological imagination to study many topics, including sociology itself! To do so, we need to ask questions such as the following: In what context did sociology begin to develop? How does sociology fit into, and relate to, the other social sciences (and what are the controversies between them)? How is research conducted by sociologists different from research in other social sciences?

The Birth of Sociology

1.3.1 Discuss the origins of sociology as a discipline.

In general, sociology and other social sciences began to develop when growing numbers of people began to turn from abstract ideas or debates (like "democracy is good" or "racism is bad") to thinking about how things worked in the real world. But the sociological imagination was not built overnight. In fact, traces of sociological thinking can be found everywhere people talk or think about their communities or institutions, but those conversations through the ages did not by themselves provoke the deeper reflections that were a part of the rise of modern social sciences. The desire to answer hard questions about the human experience with something other than pure speculation lies at the heart of the modern sociological enterprise.

The development of a new way of questioning and seeking answers to issues and problems of the modern world unfolded in fits and starts throughout the nineteenth century, but the idea that the social world could be studied with rigour and scientific methods akin to those that had been applied to the natural world took hold from the 1880s onward.

The term *sociology* was first used by the French philosopher Auguste Comte (1798–1859) in 1839. Comte thought that sociology would eventually become the ultimate science of social life, with other disciplines contributing pieces that sociology would integrate into a coherent science of society. Comte envisioned that sociological science would entail both what he called "social statics" (the study of societies as they are) and "social dynamics" (the processes of social change) (Comte, 1839–1853/2009).

As the nineteenth century wore on, a variety of new ways of studying the social world began to emerge, just as Comte predicted. At first, however, the lines between the newly emerging social scientific disciplines were very fuzzy. Key early thinkers who contributed ideas that would be very influential in the development of sociology and social theory—such as Comte himself, Adam Smith (1723–1790), Karl Marx (1818–1883), and Harriet Martineau (1802–1876)—would not call or think of themselves as sociologists.

Between 1880 and 1910, however, the social sciences began to settle down into organized bodies of knowledge and develop distinctive disciplinary profiles. For sociology, this settling down first occurred in Europe—in France and Germany. The "father of sociology," Émile Durkheim (1858–1917), founded the first European sociology department at the University of Bordeaux in 1895 and the first major European journal of sociology (*L'Année Sociologique*) in 1898. In Germany, a group of early sociologists—among them Max Weber (1864–1920)—created an influential journal called the *Archiv für Sozialwissenschaft und Sozialpolitik* (*Archives for Social Science and Social Welfare*), establishing an identity for sociology as a discipline in that country.

Historical/Corbis

The Chicago School developed many important ideas about society based on detailed studies in the city of Chicago.

On the other side of the Atlantic, a distinctively American tradition of sociology emerged around the same time, centred at the Department of Sociology at the University of Chicago, which was founded in 1895 as the first sociology department in America. Frequently taking the city of Chicago as its laboratory, the so-called Chicago School intensively studied the problems of cities and the groups of people living in them, developing a body of knowledge that remains influential to this day. Sociology became a popular and widely acknowledged field of study from the 1920s onward, with an increasingly distinctive way of understanding social life. By the time C. Wright Mills wrote *The Sociological Imagination* in 1959, sociology was one of the five major social sciences (alongside economics, political science, psychology, and anthropology). Today, as we have noted earlier in the chapter, sociologists are engaged in the study of many key societal issues and controversies, working from universities as well as inside government agencies, in nonprofit and nongovernmental organizations, and in policy and political advocacy groups.

Sociology and the Industrial Revolution

1.3.2 Explain the roles of industrialization and urbanization in the development of sociology.

While some key thinkers such as Marx, Durkheim, and Weber helped to create a new body of knowledge, great thinkers and schools alone cannot explain what helps diverse ideas come together to create a disciplined body of knowledge. As with individual lives, so too does sociology have a "social context" that shaped its growth and development. What was the social context that made people interested in this new kind of knowledge? Two critical developments spurred the social sciences in general and sociology in particular: the very rapid period of **industrialization** (the growth of factories and large-scale goods production) and increasing **urbanization** (the growth of cities) in the late nineteenth century in the United States, Europe, and elsewhere. This was a period when new technologies and innovations made possible the growth of large-scale manufacturing of consumer products, transforming economies based primarily in agriculture to those based in the manufacturing of goods. The spread of factory labour in this period of industrialization created jobs that were concentrated in **urban areas**, which are defined by Statistics Canada as those with a population of at least 1,000 and a population density of at least 400 people per square kilometre. (The U.S. Census Bureau defines urban areas as those with 1,000 people per square mile and with surrounding areas that have a density of at least 500 people per square mile.) This period of urbanization was marked by growth in the proportion of the population living in urban areas and cities—which grew rapidly in size between 1850 and 1920 in both Europe and the United States. Figure 1.3 illustrates the growth of cities and surrounding metropolitan areas in the United States during this period.

The jobs driving this growth pulled people away from farms and rural communities and provided economic opportunities for wave after wave of immigrants from other countries, who arrived in steadily increasing numbers from the 1870s until the early 1920s and continued to immigrate to North America into the 1960s.

The social changes enabled by industrialization were immense. The contexts of both individual lives and whole communities were changing rapidly. It was clear that the natural and biological sciences seemed unable to fully explain what was occurring. While chemistry and physics proved enormously useful in providing the basis for new industrial processes and could be drawn upon to explain the physical effects of the pollution spewing from the newly constructed industrial landscape, they could offer little insight into how working for wages in factories was changing the most basic human relations and group identifications. The exploding cities that developed in the United States and Europe from the middle of the nineteenth century onward were teeming with deep problems that were markedly different from those of the agricultural economies of previous centuries. To begin with, these cities were rife with high levels of poverty. The early factories paid poorly, and living in the expanding cities was often expensive, as the housing supply struggled to keep up with demand. Cities were dirty places—this was before public health and public sanitation measures had become widely implemented—and they were breeding grounds for disease, infant mortality, and early death. They were also places where crime and violence were much more common than in rural communities. Finally, they were places where

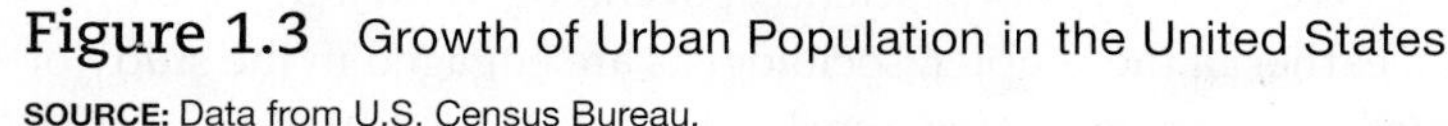

Figure 1.3 Growth of Urban Population in the United States

SOURCE: Data from U.S. Census Bureau.

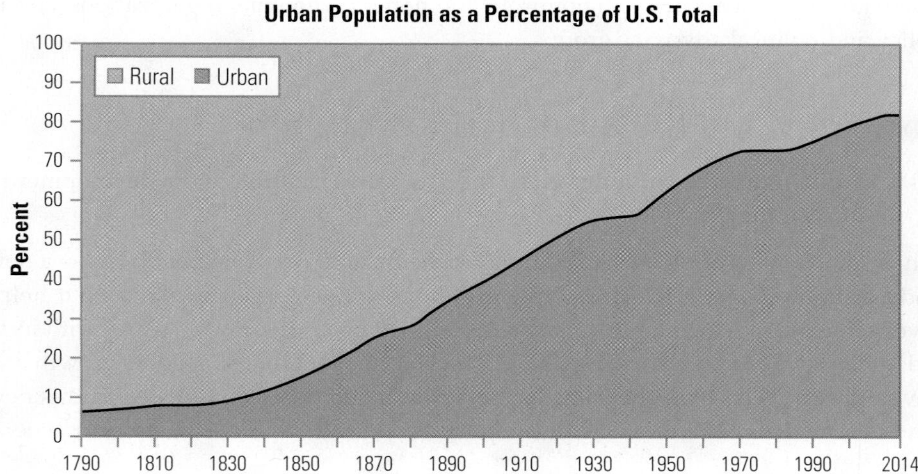

people could organize themselves to protest unpleasant conditions of life. Instead of tolerating misery alone on one's farm, now it was possible to meet and discuss problems with dozens or hundreds of people in close proximity.

In the face of these new conditions and challenges, sociology found its place as part of a broader effort to understand the sources of these emerging social challenges. Of course, sociology was not the only academic discipline to emerge from this period of social change; the other social sciences also emerged around the same time, in the late nineteenth and early twentieth centuries, and all were growing concurrent with the rise of another context—the modern research university.

Sociology's Siblings

1.3.3 Compare and contrast sociology with the other social sciences.

While all the social sciences were born from a similar impulse to understand the emerging social worlds spawned by industrialization and urban growth, there was considerable disagreement over where to go from that common starting point. So how did sociology come to differ from other social sciences? What is the nature of the sibling rivalry between them? We would point to two fundamental distinctions:

1. Sociology's concepts and theories cover a wider range of topics than other disciplines—sociologists are promiscuous in what they study.
2. Sociology's explanations of how the external world shapes the behaviours of individuals and social outcomes are broader than those of other disciplines and encompass different units of analysis. Sociologists move *from individuals to groups to institutions to global society*. Sociology is the social science discipline that is most concerned about how different parts of society link up to and mutually influence one another.

Of course, the danger in working with such a broad spectrum of topics is that it can be hard to define the parameters of sociology. As professional sociologists, the authors of this chapter are often asked this question: What exactly *is* sociology? Sometimes even professional sociologists struggle to give a short, simple answer. Unlike other social scientists, sociologists don't define themselves according to a specific arena of life. For the most part, other social scientists do. Political scientists are primarily concerned with topics that involve governments and the policies they produce. Economists are mainly concerned with individuals' economic behaviour (microeconomics) and the performance of the national (or global) economy (macroeconomics). Psychologists are interested in understanding the workings of the human mind. Anthropologists claim expertise in the practices of diverse cultures and how they vary across time and place.

Sociology cannot be categorized in the way that other social sciences often are. Sociologists can and do move into all of the areas that are the "home turf" of the other social sciences. As our name indicates, sociologists claim scientific expertise over those parts of life we call the "social" and in topics with social significance. But the "social" is a bit fuzzier as a topic and area of expertise than those studied by other disciplines. That is, most people can roughly grasp what a political scientist means when he or she studies "government" or what an economist does when researching "the economy." But sociologists often get perplexed looks when we say we study the "social world." It took one of our grandmothers 20 years to stop telling her friends that her granddaughter was a professor of "socialism" (rather than sociology). For her, this was a concrete way to make sense of the social and to translate it into something meaningful (and also a bit scary, as she was a staunch Republican!). So while sociologists' refusal to break up the world into small, narrow slices and proclaim expertise over them does cause confusion, most sociologists would have it no other way.

So how does the broad agenda of sociologists compare with other disciplines? Consider the difference between sociology and psychology. Psychology is centred on the study of the mind, the psyche, and the physical brain. Sociologists have much to learn from psychological findings, some of which we've already mentioned in this chapter. At the same time, sociologists part company with many traditional psychologists in insisting that individuals (and their minds and psyches) must also always be located in larger social contexts that are much broader than simply the family. For sociologists, it is not enough to explain individual behaviour by simply understanding the intricacies of the psyche or the cognitive processes common to all humans. Because individuals are embedded in families and communities, as well as cultural, economic, and political environments, sociologists consider human behaviour to be caused by something more than just what individual brains tell us to do. To explain why individuals do what they do, in other words, social contexts must also come into view.

A similar gap separates sociology from economics. Economists pride themselves on building and testing models of economic behaviour using clear and simple assumptions about human nature (e.g., that everything being equal, we will always act in ways that we think will enhance our self-interest and financial well-being). Their ideas, and the mathematical models of human behaviour they develop, are often elegant and lead to clear predictions that can be tested by researchers. Sociologists, by contrast, tend to believe that for all of their impressive advances, economists sometimes miss important outcomes because they don't consider a wide enough range of factors and forces affecting human behaviour. Sociologists argue that there are many things motivating individuals—altruism, self-interest, reputations, and status as well as money. While sociological theories tend to be messier and more difficult to test than many economic theories, they can also produce a wider range of possible explanations that, when successful, can produce genuinely new understandings.

Sibling rivalry aside, most social scientists today end up drawing on the ideas and insights of other fields and disciplines as well as their own. After more than a century of building their own disciplines and professional associations, in recent years the disciplines have moved to once again blur the boundaries between them. **Interdisciplinary research**, as it is known, is an increasingly central part of learning about any topic in sociology or the social sciences. Few students and scholars in any social science would be foolish enough not to draw on ideas and research from neighbouring social sciences. And sociology is perhaps the most likely to do so—it is the most interdisciplinary of all the traditional social science disciplines. Depending on the question at hand, sociologists may need to know something about the research and theories developed by economists, political scientists, psychologists, or anthropologists. We also often draw on the work of historians—a discipline that is traditionally placed in the humanities but is closely related to the social sciences and to sociology in particular. Although our main interest in this text is introducing you to sociological insights and approaches, we would certainly *not* want to leave the impression that sociology by itself has all the answers to all the questions that social scientists raise. It does not.

Sociology's Children

1.3.4 Identify some of the spin-off fields that originally started in sociology.

One interesting side note on the relationship between sociology and the other social sciences is the way in which sociology has helped to spawn a number of new areas of study. In most universities today, there are many spin-off majors and programs that largely began in sociology. This list includes such fields as criminology, gender studies, African American studies, Latino/a studies, gay/lesbian studies, urban/rural studies, organizational or management studies, industrial relations or labour studies, demography, and communication/media studies. There was once a time when much of the research and scholarship on these topics was done within sociology. But for various reasons, these subfields would eventually split off from sociology to become independent fields of study of their own (and develop their own knowledge bases and professional associations). It is, indeed, quite remarkable just how many spin-off fields originally started (at least in part) in sociology, a record of innovation and intellectual diversity of which sociologists can be proud.

It is clear that sociology has long served as an important incubator for new arenas of investigation. Even today, there are exciting new areas of study in sociology that may eventually grow into disciplines of their own. At its core, however, sociology will remain a foundational discipline for many of these interdisciplinary social sciences. And in this sense, learning the basics of sociology is an essential foundation for any one of these newer fields.

Conclusion: Looking Ahead

Our goal for this text is to provide enough background on the key areas and findings of sociological research to provide our readers with the foundation for developing your own sociological imagination. By understanding how individuals' lives are embedded in particular social contexts that are not always of their own choosing, we hope, you will learn to appreciate how personal issues that individuals face often can also be understood as larger social problems facing society.

The authors of each of the chapters in this book are writing about the topics that they do research in and teach. We believe that a collective approach to presenting the discipline of sociology provides a better way of unearthing and exciting our readers' sociological imaginations. In the course of thinking about (and teaching) the topics we are writing about, we have developed deep appreciation for the complexities, but also the excitement, of our respective topics that we hope to convey in the chapters that follow.

In order to create a unified text, we've taken a number of steps to make it easier for our readers to move from chapter to chapter. Each chapter opens with a puzzle or story that highlights one or more of the key sociological problems that will be tackled in the chapter. Following this, each chapter identifies a set of big questions that have defined the research and teaching puzzles of the field. These questions organize what follows as the authors explore how sociological thinking about each question has developed. At all points, some basic facts and data are helpful to have in hand, but at the same time we want our readers to learn to think sociologically through learning how to ask hard questions and where to look for answers.

In short, we want to stress that this text—and indeed sociology as a discipline—truly is a *project:* something we are collectively engaged in building and something for which there are relatively few completely settled answers. The problems confronted by sociologists are hard questions because there are so many things that influence individuals and group life. This is what makes sociology endlessly interesting and a sociological imagination very much worth acquiring.

CHAPTER SUMMARY

The Big Questions Revisited 1

1.1 What Is the Sociological Imagination, and Why Is It Worth Acquiring? This section introduced the concept of the sociological imagination and explored how it helps us learn to ask hard questions.

The Sociological Imagination

Looking Through a Sociological Lens

Learning Objective 1.1.1: Discuss how a sociological imagination helps to challenge stereotypes.

Engaging Our Sociological Imaginations: From Personal Puzzles to Sociological Questions

Learning Objective 1.1.2: Explain the process for forming sociological questions.

Sociological Questions: A Detailed Example

Learning Objective 1.1.3: Identify the types of questions that sociologists are particularly well equipped to explore.

The Endless Reach of the Sociological Imagination

Learning Objective 1.1.4: Discuss the wide range of topics and areas of life that sociologists study.

1.2 **What Are Social Contexts, and Why Do They Matter?** Sociology is fundamentally concerned with how we are influenced by society. All of us are situated in an array of social contexts. This section explored how these influence us and our behaviour.

Social Contexts: From Individuals to Societies

Families and Communities

Learning Objective 1.2.1: Analyze how families and communities shape the social development of children.

Identities and Groups

Learning Objective 1.2.2: Explain how our identities impact our opportunities in life.

Schools and Organizations

Learning Objective 1.2.3: Discuss how the schools and organizations we participate in shape our lives and identities.

Social and Historical Contexts

Learning Objective 1.2.4: Analyze the ways in which the social and economic context we are born into shapes the opportunities available to us.

Sociology as the Study of Social Contexts

Learning Objective 1.2.5: Explain the distinction between social interaction and social structure.

1.3 **Where Did Sociology Come From, and How Is It Different From Other Social Sciences?** This section examined the context in which sociology began to develop and explored the question of how sociology fits into, and relates to, the other social sciences.

The Sociology of the Social Sciences

The Birth of Sociology

Learning Objective 1.3.1: Discuss the origins of sociology as a discipline.

Sociology and the Industrial Revolution

Learning Objective 1.3.2: Explain the roles of industrialization and urbanization in the development of sociology.

Sociology's Siblings

Learning Objective 1.3.3: Compare and contrast sociology with the other social sciences.

Sociology's Children

Learning Objective 1.3.4: Identify some of the spin-off fields that originally started in sociology.

Learn the Terms

identity (p. 12)
industrialization (p. 18)
institution (p. 15)
interdisciplinary research (p. 20)
norm (p. 14)
social context (p. 10)
social hierarchy (p. 15)
social interaction (p. 14)
social network (p. 2)
social structure (p. 14)
society (p. 3)
sociological imagination (p. 4)
sociology (p. 3)
stereotype (p. 5)
urban area (p. 18)
urbanization (p. 18)

Chapter 2

Social Theory

by Jeff Manza, Thomas Ertman, Lynne Haney, and Steven Lukes*

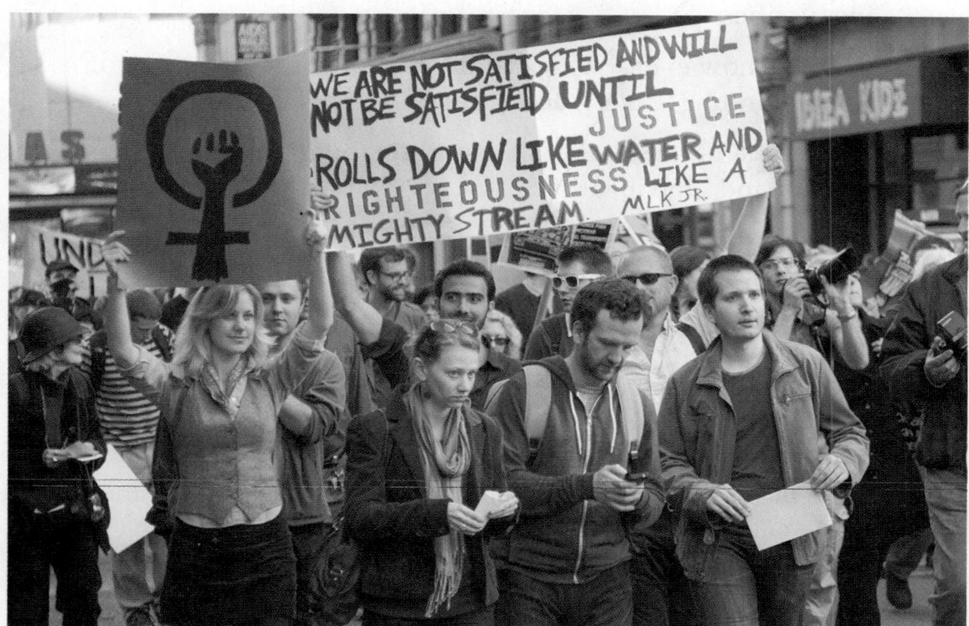

David Grossman/Alamy Stock Photo

Understanding the circumstances or conditions under which societies change is one of the three common themes that all of the major sociological theories have sought to address in one way or another.

Learning Objectives

2.1.1 Define *social theory* and describe the range of different social theories.

2.1.2 Identify the three common themes that all of the major sociological theories have sought to address.

2.2.1 Discuss why Marx believed that societies were so heavily shaped by their economic systems.

2.2.2 Analyze Emile Durkheim's explanation of what holds societies together.

2.2.3 Discuss Max Weber's contributions to our understanding of motivations for behaviour, legitimacy and authority, and status groups and social closure.

* An earlier version of this chapter was co-authored by Harel Shapira.

2.2.4 Explain how Georg Simmel's insights on social circles and social distance help us understand how individuals and groups relate to one another.

2.2.5 Explain W. E. B. Du Bois's views of the diverse ways in which racism influences the lives of African Americans and how racism produces a double consciousness.

2.3.1 Discuss the roles that norms, values, and institutions play in society, according to the theory of structural functionalism.

2.3.2 Discuss how conflict theory attempted to explain social inequalities.

2.3.3 Analyze how everyday social interaction lies at the heart of understanding society, according to symbolic interactionism.

2.4.1 Discuss neo-Marxist ideas about the capitalist state, social classes, and globalization.

2.4.2 Analyze the role of intersectionality in theories of gender inequality.

2.4.3 Explain Foucault's theory of how power operates in society.

2.4.4 Discuss how Bourdieu redefined classes and the nature of class differences.

At the heart of the sociological imagination are the theories about society that give us tools to know what to look for and think about when we seek to understand the social world. The inspiration to develop ideas into social theories can come from a wide variety of sources. One of the authors of this chapter, Steven Lukes, recounts how he was motivated to think about classical questions in social theory.

It was during a dinner conversation in Buenos Aires at the height of what was known as Argentina's "Dirty War" in the mid-1970s that I became motivated to think about morality and power. During this time thousands of people—among them trade unionists, journalists, and students—"disappeared" by orders of the Argentinean military government; that is, they were tortured and killed, often in clandestine detention centres, or in some cases simply dropped from planes into the sea. Powerful rulers and governments have resorted to torturing and killing their opponents as a way of holding on to power for centuries. When I voiced concern over what I then knew of these atrocities, my dinner companion—who was the local head of one of the world's leading news agencies—astonished me with his response. I should understand, he explained to me, that in Argentina a lower value was set on life than in Britain, from which I came.

My astonishment led me to a few questions with implications for approaching issues sociologically. In my simple disbelief of his factual claim, I first wondered on what evidence it was based. My second question was what motivated him to make this sweeping claim. As a journalist, whose task was to give an unbiased account of the local scene to the world, he seemed to be drawing on personal impressions and stereotyping prejudices. Yet he also seemed to want to offer an impartial and comparative perspective to an overheated and ill-informed visitor.

While this is not, I hasten to say, a story about good journalism, it does raise the question of what corrective procedures sociology, as distinct from journalism, can bring to overcome bias and approach objectivity in marshaling evidence. That question is general, but it is especially intriguing where values are what is at issue, for we know that what people value is shaped by societal contexts and can vary from one context to another or one culture to another. While Argentineans surely have many distinctive attitudes and customs, it was hard to imagine that caring less about their own lives was one of these. What can sociology contribute to assessing which values are variable and which are constant across contexts and cultures? We know, of course, that suicide bombers do sacrifice their lives, but to notice that is to raise the larger question of the power of ideology and the sociological task of identifying the conditions under which it can motivate individuals to such extreme behavior.

Eduardo Di Baia/AP Images

Hebe de Bonafini, the head of Argentina's Mothers of Plaza de Mayo group, whose children disappeared during the dirty war of the 1970s, leads one of the marches in Buenos Aires's Plaza de Mayo in December 1979.

Moreover, it was striking that my journalist companion avoided all mention of power relations—understandably enough, for we were in a restaurant and could be overheard. The context in Argentina at that time was, of course, extreme: a context of terror and coercion, of censorship and self-censorship, where journalists and others bit their tongues and went along with the status quo. How do we ever know what part those in power play in shaping our values, beliefs, and preferences? Sometimes what is extreme can shed light on the normal and the routine. In Argentina, the impact of those in power on ordinary lives was all too visible, if unmentioned over dinner. But how is the sociologist to investigate the less overt and more hidden operations of power in normal times and places?

The memory of this striking conversation stayed with me and played an important role in turning my attention to social theories of morality and theories about the relationship between morality and power.

Lukes's inspiration to think about how sociology could understand moral thinking exemplifies the kinds of challenges that social theorists face as they attempt to provide frameworks for understanding societies. In this chapter, we explore some of the most influential of these theories that have developed over the past 150 years.

The Big Questions

In this chapter, we explore social theory by examining four central questions:

1. **What is social theory?** Social theories enable us to see the social world in different ways. In this section, we identify three common themes that all of the major sociological theories have sought to address.
2. **How did the early social theorists make sense of the world?** The foundations of modern sociology, and social theory as we know it today, can be traced to the writings of a handful of key thinkers working in the second half of the nineteenth century and the early twentieth century. In this section, we introduce the classical social theories of Karl Marx, Emile Durkheim, Max Weber, Georg Simmel, and W. E. B. Du Bois.

3. **What innovations in social theory emerged in the mid-twentieth century?** After World War II, the interests of social theorists began to shift in new and unexpected directions, and leadership in the development of social theory and sociology as a whole passed from being located primarily in Europe to America. Here, we introduce the new directions in social theory that were embodied by functionalism, conflict theory, and symbolic interactionism.
4. **How has a new generation of social theory evolved?** Finally, we provide a brief sampling of some important new theories that have evolved since the 1960s. How have contemporary theorists built upon or transformed the work of classical and mid-twentieth century social theory?

2.1 What Is Social Theory?

Wu Kaixiang/Newscom

Seeing the Social World through Social Theory

Learning social theory is a little like putting on a pair of 3D glasses or night-vision goggles: *Theories*, like specialized glasses, enable us to see things in a different way. Theories guide, but they also provoke: They may encourage us to pay more attention to something we had ignored, ask new or unusual questions that we don't normally think about, or make arguments we so strongly disagree with that we are compelled to come up with a better approach. We don't necessarily need social theories to make observations about the world around us, but they help us know what to look for.

The ambitions of social theorists are considerable, often nothing less than providing a way to understand how societies hold together and how they organize and impact the lives of the individuals who live within them. The best and most lasting social theories have changed the way we understand societies, and the relationships between individuals within those societies, in fundamental ways. In this sense, social theory is central to the sociological imagination.

The Diversity of Social Theory

2.1.1 Define *social theory* and describe the range of different social theories.

Social theories are systematic ideas about the relationship between individuals and societies. To put it another way, they are analytical frameworks for understanding the social world. This definition is not, unfortunately, very helpful, because there is a wide variety of different kinds of social theories. Some can be very grand—seeking to explain universal features of all societies—while others are much more modest, applying only to a single topic that sociologists study, such as theories about race, gender, or religion.

Sociology is also somewhat unusual among the social sciences in having multiple and often competing social theories and theoretical traditions. By contrast, economics, for example, has long had a single dominant theoretical system that all economists (and economics students) must master. The multiplicity of theoretical traditions in sociology can be confusing at first. While it does take some effort to sort out the competing ideas and how they relate to one another, we hope to show in this chapter that there are rewards to this effort as well. In spite of the abundance of competing theoretical traditions, there is also a great deal of dialogue among theorists and theoretical traditions, and most contemporary sociologists draw from more than one tradition in their work. In this chapter, we will emphasize both the key distinctions and the vital connections as we introduce the most influential of the social theories that have appeared in the past 150 years.

Three Common Themes

2.1.2 Identify the three common themes that all of the major sociological theories have sought to address.

In spite of the diversity of social theory, there are three common themes that all of the major sociological theories have sought to address in one way or another, as illustrated in Figure 2.1 (see also Joas & Knobl, 2009, p. 18).

Figure 2.1 Three Common Themes

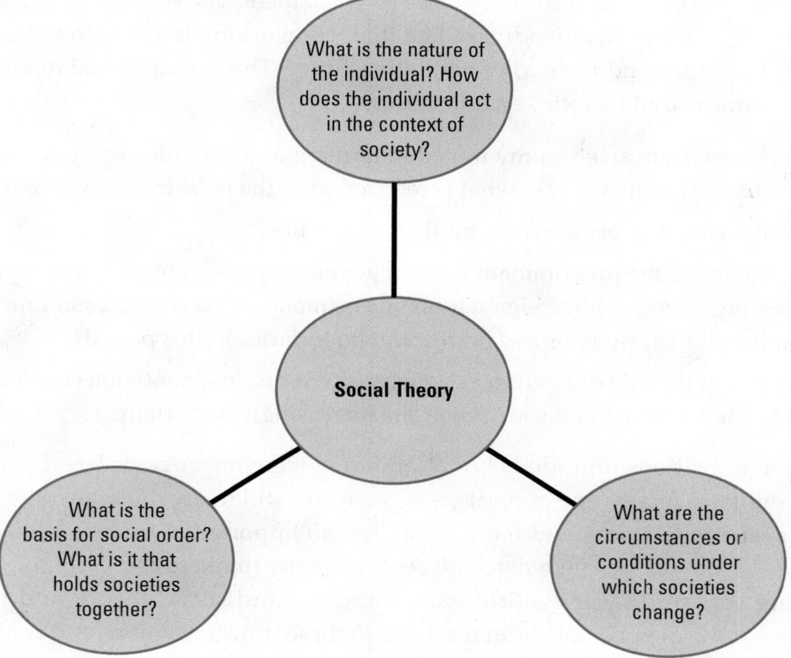
What is the nature of the individual? How does the individual act in the context of society?
Social Theory
What is the basis for social order? What is it that holds societies together?
What are the circumstances or conditions under which societies change?

Although the answers the major theoretical traditions we explore in this chapter give to these questions will vary, these three questions define the central challenges all social theories (and theorists) face.

2.2 How Did the Early Social Theorists Make Sense of the World?

Classic Image/Alamy Stock Photo

Classical Social Theory In the Late Nineteenth and Early Twentieth Centuries

The foundations of modern sociology, and of social theory as we know it today, can be traced to the writings of a handful of key thinkers working in the second half of the nineteenth century and the early twentieth century. This was a period of enormous change, characterized by four key transitions:

1. The change from an economy rooted in farming and agriculture to one based on industry and factory work (what is referred to as the *Industrial Revolution*).
2. The movement of people from rural areas to cities.
3. The change of the predominant form of government from monarchies to democracies, organized as sovereign nation-states (many of the countries in Europe established their more or less permanent boundaries in this period).
4. Changes in the role of religion in society, with a decline in religious influence on public life as nonreligious ideas became increasingly important.

These transitions unfolded slowly, and they were never complete. Even today, people still farm, many live in rural areas, there are still many undemocratic governments (even monarchies), and religion still has an important influence in many societies. But already in the late nineteenth century, many thinkers and early social scientists were sensing that the world was changing, and social theory and the new discipline of sociology emerged in response to these transformations and the sense of crisis they evoked.

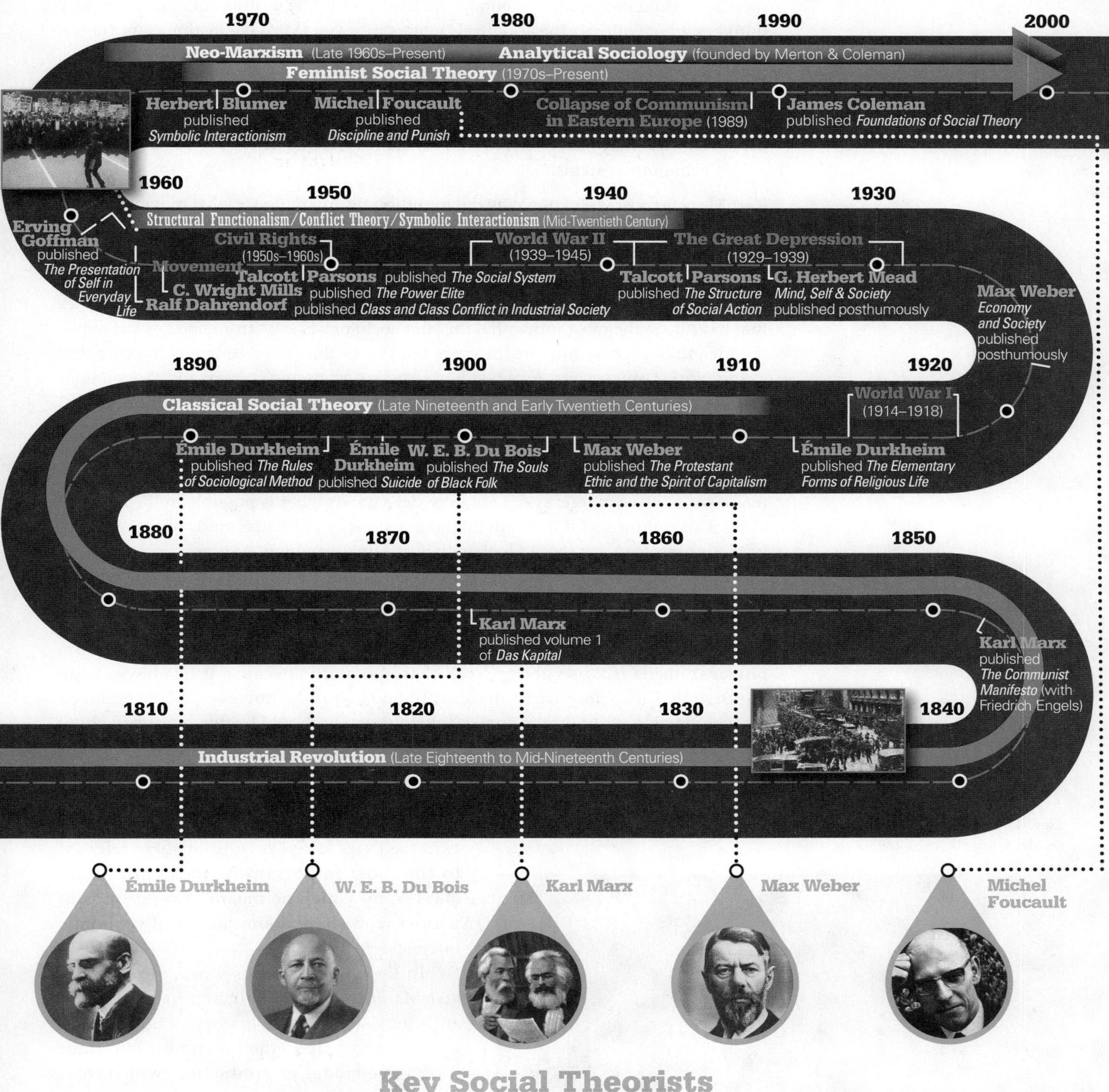

Key Social Theorists

Karl Marx (1818–1883)	**Georg Simmel** (1858–1918)	**Ralf Dahrendorf** (1929–2009)	**Erving Goffman** (1922–1982)	**James Coleman** (1926–1995)
Émile Durkheim (1858–1917)	**W. E. B. Du Bois** (1868–1963)	**George Herbert Mead** (1863–1931)	**Michel Foucault** (1926–1984)	
Max Weber (1864–1920)	**Talcott Parsons** (1902–1979)	**Herbert Blumer** (1900–1987)	**Robert Merton** (1910–2002)	

We begin our discussion of classical social theory with the writings of Karl Marx, who posed each of the three questions central to social theory in a way that many later theorists would debate and elaborate. We then turn to the writings of four other early thinkers who explored these central themes in ways that have lasting importance: Emile Durkheim, Max Weber, Georg Simmel, and W. E. B. Du Bois.

Karl Marx (1818–1883)

2.2.1 Discuss why Marx believed that societies were so heavily shaped by their economic systems.

Karl Marx is most well known as the founding figure of the socialist movement. But his theoretical and sociological writings (often written in collaboration with his friend and lifelong intellectual collaborator Friedrich Engels [1820–1895]) also ignited great debate within the discipline of sociology, and many early sociologists and theorists developed their own thinking in critical reaction to Marx. The writings of Marx that have been the most influential for later sociologists start from one key principle: the idea that the way humans produce the things they need to live is the essential foundation of any society. As a result, a society's economic system, and the relationships it creates between individuals and groups, is the defining feature of how that society works.

Because of the centrality of a society's economic system, Marx argued, human history is best understood through the history of different economic systems. He believed that a society's economic system largely determines what is possible in the realm of politics and culture, so if we want to understand why particular kinds of social or cultural ideas emerge, we should look to that society's economic system.

Why did Marx think that societies were so heavily shaped by their economic systems? His argument starts from the observation that all societies, except the simplest hunting and gathering societies, produce an economic surplus. That is, they collectively produce more goods than are required to meet their minimum physical needs *if* those goods were shared equally. Because it has never been the case that a society truly shares all goods equally, however, Marx believed that the starting point for the analysis of any society should be two questions about inequality: First, who takes possession of this surplus? And second, what means do they use to do so? Because control over the surplus gives some members of any society extra rewards not shared by everyone else, Marx suggested that in any society's economic system tensions exist between groups that give rise to conflicts and in extreme cases social revolutions. He referred to the most important of these groups as **classes**, by which he meant those groups of people who share a similar set of economic interests.

Karl Marx (1818–1865), right, and Friedrich Engels (1820–1895), left.

Interfoto/Alamy Stock Photo

In their most famous work, *The Communist Manifesto*, first published in 1848, Marx and Engels divide the history of all societies from antiquity up to their own time into three distinctive **modes of production**, which characterize the dominant economic system in a society and the classes that the economic system gives rise to: *ancient societies* based on slavery; *feudalism,* which was characterized by largely agrarian societies with a tiny group of landowners; and *capitalism,* economies organized around market-based exchange (Marx & Engels, 1848/2011).

Figure 2.2 Marx's Model of Society: Components of a Mode of Production

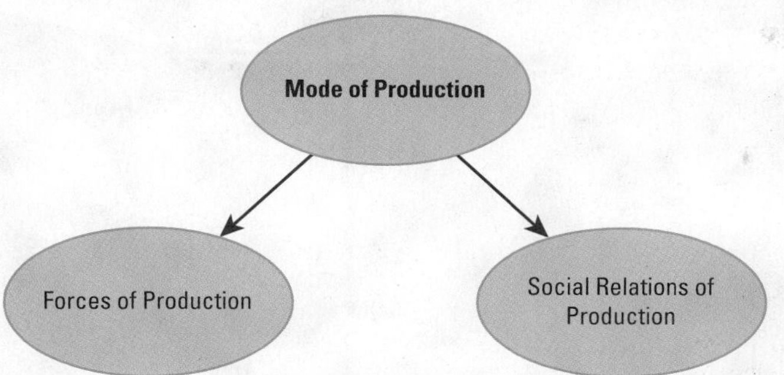

Each of these modes of production consists of two parts—what Marx calls the **forces of production**, or the technological and productive capacity of any society at a given point in time, and the **social relations of production**, which are the relationships and inequalities between different kinds of people within the economy. The forces of production can be thought of as all of the different tools people use to make things, while the relations of production are how people are organized to carry out the tasks needed to produce those things (see Figure 2.2).

Because of the overall importance of the economy in society, Marx thought that the mode of production would shape or even determine what kinds of laws and government systems were possible, as well as the kinds of ideas that people have about politics and society (Marx, 1859/1978).

Marx's analysis of the capitalist mode of production in his magnum opus, *Das Kapital* (Marx, 1867/1976) is the starting point for his analysis of modern societies, as Marx rightly anticipated that capitalism would soon become the dominant economic system around the world. At the heart of capitalist societies, Marx believed, lies the central conflict between members of two classes: the **bourgeoisie**, who possess special resources called **capital**—money or other assets that can be used for business investments—and everyone else. Possession of capital is the critical dividing line between the bourgeoisie, who can use their capital to hire other people to work for them, and the working class, or **proletariat**. Because members of the proletariat own no capital, Marx noted that they must seek paid employment in order to meet their basic needs. Marx also acknowledged that other social groups such as shopkeepers, craftsmen, and farmers occupied a space between elite capitalists and workers. However, because larger enterprises can produce more cheaply than smaller ones, Marx predicted that these intermediate groups would shrink as small producers were driven into bankruptcy and forced to join the ranks of the proletariat. Modern capitalist societies, he thought, would increasingly be polarized between a very small bourgeoisie and an increasingly large working class.

While any mode of production can sustain itself for an extended period, even centuries, Marx thought that eventually every mode of production becomes stagnant and falls into crisis, and when this happens a social revolution is likely to occur, leading to the establishment of a new mode of production. Marx argued that, in order for capitalism to arise, all of the hereditary privileges of landlords, including rules that allowed them to control the lives of agricultural workers, had to be destroyed. This revolutionary change was brought about, according to Marx, by a rising class of capitalists who demanded economic freedoms that did not exist under feudalism. Eventually, just as capitalists overthrew feudalism to create a new and dynamic economic system, Marx thought that the proletariat would create a revolution that would overthrow capitalism in favour of a **socialist society**, in which the productive forces of society are owned by everyone (not by individual business owners). They would be motivated to do so, Marx thought, because over time

Lou Linwei/Alamy Stock Photo

A factory in Zhejiang, China. Marx and Engels would not have been surprised that the Chinese economy has grown rapidly after the introduction of free-market capitalism since the late 1970s.

capitalists, in order to maintain or increase their profit, would be driven to push down the wages of workers until those workers would finally revolt. This theory is known as the theory of **class struggle**, and it is based on the idea that classes of people who are treated so differently by the economic system are inevitably going to be in conflict with one another.

The world in which we live today, especially after the collapse of communism in the Soviet Union and most other communist countries since 1989, seems far removed from what Marx envisioned. If anything, capitalism seems more entrenched than ever. But capitalism has also changed in ways that Marx and Engels did not anticipate in their writings in the nineteenth century. Capitalist societies, especially in the richer parts of the world, have developed large government-funded and -operated social programs such as social security, unemployment insurance, free or low-cost health insurance, and educational systems designed to reduce poverty and inequality even in the context of thriving capitalist economies. These economic systems have grown far more diverse, and proven far more versatile, than Marx envisioned. Marx also underestimated the willingness of capitalists to pay workers decent wages, especially when they need to recruit workers with valuable skills or keep workers satisfied. Instead of things getting steadily worse for workers, living standards have steadily risen from the nineteenth century onward.

Yet in two respects Marx's model of society and social change seems very relevant today. First, the German thinker was an early theorist of what we now call *globalization*: He and Engels anticipated the spread of the capitalist economy to the entire world in the late 1840s, a revolutionary idea at the time, and one that proved remarkably insightful in light of later developments. And the analytical tools of his social theory do provide one way of understanding the role of economic exchange in fostering globalization. Second, the failure of socialism in places like Russia and Eastern Europe, which would seem to contradict Marx's assumptions, can actually be viewed as conforming very well to what Marx himself predicted. One of Marx's most fundamental claims is that capitalism is capable of building up tremendous productive capacity, and in that way creates the conditions for socialism to become viable. Socialist leaders (in countries like Russia and China) like Lenin and Mao attempted to skip this crucial stage of development by moving from what Marx would define as a feudal mode of production directly to socialism. This proved to be impossible, and in responding to these failures leaders in these countries eventually resorted to reintroducing capitalism (as Marx might well have predicted). The resulting expansion of economic activity that the turn to capitalism has created, especially in China, has been impressive. If he were alive today, rather than seeing the failure of Communism as a repudiation of his idea, Marx would say that the true socialist revolution still lies ahead for countries like Russia and China, but only after they go through a long period of capitalist growth and development.

akg-images/Newscom

Emile Durkheim (1858–1917).

Emile Durkheim (1858–1917)

2.2.2 Analyze Emile Durkheim's explanation of what holds societies together.

The French sociologist Emile Durkheim is properly regarded as one of the founding fathers of the discipline of sociology. Like Marx, Durkheim sought to try to understand the changes taking place around him during a period of extraordinary growth and change in the late nineteenth and early twentieth centuries. Durkheim wondered how societies would continue to function in the face of these changes. Durkheim believed that the sociologist was responsible for answering these questions, almost like a doctor treating a patient—the sociologist's patient was society, and the sickness that needed to be cured was the various forms of social disorder that rapid industrialization was producing. Durkheim's contributions were many, but we will focus on three: his development of the concept of the social fact, his analysis of the roots of social solidarity, and his analysis of religion as a force in modern life.

In *The Rules of Sociological Method* (Durkheim, 1895/1982), Durkheim made a case for the need for sociology by comparing it to the sciences of biology and physics. He argued that just like biology or physics, sociology examines a force in the world that is objective and exists independent of our ability to control it. For example, just as gravity is a force that exists external to us and is not made by us, so too do social forces exist objectively in the world. We cannot defy gravity (at least not easily), but we also cannot usually defy what Durkheim (1895/1982) referred to as **social facts**—those regularities and rules of everyday life that every human community has.

Shortly after Durkheim defined the social fact, sociologists and other social scientists began to refer to them as **social forces** rather than social facts. The term *social forces* connotes something broader than what Durkheim originally meant by *social fact*, but the two are largely interchangeable. Social facts, or social forces, are "social" in the sense that they arise from human action at some point in the past, and they are "facts" or "forces" in the sense that we are born into a world where there are many rules and customs (sometimes written down, but often not) that we are obliged to obey if we are to fit in to our community and successfully interact with others.

Various everyday practices appear to us as completely natural, yet they are the result of societal forces. Marriage, for example, is both expected and valued in most societies.

elitravo/Shutterstock

How do these social forces work? In asking this question, Durkheim was on to something that would become the foundation of nearly all social theories that would follow: human behaviour is not natural but learned; in other words, we are trained, or socialized, to act the ways that we do. And for Durkheim, one of the key things involved is the **socialization** process, the way we learn how to behave in society (and all of the different situations we encounter). Among the most important of all social forces that act upon us are norms. Norms are like physical walls in constraining our actions. We may want to do something like taking an extra piece of pie, for example, but a norm against appearing to eat like a pig may stand in our way. One of the ways that we know norms exist is what happens when we violate them. Consider what happens when you break a social norm—such as talking on your phone during a movie. There will likely be a negative reaction from the other movie goers, most likely in the form of a *shush* or, if that fails, having some popcorn thrown at you or perhaps even having a security guard come and warn you. Whatever form it takes, external pressures will be exerted to stop our (poor) behaviour (in this case, directing us to turn off the phone and sit quietly).

The idea that social forces are important for their influence on individual behaviour was put to the test in Durkheim's next book, *Suicide* (Durkheim, 1897/1997), which was not only a classic demonstration of the power of sociological analysis but also a landmark in the integration of social theory and empirical research. At first glance, the act of ending one's own life appears to be the most private act imaginable, rooted in the unique details of an individual's personal life or psyche. Yet by stepping back and carefully analyzing the statistics on who commits suicide—such as variations in the suicide rate between countries, or annual and regional fluctuations of suicides within the same country—Durkheim concluded that the probability that a certain number of people will kill themselves at a given time and place is in fact very much influenced by social factors (such as religious beliefs, marital status, the country you live in, whether or not a war is being fought, and an individual's educational level).

Durkheim's insights about social forces impacting the likelihood of suicide will not help us to explain, let alone accept, a suicide committed by a friend or family member. But they do underline in striking fashion a broader truth, namely that we as individuals are embedded in a larger social world, and our likelihood of committing suicide is not entirely random.

Related to the question of the impact of social forces is one of the critical questions that occupied Durkheim throughout his career: What is it that holds societies together? This is the problem of what Durkheim called **social solidarity** (Durkheim, 1890/1997). In particular, he wondered where the shared morals and connections betw-een individuals come from. Durkheim drew a contrast between two distinct forms of social solidarity—mechanical and organic solidarity—each of which is connected with different kinds of shared morals reflecting the different kinds of societies in which they arise. **Mechanical solidarity** is the dominant form of solidarity in what Durk- heim called "primitive" societies, which are built around extended families or clans linked horizontally into tribes, such as the Iroquois or the Apache. They are characterized by a very minimal **division of labour** (or

David Keith Jones/Alamy Stock Photo

Durkheim's ideas about primitive, or tribal, societies (where he thought there was little room for individuality) were contrasted with modern societies where diversity is common. Both types of societies face the problem of creating social solidarity but do it in very different ways.

specialization of tasks), with an economic base consisting primarily of hunting and gathering or simple agriculture. By contrast, modern societies are characterized by **organic solidarity**, in which a very extensive division of labour and mutual dependence among people can be found.

How, according to Durkheim, did we move from a world of simple, "mechanical" societies (represented for Durkheim in tribal communities in which responsibility for tasks were shared) to those of today, characterized by a division of labour involving people who do lots of different things and may have little in common with one another? Durkheim argued that premodern societies were held together because people were engaged in much of the same or similar activities and, therefore, shared a worldview. Modern societies, Durkheim wrote, resemble the ways in which a living organism operates, where specialized organs work together to hold the whole together. As the populations of simpler societies expanded outward and then, running up against natural or human barriers, became denser in cities, competition for survival among their members increased. One particularly successful response to this situation proved to be specialization: individuals could acquire skills as a carpenter, stonemason, or blacksmith and make a living by specializing in one kind of labour.

So what exactly holds modern societies together? Durkheim eventually came to advance the idea that modern societies, characterized by growing diversity and complexity, still require some widely shared, sacred beliefs to hold people together. What kinds of beliefs could achieve this level of acceptance? Durkheim proposed a surprising answer: He suggested that the key to the forms of solidarity in modern societies lies in the fact that these societies guarantee individuals a measure of freedom that primitive societies did not. He even characterized this as the "cult of the individual." By this, Durkheim meant that in modern societies, we are freer to express our individual tastes, preferences, and interests because society does not seek to make everyone conform to the same set of beliefs about morality, and we perceive these individual rights as so central that they become sacred (and embedded in social institutions and the law).

As he continued to reflect on the nature of social solidarity, Durkheim developed a profound and original theory of the role religion has played in both primitive and modern societies. From his investigations, Durkheim developed a particular definition of religion as centring on the **sacred**—those objects, places, and symbols that are set apart from daily life and elicit awe and reverence, sustained by myths and rituals. The sacred for Durkheim did not require reference to the supernatural. While many sacred objects (such as the Bible or Koran) or practices (Christmas) make reference to God, there are many other things that are sacred that do not. For example, for many Americans burning or desecrating the American flag is to violate a sacred (but not religious) object. Durkheim's idea that it is social forces that create our sense of what is sacred opens the door to a whole new way of understanding religion. If religion is not the creation of God or some other supernatural force, it must inevitably be a human creation. But why is religion so common in all societies? And how, when, and why do humans come to create and recreate these sacred practices? Durkheim's answer relates back to his general interest in social solidarity: Religion helps to knit societies or groups of people together. It provides individuals with a common set of beliefs and makes both individuals and societies stronger.

Max Weber (1864–1920)

2.2.3 Discuss Max Weber's contributions to our understanding of motivations for behaviour, legitimacy and authority, and status groups and social closure.

The German sociologist Max Weber's contributions to the development of our understanding of modern societies were varied, complex, and important in ways that sociologists continually rediscover. His range of knowledge was so vast—in his writings he

Max Weber (1864–1920).

explored the history and societies of many major civilizations and religious traditions of the world, as well as such technical topics as agricultural production and prices in Prussia—that it is perhaps not surprising that his lasting contributions to social theory addressed several important issues. We will focus on three: his writings on the motives of individual behaviour, the forms of legitimate authority, and his concept of the status group and the seemingly universal process of how groups seek to monopolize opportunities for their members.

One of Weber's foundational contributions was to consider the role of individual action and behaviour as a basis for social order. Whereas Marx focused on material conditions and Durkheim on morality and social forces, Weber argued that there is something else we need to consider when we study societies: the motivations that guide individual behaviour or, in other words, the reasons we behave the way that we do. This is especially important for understanding human societies because Weber believed those motivations have changed over time.

Weber's analysis of motives stands in sharp contrast to Durkheim's emphasis on social facts, which are characterized by their objectivity and by being external to the individual. Weber argued that in order to understand the motivations for behaviour, we need to look not just at the social environment but also get inside people's heads and figure out how they interpret and give meaning to the world around them. In this way, Weber introduced a whole new dimension to the work of sociologists: interpretation of individual action. In *Economy and Society*, published shortly after his death, Weber writes that "Sociology is a science concerning itself with the interpretative understanding of social action" (Weber, 1922/1978, p. 4). This approach is known as **interpretative sociology**, a translation form of the German word *Verstehen*, which means understanding.

Weber went on to develop a typology of different kinds of social action, each differentiated by the motivations (or rationales) that guide them, as Figure 2.3 illustrates.

Figure 2.3 Weber's Typology of Motives for Action

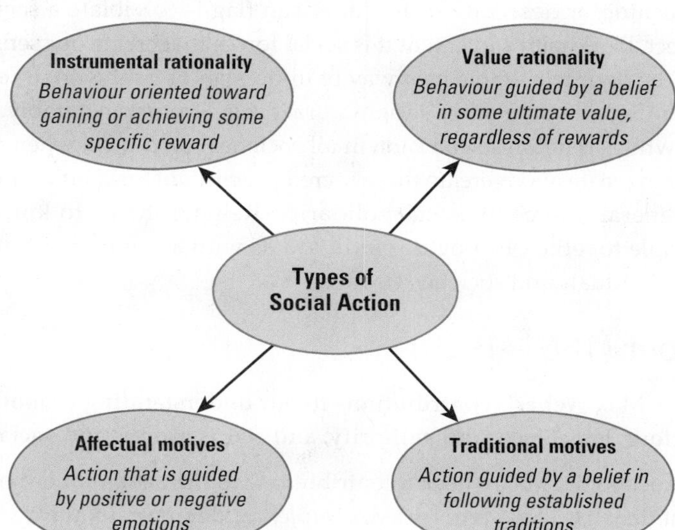

We can understand more concretely Weber's ideas about the different motives of action in terms of a specific example. Let's consider the different reasons a student might choose to attend a class in college. The instrumental reasons are pretty straightforward: A student attends class because her goal is to graduate from college, perhaps in the hopes of finding a good career and making more money than she otherwise would. Coming to class will increase her chances of getting good grades, which will lead her to graduate with a strong GPA, which will enable her to land a good job, which may enable her to make a good income. In contrast, another student could come to class guided by value-rational principles, in which case he attends class because he believes in the value of education for its own sake, without thinking about any instrumental or self-interested outcomes it might provide him. Another student might come to class guided by emotions, for example a fear that missing a class even when attendance is not required is just disrespectful or will be sanctioned by the instructor. In this case, we would say his behaviour expressed an affectual orientation. And finally, yet another student attends class because that is what her parents and grandparents did, and going to school is what she has been doing since kindergarten. It is, in other words, a tradition for which she doesn't know any better.

Library of Congress Prints and Photograph Division

In his influential book *The Protestant Ethic and The Spirit of Capitalism*, Max Weber observed that Protestantism seemed to be closely aligned to the most successful capitalist economies. Weber argued that devout Protestants believed that hard work and economic success meant that you were in God's good graces. He theorized that this was the reason that capitalism grew faster in some parts of the world than in others.

In his most famous work of interpretative sociology, *The Protestant Ethic and the Spirit of Capitalism* (Weber, 1904/2008), Weber applied his concern with individual motivations for behaviour to advance a startling theory about why capitalism appeared earlier and grew faster in some parts of the world than in others. He argued that the influence of certain religious movements—notably Protestantism—seemed to be closely connected to those places that had the earliest and most successful capitalist economies. In particular, he argued that the appearance of strict forms of Protestantism fundamentally altered market behaviour in places where they were most numerous (first in Britain, America, the Netherlands, and parts of Germany and Switzerland, and later elsewhere) because these early strict Protestants believed that it was a sign that you were in God's good graces if you became economically successful. This encouraged Protestants to work in a highly disciplined, methodical manner, and then save and reinvest whatever they earned (as opposed to consuming it). Weber believed that this gave strict Protestants an advantage over market participants from other religious groups in Europe (most notably Catholics). Eventually, the success of the strict Protestants encouraged others to assume the same work habits and investment practices if they were to survive in the marketplace. By the eighteenth century, then, a new set of distinctly modern behaviour norms ("the spirit of modern capitalism") had emerged out of what had been the religious attitudes ("the Protestant ethic") of a small minority.

A second major contribution to sociology developed in Weber's work concerns how and why people respect hierarchies and obey orders. Weber made a famous distinction between power and authority. He defines **power** as a person's ability to achieve his or her objective even if someone else wants to try to prevent it. An example of this would be when a ruler gets people to submit to his will and follow his orders by compelling them to do so through force or the threat of force. However, Weber argues that this is the exception; you can't always get your way by using force. There are far more cases where governments (or even our superiors) invoke what Weber called **authority**: the capacity to get people to do things because they think that they should abide by the commands of people above them.

Where does authority come from? Most of the time people tend to voluntarily obey orders—that is, they accept the authority of their rulers. But why? Weber explored the sources of authority by developing a theory of why and how leaders gain what he called **legitimacy**. When authority figures have legitimacy, we obey them not because of the threat of force but because we believe obeying their orders is the right thing to do. And in this way, Weber argues, the most successful political regimes are those that are able to legitimize their rule. As with Weber's basic proposition that behaviour is guided by how people interpret the world and give meaning to it, he argues that voluntary obedience to authority comes as a result of people interpreting the ruler as having legitimacy.

Weber distinguishes between different kinds of legitimacy, each connected to different interpretations of why one should voluntarily obey the ruler. Figure 2.4 illustrates these three distinct types of legitimate domination, which Weber called *traditional*, *charismatic*, and *legal-rational*.

Traditional authority seems timeless, but we know from history that kingdoms do not last forever. So how can change ever come to traditional societies, for example those that are structured around extended families and rigid status hierarchies, and have rulers who have virtually unlimited power? Weber was especially fascinated by the role played by key individual leaders whom he saw as having **charisma**. The term *charisma* is derived from a Greek word meaning "gift of grace," and Weber introduced it into the sociological study of social change. Over and over again, in traditional but also in more modern societies, according to Weber, unique individuals have claim special powers or gifts that their followers believe to be true. Most famously, these have been classic religious figures—the Hebrew prophets, Jesus, Mohammed, the Buddha—but the idea of charisma can apply to modern social and political leaders as well (for example, Gandhi, Martin Luther King Jr., or Adolf Hitler all could be said to be charismatic leaders). If such figures are to attract a following (rather than being seen as crackpots), they must demonstrate their special powers through extraordinary deeds such as miracles. Belief in a leader's charisma in turn inspires people to leave their families and status groups and instead join a new, mixed community of disciples.

Figure 2.4 Three Types of Legitimate Domination

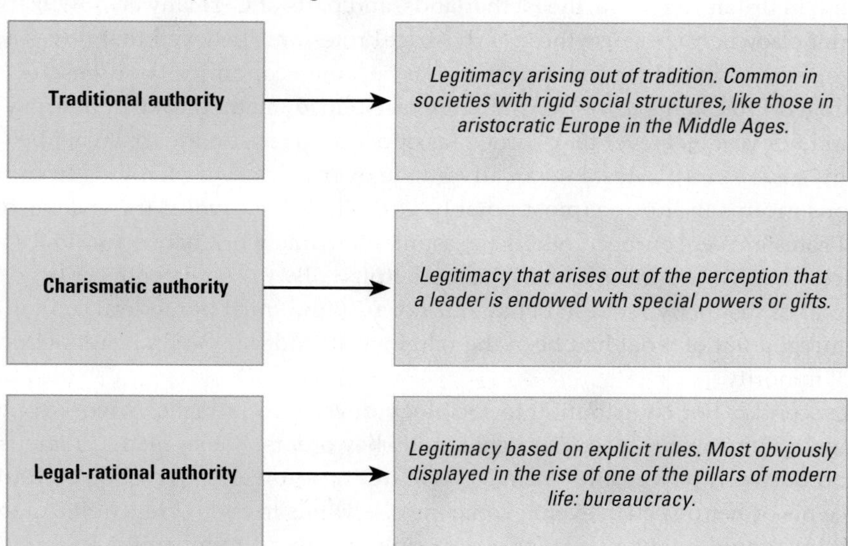

Traditional authority
Legitimacy arising out of tradition. Common in societies with rigid social structures, like those in aristocratic Europe in the Middle Ages.
Charismatic authority
Legitimacy that arises out of the perception that a leader is endowed with special powers or gifts.
Legal-rational authority
Legitimacy based on explicit rules. Most obviously displayed in the rise of one of the pillars of modern life: bureaucracy.

In this way a charismatic figure possesses the power, according to Weber, to break through the constraints of traditional authority to create new forms of legitimate domination built upon personal charisma. This authority is potentially revolutionary because the charismatic leader who calls into question traditional norms and rules proposes to replace them with new moral guidelines revealed to the leader by a higher (perhaps godly) power. Thus in the West, in Weber's view, the ever-growing number of Jesus's believers called into question traditional Roman family ties and status hierarchies by creating a community to which all—including women and slaves—were welcomed and within which all were equal. During the western Middle Ages, the Christian community was far from equal in reality, but the idea of the equality of all before God remained a powerful, radical ideal, just as did similar ideas in Islam. Various charismatic leaders in both Christianity and Islam have used these ideas to create new movements or change entire societies.

Nerissa D'Alton/Gallo images/Alamy Stock Photo

Fans attending a Lady Gaga concert may share common interests but would not be considered a status group in Max Weber's terms.

Finally, a third major contribution to social theory and sociology in Weber's writings was an important and influential theory of what he called **status groups**, groups of people with similar kinds of attributes or identities such as those based on religion, ethnicity, or race. Recall that Karl Marx had argued that classes and class conflict arising out of the economic system of any society were the central source of tension (and ultimately revolution) in any society. Weber acknowledged that economic class conflict was sometimes important, but conflicts between religious groups or racial and ethnic groups were often just as important or even more so. In contrast to economic classes, Weber emphasized that status groups are based on communities of members that share a common identity that can arise from many different sources. We all have various potential groups we could identify with; for example, on the families we are born into (and the religion and race or ethnicity our families confer upon us) or identities we develop as we get older (such as our occupation, our education, our sexuality, or communities we may voluntarily join like a neighbourhood association or a feminist activist group). But which of these statuses become a source of our conscious thoughts and actions depends in part on which are organized into communities of similar people. An individual may be a Catholic, gay, a woman, able-bodied, from California, with parents born in Mexico; she may aspire to be an actress, a volleyball player, or a fan of Lady Gaga. Which of those possible identities becomes the source of status-group membership depends in part on which have distinctive communities or organizations capable of influencing people to actively identify with them.

The Lady Gaga example also points to an important distinction between those statuses that become the basis for group conflict. Lady Gaga fans may very well consider themselves members of a group (Gaga has publicly referred to her fans as "little monsters"), but they do not participate in organized efforts on the basis of their interest in Gaga's music to claim meaningful rewards or opportunities. By contrast, one's religion, sexual orientation, gender, race, ethnicity, and disability status have been meaningful factors in access to jobs or other kinds of opportunities; in limiting what job you can aspire to, who you can date or marry, and where you can live; and in whether you have access to membership in desired social clubs or groups. Status-group struggles, Weber argued, have been an important aspect of every society's **stratification system**, that is, those inequalities between groups that persist over time. Weber did not deny that conflict between classes could be important, such as when unions demand higher wages from their employers, but he thought that Marx's emphasis on class struggle as the motor force of history neglected many other ways in which group competition and conflict influenced the process of historical change.

Weber not only advanced a broader conception of group conflict and struggle than Marx, but he also introduced an important concept for understanding *how* groups seek to gain advantage over other groups: by trying to exclude nonmembers from gaining access to opportunities. To put it another way, groups try to monopolize opportunities for their own members. He called this process **social closure**, a term that captures the various ways that groups seek to close off other groups' access to opportunities. Closure is, in short, the process by which groups seek to monopolize opportunities or rewards. Social closure can be formalized in law (such as in the American South after the Civil War, or the system of *apartheid* in South Africa, where blacks were often legally prevented from using certain public facilities, marrying whites, and living in the same neighbourhoods or attending the same schools as whites). But closure need not be written into law; it can occur in less formal ways. For example, closure of opportunities to enter the ranks of top management in large corporations for women and minorities persists even after civil rights laws were changed to give everyone equal opportunity. How? One way is that companies can change hiring and promotion policies in subtle ways to favour white men, or a certain kind of corporate culture in which women or minorities may be excluded can persist (Kantor, 1977; Dobbin, 2011).

Georg Simmel (1858–1918)

2.2.4 Explain how Georg Simmel's insights on social circles and social distance help us understand how individuals and groups relate to one another.

The German sociologist Georg Simmel was a contemporary and colleague of Max Weber, and he shared an interest with Weber in the study of groups. The social theory he pioneered, however, departed from Weber's to build upon a key set of insights about the nature of social order: Any individual stands at the intersection point of overlapping social circles, and societies are built upon these social circles (Simmel, 1964).

Georg Simmel (1858–1918).

Interfoto/Alamy Stock Photo

This insight is perhaps not surprising: Our group memberships are in many ways defining features of our lives. For example, we belong to a particular family; have groups of friends or colleagues at school or in the workplace; may also belong to a religious community, a neighbourhood association, a sports club, or a political group; and have groups of friends or acquaintances because of shared passions or hobbies. For Simmel, a key aspect of the rise of modern societies from early types of human communities was the widening of the social circles in which we could become members. Whereas in earlier times membership in a single social circle—like that centred on a local Catholic parish—might have dominated or dictated many other aspects of an individual's life, by the beginning of the twentieth century individuals had much greater freedom. They were able to choose their friends and acquaintances across different spheres of life, independent of one another, forming an intricate web of relationships, as Simmel called them. If he were alive today, of course, Simmel would have marveled at the ways that this expansion of the range of possible social circles has increased through social media (which make almost an infinite number of possibilities available to us).

In developing a theory of how individuals fit into social circles, Simmel provided a key concept for sociology—the idea of **social distance**, which is a way of describing the importance of how close to or distant from one another the individuals in groups are (this also applies to the groups themselves). Simmel famously identified a "stranger" as someone who is a member of a group but never accepted as a full member (he contrasted strangers with "outsiders" who are never part of the group at all, and "insiders" who are fully part of the group, in the "inner circle") (Simmel 1908/1971). We are all familiar with strangers in our own circles—people who are part of a group but often excluded or not invited to fully participate in group activities. Indeed, all of us have probably had the experience at one time or another of being a stranger in a group where we aspired to be an insider, undoubtedly an awkward and difficult position to be in (but a sociologically important one to understand). Simmel's insights about social distance raised larger questions about the nature of relationships between individuals and within or between groups. Social distance describes the quality of the relationships between people, and later sociologists would develop measures of the degree of closeness or distance that individuals and groups feel toward one another.

What are the implications of these insights? On the one hand, it means that as adults we enjoy an unprecedented degree of latitude in shaping our social relations according to common interests, views, and preferences. While as recently as a few decades ago members of many ethnic and religious groups came under great pressure from their families and communities to avoid close relationships with those from outside of their group, this is much less the case today (as witnessed by rising rates of intermarriage across ethnic, religious, and even national lines in both North America and Western Europe). On the other hand, the number and diversity of social circles to which greater freedom of choice permits us to belong also leads to conflicts, not only over how best to spend our time but also over values and norms of behaviour attached to particular circles that may not be compatible with one another. Thus the young corporate lawyer might have to decide, for example, whether to stay late every night at the office like other coworkers or violate this unwritten expectation of long working hours and leave earlier in order to spend more time with her partner or family (and time with one's family is also an important value). Or we may find that that the attitudes expressed by our work colleagues or the language they use violates our religious or political beliefs, and that we therefore must choose whether to give short shrift to these beliefs or speak up and object, thereby risking alienating those with whom we spend many hours daily. At any point, such conflicts may give rise to feelings of social distance or turn a potential insider into a "stranger."

Simmel noted that the way we see ourselves, and which social groups we most value, is not necessarily the same way others see us. While our family members and closest friends may be aware of all of the overlapping social groups to which we belong, and even which of those group memberships are most important to us, outsiders or passing acquaintances will most often focus on one of our multiple identities—our nationality, race, ethnic background, religion, regional origin, or place of residence—and assume it to be primary (drawing conclusions about us based on what they hold to be "average" or "common" traits of persons with those characteristics).

Simmel's work also began to bring insights from mathematics into the study of the social world, using ideas imported from geometry (and geometric space) to characterize the relationships among individuals. Simmel's insights about the formal properties of groups provided the foundation for the rise of **network analysis**, the study of how individuals are connected to other individuals and the consequences of those connections. Although the full value of these insights was not immediately clear to Simmel's contemporaries, later sociologists would recognize them as a

Figure 2.5 An Example of a Social Network

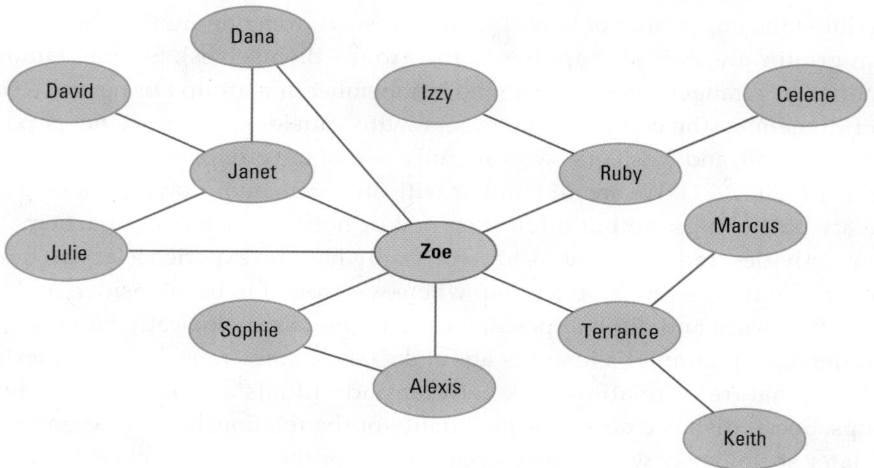

useful foundation for developing new ways of understanding society. For example, how do new ideas become popular? Often it is through **social networks**, people (including strangers) who are tied together in ways they don't typically notice. In the simple example of a social network in Figure 2.5, the lines show the ties between individuals, with Zoe indirectly connecting several different groups together through her ties.

To see more vividly how networks work, consider how rumours spread: One person may tell a close friend a secret, and if the friend tells another person (who may be completely unknown to the first person), it can begin a remarkable chain of action that can spread the secret far and wide (perhaps to the complete embarrassment of the first person). While many rumours may be harmless, the same kind of chain of interaction can spread information about a protest, whether or not a movie is any good, or how to cheat on your taxes and get away with it. With the use of mathematical tools, social network analysts have been able to generalize Simmel's insights into a wide range of different applications, from health behaviours to fads to patterns of housing segregation. It is a foundational contribution to analyzing how societies work.

W. E. B. Du Bois (1868–1963).

akg-images/Newscom

W. E. B. Du Bois (1868–1963)

2.2.5 Explain W. E. B. Du Bois's views of the diverse ways in which racism influences the lives of African Americans and how racism produces a double consciousness.

W. E. B. Du Bois's long and varied career as a social scientist, historian, journalist, essayist, and political activist (among many other activities, he was one of the founders of the National Association for the Advancement of Colored People [NAACP]) was extraordinary in many ways. Du Bois's race, however, prevented him from attaining the prestigious academic post that his penetrating scholarship would have normally entitled him to. His overriding concern as a sociologist and social theorist was the problem of race and racial inequality in American society, although his theoretical writings contained powerful insights that were relevant to all disadvantaged groups and had implications for the study of group conflict everywhere.

Du Bois's theoretical writings contained powerful insights that unmasked patterns of race and racial inequality in America but also were relevant to understanding the pathologies of prejudice and stereotyping for any disadvantaged group of people.

The dominant theories about race in Du Bois's time claimed that European whites and other racialized groups were biologically endowed differently, especially in terms of intelligence, capacity for hard work, and ability to be good citizens. These theories stressed that there were deep-seated biological reasons why European whites were superior to blacks and that the poverty and inequality experienced by blacks in North America were the result of these innate differences. If racial differences were rooted in biological differences, then it hardly mattered whether North American society gave blacks equal opportunity, as they would be fundamentally incapable of taking advantage of those opportunities.

Du Bois rejected these assertions, arguing across his 60-year career that racial inequality was not rooted in biological differences but rather manufactured by American society. He developed a theory of how **racism**—the assumption that members of a racial group are inherently inferior to other races—prevented blacks from achieving at the same level of success as whites. At every turn, throughout his career, Du Bois had to challenge the entrenched view of white superiority, which denied that racism mattered.

How did racism play this role, according to Du Bois? In his first major book, a study of the black community in Philadelphia in the late 1890s, Du Bois showed that every aspect of the lives of African Americans was shaped by the limited opportunities they were afforded (Du Bois, 1899/1995). Du Bois carried out an intensive data-collection effort, employing multiple and often innovative methods in the study. These included the use of statistical data about the neighbourhoods where Philadelphia's black population lived, what kinds of jobs they held, and how they were divided

Popperfoto/Getty Images

Du Bois's view of the "double consciousness" of African Americans was continually reinforced by the practice of segregation, which prevented blacks from participating in the mainstream of American life.

along economic lines. Du Bois supplemented this statistical portrait with interviews on a house-to-house basis, where he explored the social conditions of life in the black community beyond what statistical data could show. For example, he explored how the black poor survived on low incomes, how marriages and families were organized and functioning, and how relatively privileged blacks viewed poor blacks. The latter analysis would give rise to a concern about what Du Bois viewed as the failure of black "elites" to help poor blacks and "uplift the race," as Du Bois famously put it in a later essay (Du Bois, 1903/2008).

The role of racism in American life, and how it impacted African Americans, was dissected in a different way in Du Bois's most famous and influential work, *The Souls of Black Folks* (Du Bois, 1903/1997). Here, in a collection of essays and studies that are still widely read today, Du Bois presented more fully his view that stereotypes about blacks as lazy, unintelligent, or prone to crime were in fact the result of their place in American society. In the more sociological parts of the book, Du Bois argued that a lack of educational opportunities, not innate intelligence, produced the appearance of lower intelligence among blacks. Lack of economic opportunity, by contrast, made it appear that blacks did not work as hard as whites (a myth all the more ridiculous in the face of the back-breaking work of many southern blacks involved in agricultural or domestic labour). And he noted that because of poverty and racial segregation, African Americans tended to be concentrated in poor communities where crime rates naturally tended to be higher. In short, Du Bois argued, the social structure of American society was both the culprit and cause of the appearance of inferiority in the black community.

Du Bois's most famous concept in *Souls*, however, was a theory of how racism and social structure impacts individual blacks, producing in them what he called a kind of "double consciousness." Because of their marginalization from the mainstream of American life, Du Bois argued that unlike white Americans, blacks had to live multiple lives, one as a black person and one as an American. Further, because black Americans saw themselves as devalued in the eyes of white Americans, they suffered from having to view themselves in this way through the eyes of others. In a famous passage, Du Bois defined this double consciousness as

> a world which yields him no true self-consciousness, but only lets him see himself through the revelation of the other world. It is a peculiar sensation, this double-consciousness, this sense of always looking at one's self through the eyes of others, of measuring one's soul by the tape of a world that looks on in amused contempt and pity. One ever feels his two-ness—an American, a Negro; two warring souls, two thoughts, two unreconciled strivings; two warring ideals in one dark body, whose dogged strength alone keeps it from being torn asunder (Du Bois, 1903/1997, p. 6)

The idea of multiple selves suggested a novel way in which social structure imposes psychological costs on blacks, and it proved to be an idea that later social scientists would apply to many other disadvantaged groups.

Du Bois's writings on social structure also examined the larger context of American politics and race relations. His most important book in this vein was his study of the tragedy of the post–Civil War Reconstruction in the South (Du Bois, 1935). In contrast to the standard historical accounts of the time, which claimed the Reconstruction governments run by African Americans were corrupt and incompetent, Du Bois argued that the Reconstruction governments struggled against virulent white violence and obstructionism at every turn in their efforts to build a new political system in which African Americans and poor whites would be able to participate. While his insights were dismissed at the time, later scholarship on Reconstruction has confirmed many of the insights of Du Bois's original historical account.

2.3 What Innovations in Social Theory Emerged in the Mid-Twentieth Century?

George Marks/Getty Images

New Directions In Social Theory, 1937–1965

While the classical tradition in social theory can be seen as represented in the writings of Marx, Durkheim, Weber, Simmel, and Du Bois, the interests of social theorists began to shift in new and unexpected directions from the late 1930s onward. Leadership in the development of social theory and sociology as a whole passed from being primarily located in Europe (even the American Du Bois had been educated in Germany and was influenced by European social theorists) to America. At the centre of these new directions was the widely debated work of the Harvard sociologist Talcott Parsons (1902–1979). Parsons's effort to develop a *functionalist* theory of society sought to provide nothing less than a general theory of society built around an analysis of how the different components of society help to maintain it and keep order. Parsons's work was greeted with enthusiasm in some quarters but also spawned enormous controversy. Like Marx in the classical period, his theories would serve as a major source of critical reflection and theoretical debate for other theorists in this era. This period, which we can date from approximately 1937 (when Parsons published one of the most important books in the history of sociological theory, a two-volume study of mostly European social theorists entitled *The Structure of Social Action* (Parsons, 1937/1967) to the mid-1960s, saw both the elaboration of the functionalist model of society and the development of several key alternatives to Parsons's functionalist theory—most importantly conflict theory and symbolic interaction. In this section, we briefly discuss each of these new theoretical traditions and some of their key insights.

Structural Functionalism

2.3.1 Discuss the roles that norms, values, and institutions play in society, according to the theory of structural functionalism.

Parsons's functionalist theory of society sought to explain key aspects of social life by examining the *functions* they serve for society as a whole. It represented a grand attempt to provide a unified theory for all of sociology. Parsons argued that the key elements of any society were all organized around the broader (and often hidden) needs of the society as a whole (e.g., Parsons, 1951; Parsons and Smelser, 1956). So, for example, all societies have some kind of religion, functionalists have argued, because religion serves many useful purposes: Religious ideas and doctrines give societies a shared moral code to live by, they help people to explain the unexplainable, and they encourage social solidarity between people. Parsons eventually came to describe this theory of society as **structural functionalism**: a theory of society in which individuals, groups, and the institutions of any society are guided by an overarching social system.

According to structural functionalism, the social system contains powerful norms, values, and institutions—enduring practices of society and the organizations that manage those practices. Within the social system, individuals take on certain *roles*, such as "student" or "teacher," or "worker" or "boss," throughout life, and while in those roles they tend to act a certain way (to follow an appropriate script, like an actor). The structural functionalist theory emphasizes that norms, values, and institutions arise and persist because they prove to be good ways of maintaining social order.

While Parsons spent an enormous amount of time elaborating this framework in his later writings, examining specific norms, values, roles, and institutions, there are three critical ideas of structural functionalism to remember: (1) enduring features of society can ultimately be explained in terms of their "functional" purpose—societies develop religion, for example, as a way of creating common values or accounting for things that cannot be explained without reference to a supernatural being; (2) individuals are heavily shaped and constrained by the social system in which they are living; and (3) conflicts are minimized by the social system as individuals learn (or "know") and more or less accept their "place."

What about social change? How do societies change over time? In the structural functionalist view, social change is something that happens gradually, as norms and institutions adapt to meet new challenges or eventually are replaced altogether. In contrast to the way Karl Marx envisioned social change happening through revolutionary class struggles, Parsons and his collaborators believed that social change happened much like the theory of evolution in biology. Evolutionary biology has demonstrated that animal species adapt over time through a process of **natural selection**, where advantageous traits were selected over traits that were not, generation by generation. Parsons saw this as a useful metaphor for understanding how a society as a whole (and its component parts) evolved as well. Those features of any society that are dysfunctional are slowly weeded out in favour of those features that are helpful.

Structural functionalism seemed to provide a way of integrating the diverse elements of any society into a single, coherent theory. But, as many critics would point out, it did so only by ignoring many important aspects of contemporary societies that did not seem to fit the theory. We will consider two of the most important streams of criticism of Parsons and structural functionalism in the middle of the twentieth century in the next two sections.

Conflict Theory

2.3.2 Discuss how conflict theory attempted to explain social inequalities.

One of the major objections to functionalist social theory was that it seemed to suggest that societies are largely conflict-free places in which all of the different parts of society serve important functions and fit together more or less harmoniously. Structural functionalist theory, in its most extreme form, did indeed seem to suggest that the order-imposing elements of society (such as religion) were vastly more powerful than the conflict-generating elements, such as those arising out of the inequalities between groups that Marx, Weber, and Du Bois had seen as central to all societies. Parsons and other functionalists, by contrast, argued that these classical social theorists tended to exaggerate the role of conflict, especially insofar as social change was concerned.

A number of social theorists in the late 1950s and 1960s vigorously disagreed with Parsons, and they proposed an alternative to functionalist social theory that came to be known as **conflict theory**. Conflict theory traces its roots to Marx and Weber, and it attempts to synthesize elements of each thinker's work into a new theory of society. One of the founding figures of conflict theory, German sociologist Ralf Dahrendorf (1929–2009), argued that while Marx's view of social change based on class struggle was outdated, it was nevertheless true that many types of economic conflict still exist in the modern world and are critical components of social life (Dahrendorf, 1959). Some of these conflicts had been channeled into the relationship between unions and employers, for example, while others took place over the policies of governments—such as the taxes that corporations and rich individuals have to pay, or policies that would help poor or low-income individuals and families live better lives. Dahrendorf also argued that non-economic conflicts, such as disagreement over who has the authority to make decisions within organizations, are an often hidden but important type of conflict. The problem with Parsons's functionalist approach, for Dahrendorf and other conflict theorists, was that it neglected the critical importance of conflicts in society, thereby presenting an unrealistic image of society that exaggerated consensus and social harmony.

The most popular and influential work in the conflict theory tradition was that of C. Wright Mills (1918–1962), who wrote a series of books on class and power that argued that America in the 1950s was governed by a "power elite" that strove to protect its privileges and dominated the making of government policy (Mills, 1956). (It was Mills who invented the concept of the "sociological imagination" as a way of describing the mission of the discipline of sociology, as we discussed in Chapter 1.) For Mills, the power elite consisted of the top ranks of the leading political, economic, and military institutions in American society, and this power elite was able to exclude ordinary citizens from exerting much influence over government policies. Mills viewed the classical notion of democracy—rule by the people—as a fiction in the context of the power wielded by those at the top.

Conflict theory evolved in the 1960s to become the principal home for those sociologists seeking new ways of thinking about inequality and social injustice. The popularity of conflict theory stemmed in large part from the growing sense that functionalist theory did not seem to provide a very good way of explaining why inequalities exist within society, and at its extreme even seemed to some to justify those inequalities as functional for societies. For example, in one famous essay first published in 1945, functionalist social theorists argued that economic inequality was a necessary component of society in order to encourage the most talented individuals to pursue careers that would be the most useful for society as a whole (Davis & Moore, 1945). The authors of this paper argued that no one would undergo the long training period necessary to become a doctor unless doctors received more pay, and because societies need high-quality doctors it is necessary to provide the financial incentives to ensure an adequate supply of such people in the medical field.

By contrast, conflict theory placed these social and economic inequalities under the microscope, noting that inequalities of wealth and power are not natural outcomes but, rather, that their privileges persist because powerful individuals and groups go to great lengths to protect them. For example, some employers treat their workers poorly or may use legal or illegal means to prevent workers from organizing unions. Professions that claim to serve the public interest have developed many ways to enhance their incomes and prevent their clients from challenging them. Physicians (a profession we don't normally think of as exploiting others) created organizations like the American Medical Association that have worked very hard to ensure that the supply of doctors would be limited by law to those who complete a licensed medical school. By reducing competition, physicians are able to receive higher fees than they otherwise might.

Conflict theorists argued that inequality inevitably produces tensions between groups and individuals over who gets what. People who feel oppressed (whether via sexism, racism, economic wealth, or other forms of inequality) will eventually begin to struggle against those who take advantage of them. Sometimes these struggles happen informally (such as when workers refuse to give their bosses their best effort), while other times they are more open (such as when a union declares a strike). In highlighting the importance of inequality as a form of social conflict and struggle, conflict theory sought to revive some of the classical concerns of Marx and Weber, in particular in their respective writings on class and status-group inequality. But conflict theory never became a full-fledged system of social thought, as some of its early thinkers had thought it might. Having reminded sociologists that societies do not always function smoothly and without conflict, it was not always clear where conflict theory could go next. While conflict is unquestionably an important component of social life, a theory of conflict proved too vague to be the basis for a new social theory.

Symbolic Interactionism

2.3.3 Analyze how everyday social interaction lies at the heart of understanding society, according to symbolic interactionism.

Another critical response to functionalism that emerged in this era was known as **symbolic interactionism**, a theory of society that focuses on how people interact with one another and the role that symbols play in those interactions. While Talcott Parsons and his followers saw individuals and individual action as heavily shaped by society and its constituent parts, symbolic interactionism turns this idea on its head, arguing that social order starts from individuals and the meanings they give to objects, events, and relationships with others. Its founding theorists were two scholars who taught at the University of Chicago—philosopher George Herbert Mead (1863–1931) and Herbert Blumer (1900–1987), a sociologist and Mead's student (see Mead, 1934; Blumer, 1969).

Why does this particular cake have special meaning? Symbolic interactionists highlight the importance of the symbolic meanings we attach to objects, gestures, and conversations, which might otherwise seem like ordinary events.

Karen Mower/Getty Images

Symbolic interactionists argue that understanding everyday social interaction—including basic things such as people eating together, being in a classroom together, or greeting each other on the street—lies at the heart of understanding society, as it is through such interactions that both individual identities and societies are formed. While most sociological theories (including all of the theories we have discussed so far) focus on big-picture topics like economy, religion, politics, or society more generally, symbolic interactionism zooms in to focus on everyday human behaviour and the ways in which we interact with one another as the building blocks of society.

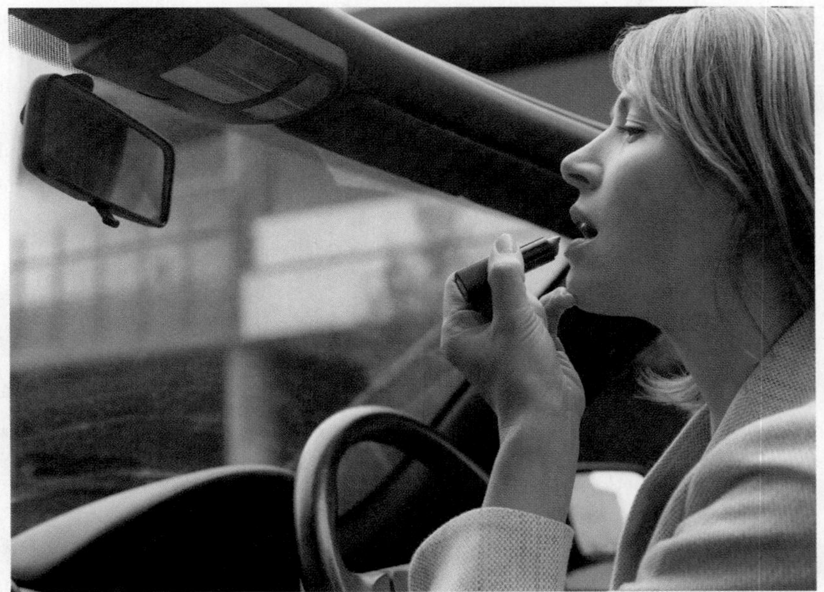

Digital Vision/Getty Images

How we "present" ourselves to others is an important aspect of how everyday life is performed. Erving Goffman compared getting ready to go out in the world as analogous to actors in a play getting ready to go on stage.

Why study everyday human behaviour? What could such everyday things as people eating together possibly tell us about society? The answer, according to symbolic interactionists, is that what distinguishes humans from other species is that in our everyday interactions we interpret and give meaning to objects, activities, and people in ways that other species do not. Mead famously argued that what distinguishes humans from animals and defines what it is to be a social being is that we are both *subjects* who act in the world as well as *objects* who exist in the world and are interpreted and defined by others. To explain this, Mead divided identities into two parts, what he called the "I" and the "Me." The Me represents the objective dimension of the self—that which is interpreted by others—while the I represents the subjective dimension of the self—in other words, that part of our self-understanding that interprets how others see us and that decides how to act based on how our actions will appear to others. In these ways, symbolic interactionists argue that our sense of self comes directly from the evaluations of others.

In his later writings on symbolic interaction, Mead's student Blumer distinguished three types of objects that can be the subject of interpretation: physical objects (a table, a tree), social objects (people), and abstract objects (ideas).

The symbolic interactionists challenged social theorists to pay more attention to the centrality of everyday acts in creating the conditions for social order. But how, a conflict theorist of this era might ask, do the powerful inequalities and distinct social roles that characterize societies impact interaction? Symbolic interactionists were very aware of this issue, noting that the evaluations and opinions of some people count more to us than others, depending on the relationship. But in each case, our behaviour is shaped by the opinions others have of us, and when we decide how to behave we consider the values of these others. In this way, inequalities penetrate our everyday interactions.

If our sense of self is determined by the opinions others have of us and we all want others to have good opinions of us, it makes sense that we will try to behave in a way that will lead others to interpret us in a positive way. This idea forms the basis of the work of a classical work by Erving Goffman, who, more than any other sociologist, popularized interactionist ideas in the 1950s and 1960s. In *The Presentation of Self in Everyday Life* (Goffman, 1959), Goffman employs the famous Shakespearean quotation that "all the world's a stage" to compare social life to theatre, arguing that our behaviours are similar to the performances of actors—like actors, we play roles, follow scripts, and have our performances evaluated by an audience (in this case, other people with whom we interact in our day-to-day lives). In this "dramaturgical" approach to social life, Goffman argues that we are constantly seeking to influence how people interpret our behaviours by strategically acting in certain ways to achieve a desired interpretation from others. Consider, for example, when we go to a job interview, we want the person who is interviewing us to think that we are organized, hardworking, and ambitious. How might we give these impressions? On the one hand, there are things we can say about ourselves, but there are also nonverbal cues that we give, as well as the way that we carry ourselves, which may signal these qualities. So we may wear a suit instead of the jeans we are more comfortable in, we sit up on the chair instead of slouching, we comb our hair in a conservative way instead of letting it go wild, and so on. In such ways, Goffman says we engage in "impression management"—strategically organizing our behaviour to communicate certain ideas about who we are.

2.4 How Has a New Generation of Social Theory Evolved?

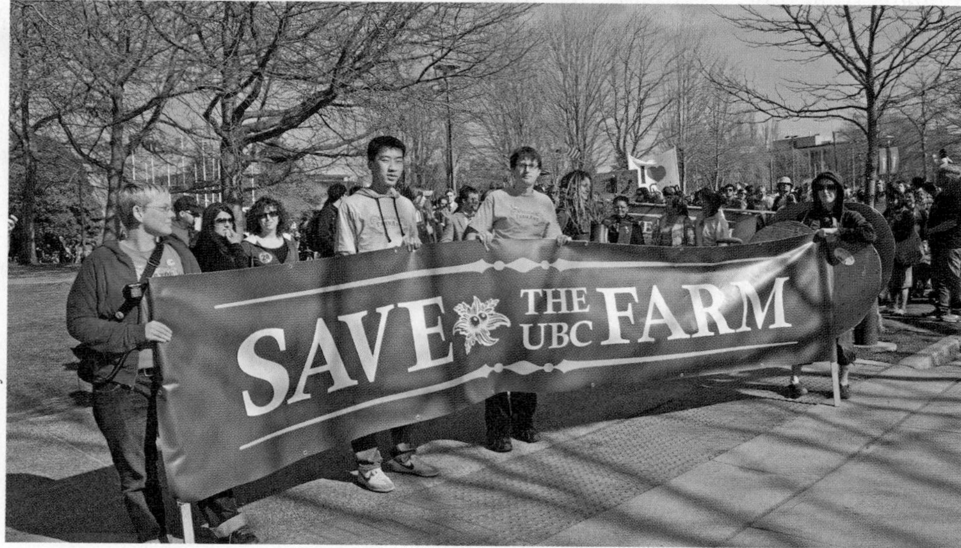

David Wei/Alamy Stock Photo

Social Theory Since The Turbulent 1960s

Sociology and the leading social theories underwent an enormous transition in the 1960s and the early 1970s as social movements around the world demanded, and sometimes won, important types of social change (Sica & Turner, 2006). This was, after all, the era of the civil rights movement, the feminist movement, the environmental movement, the anti–Vietnam War movement, and the beginnings of the gay and lesbian rights movement, among others. In this vortex, traditional ways of understanding society, including some of those that had only recently been popular, were thrown aside. For example, the dominant position of functionalism was dislodged by the late 1960s, and functionalism came to be widely (although not always accurately) dismissed as a theory that justified the inequalities of the existing social order. Conflict theory disappeared as well, replaced by other theories of inequality that emerged or reemerged in this period. Symbolic interactionism, in contrast to the other midcentury traditions, did remain vibrant, and some of the key insights of symbolic interactionists were incorporated into contemporary social theories, but even this theoretical tradition retreated to a small corner of sociology.

In the wake of the social changes brought about during the 1960s, a new generation of social theories and theorists appeared on the scene. Some had an explicit desire to connect to social movements of the times, while others sought, in different ways, to build upon aspects of the classical and mid-century traditions to develop new insights about the relationship between individuals and society, the nature of social order, and the conditions of social change. In this section, we can only provide a brief sampling of some of the most important of these theories, but we hope to indicate some of the main strands of contemporary social theory.

The Revival of Marxism

2.4.1 Discuss neo-Marxist ideas about the capitalist state, social classes, and globalization.

The older theoretical tradition of Marxism underwent a significant revival in the 1960s and afterward. A new generation of Marxist social theorists sought to update Marxism for the late twentieth century, taking into account the fact that history had not—at least up until then—worked out the way Marx and Engels had predicted it would. One central focus of what is known as **neo-Marxism** was to expand upon Marx's original ideas about politics to develop a theory of the **capitalist state**—that is, the governing institutions of a capitalist society. Neo-Marxists developed new understandings of how and why governments in capitalist societies ultimately make policies in the interests of the capitalist class, but at the same time they also began to investigate the conditions under which governments and powerful economic groups had to make concessions to the working class. For example, the capitalist state could establish social programs like pensions for the elderly, unemployment insurance, health insurance, and free or low-cost public education, programs that provide some benefits to poor and working-class people while simultaneously ensuring that capitalist firms remain profitable and the capitalist economy is able to grow.

The establishment of such programs and class compromises dramatically improved the lives of ordinary people over the course of the late nineteenth and twentieth centuries and even helped (at least according to neo-Marxists) to save capitalism from its own worst tendencies. The benefits these programs provided were seen by neo-Marxists as key to persuading the working class that it did not need socialism (Poulantzas, 1978). At the same time, however, neo-Marxists insisted that such concessions could not go on forever; at some point, their costs would become too great for capitalist economies or governments to bear. This "fiscal crisis" would ultimately open the door to the possibility of a new kind of socialist revolution (or at least make it one possible outcome among other alternatives) (O'Connor, 1973).

In addition to rethinking the classical Marxist theory of the state, neo-Marxist scholars also developed a much more elaborate understanding of the nature of social classes and the class structure within capitalist societies. Marx's two-class model—a small dominant class and a large subordinate class—clearly did not fit modern capitalist societies very well. By the middle of the twentieth century, it was obvious that the growth of a large middle class made up of professionals (such as doctors, lawyers, engineers, and teachers) and business and sales managers (who worked for large companies but did not own them) bore little resemblance to the classical proletariat that Marx envisioned. The "embarrassment of the middle classes," as neo-Marxist theorist Erik Olin Wright (1985, p. 13) put it, required a new body of theory about how modern societies are divided. Wright's effort to solve this problem argued that just as the ownership of a business is an "asset" that can be used to generate greater economic rewards (for example, when you hire people to work for you), so too are credentials (like a law degree) and supervisorial positions (in an organization) (Wright, 1985, 1997). Possession of any of these assets, Wright argued, would generate surplus income that blur the classical two-dimensional division of classes based on ownership of capital, as illustrated in Figure 2.6.

Neo-Marxist social theorists were also among the first to revive the study of capitalism as a global economic order. Immanuel Wallerstein's (1974, 2011) work on what he called the **capitalist world system** represents one widely debated example, while Robert Brenner's (2006) analysis of the global crisis of capitalism provided an alternative view. For Wallerstein, capitalism is an economic system that exists not just *within* countries but also in the economic relationships *between* countries (where rich countries are able to exploit poor countries, just as rich capitalists can be seen as exploiting workers). Wallerstein and other neo-Marxists anticipated the rise of

Figure 2.6 A New Understanding of Social Classes

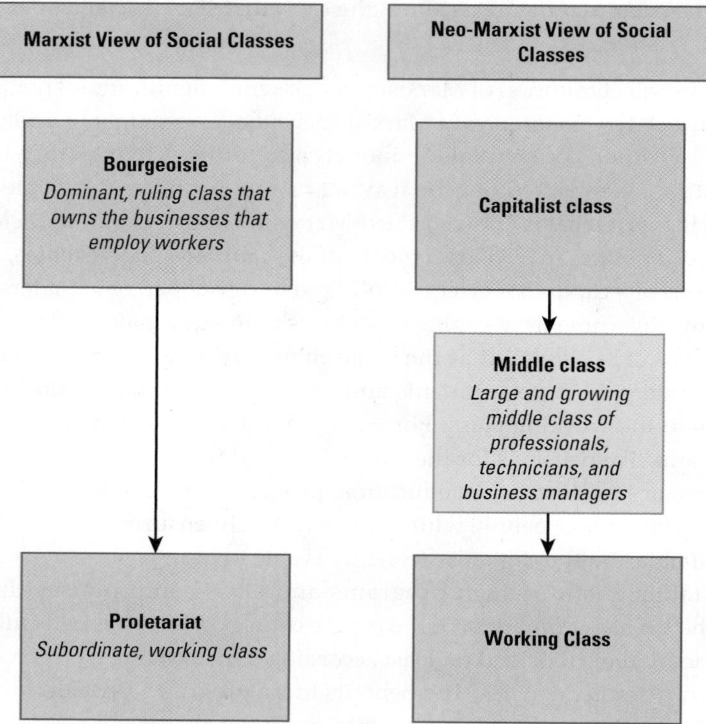

globalization—the increasing flows of goods and services across national borders—long before social scientists in other theoretical traditions began to pay attention to an increasingly global world and how the economic inequalities between countries were reproduced over time. Other neo-Marxist contributions have highlighted inherent crisis tendencies arising from unstable features of global capitalism, particularly those in the financial sector (Brenner, 2006). The banking crisis of 2007–2008, which would eventually require an enormous financial bailout by governments in the United States and elsewhere but has yet to restore rapid economic growth, is consistent with neo-Marxist predictions (although it is not yet clear whether capitalism will once again manage to save itself from being its own worst enemy).

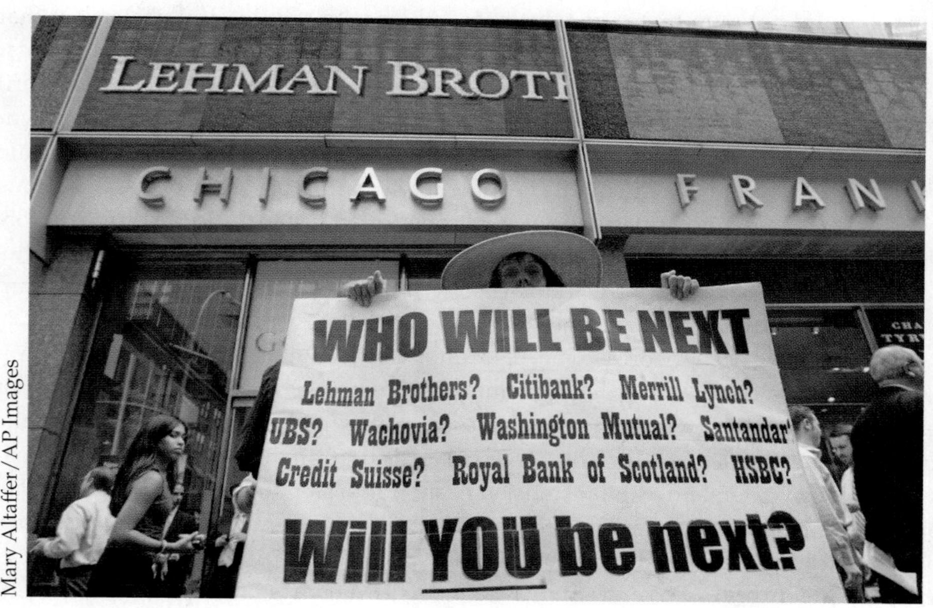

Mary Altaffer/AP Images

The tendency of capitalist economies to have periodic and often severe crises, like the financial crisis of 2008 and the economic recession that followed, are examples of why many neo-Marxists believe that a post-capitalist future is inevitable.

Feminist Social Theory

2.4.2 Analyze the role of intersectionality in theories of gender inequality.

One important limitation of neo-Marxism was that its focus on class relations and class power tended to downplay other types of inequalities. Just as Weber and Du Bois made important contributions to sociology by emphasizing the importance of status-group conflicts and racism, so too would a new generation of social theorists respond to the Marxist revival by seeking to invigorate a sociological understanding of inequalities beyond class. One such alternative was the emergence of feminist social theory. To be sure, sociologists have long been concerned about issues relating to gender (for example, in research on the family), and early women sociologists such as Jane Addams (1860–1935) combined social work activism and intellectual writings about gender issues (Addams, for example, wrote widely about prostitution). In the 1970s, however, the rise of a distinctly **feminist social theory**—which placed gender and gender inequality at the centre of its theoretical lens—challenged many of the assumptions of classical social theory for its male-centred biases.

An early and influential thinker in the development of feminist social theory was the French philosopher and writer Simone de Beauvoir (1908–1986). While Beauvoir wrote on a range of issues, from ethics and philosophy to politics, it was her work on sex and gender that made the most direct contributions to social theory. In her classic book *The Second Sex* (Beauvoir, 1952), she offers an analysis of what has come to be known as **patriarchy**—the idea that societies are set up to ensure that women are systematically controlled (and devalued). For Beauvoir, women were not born to be subordinate, but they are made to seem different and distinct from, and inferior to, men. In Beauvoir's own words, "One is not born but becomes a woman" (Beauvoir, 1952, p. 249). This idea was central to the distinction that later feminists would make between **sex**, which is a biological characteristic, and **gender**, which is the social meaning attached to being a "man" or a "woman." Beauvoir was thus one of the first theorists to insist that gender and femininity are **social constructions**—that is, societies *create* gender categories, which are not natural outcomes of biological differences– and these gendered categories are translated into enduring inequalities between men and women.

As contemporary feminist theory grew in the 1970s, it built upon and extended Beauvoir's early insights in a variety of ways. Feminist theorists share a commitment to understanding how and why the social world is designed as it is for men and women. It is possible, however, to discern three key approaches to social theory. The first approach arose as early feminist scholars began to see the social world from the perspective of women, leading them to theorize **sex differences**, or the different ways the world worked for men and women. These early works often began by making the point that most social theories had ignored women and were thus based on male realms of experience. Therefore, feminist social theorists set out to include women as the subjects of theoretical analysis. The result was often quite transformative. For instance, the sociologist Dorothy Smith (b. 1926) showed how the basis of sociology changed when women were put at the centre of the analysis: a women's perspective reveals how social science historically had systematically neglected important aspects of the experiences of women because of its male-centred bias (Smith, 1974). Echoing this, other feminist theorists analyzed how sociological inquiry would have to change if it took women seriously—from rethinking its notions of the individual to expanding its areas of inquiry to include the private sphere (such as the role of power in families).

Early feminist theorists not only rethought particular scholarly fields, they also revised theoretical traditions that crossed disciplines. One of the most important was that of **psychoanalysis** (the study of the conscious and unconscious individual mind and its influence on individual behaviour), which was quite important to some early

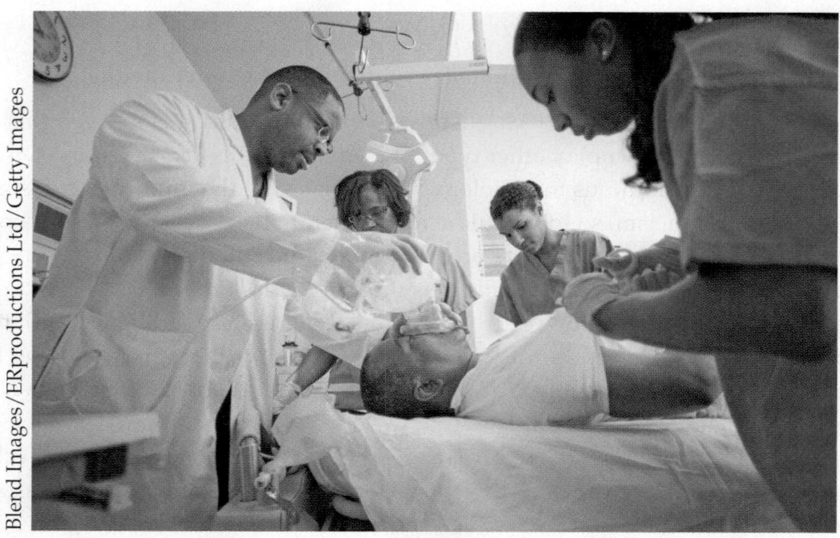

Blend Images/ERproductions Ltd/Getty Images

The continuing segregation of men and women into different types of jobs suggests the continuing power of gender in society.

feminist theorists who wanted to understand how men and women formed their senses of self. Most traditional theories of the individual in psychological and psychoanalytic theory were based exclusively on male experience. When women were brought into focus, however, those models had to change. It was argued that since women tended to develop their selves in relation to others, through their attachments and ability to care, they inevitably had different sources of identity. This insight was most famously elaborated on by the sociologist Nancy Chodorow (b. 1944), who traced the psychological basis of sex differences to the structure of the family. Drawing on psychoanalysis, Chodorow (1978) theorized that the sexual division of labour in the family, where women were primarily responsible for childrearing, created distinct development pathways for boys and girls. Thus, sex differences were rooted deep inside our heads, in our unconscious desires and emotional attachments.

Throughout the 1970s and 1980s, most feminist theorists were searching for *the* cause of gender inequality. Far too often, though, this made their theories seem somewhat simplified—as if gender inequality comes from a single fixed aspect of societies or individuals (or the relationships between individuals). Similarly, they frequently lumped all women together, ignoring critical differences among them. In the process, they tended to highlight issues of concern to privileged women—like the social isolation of middle-class housewives or the exclusion of some women from paid labour. But these were not the concerns of all women. Later feminist theorists, most notably Patricia Hill Collins (b. 1948), have paid special attention to the ways in which gender is experienced differently by different women (Collins, 1990).

From these critiques a second feminist approach to theory emerged, one that shifted from explaining sexual inequality in general to making the very existence of gender something that needed to be examined and challenged. This feminist approach explores how the categories of male and female emerge and shape social life. For instance, some feminists have explored gender dynamics in different institutions (e.g., families, schools, workplaces, churches). Others have looked at how gender "gets performed" in these social settings. So while sociologists of gender might study the division of labour in the family or at work, theorists of gender might seek to *explain* why work is divided up in gendered ways across different public and private arenas—and why we interact the way we do as women and men (Connell, 1987; West & Zimmerman, 1987).

Even more recently, a distinctive third approach has emerged in which feminist theorists have moved away from looking at gender on its own to considering it alongside other social hierarchies. This third type of feminist theory allows social life to be understood in more fluid, interconnected, and variable terms. The most influential social theorist working in this vein has been Patricia Hill Collins (1990), who has argued that the oppression black women have historically experienced requires a broader social theory of how race, class, and gender intersect to produce complex forms of inequality and injustice. Here the emphasis is on how relationships between men and women are formed in relation to multiple types of social inequalities—such as race, class, sexuality, and religion. The social world is stratified in all these ways. So when gender is constructed or performed, it is done along with these other categories. For example, the implications of gender inequality in families are very different for upper-middle-class women who can afford high-quality childcare for their children and housekeepers to clean their houses than for poor women who have far fewer such choices. This theoretical approach thus highlights the interlocking nature of inequality, or what has come to be known as **intersectionality**—a focus on the linkages among disadvantaged groups. The key innovation is to look at the way inequalities are experienced together. The experience of gender, in other words, is different for poor or rich women, white or minority women, and so forth (Crenshaw, 1991; McCall, 2005).

Michel Foucault and the Problem of Power

2.4.3 Explain Foucault's theory of how power operates in society.

If recent feminist social theorists call our attention to the multiple and overlapping forms of oppression, the writings of the French social theorist Michel Foucault (1926–1984) sought to uncover how power works in all of its many manifestations. Foucault did not fit into any of the usual disciplinary boundaries: He was a philosopher and an intellectual historian, although his writings had many implications for social theory. He wrote books on topics such as prisons and asylums, the history of madness, and a multivolume study on the history of sexuality. In contrast to the standard way of thinking about power as something that some people have (e.g., those in the government or military, the ruling class, the authority figures in important institutions) and others do not (e.g., the working class, the poor, minorities), Foucault says that power is everywhere, operating in hidden as well as open forms.

Foucault was particularly interested in the role of "discipline" across societies—both how we try to discipline ourselves and how others (and institutions) try to discipline us. Foucault explored the ways in which institutions such as schools, prisons, mental institutions, sports teams train (or retrain) individuals to conform in certain ways (including not just their minds but also their bodies). Foucault famously suggested in his book *Discipline and Punish* (Foucault, 1977) that we live in a "disciplinary society," using imagery from a proposed model prison designed by social philosopher Jeremy Bentham called the Panopticon. Placed at the centre of the prison, the Panopticon is a visual tower that allows continuous surveillance of all the inmates, with the goal of "inducing in the inmates a state of conscious and permanent visibility that assures the automatic functioning of power" (Foucault, 1977, p. 201). Foucault argued that whole societies are constructed in similar ways. He argued that we are all subjected to a disciplining power that we can't see but that is all around us.

In modern society, then, Foucault believed that discipline is both a major characteristic and a function of power. However, just as power should not be thought of as something imposed on us from above, Foucault

Foucault emphasizes the role of architecture enabling specific forms of surveillance and control. Modern technologies further the option to collect statistics on human behaviour. The collection of information is a common phenomenon in Western societies; your movement is tracked by schools, banks (as shown here), credit card companies, and, of course, government agencies.

sanjagrujic/Shutterstock

argues that everyone disciplines everyone else—from friends who make fun of each other for acting in particular ways to the ways in which we discipline our own behaviours by internalizing norms in society. Most people in America these days seem to either be on a diet or think they should lose weight, or fear that if they do not discipline their eating habits they will gain weight. When we feel guilty about certain things and monitor our own behaviour, as most of us do with respect to food, we are doing something that Foucault says is the hallmark of modern power: We become our own police agents, policing our own behaviours.

Pierre Bourdieu: A New Approach to Theorizing Social Inequality

2.4.4 Discuss how Bourdieu redefined classes and the nature of class differences.

While power and discourse were at the centre of Michel Foucault's work, his French colleague Pierre Bourdieu (1930–2002) was focused on rethinking how we understand the mechanics of social inequality. Bourdieu's insights and theoretical arguments were a direct outgrowth of his own experiences in a life marked by climbing up the French social ladder from humble origins. His social theory attempted to combine the ways in which individuals behave in the context of class differences of which they are largely unaware. In many ways, Bourdieu's focus on class follows the work of other social theorists, especially Karl Marx, who also argued that understanding classes and class conflict was the key to understanding society. However, Bourdieu makes a break with Marxist and later neo-Marxist theories of class by proposing a fundamental reconceptualization of how sociologists think about classes and the nature of class differences. Whereas Marx and other sociologists usually define classes as groups of people who share the same position within the structure of the economy (as either workers or owners of the means of production, or in terms of quantitative measures such as income), Bourdieu enlarges the definition of class to along multiple dimensions, include how people think and act in the world and the kinds of knowledge and sophistication they display. In this way Bourdieu's work combined insights from interactionists about how individuals interact with one another with theories (like Marx's) of how inequalities in economic resources influence the choices and opportunities available to all of us as individuals.

At the core of Bourdieu's analysis of society are the everyday actions or, as Bourdieu refers to them, practices, which people undertake. From how we carry ourselves when talking to people, to the different kinds of music or food that we like, to the different ways we interact with authority figures, Bourdieu argued that people act differently in the world depending upon their class location. Bourdieu says that these differences emerge from the fact that each individual has what he calls a **habitus**. Our habitus disposes us to act in certain ways in certain situations. Different people have different kinds of habituses, depending especially on their upbringing and their education. In this way, the habitus is not something we are born with but rather a set of habits that are deeply rooted in the experiences we have growing up. Bourdieu argues that because of their different upbringings, members of different classes tend to have different habituses, and this is one of the key differences between members of different classes.

To illustrate and document these class-based differences in taste and dispositions, Bourdieu turned to studying culture, specifically to the consumption patterns of members of different classes. In one of his most famous books, *Distinction: A Social Critique of the Judgment of Taste* (Bourdieu, 1979/1984), Bourdieu interviewed a cross section of French society about their tastes and preferences regarding a range of cultural products, from music to art to literature. What Bourdieu found is that people from different economic classes express different cultural tastes, and that one of the markers of belonging to one or another class is precisely that it influences the tastes and preferences of individual members of those classes regarding cultural objects. Importantly, Bourdieu argued that when we express our preference for one or another cultural object, such as one genre of music over another, we are at once indicating that we belong to one group and defining ourselves in opposition to another.

Adam Gregor/Shutterstock

Similar to Marx, Bourdieu recognizes the importance of monetary and material capital in social hierarchies. However, Bourdieu argues that other forms of capital—such as how culturally sophisticated you are, or who you know—also determine one's social class.

Building off of his recognition that people in society compete to define their tastes and preferences as better than others, Bourdieu argued that groups in society fight over not just economic resources but also cultural resources. Bourdieu expanded Marx's idea of capital (recall that Marx used the term "capital" to describe any resource that can be invested to generated monetary returns) to include not just economic capital but also other kinds of capital. Most famously, he introduced the idea of **cultural capital**, which, according to Bourdieu, refers to knowledge about what is considered "high" or respected culture, expressed most clearly in certain people's capacity to talk intelligently about art or literature; those who have cultural capital are those whom we judge to be "cultured." Importantly, although people with high economic capital often have high cultural capital, the two do not directly overlap. Consequentially, Bourdieu argued that a person's position in the social hierarchy cannot be reduced to simply the amount of economic capital he or she has but must take into account a combination of economic and cultural capital.

Bourdieu found the extended notion of capital so useful for understanding inequality that he argued that a full understanding of the social position of any individual also required examining the role of other kinds of capital, most notably what he called **social capital** (resources based on who you know and can call upon for help when you need it) and **symbolic capital** (your reputation). Membership in a group provides actual or potential resources. Durable networks of friends remain valuable throughout a person's life. For instance, one may benefit from a job reference by a college friend. Symbolic capital consists of how a person or group is judged by a particular community, often in reference to one's accomplishments. War veterans, for example, generally receive social honour.

In short, Bourdieu saw the different forms of capital as providing different pathways into the class system. Someone who has a lot of economic capital may be able to get away with a lack of symbolic capital (a poor reputation may not matter too much if you are rich) whereas someone who has a lot of cultural capital or social capital may be able to rise up in the class system even if he or she is not particularly wealthy.

Conclusion: Social Theory and the Sociological Imagination

We started from three central themes that have motivated social theorists over the past 150 years:

1. What is the nature of the individual (who are we?), and how do individuals act in the context of society?
2. What is the basis for social order?
3. What are the conditions under which societies change?

We can now see that there is no single approach that can answer these questions once and for all. This might be viewed as a source of frustration—who wouldn't want to just "know" the answer to these questions?—but it can also be a source of fruitful thought and puzzle. Put another way, the fact that individuals, societies, and social change appear differently depending on which theoretical lens you put on underscores the endless complexity of the social world.

Does this mean that we cannot choose among theories? How is it that someone—say a young sociologist—decides that one theory is better than another? In order to answer that question, it is important to understand that the history of social theory in sociology is different than the history of theories in some other disciplines, especially those in the natural sciences, where "old" theories are discarded as "new" theories arise. Instead, as we have seen, older, classical theoretical ideas continue to inform the development of new social theories. As a result, there has been a steady accumulation of more and more theory over time, as new theories pile on top of old ones. What is a new student to do?

One way of approaching this is to think about the ways that each of the major theories we have described in this chapter approaches answers to the three central questions. Here, there are clearly important differences these different starting points nevertheless still leave a couple of possibilities for choosing among social theories. On the one hand, it may be that different theories can be useful depending on what questions we are focused on. In this way, we can think of different social theories as akin to different kinds of maps. Consider the differences in Google Maps between the "map view," the "earth view," and the "satellite view." Each provides a different way of looking at a single address or location. The same analogy works for old-fashioned printed maps: We use one kind of map to help navigate the streets of one city or in driving from one place to another, a different kind of map when hiking in the mountains, and a globe when trying to locate an unfamiliar country. Each kind of map provides useful orientation for some things but not others.

But all social theories cannot be equally valid for every question we might want to examine. We have tried to point out some of the shortcomings of various theories in this chapter. In these situations, where two theories are completely incompatible on some key point of interest, a sociologist must think about how to weigh their relative merits and shortcomings. Some possible questions in such comparisons could be as follows: Which theory is more consistent with what we believe we know, or to put it another way, "the facts"? Which theory helps us ask more interesting or important questions? Which theory fits better with our own political views (or perhaps even better, which forces us to challenge those views)? In some cases, the best way to make use of different theories is to synthesize them, taking ideas from different theorists and seeing how they do (or don't) fit together.

However we come to choose the theory or theories we study or identify with most closely, all of the major social theories we have explored in this chapter provide insights into the social world and its constituent parts. And social theories are very much part of the sociological imagination: Understanding how and why social theorists have puzzled over the questions they have underscores why sociology exists in the first place. As social theory continues to evolve and develop early in the twenty-first century, we can be sure that new theoretical traditions (or revivals of older traditions) will appear to further challenge the sociological imagination.

CHAPTER SUMMARY

The Big Questions Revisited 2

2.1 **What Is Social Theory?** Social theories enable us to see the social world in different ways. In this section, we identified three common themes that all major sociological theories have sought to address.

Seeing the Social World Through Social Theory

The Diversity of Social Theory

Learning Objective 2.1.1: Define social theory and describe the range of different social theories.

Three Common Themes

Learning Objective 2.1.2: Identify the three common themes that all of the major sociological theories have sought to address.

2.2 **How Did the Early Social Theorists Make Sense of the World?** The foundations of modern sociology, and social theory as we know it today, can be traced to the writings of a handful of key thinkers working in the second half of the nineteenth and early twentieth centuries. In this section, we introduced you to Karl Marx, Emile Durkheim, Max Weber, Georg Simmel, and W. E. B. Du Bois.

Classical Social Theory in the Late Nineteenth and Early Twentieth Centuries

Karl Marx (1818–1883)

Learning Objective 2.2.1: Discuss why Marx believed that societies were so heavily shaped by their economic systems.

Emile Durkheim (1858–1917)

Learning Objective 2.2.2: Analyze Emile Durkheim's explanation of what holds societies together.

Max Weber (1864–1920)

Learning Objective 2.2.3: Discuss Max Weber's contributions to our understanding of motivations for behaviour, legitimacy and authority, and status groups and social closure.

Georg Simmel (1858–1918)

Learning Objective 2.2.4: Explain how Georg Simmel's insights on social circles and social distance help us understand how individuals and groups relate to one another.

W. E. B. Du Bois (1868–1963)

Learning Objective 2.2.5: Explain W. E. B. Du Bois's views of the diverse ways in which racism influences the lives of African Americans and how racism produces a double consciousness.

2.3 **What Innovations in Social Theory Emerged in the Mid-Twentieth Century?** After World War II, the interests of social theorists began to shift in new and unexpected directions, and leadership in the development of social theory and sociology as a whole passed from being primarily located in Europe to North America. In this section, we explored the new directions in social theory that were embodied by functionalism, conflict theory, and symbolic interactionism.

New Directions in Social Theory, 1937–1965

Structural Functionalism

Learning Objective 2.3.1: Discuss the roles that norms, values, and institutions play in society, according to the theory of structural functionalism.

Conflict Theory

Learning Objective 2.3.2: Discuss how conflict theory attempted to explain social inequalities.

Symbolic Interactionism

Learning Objective 2.3.3: Analyze how everyday social interaction lies at the heart of understanding society, according to symbolic interactionism.

2.4 **How Has a New Generation of Social Theory Evolved?** The chapter concluded with a brief sampling of some important theories that have evolved since the 1960s.

Social Theory Since the Turbulent 1960s

The Revival of Marxism

Learning Objective 2.4.1: Discuss neo-Marxist ideas about the capitalist state, social classes, and globalization.

Feminist Social Theory

Learning Objective 2.4.2: Analyze the role of intersectionality in theories of gender inequality.

Michel Foucault and the Problem of Power

Learning Objective 2.4.3: Explain Foucault's theory of how power operates in society.

Pierre Bourdieu: A New Approach to Theorizing Social Inequality

Learning Objective 2.4.4: Discuss how Bourdieu redefined classes and the nature of class differences.

Learning the Terms

authority (p. 38)
bourgeoisie (p. 31)
capital (p. 31)
capitalist state (p. 51)
capitalist world system (p. 51)
charisma (p. 38)
class (p. 30)
class struggle (p. 32)
conflict theory (p. 47)
cultural capital (p. 57)
division of labour (p. 34)
feminist social theory (p. 53)
forces of production (p. 31)
gender (p. 53)
globalization (p. 52)
habitus (p. 56)
interpretative sociology (p. 36)
intersectionality (p. 55)
legitimacy (p. 38)
mechanical solidarity (p. 34)
modes of production (p. 30)
natural selection (p. 46)
neo-Marxism (p. 51)
network analysis (p. 41)
organic solidarity (p. 35)
patriarchy (p. 53)
power (p. 37)
proletariat (p. 31)
psychoanalysis (p. 53)
racism (p. 43)
sacred (p. 35)
sex (p. 53)
sex differences (p. 53)
social capital (p. 57)
social closure (p. 40)
social constructions (p. 53)
social distance (p. 41)
social facts (p. 33)
social forces (p. 33)
socialist society (p. 31)
socialization (p. 34)
social networks (p. 42)
social relations of production (p. 31)
social solidarity (p. 34)
social theory (p. 27)
status group (p. 39)
stratification system (p. 39)
structural functionalism (p. 46)
symbolic capital (p. 57)
symbolic interactionism (p. 48)

Chapter 3

Studying the Social World

by Lynne Haney

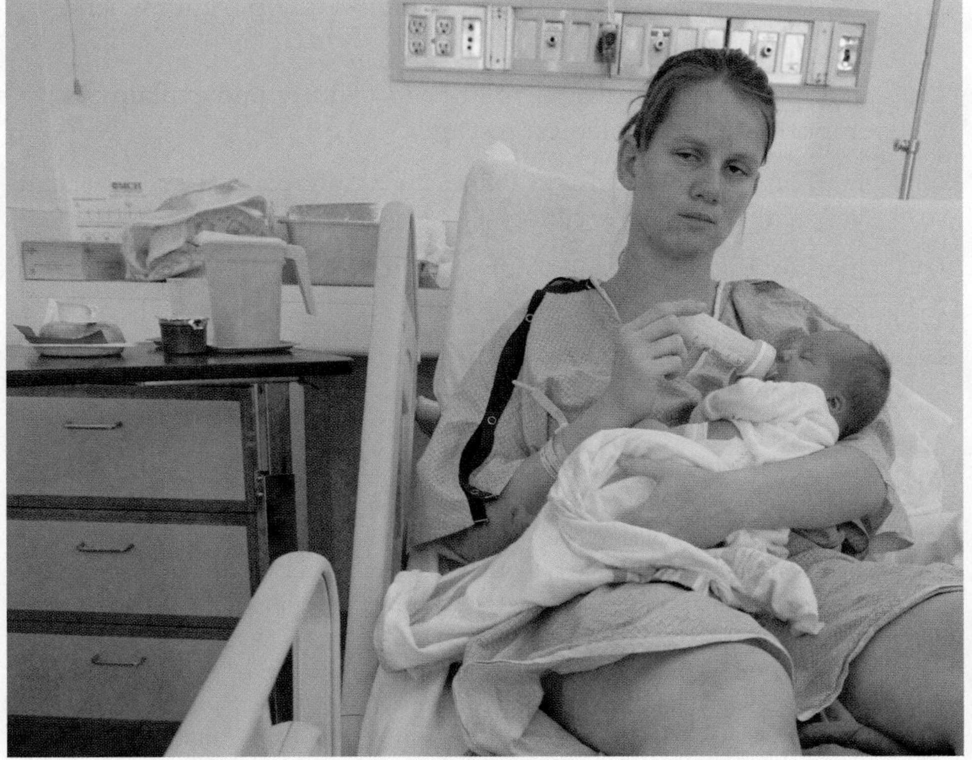

Mark Allen Johnson/ZUMA Press/Newscom

There are over 200,000 women in prison in the United States; over 70 percent of them have minor children. Many give birth to their children while in prison, which often involves being shackled to a hospital bed during childbirth—as this woman is.

Learning Objectives

3.1.1 Identify the six issues sociologists should consider to determine a research question's merit and feasibility.

3.1.2 Identify key factors that shape sociologists' choices about what to research.

3.2.1 Discuss how sociologists operationalize their research questions and distinguish between independent and dependent variables.

3.2.2 Identify the steps of the classical scientific method, and explain why sociologists might take a looser approach to research.

3.2.3 Compare and contrast quantitative and qualitative research methods.

3.2.4 Identify the key strengths and weaknesses of survey and interview methods.

3.2.5 Explain why the main strength of ethnography is also its central weakness.

3.2.6 Identify the types of research questions that are best studied from a comparative–historical perspective.

3.2.7 Explain why choosing the right research method to study motivations and behaviour is a complex process.

3.3.1 Explain sampling issues that sociologists grapple with when they begin their research.

3.3.2 Compare and contrast reliability and validity, and explain their importance in sociological research.

3.3.3 Explain why the ability to make causal inferences is so important yet challenging for sociologists.

3.4.1 Identify the goal of data analysis and describe the process sociologists use to interpret research.

3.4.2 Explain how sociologists use generalization to draw conclusions from their research.

Most of us have a clear idea about what prisons look like: located in a far-off locale, enclosed by wire fencing and concrete watchtowers, and filled with scary-looking men spending their days in tiny cells. When I entered my first prison, located in a large, dilapidated mansion on an inner-city street in northern California in 1992, as a young researcher eager to understand how women were "socialized" by the criminal justice system, a very different image confronted me. The "inmates" were young women, all official wards of the state of California, who had been sent to this prison to serve their time with their children. In place of small, dark prison cells were nicely decorated bedrooms; in place of the prison mess hall was an open, well-stocked kitchen; and in place of the barren prison recreation room was a cozy living room. Then there was daily life. It comprised not big, burly men sitting in cells but of small children running around, chased by their mothers. The only fights I ever saw were between hungry, sleepy kids and their exasperated mothers—over what the kids should eat or when they should go to bed—hardly the stuff of movies or TV shows such as *Prison Break*, *Oz*, or even *Orange Is the New Black*.

One of the most common mistakes young researchers make is to assume that our own research insights are shared by others. I made just such a mistake in this prison study—while I had been shocked by the existence of "mommy/baby" prisons, other sociologists had been writing about them for years. And whereas I was unnerved by even the idea of small children being raised in prison, other researchers seemed optimistic about the practice. These other researchers often insisted that one way to end the pains of incarceration and to stop the familial cycle of imprisonment was to keep women and children together—even if it meant bringing kids to prison. Of all these studies, the most seemingly definitive was a statistical study by the California Department of Corrections. It tracked the rearrest records of thousands of women who had done time in these prisons and found they had slightly lower repeat arrest rates than those who had served time in traditional facilities. Although the effects were small, researchers found mommy/baby prisons to be a success—and a real alternative to traditional incarceration.

The Big Questions

This chapter examines how sociologists study the social world by addressing the following big questions.

1. **Where do sociological questions come from?** We begin with the basic stages of sociological research, discussing the issues that often come up as researchers practise sociology for the first time, such as how sociologists turn their research interests into workable questions and how we know what to study.
2. **What is the best method to research different sociological questions?** Once sociologists have a working research question, they need to decide the best way to go about answering it. In this section, we examine the different types of methods that sociologists use in their research and discuss the process for determining which method is best for particular research questions.
3. **What challenges do sociologists face when collecting data?** Here, we explore some of the practical issues and challenges that surface during data collection.
4. **How do sociologists make sense of their findings?** Finally, we consider how sociologists make sure their findings are reliable and trustworthy, and how they decide what kind of general claims to draw from their research.

All of this left me wondering: Perhaps raising children in prison wasn't such a bad idea. So I returned to prison to do a more extensive study. This time I chose my sample carefully. I located my work in the state's model facility and joined its prison life. This is what **ethnographers**—researchers who enter the everyday lives of those they study in hopes of understanding how people navigate and give meaning to their worlds—do in their research. For over three years, I observed as hundreds of women and children passed through the prison's steel doors. I went to group sessions; I attended mothering classes; I taught inmates creative writing; and I went to staff meetings. By the end of the research, I was so integrated that I had keys to the prison.

Yet the more integrated into prison life I got, the more convinced I became that these were brutal, punishing places—but not in the way one might expect. The children, whom I thought would suffer most from the loss of freedom, seemed okay. With three meals a day, good childcare and education, healthcare, and other kids to play with, they were surviving life in prison fairly well. It was their mothers who were suffering. They suffered from a prison environment that stripped them of all parental power—how could they gain any maternal authority when they were ordered around and told where to go and what to do? They suffered from the loss of privacy—how could they parent when unsupervised, one-on-one time with children was not even allowed? In the end, some women became extremely anxious about their mothering; others simply collapsed under the pressure. But no one experienced the hope and optimism promised in other research accounts.

So were other researchers wrong? Not necessarily. Although we studied similar criminal justice facilities, we had different research questions, used different research methods, and collected different kinds of **data**—the facts and information used in research. Other researchers were interested in examining whether serving time with kids made it less likely for women to reoffend, so it made sense for them to track rearrest data and interview women who had reoffended. Had I been interested in this, I might have used a similar approach to my research. But I wasn't. My research questions revolved around how the women and children did time together—the practice of mothering behind bars and its implications for the mother–child bond. For this, ethnographic observation made the most sense because it gave me access to the data I needed to answer my research questions. All of this led me to paint a very different picture of these prisons and to draw very different conclusions about their possibilities and limitations.

Doing social research—whether on prisons or any other aspect of society you may want to study—raises many difficult challenges. In this chapter, we will explore those challenges and how researchers try to overcome them.

3.1 Where Do Sociological Questions Come From?

Ian Lishman/Juice Images/Glow Images

The Building Blocks of Sociological Research

Sociology and the social sciences are built upon the discoveries made by doing research on a topic. How do sociologists begin a research project? What prompts them to think something is worth studying? Our **sociological imaginations**, the way we take into account how our individual lives are impacted by social contexts, are at the centre of what prompts us to ask particular kinds of questions about the world. All sociological research shares a series of basic building blocks—ways of asking questions that arise from our sociological imaginations and our approach to concrete problems of doing research, such as collecting and analyzing data and drawing conclusions from our investigations. Good research is attentive to the particular issues that arise at all stages of the research process—and the specific research method chosen reflects the specific research question being asked in a study. The order here is critical: Sociologists first decide what they want to ask, and then they figure out the best tools and methods that can help answer those questions.

Crafting Good Research Questions From Important Topics

3.1.1 Identify the six issues sociologists should consider to determine a research question's merit and feasibility.

Few of us are ever at a loss for good topics to study. If you've found your way to a sociology course, chances are there is at least one thing about society you feel strongly about—if not many more. The challenge is not usually to find an interesting topic to investigate. The hard part is carving out a researchable question from that topic. Most often, this involves narrowing and focusing. It often will involve breaking the topic down into several parts and deciding which ones can be studied. It is a hard lesson to learn, but not all questions we are interested in can be studied.

There is no recipe for turning an interesting topic into a good research question. In general, good questions are both feasible and relevant. Feasible questions are those that can be studied given the limits of our time and resources. Feasible questions also lead us to think more specifically about a topic and to turn our ideas about that topic into a working **hypothesis**, which is the tentative prediction we have, before we begin the research, about what we are going to discover. A research question is relevant when it has the potential to tell us something about the world that we don't already know. For this reason, conducting a careful review of existing research on a topic before formulating a research question is essential. This not only helps narrow interests down to research questions, but it also reveals whether the ground to be covered is already charted territory. There is nothing worse than thinking you have an original sociological question only to discover late in the research process that others have already asked it—and have published articles and shelves of books about it. At the same time, just because someone else has done research on a topic or question you are interested in does not mean you can't re-examine it, especially if you think there is something about the earlier work that is unsatisfactory.

Although there is no easy-to-follow recipe for turning a research topic into a question, there are at least six questions sociologists should ask about a potential research question to determine its merit and feasibility (see Table 3.1).

Table 3.1 What Six Questions Should a Sociologist Ask to Determine Merit and Feasibility of a Research Question?

Question 1	**Do I already know the answer?**	Research focuses on questions for which we don't have answers. The point of social research is to ponder and then dig for information; it's not to confirm what we already know (or think we know).
Question 1: Example	What might not be known about divorce?	We know from decades of research that about half of all marriages will end in divorce. Rather than studying what's already known—how many marriages split up—focus on an aspect that we know far less about, such as the effects of divorce on children or the relationship between divorce and poverty.
Question 2	**Is my question researchable?**	Your question must be one that can actually be answered. Not even the best social researcher can answer "What is the meaning of life?" or when world peace will finally happen. Instead, ask questions that can be addressed with data that are accessible to you.
Question 2: Example	What is the source(s) of the conflict between Country X and Country Y?	Although most of us might want to know how we could stop all wars, the kind of data that might answer such a broad general question do not exist. A sociologist would be better off examining specific wars or conflicts, looking for the causes of the conflict and thinking about how that conflict may help us understand future conflicts.
Question 3	**Is my question clear?**	A clear research question uses well-defined concepts. State the question simply to ensure that anyone can understand it. In particular, make any hidden assumptions explicit. Such assumptions can be definitional, including terms or concepts we draw on without being clear about their meanings.
Question 3: Example	Are children's career aspirations shaped by their parents' occupations?	If you want to understand how parents' occupations shape their kids' academic interests, you can't just assume that the parents' occupations do affect what their kids are interested in doing. We can't take for granted that connection. Whether and how there may be a relationship is exactly what needs to be researched.
Question 4	**Does my question have a connection to social scientific scholarship?**	Decide what to research (and what questions to ask) after you are familiar with what others have already discovered. This helps you avoid repeating what has already been done; uncover specific debates about the topic; learn from the methods and approaches that other researchers have used; and discover questions or issues that previous researchers have ignored.
Question 4: Example	Do I know enough about the latest research?	While sociologists don't have to read everything before they form their research question, they need to have at least a general idea about the debates in the area of the proposed research, as well as the concepts and frameworks that structure those debates.

(Continued)

Table 3.1 *Continued*

Question 5	**Does my question balance the general and the specific?**	Good research questions should not be so broad that they can't be grasped in a meaningful way. Yet at the same time, good research questions should not be so narrow and specific that their findings, however carefully the research is done, may appeal only to us or to a very small group of people like us.
Question 5: Example	How are recent immigrants with professional degrees affected when they take service-sector jobs?	A student researcher is interested in how students who recently emigrated from Thailand to a specific neighbourhood make sense of their parents' work in service-sector jobs. This question is too narrowly focused on this student's own experience, however, so she needs to step back and reformulate it. She might instead ask how downward mobility affects recent immigrants.
Question 6	**Do I care about the answer?**	Sociologists aren't in the business of producing knowledge that no one cares about. If we don't care about our research, chances are that others won't either. Of course, there are real dangers in caring too much about our research. This can lead us to lose our distance from a topic and to become an advocate as opposed to a scientist.
Question 6: Example	Can I be very engaged in what I'm researching, yet remain objective?	The goal is to maintain a critical distance from what we study while remaining passionate about and committed to the questions we ask.

How Do We Know What to Study?

3.1.2 Identify key factors that shape sociologists' choices about what to research.

If you ask practising sociologists why they study what they study, you will likely get a long response about all of the scholarly debates that motivate them. Such explanations are surely accurate. But probe a little deeper and other influences may also come to the surface. There are endless scholarly debates and topics for sociologists to choose to study. So why do we gravitate toward some topics or questions as opposed to others? For many, the pull is personal: We find ourselves asking sociological questions that have personal significance. That significance may be direct, as when a sociologist researches something he or she has experienced firsthand, like racial inequality, religious discrimination, divorce, or educational stratification. Indeed, many sociologists have looked to their biographies to enhance their sociological imaginations and have used those imaginations to inform their research agendas. But personal influences can also be more indirect, as when a sociologist forms a research interest by observing others' experiences. For instance, people often ask me why I study incarceration. While I have never been imprisoned myself, other parts of my background shaped the interest, including many friends who got tangled up in the justice system as juveniles and adults.

For others, the pull of certain sociological questions may be less personal and more political. For instance, many sociologists are interested in questions of power and privilege because of their understandings of the causes of social inequality and because of their sense that research and knowledge can help point to better policies to address that inequality. Others grew up in periods of intense social and civil unrest that left them with an understanding of the importance of collective mobilization and an interest in studying how and when it emerges. It is not by chance that the study of social movements really took off in the 1970s, when the antiwar, civil rights, and feminist movements were at their peak, or that sociological interest in the environment has surged in recent years as more political and media attention has been devoted to issues of climate change and environmental racism.

Indeed, there are many factors that shape sociologists' choices about what to research. In this section, we will explore three key influences, as Figure 3.1 illustrates.

First, sociologists' **values**—the belief systems that shape sociologists' own views of and perspectives on the world we study—play a critical role in shaping the questions sociologists find interesting and intriguing about the social world. To say that our values influence our research questions is not, however, the same as saying that

Figure 3.1 What Influences Social Research?

SOURCE: Copyright by Pearson Education, Inc.

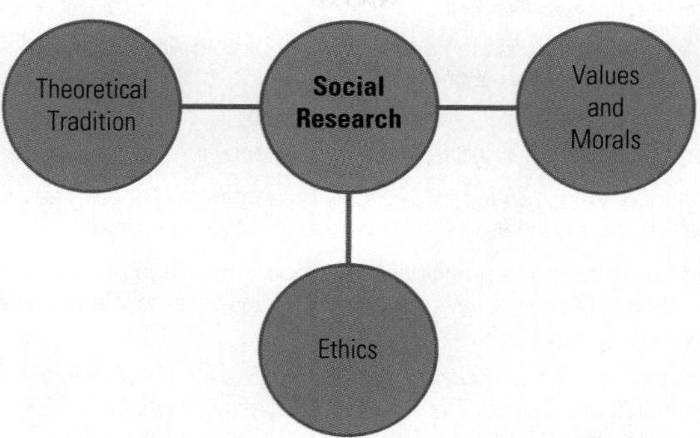

they determine our findings. Like all scientists, sociologists must remain open to all kinds of answers to our research questions—especially answers we may not like. That said, the values we bring to our research clearly motivate us to work on specific themes. For instance, if a sociologist values the democratic process, she might orient her research to examining questions about the factors enhancing or inhibiting democracy in specific organizations or countries. Or if a sociologist places high value on equality of opportunity, he might be most intrigued by research questions that focus on the policies enacted by different societies that attempt to level the playing field and give everyone an equal chance at success.

Second, sociologists typically choose to focus their research based on the *theoretical traditions* that they use to make sense of the world. There is a wide range of different theories that guide sociologists—depending on which tradition sociologists find most compelling—to ask some questions but not others. Theories are lenses through which we see the world, and the theory that guides a particular sociologist's research will have an important impact. The following examples illustrate how some of the leading theorists and theoretical traditions we introduced in Chapter 2 might approach a single topic.

For instance, many sociologists working in the tradition of nineteenth-century German theorist Max Weber see the social world as comprised of status groups; those sociologists influenced by work of nineteenth-century social and political theorist Karl Marx would be more likely to see the divisions based on social classes. And whereas a Marxian sociologist might search the world for examples of revolution, a researcher working in the tradition of twentieth-century social theorist Michel Foucault might set out to document everyday forms of resistance. Theoretical traditions thus play a critical role in shaping the questions sociologists find interesting and intriguing about the social world.

This leads to the third area of influence on social research: the **code of ethics**—a set of guidelines that outline what is considered moral and acceptable behaviour—that all scientists share (although each discipline has its own version; see Table 3.2 for ethical standards that guide sociological research). This code is especially important when the objects of investigation are real people, as they usually are for sociologists. Perhaps even more than those working in the natural sciences, social scientists must commit to protecting those we study and to not doing them any harm. Among other things, this requires us to disclose our identity as researchers and to obtain **informed consent** from our subjects by making their participation voluntary and based on a full understanding of possible risks and benefits involved. We also maintain confidentiality, guaranteeing that we will not reveal the true identities of our subjects. These commitments then shape the kind of questions sociologists can ask in our research. While we could dream up all sorts of questions we'd love to be able to research, we must consider the ethics involved in exploring them.

Table 3.2 Ethical Standards for Sociological Research

Academic organizations and institutions, such as the Canadian Sociological Association (CSA), have created ethical standards to guide sociologists' professional and research responsibilities and conduct. These standards fall into six categories.

1. Professional and Scientific Standards	The Canadian Sociological Association has issued a standard set of guidelines for use in sociological research that aims to ensure compliance with the federal government's *Tri-Council Policy Statement* (2014), and to reduce bias, dishonesty, and deception.
2. Competence	Sociologists should complete specialized training to attain competency in their areas of research.
3. Conflicts of Interest	Sociologists should not conduct research on topics that may present potential sources of conflict or bias. These might include incentives offered by companies seeking specific research outcomes.
4. Research Planning, Implementation, and Dissemination	Sociological research should be subjected to peer review, a process by which other researchers evaluate the quality of the work. The practice of peer review helps to maintain research integrity and ensures that the standards of research are upheld.
5. Informed Consent	Researchers should not expose participants to risk of personal harm. As far as possible, research should be based on the freely given informed consent of those studied. This implies a responsibility to explain, in terms meaningful to participants, what the research is about, who is undertaking and financing it, why it is being undertaken, and how it is to be disseminated. Colleges and universities have institutional review boards (IRBs) that oversee research involving human subjects. The boards review projects, assess potential harm to research subjects, and recommend how to revise the project to protect subjects. Standard IRB rules state that subjects must receive verbal and/or oral explanation of the project and that they retain the right to stop or leave the research project at any time.
6. Confidentiality	In almost all cases, sociologists conducting research must adhere to standards that ensure the confidentiality of their subjects.
7. Aboriginal Peoples	Researchers are also subject to special guidelines for research involving First Nations, Inuit, and Métis peoples of Canada.

SOURCE: Based on *Statement of Professional Ethics*, by the Canadian Sociological Association, 2012, Mississauga: Canadian Sociological Association (http://www.csa-scs.ca/files/www/csa/documents/codeofethics/2012Ethics.pdf), and the *Tri-council Policy Statement: Ethical Conduct for Research Involving Humans* (2nd ed. [*TPS2*]), by Canadian Institutes of Health Research, Natural Sciences and Engineering Research Council of Canada, Social Sciences and Humanities Research Council of Canada, 2014, Ottawa: Secretariat on Responsible Conduct of Research (http://www.pre.ethics.gc.ca/pdf/eng/tcps2-2014/TCPS_2_FINAL_Web.pdf).

So while a sociologist might want to ask questions about how and when people acquiesce to authority—as social psychologist Stanley Milgram did in a classic 1950s study that pretended to have his subjects administer electric shocks to others when ordered to do so (Milgram, 1963)—this might be considered harmful and detrimental for research subjects today. Or if a sociologist wanted to study the experience of prison—as Philip Zimbardo and Craig Haney did in their early 1970s Stanford Prison Experiment that turned young students into guards and prisoners (Haney, Banks, & Zimbardo, 1973)—this would most likely be considered out of bounds and dangerous for participants today.

Of course, researchers are not always aware when their questions could jeopardize their subjects' well-being. When both the Milgram and the Haney–Zimbardo studies were conducted, the researchers did not anticipate how much harm their studies would inflict on participants. Moreover, what constitutes "harm" can change and has changed over time—in both cases, researchers worked within the acceptable protocols of their universities. Today, to help researchers foresee any potential dangers and to safeguard the ethical standards of their work, **institutional review boards (IRBs)** operate at most universities and are required at all universities that receive research funds from the federal government. These boards review researchers' proposals before any work can begin in order to assess their potential harm and the benefits of the research for participants. They also evaluate whether ethical procedures will be in place and followed by researchers. In Canada, the second edition of the *Tri-Council Policy Statement: Ethical Conduct for Research Involving Humans* (2014), known as *TCPS 2* or the Policy, is a joint policy of three federal research agencies: The Canadian Institutes of Health Research (CIHR), the Natural Sciences and Engineering Research Council of Canada (NSERC), and the Social Sciences and Humanities Research Council of Canada (SSHRC) govern universities and colleges that receive federal funding. Needless to say, such reviews have influenced the questions sociologists ask. Consciously and unconsciously, sociologists end up steering themselves away from those areas they know will encounter problems in these boards, like electroshock studies of authority and simulated prison experiments. A number of social scientists have been critical of special guidelines that require researchers to allow research subjects to participate in the interpretation of the data and in the review of research findings before the completion of publications resulting from the research.

3.2 What Is the Best Method to Research Different Sociological Questions?

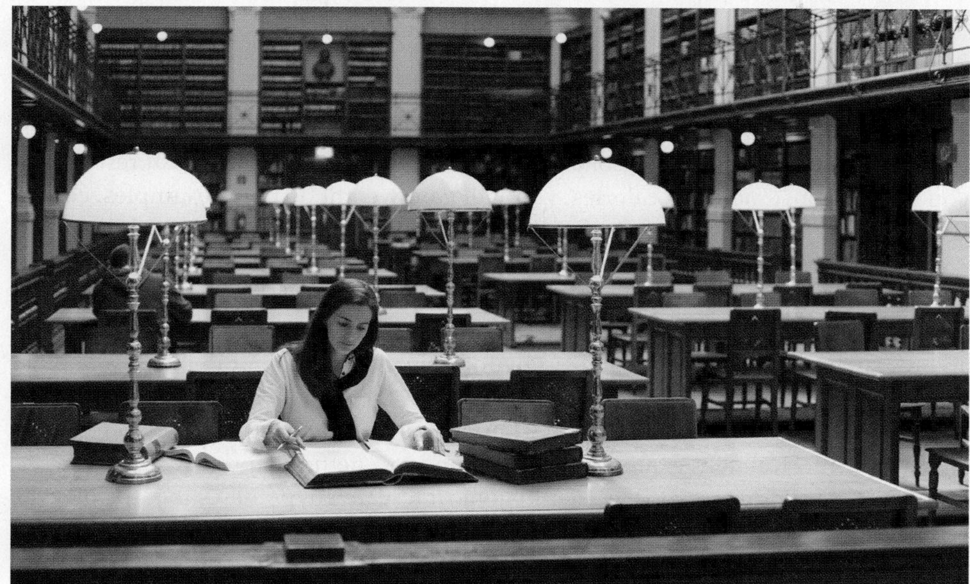

Lichtmeister/Shutterstock

Sociological Research Methods and Challenges

Once we have worked through all of these questions and have at least a working version of a research question, we need to decide on the best way to go about answering it. This implies deciding on a research method and a research design. This is the "who, what, where, when, and how" stage of the research process. It's when we decide who or what to study. It's when we decide exactly how many people, places, or things to include in our research project. It's when we decide where to locate our research, in terms of both time and place. It's when we decide when to conduct the research and for how long. It's when we decide if we will do a comparison and, if so, what it will consist of.

Getting Started

3.2.1 Discuss how sociologists operationalize their research questions and distinguish between independent and dependent variables.

Answering these "who, what, where, when, and how" questions will help researchers to **operationalize** their research, that is, specify the operations and techniques that will be used to examine the concepts that are the focus of the study. And it's when we decide how to measure our variables—those factors, attributes, or phenomena to be studied. Most commonly, researchers seek to separate the **dependent variable(s)** from the **independent variable(s)**. Independent variables are those factors we think influence or cause a particular outcome or dependent variable. If there is a relationship between an independent and a dependent variable, we expect that when the independent variable changes, the outcome (dependent variable) will change as well. For example, based on a lot of research we think that for most people, most of the time, finishing college or getting more years of schooling or training will increase their income.

Figure 3.2 A Hypothesis About Crime

SOURCE: Copyright by Pearson Education, Inc.

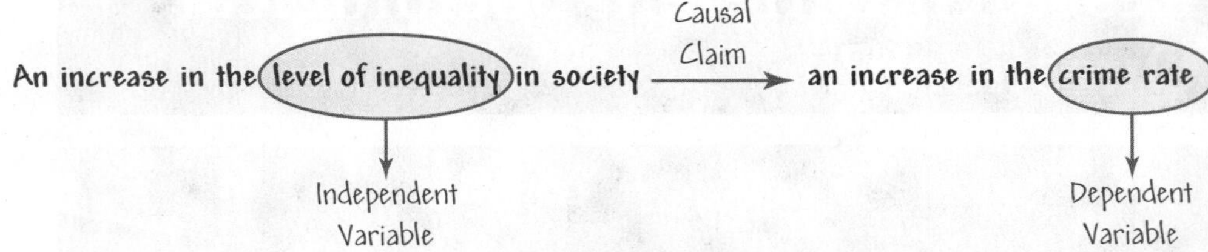

Or, as we know from both personal experience and established medical research, if you start to consume more calories, you will gain weight. In these examples, education and calorie consumption are the independent variables, and income and weight are the dependent variables. Figure 3.2 shows another example of a research hypothesis, concerning crime.

Being clear about what factors are causing what outcomes is central to beginning any research project and developing a hypothesis that can be put to the test. In most cases, sociologists start from an intuition or from their review of previous research about what independent variables may be causing an outcome they are interested in studying. Unfortunately, examples like the impact of getting more education or consuming more calories are much easier than most research hypotheses that sociologists actually consider, and even those seemingly simple examples may have more complexity than you might think at first glance. For example, if athletes in heavy training begin consuming more healthy calories as part of a program to expand their lean muscle mass, they may actually lose weight. In the real world, there are usually many possible independent variables, and those variables may influence each other as well as the dependent variable. In the case of crime, for instance, we know that younger people (for example, between the ages of 15 and 30) are more likely to commit crimes. Perhaps because of a "baby boom," higher crime rates may be caused not by inequality but rather because there is a larger proportion of young people in the general population.

The Classical Scientific Method of Research

3.2.2 Identify the steps of the classical scientific method, and explain why sociologists might take a looser approach to research.

The logic underlying any research, from beginning to end, can vary. But sociologists and other scientists often try, as much as possible, to remain true to the classic steps of the **scientific method**, which are detailed in Table 3.3.

Table 3.3 What Are the Steps of the Scientific Method?

Step 1: Formulate a research hypothesis	Formulate research questions and hypotheses based on previous scholarship.
Step 2: Predict the relationship between the independent and dependent variables	Identify the variables that are key to the hypothesis, and predict relationships among those variables (with one or more independent variables predicted as influencing a dependent variable).
Step 3: Find existing data or collect new data	Identify a source of data that you can use to test the hypothesis. If no existing data can be found, you must collect your own data on each of the variables.
Step 4: Analyze data	Once the data are collected, analyze the data to determine whether the relationship researchers hypothesized between the key variables held up.
Step 5: Draw conclusions	Finally, draw empirical and conceptual generalizations from the data and write up the results.

It is important to be familiar with the steps of the scientific method, but it is also important to note that in the real world of research, a somewhat looser approach to the process of discovery is often necessary. Sociologists may cover each of the steps in the classical scientific method, but sometimes in a slightly different order, depending on the research project and how it develops. For example, while in many cases sociologists may have hypotheses, sometimes they work with hunches based on observation or experience, or bold guesses about what they think they might find, instead of a clearly defined hypothesis. Often, it is only after working with data that hypotheses begin to emerge. Further, some research questions are impossible to organize neatly into a set of relationships between variables. In that case, sociologists may opt to remain more flexible about what they are looking for, allowing the people they observe and interview to help define key issues and problems. Or they may begin by collecting information on several issues until they decide which they want to focus on. All of these examples suggest that in the real world of research, sociologists and other social scientists will go back and forth between the steps of the classical scientific method. They will return to their questions for refinement and specification once the research is underway. Knowing the steps of the classical method of scientific research is important, but at the same time good researchers should continually reflect on what they are doing and change course when they sense it is necessary. It might be nice if research could be conducted like following a recipe, but it is usually much more complicated.

Quantitative Versus Qualitative Research Methods

3.2.3 Compare and contrast quantitative and qualitative research methods.

Two broad types of research are employed by sociologists: quantitative research and qualitative research. While these types of research are subject to similar rules about research design, they are in many ways different from one another. At the heart of the difference between the two types of research methods is the kind of data they rely upon to draw conclusions. **Quantitative research** relies upon data that are statistical in nature, for example, data that come from the census or other government surveys, or polls or surveys conducted by social scientists, or any kind of information that can be put into numerical form (such as "How many times does the typical police officer in a city stop a white male versus a young Aboriginal male?"). Quantitative research takes raw data that come in a numerical form and uses it to analyze how one or more independent variables are related to a dependent variable that is also measured numerically. **Qualitative research**, by contrast, relies on words or detailed interviews with informants, direct observations, historical records, or even pictures as data. Qualitative research usually involves the analysis of large amounts of textual material by a researcher, whereas quantitative research involves the use of statistical methods to examine the numerical data used in the study. To complicate matters further, some researchers use evidence that is both qualitative and quantitative; they employ what is known as **mixed-method research**. In such studies, the researcher (or research team) hopes to gain different insights into a question by combining numerical and textual evidence.

Sociology is unique within the social sciences in that it encompasses a range of acceptable research methods. We will focus our discussion in the next sections on three of the most common: one method (interviews and surveys) that can be done either qualitatively or quantitatively and two methods (comparative–historical and ethnographic) that are usually done qualitatively.

How do we know what method is best for a particular study? The starting point is to think about what kind of evidence is needed to answer the question we have posed. Can the question be answered by surveying large numbers of people and comparing the responses of different groups? Or it is best addressed by talking directly to a subsample of these people, perhaps in more depth and for a longer period of time? Or is it best addressed by observing them and watching them interact? Or can the question be captured by looking at similar or different groups of people in other times and places? The decision about which method should be used must always be based on the research question—methods are means to an end, not an end themselves.

Just as the choice of a research question leads to a specific research method, the choice of a method implies specific research challenges. So while all research has its dilemmas, different methods highlight different dilemmas. To provide a concrete sense of this as well as a feel for what each of the main sociological methods actually involves in practice, in this section we discuss one of the main issues confronting sociologists using each method—including examples of how they grappled with it. How hard is it for historical sociologists to select their cases? How tricky is it for interviewers to draw their samples? And how difficult is it for ethnographers to theorize and generalize from their work?

Survey and Interview Methods and the Dilemmas of Design

3.2.4 Identify the key strengths and weaknesses of survey and interview methods.

Interviews are a basic and widely used type of sociological research. They come in many shapes and sizes. The most common type of interview is the **survey**, which is a questionnaire that asks standardized questions of large groups of randomly chosen people. These questions can be asked in person, on the phone, by mail, or increasingly on the Internet. (Surveys are also sometimes called *polls*, although the term *poll* primarily refers to surveys usually done on the phone and conducted by media or political organizations with less rigorous methods than academic or government surveys.) Because surveys can be used to collect information about any aspect of social life of interest to the investigator, including information about such topics as jobs, families and family life, health, education, wealth and income, and religious and political attitudes and values, it is hardly surprising that surveys are so widely used to answer research questions. Surveys have been in wide use since the 1930s, when social scientists first figured out how to design a survey at reasonable cost that would provide valid information about an entire population.

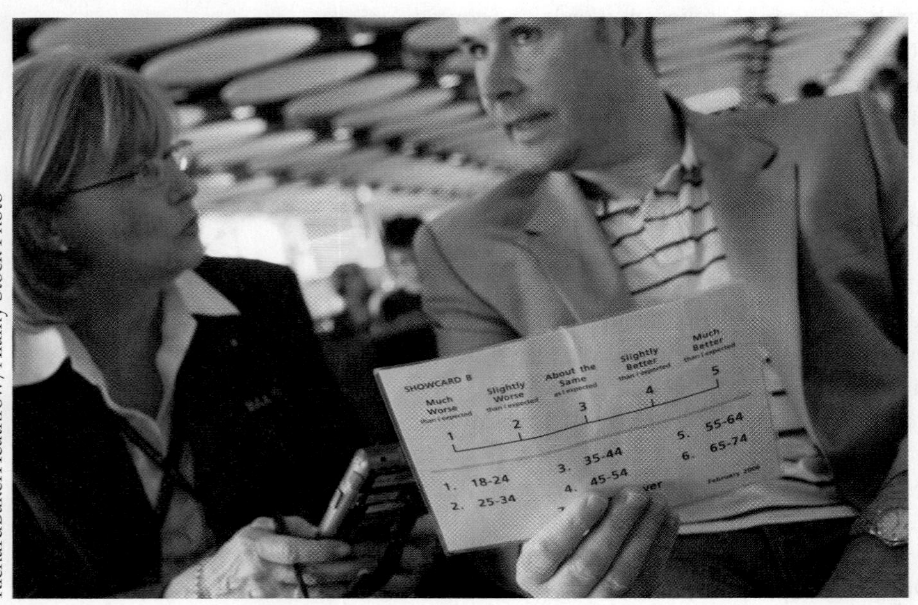

With the proliferation of cellphones and online communication, survey researchers are confronting new obstacles to obtaining a diverse, representative sample.

RichardBakerHeathrow/Alamy Stock Photo

In a typical survey, respondents are asked identical questions, and they are generally required to choose among the answers provided to them. These are called *closed-ended surveys*. But there are also other kinds of surveys that include some *open-ended responses*, in which interviewees provide answers to questions in their own words. There are even surveys where researchers deliberately vary the wording of some questions to see whether those changes influence the responses people give.

Surveys are very good at generating data about an entire population. The most famous survey in Canada is the census, conducted every five years by Statistics Canada;

most households receive a short-form census, and a smaller number receive a long-form version that gathers more detailed information. The census and other government surveys are essential tools for researching many social science questions and for informing governments' social policies. For example, if you want to know how many children the average family has, or how Canadians are living in single-parent families, or what percentage of people in your hometown have university degrees, data from the census can provide the answer. The census is unique in that it literally attempts to gather responses from every single household in Canada (and, as a result, costs billions of dollars to collect). The census is very limited—by law—in the kinds of information it can collect. Essentially, it can gather only basic information about each household. Filling out the census is mandatory, and failure to comply is punishable by law.

Statistics Canada also carries out a National Household Survey (NHS) once every five years that is designed to complement the census. The National Household Survey encompasses interviews with about 30,000 households and provides information about the demographic, social, and economic characteristics of people living in Canada. In 2011, the federal government cancelled the long-form census and substituted the (voluntary) NHS, giving rise to considerable controversy in Canada. Critics pointed out that by cancelling the long-form census, the Harper government stripped Canadians of the capacity to gather information about their population in an age of information. The decision took its toll on Statistics Canada and on sociologists who rely on accurate data for making a wide range of policy recommendations. The fact that the 2011 NHS was voluntary made evidence-based predictions about social trends and comparative analyses less accurate. The NHS was made mandatory by the Liberal government of Prime Minster Justin Trudeau in 2016.

These large, government-run surveys are valuable for many research questions, but social scientists often want to know much more than the information available in some government surveys. For example, many want to know far more about people's family and work history, mental health, political affiliations, and opinions about a wide range of issues. For this kind of information, more specialized surveys are needed. Some of the most useful of these researcher-driven surveys are carried by groups of investigators, such as the **General Social Survey**. The two primary objectives of the General Social Survey (GSS) are to gather data on social trends in order to monitor changes in the living conditions and well-being of Canadians over time and to provide information on specific social policy issues of current or emerging interest. A specific topic is usually repeated every five years. These surveys are now very valuable for historical reasons, as they allow researchers to investigate social and political trends over long historical periods by comparing answers to the same questions over time. But these broad general surveys are often not very useful for answering more specific research questions. For this, researchers must design and carry out their own investigation, creating original questions for the population they are attempting to study.

Surveys are valuable for many purposes, but they have some limitations as well. For example, they typically constrain the kinds of answers that can be given, and they don't allow those being interviewed to elaborate on or explain their answers (since doing so could turn a 20-minute survey into a much longer interview). For many research questions, that is not necessarily a limitation, but if you want to know about *why* people think the way they do, or *why* they act in the manner that they do, or if your research question concerns how and what people *feel* about various situations or events, the limitations of the survey format can become overwhelming.

Related to surveys, but different in many ways as well, are **in-depth interviews**, in which respondents are asked questions about a topic without using standardized answer formats. The format of the in-depth interview gives researchers much more freedom to ask about whatever they are interested in—and to follow up when more detail is needed or appropriate. Interviewees are also free to elaborate on their answers. Although both surveys and in-depth interviews gather data from the answers provided by the interviewee, these methods have important differences. A survey is typically shorter, often lasting only 20–25 minutes (although the GSS takes about 90 minutes to complete). In contrast, in-depth interviews tend to last much longer. The typical length of in-depth interviews, the time required, and the cost of transcribing and analyzing them mean that most research based on in-depth interviews will have far fewer cases.

As a sociological method, surveys and interviews share some key strengths and weaknesses. Their main strength is their ability to learn facts about large numbers of people (through surveys), and to understand how people make sense of their worlds (through in-depth interviews). For example, surveys allow us to know how many young college graduates are unemployed, how many people have moved to Canada from other countries, how many people own their own home, and how many people are living in poverty. Without surveys, we would know far less about society than we do. Surveys can also ask people about their beliefs and attitudes on a wide range of subjects. But there is often no better way to determine how people understand their lives and experiences than by asking questions in longer, in-depth interviews. In-depth interviews also allow sociologists to give ordinary people the opportunity to bring their experiences to bear on social science research.

Despite the vast utility of surveys and interviews, with these strengths come challenges. Surveys are often expensive and time-consuming to conduct. Designing a survey or conducting an interview takes great skill and practice, and much time and effort can be wasted if the survey or in-depth interview is not well designed at the beginning (and sometimes that is difficult to know until you actually start the research). In-depth interviews face special problems as well: It is always challenging, for example, to conduct interviews with someone you do not know and to ask them questions about potentially sensitive issues. And then there are the complexities of making sense of and analyzing all the data from these interviews, which can often yield hundreds of pages of transcripts and quotations from respondents. Finally, both surveys and in-depth interviews face the potential problem that what people say about themselves or their actions is not always entirely accurate. Survey respondents or interviewees in an in-depth interview may be uncomfortable revealing things about themselves that the researcher is interested in. There are many reasons why respondents may not always be reliable: They may be embarrassed, they may be concerned about appearing violate some established social norm in answering questions, or they may simply be confused about the question itself and give incomplete or misleading answers as a result.

Ethnographic Methods and the Challenge of Theory

3.2.5 Explain why the main strength of ethnography is also its central weakness.

If people don't always do what they say—or can't tell an interviewer what they really think and how they actually behave in different settings—what is a researcher to do? Overcoming this problem is one reason why direct-observation research—known as **ethnography**—has long been a prominent and widely used method for conducting sociological research. Ethnographers get inside the worlds they study, up close and even as direct participants. Critical to doing ethnographic research is the decision about where to locate these observations—that is, in what "site" ethnographers think the phenomenon they are interested in can be found. Then, once "in the field," they need to decide who, where, and what to observe. Ethnographic researchers are always asking themselves if they should include different kinds of observations, or if they should expand the kind of people and interactions they are focusing on. Because their work is typically centred in one place, a major challenge arises as researchers try to make sense of their data and figure out whether and how their research applies to contexts other than the one they studied.

As with interviews, there are many types of ethnographic research. Ethnographic research was pioneered by anthropologists, who often carry out their research in foreign environments to understand different cultural practices and social norms. Sociological ethnographies, by contrast, typically involve research conducted in contemporary settings. Almost any social setting can be the subject of ethnographic research. Families, neighbourhoods, schools, companies, government offices, public washrooms, social movements, and many other places and organizations have been the subject of prominent ethnographic research. For instance, one recent ethnographic study examined how the "party culture" in modern universities impacts students' overall university experience and their future pathways (Armstrong & Hamilton, 2012). These sociologists spent a year living on a dormitory floor at a Midwestern university, getting to know each of the 53 students living on the floor, and then following them through their university years and then into post-university life. Through this deep immersion in the lives of a handful of students, the authors were able to observe aspects of the lives of these students that would not likely have surfaced during a survey or in-depth interview.

MIXA/Getty Images

Some ethnographers immerse themselves deeply in the culture or subculture they are studying. Others observe people in contexts they are familiar with, such as an ethnographer who studies how people interact in a nail salon.

Ethnographic research can be viewed as a continuum (Luker, 2010). On one end are delineated observations in contexts researchers are fairly familiar with and on questions that are clearly defined, such as in research by an ethnographer who goes out to study how men interact in a local barbershop in Calgary or by a researcher who studies how women negotiate the dynamics of power and beauty in local nail salons in Toronto. On the other end is total immersion in another culture or subculture for long periods of time, such as by an ethnographer who heads off to Rwanda to study postgenocidal society or an ethnographer who observes the religious practices of Muslim women in Eastern Europe. Most ethnographic work in sociology falls someplace in the middle, with researchers documenting the patterns, processes, and practices of everyday life both of those they may be familiar with and of those who may be far more unfamiliar.

The real strength of ethnographic research is that it can produce some of the richest, most nuanced accounts of social life. Done well, ethnography transports us to places and spaces we don't normally have access to, from the inside of prison cells to the dealings of street gangs to the struggles of homeless heroin addicts to the trials and tribulations of fashion models. It can provide **thick descriptions** (Geertz, 1973) of the people living in those spaces—that is, rich and detailed descriptions of the ways they make sense of their lives, from the perspective of those people themselves. Ethnography is the ideal method to use for getting at *practice*—the point where words and actions collide, and frequently diverge. Instead of taking people's words at face value, ethnographers are able to link words to the way people act, a connection that frequently leads to fascinating examples of inconsistency—which can tell us an enormous amount about social life.

A great example of this inconsistency between what people say about their actions and their actual behaviour, and of how ethnographic research can provide a much more accurate picture than surveys, can be seen in Meg Luxton's (1980) research in a book called *More Than a Labour of Love,* in which she combined participant observation and in-depth interviews to describe the unpaid and unrecognized work that women do in their homes caring for children and partners and maintaining the house to show how women's unpaid labour is necessary and central to the economy. Arlie Hochschild's book called *The Second Shift* (1989) provides another good example of ethnographic research. Researched and written in the late 1980s, the book remains unusual for its combination of interviews with and observations of couples, focusing on how they manage the tensions between work and family. What Hochschild found is fascinating: The way couples represented what went on in their homes almost always differed from what Hochschild saw in their homes. In some cases the couple claimed to be "traditional"—with the husband taking care of the world of paid work and the wife the domestic arena of unpaid labour—but then in everyday life, Hochschild watched as the men did a considerable amount of the cleaning, shopping, and household organizing. In other cases, she found the opposite: Couples claimed to have an equal division of labour outside and inside the home, yet their lives revealed something else. Their interview proclamations were contradicted by sound of the wives' feet as they ran around the house cooking, cleaning, and caring for the kids while their husbands watched television or worked on their cars. Faced with the differences between words and action, Hochschild was able to analyze what she called "family myths," the complex ways couples smooth over the gap between what they would like from their relationship and what they actually get from it. Now decades old, the account still provides an insightful analysis of the workings of these myths and still shows the importance of observing what people do, and not only what they say.

The irony, however, is that ethnography's main strength can also be its central weakness. In the process of producing thick descriptions of interesting aspects of social life, ethnographers can sometimes lack analytical focus or theoretical relevance. Some ethnographers seem reluctant to conceptualize or theorize from their data. While this was not true in Hochschild's case—in part because her empirical findings about the discrepancies between words and actions were confirmed by many other kinds of data—some ethnographic studies are plagued with an inability to generalize beyond their specific fields. Indeed, generalizing from ethnographic data can be particularly thorny. Ethnographers can find it hard, if not impossible, to claim that their case is truly representative of a larger trend or issue, particularly if they fail to critically analyze or observe contradictions in the claims made by their research subjects. They can find it hard, if not impossible, to move beyond the places and everyday lives they are embedded in and to analyze them in terms that would seem foreign to those lives. And they can find it hard, if not impossible, to make broad points from the small, local contexts ethnographers tend to research. All of this can leave ethnographers wary of using their work to engage in the larger theoretical and conceptual debates of sociology.

Of course, the ability of ethnographers to provide very detailed accounts of local settings is not considered a weakness by everyone. In fact, some embrace and celebrate this aspect of ethnographic work. Clifford Geertz (1973), the famous anthropologist who came up with the term *thick description* to describe what ethnographers do, saw it as an asset of the method—a way for social scientists to render what he called an "understanding of understanding" (Geertz, 1983, p. 5). More contemporarily, there are some ethnographic studies whose goal is simply to offer new and different descriptions of social life. One of the best, most prominent examples of this is an ethnographic account of homeless street book vendors and magazine sellers in New York City, a tour de force of detail and insight into what everyday

Figure 3.3 The Extended Case Method

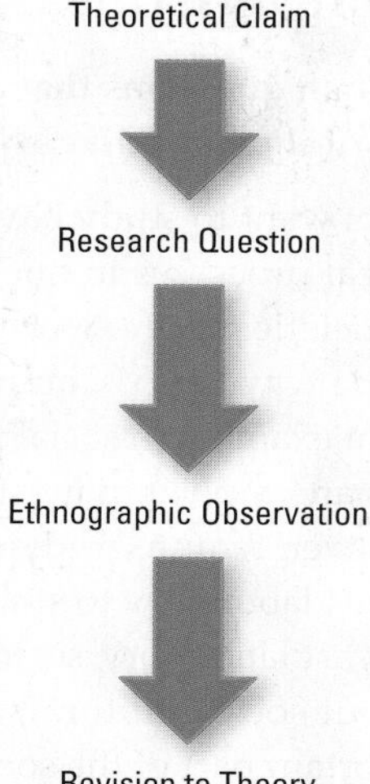

life on the street looks and feels like for these men: the indignities they suffer, the meanings they make, the ways they attempt to protect their sense of self, and the strategies they use to maintain a "moral order" on the street (Duneier, 1999, p. 9). And while no one can read this study and not learn an enormous amount about how men like this live and survive, there is not much in the way of explanation or theory in the account. There is not even very much about what others have found in studies of similar topics. In fact, Duneier almost explicitly rejects using theory even to organize his account, opting instead to divide up his story according to the different types of men on the street and the different labour they engage in. Hence, ethnographies in the tradition of studies like these are so engaging and so captivating that they reveal the power of good thick description, yet they can also leave readers without a sense of what these men's lives tell us about broader sociological concepts and theory.

For this kind of analysis, there are other ethnographic traditions. There are those ethnographers who try to move beyond descriptive accounts of specific locales to connect their ethnographic insights to larger sociological debates and theoretical questions. For instance, sociologist Michael Burawoy has oriented his career to debunking the idea that ethnography cannot be used to engage theoretical questions. To do this, he has developed the **extended case method**, a way of doing ethnography that emphasizes its contribution to social theory (Burawoy, 2009). A simple diagram of how this method works can be seen in Figure 3.3.

As Burawoy points out, an ethnographic site need not be representative of a large social process to extend the reach of theory. It need not cover lots of randomly sampled cases to contribute to social theory. Instead, he insists that ethnographers can and should be theoretically focused from the start of their research: When they head out into the field, they should go armed with concepts and theories they want to hold up to the social world. Because the real world is almost always more complex than our theories of it, an ethnographer's job is to revise social theory in light of what he or she observes in that world. Rather than striving for thick description, these ethnographic accounts aim for theoretical reconstruction. The books and articles written in this ethnographic mode reveal its payoffs. From Burawoy's own work on the relationships between managers and workers in factories in the United States and Eastern Europe to his students' work on everything from HIV activists to housekeepers to welfare workers to Chinese assembly-line workers, many broader theoretical questions have emerged (see Burawoy, 2009; Burawoy, Blum, et al., 2000; Burawoy, Burton, et al., 1991).

Comparative–Historical Methods and the Complexity of Comparisons

3.2.6 Identify the types of research questions that are best studied from a comparative–historical perspective.

Some of the questions sociologists want to study have an important time dimension; they involve history and historical processes in one way or another. In other cases, comparisons—either between societies in the world today or between societies at earlier points in time—may be the way to go. **Comparative–historical research** is a qualitative method of analysis that examines a social phenomenon over time or in different places. While comparisons are implicit in most social research, some questions are particularly well suited to or even require studying from a historical perspective. History provides a remarkably vast laboratory to study large-scale processes of social change. Not surprisingly, in this vast laboratory, sociologists have found ways of testing theories and hypotheses about social, cultural, and political change. Historical research has always been an important part of the sociological tradition.

Sociologists who study history do so in ways that are often quite different from those of historians. Historians are typically experts in a particular time and place—such as nineteenth-century England, czarist Russia, Nazi Germany, and so forth—and most of their research centres on issues in their area of specialization. By virtue of their deep immersion in a particular context, historians are able to capture nuance and detail in ways that most historical sociologists would not. By contrast, sociologists who study history typically do so to make *comparisons* over time and context. They are not necessarily experts in any one time period or place; rather, they take advantage of the variations in time and place to make sense of the larger patterns that the study of history affords.

Charles Tilly's theory showed that protests were not random or irrational eruptions but rather developed in particular contexts such as periods of political turmoil.

Interfoto/Alamy Stock Photo

Although they may draw on the findings of historians to develop their conclusions, historical sociologists have also been very innovative in constructing new sources of data that allow for surveys and comparisons over time. For example, the influential work of Charles Tilly (1929–2008) developed a method for reconstructing the history of the protest movements of ordinary citizens over long historical periods in countries like France and Britain by coding newspaper reports, including those in small, obscure local papers (e.g., Tilly, 1986). Matching these records to other social and economic data, Tilly was able to develop a theory of the cycles of protest over time that showed that protests were not random or irrational eruptions but rather developed in particular contexts such as food shortages, wars, and periods of political turmoil.

Several different kinds of historical comparisons are possible. Research within a single country—for example, comparing neighbourhoods, cities, or provinces within Canada, or specific institutions in different historical periods—is a common type of comparative–historical investigation. By contrast, **cross-national comparisons** typically have as their goal explaining the differences between countries, such as understanding why some outcome is observed in one country and not another.

In order to explore how comparative–historical research is conducted, let's examine in a bit more detail one classical piece of scholarship, Max Weber's *The Protestant Ethic and the Spirit of Capitalism* (Weber, 1904/1976. Weber's *Protestant Ethic* is one of the true classics of the social sciences. Weber's starting puzzle was that he wanted to know why capitalism as an economic system was thriving in some parts of Europe but not others. He noted, for example, that in his native Germany some parts of the country were much more economically advanced than others. How could he study this phenomenon, and what might provide an answer to his puzzle?

Weber noticed one important difference between the regions of Europe that were the most economically successful and those that were further behind: The advanced regions tended to be areas where Protestants were dominant. In the long history of religion in Europe, the struggle between Catholics and Protestants had produced an uneven map of religious influence. Catholicism retained its historic influence in many parts of Southern Europe, such as Spain, France, and Italy, whereas Protestantism was the dominant religion in most parts of Northern Europe. A few countries, like Germany, were divided regionally, with Protestants controlling some areas and Catholics others. The United States was another country where Protestants were numerically dominant (indeed, some of the early settlers in America practised a kind of extreme form of Protestantism that faced persecution in Europe).

Having made this discovery, Weber then had to try to account for why Protestantism might have been associated with the early rise of capitalism. This led him to dig into the relationship between the views of key figures in the history of Protestantism (especially Martin Luther and John Calvin) and their more modern followers (including Benjamin Franklin in the United States), whom Weber saw as popularizing economic doctrines that connected Protestant religious beliefs to the promotion of individual virtues like thrift and saving that were beneficial for capitalism as an economic system. Weber concluded that a critical aspect of Calvin's form of Protestantism was this: Being economically successful was a way of demonstrating your worthiness to God, whereas consuming whatever you had was a sign that you were not one of the select who would be sent to Heaven.

Scholars have been debating the arguments and evidence that Weber presented ever since. For example, Weber wrote before Western scholars had a good understanding of the Muslim world (which included pockets of early capitalism), and he may have missed some important religious differences even in Europe. Nevertheless, by using historical variation to test a theory about the importance of religion, Weber showed how sociologists can draw upon history to test important propositions about society.

The ultimate goal of research is to find a way to present sociologists' most interesting findings to others in the hopes of advancing our knowledge of the social world. This is a goal all social researchers strive for, regardless of the questions they ask or the methods they use. Much of this section has stressed the differences between methods—how different questions imply different methods and how different methods involve different challenges and dilemmas. Yet the project of social research unites more than it divides: All sociologists want to ask innovative questions and develop new puzzles about the social world. We want to solve those puzzles by gathering data and writing up the results in ways that are convincing, intriguing, and provocative. And we want our solutions to prompt others to ask better questions in their own research and to add to the development of the sociological imagination.

Matching the Question With a Method

3.2.7 Explain why choosing the right research method to study motivations and behaviour is a complex process.

So far, we've explored several of the most prominent methods used by sociological researchers. But how do we know what method is the best to use? Sometimes the choice is obvious: When a research question centres on patterns of behaviour among large groups of people, survey methods are usually the best bet. For instance, if you wanted to know how crime affects communities, you might use statistical methods to chart inhabitants' well-being in high-crime neighbourhoods, as sociologist Patrick Sharkey did in his study of the school performance of kids living in areas marked by violence (Sharkey, 2012). But when the question is about the thought processes that lead people to have certain opinions or engage in certain behaviours, those questions usually require in-depth interviews, like the questions asked by sociologist Kathleen Gerson (2011) in her study of how young people negotiate their relationship ideals and expectations in a world of changing gender roles. And if the question has more to do with how people interact and less with how they say they interact—like my questions about how women and children do time together in prison—then ethnographic observation is often the way to go.

In some cases, the decision about which research method to employ is less obvious. Indeed, many studies go wrong precisely by choosing the wrong method to study the problem: They ask a good, clear research question grounded in the existing scholarship, but they end up collecting data that don't help answer it. For example, whenever I teach a research methods course, inevitably several students will want to study gender differences in romantic relationships. Usually, they want to know something about how men and women act differently in their relationships—whether men are more distant and withdrawn (from Mars) and women are more open and connected (from Venus). And usually these students start off planning to use interview methods, largely because those seem most familiar to them.

Then they inevitably encounter problems with the question/method choice: First and foremost, asking interview questions about motivations rarely gets at actual behaviour. What people say about what they do in relationships may have nothing to do with how they really act in them. For instance, research shows that, when interviewed, married men almost always overestimate how much housework they do, while married women exhibit the opposite reporting error, claiming to do less housework than they actually do. And this is not because either group is being consciously deceptive. We all have powerful scripts we tell ourselves about how and why we act like we do, especially when it comes to emotionally laden things like romantic relationships. So while interviews are often a great way to capture those scripts and opinions, they are not the best way to learn about what men and women actually do in their relationships—much less the invisible influences that shape those behaviours.

The reverse problem can also surface—that is, when a researcher wants to study individuals' opinions about something and tries to do so by observing behaviour. Over the years, I have had many students interested in knowing what young people think about interracial dating. Their hypothesis is usually that attitudes toward interracial dating have changed, and thus they want to test their hunch. So they propose observing women and men as they date. I've had students propose to do ethnographic work in university parties, campus groups and clubs, and bars (if they are of legal drinking age, of course)—all with the intention of observing young people's dating interactions to see if they approve or disapprove of interracial romantic relationships and encounters.

What's the problem with this? Quite simply, looking at behaviour doesn't allow researchers to say much about opinions or motivation. People are complicated. They often act in ways that are inconsistent with their ideas and opinions. This is especially true when it comes to dating and sexuality, since we often have powerful beliefs about what we should and should not be doing—beliefs that can shape what we are able to admit to actually doing. So let's say these students saw people of different races talking and flirting. Would that tell the student researchers anything reliable about people's views of interracial dating? Not really. Just as we can't assume that opinions lead clearly to behaviour, there's a danger in reading opinion from actions. If we want to study opinions, we need to ask respondents about them; if it's motivations we are after, we need to go out and observe real behaviours and interactions.

Hence, choosing a research method is a complicated and complex process; it requires considerable thought, and some experience through trial and error also helps. It requires good logic and analytical skills to foresee what kind of evidence is needed to answer a research question. But it also requires an honest assessment of what kind of person the researcher is. Extremely shy sociologists (they do exist) are perhaps best advised not to carry out in-depth, face-to-face interviews. Socially awkward sociologists (they also exist) would perhaps not make the best ethnographers because that method requires lots of social interaction and rapport building. And those researchers who are allergic to math might want to stay clear of statistical work with large surveys and data sets.

3.3 What Challenges Do Sociologists Face When Collecting Data?

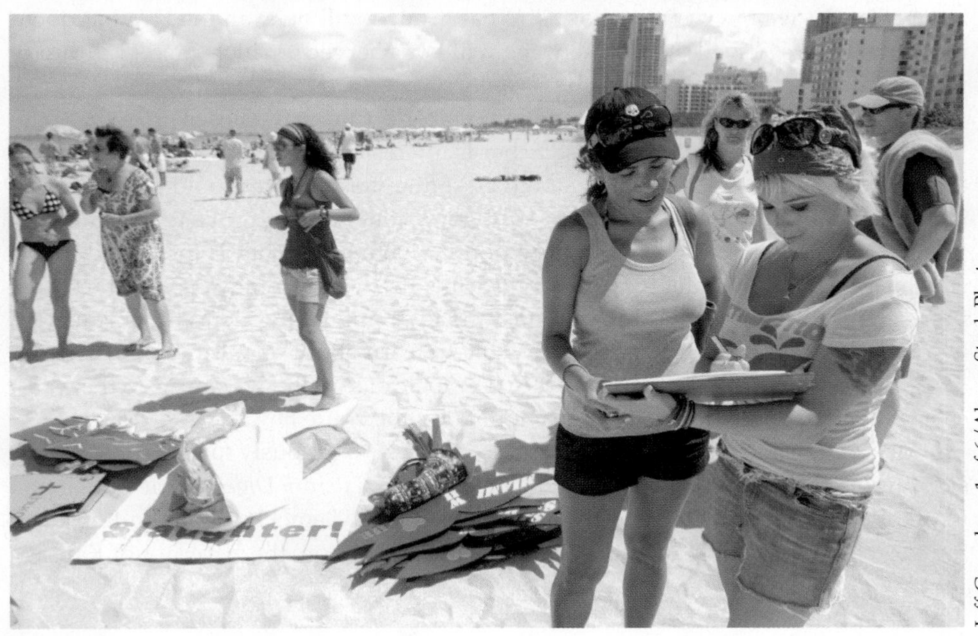

Jeff Greenberg 1 of 6/Alamy Stock Photo

The Challenge of Data Collection

Once our questions are defined and narrowed and our research method is selected, sociologists begin collecting data. We search for evidence that helps to answer the question. This is the stage when researchers must deal with the nuts and bolts of research. That may sound dull, but it is also when sociologists sometimes discover new things about the social world. Of course, the process of discovery looks different depending on the research method being used. Sociologists who rely on survey data must either conduct those surveys or work with data already collected in large data sets (such as the census, the NHS, GSS, or other existing surveys available to researchers). The same is true of those who use already-collected administrative data or information collected by other large institutions, like schools, the criminal justice system, the police, welfare agencies, and other governmental bodies. These sociologists must make sure the administrative data are complete, inclusive, and comprehensive—particularly because those data have usually been compiled by administrators rather than social scientists. Other sociologists recruit respondents and conduct in-depth interviews with them. Still others set off to work and live among those being studied for participant observation. And yet others head off to the archives to analyze past events and to unearth their contemporary relevance. In this section, we will explore in more detail some of the challenges all of these methods of research face.

Sampling Issues

3.3.1 Explain sampling issues that sociologists grapple with when they begin their research.

One of the most critical problems all sociologists face, regardless of the method they use, is the problem of how to draw a proper **sample** to study. Sampling is the process of identifying the subjects a researcher will study. Why not just study everyone or everything that could possibly be relevant for your project? The short answer is that researchers almost never have the time and resources to study everybody and everything we might be interested in knowing about. Only the federal government, spending millions of dollars to carry out the national census every five years, can conduct a survey of all Canadians—and even the census misses some people despite all efforts. So, inevitably, we must make choices: What groups will be examined? What documents will be reviewed? Which settings will be observed? Which smaller group of people will be interviewed in depth?

A valid sample is one in which the subjects (or documents) chosen are representative of the entire population the researcher is interested in studying. In other words, the findings on the smaller group should be similar to what we would expect to find if we magically had the resources to study everyone in the group. Whether or not a sample is representative of the entire population a researcher is interested in is a critical issue that can undermine the value of an otherwise carefully designed research project. There are no standard or easy answers to sampling questions, but fortunately, by following some basic rules, it is possible to learn about an entire population by studying only a much smaller subset of it. The logic of sampling is similar to the way a chef tests the soup by tasting a small amount (not the entire bowl).

Making mistakes at the sampling stage can lead to seriously false results. A classic example occurred in 1936, when the magazine *The Literary Digest* carried out a poll to predict the presidential election that year (in which Democrat Franklin Roosevelt ran for reelection against Republican candidate Alf Landon, the governor of Kansas).

Marcell Mizik/Shutterstock

luchschen_shutte/Fotolia

The logic of sampling is similar to a doctor's taking only a single test tube of our blood to examine for a whole range of possible problems.

The magazine sent out ballots to two groups: car owners and people who had telephones. Ten million ballots in all were sent out, and 2.4 million were returned. The results predicted a huge victory for Governor Landon. The *Digest* pronounced with great fanfare and publicity that Landon would win the election with 57 percent of the vote and 370 electoral votes (*Literary Digest*, 1936). On election day, however, Roosevelt crushed Landon, winning over 60 percent of the popular vote, and Landon received a grand total of exactly 8 electoral votes. The resulting embarrassment contributed to putting *The Literary Digest* out of business. How could the opinions of 2.4 million *Digest* readers have been so wrong? There were a number of problems with the sample used by the magazine. First, in 1936, in the middle of the Great Depression, people who owned cars and had telephones in their homes were on average significantly more affluent than other Americans. Because Landon, the Republican candidate, appealed to richer people, the sample was not representative of the entire United States. A much smaller percentage of poor and working-class people received ballots than were in the entire population. Second, because there was no follow-up once the ballots were mailed out, only people who were motivated to go to the trouble of returning the ballot without being reminded or prodded participated. For whatever reason, Landon voters were simply more motivated to return *The Literary Digest* ballot than were Roosevelt voters. This magnified the problem with the sample.

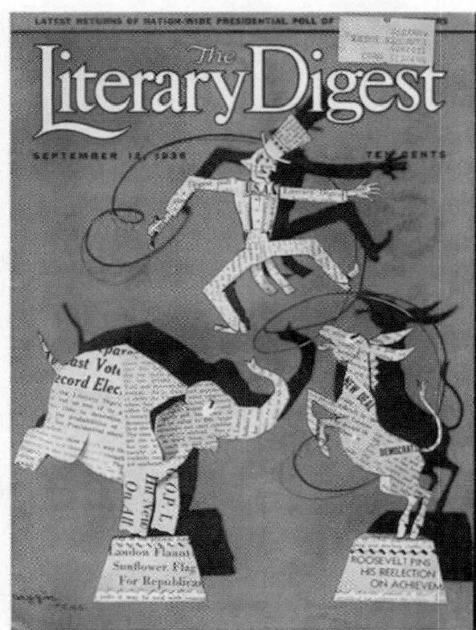

Library of Congress Prints and Photograph Division

In 1936, *The Literary Digest* conducted a poll that predicted a landslide win for Kansas governor Alf Landon against the incumbent, President Franklin Roosevelt. The magazine made several critical errors when selecting its sample, and the embarrassing error ultimately put *The Literary Digest* out of business.

Today, modern pollsters and survey researchers can usually predict the results of presidential elections within 1 or 2 percentage points by interviewing as few as several hundred people. How do they achieve this? Instead of drawing their sample of people to interview from a skewed list (like *The Literary Digest*'s use of car and telephone registry records), they are careful to draw a **representative sample** in which each member of population has an equal likelihood of being contacted. As a result, this small subset can, like a test tube of blood, approximate the entire population. In fact, a well-drawn sample of as few as 700 to 800 people can produce a reasonable approximation of a very large population (even the entire population of the United States—over 320 million people). Researchers also contact the people chosen to participate in the poll more than once if they don't connect or agree to participate the first time. This helps to minimize the other source of bias in the *Literary Digest* poll: People who eagerly volunteer to participate may be different from those who are more reluctant, but sometimes a reluctance to participate can be overcome by a determined interviewer.

In 1936, George Gallup, a little-known statistician from Iowa, conducted a survey regarding the upcoming U.S. presidential election between Franklin Roosevelt and Alf Landon. Unlike most of the other surveys that were taken by leading magazines and newspapers, Gallup's survey correctly predicted that Roosevelt would win. Following this success, Gallup grew to prominence, and the Gallup Poll would soon become the most utilized tool for measuring the U.S. public's attitudes. One of the most remarkable features of the Gallup Poll is that it has allowed us to track significant changes in U.S. public opinion over time.

However, in order to conduct a valid survey or poll, a variety of steps are needed. In general, the key to drawing a good sample is to use some type of what is known as true **random sampling**, in which everyone or everything being studied has an equal chance of being selected for study and each subject is selected entirely at random. For example, if a researcher has a list of the entire population he or she wants to sample, taking every third name (or fifth, or hundredth, or some other randomly chosen but systematically sampled number) will produce a truly random sample. Of course, social scientists use far more sophisticated methods for securing random assignment with very large populations, where a single list of all people does not exist. One widely used approach is to have a computer randomly dial phone numbers so that everyone who has a phone is equally likely to be contacted—and a phone is something that virtually all adult North Americans have.

Even when a random sample of people is contacted, however, there is a very strong possibility that biases will emerge. Recall the second problem of the *Literary Digest* poll: Landon voters were simply more likely to return the ballot than were Roosevelt voters. Similarly, not all people are equally likely to respond favourably to a researcher's request to be studied, even after they have been asked repeatedly or offered incentives to participate. In this way, the social sciences are very different than the natural sciences, where research "subjects" do not have the ability to refuse to participate! Today, cellphones are replacing home phones, particularly among younger people, who may then be systematically excluded from a random sample that relies upon the home telephone to randomly sample the population.

Because it is often the case that some kinds of people who are asked to do an interview are more likely to agree to participate or are more easily contacted through conventional means, sociologists must frequently rely on statistical adjustments known as **weighting**, in which they attempt to make sure that the characteristics of their sample reflect those of the total population they are studying. They do this by giving individuals from groups underrepresented in the sample a slightly higher "weight"—that is, their answers to each question are given slightly more value than those of groups that are sampled in the right proportion. Here is an example: If a sociologist is interested in understanding all college students' dating practices and 60 percent of college students are female, this gender disparity should be reflected in the sample because gender is surely relevant to a study of dating practices. If, however, the initial sample of college students yielded interviews with respondents who were evenly split between men and women, the researcher has undersampled women. One way to adjust for this is to give a little extra weight to the responses of each of the women who did respond, so that overall their views end up being 60 percent of the total. On the surface, this may seem unwise or even unfair. Why should any respondent's answers be given more weight than anyone else's? But if we are worried about our sample being representative of the population we are trying to study (in this case, all college students), we get closer to the true population by using statistical weighting to adjust the sample.

When it comes to doing in-depth interviews, the problem of drawing a sample gets more complicated. Clearly, no one researcher, or even a large team of researchers, can complete long interviews with enough respondents so that everyone in an entire large population has an equal probability of being selected. But that does not mean that in-depth interviewers can just talk to anyone and get valid results. Attempting to approximate a representative sample is tricky, but it is possible to come close.

Decisions about choosing a sample and getting participation affect virtually all sociological research, not just surveys. In particular, the issues of **access** and resources are always critical. If planning an original survey, do we have access to the resources necessary to contact a sufficiently large group of people to be representative of the entire population? Or if we are doing comparative–historical research, are the documents that we can find in archives sufficiently complete and representative of what was really going on to allow a researcher to draw conclusions from them? If we are relying on in-depth interviews, can we locate and persuade enough subjects to participate? Or if we are doing ethnographic research, can we get access and permission to study in settings that encapsulate the processes we are most interested in? Sociologists can dream up the perfect population, archive, or setting from which to address our research questions, but that population and setting might be completely inaccessible to us. This is why there are so few studies of the very rich and influential—it is close to impossible to get them to give researchers unfettered access to their lives. The same is true of interview studies of this demographic. Even historical studies of the rich and famous are few and far between because they often have the ability to protect and control what is written about them long after they were alive.

So sociologists work with what we can get. For survey researchers, this might mean settling for a data collection that only approximates the target population or includes only those survey questions that can be asked in a relatively short amount of time (to hold down the costs of the survey). For historical sociologists, it might mean working with documents that only indirectly relate to the events or actors being studied. And for an ethnographer, it might mean working in a setting where some but not all of the processes to be analyzed are at play. Even then, gaining access to sociological data can be quite a challenge and requires some good negotiating skills on the part of researchers. This is because most social research implies imposing on others' lives and asking people to tolerate disruptions caused by us, whether for the hour it takes to complete a survey or the afternoon it takes to give an in-depth interview or the months and years of being observed.

Issues of Reliability and Validity

3.3.2 Compare and contrast reliability and validity, and explain their importance in sociological research.

When collecting data, all sociologists, regardless of the specific method they use, tend to obsess over issues related to the reliability and validity of the information they gather. While these two concepts are related, sociologists tend to think of them in distinct ways. When sociologists talk about **reliability** in measurement, they want to know whether if they used the same measurement technique in an additional study, they would end up with similar results. If the results can indeed be **replicated**—that is, the same results can be found by more than one researcher—we say that the results are reliable. However, reliability does not necessarily mean that the measurement correctly reflects what the researcher is trying to uncover. One can get the same measurement again and again, but the results might not mean what the researcher thinks they mean. For instance, most white Americans do not want to appear to be racist and so may consistently provide favourable answers to survey questions about their willingness to send their children to schools with a high percentage of black children. But in their actions, they may choose to move to largely all-white suburbs. In such a case, the results from the survey question are reliable, but there is something wrong. The researchers are not actually measuring what many white American parents are really doing. The concept of **validity** captures this—namely, whether the measurement a researcher is using is actually accurate. If the measurement reflects what the researcher is hoping to understand about the social world, we say the results are valid.

To better understand these important concepts, let's consider an example. Sociologists who study race and racism have found that in using surveys or in-depth interviews to learn about whites' views about black peoples, whites consistently give interviewers responses that are not consistent with their actual behaviour. In particular, whites consistently tell interviewers that they think the best qualified person should get a job regardless of their race. This is a reliable result—people say they believe in equal opportunity almost no matter how you ask the question. But is it valid? Researchers have found, for example, that even white employers who express support for equal opportunity will favour white applicants over black applicants with identical résumés (Pager & Quillian, 2005). In other words, questions about equal opportunity may reliably suggest support, but those answers may not be valid.

The Complications of Causality

3.3.3 Explain why the ability to make causal inferences is so important yet challenging for sociologists.

One of the biggest worries for sociologists, particularly for those conducting statistical analysis, is developing techniques to improve their ability to make causal arguments. The concept of **causality** is central to sociological research. Sociologists interested in understanding the world or informing social policy often want to go beyond simply documenting that two social phenomenon appear together—in other words, that they "co-vary" with each other. This is what sociologists call **correlation**. An obvious example of this is the relationship between income and education—they are correlated in that higher income is associated with higher education. Put another way, those who are richer tend to be better educated. These social attributes vary together; a change in one is linked to a change in the other. But how are they linked? What is actually causing the higher incomes received by those with more education? To answer this, sociologists often need to know if it is likely that one thing is caused by another. That's what **causal inference** is all about. And it's not easily done. Figure 3.4 gives you a closer look at the distinction between correlation and causation.

To illustrate the challenges of establishing causality, let's look at one area of research that not only has been a prominent focus of sociological attention but also is familiar to all twenty-first-century students: educational achievement as measured by standardized test scores. Sociologists have a long tradition of attempting to understand variation in student test scores and why some groups of students do better on these tests than others.

While schools and governments began widely using test scores to assess individuals and schools early in the twentieth century, the most important contributions of sociologists were made in the past half century. For example, in the United States after the passage of the Civil Rights Act of 1964, Congress explicitly required the government to "conduct a survey and make a report to the President and the Congress, within two years of the enactment of this title, concerning the lack of availability of equal educational opportunities for individuals by reason of race, color, religion, or national origin in public educational institutions at all levels in the United States." A prominent sociologist, James Coleman, was put in charge of the effort. Researchers in the fall of 1965 collected and processed 639,650 surveys and, remarkably, by the summer of 1966 completed and distributed a report of approximately 1,000 pages, which came to be known as the Coleman Report (Coleman et al., 1966/1974).

Coleman and his associates had student surveys that included test score items. Based on this information, they explored how student background and school characteristics were related to test score performance. At the time, many individuals assumed that differences in test score results were likely the product of inequalities in school resources—that is, many members of Congress and the public worried that African American students were often placed in schools with inadequate science labs, libraries, and other resources that inhibited their academic achievement. If you looked simply at test score results in poor or wealthy schools, you would find just that pattern. Test scores were higher in schools with more resources.

However, analysis in the Coleman Report demonstrated that this relationship between school resources and student test scores was largely a spurious one. When two factors seem to move in the same direction but both are themselves caused by something else (i.e., a third factor), sociologists refer to the apparent relationship between the first two factors as a **spurious relationship**. Coleman and his colleagues showed that such was exactly the case with the relationship between educational resources and student test scores. Specifically, Coleman demonstrated that while it looked like one caused the other, in fact other factors—namely, family background and the racial composition of schools—were behind the relationship. If you wanted

Figure 3.4 Correlation, but Not Causation

Does the number of countries in the world cause global warming? Since 1945, many new countries have been established and recognized by the UN. Since 1945, average temperatures across the globe have increased. Graphed together, there appears to be a correlation between the increasing number of countries and global warming. However, no scientist believes that the fact that the world has more recognized countries than before is a cause of global warming. Instead, climate scientists point to the increase in emissions as the cause of global warming.

SOURCE: From About.com, 2009; GISS/NASA, 2012.

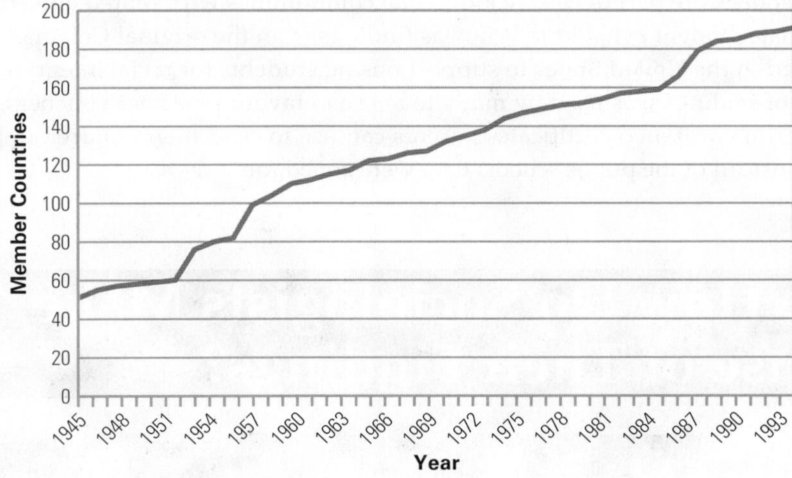

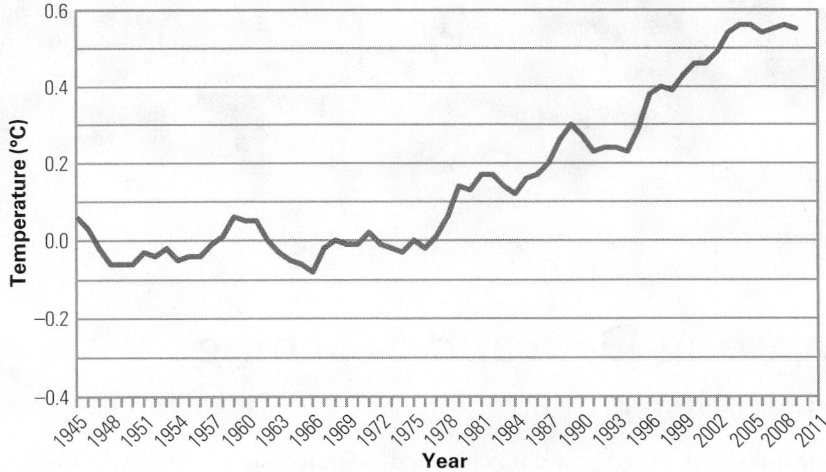

to reduce inequality in student outcomes, equalizing funding would not do much. Instead, one would have to begin to better racially integrate U.S. public schools so that the school peers of African American students more closely resembled those of a typical white student.

The Coleman Report, however, was based on data with a serious limitation: They were **cross-sectional**—that is, they were all collected at one point in time. How could one hope to get at what caused what when both things examined were being measured simultaneously? By 1980, Coleman and other social scientists had convinced the government that what was needed was **longitudinal** data, which are collected over a long period of time, to address these questions more productively. A new data set was collected that interviewed a random sample of Grade 10 students every two years as they grew older. With students followed over time, sociologists were able measure how much individual test scores improved between Grades 10 and 12 and beyond.

This change in methods allowed researchers to more accurately identify the effects of school on student academic achievement. Rather than trying simply to adjust test scores for social background as had been done in the Coleman Report, social scientists were now able to see how much growth in test scores occurred in different school settings. In analyzing this new longitudinal data, Coleman and his colleagues found that students in Catholic schools learned more than similar students in public schools (Coleman & Hoffer, 1987). Coleman thought that this was most likely due to better discipline in Catholic schools, resulting from the fact that parents and students in these schools were part of closely knit social communities with shared agreement on appropriate student behaviour. Whereas findings from the original Coleman Report were used in the United States to support busing students for racial integration, this new set of findings was used by many to argue in favour of school vouchers, which are government-issued certificates parents can use to send their children to private schools instead of the public schools they were zoned for.

3.4 How Do Sociologists Make Sense of Their Findings?

Alex Williamson/Alamy Stock Photo

Analyzing Data and Reaching Conclusions

With our questions asked and data collected, sociologists are finally in the position to make sense of what we have found. This stage of the research process is called **data analysis**—when we interpret the information we've collected and look for patterns in it. Some sociologists wait until this stage before they do any analytical work. Those who work with survey data, for instance, rarely stop midway to analyze only a subsample of their subjects. Instead, they tend to wait until all the data are in to begin analyzing them and drawing conclusions from them. Yet with other methods, it is essential that analysis occur while the data are being gathered. For ethnographers—especially those who spend years in the field—it would be a disaster to wait until all observations are made before analyzing them. Facing hundreds of pages of unanalyzed field notes would overwhelm even the most experienced researcher. The same is true of historical sociologists who spend months or even years in the archives; waiting until they are confronted with thousands of archival documents would be a disaster. Thus, along-the-way analysis is critical for many research projects.

In this section, we examine some of the issues that commonly occur when sociologists try to make sense of their data.

How Do the Puzzle Pieces Fit Together?

3.4.1 Identify the goal of data analysis and describe the process sociologists use to interpret research.

Whichever logic a sociologist uses, the goal of data analysis is the same: to figure out how the pieces of the empirical puzzle fit together and what the completed puzzle tells us about the social world. Indeed, we can think about data as pieces of a larger puzzle—and the job of the researcher is to put them together into patterns and make research conclusions. But for anyone who has struggled with a thousand-piece puzzle, it is clear that the process of making it whole can be very difficult. Sociologists have many strategies to aid them here. First, in most projects researchers engage in some form of **data coding**—that is, organizing the data according to key categories and concepts. Transforming raw data into a usable format is a key part of beginning to analyze that data. For example, those doing statistical analysis must first put their data into a form that is computer usable—standardizing the raw data, usually by assigning numbers to them, and also looking for obvious errors, a process known as "cleaning" the data.

Because most interviewers, ethnographers, and historical sociologists collect primary-source data, or their own data, they must do their own coding. In the past, this would have been done by hand; fortunately, a variety of software packages are now available that make it infinitely easier to work with most kinds of data. Still, even with computer-assisted data analysis there is much to be done. On the one hand, a specific code has to be used classify a specific piece of data. Those codes then become the mechanism through which the data are sorted, systematized, and arranged. It is the way data are categorized across cases. Figuring out an appropriate coding scheme is a critical step to finding what is in those thousands of documents or pages of interview transcripts.

Once our data are coded, sociologists usually do more analytical work before making research conclusions. This work involves making sense of the data and breaking them down to see emergent patterns. For those who think visually, **data displays** can be a useful way to go about this. These are visual images of the patterns forming in the data. They are ways to represent the data; they are visual summaries of what has been found. Such displays include diagrams, flowcharts, typologies, tables, and matrices. Even if these visuals never make it into the final research product, their importance lies in the process of constructing them and in drawing out the connections being made across the data as well as the patterns that still need to be fleshed out.

For those who tend to think verbally, **research memos** can serve a similar purpose. These are extended versions of research notes, usually organized analytically, that allow researchers work through their findings and supporting evidence, as well as to make sure the analytical forest is not lost amid all the trees of data.

What Do Our Conclusions Tell Us About the Social World?

3.4.2 Explain how sociologists use generalization to draw conclusions from their research.

In the end, the goal of all research is to reach reliable and valid conclusions. In the final step of any project, sociologists have to go back to the research question they began with and figure out how the empirical patterns that they uncovered help to answer it. Put another way, they strive to make general claims about the issues posed by their research question. Yet **generalization** is a tricky thing in much sociological research. On the one hand, as sociologists we don't want to limit our conclusions only to the specific sample of people, places, or things we studied directly; we also want to form conclusions from those samples to say something overall about broad social patterns. But in doing this, we need to make sure we don't overextend our claims; we must be careful that the conclusions drawn from the data are reliable and valid.

So sociologists proceed with caution as they turn to writing up their results. All researchers would love to have "proven" some new hypothesis or finding that will change the way we think about the world. Some have conducted their research in a way that allows them to claim **empirical generalizability**—they apply conclusions from their findings to a larger population. If the sample was big enough and drawn randomly, these sociologists feel confident generalizing from a part to the whole. Other sociologists who did not work with a big national data set, and who were unable (or unwilling) to sample randomly, cannot make those kind of empirical claims. So they tend toward **theoretical generalizability**—they apply conclusions from their findings to larger sociological processes. To use one sociologist's phrasing, they "bump up a level of generality" to bring their findings to bear on a broader concept or theory (Luker, 2010). Whatever level a sociologist decides to generalize to, we all strive to address the "big questions" in the social sciences—questions that we will outline and discuss throughout this text.

Conclusion: Thinking Critically About Research

Now that we have introduced the kinds of methods that sociologists use in their research, you are in a position to bring critical insights to bear on all of the research you will read about in this text and even to think about how you might design your own research project. Whether the research is on the family, culture, race and ethnicity, religion, power and politics, or the environment, the methodological issues guiding the research reported are always the same: What was the research question? Was the method used appropriate for addressing the question? Were the data collected systematically? Were the findings reliable and trustworthy? And what's the larger take-away from the work? What does it teach us about the larger world we live in?

CHAPTER SUMMARY

The Big Questions Revisited 3

3.1 **Where Do Sociological Questions Come From?** We began the chapter with the basic stages of sociological research, discussing the issues that often come up as researchers practise sociology for the first time, such as how sociologists turn their research interests into workable questions and how we know what to study.

The Building Blocks of Sociological Research

Crafting Good Research Questions From Important Topics

Learning Objective 3.1.1: Identify the six issues sociologists should consider to determine a research question's merit and feasibility.

How Do We Know What to Study?

Learning Objective 3.1.2: Identify key factors that shape sociologists' choices about what to research.

3.2 **What Is the Best Method to Research Different Sociological Questions?** Once sociologists have a working research question, they need to decide the best way to go about answering it. This section examined the different types of methods that sociologists use in their research and discussed the process for determining which method and design is best.

Sociological Research Methods and Challenges

Getting Started

Learning Objective 3.2.1: Discuss how sociologists operationalize their research questions and distinguish between independent and dependent variables.

The Classical Scientific Method of Research

Learning Objective 3.2.2: Identify the steps of the classical scientific method, and explain why sociologists might take a looser approach to research.

Quantitative Versus Qualitative Research Methods

Learning Objective 3.2.3: Compare and contrast quantitative and qualitative research methods.

Survey and Interview Methods and the Dilemmas of Design

Learning Objective 3.2.4: Identify the key strengths and weaknesses of survey and interview methods.

Ethnographic Methods and the Challenge of Theory

Learning Objective 3.2.5: Explain why the main strength of ethnography is also its central weakness.

Comparative–Historical Methods and the Complexity of Comparisons

Learning Objective 3.2.6: Identify the types of research questions that are best studied from a comparative–historical perspective.

Matching the Question With a Method

Learning Objective 3.2.7: Explain why choosing the right research method to study motivations and behaviour is a complex process.

3.3 **What Challenges Do Sociologists Face When Collecting Data?** This section explored some of the practical issues and challenges that surface during data collection.

The Challenge of Data Collection

Sampling Issues

Learning Objective 3.3.1: Explain sampling issues that sociologists grapple with when they begin their research.

Issues of Reliability and Validity

Learning Objective 3.3.2: Compare and contrast reliability and validity, and explain their importance in sociological research.

The Complications of Causality

Learning Objective 3.3.3: Explain why the ability to make causal inferences is so important yet challenging for sociologists.

3.4 **How Do Sociologists Make Sense of Their Findings?** This section considered how sociologists make sure their findings are reliable and trustworthy and how they decide what kind of general claims to draw from their research.

Analyzing Data and Reaching Conclusions

How Do the Puzzle Pieces Fit Together?

Learning Objective 3.4.1: Identify the goal of data analysis and describe the process sociologists use to interpret research.

What Do Our Conclusions Tell Us About the Social World?

Learning Objective 3.4.2: Explain how sociologists use generalization to draw conclusions from their research.

Learn the Terms

access (p. 84)
causal inference (p. 86)
causality (p. 86)
code of ethics (p. 67)
comparative–historical research (p. 78)
correlation (p. 86)
cross-national comparison (p. 78)
cross-sectional (p. 87)
data (p. 63)
data analysis (p. 88)
data coding (p. 89)
data display (p. 89)
dependent variable (p. 69)
empirical generalizability (p. 90)
ethnographers (p. 63)
ethnography (p. 74)
extended case method (p. 77)
generalization (p. 89)
General Social Survey (p. 73)
hypothesis (p. 65)
independent variable (p. 69)
in-depth interview (p. 73)
informed consent (p. 67)
institutional review board (IRB) (p. 68)
longitudinal (p. 87)
mixed-method research (p. 71)
operationalize (p. 69)
qualitative research (p. 71)
quantitative research (p. 71)
random sample (p. 83)
reliability (p. 85)
replicated (p. 85)
representative sample (p. 83)
research memo (p. 89)
sample (p. 82)
scientific method (p. 70)
sociological imaginations (p. 64)
spurious relationship (p. 86)
survey (p. 72)
theoretical generalizability (p. 90)
thick description (p. 75)
validity (p. 85)
value (p. 66)
weighting (p. 84)

Chapter 4

Social Interaction

by Harvey Molotch

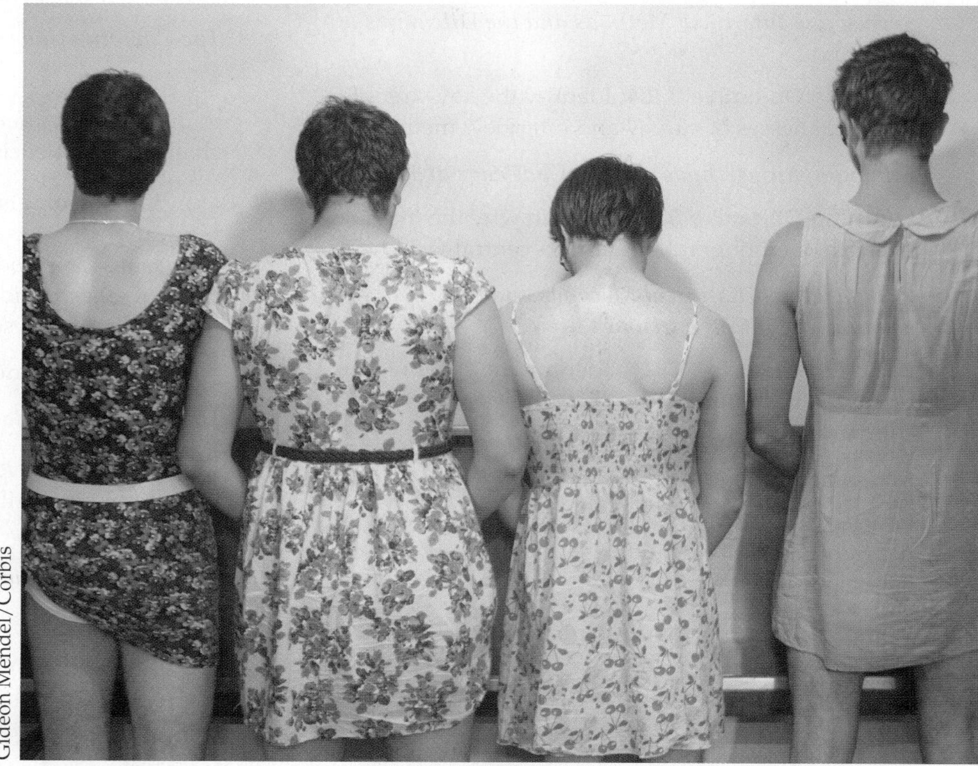

Gideon Mendel/Corbis

While it may seem to be an unusual setting to study sociology, we can learn a lot about social interaction in the public restroom.

Learning Objectives

4.1.1 Explain how the opinions and judgements of others shape our identities.

4.1.2 Compare and contrast the roles that significant others, reference groups, and generalized others play in guiding our behaviour and in shaping our sense of self.

4.1.3 Discuss how we differ in the ways we present ourselves to others.

4.2.1 Explain how context gives meaning to words and situations.

4.2.2 Explain how conversation patterns can demonstrate social competence.

4.2.3 Discuss how individuals manipulate emotion in social interaction.

4.2.4 Analyze the impact of digital communication technologies and social media on our methods of self-presentation.

4.2.5 Identify some of the methods we use when interacting in public.

4.3.1 Identify the causes of role conflict.

4.3.2 Explain how a self-fulfilling prophecy can influence label formation.

4.3.3 Identify the role of informal rules in social interaction.

4.3.4 Explain what makes people conform and how conformity impacts how we live together.

The public restroom might be the last place you would expect to learn about the ways people think and interact with others. We spend our days carefully managing how we present ourselves and interact with others in all different kinds of social situations. But nowhere is the presence of others felt more strongly than in a public restroom, making it an interesting place to learn about social interaction. What happens in the public restroom provides clues about how we achieve and safeguard our own identity, always in ways appropriate to the context we are in. The public restroom shows the intensity of the stakes in getting things right, and maybe this justifies, even invites, bringing it up as an academic topic.

The specific restroom predicament is that we humans need to eliminate our own body waste, but that process is somewhat animalistic. It conflicts with our efforts to show ourselves as civilized. We must do it, but unlike other creatures in the animal kingdom, our culture intervenes to shape what it means to perform this so-called natural act. We notice who is present and where and how they look—at themselves and at us. We manage in tiny, moment-by-moment ways what others see and hear, looking inward and outward at the same time. A casual touch or accidental bump registers immediately, just as we acutely pick up on gestures, sounds, and movements.

Among the reasons the stakes are so high is that, in sociologist Erving Goffman's famous terms, the bathroom is part of our "backstage" where we set up our "presentation of self" (Goffman, 1959). Usually, we are in the privacy of our own home when we perform these core personal activities. In contrast, the public restroom is not private. So besides avoiding the usual public embarrassments—slipping on the floor, crying out loud, wearing mismatched socks—we take on other worries about giving away something so private: There should be no suspicious soiling or water splash on our clothes. Indeed, there should be no evidence at all of where we've been or what we've done. And while on task inside the restroom, we must carefully monitor what we expose and to whom. To mess up in any of these matters would risk spoiling our identity, maybe even implying we were not decent or competent in other regards as well.

One way we avoid such labels is through our specific cultural knowledge of what to do and when. This includes smoothly working the hardware and equipment at hand—sinks, toilets, toilet paper, and stall doors—as well as the social aspect. We ordinarily do not fumble with doorknobs or shout approval at the sound of another person's defecation. We follow the rule of respecting separate rooms for women and men without being told by a police officer to do so. If one is available, men choose a urinal that is not adjacent to one being used by a stranger.

The Big Questions

In examining how humans develop a sense of self through social interaction, our discussion is guided by exploring the following big questions:

1. **How do we develop a sense of self?** Each of us has a unique identity. But is this sense of self a single thing, or is it a process of interaction? In this section, we examine how we know ourselves through the reflections of ourselves that mirror back others' opinions of us—the "looking glass" of others.
2. **How do we make sense of our worlds?** Human beings have specific methods for demonstrating competence as interacting members of society. In this section, we explore how the sociological field of ethnomethodology examines these methods.
3. **What challenges do we face as we move from one social context to another?** The social self is not fixed but is always changing, which can sometimes bring challenges. Here we examine what happens when individuals experience role conflict and how informal rules and our keen awareness guide our behaviour. We also look at how and why people conform, and what consequences conformity has on how people live together.

Imagine the problems for visitors from a part of the world where things are different. In other countries, people may squat over an opening—a superior arrangement both in sanitary and physiological terms compared to the chair-sit of the Western world. They may cleanse themselves not with toilet paper but by using water piped into the stall that they can spray at fouled body parts. Women and men may share facilities by using them at different *times* instead of having different *places*. And what a contrast all of it is with the practices in the Roman Empire, where citizens did their business with as many as 80 to 90 individuals sitting adjacent along a room's perimeter, open to one another and apparently speaking about issues of the day. Speaking for myself, I would be culturally lost and quite disturbed to be so exposed.

Besides worry about germs, something common among modern restroom users, there is concern about social contamination. The very presence of the wrong kind of person, one imagined as inappropriate for social interaction, is a pollutant. In India, this means avoiding persons of the lowest caste (whose role is, among other lowly tasks, cleaning toilets); in countries like Canada, those who appear unkempt or disorderly may generate worries about their being too nearby. Some people will not enter a restroom with a homeless person inside and avoid sharing one with any of those too far below their own social standing.

Our behaviour in public restrooms is heavily influenced by gender. In their respective restrooms, men and women behave differently, much beyond constraints imposed by biological variation. Men, for example, virtually never have conversation from stall to stall (women apparently do so on occasion) and converse only in very constrained ways at the urinals. They take pains to keep their eyes straight ahead, never looking at the exposed anatomy of another man *and not looking like they are trying not to look* at another man's anatomy. Yet women are more at ease. They report that restrooms are where they go to chat. It is where, they sometimes say, they learned as girls how to groom themselves, hold their bodies, use menstrual products, and adjust their clothes—with pals and relatives fussing around them with help and suggestions (Saurez, 2008). Whether male or female, in choosing the "right" room and then engaging in practices appropriate to that room, users reinforce their unique identity as a particular kind of person, namely a man or woman, and one who grooms him- or herself and handles the presence of others in a specific way.

As the example of the public restroom suggests, our actions are guided by the watchful judgements of those who matter to us, even strangers. This chapter examines how we can each be distinctive individuals yet subject to the influence of others. How can there be, sociologists ask, both individual identity and also conformity? And just how does all this get accomplished in human interaction?

The answers, as it turns out, come not from thinking of "individual" and "society" as opposite or even separate things at all. Instead, an individual and her or his society influence one another continuously through history and constantly from moment to moment. It happens—and this is a fundamental starting point for understanding human beings—through how we interact and how we think. Here is the key: We introspect, and we do it with the help of other people.

4.1 How Do We Develop a Sense of Self?

Ros Drinkwater/Alamy Stock Photo

The Social Self

We have the ability to think not just about objects before us, like a banana or a mate, but about our very selves. Not even smart and sensitive French poodles can do that. Like other nonhumans, intelligent dogs are driven by instinct rather than introspection, which is why they pee all over town even when they will get the same amount of food and love by going only once or twice and only in one spot. The remarkable human capacity for consciousness of *self* becomes the vehicle through which we take our actions, interpreting and evaluating everything that comes our way, including other people.

The social self is the only kind of self there can be: *The self is not a thing, but a process of interaction*. This important school of thought in sociology, based in the thinking of the early-twentieth-century philosopher George Herbert Mead, is called *symbolic interaction*, or just interactionism, and it guides ideas for this chapter. Central to this line of thinking is the idea that an individual's personality, preferences, ideas, and so forth are constructed and shaped by and through communication with both others and his or her self.

The Looking-Glass Self

4.1.1 Explain how the opinions and judgements of others shape our identities.

The concept of the **self**—that is, one's own identity and social position, as made and reformulated through interaction—is so basic that if it becomes too hard to achieve, even physicality becomes problematic. For example, we know from studies of orphanages that babies have a hard time surviving biologically without social stimuli. In a classic 1945 study, the psychoanalyst René Spitz compared the babies and small children in an orphanage to those in a nursery for the children of incarcerated mothers. Caring professionals staffed both facilities, which were clean, warm environments where the babies received good medical attention and nutritious food. But there were differences. In the nursery (but not the orphanage), the infants could see everything and each other right through the bars of their cribs. They could see the bustle of attendants and visitors going about their business all around them. The biggest medical problem in the nursery was the common cold, and the infants were otherwise healthy and happy.

Meanwhile, in the orphanage, the babies were separated from the staff most of the time and only had human contact when being fed or changed. They lived in cubicles, making it impossible to see each other, and their cribs had solid sides so they could not even see out of them. The result, wrote Spitz, was that "each baby lies in solitary confinement up to the time he is able to stand up in his bed" (Spitz, 1945). Unlike those in the nursery, the orphanage infants suffered emotionally and physically. They became progressively more withdrawn and more susceptible to hosts of chronic maladies as they grew. Forty percent actually died within two years of Spitz's first observations. He concluded that the poor emotional and physical health of the orphanage babies was caused by a lack of social contact with others. When the orphanage switched cribs and caregivers started interacting with children, mortality sharply declined.

Deprived of social interaction, prisoners fare poorly in solitary confinement.

Thinkstock Images/Getty Images

Adults do not fare much better in solitary confinement. In Canadian prisons, it is common to discipline inmates by sending them "to the hole" for weeks, months, and even years for breaking rules. In windowless cells, prisoners' food may be delivered through a slot in the door, and if they are allowed visitors at all, these may be restricted to videoconference. In what psychologist Craig Haney dubbed the supermax prison, inmates are typically confined to their cell for 23 hours a day and effectively denied contact with other humans. Without real social contact, prisoners' mental health falls apart. The minds of some begin to grind to a halt with confusion, lethargy, and inability to concentrate. The minds of others go wild with hallucinations, paranoia, and intense anxiety. That's why, in search of basic social contact, some may resort to tapping on the pipes and air ducts running through their cells just to be acknowledged by someone else who might tap back (Haney, 2003). Or they commit suicide.

So where does this need for social contact that looms so large and can be a matter of life or death itself come from? We really only know ourselves—even that we exist—through the eyes of other people. The actions we take, the expressions we use, and the gestures we make enlist evaluations from those around us. Those others tell us, not necessarily with explicit words, what we are—and we interpret their evaluations as representing our being. It starts, of course, with our parents or other caregivers who can't help but notice our early babbling and silly movements. Their smiles and frowns become the stuff that gives us an early sense that we even exist. From then on feedback comes about what *type* of person we are, including how good or bad.

The judgements accumulate throughout our lives as we gather playmates, siblings, friends, teachers (sometimes psychiatrists and police)—a stream of judges and judgements that fill in our sense of our own being. Are we clever? Pretty? Short or tall? Nice or selfish? We are, in effect, asking all these things all the time, and others are providing the answers. We know ourselves through the "looking glass" of others that mirror back to us the impressions we create. The term **looking-glass self** was coined by sociologist Charles Horton Cooley in 1902 to emphasize the extent to which our own self-understandings depend on how others view us. Interaction makes our world go round.

Looking for approval becomes truly motivating. If there is a fundamental human instinct, this is it. Because we want to belong and make connections with others, we try to anticipate what will be made of what we do. We have the ability to, in the lingo of sociology, "take the role of the other." This allows us to conform to others' expectations because we can imagine how they will receive what we do or say. And those others shape their behaviours in light of their expectations of how we will receive them. It becomes a complicated system of interactions across a wildly complicated array of people in direct and indirect communication. This is a key setting, sociologically speaking, where conscience and guilt come from. We don't want to let others down. We really do want to satisfy their expectations for us because that is also the way to create a positive sense of one's own being and to socially belong and be connected in positive ways with others. Even if it is only indirect contact through things we have read, seen on television, or picked up on social media, we take note and gain some understanding of what we need to do to please and to fit into social behaviour expected by others.

Significant Others, Reference Groups, and Generalized Others

4.1.2 Compare and contrast the roles that significant others, reference groups, and generalized others play in guiding our behaviour and in shaping our sense of self.

We know that we are motivated by the approval of others, but do all others matter to us equally? Sociologists try to determine how other people, by virtue of their social location, do or do not matter to us. We take some people and types of people more seriously than others, which is evident in the ways we defer to them and seek their approval. Homeless street people, for example, do not count for as much as those able to present themselves in a higher-status way.

At the individual level, sociologists, following in the footsteps of George Herbert Mead, use the term **significant other** to denote individuals close enough to us to have a strong capacity to motivate our behaviour. Almost everyone has more than one significant other in the sociological sense.

Sometimes individuals have a more or less similar level of significance because of their common membership in a relevant social category. Doctors are alert to the opinions of other doctors. They are not as dependent for their sense of self on the viewpoints of say, the custodial staff. University students are likely interested in the opinions more of their fellow students than of those they once knew who left high school without going on to higher education. In figuring out how we are doing, we *reference* others whose social positions and preferences makes them especially relevant to our own sense of worth. Sociologists call these groups that influence our behaviour **reference groups**. Each of us has our own set of these groups, and we tend to stick with our reference groups in part because, once we are in, we spend our time doing things that people like us do alongside other people who do them. We model our

The generalized other is social control exercised by commonsense understandings of what is appropriate in a specific time and place.

Terry Harris/Alamy Stock Photo

behaviour on such individuals, and sometimes there are particular individuals in the group who may function as **role models**. They have disproportionate influence as we imitate how they move, dress, and carry out life.

We are each associated with a number of reference groups, even at the same time. For some of us this is made vivid through online social networking sites: We are located in webs of groups that are themselves clustered around commonalities of age, taste, or status. Others we know share some of the same linkages; our list of groups and their lists have high overlap. Those we friend, they friend. Clubs we join, they join. Their influence on us is likely to be particularly strong compared to, say, an acquaintance who hardly knows anyone else we know or does any of the things we do. While we may of course develop bonds to such outsiders, sociologists who study social networks found that these relationships tend to be few in number and dissolve more quickly than relationships with those in groups having multiple links into our own social circles and interests (McPherson, Smith-Lovin, & Cook, 2001). Birds of a feather do stick together and keep at it; if they leave, it is an unstable departure.

Some of our ties are far more general than our immediate social networks, whether face to face or electronic. Grounded in the larger cultures in which each of us participates, people have a sense of what everyone knows to be appropriate as proper behaviour. For example, in North America no one goes about her or his business in public while naked. Wearing clothes is so commonly understood that there generally does not need to be a rule about it; it's just taken for granted. Also, we do not eat dogs or insects. We all know these things and risk making a severely bad impression if we transgress. Sociologists call this social control exercised by commonsense understandings of what is appropriate in a specific time and place the **generalized other**. We walk around with all kinds of unspoken knowledge of do's and don'ts without much understanding or need to consult where we got them. We just do it. Virtually all the significant others do it; all the role models do it, and the reference groups too.

Life's a Stage

4.1.3 Discuss how we differ in the ways we present ourselves to others.

We are always, in a sense, on stage—performing the self in the spotlight of others. We need approval not just as some kind of bonus for a nicer life. We need it to *be*. The show must go on, and the show is our life.

Evidence of how carefully we consider which parts of ourselves to share can be found by examining the stuff we carry around each day. Ethnographer Christena Nippert-Eng (2010) likened our wallets and purses to toolkits for managing the multiple faces we show to others. Business cards, if we have them, are meant for just about anyone we might meet. They are props on our most public stage. But more personal things in the same wallet, such as a drug prescription, may be kept secret from our closest friends yet shared with any random employee of a pharmacy. While we all conduct life through these multiple faces, Nippert-Eng found that different people think differently about what they are willing to share. Some would be horrified to let others see the receipts in their wallets, but others do not worry about what these slips of paper might reveal. We think differently from one another about what aspects of our identities we are willing to show, and exactly how.

While we all share the fact that we live as if on stage, we are not all the same. Whereas a geneticist might think we are each unique because of our biological codes, a sociologist views each of us as different because no one has had the same set of social interactions. Each of us bounces, searches, lurches, and passes through particular settings, interacting with a different array of individuals and expectations throughout the day. There are overlaps, especially among those with common origins and similarities of gender, class, or ethnicity, but never in a way that creates identical individuals.

It also follows that we are always changing. Because the process never stops and our circumstances keep shifting, we constantly alter identity over time, even if only in tiny ways, even from minute to minute or hour to hour. Sometimes we are Canadian; sometimes we are Irish Canadian or African Canadian. Sometimes we identify ourselves by our occupation ("I am a lawyer"), other times by hobbies or passions ("I am an activist" or "I am a Blue Jays fan"). As we act in the world and the world responds to us, we become different selves—including how "good" or "bad" we take ourselves to be and in just what ways.

4.2 How Do We Make Sense of Our Worlds?

D. Hurst/Alamy Stock Photo

People's Methodology

So now we know that social interaction forms the individual. But then what? What underlies the capacity to make this happen? At the most basic level: How do individuals demonstrate competence as interacting members of society? How do we show that we are safe to be around and capable of sharing in social life? Some sociologists, influenced by interactionism but branching out in some new directions from it, study this problem with precise observations and experiments. It turns out that human beings have specific methods for interacting with others, and that people all over the world, regardless of culture or historical moment, use these same methods. That at least is the perspective of the influential sociologist Harold Garfinkel (1967), the inventor of a sociological subfield he called **ethnomethodology**—the study of people's methods.

Context, Context, Context

4.2.1 Explain how context gives meaning to words and situations.

What do those methods look like? One of them—a kind of master method—is that people persistently and intensively take context into account. So even a word that may seem straightforward, such as *kill*, gets its meaning from context. When we hear a phrase like "I'll kill you," it matters whether it is a child tickling her brother, a teenager whose sister ruined her new sweater, or an interrogator in a secret prison. The participants in "I'll kill you" draw on context to figure out what it really means at that particular moment. The setting doesn't just adjust the meaning of the word *kill*; it can radically alter it—teasing a laughing child versus threatening an archnemesis, for example. There is no freestanding meaning; people always construct meaning by drawing on social context.

There are other methods that follow from taking context into account, like not demanding that people provide absolutely complete responses to the questions we ask them. Instead, drawing on context, we have a sense of how much there should be and let it go at that. Otherwise, those answers could go on infinitely. So when we ask someone, "How are you?" we ordinarily don't want to know their body temperature, for example (unless, of course, they have a fever). Given the context, we let it pass, maybe with just "fine" or "okay." Of course, what is or is not the appropriate answer varies according to who is asking and under what circumstances: Our doctor might really want to know our body temperature, and our best pal may want to know how we're getting along with our boyfriend or girlfriend. It all depends, and in pretty exact ways, on who is doing the asking, who is doing the answering, their relationship, and the specific occasion. And we generally understand this and act accordingly; it is our method.

Conversational Precision

4.2.2 Explain how conversation patterns can demonstrate social competence.

We can see people's methods in action in a conversation—any conversation. Without being fully aware that they do so, people fit each utterance in a precise way to the ongoing flow of what the other is saying. Sociologists who study such ordinary talk learn exactly how turn taking, the fundamental basis of conversation, can occur, and how people use careful tactics to allow it to happen.

We notice the slightest forward nod of the head as signalling that somebody wants a turn—and we often defer to it by becoming silent ourselves. We pick up on silence. It only takes three-tenths of a second before a conversationalist notices that nothing is happening and thus there is an opportunity to come in, like the way a jazz performer can "feel" a signal to come in on a beat—or make that three-tenths of a second of silence to notice that something *is* happening. Sociologist Emanuel Schegloff, of the University of California–Los Angeles (UCLA), learned that even very brief silences are in fact information (Schegloff, 1996). So if you ask somebody on a date, if the answer is going to be "yes," the yes happens immediately—within a split second of the request or even overlapping the end of it. But if the answer is going to be "no," the answer comes with a delay, indeed *through* the delay. A tiny silence serves notice of the bad news that's coming. Or the "no" can be detected in little words and utterances that sort of waste time, like "uh" or "well" or "gee" or even a string of all of them—a turn-down in process.

Here is an actual example (Davidson, 1984)—it might be helpful to read it aloud with someone else:

EDNA: Wanna come down and have a bite of lunch with me? I got some beer and stuff.

NANCY: Well, you're real sweet, hon. Uhm. Let—I have—

EDNA (coming in on Nancy's "Let"): Or do you have something else t—

NANCY (coming in at the middle of Edna's "else"): No, I have . . . to uh call . . . Bob's mother.

One of the nice things about saying "no" in convoluted ways is that the questioner can reframe the request, maybe adding something like "or do you have something else to . . ." (as Edna does). Often, saying no in a roundabout way takes some of the sting out of rejection. We do this for each other all the time. This method, and many others like it, helps us build a sense of safety and solidarity even when we can't agree to one another's requests. We help each other "save face," as we sometimes say, and retain a more positive sense of self. And it can happen only because of the remarkable capacity we have for sensing the very small moves we all make. Even when we argue with others, we tend to maintain these types of "practical ethics." It builds a sense of safety and solidarity with other human beings even when we can't agree on the substance.

People take turns because simultaneous talk is almost impossible to maintain (try it with a friend and you'll see). Somebody has to bow out, and they almost always do within seconds of the start of an overlap. Sociologists refer to this kind of response to conversation disruption as a *repair*, a way one of the speakers helpfully acts to safeguard the interaction (Schegloff, 2000). It turns out that we are all active in doing such repairs, but some of us are more ready to do it than others.

Sociologists have discovered some patterns to who gives in. Allowing of course for some frequent exceptions, men, quite counter to the stereotype of being "strong and silent," interrupt women more than the reverse. Should both be speaking simultaneously, it is the women who most often relent. Doctors interrupt patients more than patients interrupt doctors—except when the doctor is a woman; then the pattern becomes more equal (West, 1984). Adults interrupt children more than children interrupt adults, something that goes against the common assumptions (certainly that of parents) (West & Zimmerman, 1977).

So the process is not necessarily democratic. Besides the gender and age difference, bosses—it will not be surprising to learn—show their power in talk, something employees may pick up on in sensing their employer has "talked down" to them. Conversational inequalities, precisely because of the subtleties involved, are sometimes hard to notice or at least describe by those taking part. But they are important not just because being interrupted, for example, is insulting. When someone lacks access to a conversational turn, they miss the opportunity for their opinions to count. They have less capacity to help create the reality that they and others live by.

Emotion

4.2.3 Discuss how individuals manipulate emotion in social interaction.

Another method people use in social interaction is emotion. Emotions are not, as the stereotype might imply, utterly beyond our control. Sometimes we speak of emotions as "outbursts"—laughs and cries that break out contrary to anyone's intentions. But for sociologists, emotions are also performances we arrange for specific purposes, although the specific content of the display varies by context.

Kcna Kcna/Reuters

At the funeral for North Korea's ruler Kim Jong-il, people wailed with grief. How do societies differ in the way individuals express emotion? How do specific occasions call out particular ways of expressing emotion?

Who should cry differs from society to society. In some cultures and some situations, people who fail to cry are thought to be inappropriate; they "should" do so at the death of a loved one. Certainly, they should not laugh on such an occasion, although in some settings of the world (New Orleans or Bali), it can certainly be appropriate to *dance* at funerals. At football (what North Americans call soccer) matches in Europe and South America, disorderly mayhem and interpersonal belligerence occur with some frequency; in North America such behaviour is much less frequent. Yet rates of violent crimes in the United States, including "crimes of passion," are higher than in most parts of the world. Somehow there are conventions of time and place for exhibiting aggression and emotional breakdown toward others.

At a more micro level, sociologists studying fights and conflict notice how contestants carefully fit their threats and gestures into a script of calls and countercalls that all parties understand ("oh yeah?" "says who?"). University of Pennsylvania sociologist Randall Collins calls such strings of events "interaction ritual chains." By looking systematically at confrontations among people on the street or in other settings, Collins saw how seldom individuals come to blows. This is because, in the great majority of instances, the participants know that their own bluster and rant, as well as that of their opponent, is theatrical. And besides, most people have no idea how to fight physically; we are afraid of one another. So we look for ways to end the argument without resorting to violence—and socially talented as we all are, we find them. People only *appear* to be out of control (Collins, 2008).

Bursts of laughter alongside others are, as UCLA ethnographer Jack Katz argues, also displays of how context affects emotion and its display. By studying families looking at each other in funhouse mirrors, Katz discovered that unlike conversation, where turn taking is the rule, in laughter everyone can get in on the action all at once. Others may invite us into laughter with a chuckle, but when we all laugh together, we laugh also in collective agreement that something warrants abandoning our façades of emotional reserve. Together, our laughter affirms one another's emotion, our togetherness in feeling that emotion, and that it is safe to express that emotion with loud yelps and unconventional bodily movement (Katz, 1999). In contrast to conversation turn taking, it would be considered odd, even disruptive, to hold off one's laugh until the prior laugher was finished.

One way to understand the social nature of emotion is to study how audiences interact with those who perform on stage. We excite each other. Appreciating a performance with others of like mind and spirit is *rousing*. After going to a concert, we sometimes remark not just about the performer but also about the audience. And indeed, performers acknowledge that they feed off the audience in front of them just as the audience feeds off the performer. It becomes a cycle of mutual reinforcement.

Again, people fit their response to the conditions at hand. One does not hoot and holler at a Catholic Church mass, and one does not remain somber and still at a rock concert. To do either would be an offence not just to those on the stage but also to one's compatriots in the audience. We need each other to build a common experience, and the greater the mutual appreciation, the greater the show. We like it when someone knows how to rouse us in the crowd. If nothing like this happens, it is disappointing. There is a "collective effervescence," as Émile Durkheim (1912/1995, p. 228) famously called it in 1912, when audience members egg each other on. As in a frequent sociological dynamic, people change the situation that changes them.

The British sociologist Max Atkinson (1984) studied a version of all of this in a very precise way. Atkinson recorded speeches being made by British politicians at party rallies, paying close attention, split second by split second, to what the speakers were doing and how their audiences responded. Using a decibel meter, he measured the volume of audience applause and how long each round of applause lasted, including the clapping interruptions during the speech itself. Atkinson learned that applause happens in bursts, quickly rising to a crescendo in about one second before gently levelling off (see Figure 4.1).

We all know the embarrassment of applauding alone—of not knowing, for example, that a symphony has a series of movements and that one should wait until the end of the last one before clapping. Regular symphony goers learn the ropes and avoid the stigma. But in other situations, such as being at a political speech, knowing when to let loose can be more ambiguous.

So Atkinson learned that the talented speechmaker provides audience members with cues that tell when to applaud—moments when they can presume others will be applauding with them. As one example, Atkinson learned that effective orators speak in threes—"of the people, by the people, for the people." When these are aligned with the right kind of intonations, audience members will respond appropriately and clap at just the right moment and together. Sometimes we say people who can generate such a response are charismatic. We think that there is some trait deep within them that causes others to respond with obedience or enthusiasm—as if they have magic or some kind of spiritual gift not found in ordinary human beings. In reality, Atkinson argues, good orators have simply mastered the art of knowing what people need to act together. The art of working a crowd is a social skill that can be very effective at parties, at meetings, or anywhere else interaction occurs. We all, with one degree of success or another, "work the crowd," and the crowd indeed wants to be worked.

Figure 4.1 Applauding Together

Using a decibel meter and sound recordings, sociologist Max Atkinson found that applause started very fast (reaching its full crescendo in about a second) and remained level for about 5.5 seconds before trailing off fairly fast. This suggests how strongly people work to coordinate their applause with one another, careful to start clapping at the "right" time and careful to stop when it seems others are stopping as well.

SOURCE: Adapted from *Our Master's Voices: The Language and Body Language of Politics* (p. 24), by Max Atkinson, 1984, London: Methuen.

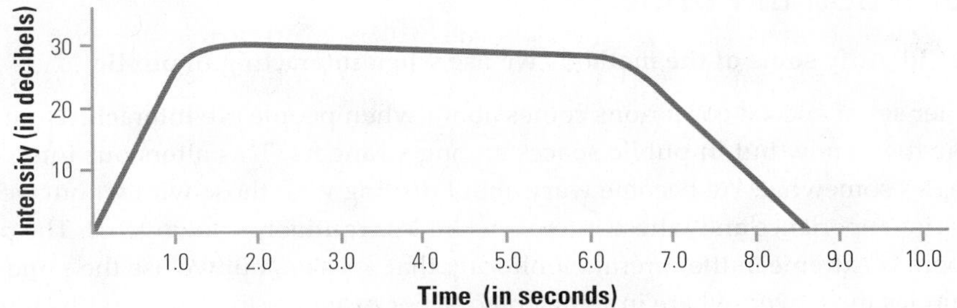

Self-Presentation in a Digital Age

4.2.4 Analyze the impact of digital communication technologies and social media on our methods of self-presentation.

We strive to use the same techniques as communication moves to other media. Social media, of course, change some of the details of the patterns of interaction, but these patterns have many of the same features. When we fret over our Facebook profiles, arranging and rearranging the details, we are manipulating our presentation of self in ways that Goffman would immediately recognize. Based on others' responses or lack of responses, we alter our pages accordingly. We can see, in this e-version of our self-presentation, once again how much people yearn for the approval of others and work social media to bring it about.

This goes on even as we figure out some rudimentary ways of compensating for a lack of face-to-face interaction. Sociologists studying a group of other researchers communicating mostly by e-mail found, indeed, that the participants often got confused about one another's meanings (Menchik & Tian, 2008). They didn't catch each other's tone and spent a great deal of time clarifying how they intended their words to be heard. One round of e-mails got particularly heated when one of the participants seemed to imply another had engaged in plagiaristic behaviour (a very critical allegation for these academics), giving rise to offence. The person who sent that e-mail then wrote to all:

> *I wrote, "I think it would appear plagiaristic" (though I failed to put the word 'plagiaristic' in quotes as I had intended). A careful reading of this, I believe, is that I am not absolutely certain and I am not calling Victor a plagiarist as he seems to imply. . . .* (Menchik & Tian, 2008, p. 343)

Other kinds of communication via social media can have similar issues. For example, posting photos or videos can produce misunderstandings, and text messages and the 140-character limit on Twitter encourage short but sometimes misleading forms of communication.

To combat this possible miscommunication, people often incorporate little signs to clarify how they want their words to be understood. Sometimes, this means words in all capital letters to show emphasis, or quotation marks to show some qualification; other times it means a smiley face, ":-)" or another kind of emoticon. People might sign off by saying what city they are in as a signal that they are travelling (so maybe were less available), in a different time zone, busy with something unusual, or about to get on a plane. So social media users are creative in figuring out ways to adjust to the technology, increasing their clarity and lessening the likelihood of being misunderstood (Menchik & Tian, 2008). As we see, changes in how we communicate stimulate new ways to send social signals. But they are not a complete substitute for real person-to-person communication and indeed show us what we are missing when we make the switch from being there to relying on media technology. Indeed, much e-mail involves making arrangements for face-to-face interaction, especially when matters become emotionally or logistically complex.

Interaction in Public

4.2.5 Identify some of the methods we use when interacting in public.

Another set of special conditions comes about when people are interacting not with people they know but in public spaces among strangers. This alters our interaction strategies somewhat: We become wary about dealing with those with whom we may lack prior experience and whose intentions are less routinely known to us. The public restroom is extreme in the careful monitoring that goes on, but we use the same basic techniques most everywhere in public places. For example, in dealing with strangers pretty much anywhere, we glance at faces, but only for a fleeting moment. To do otherwise implies that we have some special business with them or may even be attracted to them. If that is not plausible, we may be perceived as a threat or as weird or crazy. So in Goffman's terms, the parties solve the problem by mutually "dimming the lights" as their paths cross. They engage in **civil inattention**—ignoring each other to an appropriate degree although noticing that the other is present. In this way, dozens and dozens, maybe even hundreds and hundreds on city streets and crowded campus walks, see and hear each other without being a needless bother or stirring up anxiety. According to one of the great social thinkers, German theorist Georg Simmel, *inattention*, especially in dense places, is precisely what makes social life in large cities possible (Simmel, 1950).

Randy Duchaine/Alamy Stock Photo

It is not always rude to ignore someone. If you see a friend it might be rude to not say hello. But it might also be rude to start talking to random strangers. By engaging in civil inattention, we can politely ignore others in public places.

The next time you enter a bus or movie theatre, or another place where strangers sit together, you are likely to see civil inattention in action. As people search for a seat, they look at the empty chairs, not the faces of others already sitting. Everyone may be drawn toward a particular region of the space, like the middle rows of the theatre, but as more people file in one at a time or in groups, they are likely to take seats that are not directly next to strangers. If they did, it would be considered odd—almost as bad as a man choosing the adjacent urinal when others are available. The person the newcomer sat next to might be alarmed. So without any sign that we are paying any attention to those around us, we navigate to a place where others have a bit of space from us, and we from them. But when there are not so many open spaces, the seats next to strangers become fair game. Even then, however, we usually do not pay obvious attention to those strangers right next to us.

Sometimes our public performances are imperfect—but we have remedies. One famous and simple method is to just say, "oops" or "sorry." Goffman made a big deal out of *oops*. By blurting out this one syllable, not even really a word at all, I can signal that all is okay, the world is functioning in a more or less reasonable way, and I have not gone out of role or out of my mind (Goffman, 1978).

But just as there are rude interrupters, sometimes people are not very nice in how they deploy their demeanour, and it is not due to being clumsy or socially unskilled. Individuals may deliberately not avert their glance. Schoolyard bullies may stare down their victims as a form of intimidation. If a stranger sits next to me on an otherwise empty bus and proceeds to stare at my face, all the right alarms go off because something is going very wrong.

Ethnographer Mitchell Duneier and I analyzed troubles that happen between street people and those they bother with requests for small change or call out to for other reasons (Duneier & Molotch, 1999). Most of us know the experience of being asked for money by strangers. Often those who ask do not observe the fine points of conversation. They approach us even when we do not signal that we want to talk. In that regard, they pay us no mind. They may blurt out their request and do not seem to register the fact that we are not showing any interest. They do not modify their question to avoid our having to give a flat-out "no." They may force the issue and require us to be rude. And that is something people do not like to do to one another. We are upset precisely because we are forced to behave in an uncivil way.

Duneier and I noticed problems in particular with women passersby. The men on the street routinely remark on their bodies and how they look and try to entangle them with questions. Duneier recorded one such set of interactions in New York in the year 1999 (see Duneier & Molotch, 1999, p. 1277), between a man named Mudrick and a woman passerby:

MUDRICK: Hey pretty. (0.8 of a second goes by)

WOMAN (flatly): Hi how you doin'.

MUDRICK (coming in on "doin'"): You alright? (2.2 seconds go by)

MUDRICK: You look very nice you know. I like how you have your hair pinned. (0.8 of a second goes by)

MUDRICK: You married?

WOMAN: Yeah.

MUDRICK: Huh?

WOMAN: Yeah.

MUDRICK (interrupting): Where the rings at?

WOMAN: I have it home.

MUDRICK: Y' have it home?

WOMAN: Yeah.

MUDRICK: Can I get your name?

MUDRICK: My name is Mudrick, what's yours?

We see here the tactics at work that many of us find so difficult. Timing is everything. The woman responds to Mudrick's initial greeting, but only after what is, in conversational terms, a lengthy silence of nearly a second. And her "how you doin'" is said as a statement, not a question. Both are signs that she wants the conversation to stop there. Mudrick ignores the signals as he delivers a follow-up attempt at further conversation (line 3) before she even finishes her response. The woman does not respond as more than two seconds pass—an eternity. Mudrick tries again with another compliment, followed by yet another barrage of questions. The woman gives some responses, but each of her responses signals a desire to end the conversation. Mudrick is still asking questions as the woman walks away.

When people pay a compliment or ask a question, they almost always get a response, and get one pretty quickly if they have a willing conversation partner. But people may signal they don't want to talk through pauses and nonresponses, what conversation analysts call *disaffiliative gestures*. Mudrick not only ignores those signals the woman gives, but he also ups the ante with even more intrusive questions. The woman's disaffiliative gestures escalate until she does something rude by not responding at all to repeat questions—just as she was a bit rude in the first place by not really taking up Mudrick's efforts to converse.

The way Mudrick forces the woman to be really rude by ignoring her signals to end the conversation is what Duneier and I called *interactional vandalism* (Duneier & Molotch, 1999). An offence takes place, but one that is very subtle. When it happens to us, we are aware of a problem, but without the kind of painstaking sociological observations carried out by Duneier, it is hard to pin down. We see from the start that Mudrick does not count for much to the woman, and this had something to do with the bad footing on which the whole thing began. If it had been the mayor of New York or a movie star being abrupt, she might have gone along even if she was spoken to in the same way. This tells us that besides the intricacies of conversational technique, people put up with more from others depending on the kinds of statuses in play and how individual identities are socially categorized, with street people way down on the totem pole.

4.3 What Challenges Do We Face as We Move From One Social Context to Another?

Kaiser/Agencja Fotograficzna Caro/Alamy Stock Photo

Shifts and Dilemmas

Our social selves are always set up for potential change as we move from one social location to another. And as we move between these social contexts, we sometimes encounter difficulties in deciding how to act.

Status and Role Change

4.3.1 Identify the causes of role conflict.

One type of challenge comes from the fact that we enter into different life statuses as we age or just change our life situation. A **status** is a distinct social category that is set off from others and has associated with it a set of expected behaviours and roles for individuals to assume. Each of the status changes brings different types of groups, and the expectations they have for us, into play. In terms of educational status, we move from being elementary school students to high school students and then university students; on the personal front, we become girlfriends or boyfriends, husbands or wives, parents, business managers, professionals, or employees (of course, many of these statuses overlap). Of interest to sociologists is that these different statuses each come with a set of roles *others* expect us to perform. Think of there being a menu of statuses, each with accompanying societal expectations.

So the readers of this text are students, and students are supposed to fulfill certain expectations, or **roles** or role sets, as students: respect the teacher, show up for lecture, keep one's hands to oneself while sitting in the classroom, complete assigned papers, and take exams. Because students do generally conform, life in the college or university classroom is pretty stable and looks a lot different than life in a mosh pit. And so it goes: What is appropriate for a funeral director differs from that for a lawyer, for a teenager from that for a husband, for a restaurant chef from that for

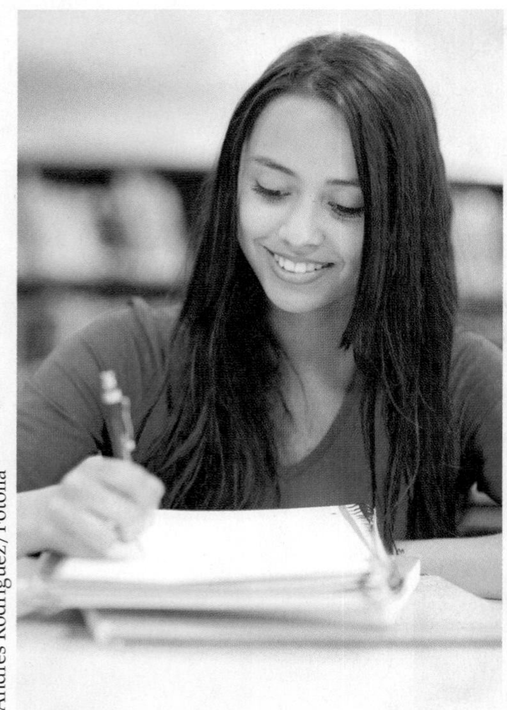

Sometimes our role as student conflicts with fulfilling the expectations of a friend. As a student, we want to fulfill our teachers' expectation that we keep up with assignments and prepare for tests. But our best friend is having a crisis and needs our help. Which role are we supposed to fulfill?

a physician. If the doctor really made us the chicken soup she suggests we drink, we would find it creepy.

Sometimes we will experience **role conflict**—fulfilling the expectations of one of our roles conflicts with meeting the expectations of another. Most of us have experienced this uncomfortable situation when our role as son or daughter conflicts with fulfilling the expectations of a friend. As a son or daughter, we want to fulfill our parents' expectation that we come home for a grandmother's birthday, but our best friend needs our help during a move to a new apartment. We are damned if we do and damned if we don't.

Inconsistent demands arise in many different situations because of the variety of reference groups exerting influence on us. For example, it may be important for certain types of working-class youths to satisfy peer-group expectations that are not consistent with those of school authorities. Sociologists who study delinquency, for example, have found exactly this kind of conformity dilemma. A teenager's peers may encourage kinds of behaviour frowned upon by adults, leaving the teen in a complicated situation of trying to fulfill two different roles. If the teen chooses to engage in delinquent behaviour, it is not that she or he is a nonconformist; rather, she or he is conforming to groups who are devalued by those with authority. This type of conflict is intensified when the police or other officials try to assert control, but the issues are the same.

Labelling

4.3.2 Explain how a self-fulfilling prophecy can influence label formation.

However similar people are in the fact that they conform, they are made different depending on others' opinions of the groups with which they identify. Sociologists have long been concerned with people regarded as a problem by dominant members of society, often referred to as **deviants** by those who make the rules and express opinions about behaviours they find troubling. According to the sociological school of thought called *labelling theory*, so-called deviants come about because there is a person or group that can serve as the object of the label "deviant" and an individual or institution that can put the label on and make it stick. Sociologists long ago stopped believing it was useful to think of people like criminals or most of the so-called insane as essentially different from others. Indeed, it was once common to regard people like divorced women and gay and lesbian individuals as deviant, even criminal or diseased in the case of homosexuals. We no longer think this way, and we understand these labels to have been conventions of their time and place but not accurate descriptions corresponding to the nature of the individuals involved.

One consequence of being labelled (whether the label makes sense or not), some versions of the theory say, is that the individuals so identified in fact change their conduct and embrace the very behaviour that led them into the deviant category in the first place. So the kid who is told he is no good links up with others told the same thing. Whatever their common bonds before, they now at least share a label—presto, a gang. Their networks may start to overlap, especially if they are put in the same detention centres or programs. The boys provide mutual social support and clear the way for, even value, the disapproved behaviour. Just as the nice kids evolve into virtual saints, so it is that others fulfill the expectations of delinquents, rebels, or bad girls. This is an example of what the sociologist Robert Merton called a **self-fulfilling prophecy** (Merton, 1968, p. 475). Something becomes true because people say it is true.

University of California–Santa Barbara professor Thomas Scheff studied how this works in a mental hospital. Some people fight against the label of "crazy" but may face an uphill battle as everyone around them pressures them to accept it (Scheff, 1999).

Their diagnosis, after all, rests on a whole set of labelling institutions, largely held to be legitimate, of doctors, nurses, and the institution. The patients often learn, according to Scheff, that the best route to being released from treatment is to acknowledge the judgements of others that they are crazy.

But quite apart from the labelling apparatus, people inside a mental institution may indeed be about as normal as anyone else. To test this idea, psychologist David Rosenhan sent his research assistants, all with no history of mental health issues, to present themselves to different psychiatric hospitals and tell a single lie: that they were hearing voices in their heads. The people on duty diagnosed all of them as having psychiatric disorders and admitted them to the hospital. Once in the hospital, the undercover assistants told everyone, doctors and nurses included, that they had no more symptoms, and they continued acting normally. Some of the researchers were held for months (this is research commitment!), and none were released by the hospital until they agreed that they indeed had a mental illness (Rosenhan, 1973). Sometimes even our freedom depends on agreeing to the labels placed on us.

The Rosenhan study—published under the title "On Being Sane in Insane Places"—did lead to some reform, and many took to heart the dangerous power of labelling in psychiatric (and other) institutions. In an example of how social research can lead to policy change, it (along with the writings of Scheff and of Goffman) became part of the deinstitutionalization movement that led to the closing of many psychiatric hospitals and their replacement (alas, often not fulfilled) by community-based treatment facilities.

Rule Use

4.3.3 Identify the role of informal rules in social interaction.

Even those of us not in mental institutions are surrounded by organizations we have to answer to, and they all have their rules. These rules often are explicit (such as laws or institutional regulations), but they can also be informal and include norms and expectations for individual behaviours. We must enact our various statuses and roles within the businesses, government agencies, and schools where we make our living, buy our stuff, and get our housing. In doing so, we also have some tricky manoeuvring to do.

Consider, for example, the way we understand and deal with rules that are supposed to determine how we relate to each other. Let's get back to *kill*. The Bible is explicit: Don't do it. The law says the same. But only a jerk would reprimand somebody who swats a mosquito or shoots a rattlesnake about to bite the baby. We might have to kill the person getting ready to throw a bomb in a theatre. If we are on active duty in the military, it is not acceptable to denounce someone (at least someone on your side) who is prepared to kill others. So even this most important of rules requires human interpretation. And that is just what happens, whether in everyday life or in a large-scale organization: interpretation, interpretation, interpretation.

Here's an example quite common to ordinary life, one that we witness all the time in places like restaurants or the airport : "first come, first served." But if a huge celebrity like Lady Gaga or Hilary Clinton wants some service, any competent receptionist would not make her wait in line before being served. And this revision is not limited to celebrities. The sociologist Don Zimmerman studied how receptionists handle clients in a welfare agency, finding that they continuously modified the "first come, first served" rule in order to keep the overall operation running smoothly (Zimmerman, 1970). If there are screaming children, they and their parents get taken ahead of others to curtail the deafening noise that would inhibit anyone from getting work done. If somebody came in who was visibly ill, disorderly, or injured, they would get early attention, even if it was to call in help from the outside, like police or an ambulance.

Similarly, although there may be no official rule that instructs the doctors in busy emergency rooms to make drunken alcoholics wait longer for care (even risking their lives), medical personnel will likely give preference to a more innocent individual, maybe an elderly person hit by a car or a suffering child (Sudnow, 1967). Each of us judges the context and uses the amazing human capacity to scan organizational and individual needs to come up with the appropriate behaviour by bending the rules.

Sometimes we invoke what sociologists have called informal rules that exist alongside the official ones, notions like "respect the needs of children," perhaps. We may use some informal rules to explain to others (or even to ourselves) after the fact that we "really" were not breaking a rule, just following a different one. For example, as I learned in researching the New York subways, train conductors and other workers explain that they rarely report suspicious packages to their supervisors, as they are supposed to do, because that would slow down the system, and that, in turn, would defeat the more informal rule that it is their job to keep the trains running on time.

What really makes us competent members of society is not so much knowing all the rules (formal or informal) but rather knowing what to do on particular occasions given what is expected of us. We don't so much follow rules as use them to make what we did appear both to ourselves and to others as a rational and appropriate action. We act to maintain the normalness of the world so we can all move forward. It's kind of like saying "oops" or "sorry" so people will know things are pretty much OK.

There are people who seem unable to function in this way; they have trouble taking context into account. They insist on "going by the book." When we meet them in real life, they strike us as silly or severely incompetent. We have all come across such extremely annoying people. They seem to lack proper discretion. Garfinkel referred to such individuals as "judgmental dopes" (Garfinkel, 1967, chap. 2). This makes them difficult as coworkers, as neighbours, or even as friends. They may literally live in communities, but they are more like ants in the anthill than humans who interpret and know, as we often say, "it all depends."

On occasions when people do follow the rules in literal ways, everything can easily get screwed up. For example, to cause disruptions, labour unions sometimes call on the rank and file to "work to rule." It is a call to go by the book—exactly. This means not taking the kind of shortcuts that allow the work to actually get done. It is a good union tactic because the only response for employers is to insist workers go back to their old ways of *not* strictly following procedures, an awkward stance for management to take. In one recent study of an Idaho sawmill, an employee in a work-to-rule action left a fire burning in an expensive piece of machinery and walked away to make it to a "mandatory" safety meeting on time (Richardson, 2009). After the protest period, workers returned to the ordinary ways of working, acknowledging that a fire was a good exception to the "mandatory" requirement, to get it all done.

Conformity Experiments

4.3.4 Explain what makes people conform and how conformity impacts how we live together.

Just how people conform to their social circumstance has fundamental consequences for how people live together. Social scientists sometimes set up laboratory experiments to see how people interact under one condition or another, in particular the way they do or do not go along with social pressure. It is almost like a laboratory for rats, except that the experimenter watches people instead of some other kind of animal. Unlike when we watch other animals, we get to see how the special human capacities for social awareness enable manipulation, conformity, and sometimes also resistance. The stakes can be high.

What does it take, an experimenter asks, to get people to give an obviously wrong answer to an easy and factual question? Not much, as it turns out. A social scientist named Solomon Asch, in a classic midcentury study, presented individuals with a line drawn on a card and asked them to choose from among three lines drawn on another card the one that matched it most closely in length (see Figure 4.2). It was pretty simple to do because one of the lines indeed matched perfectly. Asch staged groups of five to

Figure 4.2 The Asch Conformity Experiment

Solomon Asch showed groups of research subjects two cards like these. He asked them to match the line on card 1 with one of the same size on card 2. Asch's research collaborators were secretly mixed in with the research subjects and sometimes agreed that the wrong lines matched. Asch found that the naïve subjects went along with the research collaborators about one-third of the time, and approximately 75 percent conformed to the research collaborators' wrong answer at least once.

SOURCE: Adapted from "Opinions and Social Pressure," by Solomon Asch, 1955, *Scientific American, 193*, p. 3.

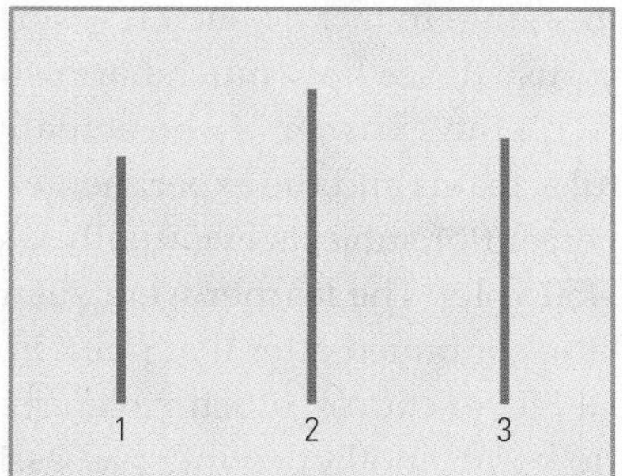

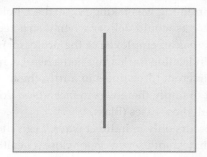

seven people to make the call. But except for one person in each group, the participants were, in fact working with the experimenter. Only one individual in each group was naïve. After a few warm-up runs, where everyone provided the same correct response, the clued-in participants gave consistently wrong answers. Conformity started happening, with naïve subjects (127 males were used) agreeing to a wrong answer *37 percent of the time*. Three-quarters of them conformed at least once, 5 percent conformed every time, but about 25 percent never did (Asch, 1955). So there we have it: Group pressures can change people's behaviours or thoughts in many—but not all—instances.

In various versions of this experiment, some conducted by other researchers following in Asch's (1955) footsteps, it was possible to change the specific conditions to see what causes conformity to rise or fall. One striking finding is that a single ally strongly influences results. If the experiment permitted one person to join the naïve subject in reporting an accurate result, the impact of a majority opinion to the contrary lost much of its power. This implies the importance of people having even just one other person in support. It is much easier to "go against the world" if you have a companion, whether it is a companion in love, or crime, or truth.

These kinds of experiments have their critics. Real life might be different, say the skeptics. And we do not know if those taking part in the experiment really believed that the group was right, only that they *reported* wrong answers to the experimenter. Even so, saying things you don't believe is also conforming and has effects: If nobody says the emperor has no clothes, it makes it easier for the emperor to continue to rule even though he is naked—or to use a more dramatic example, if no one says anything when a dictator decides to use police and military power to kill large numbers of citizens, the killing will go on and on. And the experimental results, it could be argued, are especially impressive given that the research subjects had no good reason to lie other than the pressure to conform. In real life, we really are trying to gain other people's favour. We may not want to go against significant others and reference group members who could fire us from our jobs, flunk us in our courses, or put us in prison. That people will go along to get along when nothing is at stake explains why they do so when there are strong reasons for compromising the truth.

An even more severe lesson from the social science laboratory is that when conditions are right, people—ordinary people—will harm other ordinary people, perhaps even kill them. Inspired by concerns about major real-life situations, the Yale social psychologist Stanley Milgram (1963) wanted to learn the conditions that might cause otherwise respectable individuals to harm one another, merely because they were asked to do so. Milgram conducted his experiments in the post–World War II period when the Holocaust was fresh in people's minds. Some were speculating that the Germans blindly followed Hitler because of some peculiar attribute of the German personality, or at least particular patterns distinct to German culture. Repeated in various settings besides the original version at Yale University, Milgram's so-called obedience studies revealed the Germans who followed orders in World War II to be not so special in these regards.

In his experiment, Milgram (1963) induced his subjects (sometimes college undergraduates) to deliver what they thought were painful, even fatal, electrical shocks to a stranger who had given a wrong answer in what they were told was some kind of learning training. In fact no such learning training was taking place; the whole thing was just a ruse to see how much harm subjects would deliver when instructed to do so. Even with the "learner" (who actually was an employee of the professor) letting out painful screams and the experimenter indicating the learner had a heart condition, over 60 percent of subjects eventually delivered, three times in a row, the last-stage shock of 450 volts. The learner went silent to imply there was in fact a fatal dose, but the shocking continued after that point in all these cases (Blass, 1999).

In real life, of course, much violence occurs only in indirect ways. Legislators say it's okay to bomb another country, assassinate another person, or close a health clinic down—without ever getting close to the bodies or being on the scene. Those situations, like the extreme case of the Nazis, do not involve direct aggression but only indirect bureaucratic action. Many conclude from the Milgram results that it could happen here and in our own time.

Another famous study followed up on the problem of obedience a few years later. Twenty-four Stanford undergraduate men were recruited by Professor Philip Zimbardo (2007) to live in a mock prison. They were randomly assigned roles either as prisoners or guards. Psychologists had selected them out of a total of 75 volunteers because they were deemed the most psychologically stable and healthy. In many cases, the guards became intensely sadistic, humiliating their prisoners, forcing them to go naked, and limiting their capacities to urinate or defecate. Early on the prisoners rebelled but then, after their rebellion failed, submitted to gross abuse. Several had emotional breakdowns, and about a third were judged to have had strongly negative psychological effects. Despite the fact that it was all make believe, the prisoners became radically dependent on their guards' attitude toward them. Some became supplicants, weeping and trembling in the face of those on whom they bestowed authority.

The consequences of the experiment were so intense that Zimbardo had to shut it down after only the sixth day of what was supposed to be a two-week run. Five students had quit rather than go through with even the six days. It became apparent that Zimbardo was risking the mental health and perhaps long-term well-being of others. That people would so readily accept a social role and so fervently conform to the expectations surrounding it provides sobering information about how far people will go to conform to their role set, with perhaps catastrophic consequence.

Zimbardo (2007) noted, in connection with U.S. guards' sadistic treatment of Iraqi prisoners at Abu Ghraib, that his experiments were only too relevant to real life and the extremes to which otherwise normal people will go if supported by role expectations and the right (that is, wrong) kind of social context.

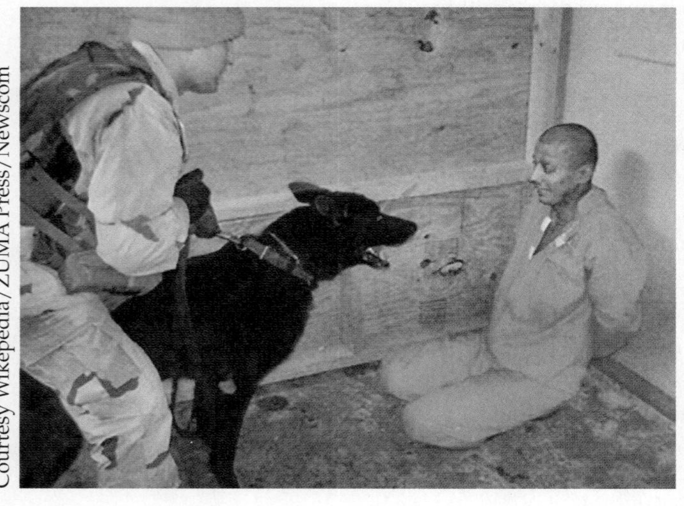

Courtesy Wikepedia/ZUMA Press/Newscom

We can start to understand how face-to-face interactional systems can build up group loyalties, which can follow along ethnic, racial, or national lines. Unlike those among the Stanford students, these demarcations are not randomly assigned, and as is the case with race, for example, individuals have little choice in how they start the process. People really are born into particular groups and have to deal with how others react to those identities.

I act out to satisfy my reference group, and this can put me in opposition to yours. People link up and cast others away as deviant or different in some lesser or dangerous way. But like fish that live in the same school and never even get out of the water, sometimes they do not know that another world is possible—where people have different beliefs and judgements that, in their context, make sense. Our deviance is their normal and vice versa. Other people's ways of life, if known at all, are inferior or maybe even evil—in part just because they are different. Those who belong to groups at the top of the structure have special capacity to demean and punish those below, whether within their same community or in societies farther afield.

Conclusion: What We Know and What We Don't Know

Interactionism provides us with the tools for understanding the social self. Interactionism posits that meaning is produced through interactions between individuals, and thus it introduces the presence of others to understand what an individual is. For each of us, those relevant others differ, and this helps create uniqueness. At the same time, these unique individuals must gain approval from at least some people and groups to have a positive sense of self and to be able to function in the world. To achieve these ends, people have all sorts of artful techniques to know exactly what to do and under what conditions. We read contexts, we use exacting precision as we converse, and we play our emotions to fit the conditions at hand. We do not simply obey rules but creatively interpret them to make them work for ourselves and the organizations that, for better or worse, we come to serve.

This interaction creates not only distinctiveness but also conformity. At the individual level we can be challenged to conform to inconsistent demands coming from opposing parties. It can mean trouble for whole groups who get labelled as deviant because of the relevant others and reference groups that shape their identity and destiny. At the macro level, terrible danger can arise when people conform in ways that create harm and havoc on a mass scale (as the Milgram and Zimbardo experiments vividly demonstrate). Building a society that gives people a sense of their own dignity while at the same time doing the least harm to others is a huge challenge. Many of the important dramas of world history reveal instances when we did not get it right.

Sociology still has some explaining to do; while we have concepts that explain the overall order, we have trouble with the exceptions. So although most people conform to society's laws and accepted codes, some are renegades. One-fourth of Asch's subjects would not conform; five of Zimbardo's dropped out. In the Milgram experiment, not only were there people who would refrain from giving the fatal shock (about one-third), but there was a scattering of subjects who walked out early on. Given how much people usually conform to the social circumstances at hand, we do not have a strong explanation for those who do not go with the flow. We don't know why some Germans risked their lives to hide Jewish families from the Nazis or, at a different part of the moral spectrum, what mix of social factors could produce an individual who would mow down strangers at a shopping mall or students on a college campus.

Nor do we have a firm understanding of why some individuals, of whatever background and circumstance, seem more interactionally creative than others. They can work a room, work an audience, and work their lives in ways that overwhelm others of similar sociological location. Labels, especially negative ones, may come their way, but they do not often stick.

Maybe having such strengths could enable people to lead beneficial social and political movements as well as more satisfying personal lives. If we could find ways to "bottle it," maybe working with like-minded scholars from psychology, we could conceivably encourage, through childrearing and education, more of these people into being.

CHAPTER SUMMARY

The Big Questions Revisited 4

4.1 How Do We Develop a Sense of Self? Each one of us has a unique identity. But is this sense of self a single thing, or is it a process of interaction? In this section, we explored how we know ourselves through the reflections of ourselves that mirror back from others' opinions of us—the "looking glass" of others.

The Social Self

The Looking-Glass Self

Learning Objectives 4.1.1: Explain how the opinions and judgements of others shape our identities.

Significant Others, Reference Groups, and Generalized Others

Learning Objectives 4.1.2: Compare and contrast the roles that significant others, reference groups, and generalized others play in guiding our behaviour and in shaping our sense of self.

Life's a Stage

Learning Objectives 4.1.3: Discuss how we differ in the ways we present ourselves to others.

4.2 How Do We Make Sense of Our Worlds? We all have specific methods for demonstrating competence as interacting members of society. In this section, we explored how the sociological field of ethnomethodology examines these methods.

People's Methodology

Context, Context, Context

Learning Objectives 4.2.1: Explain how context gives meaning to words and situations.

Conversational Precision

Learning Objectives 4.2.2: Explain how conversation patterns can demonstrate social competence.

Emotion

Learning Objectives 4.2.3: Discuss how individuals manipulate emotion in social interaction.

Self-Presentation in a Digital Age

Learning Objectives 4.2.4: Analyze the impact of digital communication technologies and social media on our methods of self-presentation.

Interaction in Public

Learning Objectives 4.2.5: Identify some of the methods we use when interacting in public.

4.3 What Challenges Do We Face as We Move From One Social Context to Another? The social self is not fixed but is always changing, which can sometimes bring challenges. This section examined what happens when we experience role conflict and how informal rules and our keen awareness guide our behaviour. We also looked at how and why people conform and what consequences conformity has on how people live together.

Shifts and Dilemmas

Status and Role Change

Learning Objectives 4.3.1: Identify the causes of role conflict.

Labelling

Learning Objectives 4.3.2: Explain how a self-fulfilling prophecy can influence label formation.

Rule Use

Learning Objectives 4.3.3: Identify the role of informal rules in social interaction.

Conformity Experiments

Learning Objectives 4.3.4: Explain what makes people conform and how conformity impacts how we live together.

Learning the Terms

civil inattention (p. 105)
deviant (p. 108)
ethnomethodology (p. 100)
generalized other (p. 98)
looking-glass self (p. 97)
reference group (p. 97)
role (p. 107)
role conflict (p. 108)
role model (p. 98)
self (p. 96)
self-fulfilling prophecy (p. 108)
significant other (p. 97)
status (p. 107)

Chapter 5
Social Structure

by Jeff Manza*

Roger-Viollet/Bilderwelt/The Image Works

Jewish children waiting for lunch in the Lodz ghetto in Poland, 1942. Because of the German government's attempt during World War II to kill all Jews in Europe, many of these children would have later died in concentration camps.

Learning Objectives

5.1.1 Explain how social structure is similar to the structure of a tall building.

5.1.2 Identify the two key components of social structure.

5.2.1 Distinguish between roles we choose for ourselves and social hierarchies.

5.2.2 Explain how social hierarchies arise and persist.

*An earlier version of this chapter was coauthored with Harel Shapira.

5.2.3 Discuss the roles that power and privilege play in social hierarchies.

5.2.4 Explain the impact that population size has on the ways in which groups within a social hierarchy relate to one another.

5.3.1 Distinguish between social norms and formal rules of behaviour.

5.3.2 Explain the process of institutionalization and identify examples of common practices that have been institutionalized.

5.3.3 Explain why large formal organizations are critically important to the overall structure of a society.

5.4.1 Discuss how socialization contributes to the creation of roles and norms.

5.4.2 Discuss how social structure exerts influence over our interactions with others.

5.4.3 Discuss the relative impact of social structure versus individual choice.

5.5.1 Explain how past outcomes impact present choices.

5.5.2 Analyze the power of path-dependent processes.

Inge Deutschkron was born in 1922 and grew up in a socially mixed neighbourhood in the north of the German capital of Berlin. Her father, Dr. Martin Deutschkron, belonged to a high-status group in Germany because he held a doctoral degree and taught at an elite secondary school. Despite his social standing, Inge's father was a socialist, believing that modern society should be far more egalitarian than capitalism normally allows. Martin and his wife sympathized with unions and laboured tirelessly for the Marxist-inspired Social Democratic Party, sometimes taking young Inge along to meetings and demonstrations.

In January 1933, Adolf Hitler's Nazis came to power in Germany. Shortly thereafter, Inge's father was dismissed from his teaching position as an enemy of the Nazi regime because of his political views. But there were worse things to come for the family. On March 31, 1933, Inge's mother sat the 10-year-old down and revealed to her something she could barely comprehend: The country's new rulers considered her Jewish, and she could expect to be persecuted for this. This news came as a surprise to the young girl, as religion had played no part whatsoever in her upbringing. Had she lived in a different time or place, it is likely that her Jewishness would have played little or no role in her life. Yet for the Nazi government, Jewishness was a matter of "racial" identity that one was born with and could not escape. Because Inge's grandparents were Jewish, she was considered Jewish as well. It had nothing to do with how she felt as an individual; despite her upbringing in a nonreligious household, the Nazi government viewed her as a member of an alien people locked in an eternal struggle with German "Aryans." Although her father managed to flee in 1939 to England, Inge and her mother remained trapped in Berlin, threatened after 1941—like all other people classified as Jewish—with deportation to concentration camps and a near-certain death (6 million Jews in all died in the camps). With the help of a network of sympathetic fellow citizens, however, she and her mother miraculously survived underground in Berlin—the heart of Hitler's Third Reich—until the end of the war. In February 1945, they took advantage of the destruction and occupation of many cities in Germany to pass themselves off as refugees who had lost their identity papers. Yet even this return to a "legal" German identity nearly proved fatal when Russian soldiers reached greater Berlin in April 1945 and could see Inge and her mother only as members of a hated nationality (German). Only after they could produce Nazi documents attesting to their Jewishness were they protected, and even granted the privileged status of "victims of fascism" (Deutschkron, 1989).

The Big Questions

In this chapter we explore the concept and importance of social structure by examining five central questions:

1. **What is social structure?** Why do sociologists reject the view that the world is simply made up of a collection of individuals? In this section, we introduce the concept of social structure. Although social structures are normally hidden from view, they are essential to making social life possible. The key elements of social structure (roles and hierarchies, norms and institutions) are introduced.
2. **How do roles and social hierarchies shape our life chances?** The social structure of any society consists of a wide range of different roles and social divisions, or hierarchies, between groups. In this section, we will explore where these various roles and social hierarchies come from and why they matter.
3. **How do norms and institutions influence social life?** A society's social structure also contains an elaborate set of norms and institutions. In this section, we will explore some of the central aspects of norms and institutions and why they influence our behaviour.
4. **How do social structures influence our daily lives and social interactions?** Where do the identities and roles that are so important for social interaction come from? How do changes in social structure influence social interaction? Does acknowledging the existence of social structure mean that we have limited free will?
5. **Why are social structures slow to change?** What are the forces that that make social structures endure? Why is change such a slow process?

Born in 1922, Inge Deutschkron and her mother of Jewish ancestry miraculously survived living underground in Berlin at the heart of Hitler's Third Reich until the end of the war.

Franka Bruns/AP Images

The story of Inge Deutschkron, described in her best-selling memoir (Deutschkron, 1989), illustrates in a particularly graphic way how social forces outside the control of individuals can dramatically shape lives and fates. The way Inge's family members were forced to see themselves and were seen by others was determined by social and political factors entirely beyond their control (in this case, the Nazi government's imposition of a system of racial classification that turned the secular Deutschkron family into Jews). For millions in 1940s Europe, this act of social classification would prove to be a matter of life and death. Of course, most people have not been subjected to arbitrary racial laws or the whims and injustices of a dictatorial state like the victims of the National Socialism era in Germany. But in many other everyday ways, the **social structures** in any society exert powerful influences over individuals and social interaction: They set limits on our choices and opportunities, they enable and motivate us to do some things and not others, and they make some outcomes much more likely than others. Social structures are often mysterious and hard to see, but they are also truly very powerful, enduring, and slow to change. As we will explore in this chapter, understanding the social worlds that humans inhabit requires us to consider the impact of social structure on the lives of individuals.

5.1 What Is Social Structure?

Stephen Barnett/ImageState/Alamy Stock Photo

Social Structure as the Context of Human Action

Social structure is a term that is fundamental to the entire way sociologists understand social life. But not everyone agrees that social structure does, in fact, exist. British prime minister Margaret Thatcher once famously declared that "There is no such thing as society." By this she meant that the notions both of "society," used in everyday conversations, and "social structure," in the research and writings of sociologists and other social scientists, were a myth, a vague idea that could be used as a way of making excuses for bad individual behaviour or disappointing outcomes. For example, to say that criminals are "made," not "born," suggests that society, not the individual offender, is responsible for criminal behaviour. Thatcher preferred the idea that it is always individuals who are entirely responsible for their own behaviours and their successes and failures in life. While sociologists do agree that individuals have room to shape their own destiny, they would strongly disagree with Thatcher that individuals are not heavily influenced by social structure as they interact with others and go about their daily routines.

Defining Social Structure

5.1.1 Explain how social structure is similar to the structure of a tall building.

Let's start with a straightforward example. If you are born into a poor family, it is much more likely that you will be poor as an adult than if you are born into a rich family. Why? Margaret Thatcher's answer is that it comes down to the personalities and actions of each individual: The rich adult has a better work ethic and simply worked harder or took advantage of opportunities better than the poor adult did. For sociologists, however, the answer is much more complicated. The external influences that provide the context for individual and group action contribute to helping the rich child become a rich adult and also make it much more difficult for the poor child to become a rich adult. Rich children are far more likely to have opportunities for intellectual growth (such as travel to foreign countries, attending very good private schools, or having tutors and other forms of special help along the way). They are more likely to meet or know people who will help them find their place in the world (like private-school counsellors who help place students in the best possible college or university, or family friends who may help in landing a great job). The poor child, by contrast, typically enjoys few or none of these resources.

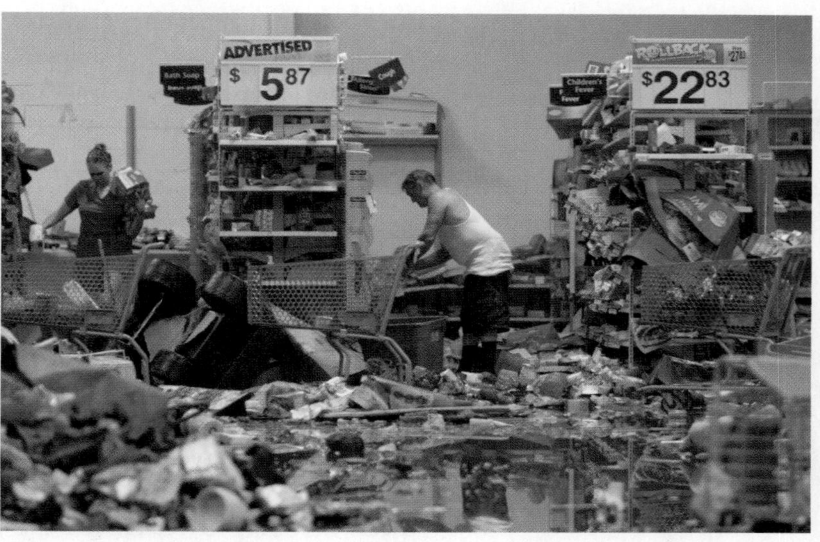

Magnum Distribution/Magnum Photos

When social structures break down, so does social order. A powerful example of this was during Hurricane Katrina, when lootings and crime skyrocketed in New Orleans. Have you ever been in a situation when you felt like the social structure was weak or falling apart?

What exactly is *social structure*? As we saw in Chapter 1, sociologists use the concept of social structure to describe the diverse ways in which the rules and norms of everyday life become enduring patterns that shape and govern social interactions. The sociological definition of social structure attempts to capture the many elements of society that have power over us, that exist separately and independently from individuals while playing a role in influencing both our individual actions and the nature and outcomes of social interactions between individuals and groups. In the example above, the rich child benefits by her place in the social structure, while the poor child suffers. Because of these social structures, the odds of adult success are dramatically higher for the rich child.

Social structures range from the norms governing interactions between friends or lovers to the global environment in which whole countries and their governments make decisions about war and peace. Social structures are all of the elements of society that provide the regular patterns that we can all count on or anticipate in our daily lives as well as inside those groups and organizations we participate in. We don't always think about *all* of the reasons why, at any point in time, of the many possible types of actions we might take, only a few are realistically possible. How do social structures influence the simple act of crossing the street?

We feel comfortable and safe walking across the street when the light is green because we are confident that cars will stop and not run us over. But once we stop to think about *why* we have such confidence, we can see that there are a lot of hidden factors at work. Laws that would severely punish a driver are perhaps the most important, but those laws and punishments require a whole complex legal system to enforce them and to convince drivers to take them seriously. There are also norms and courtesies that help, especially when the situation is less cut and dried (for example, when a car is turning a corner where there is no light and you are in the middle of the street). To be sure, thousands of pedestrians are killed each year, but the number would be drastically higher in the absence of laws, rules, and norms that guide pedestrians and drivers. In short, social structures provide the backdrop for action of all kinds, operating in the background of social life and exerting powerful influence over individuals, groups, and organizations.

Like anything that is normally hidden from view, it is often only when social structure is *absent* that its importance becomes clear. We've all seen movies and TV shows or read novels about situations where social structures completely break down—for example, in the aftermath of a nuclear war, a mammoth plague, or a shattering natural disaster, or even in horror films where zombie-like creatures have taken over the world. In fictional accounts such as these, individuals or characters have to make do without the order normally provided by social structure. Dramatic fictional renderings like these play off a very real idea: that underneath everyday social life is a foundation that makes social order possible.

One of the most important aspects of any structure, physical or social, is that it endures over time, even as other things change around it. A building provides a good example of how physical structures work and helps us think about social structures as well. A tall, old building will have many different occupants over the years, each doing different things (and living very different lives). But unless the building meets the wrecking ball, it will continue to exist even as all of its occupants change or its exterior or interior is renovated. This is also true of social structures. Social structures, over time, give social life a regularity that it might not otherwise have. Human beings are born, live, die, and are replaced by new people, but the social structures governing those lives remain in place. Historical changes do occur, sometimes even revolutions that can bring about big changes in social structures, but most of the time changes to social structures happen slowly and modestly. The very persistence of social structures—and their durability—is an important part of what gives them their power. We will explore this idea in more detail later in the chapter.

Key Components of Social Structure

5.1.2 Identify the two key components of social structure.

Although the concept of social structure is a bit challenging to define, we all know about the existence of social structures in one way or another, once we start thinking about them. Poor people "know" that the world is stacked against them, and the rich "know" they have a lot of advantages (even if they sometimes prefer to think that isn't true). College and university students "know" that if they complete their degree they will have better life opportunities than if they flunk out. We all "know" that we are supposed to show respect to our teachers, doctors, judges, ministers, and the prime minister. And we are all at least somewhat attuned to the ways social structures are slowly changing—just think about the types of jobs and careers that will be opening up in the future versus the kinds of jobs and careers that were common 50 or 100 years ago. You would have to be blissfully unaware of what is going on in the economy right now not to know that the job market is changing very rapidly and that change in the economic structure of modern societies will have a considerable impact on everyone.

There are many elements to a society's social structure, and sociologists sometimes disagree about what is "structural" in a society and what is not. But as a general starting point, it is helpful to distinguish two key related, but distinct, components roles and social hierarchies, and norms and institutions as Figure 5.1 illustrates.

Both of these components, individually and in combination, make up the essential core of what sociologists mean when they refer to *social structure*. To get a better grasp on them, we will discuss each component separately in the next two sections before exploring how they are connected in their impact on daily life and social interaction.

Figure 5.1 Key Components of Social Structure

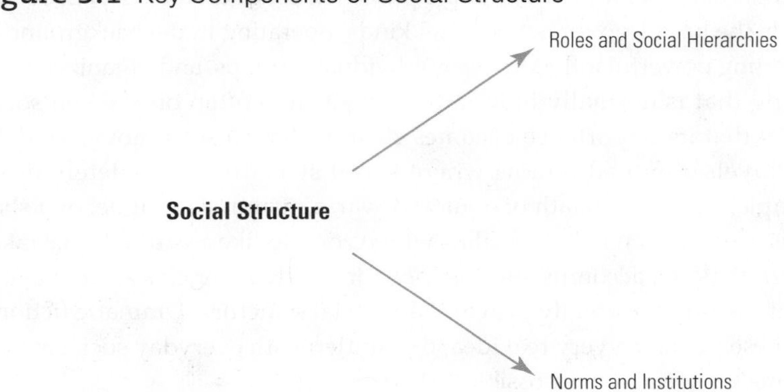

5.2 How Do Roles and Social Hierarchies Shape Our Life Chances?

A. Astes/Alamy Stock Photo

The First Dimension of Social Structure: Roles and Social Hierarchies

Roles and social hierarchies are critical components of a society's social structure. Let's look at how they shape our lives.

Roles

5.2.1 Distinguish between roles we choose for ourselves and social hierarchies.

Any modern society contains within it a complex set of social positions, and even some of the earliest human societies contained a number of different positions (such as "chief" and the "shaman," or medicine man). We use the term **role** to describe the rules and expectations that are associated with different positions. Every role we can think of—child/parent, doctor, sorority member, garbage collector, director, assistant to the director, priest, counsellor, roommate, subcontractor, chairperson, fan, subway rider, teammate, and on and on—has a distinct set of expectations and rules associated with it. When we take on a role, like an actor in a play, we are expected to perform it in a certain way. We often have some flexibility in exactly how we perform the role (just as different actors playing the same role will do it somewhat differently), but we are also heavily constrained in what we can (and must) do while in the role because of its script.

Once we reach a certain age, we all begin to play multiple roles. We even switch from one role to others throughout the day. For example, when we wake up we may be either parent or child. When we leave for the day, we assume the role of "driver" if we drive a car, or "rider" if we use public transportation, or "bike rider" if we use a bicycle. When we get to our destination, let's say, school or work, we then take on other roles (student, teacher, boss, worker, etc.). The importance of these roles can perhaps be seen most easily in the ways that occupying a particular role changes our behaviour

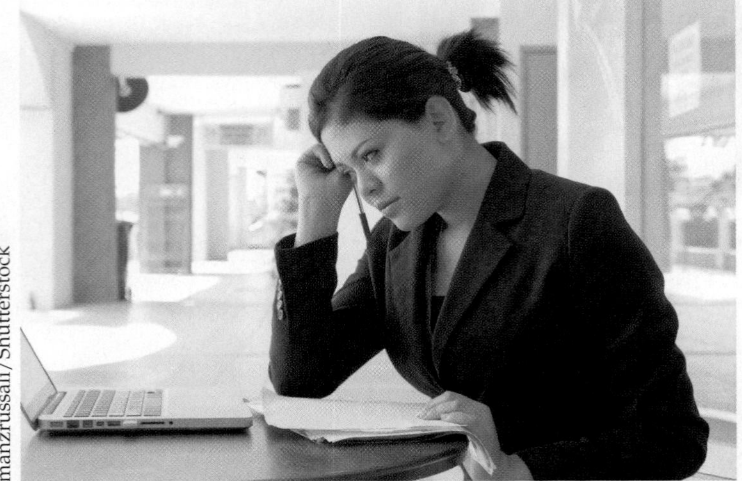

manzrussali/Shutterstock

As we become adults, we will take on many new roles that entail important responsibilities—not just to ourselves, but to others (such as employers and children) as well.

over the course of our lives. As we age throughout our lives and shift from one stage of what sociologists call the **life course** to another, we are supposed to transition between roles. In other words, we are expected to "grow up" (it is very embarrassing for an adult to be called a "child"). In the process of moving from one life stage to another, we are expected to alter our behaviour to fit new roles.

One critical aspect of taking on any role is that our behaviour changes as a result. As we shift from toddler to kindergartener to high school student to university student to graduate student, we are expected to behave differently, becoming (hopefully) more mature and independent at each stage. Some of the roles we play may change throughout the day—a simple example would be when we switch from being a driver to becoming a pedestrian as we exit our car and begin to walk. In simple cases like this, universal rules and expectations that apply to everyone, no matter who they are, govern the role (e.g., do not drive through a crosswalk when a pedestrian is in it, or do not jump in front of an oncoming car in the middle of the street). But more permanent roles often require challenging shifts in behaviour that can be costly. The factory worker who is promoted to become a supervisor at the same workplace has to adopt a different persona, going from a coworker to someone who has to sometimes make hard and perhaps unpopular decisions concerning former coworkers that he or she now supervises.

Before we leave our discussion of roles, it is important to make a distinction between roles that are assigned to us (such as "child") and roles that we obtain through deliberate action or achievement (such as "boss," "parent," "NHL hockey player," or "pharmacist"). Many of the most important roles arise out of longstanding inequalities (or hierarchies) in society, such as those based on race or ethnicity (whether you are "white," "black," "South Asian," etc.), gender, nationality (for example, "Canadian," "Argentinian," "Chinese"), and religion—all roles into which we are (usually) born.

While some roles—like being a driver or a pedestrian—may not have clear differences of status built in, many other roles do. Roles that come with varying amounts of power and privilege are better described as **social hierarchies**: important and enduring social positions, ordered from high to low, that grant some individuals and groups higher status and more power than others depending on where they stand in that hierarchy. We turn now to an analysis of these hierarchies.

Social Hierarchies

5.2.2 Explain how social hierarchies arise and persist.

Every society in the world today contains many types of social hierarchies. Hierarchies can be based on almost any way that people divide themselves into groups or categories, and members of one group or category are accorded more status, opportunities, power, or authority than others. Recall our example of Inge Deutschkron from the chapter's introduction: Once young Inge and her family were declared Jewish, they suddenly were placed at the bottom of a (deadly) social hierarchy. Some hierarchies are more important than others (and most do not lead to genocide), but taken as a whole, they are a critical source of what gives social structure its meaning.

Social hierarchies arise and persist in any situation in which members of one group are able to use their possession of some *asset* or *attribute* as a basis for claiming special advantages over others who do not possess it. The asset in question can vary widely, as the following examples suggest. An asset might be something individuals are born with, like their skin colour or gender. It might be something they are usually born into but can change in adulthood, such as membership in a particular religious denomination. Or it could be something they attain later in life, such as education or having the resources to start a business and hire others.

Jin Liangkuai/Xinhua/Landov

Evidence that men continue to dominate the most desired positions is a source of gender conflict in the workplace, and one that impacts the lives of all women who seek entrance into top managerial positions.

Both individuals and societies as a whole are impacted by social hierarchies. As an individual, where you fall in the social hierarchies in your society likely either enhances or diminishes your chances for achieving what you hope out of life (and may even limit your aspirations). For societies as a whole, hierarchies are most important because they can generate enormous tensions and conflicts between dominant and subordinate groups, conflicts that may in some cases become violent. The general requirement of having to defer to or show respect for higher-status people (and the disgust that may sometimes entail) is an example we are all familiar with, and one that can easily generate tensions. Indeed, whenever social hierarchies allow dominant groups to get more of something that is valued than subordinate groups, it is hardly surprising to find subordinate groups wanting to challenge the situation. In such cases, the more powerful group will try to resist demands for change, and will often succeed. Examples are everywhere. For example, the gender hierarchy has long been one basis for exclusion of women from the opportunity to compete equally with men in the labour market, including for top management positions in large corporations. In spite of a powerful feminist movement and decades of efforts to provide equal opportunities for women, a "glass ceiling" still appears to exist when it comes to the most desired positions of power and authority.

The *glass ceiling* is a metaphor used to describe the relatively slow progress women have made moving into high-level executive positions. Corporations now willingly hire women to work in the lower rungs of management, but when it comes time to promote, women remain disadvantaged. Currently (in early 2015), only 25 of the Fortune 500 companies are run by women, nearly five decades after the principle of gender equality was fully established in North American law with the passage of the Bill of Rights in Canada in 1960 and the Civil Rights Act of 1964 in the United States. Male executives and corporate boards continually find ways to limit the opportunities for upward mobility of women in large corporations. Despite the exclusion of women from the most desired positions of power and authority, there are those who have succeeded in breaking through the barriers. Two examples are Angela Merkel, who became the first female chancellor of Germany in 2005, and Michaëlle Jean, who became the first governor general of Canada of Caribbean origin in 2005. Jean came to Canada as a refugee from Port-au-Prince, Haiti, in 1968 and worked as a broadcast journalist before becoming Canada's third female governor general.

We turn now to two key issues related to social hierarchies—power and group size—that influence how social hierarchies impact individuals and societies.

Power and Privilege in Social Hierarchies

5.2.3 Discuss the roles that power and privilege play in social hierarchies.

The case of the glass ceiling highlights the ways in which social hierarchies involve **power**—the ability to influence the behaviour of others—and **privilege**—the ability

Bruce Roberts/Science Source

History is filled with examples of the power imbalance within social structures. It can be seen in the capacity of the powerful to influence the behaviour of others, including establishing laws that will exclude subordinate groups and reproduce the power inequality.

or right to have special access to opportunities or claims on rewards—by which a dominant group seeks to monopolize opportunities and control rewards or at least prevent its existing privileges from eroding. Subordinate groups, by contrast, are subjected to inferior status and limited opportunities. The most common mechanism through which privilege is maintained is **discrimination**, where a dominant group uses either legal or informal means to control opportunities and reduce or eliminate challenges from subordinate groups. Legal means of exclusion—where one group is prevented by law from attaining certain kinds of valued positions—are blunt and powerful. The rules of social hierarchies become most visible and have their biggest impact when they are explicit and clear to everyone and when the sanctions for violating them are most clear. Consider this example: Imagine that it's the 1950s and you're somewhere in the American South, let's say, Alabama. And let's say you are African American, and you need to go to the bathroom or find a restaurant to eat in. Your choices are limited because of certain features of the social structure—in this case, race and racism—that are in place, resulting in laws that prevent you from using bathrooms or restaurants reserved for whites. Other laws that were common in Southern states limited your right to attend the schools of your choosing, marry whom you wanted, or compete for jobs on equal terms with white workers.

But such laws and rules blatantly violate fundamental ideas about equality in modern democratic societies. Not surprisingly, they were and are subject to powerful challenges by subordinate groups for precisely that reason. Challenges have come both from **social movement** protests—collective action aimed at bringing about some kind of change, like the civil rights movement and the women's movement—and from legal and political challenges brought by those groups or individuals. These challenges have often succeeded in eliminating the legal foundation for one group using the law to make another subordinate. However, just because explicit legal restrictions on subordinate groups disappear does not mean that social hierarchies and the inequalities associated with them suddenly cease to exist. The persistence of the glass ceiling in business is but one of many examples. Dominant groups can still assert their power through a variety of informal means that do not rely on formal laws. One of the most important of these is the development and deployment of negative *stereotypes*, which are false or exaggerated generalizations about a subordinate group applied to all members of the group. Examples of classic negative stereotypes include the idea that some groups are lazy, are unintelligent, are prone to criminal activity, are better suited for caring work than high-paying professional employment, have bad attitudes, or lack ambition. Any of these stereotypes, if widely held by members of the dominant group and others in society, justify continuing discrimination against subordinate groups *even if* formal legal equality is achieved. For example, laws can be passed that require employers to consider all applicants for jobs equally. But if employers hold negative stereotypes about subordinate groups, research suggests, they will consistently favour members of the dominant group in making decisions about whom to hire. One way to examine this is to look at differences in outcomes, for example, income, for members of different groups working in the same occupation. When we do this, we can begin to see how informal means of discrimination against subordinate groups persists. Table 5.1 shows the difference in wages of men and women and of whites and blacks who are working full-time in the same occupation in the United States.

By looking at wage differences within the same occupation, we can see how even women and blacks who attain the same occupation as men and whites, respectively, can be denied access to the most attractive or well-paying opportunities for workers in that occupation.

Table 5.1 Inequality in Income by Gender and Race Within the Same Occupation (U.S. dollars)

Occupation	Men's Median Yearly Wage	Women's Median Yearly Wage	Gender Pay Gap	Occupation	White Median Yearly Wage	Black Median Yearly Wage	Racial Pay Gap
Lawyer	$106,860.00	$85,072.00	$21,788.00	Lawyer	$109,900.50	$84,536.77	$25,363.73
Computer systems analyst	$76,804.00	$65,208.00	$11,596.00	Computer systems analyst	$70,722.40	$61,599.46	$9,122.94
Chief executive	$118,300.00	$89,960.00	$28,340.00	Chief executive	$112,174.50	$79,174.80	$32,999.70
Physical scientist	$79,144.00	$60,892.00	$18,252.00	Physical scientist	$69,095.76	$58,605.43	$10,490.34
Accountant	$70,200.00	$51,792.00	$18,408.00	Accountant	$55,912.38	$38,751.00	$17,161.38
Social worker	$44,512.00	$43,940.00	$572.00	Social worker	$39,034.18	$38,437.77	$596.41
Public relations specialist	$70,252.00	$51,428.00	$18,824.00	Public relations specialist	$52,433.21	$48,255.77	$4,177.44
Designer	$53,456.00	$44,460.00	$8,996.00	Designer	$38,842.32	$36,137.33	$2,704.99
Patrol officer	$52,832.00	$42,380.00	$10,452.00	Patrol officer	$57,929.12	$52,862.93	$5,066.19
Chef	$30,264.00	$24,024.00	$6,240.00	Chef	$30,155.32	$26,147.67	$4,007.65
Janitor	$26,572.00	$21,216.00	$5,356.00	Janitor	$20,284.18	$18,892.71	$1,391.47
Advertising sales agent	$49,140.00	$43,784.00	$5,356.00	Advertising sales agent	$48,282.54	$38,228.10	$10,054.44
Nurse	$56,416.00	$53,140.00	$3,276.00	Nurse	$54,138.83	$42,194.18	$11,944.65

SOURCE: U.S. Census, 2012

Group Size and Social Hierarchies

5.2.4 Explain the impact that population size has on the ways in which groups within a social hierarchy relate to one another.

One of the most important but often ignored aspects of the social hierarchies of any society is how the relative size of various groups competing for desired positions or opportunities influences the relationship between them. The most important kinds of desired positions at issue include jobs and economic opportunities, as well as opportunities in the educational system. Because the key social groups competing for these desired positions—for example, those based on race, ethnicity, religion, or nationality—will inevitably change in size over time, competition and conflicts between groups may increase. For example, when a subordinate group becomes more numerous, members of a dominant group may begin to feel more threatened than before. In this way, population factors—in particular when groups change size—are a key part of why and when social hierarchies produce conflict.

The most common way in which the size of social groups changes over time is the result of *immigration,* when individuals and families move to take up residence in a new country. Most countries around the world allow some people born in other countries to move to and live in their country, and both Canada and the United States have often been world leaders in welcoming people from other places. When immigration first increases, the flow of immigrants from a particular country or region of the world to a new place may be just a trickle, and hardly anyone notices their presence. But as immigrants settle into their new country, they often encourage other family members and friends to join them in the same community. Over time, people from these new places may become more numerous and cluster in the same areas, and can seem threatening to those who lived there before. When this occurs, competition for jobs, housing, and places in schools may begin to occur. All of sudden, members of the native group may begin to feel that the immigrants are posing a threat to their way of life. And they may begin to explicitly seek to exclude immigrants from opportunities by employing stereotypes and other forms of active discrimination, or pushing for the government to pass laws that will limit the flow of immigrants into the area.

Another way in which population changes can become critically important for the life chances of individuals occurs as economies evolve and the overall mix and types of jobs begins to shift. Economies, especially in the period since the Industrial Revolution, do not stand still. They are in constant motion because of new technologies, new types of consumer demands, and the discovery of new kinds of raw materials for producing goods. The process of creation and destruction of jobs represents a powerful source of social structure change. And the impact is very uneven: While usually benefitting some individuals and societies as a whole, these changes can also harm many people.

Three critical long-term economic trends have fundamentally transformed societies around the world, including Canada and the United States. The first of these trends—the long-term decline in agricultural production and employment, and the rise of manufacturing jobs—is what is known as the Industrial Revolution. It occurred at a very rapid pace in the late nineteenth and early twentieth centuries in North America and Europe, and later in other parts of the world (and is just beginning in still others). The most important change in the social structure of mid-nineteenth-to mid-twentieth-century North America was the decline of the central role of agriculture in the economy. For most of the nineteenth century, most North Americans worked on small farms that either they or someone else owned (including the majority of the U.S. slave population before the American Civil War). Many others did jobs that were related to agriculture—providing farmers with supplies or transporting and selling farm products in cities. By the early part of the twenty-first century, however, agricultural work was replaced by service work, as Figure 5.2 highlights.

So where did all of these former farmers go? The short answer is that the enormous growth of manufacturing provided new opportunities for both citizens and new immigrants in North America's booming late-nineteenth- and early-twentieth-century cities, reflecting a second major economic shift in North American history. Manufacturing jobs were the primary source of employment growth in the North American economy between the 1850s and the 1960s. If the typical North American worker in 1850 was a farmer, in 1950 he (and full-time workers were at that time were still mostly men) worked in a factory. Employment in manufacturing skyrocketed in

Figure 5.2 Declining Farm Employment in Canada

SOURCE: From "Farmers Leaving the Field," by Geoff Bowlby, 2002, *Perspectives on Labour and Income* (online ed., Chart A), *3*(2) (http://www.statcan.gc.ca/pub/75-001-x/00202/6086-eng.html). Copyright by Statistics Canada, Client Services Division. This does not constitute an endorsement by Statistics Canada of this product.

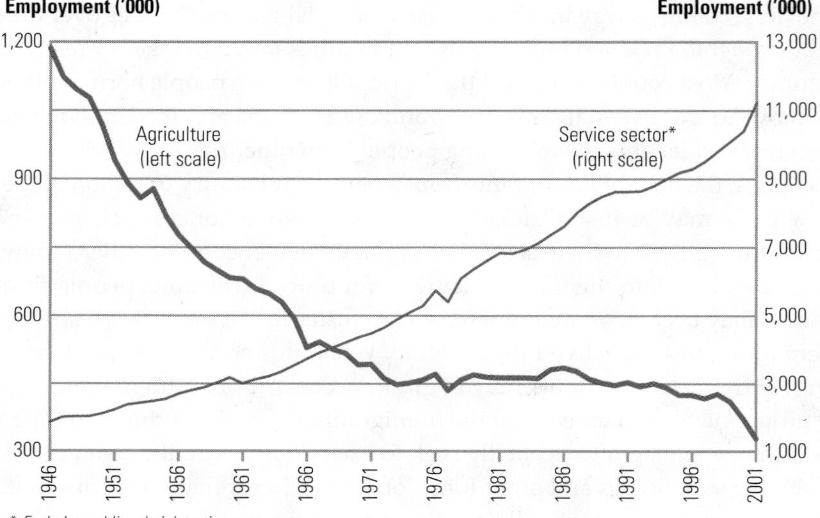

the early decades of the twentieth century, and entire communities were built around large factories and sometimes a single dominant manufacturing industry. Opportunities for employment in North America's rapidly growing manufacturing sector were important factors encouraging Europeans and others to move to North America before World War II. The most famous of these industrial centres dominated by manufacturing was the concentration of the automobile industry in Detroit, but there were many others as well: Steel dominated in Hamilton and Sault Ste. Marie, Ontario; Pittsburgh, Pennsylvania; and Gary, Indiana. Shipbuilding drove the economy in Montreal, Quebec. Meatpacking employed large numbers in Winnipeg, Manitoba, and Chicago, Illinois, while the rubber industry spurred economic growth in Akron, Ohio, and grain milling in Buffalo, New York. Transportation hubs for manufacturing companies came to dominate places like New Orleans, Louisiana. All of these cities and regions prospered as demand for manufactured products grew both in North America and around the world.

Beginning in the 1970s, however, employment in manufacturing began a steep and seemingly irreversible decline, as Figure 5.3 shows. While the causes of the decline in manufacturing jobs in recent decades have been widely debated, one key factor that all analysts agree on is that major technological advances both displaced human workers and made it possible for manufacturing companies to efficiently produce in countries where wages were far lower than in Canada and the United States, such as China. Most of the consumer goods we buy today are largely assembled outside of North America. What has replaced those manufacturing jobs?

The third critical long-term economic trend that has transformed Canada and the United States and other societies around the world is the dramatic rise in employment in white-collar, knowledge-based occupations, a dynamic that accelerated in the second half of the twentieth century and continues today. The new jobs that have been created since the 1970s have primarily been in the so-called *service sector*, a term used to describe a wide range of industries that include finance, real estate, professional and personal service of all kinds (ranging from expensive lawyers and doctors to child- and elder-care workers), sales jobs of one kind or another, and emerging knowledge-based occupations in computers and information technology (including IT professionals, repair technicians, and software and hardware designers). These shifts have expanded the number of desirable jobs, but the overall mix of jobs also includes a growing number of "bad" jobs, such as service and maintenance work, call-centre work, janitorial services, personal and household service work, and fast food

Figure 5.3 Manufacturing Employment in the United States (in millions)

SOURCE: U.S. Bureau of Labor Statistics

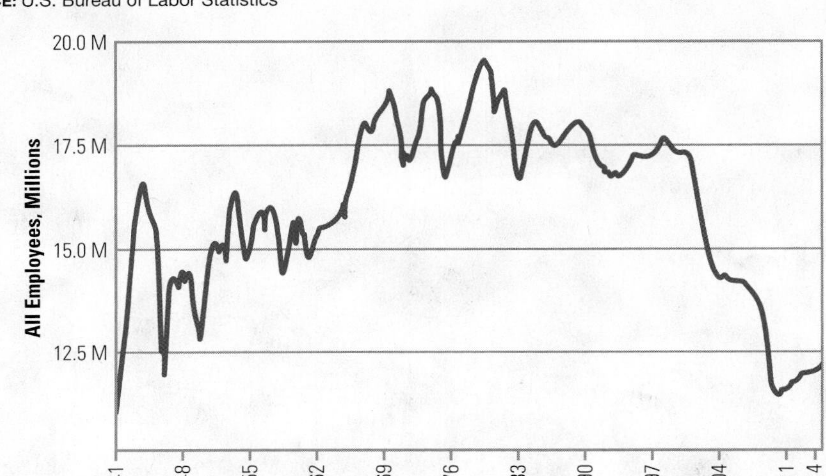

restaurant work; these jobs pay low wages and offer few opportunities for advancement (Wright & Dwyer, 2003).

The consequences of these population changes for individuals and families were immense, and entire communities have been affected as well. For example, someone born in a working-class community in 1940, growing up with the expectation of working in a factory, could expect to find a decent job in his or her late teens or early 20s (say, around 1960). But 20 to 25 years later, in middle age, those factory jobs were rapidly disappearing. Millions and millions of factory workers lost employment in this period and struggled to find similar-paying jobs, and young people entering the labour market without university degrees struggled to find jobs similar to those of their parents. It's not hard to see how painful these shifts were. If you were in your 40s and 50s and had spent a lifetime acquiring the knowledge to be a skilled factory worker, and suddenly there were no jobs for someone with your skills, what could you do?

Cities and communities dependent on manufacturing jobs have been hit very hard. Nowhere is this more extreme than in Detroit, Michigan, once the home of the auto industry. Today the city of Detroit has only a handful of automobile manufacturing jobs left. While a new economy based on service-sector work has grown, it remains very small in comparison to what it once was, and many people whose lives were built on working in the auto factories are simply unable to transition into these different jobs, which require different skills. Once an emblem of economic strength, Detroit now symbolizes the impact of the changing economic system.

The decline of manufacturing jobs, in Detroit and elsewhere, has meant that higher education is an increasingly important means for achieving quality employment and income. When manufacturing employment was abundant, a high school education was frequently adequate to find a job that paid a good income. Today, an individual with only a high school education is at a severe disadvantage in competition for better-paying jobs in the service-sector economy, where knowledge and credentials are increasingly important. Just as during the transition from farming to manufacturing, economic changes have rendered one type of skill set less valuable than other skills; in recent years, knowledge acquired through education is increasingly critical (Goldin & Katz, 2008).

5.3 How Do Norms and Institutions Influence Social Life?

Tom Mackie/Alamy Stock Photo

The Second Dimension of Social Structure: The Powers of Norms and Institutions

The second major dimension of social structure is rooted in the norms and institutions that influence social life. Social norms shape the way we interact with one another by providing a complex set of rules we are supposed to know and follow—in other words, they are scripts for everyday action. Norms also guide the behaviour of groups and entire organizations. Institutions turn norms into enduring customs of social life by creating formal organizations such as schools, churches, and governments that regulate and enforce the norms and customs in particular fields of human activity. Whether we are discussing institutions in terms of enduring customs or the concrete organizations they may give rise to, institutions are critical to how the social world is organized.

Norms and Rules

5.3.1 Distinguish between social norms and formal rules of behaviour.

Let's start with some basic building blocks. As the unwritten rules of society, norms tell us what is and is not appropriate in any situation, and they provide guidance for selecting courses of action. In this way, norms are related to formal rules of behaviour, like laws and written guidelines, even though norms are generally not written down anywhere. Rules are more formal, explicit guidelines for behaviour. Norms, by contrast, are somewhat more ambiguous (although written rules are often ambiguous as well). Norms are things we just know, whereas rules are things we may have to refer to a rulebook, handbook, or legal code to find. Sometimes the distinction between the two is fuzzy. Here are some examples of formal rules versus social norms: Drivers are required to stop and wait for pedestrians to cross inside a crosswalk. If the pedestrian is outside the crosswalk, however, the formal rules are ambiguous (the driver is responsible for avoiding an accident, but the pedestrian is responsible for not walking across the street in front of a car). Social norms are at play here. It would be polite for the driver to wave the pedestrian across. Similarly, civility, or being respectful in accordance with the system you wish to master, leads to greater success. Institutions such as the university reward civility exercised in the classroom and in students' interactions with their professors. In order to be successful in an institution, students must learn to master the informal norms of civility and develop these professional skills for academic success. Canadian sociologists Kevin D. Haggerty and Aaron Doyle sought to clarify the expected norms for success in graduate school in their book *57 Ways to Screw Up in Grad School* (2015). As graduate directors of sociology programs themselves, they had witnessed graduate students make a number of common blunders that undermined their success and limited their chances of landing a job and having a rewarding career afterwards. By setting out the unwritten rules of graduate school (norms), Haggerty and Doyle provided a blueprint for mastering the expectations of the institution, showing that success is about much more than completing the official requirements. Success also depends upon mastering the informal practices and rituals of graduate school.

Norms and formal rules and laws are important, but they are also regularly violated (even criminal laws). Who among us has not committed acts that were, or could under certain circumstances be considered, inappropriate or perhaps even criminal? Most of the time we can get away with petty violations of rules and norms; but there can be costs to such violations when someone in a position of authority chooses to enforce norms or rules. When rules are formalized into law, their violation can carry explicit sanctions (even up to and including jail or prison sentences). But even violating routine norms can be consequential. Those who do not act in accordance with basic norms may be thought of by others as "weird" or abnormal and may be shunned in some way. To see that this is true, just try doing some small thing that violates a basic norm, like getting too close to someone when you talk to them, refusing to stop shaking someone's hand, or talking loudly in the movie theatre, and see what happens. Because there are consequences that follow from even routine violations of social norms, we all have powerful incentives to follow the basic rules and norms.

Norms and rules are one critical way in which social structures gain power over us as individuals. We seem to be free to do what we want in most situations, except that there are usually clear norms and/or rules that guide or tell us what we should be doing (and how we should be doing it). We usually don't know where those norms or rules come from; they are just there. The great French sociologist Émile Durkheim (1895/1982) called these **social facts**—those parts of society that are independent of individuals but exert a force over us. We are powerless in part because no one individual can change the norms or rules very quickly, even ones that are irrational or harmful. Norms and rules tend to change very slowly, if at all.

Institutions and the Patterning of Social Life

5.3.2 Explain the process of institutionalization and identify examples of common practices that have been institutionalized.

While norms and rules are powerful, they become truly significant when they come to be incorporated in one of the major institutions in society. Institutions emerge whenever groups of people begin to try to formalize something that individuals were already doing informally—an important norm, rule, or common practice already in society. This process of **institutionalization** is complex, and institutions usually come into existence slowly, often taking decades or even centuries to take shape. Humans build institutions for many reasons, but most importantly to try to ensure that things are done a certain way and that there is continuity over time. Institutionalization often includes the establishment of organizations that are designed to enforce or execute the now formalized norms and rules, and inside these organizations, roles for administering the rules and norms come to be assigned.

This may sound a bit abstract, so let's take a concrete example: the case of religion. For vast stretches of human history people would gaze at the sky and wonder what it all meant. At different moments in different places, however, some people began to develop more systematic ways of thinking about the wonders of nature and the place of human beings in the world. They began to develop ideas and theories about how the world began and the possibility of a higher being that might have created it. Eventually, people began to create lasting ideas about the gods, and began choosing particular people to teach others about those gods. At some point, they began creating specific sacred places where religion and religious rituals could be enacted (including temples, mosques, and churches). As formal roles, rules, and rituals were introduced, from one generation to the next or from one group of people to another (sometimes by wars), religion slowly came to be institutionalized, and religious organizations began to take shape. Over time, religious texts began to appear, and the permanent rituals and rules that members of the religion were expected to follow became established.

Another example of the process of institutionalization can be seen in the development of schools and educational systems. Teaching and learning have existed from the beginning of human civilization in some form. Parents would educate their children as best they could to do whatever was necessary to survive: for example, teaching children how to hunt, gather food that was safe to eat, or grow food (agriculture). Even small nomadic tribes and the very earliest human settlements developed ways of passing knowledge from one generation to the next; it is impossible to manage human life without the transmission of knowledge. But much of that kind of teaching and learning is rather different from what we think of when we talk about education today. At some point, these civilizations got the idea that learning could be facilitated by bringing children together in groups. Eventually, the first schools appeared and began to establish a concrete **curriculum,** which is the structure of coursework and content of a sequence of courses making up a program of study in a school or school system. It was at this point that learning truly began to become institutionalized. Interestingly, many of the earliest schools were founded by religious orders wanting to train future religious leaders. Only later did members of elite families begin to see schools as places that could effectively teach their children the arts and knowledge of upper-class life, and it was still much later that, with the rise of mass universal schooling, formal education spread to all children.

Library of Congress Prints and Photographs Division

Education became institutionalized as the first schools began to appear and a formal curriculum was established.

The institutional system of any society extends far beyond religion and education. Every chapter in *The Sociology Project* explores in detail one or more major institutions: family institutions, urban institutions, political institutions, law and criminal justice institutions, medical institutions, government institutions, economic institutions, global institutions, and so on. But even in a long book, we aren't able to discuss all of the institutions in society.

It is important to keep in mind that, although they are very powerful in providing an organizational framework for the social world, institutions are ultimately the creations of human beings, and as such they can be, and sometimes are, reformed or reinvented over time. The current struggle over the institution of marriage is a good example. As gays and lesbians are granted the same rights to marry as heterosexuals in Canada, the United States, and other countries around the world, the impact on our entire conception of marriage and intimate relationships—and the institution of the family more generally—is slowly changing. No longer is marriage always between a man and a woman, at least in most places. Because institutions can be designed to foster more or less equality between members of different groups in a social hierarchy, as the example of same-sex marriage suggests, institutional inequality is a constant source of conflict. For example, educational institutions can be explicitly designed to discriminate against girls, as is still the case in some countries, or against racial, ethnic, or religious minorities. Challenging institutional practices is an important way in which subordinate groups try to gain more equal status. Returning to the marriage example, for much of human history, the law and practice of marriage often provided definite advantages to men. In Canada, until the latter part of the nineteenth century, married women could not own property in their own name. Sexual violence against women, especially if it occurred inside a marriage, was rarely, if ever, treated as criminal by courts of law, as rape. Today marriage and divorce laws are far more egalitarian between the genders, although that is not the case in all countries around the world.

Large Organizations and Governments as Institutions

5.3.3 Explain why large formal organizations are critically important to the overall structure of a society.

Large formal organizations—groups of people acting together in pursuit of some common goal—are important elements of the overall institutional context in any society.

Everywhere we look there are large, powerful organizations that seem entrenched and permanent. Among the most important of these organizations are the economic institutions of society (and all of the economy's various components, such as large companies and the marketplaces they operate in), the government (and all of its many bureaucracies and agencies, including the military), religious organizations (including all of the major religious denominations, such as the Catholic Church, the various Protestant denominations, the Mormon church, Islam, and so forth), educational organizations, medical organizations such as hospitals, and many others. The power and reach of large organizations are often immense, impacting individual lives in many ways.

In particular, the institutions of the government are vital parts of the overall social structure. Because, in many respects, governments stand above the other institutions of society, when the government acts it has enormous powers not shared by any other institution. Sociologists refer to the government, in this sense, as the *state:* that is, the range of government and legal branches, including agencies and offices of government, lawmaking bodies (e.g., legislatures), the legal system, the military, and even the constitution itself. National constitutions provide not only the basis for government power and its limits but also the ultimate legal foundation for all social action. The power of state institutions to change the lives of individuals is easy to see when we think about dramatic cases like Hitler's Nazi government in Germany in the 1930s and 1940s, under which Inge Deutschkron lived. Brutal dictatorships often literally choose who gets to live and who must die. Joseph Stalin, the dictator of the Soviet Union at the same time that Hitler ruled Germany, was said to have had as his bedtime reading a list of Communist Party members marked for death; he would go through the list and mark off those who were to be executed and those who were to be sent to prisons in the outer reaches of the Soviet Union or left alone (Khlevniuk, 2008). But not only dictatorships claim the right to kill their own citizens: In the United States, the Obama administration ordered and carried out the 2011 execution, without trial, of an American cleric named Anwar al-Awlaki, living in Yemen, who was accused of organizing terrorist activities (Savage & Baker, 2013).

These examples are extreme, but all modern states have enormously significant powers. Governments can make policies that help determine things like the wealth and income gap between individuals, how many people will be allowed to live in poverty, how much damage to the natural environment will be allowed, and many other aspects of our lives.

5.4 How Do Social Structures Influence Our Daily Lives and Social Interactions?

Michael Chamberlin/Shutterstock

The Context of Social Interaction

One of the important questions to consider about social structures is exactly how they penetrate into our thoughts, actions, and interactions with others. Why, when, and how do social structures shape our daily lives? Are social structures all-powerful? In this section we consider some of these issues.

Socialization

5.4.1 Discuss how socialization contributes to the creation of roles and norms.

If roles, hierarchies, norms, and institutions are so important in shaping our identities and social interactions, how do we learn them? The short answer is that through our participation in various institutional settings, by experiencing different roles, and by being exposed to the power of social hierarchies throughout our lives, we learn about and (usually) are compelled to adapt to the basic norms and rules of the society we live in.

At the heart of the transmission of ideas about the importance of conformity in our participation in social life is what is known as socialization. **Socialization** is the process through which we are trained and learn how we are expected to behave in society or in particular social settings. It is how we come to understand the expectations and norms of our groups. Throughout our lives, we are constantly being socialized to behave in certain ways (or to not behave in others). The process begins in families, where parents attempt to teach their children a wide range of rules and norms and more generally how to apply them. We also learn by practising; the first time we attempt to do something the "right" way, we may mess it up, but eventually we should get the hang of it. Our parents play key roles early on in teaching us how to do things, beginning right at birth. When a baby sitting in a high chair picks up her food and throws it on the ground and is greeted with a "no" from her parents, she is receiving an early message about the importance of being neat and handling food appropriately.

Socialization continues at every stage of the life course and involves learning from many different people, groups, and organizations. Children play games, and these games sometimes involve role playing of one kind or another where children "practise" being adults (Corsaro & Eder, 1990). Developmental psychologists find that these games are important because they teach children the importance of subscribing to an assigned role, even if only for the purposes of the game at hand. As they get older, children move from play to structured learning environments. Here, among other things, they learn about rules and the need to conform to rules in places like day cares, schools, and the various group activities (including sports) that they participate in. As children grow up and begin to organize their own relationships with other children, they have to learn things like how to get along and interact with others. As they move through school, they learn how to do things that will be rewarded—like how to take a test or how to write a paper—and their success in mastering these activities goes a long way toward determining their outcomes in life.

Learning new skills and adapting to new situations is something that we all have to do throughout our lives; socialization is a never-ending process. Taking a new job, participating in a new activity or hobby, making new friends and entering a new circle of people, or joining a new kind of organization all require the acquisition of new skills and ways of handling ourselves. As we take on new roles, we have to learn new guidelines and rules. There is a saying that "you can't teach an old dog new tricks"; however accurate it may be for dogs, it doesn't apply to humans very well. We continue learning and adapting to new situations until the end of our lives. For example, older people who move into elder-care facilities learn to follow the rules of the facility fairly quickly, even though they have lived independently for their entire adult lives.

Socialization works in large part because the human mind is capable of learning and remembering immensely complicated rules. A simple, but nearly universal, example of how individuals adapt to new situations occurs is learning how to drive. Driving is not at all the simple process many think it is—cognitive psychologists have shown that learning to drive is mentally challenging in many ways—but it is a skill that almost everyone can eventually master with enough practice. Driving requires us to learn a large set of rules and to be able to apply them in making split-second decisions where mistakes can have large consequences. Our ability to learn those rules and apply them correctly (at least most of the time) is critical to what makes car travel as (relatively) safe as it is. Learning how to date is another common new situation that almost everyone must pass through. If learning how to drive is something that almost everyone masters, dating is such a complicated ritual, with so many subtle and hard-to-grasp mechanics, that evidently many people never learn to do it very well.

Social Structure and Social Interaction

5.4.2 Discuss how social structure exerts influence over our interactions with others.

We are now in a position to examine the multiple ways in which social structure exerts influence over our interactions with others. Through socialization and daily practice, we absorb the rules and norms that are associated with social structure. As we take on new roles, we adapt to the expectations of those roles. We learn about hierarchies and appropriate deference to people in positions of authority. We also learn biases and stereotypes about different groups, and if we are not careful (and do not exercise our sociological imaginations), we will come to adopt those stereotypes, which may subsequently guide (in subtle or explicit ways) our behaviour toward others. In the course of conforming to the rules and norms imposed by social structure in our interactions, we make a small contribution toward reproducing social structure!

In Chapter 4, we discussed a number of different examples of how our daily interactions with others are shaped by norms and social rules. But the influence of social structure does not stop there. What happens when we consider interactions within and between organizations? Most organized group activities are governed by internal and external rules of various kinds that shape what they do. Consider professional hockey. There is a set of rules that governs play; these rules are established by the governing body of the sport (the National Hockey League, in this case), which can be thought of as playing a role similar to that of a society's government. Within the rules established and enforced by the NHL, teams (organizations) select players and coaches, and coaches (leaders) have developed a small number of different ways to organize play. On the ice, a hockey team consists of different players assigned different responsibilities based on the

Multiart/Fotolia

Learning how to be a parent is one especially complicated role many people take on. Reading a book on parenting, or having a nurse at the hospital provide a few instructions on how to breast-feed your child and change his or her diaper, can only help so much. Parents learn how to care for their children by practising and talking to other parents as well as teachers, counsellors, and perhaps their own parents. While what it means to be a "good" parent is widely debated, almost all parents do many caring and good things for their children and try the best they can within the limits of their resources.

positions that they play and the plan designed by their coaches. There's the goalie, centre, left and right wings, left and right defence, and so forth. Each of these players, as a result of the position he or she occupies and the team he or she plays for, has a specific *role* to play. That is, each of them is expected to do certain things: If you're the goalie, you'd better stop the puck, and if you're playing left or right wing, you'd better be able to shoot the puck. To be sure, individual players have different ways to perform their jobs, and variation in how well they succeed is what determines which players are "great" and which are less so, but the jobs and tasks they perform are still all conducted within the broader rules associated with a particular role.

modestil/Fotolia

Hockey provides a good example of how social structures guide our interactions with others. On the ice and off, each member of the team as well as the coaches have specific roles to play, all of which are governed by the rules of the sport.

Social Structure and Individual Free Will

5.4.3 Discuss the relative impact of social structure versus individual choice.

We've seen that social structures are powerful. Indeed, sometimes when social scientists write about the powers of structures, it may appear as if they are *too* powerful, with individuals almost becoming robots who fulfill roles and act according to scripts handed down to them. They fill positions in the society but are entirely replaceable by other individuals and have little control over the worlds they inhabit. It can almost seem as if individuals have no free will of their own, no capacity to choose how to act. If this were the case, society would just reproduce itself in the same shape over and over, creativity would not exist, and nothing would ever change. But we know from our own experiences that this is not true. Of course we have some choices about what we can do, about how we behave and what course of action we might take. And, surely, things can change as a result of human action. Just think of the civil rights movement or the more recent uprisings in support of democracy in the Middle East; revolutions happen, new laws are passed, old ones are overturned, and social hierarchies change shape.

Plenty of everyday examples from our own lives make the same point. For example, we can readily observe that two people will often behave very differently even when they find themselves in the same situation. This will be true even if they live in the same society and face the same rules and norms governing their behaviour. Take two people who hear someone cry out for help: One may intervene, while another may simply ignore it. Take two investment bankers facing a shortfall in a large investment fund: One may try to raise more money from other investors, while the other may illegally move funds from other accounts to cover the losses. A huge body of research makes this point over and over again: People are not robots. They will respond in different and occasionally unpredictable ways, depending on the choices and opportunities confronting them. Such examples and evidence from experiments suggest that people do indeed have some significant measure of individual choice. Philosophers of free will can rest easy; the sociological account of social structure does not mean that all individual choice is irrelevant!

5.5 Why Are Social Structures Slow to Change?

Andersen Ross/Blend Images/Getty Images

The Endurance of Social Structures

One of the hallmark features of social structures is their endurance. People come and go, but social structures continue to operate more or less as they always have. This raises an important question: Why are these social structures so persistent? Or to put it more bluntly, why do those parts of the social structure that many people come to think are unfair persist? There are a number of answers to these questions that we will explore in this section, beginning with the process known as path dependency.

Change is difficult, as August Dvorak learned in 1936 when he created the Dvorak keyboard. Although its layout is more efficient and easier to use than the standard QWERTY keyboard, very few people use it today.

Editorial Image, LLC/ Alamy Stock Photo

Jeffrey Banke/Fotolia

Path Dependency

5.5.1 Explain how past outcomes impact present choices.

Social structures persist in part because earlier developments and institutionalization make it much easier for individuals to work within them than to try to rip them apart. This process is commonly known as **path dependency,** a term sociologists use to describe the ways in which outcomes of the past impact actors and organizations in the present, making some choices or outcomes logical and others illogical. A classical example of this is the QWERTY keyboard. Nobody in their right mind today would invent an English-language keyboard laid out the way the keys are, with many of the most commonly used letters placed in hard-to-reach locations. Yet attempts to replace the QWERTY keyboard have always failed. Why? One answer is simply that in order to use any keyboard, more or less everyone learns to navigate the QWERTY layout. Switching to a better-designed and more efficient keyboard layout, like the system designed by August Dvorak in 1936 (see the photos), will be initially time consuming and costly, and even if you were willing to master the other keyboard, every time you use a friend's computer or any device like a smartphone that has a QWERTY layout, you would have to unlearn your new keystrokes and go back to the QWERTY. And if you practised enough on the new machine, your fingers would develop a different kind of muscle memory that would make it hard to go back and forth. So instead of switching to a new keyboard, we struggle with the one we are used to.

Path dependency, as the QWERTY example suggests, rests on the idea that any path, once adopted, is extraordinarily difficult to reverse (Pierson, 2000). In other words, what has happened in the past sets limits on what is possible today or in the future. Path dependency is a historical process, one that is closely tied up with how and why particular norms and institutions come to be established, and, once established, are difficult to change. Studying the development of many institutions over long historical periods suggests a rough model that is displayed in Figure 5.4. For long periods of time, there may be many different ways of doing things, and no one approach is dominant. Indeed, in the early phase of the development of any component part of the social structure, a disorganized and seemingly random process of human interaction may exist. Almost anything goes. It takes time for norms and institutions to take root and develop. But at some critical point, things begin to change, often in response to a single key event that establishes a new norm, rule, or way of doing things, and institutions may emerge to organize and maintain it. This phase is sometimes described as the "critical juncture," in that the range of possible actions begins to narrow. Finally, as more and more people and groups get used to doing things a certain way, a third phase can emerge, known as the "lock-in." From that point on, changes will be sharply limited by the rules, norms, and institutions that are now firmly in place and difficult to dislodge. Figure 5.4 provides a hypothetical visual image of how path dependency develops, as the wide range of possibilities in phase 1 gradually narrows and then finally "locks in" in the third phase.

How Social Structures Persist

5.5.2 Analyze the power of path-dependent processes.

The idea of path dependence is important, but we need to develop an understanding of why it is so powerful. What are the processes and mechanics of path dependence? Social structures tend to persist over time for a number of concrete reasons. An important place to start is with individuals: We all play a role in reproducing social structure through everyday actions that conform to existing norms, expectations, and institutional rules. When we obey the commands of hierarchy without challenging it, we tacitly accept that heirarchy as reality and inadvertently help to maintain it. We don't realize it unless we think about it, but by simply following the scripts and rules that social structure provides in our daily actions and interactions, we are helping to reproduce social structure. When we refer to someone as "Dr. Smith" rather than "Ms. Smith," we are confirming the special status of "Dr. Smith" and the institutions that have conferred status and title on her.

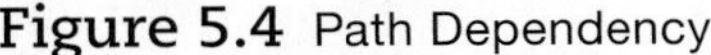

Figure 5.4 Path Dependency

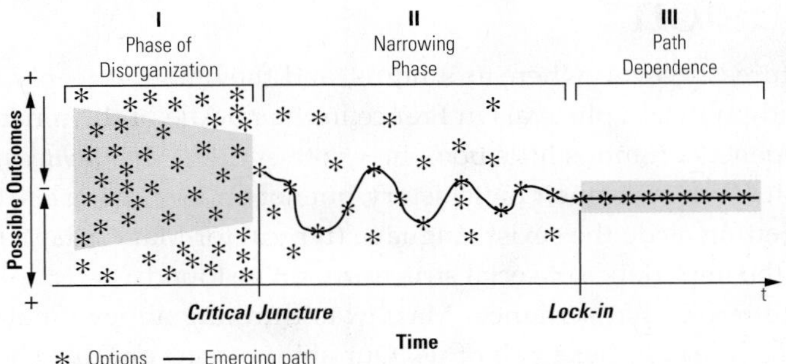

Gianni Muratore/Alamy Stock Photo

We follow social scripts when we go through security at airports.

When we stand in line without cutting, we are confirming the norm of "waiting for your turn." A wide variety of ordinary things we do with little or no thought help to reinforce social structure, as the following examples suggest.

Another reason social structures persist is political: Once a particular element of social structure comes to be established, be it either roles/hierarchies or norms/institutions, it may generate its own **interest groups**, that is, organizations established to promote the concerns of a group or business corporation that are related to a particular set of rules or policies. These interest groups will fight to protect and extend existing social arrangements when they are viewed as beneficial to the organization's members. We've already discussed how this works in the maintenance of social hierarchies, where members of a dominant group have strong incentives to organize themselves to maintain their privileges.

Similar dynamics exist in social institutions. For example, institutions create jobs, and the workers in those jobs have incentives to try to maintain the institution. Proposals to cut the budgets for any of the organizations in an institution field—such as schools, the military, prisons, and so forth—are routinely met with strong opposition from those who have jobs and currently draw an income from the institution. Similarly, even people who do not work for the institution but benefit from it in some other way will often resist any changes to it. Cuts to the police force may be opposed not just by police officers, but also by citizens who fear an increase in crime. When a local school is threatened with closure, members of the community, not just the teachers, can be counted to rally in support.

Finally, and perhaps most importantly, social structures also persist simply because there is often broad public support for existing roles/hierarchies and norms/institutions, or fear of the consequences of dramatic change. We are frequently more comfortable living within the worlds we know and trying to make them better in small ways, however much they may make us grumble and complain, than opting for something radically new. The expression "you are better off with the devil you know than the one you don't" is the commonsense version of this idea, and it expresses a powerful reality that social psychologists have called *risk aversion* (Kahneman, 2011). Of course not everyone feels completely averse to change all the time, and under extreme or unusual conditions, large numbers of people can and sometimes do opt to try to tear down parts of the social structure rather than reform it. But most of the time, however often we might complain about it, we tend to accept the status quo or try to reform in small ways the parts that are not working rather than trying to tear it down.

Conclusion

Social structures are everywhere around us, and they matter deeply. Writing about the social and political upheavals in France in the middle of the nineteenth century, Karl Marx opened a famous little book he wrote entitled *The Eighteenth Brumaire* by declaring that "Men make their own history, but not under circumstances of their own choosing." Setting aside the sexist language (typical for Marx's day), few clearer expressions of the importance of social structures can be found.

When he wrote that sentence, Marx was thinking about nineteenth-century France, but his idea applies to all of us. Our ability to act and the choices we make are always limited by the circumstances in which we find ourselves. We noted in this chapter's introduction that Inge Deutschkron would not have been Jewish but for the rise of Adolf Hitler and the Nazi government's racial laws. She did not become Jewish because she suddenly discovered religion. Rather, she was forced to completely alter her life and her self-understanding and identity because of an arbitrary and external decision imposed upon her. There are many similar examples all around us that we can begin to notice once we understand the logic of social structure. Throughout our lives, we are continually making choices shaped by existing roles and hierarchies on the one hand and existing norms and institutions on the other.

Fortunately, social structures that are in conflict with emerging societal realities or the needs of ordinary people can change, even if slowly. If we go back far enough and study social structures historically, we will find many examples of how hierarchies and institutions have changed more dramatically over time. Throughout the rest of *The Sociology Project*, we will be considering important changes to social structure in different areas of social life. For example, we will discuss how the racial hierarchy has proved permeable and has shifted over time in much more detail in Chapter 10. In Chapter 11, we consider a variety of ways in which gender and sexuality have also shifted over time; society is becoming somewhat more egalitarian between men and women, and in a process that is ongoing, more accepting of gays and lesbians and nontraditional forms of sexual and social intimacy. In other chapters, we will look at how the market economy has changed in dramatic ways (Chapter 8) and at how schools (Chapter 14), religious institutions (Chapter 13), immigration (Chapter 10), medicine (Chapter 15), and criminal justice (Chapter 16) have all evolved in important ways over time.

For now, however, we can note one very important general point. Behind many of the most important changes to social structure are politics: subordinate groups demanding fairer or more equitable treatment and institutions responding to their members' demands to respond to changes that occur elsewhere in society. The powerful usually can protect their interests in maintaining the status quo, but sometimes subordinate groups win changes. In particular, when subordinate groups organize themselves into *social movements*, a topic we treat in detail in Chapter 17, they are in a better position to challenge hierarchies in various ways.

Understanding social structures is central to the larger project of the sociological imagination. Sociologists pay so much attention to trying to understand the different elements of social structure, and where and why they limit the possibilities for improving the human condition, out of a recognition that only by understanding these underlying structures can we develop appropriate understandings and make meaningful progress in addressing the pressing social problems of society.

CHAPTER SUMMARY

The Big Questions Revisited 5

5.1 **What Is Social Structure?** Why do sociologists reject the view that the world is simply made up of a collection of individuals? In this section, we introduced the concept of social structure and explored how it is very much like the structure of a tall building—normally hidden from view, but essential to what is possible to build. The key elements of social structure (roles and hierarchies, norms and institutions) were introduced.

Social Structure as the Context of Human Action

Defining Social Structure

Learning Objective 5.1.1: Explain how social structure is similar to the structure of a tall building.

Key Components of Social Structure

Learning Objective 5.1.2: Identify the two key components of social structure.

5.2 How Do Roles and Social Hierarchies Shape Our Life Chances? The social structure of any society consists of a wide range of different roles and social divisions, or hierarchies, between groups. In this section, we explored where these various roles and social hierarchies come from and why they matter.

The First Dimension of Social Structure: Roles and Social Hierarchies

Roles

Learning Objective 5.2.1: Distinguish between roles we choose for ourselves and social hierarchies.

Social Hierarchies

Learning Objective 5.2.2: Explain how social hierarchies arise and persist.

Power and Privilege in Social Hierarchies

Learning Objective 5.2.3: Discuss the roles that power and privilege play in social hierarchies.

Group Size and Social Hierarchies

Learning Objective 5.2.4: Explain the impact that population size has on the ways in which groups within a social hierarchy relate to one another.

5.3 How Do Norms and Institutions Influence Social Life? A society's social structure also contains an elaborate set of norms and institutions. This section explored some of the central aspects of norms and institutions and why they influence our behaviour.

The Second Dimension of Social Structure: The Powers of Norms and Institutions

Norms and Rules

Learning Objective 5.3.1: Distinguish between social norms and formal rules of behaviour.

Institutions and the Patterning of Social Life

Learning Objective 5.3.2: Explain the process of institutionalization and identify examples of common practices that have been institutionalized.

Large Organizations and Governments as Institutions

Learning Objective 5.3.3: Explain why large formal organizations are critically important to the overall structure of a society.

5.4 How Do Social Structures Influence Our Daily Lives and Social Interactions? Where do the identities and roles that are so important for social interaction come from? How do changes in social structure influence social interaction? Does acknowledging the existence of social structure mean that we have limited free will?

The Context of Social Interaction

Socialization

Learning Objective 5.4.1: Discuss how socialization contributes to the creation of roles and norms.

Social Structure and Social Interaction

Learning Objective 5.4.2: Discuss how social structure exerts influence over our interactions with others.

Social Structure and Individual Free Will

Learning Objective 5.4.3: Discuss the relative impact of social structure versus individual choice.

5.5 Why Are Social Structures Slow to Change? Why and how do social structures change? In this section, we explored the forces that hold societies and social structures together and why change in social structure is relatively slow.

The Endurance of Social Structures

Path Dependency

Learning Objective 5.5.1: Explain how past outcomes impact present choices.

How Social Structures Persist

Learning Objective 5.5.2: Analyze the power of path-dependent processes.

Learning the Terms

curriculum (p. 131)
discrimination (p. 124)
institutionalization (p. 130)
interest group (p. 138)
life course (p. 122)
path dependency (p. 136)
power (p. 123)
privilege (p. 123)
role (p. 121)
social fact (p. 130)
social hierarchy (p. 122)
socialization (p. 133)
social movement (p. 124)
social structure (p. 117)

Chapter 6
Culture, Media, and Communication

by Eric Klinenberg*

Despite the stereotype that living alone is an isolating experience, more and more Americans are choosing to live alone.

Learning Objectives

6.1.1 Define culture from a sociological perspective.

6.1.2 Explain how a group's symbols can be considered its culture, and give examples of collective symbols of contemporary North American culture.

6.1.3 Describe how our values and beliefs influence how we live our lives.

*An earlier version of this chapter was co-authored by David Wachsmuth.

6.1.4 Explain the ways in which culture is a form of communication.

6.2.1 Discuss the role that culture plays in establishing group style, and explain what distinguishes a subculture from the mainstream.

6.2.2 Discuss the concept of "culture wars" and explain the importance of practising cultural relativism in a multicultural North America.

6.2.3 Explain what produces and reproduces national cultures, and what effects they have.

6.3.1 Define cultural capital and discuss ways North American elites have become cultural omnivores.

6.3.2 Analyze how money and culture reproduce status over the long term.

6.4.1 Analyze how the concept of the public sphere explains how culture is produced in society.

6.4.2 Compare and contrast the cultural industry and the cultural democracy perspectives.

6.4.3 Discuss the ways in which communication changes with the form or medium.

6.5.1 Explain the role that the media play in making the news.

6.5.2 Identify three trends in the media landscape that have put commercial pressure on journalism.

6.5.3 Discuss the ways the Internet has created new opportunities and dangers for the free media and for democracy.

More people live alone now than at any other time in history. In prosperous American cities—Atlanta, Denver, Seattle, San Francisco, and Minneapolis—40 percent or more of all households contain a single occupant. In Manhattan and in Washington, DC, nearly one in two households is occupied by a single person. In Paris, the city of lovers, more than half of all households contain single people, and in Stockholm, Sweden, the rate tops 60 percent. The decision to live alone is increasingly common in diverse cultures whenever it is economically feasible.

The mere thought of living alone once sparked anxiety, dread, and visions of loneliness. But those images are dated. Now the most privileged people on earth use their resources to separate from one another, to buy privacy and personal space.

How has this happened? At first glance, living alone by choice seems to contradict entrenched cultural values—so long defined by groups and by the nuclear family. But after interviewing more than 300 "singletons" (my term for people who live alone) during nearly a decade of research, it appears to me that living alone fits well with modern values (Klinenberg, 2012). It promotes freedom, personal control, and self-realization—all prized aspects of contemporary life. It is less feared, too, than it once might have been, for the crucial reason that living alone no longer suggests an isolated or less social life.

Our species has been able to embark on this experiment in solo living because global societies have become so interdependent. Dynamic markets, flourishing cities, and open communications systems make modern autonomy more appealing; they give us the capacity to live alone but to engage with others when and how we want and on our own terms. In fact, living alone can make it easier to be social because

The Big Questions

1. **What is culture?** When sociologists talk about culture, they refer to a shared system of beliefs and knowledge, more commonly called a system of meaning and symbols; a set of values, beliefs, and practices; and shared forms of communication.
2. **How does culture shape our collective identity?** Cultural practices both reflect and define group identities, whether the group is a small subculture or a nation.
3. **How do our cultural practices relate to class and status?** People's cultural habits help define and reproduce the boundaries between high status and low status, upper class and lower class.
4. **Who produces culture, and why?** The cultural field is the place for creativity and meaning making. But it is also a battlefield: Who controls the media and popular culture, and what messages they communicate, is central to how social life is organized and how power operates.
5. **What is the relationship between media and democracy?** The media are arguably the most important form of cultural production in our society. The news is vital to democracy, and new ways of participating in the media are changing how democracy works.

single people have more free time, absent family obligations, to engage in social and cultural activities.

Compared with their married counterparts, single people are more likely to spend time with friends and neighbours, go to restaurants, and attend art classes and lectures. Surveys, some by market research companies that study behaviour for clients developing products and services, also indicate that married people with children are more likely than single people to hunker down at home. Those in large suburban homes often splinter into private rooms to be alone. The image of a modern family in a room together, each plugged into a separate reality—be it a smartphone, computer, video game, or TV show—has become a cultural cliché. New communications technologies make living alone a social experience, so being home alone does not feel involuntary or like solitary confinement. The person alone at home can digitally navigate through a world of people, information, and ideas. Internet use does not seem to cut people off from real friendships and connections.

All signs suggest that living alone will become even more common in the future, at every stage of adulthood and in every place where people can afford a place of their own. Modern culture has shifted in ways that have made this dramatic change in the way we live possible. In this chapter, we will explore the sociology of culture and look more carefully at how these changes in culture and communication are changing the way we live our lives. One important part of the sociology of culture involves studying people's daily routines and practices. Another involves examining the values, social norms, and collective beliefs that make some behaviours acceptable and others suspect. Fortunately, the search for this kind of information is as rewarding as its discovery, which explains why the sociology of culture is one of the fastest-growing parts of the field today.

6.1 What Is Culture?

National Geographic Image Collection/
Alamy Stock Photo

The Many Meanings of Culture

The latest song by Beyoncé, a performance of the opera, our assumptions about monogamy, a series of posts on Twitter, a headline in the newspaper, the reason one person sleeps in and another wakes up early: these are all examples of culture. People use the word *culture* to refer to all sorts of things, from art to traditions to individual learned behaviour. In everyday language, *culture* is often a synonym for art or artistic activities, as indicated by the expression "getting some culture," or a synonym for refined taste, as when we call a person "cultured." These are certainly two of the ways that sociologists use the word, but there are a number of others. In fact, as one writer puts it, "culture is one of the two or three most complicated words in the English language" (Williams, 1976, p. 87).

The modern Western history of the concept of culture begins with the rise of world travel in the eighteenth and nineteenth centuries, when merchants from Europe came into contact with non-Europeans for the first time. These merchants were struck not only by the physical differences between themselves and the non-Europeans, but also by the differences in how they behaved. This included everything from how they dressed to the way their families were organized. In an attempt to make sense of these differences, scientists in the nineteenth century connected the physical differences with the behavioural differences, arguing that people's biology—and particularly their race—determined how their societies were organized.

Toward the end of the nineteenth century, anthropologists began to criticize this idea and instead argued that it was not race that was responsible for these differences but something else—something that was not hereditary but rather learned, something that was not natural and biological but rather socially produced. That something was culture. These days, the argument that the differences between groups of people are more than just biological, and that we learn how to behave, seems obvious. But at the time, it was an important discovery.

From this early research came some basic conclusions about culture. First, culture is a characteristic not of individuals but of groups. Second, culture is a way of understanding differences between groups and similarities within groups. Last, culture is an aspect of social life that is different from nature or biology. Indeed, what makes culture a social phenomenon is precisely that it is not natural. While it's difficult in practice to draw a line between nature and culture, sociologists now recognize that certain biological things about humans are relatively constant throughout history (for example, everyone gets hungry), while cultural things are not (for example, the kind of food we eat and how we eat it).

Defining Culture

6.1.1 Define culture from a sociological perspective.

In the early twentieth century, sociologists and anthropologists generally defined culture as the entire way of life of a people. If you were transported back to ancient Rome, what kinds of things would you need to fit in? You would certainly need language and information about art, customs, and traditions. But you would also need all sorts of material objects, including clothing, tools, and a house. This was all considered part of a society's culture: both material and nonmaterial aspects.

Today, when sociologists talk about **culture**, they are usually referring to three things: a shared system of beliefs and knowledge, more commonly called a system of meaning and symbols; a set of values, beliefs, and practices; and shared forms of communication (Sewell, 2005). We will explore each of these components of culture in the next three sections.

Culture as a System of Meaning and Symbols

6.1.2 Explain how a group's symbols can be considered its culture, and give examples of collective symbols of contemporary North American culture.

Every society is full of **symbols** that communicate an idea while being distinct from the idea itself. Some are straightforward: For example, in contemporary North American society, a red heart implies love and a green traffic light tells you that you are allowed to drive. Other symbols are less obvious: When a car commercial shows a car driving off-road at high speeds, it is likely that the advertiser is trying to make you think about freedom and excitement and associate those ideas with the car. A national flag might have a number of different meanings for different people. Symbols, whether simple or complex, are things that communicate implicit meaning about an idea. Taken together, a group's symbols are an important part of its culture.

We can analyze and interpret collective symbols to learn about particular cultures. The anthropologist Clifford Geertz demonstrated the idea that culture is a system of collective meaning by analyzing a Balinese cockfight in 1950s Indonesia (Geertz, 1972). Cockfights—boxing matches between roosters—were outlawed by the national government but were still important events in local communities. Multiple pairs of birds would fight over the course of an afternoon, and hundreds of residents would watch, cheer, and place bets. Geertz studied the cockfight the way a student of literature might study a novel, as an object full of symbols needing to be interpreted. For example, Geertz found that participants in the cockfights often gambled far more money than seemed to be rational from an economic perspective. He concluded that the betting wasn't just about winning or losing money; it was a way of indicating and reworking status hierarchies (those who bet aggressively and were successful were simultaneously securing and displaying high status in the eyes of other participants). The cockfights allowed the Balinese to collectively interpret their own status hierarchies: "a story they tell themselves about themselves" (Geertz, 1972, p. 26).

The collective rituals we display in our cultural events, such as this cockfight in modern Indonesia, can demonstrate shared values. What cultural events could reveal shared Canadian values?

Paparazzi by Appointment/Alamy Stock Photo

Symbols always exist in specific social contexts—a green traffic light would be mysterious to someone raised in a society without cars, for example, while most of us would find the rituals of a Balinese cockfight equally mysterious. For this reason, studying symbols helps us understand things about society that are not often discussed, such as distinctions of honour, inequality, and competition. For instance, if Geertz had asked them directly, the Balinese cockfighters would not have told him that betting was more a status issue than a financial one. That was something that he could perceive only through careful observation of a place that he had moved to and a group that he had gotten to know well. This research method, based on lengthy and intimate observation of a group, is called *ethnography*.

How could we use Geertz's insights to interpret the collective symbols of contemporary North American culture? In the place of a cockfight, we could study the Super Bowl—the most-watched cultural event in North America, which features familiar rituals and symbols such as betting on the outcome, Super Bowl parties with friends and family, an elaborate half-time show, and blockbuster television ads. But collective symbols don't have to be massive spectacles to be meaningful. Nowadays we might focus on different cultural events, such as trending video clips on YouTube. From music videos to people filming their cats to back-and-forth video debates about politics or technology, sites such as YouTube display our new collective symbols by allowing people to share and interpret culture together (Burgess & Green, 2009).

Culture as a Set of Values, Beliefs, and Practices

6.1.3 Describe how our values and beliefs influence how we live our lives.

Consider again the Super Bowl. The rituals we described above are more than cultural symbols; rather they also demonstrate common **values**—judgements about what is intrinsically important or meaningful—such as patriotism, competitiveness, and consumerism. But how does such collective meaning and its expression help to shape our social behaviour? Is culture just a set of values and beliefs, or does it actually influence how we live our lives? In other words, how is culture actually practised? The answer is that culture influences the kinds of decisions we make in our lives, whether or not we are aware of it.

The way we eat is an example of the kind of habitus we develop. In particular, think about how you hold a fork and a knife. Some people hold a fork upside down in the left hand, with the tines facing downward. Others hold a fork in the right hand and use the tines in a scooping fashion. People often label these behaviours with class distinctions as well.

George Doyle/Getty Images

The influential work of French sociologist Pierre Bourdieu developed an analysis of how culture works in this way. Bourdieu argued that we all develop certain sets of assumptions about the world and our place in it: our tastes, preferences, and skills. In the course of growing up and socializing with other, we also develop habits—what Bourdieu called **habitus**—that become so routine we don't even realize we are following them (Bourdieu, 1992).

Bourdieu's concept of habitus helps explain how our future choices and opinions are always guided by our past experiences. Someone raised in a wealthy family in the upscale Toronto neighbourhood of Rosedale will have no trouble fitting in at a fancy dinner party but perhaps quite a bit of trouble fitting in on a farm, while someone raised on a farm will have the opposite experience. But people are exposed to all sorts of different cultural systems and forms of meaning, after all. So how is it that you choose to act one way at one time and a different way at another? One way to answer this question is to think of culture as a **tool kit**—a set of ideas and skills that we learn through the cultural environment we live in and apply to practical situations in our own lives (Swidler, 1986).

If a friend introduces you to someone, how do you behave? If you're single and interested in flirting, you'll draw on one set of cultural tools you've developed; if you're just trying to be polite, you'll draw on a different set of tools. Just as a car mechanic has a box of tools at her disposal for fixing a variety of problems, people have a kind of tool kit of behaviours and opinions that they apply to different situations they find themselves in. Some people will have better tools for certain situations, and some people will have better tools for others. What's more, even though people immersed in the same cultural environments will tend to have similar cultural tools in their tool kit, they probably will have quite different levels of expertise and familiarity with the tools. So two people who hang out in similar social circles might have the same basic set of conversational tools in their cultural tool kits, but the one who keeps to himself will be less comfortable using them than the one who frequently chats with people she doesn't know very well.

One researcher studying love found that the two most important cultural tools are the idea of love as a voluntary choice and the idea of love as creating a set of commitments to another person (Swidler, 2003). Most North Americans have both of these tools, or ways of understanding love, available to them. But their personal backgrounds will affect which one they tend to rely on and which one they are more competent with. Your own past experiences with love might make you leery of thinking of it in terms of commitment, so this will change how you navigate future romantic encounters. Or you may not have had much experience with commitment, such that when you try to use that cultural tool, you don't do a good job of it. From this perspective, culture does not just establish differences in how we interpret the world and give it meaning but rather influences what kinds of strategies and actions are practically available to us.

Culture as a Form of Communication

6.1.4 Explain the ways in which culture is a form of communication.

Both culture as a system of meaning and symbols and culture as values, beliefs, and practices describe forms of *communication*, which is the sharing of meaningful information between people. One important way this occurs is through language. **Language** refers to any comprehensive system of words or symbols representing concepts, and it does not necessarily need to be spoken, as the hundreds of different sign languages in use around the world suggest. Culture and language are closely related. The ancient Greeks called the supposedly uncultured peoples they encountered "barbarians," which literally means people who babble—who have no language.

Researchers have disagreed over the years as to the importance of language for culture. At a basic level, language is a **cultural universal,** a cultural trait common to all humans: As far as we know, all human societies throughout history have used language to communicate with each other. Some linguists have even argued that language is the fundamental building block of thought—that if you don't have a word for something, you literally can't think it. The implication of this view is that a group's language is directly responsible for many of its cultural symbols and practices. A simple example is the distinction between two different words for "you" in French: an informal *tu* and a more formal *vous*. English used to have a similar distinction (*thou* versus *you*), but it died out over time. As a result, English speakers would possibly place less emphasis on formality in their communication with each other and hence in their group culture. But just because people speak the same language does not mean they share the same culture. Canadians and Americans both speak

English, but of course there are many cultural differences between (and within) the two countries. Now most linguists and cultural sociologists believe that language *influences* culture without completely determining it. So while English no longer has an informal *you* and a formal *you*, this doesn't mean that all our conversations are informal. Instead, we have developed different ways of communicating those concepts, such as the frequent use in the American South of *ma'am* and *sir* when speaking to an elder.

Communication can occur between individuals, or it can occur at large within society—what is normally called **mass communication**. In recent history, mass communication has occurred primarily through the mass media: television, radio, and newspapers. At the mass media's peak, tens of millions of Americans watched the same nightly news broadcasts, and millions read the same daily newspaper in large metropolitan areas. To be sure, even prior to the emergence of the mass media, meaning was still communicated on a large scale, just not quite as large or as quickly; the Balinese cockfight could be considered a form of mass communication at a smaller scale, for example, as could a minister giving a sermon to a large congregation.

The Internet has emerged as the main medium for mass communication today. People increasingly access traditional media sources online via newspaper websites or video sources such as Hulu and YouTube. In so doing, they also transform formerly passive media consumption (as represented by a printed newspaper or television news) into something they can participate in by writing comments, reposting stories, and creating their own mashups. Old media and new media now blur together (Jenkins, 2006). But the Internet has also created a whole new set of communication possibilities only loosely tied to previous forms of mass communication, most notably through social networks and instant messaging.

Social media have altered the way children, adults, and (increasingly) the elderly engage with each other, both online and in person and at distances near and far. These new forms of communication have changed the ways corporations as well as anticorporate activists operate, the ways that charitable organizations raise funds (especially after a catastrophe), the ways that political officials campaign and govern, and the ways that social movements organize. Social media have affected the ways we get, and sometimes even make, news and entertainment. Cultural sociologists are curious about how and to what extent social media have transformed everyday life for people at different ages and in different places, as well as about how the rising use of social media will affect our interest in other kinds of media, from newspapers to telephones and radios to books.

The social theorist Manuel Castells argued that we are participating in a new form of Internet-centred communication that he called mass self-communication because it can potentially reach a global audience but its content is often self-generated and self-directed (Castells, 2009, p. 58). In other words, the Internet offers both the large-scale and ever-present nature of the mass media and the individualized content of interpersonal communication. As Figure 6.1 illustrates, the use of social media has exploded over the past decade, such that it rivals the scope of the traditional media.

How are the Internet and mass self-communication changing cultural systems and practices? If the constant flow of communications, information, and entertainment online makes it difficult to focus, does this also mean that our work and our relationships will suffer? Will our accumulation of Facebook friends be offset by a loss in deep friendships, or does connecting through social media make us more likely to spend time with others offline? Will our ideas become more superficial because we'll lack the attention span necessary to develop them? Will we lose interest in certain cultural genres—traditional news reporting, literary novels, nonfiction books—in

Figure 6.1 The Social Media Explosion

This graph shows the percentage of U.S. Internet users in each age group using social networking sites, from 2005 through 2013.

SOURCE: Based on information from the Pew Research Center (http://www.pewinternet.org/fact-sheets/social-networking-fact-sheet/).

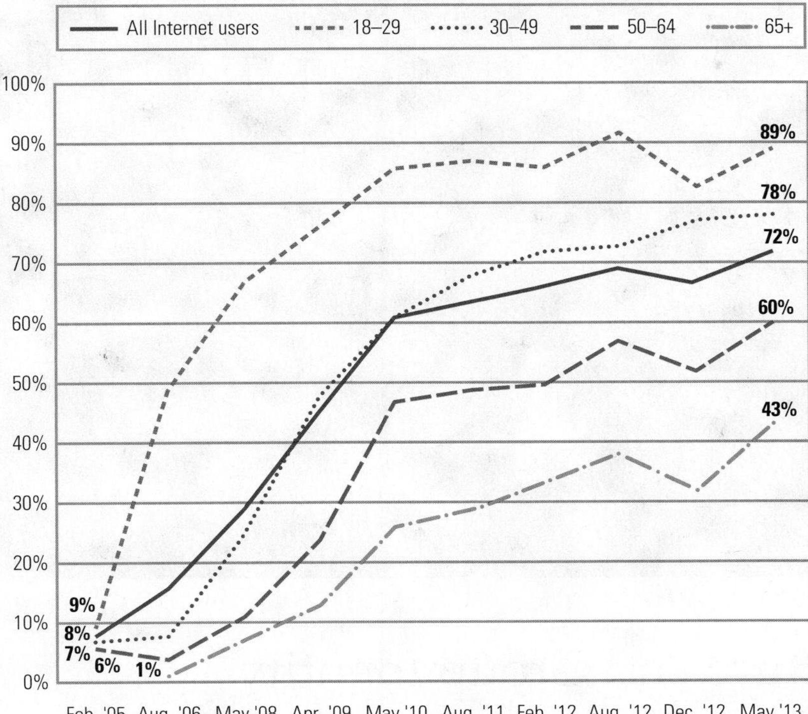

favour of others—news briefs, pulp fiction, video games—that either require less of our minds or deliver more immediate rewards?

It's hard to know for sure: When it comes to information and communication, the last few decades have probably been the most rapid period of transformation in history. Access to technology is creating new types of divisions of haves and have-nots, in the form of the social, economic, and cultural gap, known as the **digital divide**, between those with effective access to information technology and those without such access. This is the divide between those who are connected and those who are not; between those with high-speed access and those in the slow lane; between those with the education and media literacy to navigate around the more innovative and independent sites and those who mainly visit the big commercial sites (Klinenberg, 2007); between "digital natives" born into the age of the Internet and older "digital immigrants" who have to try to keep up with the changes (Palfrey & Gasser, 2008). Canada is one of the most connected countries in the world, but the digital gap persists for those who are poor and those who live in remote and rural areas. Only 27 percent of remote northern communities have Internet access. For example, Canadians in Nunavut, a region with just 36,000 residents spread across a land mass nearly three times the size of Texas, have the worst levels of connection in Canada (Freeman, 2014).

As computers and the Internet become more important to everyday life around the world, understanding the causes and effects of the digital divide (Norris, 2001) will be one of the most important tasks for sociologists of culture and communication.

6.2 How Does Culture Shape Our Collective Identity?

Frans Lemmens/SuperStock

Culture and Group Identity

We all think of ourselves as belonging to many different groups. Some of these groups are relatively easy to define—for example, nationality or religion—but others are less clear. Are football fans a group? What about university students? If so, how can you tell? More fundamentally, what makes up group identity, and how do sociologists study it? It turns out that culture is central to group identity—both in defining a group and in maintaining it. Some scholars even suggest that we should use the word *culture* only to refer to differences and similarities that form the basis for groups coming together or clashing with each other (Appadurai, 1996, p. 13).

Mainstream Culture, Subcultures, and Countercultures

6.2.1 Discuss the role that culture plays in establishing group style, and explain what distinguishes a subculture from the mainstream.

In the absence of clear ways to define where one group ends and another begins, we need to take our cues from shared behaviours. One way of thinking about identity in cultural terms is through the concept of **group style**, or the set of norms and practices that distinguishes one group from another (Eliasoph & Lichterman, 2003). Different groups have different *norms*, or shared assumptions about correct behaviour. Because most of us belong to many groups (for example, our school, our national identity, and our gender), we learn to adopt the right style for the right occasion. Adopting the right style is not always a simple matter, though—think of how difficult it would be to fit in if you were suddenly transported to a different time or place. Group style is thus a way for people to communicate belonging or not belonging. According to this account of identity formation, culture is a practice of communication.

Mainstream culture—the most widely shared systems of meaning and cultural tool kits in a society—is expressed in the activities and norms of many groups. The Chamber of Commerce, established religious groups, alumni associations, sports teams, civic organizations, and many other such groups accept and embrace the mainstream culture in one or another aspect of their activities. But some groups deliberately set themselves off from mainstream culture. In North America, well-known examples include hippies in the 1960s and online gamers in the 2000s. Contemporary sociologists refer to such groups as **subcultures**, or relatively small groups of people whose affiliation is based on shared beliefs, preferences, and practices that exist under the mainstream (literally *sub*cultures) and distinguish them from the mainstream. Other examples might include rock climbers, hunters, ballroom dancers, and chess players. Sociologist Claude Fischer (1975) claimed that subcultures are most likely to emerge in cities, where—unlike in small towns and traditional villages—the large, concentrated population allows many such groups to flourish. Some subcultures may have a clearly articulated sense of common purpose or definition, while others may be only loosely connected by mutual interests.

Paul Carstairs/Alamy Stock Photo

Countercultures such as punks use their appearance and behaviours to deliberately set themselves off from mainstream culture. What are other examples of contemporary "resistance through rituals"?

While subcultures often exist in harmony with mainstream culture—there's nothing socially threatening about rock climbers, for example—cultural-studies scholars in the United Kingdom argued that some subcultures express differences in political and economic power and that setting yourself apart from the cultural mainstream is often an act of "resistance through rituals" (Hall & Jefferson, 1975). This type of subculture is usually called a **counterculture**—a group whose ideas, attitudes, and behaviours are in direct conflict with mainstream culture and who actively contest the dominant cultural practices in the societies of which they are a part. Some recent or current countercultural groups include antigovernment militias, the U.S. Tea Party, Idle No More, and the Occupy movements. Sociologists consider culture an arena of struggle within which different mainstream cultures, subcultures, and countercultures are unequally ranked and often stand in opposition to another, each fighting for supremacy in determining what counts as culture and seeking to reap the rewards that come from it (Clarke, Hall, Jefferson, & Roberts, 1975, p. 11).

Is There a Dominant Culture in North America Today?

6.2.2 Discuss the concept of "culture wars" and explain the importance of practising cultural relativism in a multicultural North America.

It only makes sense to speak of subcultures and countercultures when there is a dominant mainstream culture that they can challenge. Is there a single mainstream culture in North America in the twenty-first century?

The Italian revolutionary and Marxist theorist Antonio Gramsci famously argued in the 1930s that the dominant economic classes in any society attempt to maintain their power by encouraging certain moral and cultural understandings that are favourable to them. The process by which powerful groups gain legitimacy and hold power based on establishing or reinforcing widely shared beliefs about what is right or wrong, proper or improper, valuable or not, is called **hegemony**. When these views become taken for granted, they can help to reinforce the dominant group's authority. For example, in North America today, it's common sense to think that people should work in order to earn enough money to live, that those who work harder or better will get ahead, and that people who choose not to work should only be entitled to the bare minimum of financial support. But such commonsense notions could easily be said to serve the interests of wealthy business owners, who need to find hard workers for their businesses to succeed. Gramsci argued that movements seeking to radically transform a society needed not just to win political power but to overthrow cultural hegemony—to fight common sense with good sense. Culture, in other words, is not just entertainment; it's an arena of perpetual conflict.

These days, such cultural conflicts usually refer to arguments over the proper role of family and religious values in certain questions of state policy: abortion rights, immigration rights, and gay rights are three of the most important. The American sociologist James Davison Hunter argued in the early 1990s that people tended to line up on the same sides on many of these issues—positions he labelled "progressive" and "orthodox"—and that being progressive or orthodox didn't necessarily correspond to social class or political affiliation. The main battle lines of American electoral politics, he concluded, were shifting from economic questions to moral questions, and he even claimed that these conflicts over family and religious values were so intense as to constitute **culture wars** (Hunter, 1991). Like Americans, Canadians can also be divided into two clear-cut political cultural camps, with one taking a conservative position and another taking what is usually called a liberal or progressive position. The issues include abortion, funding for the CBC, capital punishment, guns, the Middle East, evolution, law and order, French language rights, and Indigenous self-government (Caplan, 2010).

Although the idea of culture wars may seem to be a useful way of capturing conflicts that often become very heated, it assumes that there are two dominant cultures squaring off against each other: a liberal culture and a conservative culture. This is at odds with another important way to describe the contemporary group-identity landscape of both Canada and the United States: multiculturalism. **Multiculturalism** refers to beliefs or policies promoting the equal accommodation of different ethnic or cultural groups within a society. In Canada, Quebec was recognized as a "distinct society" as a precondition for participating in constitutional talks in 1985. Both the Meech Lake Accord (1987) and the Charlottetown Accord (1992) proposed a distinct society clause in the constitution. The purpose of recognizing Quebec as a distinct society within a nation was to highlight its majority French-speaking population, culture, and civil law tradition.

Societies with large immigrant populations, such as Canada and the United States, will contain people of different cultural and religious backgrounds, creating new and more varied types of cultural conflicts than the culture wars theory suggests. Statistics Canada (2010) projected that by the year 2031, between 25 percent and 28 percent of the population could be foreign-born. About 55 percent of this population would be born in Asia. This population is projected to increase approximately four times faster than the rest of the population. Explore these anticipated demographic changes in Canada in Table 6.1.

For some observers, the current challenge of immigrant cultures and multiculturalism will eventually go away, as immigrant groups properly adopt mainstream values. Historically, the standard metaphor for this process is associated with the United States and is referred to as the *melting pot*, the idea that although immigrants come from all sorts of diverse cultural backgrounds, they will eventually be assimilated into society until they become, at some point, genuinely American. The history of white immigrant groups from Europe in the late nineteenth and early twentieth centuries seems to confirm this idea. But the melting pot concept is a controversial one today; it is often seen as an example of **ethnocentrism**—an inability to understand or accept cultural practices different from one's own. The idea that every immigrant group must become "American" is no longer widely accepted. Unlike the United States, Canada's official policy of cultural accommodation seeks to promote the equal celebration of racial, religious, and cultural diversity.

Table 6.1 Proportion of foreign-born and visible minority populations by census metropolitan area, 2006 and 2031 (reference scenario).

The demographic character of Canada is expected to change dramatically by 2031.

	Foreign-born		Visible minority	
	2006	2031	2006	2031
	% of population			
Canada	**20**	**26**	**16**	**31**
Abbotsford–Mission	24	29	23	39
Barrie	13	13	6	11
Brantford	12	13	5	10
Calgary	24	30	22	38
Edmonton	19	22	17	29
Greater Sudbury	7	5	2	5
Guelph	20	25	13	25
Halifax	7	11	7	12
Hamilton	24	27	12	25
Kelowna	15	14	5	10
Kingston	12	14	6	11
Kitchener	23	28	14	28
London	19	23	11	22
Moncton	3	5	2	5
Montréal	21	30	16	31
Oshawa	16	19	10	21
Ottawa–Gatineau (Ottawa part)	22	29	19	36
Ottawa–Gatineau (Gatineau part)	8	15	6	14
Peterborough	9	11	3	8
Québec	4	7	2	5
Regina	8	10	7	12
Saguenay	1	2	1	2
Saint John	4	6	3	8
Saskatoon	8	10	6	13
Sherbrooke	6	11	4	10
St. Catharines–Niagara	18	19	7	14
St. John's	3	4	2	5
Thunder Bay	10	8	3	7
Toronto	46	50	43	63
Trois-Rivières	2	5	2	4
Vancouver	40	44	42	59
Victoria	19	20	10	17
Windsor	23	28	16	33
Winnipeg	18	24	15	27

SOURCE: Adapted from "Projections of the Diversity of the Canadian Population," by Statistics Canada, *The Daily*, March 9, 2010 (http://www.statcan.gc.ca/daily-quotidien/100309/t100309a1-eng.htm). Copyright by Statistics Canada, Client Services Division. This does not constitute an endorsement by Statistics Canada of this product.

The problem with ethnocentrism is that it leads us to make incorrect assumptions about others on the basis of our own experience. If Geertz had observed the Balinese cockfight from an ethnocentric point of view, he simply would have concluded that many Balinese made risky and irresponsible bets. Or imagine if you went to a Chinese restaurant and concluded that the owners must not have heard about forks and knives because they brought you chopsticks. Although we have all been raised in specific cultural contexts that will influence our thinking in unacknowledged ways—and so we can never escape ethnocentrism entirely—these kinds of assumptions make it difficult to understand other cultures with any kind of depth. We will misinterpret shared meanings or fail to grasp what is important in a given situation. For this reason **cultural relativism**—evaluating cultural meanings and practices in their own social contexts—is central to the sociological imagination. For example, Geertz tried to discover not the cultural significance of the Balinese cockfight in general but rather its significance *for the Balinese*. When we travel to foreign lands, we will have a much more enriching experience trying to understand what we observe if we try not to compare it to our own world but rather to understand it on its own terms. Thus, cultural relativism is the opposite of ethnocentrism.

National Cultures

6.2.3 Explain what produces and reproduces national cultures, and what effects they have.

Even in the era of globalization, the most important group identity in the modern world is surely the nation. The entire world is divided into nation-states, and most people are citizens or subjects of a single one of them. So it is not surprising that **national culture**, the set of shared cultural practices and beliefs within a given nation-state, is an important principle for sociology. Are there differences in cultural norms, assumptions, and identities between different nations? If so, what are they, what produces and reproduces them, and what effects do they have? These are the questions that sociologists try to answer about national cultures.

Today it seems obvious that the world should be divided into nations and that people should think of themselves in these terms: I'm American and you're Canadian, she's British and he's Chinese. But it wasn't always so. The rise of **nationalism**—the fact that people think of themselves as inherently members of a nation and often take pride in that identity—is a relatively recent phenomenon in world history. Quebec nationalism led to the province's recognition as a distinct society within a nation. National communities became possible only with the origination of *print capitalism*—the mass production of books and then newspapers written in local languages for simultaneous mass consumption by an increasingly literate public (Anderson, 1991). When French people read French newspapers and German people read German newspapers, they not only learn what's happening in their respective countries; they also confirm their membership in a shared national culture. Even today, when newspaper readership is on the decline, other forms of shared media consumption follow the same pattern. A study of the geography of Twitter, for example, found that people's networks are generally national and unilingual—although in theory your experience of Twitter could be truly global, in practice it is likely to reinforce your sense of belonging to a certain nation (Takhteyev, Gruzd, & Wellman, 2012).

Members of nations share an assumption of commonality with each other, even though they come from diverse class and ethnic backgrounds and most will never meet. In a country like the United Kingdom, with a strong national government and a common language, this is a plausible enough assumption. But what about Indonesia, composed of 13,000 islands and home to over 700 languages? With the notable exception of some separatist regions at the periphery, Indonesians generally also imagine themselves to be a single national community. And importantly, they view their community as limited, as one among many. A national community is not like a religious community, whose practitioners may hope to convert the entire world to their faith. Indonesians don't want to make all Italians Indonesians.

In contemporary life, cultural sociologists generally take nations for granted, the same way we all do, and many of them study the differences between national cultures: What makes national cultures different from one another, and what are the

Figure 6.2 Measures of Differences Between Nations

As these graphs illustrate, there are notable differences between people of different nations on some basic cultural attitudes.

SOURCE: Based on data from *Television Audience Report, 2010–2011*, by Nielsen, 2011 (http://www.nielsen.com/us/en/insights/reports/2011/television-audience-report-2010-2011.html).

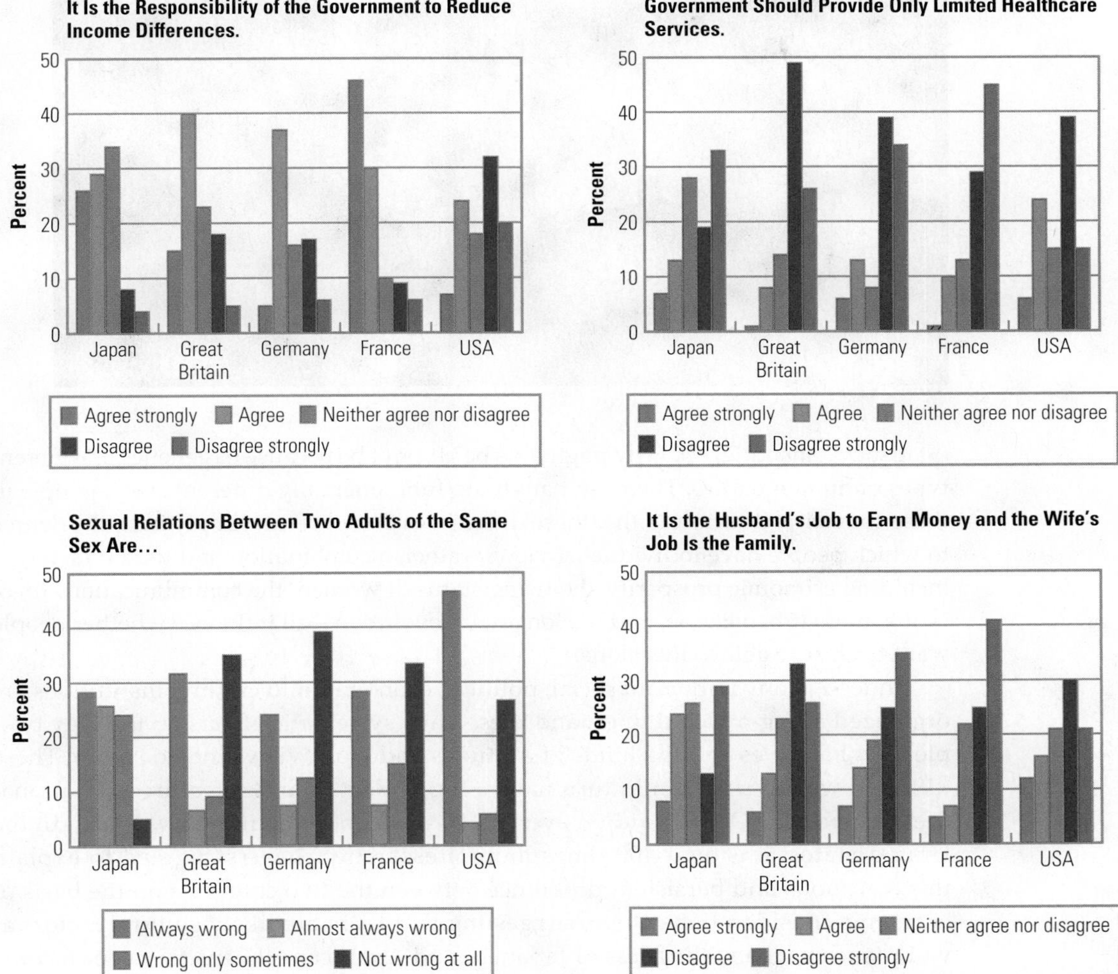

implications of the differences? Before we turn to a discussion of the complexities, examine the data in Figure 6.2 about the large differences between people of different nations on some basic cultural attitudes.

To take one of the most widely believed differences as an example, Americans are thought to be more individualistic than people in other countries. Compared to people in other rich countries, Americans are more likely to believe that individuals should take care of themselves rather than look to the government to support them (Brooks & Manza, 2007). In contrast, Canadians are thought to be more collectivist because they recognize and value the role of government, particularly to provide healthcare, keep order and peace, and provide certain other universal benefits such as maternity leave and day care.

But the importance of individualism is complicated. Consider the cultural shift we noted in the beginning of the chapter—the rise of people who choose to live by themselves. In spite of their apparent individualism, Americans are actually far less likely to live alone than are residents of apparently less individualistic nations, such as Sweden, Norway, Finland, and Denmark (Klinenberg, 2012). In Canada today, one-person households make up 27.6% of all homes, a threefold increase since 1961

Preschools follow very different educational approaches in different countries. Why is preschool an important place to study national cultural differences?

Stuart Bay / Alamy Stock Photo

(Statistics Canada, 2012). Why might this be? It can't be because of genetics or different types of human nature: There isn't anything fundamentally different about people in these countries. It turns out that these differences do not result simply from the degree to which people have individualist views; rather, a combination of different factors—including economic prosperity, the rising status of women, the communications revolution, mass urbanization, and the longevity revolution—all influence whether people want to and are able to live alone.

Indeed, many important social, political, economic, and cultural institutions are organized along national lines, and these have systematic effects on the way people live their lives and the kinds of attitudes and worldviews they develop. These different worldviews can in turn have a big impact on other features of national life. In Japan, CEOs are paid on average 16 times more than their workers; in the United States, it is over 400 times more. Researchers have struggled to explain this enormous and persistent difference between the two countries on the basis of economic considerations alone, suggesting that there are likely cultural factors at work (such as the willingness of Japanese and American citizens to accept income disparities).

One important area of research is early childhood, because it is when we are children that many of our cultural assumptions are formed. One study of preschools in Japan, China, and the United States revealed the very different roles that preschools play in forming cultural identities in these three countries (Tobin, Wu, & Davidson, 1989). By recording classroom activities and then discussing the videos with teachers and parents, the researchers found that U.S. preschools put heavy emphasis on creativity and respect for the children as individuals. In China the emphasis was on instilling order and discipline in the children, an understandable objective in the context of China's single-child families where "little emperors" are often seen as spoiled by their parents and grandparents. In Japan, meanwhile, educators left children to their own devices to a much greater degree than in the other two cases, forcing them to learn to get along respectfully with others.

These might seem like stereotypes, but that's exactly the point. If there are durable differences in cultural norms between different countries, we would expect to find evidence of them in institutions such as preschool. As the authors of the preschool study indicate, preschool both *reflects* national culture—because teachers and parents are influenced by certain ideas and try to pass them along—and helps *reproduce* it—because children inherit these same ideas.

6.3 How Do Our Cultural Practices Relate to Class and Status?

Robert Harding World Imagery

Class, Status, and Culture

How do you know whether people are wealthy or powerful? You can't see their bank accounts or know who is in their phone address books. The chances are that you can make an educated guess because of cultural signs: the way they dress, how they speak, the sports they play, the music they like, the kinds of things they like to do: in short, their **taste**—their cultural preferences. Although we normally think about social class in mainly economic terms, taste—and culture more broadly—plays a crucial role in setting and maintaining class distinctions.

Cultural Capital

6.3.1 Define cultural capital and discuss ways North American elites have become cultural omnivores.

Contrary to popular assumption that it is the land of opportunity, North American societies are intensely class-bound. Someone who is born into the working class is very likely to stay working class for her entire life, and the same is true for someone born into the upper class. One way of understanding why that is the case is to think about the kinds of resources people can bring to bear in their lives. One kind of resource is money and other economic assets; another is social connections and networks of friends and acquaintances. Bourdieu referred to these as *economic capital* and *social capital*, respectively. He also suggested that there is a third type of resource important for determining class position: In addition to the money you have and the people you know, your success in life is also influenced by your **cultural capital**. This is your education, tastes, and cultural knowledge and your ability to display sophistication (or a lack thereof) in your speech, manners, and other everyday acts. Bourdieu argued that your cultural capital, as much as your wealth or connections, confers on you higher or lower status in the eyes of others (Bourdieu, 1984).

We use our cultural capital all the time in interactions with others and often don't even realize we are doing so. Others size us up the moment we open our mouths and start offering opinions or thoughts about the world around us. Bourdieu did not consider public or over-the-top displays of status symbols to be an important form of cultural capital; instead, he emphasized the various ways that people display taste in everyday life. Discussing why you enjoyed the Spanish director Pedro Almodóvar's latest film, for example, signals to others that you have good taste in movies. Taste also implies distaste; if the person you are talking to doesn't know who Almodóvar is, you are likely to make negative judgements about his or her own tastes and status. Even if you don't *consciously* judge other people on their tastes, the chances are that tastes will

Russell Gordon/Danita Delimont, Agent/Alamy Stock Photo

Cultural capital is only valuable if it is rare or hard to obtain. Now that the middle class can easily buy modernist furniture at Ikea, that kind of furniture is no longer an important status symbol in and of itself. We now have new divisions, by brand. IKEA could be considered low-brow modern, while the much more exclusive furniture sold at Herman Miller is considered high-brow modern.

influence the kinds of people you want to spend time with or avoid. Tastes, therefore, help maintain status boundaries between different groups (Holt, 1997).

Cultural capital requires scarcity: Cultural experiences that everyone can share cannot serve as the basis for status distinctions. Before the Swedish home-products company IKEA began to sell its inexpensive furniture, the aesthetic it applied (minimalist Scandinavian modernism) was considered a sign of high status. But because the middle class can afford IKEA furniture and shops there extensively, this aesthetic is no longer an embodiment of significant cultural capital. The issue is not money but difficulty: In order to provide a basis for signalling distinction, high-status cultural consumption must not be easy to participate in, and if it becomes easy it will stop being high status.

How does this notion of cultural capital apply to contemporary life in North America? In his study of cultural capital in France, Bourdieu emphasized that upper-class groups tend to appreciate high culture and arts in ways that ordinary working people cannot. But North American societies have a more pervasive mass culture than many other societies, one in which people of many different classes may listen to similar music or enjoy similar kinds of music or television. Recent research has suggested that North American elites are less snobbish than those in other countries and are increasingly behaving as **cultural omnivores** who demonstrate their high status through a broad range of cultural consumption, including low-status culture. Highly educated North Americans today are more likely than average to consume not only high culture but popular culture as well. It is a sign of distinction to have wide-ranging tastes, such as an appreciation for sports and modern dance, hip-hop as well as classical music, and so forth (Kahn, 2009; Peterson & Kern, 1996). Yet we shouldn't overstate the inclusive nature of elite tastes. While, for instance, some cultural elites show a fondness for country music (a low-status genre more associated with the working class), the type of country music elites generally enjoy is not the commercial country of Shania Twain or Garth Brooks but rather more alternative country acts such as k.d. lang, The Sadies, or The Rural Alberta Advantage (Holt, 1997).

How Culture Reproduces Class

6.3.2 Analyze how money and culture reproduce status over the long term.

An important topic for sociologists concerned with power and inequality is the process that causes class boundaries and distinctions to be maintained over time, known as **class reproduction**. There are lots of reasons why some people are rich and others poor, but how do those boundaries get maintained in the short term, as well as over the longer term? Bourdieu's theory of cultural capital examines how, in countless everyday interactions, we remind ourselves and others about our relative statuses, and this helps to ensure that our status differences persist. But what explains class and status reproduction over the long term and across generations? For example, why are middle-class children likely to grow up into middle-class adults and working-class children likely to grow up into working-class adults?

One obvious answer is money: Wealthier families will have an easier time affording private schools, SAT preparation courses, university tuition, and personal tutors, and they will also likely leave sizeable inheritances to their children. But money explains only part of the story: Sociologists have shown that people make meaningful choices about how to live that are limited but not solely determined by their economic circumstances. The question of how and why we make the choices we do is what culture helps to explain.

For example, in one famous study the sociologist and ethnographer Paul Willis (1977) followed a set of boys from working-class homes in a British industrial town in the 1970s. They frequently behaved badly in school, were rebellious, and didn't seem to care much about their futures. A standard opinion at the time was that such cases were simply people failing to make the right choices to get ahead in life. But Willis found it was quite the opposite: The boys' apparently unproductive behaviour in school was in fact their way of adapting to their class circumstances. The same attitudes that got them in trouble with their teachers turned out to serve them very well in factory work a few years later, where standing up to authority and not working hard on command helped workers gain collective leverage against their bosses. The rebellious boys were learning how to be working-class men.

A more recent study by sociologist Annette Lareau compared middle-class and working-class families in the United States to see how different class positions affect parents' approaches to childrearing and what the implications of the differences are for children's futures. During the study, it became clear that there were two quite different approaches. Middle-class parents followed an approach of *concerted cultivation*, actively fostering their child's talents and intervening on their behalf, thereby instilling a sense of entitlement. Working-class parents, by contrast, followed an approach of *accomplishment of natural growth*, caring for their children but leaving them to fend for themselves socially, thereby instilling a sense of constraint (Lareau, 2003). The middle-class children's sense of entitlement will make it more likely that they push to succeed socioeconomically when they are older, while the reverse is true of the working-class children's sense of constraint, making it more likely that as they get older, the children will stay in the class they were born into.

The implication of both of these classical studies is that class is reproduced not only through the money you (or your family) have but also through the culture you learn and practise growing up.

6.4 Who Produces Culture, and Why?

Megapress/Alamy Stock Photo

The Conditions of Cultural Production

In 1845, Karl Marx and Friedrich Engels argued that the people who have the most wealth and power in a society generally also have the greatest ability to produce and distribute their own ideas and culture (Marx & Engels, 1845/1972). In nineteenth-century Europe, these people were capitalists, such as factory owners and bankers, who valued their rights to own private property and their freedom to run their businesses as they saw fit. By using their influence with newspaper owners, politicians, and some intellectuals, they were able to make liberty and freedom the dominant ideas of the age.

Marx and Engels's argument suggests that cultural production is a historical phenomenon. Ideas and fashions don't just change randomly over time; they also respond to other changes in a society's political and economic circumstances. At the same time, in the nineteenth century it was much more difficult to spread ideas than it is today. Printing presses were expensive, and much of the population was illiterate. Today, with the Internet and social media, do powerful people and classes still have control over the production of culture? Does Gramsci's notion of hegemony adequately characterize the cultural environment of the twenty-first century? Sociologists of culture are paying increasingly careful attention to the changing *conditions of cultural production:* Who controls the production of ideas in society, and to what ends?

The Public Sphere

6.4.1 Analyze how the concept of the public sphere explains how culture is produced in society.

A basic premise of public life in a democracy such as Canada is that everyone is allowed to participate in the discussions, debates, and elections that decide who shall govern. In theory, all citizens over 18 can vote, run for public office, or start a political organization to try to convince other people of their point of view. This vision of equal participation in political life is a powerful one, and it centres on the idea that there exists what German sociologist Jürgen Habermas described as the **public sphere** (Habermas, 1962/1989). According to Habermas, when private citizens assemble in groups (wherever that might be) to confer about matters of general interest, they are engaging in critical activities for democratic life. In an ideal public sphere, citizens set aside their own interests, as well as their wealth and status, and meet as equals to collectively debate and generate ideas about how to govern collectively. And individuals have influence only because of the power and value of their ideas.

In eighteenth-century Europe, when the public sphere began to emerge, it was centred in a range of institutions such as newspapers, pubs, social clubs, and coffee shops—in short, any location where people could gather and discuss the news of the day. The public sphere stood apart from the state and offered citizens a way to criticize and influence the government, which was a novel idea in an age of absolute monarchies. In modern welfare states such as Canada, the public sphere is where different social groups organize to become political actors and compete for influence. Environmental activists and interest groups such as the Canadian Association of Petroleum Producers are examples of the kinds of groups that are prominent in today's public sphere. An important way they compete is by trying to shape public opinion through the production of ideas, for example in newspapers, on television, and with advertising. In contemporary societies like Canada, the public sphere is increasingly becoming organized online, and in particular through social media.

However appealing the image of the ideal public sphere may be, in practice public participation is massively unequal. Many people choose not to have any interest in politics or to vote in elections. Further, it is very hard to attract an audience for your ideas if you don't have a fair amount of money backing you. For example, in the United States, the Tea Party movement has received many millions of dollars in funding from a small number of wealthy conservatives, while Occupy had to rely on much smaller amounts of money, generally from small donations. As a result, the Tea Party has been able to spend more money on advertising and promotion, on bankrolling its preferred political candidates, and on other activities that give its members influence in the public sphere, while Occupy disappeared fairly quickly. In general, sociologists argue that the same things that give some people power over others in private life—such as race, gender, class, and education—will give some people more influence in the public sphere (Fraser, 1992).

Another problem with the ideal image of the public sphere is that that there has never been one overarching public sphere; rather, various social groups—and subcultures—have frequently constituted their own **counterpublics**, alternative public spheres through which they produce and circulate their own values, beliefs, and ideas. Factories and unions produced one kind of counterpublic in the first half of the twentieth century, and the networks of black churches that formed the backbone of the civil rights movement and the gay liberation activists who gathered in bars and clubs are also examples of Northern American counterpublics.

Fragmented publics do not necessarily need to be subordinate, either: The concept can apply to any subculture. One researcher describes the users of social networking sites such as Facebook as constituting a **networked public**, or online public sphere. Networked publics attract participation from teenagers in particular because of things they offer that face-to-face public settings cannot. Social networking allows persistence (you can browse through your friends' profiles and message histories years after initial friend requests and conversations), searchability (you can seek out other people with similar interests and connect with existing friends regardless of geographical proximity), replicability (it is hard to distinguish the "original" from the "copy" when copy-and-paste is ubiquitous), and invisible audiences (much of our activity on social networks is potentially being observed by people we don't know, and perhaps at totally different times), and these features make networked publics distinct public spheres (Boyd, 2008). Regardless of whether there is one public sphere or many, the concept of the networked public forces us to think broadly about how ideas and culture are produced and how people participate in that production.

The Culture Industry Versus Cultural Democracy

6.4.2 Compare and contrast the cultural industry and the cultural democracy perspectives.

Who controls popular culture today, and who benefits from it? Is it the corporations that produce it at a profit, or the public who consumes it, shares it, and enjoys it? If record labels, movie studios, and advertising agencies heavily push the latest songs and movies, when we enjoy them are we dupes or are we exercising cultural free will? Sociologists have been largely split on these questions between two perspectives: one that sees popular culture as an industry and one that sees popular culture as a democratic arena—a cultural public sphere.

Writing after World War II, the German sociologist and philosopher Theodor Adorno argued that the popular culture that dominates the public sphere encourages a passive, conservative public. He was referring to popular music, movies, and other types of mass culture, all of which he labelled the **culture industry** (Horkheimer & Adorno, 1947/2002). His chief complaint was that popular culture encourages audiences to passively consume what they are watching, reading, or listening to rather than participate or engage creatively with the work. The kind of culture that the culture industry produces is standardized, is commoditized, and does not challenge the status quo; at the end of the day, it is advertising rather than art.

Other sociologists have argued that Adorno's critique of popular culture (along with others like it) was too pessimistic. They instead believe that popular culture provides an arena through which we all debate the meaning of the good life and the conditions for attaining it—an explicitly cultural version of Habermas's public sphere. One response, for example, to Adorno's claim that most people passively receive the culture that is offered to them is that popular culture is user driven. Cultural producers want to attract an audience, so they tailor their art to reflect popular preferences (Gans, 1999). Movie studios wouldn't keep releasing the same kind of movies if people didn't want to watch them, and when people vote with their time and money by choosing not to watch a certain kind of movie, studios will probably stop making that kind of movie. According to this perspective, popular culture is an element of *cultural democracy*. In the cultural marketplace, lots of different tastes—including those of subcultures, such as hip-hop, that elites disapprove of—are accommodated. Different cultural styles exist "because they satisfy the needs and wishes of some people, even if they dissatisfy those of other people" (Gans, 1999, p. 91).

The Medium Is the Message

6.4.3 Discuss the ways in which communication changes with the form or medium.

Debates over whether popular culture is an industry, a democracy, or something else focus not only on the content of popular culture but just as often on its form. If the same content is broadcast on cable TV and on Twitter, will it communicate the same thing? The answer from communications theory is that it won't. As the Canadian media theorist Marshall McLuhan famously declared, the medium is the message (McLuhan, 1964). By this, McLuhan meant that different media encourage different ways of communicating, of organizing power, and of centralizing or decentralizing social activity.

Compare listening to a news bulletin on the radio with reading the same news on a website. There are some obvious differences: For example, when you hear the news on the radio, you hear only what the announcer says, while on a website you have the opportunity to follow hyperlinks and look up unfamiliar things on Wikipedia. In this respect, the web offers a richer experience than the radio. But there are some other differences that may not be as obvious. On the radio you can't follow hyperlinks, but you also have a harder time skimming the material the way you can on a website. Radio dominates one of your senses—hearing—and prompts you to devote most of your attention to receiving and processing the information you are hearing. A website, by contrast, provides you with a more ambiguous sensory experience. There might be sound and video on the webpage, but there might be just text. You might be listening to music in the background, or you might have an instant messaging window open simultaneously. Reading news on a website requires more of your direct engagement than listening to the radio does. Different forms of communication can thus provide very different experiences even when communicating the exact same content.

Cultural production in North America is increasingly occurring online. But an arguably greater transition was from the age of typography to the *age of television* (Postman, 1985). From the sixteenth century until midway through the twentieth century, discussions of public issues in the West were primarily based in the written word and in this sense biased toward careful and considered thought. Personal communication, for example, largely occurred via letters, which took a long time to write and be delivered, encouraging people to thoughtfully consider what they wanted to say. Similarly, large-scale communication occurred through books and pamphlets, which also encouraged thoughtfulness. Beginning in the 1950s, however, public communication increasingly shifted toward television. TV became the primary way in which people got their news about the world. According to some communications scholars, this age of television led to a decline in the quality of public discourse. How much of what we see on the news has any actual relevance for our lives in the sense that it will cause us to make different decisions? Endless reporting of distant natural disasters, for example, is irrelevant to our daily lives, and this helps promote a loop of impotence because we become used to passively receiving information without expecting to be able to act on it in any meaningful way. What's more, the information we receive through television tends to arrive in a series of short, disconnected sound bites, which make it difficult for us to put it in any coherent context. Ultimately, the bias of television as a medium is toward stimulation and entertainment, possibly at the expense of understanding.

Do we still live in the age of television? Things have changed since the 1980s, when the Internet existed only in a few laboratories and no one had cellphones. Our media consumption habits have changed as well. Today, no single medium of communication dominates the way television did for most of the second half of the twentieth century. One particularly striking change in media consumption is the increase in cultural multitasking—for example, when you watch TV, how often are you also checking Instagram, browsing the Internet, or texting with a friend? The contemporary media environment is a "torrent": a nonstop flow of information that we rarely if ever disengage from. The torrent doesn't so much command our active attention as it forms a sensory background for our lives (Gitlin, 2007). As we all live our lives in an increasingly online and interconnected fashion, just how cultural production continues to change in the years ahead will be a crucial question for both sociologists and the public at large.

6.5 What Is the Relationship Between Media and Democracy?

Kathy deWitt/Alamy Stock Photo

Media and Democracy: A Changing Landscape

It has long been obvious that how the news is presented is vital to how citizens develop their social and political views about the world. In this sense, the news media are a key element of the larger impact of culture in society. Writing nearly 100 years ago, the famous journalist Walter Lippmann was skeptical of the media's ability to provide the public with the information necessary for a democracy. He argued that "news and truth are not the same thing." Democracy requires truth, but the news can only describe and discuss events from day to day. Lippmann believed that democracy required a collective intelligence, which could only be had with extensive social organization, and that here the press could play only a small part, although a necessary one (Lippmann, 1922, p. 358). The media are arguably the most important form of cultural production in our society, and if we want to understand the broader impact of culture in society, it is important to consider how the media relate to democracy (a topic we broached in the previous section when we introduced the concept of the public sphere). In this section, we consider that relationship.

Making the News: The Media as a Cultural System

6.5.1 Explain the role that the media play in making the news.

Journalism—the production and dissemination of information of general public interest—is above all else a form of cultural communication. But sociologists of the media are in broad agreement that the news does a lot more than just pass along facts to the public. By deciding what to cover and how to cover it, journalists don't simply report on the news: They actually help to create and change it (Schudson, 2003, p. 11).

How does the news have this kind of power, and is it a good thing? There are plenty of concerns about the power of the media. Common liberal critiques suggest that the mass media support corporate power, militarism, and the interests of the wealthiest. Common conservative critiques suggest that the media make the culture more liberal and spread feminism, environmentalism, and the acceptance of homosexuality. Political insiders on all sides believe the media exert a kind of *agenda-setting* power that can change the course of political events.

The problem with these debates is that it is difficult to prove that the media actually have this influence. There are anecdotes on both sides. For example, one famous example of apparent media influence was during the Vietnam War. Until 1968, TV news coverage was favourable to the war, sanitizing violence and especially U.S. casualties. That changed in 1968, most famously with CBS news anchor Walter Cronkite's February editorial calling for negotiations with the Viet Cong, and the popular narrative is that media criticism of the war prompted a turning point in galvanizing opposition to the war. An example of the opposite situation occurred in the aftermath of the terrorist attacks of 9/11, when relentless media coverage of the bombings led to overwhelming public support for going to war against the perceived perpetrators, in Afghanistan and later in Iraq (even though there was no evidence that the Iraqi government had any involvement). These examples suggest that when it comes to the most important decisions governments make—even those concerning war—the media can exert considerable influence.

Yet such dramatic examples may overstate things. People get their information about the world not just from what they hear in the media but also from talking to other people, from the views expressed in groups they may be a member of (for example, their synagogue, mosque, or church), and from ideas they may have learned in school or through their own personal experiences. Because the media are so visible and audible, they are presumed to be important forces in society. But if the public doesn't passively receive whatever the media tell it, how do the media have influence? According to media scholar Michael Schudson, the media act as a cultural system: They set the context for making events in the world intelligible. They do this by helping construct a community and a public conversation. Regardless of your opinions on a given issue, when you hear about it in the news, you are more likely to treat it as an event of importance. This is why public relations experts say, "There's no such thing as bad press." The news amplifies issues and makes them publicly legitimate.

Corporate Media Concentration

6.5.2 Identify three trends in the media landscape that have put commercial pressure on journalism.

One of the premises of the free press in a democracy is that citizens will be exposed to a variety of perspectives and sources of information in order to participate meaningfully in public life. But just six corporations own most of the media in Canada: Bell, Rogers, Shaw, Newcap, Quebecor, and the government-funded Canadian Broadcasting Corporation (CBC). How much choice do media consumers actually have?

Three trends in the media landscape have put commercial pressure on journalism. The first is consolidation: Fewer and fewer corporations own more and more of the media outlets in a given market. Canada has the most concentrated TV ownership of any G8 country. Consolidation limits consumer choice—in an extreme case, the corporation Clear Channel once owned all the commercial radio stations in the city of Minot, North Dakota. This is a monopoly and is still comparatively rare, but oligopolies (markets controlled by a handful of firms) are now the norm in the media. Consolidation also makes it difficult for new entrants to break into the market, increasing the likelihood that the media market will stay dominated by the same players.

A second trend is conglomeration, which describes a firm controlling multiple types of media functions. For example, the Walt Disney Company, one of the big six U.S. media corporations, owns ABC, ESPN, hundreds of radio stations, and various print media operations. When Disney has a new movie to release, it can rely on its subsidiaries to promote the movie on its stations and television programs, and to ensure that the coverage is positive. This is called *synergy*, and Disney is the master of synergy.

The final trend is hypercommercialism. It has long been standard for movies to feature some sort of product placement—advertising where shots or mentions of a product are integrated into the movie itself as opposed to a separate ad. But product placement has soared to new heights in recent years and shows no sign of abating. The 2010 romantic comedy *Valentine's Day*, for instance, featured product placements for 60 different products—one every 125 seconds! This is an example of hypercommercialism, and it is a defining feature of today's corporate media—blurred lines between advertising and editorial content in newspapers; the ubiquity of outdoor advertising; the spread of media companies into retail businesses, such as the ESPN Store; and sponsored programming, such as the corporate naming of nearly all professional sports venues.

An example of hypercommercialism is sponsored programming, such as the corporate naming of nearly all professional sports venues.

Torontonian/Alamy Stock Photo

These three trends have put enormous commercial pressure on journalism (McChesney, 1999). Within the bounds of profitability and corporate acceptability, the media produce a wide range of content; outside of these bounds, however, very little is likely to appear.

Media, Democracy, and the Internet

6.5.3 Discuss the ways the Internet has created new opportunities and dangers for the free media and for democracy.

The notion that the press is vital to democracy is an old one. But the relationship between the media and democracy looks different in the age of corporate media consolidation and digital technologies. Corporate consolidation means that media are less responsive to the local communities that they serve, and the quality of democratic politics and cultural life suffers as a result (Klinenberg, 2007, p. 26). Less local staffing, less local news gathering, and less interaction with the local community means less ability to play the democratic role that many observers would like to see.

At the same time, people are fighting back, and they're increasingly doing so online. Citizen journalism has exploded in the last decade, in large part because barriers to entry are so low. In the mid-1990s, a group called Radio Mutiny set up an unsanctioned pirate radio station in West Philadelphia as a challenge to corporate media, but doing so took nine months of hard work to build the transmitter (Klinenberg, 2007). Setting up a blog, by contrast, takes only a minute or so. The Internet has lowered the bar for entering the public sphere, allowing the people formerly known as the audience to assert their own voices, if not nearly as forcefully as the conglomerates such as Clear Channel, Disney, and even Google.

The most spectacular incidence of Internet activism and democracy in recent years is the 2011 Arab Spring uprising in the Middle East, and particularly the mass Tahrir Square demonstrations in Egypt that overthrew the government of dictator Hosni Mubarak. Across the region, people protested against their governments, most visibly by gathering in large numbers in public squares. Within a few months, four national governments were forced from power, and a number more only narrowly avoided that fate. Here social networks, and in particular Twitter, were often held to be crucial to activists' organizing efforts by allowing people to coordinate their protests and get up-to-the-minute information on what was happening elsewhere. At the same time, governments in Egypt and other parts of the Middle East also used social media in their attempts to repress the civilian uprising.

Despite the ongoing development of grassroots and citizen-led media activism, it would be a mistake to view the Internet as the remedy for the troubles of the contemporary media landscape. Although it empowers people to easily post and share content with each other, setting up a blog is of course no guarantee that anyone will read it. There is evidence that readership online follows roughly the same pattern as readership offline—a large majority of people get their news from a tiny number of sites, while most sites get virtually no traffic at all (Hindman, 2008). Moreover, the Internet has not necessarily made it any easier to monitor the activities of the powerful—a key traditional role of journalism. And corporations are increasingly finding ways to subvert the apparently democratic nature of social media by hiring people to post and monitor content. Finally, the actual efficacy of online activism, for example in the Arab Spring, has yet to be proven. There is no doubt that activists are using Twitter as a key tool for communication and mobilization, but we don't yet know if this actually makes a difference to the outcomes. It is more realistic to say that the Internet has created both new opportunities and new dangers for the free media and for democracy.

Conclusion

It is the nature of culture that it changes dramatically over time and across locations. The collective meaning and shared rituals of the Balinese cockfight from 50 years ago would probably be scarcely recognizable to contemporary Indonesians, and no doubt the culture of early-twenty-first-century North America will seem equally strange to Canadians and Americans in 50 or 100 years. What would be truly shocking is if culture stayed the same.

But even compared to a baseline of ongoing cultural change, it is fair to say that a dramatic cultural transformation has been occurring in recent decades in North America and throughout the world with the rise of the Internet and global cultural flows. Many of the most pressing questions for the sociological study of culture in coming years will likely be concerned with the implications of the Internet and other new forms of interconnectivity that social media in all its forms has begun to deliver.

We shouldn't make the mistake, though, of assuming that the increasing prominence of the Internet in society means that all of our important cultural questions will be online ones. The persistence of offline forms of social life—street life, public performances, print media, poorer communities that do not have easy access to the necessary technology, and more—in an online world will be an increasingly urgent focus of research and public policy. Will the digital divide get wider or narrower in years to come, and what will be the implications for cultural production, communications, and democracy?

CHAPTER SUMMARY

The Big Questions Revisited 6

6.1 What Is Culture? This section explored how sociologists talk about culture as a shared system of meaning and symbols; a set of values, beliefs, and practices; and shared forms of communication.

The Many Meanings of Culture

Defining Culture

Learning Objective 6.1.1: Define culture from a sociological perspective.

Culture as a System of Meaning and Symbols

Learning Objective 6.1.2: Explain how a group's symbols can be considered its culture, and give examples of collective symbols of contemporary North American culture.

Culture as a Set of Values, Beliefs, and Practices

Learning Objective 6.1.3: Describe how our values and beliefs influence how we live our lives.

Culture as a Form of Communication

Learning Objective 6.1.4: Explain the ways in which culture is a form of communication.

6.2 How Does Culture Shape Our Collective Identity? This section explored how cultural practices both reflect and define group identities, whether the group is a small subculture or a nation.

Culture and Group Identity

Mainstream Culture, Subcultures, and Countercultures

Learning Objective 6.2.1: Discuss the role that culture plays in establishing group style, and explain what distinguishes a subculture from the mainstream.

Is There a Dominant Culture in North America Today?

Learning Objective 6.2.2: Discuss the concept of "culture wars" and explain the importance of practising cultural relativism in a multicultural North America.

National Cultures

Learning Objective 6.2.3: Explain what produces and reproduces national cultures, and what effects they have.

6.3 **How Do Our Cultural Practices Relate to Class and Status?** In this section, we discussed how people's cultural habits help define and reproduce the boundaries between high status and low status, upper class and lower class.

Class, Status, and Culture

Cultural Capital

Learning Objective 6.3.1: Define cultural capital and discuss ways North American elites have become cultural omnivores.

How Culture Reproduces Class

Learning Objective 6.3.2: Analyze how money and culture reproduce status over the long term.

6.4 **Who Produces Culture, and Why?** The cultural field is the place for creativity and meaning making. But it is also a battlefield. In this section, we explored who controls the media and popular culture and what messages they communicate.

The Conditions of Cultural Production

The Public Sphere

Learning Objective 6.4.1: Analyze how the concept of the public sphere explains how culture is produced in society.

The Culture Industry Versus Cultural Democracy

Learning Objective 6.4.2: Compare and contrast the cultural industry and the cultural democracy perspectives.

The Medium Is the Message

Learning Objective 6.4.3: Discuss the ways in which communication changes with the form or medium.

6.5 **What Is the Relationship Between Media and Democracy?** The media are arguably the most important form of cultural production in our society. This section examined the media's relationship to democracy and the new ways in which it is changing how democracy works.

Media and Democracy: A Changing Landscape

Making the News: The Media as a Cultural System

Learning Objective 6.5.1: Explain the role that the media play in making the news.

Corporate Media Concentration

Learning Objective 6.5.2: Identify three trends in the media landscape that have put commercial pressure on journalism.

Media, Democracy, and the Internet

Learning Objective 6.5.3: Discuss the ways the Internet has created new opportunities and dangers for the free media and for democracy.

Learn the Terms

class reproduction (p. 158)
counterculture (p. 151)
counterpublic (p. 161)
cultural capital (p. 157)
cultural omnivore (p. 158)
cultural relativism (p. 154)
cultural universal (p. 147)
culture (p. 145)
culture industry (p. 161)
culture wars (p. 152)
digital divide (p. 149)
ethnocentrism (p. 152)
group style (p. 150)
habitus (p. 146)
hegemony (p. 151)
journalism (p. 164)
language (p. 147)
mainstream culture (p. 150)
mass communication (p. 148)
multiculturalism (p. 152)
national culture (p. 154)
nationalism (p. 154)
networked public (p. 161)
public sphere (p. 160)
subculture (p. 151)
symbol (p. 145)
taste (p. 157)
tool kit (p. 146)
value (p. 146)

Chapter 7

Power and Politics

by Steven Lukes and Jeff Manza

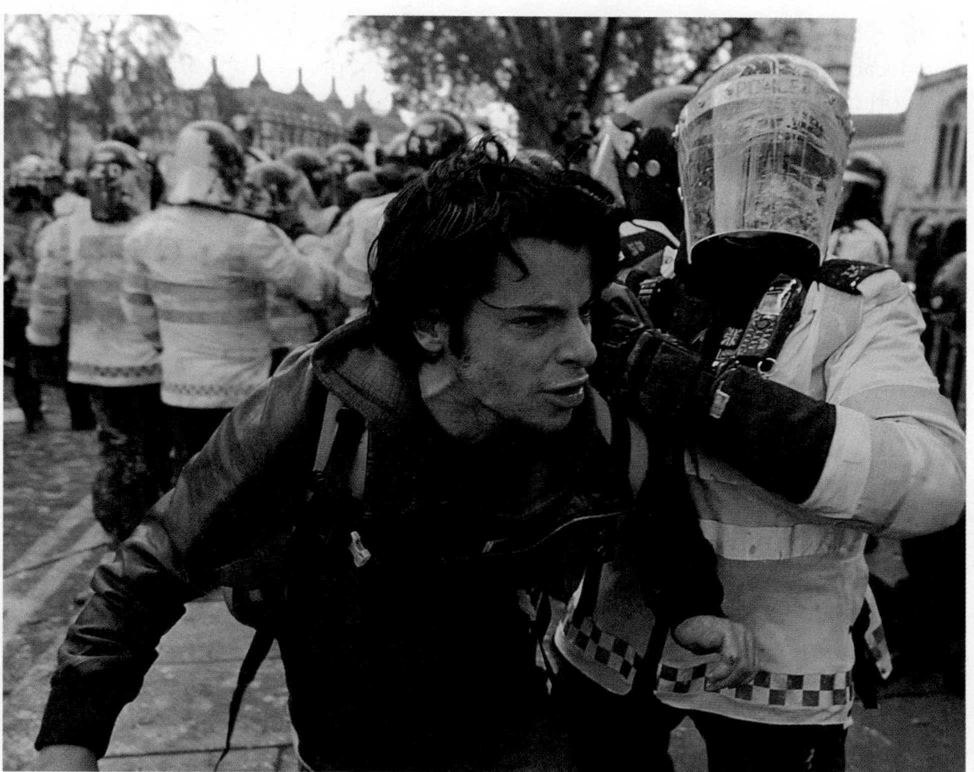

Robert Munro/Alamy Stock Photo

In Parliament Square, London, a protestor is detained by police following clashes during student demonstrations over the proposal to triple university tuition fees. Why are protests like this one so unusual?

Learning Objectives

7.1.1 Identify who has power in the one-dimensional view.

7.1.2 Explain the role of agenda setting in the second dimension of power.

7.1.3 Discuss the various ways in which the workings of power can be hidden.

7.2.1 Define the state and explain how it regulates the economy.

7.2.2 Explain how the state influences who gets what government services.

7.2.3 Discuss how and why states tend to adjust their policies to support the goals of powerful business interests, and identify exceptions.

7.3.1 Discuss what tax policies and antipoverty programs tell us about how power is distributed in North America.

7.3.2 Explain how agenda setting occurs.

7.3.3 Analyze views on policies involving income inequality and the redistribution of wealth.

The decade of the 1960s is famous today as a period of protest and turmoil all around the world. In the United States, protests against the Vietnam War were reaching their peak, and other kinds of social movements were also sprouting up, especially on college campuses. One particularly dramatic set of protests took place at Columbia University in New York City in April 1968. Student rebels, demanding a variety of changes in the governance of the tradition-bound Ivy League campus, had taken over the office of university president Grayson Kirk. After the students had occupied the office for several days, police officers stormed President Kirk's office and forced them out. Here is how one observer described the scene:

> *One and a half hours after the President's suite had been cleared of student demonstrators, Grayson Kirk stood in the center of his private office looking at the blankets, cigarette butts and orange peels that covered his rug. Turning to A. M. Rosenthal of the* New York Times *and several other reporters who had come into the office with him he murmured, "My God how could human beings do a thing like this?" It was the only time, Truman [Kirk's dean] recalled later, that he had ever seen the President break down. Kirk's windows were crisscrossed with tape and on one hung a large sign reading "Join Us." His lampshades were torn, his carpet was spotted, his furniture was displaced and scratched. But the most evident and disturbing aspect of the scene was not the minor damage inflicted by the students. The everything-in-its-place decor to which Kirk had grown accustomed was now in disarray—disarray that was the result of the transformation of an office into the living quarters of 150 students during the past six days. (Avorn, 1968, p. 200)*

Commenting on this report, the famous sociologist Erving Goffman wrote:

> *The sociological question, of course, is not how could it be that human beings would do a thing like this, but rather how is it that human beings do this sort of thing so rarely. How come persons in authority have been so overwhelmingly successful in conning those beneath them into keeping the hell out of their offices? (Goffman, 1971, p.)*

Goffman's astute observation highlights a critical question for the sociologist studying power and politics: Why is it that, in most times and places, people accept injustice and learn to live with it? Why don't the vastly larger poor and middle classes demand a greater share of societal wealth?

In this chapter, we will explore these questions by examining power and its political underpinnings. Power is a complex idea. We are often not fully aware of the impact that power has on us, and sometimes we are not aware of its operation at all. Sometimes we can be mistaken about the causes of what afflicts us, and we may see power at work when it is not, attributing our misfortunes to conspiracies of one sort or another. One huge task for the sociologist studying power is to shed light on power at work. What are its typical *mechanisms*, or modes of operation? Why do we sometimes go along with relationships or support government policies that work against our interests? Does power influence our compliance, and, if so, how is our compliance secured? And where does power lie? Who has power? Are we looking for individuals, or groups, or impersonal institutions? Are the answers to such questions always obvious? As we will see, power is most effective when it is least observable to participants and observers alike. And if that is so, then the task facing the sociologist of power is all the more daunting.

The Big Questions

In this chapter, we explore three central questions.

1. **What are the distinct forms of power?** In this section, we explore the three dimensions of power, using a sociological lens to examine not only the most visible ways in which power is expressed but also its more subtle forms.
2. **What is the state, and how does it distribute power in a society?** Here, we examine the institutions of power, which sociologists refer to as *the state*. We explore how and why states matter in the distribution of power, and why states tend to promote the interests of the powerful.
3. **Who has power in North America today?** Our discussion of the dimensions of power and political institutions leads us to an examination of the Canadian political system. How is Canada different from other, similar countries in the way power is distributed in national politics?

AP Images

Student rebels assist each other in climbing up into the offices of Columbia University president Grayson Kirk at the campus in New York City, April 24, 1968.

7.1 What Are the Distinct Forms of Power?

Ben Stansall/Getty Images

The Three Dimensions of Power

Power in the most general sense simply means the capacity to bring about some outcome; in other words, either to effect changes or to prevent changes from occurring. In social and political contexts, the effects of power will be those that are significant to people's lives. When these effects of power negatively affect someone's interests, we can speak of power being held or exercised *over* them. In such cases, the sociologist's quest is to try to reveal what this involves. There are also other ways of identifying social and political power: for instance, as *collective* power to achieve shared goals (as when people cooperate to promote a cause or a campaign) or as *positive* power, where power serves others' interests (as, ideally, parents, teachers, doctors, philanthropists, and social workers are supposed to do).

In this chapter, we will first focus on what is involved in having and exercising power over others and then turn to an analysis of how power over others can be extended to the capacity to achieve goals through the political system.

It is useful to think of power as containing three distinct "dimensions," as Table 7.1 illustrates. The first of these dimensions—the one-dimensional view—involves situations where we can see power at work when one party prevails in a conflict. A second dimension of power involves the ways in which those with power prevent or deflect

Table 7.1 The Three Dimensions of Power

	First Dimension	Second Dimension	Third Dimension
Power of A over B	A has superior resources and wins open conflicts.	A constructs or benefits from barriers that prevent B from challenging A's position or even raising a challenge in the first place.	A influences B to support or think the way A does, even when it is not in B's interests to do so.
Powerlessness of B versus A	B has few resources to win open conflicts.	B fails to get its challenge to A to be taken seriously, or B is so frustrated by lack of power that B fails to issue a challenge to A.	B comes to believe in A's ideas even when it is not in B's interests to do so.

SOURCE: Adapted from *Power and Powerlessness: Quiescence and Rebellion in an Appalachian Valley*, p. 21, by John Gaventa, 1980, Oxford: Clarendon Press.

challenges to their authority from arising in the first place. Finally, a third dimension occurs when those with power are able to convince those without that their views are correct and should be accepted or assumed to be correct. In this case, power may appear completely invisible.

The One-Dimensional View of Power

7.1.1 Identify who has power in the one-dimensional view.

The most straightforward situation where we can see power at work is one where there is a conflict between two or more individuals or groups and one of them prevails. Let's call the more powerful individual or group "A" and the less powerful individual or group "B." There are countless examples of power at work in this observable form, involving conflict over an issue or issues for which the participants have interests that are in contention. The conflict can be interpersonal—between lovers or within families—or it can occur within or between organizations. It can even exist between countries.

A bully in the schoolyard, a mugger in the street, a landlord versus a tenant, a struggle between employers and unions over wages, a group of people rising against a dictatorship, a country locked in civil war or at war with other countries—all of these involve power in a directly visible form. Sometimes, the balance of power can shift and the usually powerless agent can gain and sometimes exercise power. In some cases, the power of the powerful is illegitimate (such as the bully or the mugger), sometimes legitimate (the landlord's rent might be legal and fair), and sometimes (as, for example, in a war within or between countries) what is right and wrong itself may be what is at issue (that is, whoever wins a war gets to write history).

Power is often exercised just by following the "rules of the game." For example, when companies compete for market share in selling some good or service, they are playing by the rules of the economic game. When a group of legislators wins a vote, they are using the rules to compete (and win) in the political game. But in other cases, those who win may do so not by *following* the rules of the game but rather by *manipulating* them in some way. Using threats or bribes to get what you want are examples of how someone or some group can gain power by breaking the rules.

But exercising power by breaking the rules of the game is an uncertain undertaking. For example, when threats of violence escalate into the actual use of force, it means that the mere threat itself has failed. The use of force often signifies weakness. For example, when governments headed by dictators face social rebellions, as we saw in some of the Arab Spring protests in the Middle East in 2011, they often use military force to try to stop the protests. This may stop or slow down the protests, but in many cases these governments will eventually fall if protests continue to grow and if force is not enough to intimidate people into ending their protests. Indeed, using force over and over is rarely sustainable over the long haul. If the more powerful A must use force against the less powerful B, A has not succeeded in getting B to comply but only to temporarily give in.

In a display of one-dimensional power, antigovernment protestors demonstrate in the streets of Syria demanding the ousting of President Bashar al-Assad.

Ali Bitar/UPI/Landov

The Two-Dimensional View of Power

7.1.2 Explain the role of agenda setting in the second dimension of power.

Treating power as a one-dimensional process focused only on outcomes when there is conflict ignores the fascinating puzzle of why some important issues or ideas never come up for discussion or debate in decision-making arenas. We can define a second dimension of power in which a power holder (A) prevents a subordinate group or individual (B) from raising issues that would challenge A's power. Power in this second dimension refers to the ability of some actors to prevent others from ever getting alternative ideas proposed or considered in the first place. This process, like one-dimensional power, is present at all levels of social life, from interpersonal relationships to international relations between countries. It is the power to decide what gets decided. But it is usually less visible than the overt conflicts that typify the first dimension of power.

At the heart of the second dimension of power is the process of **agenda setting**—the act of consciously or unconsciously averting the challenge of potential issues that the more powerful actor would rather avoid. The ability to control or set the agenda is a critical resource of power whether we are talking about relationships between couples or families or in Parliament or the United Nations. When power is exercised through agenda control, the *grievances* of excluded or marginal groups can be denied a hearing. There are a variety of ways agenda control can be achieved, the most common being the literal manipulation of agendas through the control of procedures, thereby affecting what gets discussed and decided. For example, if a city council does not want to respond to a citizen's complaints that streets are not being cleared of snow fast enough, the council may try to avoid holding hearings to learn more about the issue.

This second dimension of power requires us to stretch our understanding of what issues are important where power may be at stake: They are not *just* those that are the subject of open conflict but *also* those that are prevented from becoming the subject of challenge. Small children might prefer that more of the family budget be spent on candy than on vegetables or that more (or less) time be spent with relatives, but parents typically do not let small children have much say over what kinds of foods the family buys or how many times the family visits relatives. In this way, the parents control the agenda for discussion without the child even necessarily being aware of it. The same kind of dynamic arises in politics. Researchers have puzzled over why some topics are the focus of intense discussion and debate while other equally or even more important topics are ignored. Why do some issues become widely discussed social problems, while other equally pressing issues do not?

Among the most important examples of this, from a sociological perspective, is the relative lack of attention to issues surrounding the persistence of poverty, racism, and rising inequality versus the enormous amount of attention given to the health and well-being of big business, banks, and corporate profits. For example, every print newspaper in North America has a section devoted to business, covering the comings and goings of business executives and the profitability (or lack thereof) of various local and national companies, and every day the ups and downs of the stock market are widely covered. But there is no comparable devoted coverage of the daily grind of poverty, or the insecurity faced by millions of North American families, or the trials and tribulations of the groups that try to represent the interests of the poor.

The study of agenda setting has paid special attention to the mass media (such as television, newspapers, talk radio, and online news sites) as crucial sites where the second dimension of power operates. When the media gives a large amount of attention to a particular issue, it becomes much more likely that that issue will receive the attention of politicians and policymakers. The fact that coverage of big business is so pronounced is perhaps unsurprising once we observe that most important media outlets are themselves owned by corporate entities or conglomerates. The search for profit in the news media is also a critical factor determining what we read or watch. Much of the focus of the media today is driven by editors' perceptions of what sells—that is, what citizens are most interested in reading about. For example, there is an old saying that "if it bleeds, it leads": Sensational stories about murders and other violent crimes (and usually the more gory the better) have always generated a lot of attention. Celebrities and celebrity gossip also generate intense fascination. The celebrity in trouble with the law, or celebrity couples falling in and out of love or marriage, can be sure to provoke especially intense coverage, with only the names changing from year to year. By contrast, the media usually pays much less attention to those who challenge the status quo and seldom provides opportunities for challengers to reach other like-minded people.

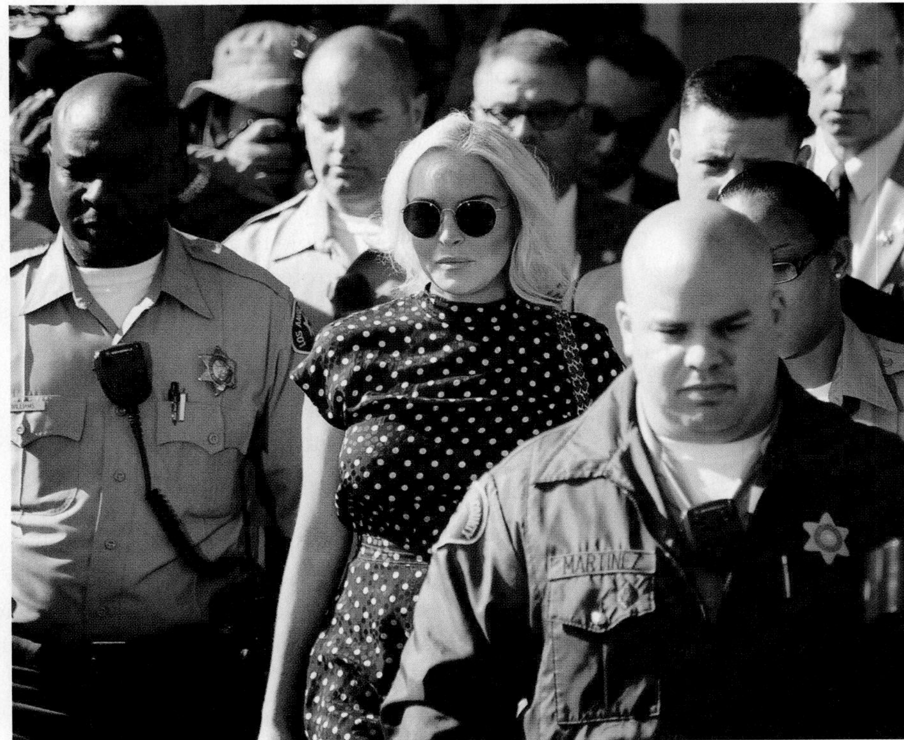

News stories about celebrities, like Lindsay Lohan (shown here), always generate intense fascination in the media. Why do these types of news reports get so much more attention than reports about wars or poverty?

The Three-Dimensional View of Power

7.1.3 Discuss the various ways in which the workings of power can be hidden.

The first and second dimensions of power are important, but they do not exhaust the possibilities. Seeing power three-dimensionally involves understanding the various ways in which its workings can be hidden from the view of those subject to it and perhaps even from those who possess power. A third dimension of power operates when a powerful actor can persuade a weaker actor to adopt beliefs or behaviours that serve the interests of the powerful. Power can, in some cases, result from the *anticipation* by others of what they believe the powerful would do if they were not to comply with their interests.

Research on power has demonstrated that in many contexts people will defer to, or are even attracted toward, those with power. The power of wealth, privilege, and **status**—the prestige accorded to individuals and to important social or economic roles—is often at work without the powerful having to lift a finger to exercise it or even being conscious of its impact or its reach. Many of us behave differently in the presence of the powerful or famous than with other people. When the boss visits the office or when a celebrity walks into a restaurant, we may make extra efforts to try to ensure their happiness. These powerful people do not even need to assert their authority to secure respect or obedience from others.

A three-dimensional view of power questions the notion that whenever conflict is absent, people are content. The most effective—and potentially the most sneaky—use of power is to prevent conflict from arising in the first place by

Charles Wilson, then president of General Motors (GM), declared, "What is good for General Motors is good for America," during congressional testimony in 1953. But do all citizens benefit from policies that make GM more profitable?

persuading B that whatever A wants is in B's best interests. Power holders may attempt to gain consent for their power by shaping the perceptions and beliefs of the powerless. Where the powerful are in the business of preserving and protecting the status quo, the effects of such power are to encourage people to accept their role in the existing order of things—perhaps because they cannot imagine any alternative, or they see the status quo as impossible to change, or they see it as divinely ordained and beneficial. All of these reasons have been invoked to encourage ordinary people to accept the rule of kings or dictators. But just because people don't actively protest against a dictator or king does not prove that their apparent consent is not the outcome of power. To assume that the absence of a grievance is the same thing as genuine consensus rules out the possibility of manipulation in how people think.

The powerful are often in a position to prevent change by exploiting their power in an attempt to shape perceptions and get people to accept as true all kinds of mythical and simplistic versions of reality. Those in power may do this by playing not only on their followers' fears, prejudices, and limited information but also on the many ways in which people are susceptible to biased and/or faulty reasoning. In the most extreme form, such as propaganda issued by a dictator's government, the attempt at persuasion is open and direct. But persuasion can be more subtle and need not be deliberately engaged in, and it can coexist with power in the first and second dimensions. For example, the threat of a punishment and the offer of a reward can be combined. Bosses may try to persuade their workers not to go on strike by offering them a modest pay raise or some other benefit while holding out the threat that the business will be moved or that workers will lose their jobs if they do go on strike, and at the same time co-opting their leaders and benefiting from "symbolic power" that appeals to workers' patriotism or their loyalty to their company (or both).

The three-dimensional view enables us to see that power over others is not always simply a matter of being able to prevail over them when conflicts of interest occur, or even to set the agenda of what such conflicts are about. It can also consist of being able to secure the dependence, allegiance, or compliance of others. That compliance may occur without the powerful needing to act, and it can exist without conflict when the powerful shape the preferences of others in ways that work against their interests. The third dimension of power, in other words, reveals itself when the powerless embrace the interests of the powerful as their own. Consider the famous slogan uttered by Charles Wilson, then president of General Motors (GM), during congressional testimony in 1953, when he declared, "What is good for General Motors is good for America." All citizens benefit, in other words, from policies that make GM more profitable. What Wilson had in mind when he made this statement was that when GM is profitable, it will hire more workers and generate more business for the subcontractors who supply GM with parts used in the manufacture of automobiles. But GM—or any large corporation—does not exist only to provide jobs for North American workers; it also tries to maximize its profits and payouts to its shareholders. In order to maximize profits, GM has an interest in trying to keep the wages it pays its workers as low as possible, to have minimal regulations applied to its products, to try to pay as little in corporate taxes as it can, to not have to spend large sums to reduce the pollution it causes, and so forth. None of these things are likely to be in the general interests of all citizens or even of all GM workers not in the top management of the company.

Thus far, we have suggested that a sociological understanding of power compels us to examine not only the most visible ways in which power is expressed but also its more subtle forms. Power may be revealed in open conflict, but it may also reflect the ability of a power holder to keep challenges from arising in the first place or even the capacity of a power holder to convince subordinate groups that it is in their interests to support the existing arrangement.

7.2 What Is the State, and How Does It Distribute Power in a Society?

Adwo/Fotolia

The Institutions of Power

Power in all of its forms can be expressed in any setting in a multitude of ways. A parent, a teacher, a small business owner, and a religious leader may all have some kinds of power, but power is consequential on a grand scale when the government is involved. Governments make laws, spend large sums of money on a huge number of areas, tax individuals and companies, and prepare for (and sometimes go to) war. Large government **bureaucracies** define policies and procedures, and issue and administer regulations that are to be adhered to by others. Courts and legal institutions interpret and enforce laws and government policies (and sometimes find those policies unconstitutional). Taken as a whole, these institutions are supposed to make our lives better, but they also have a huge impact on the overall distribution of power in any society. We now turn to an examination of these institutions and the question of who gets what from government.

What Is the State?

7.2.1 Define the state and explain how it regulates the economy.

Sociologists use the term **the state** to refer to all of the formal political institutions of any society. In Canada these include the three branches of government (the executive, legislative, and judicial branches), as well as all of the bureaucracies that support the work of each branch. Other government institutions at lower levels of administration—such as local governments or intermediate regional governments (like the "state" government in California or Texas, or provincial governments in Canada)—can also be considered part of the state, but in this chapter we will focus on federal political institutions.

It is important to note that the state is not simply just an elected government, like the Liberal government or the House of Commons. Although elected officials are certainly key parts of the state during the time they hold office, the state in Canada also includes the queen (our head of state, represented in Canada by the governor general) and the Senate, as well as the legal system (and the courts that enforce the law), the military, and those permanent bureaucracies that remain in place regardless of who is the head of the current government. In the United States, for example, a new president appoints a few thousand senior administrators and staff on taking office, but the entire U.S. federal government employs over 3 million people. Most of these employees remain in office no matter who is president. Similarly, judges are often appointed for long terms or for life and are not dependent on who holds elected office. In Canada, when the prime minister leaves office and a new government is elected, those permanent bureaucracies continue doing what they were before the change in elected government. This is one reason why bringing about change in federal politics—irrespective of which major party is in office—is often difficult to achieve.

What are the powers of the state? Adam Smith (1723–1790), the great theorist of the emerging system of capitalism in the eighteenth century, famously described capitalism as an economic system governed by the "invisible hand" of the free market, in which successful entrepreneurs and efficient producers would be rewarded and those with bad ideas or products competed out of business. This imagery, although not at all representative of Smith's more complex views, has proved a remarkably powerful one over the nearly 250 years since Smith's famous work *The Wealth of Nations* was first published in 1776. But that image is fundamentally misleading in several critical respects, which Smith himself noted elsewhere in his magnum opus. For example, in order for markets to function properly, the state has to provide a wide range of legal guarantees and rules, and must have the capacity to enforce those rules when they are violated. For example, market exchanges rely on contracts. A contract exists when one person agrees to provide a certain good at a certain price and the other person agrees to pay that price. As long as both parties do what they promise, the terms of the contract are fulfilled and everyone is more or less satisfied. But what happens when one party fails to do what it promises? It is ultimately state institutions—sometimes the courts, sometimes government agencies—that normally provide the necessary assurance that if one party fails to live up to its contractual commitments, it will be penalized (this is not true, of course, for illegal organizations like the Mafia, which have their own methods of enforcing rule violations that do not rely on the state). For most individuals and business organizations, however, the critical backing provided by the state makes contractual exchange possible.

Laws and regulations exist to prevent companies from falsely advertising their products, such as labelling nonorganic food products organic.

allesalltag/Alamy Stock Photo

The role of the state has grown over time to include a wide range of other supports that help make both the economy and society work. One of the most important thing states do is *regulate* the economy in ways that try to provide a level playing field for all participants and to prevent economic actors from harming innocent third parties. Here are examples of important regulatory policies designed to protect citizens from being harmed by economic actors that all modern states have some version of:

- Laws and policies that prevent large corporations from taking advantage of their size to cut special deals with suppliers or using their size to drive competitors out of business and create uncompetitive monopolies (for example, in the 1990s when the Microsoft Corporation provided low-priced operating software for new computers but then made it difficult for consumers to run non-Microsoft programs).
- Laws preventing stock market traders from using insider knowledge to unfairly profit (for example, if employees at a company know of a new product that will increase the value of the firm's stock, they are not entitled to use that knowledge to buy up the company's stock in advance of the new product's release and later sell at a profit).
- Laws and regulations that prevent firms from making false advertising claims about their products (for example, not allowing a food manufacturer to call nonorganic food products organic).
- Laws and regulations that require companies to meet minimal standards in terms of safety for workers and consumers (for example, laws barring a clothing manufacturer from making clothes that might catch on fire).
- Laws and regulations that make companies or individuals compensate innocent third parties when their actions cause harm (for example, if a company's factory creates pollution that damages the health of families living nearby).

These examples are just some of the many ways that modern states act to try to solve some of the problems and limitations of a market economy. In each of these cases, one can argue that the regulations are in the general interests of the broad public: They make sure that there is competition between firms, and protect consumers and innocent third parties. These policies also give individuals who want to start a business a reasonable expectation that if the goods or services they provide are of high enough quality, they will be able to compete against existing businesses on fair terms.

The state also provides much needed infrastructure for the economy to work. The state funds and operates most of the schools where future workers learn to read, write, and think. It builds and maintains the roads, bridges, and trains that businesses use to transport goods to markets. It operates the airports and regulates the skies so that planes do not crash into each other. It runs the military and the police. It provides healthcare and old age income for elder workers who can no longer work so employers don't feel obligated to keep them employed. Indeed, the list of things that "big government" does that make possible so many other beneficial activities is so long that it is virtually impossible to imagine a modern economy—or society—without it.

Why States Matter in the Distribution of Power

7.2.2 Explain how the state influences who gets what government services.

The policies and programs adopted and maintained by the state are hugely important in many different ways, but they can be designed in ways that help some people more than others. Policies could, for example, be designed to ensure that poor families receive a greater share of the economic pie, or, by contrast, they can be designed to allow the rich to maintain or even increase their share of wealth. These policies, known as *tax and transfer policies*, are especially important for the distribution of income and wealth. All governments must tax their citizens to pay for government services, but whether the rich will pay a higher share than the poor varies widely across countries and over time.

Taken as a whole, *who gets what* is at least partly determined by the policies of the governmental agencies. Here are a few of the many examples of how states impact who gets what in any society:

- States set or alter the rules of the game within which individuals and groups contest each other for power—policies can favour big business, small business, farmers, or workers and unions, but not everyone at the same time. For example, states decide whether or not employers have to take special precautions to ensure their workplace is safe, or whether water in areas that don't get much rain will go to farmers or to urban areas, and a vast number of similar decisions.
- States allocate a huge amount of resources and income through various kinds of spending programs, collectively known as the **welfare state**. These programs include pensions for the elderly (primarily known as Old Age Security in Canada), unemployment insurance, welfare programs for poor families, and many other such social programs.
- States decide who bears the burdens of paying for all government public spending programs, primarily through their tax policies (for example, should tax burdens be equal for everyone, or should the rich pay a higher percentage, or should companies be taxed on the profits they earn?).
- States have the power to decide such life-and-death matters as whether a country goes to war (and who has to fight that war) or whether the death penalty is legal (and whether the government is allowed to kill). Other life-defining public policies include whether or not food and housing shall be provided to those who cannot afford to pay for it themselves. Should those who are truly destitute be given the means to survive or not?

In each of these policy areas, states make choices that impact the distribution of power across the entire society. In many important ways, states provide the institutional backdrop for market economies to function and directly or indirectly ensure that investments can be made profitably. Sometimes states will directly intervene on behalf of the powerful, especially in periods of political conflict and stress. But states are not simply tools of the ruling classes of a society. States also make policy decisions, as we will see, that can empower the poor and help the disadvantaged obtain a greater share of the benefits of economic growth.

Promoting the Interests of the Powerful?

7.2.3 Discuss how and why states tend to adjust their policies to support the goals of powerful business interests, and identify exceptions.

In this section, we will examine some general reasons why states more often than not adopt policies in the interests of the powerful. Why might this be the case? Or more specifically, how and why do states tend to adjust their policies to support the goals of powerful business interests over ordinary people?

Social scientists who have studied this question have proposed two broad sets of answers. The first view is what we might call the *business confidence* theory of the state (Block, 1987). It holds that whatever the preferences of government officials (for example, whether a Liberal or a Conservative is prime minister), the state as a whole has a powerful incentive to make sure that big business interests have the confidence and security they need to want to make investments that will create jobs and produce economic growth. When entrepreneurs and business executives think that business conditions are not favourable, their willingness to invest declines. Because the overall health of the economy is so important, states are driven to adopt policies that will convince business leaders that the economy will remain healthy in the near future. In the era of economic globalization, maintaining a healthy business environment at home is important for discouraging companies from moving abroad, or alternatively, for encouraging foreign companies to invest in your country. A newly elected government has to take these issues into consideration.

The second argument for why states tend to promote the interests of the powerful focuses on the relative political power of different groups in democratic political systems, which can vary over time but often provide more affluent individuals and corporations privileged access to government officials (Domhoff, 2006; Hacker & Pierson, 2010). Large corporations and rich individuals simply have more resources to influence political life than do other groups representing working-class and middle-class people. For example, rich individuals and corporations will try to influence elections and election outcomes by donating large amounts of money to candidates they favour, but they also gain close connections to these candidates and office-holders, who need those donations to win office in the first place. As a result, corporate executives and rich individuals are also far more likely to have access to politicians than are poor or middle-class people. They tend to travel in some of the same circles and clubs, and their donations will open doors when something of importance is being debated and discussed. The upshot of this disproportionate influence is that policies will often tend to favour the interests and preferences of the powerful and well organized. As we will see in the next section, there is plenty of evidence in support of this argument.

Taken together, these two theories tend to suggest that policy will always favour the powerful. But exceptions do occur; sometimes the powerless get what they want instead (Piven & Cloward, 1997). In the late 1920s, a range of new government programs were adopted in the wider context of the First World War, which had emphasized the negative effects of industrialization and urbanization in Canada. With the rise of Western, farmer-based political parties in Canada, Old Age Security was adopted to offset the negative effects of the market economy, particularly for the elderly and women who had lost husbands and sons during the war. Later, in the 1960s, Lester B. Pearson's Liberal government would also implement student loan programs to encourage wider access to post-secondary education, along with universal healthcare and the Canada Pension Plan. These examples suggest that it is hardly the case that the powerful always win. When the poor are well organized into social movements, they can sometimes exert influence over the direction of policy. If there is one thing that both the 1920s and 1960s had in common, it is that in both eras, large social movements (of mostly farmers, trade unions, and the unemployed in the 1920s, and of those who participated in the civil rights movement in the 1960s) changed the context of political power.

But large social movements of the poor or working class are relatively rare. How is power distributed in more normal circumstances? What role does the state play? We turn to a more specific examination of that question in the next section of the chapter.

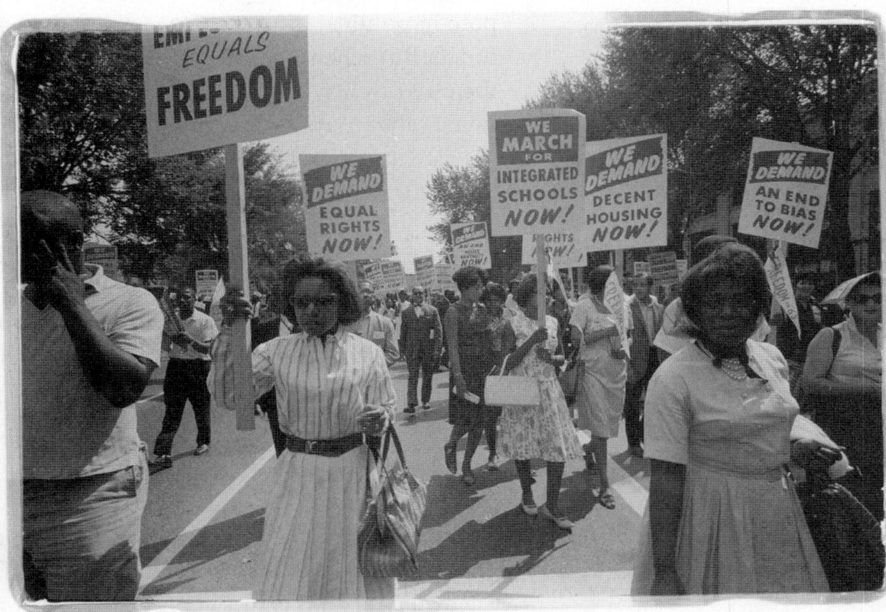

The civil rights movement pushing for the integration of schools in the 1960s helped change the context of political power in the United States.

Library of Congress Prints and Photographs Division [LC-DIG-ppmsca-03128]

7.3 Who Has Power in North America Today?

Adrian Wyld/Associated Press

Power in North America

A sociological analysis of power provides a different way of understanding North American politics than what is typically reported in the news media. Ordinarily, we think or hear only about the first dimension of power: who wins elections (or who is ahead in the polls leading up to an election); the outcomes of debates over the passage of particularly important laws or government programs; or conflicts over foreign and military policy. Most of what we read about national politics involves such openly contested conflicts over public policy decisions. These are important aspects of any **democracy**, a political system in which all citizens have equal rights to participate in political life (to vote, to run for office, to have freedom of expression, and so forth). But when we inspect North American democracies more closely, we also find the other dimensions of power shaping political outcomes in complicated ways that do not always reflect the political equality model of how a democracy is supposed to operate. In this section, we will discuss how the government operates by examining each of the three dimensions of power.

Who Wins? Policy and Politics in the First Dimension

7.3.1 Discuss what tax policies and antipoverty programs tell us about how power is distributed in North America.

The first dimension of power in North American politics concerns the question of who wins (or more specifically, who can achieve their goals) when there is open conflict. In many cases, at least in recent years, these conflicts have sometimes put most or all conservatives on one side and most or all liberals on the other side of the conflict. Other issues are more complicated and do not always cleanly break along party lines. When the issues under discussion become especially heated—for example, during the expense claim controversy about the spending habits of Conservative-appointed senators Pamela Wallin and Mike Duffy in the fall of 2013—the debates in the media that ensue hold everyone's attention for a brief period. Most of the time, however, the issues being discussed and debated in Ottawa are obscure to most Canadians. On most issues, only professional policy analysts and political insiders fully understand all of the details of policy proposals and appreciate what it is at stake. Many important decisions are made largely outside of the public's view.

When it comes to the national politics of the first dimension of power, a sociological perspective urges that we take a step back from a narrow focus on these day-to-day conflicts to ask: What are the broad patterns buried in these outcomes? We do not have enough space in this chapter to consider a wide range of political outcomes from open political conflicts, but we can focus on a set of policies that are among the most important: policies that impact the distribution of wealth and inequality. More specifically, we will focus on two: (1) *tax policies*, especially some of the political changes in the ways taxes are paid that have enabled the super wealthy to take home a much greater share of the economic pie than they do in all other rich, democratic countries most like Canada and the United States; and (2) *antipoverty programs*, or more specifically, why it is that the policies of the North American governments do the least, of any of the rich countries most similar to us, to reduce poverty and help families live in a minimally acceptable way.

Beginning with taxes, both Canada and the United States have an extraordinarily high concentration of income and wealth at the very top. Canada's tax policy disproportionately benefits the wealthy. Tax policy is one of the most powerful public policy tools of government because it allows states to redistribute resources and reduce inequalities. Changes to the Canadian tax system since the mid-1990s have reinforced income inequality, and tax cuts have disproportionately benefited the wealthy (Lee & Ivanova, 2013). Canada's corporate income tax rates are among the lowest of the G8 countries. In the United States, the top 1 percent of households received nearly 24 percent of all income in 2007 (declining slightly to 22 percent in 2013, but up from about 8 percent in 1970); the top 10 percent received about half of all income in recent years, while the remaining 90 percent of all families received the other half of all income. (For details about the high levels of inequality, and how much greater it is in the United States than in other countries, see Chapter 9.)

Why is it better to be really rich in North America now than, say, 40 years ago? Or why is it better to be rich in the United States than, say, Germany? The short answer is because of important policy changes that have altered the way incomes and wealth are distributed and consumed. The political organizations of the upper class have successfully convinced Congress and various presidents to make it easier for them to retain most of their income and wealth and to pass on nearly all of it to their children or favourite charity when they die. The most obvious way this has been achieved is through changes to the tax system; that is, how much tax citizens in different income brackets are required to pay. The tax rate on earnings above a certain amount of income becomes a crucial factor in whether or not the rich will have more than everyone else or a *lot* more than everyone else. Canada and the United States, like all rich countries, have long had a **progressive income tax system** in which the upper class is expected to pay a greater share of their income in taxes than the middle class. The logic is that those who have higher incomes can afford to contribute a somewhat higher share to pay for government programs that benefit everyone; an extra dollar for a billionaire is surely less valuable than an extra dollar for a poor family. This logic is common to all democratic societies, and public opinion polls show that North Americans support requiring the rich to pay higher tax rates than everyone else (McCall, 2013).

But in spite of this commitment to a progressive system of taxation, tax burdens on high earners have declined dramatically in the past 30 years in countries such as the Canada and United States. Figure 7.1 tells the remarkable story of the American

Figure 7.1 Tax Rate on Highest-Earning Americans

SOURCE: Based on data from Citizens for Tax Justice, 2011.

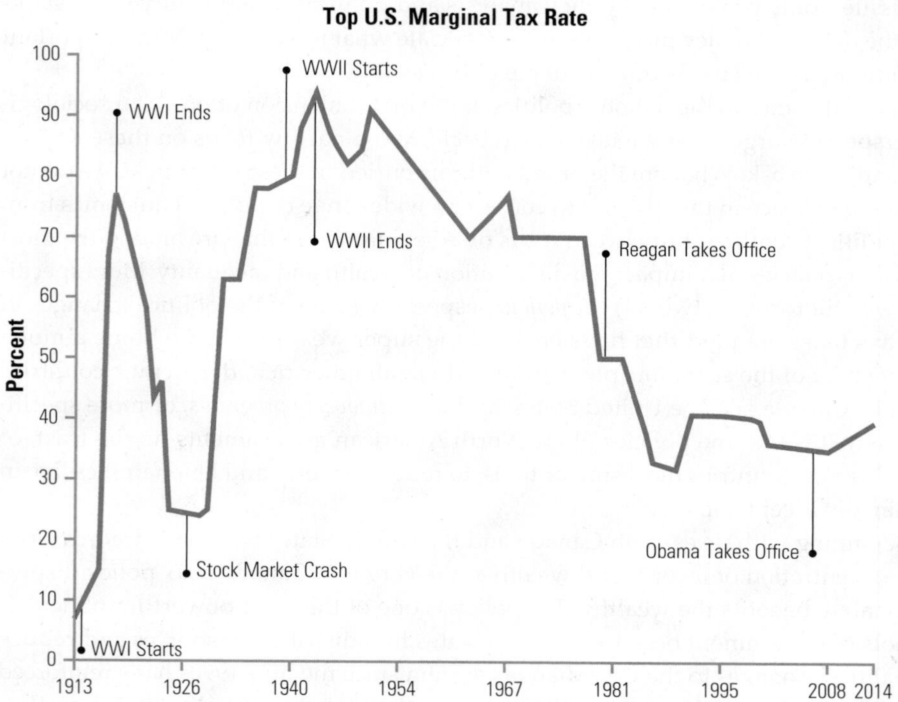

history of tax rates on high incomes. At the end of World War II (when especially high taxes were adopted to help pay for the war effort), the highest earners were paying over 90 percent of their earnings above the top threshold (in 1944, that was $200,000). In the early 1960s, the top rate was reduced to around 70 percent of earnings above the highest bracket (in 1964, that amount was $400,000). It was lower but still about twice as high as it has been since the mid-1980s. In the early 1980s, in two dramatic waves of tax cuts on high earnings during the presidency of Ronald Reagan, the rich saw their tax rates fall below 30 percent. The bracket bumped up a bit in the early 1990s under presidents George H. W. Bush and Bill Clinton, settling at 39.6 percent today for incomes above $400,000 (or $450,000 for married couples). In the United States, the tax rate on high earners is also significantly lower than in other rich democratic countries such as Canada.

Other changes to the tax code in the United States in recent decades enable the super rich to pay much less than the official tax rate would suggest. For example, they often not only have high earnings but also typically receive considerable income from investments. Much of this investment income is treated differently from other kinds of income and may be taxed at a rate as low as 15 percent (the so-called capital gains tax rate). The wealthy can also shelter other earnings from taxation, reducing the overall tax rate paid by rich families. Commonly known as *loopholes*, these tax breaks are useless for the vast majority of American families but extremely valuable for the very rich. For example, many of the very wealthiest Americans make liberal use of offshore tax shelters, by creating investment schemes in little countries like the Cayman Islands that have no income tax, as a way of avoiding or radically reducing taxes they would otherwise pay to the American government. Wealthy individuals and families can afford to employ lawyers and tax accountants skilled in the manipulation of these rules to seek every possible vehicle to reduce their tax rate, something that ordinary Americans would not be able to do (Winters, 2011).

Compared to the United States, Canada has a more progressive tax policy for personal income. High-income Canadians as a group pay higher income taxes than other Canadians, but they have much more disposable wealth. According to Statistics Canada, in 2004 the top 5 percent of tax filers received 25 percent of income and paid 36 percent of income and payroll taxes. In contrast, the bottom 95 percent of the tax filer population received 75 percent of income and paid 64 percent of taxes (Murphy, Roberts, & Wolfson, 2007). Seven years later, according to Statistics Canada's 2011 National Household Survey, the top 10 percent of earners received 28.1 percent of all income in Canada but paid 42.1 percent of all income taxes (Grant & Curry, 2013). In Canada, then, the highest earners pay a greater share of income tax than their share of the total income. However, in the top 0.01 percent, about 100 tax filers paid no taxes in 2004. Tax deductions, such as business losses and gifts to the Crown, are responsible for a number of these situations (Murphy et al., 2007). The differences between Canada and the United States are most striking at the upper end of the earnings spectrum. These differences grow even larger the higher up the income spectrum you look. For example, among the top 0.01 percent of the tax filer population, the average American family income was $25.8 million, over three times the Canadian figure of $8.4 million (Murphy et al., 2007).

Recently, billionaire investor Warren Buffett highlighted just how tax loopholes and reduced rates on certain kinds of income can benefit the wealthiest Americans (Buffett, 2011). He noted that he paid federal income taxes at a lower rate—about 18 percent on his 2010 income—than did his secretary and other lower-level employees at his firm, Berkshire Hathaway. The very wealthy 2012 Republican presidential nominee Mitt Romney similarly revealed, when he released his tax returns during the campaign, that he was paying less than 15 percent of his income in federal taxes.

Just as wealthy individuals and families have benefited from many changes in the tax laws over the past, so too have corporations. Private companies now pay much less in taxes than they used to. Not only has the overall rate of corporate taxes fallen, but many industries have also enjoyed special tax deals that allow them to pay even lower rates. For example, the oil industry has regularly received special tax breaks and loopholes, ostensibly to encourage these companies to drill for more oil, even as oil prices have soared and oil company profits reach record highs.

Even the lower rates of corporate taxes paid today do not tell the whole story. In fact, yet more loopholes enable some corporations to reduce their taxable income down to nothing. The all-time champion of avoiding corporate taxes appears to be General Electric (GE), known for its household appliances like refrigerators and light bulbs, and more recently for green-power products as well as its finance arm, GE Capital. In the 1980s, GE so successfully avoided paying taxes that then-president Ronald Reagan (who was earlier in his life a paid spokesperson for GE and in general opposed high government taxes) ordered his staff to try to close some of the loopholes GE was using to avoid taxes. But the company is a powerhouse in Washington, DC, and it has persisted in managing to pay very low taxes. The *New York Times* reported that in 2010 GE managed to pay *no* corporate income taxes at all, despite making $14 billion in profits across the world. (GE does pay sales taxes and Social Security taxes.) GE's tax lawyers and accountants, many of whom formerly worked for congressional tax committees or the Internal Revenue Service, aggressively use a variety of tax shelters to reduce profits, and the company further lobbies Congress each year for special tax breaks often buried in legislation and unnoticed by the media or the public. GE's successful avoidance of all corporate income taxes may be extreme, but any corporation can reduce its tax bill by using similar strategies (Kocieniewski, 2011).

Under the Conservative government of Stephen Harper, Canada cut corporate tax rates similar to the way the United States did under the Reagan and Clinton administrations. In 2000 the combined federal–provincial corporate tax rate was 42 percent.

Figure 7.2 Federal Corporate Tax Rate on General Income

SOURCE: Based on data from *What Did Corporate Tax Cuts Deliver? A Background Report for Corporate Tax Freedom Day 2013*, by the Canadian Labour Congress, January 2012, Ottawa: Canadian Labour Congress (http://canadianlabour.ca/sites/default/files/media/what-did_corporate_tax_cuts_deliver-2014-en-web.pdf).

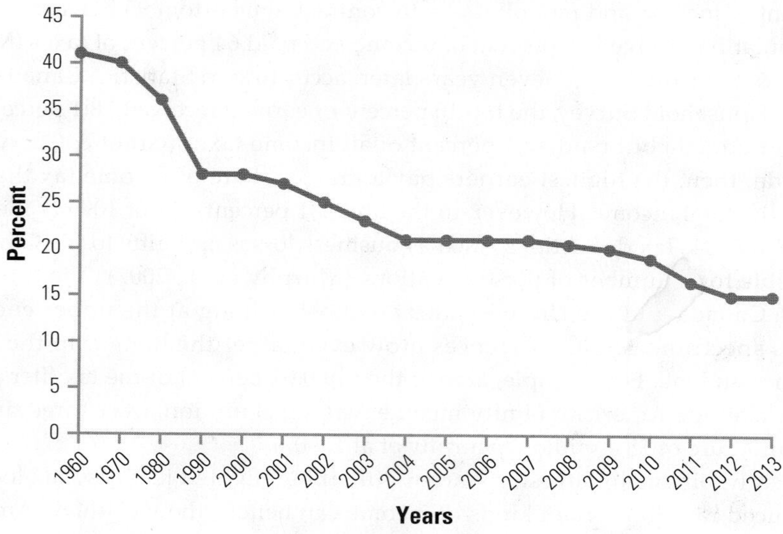

By 2012 the combined rate had fallen to 28 percent (Canadian Labour Congress, 2012). Private companies now pay much less in taxes than they used to. Figure 7.2 shows the dramatic changes in statutory federal corporate income tax rates since 1960. Rates have fallen from 41 percent to just 15 percent in January 2012. Big cuts were made under Liberal governments in the first part of the twenty-first century (from 28 percent to 21 percent) and then under the Harper Conservative government (21 percent to 15 percent). The argument in favour of corporate tax cuts has been that increased corporate profits would be reinvested in company operations thereby contributing to the economy and job growth. Instead, tax cuts have led private companies to hoard cash reserves (Canadian Labour Congress, 2012). Fourteen percent of all income in Canada is now received by the top 1 percent of the population, up sharply from the 8 percent they received in the 1980s (Broadbent Institute, 2014).

Even the lower rates of corporate taxes paid today (as shown in Figure 7.2) do not tell the whole story. According to the Canadian Labour Congress (2012, pp. 5–6), Statistics Canada data reveals that non-financial corporations have seen an increase of more than 200 percent in their cash reserves over 10 years. In 2011 the cash reserves of non-banking corporations increased by $72 billion from $503 billion in reserves to $575 billion by the end of 2011, which is enough to pay off the federal national debt ($33.4 billion in 2011). Rather than invest profits in the Canadian economy, non-financial corporations have been hoarding money. This has been very costly in terms of foregone government revenues.

Reduced tax burdens allow corporations to retain more of their earnings, and in recent years they have lavished pay and other perks (including generous stock options) on their top managers. We know most about the compensation of the chief executive officers (CEOs) of companies, as firms are required to report the annual incomes of their CEOs. This requirement produces very clear information about the trends over time. From the 1930s through the 1970s, CEO compensation averaged (in 2010 dollars, adjusted for inflation) about $1 million per year. That was a lot of money then, but compensation began to shoot up in the 1980s and 1990s. As Figure 7.3 shows, by 1995, the CEO-to-worker compensation ratio had grown to more than 120 to 1, and by 2005, the highest compensation had reached $9.2 million

Figure 7.3 Average Annual CEO Compensation Compared to Average Worker Compensation

SOURCE: Adapted from Lawrence Mischel and Josh Bivens, "Occupy Wall Streeters are right about skewed economic rewards in the United States," Economic Policy Institute Briefing Paper #331, 2011.

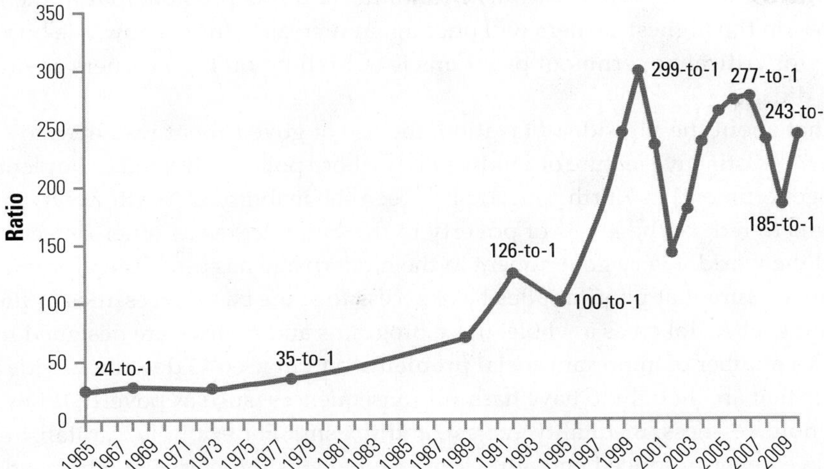

(a 900 percent increase) and was only slightly lower at $8.5 million after the recession of 2007 and 2008 (Mischel, Bernstein, & Shierholz, 2009). In recent years, CEO compensation is about 250 times more than what the average worker earns, more than a tenfold increase from the 1960s.

A similar picture exists in Canada, where the CEO Elite 100—the 100 highest paid CEOs of companies listed on the Toronto Stock Exchange Index (TSX Index)—earned 27 percent more in 2011 than in they did in the previous year, averaging $8.38 million in 2010, up from $6.6 million in 2009. In contrast, the average Canadian working full-time earned $44,366 in 2010. By 2011 the average Canadian salary had increased only 1.1 percent. When adjusted for inflation, average Canadians working full-time earn less than they did in the 2008–2009 fiscal year. Figure 7.4 shows the average salaries of the CEO Elite 100 in comparison to the average salary of a full-time worker and a full-time minimum-wage worker in Canada (Mackenzie, 2012, p. 5). In 1995 the average pay of the highest paid 50 CEOs in Canada was 85 times that of the average worker. By 2010 this group's average pay had risen to 255 times that of the average worker (p. 7). This signals an alarming increase in economic inequality in Canada since the mid-1990s, when government tax policies began to favour the top income earners.

Figure 7.4 Canada's Top Paid CEOs and the Rest of Us

SOURCE: Data from *Canada's CEO Elite 100: The 0.01%*, Chart 2, p. 5, by Hugh Mackenzie, January 2012 (http://www.policyalternatives.ca/publications/reports/canada%E2%80%99s-ceo-elite-100).

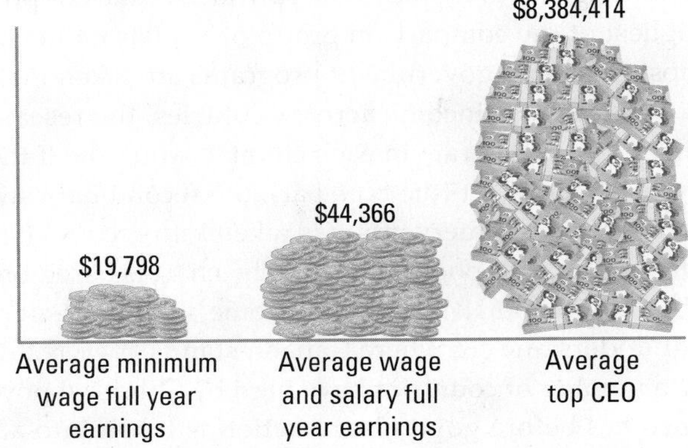

Looking at the big picture, we would argue that in the fight over how the benefits of economic growth are distributed, dramatic changes in individual and corporate tax rates indicate that in recent decades rich individuals and families, as well as large corporations and their top executives, have been winning. The struggle over who should pay what taxes will continue, and it is possible that in the future tax rates on the highest earners will once again increase. But for now, the burden of paying for critical government programs is not falling on high earners as much as it once did.

What about the flip side of taxation, the use of government resources to reduce poverty? A distinctive feature of **public policy** (those policies adopted or implemented by the government) in North America has been the inability of North American governments to reduce the levels of poverty to the same degree as other rich countries around the world. Every government in the modern age has established programs to try to make sure that poor families have access to some basic necessities of life, like food and shelter. Taken as a whole, these programs and policies are designed to help address a number of important **social problems**, a term used to describe a wide range of issues that are thought to have harmful consequences (such as poverty, crime, drug abuse, homelessness, inequality, racism, and sexism). For example, capitalist economies have never produced enough decent-paying jobs for everyone who needs one, inevitably leaving some individuals and families in poverty. Antipoverty programs operate as a kind of insurance program for misfortune. Adults (and their children) may fall into poverty for any number of reasons: inability to work because of a physical or mental disability or an extended illness or accident, the economy being in recession and unemployment being high, or just plain bad luck. Because we can't know in advance who among us will end up homeless and destitute, we all contribute a little to provide protection for those who do end up in that state. Antipoverty programs also attempt to give poor children the same opportunity as middle-class children to succeed in life. The logic is that poor children who are poor through no fault of their own should not be held back as a consequence, and that by providing poor children with the opportunity to succeed, we provide the resources for them to make a better life for themselves as adults and for their children.

Although every country has welfare-state programs designed to reduce poverty, some do it a lot better than others. We now know that in rich countries it *is* possible to dramatically reduce the number of children and families living in poverty, if government programs make a commitment to doing so. How do we know this? A number of scholars have studied the problem, using very carefully developed data about household income and living standards to be able to compare across countries. Using a standard definition of poverty and comparing Canada and the United States to other rich countries, we can look at the data and see that, in fact, the United States and, to a lesser extent, Canada do very badly in comparison to the rich democracies most like us (Smeeding, Robson, Wing, & Gershuny, 2009).

The bar graph in Figure 7.5 displays the raw facts: Rates of poverty in Canada are among the highest of the comparison group of similar nations, although interestingly this is most clear *after* government programs are taken into account. Using comparable data about family income across countries, the researchers estimated what the (hypothetical) poverty rate in each country would be if there was no government policy to try to correct it (the blue bar); the second bar estimates the *actual* poverty rate once government intervention is taken into account (such as programs that provide welfare benefits to poor families). The chart is based on truly comparable data from each country and all sources of income, an important point that makes it a unique way of understanding where Canada stands. Two results are of special importance. First, a number of countries have high hypothetical poverty rates based just on market incomes before government action is taken into account. In some cases, this is larger than Canada's. Second, few countries in this comparison group

Figure 7.5 Pre-Tax and Post–Tax Transfer Poverty Rate

SOURCE: Based on data from *Income Poverty and Income Support for Minority and Immigrant Children in Rich Countries* (Luxembourg Income Study Working Paper No. 527), by Timothy Smeeding, Karen Robson, Coady Wing, and Jonathan Gershuny, December 2009 (http://www.lisdatacenter.org/wps/liswps/527.pdf).

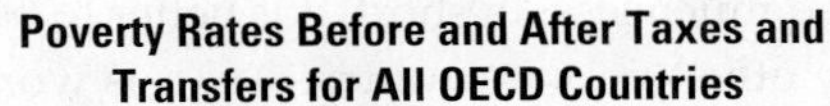

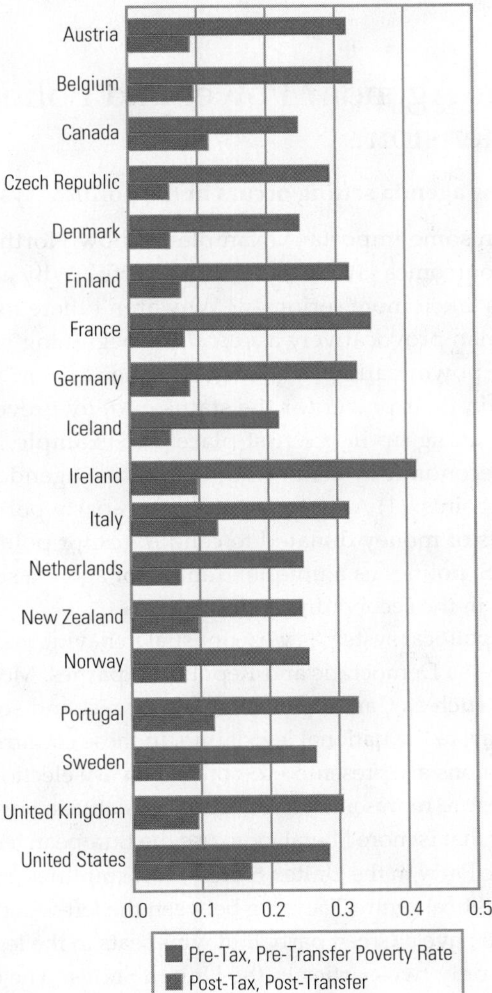

do as little as Canada and the United States to reduce poverty; notice that for both countries there are only modest differences between the poverty rates before and after government intervention, whereas in other countries a significant difference exists. In other words, public policy does less to reduce poverty in Canada and the United States than in other countries. It's especially instructive to compare ourselves to the United Kingdom, a country very similar to our own. If people in the United Kingdom had to live solely on what they earned, without any help from public programs, there would be an even higher rate of poverty than in Canada. But the United Kingdom dramatically reduces its poverty rate (by over 50 percent) through its various antipoverty programs.

Looking at the first dimension of power, what can we say about who wins overall? In other words, who is able to exert their will in order to prevail in national politics? We cannot possibly examine all of the policy controversies and outcomes that take place. In any given year, there are literally hundreds of important issues that come up for discussion and debate and are decided in Parliament or by the Supreme Court. But our more limited survey of two important areas of public policy—poverty and inequality—suggest that compared to the nations most similar to Canada and the United States in terms of wealth, economic development, and longstanding democratic government, we would have to conclude that powerful actors appear to prevail more often, and receive far more rewards when they do, than in other countries, while the poor are helped much less. In short, it is better to be rich in Canada and the United States than in any other similar country, and it is worse to be poor than in any most similar country.

Who Sets the Agenda? Power and Politics in the Second Dimension

7.3.2 Explain how agenda setting occurs in the political system.

We have now seen some important examples of how North American tax policies produce concrete outcomes that reward the powerful. Why aren't other approaches, ideas, and policies taken more seriously? Why aren't there more challenges to those in power, as Goffman provocatively asked at the beginning of this chapter? The second dimension of power calls our attention to the ways in which powerful actors sometimes maintain their power (or the status quo) by preventing certain issues or challenges from coming up in the first place. For example, several features of the U.S. political and economic system combine to set an agenda. In particular, we will highlight two key points: (1) America's unique two-party political system and (2) the enormous amounts of money donated to candidates for political office in American politics. Taking U.S. politics as a unique example of agenda setting, we will examine power and politics in the second dimension.

The American political system is very unusual in having just two major parties who contend for office—the Democratic and Republican parties. Most democratic countries around the world, such as Canada, have at least three, and sometimes four or more, parties who win seats in the national legislature. In these countries, a much wider range of options and opinions are presented to voters at every election, and a wider range of opinions and parties are represented in national legislatures. For example, in most countries there is a party that is more liberal, or to use the European term, "social democratic," than the Democratic Party in the United States. Most countries also have a political party that occupies the political centre, standing between the left-wing and right-wing parties. Many countries also have a Green party that wins seats in the legislature.

Why are there only two parties in the United States? The electoral system established by their constitution—in which the candidate (and party) winning the most votes in a single district wins the seat—makes it virtually impossible for third parties to gain traction. By contrast, systems of **proportional representation (PR)**, found in one form or another in most other democratic countries, allow minority parties to gain representation based on the share of the vote they win.

In PR systems, voters select a party, not a candidate. The proportion of votes received by each party translates into seats in the national parliament. In many cases, a party receiving as little as 5 percent of the vote will receive seats in the legislature and gain a foothold in the political system. In the United States, by contrast, only the candidate winning the most votes in a congressional district or state wins a seat in the House or Senate, respectively. As a result, a new political party seeking to build support cannot do so gradually (as under PR systems) by electing a few representatives and building a reputation with voters. Regional third-party efforts—most notably the Populists of the late nineteenth century in parts of the American South and the Midwestern Progressives in the twentieth century—have occasionally been viable for a period of time, winning some seats in Congress. But these efforts are relatively easily turned aside by the major parties and their voters co-opted into one or the other of the major parties. The two-party system had become firmly established by 1840, and there has been only one successful example of a third party entering the political system and displacing one of the dominant parties since then: The Republican Party was founded in 1854 during the intense conflicts of the pre–Civil War era (Abraham Lincoln won the presidency on a Republican ticket). The Republicans became the main opposition to the Democrats, displacing the Whig Party when it fractured over the issue of slavery. In all other cases in American politics, however, third parties have failed.

The range of viable political parties in other democratic countries has important consequences for how agendas are set and what kinds of political issues are discussed in the media and in their national legislatures. Imagine how different Congress might be today if libertarian, socialist, and Green parties all won seats in Congress alongside the Democratic and Republican parties. In such a case—which would be similar to what happens in many European countries—there are simply more political positions under discussion. It is also likely that no one party would have a majority of seats, and winners would have to form a coalition of parties in order to govern (thus encouraging a wider range of discussion and compromise than a two-party system requires). A multiparty system also changes the nature of electoral campaigns, where citizens have a wider menu of options to consider (and a wider range of opinions are expressed). The daily coverage of political life in the media (such as on political talk shows on television) is also very different. When there are only two significant political parties, by contrast, the effort to be balanced is much easier: You only need to hear from two different parties, two different points of view. A more complex political environment prevents the kind of "he said/she said" of today's political discourse in the United States, where there are only two viable political parties.

In addition to its two-party system, American politics are also exceptional in the amount of money that is available to, or must be raised by, candidates for political office. Not surprisingly, most of the money given to support candidates running for office comes from wealthy individuals and large corporations and business groups. In recent decades, incentives for political candidates to seek funding have increased dramatically. Political strategists and campaign managers have reached a consensus that high-spending media campaigns are the most efficient way to reach voters and that serious candidates for office need to raise funds. Where does this extraordinary flow of political money come from? Contributions come from either individual donors or political action committees (PACs) organized by a wide range of individual businesses and business associations, unions, and ideological groups such as the National Rifle Association or Emily's List (a group that works to elect prochoice Democratic women). PAC contributions can be reasonably divided into three broad categories: business-related (including both business PACs and individual executives working for large corporations), labour, and ideological PACs (with the latter running the gamut from far left to far right). By an enormous and growing margin, contributions from businesses vastly outstrip contributions by unions, reaching a ratio of 19:1 in the 2012 U.S. election.

In Canada, corporations and unions have been prohibited from making donations to political parties since 2004. Taxpayers no longer fund election campaigns since the Conservative government phased out government subsidies to political parties in April 2015. These per-vote subsidies were designed to level the playing field for political parties. With the elimination of the per-vote subsidy, Canadian political parties now rely more heavily on private donations that are subsidized through tax credits. Powerful Canadian business families make large tax-deductible political donations. The Conservative and Liberal parties receive the largest private donations from wealthy business owners. For example, the Beaudoin family of Quebec, who own the controlling interest in Bombardier Inc., donated a total of $200,000 in 2013 with the largest share going to the Liberal Party ($132,000) and a smaller share going to the Conservative Party ($81,000). The Conservative Party of Canada receives a larger share of donations than both the Liberal and New Democratic parties combined. During the 2011 election campaign, repeat donors gave the Conservative

Party more than $14.5 million dollars, nearly double what they gave to the Liberal Party (*The Globe and Mail*, 2015).

Why has the amount of money being contributed to candidates for political office grown so much? One answer is that the vast increase in wealth at the top has expanded the resources for the rich to invest in the political system. Rising household affluence creates a similar dynamic. Giving among the wealthy for all purposes—civic, charitable, and religious as well as political—has increased in this era of rising inequality. While much of this giving may have benign political consequences, no such simple conclusions would be appropriate when it comes to political money. By donating large sums of money to those political parties most likely to represent their interests over others, powerful business owners are able to set their own agendas in the political realm and influence social and economic policies in both Canada and the United States.

The Third Dimension: Do North Americans Believe in Policies Benefiting the Powerful?

7.3.3 Analyze views on policies involving income inequality and the redistribution of wealth.

Government policies that allow the very rich to earn and keep most of their exceptionally high and growing incomes while poor and working middle-class families see few of the benefits of economic growth of the past 30 years would seem to not be in the interests of most North Americans. Some would add that the failure to tax the rich and large corporations more extensively means doing less to lift children and families above the poverty line, having schools and universities that are not as good as they might be, having fewer police officers and firefighters, and not repairing or maintaining streets and bridges and public parks as much as we might. The very richest people need not worry about these things—they can send their children to top private schools and can afford to live in communities that provide a high level of security far from the sources of pollution and crime. But what about everyone else? Why do they not always insist that they have access to the same quality schools, safe communities, and healthcare as the rich?

These are the tensions that become obvious when we examine power three-dimensionally. The question then becomes: Do Canadians hold views that favour public policies beneficial to very rich Canadians? As we have noted, this is the most challenging part of studying power, and one that necessarily becomes controversial when we consider what, exactly, is in any one individual's or group's best interests. The challenge of studying the third dimension of power may involve knowing things that are impossible to know (such as what we might think if we were fully informed about the impact of government policies).

Several decades of social science research on what the public thinks about government and public policies give us one way of beginning to answer the question. Scholars who conduct opinion *surveys*—or polls—of a *representative sample* of North Americans provide one type of evidence for studying how people reason about their underlying beliefs or preferences. The term used to characterize the results of opinion surveys on social and political issues is **public opinion**. While these methods are not perfect for examining the third dimension of power—most polls and surveys provide limited opportunity for a more detailed examination of how people think—they do provide at least a first look at the issue.

These questions may be further considered in relation to Canadians' attitudes about inequality and public policies designed to reduce inequality and poverty. What do we know from research on public opinion in these areas? An opinion poll conducted online between September 10 and 23, 2014, by the Broadbent Institute revealed a number of key findings related to Canadians' attitudes about the role of the state with respect to income inequality and the redistribution of wealth:

- Canadians *think* the wealthiest fifth—or top 20%—of Canadians hold more than half of the wealth in the country (55.5%) and that the poorest fifth—or bottom 20%—hold less than 6%. (In actuality, according to Statistics Canada's Survey of Financial Security [Statistics Canada, 1999, 2005, 2012] the wealthiest hold more than two-thirds (67.4%) of the wealth, while the poorest fifth of Canadians own no share at all.)
- Canadians think that the wealthiest 20% should hold only 30.3% of all the wealth and that the poorest fifth should hold 11.5%.
- Canadians think the ideal would be if the middle fifth held 23.7% of wealth, a very different picture from the 9% the middle currently holds.
- The desire for a more equitable distribution of wealth holds regardless of demographics or past political preferences, including those who voted for the Conservative Party in 2011.
- A large majority—four out of five Canadians, or 80%—believe the gap between the rich and everyone else has widened over the last decade. Yet large majorities, regardless of demographics or political preference, also believe that the federal government can and should do something to reduce inequality.
- Canadians across demographics and political preference expressed their support for a range of progressive policies in order to achieve greater economic equality.

As Figure 7.6 reveals, Canadians are concerned about the problem of **widening income inequality**. The Broadbent Institute survey found that 77 percent of Canadians think that the widening gap between rich and poor undermines Canadian values and that the majority of Canadians are willing to pay more to protect social programs. What is more, this commitment to reducing income inequality is not

Figure 7.6 How Much Should the Government Do to Reduce the Gap Between the Rich and the Rest?

SOURCE: From *The Wealth Gap: Perceptions and Misconceptions in Canada*, Figure 3, p. 10, by the Broadbent Institute, December 2014 (https://d3n8a8pro7vhmx.cloudfront.net/broadbent/pages/31/attachments/original/1430002077/The_Wealth_Gap.pdf?1430002077). Copyright by The Broadbent Institute. Used with permission.

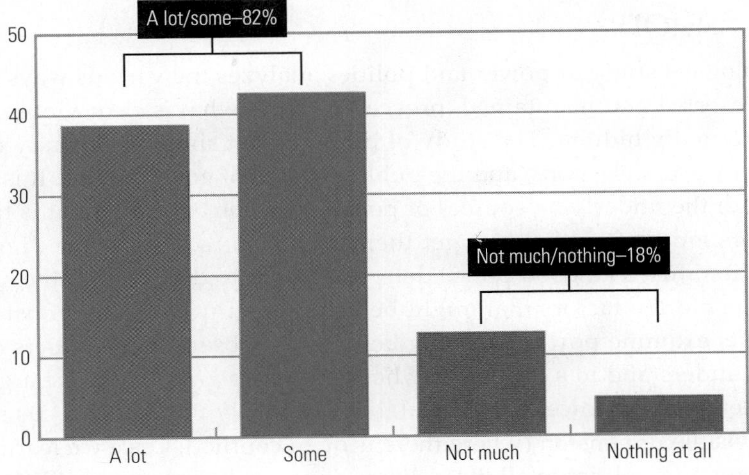

a left–right ideological issue—support for reducing income inequality cuts across political party lines. When it comes to the desire to protect public services and reduce income inequality, Canadians are more united than we are polarized. Support for government action to reduce income inequality crosses all geographic divides, income levels, and gender or age differences. Few Canadians find it acceptable that income inequality is getting worse and that our governments are doing nothing about it.

Only a small minority of Canadians (20%) believe that there is nothing wrong with a widening income gap. An overwhelming majority of Canadians (83%) are in favour of increasing income taxes on the wealthiest, and three-quarters of Canadians (73%) support the idea of increasing income tax on corporations by bringing them back to 2008 levels—even a majority of conservatives support this issue (Broadbent Institute, 2014).

Canadians are willing to pay higher taxes to protect programs they value, which in turn would help reduce income inequality. A survey conducted by the Broadbent Institute in 2012 as part of its equality project asked, "Would you personally be very, somewhat, not very or not at all willing to pay slightly higher taxes if that's what it would take to protect our social programs like health care, pensions and access to post-secondary education?" Two-thirds (64%) of Canadians said yes. Almost one-quarter (23%) are "very willing" to pay more taxes to save social programs; 41 percent are "somewhat willing" to pay slightly more tax. Clearly, the results show that Canadians are willing to do their part to support public services, if the government takes a reasonable approach to taxation (Broadbent Institute, 2012).

Despite this support for government policies that reduce income inequality, Canadians have elected governments at both the federal and provincial levels who support the interests of wealthy business owners over those of the majority of Canadians. The gap between the rich and the poor has widened in North America since the 1980s. Given that wealthy Canadians exercise political influence through large campaign donations to the Conservative and Liberal parties (both of which have implemented large tax cuts in past decades), we can begin to see the dynamics of power as it operates in the third dimension. When surveyed, Canadians *say* that they want governments to implement policies that reduce income inequality, but voters routinely elect governments whose policies benefit only the wealthy few. Thus, when it comes to what Canadians *do*, rather than what they *say*, there is evidence to suggest that they believe in the ideas promoted by the wealthy, when it is not in their interests to do so.

Conclusion

The sociological study of power and politics analyzes the various ways in which power is exerted and maintained, proceeding from what is clearly observable to what is normally hidden. The study of power is not simply the study of public debates, votes and elections, and the public policies of governments. It is *also* concerned with the underlying sources of political outcomes and how it is that powerful actors more often than not get their way. This requires some digging and investigation: Just as a good police detective needs to dig beneath the surface to explore the hidden factors that might be behind a murder, so too must political sociologists examine power by going beyond the observable conflicts of political life to understand in a deeper way how power operates. We have argued that three dimensions of power are central, but ordinarily the media focus solely on the most visible dimension (where there is open conflict). Once we learn to think about power and politics in all three dimensions, we have learned a different way of thinking about political life. It is, in short, an application of the sociological imagination to the study of power.

Because power and power relations are such a pervasive aspect of social life, the study of power has to be considered a central task for all of sociology (and for all citizens). Armed with the approach we have outlined here, many questions, challenges, but also opportunities open up for all of us—students, citizens, workers, parents, retirees—to think about what might be done to make democracy in Canada and elsewhere work better. We have mostly focused on party politics in North America, but power can often be studied and, where appropriate, more easily challenged at lower levels of societies. In our towns and cities, workplaces and other organizations, or even in our own families, power can be analyzed in terms of three dimensions and how they reinforce one another. And analysis is always the precursor to effective change.

CHAPTER SUMMARY

The Big Questions Revisited 7

7.1 What Are the Distinct Forms of Power? In this section, we examined the three dimensions of power, using a sociological lens to examine not only the most visible ways in which power is expressed but also its more subtle forms.

The Three Dimensions of Power

The One-Dimensional View of Power

Learning Objective 7.1.1: Identify who has power in the one-dimensional view.

The Two-Dimensional View of Power

Learning Objective 7.1.2: Explain the role of agenda setting in the second dimension of power.

The Three-Dimensional View of Power

Learning Objective 7.1.3: Discuss the various ways in which the workings of power can be hidden.

7.2 What Is the State, and How Does It Distribute Power in a Society? In this section, we examined what the institutions of power (the state) actually do. We also explored why states matter in the distribution of power and why states tend to promote the interests of the powerful.

The Institutions of Power

What Is the State?

Learning Objective 7.2.1: Define the state and explain how it regulates the economy.

Why States Matter in the Distribution of Power

Learning Objective 7.2.2: Explain how the state influences who gets what government services.

Promoting the Interests of the Powerful?

Learning Objective 7.2.3: Discuss how and why states tend to adjust their policies to support the goals of powerful business interests, and identify exceptions.

7.3 Who Has Power in North America Today? Finally, our discussion of the dimensions of power and political institutions led us to an examination of the Canadian political system.

Power in North America

Who Wins? Policy and Politics in the First Dimension

Learning Objective 7.3.1: Discuss what tax policies and antipoverty programs tell us about how power is distributed in North America.

Who Sets the Agenda? Power and Politics in the Second Dimension

Learning Objective 7.3.2: Explain how agenda setting occurs.

The Third Dimension: Do North Americans Believe in Policies Benefiting the Powerful?

Learning Objective 7.3.3: Analyze views on policies involving income inequality and the redistribution of wealth.

Learn the Terms

agenda setting (p. 174)
bureaucracy (p. 177)
democracy (p. 182)
power (p. 172)
progressive income tax system (p. 183)
proportional representation (PR) (p. 190)
public opinion (p. 192)
public policy (p. 188)
social problem (p. 188)
state (p. 177)
status (p. 175)
welfare state (p. 180)
widening income inequality (p. 193)

Chapter 8
Markets, Organizations, and Work

by Richard Arum and Jeff Manza*

RosaBetancourt 0 people images / Alamy Stock Photo

Founded by Canadian businessman Chip Wilson, Lululemon is one example of an entrepreneurship that has made it big. Since its opening in 2000, Lululemon, which sells upscale yoga-inspired athletic apparel, has grown from one store in Vancouver, BC, to a corporation with hundreds of stores across North America.

Learning Objectives

8.1.1 Identify alternatives to market capitalism and discuss the pervasiveness of markets in modern societies.

8.1.2 Explain how sociologists define markets differently than economists.

8.1.3 Explain how social networks influence markets.

8.1.4 Explain how power influences markets.

8.1.5 Explain how cultural knowledge influences markets.

*An earlier version of this chapter was coauthored by Abby Larson, Michael McCarthy, and Christine Baker-Smith.

8.2.1 Explain how organizations can form, transform, and survive over time.

8.2.2 Identify the benefits and limitations of bureaucratic processes and regulations.

8.3.1 Discuss how an organization's structure and niche may contribute to its success or its failure.

8.3.2 Explain organizational isomorphism and identify the differences among three types: coercive, normative, and mimetic.

8.4.1 Explain how workplaces and the type of work people do changes over time.

8.4.2 Discuss how organizations develop and manage the labour process and their workers.

When we think about companies in North America, names like Walmart, Google, Apple, or Bombardier come to mind. But of the nearly 6 million U.S. companies with employees, just over 5 million are small businesses owned and operated by someone who employs less than 20 people. Entrepreneurship fascinates people for many reasons. Small businesses significantly contribute to the economy. Most of us know family members or friends who work for themselves. And entrepreneurship and self-employment are aligned with many North Americans' hopes and dreams: to tell an employer to take this job and shove it, to be one's own boss, to build something from scratch. Yet while many people do start businesses or work for themselves at some point, most do not last in this status for long. Most start-up businesses typically fail within the first few years.

In 2009, as part of a larger research project, we asked American university students in their senior year about their entrepreneurial aspirations, and then we followed up with this nationally representative group of students after graduation. During their senior year, 5 percent of students reported that they planned to own their own businesses within two years of completing college, while fully 36 percent of respondents reported that they aspired to be entrepreneurs at some point in their lives.

Although in the year or two after graduation only 2 percent of graduates in our study actually ended up fully immersed in self-employment, it turns out that the students' estimate of being self-employed at one point in their lives is not far from what we would expect from U.S. data. About 20 percent of American men and women have been self-employed by the time they are in their early 30s, and more than 30 percent have been self-employed by the time they are in their early 50s.

Our research also explored how the character of self-employment has changed dramatically in recent decades in the United States. While self-employment had been in decline in most developed economies throughout the twentieth century, and many social scientists believed that it was likely to disappear altogether in the face of markets increasingly dominated by large companies, self-employment surprised many social scientists by reemerging and beginning to grow in the last quarter of the twentieth century. When we looked closely, we found an additional surprise. Traditional self-employment—an activity dominated by small shopkeepers, restaurateurs, and craftspeople—is still declining. But new forms of self-employment emerged to replace it. In particular, two types of self-employment are growing: professional freelancers (including consultants, artists, designers, and writers, who value independence and flexible job hours) and low-income, marginal, informal forms of self-employment, such as in-home childcare or day labour.

Figure 8.1 Self-Employment in Selected Countries

SOURCE: Based on data from *The Reemergence of Self-Employment: A Comparative Study of Self-Employment Dynamics and Social Inequality*, by Richard Arum and Walter Müeller, Princeton, NJ: Princeton University Press, 2004.

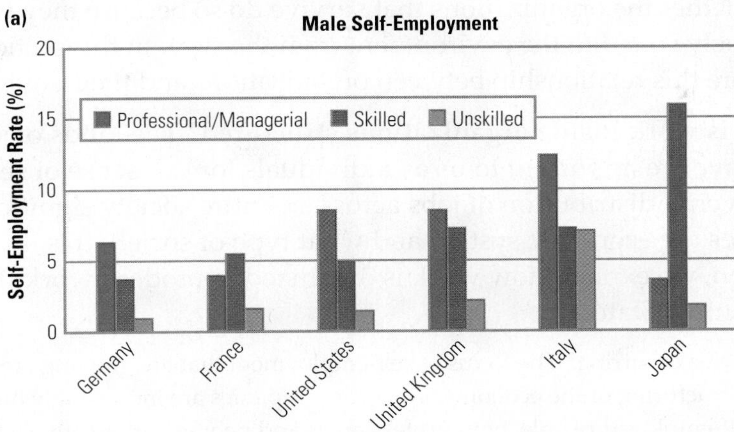

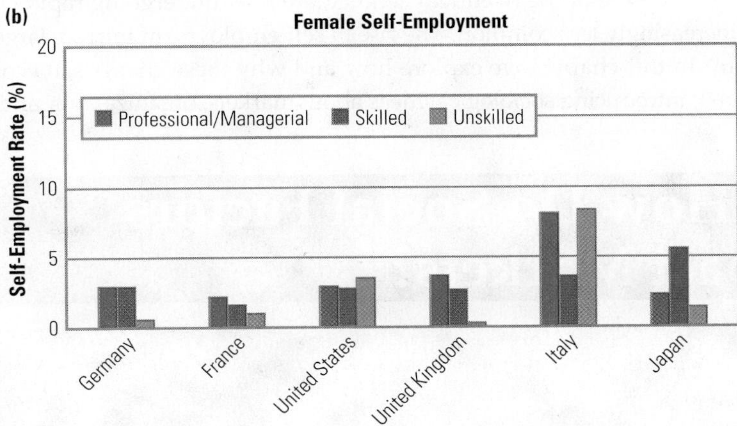

Although professional and unskilled forms of self-employment are increasing for both men and women in most settings, it is interesting to see how much rich countries differ in the extent to which traditional forms of self-employment are prevalent, as you can see in Figure 8.1.

The Big Questions

1. **How do social factors impact markets?** We live in what is sometimes called the "age of the market," and sociologists are increasingly aware that markets are part of the social structure of society. In this section, we explore how a sociological understanding of markets differs from an economic understanding.
2. **Why are organizations important for social and economic life?** To gain a deeper understanding of how modern economies work—and ultimately how social forces influence the economy as a whole—sociologists place considerable importance on analyzing the organizations that exist within markets.

3. **What is the relationship between organizations and their external environments?** The ecological framework of organizational sociology challenges whether organizations actually adapt to their environment or whether the organizations that survive do so because they were uniquely suited to the environment from the start. In this section, we explore this relationship between organizations and their environment.
4. **How is work inside organizations structured?** The kinds of jobs we have are important to us as individuals for our sense of self. But the overall distribution of jobs across an entire society significantly defines the economic system and what type of society it is. In this section, we explore how work is organized in modern workplaces in the United States.

Why is this occurring? The forms of self-employment that are growing are related to a larger restructuring of the economy, in which companies are increasingly outsourcing work to self-employed people, both professionals and people with relatively few skills. Stable organizations and individual careers inside those organizations, which were so common in the middle of the twentieth century, are now undergoing rapid change and becoming increasingly less common. The rise in self-employment mirrors larger shifts in the economy. In this chapter, we explore how and why these changes in economic life have occurred, introducing sociological ideas about markets, organizations, and work.

8.1 How Do Social Factors Impact Markets?

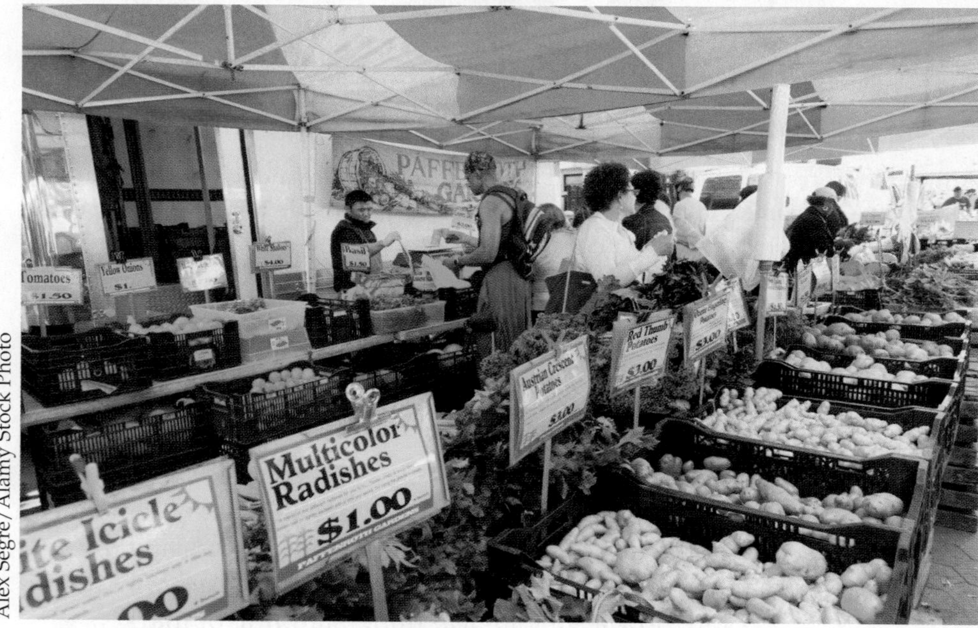

Alex Segre/Alamy Stock Photo

The Creation and Functioning of Markets

We live in what is sometimes called the "age of the market." **Markets**—places where buyers, sellers, and producers engage in exchange of commodities and services—are the foundation of economic life. There is an increasing awareness among sociologists that markets are at heart of the social structures that provide the architecture of modern societies.

The Pervasiveness of Markets

8.1.1 Identify alternatives to market capitalism and discuss the pervasiveness of markets in modern societies.

For much of the twentieth century, the universal centrality of markets was challenged by the alternative economic system in communist countries. Following the Russian Revolution in 1917 and the establishment of communist governments first in the Soviet Union and later in Eastern Europe, North Korea, and Cuba, alternatives to market capitalism as a way of organizing a country's economy existed. While these governments professed an ideological commitment to communism—that is, a society organized without private property and based on the principle that individuals should be able to consume societal resources based on their needs, not their ability—in practice, the government controlled almost all forms of economic activity. The socialist economies of the twentieth century in the Soviet Union, Eastern Europe, and elsewhere were driven by **central planning**, in which the government decided what kinds of goods and services would be produced and how much they would cost. For a time, centrally planned economies appeared to be doing reasonably well; in the 1960s and 1970s, there were debates among economists and other observers about whether **capitalism** (an economic system based on private property and market exchange) or **socialism** (an economic system where the government owns property and controls production) was superior. But a long period of stagnation and decline of socialist economies beginning in the 1970s, coupled with the lack of democracy in these societies, led to their downfall in the late 1980s and the collapse of the Soviet Union in 1991.

Today, the idea that a centrally planned economy is a viable alternative to market capitalism has virtually disappeared. Almost every arena of social life has a market attached to it. People can buy all of the necessities of life for a price. Even babies and new organs can be purchased, although these practices may be questionable and illegal. Buyers can even pay to have their bodies frozen until some future time when (it is hoped) they can be brought back to life. **Entrepreneurs**—people who start or invest in businesses—are constantly inventing new products and ways to sell goods and services to potential buyers.

Many economic sociologists who study markets have noted that markets are increasingly penetrating areas of social life that were once considered outside of the market domain. Even the most intimate spaces of individuals' lives now have markets available. For centuries most families cared for their own children. More recently, however, that has changed. Affluent families frequently hire others to take care of their children, prepare their meals (at home or at restaurants), clean their houses, take care of their yards, and provide home security. Even middle-class and relatively poor families use some of these same services (e.g., childcare). Sociologist Arlie Hochschild (2012) recently analyzed even more dramatic examples of the outsourcing of our lives. For example, some specialists help people find lovers, "nameologists" help parents choose children's names, and "wantologists" help people figure out what they want out of life. One thing is certain: Markets are pervasive in our daily lives. Think about the markets you encounter on a daily basis. Do you rent an apartment or own a house? What did you eat for breakfast? Did you listen to music or news online? Check your e-mail? Send a text message? What did you wear? How did you get to class or work? All of these involve markets.

The pervasiveness of markets can be seen in other ways. Consider how important functions of government that were previously handled only by government employees are increasingly being subcontracted to private entrepreneurs. The U.S. federal government, for example, has used private military contractors to join American soldiers on the ground in recent wars, and the Canadian government uses private contractors to produce ammunitions, outsourcing to the market part of the task of war-making. Local governments have also sought to cut their costs by hiring private firms to handle what was formerly done by government employees. The municipal government in Sandy Springs, Georgia—a city of 94,000 people—has taken this to an extreme, subcontracting almost all traditional government functions to private companies, including its local court system, where a judge who is paid $100 an hour presides. The city directly employed just seven full-time workers in 2012 (Segal, 2012). Canadian cities such as Winnipeg, Regina, and Saint John have considered public–private partnerships for their drinking water and waste treatment systems. French water profiteer Veolia has entered into multimillion-dollar contracts with various North American municipalities to provide infrastructure in exchange for private control over water.

So ubiquitous are markets in our society as a means by which to organize social behaviour that we do not often give them much thought. They are a taken-for-granted part of how we live our lives. But it is exactly for this reason that we need to examine them with the tools of the sociological imagination.

Defining Markets

8.1.2 Explain how sociologists define markets differently than economists.

What is a market? The answer may seem intuitive—one of those "you know it when you see it" kind of things—but on closer inspection it is a bit more complicated. The stock market is one kind of market we all hear a lot about. Movies showing the frenetic shouts of traders on Wall Street as they hustle to buy and sell shares in companies for profit represent one image of financial markets, and the daily (or even hourly) news reports on the ups and downs of the stock market suggest that this particular market must be important indeed. But there are also a lot of markets that appear more ambiguous. Consider the case of a free online dating site. Is that also a market? Certainly there are "buyers" (people who respond to ads) and "sellers" (those who put up profiles seeking dates). But no money changes hands. What about services that facilitate housing exchanges for vacations (where homeowners "trade" their house or apartment for someone else's, giving both parties free vacation housing)? Consider the annual cultural festival Burning Man, held in the Nevada desert. Once you have purchased your ticket and have travelled to the festival, there are both formal and informal rules against the exchange of any currency, and all goods and services are exchanged through a barter economy only. Do markets operate there?

These examples highlight the complexity of defining what we mean by the term *market*. In classical economic theory, a market implies an exchange of goods and services between buyers and sellers. In this definition, exchanges can happen in the blink of an eye (when we hand over money or click a computer screen), and the demand determines the price of the good or service being exchanged. Both buyer and seller assume they have knowledge about the good or service being traded. Economists call this perspective on markets the **rational-choice perspective**, and it is powerful because it relies on a simple set of assumptions about what motivates individuals and organizations as they enter into market exchanges: Everyone simply wants to be better off.

Social forces support market exchanges even in alternative countercultural settings, like the Burning Man festival held once a year in the Nevada desert.

Brad Horn/AP Images

Missing from the standard economists' definition, however, are many of the concerns and considerations about social forces that sociologists always think are also important for understanding how social interaction in markets operate. In particular, sociologists have proposed expanding the classical economists' definition of the market to include other motivations: What is necessary for these exchanges to occur? How do buyers and sellers find each other? How do people know that they won't be cheated, or to put it another way, what enables trust between market participants who do not know each other? What role does power play in the market? And, finally, when are market exchanges influenced by the different amounts of power held by market participants?

The sociological approach views markets not as random, one-shot exchanges between a buyer and seller but rather as part of *repeated* interactions that people carry out according to formal and informal rules. For a market to exist, there must be shared understandings about what kinds of commodities will be traded, who can trade, and how the trades take place. And for this to happen, important societal institutions—such as governments and laws—as well as norms of appropriate behaviour come into play. Indeed, without all of these other forces, market exchanges would often be impossible or very limited. To make our sociological understanding of the market more specific, we'll concentrate on three critical social factors that influence how markets work: (1) social networks, (2) power, and (3) culture.

Social Networks

8.1.3 Explain how social networks influence markets.

Today, the term *social network* is widely associated with technological platforms that connect individuals and facilitate the exchange of information and, increasingly, goods and services (Facebook, Twitter, and a myriad of other social media sites). When sociologists talk about **social networks**, however, they are also interested in a much broader set of social relationships: the ties between people, either through family/kinship relationships or through relationships involving friends, colleagues, classmates, or even friends of friends. Whereas classical economic theories view markets as ruthlessly impersonal, sociologists argue that connectivity between people is an important part of how market exchange happens.

In his bestselling book *The Tipping Point*, Malcolm Gladwell (2000) uses the story of Paul Revere to illustrate why social networks matter. On the night of April 18, 1775, two prominent men set out on horseback to warn Boston-area residents that the British army was on its way and the Revolutionary War was underway. William Dawes rode to the south, where he knew very few people. Little came of his otherwise heroic effort. Revere, in contrast, rode to the north, where he was well known. Revere was able to alert his friends and associates, and they alerted others, and in short order a small army was created to fight the British forces. If Dawes had been able to take advantage of his social networks as Revere had, would Dawes have been remembered as a hero instead?

People who study markets through the lens of networks tend to argue in a similar fashion that economic activities, including market activities, are often built on kinship and friendship, and trust and goodwill, initially between people who know each other. Markets often need these social ties to establish levels of trust necessary to carry out economic exchange. These ideas were famously theorized by the sociologist Karl Polanyi (1944/1957), who argued that economic action is *embedded* in social interactions—economic exchange takes place within the context of socialized life. People often buy and sell from people they already know.

Consider this example: Sociologists who have studied banks and loans have found that while large corporations may be able to court a number of banks to secure loans, the fact of having done business before often influences preferences (Uzzi, 1999). While one might anticipate that a business that discovered lower interest rates from another bank would immediately switch banks, many businesses will prefer to stay with the bank that they know and to ask that bank for lower rates. Developing a relationship with a bank over time can have advantages on both sides. For example, having a history of trust built up may provide a certain level of wiggle room for the business when it comes time to negotiate the terms of the loan, as the bank has information about the trustworthiness of the business.

Social networks have proven especially important for the ways they spread information related to markets. One famous example of how connections matter for economic outcomes can be found in a line of work established by Mark Granovetter in the 1970s, showing that someone's chances of getting a job are highly influenced by who they know (Granovetter, 1973). Studying how people found jobs in the Boston area in the early 1970s, Granovetter interestingly discovered that it wasn't someone's first-degree connections (the people that one knows personally) but rather second-degree connections—friends of friends—who were most helpful for securing new jobs. Later research has found mixed results for this specific argument. But the general point that Granovetter was making—that hiring does not simply involve an employer choosing from among the best available applicants but rather that referrals and recommendations from friends and acquaintances play a vitally important role as well—remains central to how we understand the hiring process.

Social networks potentially matter a great deal for how individual careers develop, either inside a company or when moving from one job to another. Managers inside companies may promote the "best" people on staff, but how do they decide who that is? In part, they often think the people they consider friends, or enjoy being around, are the people most qualified for promotion. Or, perhaps more likely, they will hire or promote someone who has been recommended to them by someone they trust. And moving from one job to another, or finding opportunities, is often facilitated by whom you meet in your current job. As people move to new companies and become involved in hiring, they often look to former colleagues and people they know as potential hires. In many professional and managerial occupations, paid intermediaries known as "head hunters" or executive search firms help companies identify and recruit top employees from other firms (or help individuals seeking such positions find them), but direct or indirect knowledge through social networks is often just as effective. In this way, the search firm creates networks that companies (or individuals) may not have found on their own.

One prominent scholar of social networks gives an example from his own network to show how career advancement can work and how you can map your own social network (Uzzi & Dunlop, 2005). Some people in your network can be *superconnectors*, that is, people who introduce you to two or more important people. As Table 8.1 reveals,

Table 8.1 Mapping a Social Network (for Professor Brian Uzzi, Northwestern University)

Name of Contact	Who Introduced You to the Contact?	To Whom Did You Introduce the Contact?
Mark Granovetter	Me	
Greg Duncan	Steve Alltop	
Deb Gruenfeld	Me	
Henry Bienen	Steve Alltop	
John Wolken	Mitch Petersen	

SOURCE: Brian Uzzi and Shannon Dunlap 2005, p. 56, How to Build Your Network. Harv Bus Rev. 2005 Dec;83(12):53-60, 151. Used with permission.

Uzzi showed that Steve Alltop is one of his superconnectors. Alltop introduced Uzzi to both Greg Duncan and Henry Bienen, people important for Uzzi's career. Because of their value to others, superconnectors are often held in very high regard. What else does this table show regarding Uzzi's social network?

Understanding your own social network, and thinking about the people who have had the biggest impact on your life so far (and how you may or may not have helped them), is a very useful exercise.

Markets and Power

8.1.4 Explain how power influences markets.

In the classical economic view of markets, who the buyers and sellers are should not matter. Buyers simply look for the best quality product at the lowest price they can afford without caring who is selling it to them, and sellers simply try to maximize their sales to any buyer(s) they can find. On this basis, some economists have argued that markets are the great equalizer. Gary Becker, a Nobel Prize–winning economist who studied human behaviour through the lens of the market, famously argued that because markets treat everyone the same, common types of discrimination such as racism or sexism will eventually disappear (Becker, 1976). But when sociologists study how markets actually work, as opposed to how they should work in theory, researchers tend to find that people's biases impact how people behave in the market. It is by now thoroughly established, on the basis of decades of research, that employers do not treat all potential job applicants simply on the basis of merit but also tend to look at demographic characteristics such as age, gender, race, and ethnicity of a job applicant. Whites are less likely to purchase identical products from a black person than from a white person (Doleac & Stein, 2010). White cab drivers are less likely to pick up a black rider than a white rider (Gambetta & Hamill, 2005). In short, there is plenty of evidence that markets are entirely capable of discriminating against some groups.

Power influences markets in many ways. Consider the importance of power relationships between firms operating within the same market. It is well known, for example, that larger firms can often get better deals on the same product than smaller firms—something Walmart has employed to great effect. By getting better deals from suppliers, they can undercut smaller competitors' prices (Lichtenstein, 2009). Another example: During the financial crisis of 2008, the auditing industry provided special protections to their best clients. Auditing firms perform what is called due diligence, an investigation from an allegedly disinterested review of a company's financial books, and those reports are used to provide potential investors with information about the health of the company. In recent years, a number of corporate accounting scandals have been in the news, many in relation to the financial industry. In the aftermath of that crisis, it became clear that large, powerful firms often can manipulate the reports of allegedly independent auditing firms to get favourable reports even when investments are in trouble. Why do auditors do this? With millions of dollars in fees at stake, it's perhaps not surprising that large investment banks are treated very differently from small businesses.

Here is another example of how power operates in financial markets: Financial markets—especially electronic ones—are often portrayed as perfect markets because they are anonymous. In a perfect market, supply and demand come together regardless of the traders' personal characteristics (e.g., wealth, race, gender), and power does not affect the workings of the market. Among many others, journalist Michael Lewis contested this view. He referred to the stock market as "rigged," pointing out the powerful position high-frequency traders (HFTs) take in today's

Mark Oleksiy/123RF

Journalist Michael Lewis views electronic financial markets as being "rigged" in favour of the few organizations that can afford to buy the technology and pay highly skilled computer programmers.

financial markets. In just milliseconds (a thousandth of a second), fibre optic cables link superfast computers to brokers who are able to intercept and buy orders from market participants who do not possess the same technologies. Brokers then sell the shares back to the other participants at a higher price and pocket the margin. This trading strategy is available only to very few organizations in financial markets—those that can afford both to buy the technology and to pay highly skilled computer programmers. Hence, according to Lewis, financial markets discriminate among participants based on their resources (Lewis, 2014).

Culture

8.1.5 Explain how cultural knowledge influences markets.

There are other important aspects of markets that are not normally visible to participants. In particular, the informal rules that govern how people behave in markets are key to how markets work. Without common understandings about how market interactions are supposed to operate, it would be very difficult for successful exchanges to occur. In studying how markets work, sociologists have thus found that it is important to look closely at the underlying rules that participants must know (or learn).

When we think of market rules and regulations, it's easy to think of the formal rules and laws established by the government. For example, a common rule prohibits insider trading. In other words, if a member of a company has information about the company's strategy or knows, for example, that the company is going to be sold soon, he or she is not legally permitted to trade that company's stock using information that only someone on the "inside" would know. This rule exists to help create an equal playing field among market participants who would not have this kind of insider information. Governments set many of the rules of the game, and these guidelines are essential for creating and sustaining markets.

But most of the rules that govern market behaviour are not formal or even explicit rules; rather, they are informal and taken for granted by the participants. These informal rules are as much part of the market as the formal rules, and participating in a market requires knowing both sets. For example, we are all familiar with the dating market, where unspoken rules have to be mastered. Those rules include how and when to express interest in someone else or demonstrate appropriate levels of enthusiasm. But knowing whether and how you can bargain for the best deal with someone else in a market situation (let's say, with an employer, when you are negotiating a salary) is an important type of normally hidden, but often crucial, cultural knowledge. If you master the art of negotiation, you will make more money over the course of your career than you otherwise would.

Most of the time, we buy things from stores or companies we know, and the price is marked and can be easily compared to other similar products or stores. But what about when we are shopping at a flea market, a farmers' market, or a garage sale? At the Grand Bazaar market in Turkey, many complicated rituals are typically interacted when we are buyers and sellers attempting to negotiate what we want.

Agencja Fotograficzna Caro/Alamy Stock Photo

8.2 Why Are Organizations Important for Social and Economic Life?

Zuma Press, Inc/Alamy Stock Photo

Organizations in the Modern World

When we say that we live in the age of markets, we have to add one important caveat: These markets are not typically just made up of a bunch of individuals selling goods to other individuals. Rather, contemporary markets contain within them a variety of organizations, large and small, that shape the boundaries of most markets. In almost everything we do, we encounter an organization, and an almost endless array of organizations impact our daily lives—hospitals, day-care centres, schools, churches, businesses, and government. Virtually every market has a set of key organizations that operate within it in both competitive and noncompetitive ways. To gain a deeper understanding of how markets and modern economies work—and ultimately how social forces influence the economy as a whole—sociologists have placed considerable importance on analyzing how organizations work. What role(s) do organizations play in your daily life?

What exactly is an **organization**? It can be defined as a group engaged in a specific activity that has an identifiable purpose or goal and that has an enduring form of association that is independent of the people involved in it at any one moment. In other words, an organization has to be something more than just a collection of individuals doing the same thing; a group of friends going fishing is not an organization, but a company that farms fish and sells them to supermarkets is.

Given this admittedly broad definition, it is no surprise that there are many different types. Organizations can be huge (e.g., the Canadian government, Walmart) or as small as three or four people (if they have established some procedure for keeping things going even if one or more of the members have to be replaced). In spite of such vast differences in the size and scale of organizations, sociological research has found that they typically have many things in common. In this section of the chapter we discuss several of these well-established common features.

Organizational Persistence

8.2.1 Explain how organizations can form, transform, and survive over time.

One nearly universal finding about organizations, and one that provides an important clue to understanding how they work, is that once established, organizations tend to persist. This holds true even in the face of important challenges to their existence. A famous organization is the March of Dimes, a charitable organization established in 1938 by President Franklin Roosevelt and others to fight polio, a medical condition that could

JC Olivera/STR /Contributor/Getty Images

Education regarding an illness can force charitable organizations to redefine their missions.

cripple an individual. (Roosevelt himself was a victim of polio.) The organization began with one simple request: Donate a dime to help the fight against polio. In 1955, a new vaccine (known as the Salk vaccine) was approved for use, and it proved so successful that it essentially eliminated polio. The organization had achieved its goals. So did the March of Dimes go out of business? No. After a long internal discussion, in 1958 the organization's leaders decided to look for new medical conditions to fight by raising money from the public, ultimately changing the mission to fighting birth defects and other childhood diseases. It has since expanded into an all-purpose health research organization that operates in the U.S., Canada, and other countries around the world (Rose, 2003).

Why does an organization like the March of Dimes persist even when its original mission has been completed? One reason is that the people who are involved have a strong interest in the organization's survival. Employees who work for an organization, for example, want the organization to survive so they keep their jobs. An organization also may have a name and a reputation that is well known to others. That name brand usually is valuable, and rather than going completely out of existence an organization may survive by being absorbed into (or bought by) another organization.

Most importantly, organizations (especially as they grow) tend to develop into **bureaucracies**, where rules are written down and defined roles of members of the organization are made clear. Once a bureaucratic form emerges, an organization is on the road to establishing a long-term presence. In a bureaucratized organization, people can join and leave the organization, but the organization itself persists because it has established operating principles and procedures that do not rely on particular individuals to maintain it. In these cases, the organization has now become more than the sum of all of the individuals within it.

The famous case of Apple Computer provides a good example of how bureaucracies develop as organizations grow (even in the computer industry, which prides itself on avoiding bureaucracy!). Although the story of Apple Computer is frequently presented as a story about the brilliant business acumen of CEO Steve Jobs (the visionary who combined a fascination with both technology and design with a willingness to explore new products), Apple is also a fairly typical story of an organization that evolved (successfully, in this case) over time from a small organization created by a couple of individuals to a larger, bureaucratic organization. Founded in a garage in Palo Alto in 1977 by two young computer enthusiasts, Jobs and Steve Wozniak, Apple produced the first commercially successful personal desktop computer (the Apple II) and in 1984 launched the Macintosh computer, which would be one of the company's staple products. But it was not a story of one success after another. Apple made many wrong turns along the way (including, at one point, firing company founder Jobs, introducing failed products, and seeing declining market share for its personal computers). The company's survival during its ups and downs in the 1980s and 1990s, before the introduction of its breakthrough products in the late 1990s and 2000s such as the iPod, the iPhone, and the iPad, hinged in large part on the creation of an organizational structure that had the resources and stability to cushion the ups and downs of its business. Perhaps if Jobs had not returned to Apple, it would have remained a much smaller company or even gone out of business. But either way, its evolution makes it a dramatically different type of organization today than when Jobs and Wozniak founded it.

The Downside of Bureaucracy

8.2.2 Identify the benefits and limitations of bureaucratic processes and regulations.

While the process of bureaucratization of an organization can provide strength and stability, it can also create complex new problems for how decisions get made. We have a number of shorthand expressions for these problems: Bureaucracies, as we all know, are famous for "red tape," for being "inefficient," and for being "bloated" and ineffective. Calling someone a "bureaucrat" can often be an insult. Let's probe these issues a bit further.

To ensure stability and predictability, organizations rely strongly on rules and regulations. Sociologist Max Weber, observing the German civil-service sector in the early twentieth century, provided the single most influential description and analysis of bureaucratic organizations (Weber, 1922/1978). The move of any organization toward a bureaucratic form, Weber thought, was a necessary response to the complexities of modern large-scale markets and big governments. An organization that embraced bureaucratic means was attempting to find ways to allocate resources and make decisions more efficiently than it otherwise would. The hallmark of a bureaucracy, according to Weber, was the existence of formal procedures and rules, which are supposed to ensure both consistency (the same problem or task is addressed the same way each time) and accountability (individuals in the bureaucracy are accountable to those above them). Bureaucracy, Weber thought, was an inevitable feature of the modern world. Yet Weber also saw many negative aspects of bureaucracies. While undertaken with efficiency as the end goal, the bureaucratic form of organization also creates stifling routines and boring jobs, and makes it more difficult for individuals within a bureaucratic organization to be creative and innovative; bureaucracy can also make it more difficult for an entire organization to respond to changes in the environment in which it operates.

Weber's theory of bureaucracy emphasizes three central features. First, bureaucracies establish positions of authority that are hierarchically organized—that is, the higher up you go in a bureaucracy, the more authority is vested in that position. Bureaucracies are hierarchically organized so that there is a chain of command, and everyone working in the bureaucracy is responsible to the office above him or her. (Even the president or CEO of an organization is typically responsible to an outside board of some kind.) Second, written rules define the scope and responsibility of each position within a bureaucratic organization. Each employee is expected to perform those (and only those) roles. Third, while organizations may have volunteers, they are only properly considered bureaucratic when the decision-making officers of the organization are full-time, salaried positions.

Weber's classical theory captured many of the key features of the bureaucratic organizations that were growing rapidly in the late nineteenth and early twentieth centuries. But Weber missed a few things. In particular, he focused on the formal aspects of bureaucratic organizations, but did not analyze the informal aspects of how bureaucracies actually work. Later critics and researchers who have studied many organizations in both the for-profit and not-for-profit sectors have noted just how often bureaucratic organizations deviate from their formal rules. Rules are routinely broken or ignored and often can prescribe what someone does in an actual job only in a vague way. Bosses are only sometimes able to effectively supervise their subordinates. Bureaucratic officials are also self-interested in ways that Weber's model did not anticipate. For example, bureaucrats often seek to increase the amount of resources available to their unit, whether or not that is the wisest use of the organization's resources. Having a bigger budget under their control provides many benefits, even if the money might have been better spent somewhere else in the organization.

In the real world, then, bureaucracies are often messy places where rules and regulations are difficult to define and implement. Organizational decision-making seldom follows a clear path. **Loose coupling** is one way many managers within bureaucratic organizations try to disentangle themselves and their unit from irrational rules and regulations or to implement those rules in creative ways that make sense. In sociological terms, loose coupling decentralizes decision-making and permits multiple approaches within the same bureaucratic organization to emerge. Loose coupling is evident in many different organizational environments. It has both positive and negative elements. It can be valuable because it provides organizations with the flexibility to manoeuvre as challenges arise. For example, a few years ago the New York City Department of Education mandated that schools adopt a zero-tolerance policy for student possession of cellphones on campus. The district policies required that all student cellphones be confiscated and held until parents were notified and came to school to pick up what had been defined as contraband. Administrators and teachers in many schools, however, understood that while the intention of the policy was perhaps laudable, attempts at implementation would at best be laughable. In many schools, students had cellphones with the full support of their parents, who used these devices to keep in touch with them. Confiscating phones of the entire student body and summoning a mob of irate parents would not have been effective practice.

But loose coupling has downsides. For example, it can't go so far as to allow principals and schools the freedom to disregard federal rules requiring standardized testing, without putting federal funding in jeopardy. More generally, too much loose coupling within an organization can mean that overall objectives can never be properly implemented or that individual units will tend to be in conflict and competition with each other. But large bureaucratic organizations need some room for loose coupling to avoid the worst consequences of bureaucratic inefficiencies or one-sided rules that don't fit in some cases. The key is to find the right balance, which is never easy and can change in a short period of time.

8.3 What Is the Relationship Between Organizations and Their External Environments?

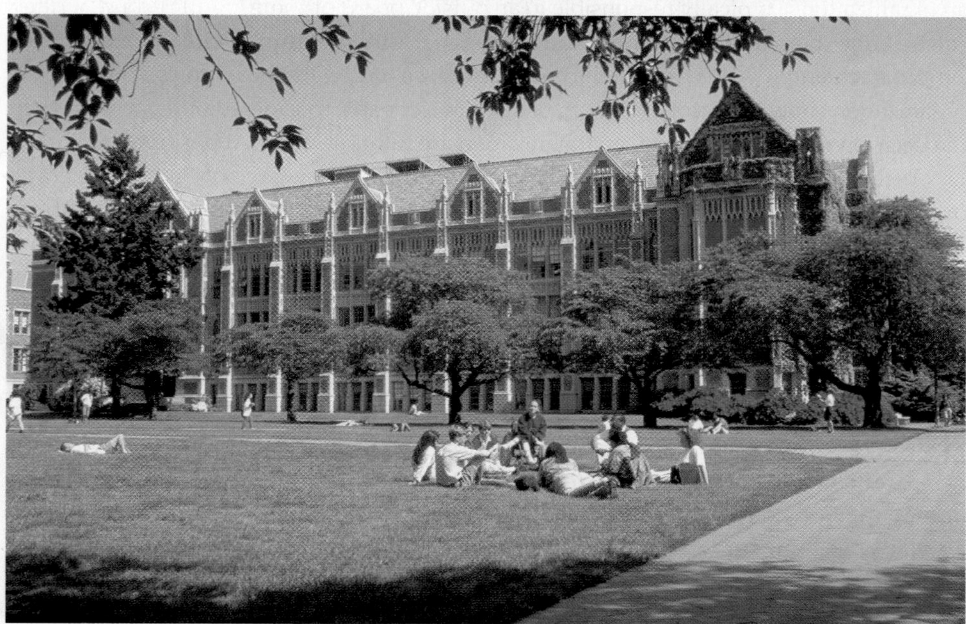

Jonathan Nourok/PhotoEdit, Inc.

Organizations and Their Environments

The sociological imagination, as we have discussed throughout this book, urges us to look at the social contexts in which individuals and groups—and now organizations—interact. Like individuals and groups, organizations operate in the context of a larger environment, but one consisting of other competing firms, government policies and legal requirements, and sometimes unions. In an increasingly global world, organizations face pressures (but may also have opportunities) that may arise from developments happening a long way from their headquarters. Just as individuals are affected by their environments, so too are organizations.

To better understand this, it may be useful to start with an analogy with nature. Every animal, plant, or other organism lives within a particular natural environment. Evolutionary theory teaches us that the environment influences not only the life and death of any organism, but also the ways in which the organism changes across generations. Like organisms, organizations depend on their surroundings to provide resources necessary for survival. Where an animal might depend on its environment to provide food and water, an organization depends on it for economic, social, and political resources. Without these resources the organization will perish. This ecological metaphor is useful for understanding how organizations work. In this section of the chapter, we consider some classical ideas about organizations and their environments that have grown from this analogy.

Organizational Structure

8.3.1 Discuss how an organization's structure and niche may contribute to its success or its failure.

An ecological approach to understanding organizational structure raises these questions: Do successful organizations continually adapt to the environments in which they operate? Or do they survive because they were uniquely suited to the environment from the start? Either way, organizations must have features that are suitable for their environment if they are to stay alive and prosper. Large organizations do sometimes go out of business or shrink and change dramatically. Generally, the organizations that survive and thrive over time have created an internal culture that is a good match to their environment, one that makes it possible to change as the external environment evolves (Hannan & Freeman, 1989). But many organizations have developed internal cultures that resist change, perhaps because their bureaucratic rules are too rigid. Strong resistance to change is referred to as **structural inertia**, and it can be terminal if the environment dramatically changes and the absence of adaptation leads to organizational mortality.

It is not hard to see why structural inertia occurs. An organization that is successful early in its history has little reason to change. As the expression goes, "Why fix what isn't broken?" But structural inertia may also prevent the organization from surviving at some point. How would this happen? Though structural inertia is necessary, once it is set in place it is difficult to change. Think of the *Titanic*, a luxury cruise ship that tragically sank in the Atlantic in April 1912. The first of its kind when built, the ship's massive size made it great, but its size also contributed to its inertia, thereby rendering it unable to avoid hitting an iceberg. As organizations become successful, they can become like the *Titanic*—the very things that won them success may actually make them eventually fail. The history of business organizations is littered with successful firms that are now bankrupt because they could not adapt to oncoming challenges despite their initial success.

How do organizations survive in the face of competition? Although situations can be unique, the most common way that an organization competes is to identify and fulfill a **niche** (a distinct segment of a market or social process) for which the organization's services or products are in demand. A niche might provide high-end (expensive) products or services to a small group willing to pay very high prices for the "best," cheap goods and services to a larger group, or a good or service that no one else is currently providing. Though there will still be competition from similar organizations, an organization that is effective at identifying and servicing a unique niche will usually do well, at least as long as that niche exists.

The competition to control a niche is easiest to imagine among for-profit organizations, but we can see the same thing if we look at nonprofit organizations. Take, for example, higher education. All of the organizations in higher education (such as the University of Toronto, Mount Allison University, the University of Northern British Columbia, or the privately funded Quest University) attempt to create for themselves a unique niche that appeals to certain kinds of students. By identifying a particular market of students that the institution can serve, a school limits the amount of competition it must face to survive in its environment.

Take, for example, the difference between a small university in one province (such as the University of Northern British Columbia) and an elite Ivy League university in another province (such as McGill University). While the small university has institutional competition in the form of similar schools, its identification as a regional, undergraduate institution allows it to limit the demands placed on it and its competition for survival. For the most part, the University of Cape Breton does not need to compete with ivy league universities like the University of Toronto for the same students. Students interested in or able to afford attending Ivy League universities in Canada are likely to be somewhat different than their peers who choose among only small undergraduate schools during their university application process. They may have different goals, different resources, and other features.

A small university in one province, for example, may have a much more specified array of majors than an elite Ivy League university—a regional university in one province might have majors in veterinary medicine, business, and the like, while a large research intensive university like the University of Toronto or private ivy league universities in the U.S. may focus more on graduate and professional training such as law or medicine. Different types of students are drawn to each of these types of schools. Similarly, while the small university does not need to compete as heavily with large research-based universities for its applicants once it has its own niche, it also reduces the actions demanded of it by limiting the types of people it serves.

By clearly identifying itself as one that serves students who are interested in particular levels of study or specific programs, the small university has provided itself with the freedom to put resources into these specific majors by providing focused education that prepares students for answering the specific needs of the regional economy. For example, Brock University, located in the heart of wine country on the southern Ontario Niagara peninsula, offers a variety of specialized programs in oenology and viticulture to prepare graduates for work in the wine production industry. These resources then give the institution a stronger ability to compete for organizational survival against those that are outside its niche but still in the larger institutional environment, like large research-intensive universities.

Organizational Similarity

8.3.2 Explain organizational isomorphism and identify the differences among three types: coercive, normative, and mimetic.

While organizations compete, one of the most well-established sociological findings about organizations is that over time successful organizations in the same field will tend to look a lot like each other. In spite of the endless array of organizations in the modern world, there are many common features that make them easy to recognize or understand. For example, think about high schools. There are obvious differences between public and private high schools, between affluent private schools and impoverished public ones, or between high schools that have a large percentage of immigrant students versus those that do not. Despite these differences, almost all of these schools are organized in a very similar way. They have principals who administer the school, they offer the same core subjects, they have more or less the same kinds of sports teams and physical education systems, they organize the day into periods where students move from class to class and work with different teachers, and so forth. Experimental schools vary some of these dimensions but rarely depart too far. Why are there so many similarities in the ways organizations (like high schools) operate?

gyn9037/Shutterstock

Pressure for disability accommodations can take many forms.

Let us begin with a concrete example. In Canada, human rights legislation across all provinces and territories declares that those citizens with disabilities should have the same access to physical spaces such as buildings and bathrooms as their non-disabled peers. Each provincial act includes a set of rules for the physical buildings in which organizations operate. These rules and regulations mandate that certain facilities in every commercial and public-service building be accessible to all individuals, including those who are challenged with a mobility disability. Organizations then have to modify their physical structures to comply with these rules. Modification of a building by adding additional wheelchair ramps, elevators, handicap-accessible bathrooms, and the like, however, is very expensive and time consuming, and the likelihood of being caught for failing to comply is low. Nonetheless, researchers have found that most large organizations make a serious effort to comply. Why?

There are several reasons an organization might comply with the demands of increasing accessibility, all of which are related to a sociological concept called **organizational isomorphism**. *Isomorphism* refers to the process whereby organizations in the same field tend to become increasingly similar to each other over time (DiMaggio & Powell, 1983). Isomorphism is a complicated word and concept—definitely hard to pronounce (eye-so-more-fizzum)—but it is an important and valuable term to try to grasp and remember. The phenomenon of isomorphism has been found repeatedly in research across a wide range of organizations and industries. So why might organizations in the same field, market, or industry become more similar over time? The most straightforward way this occurs is when organizations are pressured to comply with certain legal regulations or requirements (such as the legal requirements that all buildings must provide wheelchair access). When applied to all organizations in the field, **coercive isomorphism** occurs. In this case, these organizations are compelled to take the same actions to avoid facing consequences that might include being sued by a customer or being fined by a government agency.

But compulsion is hardly the only way isomorphism occurs. There are two other reasons an organization might adopt similar behaviours or policies. Imagine that an organization, in response to the human rights law, must make a significant investment in making physical building changes. While these expenses may be considerable, the damage that could be done to the organization's legitimacy by *not* complying might be even greater. Imagine if protestors in wheelchairs began picketing in front of the organization's headquarters because it refused to provide access for disabled persons. That would clearly not be a good thing for the organization's reputation.

However, if an organization moves quickly to promote equal access, it may be able to advertise itself as especially fair, sensitive, and responsive (and perhaps even imply that its competitors are not). In recent years, many companies have voluntarily adopted "green" practices and asserted they are environmentally sensitive organizations. Employers within the organization often have expectations—learned in schools or from professional associations—about what the organization should do. Responding to these kinds of (positive or negative) expectations is what is known as **normative isomorphism**: The organization is responding to pressures that are exerted on its legitimacy. Here the word *normative* indicates the general feelings or expectations of the people that the organization serves (for example, employees and customers or clients). Failing to attend to those expectations and needs of its supporters, the organization would fail to address the normative environment in which it lives and, thus, would potentially lose its legitimacy within that environment.

Now let us assume the organization feels pressure both legally and from wanting to allow disabled attendees entrance to their building (or avoid appearing insensitive). Then what? How does it know which type of modifications would be appropriate to build? Facing this uncertainty, it might look at what other organizations are doing and then do something similar. In this way, the company is engaging in what is known as **mimetic isomorphism**, which means it literally imitates or mimes the practices of other organizations. By making itself look like all the others, the organization does not attract negative attention that might call its legitimacy into question. Inside organizations, the practice of keeping an eye on competitors to see how they do things—the study of "best practices" in an industry—is an example of mimetic isomorphism.

8.4 How Is Work Inside Organizations Structured?

Bloomberg/Getty Images

The Division of Labour in Modern Societies

One of the most important things that markets and organizations do is provide jobs and economic opportunities for individuals. Most people below retirement age earn either a wage paid by an employer or income from self-employment. In 1970, hours worked per person were similar in Western Europe and North America. Today,

Figure 8.2 Average Hours Worked in a Calendar Year

SOURCE: Gertler, Mark, and Kenneth S. Rogoff, eds., *NBER Macroeconomics Annual* 2005, Figure: Average hours worked in a calendar year., © 2006 Massachusetts Institute of Technology, by permission of The MIT Press.

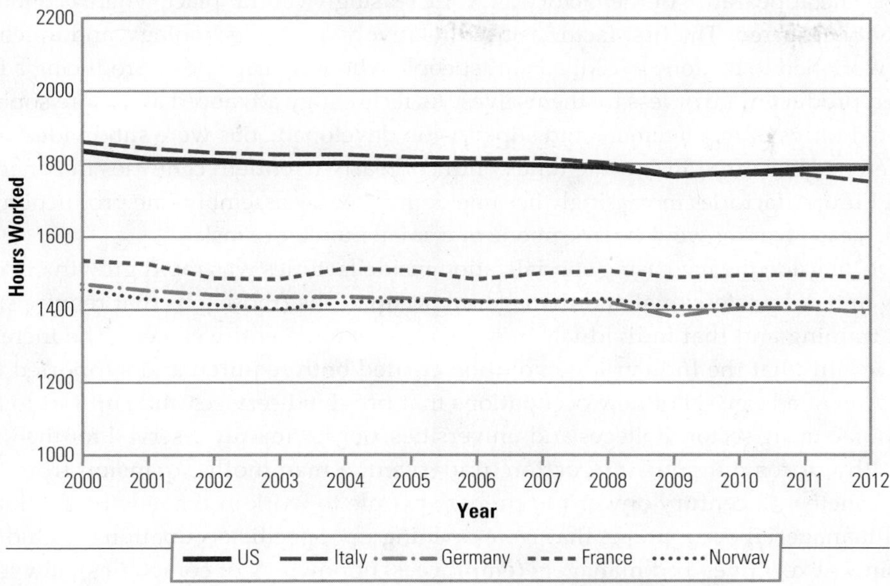

however, the average full-time worker in the United States works about 150 hours more than the average number of hours worked per year by full-time workers in other similar countries, about an extra month of work time (see Figure 8.2). If the typical American worker sleeps about 8 hours a night and takes two weeks of vacation a year, he or she is spending 30 percent of his or her waking hours at work. Similarly, in Canada, the amount of time workers spend in paid employment increased dramatically between 2001 and 2012. In 2001, 55% of men and 39% of women reported working more than 45 hours per week. By 2012, 68% of men and 54% of women reported working more than 45 hours per week (Duxbury & Higgins, 2012).

Given the amount of work the average adult does, it should hardly come as a surprise to learn just how important work is for our sense of self. The overall (or aggregate) distribution of jobs across an entire society significantly defines the economic system and what type of society it is. All societies have a **division of labour**, in which some people do some things and other people do other things. Imagine you were dropped down in a strange place and asked to figure out what kind of society you were observing. Two things you might want to know would be: What jobs do people have here? What is the division of labour in this society? Hunting-and-gathering societies and agrarian societies, past and present, are defined by the basic fact that most individuals are engaged in those activities. They have a relatively simple division of labour. By contrast, contemporary advanced societies like the United States and Canada are defined by a complicated division of labour in which there are hundreds of different kinds of jobs in a bewildering array of organizational settings.

Increasing Specialization in the Division of Labour

8.4.1 Explain how workplaces and the type of work people do changes over time.

How is work organized in modern workplaces, and how has it changed over time? The specialization of tasks within and between organizations, and among workers toiling within organizations, provides a useful starting point for thinking about work in contemporary and earlier societies.

Since the mid-nineteenth century, there has been an explosion in the types of jobs people could do. The **Industrial Revolution**—the rise of large-scale production of goods and products for mass markets—revolutionized the nature of work because it led to the appearance of the factory as an increasingly central place where economic activity occurred. The first factories used relatively simple technology, and much of the work had to be done by skilled craftspeople who were capable of producing a finished product more or less by themselves. As technology advanced and more sophisticated forms of management and supervision developed, jobs were subdivided into different specialties. In the late nineteenth and early twentieth centuries in America and Europe, factories increasingly became dominated by assembly-line production, in which each worker would perform one or a small number of tasks.

Alongside the increasing specialization inside factories was rapid growth of both new and old professional and managerial **occupations** (those jobs that require special training and that individuals may perform over an entire career). The increasing wealth that the Industrial Revolution created both required and supported the creation of a large set of new occupations that provided services and support to the manufacturing sector. Colleges and universities, once primarily reserved for the very wealthy or for religious instruction, underwent a mammoth expansion from the late nineteenth century onward to prepare people to work in the new professional and managerial occupations that were opening up. Specific occupations, including business executives and managers (employees, not owners of companies), lawyers, accountants, and professors and teachers, expanded rapidly.

The continuing growth of specialization in occupations has continued to the present. Statistics Canada has a detailed job classification system that identifies over 17,000 different job titles. Reviewing the list, we find some remarkably fine-grained distinctions that would have little meaning to an outsider but are entirely comprehensible to those working in the area.

The Labour Process

8.4.2 Discuss how organizations develop and manage the labour process and their workers.

The vast number of jobs might seem to imply that only specialists can perform those jobs. But most occupations are performed inside organizations and are controlled in a variety of ways by the supervisors and managers who oversee individual workers. The **labour process** is the term that sociologists have developed to describe how jobs are organized and controlled by managers from above. The study of the labour process attempts to open up the workplace by examining how workers actually do their jobs, how managers and supervisors try to control and direct them, and how the relationships between the two unfold. It represents another way in which the sociology of the economy moves into areas to which classical economics paid relatively little attention. For classical economists, problems such as getting workers to cooperate as a team or not letting them goof around too much while on the job were not a central concern, but organizations face these problems all the time.

Monitoring work increases productivity, although it can also produce resistance, as researchers learned during the Hawthorne studies, conducted during the 1920s and 1930s.

Allan Cash Picture Library/Alamy Stock Photo

Early research into the labour process attempted to understand why some workplaces were more productive than others. In the famous **Hawthorne studies** in the 1920s and 1930s, Harvard industrial sociologist Elton Mayo and his associates conducted a variety of experiments with different teams of workers. The studies aimed to identify what factors might induce workers to produce more output in the same amount of time. Among other things, the researchers found that cooperation between the workers was especially important for increasing productivity. The act simply of systematically observing workers for the project also led to improved productivity.

Since the 1960s, however, questions about how to make work more efficient have tended to fall to engineers and business management scholars. The sociology of work and the labour process has instead come to focus on a very different set of questions about the organization of the labour process. An important shift was marked by the appearance of a book entitled *Labor and Monopoly Capital* by Harry Braverman (1974). This widely discussed study argued that to maximize profits, capitalist firms and their managers are continually driven to reduce their employees' ability to control what they do on the job. Braverman pointed to the rise of **scientific management**, a late-nineteenth-century and early-twentieth-century movement sparked by the writings of Frederick W. Taylor, an early industrial engineer, as central to modern management strategies. Scientific management is premised on the idea that managers need to figure out how to understand and control what the workers under them are doing. Instead of allowing workers to decide how something should be done, or done differently, managers should control those decisions and keep workers focused on precise tasks. The pinnacle of scientific management is the well-developed **assembly line** system of production, in which every task a worker must perform is completely scripted. Henry Ford, the founder of the Ford automobile company in Detroit, was among the first to implement fully such a design early in the twentieth century, and his assembly line was much copied all over the world.

The workplace Braverman described was one in which workers faced a steady process of **deskilling**, in which jobs are made ever more simple and workers become more interchangeable. In this way, management seeks to block or prevent workers from having the upper hand because they, rather than management, know how to "get the job done."

Take, for instance, the craft of shoemaking. Prior to the development of capitalism, Braverman argued, a shoe was typically made in its entirety by a craftsman known as a cordwainer (i.e., a shoemaker). A single person would make the pair from start to finish. In order to mass produce shoes in an efficient way, shoe companies and their managers had to study and break down each step in the process and assign each to a different person on a factory assembly line (today usually in a place like Vietnam or China). These modern factory workers probably do not know how to make the shoe in its entirety (including how to make the raw materials as well as how to assemble the entire shoe). Their individual tasks at work are heavily routinized and fairly easy to learn. The workers in such a factory are easily replaceable and have a weak position to resist what management wants as a result.

Braverman's thesis generated an enormous amount of debate about the extent and depth of deskilling in modern workplaces. Some sociologists argued that industrialization has had a more complex pattern. While some jobs clearly were being deskilled, there were also *new* types of jobs that required more skills than the jobs they replaced. And modern technology has in many cases increased the amount of skill required in particular jobs (for example, requiring knowledge about computers that

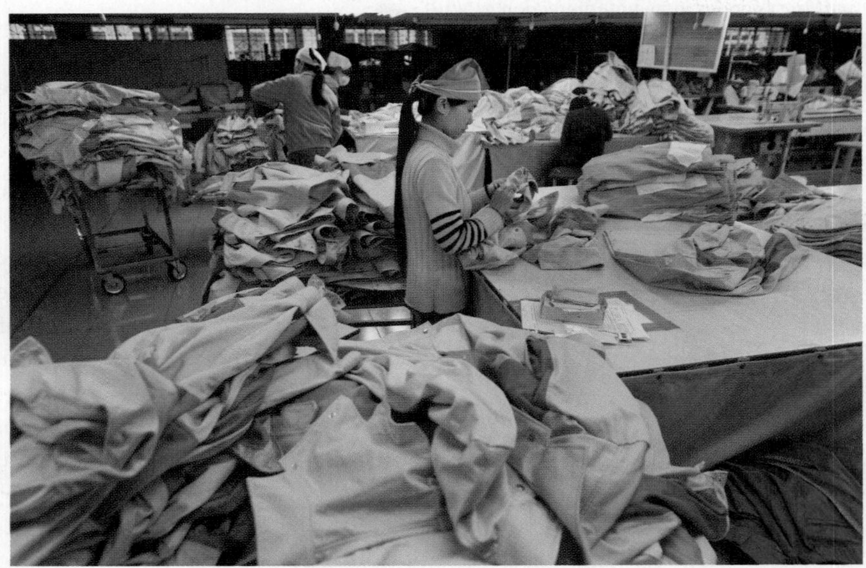

Assembly-line workers, such as those in this shoe factory, are easily replaceable because their tasks are routinized and easy to learn.

Ton Koene/VWPics/Alamy Stock Photo

Figure 8.3 Growth of High- and Low-Quality Jobs in 1960 and 1990 in the United States

NOTE: Jobs grouped into 10 categories based on analysis of relative quality; 1 = lowest; 10 = highest.

SOURCE: Based on "The American Jobs Machine: Is the New Economy Creating Good Jobs?" 2000, by Erik Olin Wright and Rachel Dwyer, *Boston Review 25*(6).

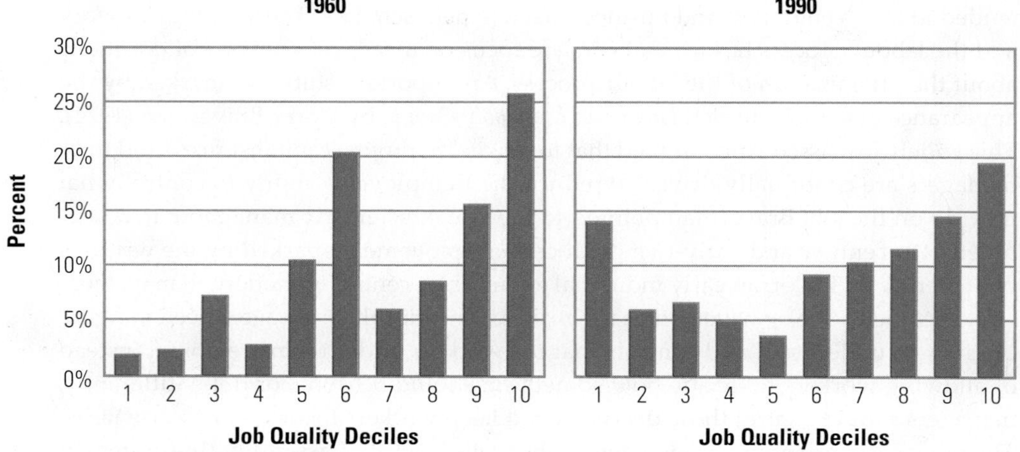

direct robots). Indeed, if we look at the overall pattern of job growth over time, it does seem clear that there has been a long-term shift toward jobs that require *more* skill and *more* education, not less—one reason the income differences between university graduates and those without university degrees has been growing in recent years (Goldin & Katz, 2010). Two sociologists who tested this proposition came to exactly this conclusion. Grouping all job titles into 10 categories ranging from the least skilled to the most skilled and asking where job growth is occurring across these categories, they found that in the 1960s, the pattern of fastest growth was for the most skilled job categories (8–10), and the lowest growth was at the bottom (Wright & Dwyer, 2003).

Observe the differences between job quality deciles over several decades in Figure 8.3. The 1960s were a time of solid economic growth in North America, and one characterized by strong growth in more skilled jobs. What about the 1990s, another period of solid (even spectacular) economic growth? Here, the authors find a more mixed pattern, in which the fastest-growing occupations are those at the top (10), but the second-fastest-growing title is at the very bottom (1), followed by the medium- to higher-skilled categories (6–9). On balance, though, there is little evidence that workers are being pushed into the least skilled (or most deskilled) jobs.

Other research that has examined either specific occupations or workplaces paints a much more nuanced picture of the relationship between the skills of workers and management's attempts to squeeze as much out of their workers as possible (Vallas, Finlay, & Wharton 2009). For example, many kinds of skills that workers develop in their jobs are not easily measured but important. An assistant who can anticipate what the boss needs ahead of time, the restaurant cook who has learned how to substitute one ingredient for another when supplies run short without ruining the flavour of a dish, an auto mechanic who can solve a new problem she has not seen before, or a teacher who can sense when a student is not understanding some key point—all possess important skills that require the ability to respond to problems that even the most elaborate program of scientific management cannot anticipate or control. While many jobs may not require or enable an individual worker to become true craftspeople, this does

Sam Dao/Alamy Stock Photo

For those in professional jobs—especially in computing, business, law, medicine, and administration—increasing attention has been devoted to designing "alternative" workplaces that stress cooperation and interaction. At the forefront of this are the work campuses created by many high-tech companies.

Randy Duchaine/Alamy Stock Photo

not mean that there are not still important skills and knowledge being applied in everyday labour.

Ongoing changes in the organization of work and the labour process are reflected in the new workplaces of the twenty-first century. As we noted earlier in the discussion of organizations, increasingly, the large assembly-line factory in which an individual worker performs a single task (or set of tasks) is being replaced by workplaces where cooperation among workers is encouraged and jobs are more interchangeable and interconnected. This change is still ongoing, but it represents one of the most important shifts in the nature of work since the advent of the modern assembly line in the age of Ford.

Conclusion: Markets, Organizations, and Work in the Twenty-First Century

Using a sociological imagination to examine the interrelationships among markets, organizations, and work, we have noted throughout this chapter many ways in which important changes now are underway in advanced economies. We began by noting how market forces are penetrating many arenas of social life that were once handled by individuals, families, churches, or other social organizations. Markets are also growing into arenas where governments once held monopolies. To say that we live in the "age of the market" reflects its growing penetration into new areas of social life.

Work and organizations are not immune to these pressures and are changing as well. The organizations that are adapting best to this new environment often have loose coupling—the weakening of the relationship between executives at the top and the rest of the firm—in their organizational form. At the centre of this alternative type of organization is the idea that bureaucracies tend to stifle creativity; therefore, it is better to create organizations where members share tasks and responsibilities, and all participate in management to some extent. Further, work teams operating independently of one another may come up with innovations more rapidly than the classical bureaucratic firm. Some of the most common examples can be found in the high-tech sector. At firms like Google, Facebook, and many start-up companies in the sector, instead of a chain of command there are often a bunch of different work teams, typically with about three to seven members, who work together on various projects.

No one member of the team is irreplaceable, and the team takes advantage of its collective intelligence. The team has to report to higher management, and at some point if nothing is accomplished the team is broken up and members are reassigned to other, more productive units.

This does not mean that all of the insights of organizational theory that we have discussed in this chapter are going out the window. Quite the contrary: The pressures to emulate one another—what sociologists call isomorphism—appear to be driving some of the ongoing changes in work and organizational forms we have observed. For example, when one company or organization figures out how to cut its costs or implement a new style of workplace organization, other firms study that change and may implement it as well. Change is happening, but not in a random way.

Finally, the world of work is changing. For much of the second half of the twentieth century, most workers enjoyed some measure of job security and opportunity within the firms they worked. Today, however, young people entering the labour market can anticipate having to change jobs every few years, and the possibility of periods without work (and income) have been increasing. The twenty-first-century world of work is a dynamic one, and inefficient firms and industries will not be able to survive for long periods of time. There may be certain advantages to consumers in this new environment, but the emerging model of rapid change can impose real costs on individual workers and their families.

CHAPTER SUMMARY

The Big Questions Revisited 8

8.1 *How Do Social Factors Impact Markets?* We live in what is sometimes called the "age of the market," and sociologists are increasingly aware that markets are part of the social structure of society. In this section, we explored how a sociological understanding of markets differs from an economic understanding.

The Creation and Functioning of Markets

The Pervasiveness of Markets

Learning Objective 8.1.1: Identify alternatives to market capitalism and discuss the pervasiveness of markets in modern societies.

Defining Markets

Learning Objective 8.1.2: Explain how sociologists define markets differently than economists.

Social Networks

Learning Objective 8.1.3: Explain how social networks influence markets.

Markets and Power

Learning Objective 8.1.4: Explain how power influences markets.

Culture

Learning Objective 8.1.5: Explain how cultural knowledge influences markets.

8.2 *Why Are Organizations Important for Social and Economic Life?* To gain a deeper understanding of how modern economies work—and ultimately how social forces influence the economy as a whole—sociologists place considerable importance on analyzing the organizations that exist within markets, a topic explored in this section.

Organizations in the Modern World

Organizational Persistence

Learning Objective 8.2.1: Explain how organizations can form, transform, and survive over time.

The Downside of Bureaucracy

Learning Objective 8.2.2: Identify the benefits and limitations of bureaucratic processes and regulations.

8.3 *What Is the Relationship Between Organizations and Their External Environments?* In this section, we explored the relationship between organizations and their environment. Do organizations actually adapt to their environments, or do the organizations that survive do so because they were uniquely suited to the environment from the start?

Organizations and Their Environments

Organizational Structure

Learning Objective 8.3.1: Discuss how an organization's structure and niche may contribute to its success or its failure.

Organizational Similarity

Learning Objective 8.3.2: Explain organizational isomorphism and identify the differences among three types: coercive, normative, and mimetic.

8.4 ***How Is Work Inside Organizations Structured?*** In modern societies, jobs are specialized and have distinct labour processes associated with them. In this section, we examined various theories about job specialization and the management of the labour process.

The Division of Labour in Modern Societies

Increasing Specialization in the Division of Labour

Learning Objective 8.4.1: Explain how workplaces and the type of work people do changes over time.

The Labour Process

Learning Objective 8.4.2: Discuss how organizations develop and manage the labour process and their workers.

Learn the Terms

assembly line (p. 217)
bureaucracy (p. 208)
capitalism (p. 201)
central planning (p. 201)
coercive isomorphism (p. 213)
deskilling (p. 217)
division of labour (p. 215)
entrepreneur (p. 201)
Hawthorne studies (p. 216)
Industrial Revolution (p. 216)
labour process (p. 216)
loose coupling (p. 210)
market (p. 200)
mimetic isomorphism (p. 214)
niche (p. 211)
normative isomorphism (p. 214)
occupations (p. 216)
organization (p. 207)
organizational isomorphism (p. 213)
rational-choice perspective (p. 202)
scientific management (p. 217)
socialism (p. 201)
social network (p. 203)
structural inertia (p. 211)

Chapter 9

Social Stratification, Inequality, and Poverty

by Florencia Torche, Richard Arum, and Jeff Manza

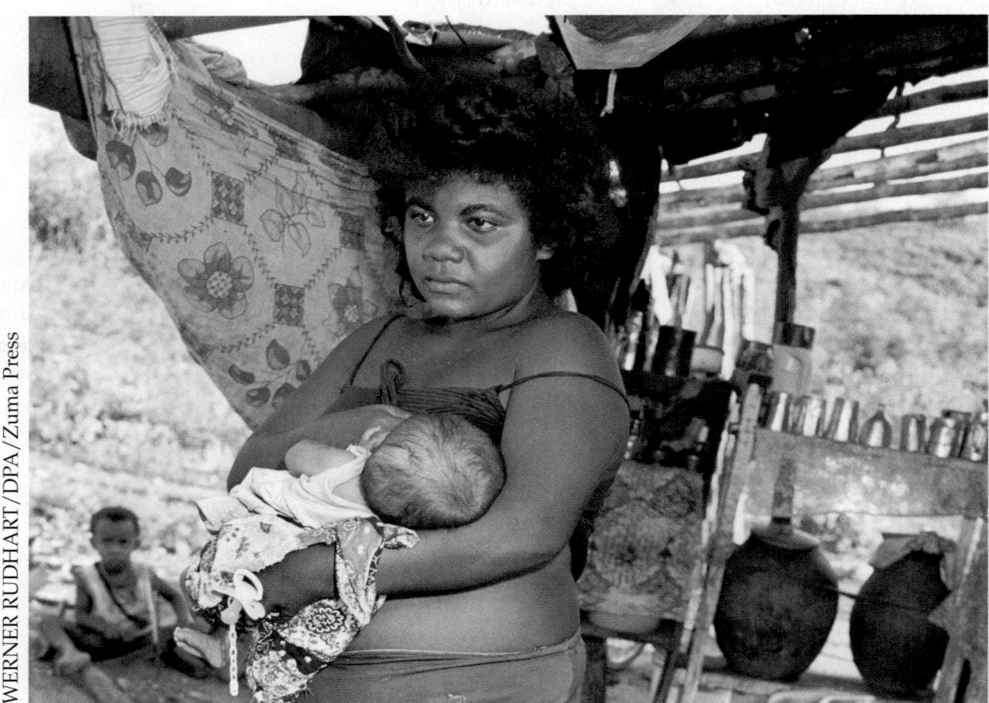

WERNER RUDHART/DPA/Zuma Press

Poverty affects children even before they are born, in visible ways such as lack of food and healthcare, and in less visible ways such as maternal stress.

Learning Objectives

9.1.1 Define *inequality* and explain how the form and level of inequality has varied throughout history.

9.1.2 Compare and contrast income and wealth as measures of economic inequality.

9.1.3 Define *class* and identify what constitutes a social class.

9.2.1 Discuss trends in income inequality and compare inequality in Canada and the United States to that in other countries around the world.

9.2.2 Identify factors explaining why economic inequality in North America has increased since the 1960s.

9.2.3 Describe who constitutes the "1 percent" in North America.

9.3.1 Define *social mobility* and describe how inequality of opportunity is measured.

9.3.2 Compare and contrast chances for social mobility in the United States to other countries such as Canada and Norway.

9.3.3 Identify factors that affect how much social mobility exists in a society.

9.3.4 Discuss the relationship between education and social mobility.

9.4.1 Distinguish between absolute and relative measures of poverty.

9.4.2 Identify factors that increase the likelihood of poverty.

9.4.3 Compare and contrast the level of poverty in North America to that in other regions.

9.4.4 Explain the impact of growing up in poverty on children.

9.4.5 Discuss the problem of homelessness and identify some contributing factors.

How does growing up poor impact children? We would like to think that all children have an equal chance to succeed in life. How true is this? This is a question that social scientists have been especially interested in examining in recent years. Despite the levels of wealth and economic productivity that capitalist societies have achieved, many families continue to live in poverty, in many cases lacking the resources to meet their everyday needs. And evidence is accumulating that children are especially harmed by poverty, sometimes in subtle and hidden ways. One of these ways is that the stress of a mother's poverty may be toxic to her child even *before* birth. Until recently, researchers believed that the fetus was fully isolated from its environment by the placenta, which would shield it from any damaging exposures. We now know that this is not the case. Researchers have confirmed, for example, that alcohol, tobacco, and drug use during pregnancy can affect the fetus. But what about the stresses caused by poverty? Is it possible that the stress faced by mothers living in poverty can affect the fetus, just like smoking or drug use? If so, it would suggest that the impact of poverty goes well beyond the lack of material resources.

The ideal research design to study the impact of stress during pregnancy would involve assembling a group of pregnant women and giving stress to half of them selected at random (treatment group) while not giving stress to the other half (control group). Of course, for ethical reasons, this sort of experiment is not possible. But in 2005, an earthquake in Chile provided an alternative strategy to assess the impact of stress. Because the earthquake came unannounced, and because it affected some Chilean cities but left others untouched, it created a kind of natural experiment similar to what might have happened if we had assigned added stress to only some pregnant mothers. In other words, those women who happened to experience the earthquake were, like poor mothers everywhere, exposed to extra stress during their pregnancy, while others who happened to live in areas far away from the earthquake served as the control group for the study. By comparing these two groups of pregnant women, Florencia Torche was able to measure the effect of stress separate from other factors usually associated with it.

The findings were striking. Babies exposed to the earthquake in the first trimester of gestation were far more likely to be born preterm and low weight, two conditions that have been shown to have very serious consequences. Babies born preterm require much more medical attention and are at a higher risk of dying in the first year of life and of experiencing health, developmental, and cognitive problems later on if they survive. And this is only an extreme impact; other, less obvious negative consequences of being exposed to stress can be found among a much larger group of babies in the study.

The Big Questions

1. **What is inequality?** At the heart of the study of social stratification is the concept of inequality. We know that some people simply have more than others. But why? Has the enormous gap between rich and poor always existed? What is the sociological concept of class, and does it help us understand inequality? We examine all of this in the first section of the chapter.
2. **Why is North America so unequal?** Inequality in both Canada and the United States today is about as high as it has been since we started measuring it in the early twentieth century, and poverty rates have remained persistently high as well. How do Canada and the United States compare with other developed countries? Does North America have more people living in poverty than other countries? Why is North America so unequal?
3. **Do we all have an equal opportunity to succeed in life?** Social mobility, which refers to the movement of individuals from their family's social position to their own social position in adulthood, is one of the most important topics in the study of social stratification. Inequality of opportunity arises whenever some individuals or groups have privileged access to better jobs and/or schools by virtue of the family they were born into. In this section, we examine how social mobility is measured, why countries differ in opportunity, and the relationship between education and mobility.
4. **How much poverty exists in North America and around the world?** Poverty is a complicated concept. Beyond a minimum of resources to ensure subsistence, it is difficult to define what our "basic" needs are. In this section, we examine two ways of viewing poverty and examine how much poverty there is in the United States and in other countries around the world. We also look closely at the problem of childhood poverty.

Why did the earthquake affect the chances of being born preterm? The most likely explanation is that the acute stress elicited by the earthquake has an effect on the placenta. Basically, stress sends a message to the fetus that says, "The outside world is not too safe, so you should get out as soon as possible." This sets a biological clock for early delivery. Because premature birth predicts developmental problems later on, this study strongly suggests that being exposed to a stressful environment due to poverty even before birth may have a negative effect on a child's outcomes. Given strong evidence that poor mothers have more stressful pregnancies, this leads to a very troubling conclusion: Even before they are born, poor children are much more likely to be exposed to stress that impacts their development in the womb, and that stress is very damaging and will have lifelong impacts. This is, as we will see, just one of the many ways in which poverty and inequality have negative consequences for individuals and society as a whole.

This research suggests but one of the many complex ways in which inequalities in any society can have hidden as well as more obvious consequences. A central value in all modern democratic societies is the idea of "equality of opportunity," which means that everyone, regardless of the resources of the families they are born into, has an equal chance at succeeding in life. But the fact that poverty handicaps children from conception and results in cumulative disadvantages as they grow up raises serious questions about the ability of these societies to achieve full equality of opportunity. In this chapter, we will examine why inequality exists, how it is maintained over time, and what the consequences of inequality are for society.

9.1 What Is Inequality?

Dhoxax/Shutterstock

Inequality: An Introduction

The sociological subfield of **social stratification** examines inequalities among individuals and groups. It is the systematic study of inequality. In this chapter, we will explore how sociologists think about inequality and poverty, and we also consider the puzzle of why there is so much poverty and inequality in places like the United States, in spite of the fact that it is among the richest countries in the world. In order to do that, we will need to make comparisons to the past as well as to many other countries around the world. In this section, we introduce the concept of inequality.

A Brief History of Inequality

9.1.1 Define *inequality* and explain how the form and level of inequality has varied throughout history.

Some people have more than others. **Inequality**—the unequal distribution of valued goods and opportunities—is a feature of virtually all known human societies. But throughout history, the form and level of inequality have varied widely. Primitive hunting and gathering societies, for example, typically shared their limited food supplies and resources among all members of the tribe more or less fairly, although decision-making powers might be exercised by tribal chiefs and special privileges were given to the medicine man (known as the *shaman*). In these primitive communities, mere survival was often in question, and there was little, if any, surplus left over after basic necessities were met. Without significant opportunities for some individuals to gain at the expense of others, there was relatively little possibility for significant inequalities to emerge.

As more complex societies and communities began to appear, and as desired objects not necessary for survival began to be invented and created, the first tribal "Big Men" emerged. A Big Man is someone who, whether because of physical strength or cunning, is able to hoard desirable goods and accumulate more status and power within the tribe or community than others (Flannery & Marcus, 2012). Big Men developed ways of showing off their wealth to establish their higher status within the tribe, for example, by building bigger huts or shelters, displaying jewellery or other special goods at ceremonies, or being able to take in multiple wives.

As more settled agricultural communities began to form, somewhere around 12,000 years ago, the possibilities of entrenching inequality first began to be possible. In particular, the establishment of **slavery** was an important landmark. Slaves are individuals who are compelled to work for others. A slave system facilitates the creation of wealth (which slaves do not share in) for the slave owners and creates a divide between humans living in the same vicinity. This was true in the slave societies of the ancient world, for example in ancient Egypt, where slaves were employed to build monuments to rulers, and famously in ancient Athens and the Roman Empire. But slavery would persist throughout history (and indeed, in small pockets, still exists today), most often in societies or places where agriculture is a primary type of economic activity.

While slavery produces an extreme form of inequality, two other types of inequality developed throughout the world prior to the advent of capitalism in the eighteenth and nineteenth centuries. One historical source of wealth accumulation involved traders who acquired desired goods in one place and sold them at a profit in another. Some of the merchants living in the cities and urban settlements of the Middle Ages (ca. 500–1500 CE), for example, were able to become rich by buying and selling goods, although this sort of wealth accumulation goes back even earlier. As armies and governments began to develop and expand, the desire to conquer other lands and capture valuable goods and resources or enslave the conquered peoples allowed some rulers and their favoured supporters to become wealthy.

But the most common and important source of inequality prior to the rise of capitalism arose from land ownership under a system known as **feudalism**. Feudalism refers to a social order based on agriculture in which those who own land (landlords) are entitled to receive the products of the labourers, or **serfs**, who are legally obligated to work for the landlord (but not otherwise enslaved). The largely agrarian settlements and societies of the Middle Ages were places where a handful of landlords were sometimes able to accumulate considerable fortunes (as we can see today in the grand castles that have survived from that era). Their ownership of large swaths of land permitted them to lease it out to serfs, who would typically become indebted to the lord and obligated to continue working the land. The vast majority of human beings lived, for centuries, on the verge of starvation and indeed died very young (the life expectancy at birth in medieval England was about 30 years; today it is around 80 years in Canada, the United States, and similar rich countries). The tiny stratum of economic elites in these societies generally lived apart from the rest of the population, sometimes in grand castles or gated estates, and there were no significant numbers of people in "middle" classes like those of today. Prior to the Industrial Revolution, the vast majority of people around the world toiled hard and died young by today's standards, and they enjoyed few luxuries.

The system of inequality as it has evolved over the past 250 years is much more complicated. The Industrial Revolution allowed rapid and sustained economic growth; societies as a whole got richer, and within them vastly greater inequalities emerged. The changes were dramatic. Between 1500 and 1820 CE, average annual incomes around the world grew from $545 to $675, a very modest change. But in areas where the Industrial Revolution was taking off, the change was more dramatic. In the 130 years between

Figure 9.1 Comparative Levels of Per-Person Income Per Capita

SOURCE: Based on *Monitoring the World Economy, 1820–1992* (Fig. 1–4), by Angus Maddison, 1995, Paris: OECD.

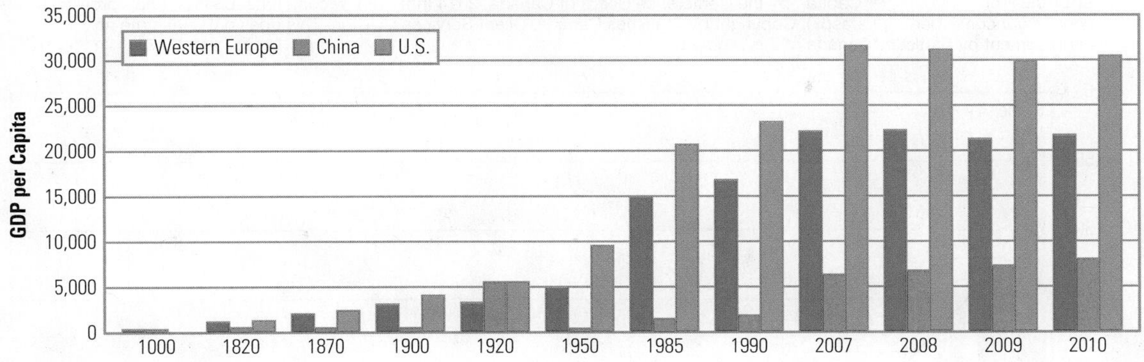

1820 and 1950, average incomes in Western Europe increased four times. And in just the 40 years between 1950 and 1990 they increased almost 3.5 times as much (average incomes in Europe have continued to rise since then). The pace of change and improvement in living standards have accelerated in recent years. Figure 9.1 illustrates the historical rise of income in Western Europe and the United States in comparison to China. The figure indicates the average income per person, adjusted for inflation, in the most developed countries in the world at each point in time (Maddison, 1995). The United States and Canada were similar to Western Europe until around 1870, after which both countries began to become richer faster, going from a per capita income of approximately $2,400 (U.S.) and $1,600 (Canada) per person in 1870 to $5,500 (U.S.) and $3,800 (Canada) in 1920, $9,500 (U.S.) and $7,200 (Canada) in 1950, and $23,000 (U.S.) and $18,000 (Canada) in 1990. To gain further perspective, we can compare Western Europe with China; through 1300 CE, the two regions had similar levels of income (with China leading for much of the period before), but they then began to diverge substantially as the take-off period for Western Europe and the United States began. Although Canada's per capita income has increased considerably over the past 250 years, it has grown more slowly than that of the United States. By 2013, Canada's national income grade was "C," along with other countries such as Australia, the Netherlands, Ireland, Sweden, and Germany. In comparison, Norway and the U.S. had income grades of A. Only the province of Alberta scored an income grade of A+ due to its resource boom, which helped lift levels of per capita income (Conference Board of Canada, 2014). Figure 9.2 illustrates the grades assigned by the Conference Board of Canada to various countries and Canadian provinces in 2013.

These per capita income figures are impressive, but they highlight just how unequal North America has become. The average income per person (for both children and adults) is currently around $25,000 in Canada and $31,000 in the United States. This implies that the average family of four would have an income between $100,000 and $124,000. But we know that is high; a family of four with an income of $100,000–$124,000 would be among the top 10 percent of all North American families, not around the middle. The reason for the disparity is the difference between the **median**

As this image suggests, under feudalism, landlords often built large homes (or even castles) and could afford many servants and other luxuries, while generations of serfs who worked the land barely had enough to survive.

North Wind Picture Archives/Alamy Stock Photo

Figure 9.2 Income Per Capita, Provinces and International Peers, 2013

($US at 2005 purchasing power parities and 2005 prices)

SOURCE: From "Income Per Capita," by the Conference Board of Canada, 2014 (http://www.conferenceboard.ca/hcp/provincial/economy/income-per-capita.aspx). Copyright by Statistics Canada, Client Services Division. This does not constitute an endorsement by Statistics Canada of this product.

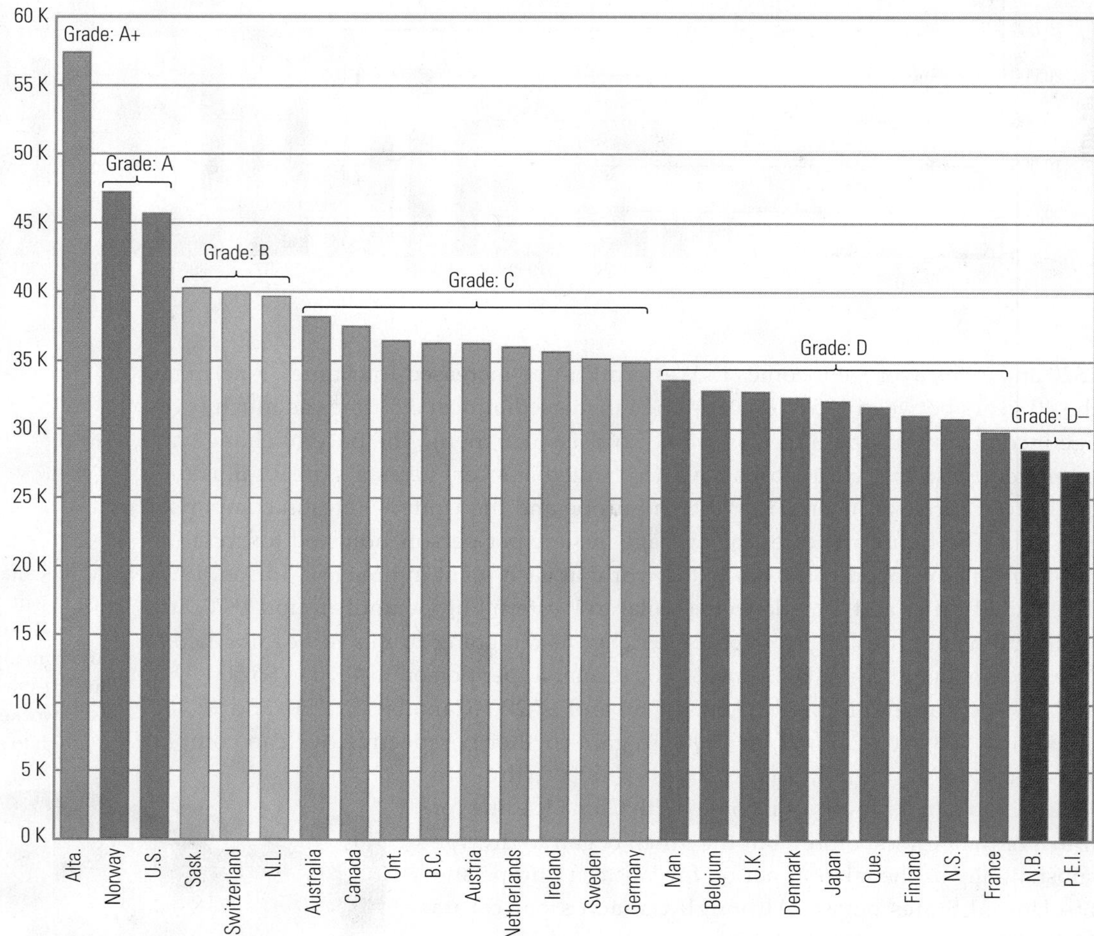

(the individual or family exactly in middle, where half of all such families are above and half are below) and the **mean** (or average). The median family income in the United States in 2009 was around $60,088, and in Canada it was around $68,000; this is vastly below the $100,000–$124,000 suggested above. How can this be? Why is the gap between the two statistics so large?

The short answer to understanding the difference between mean and median income is that because the gap between the very richest individuals and families and everyone else has grown enormously in recent years, the mean (average) income has risen much faster than the median. To understand the difference consider this scenario: There are five people in a bar, each earning around $50,000 a year, so their average income is $50,000; suddenly Bill Gates walks into the bar, and the average income in the bar increases massively even though the first five people have not changed jobs. In that case, the median gives a much better sense of how much the bar patrons are actually earning. Average incomes have risen, but largely because the top earners are earning more.

If we look globally, it is beyond doubt that those individuals and families who enjoy extraordinary wealth today are richer than the rich at any other point in human history. *Forbes* magazine does an annual survey of the richest people in the world. Topping *Forbes*'s analysis of the richest individuals in the world in 2014 was Microsoft founder Bill Gates, who was estimated to have a net worth of $76 billion. Next in line was the Mexican telephone mogul Carlos Slim Helú, who was estimated to have a net worth of $72 billion. The next two richest people—Spanish fashion retailer Amancio Ortega Gaona and American investor Warren Buffett—possessed an estimated $64 and $58 billion in wealth, respectively. Canada's richest family, the David Thomson family, joined the list at number 35 with a net worth of approximately $17.5 billion (Brown, 2014). Across the globe, the rich have gotten richer, and today they collectively control an enormous share of the world's wealth. It's a good time to be super-rich. One key report by a leading team of wealth investigators (Credit Suisse, 2013) shares these astonishing findings, for example:

- Almost half of all the wealth in the world is controlled by the top 1 percent of the world's population.
- There are over 1,000 billionaires in the world, about half of whom live in North America.
- The bottom 50 percent of the world's population has the same total wealth as approximately the 80 richest people in the world, and one projection suggests that in the next few years, the world's richest 1 percent will own more than the bottom 99 percent combined (Oxfam, 2015).

Measures of Economic Inequality: Wealth and Income

9.1.2 Compare and contrast income and wealth as measures of economic inequality.

In what specific ways are societies unequal? Social scientists have focused most of their attention on two critical measures of inequality: income and wealth. These are fundamentally different measures, and it is important to understand the difference. **Income** refers to the receipt of money or goods over a particular accounting period (such as hourly, weekly, monthly, or yearly). There are multiple possible sources of income: earned income from a regular job, income received from investments or ownership of income-generating properties or businesses, income transfers from the government, income received from family or friends (inheritances or gifts), and illegal or "underground" earnings (such as from crime or informal and untaxed work or business activity). Most people, before retirement age, receive most or all of their income from their job, but some have multiple sources of income.

Wealth, which refers to the net value of the assets (that is, assets minus debts) owned by individuals or family, is an alternative measure of household resources. The most commonly owned wealth asset is real estate. Approximately two-thirds of North Americans own the primary residence in which they live. Because homes tend to increase in value over time, home ownership has historically been the primary way that families with modest incomes can accumulate wealth (by buying a house and living in it for many years while it appreciates in value). A smaller subset of the population owns **net financial assets (NFAs)**. These include the total value of savings, investments, retirement accounts, and other convertible assets (less outstanding debts). While most families have savings accounts, far fewer have NFAs that are substantial. The median family has NFAs of $21,200 in 2013, but many families have little or no financial assets including savings for retirement (Brandon, 2012; Bricker et al., 2014). Wealth differences between individuals and groups are often far larger than income differences (Keister, 2006). Figure 9.3 illustrates wealth inequality in the United States between 1983 and 2007 (the non-home wealth excludes the ownership of real estate).

We can also consider other measures of well-being, and it is good to be aware of these. The most important of these alternative measures are **consumption** (how much an individual or family actually consumes in a month or a year, which may not directly correspond to their income if they are able to borrow money), health and well-being, and opportunity (a concept we discuss in much more detail later in the chapter).

Figure 9.3 Wealth Inequality

SOURCE: Based on data in *Recent Trends in Household Wealth in the United States: Rising Debt and the Middle-Class Squeeze—An Update to 2007* (Working Paper no. 589), by Edward N. Wolff, 2010, Annandale-on-Hudson, NY: Levy Economic Institute of Bard College.

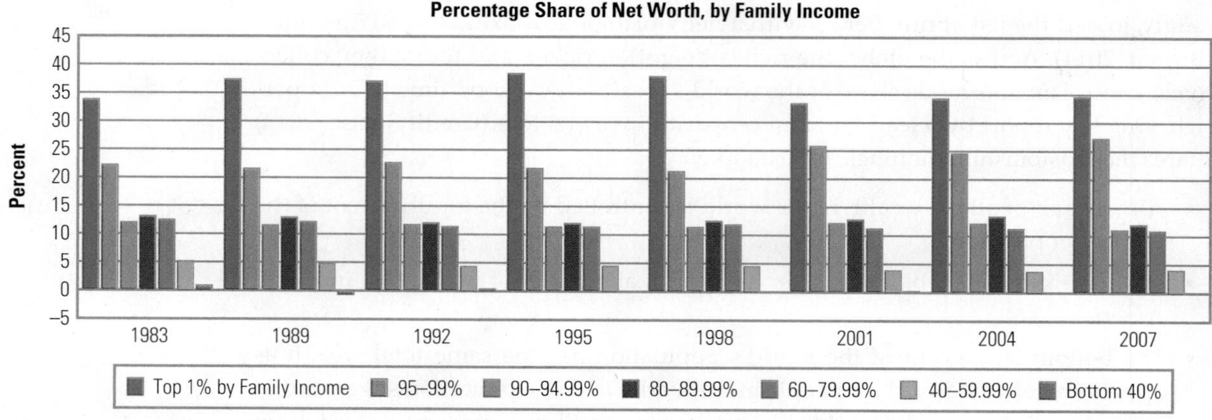

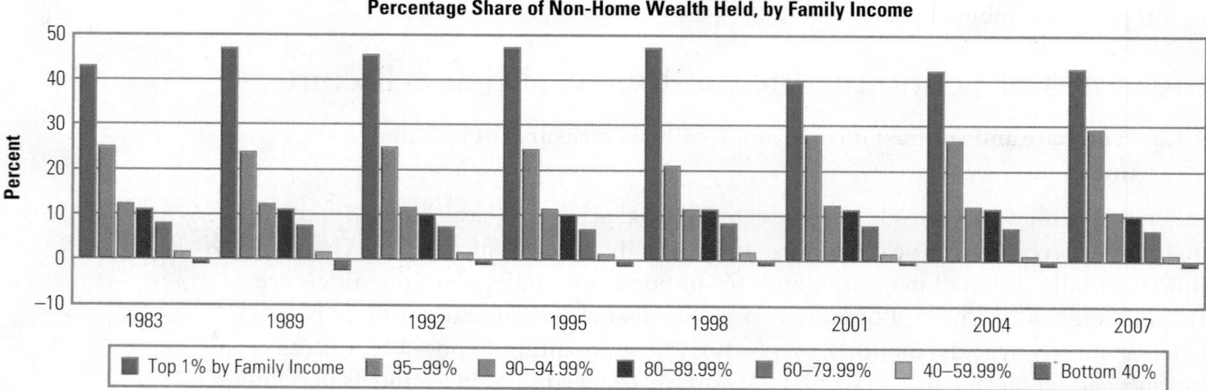

But most research and policy-making debates centre on income and wealth, so that will be our focus in the rest of this chapter.

Inequality by Class

9.1.3 Define *class* and identify what constitutes a social class.

The system of inequality today does not, of course, consist only of the rich and everyone else; sociologists have developed a variety of tools for understanding inequality across the entire range of income and wealth. In most countries, and indeed all of the developed countries most similar to Canada and the United States, there is a large **middle class**. If we think just about income, in this middle class are people working for a wide range of businesses in mostly professional, technical, or managerial jobs, or small business owners running modestly successful businesses. Those who have manual jobs, such as skilled factory workers, can also earn incomes that put them in the middle class, although that is much less common. Middle-class people and their families enjoy enough income to allow them to buy homes, cars, computers, and large televisions, and have savings and retirement accounts.

But the concept of "middle class" that many people think about is rather vague. How exactly do sociologists conceptualize what is meant by the middle class, and more specifically, what do they mean by class? Sociologists use the term *class* in general to identify groups of people in similar social and economic positions, who have similar opportunities in life, and who would benefit (or be hurt) by the same kinds of government policies. Classes are groups, not individuals (although individuals make up classes), and it only makes sense to think about classes in relation to each other. Using the concept of class to understand some of the broad patterns of inequality in North America can be useful beyond what we can learn by studying individuals and families.

What makes up a class? There is disagreement about how to define classes, and sociologists disagree about how many different classes there are. But most agree that classes are made up of people sharing a similar economic situation who (1) have conflicting economic interests with other classes (for example, workers want more pay while business owners want to hold down workers' pay to increase profits); (2) share similar **life chances** (that is, members of the same class are likely to have similar incomes and opportunities as they move through life); (3) have similar attitudes; and (4) have the potential, at least, to engage in collective action (such as when workers organize a union).

Class analysis is the study of how, when, and where classes exist along these four dimensions. Classes become more visible when there are sharp differences between them on some key political controversy or in periods of sharp economic grievances. This is most vivid in a situation where revolutionary change is in the air and large numbers of people demand a more equal distribution of economic goods and opportunities. But revolutions and other types of collective action by entire classes are relatively rare. What about everyday life?

bart78/Shutterstock

One way in which social class becomes visible is when comparing consumer behaviour. Certain products serve as status symbols that reflect one's social standing. Members of higher social classes, for example, are able to buy luxury products, such as expensive or exclusive cars and fashion items.

Karl Marx introduced the concept of class in his many economic and political writings in the nineteenth century and most famously in *The Communist Manifesto*, coauthored with Friedrich Engels (Marx & Engels, 1848/1983). Marx's concept of class built on the idea that as a result of its economic system, any society has a single, critical division between two classes (one dominant, one subordinate). Marx thought that in capitalist societies the most important class distinction was between business owners (or what Marx and Engels called the **bourgeoisie**) and workers who do jobs for pay (a group they referred to as the **proletariat**). Other classes could exist, but they were of minor (and declining) importance. But since Marx wrote in the nineteenth century, it has become clear that only a much broader notion of class can provide a meaningful description of contemporary capitalist societies. Various middle-class groupings—such as business managers, professionals, and those who are self-employed—are not usefully lumped together with factory workers, sales workers, or the baristas at Starbucks. Any sophisticated theory of class will need to attend to the groups in the middle.

But to ask the question "What is middle about the middle classes?" (Wright, 1986) is to raise a whole host of problems for the concept of class. There have been three broad solutions to this problem. The first solution is to distinguish classes based on income (as noted earlier). Those with high incomes belong in one class, those with incomes near the median are in the middle class, and those with low incomes are in the lower classes. Simple, right? But the problem with using income to define classes is that there are no clear-cut boundaries between classes (do we really think that having an annual income of $79,000 places a person in the middle class, while an income of $80,000 places another person in the upper class?). Further, sociologists have argued that more important than the amount of income is the *source* of income. *How* people earn gives us a better way of predicting how people will behave, who their friends are, and what kinds of opinions they may hold. For example, a part-time community college instructor may have the same *current* income as the unionized janitor who cleans up at the end of the day. But, having earned advanced degrees and possessing a different skill set than the janitor, the community college instructor is likely to have very different friends, ideas about what is just and fair, and, perhaps most importantly, the potential to earn far more income over her life than the janitor, irrespective of their current (similar) incomes. The sociological concept of class attempts to capture these varying life chances in dividing society into class locations, so most sociologists conclude that income alone is not the best way to think of what we mean by classes.

A second approach to class that some analysts employ is to move in the opposite direction from a simple income measure and utilize a much broader definition of class based on components such as education, income, and current occupation. Using this approach, researchers can construct a score for an individual's **socioeconomic status (SES)**. The basic premise of the SES approach is that by combining a number of different attributes of any individual, we can properly place him or her in relation to others and assign him or her to a class. While different weights can be assigned to each, one basic decision rule is that someone scoring high on all three dimensions (income, education, occupation) is "high SES," someone scoring low on all three is "low SES," and everyone else is somewhere in the middle (or "middle SES").

SES is useful for many purposes and generally does a better job than simple income measures to distinguish among people for research purposes. But a key aspect of class theory is that members of the same class should have some context for acting together to try to improve their lot in life in some way. People in the same SES location are not ever likely to act together on that basis (have you ever seen someone holding a sign at a protest saying "low SES people unite"?).

A third approach to class, and the one favoured by most sociologists, is to focus on each person's occupation in adulthood. Following Marx, this approach views the place of each individual in the economic system as crucial. And unlike income or SES, there are many examples of occupational groups having similar political views and acting together to push for higher wages or to change government policies (e.g., in unions or professional associations like the American Bar Association or the Canadian Medical Association, and for the capitalist class, there are the Chamber of Commerce and other business associations). Most of the occupation-based approaches divide different occupations into a small group of distinct classes that have similar kinds of life chances, organizations, and (less often) social and political viewpoints. The most popular of these schemes is that of sociologists Robert Erikson and John Goldthorpe (1992), who have identified five core classes displayed (in a slightly simplified way) in Table 9.1. The Erikson–Goldthorpe scheme makes distinctions between those individuals who own their own businesses (or are self-employed) and those who work for someone else. Among those who are employed, distinctions are made between those who have jobs that either entail supervising others or require employer trust (what they call "the salariat") and those that do not; between those involving manual work or not; and, among manual workers, those that require special skills and training versus those that do not. Table 9.1 shows some of the representative types of occupations falling into each category.

Table 9.1 The Erikson–Goldthorpe Class Scheme

Salariat/Service Class: Professionals, managers, and administrators; higher-grade technicians; supervisors of nonmanual workers
Routine Nonmanual Workers: Nonsupervisorial employees in administration and commerce positions; sales workers; secretaries, clerks, and other rank-and-file white-collar workers
Petty-Bourgeoisie: Business owners (other than farm); self-employed workers and consultants; artisans, etc.
Farm Owners: Farmers and ranchers (landowners)
Skilled Workers and Supervisors: Skilled manual workers; supervisors of manual workers (foremen); lower-grade technicians/repairmen
Nonskilled Workers: Semi- and unskilled manual workers
Farm Labourers: Farm and ranch employees

SOURCE: From *The Constant Flux: A Study of Class Mobility in Industrial Nations* (Table 2.1), by Robert Erikson and John Goldthorpe, 1992, Oxford: Clarendon Press.

9.2 Why Is North America So Unequal?

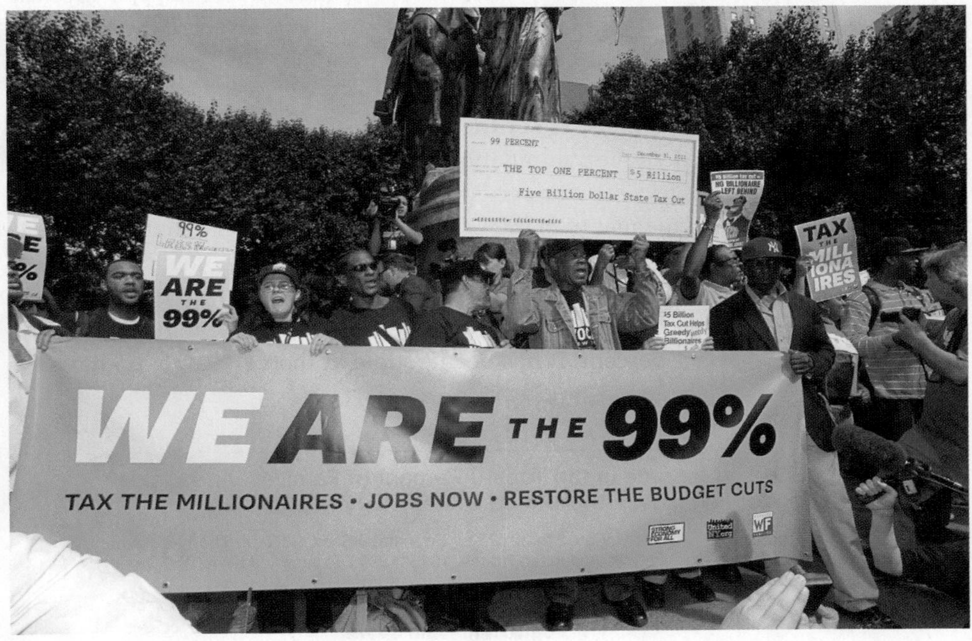

Tom Zuback/Alamy Stock Photo

Unequal North America in Comparative Perspective

Today, economic inequality in both Canada and the United States is about as high as it has ever been, at least since good data about incomes became available in the early twentieth century and we have been able to measure it. Inequality is also, as we shall see, higher in the United States than in any other rich, democratic country (although there are less developed countries that have more inequality). In spite of its enormous wealth, the United States has more people living in poverty than most other similar countries. These two facts are both of considerable importance, requiring us to think hard about how and why America in particular is so unequal.

Trends in Income Inequality in North America and Around the World

9.2.1 Discuss trends in income inequality and compare inequality in Canada and the United States to that in other countries around the world.

When did inequality start increasing? Is this a new trend, or has inequality always been high? One method that researchers have used to measure long-term trends in inequality is to examine the share of total national income that goes to different groups in the country. In a perfectly **egalitarian** (equal) society, the income share of the wealthiest one-tenth of families, for example, will be exactly 10 percent of the national income. The higher the income share of the wealthiest group, the more inequality there is.

Researchers have been able to examine tax returns as a source of information about income in order to measure income inequality in the United States since 1917, soon after the federal income tax was established permanently by the 16th Amendment of the U.S. Constitution. Because in the United States everyone has to file a tax return, even if they do not pay taxes, it is possible to track the incomes of all U.S. families over a long historical time period. The pioneering and important work of economists Thomas Piketty and Emmanuel Saez (2003) has led the way in uncovering those trends. What does their analysis show? Explore the graphs in Figure 9.4 highlighting important research on the trends in income inequality and its consequences.

As we can see, the income share of the wealthiest groups in the United States has always been higher than their population share, but *how much more* has changed considerably over time. The post-war period from the 1940s to the 1970s marks a historical low in the level of inequality in the United States. In the 1960s, only about one-third of the total income in the country went to the wealthiest one-tenth of families, and the top 1 percent received about 8 percent of all income. By 2012, the top 1 percent of families was earning almost 23 percent of all income! Even more remarkable is the fact that within the top 1 percent, it has been people at the very top who have the

Figure 9.4 Share of Income in the Top 10 Percent of Families, and Inside the Top 1 Percent of Families in the United States, 1917–2010

SOURCE: Based on "Tables and Figures: Updated to 2012," by Emmanuel Saez, 2012, in Thomas Piketty and Emmanuel Saez, "Income Inequality in the United States, 1913–1998," *Quarterly Journal of Economics, 118* (http://elsa.berkeley.edu/~saez/).

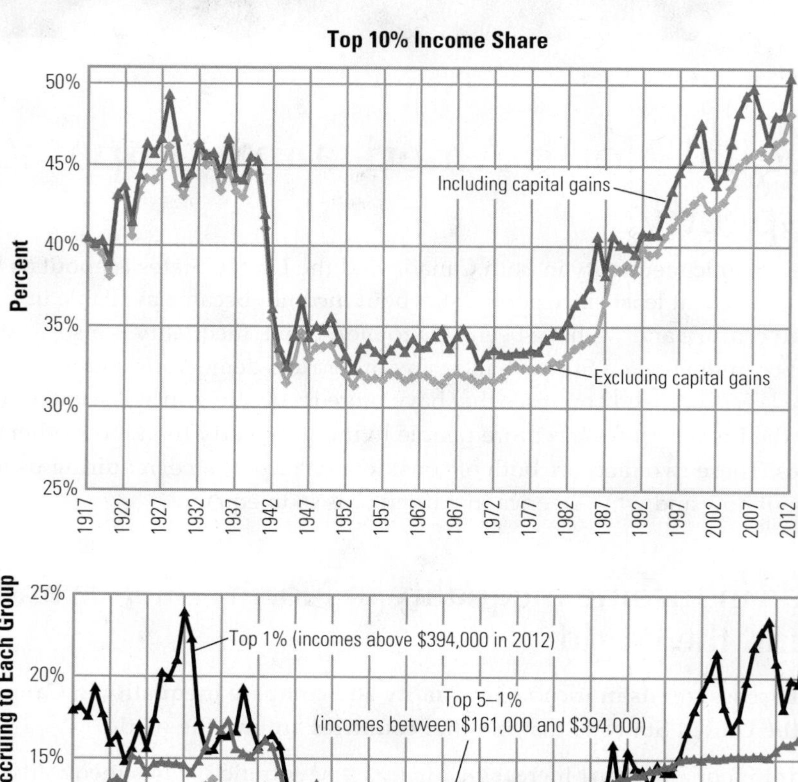

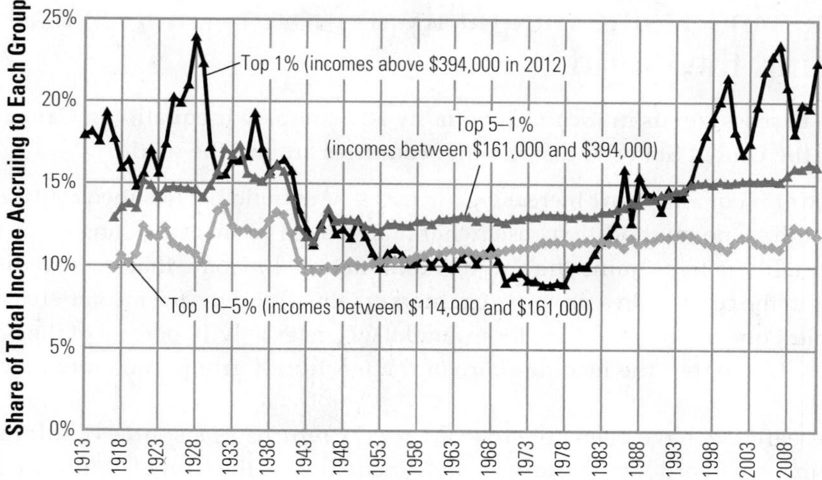

highest earnings and whose incomes have grown the fastest (so those lucky families at the .995 percentile—the top one-half of the top 1 percent—have done much better than those merely at the .990 percentile).

In Canada, income inequality is less pronounced than in the United States, although it has been increasing in the past 20 years. Canada now ranks 12th out of 17 peer countries. Another way of tracking income inequality is to divide the population into five groups (quintiles) from poorest (bottom quintile) to richest (top quintile), and then calculate the share of income that accrues to each group. If each of the five income groups has the same share of total national income—that is, 20 percent—the distribution could be described as equal.

The pie chart in Figure 9.5 shows the share of national income going to each quintile in 2010 in Canada. The richest income group (top quintile) has by far the largest share of Canada's economic pie—with 39.1 percent of total national income. This richest group is the only quintile to have increased its share of national income over the past 20 years—from 36.5 percent in 1990 to 39.1 percent in 2010. All other quintile groups have lost share, including middle-income groups (Conference Board of Canada, 2013).

How different is the level of income inequality in the North America compared to other countries around the world? See Figure 9.6 for some details.

As Figure 9.6 reveals, the level of inequality in the United States is twice as high as that in Sweden (a very egalitarian country) and about one-third higher than most other European countries. This is instructive in that these are countries that have similar levels of economic development as well as similar educational systems and democratic political institutions. The United States is the most unequal country of the developed world, and the difference from other countries is very substantial. Canada, in contrast, has a level of inequality similar to that in many European countries, as well as Australia and Taiwan. Indeed, to find countries with *more* inequality than the United States, we would have to include in the comparison group a couple of countries in Latin America and Africa that have extremely high levels of inequality (South Africa and Namibia are the most inegalitarian countries in the world).

Figure 9.5 Share of Canadian Wealth by Quintile

SOURCE: Conference Board of Canada, 2013. http://www.conferenceboard.ca/hcp/details/society/income-inequality.aspx. Used with permission.

Richest Group Accounts for the Largest Share of Canadian National Income, 2010 (share of national adjusted after-tax income by income quintile, per cent)

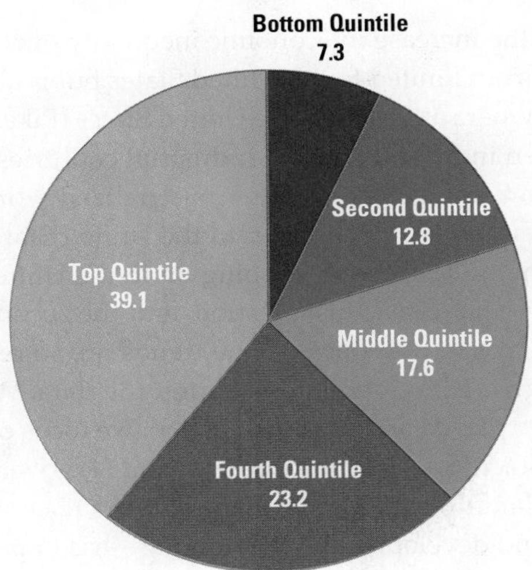

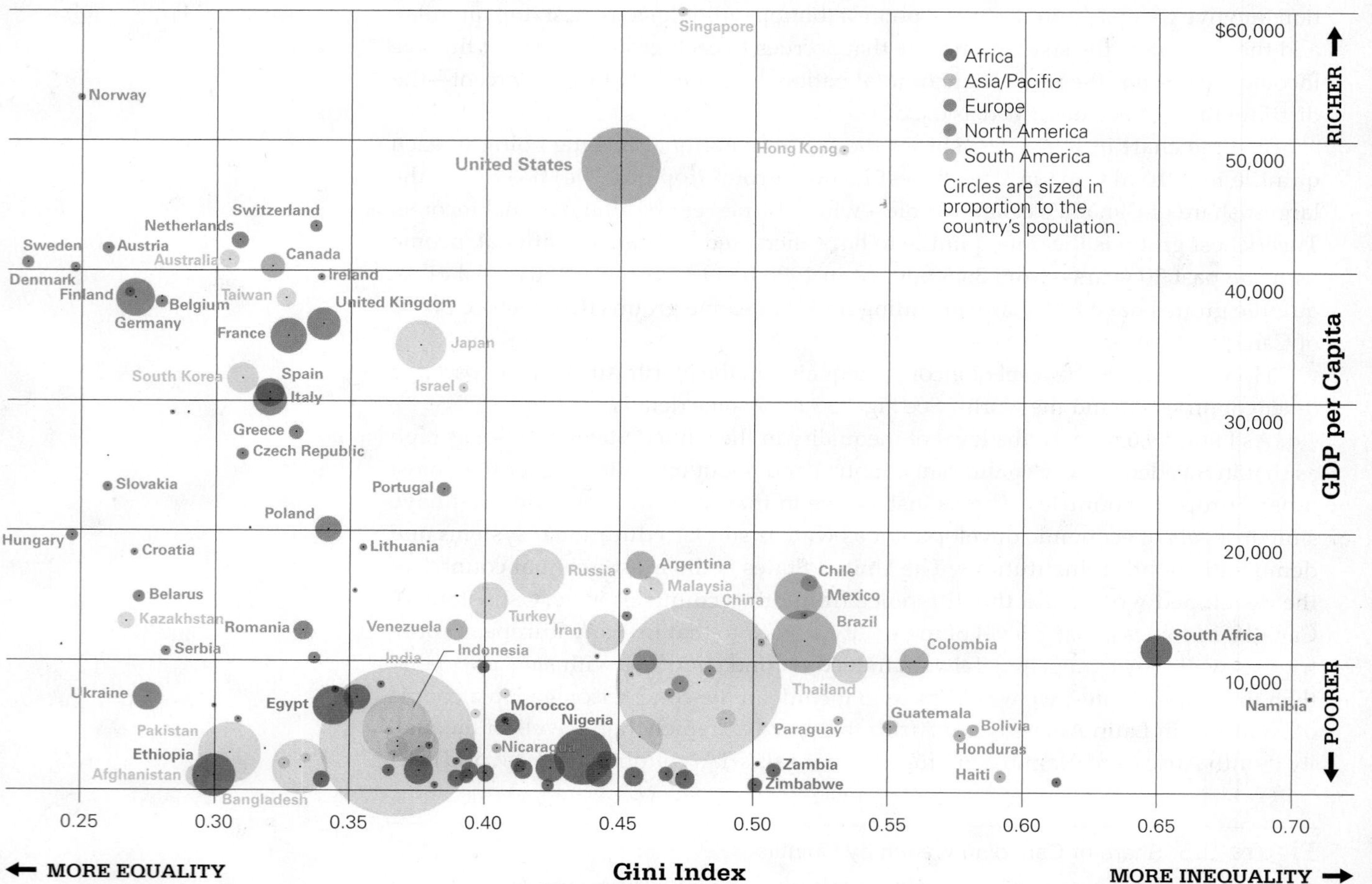

Figure 9.6 Income Inequality Around the World

Developed by Italian statistician and sociologist Corrado Gini, the Gini index is the most commonly used measure of overall income inequality. The index ranges from 0 to 1, where 0 indicates complete inequality (one family gets all the income, and all other families get nothing). The larger the Gini coefficient is, the more inequality there is.

SOURCE: Based on data from U.S. Census Bureau, 2012; *C.I.A. World Factbook*, by United States Central Intelligence Agency, 2011, New York: Skyhorse.

Why Did Inequality Increase?

9.2.2 Identify factors explaining why economic inequality in North America has increased since the 1960s.

Which factors explain the increase in economic inequality over the last decades? The increase in inequality is not limited to the United States but is also happening in other countries, although nowhere as fast as in the United States (Piketty, 2014). The fact that inequality has also risen in most advanced industrial countries suggests that at least some of these factors are shared across the industrialized world. However, the fact that inequality is higher and has risen faster in the United States than in other countries suggests that something different is going on in the United States. Researchers are hard at work trying to address this question, and the accounts they have offered so far are still preliminary, in part because the trends are so recent but also because researchers have disagreed about how to interpret the data. We do know, however, that several factors have played a role. In this section, we focus on four: (1) technology, (2) the decline of manufacturing, (3) globalization, and (4) government policies.

One possible explanation for rising inequality focuses on how technology—especially the growth and development of computing—has impacted society. From the 1970s onward, Canada and the United States and other rich countries have experienced major technological advancements. There was a time not so long ago when nobody used computers and when face-to-face meetings or typed letters instead of e-mail and smartphones were the norm for communication.

Technology matters for inequality because it complements some jobs while replacing others. In other words, the impact is uneven. For example, changes in computer technologies have dramatically reduced the need for bank tellers (an occupation that requires middle-level skills), allowing customers to make financial transactions through ATMs or online; technology has also given online access to banking records. At the same time, these improvements in computer technology have increased the need for a new type of banker: financial analysts, who usually have an MBA or at least a BA. In general, technology complements jobs that require higher levels of education—especially a university degree or more—while it tends to replace jobs with middle and lower levels of education. As a result, having a university degree or more pays off more than ever before if you live in the US—the so-called **university wage premium**—whereas people with less than a university degree have seen their earnings decline or have increasing trouble finding good jobs.

What has happened in the United States in the last few decades is that higher education has not expanded at the pace required by technological change. As a result, people who have a college degree have become scarcer relative to the needs of the economy, and because of their relative scarcity they have been receiving higher salaries. As two economic historians have put it, a dynamic economy is characterized by a "race between education and technology" (Goldin & Katz, 2010). If technology advances faster than the educational system can produce trained workers, then the educational premium increases. This, some researchers argue, is what has happened in the United States since the 1980s. (Many recent college graduates, since the recession that began in 2007, may puzzle over this claim, as unemployment has grown and it is harder even for college graduates to find good jobs. But we are describing a much longer trend and one that is likely to continue once the North American economy starts growing again.) According to a recent Statistics Canada Labour Force Survey, the university wage premium has narrowed in recent years due to increases in economic activity fueled by the oil boom, especially in Alberta. The demand for unskilled labour beginning in 2000-2002 tended to reduce wage differences across education levels, especially for young men. At the same time as wages for young men with high school educations increased, the wages of young men with bachelor's degrees employed full time either declined or

Table 9.2 Average real wages of full-time employees aged 20-34, 2000 to 2002 and 2010 to 2012

	MEN		WOMEN	
	High School Diploma	**Bachelor's Degree**	**High School Diploma**	**Bachelor's Degree**
		2002 Dollars		
Panel 1: Average real weekly wages				
2000 to 2002	616	874	468	730
2010 to 2012	668	861	519	761
		Percentage Points		
Percentage change	8.5	−1.5	11.0	4.3
		2002 Dollars		
Panel 2: Average real hourly wages				
2000 to 2002	14.92	21.88	12.21	19.09
2010 to 2012	16.26	21.82	13.57	20.07
		Percentage Points		
Percentage change	9.0	−0.3	11.1	5.1

SOURCE: Statistics Canada, Labour Force Survey. Catalogue no. 11F0019M - No. 360. Reproduced and distributed on an "as is" basis with the permission of Statistics Canada.

grew only moderately. Increases in minimum wages in some provinces also reduced the wage differences across education levels, especially for young women. Despite the narrowing of the wage gap between the high school educated and the university educated, those with university educations have higher rates of full time employment and unionization that can lead to greater income over time.

Table 9.2 shows the average real wages of full-time employees aged 20–34, from the 2000-to-2002 period to the 2010-to-2012 period. The table reveals that education did not lead to greater wage gains in the short term, particularly for young men. Those with a university degree still earn more than those with a high school diploma but not by as much as in the earlier period (Frenette and Morissette, 2014).

A second set of factors contributing to inequality concerns the changing mix of jobs and opportunities in the late twentieth and early twenty-first centuries. Developed countries like Canada and the United States have undergone a steady decline in industrial or manufacturing jobs. This process, known as **deindustrialization**, has had a number of important consequences. In 1950, almost 40 percent of all jobs were in industry and manufacturing, and wages for experienced manufacturing workers were relatively high. Today, only 20 percent of jobs are in manufacturing, and the constant threat of moving jobs to other countries has helped hold down wages for manufacturing workers. For many workers, this process of deindustrialization has meant replacing good jobs with bad ones—jobs that pay less, offer fewer benefits such as healthcare and pensions, and are more likely to be part-time. For example, some jobs that have been growing in recent years—like food preparation workers, security guards, childcare workers, customer service representatives, healthcare aides, and cashiers—are all low-wage jobs but ones that an increasing number of people work in.

Why have manufacturing jobs disappeared so rapidly in Canada and the United States and other countries? The heart of the answer is not that there is less manufacturing being done in the world but rather that it is increasingly being done elsewhere, in places where workers will accept lower wages and companies can, as a result, make higher profits. At the centre of this important change is **globalization**, which involves the growing permeability of national borders and the increase in flows of goods, services, and even people across national borders. One of the most important aspects of globalization is the increasing *trade* between countries, which results in cheaper imported goods from these countries and often allows companies to relocate manufacturing jobs to other countries. Because developing countries can often manufacture products at lower cost than richer countries, trade can depress the wages of low-skill domestic workers who produce these goods. In many well-documented cases, these lower costs are often the result of **sweatshop** conditions, workplaces that are characterized by extremely low wages and poor or unsafe working conditions and that in some cases employ children.

Globalization has also led, in short, to what is known as **outsourcing**—the contracting of parts of the production process to another party, often abroad, such as when the customer service representative who helps you with your credit card bill issue does so from India. Outsourcing is extremely common in manufacturing, where different components can be made in different places with only final assembly taking place in North America. As *New York Times* columnist Thomas Friedman (2012) has suggested, the world is now so thoroughly integrated that products are imagined, designed, built, and marketed through global supply chains, wherever cheap productive and organizational talent is available. Products are not "Made in North America," even if final assembly takes place there. Rather, they are "made in the world."

Take Apple Computer as an example. A few years after Apple began building the first Macintosh computer in 1983, the late Steve Jobs bragged that it was "a machine that is made in America." In 2011, all of the 70 million iPhones, 30 million iPads, and 59 million other hardware products Apple sold were manufactured overseas. Many of these popular products are made by an enormous Taiwanese multinational manufacturing company called Foxconn, in a complex of factories located in Shenzhen, China, that employs over 300,000 workers. At these plants, Apple products are made by workers who labour long hours for low pay under demanding and sometimes risky conditions. According to a recent *New York Times* report, an explosion killed two workers and hurt a dozen in a Foxconn plant in Chengdu, China. In Wintek, another Apple manufacturing partner in China, hundreds of workers were injured after being ordered to use toxic chemicals to clean the iPhone screens, highlighting a record of poor safety procedures at these factories that has long been documented (Duhigg & Barboza, 2012).

Deindustrialization is a critical piece of the larger pattern of **economic restructuring**, which refers to changes that have taken place since the 1970s in the way the economy, firms, and employment relations are organized. The post–World War II decades of the 1950s and 1960s were characterized by an organizational type in which many employees, once hired, were offered long-term job stability and protected from economic volatility. A deep economic recession in the early 1970s shook this system. Based on a desire to cut costs and increase profits, firms increasingly sought to squeeze their workers and make terms of employment more flexible. For example, it became much easier for employers to dismiss employees, to reduce benefits, and to avoid having to bargain with unions. The cumulative impact of economic restructuring can be seen most clearly in the flattening out of wages for workers in the middle and lower half of the American economy. Figure 9.7 illustrates the grim details.

Finally, we can look to government policies as a contributing factor. So far we have focused on economic changes in driving the overall pattern of income inequality, but the pattern is also very much the result of government policies. The most important of these policies is taxation (that is, the amount of taxes everyone has to pay on their incomes), while for the very poor the failure to raise the minimum wage has been especially consequential.

Taxes have a big impact on the overall level of inequality in a society because of their impact on high earners (and also because taxes are used to pay for government programs that support the poor, the elderly, the disabled, and other disadvantaged individuals and families). A **progressive tax system** is one in which tax rates are higher on richer people than poorer people, with the idea being that it is fairer to

Figure 9.7 Average Hourly Wage and Productivity, 1947–2009

The vertical axis in this graph indicates an index, which has its base in 1947. This means that both productivity and hourly wage are measured in comparison to their respective value in the base year. Productivity is a measure of the net economic output per worker per hour. The graph shows that, after nearly two decades of simultaneous growth of productivity and wages, wages have stagnated since the 1970s, reflecting the restructuring of American firms. However, productivity kept rising and, as indicated in the graph, the average worker was far more productive in 2010 than the same worker would have been in 1970. What does this say about income inequality? It means that workers, on average, receive a smaller share of their average economic output than four decades ago.

SOURCE: *The State of Working America*, Economic Policy Institute (http://stateofworkingamerica.org/chart/swa-wages-figure-4u-change-total-economy/). Used with permission.

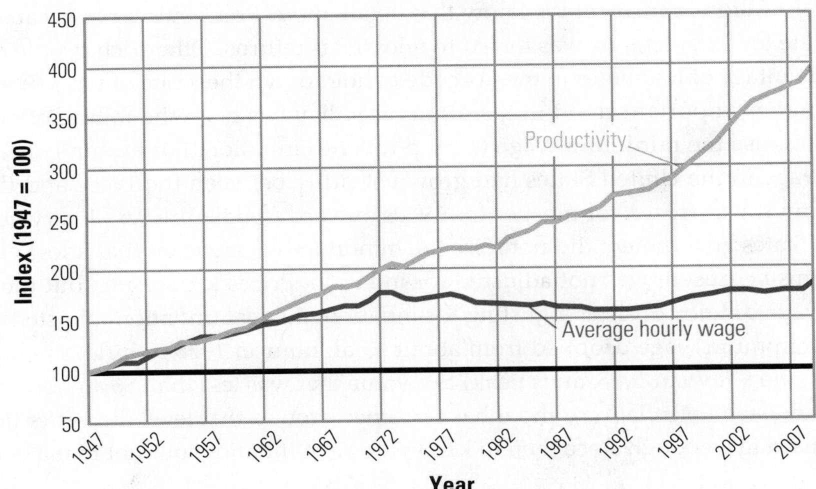

Figure 9.8 Top Marginal Tax Rates, United States, 1960–2011

Top marginal tax rates refers to the rate that applies to the wealthiest taxpayers.

SOURCE: U.S. Department of the Treasury, 2011.

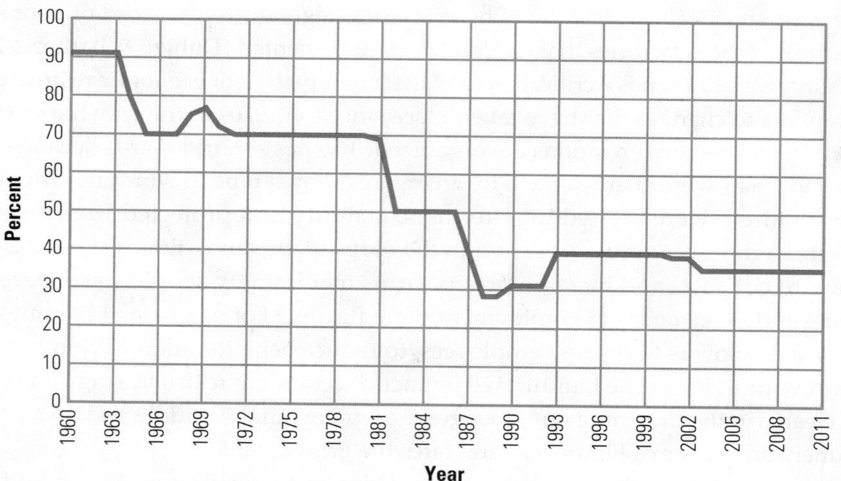

ask those who can afford to pay more to do so. Many tax systems around the world, including in the United States, are progressive. Some have argued that if tax rates on the rich are high enough, the rich will constrain their incomes (why try to earn more if you are going to give most of it back in the form of taxes?). Of course, it is never that simple; because the tax code contains a large number of deductions and exemptions, the actual rate paid by high earners (who typically employ a small army of tax lawyers and consultants to reduce their tax burdens) is always lower than the official rate. Still, the federal income tax rates paid by the highest-earning Americans have fallen dramatically over time, from over 90 percent to 39 percent today. To see this evolution, explore Figure 9.8. In contrast, in Canada, where income inequality is less pronounced than in the United States, Canadian high-income earners pay higher rates of income tax. Canadian high-income earners are getting richer, but they are also paying an increasing share of total personal income taxes. Nearly one-third of those Canadians in the top 0.01 percent had a tax rate of 40 percent, although some paid as little as 10 percent, and some paid no taxes at all in 2004 (Statistics Canada, 2007).

Figure 9.8 shows the official rates, not the rates that people actually pay. It is important to note that the tax rate does not fully apply to many high earners, who are able to shield much of their earnings from some or even all taxation. For example, 2012 Republican presidential candidate Mitt Romney, who has an estimated net worth of $250 million, paid just 13.9 percent of his income in federal taxes in 2010 on more than $21 million in income. We know this detail about Romney's taxes because, as a candidate for president, he was forced to release his returns. Other rich people quietly take advantage of loopholes in the tax code to hold down their rate of tax.

Another important trend in government policy has been the failure of governments to raise the **minimum wage** to keep up with inflation. For example, the minimum wage in the United States had grown steadily between the 1940s and the late 1960s, but it was frozen for most of the 1980s onward (see Figure 9.9). Every year the United States government did not raise the minimum wage meant that it lost value in real terms because it was not adjusted for inflation. Prices kept rising, but the minimum wage did not. So after adjusting for inflation, the real (inflation-adjusted) value of the minimum wage dropped from about $9 an hour in 1978 in inflation-adjusted dollars (and $10.79 in 1968, at its peak) to a value that was less than $6 an hour in 1990 (again adjusted for inflation), and it has remained around that level thereafter (having been raised just enough since then to keep pace with inflation, but not to make up for

Figure 9.9 The Declining Value of Minimum Wage in the United States, 1960–2009

SOURCE: Economic Policy Institute (http://www.epi.org/publication/state_of_working_america_preview_the_declining_value_of_minimum_wage/). Used with permission.

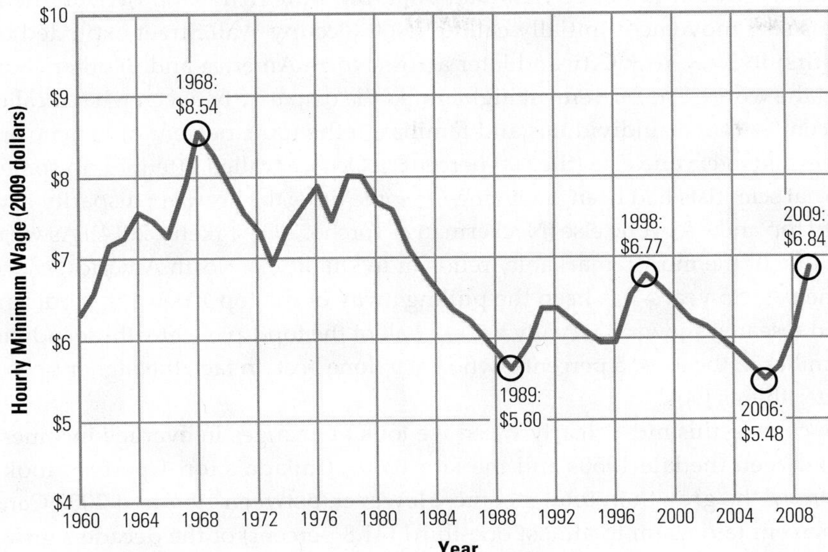

past losses). The real Canadian minimum wage (in 2013 dollars adjusted for inflation) has changed very little since the 1970s. Researchers for Statistics Canada found that since 1975 the average minimum wage has varied between $7 and $11; it peaked in 1975 and 1976. The average minimum wage declined to under $8 in the mid-1980s and then changed very little until 2005, when it began rising again slightly. In 2010, the average minimum wage reached approximately $10 and remained at that level until 2013 (Galarneau & Fecteau, 2014).

What are the consequences of minimum wage policy on inequality? The stereotypical portrait of the minimum wage earner is a teenager working for pocket money, but in fact, both women and youth are overrepresented as minimum wage earners. Approximately 60 percent of all minimum wage earners across all age categories are women, who make up approximately 50 percent of the working population (Statistics Canada, 2010). The percentage of women earning minimum wage in Canada increased from 6 percent in 1997 to 8 percent in 2013, while the percentage of men earning minimum wage increased from almost 4 percent in 1997 to 5.5 percent in 2013 (Galarneau & Fecteau, 2014).

Teenagers are most affected by increases in the minimum wage because they make up the largest group of minimum wage earners. In Canada, 50 percent of minimum wage earners are between the ages of 15 and 19, and 13 percent are between 20 and 24, so more than 60 percent of minimum wage earners are under 25. Those earning minimum wage are also most likely to be the least educated: The proportion of minimum wage employees with less than a high school diploma was 20 percent, compared to less than 3 percent of minimum wage employees with university degrees (Galarneau & Fecteau, 2014).

Even if the minimum wage affects only a small proportion of the working population, it matters for inequality because it affects the well-being of families at the bottom of the income distribution *and* because many workers are paid just over the minimum wage (so when it does not go up, those workers are not likely to see any increases either). Increasing the minimum wage can automatically increase the proportion of working people paid at this level because some of the employees whose wages were formerly above the old minimum wage level are now paid at the new rate along with those who were already earning minimum wage (Galarneau & Fecteau, 2014).

The 1 Percent

9.2.3 Describe who constitutes the "1 percent" in North America.

Most people would rather be rich than poor. But how rich is too rich? In the fall of 2011, a social movement initially calling itself Occupy Wall Street exploded on the scene, first in New York City and later across North America and in other countries around the world. The movement highlighted the disparity between what it called the "1 percent"—that is, individuals and families in the top 1 percent of income and/or wealth—and everyone else (the "99 percent"). Occupy called attention to something that social scientists had been analyzing for some time: the growing disparity between the very top and everyone else (Neckerman & Torche, 2007; Piketty, 2014). As we noted above, one of the most remarkable trends in inequality in North America, especially over the past 25 years, has been the pulling away of the top 1 percent. And, as more detailed research shows, it is really the top half of the top 1 percent—those individuals and families in the top 0.5 percent—who have done best. In fact, the higher up you go, the better things look.

We can see this most clearly when we look at changes in average incomes over time. Between the late 1950s and the late 1960s, Canada's top 1 percent took only 8 percent of the growth in total income. However, between 1997 and 2007 Canada's top 1 percent laid claim to almost one-third (31.8 percent) of the decade's growth in total income. Here we can see that growth in average incomes has collapsed while incomes for the top 1 percent have continued to soar (Yalnizyan, 2010).

For a closer look at just how well the very richest have been doing, Table 9.3 displays this picture starkly for the year 2007 (again drawing from the important work of economists Piketty and Saez). The "material power index" is a way of calculating how much more material resources different groups have. In developing this measure, political scientist Jeffrey Winters (2011) has concluded that the gap in power between rich and poor in the contemporary United States is probably greater than that between the richest families in Ancient Greece and Rome and the slaves of those societies!

So who are the people at the very top, the so-called one percenters? Do they work, or did they inherit their money? For those who work, what kinds of jobs do they have? How different are the group of people in the entire top 1 percent, as opposed to the top 0.1 percent (or the top tenth of the top 1 percent)? Three economists have studied this question using data from U.S. tax returns filed in 2004–2005 (Bakija, Cole, & Heim 2012). Perhaps somewhat surprisingly, only 6 percent (of the

Table 9.3 Material Power in the United States, Based on 2007 Incomes

Threshold of Taxpayers	Number of Taxpayers	Average Income	% of All Income	% Income Cumulative	Material Power Index
Top 400	400	$344,800,000	1.6	1.6	10,327
Top 1/100th of 1%	14,588	$26,548,000	4.5	6.1	819
Top 1/10th of 1%	134,888	$4,024,583	6.2	12.3	124
Top half of 1%	593,500	$1,021,643	7.0	19.3	32
Top 1%	749,375	$486,395	4.2	23.5	15
Top 5%	5,995,000	$220,105	15.1	38.6	7
Top 10%	7,493,750	$128,560	11.1	49.7	4
Bottom 90%	134,887,500	$32,421	50.3	100.0	1

NOTE: Based on United States Internal Revenue Service tabulations of individual income tax returns for 2007, CPS-estimated number of potential tax units, and National Income Accounts total income figures. Income includes realized capital gains. Each income level is exclusive of the category above it. Average income of the top 400 taxpayers is from the Internal Revenue Service (2009). The total number of taxpayers filing returns in 2007 is 149,875,300, and the total reported gross personal income is $8,701 billion.

SOURCE: Jeffrey Winters, 2011, *Oligarchy*. Reprinted with the permission of Cambridge University Press.

top 0.1 percent; it is 7 percent if we look at the entire top 1 percent) are not working. The vast majority of high earners do have jobs, as opposed to living off inheritances (although many combine working income with income from investments of various sorts). Two occupations stand out: executives and high-level managers (41 percent of the top 0.1 percent and 30 percent of the top 1 percent); finance (18 percent of the top 0.1 percent and 13 percent of the top 1 percent); and then a scattering of high earners in many different occupations including law, medicine, real estate, arts, media and sports, and entrepreneurs (business owners). The growth in pay received by top company executives has received a great deal of attention and discussion in recent years, and for good reason. In 1965, the average top executive made about 20 times as much as the average-paid worker at a large company; in 1978, it was 30:1. In other words, top executives were paid a lot more than the typical worker at these companies, but the gap was a small fraction of what it is today. In 2013, the average top executive made 296 times as much as the average worker in the same company (Mishel & Davis, 2014).

Looking at Table 9.4, several other interesting observations stand out. For one thing, the differences in the occupations between the top 1 percent and 0.1 percent are interesting to note; as we move downward to look at the entire top 1 percent, we see some occupations like those in the medical field (mostly doctors) increasing dramatically (from 4.4 percent of the top 0.1 percent to fully 15 percent of the top 1 percent). There are also a scattering of new occupational fields that appear, such as blue-collar workers and government employees. It may be surprising to see people working in these occupations as earning extremely high incomes, but keep in mind that very, very few blue-collar or government employees earn incomes that put them in the top 1 percent, and even in jobs such as this there are only a handful of people with very specialized skills or abilities that enable them to earn very high pay.

Table 9.4 Occupations of the Top 1 Percent and Top 0.1 Percent of Income Earners

This table shows the occupations reported on the tax returns of the highest earning Americans, in the top 0.1 percent and the top 1 percent. Executives and financial professionals are more common at the very top (almost 60 percent) than in the less rarefied and larger group in the top 1 percent, where physicians, lawyers, computer/math/engineering, and skilled sales professionals are more highly represented.

	Top 0.1%	Top 1%
Executives, managers, supervisors (nonfinance)	40.8%	30.0%
Financial professions	18.4	13.2
Not working	6.3	7.4
Lawyers	6.2	7.7
Real estate	4.7	3.9
Medical	4.4	14.4
Entrepreneur	3.6	2.8
Arts, media, sports	3.1	1.7
Computer, math, engineering, technical	3.0	4.2
Business operations	2.2	2.8
Skilled sales (except finance or real estate)	1.9	3.7
Professors and scientists	1.1	1.8
Farmers and ranchers	1.0	0.8

SOURCE: Based on *Jobs and Income Growth of Top Earners and the Causes of Changing Income Inequality: Evidence from U.S. Tax Return Data*, unpublished paper by Jon Bakija, Adam Cole, and Bradley Heim, 2012, Department of Economics, Williams College (http://econ.williams.edu/people/jbakija).

9.3 Do We All Have an Equal Opportunity to Succeed in Life?

Monkey Business/Fotolia

Inequality, Education, and Social Mobility

So far we have discussed inequality in terms of income and wealth. But this is only part of the story. One important type of inequality is **inequality of opportunity**—which refers to the ways in which inequality shapes the opportunities for children and young adults to maximize their potential. Equality of opportunity would exist in a world where all children have similar chances to succeed in life, regardless of whether they were born in wealthy or poor families. If everyone, regardless of their social background, has similar chances of success in life as an adult, we could say that opportunities are truly equally distributed, and only merit and hard work are rewarded. If, in contrast, an individual's chances to do well in life depend on the advantages (or disadvantages) of the family and circumstances he or she was born into, then we can say opportunity is unequally distributed. This is one of the most important topics in the study of inequality and social stratification.

Measuring Opportunity: The Concept of Social Mobility

9.3.1 Define *social mobility* and describe how inequality of opportunity is measured.

While most North Americans accept some degree of inequality in outcomes as an inherent feature of a capitalist economy, there is broad support for the ideal of equality of opportunity. Most of us believe very strongly, for example, that children should have the opportunity to flourish even if they are born into families with limited resources. This idea is part of what is known as the "American Dream" of equal opportunity for all. Politicians and social theorists have also sometimes called for equality of opportunity on the grounds that it benefits society: If poor children have no chance to succeed in life, their talent and potential contributions will be lost, and this is inefficient for the society as a whole.

Measuring opportunity in any society is not a simple research question. Whereas we can measure other kinds of inequalities—income, wealth, consumption, even well-being—in relatively straightforward ways (even if the details are complicated!), there is no single, obvious way of determining how much opportunity individuals really have. The solution that social scientists have settled on is to examine what is known as **social mobility**, or more specifically, the pattern of intergenerational inheritance in a society. Social mobility is a measure of the extent to which parents and their children have similar or different social and economic positions in adulthood. A high-mobility society is one where there is relatively little connection between parents' and children's place in life. By contrast, when there is a relatively close connection between parents and their children's positions when children reach adulthood, social mobility is low. A high-mobility society approximates the ideal of equality of opportunity; in such a society, where a child ends up in life is determined largely through her or his own achievements. An immobile society, by contrast, is one where your chances are largely determined at birth; in extreme cases, immobility creates a **caste society**, one in which the advantages or disadvantages of birth determine fully your social position (such as was traditionally the case in India, where being born into a lower caste meant no chance to move into a higher caste).

In other words, in a perfectly mobile society, parents' resources would be completely irrelevant for children's outcomes; that is, everyone would have the same chances of succeeding in life regardless of their family background. In a perfectly immobile society, however, chances of success would be entirely determined by parental resources. Children of poor parents would grow up to be poor, while children of rich parents would grow up to be rich. In the real world, all societies fall somewhere in between these two extremes. To study where different societies fall, we ask the question: To what extent do family resources (that is, who your parents are) determine how well you will do in life?

Accounts of individual social mobility often focus on individual effort and ability. Stories about mobility usually highlight exceptional individuals who overcome massive difficulties and experience upward mobility—the "rags-to-riches" story—and, less frequently, individuals who decline in spite of the many opportunities they had and experience downward mobility. Countless movies and novels have portrayed these situations. These anecdotal cases often highlight the extent to which individual upward and downward mobility can be linked to specific individual attributes: hard work overcoming disadvantage, drug abuse offsetting privilege, and so forth. But these individual stories aside, there are patterns that we can observe across different societies that suggest that mobility is not simply an attribute of individuals and their successes or failures. We explore this in more detail in the next section.

Social Mobility in Comparative Perspective

9.3.2 Compare and contrast chances for social mobility in the United States to other countries such as Canada and Norway.

One way in which social scientists measure social mobility in different societies is by identifying the strength of the **association**—that is, the relationship between two variables that change together—between parents' social standing (which could be measured based on income, occupation, or other measures of social standing) and their children's outcomes as adults. An association of zero means that there is literally no connection whatsoever between parents' income and children's income (or parents' and children's occupation, or education, or other measure of success). Thinking about income, if parents' income does not make any difference to how small or large their children's income will be, we can say that a situation of *perfect mobility* exists. An association of one, in turn, means that parents' income fully determines children's income.

Figure 9.10 Intergenerational Association of Earnings in the United States and Other Advanced Industrial Countries

SOURCE: Based on data from *How Much Can We Learn From International Comparisons of Social Mobility?* (Working Document), by Jo Blanden, 2009, Centre for the Economics of Education, London School of Economics (http://cee.lse.ac.uk/ceedps/ceedp111.pdf).

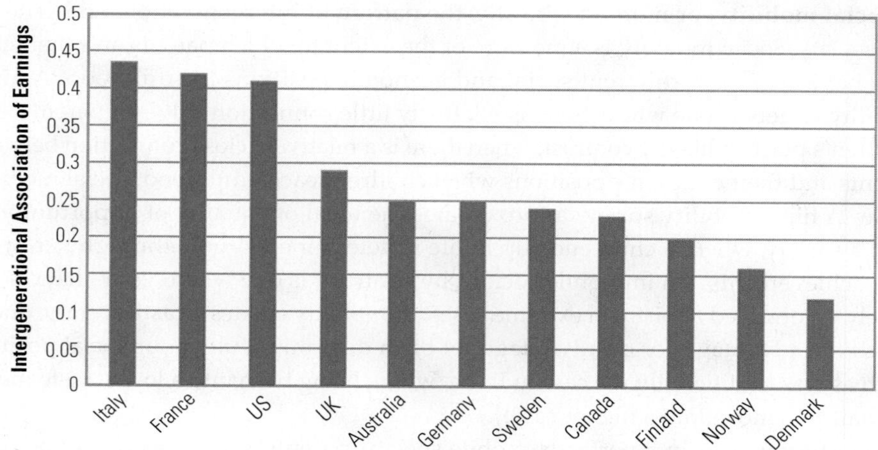

In that situation, which is one of perfect **immobility**, if your parents have an income that is, say, 50 percent higher than the average income, you too as an adult will have an income 50 percent higher than the average.

Figure 9.10 displays the association of parents' and adult children's earnings in Canada, the United States, and other advanced industrial countries for which we have comparable data. As the figure shows, the chances of mobility vary substantially across countries. Countries such as Italy, France, and the United States have relatively high intergenerational association, that is, lower mobility on this measure. At the other extreme, Nordic countries such as Denmark, Norway, and Finland have weaker associations between parents' and children's income, indicating higher chances of mobility. For example, the intergenerational association in Norway is .16. That means that, on average, Norwegian parents pass on 16 percent of their economic advantage (or disadvantage) to their kids. For example, a Norwegian parent who earns $100,000 more than the mean income will, on average, have kids who will earn $16,000 more than mean. The intergenerational correlation of .23 in Canada means that if your earnings are $100,000 higher than the mean, then your kids will, on average, make $23,000 more than the mean. Figure 9.10 reveals some troubling evidence about the state of social mobility in the United States.

The intergenerational association of .41 in the United States means that if your earnings are $100,000 higher than average, then your kids can expect to make $41,000 more than the mean (of course these are averages; there will be a lot of variation from one family to the next). That is vastly more than in Norway or Canada and many other countries. Your success (or difficulties) in life are much more closely related to your parents in the United States than elsewhere. There are other rich countries, especially in Southern Europe, that also have rates of social mobility similar to those in the United States.

Measuring social mobility through the association of earnings between parents and their adult children in the developing world is more challenging because quality data on both parents and adult children are scarcer. But we do have some high-quality research on a number of countries in Latin America. Based on the best available estimates, the intergenerational association is much higher in countries such as Brazil, Chile, or Mexico than in very rich countries, reaching values between .5 and .6.

This means that, on average, parents pass along more than half of their economic advantage (or disadvantage) to their children (Torche, 2014).

Factors Influencing Mobility

9.3.3 Identify factors that affect how much social mobility exists in a society.

What specific factors affect how much mobility exists in a society? This is also not an easy question, as researchers have found that a large number of different factors influence social mobility. For example, the amount of mobility will depend on what goes on inside families and how individuals are slotted into jobs within the **labour market** (the process by which employers hire individual workers). In a context where good jobs are expanding, upward mobility is more likely than in a society where good jobs are declining. Perhaps most importantly, however, the policies that governments adopt are very important, especially in relation to the education system. And these factors also overlap.

Families matter because parents play a large role in shaping how much education and other social and intellectual assets children acquire, and it is education and other assets that will determine children's incomes. If a society's education system is very limited, no matter what kinds of efforts parents make to encourage their children, it may not lead to better educational outcomes. Labour markets—the way workers are hired and promoted—matter because it is in the labour market that education pays off in economic terms. Government policies matter because government regulates both labour markets and educational systems. Governments decide whether and to what extent disadvantaged children should get compensatory assistance, which may help them overcome disadvantages associated with their family background. Governments also decide how equal schools are in rich and poor areas and how much support students receive for going to community colleges and universities.

These three factors—families, labour markets, and government policies—are all highly correlated with the level of inequality children face when they are growing up. High inequality of opportunity usually means that advantaged families can invest much more than disadvantaged families in their children's education and that the quality of schools that wealthy children attend will be much better than schools serving poor children. High inequality is also closely related to a high payoff of having a university degree. And high inequality is related to the role of the government. If the government has a weak system of policies to compensate for the disadvantages that poor children face, these children will have much less opportunity to succeed as adults (thus reinforcing inequality).

Social scientists have shown that the overall level of inequality of conditions in a country is indeed typically related to the level of intergenerational mobility (or equality of opportunity) in that country. Specifically, higher inequality overall is associated with lower mobility. Figure 9.11 plots the level of inequality when children were growing up in each country on the x axis (the horizontal axis) against the intergenerational earnings association on the y axis (the vertical axis). As we can see, countries with higher levels of inequality display stronger intergenerational associations between parents' income and children's earnings. In contrast, mobility is much higher in low-inequality countries.

Figure 9.11 suggests a clear relationship between inequality and mobility. We cannot, however, jump to the conclusion that high inequality *causes* low mobility. There may be other factors that produce both inequality of conditions and low intergenerational mobility. The figure, however, does suggest that a society's overall level of inequality plays an important role and helps to explain the differences in mobility between countries.

Figure 9.11 Relationship Between Income Inequality and Mobility in Selected Countries, Around Year 2000

SOURCE: From "Inequality from Generation to Generation: The United States in Comparison," by Miles Corak, in Robert S. Rycroft (Ed.), *The Economics of Inequality, Poverty, and Discrimination in the 21st Century*, 2013, Santa Barbara: ABC-CLIO (http://milescorak.files.wordpress.com/2012/01/inequality-from-generation-to-generation-the-united-states-in-comparison-v3.pdf). Copyright by ABC-CLIO LLC, 2013. Used with permission.

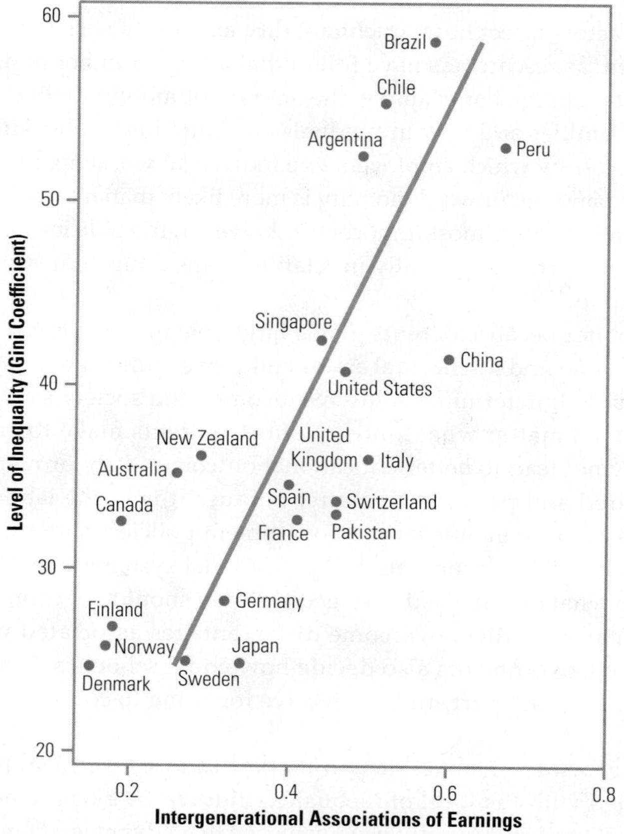

Education and Social Mobility

9.3.4 Discuss the relationship between education and social mobility.

Sociologists have emphasized the primary role of education in understanding social inequality and how individuals move in and out of poverty from one generation to the next. In all complex societies, privileged, high-status positions by definition are scarce—that is, after all, what makes them privileged. The existence of high-status positions in a society is possible only when there are also lower statuses—less privileged ones. What sociologists have discovered is that in modern societies, these privileged positions are rarely directly inherited by children of the upper class; rather, they are allocated principally through education systems. Upper-class parents are (almost always) unable to directly transfer privileged occupational positions to their children; a doctor or lawyer cannot simply pass on the family business to her child unless the child can get into and through medical school or law school. Instead, these parents invest for decades in their children's education in the hopes that similar occupational opportunities will be conferred indirectly.

To understand this important insight into how education and social inequality are linked, it is worth reviewing how sociologists have emphasized different aspects of this relationship over the past century. Education has a dual character with respect to attaining privileged, high-status positions. On the one hand, education systems can function to challenge other traditional forms of allocating privileged positions in society.

In traditional societies, for example, occupations are often simply passed on from parent to child. If a father was an agricultural labourer, his sons would also likely be agricultural labourers. The establishment and spread of public education broke down these traditional forms of occupational inheritance and substituted a new way of deciding who will get what. Educational systems do this through what are known as principles of **meritocracy**, a system where rewards and positions are distributed by ability, not social background or personal connections.

Education systems, however, can also be used to maintain and preserve privileged access to scarce positions if families with more resources are able to invest in more or better education for their children, for example by moving to a better neighbourhood or paying for private school or private tutoring. Furthermore, educational systems produce credentials, and groups can use these credentials to separate those with privilege from those without. In modern societies, high-status positions increasingly require educational credentials. It no longer matters how good you are at a particular thing—for example, teaching or healing people; without the proper educational certificate, you are typically denied access to privileged jobs such as being a doctor or university professor.

Sociologists recognize that schools play a fundamental role in society, not simply by training individuals for employment but also by working to select those who will be granted access to more desirable occupations. To the extent that schools facilitate the movement of talented individuals from lower social origins to privileged occupations, sociologists consider the society "open" rather than "closed." When individuals from disadvantaged socioeconomic backgrounds attain privileged occupational positions with associated higher social rewards (such as status, prestige, and income), social mobility has occurred. Sociologists have repeatedly demonstrated that schools play a critical role in either blocking or facilitating social mobility.

9.4 How Much Poverty Exists in North America and Around the World?

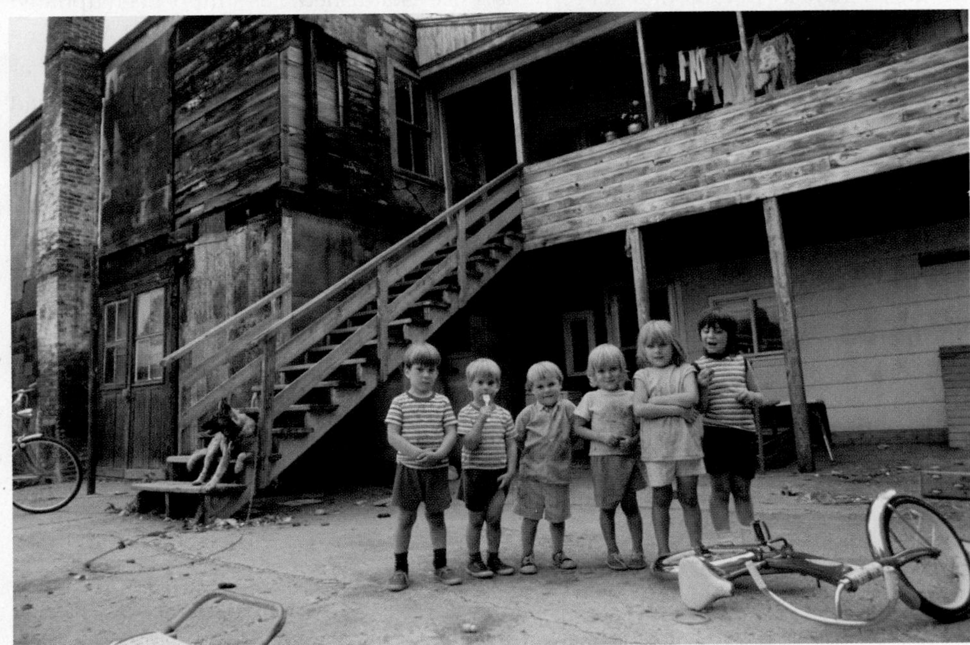

Nathan Benn/Alamy Stock Photo

Life at the Bottom: The Problem of Poverty

Poverty is a complicated concept. In the simplest of terms, it is a condition that involves the inability to afford basic needs such as food, clothing, shelter, and healthcare. But beyond a minimum of resources to ensure subsistence, it is difficult to define what basic needs are. Adam Smith, the founding father of economics, wrote the following in his classic 1776 book *The Wealth of Nations*:

> *A linen shirt is, strictly speaking, not a necessary of life. . . . The Greeks and Romans lived, I suppose, very comfortably though they had no linen. But in the present times, through the greater part of Europe, a creditable day-labourer will be ashamed to appear in public without a linen shirt, the want of which would be supposed to denote that disgraceful degree of poverty which, it is presumed, nobody can well fall into without extreme bad conduct.* (Smith, 1776/1976, p. 466)

It may be the case that having a cellphone today is as necessary as having a linen shirt was in the late eighteenth century, when Smith was writing. What about a car? A computer? It is entirely possible to argue that, given the importance of transportation (particularly where mass transit options are limited) and access to information and communication that are crucial for finding a job or going to school, such items are indeed basic needs.

Different Measures of Poverty

9.4.1 Distinguish between absolute and relative measures of poverty.

The official method by which the federal government measures poverty in the United States is by setting an income threshold—the minimum income necessary to afford basic necessities. This threshold is called the *poverty line*. But how is that minimum income determined? The story is a fascinating one, with major implications for how we understand and discuss poverty. The official poverty line was defined for the first time in the mid-1960s as part of a major government effort to reduce the amount of poverty in the United States (what came to be known as the War on Poverty). The task was assigned to an obscure official in the Social Security Administration named Mollie Orshansky in 1963, and her formula, once established, has simply been updated each year to take inflation into account. Orshansky reasoned that the typical American family spent about one-third of its income on food at that time. With what she calculated to be the cost per person of a nutritionally minimally adequate diet multiplied by three, a family (or individual) would have an adequate amount to live on (and not be in poverty). The poverty line varies by family size and is adjusted each year. In 2012, for example, the poverty line for a family of four was $23,492. So families of four people with an income less than $23,492 were considered poor. The poverty line for a person living alone was $11,720. Using the official definition, in 2013, about 15 percent of Americans lived in poverty (more than 45 million people, out of a total population of approximately 313 million). Table 9.5 summarizes the poverty line for various household types in the U.S.

This measure of poverty the U.S. government employs has not been changed since the 1960s (except for adjusting for inflation). Many criticisms have been raised of this measure: For example, it accounts for some kinds of income that poor people may receive, like food stamps, but does not take into account taxes they pay or adjust for differences in cost of living across states or cities. Unlike the United States and other countries, Canada has no official measure of poverty. Instead, Statistics Canada produces three main measures of low income: the **Low Income Cut-Off (LICO)**, the **Low Income Measure (LIM)**, and the **Market Basket Measure (MBM)**. These measures are

Table 9.5 Poverty Line for Various Household Types

U.S. Census Bureau Poverty Thresholds, 2012	
Size of Family Unit	**Poverty Threshold**
One person (unrelated individual)	$11,720
Under age 65	11,945
Age 65 or older	11,011
Two people	14,937
Householder under age 65	15,450
Householder age 65 or older	13,892
Three people	18,284
Four people	23,492
Five people	27,827
Six people	31,471
Seven people	35,743
Eight people	39,688
Nine people or more	47,297

SOURCE: From *Weighted Average Poverty Thresholds, 2012*, by the U.S. Census Bureau, 2013. Copyright by the U.S. Census Bureau.

considered to be indicators of the minimum income necessary to afford basic necessities. It is generally agreed that poverty refers to the intersection of low income and other dimensions of social exclusion including access to adequate housing, transportation, healthcare services, and other socially valued goods and services. Measures of poverty can either be *absolute* or *relative* measures.

Many European governments use a measure of **relative poverty**, which attempts to capture changes in living standards. The most common definition of relative poverty describes it as having a family income below 50 percent of the median income (the median is the midpoint of the income distribution in the country, with half of the population above and half below). The median income serves as a benchmark of what is common or typical in a society, so being 50 percent below the median means being significantly disadvantaged in comparison with other members of society. The idea of relative poverty is that someone who makes less than half the median income is excluded from the shared benefits of society. A relative measure of poverty is in fact a measure of inequality because wider economic disparities will result in a larger proportion of families living far below the median income. The official definition of poverty used by the United States government is a measure of **absolute poverty**, one that attempts to define the minimum amount of income necessary to meet basic needs, but one that does not adjust for changes in living standards. Using a relative measure of poverty, millions more would be considered poor in the United States. However it is measured, though, poverty is unquestionably a major problem in the United States.

Poverty in Canada: Who Are the Poor?

9.4.2 Identify factors that increase the likelihood of poverty.

The oldest and most commonly used measure of poverty in Canada is the Low Income Cut-Off (LICO) published by Statistics Canada for 35 different regions in Canada. Statistics Canada's after-tax LICO is a level of income at which point a family spends 63.6 percent or more of its income on food, shelter, and clothing. The Low Income Measure (LIM) is a purely relative measure of poverty used for international comparison. The LIM defines low income as being much worse off than the average and is calculated as having less than 50 percent of median household income in a given region. The Market Basket Measure (MBM) is an absolute measure that attempts to estimate the amount of income needed by a household to meet basic needs defined as community norms. The MBM establishes the level below which a household does not have the income to purchase a specific basket of essential goods and services including nutritious meals, personal-care items, and household supplies. The MBM is calculated for specific regions and takes local conditions and costs into consideration (Citizens for Public Justice, 2013).

Figure 9.12 shows the poverty rates and poverty line for various regions and communities across Canada in 2011 based on all three definitions of poverty. As we can see, the percentage of people living in poverty varies according to region and according to the measurement used to calculate low income. If we rely on the LICO measure for a family of four, we can see that 6.5 percent of the Canadian population lived at or below the poverty line in 2011. This percentage increases when using the MBM measure to 8.9 percent, and to 9.8 percent when using the LIM measure. Poverty rates are higher in the major metropolitan cities of Vancouver and Montreal, where the cost of living and median incomes are much higher than smaller prairie cities such as Saskatoon and Winnipeg. Rates of poverty depend upon the measure one uses. If we rely on the Low Income Measure (LIM), the average poverty rate in Canada has hovered around the 12–13 percent mark since 1981, except for a dip down to 10.5 percent in 1989 (Citizens for Public Justice, 2013, p. 9). Using the after-tax Low Income Cut-Off (LICO) measure, average poverty rates in Canada have declined from 11.6 percent in 1981 to 8.8 percent

Figure 9.12 Poverty Rates and Lines by Selected Communities, 2011

SOURCE: "Poverty Rates and Lines by Select Communities," p. 7 in Citizens for Public Justice, 2013, *Poverty Trends Highlights: Canada 2013* (https://www.cpj.ca/poverty-trends-highlights-canada-2013). Used with permission.

Remember that the average poor household in Canada relies on an income that is 33 per cent below the poverty line.

Low income measures only capture material dimensions of poverty; poverty also manifests itself in other ways including social exclusion, diminished well-being, and stress.

Poverty rates and lines in select communities in Canada, 2011

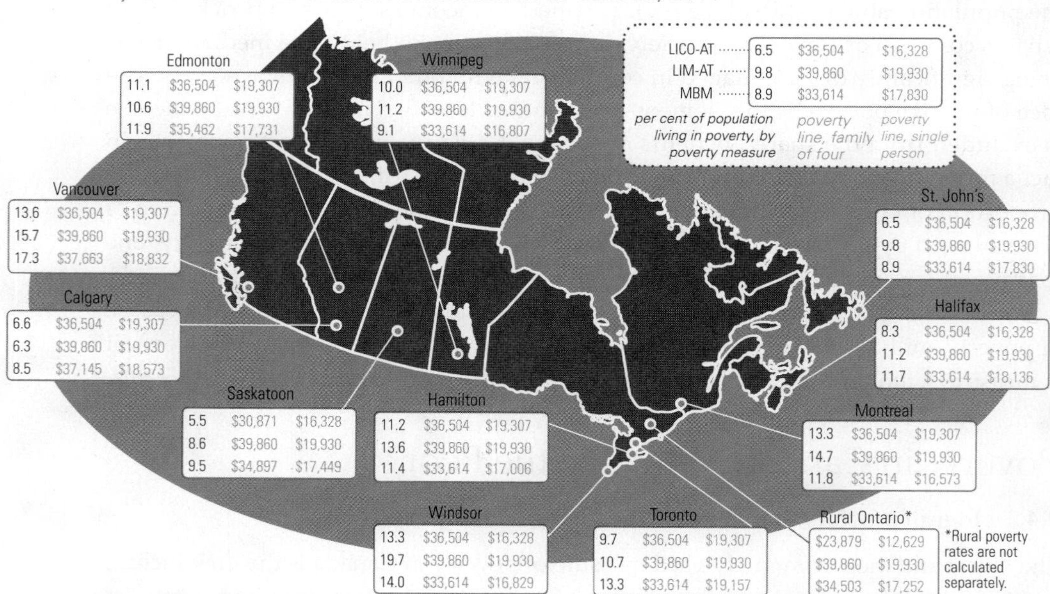

Here's how the MBM for a family of four in Toronto is calculated:

- Food = $813/month
- Shelter (incl. utilities) = $1,123/month
- Transportation = $366/month
- Clothing = $157/month
- All other expenses = $732/month

Based on your own experience and budget, do the poverty line examples seem low, high, or about right? Which measure do you think is best?

in 2011 (p. 9). These figures can be much higher for those age 65 and older, as well as for children and particularly those living in lone-parent families. Overall, however the poverty rates for these cohorts have declined *significantly* since 1981.

Even though people living in poverty are diverse, there are a number of factors that increase the likelihood that someone will be poor. Among these, the most important are education, employment status, minority status, age, and family structure. Education matters because, as we have discussed, schooling is an important determinant of the skills that people can sell in the market in exchange for a wage. Having less than a high school diploma puts anyone at higher risk of poverty. Employment status and type of job are basically the outcome of education and other skills and other assets. Having and maintaining a job that pays wages higher than the poverty line will keep anyone out of poverty. But there have never been enough jobs for all who want and need one, and even full-time jobs at the minimum wage are not enough to lift a family out of poverty. So those who either do not have jobs or have very low pay will be poor. Aboriginal status also matters in Canada. The overall prevalence of low income is significantly greater among Aboriginal people than among the non-Aboriginal population. Of those with Aboriginal identity living in private households, 18.7 percent who live in families and 42.8 percent who are unattached individuals experienced low income in 2005 (Collin & Jensen, 2009, p. 16). By contrast, among non-Aboriginal people, low-income rates were 8.4 percent for individuals in economic families and 28 percent for unattached individuals that same year (p. 17). As Chantal Collin and Hilary Jensen have shown, the situation is worse for Aboriginal children. A large proportion of young Aboriginal children (under six years of age) live in low-income families, particularly in urban areas. In 2006, 49 percent of young First Nations children living off-reserve were members of low-income families, a proportion that rose to 57 percent in census metropolitan areas. The same year, 32 percent of young Métis children, of whom 42 percent were living in census metropolitan areas, lived in low-income families. Among young non-Aboriginal children, the average low-income rate was 18 percent, rising to 21 percent in census metropolitan areas (p. 19). Finally, family structure also matters. Families in which there is a single parent—usually a female—are much more likely to be poor. This phenomenon has been called *feminization of poverty*, and it highlights the difficulties of complementing the roles of primary caregiver and provider on a single income.

One widespread belief about the poor is that most do not have jobs. This is not true. In fact, most of the people living in poverty engage in the labour market at least some of the time. Most of the working poor have strong attachments to the labour market, 76 percent reporting full-time, full-year work in 2001. These individuals earned, on average, $12.00 per hour, which was 50 percent higher than the highest minimum wage in Canada at that time. One-third of the working poor were employed in the sales and services sector. In 2007, 5.9 percent of working families in which the main income recipient had 910 hours or more of paid work that year lived on a low income. This was a decline from 7.3 percent in 2006 and was significantly lower than in 2000 (8.3 percent). In 2007, working poor families accounted for 31 percent of all low-income families (Collin & Jensen, 2009, pp. 25–26).

These statistics highlight the fact that many poor people in Canada are engaged in the labour market. They are known as the **working poor**, people who cannot make enough income to be free from poverty even if, as many do, they work full-time. How can this be? Many jobs simply do not pay enough to lift people working in them above the poverty line. But this is not all. For the working poor, poverty is not just about low income. Low-paying jobs are often unstable, and many people working in these jobs work on a temporary or part-time basis. Such jobs are not secure enough to build economic security, save money, and plan for the future. Even those families that are usually above the poverty line may be very vulnerable to economic and family circumstances. A recession, a divorce or spousal abandonment, or a severe illness can change the picture for families living close to the poverty line in ways for which middle-class families have more of a cushion. Most poor families have very little in the way of savings to fall back upon in the event of any crisis. They live, in short, at the edge of insecurity.

Poverty in International Comparative Perspective

9.4.3 Compare and contrast the level of poverty in North America to that in other regions.

Is the level of poverty in North America comparable to other advanced industrial countries? On the one hand, all of the rich countries have experienced similar economic trends in terms of deindustrialization and economic restructuring, which suggests they are likely to have levels of poverty that should be broadly similar. But on the other hand, the U.S. policies toward poverty reduction are quite different from the policies of other countries in Western Europe, Canada, or Australia. The United States spends less to directly alleviate poverty through welfare programs than any other wealthy country, although the United States does spend a lot on education relative to other countries (Garfinkel, Rainwater, & Smeeding, 2010).

Comparing poverty levels across countries is no easy task. It requires a common measure of income, a common poverty line, and a way to make currency similar across nations. One important comparative study has undertaken this task to compare 11 advanced industrial countries (Smeeding, 2006). In order to compare poverty, the author uses both an absolute poverty line, such as the one used in the United States, and a relative poverty line, such as the one used in Western Europe. He also distinguishes between "market" income (what is received from earnings) and "disposable" income (what families have to spend after taking taxes and government programs into account), two different ways of conceptualizing what families have to live on. Taking everything into account, the answer to how the United States compares to other countries is somewhat complicated, but in terms of disposable income, poverty is higher in the United States than in other rich countries and more than twice as high as in many other countries. Canada ranks 5th after the United States, Ireland, Italy, and the United Kingdom. Figure 9.13 shows the comparison across 11 countries in 2000.

Figure 9.13 Relative and Absolute Poverty Rates in 11 Advanced Industrial Countries

SOURCE: Based on data from "Poor People in Rich Nations: The United States in Comparative Perspective," by Timothy Smeeding, 2006, *Journal of Economic Perspectives*, *20*(1), pp. 69–90.

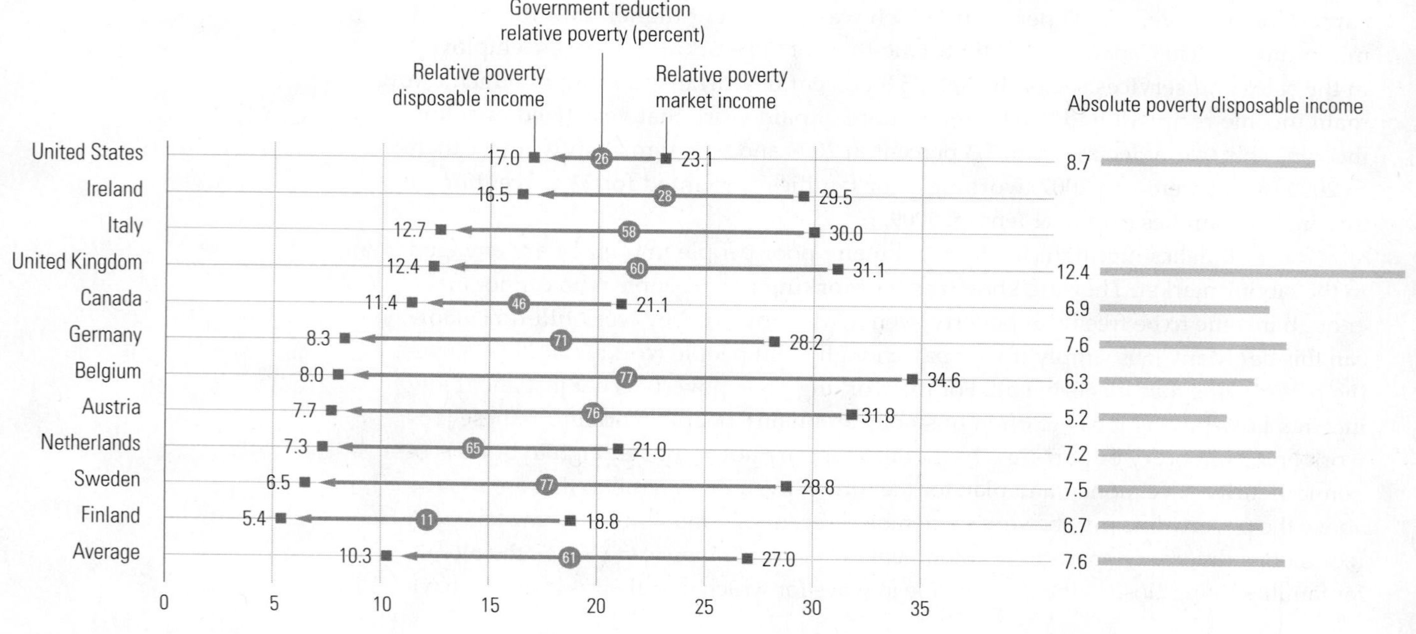

What is interesting to note in Figure 9.13 is that if we look at the right side, the poverty rate based on market incomes would be *lower* in the United States than many other countries, but because the U.S. government does relatively little to help poor families in comparison with other countries, the percentage of poor families declines only from 23.1 percent to 17 percent (it goes from 34.6% in Belgium to 8%, and on average of all these countries it goes from 27.0% to 10.3%).

In case this result might reflect the use of a relative measure, we can also compare absolute poverty rates in different countries. The bar graph on the right of Figure 9.13 uses the official poverty line in the United States for every country. Here again, the United States has a significantly higher poverty rate (although it is higher in the United Kingdom). These data suggest, then, that one important reason for excess poverty in the United States is that the government is doing far less to reduce poverty than most other countries. Using an absolute standard that captures a comparable income threshold across countries, poverty is lower in Canada than the United States and many other advanced industrial countries. These data suggest, that one important reason for the lower poverty in Canada relative to the United States is that policy is doing far more to reduce poverty.

Poverty and Children

9.4.4 Explain the impact of growing up in poverty on children.

A particularly important concern that social scientists and government officials have about poverty is how it impacts children. Why is childhood poverty a powerful predictor of poverty in adulthood? Childhood poverty creates a vicious cycle that reproduces disadvantage across generations. Poor households tend to have more children than wealthy households, and poor children are more likely to live with a single parent than nonpoor children; these tendencies contribute to the high percentage of children living in poverty. The high percentage of children growing up in poverty is worrisome for many reasons. Let's look at some of these:

In some cases the reason is obvious. Lack of basic nutrients, shelter, immunization, and access to healthcare is detrimental to children's development. When extra money prevents hunger, homelessness, or buying medicine and other necessities, it can make a huge difference in the lives of children.

But the detrimental consequences of poverty are not limited to cases of extreme deprivation. As researchers in the social and biological sciences have shown, living in poverty is an important source of stress, and stress is extremely bad for children (as we also noted in the introduction). Poverty is not just about the inability to afford things. Poverty is also usually associated with exposure to environmental toxins, neighbourhood violence and insecurity, anxiety about making ends meet, difficulties in accessing institutional services such as healthcare or schools, and many other stressors. Poverty and its attendant stressors can shape the neurobiology of the developing child in powerful ways, which may compromise cognitive development and concentration, thus affecting school attainment. This is a direct effect of poverty on the child. Poverty is stressful for parents too, and it may affect the investments of time and resources that parents make in children, as well as parents' interactions with children. This is an indirect effect of poverty on children—stress takes a toll on parents, which in turn will affect children's learning and development.

Homelessness

9.4.5 Discuss the problem of homelessness and identify some contributing factors.

One of the most extreme forms of poverty is **homelessness**—literally, the lack of permanent shelter to live in. Homelessness is a significant social problem in many parts of the world, including Canada. Individuals and families can become homeless for any number of specific reasons, including wars and violent conflicts that can in some cases create millions of refugees. But under more normal circumstances, the one nearly universal reason for homelessness is extreme poverty (although other problems such as mental illness or personal disasters are significant). Most people who become homeless will not remain so indefinitely, but even brief periods of homelessness can be devastating. Life on the streets and even in homeless shelters can be dangerous, and not having a regular address makes many aspects of daily life difficult.

The problem of homelessness in Canada grew considerably between the 1970s and 2000s, when the closing down of mental hospitals, decline of social programs for the poor, de-funding by the federal government of low-cost housing in urban areas, and rise in unemployment among high-risk groups combined to increase the number of people without regular residences. While a variety of government programs aimed at reducing homelessness have stabilized and reduced the size of the homeless population since the early 1990s, the problem has hardly been eliminated. It is estimated that approximately 30,000 people are homeless in Canada on any given night (Gaetz, Donaldson, Richter, & Gulliver, 2013).

Although homelessness is most common among single men, the lack of a regular dwelling creates especially significant hardships for families with children and is yet another example of how poverty impacts the innocent young. Using a broader definition of homelessness that includes doubling up with family or friends, it has been estimated that some 1.5 million children experience homelessness in the United States at some point during a given year, a number that is particularly disturbing given the strong evidence of high levels of stress and dislocation homelessness causes for children (Bussuk, Murphy, Coupe, Kenney, & Beach, 2011).

Conclusion: Should We Be Concerned About Excessive Inequality?

To what extent does inequality matter? The simplest answer to this question is the most straightforward: Higher levels of inequality mean that the poor have fewer resources to acquire needed goods and services than they would in more egalitarian countries. At the same time, the lives of middle-class families have stopped improving as they did for much of the twentieth century while the very richest individuals and families have received almost all of the benefits of economic growth. This is a vitally important fact in its own right. The further down the income distribution you look, the more difficult it becomes for families to meet basic needs, and for the past 35 years there have been very few improvements in living standards for most American families. This has not been the case in Canada, where government policies have worked to reduce the number of Canadians with low incomes over the same time period. Nevertheless, income inequality has increased in Canada. The fact that the rich are absorbing a larger share of the total income being produced in North America and many other parts of the world makes it difficult for families who live in those countries with high income inequality to address basic needs or to envision a brighter future for themselves or their children.

But beyond the consequences of rising inequality for household well-being and shared prosperity, what else can be said? We've discussed in this chapter how economic inequalities are related to child development, education, and social mobility into adulthood, but are there other consequences? A few issues are worth paying attention to. One is political. Every adult citizen has one and only one vote, but there are other ways to influence political outcomes that can enable those with money to exert influence. Perhaps the most important of these is by donating volunteer time or money to candidates for political office, which has increased dramatically in recent decades. As rising wealth at the top makes it easier for affluent individuals to "invest" in the political system, this may be harmful to the country as a whole: The interests and concerns of the rich are not necessarily the same as those of everyone else (see Chapter 7 for more details).

Another issue to consider is the fact that societies with high levels of overall economic inequality have appeared, in a number of studies, to have poor overall societal health, while societies that are more equal seem to have better health. The main reasons researchers have suggested to explain this finding are that rich people are in a position to access better healthcare than they otherwise would, potentially squeezing out poorer people who are less likely to have coverage for healthcare (in the United States), and, further, that the stress associated with poverty or low income causes additional health problems (Wilkinson, 2006). In Canada, lack of access to healthcare in remote regions and on Aboriginal reserves has led to poorer health outcomes in these regions.

Another, more subtle consequence is that inequality may change our preferences and desires in ways that are unhealthy. In particular, the desire to keep up with the rich when it comes to consumption may be pushing us to consume more stuff than we really need. To the extent that people look up to others who have more than they do, people will never feel completely satisfied with the possessions they do own, and they want more. This has become a problem because many North American families are taking on ever-higher levels of debt to try to attain such goods. "Luxury fever" also impacts subjective well-being—we are never fully satisfied with what we have when we hear or read about the lives of the rich (Frank, 1999). Even though North Americans have a higher average income than virtually all other countries in the world, international surveys show that North Americans are not as satisfied as we would expect. High levels of income inequality are the most likely culprit (Oishi & Diener, 2011).

Inequality is always going to be with us, but the *amount* of inequality that a society allows is not set in stone. As we have seen throughout this chapter, governments *can* choose to adopt policies that can reduce the amount of income and wealth controlled at the very top, and they *can* choose to adopt policies that will reduce the number of people living in poverty. Many very successful and rich countries have made those choices. Canadian government policies over the past three decades have consistently reduced the proportion of people living below the Low Income Cut-Off in all categories. Nevertheless, the situation faced by Canadian children who are vulnerable to poverty has changed very little in recent decades in comparison to well-off children, whose economic situation improved significantly. In comparison, the United States has accomplished much less through policy changes. America has high levels of poverty and inequality, and government policies of recent decades have done little to ensure that the benefits of economic growth are shared more equitably among the entire population.

CHAPTER SUMMARY

The Big Questions Revisited 9

9.1 What Is Inequality? At the heart of the study of social stratification is the concept of inequality. In this section, we explored the history of inequality and the ways societies and thinkers have typically justified inequality. We also discussed the sociological concept of class.

Inequality: An Introduction

A Brief History of Inequality

Learning Objective 9.1.1: Define *inequality* and explain how the form and level of inequality has varied throughout history.

Measures of Economic Inequality: Wealth and Income

Learning Objective 9.1.2: Compare and contrast income and wealth as measures of economic inequality.

Inequality by Class

Learning Objective 9.1.3: Define *class* and identify what constitutes a social class.

9.2 Why Is North America So Unequal? Inequality today is about as high as it has ever been since we started measuring, and poverty rates have remained persistently high. In this section, we compared Canada and the United States with similar developed countries and asked why North America is so unequal.

Unequal North America in Comparative Perspective

Trends in Income Inequality in North America and Around the World

Learning Objective 9.2.1: Discuss trends in income inequality and compare inequality in Canada and the United States to that in other countries around the world.

Why Did Inequality Increase?

Learning Objective 9.2.2: Identify factors explaining why economic inequality in North America has increased since the 1960s.

The 1 Percent

Learning Objective 9.2.3: Describe who constitutes the "1 percent" in North America.

9.3 **Do We All Have an Equal Opportunity to Succeed in Life?** Social mobility is one of the most important topics in the study of social stratification. In this section we examined how social mobility is measured, why countries differ in opportunity, how North America compares to other countries, and the relationship between education and mobility.

Inequality, Education, and Social Mobility

Measuring Opportunity: The Concept of Social Mobility

Learning Objective 9.3.1: Define *social mobility* and describe how inequality of opportunity is measured.

Social Mobility in Comparative Perspective

Learning Objective 9.3.2: Compare and contrast chances for social mobility in the United States to other countries such as Canada and Norway.

Factors Influencing Mobility

Learning Objective 9.3.3: Identify factors that affect how much social mobility exists in a society.

Education and Social Mobility

Learning Objective 9.3.4: Discuss the relationship between education and social mobility.

9.4 **How Much Poverty Exists in North America and Around the World?** Poverty is a complicated concept. Beyond a minimum of resources to ensure subsistence, it is difficult to define what our "basic" needs are. In this section, we examined two ways of viewing poverty and just how much poverty there is especially in the United States and in other countries around the world. We also looked closely at the problem of childhood poverty.

Life at the Bottom: The Problem of Poverty

Different Measures of Poverty

Learning Objective 9.4.1: Distinguish between absolute and relative measures of poverty.

Poverty in Canada: Who Are the Poor?

Learning Objective 9.4.2: Identify factors that increase the likelihood of poverty.

Poverty in International Comparative Perspective

Learning Objective 9.4.3: Compare and contrast the level of poverty in North America to that in other regions.

Poverty and Children

Learning Objective 9.4.4: Explain the impact of growing up in poverty on children.

Homelessness

Learning Objective 9.4.5: Discuss the problem of homelessness and identify some contributing factors.

Learn the Terms

absolute poverty (p. 251)
association (p. 245)
bourgeoisie (p. 231)
caste society (p. 245)
class analysis (p. 231)
consumption (p. 229)
deindustrialization (p. 238)
economic restructuring (p. 239)
egalitarian (p. 234)
feudalism (p. 226)
globalization (p. 238)
homelessness (p. 255)
immobility (p. 246)
income (p. 229)
inequality (p. 225)
inequality of opportunity (p. 244)
labour market (p. 247)
life chances (p. 231)
Low Income Cut-Off (LICO) (p. 250)
Low Income Measure (LIM) (p. 250)
Market Basket Measure (MBM) (p. 250)
mean (p. 228)
median (p. 227)
meritocracy (p. 249)
middle class (p. 230)
minimum wage (p. 240)
net financial assets (NFAs) (p. 229)
outsourcing (p. 238)
progressive tax system (p. 239)
proletariat (p. 231)
relative poverty (p. 251)
serf (p. 236)
slavery (p. 226)
social mobility (p. 245)
social stratification (p. 225)
socioeconomic status (SES) (p. 232)
sweatshop (p. 238)
university wage premium (p. 237)
wealth (p. 229)
working poor (p. 253)

Chapter 10
Race and Ethnicity

by Ann Morning* and Guillermina Jasso**

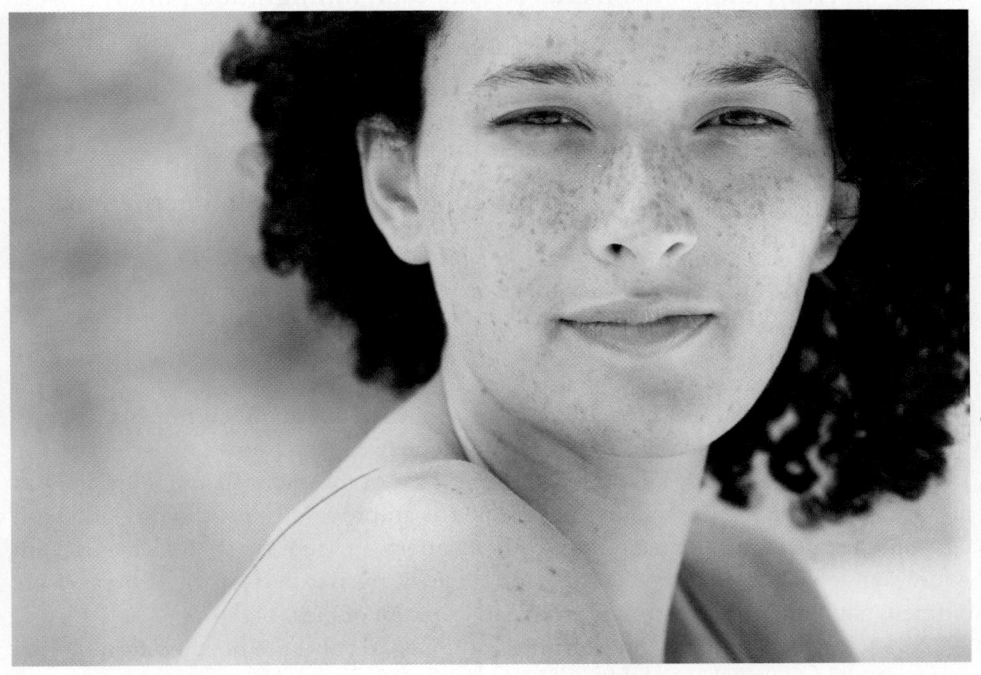

Alix Minde / AGE Fotostock

Today, experts in the social and natural sciences debate whether the distribution of human biological characteristics around the world—like dark skin, light hair, or particular genetic traits—can be mapped onto the three or four racial categories that European scientists invented in the 1700s.

Learning Objectives

10.1.1 Compare and contrast contemporary sociologists' and Max Weber's definitions of race and ethnicity.

10.1.2 Discuss key distinctions between race and ethnicity.

10.1.3 Distinguish racial labels from ethnic ones.

10.2.1 Explain how changing North American definitions of who counts as white support the constructivist view of race.

10.2.2 Analyze the arguments against a biological determination of race.

10.2.3 Discuss how race is understood differently around the world.

*An earlier version of this chapter was coauthored by Nandi Dill, Rachel Garver, and John Halushka.
**An earlier version of the immigration content was coauthored by Leslie-Ann Bolden, Carse Ramos, and Harel Shapira.

10.3.1 Discuss the roles of prejudice, stereotyping, and discrimination in the sociological definition of racism.

10.3.2 Explain how people can be socialized into racism.

10.4.1 Discuss immigration as part of the fabric of social life and how it is becoming increasingly important in the twenty-first century.

10.4.2 Examine how societies seek to limit or regulate immigration and emigration.

10.4.3 Identify the six main eras of Canadian immigration policy.

10.5.1 Analyze the factors that influence the desire to move.

10.5.2 Distinguish between a mover and a stayer.

10.5.3 Analyze the dilemmas that immigrant families face.

10.5.4 Discuss what happens to the children involved in international migration.

10.5.5 Analyze the social and economic benefits and costs of immigration.

What exactly is race? Does biology play a role in it? What about culture? Is it something that people invented, or has it always been part of the human experience? The study of race and ethnicity has long been central to North American sociology and has also featured prominently in other fields, such as anthropology, psychology, and biology. But in spite of this longstanding scholarly attention, we have yet to come up with widely agreed-upon definitions of *race* and *ethnicity*. Even experts struggle to precisely define what they mean when they invoke the concept of race.

About 10 years ago, I (Ann Morning) travelled around the northeastern United States to interview anthropology and biology professors about how they understood the concept of race. What I found surprised me because it ran counter to what many of my graduate school professors had told me—that social and natural scientists today all agree that race is a human invention without any basis in biological characteristics. When I actually spoke with anthropologists and biologists, though, it immediately became clear that their views on race varied a great deal and hardly reflected the consensus that my graduate school advisors presumed.

One of the discoveries that intrigued me the most was the way they used *me*—or, more specifically, my physical appearance—to back up their views. In several instances, the professor I was interviewing would say something about *my* race in order to support his or her definition of the term in general. What struck me most, though, was that even with the same "data" at hand—namely, me and my physical features—these academics came up with wildly different interpretations of race.

In one of my very first interviews, a cultural anthropologist at a large urban public university asked me how I identified myself in racial terms. It's a question I'm used to because, with my African, European, Asian, and American Indian ancestry, people are often curious about my background. The anthropologist's reaction was to use me as evidence that race does not really have any biological underpinning. "You're a perfect walking example of why [race] doesn't work," he concluded. "I just wonder, looking at you," he went on, "how anybody could maintain that there are these hard and fast races. . . ."

A few weeks later, a biology professor at a state university explained to me how race might come up in a lecture on genetics. Skin colour, he suggested, "could be used as an example of quantitative genetics . . . The general thought is that by and large,

The Big Questions

1. **What is the difference between race and ethnicity?** More often than not, the words *race* and *ethnicity* are used interchangeably, as if they mean the same thing. And indeed they have more than a passing resemblance. But sociologists make clear distinctions between race and ethnicity, and use the two terms to describe different kinds of categories and identities.
2. **Is race real?** If there's one thing academics agree on, it is that race is real. Where they part ways is on the question of whether race is anchored in deep-seated physical differences between individuals or is an invention that is not determined by human biology but that nonetheless is "real" because it has an unmistakable impact on daily life.
3. **What is racism?** In classroom discussions of race and ethnicity, students often preface their comments with phrases like "I don't know if I should say this, but . . ." or "I'm not sure what the right term for this group is, but. . . ." Concern about the "political correctness" of our ideas, speech, and behaviour is a prominent feature of both public and private conversations on race today. Sociologists have thought a lot about prejudice and discrimination, providing ample food for thought on racism.
4. **What is immigration, and how do governments regulate it?** What kinds of things do sociologists study when they study immigration, and why is the study of immigration important for understanding the world we live in? In this section, we examine the basic concepts, history, and ideas in the study of immigration.
5. **Why do people move, and what are the consequences?** People move for many reasons, but the most fundamental of these is the desire to make a better life for themselves and their children. Sociologists are interested in the characteristics of both those who move and those who stay, as well as the countries they come from and the countries in which they settle. Distinguishing between these different categories of people and places provides important insights into the dynamics and consequences of the migration process.

although there are some environmental influences, there are four sets of genes which determine skin colour." Peering over his glasses at me, he mused, "I take a look at you, and you might have—don't be offended—you have, if there are four . . . that means there are eight genes, and I would say you have three or four black genes and four or five white genes . . . just on skin colour." In contrast to the cultural anthropologist who felt that my appearance disproved the existence of races, this biologist thought I was a textbook example of how race is rooted in DNA.

Finally, one rainy afternoon a physical anthropologist at an Ivy League university gave me a tour of his large laboratory, pointing out various human skeletons and the traits he argued reflected their racial heritage. Soon our talk turned to the uncertainty involved in determining race from skeletal remains. "Environments have changed enormously," the anthropologist explained. "There's been more intermixing." Then he turned to me and said, "I mean, if you give me your skull and so forth, and I look at your nasal aperture, I'm not going to have a clue that you have any black ancestry." But then he corrected himself: "Now I might, given your teeth, because they're large."

As these anecdotes drawn from my research suggest, contemporary scientists' ideas about race—and what it has to do with biology, society, or anything else—span a wide spectrum. A cultural anthropologist who thought it was impossible to identify clear-cut races (and thus that they do not exist) disagrees sharply with the biologist who thought that race could easily be traced back to an individual's genetic profile. For me, these encounters sum up a fundamental characteristic of today's scientific perspectives on human difference: Even thoughtful and highly trained specialists, working with the same data, have yet to reach a consensus on the basic question of what race is. It is hardly surprising that everyone else struggles with these issues as well.

10.1 What Is the Difference Between Race and Ethnicity?

Gino Santa Maria/Fotolia

Understanding Race and Ethnicity

Sociologists share fairly precise understandings of both race and ethnicity. Yet the sociological distinction between the two terms runs counter to everyday practice, where *race* and *ethnicity* are often used as synonyms for each other. People from all walks of life—journalists, teachers, doctors, advertisers, and politicians—routinely use the two terms interchangeably.

Why do we often tend to treat race and ethnicity as the same thing in everyday conversations? Sometimes the term *ethnicity* is seen as a polite replacement for *race*—a way to avoid using a term that is associated with racism and racial inequality. The confusion between race and ethnicity is in part due to the fact that, at their core, the two concepts have a great deal in common. Both are systems for classifying human beings into groups based on shared ancestry. The crucial distinction between them lies in the different kinds of characteristics that are used to assign people to ethnic or racial groups.

Except for Aboriginal peoples, a person's ethnic or cultural identity is usually associated with ancestors who first came to the North American continent. The Canadian census collects information about the Aboriginal population by identifying common descent using the categories of ethnic origin, Aboriginal identity, Registered or Treaty Indian, and member of an Indian band or First Nation.

Sociological Definitions of Race and Ethnicity

10.1.1 Compare and contrast contemporary sociologists' and Max Weber's definitions of race and ethnicity.

Max Weber (1864–1920), one of sociology's founding figures, was also one of the first sociologists to define ethnicity and race. Weber described ethnic groups as "those human groups that entertain a subjective belief in their common descent," adding that "it does not matter whether or not an objective blood relationship exists" (Weber, 1922/1978, p. 389). The most striking aspect of Weber's definition is that the key ingredient for ethnic membership is *belief* in shared descent. The subjective dimension of ethnicity would go on to become a central fixture of later sociologists' thinking.

Weber did not portray race as equally subjective, however. Instead, like most scholars of his era, he felt that races stemmed from "common inherited and inheritable traits that actually derive from common descent" (p. 385). This view of race is called **essentialism**; that is, it presumes that an individual's identity depends on fundamental and innate characteristics that are deep-seated, inherited, and unchangeable. These traits are thought to be part of people's "essence," their very being. Whereas Weber observed that many different characteristics or experiences could serve to indicate who belonged to which ethnic group—including physical resemblance, historical memories, and common cultural practices—he believed that it is physical makeup alone that determines an individual's race. In a nutshell, ethnicity is based on people's cultural practices, and race is based on their biological traits.

Not all early sociologists held an essentialist view of race. Across many books and essays examining racial oppression in America, W. E. B. Du Bois (1868–1963) challenged the view that distinctive traits had a biological component common to all African Americans and that those traits could be determined by examining how blacks in America live and work. Du Bois argued that the racism so prevalent in American society in the late nineteenth and early twentieth centuries made it impossible for blacks to find jobs or achieve success in the way that whites could. High unemployment among African Americans did not mean that blacks were lazy. The reluctance of white employers to hire blacks created some of the very "facts" used to confirm the stereotype about laziness.

While contemporary sociologists share Weber's view of ethnicity, most reject his definition of race in favour of the position Du Bois advocated. Sociologists today believe that racial identification is as subjective a process as ethnic classification. The major difference between race and ethnicity lies in the basis on which group boundaries are drawn. In other words, we look for different clues or signs when we think about people's ethnicity as compared to their race.

Why exactly do contemporary sociologists reject Weber's description of race as an identity based solely on inherited physical traits? The difference in viewpoints is subtle but meaningful. In a sense, today's sociologists have taken to heart Weber's message about the subjectivity of group definitions and have come to believe that even our perceptions of biological similarity are subjective. So our racial classifications are based not on some objective measure of physical resemblances (as Weber claimed) but rather on our beliefs and socially influenced perceptions of which kinds of people are biologically similar and which are different.

A useful illustration comes from the United States' one-drop rule, a custom that became enshrined in many state laws around the turn of the nineteenth century.

According to this longstanding method of identifying a person's race, someone with one black grandparent and three white grandparents is a black person because so much as a "drop of black blood" means that a person somehow has more in common with blacks than with whites. This is the same reasoning that leads us to label President Obama black even though his mother was white. Clearly, there is no natural biological rule that makes him more black than white. Instead, there are social rules—cultural customs—that determine how we classify people by race and even how we "see" race. In both Canada and the United States, to be federally recognized as an "Indian" an individual must be able to comply with strict standards of government regulation (Lawrence, 2003, p. 3). According to the Constitution Act, 1982, Section 35(2), the term *Aboriginal peoples* "includes the Indian, Inuit, and Métis peoples of Canada." The Canadian government classifies persons of Aboriginal ancestry in relation to three variables: Aboriginal group, Registered or Treaty Indian status, and membership in a First Nation or Indian Band (Statistics Canada, 2015). Prior to the colonization of the Indigenous peoples of the Americas, the descriptor *Indian* was meaningless. It was through external regulatory laws that this common identity became imposed as a natural category of existence (Lawrence, 2003, p. 4). According to Bonita Lawrence, "settler governments in North America usurped the right to define Indigenous citizenship, reducing the members of hundreds of extremely different nations, ethnicities, and language groups to a common raced identity as 'Indian'" (pp. 3–4).

Immigration is particularly important for the history of North American society. Nearly all of us have an immigration story. The sole exceptions are the descendants of the native peoples of the global North and the global South, but even these "native" peoples are themselves descendants of migrants from several thousand years ago. Today, every country in the world has a significant immigrant population, and in many countries more than 1 in 10 (or even 1 in 5) people were born in another country. In spite of the nearly universal nature of the immigrant experience, and its continual growth in recent years, social and political controversy over rising immigration has increased worldwide. Part of the reason for the tensions around immigration is that it brings with it important changes to any society. This chapter explores the issues associated with the movement of people across borders.

In this chapter, we define **ethnicity** as a system for classifying people who are believed to share common descent based on perceived cultural similarities. We define **race** as a system for classifying people who are believed to share common descent based on perceived innate physical similarities. Framing the two concepts in this way makes clear how much they have in common, but it also highlights the fundamental difference between them.

Key Distinctions Between Race and Ethnicity

10.1.2 Discuss key distinctions between race and ethnicity.

Contemporary sociologists have written extensively on the similarities and differences between the concepts of race and ethnicity.

One of the first things that researchers have identified is that in any given place, the notions of race and ethnicity may not be equally important for people (Cornell & Hartmann, 2007). Another key difference is that racial categories tend to be imposed on individuals or groups by others, while ethnic labels are more likely to be chosen for themselves by the individuals or groups concerned. This contrast can be described as external versus internal classification. The concept of race gained much of its power and reach from Europeans' imperial encounters with Africans, Asians, Indigenous peoples of the Americas, and others, beginning in the fifteenth century. Prior to that, Western medieval societies were divided by religion (i.e., Christians versus non-Christians), and going back even further, the ancient Greeks distinguished between themselves and "barbaric" people; but a colour-coded hierarchy of race as we understand it today did not yet exist in the Western imagination. It was not until European explorers, armies, clergy, and settlers sought to dominate people across the globe that the race idea formed. Europeans came to believe that the differences they observed in appearance and behaviour between themselves and others could be explained by intrinsic, racial characteristics. Equally importantly, they were persuaded that races fell along a hierarchy in which they occupied the top rung, so European domination and colonization of others was only natural. Beliefs about racial difference then grew out of a context of conquest, exploitation, and enslavement and were further cultivated to justify power inequalities.

A similar modern example can be seen in the creation of the "Hispanic" category by the United States government to characterize people from many different countries in Central and South America. Although the government considers Hispanics to be an ethnic and not a racial group, they have effectively been "**racialized**" into being considered by many to be a race comparable to whites or blacks. Yet the very notion of a Hispanic race—or even a Hispanic ethnicity—is a very recent one, stemming from the federal government's attempts in the 1960s and 1970s to develop a set of official racial classifications (Graham, 2002). Before then, it was not obvious that people from Central America, like Mexicans and Guatemalans, had much to do with people from the Caribbean, like Cubans and Dominicans, let alone with people from South America, like Peruvians and Argentines. So, although they did not choose or invent the label for themselves, people with origins in any of these places now find themselves in a society in which, regardless of how they prefer to identify themselves, they are labelled by the government, other institutions, and other people as Hispanic.

Distinguishing Racial and Ethnic Labels

10.1.3 Distinguish racial labels from ethnic ones.

So how can we tell which groups are ethnic and which are racial? Any list or taxonomy depends entirely on time and place. In my research on censuses conducted around the world (Morning, 2008), I discovered that the official racial and ethnic categories used by different countries to classify their populations vary widely. In Guatemala, ethnic groups on the census include "Garifuna" and "Ladino" people; in Bulgaria, the main categories are "Bulgarian," "Turkish," and "Gypsies." The New Zealand census classifies people as "New Zealand European," "Maori," "Samoan," "Tongan," "Chinese," and "Indian" (among others), while Sri Lanka recognizes ethnic groups like "Sinhalese," "Sri Lanka Tamil," "Indian Tamil," "Sri Lanka Moor," "Burgher," "Malay," "Sri Lanka Chetty," and "Bharatha."

Despite such immense local variation, there is a rule of thumb we can use to distinguish racial labels from ethnic ones. Race is anchored in colour terms—like "black" and "white"—that denote vast, continental groupings that include millions if not billions of people. "Black" might refer to people from sub-Saharan Africa or the Caribbean or Australia, "white" to natives of Europe. Even if they are not frequently used today, colour terms like "red," "yellow," and "brown" refer to similarly large-scale groups: Indigenous (or native) peoples of the Americas, Asians, and Hispanics.

In contrast, ethnic groups tend to be much smaller in size and associated

Native Americans, such as the Hopi, are regarded as a distinct ethnic group in the United States, even though their ancestors were native to the area.

Julien McRoberts Danita Delimont Photography/Newscom

with local, national, or regional geography rather than with continents. It is not surprising, then, that different countries recognize startlingly different sets of ethnicities; they are concerned with groups that differentiate themselves within national borders.

Sometimes these ethnic groups are considered native to the area, like Hopi or Navajo people in the United States; other times they are recognized to be descended from immigrants, like Korean Canadians, German Canadians, and South Asian Canadians. Yet often the historical distinction between native and migrant is murky. When the United States annexed large swaths of Mexican territory in the nineteenth century, many people went overnight from being residents of Mexico to becoming residents of the United States. Were these Mexican Americans then an immigrant or a native ethnic group? Similarly, when settler governments colonized what eventually came to be known as Canada, the inhabitants came to be known as "Indians" and were distinguished from the European settlers on the basis of skin colour and cultural practices.

10.2 Is Race Real?

Malcolm Fairman/Alamy

The Social Construction of Race

Sociologists often describe race as a **social construct**, or a social phenomenon that was invented by human beings and is shaped by the social forces present in the time and place of its creation. The idea of *invention* often leads people to assume that something that is socially constructed is not real. But since when are social inventions not real? Thomas Edison invented the light bulb, but it is real. Steve Jobs invented the iPad, and it is real. Similarly, the belief that human beings come in four or five colours or flavours called "races" is invented—but as long as people and governments act as if these ways of characterizing people are meaningful, they are real. Or, to put it differently, races are real—but they are not biological. They are real social groupings that have real effects on people's lives. The **constructivist** view of race used by sociologists today—that is, the argument that racial categories are social creations, not biological facts—can be contrasted with the *essentialist* view of race, which asserts that there are enduring differences between races that are rooted in biological sources and do not change from one generation to the next.

Race and Society

10.2.1 Explain how changing North American definitions of who counts as white support the constructivist view of race.

To say that race is socially constructed means several things. First is the idea that race is a classification system that is invented, created by human beings, and therefore something that is made rather than something that is natural or biological. Second is the perspective that it is *socially* created—not the work of a single individual but rather the product of masses of people who form a society. In that sense, race is a lot like language: No single person invented English or Spanish or Korean, but languages are real social phenomena that millions of unnamed people have shaped. Third, the social foundation of race implies that as societies change, so do their ideas about race. Many sociologists, historians, and anthropologists investigate just how societal factors—such as economic conditions and organization, shifts in cultural values, or political upheavals—influence beliefs about race.

One puzzle that has fascinated researchers is how North Americans' ideas about who is white have changed over time. Many people whom we consider to be white today would not have been classified as such a century ago. Irish, Italian, Jewish, and other European ancestries were routinely excluded from the white category. The historian Matthew Frye Jacobson (1998) argues that the massive wave of European immigration to North America over the period of roughly 1880 to 1920 had a major impact on who was considered white. If whiteness had seemed self-evident when the European-origin population of North America was largely of English descent (though with Irish, Scottish, Dutch, German, and French members as well), its boundaries were much less clear when immigrants began arriving from places like Poland, Italy, Greece, Hungary, and Russia in the late nineteenth century. As a result, politicians, scientists, and everyday people started to view the newcomers as members of separate races, distinct from—and inferior to—"true" whites, who were of northwestern European origin.

Changing definitions of who counts as white lend powerful support to the constructivist view of race. If race were simply a matter of our physical makeup, the boundaries of the white category would not have shifted so dramatically over the last 200 years; people's bodily characteristics have not changed over that time. What changed instead were beliefs about who belonged to what race as people went about constructing and reconstructing race categories.

Race and Biology

10.2.2 Analyze the arguments against a biological determination of race.

The hardest thing for most people to accept about the constructivist perspective on race is that it seems to contradict what they see with their very own eyes. How can anybody claim that race is not a biological fact when we can easily "see" race? Every day we come across people whom we can immediately identify in racial terms, for example as white or Asian.

The simple answer is this: We can easily spot surface physical differences between people. But the ways in which we then assign people to racial groups is purely a matter of *socialization*—that is, of having been trained (consciously or not) to pick out particular bodily characteristics and then associate them with particular groups.

Consider the following very simple example. Pretend you are in a laboratory with a researcher who puts three coloured blocks in front of you—red, yellow, and blue—and asks you to divide them into two groups. You might decide that red and yellow go together, while blue remains its own category, or perhaps you might choose to group red and blue together, leaving yellow on its own. There is no obvious similarity here, no clear-cut grouping of which two colours go together. But if every time you make a choice, the researcher corrects you by putting the yellow and blue blocks together and leaving the red apart, you will learn very quickly that the colours yellow and blue fit together. From that point forward, you will easily be able to classify yellow and blue—but not red—as part of the same group, even when you're asked to sort toy cars or beach balls instead of blocks. Matching items to groups based on colour will become an automatic reaction you don't even have to think about; after a while, it will seem natural that yellow and blue go together, but not red.

Race works the same way. We grow up learning to look for certain pieces of information about a person's body (notably skin colour, hair colour, hair texture, and eye colour and shape), while disregarding other things, like height, weight, ear shape, and hand size, to come up with an idea of which race they belong to. And, today, at least, we're usually right: The race we think the person belongs to is in fact the race with which he or she identifies. But that does not mean that our racial classification of others, and their racial identification of themselves, is based on some innate racial characteristics they possess and that we simply observe. Instead, it's more like a situation in which, instead of blocks, we have yellow-coloured, blue-coloured, and red-coloured people, and we've all been trained to think of the yellow and blue people as being in a different category than the red ones. In other words, both the observers and the observed share exactly the same mental rules of who belongs to what race. But that does not mean there is anything natural or necessary about blues and yellows being matched together, or about reds being held apart. Human beings vary in their surface (and other) biological traits as we move around the world, and we are very good at spotting physical differences between the members of our species.

We can generally see physical differences between Norwegians and Italians, Italians and Nigerians, Nigerians and Ethiopians, Ethiopians and Indians, and Indians and Koreans. We can even see physical differences between siblings! But we don't generally consider those differences to indicate that a brother and sister are members of different races. Similarly, we may or may not consider the physical differences we notice between different groups around the world to reflect racial differences. For example, we can see surface differences between Norwegians and Nigerians and Koreans, and indeed we usually consider them to be members of different races. In these examples, racial difference maps onto observable physical difference. But in other cases, like the comparisons of Norwegians to Italians, or Nigerians to Ethiopians, or Indians to Koreans, we see physical differences between them but classify them as members of the same racial group. Despite their distinctive surface characteristics, in North America today Norwegians and Italians are considered to be racially white, Nigerians and Ethiopians black, and Indians and Koreans, Asian. It is not biology that dictates that Indians and Koreans are members of the same race while Ethiopians are not, but rather socially created and widespread rules for grouping people.

In the last few decades, some scientists have argued that even if surface physical features are not a reliable indicator of race, patterns in our DNA reveal the existence of human racial groups. This assumption underpins criminal forensic experts' analysis of DNA evidence (extracted from crime scene specimens like blood or saliva) to try to guess the perpetrator's race. It is also behind the new pastime of genetic genealogy, where companies analyze their clients' DNA to estimate the racial makeup of their family tree. But just as in the case of sorting blue and red blocks, racial analysis of DNA starts with man-made rules for assigning individuals to racial groups. Before looking at a customer's—or a suspect's—DNA sample, scientists have to decide which characteristics of the DNA will be indicative of which kind of racial ancestry. And to do that, they have to come up with a list of which race(s) they believe are out there, and then sample individuals from those assumed races to find out what kinds of genetic characteristics they typically have. In the United States, genetic genealogy firms generally try to identify European, African, or East Asian ancestry. In the United Kingdom, where much of this forensic technology was developed, the categories of interest are "Caucasians, Afro-Caribbeans, and Asians from the Indian subcontinent"

(Evett, Gill, Scranage, & Weir, 1996, p. 398). In both cases, scientists divide humankind into racial categories that are familiar, given their society's histories. But the technology could be used with any kind of geography-based grouping—even a simple division of human beings into "red" and "blue" races. Once two or more categories have been created, and individuals have been selected to provide representative DNA for each of those categories, then it is simply a matter of working through a statistical algorithm for assessing how similar the particular customer's (or suspect's) gene variants are to those typically found within the "red" or "blue" sample. Crucially, the genetic genealogy companies' estimates can never be disproved or properly assessed: If you are informed that your ancestry is 30 percent African, 40 percent Asian, and 30 percent European, what independent and reliable data can you use to verify this statement?

For many people, the constructivist view of race is hard to truly grasp because it flies in the face of what we think we see and know. Its basic premise is that even though we may *think* race is grounded in human biology, it isn't really—it just claims to be.

Race and Place

10.2.3 Discuss how race is understood differently around the world.

The sociological view that race is socially constructed is grounded in a comparative (or cross-national) perspective. Depending on location, the *race concept*—people's beliefs about race, including their notions of which groups are races and who belongs to which race—has emerged in different forms at different times, or perhaps not at all. Because Western scholars have focused less on societies outside Europe and North America, the study of race thinking elsewhere is still in its infancy. But the research that has been done in this area offers some fascinating insights on how race can be imagined differently across the globe.

One question that researchers ask is how we can explain the noticeable variations in the way people around the world think about race. One study of West Africa found that local racial groupings like black, white, and red had little to do with individuals' surface physical appearances but instead were based on whether individuals were believed to have noble ancestry, which in this context meant Arab heritage (Hall, 2011). Similarly, as the following photo shows, Brazilians do not link physical appearance to racial group the same way North Americans do; in Brazil, dozens of racial labels exist to classify people based on very specific combinations of skin colour, hair colour, hair texture, facial features, and so forth. As a result, full siblings can be of different races in Brazil, a situation that is unthinkable by North American standards.

In Brazil, race labels are meant to give more specific details about people's appearance in terms of facial traits, skin colour, eye colour, hair colour, and hair texture. This focus on physical appearance means that a person's race depends on how he or she looks as much as if not more than on his or her ancestry. As a result, even full siblings can be considered to be of different races in Brazil. Would you say that the members of this Brazilian family all belong to the same race?

Homer W Sykes/Alamy

Scholars have noted that while contemporary North Americans attribute racial differences to genes, people elsewhere (and at different times) have thought of racial difference as residing in the blood, or the mind, or the soul (Nelkin & Lindee, 1995). What causes the race concept to take on such different forms? To date, researchers have concentrated on two types of explanations for such variations in race thinking. The first is that as the Western race concept spread across the globe in the wake of imperial conquest, it blended with local traditional beliefs and prejudices to create many new versions of race (Dikötter, 2008). For example,

South Koreans' ideas of race today likely reflect a mixture of ideas brought by U.S. military personnel stationed there since the mid-twentieth century, historical Korean and Japanese colour preferences, Confucian beliefs about groups' proper places, and longstanding images of Korea as a nation based on shared blood (Kim, 2008).

The second approach for explaining local variants in ideas about race tends to focus on demographic, economic, and political factors. Why, for example, have Americans traditionally classified people with white and black ancestry as black, while Australians thought that mixture between whites and Aboriginal people would result in white, and not native, descendants? A key difference lies in the economic roles that European settlers expected African Americans and Aboriginal Australians to play. Because black slaves in the United States were a source of free labour, it was in white Americans' best interest to increase their numbers, and the one-drop rule of treating mixed-race people as black was one way to add to the black population. In contrast, for white Australians, Aboriginal people represented a source of free land, but to successfully occupy that land, they had to empty it of Aborigines. For the European settler community in Australia, then, it was preferable to erase the Aboriginal population by absorbing it into the white one—or by removing it and concentrating it on undesirable lands (Wolfe, 2001). Again, there is nothing natural or inevitable about the way human beings have created racial categories; the conventions and classifications we come up with are reflections of the social, economic, and political worlds we live in.

10.3 What Is Racism?

Heather Coit/AP Images

Contemporary Racism

North Americans use the word *racist* or *racism* to describe an astonishingly long list of things. In addition to labelling individual people racist because of things they say or do, we also talk about ideas, speeches, sermons, movies, songs, books, policies, laws, and even political parties as being racist. Whether something or someone is racist is often the subject of heated debate. Are laws making unauthorized immigration a crime racist? Are sports mascots and team names representing Indigenous persons racist? Is it racist to oppose affirmative action policies? Such controversies stem in part from the lack of an explicit, widely shared notion of what racism is.

How Do Sociologists Define Racism and Discrimination?

10.3.1 Discuss the roles of prejudice, stereotyping, and discrimination in the sociological definition of racism.

For sociologists, the term **racism** includes two phenomena: *prejudice* and *discrimination*. **Prejudices** are negative beliefs, feelings, or attitudes held about entire groups. They are broadly applied and are based on subjective and often inaccurate information. Prejudices involve prejudgments of individuals based on **stereotypes**, which are simplified generalizations about a group. These blanket images are hard to change because, as psychologists have shown, we tend to look for and remember information that seems to confirm our stereotypes while ignoring or dismissing information that does not support them.

Discrimination differs from prejudice in that it involves actions rather than beliefs. It includes any behaviour that harms individuals or puts them at a disadvantage on the basis of their group membership. Discrimination maintains and reinforces social hierarchy by keeping subordinate groups from advancing. This can vary in degrees of severity. The mildest form of racial discrimination is the use of negative words or phrases in reference to a particular group. While names or phrases may be hurtful or even work toward perpetuating stereotypes, they usually do not impact people's life chances directly. A more extreme type of discrimination involves placing limits on people's opportunities based on their racial group. This involves preventing specific racial groups from equally accessing schools, employment, housing, and other institutions that are part of membership and participation in society. At its most extreme, discrimination can take the form of violence against an individual or members of a racial group. From the Civil War on, for many decades, **lynching** was an act of violence used primarily to intimidate, punish, and terrorize blacks in the American South. Many other societies, such as South Africa, Rwanda, and Bosnia, have also experienced violent forms of racially and ethnically charged discrimination, including **genocide**, which is the deliberate and systematic killing of a category of people.

Acts of racial or ethnic discrimination can be classified as individual or as institutional and structural. **Individual discrimination** is an action carried out by an individual or small group that harms one or more individuals based on their group membership. An employer refusing to hire blacks, a landlord who does not rent apartments to Mexican Americans, and a group of teenagers who paint swastikas on a Jewish synagogue are all examples of individual-level discrimination. In these cases, individuals or small groups take purposeful actions to negatively affect members of specific racial or ethnic groups.

Discrimination may not always be intentional, however. Recent psychological research suggests that our behaviours are influenced by many kinds of **implicit prejudice** (also called *unconscious prejudice*), involving stereotypes that can be activated in our minds without our being aware of them (Greenwald & Banaji, 1995). Even people who consciously reject racial stereotypes may nonetheless be influenced by them. Psychologists have discovered this through various experiments, the most well-known of which is the Implicit Association Test, which you can take for yourself at http://projectimplicit.net. This test has repeatedly shown that when given a task to complete, people are generally slowed down if it involves recognizing non-stereotypical associations (such as matching the words "black" and "pleasant") and can usually speed up when required to make stereotypical matches (such as "white" and "pleasant"). Although negative implicit bias is widespread—nearly 85 percent of whites taking the test are estimated to have some degree of unconscious racial prejudice—research suggests it can be reduced through introspection and positive exposure to the target group, in much the same way that thought exercises and habituation can help people control powerful emotions like fear and anger. In fact, implicit prejudice may be to emotion what explicit (or conscious) prejudice is to thought (Quillian, 2006). Implicit bias seems to come into play when it is difficult for individuals to regulate themselves (for example, in split-second decisions or through their body language), whereas explicit prejudices may have a greater impact on deliberate or premeditated actions (like a speech). Recent tragedies where police offers have fatally shot unarmed black men raise distressing questions about how important implicit prejudices may be.

People are not the only actors who may discriminate, however. Sociologists maintain that institutions can also be discriminatory. **Institutional (or structural) discrimination** occurs when the actions or policies of organizations or social institutions exclude, disadvantage, or harm members of particular groups. Jim Crow—a system of laws and social norms that governed interactions between blacks and whites in the American South in the early twentieth century—represented an institutionalized system of discrimination. Schools, housing, transportation, and public facilities all formally engaged in discriminatory practices by keeping blacks and whites separate and in grossly unequal facilities. South Africa's system of apartheid is another example of this institutional form of discrimination where whites were able to secure their social position by excluding nonwhites from the majority of institutions.

As in the case of individual discrimination, institutional discrimination may or may not be intentional. An example of intentional institutional discrimination would be the Dominion Elections Act, which up until 1948 made race a ground for exclusion from voting in a federal election. Similarly, in British Columbia the Provincial Elections Amendment Act of 1947 gave voting rights to all except Japanese and Indigenous persons but at the same time removed the franchise from Doukhobors, Hutterites, and Mennonites unless they had served in the armed forces. Unintentional discrimination occurs when institutions adopt policies that have a disparate impact on different populations. For example, many school dress codes in North America prohibit all students from adopting certain hairstyles that are popular mostly among specific ethnic groups, or from wearing clothing such as shirts with spaghetti straps or skirts above a certain length. These seemingly neutral policies affect minorities and girls, and are therefore a form of unintentional discrimination.

Why Does Racism Occur?

10.3.2 Explain how people can be socialized into racism.

Some of the earliest research on prejudice and discrimination was conducted by psychologists, who saw racism as an expression of particular personality disorders. Yet such psychological approaches to prejudice came to be criticized for overlooking the social contexts that give shape to the beliefs and behaviours that underlie racism. Moreover, because these early theories treated racism as if it were an abnormal and thus unusual condition, they were inconsistent with the fact that historically, large numbers of Americans have held prejudices and acted in a discriminatory fashion. To put it another way, when large numbers of people in a particular time and place express similar views about a racial or ethnic group, it is hard to ascribe those views to individual personality disorders.

Accordingly, sociologists have sought to develop theories of racism that pay attention to the role of social rules and guides to behaviour that vary across social contexts. These theories consider the type of situations where norms are in place that could encourage or give rise to prejudicial beliefs or discriminatory acts. Through socialization, people learn the norms that operate in an environment or society at large. Research has shown that even very young children absorb racial prejudices and act upon them—for example, when choosing play partners (Van Ausdale & Feagin, 2001). For that matter, sociologist Osagie Obasogie (2014) has shown that blind people—who cannot see the visual cues like skin colour that we rely on to identify a person's race—nonetheless learn from their sighted family and friends to make distinctions between members of different races. Far from being "colour-blind," they are often taught to look down on and avoid people of other races, even when it means refusing valuable assistance or rewarding friendships. In short, people learn from those around them to think and act in a racist fashion—they are socialized into racism.

The challenge remains, however, to explain why racism comes to permeate a given society in the first place. Sociologists have responded to this challenge by highlighting the connection between racism and power. Whether we think of the origins of racial thinking in contexts of imperialism and slavery or in more contemporary manifestations like the official racial segregation of U.S. schools until the 1950s (and widespread unofficial segregation since), it is evident that racist exclusions and handicaps both reflect and perpetuate imbalances in the amount of power that different groups hold. Race-based hierarchies do not occur by chance but rather are the product of human efforts to acquire and preserve social privileges. We can ascribe racism to groups' sustained efforts, conscious and unconscious, to shore up their own status in society.

The intermingling of different populations of people around the globe is by no means a modern phenomenon. People move, or are forced to move, for a variety of social, political, and economic reasons, as we shall see below. According to Anthony Giddens and Philip Sutton (2012), **diaspora** describes the process whereby ethnic populations have dispersed around the globe from their homelands, often under forced conditions. One example of a diaspora is the African or black American diaspora that resulted from the forced migration of slaves to the Americas and elsewhere. In the following section, we examine the linkage between race, ethnicity, and migration in the context of immigration. In doing so, we can also examine how bigotry and intolerance have been politically and economically motivated and have enabled certain groups of people to exercise and maintain power over others. By examining immigration policy, for instance, we can see how British and French colonialists were better able to achieve power through racist and exclusionary policies.

10.4 What Is Immigration, and How Do Governments Regulate It?

Torontonian/Alamy Stock Photo

Immigration: A Sociological Perspective

People move for many reasons. They grow up in one town, may go somewhere else for university, and may move to yet another place to work. Some people are forced to leave their homes because of war, economic hardship, or natural disasters. Others relocate to join loved ones (such as children, parents, or romantic partners). But whatever the underlying reasons and whatever the distance travelled, whether from one city to another or from one country to another, the movement of people is a fundamental feature of our world. Indeed, from the earliest human migrations out of Africa, there have always been substantial numbers living away from the place where they were born. This continues to be true today. In 2010, about 216 million lived outside the country where they were born (World Bank, 2011a). Who are they? Why do they move? And where do they go? In this chapter we explore these questions, using sociological perspectives and imagination to understand immigration and its impacts.

Understanding Immigration from a Sociological Perspective

10.4.1 Discuss immigration as part of the fabric of social life and how it is becoming increasingly important in the twenty-first century.

Migration is the process by which individuals move from one place to another. The idea that migration is a *process* provides the foundation for a sociological approach to immigration as a whole. To think of migration as a process is to think of it not simply as a single event but rather as a long unfolding that takes place over time—starting with the initial idea, continuing with the planning stage, then the actual migration, followed by short-term and long-term impacts and consequences. Although migration is one process, sociologists sometimes distinguish between **emigration**, the act of leaving one place, and **immigration**, the act of arriving and settling in another. In order to understand migration we need to consider this long unfolding process and, importantly, the conditions and characteristics not only of individual migrants but also of the places they leave from and go to.

Taking into account the larger social context, including the economic and political situation a potential migrant faces, is the second element of the sociological approach to immigration. Certainly, the decision to emigrate and the consequences of immigrating result from individual motivations and personalities; however, the decision to emigrate also depends on the laws, policies, and social customs of different countries. Individual motivations are important, and a basic factor in migration is that people are seeking to make better lives for themselves. But, of course, sociologists assume that everyone wants a better life, so we must ask: Why do some people desiring a better life move, while others do not? How does moving from one place to another make it more possible for some people to secure better lives? Why do some people who live in one place tend to migrate more than people from other places? And, finally, why do people from certain places tend to migrate to specific places? Connected to the focus on process and the examination of both emigration and immigration, sociologists distinguish between **receiving countries** (host or destination countries where migrants go) and **sending countries** (countries from which migrants originate). As you can see in Table 10.1, some countries have high numbers of emigrants (sending countries) while other countries have high numbers of immigrants (receiving countries), and some have significant numbers of both.

The United States, the destination of some 40 million migrants, is the top receiving country, and Mexico, the origin of almost 12 million migrants, is the top sending country. Saudi Arabia, Canada, Spain, Australia, and the United Arab Emirates also stand out as major receiving countries, while China, Bangladesh, the Philippines, Turkey, and Egypt are major sending countries. Some countries have both immigration and emigration streams. These include Russia (with 12.3 million immigrants and

Table 10.1 World Migration: Major Sending and Receiving Countries in 2010

Country	Millions of Persons
A. Top 15 Sending Countries	
Mexico	11.9
India	11.4
Russian Federation	11.1
China	8.3
Ukraine	6.6
Bangladesh	5.4
Pakistan	4.7
United Kingdom	4.7
Philippines	4.3
Turkey	4.3
Egypt	3.7
Kazakhstan	3.7
Germany	3.5
Italy	3.5
Poland	3.1
B. Top 15 Receiving Countries	
United States	42.8
Russian Federation	12.3
Germany	10.8
Saudi Arabia	7.3
Canada	7.2
United Kingdom	7.0
Spain	6.9
France	6.7
Australia	5.5
India	5.4
Ukraine	5.3
Italy	4.5
Pakistan	4.2
United Arab Emirates	3.3
Kazakhstan	3.1

SOURCE: From *Migration and Remittances Factbook 2011*, by World Bank, 2011, Washington, DC: World Bank. Copyright by World Bank Group.

11.1 million emigrants—due no doubt to population shifts since the fall of the former Soviet Union), Germany, India, the United Kingdom, Ukraine, Pakistan, Kazakhstan, Italy, and France (which, with 1.7 million emigrants, does not make the top 15 sending countries). Later in the chapter, we examine in greater detail why it is that some countries are sending or receiving countries (or both), but for now, keep in mind that migration in the world is not random but rather highly *patterned*; that is, it has an order and particular shape, with some people and places having a greater likelihood than others to be involved in migration.

Restricting Immigration

10.4.2 Examine how societies seek to limit or regulate immigration and emigration.

As individuals and families move from one place to another, their comings and goings are not always happy or even legal. Indeed, throughout history, many societies have sought to limit or regulate both immigration and emigration. Regulations on emigration range from absolute prohibition on people leaving (as in the communist countries of Eastern Europe during the years of the Cold War, roughly 1948–1989), to restrictions on certain groups of people (such as Jews in Germany during the period of Nazi rule between 1933 and 1945), to enforced departure or exile (as in the case of Dante, condemned in 1302 to perpetual exile from his native Florence). The Berlin Wall—built in 1961 as a barrier between West Berlin and both East Berlin and the surrounding East German territory—is a prominent symbol of the efforts of governments to keep people from leaving. More recently, many countries have been concerned about **brain drain**, the departure of well-educated and skilled citizens to other countries where they can use their skills more productively and make more money. Countries have adopted a variety of strategies to discourage their most skilled younger people from leaving. Many such initiatives are aimed at improving economic growth in the hope that more job opportunities will improve retention rates. Countries also sometimes focus on members of the country's diaspora (people settled far from their homeland), hoping to entice them to return to the origin country.

Throughout history, groups and societies have also sought to regulate immigration. As with emigration, such regulations range from absolute prohibition (preventing anyone from entering a country) to enforced importation (as in the great slave migrations of the eighteenth and nineteenth centuries). In between these extremes lie the elaborate regulations common today throughout the world, which reject some immigrants outright and admit others under a variety of provisions for temporary or permanent stays. For both temporary and permanent residence, there is an intricate system by which foreign-born persons become eligible for a **visa**—the authorizing entry document. The decision about who is entitled to a visa becomes a critical part of immigration policy.

These regulations, at both exit and entry, represent a major element in understanding migration not only as an individual decision but also as movement subject to government policies and social and economic forces. On the one hand, when analyzing immigration sociologically we need to think about the social, economic, and political situation of both the sending country and the receiving country, but we also need to think about **emigration and immigration policies**, the set of rules and regulations established by each country with regards to the movement of people across borders. Although a person may wish to leave a country, leaving may be prohibited or the choice about where to go may be highly constrained. In the next section, we highlight these issues by considering the history of immigration policy in Canada.

Immigration in Canada

10.4.3 Identify the six main eras of Canadian immigration policy.

According to Alan Green and David Green (1996, p. 3), "Immigration policy in Canada is a complex entity consisting of an interconnected set of guidelines, regulations and actions by government agents. It is often difficult to determine what the main goal of the policy is, especially since so much of it is set out of the public eye." There are three main categories of immigration in Canada: the social category, or family class; the humanitarian category, or refugee class; and the economic category, or skilled worker and business class. Under the **family class**, permanent residents can apply to sponsor family members to immigrate to Canada. Under the **refugee class**, people from war-torn countries can apply for protection from persecution on humanitarian grounds. Skilled workers and business owners can apply for immigration to Canada under the **economic class**. Within each of these classes there exists a points system for qualification. The **points system** awards points based on language skills, education, age, income and wealth, investment potential, and employment.

WHITE SETTLER SOCIETY, 1600s–1800s The first settlers to come to Canada in the early 1600s were not immigrants but rather **colonists** who came to expand the French and British empires. Fur-trading enterprises like the Hudson's Bay Company established outposts and bartered with Indigenous peoples, who supplied most of the fur (Hale, 2013, p. 596). Until the 1960s, the image that Canada projected of itself was one of two founding nations, based on the notion that French and British peoples built this country. This is historically inaccurate: The establishment of the nation of Canada depended upon Indigenous peoples' cooperation with early **white settlers**. This cooperation resulted in Indigenous people losing their lands through deceitful treaties and their culture through the **residential school system** (Tepperman, Albanese, & Curtis, 2012, p. 252).

In this context, the early rules governing immigration were designed primarily to prevent diseases from entering Canada. Limits were placed on how many people could be transported on non-cargo ships at any one time. Few restrictions were placed on who immigrate to Canada until the twentieth century, when the Canadian government began to adopt **exclusionary immigration policies**. See Table 10.2.

EARLY-TWENTIETH-CENTURY IMMIGRATION, 1880s–1915s Immigration has been an important component of demographic growth throughout Canada's history as a nation-state. Before World War I, immigration was a tool for economic development. Immigration was used by white settlers to fill so-called *open lands* and provide a skilled labour force for national expansion of the economic infrastructure. Early-twentieth-century immigration in Canada began with the arrival of nearly 42,000 immigrants in 1900, mainly from the United States and Britain. This number rose to

Table 10.2 Did You Know?

Did you know…
• In 1604, the first European settlement north of what is now Florida was established by French explorers Pierre de Monts and Samuel de Champlain, first on St. Croix Island (in present-day Maine), then at Port-Royal, in Acadia (present-day Nova Scotia).
• The **Acadians** are the descendants of French colonists who began settling in what are now the Maritime provinces in 1604.
• Most French-speaking Quebecers are descendants of 8,500 French settlers who arrived in the 1600s and 1700s.
• The Loyalists came to Canada from the United States in 1776, to escape the American Revolution. They were of Dutch, German, British, Scandinavian, Aboriginal and other origins and from Presbyterian, Anglican, Baptist, Methodist, Jewish, Quaker, and Catholic religious backgrounds.
• When Canada became a country in 1867 our first prime minister was, of course, an immigrant. **Sir John Alexander Macdonald,** was born in Scotland on January 11, 1815, and he came to Upper Canada as a child.
• The Dominion Lands Act was the 1872 piece of legislation that granted a quarter section of free land (160 acres or 64.7 hectares) to any settler 21 years of age or older who paid a $10 registration fee, lived on his quarter section for three years, cultivated 30 acres (12.1 hectares), and built a permanent dwelling.
• Between 1901 and 1914, over 750,000 immigrants entered Canada from the United States. While many were returning Canadians, about one-third were newcomers of European extraction—Germans, Hungarians, Norwegians, Swedes, and Icelanders—who had originally settled in the American West.
• Before 1914, some 170,000 Ukrainians, 115,000 Poles, and tens of thousands from Germany, France, Norway, and Sweden settled in the West and developed a thriving agricultural sector.
• Between 1928 and 1971, one million immigrants came to Canada through Pier 21 alone.
• By the 1960s, one-third of Canadians had origins that were neither British nor French, and took pride in preserving their distinct culture in the Canadian fabric.
• Today, most immigrants come from China, Philippines and India.
• The proportion of foreign-born Canadians was 19.8% in 2006.
• 24% of Canada's population speaks languages other than English and French.
• Since the fertility rate in Canada is only 1.68 children per female, the majority of Canada's population growth is due to immigration.

SOURCE: From *Backgrounder: Facts on Canadian Immigration History*, by Citizenship and Immigration Canada, June 27, 2011 (http://www.cic.gc.ca/english/department/media/backgrounders/2011/2011-06-27.asp). Copyright by the Government of Canada.

over 400,000 in 1913, accounting for 44% of Canada's net population growth. By 1911, 41% of the population of Manitoba, 50% of the population of Saskatchewan and 57% of the population of Alberta and British Columbia was made up of immigrants (Boyd & Vickers, 2000, p. 3).

THE WARS AND THE GREAT DEPRESSION, 1915–1946 The Great Depression and the Second World War curtailed immigration to Canada significantly. This decline in immigration in the 1930s and 1940s led to a net loss in population as people migrated to the United States in search of employment. Britain continued to be the leading country of origin for immigrants, but this pattern soon shifted to include Germany, Russia, the Ukraine, and Eastern European countries, including Poland, Czechoslovakia, and Hungary. War-related measures restricted the attempts of Jewish refugees, who were fleeing the Holocaust regime of the German government, to come to Canada (Boyd & Vickers, 2000, pp. 6–7).

POST-WAR EXPANSION YEARS: 1946–1970 Following Germany's surrender to the Allied troops in 1945 and Japan's surrender later that same year, the Canadian economy and immigration expanded significantly. Post-war immigration in North America included people who had been displaced from their homelands by the war as well as the foreign-born wives and children of those service personnel who had served abroad (Boyd & Vickers, 2000, p. 7). Europe and the United Kingdom accounted for the vast majority of immigration to Canada. According to Monica Boyd and Michael Vickers, "During this time, net immigration was higher than it had been in almost 50 years, but it accounted for no more than 30% of total population growth between 1951 and 1971" (p. 7).

HUMANITARIAN MEASURES: 1970–2001 The Immigration Act of 1978 introduced humanitarian-based efforts allowing refugees to enter Canada under a new category of immigrant. These measures resulted in the diversification of the Canadian population as more people from war-torn African countries, as well as Asia and the Indian subcontinent, began to arrive. According to Boyd and Vickers (2000, p. 9), "Each successive Census recorded declining percentages of the immigrant population that had been born in European countries, the United Kingdom and the United States. . . . By 1996, 27% of the immigrant population in Canada had been born in Asia and another 21% came from places other than the United States, the United Kingdom or Europe."

Since the 1970s, Canada has adopted an official policy of **multiculturalism** aimed at affirming the value and dignity of all Canadian citizens regardless of their racial or ethnic origins, their language, or their religious affiliation. This policy of multiculturalism differs from the U.S. policy of **assimilation** in that it encourages all citizens to maintain and celebrate their cultural heritage rather than assimilate into one big melting pot.

SECURITY MEASURES: POST–9/11 Immigration policies have undergone important changes since the terrorist attacks of September 11, 2001. Shortly after these attacks, North American governments passed a number of measures to make it more difficult for people around the world, but especially from countries with large Muslim populations, to travel to Canada and the United States or to obtain visas for short- or long-term residence. Enhanced monitoring of foreigners who do gain entry from these countries has also increased significantly in recent years. These measures have raised important questions about how open North America intends to be in the future.

After 9/11, the Canadian government adopted the use of the **security certificate** to detain and deport permanent residents and foreign nationals using secret evidence that even the accused is not allowed to see. Security certifications are a mechanism available under the Immigration and Refugee Protection Act that allows the Canadian Security Intelligence Service (CSIS) to collect intelligence about a foreigner living in Canada who they believe is a national security threat. They cannot be used

Table 10.3 The Secret Trial Five

The Secret Trial Five
Hassan Almrei Almrei, a Syrian-born refugee, had been in custody since October 2001, after CSIS accused him of links to al-Qaeda. He was freed to a strict house arrest in January 2009. A federal judge then struck down the security certificate, essentially freeing Almrei in December 2009.
Adil Charkaoui The Morocco-born permanent resident was arrested in May 2003 on suspicion of links to al-Qaeda. Two years later, he was released on tight bail restrictions. The Montrealer is a teacher and father of three.
Mohamed Harkat An Algerian refugee living in Ottawa, where he worked as a gas station attendant, Harkat was arrested in December 2002 and held for 3½ years before release on bail in June 2006.
Mahmoud Jaballah The Egyptian-born man was released from custody in 2007 after being held for six years. He was teaching at a Muslim school in Toronto when arrested in 2001 over alleged links to Egyptian terrorist group Al Jihad. It was the second time he was arrested on a security certificate. The first was in 1999, but was quashed.
Mohammad Mahjoub Also an Egyptian, he's accused of links to al-Qaeda leader Osama bin Laden. The Federal Court ordered his release in early 2007, nearly seven years after Mahjoub's arrest on a security certificate issued in May 2000. On March 18, 2009, however, a federal court judge returned him to custody upon Mahjoub's request, which was in protest against his "oppressive" bail conditions.

SOURCE: From "Security Certificates and Secret Evidence," *CBC News*, August 21, 2009 (http://www.cbc.ca/news/canada/security-certificates-and-secret-evidence-1.777624). Copyright by CBC. Used with permission.

on Canadian citizens (Chipman, 2013). Security certificates have been part of the Canadian immigration regime since 1978. The use of security certifications has come under increased scrutiny, particularly in the post-9/11 period. The detention by the Canadian government of the men involved in what is known as the Secret Trial Five (Hassan Almrei, Adil Charkaoui, Mohamed Harkat, Mahmoud Jaballah, and Mohammad Mahjoub) drew criticism from international and human rights groups because the accused have been denied due process and face **deportation** to Morocco, Algeria, Syria, and Egypt, where they could face torture (CBC, 2009). See Table 10.3.

10.5 Why Do People Move, and What Are the Consequences?

Library of Congress Prints and Photographs Division [LC-USZ62-20621]

Self-Selection, Push and Pull Factors, and Migration Dynamics

People consider moving across borders for many reasons. Perhaps most fundamentally, moving may provide a better life for migrants and their children. The central way that sociologists approach the question of why people move, however, is to examine the potential gains migrants make between their expected well-being in the sending country versus the life they envision for themselves or their families in the receiving country. The outcome of this comparison depends jointly on the potential migrant's own characteristics and on the characteristics of both the sending country—including its push factors—and the receiving country—including its pull factors. **Push factors** in the home country are those that drive people to leave, while **pull factors** in the receiving country are those that attract people to go there. Some push factors include economic hardship or political strife in the sending country. Simultaneously, pull factors include the economic and political characteristics of the receiving countries. For some people, there will be a benefit from migration, and for others there will not. To illustrate, a key comparison is between expected wage in the origin country versus the expected wage in the destination country (adjusted for purchasing power); countries differ in how they reward skills and occupations, so some individuals will benefit economically from a move and others not, and among those who benefit, some will benefit more than others.

Further, countries are connected to one another in many different ways. For example, people from Mexico are more likely to go to the United States than to Europe not only because there are higher wages in the United States but also because the two countries share a nearly 2,000-mile land border and a long history, with their peoples and economies connected to each other in many ways. Mexico and the United States are strong trade partners; the United States is Mexico's largest trading partner, buying 77.5 percent of Mexican exports in 2012, and Mexico is the third largest buyer of U.S. exports. The United States has many companies based in Mexico and a high degree of investment there. Thus, people in each country have many business or professional colleagues, friends, and family members in the other country.

The Desire to Move and Migrant Energy

10.5.1 Analyze the factors that influence the desire to move.

Although migration is a universal phenomenon, most people will not move to another country. The *desire to move* and the **migrant energy** it unleashes vary in strength. Some people may want very much to move, others may want a little to move, and others may not want to move at all. Persons with a high desire to move (with large amounts of migrant energy) are said to be positively **self-selected** for migration. In other words, those who choose to migrate are often those who are the most positively disposed to their new country and have very strong levels of determination to succeed.

To understand what factors impact the desire to move, sociologists link it to other personal characteristics, such as earnings or health. We ask, for example, is the desire to move stronger among the rich or the poor? Among the healthy or the unhealthy? The answers to these questions help illuminate the reasons why some people make the decision to move while others do not. If in a sending country the desire to move is strongest among the highly skilled, we say that selection on skill is positive, and if the desire to move is strongest among the unskilled, we say that selection on skill is negative. Similarly, if the desire to move is strongest among the healthiest, we say that selection on health is positive; and if the desire to move is strongest among the unhealthiest, we say that selection on health is negative. The type of selection helps illuminate the characteristics and dynamics of different migration flows.

Sociologists and other social scientists sometimes isolate one force or one dimension and explore its dynamics in the migration process. Freedom from want is a good example. Many theories of the migration process begin with the assumption that people move to maximize their well-being and, more specifically, that well-being varies with the difference between the wage in the sending country and the wage in potential receiving countries, after the costs of migration. In other words, migrants consider whether their economic circumstances would be better in a new country if they could move there. Consequently, the higher the cost of migration, the greater the required improvement in the wage.

Whatever the migration dynamic may be, once set in motion, it often acquires a life of its own. This can happen in several ways. First, there is habit. For example, if a young man's father and grandfather both went abroad every year to work in the harvest, it becomes an expectation, perhaps even a norm, that the young man will do the same. Second, the costs diminish with each generation because crucial information can be passed from parent to child. These and other mechanisms may intensify as networks of migrants form and enlarge (Massey et al., 1993).

Movers and Stayers

10.5.2 Distinguish between a mover and a stayer.

From this landscape of the search to make life better, we can isolate and examine the processes set in motion. Consider again the fact that not everyone with a high desire to move will actually move, and some with low desire to move will in fact move. Why? There are two sets of reasons. First, recall our earlier discussion of government policies on exit and entry. Some individuals may be barred from leaving the sending country or entering the receiving country. Others may be forced to leave the sending country or to enter the receiving country. Second, family dynamics intervene, forcing some persons to move or making it impossible for others to move, however great their desire to move (Mincer, 1978).

Social scientists have found it useful to distinguish between **movers** (those who migrate to the destination country) and **stayers** (those who stay in the origin country). Linking movers and stayers to the desire to move yields what economist Jacob Mincer (1978) called *tied movers* and *tied stayers*. Thus, the set of movers is diverse in that it includes both movers-at-heart (with high desire to move) and tied movers (with low desire to move). Similarly, the set of stayers is diverse in that it includes both stayers-at-heart (with low desire to move) and tied stayers (with high desire to move).

Immigration is controversial around the world because it has wide-reaching effects on the sending country, on the receiving country, and on individuals and families in both countries, including natives, immigrants, and the children of immigrants. Social scientists and government officials have spent a great deal of time trying to estimate both the benefits and costs of immigration for receiving countries like Canada and the United States. Sociologists are also particularly interested in the impact of immigration on families and children.

Shown here, an immigrant woman works in a bakery in Florida. One of the great puzzles of immigration research is why some people choose to move to a foreign land while other, similar people do not.

Jeff Greenberg/The Image Works

Immigration Dilemmas for Families

10.5.3 Analyze the dilemmas that immigrant families face.

To appreciate the complexity of the process for families and the effect of financial resources, consider two families from the Dominican Republic: Family A and Family B.

In Family A, the wife is a physician and the husband is a software engineer with a baccalaureate degree who was sponsored by a U.S. firm for an employment visa. They have two children, a five-year-old and a six-month-old infant. Both the wife and the two children were included on the husband's visa application as accompanying family members. After all the requisite documents were collected (including national identity cards, police records, and military service records) and the family was interviewed, they obtained visas. For this family, the process was smooth. They arrived in 2008 and settled in an affluent suburb in New Jersey. Eventually they had a third child. The total duration of the visa process was about three years.

Contrast this story with Family B. The husband is a welder and the wife a bank teller. They had hoped that his occupation would qualify him for a visa in the subcategory for skilled workers. However, no opportunity ever materialized. They became eligible, however, when the wife's brother, a naturalized U.S. citizen, offered to sponsor her. To prepare for their visas, they collected all the same documents that Family A had collected, including birth certificates for their three children—ages 17 (girl), 13 (boy), and 6 (girl). Additionally, however, because the visa is in a family-sponsored category rather than an employment-based category, the United States Citizenship and Immigration Services requires that a sponsor sign an affidavit of support. (To prove that the sponsor is financially responsible for the applicant, the supporting paperwork must show that the household income is equal to or higher than 125 percent of the U.S. poverty level for the household size.) After much figuring and calculating and searching for a joint sponsor, the family concluded that the financial requirements for the whole family could not be met. Reluctantly, and sadly, they decided to leave their three children with the children's grandparents in the Dominican Republic. The couple arrived in New York City in 2008 and moved into the predominantly immigrant neighbourhood of Washington Heights. For them, the visa process lasted 12 years—9 years longer than for Family A (because the visa queue is so much longer in the family-based categories than in the employment-based categories).

The couple's options for bringing their children changed. Now the children in Family B could no longer be brought as accompanying children; they would have to be sponsored. There would be a wait for visas to become available. So the couple set out to work as hard as possible to accumulate the financial resources to sponsor their children and qualify financially for the affidavit of support. The children's priority date was February 15, 2010, and visas became available in July 2012. Unfortunately, the eldest daughter married, losing her eligibility. Also, the couple was unable to find the resources to sponsor both of the two younger children. The family faced the wrenching decision: Which child could they bring to the United States—the middle child or the youngest?

The couple decided to bring their middle son, who showed great promise as a student. This child attended school and worked part-time in the neighbourhood grocery store to supplement the family's income to satisfy the financial requirements for bringing the youngest child. But there was a pervasive grief in the family because there was no visa category available for the eldest daughter—no pathway for the married child of a lawful permanent resident. Only if one of the parents naturalized would it become possible to sponsor her as the married child of a U.S. citizen. The couple would not even become eligible to naturalize until 2013, and they worried that they will not yet have the requisite English language skills.

There is a note of joy, however. While in the United States, the couple had a fourth child. This is a golden child, a U.S. citizen by birth. The family is blended—and divided. Around this time, the grandparents in the Dominican Republic experienced some health problems, and the couple started to think they should bring their third child, now 10 years old. But how? They could not yet sponsor her immigration because they could not meet the financial requirements. The family continues to hope that somehow they will find the resources or that the rules will change or that they will find a new joint sponsor.

There is a further lingering regret. If the family could have immigrated when it first applied, all the children would be completely fluent in English and speak it without an accent. But the long waits for numerically limited family visas and the financial requirements made that impossible. With every passing day, the dream fades.

Notice how vastly different the two scenarios are, and notice the part played by money. The second family's story could have been as short as the first's had they secured the resources to satisfy the financial requirements for bringing all three of their children as accompanying children when the adults obtained lawful permanent residence—when it was straightforward to bring them, the children were all still young and unmarried, and there was no further wait for a numerically limited visa.

The irony is that family reunification is the cornerstone of U.S. immigration law, and yet the many complexities in the law, the many moving parts, often serve to divide families. The further irony is that the United States has long celebrated its welcoming of the poor but now makes it extremely challenging and, in many cases impossible, for poor people to come to the United States legally.

Children of Migration

10.5.4 Discuss what happens to the children involved in international migration.

What about the children of families that migrate? The distinct sets of children affected by international migration are as follows: (1) foreign-born children living with their foreign-born parents; (2) native-born children living with their foreign-born parents; (3) foreign-born children living in the sending country, including (a) those left behind by parents who are in the receiving country and (b) those living with their foreign-born parents but who already have a link to the receiving country (such as being in the queue for a numerically limited visa); and (4) native-born children living in the parental origin country, including (a) those sent by parents who are in the receiving country to be raised in the sending country and (b) those living with their foreign-born parents who have no intention of returning to the receiving country. Each of these sets of children has been studied and discussed by sociologists and other social scientists.

Much attention has been paid to children living in the receiving country that were born to foreign-born parents—the **second generation**. These children are citizens from birth, raised in the receiving country, heirs to both the parental migrant energy and all the opportunities of the new country. A large research literature indicates that these quintessential second-generation children do better than their parents.

Indeed, classically, they have outperformed their parents—and they have tended to outperform the third, fourth, and later generations that follow them. Many of the great scientific and artistic advances in Canada and the United States have been made by these second-generation children. Why has this so often been the case?

To understand the second-generation effect, it is important to understand the conditions under which it can be expected. Some immigrants come from countries where they were unable to develop their potential, so that they have lower schooling and fewer skills than they would have obtained under more favourable circumstances. As a result, it is completely natural that their children, inheriting similar potential but placed in a situation where they can develop that potential, will outperform the parents. Moreover, the children inherit at least a portion of their parents' migrant energy; therefore, they will outperform third- and higher-generation children of similar potential.

The great migration at the turn of the twentieth century brought to North America immigrants who for reasons of poverty or religion or gender were severely underschooled—brilliant men who had left school in the third grade to fend off starvation, brilliant women who were illiterate. It is no surprise that some of their offspring would become great scientists, musicians, and writers, including a few very famous sociologists we have read about in this book.

But much has changed in the past 100 years. In particular, both Canada and the United States today increasingly favour the immigration of the wealthy and highly skilled. So what would one expect today? First, the children of highly educated parents will be much less likely to outperform their parents. How can they? If their parents have PhDs, what can they do to outschool their parents? Moreover, they have attenuated migrant energy; no matter how much of it they inherit, it cannot match the migrant energy of the actual migrants. Second, however, they are likely to outperform third- and higher-generation counterparts of the same potential because they do inherit some of their parents' migrant energy.

Pictorial Parade/Staff/Getty Images

Robert K. Merton (1910–2003), one of the most distinguished sociologists in the twentieth century, was a second-generation immigrant. Merton's Yiddish-speaking Jewish parents moved to the U.S. from Russia in 1904, settling in Philadelphia, where Merton was born and raised.

A recent study of the 8- to 12-year-old American children of immigrants in the New Immigrant Survey compared English fluency between children born in the United States and children brought before the age of four (Jasso, 2011). The children born in the United States had a significantly higher probability of being fluent in English than those who immigrated at a young age.

Another question concerns the effects on children of growing up in unauthorized status or with parents who are unauthorized (illegal immigrants). For many families, this is an indefinite condition, with some or all family members unauthorized and no remedy in sight. Research on children ages 8 through 12 found that the probability of being fluent in English was higher among children whose parents had illegal experience than among children whose parents had never been unauthorized (Jasso, 2011). Why would having parents with unauthorized status have a positive effect on children's fluency in English? One possible reason is that children who have seen the hardships of illegality are equipping themselves for their new life. Another is that they may have gained English fluency by translating for their parents (Valdés, 2003).

Sociologists also carefully study families in which parents live in Canada or the United States but leave their children behind in the origin country or send their North American–born children back to the home country. Why would a child be left behind? There are several reasons. First, as mentioned above, some visa categories do not provide visas for the children of new immigrants; examples include Canada's Live-In Caregiver Program, which does not allow migrant workers to bring their children with them to Canada. The women working as live-in nannies for Canadian families send remittances home to support their children and extended families. Migrant remittances, discussed below, have a significant financial impact on both sending and receiving countries.

Social and Economic Benefits and Costs

10.5.5 Analyze the social and economic benefits and costs of immigration.

When migrants leave their hometown and country of origin, they take their skills and abilities to another place. They also often leave behind relatives and friends—sometimes close family members like spouses and children. Whether the trip is temporary or permanent, migrants often provide monetary gifts, bequests, loans, or other financial help to those left behind. Indeed, often the very purpose of the migration is to obtain financial resources to support the family in the origin country. These transfers are known as **migrant remittances**, and they constitute an extremely important source of income for individuals, families, and households around the world and especially in developing countries (Maimbo & Ratha, 2005; Rapoport & Docquier, 2006; World Bank, 2011a).

The World Bank (2011a) estimates that worldwide remittance flows exceeded about $440 billion (U.S. dollars) in 2010. The United States was the top source, with $48.3 billion in recorded remittances. About $325 billion went to developing countries. As the World Bank (2011b) notes, "remittances sent home by migrants to developing countries are three times the size of official development assistance and represent a lifeline for the poor."

Remittances sent back home represent only one of two directions of monetary and nonmonetary flows. Money and goods are also sent from the origin country to assist migrants in the destination country, for example, to pay college tuition, buy a home, start a business, or make a film. Accordingly, the broader term **transfers** is used to denote flows in both directions. To illustrate, migrants in the United States send remittances to other countries—estimated by the World Bank (2011a) at $48.3 billion in 2010. At the same time, international students and others living in the United States—temporarily or permanently—often receive allowances and other financial assistance from their family abroad. An extreme case of such financial help involves the most expensive apartment ever sold in New York City (at the time of the sale), purchased in March 2012 for $88 million for a student from Russia (Barrionuevo, 2012).

Sociologists and other social scientists study migrant remittances, attempting to understand three main things: (1) the amounts of transfers in both directions; (2) the determinants of sending or receiving transfers; and (3) the consequences of remittances for individuals, households, and countries. With respect to the magnitude of remittance flows, researchers almost universally believe that the true size, including unrecorded flows through both formal and informal channels, is larger than the recorded flows (World Bank, 2011a). Recorded statistics, incomplete though they may be, provide a window into remittance flows. Table 10.4 reports the top 15 remittance-sending and remittance-receiving countries. As shown, besides the United States, other countries in the top five remittance-sending countries are Saudi Arabia, Switzerland, Russia, and Germany. The top five remittance-receiving countries are India, China, Mexico, the Philippines, and France. India and China have large populations, and, not surprisingly, remittances received exceed $50 billion each, more than twice the remittances received by the much smaller Mexico and Philippines.

The second focus among researchers pertains to the link between the characteristics of migrants and whether they send transfers and remittances (and if so, in what amounts). Ideas about altruism and about familial contracts and insurance permeate the research literature. Two key findings have been established. First, temporary

Table 10.4 Migrant Remittances: Major Sending and Receiving Countries, 2010

Country	Billions of U.S. Dollars
A. Top 15 Sending Countries	
United States	48.3
Saudi Arabia	26.0
Switzerland	19.6
Russian Federation	18.6
Germany	15.9
Italy	13.0
Spain	12.6
Luxembourg	10.6
Kuwait	9.9
Netherlands	8.1
Malaysia	6.8
Lebanon	5.7
Oman	5.3
France	5.2
China	4.4
B. Top 15 Receiving Countries	
India	55.0
China	51.0
Mexico	22.6
Philippines	21.3
France	15.9
Germany	11.6
Bangladesh	11.1
Belgium	10.4
Spain	10.2
Nigeria	10.0
Pakistan	9.4
Poland	9.1
Lebanon	8.2
Egypt	7.7
United Kingdom	7.4

SOURCE: From *Migration and Remittances Factbook 2011*, by the World Bank, World Bank, 2011, Washington, DC: World Bank.

migrants are more likely to send remittances. Second, sending remittances seems to be unresponsive to external shocks such as economic recessions. Finally, the patterns of results suggest that sending remittances may be usefully interpreted as part of a familial contract.

What about effects of remittances? There is little doubt that remittances improve the daily lives of recipients. Remittances can be used to pay utility bills, send children to school, improve housing, obtain medical care, or purchase vehicles. For many receiving families, those funds are the difference between solvency and extreme poverty. Other questions pertain to the effect of remittances on a country's development, its economic growth, and economic inequality. Hillel Rapoport and Frédéric Docquier (2006) conclude that the overall effect of remittances on immigrants' sending countries' long-run economic performance is positive. Especially for poor countries, remittances sent back provide a valuable infusion of resources that enhance living standards.

Conclusion: Developing a Sociological Imagination on Race and Ethnicity

In trying to uncover the cultural and structural forces that shape our lives, even when we are not aware of them, sociologists often come up with answers that are not intuitive, because they go against the grain of common sense. The study of race, ethnicity, and migration is a good example. *Race* is an everyday term for North Americans, and one that we usually think is a straightforward descriptor of people's physical characteristics. What sociology tells us, though, is that there are no such simple, obvious groupings of human beings based on bodily traits and that labels like "black" and "white" tell us more about the way societies choose to classify people than they do about the individuals who get assigned to these categories. Similarly, how and why people migrate from one place to another is shaped by government policy that often intentionally discriminates against certain kinds of immigrants who are deemed to be undesirable on the basis of ascribed racial and/or ethnic classifications. In this area, as in so many others, developing a sociological imagination means looking beyond widespread beliefs that are too often taken for granted.

David R. Frazier Photolibrary, Inc./Alamy

Immigrant workers, even many of those earning low wages, such as this migrant worker in Oregon, will often send money back home to help family and friends.

CHAPTER SUMMARY

The Big Questions Revisited 10

10.1 What Is the Difference Between Race and Ethnicity? In this chapter, we explored how the words *race* and *ethnicity* are often used interchangeably, as if they mean the same thing. Sociologists make clear distinctions between race and ethnicity, and use the two terms to describe different kinds of categories and identities.

Understanding Race and Ethnicity

Sociological Definitions of Race and Ethnicity

Learning Objective 10.1.1: Compare and contrast contemporary sociologists' and Max Weber's definitions of race and ethnicity.

Key Distinctions Between Race and Ethnicity

Learning Objective 10.1.2: Discuss key distinctions between race and ethnicity.

Distinguishing Racial and Ethnic Labels

Learning Objective 10.1.3: Distinguish racial labels from ethnic ones.

10.2 Is Race Real? In this chapter, we analyzed the question of whether race is anchored in deep-seated physical differences between individuals or is an invention that is not determined by human biology but which nonetheless is "real" because it has an unmistakable impact on daily life.

The Social Construction of Race

Race and Society

Learning Objective 10.2.1: Explain how changing North American definitions of who counts as white support the constructivist view of race.

Race and Biology

Learning Objective 10.2.2: Analyze the arguments against a biological determination of race.

Race and Place

Learning Objective 10.2.3: Discuss how race is understood differently around the world.

10.3 What Is Racism? In this chapter, we examined how political correctness of our ideas, speech, and behaviour is a prominent feature of both public and private conversations on race today. Sociologists have thought a lot about prejudice and discrimination, providing ample food for thought on racism in contemporary North America.

Contemporary Racism

How Do Sociologists Define Racism and Discrimination?

Learning Objective 10.3.1: Discuss the roles of prejudice, stereotyping, and discrimination in the sociological definition of racism.

Why Does Racism Occur?

Learning Objective 10.3.2: Explain how people can be socialized into racism.

10.4 What Is Immigration, and How Do Governments Regulate It? What kinds of things do sociologists study when they study immigration, and why is the study of immigration important for understanding the world we live in? In this section, we examined the basic concepts, history, and ideas in the study of immigration.

Immigration: A Sociological Perspective

Understanding Immigration from a Sociological Perspective

Learning Objective 10.4.1: Discuss immigration as part of the fabric of social life and how it is becoming increasingly important in the twenty-first century.

Restricting Immigration

Learning Objective 10.4.2: Examine how societies seek to limit or regulate immigration and emigration.

Immigration in Canada

Learning Objective 10.4.3: Identify the six main eras of Canadian immigration policy.

10.5 Why Do People Move, and What Are the Consequences? People move for many reasons, but the most fundamental of these is the desire to make a better life for themselves and their children. In this section, we looked at the characteristics of both those who move and those who stay, as well as the countries they come from and the countries in which they settle. Distinguishing between these different categories of people and places provides important insights into the dynamics of the migration process.

Self-Selection, Push and Pull Factors, and Migration Dynamics

The Desire to Move and Migrant Energy

Learning Objective 10.5.1: Analyze the factors that influence the desire to move.

Movers and Stayers

Learning Objective 10.5.2: Distinguish between a mover and a stayer.

Immigration Dilemmas for Families

Learning Objective 10.5.3: Analyze the dilemmas that immigrant families face.

Children of Migration

Learning Objective 10.5.4: Discuss what happens to the children involved in international migration.

Social and Economic Benefits and Costs

Learning Objective 10.5.5: Analyze the social and economic benefits and costs of immigration.

Learn the Terms

assimilation (p. 278)
brain drain (p. 276)
colonist (p. 277)
constructivist (p. 266)
deportation (p. 279)
diaspora (p. 273)
discrimination (p. 271)
economic class (p. 276)
emigration (p. 274)
emigration and immigration policy (p. 276)
essentialism (p. 263)
ethnicity (p. 264)
exclusionary immigration policy (p. 277)
family class (p. 276)
genocide (p. 271)
immigration (p. 274)
implicit prejudice (p. 271)
individual discrimination (p. 271)
institutional (or structural) discrimination (p. 272)
lynching (p. 271)
migrant energy (p. 280)
migrant remittances (p. 285)
migration (p. 274)
movers (p. 281)
multiculturalism (p. 278)
points system (p. 276)
prejudice (p. 271)
pull factors (p. 280)
push factors (p. 280)
race (p. 264)
racialized (p. 265)
racism (p. 271)
receiving countries (p. 274)
refugee class (p. 276)
residential school system (p. 277)
second generation (p. 284)
security certificate (p. 278)
self-selected (p. 280)
sending countries (p. 274)
social construct (p. 266)
stayers (p. 281)
stereotype (p. 271)
transfers (p. 285)
visa (p. 276)
white settlers (p. 277)

Chapter 11

Gender and Sexuality

by Paula England

Juice Images/Alamy Stock Photo

Ideas about gender are often closely linked to cultural expectations. How do cultural ideas influence how women and men believe they are supposed to act at work, in social gatherings, or in the types of relationships they have?

Learning Objectives

11.1.1 Distinguish the concepts of sex and gender and explain how gender is socially constructed.

11.1.2 Describe the process of gender socialization.

11.1.3 Explain how gender differences vary by setting and time.

11.1.4 Discuss the role of stereotypes in constructing social expectations of gender.

11.2.1 Discuss reasons for the dramatic increase in women's employment and education since 1960.

11.2.2 Describe occupational sex segregation and explain the gender pay gap.

11.2.3 Discuss the impact of the gender revolution on men's roles.

11.3.1 Discuss the relative influence of biology and society on sexual orientation.

11.3.2 Discuss the impact of biology and society on sexual behaviour.

11.3.3 Identify the challenges that lesbian, gay, bisexual, transgendered, and questioning individuals encounter.

11.4.1 Discuss how attitudes toward premarital sex and the context in which it typically occurs have changed over the last 50 years.

11.4.2 Discuss changing rates of births outside of marriage.

11.4.3 Discuss the role that gendered expectations play in sexual and romantic behaviour.

In 2014, women held CEO positions at 25 Fortune 500 companies. Women have headed companies like Yahoo, PepsiCo, Xerox, and Hewlett Packard, achievements few dreamed possible just decades earlier (Catalyst, 2014). These women, and many of today's women leaders in other fields, exude confidence and assertiveness. Naturally, we would assume these qualities would extend from a woman's professional life to her personal life, but do they?

Can a woman be a strong leader, communicator, and innovator at work and also feel like asking a man on a date is inappropriate because of her gender?

A few years ago I was conducting research on sex and relationships among university students in the United States. During one of my interviews I met Janine, a graduate student studying for her master's in business administration (MBA). As we spoke about dating, relationships, and sex, she expressed her preference for traditional dating rather than "hooking up." Janine took great pride in waiting for men to ask her on dates. Her reasoning for never asking men on dates was that she believed men wouldn't see her as "relationship material" if she did. What a paradox, I thought—a woman who feels absolutely entitled and confident about scaling upper management, which was off-limits to women a few decades ago, but who wouldn't even consider asking a man on a date. Clearly, some things have changed and others have stayed the same!

In this chapter we will consider patterns and change in both gender and sexuality. The term **gender**, as used by sociologists, refers to the way in which social forces structure how being male or female affects what is expected of you, how you are treated, what opportunities you have, and the results for individual men and women. We will also examine sexuality and how sociologists study it, because the topics of gender and sexuality are related in several ways. We will discuss cultural ideas about how women and men are supposed to act—at work and in social gatherings as well as in romantic and sexual relationships. We will also explore sexual orientation, including same-sex romantic relationships, in our society.

The Big Questions

From the early writings of the founding sociologists over a century ago until about 1970, not many sociologists studied gender or sexuality. These topics were seen as more in the realm of nature than society. But since about 1970, sociologists have used their methods and approaches to study these topics. In this chapter, we will examine how sociologists answer the following big questions about gender and sexuality:

1. **Where do gender differences come from?** In this section we will explore gender differences and examine their origins, with a focus on what sociologists have shown.

2. **How have the lives of women and men changed in the last 50 years?** Women's lives have changed so much in the last 50 years that we often call the changes a gender revolution. Here we explore some of these changes, as well as how they have affected men's lives.
3. **How are our sex lives shaped by biology and society?** There is no question that sexual attraction and behaviour are affected by biology, but, as we will see in this section, they are also strongly affected by social construction.
4. **How has sexual behaviour changed in the last 50 years?** Sexual behaviour of young unmarried adults has changed substantially over the last several decades, but what about the extent to which sexual and relational behaviour is affected by gender norms and inequalities? In this section we will explore sexual behaviour as well as gender inequalities in the sexual realm.

11.1 Where Do Gender Differences Come From?

Marmaduke St. John/Alamy Stock Photo

Gender Differences

All around us we see differences between the way men and women (or boys and girls) dress, the activities they engage in, and what they say they want. More boys than girls play certain sports, more girls than boys play with dolls, many university majors and occupations contain either mostly men or mostly women, and more women than men are stay-at-home parents.

But sometimes we exaggerate the size of these differences. Take, for example, the common belief that males score higher than females on standardized math tests. One way to quantify this is by computing the difference between the average (also called the *mean*) male and female scores. In 2012, data on the mathematics part of the SAT Reasoning Test that many students take to apply to colleges and universities in the United States, men's average score, on a scale from 200 to 800, was 532, and women's was 499, with a difference of 33. (Canada does not have university admissions tests;

Figure 11.1 Male and Female Distributions and Means on the SAT Test

SOURCE: Based on data from the College Board, 2012 (http://media.collegeboard.com/digitalServices/pdf/research/Total-Group-2012.pdf).

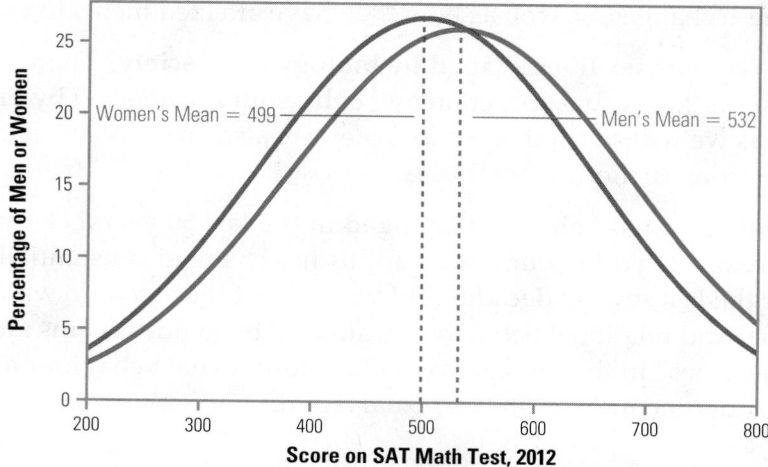

many readers of this book will not have taken the SAT unless seeking entry to a U.S. university). Another way sociologists examine the gender difference is to plot the whole distribution of scores for each sex, showing the percentages for men and women at each score. Figure 11.1 shows both the male and female means and the whole male and female distributions for the 2012 SAT Math Test. Each of the two curves has a large bulge in the middle, which tells you that more people score in the middle of the distribution than at either extreme. The male mean (at the centre of the male distribution) is a bit higher than the female mean. But the figures also show how much the two distributions overlap, and that the mean difference looks rather small compared to the amount of overlap. Thus, even on a characteristic where one sex has a higher average, there will be many members of the sex with the higher average who are below the average of the sex with the lower average. This point is critical to keep in mind so as not to exaggerate gender differences.

In the rest of this section, we will explore some of the main factors affecting gender.

Sex Versus Gender: The Social Construction of Gender

11.1.1 Distinguish the concepts of sex and gender, and explain how gender is socially constructed.

When men and women really do differ, what shapes these differences? Many people believe that sex differences in behaviour and preferences are "natural," caused by biological differences such as differences in hormones, anatomy, or brain structure. There is some truth to this. A person's **sex** is a biological matter. Humans group into two sexes, where males and females differ in anatomy, chromosomes, and average levels of certain hormones. But it is also true that men and women overlap on many of the defining characteristics, and some people, called **intersex individuals**, are born with some defining anatomical characteristics of each sex.

One example of a biological influence is the evidence that testosterone, a hormone present in both men and women but generally in much greater amounts in men, encourages some kinds of aggressive or dominance-seeking behaviour. This suggests that the higher levels of aggressive behaviour that we see in men, on average, are caused in part by the fact that men have higher testosterone levels than women. Yet causation is not just one-way, from hormone to behaviour; changes in the social environment can also change testosterone levels. For example, one study showed that men's testosterone levels increase before a competitive athletic event, and those of the winners stay elevated afterward, while the testosterone levels of the losers drop afterward (Mazur & Booth, 1998). Another biological difference is that only women can breastfeed infants. But men participate much more in infant care in some societies than others, showing that society also has an effect.

Robert Harding World Imagery

Fathers of the Aka tribe in West Africa spend more time in close contact with their infant children than in any other society, indicating that society can play a role in influencing sex differences.

When sociologists talk about gender, they focus on the ways that social forces create differences between men's and women's behaviour, preferences, treatment, and opportunities, and the characteristics of men and women that reflect these forces. While biology clearly has a role in such differences, research in sociology has shown that social arrangements have powerful effects on differences between men and women. The entire system of social processes that create and sustain gender differences and gender inequality is often referred to as the **social construction of gender**. Societies have a broad gender system that consists of interactions in small groups in which what is expected of a person and is rewarded depends upon his or her sex, and institutions like schools, churches, corporations, or governments set policies or rules that affect males and females differently (Risman, 2004). To the extent that men have more power than women in politics, the economy, and the family, the gender system is called **patriarchy**.

One interesting group of people challenges many of our assumptions about sex and gender and how they go together. **Transgendered** individuals are those who were assigned one sex category at birth, based on the usual anatomical criteria, but feel strongly that they belong in the other sex category. Some undergo surgery to correct this perceived incorrect assignment. Transgendered people are often subjected to extreme ridicule and even violence because of the actions of people who are intolerant of those who challenge the notion that one's sex is something fundamental and unchanging. Sometimes the term *transgender* is used to refer to a broader group of people who change or challenge sex or gender categories—perhaps dressing conventionally male while being in a female body (or vice versa) or rejecting the need to look male or female in dress and style altogether (McKenna & Kessler, 2006). This challenges people's belief that sex and gender are binaries—having only two categories.

Gender Socialization

11.1.2 Describe the process of gender socialization.

One way that gender is socially constructed is through *socialization*, a concept we have explored in more detail in Chapter 5. Socialization is the means by which members of a society are taught its norms and practices. Some of what gets taught is conventions about gender—what boys should do differently than girls or women differently than men.

Parents are important agents of socialization. Most parents dress boys and girls differently, decorate their rooms differently, have different aspirations for them, and give them different toys. Parents' socialization practices have changed in that girls are now encouraged to take part in a broader range of activities. For example, many parents now encourage their girls to play sports and give them what used to be thought of as boys' toys, such as Lego and racing cars. But not many parents have started to give their boys dolls. Studies show that fathers—more than mothers—are particularly discouraging of boys doing anything that they see as feminine, like playing with dolls or ballet dancing (Maccoby & Jacklin, 1974). Peer groups are also agents of socialization. Male peer groups often ostracize boys who are not seen as stereotypically masculine enough and ridicule boys believed to be gay (whether they are or not) (Pascoe, 2007).

Another important agent of socialization is the mass media—popular music, movies, television shows, Internet sites, and advertisements. Most of us see and hear hundreds

katrinaelena/Getty Images

Parents are powerful agents of gender socialization. Most parents dress boys and girls differently, for example.

of media messages every day. In movies and television, women portrayed in romantic roles are almost always young and thin and look like models. In contrast, men can be cast in a romantic role even if they are older and heavy. Ads typically show women rather than men doing housework. Men are seen in powerful roles in the economy, politics, and athletics. Some of this simply reflects the current social reality, but men and women are portrayed in a narrower range of roles in the media than they take in real life (Holtzman, 2000).

Socialization not only affects children but continues through adulthood as those around us continue to affect us, we continue to see and hear media images, and we are affected by major institutions such as religion and government.

Variation in Gender Differences

11.1.3 Explain how gender differences vary by setting and time.

There are two main reasons why we know that many of the typical differences we observe between men and women are, at least in part, socially constructed. First, these gender differences vary between different social settings—that is, between different cultures and even between different situations within one society. Second, gender arrangements have changed over time. For example, the proportion of married women with young children who hold paid jobs has increased dramatically. If biology were driving all the differences between men and women, we would not expect things to vary by the social setting or change over time.

One example of gender changing between different social settings is that men and women conform more closely to norms of masculinity or femininity when they are aware of being watched. Look at the data from one revealing study: One research team asked university students to play a video game in which they first defended and then attacked by dropping bombs. The number of bombs a student dropped in the video game was taken as a measure of aggressive behaviour. The researchers were interested in whether there were gender differences in aggression because most people think of men as more aggressive than women, and some past studies have found this sex difference (Hyde, 1984, 2005). But how much of that difference is just a matter of people doing what others expect of them rather than enduring differences in preferences? To find out, the researchers randomly assigned half of the students who had agreed to be in their study into each of two groups. As long as a truly random process is used, this guarantees that the two groups should be equivalent on just about anything before the treatment. In this **random-assignment experiment**, participants in one group were led to believe that their actions during the video game would be monitored by the researcher. The other group received a different treatment; they were given the impression that no one would be monitoring their games. Among this second group, men did not drop any more bombs than women. In the first group, the group that believed they were being watched, men dropped significantly more bombs than women (Lightdale & Prentice, 1994).

As Figure 11.2 illustrates, the researchers concluded that gender-stereotypical behaviour is more likely to happen when people believe that they are being watched. Of course, people are being watched by others in a good deal of their life—in school, at home with family, at work, at social gatherings, or out on the street. This suggests that some of how women and men act results from trying to live up to what they think others expect from someone of their sex. Apparently, this social pressure, even with no rewards or punishments, has an effect. Although this study only focused on aggression, you can imagine all sorts of other gender differences that social expectations might affect.

Figure 11.2 Average Gender Differences in Aggression in Monitored and Unmonitored Conditions

SOURCE: Data from "Rethinking Sex Differences in Aggression: Aggressive Behavior in the Absence of Social Roles," by Jenifer R. Lightdale and Deborah A. Prentice, 1994, *Personality and Social Psychology Bulletin, 20*, 34–44.

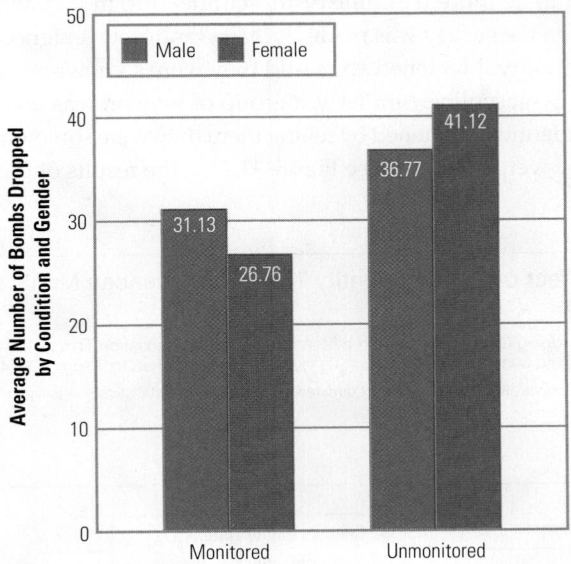

The Impact of Stereotypes

11.1.4 Discuss the role of stereotypes in constructing social expectations of gender.

Some social expectations are based on **stereotypes**, beliefs about a group that are often untrue or exaggerated as a description of the group. These beliefs are then applied to individual members of the group, for whom they may not be true at all. Educators worry about the stereotype that girls and women perform worse in math because math is so crucial for many technical majors and careers. Men do better on the SAT Math Test, on average, as we saw in Figure 11.1. But a recent review of many studies showed that most other standardized math tests show only small gender differences, with the average differences virtually disappearing on most tests but the SAT since the 1990s (Hyde, Lindberg, Linn, Ellis, & Williams, 2008). Despite the lower average scored by girls on some standardized tests, when they take math classes in high school or university, girls average higher grades than boys, mainly because they study more (Dee, 2007; DiPrete & Buchmann, 2013).

Researchers have wondered if exposure to the idea that men perform better at math helps to produce the very reality it claims to merely describe. To find out, one researcher randomly assigned male and female university students to two groups—one in which they were told that men perform better on tests, on average, and one in which they were told that there is no average gender difference on such tests. Then male and female participants were asked to assess their own skills on a scale. In the group that had been told that men perform better, women assessed themselves lower on the scale than men did, but this difference was smaller in the group told there is no gender difference (Correll, 2004).

Another experiment randomly assigned two groups in the same way and then asked each group to take a math test. In the group told that men perform better, the male students scored higher, on average, than the females, but in the group told that there is no gender difference in the population, the men and women scored the same (Spencer, Steele, & Quinn, 1999). In these studies, we see that what people hear from others about whether their sex is better at something affects their confidence and even their actual performance—and this is true even if the generalization they are told is untrue. Thus, stereotypes that are untrue or exaggerated will tend to produce the very difference they claim is true, even if the difference didn't exist before.

Social context can also determine how "macho" men act. A team of sociologists showed this in a recent experiment in which male and female university student participants were randomly assigned to two groups. First, the students were given a gender identity survey. Then they were given feedback on whether their answers to the survey showed them to be more feminine or masculine. But, in fact, what they were told about their scores on the survey was made up. Men randomly assigned to the group having their gender identity threatened were told they were somewhat feminine; the others were told they were masculine. Similarly, a group of women was randomly assigned to have their gender identity threatened by telling them they were somewhat masculine, with the others told they were feminine. See Figure 11.3 for the results of this intriguing study.

Figure 11.3 Effect of Gender Identity Threat on American Men's and Women's Reported Attitudes

SOURCE: Data from "Overdoing Gender: A Test of the Masculine Overcompensation Thesis," by Robb Willer, Christabel Rogalin, Bridget Conlon, and Michael T. Wojnowicz, 2011, *American Journal of Sociology, 118*(4), 980–1022.

NOTE: All differences between the "threatened" and "not threatened" conditions are statistically significant for men. None are significant for women.

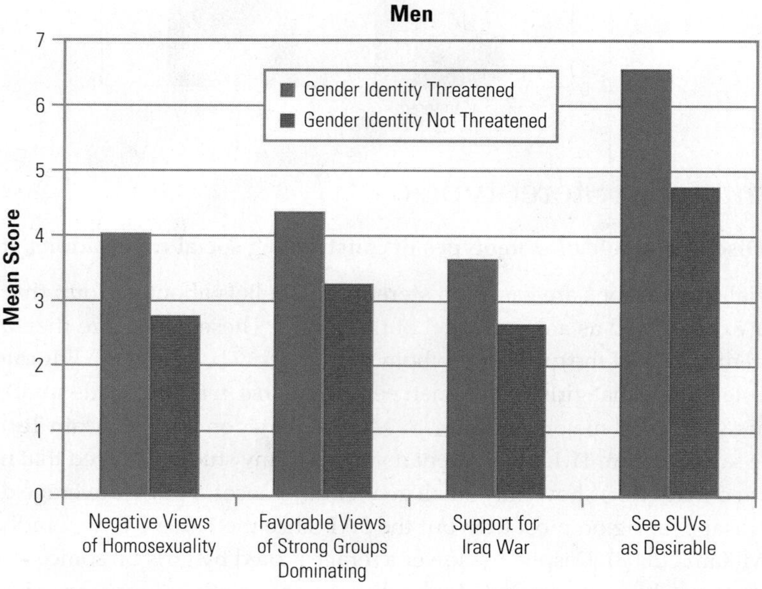

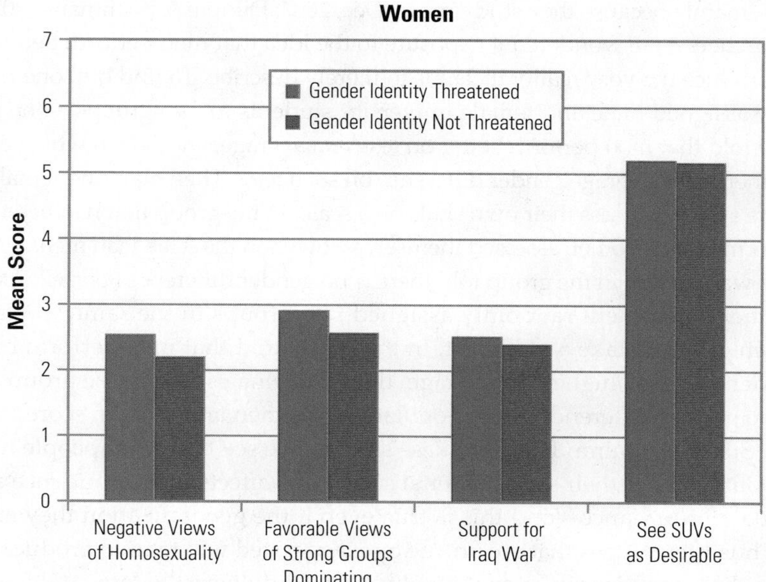

What was interesting was the effect on men of being told they were feminine rather than masculine. When the participants were given a second survey, these men expressed more negative views of homosexuality, more favourable views of strong groups dominating weak groups, more support for the Iraq War, and more favourable views of SUVs (Willer, Rogalin, Conlon, & Wojnowicz, 2013). Interestingly, women's attitudes on the second survey weren't significantly different for those told they were feminine and masculine.

The authors concluded that men desire to appear masculine, and if they have reason to think others doubt their masculinity, they redouble their efforts to engage in behaviour culturally coded as masculine. Women seem to be less worried about how feminine they appear, reflecting less social pressure on them to act feminine.

These studies do not necessarily prove that biological influences have no impact on gender differences. But, because the studies show that gender differences fluctuate depending on the social situation, we can be sure that some of the differences we observe come from social forces. In addition, the fact that gender inequality has changed over time is further evidence that gender is at least partly socially determined and that biology does not completely dictate destiny. Next, we will examine these changes.

11.2 How Have the Lives of Women and Men Changed in the Last 50 Years?

Enigma/Alamy Stock Photo

The Gender Revolution

Women's lives have changed so much in the last 50 years that we often call the changes a gender revolution. Most of the changes consist of ways in which girls and women have taken on activities and roles previously limited mostly to men.

More girls than ever are playing on sports teams, more girls hold offices in student government than previously, more women than men now get university degrees, women's employment has increased, some women have moved into traditionally male professions, women hold some elected offices in provincial legislatures and Parliament, and some women retain their birth-given last name when they marry. When Justin Trudeau was elected prime minster of Canada in 2015, he appointed a gender-equal cabinet made up of 15 women and 15 men. When asked why, he famously quipped, "Because it's 2015." In this section, we look more closely at a few of these changes in women's lives, as well as how these changes have affected men's lives since the 1970s.

Rising Women's Employment and Education

11.2.1 Discuss reasons for the dramatic increase in women's employment and education since 1960.

Of all the changes in the lives of women over the last several decades, the biggest is the increase of women in the paid workforce. Even married women with small children now hold jobs outside the home at high rates. Figure 11.4 shows the percentage of men and women in Canada who were employed from 1976 to 2005, among adults 25 to 54 years old. (People are counted as employed if they held a paying job any time in the last year.)

Men's employment declined slightly. Women's employment, which had been rising slowly most of the century, rose dramatically between 1972 and 1990 and then plateaued, with only a slight increase since then. Yet it levelled off at a fairly high point, with over 70 percent of women employed. While women's employment is still lower than that of men (whose rates are 80 to 90 percent), the two sexes have converged substantially.

The two main reasons that women's employment increased were economic. First, as wages increased during the 1960s and 1970s, so did the incentive for women—or couples—to decide in favour of a woman working for pay (Bergmann, 1986). In addition, the economy changed to include a higher share of jobs in service work (jobs like secretary, receptionist, nurse, and store clerk), which had always employed many women. As the demand for service workers rose, more opportunities became available for women (Oppenheimer, 1970). One result of this growth of women's employment is that many families that include a husband and wife are now dual-income families.

Figure 11.4 Percentage of Men and Women Employed, Canada, 1976–2005

SOURCE: Adapted from *Labour Force Survey*, by Statistics Canada, 2005, Ottawa: Statistics Canada. This does not constitute an endorsement by Statistics Canada of this product.

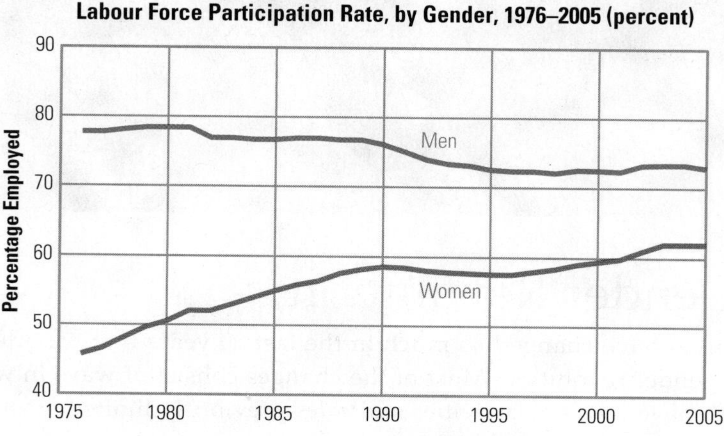

According to René Morissette, Garnett Picot, and Yuqian Lu (2012, p. 2), in Canada, "The period from 1998 to 2011 marked a recovery in the wages of younger workers [wages had fallen briefly in the mid-1990s]. From 1998 to 2011, average hourly wages of young men increased by 10% while those of men aged 45 to 54 grew by 3%. The corresponding numbers for women were 14% and 10%, respectively." In the United States a typical worker's hourly pay increase lagged far behind the increases in productivity (defined as improvements in the amount of goods and services produced per hour worked). Between 1948 and 1973, the average hourly wage increased by 91 percent, roughly in line with a 93 percent increase in productivity. However, between 1973 and 2013 a typical worker's hourly pay increased only 9 percent while productivity increased by 74 percent. In other words, American workers produced much more, but their pay did not increase proportionally (Mishel, Gould, & Bivens, 2015). In fact, the earnings of men who have no more than a high school education—who often work in factories, as drivers, or in construction—have decreased, which has encouraged employment of their wives. Men in managerial and professional jobs (like lawyers and engineers) have seen their pay increase more than the cost of living, yet the typically well-educated wives of these men have increased their employment dramatically as well (Juhn & Murphy, 1997). Laws against sex discrimination have made it more possible for well-educated women to achieve high-level careers. The **feminist movement** encouraged these laws and their enforcement, which encouraged many women to have a career as well as a family.

If we go even just as far back to 1990, 14 percent of Canadian women between the ages of 25 and 54 had a university degree. As Figure 11.5 shows, women steadily increased their share of degrees over time. By 2009, 28 percent of the same age group of women had a university degree. Among younger women the numbers are even higher: In 2009, 34.3 percent of women between 25 and 34 had a university degree compared to 26 percent of men in the same age group. Similar trends are occurring in many countries around the world. For instance, among African Americans, women are an even higher percentage of graduates (McDaniel, DiPrete, Buchmann, & Shwed, 2011). The fact that more women than men obtain a university degree reflects the facts that girls, on average, study a bit harder and get higher grades in elementary and high school, that they like school better, that fewer of them have discipline problems in school, and that fewer are involved in crime

Figure 11.5 Distribution of Women Aged 25 to 54, by Highest Level of Educational Attainment, Canada, 1990 to 2009

SOURCE: Adapted from *Women in Canada: A Gender-Based Statistical Report* (chart 1, p. 6), by Martin Turcotte, 2011, Ottawa: Minister of Industry (http://www.statcan.gc.ca/pub/89-503-x/2010001/article/11542-eng.pdf). Copyright by Statistics Canada, Client Services Division. This does not constitute an endorsement by Statistics Canada of this product.

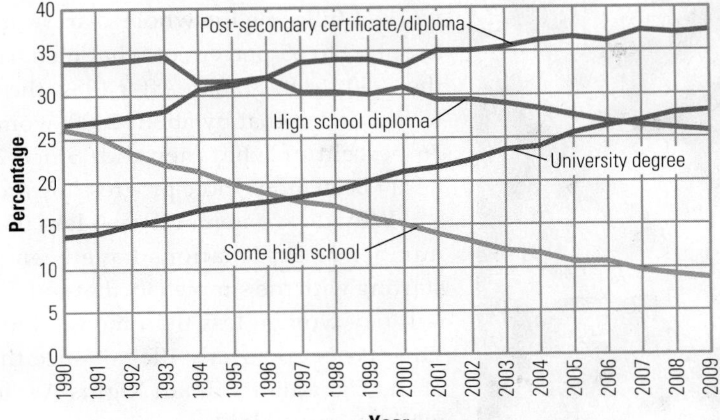

(DiPrete & Buchmann, 2013; Steffensmeier & Allan, 1996). However, on average, boys have been more involved in crime and have received slightly lower grades than girls for decades, so these facts alone cannot explain the dramatic shift. Researchers are still trying to figure out why the gender gap favouring university degrees for men has reversed to one favouring university degrees for women. They suspect that one reason is that, even when girls were performing better in high school, parents prioritized paying for sons to attend university in the era when most women became full-time homemakers. Today both young men and women plan to work for pay during much of their future lives, so now girls doing as well as their brothers are just as likely to go to university, and if they are doing better, they are more likely to complete university.

Change in Women's Jobs and in the Pay Gap

11.2.2 Describe occupational sex segregation and explain the gender pay gap.

In the past, many women worked in traditionally female occupations such as maid, secretary, nurse, or teacher. But since about 1970 an increased number of women have entered traditionally male fields, becoming managers, lawyers, doctors, engineers, or professors, and more women have enlisted in the military. Sociologists measure **occupational sex segregation** with an index that ranges from 100 for complete segregation (all occupations are either 100 percent male or 100 percent female) to 0 for complete integration (each occupation has the same percentage of females as the paid workforce as a whole). Using this measure, occupational sex segregation declined substantially in the 1970s and 1980s but has declined more slowly since then (England, 2011).

Women with bachelors and graduate degrees have entered traditionally male occupations much more frequently than women graduating only from high school. In most countries, the male jobs not requiring a university degree—such as carpenter, welder, electrician, or truck driver—have seen only small numbers of women join their ranks. In less affluent, developing nations, women are more likely to choose traditionally male majors like natural science and engineering (Charles & Bradley, 2009).

Despite some integration, jobs remain quite sex segregated. This is partly because socialization still encourages young men and women to aspire to different jobs. Another factor is hiring discrimination. Although it has been illegal in Canada to refuse to hire people for a job because of their race or sex since the Employment Equity Act passed in 1986, the law has not entirely ended discrimination.

Women's earnings have also increased relative to men's. Figure 11.6 shows the median women's earnings as a percentage of the median men's earnings for each year. (The median for either sex is the level where half the people of that sex are below it and half are above.) The figures include only those who worked full-time the whole year. Women earned about 60 to 65 percent of what men earned from the 1950s to the 1980s. After 1980, the gap began to narrow, so that by about 2000, women earned 76 percent of what men did. Since 2000 there hasn't been much more progress toward equality.

Why do women still earn less than men? A number of explanations have been proposed, starting with the simple fact that some employers still pay women less than men in the same job. This has been strictly illegal since the passage of the Canadian Human Rights Act in 1977 (as well as equivalent provincial and territorial

In the last 40 years, occupational segregation has declined significantly. One example of this is that more women have entered into engineering, still a largely male-dominated field.

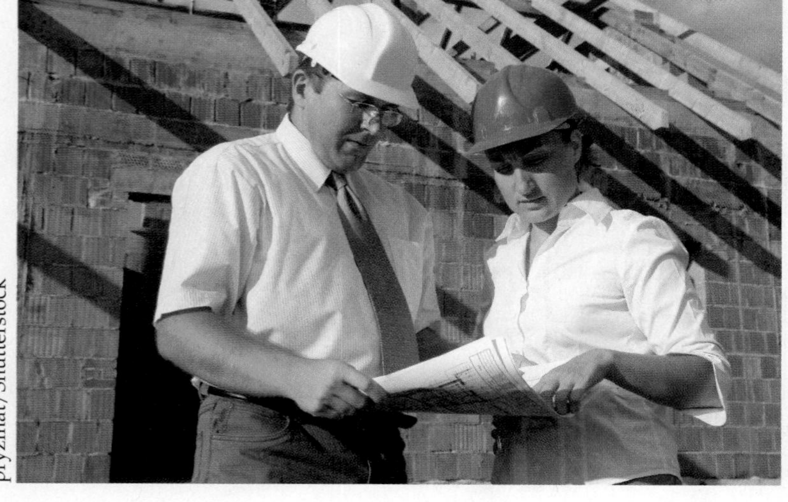
pryzmat/Shutterstock

Figure 11.6 Median American Women's Annual Earnings as a Percentage of Men's

SOURCE: Institute for Women's Policy Research, 2011. Used with permission.

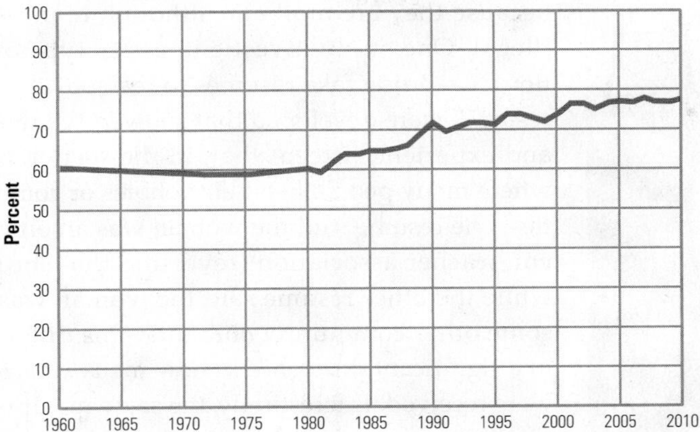

legislation), unless the difference is based on seniority, performance, or some factor other than sex itself. But it sometimes happens. Because of cultural messages that women should be modest while men should promote themselves, women may negotiate less strongly for pay (Babcock & Laschever, 2003). Other times, employers simply offer women less. Another explanation is that employers pay people more when they have more years of experience, and women are more likely than men to have dropped out of paid employment for a time to take care of children.

Another key factor in the pay gap is that women are concentrated in lower-paying occupations. Some of this is because women choose occupations—for example, those helping people—that pay less than other jobs requiring the same amount of education. This may reflect different socialization by gender. Another part of the concentration of women in lower-paying jobs is that, as mentioned earlier, some employers discriminate against women when hiring in higher-paying jobs, leaving the women no choice but to seek lower-paying jobs (Reskin, 2000).

Additionally, employers often set lower pay rates in jobs filled mostly by women than in different jobs requiring the same amount of education but filled mostly by men (England, 1992; Levanon, England, & Allison, 2009). For example, secretaries (mostly women) in some organizations earn less than assembly workers on the factory line or janitors (mostly men) even though the secretaries need as much education and as much (though different kinds of) skill.

Why do employers fail to pay mostly female jobs as much as comparably demanding yet different male jobs? Research that I conducted some time ago convinced me that employers often do this out of a biased perception that whatever is done by women must be easier and not as important for the company. Often the bias is unconscious, but many researchers see it as a form of discrimination. While this is not recognized as illegal discrimination in U.S. federal law (England, 1992), it is in some other nations. If an employer won't hire someone into a particular job because she is female, or pays a woman less than a man in the same job when their seniority and performance are equal, the employer is violating U.S. law. In Canada, the federal government is required to be preferential toward certain minority or underrepresented groups when it hires for all positions. But North American laws do not cover setting lower pay levels in particular jobs because they are filled largely with women, even though there is evidence that employers do this. Gender-based pay discrepancies result in significant losses for women when they reach retirement age because they end up with fewer dollars in their pension funds after decades of savings relative to men. Dr. Ursula Franklin, a famous research physicist who taught at the University of Toronto for over 40 years, won a pension settlement with the

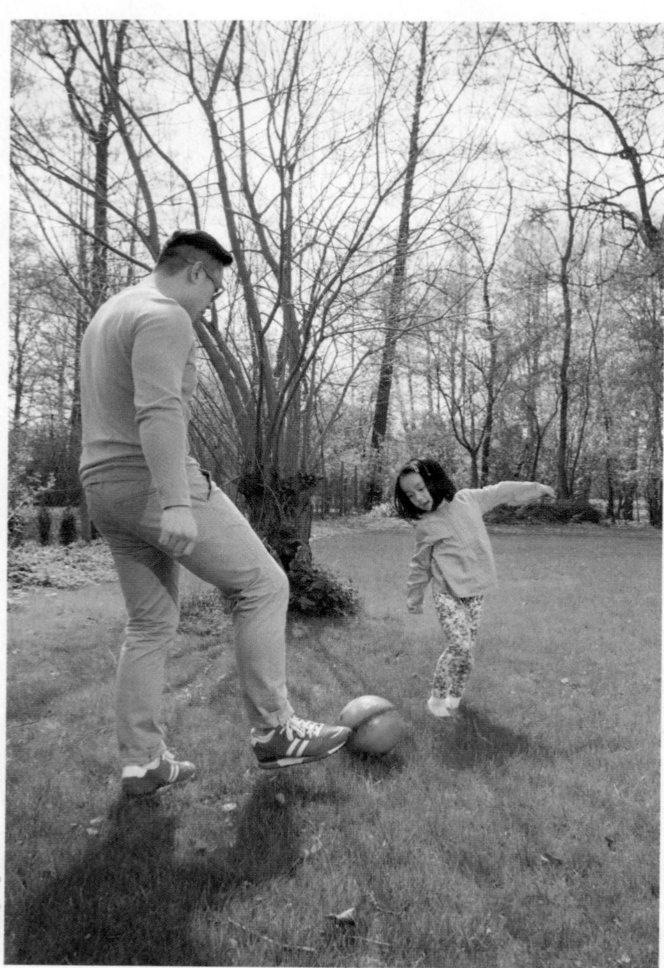

Employed fathers spend more time caring for their children than they did 50 years ago, but so do employed mothers, and women's hours of paid work have increased much more than men's hours of household work. Why do men's roles seem to be more resistant to change than women's?

University of Toronto because she had been underpaid relative to her male counterparts for decades.

Some employers discriminate against women simply because they are mothers, although in most cases this is illegal. One study investigated this type of discrimination by sending fake résumés to real job ads. Two identical résumés were developed that showed the same credentials and experience except that, in the section of the résumé where many people list their hobbies or community activities, one résumé said the woman was an officer in the parent–teacher association (revealing that she is a mother), while the other résumé said the woman was an officer in some other community club. Just this difference resulted in a significant difference in how many calls for interviews were received. Interestingly, the same manipulation to fake men's résumés showed no fatherhood penalty (Correll, Benard, & Paik, 2007).

Some of these factors in the gender pay gap are also factors in why the pay gap is smaller than before. Women's employment has become more continuous, with more women staying employed when they have small children, so the average woman's years of job experience are now closer to those of the average man. Because salaries tend to increase with more years of experience, this convergence between men's and women's years of experience has reduced the pay gap. As more women than ever have chosen traditionally male high-paying fields, such as law, medicine, and management, this has increased women's pay relative to men's. Also, enforcement of antidiscrimination law has reduced employer discrimination. All these factors have contributed to the reduction of the gender pay gap. But progress toward gender equality in employment, occupations, and pay has slowed down since the 1990s. Figure 11.6 shows this slowdown for pay equality. Interestingly, it was around the same time that attitudes about gender, which had become more egalitarian among both men and women in the 1970s and 1980s, moved in a more conservative direction (Cotter, Hermsen, & Vanneman, 2011).

The Impact on Men

11.2.3 Discuss the impact of the gender revolution on men's roles.

The gender revolution has also impacted men's and boys' lives. Since the 1970s, married men have begun spending substantially more time with their children and doing a bit more housework. In this way their roles expanded to take on some traditionally female activities, parallel to the way more women moved into traditionally male activities. But what is striking is how asymmetric these changes were. Men moved much less into what had been women's arenas than vice versa. In fact, probably the larger change for boys and men was not taking on formerly female activities but how all the movement of girls and women onto what had been their turf impacted them. Let's look at how these changes affected men's lives.

We saw that women's employment increased dramatically, especially from the 1970s to about 1990. As this happened, men's attitudes, like women's, became more accepting of female employment (Cotter, Hermsen, & Vanneman, 2011). But men didn't move in large numbers into being full-time homemakers; we saw in Figure 11.4 that

80 percent of all men are still employed. Indeed, norms of masculinity seem relatively unchanged in insisting that married men are supposed to have a job—so much so that when men aren't employed, couples more often divorce (Sayer, England, Allison, & Kangas, 2011). Even if norms had shifted to make men's employment more optional, it would have been impractical in most couples for the husband to become the homemaker, as the wives entering employment typically didn't make as much money as their husbands, so families would have taken a reduction in pay if men quit their jobs.

Many advocates of work–family balance and gender equality have hoped that more couples could have each partner employed half the time while they share childrearing and household work relatively equally. But that is very difficult to do without financial sacrifice in the North American economies. In all countries in the European Union, the law requires that employers pay part-time workers the same amount per hour as full-time workers in the same job. But in North America, employers do not have that constraint, and part-time jobs typically pay substantially less per hour than the same job done a full 40 (or more) hours per week; part-time jobs also often provide no added benefits. Thus, few couples could move from one full-time earner to each partner working half-time without a loss in income. For all these reasons, the biggest change for men as a result of women's increased employment was not that more men started staying home or working part-time but that many of them got used to being part of a two-income couple. The obvious benefit of this for men is that they share in the increased earnings that result. But it also means that women are more able to support themselves and more apt to leave unhappy marriages (Sayer et al., 2011).

With more women working for pay, women also don't have as much time for housework, so we might expect that women would look to men to do more housework and childcare than before. Employed fathers increased the time they spent caring for children substantially, but so did mothers (Bianchi, Robinson, & Milkie, 2006). Men's housework on average did increase, but only by a small amount, as Figure 11.7 reveals. Between 1965 and 1995, on average, married mothers decreased

Figure 11.7 Husbands' and Wives' Weekly Housework Hours, United States, 1965–2010

SOURCE: From "Gender Equality: Family Egalitarianism Follows Workplace Opportunity," by Philip Cohen, 2013, June 7, Council on Contemporary Families (https://contemporaryfamilies.org/gender-equality-family-egalitarianism-follows-workplace-opportunity); based on data from "Housework: Who Did, Does, or Will Do It, and How Much Does It Matter?" by Suzanne M. Bianchi, Liana C. Sayer, Melissa A Milkie, and John P. Robinson, 2012, *Social Forces, 91*(1), 55–63.

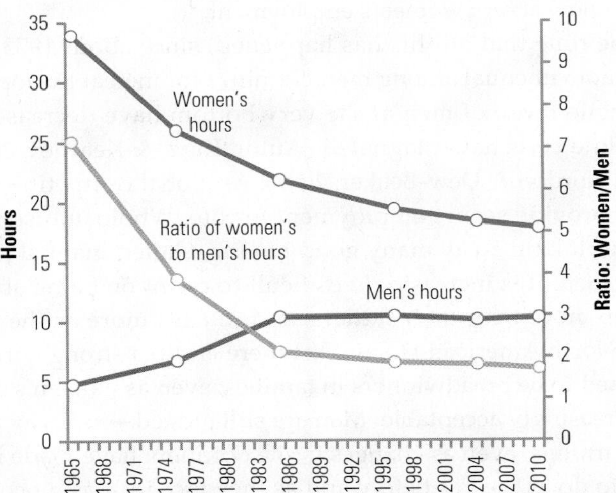

their housework by 15 hours per week, mainly because more of them took jobs, but married fathers increased their housework by only 5 hours per week (Bianchi, Robinson, & Milkie, 2006). Since then, there has been virtually no change. Working women continue to do nearly twice as much housework as their husbands (Bianchi, Sayer, Milkie, & Robinson, 2012). Women have thus entered traditionally male spheres (in this case employment) more than men have taken on traditionally female activities.

As more women chose traditionally male fields of study in university, and careers previously filled mostly by men, very few men decided in favour of traditionally female majors, like elementary education, and only a trickle of men moved into occupations filled mostly with women. Thus, the desegregation of occupations and fields of study was a largely one-way street, with women moving into traditionally male fields while few men entered traditionally female fields (England, 2010a).

Men didn't enter female-dominated occupations in large numbers for several reasons. One is that these occupations, as we saw earlier, often pay less than male-dominated occupations—even when you compare jobs requiring the same amount of education. Second, as boys their socialization often encouraged "guy" hobbies and activities more consistent with jobs such as athletic coach or engineer than preschool teacher or fashion designer. In addition, the social stigma of doing anything that makes a male seem feminine is much greater than any parallel stigma of females engaging in male-identified activities. It has long been a feature of our culture that males are ridiculed for doing anything seen as feminine. Thus, men risk both lowering their income and being stigmatized if they undertake activities and jobs thought of as feminine. Some still do so because of a real sense of calling in a caring profession or because some unusual life circumstance brought them into a nontraditional role. While they may earn less than if they chose a more male-dominated field, just as women do, research shows that men are not treated worse than women within the female jobs but, if anything, tend to be welcomed and rise to the top of these fields (Budig, 2002).

In sum, the large changes in gender roles of the last 50 years have moved men into what had been female realms much less than they have moved women into previously male-dominated activities. It has been less appealing for men to enter traditionally female activities such as childcare, homemaking, and female occupations because these occupations often pay less than traditionally male occupations, and such moves are much more stigmatized than women taking on male roles. Of course, the changes in girls' and women's lives have created changes for boys and men. Boys have had to get used to girls competing with them more openly in school, and men find women competing for the same types of jobs they have. Men have gotten used to employed wives, and most now accept women's employment.

At the same time that all this has happened, since about 1973, earnings have become much more unequal among men. Earnings for men at the top have increased enormously, while those of men at the very bottom have decreased and those of men in the middle class have stagnated (Autor, Katz, & Kearney, 2008; Eckstein & Nagypal, 2004; Gordon & Dew-Becker, 2007). As global competition has increased, few employers provide secure employment for life. Whole industries have moved largely overseas, taking away many good-paying, skilled manual jobs in factories. Thus, for most men, it is increasingly difficult to count on being able to hold a job steadily, to earn more than their fathers, and to earn more as they get older—all features of the North American Dream. Yet there is still a strong norm that suggests men are supposed to be breadwinners in families, even as women's sharing this role has become increasingly acceptable. Men are still judged—in a way that women are not—by their earnings, even as changes in the economy have made it more difficult for many men to do as well as before and as they face increasing competition from women who have equal education.

11.3 How Are Our Sex Lives Shaped by Biology and Society?

ames Atoa/Everett Collection/Newscom

Sexuality

We've already examined many aspects of men's and women's lives, but we've so far ignored one key area: sexuality. We often think of sex as an entirely natural, biological matter, not socially constructed at all. It seems biological because nonhuman animals as well as humans have sex, and the age at which we are interested in sex is affected by hormones. There is no question that sexual attractions and behaviour are affected by biology, but, as we'll consider in this section, they are also strongly affected by social construction (Gagnon & Simon, 1973).

For example, social norms regulate fine details about what appearances are seen as sexually appealing or disgusting. In China prior to 1920, many upper-class girls' feet were bound, a painful process that stunted their growth; men evidently found tiny feet sexually alluring (Mackie, 1996). Today's notion that ultrathin women are the most beautiful would mystify people in many cultures, where such women would be seen as unhealthy and not sexy at all! In Mauritania, a country in West Africa where among some groups fatness is considered beauty, many young girls are force-fed to become fat enough to attract a mate (Waterlow, 2013).

Societies also put many restrictions on sex. In some societies, homosexual behaviour is illegal and punishable by prison time (Ottosson, 2010), while, by contrast, the right to same-sex marriage is protected by law in some countries around in the world. Premarital sex and childbearing have been stigmatized in some historical periods, and still are today in some nations, but they are extremely common in other societies. In this section we will explore these and other social influences on sexuality.

In the "Long Neck" tribe in northern Thailand, women are seen as more beautiful if they have long necks, and some take drastic measures to achieve this beauty. What drastic measures do North American women take to alter their bodies?

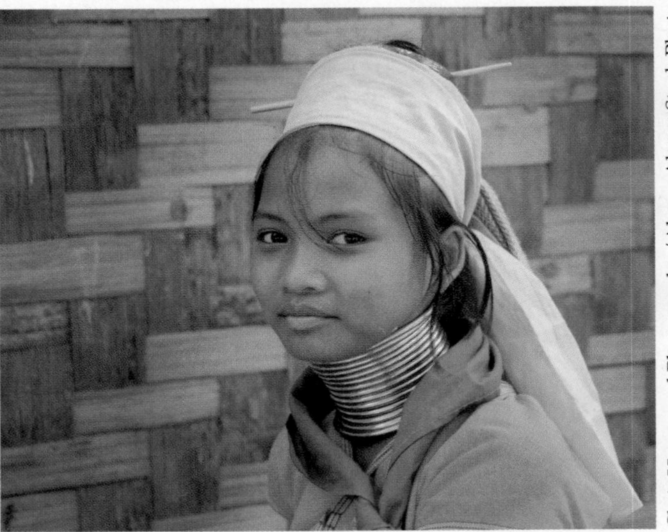
Chris Hammond Photography/Alamy Alamy Stock Photo

Sexual Orientation

11.3.1 Discuss the relative influence of biology and society on sexual orientation.

The term **sexual orientation** refers to whether individuals are attracted to members of the other sex, the same sex, or both. Today we use the medical terms *heterosexual*, *homosexual* (although homosexual women are increasingly referred to as *lesbians* and men as *gay*—sometimes the term *gay* is also used to describe either men or women who have sex with members of their own sex), and *bisexual* to describe three dominant sexual orientations. But not everyone fits neatly into one of these three categories. One researcher writing decades ago suggested that there was a continuum from homosexual to heterosexual and that people could be various places along this scale (Kinsey, Pomeroy, & Martin, 1948/1998; Kinsey, Pomeroy, Martin, & Gebhard, 1953/1998; Sell, 1997). A recent study followed women who, at the beginning of the study, identified as something other than heterosexual. The study found that about two-thirds of these women shifted the sexual orientation they identified with over 10 years. They moved in all directions between identifying with the labels *lesbian*, *bisexual*, and *heterosexual*, and even preferring no label. Also, the study showed that behaviour (which sex one has sex with), attraction (which sex one is attracted to), and identity (whether one refers to oneself as lesbian, bisexual, or heterosexual) are not always consistent (Diamond, 2008).

An interesting question is where our sexual orientation comes from. As with other aspects of sex, there is evidence that both biology and society have their effects. Evidence that genetics affect sexual orientation comes from research on twins and other siblings. Researchers asked samples of gay men or lesbians, some of whom were twins, about the sexual orientation of their siblings. They compared how often same-sex siblings—including identical twins, fraternal twins, and adoptive siblings—of gay or lesbian individuals were also homosexual. Siblings differ in their degree of genetic relatedness—with identical twins having identical genes, fraternal twins being as related as nontwin siblings, and adoptive siblings being the least genetically similar. The researchers found that a higher percentage of the identical twins of gay men were also gay, compared to a lower percentage of the fraternal twins of gay brothers and an even lower percentage of the adoptive brothers of gay men. A similar pattern was found for women (Bailey, Dunne, Nicholas, & Nicholas, 2000; Bailey & Pillard, 1991; Bailey, Pillard, Neale, & Agyei, 1993). On the one hand, the study proves that genes don't entirely determine sexual orientation because even among identical twins, when one twin is gay or lesbian, most of the time the other is not. Because identical twins are genetically identical, if they don't have the same sexual orientation, something else from their social experiences must explain their differences (Stein, 2001). On the other hand, the study shows that there is some influence of genes on sexual orientation as the finding is that siblings who are more genetically related are more similar in sexual orientation than siblings who are less genetically related.

Sexual Behaviour

11.3.2 Discuss the impact of biology and society on sexual behaviour.

How do biology and society affect other aspects of our sexual behaviour? A big debate in this area is whether men like casual sex more than women, and, if so, if this is because of some biological difference or a result of social influences (Schmitt, 2003). Evolutionary theories say that this is a gender difference that we would expect to have evolved millennia ago. According to these theories, in any population, variation in genes occurs at random. Some of the randomly occurring new genes lead to things that enhance survival, others hurt survival, and still others are neutral. Over many thousands of years, the genes that enhance survival will be more represented in the population because the people (or other animals) with these genes are more likely to survive long enough to reproduce, and their descendants will carry those genes.

If there are sex-specific genes, then genes that helped women to produce offspring that survive will be carried in women today, while genes that helped men produce offspring that survive will be carried in men today. Because a woman carries a fetus for nine months, her number of surviving children will not be enhanced much by frequent sex with multiple partners. But this is different for males, who could potentially impregnate many women in the nine-month period it takes a woman to gestate one child. Thus, any combination of genes that encouraged frequent, casual sex would increase men's number of offspring and the representation of this combination of genes in the future gene pool. But it probably would not increase women's. According to one evolutionary theory, this is why evolution led to more preference for casual sex among men (Buss, 1994).

Frilet Patrick/hemis.fr/Alamy Stock Photo

Nightclubs and university parties often feature women showing more skin than men. Why is this?

Even if evolution is one factor in why men seek casual sex more than women, sociologists also point to a social factor. Our culture features a **double standard of sexuality** (Crawford & Popp, 2003; England, Schafer, & Fogarty, 2008; Kreager & Staff, 2009). This is the tendency to judge women more harshly than men for having casual sex. One piece of evidence that a double standard is in play is that we have many more pejorative terms to refer to women who we think have sex too casually—terms like *slut* or *whore*—than we have for men doing the same thing. Many men engage in the same behaviour, but we are less likely to call them similar names. There are some terms like this to refer to men (such as *man whore* or *player*), but they seem less consistently negative. Indeed, within male peer culture, being a player is often a positive source of status. Recognizing the double standard, sociologists point out that women are more motivated than men to avoid casual sex because it does greater damage to their reputations. It is not entirely a matter of a biologically dictated lack of interest.

One way that we know biology has some relevance to sex is that among youth of the same age, those who are experiencing puberty and have the associated increases in certain hormones are more likely to have sexual fantasies and engage in sexual behaviour. But the same study that shows this also shows that social factors are relevant as well. For example, youths brought up in religious households that discourage early sex are less likely to engage in such behaviour (Udry, 1988). Further evidence of social influences on sex is the fact that the prevalence of sex before marriage has changed quite drastically in most modern societies, as we'll discuss later.

Sexual Minorities

11.3.3 Identify the challenges that lesbian, gay, bisexual, transgendered, and questioning individuals encounter.

The term **sexual minority** refers to anyone who is not heterosexual or who is transgendered (having changed their sex or gender from what was assigned to them at birth). To understand what it means to be a member of a sexual minority, consider the situation of a hypothetical 17-year-old named Tom, who has just recently begun to identify himself as gay. If Tom is typical of the young gay men interviewed in one study, he was first aware of attractions to other males at age 8, first knew the meaning of the term *homosexual* at age 10, first applied the term *homosexual* to his own attractions at age 13, and first had sexual contact with another male at 14, yet he didn't think of himself as gay until age 17, won't tell any of his friends he is gay until age 18, and won't tell his family until age 19 (Savin-Williams, 1998). Why the secrecy and the delay in squaring one's identity with one's urges? The answer lies in the messages about sexual orientation that one gets from social experiences growing up. This is called **heteronormativity**, a situation where the culture and institutions send the message that everyone is heterosexual, or at least that this is the only normal way to be.

To see what heteronormativity is like, consider all the experiences our hypothetical young man is likely to have had growing up. Tom listens to rock music, and most of the songs are about sex or romance between men and women. The plots of most television shows or movies feature romances or sexual escapades between men and women. In his high school, bias against gays abounds (Pascoe, 2007). His male friends frequently insult each other with the term no one wants to be called ("fag"), and another common put-down is "You're so gay!" Tom was never on the receiving end of these insults, and he doesn't want to be, either; that's one reason he doesn't want to tell people at his high school that he is gay. He also hears friends say no homo" jokingly when they are touching each other. At his family's church, nothing is said pro or con about homosexuality, but his friend who belongs to a more conservative church says that, at his church, the preacher talks about the evils of being gay from the pulpit. Tom reads that same-sex marriage is being legalized in many states, but the only weddings he or his parents have been to involve a man marrying a woman. He has never met a married couple consisting of two men. He certainly can't imagine gaining popularity, and figures he might invite ridicule if he asks a boy to his senior prom. It is little wonder that Tom gets the impression that his same-sex attractions are something to hide. His experience is typical of young people growing up gay, lesbian, or bisexual. You can see from Tom's example some of the difficulties of growing up as a member of a sexual minority in a heteronormative environment.

But some members of sexual minorities experience even worse things. Those who show affection for someone of the same sex are often ridiculed by youth peer groups, regardless of whether they appear masculine or feminine. Some employers refuse to hire those they think are gay or fire people upon discovering it. Such discrimination, even if completely open, has been banned by Canadian human rights legislation since 1996, when sexual orientation was added as one of the prohibited grounds of discrimination. In addition, section 15(1) of the Canadian Charter of Rights and Freedoms guarantees that every individual is to be considered equal regardless of religion, race, national or ethnic origin, colour, sex, age, or physical or mental disability. Surveys conducted by U.S. sociologists indicate that nearly half of people belonging to a sexual minority report that they experienced some kind of discrimination in housing or employment based on sexual orientation, about 40 percent report being threatened with violence, and about 80 percent say they have been verbally harassed because of their sexual orientation. Terms used for any of these kinds of bias directed at a person because of their sexual orientation are **heterosexism** and **homophobia**; these terms are often used interchangeably. Probably as a result of these various forms of ridicule and harassment, gay and lesbian youth are two to three times as likely to commit suicide as heterosexual youth (O'Brien, 2000). If one dresses or looks in a way that social norms see as more appropriate for the other sex, one may be stigmatized and sometimes even visited with violence in school or on the street, whether or not one is actually gay or lesbian.

Despite this grim picture of what a young person growing up as a member of a sexual minority has to face, the scene has changed substantially over the last few decades, due in part to a social movement for gay rights (Armstrong, 2002) and to a change in public opinion toward more tolerance of sexual diversity. The gay rights movement has sought to make gay, lesbian, bisexual, and transgendered people appear as individual human beings rather than as negative stereotypes, to support legislation against various sorts of discrimination based on sexual orientation, and to get rid of legislation that explicitly forbids sexuality or marriage between those of the same sex.

Many things have changed in a way more friendly to the lives of sexual minorities. Same-sex activity is no longer a crime, and discrimination on the basis of sexual orientation is banned across Canada. The Canadian military dropped its ban on service by gay and lesbian soldiers in 1992 (this ban was lifted in the United States in 2011). The Netherlands became the first country to allow same-sex marriage in 2001, and since then Belgium, Spain, South Africa, Norway, Sweden, Portugal, Iceland, and Argentina have followed suit. Same-sex marriage is legal in both Canada (2004) and the United States (2015) since both countries' highest courts declared civil unions a protected civil right. Most colleges and universities have lesbian, gay, bisexual, transgender, and questioning (LGBTQ) centres providing services and a place to socialize. Many cities have such centres as well. Some high schools have Gay–Straight Alliance groups. There are newspapers and magazines directed at the LGBTQ community. There are neighbourhoods, sometimes called *gaybourhoods*, with high concentrations of sexual minorities in one area of some large cities. Some gay college and professional athletes have "come out"; in 2013, veteran NBA player Jason Collins announced he was gay, and in 2014 Michael Sam became the first openly gay football player to be drafted by an NFL team.

11.4 How Has Sexual Behaviour Changed in the Last 50 Years?

Glow Images

The Sexual Revolution and Beyond

Over the last 50 years, sexual behaviour of young unmarried adults has changed substantially. There has been some, but much less, change in the practices of married couples. In this section, will we explore changes in attitudes in the practice of premarital sex and in births outside of marriage. We will also explore persisting gender inequality in sexual relationships and generational differences in sexual behaviour.

Premarital Sex

11.4.1 Discuss how attitudes toward premarital sex and the context in which it typically occurs have changed over the last 50 years.

To look at changes in sexual behaviour, it is best to rely on data from surveys that used **probability sampling**. This method of drawing a sample to survey from the population ensures that everyone has an equal probability of being in the sample, so we can be sure that it is representative of the population. Surveys using probability sampling have asked respondents about the age at which they first had intercourse and the age they first married, if they have. These surveys paint a picture of a substantial increase in the proportion of North Americans having sex before marriage. Among people coming into adulthood after the 1960s, 90 percent or more have had premarital sex; it has become accepted in most groups in North American society (Finer, 2007). In some religiously conservative groups (Christian, Jewish, or Muslim), young people are taught to avoid premarital sex, and some even take virginity pledges. However, studies show that a teen's religious denomination doesn't have much effect on whether he or she has sex. Instead, more religious youth from almost any denomination or faith tradition tend to start having sex later (Regnerus, 2007).

Although many North American high school students have sex, many North American parents disapprove. One study compared attitudes of American and Dutch middle-class parents by interviewing parents of 16-year-olds in both nations. The researcher asked parents how they would feel about their son or daughter having a girlfriend or boyfriend sleep overnight in the family's home. Almost all Dutch parents said this was okay. They thought sex should be in a relationship with a nice person and saw sex as a natural and appropriate progression of a relationship. They preferred to have their teen child have sex at home in a safe, comfortable place. They wanted to talk to their child about using protection from sexually transmitted infections (STIs) and pregnancy. In answer to the same question, almost all the American parents said they were vehemently against their child having sex. They expressed concern that kids who have sex are driven by "raging hormones," not making considered decisions. They saw teen sex as the outcome of a "battle of the sexes" rather than envisioning a caring relationship among the teens. Even if they knew that sex was common and their own child might be doing it, most didn't want to approve of it in their own home (Schalet, 2011).

For people coming of age in the 1960s through the 1980s, the proportion of those having premarital sex increased, and, as Figure 11.8 shows, the median age that people first had sex outside marriage decreased from age 20 to 17. But more recently, since the late 1980s, the trend has reversed. That is, the proportion of teens having sex by

Figure 11.8 Median Age of Premarital Sex for U.S. Teens

SOURCE: From "Trends in Premarital Sex in the United States, 1954–2003," by Lawrence B. Finer, 2007, *Public Health Reports, 122*, 7–78.

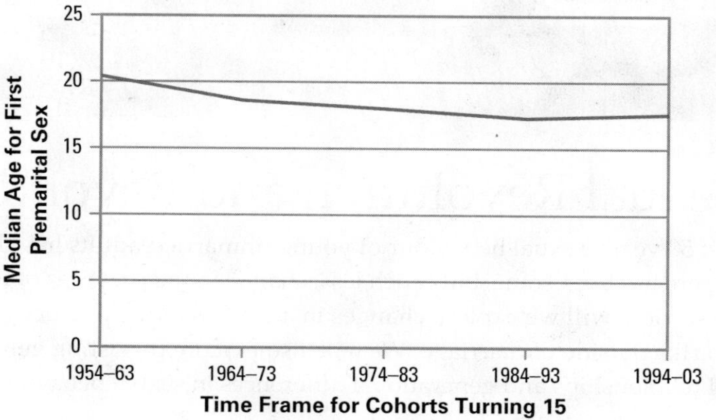

Table 11.1 Percentage of Canadian Youth Aged 15–17, 18–19 Reporting Ever Having Sexual Intercourse, 1996/1997, 2003, 2005, 2009/2010

Age Group	1996/1997	2003	2005	2009/2010
15–17	32%	30%	29%	30%
18–19	70%	68%	65%	68%

SOURCE: Based on data from "Sexual Behaviour and Condom Use of 15- to 24-Year-Olds in 2003 and 2009/2010," by M. Rotermann, 2012, *Health Reports, 23*(1), 1–5.

a given age has decreased. For example, in 1988, 51 percent of female teens 15 to 19 had had intercourse at least once, but among those the same age in 2006–2010, only 43 percent had had intercourse (Martinez, Copen, & Abma, 2011).

In Canada we find that the percentages of Canadian young people in the 15–17 and 18–19 age groups who reported ever having sexual intercourse remained remarkably stable from 1996/1997 to 2009/2010 (Rotermann, 2008, 2012 (see Table 11.1 for more details). In response to the question "Have you ever had sexual intercourse?" Thirty percent of 15- to 17-year-olds and 68 percent of 18- to 19-year-olds reported that they had had intercourse (Roterman, 2012). These percentages have remained remarkably stable over the time period. In sum, while less than half of Canadian teens report having intercourse before age 18, more than two-thirds do so before age 20.

While premarital sex has become almost universal, what has changed over time is the context in which it typically occurs, with the acceptable contexts becoming more casual. In the 1950s and 1960s, those who had premarital sex often did so only with the person they later married. In the 1970s, sex became common in relationships, and since then, young couples in relationships have increasingly become involved in **cohabitation**, the term that sociologists and demographers use to describe the act of living together as an unmarried couple. These relationships may be serious enough that couples are considering marriage, or they may involve couples who are not engaged but just dating and who cohabit for practical reasons, such as to save money by sharing rent. It is only in recent decades that sexual activity has become common in casual liaisons where there is no expectation that either party expects a relationship to ensue. Youth culture uses different terms to refer to such a liaison, one of which is **hookup**.

On college and university campuses today, when students say they "hooked up," this can mean anything from just making out to having intercourse. In an online survey I conducted with students at over 20 colleges and universities, one of the questions asked students whether they had ever hooked up in college or university with someone with whom they were not in a relationship. Those who said yes were asked to report on what happened sexually in their most recent hookup. Figure 11.9 shows what percentage was

Figure 11.9 How Far College Students Went on Their Most Recent Hookup

SOURCE: Based on data from the *Online College Social Life Survey*, by Paula England, 2010.

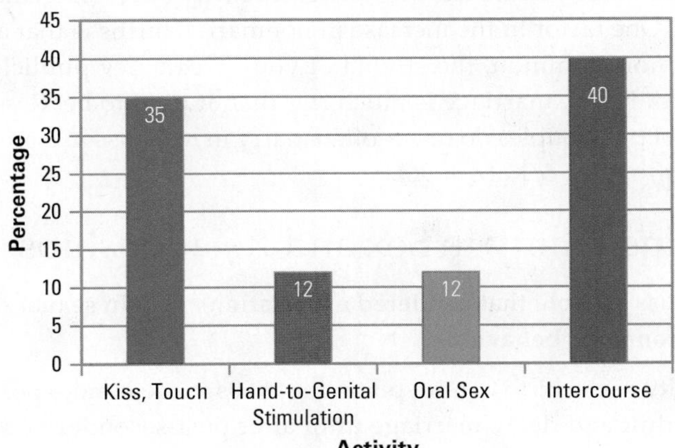

Gianni Muratore/Alamy Stock Photo

In your experience, do hookups often lead to relationships?

in each category, where hookups were classified by how far students went sexually (so, for example, if you made out and had intercourse, you were classified as having intercourse).

Figure 11.9 shows that 40 percent of hookups involve intercourse. These are often cases where the couple had hooked up together before. Thirty-five percent of hookups involved no more than kissing and nongenital touching. Most hookups were with someone the student already knew at least moderately well. Qualitative interviews I did with students showed that while many hookups led nowhere, some relationships started with hookups, sometimes with one or more dates between hooking up and defining the relationship as exclusive (England, Schafer, & Fogarty, 2008).

Births Outside of Marriage

11.4.2 Discuss changing rates of births outside of marriage.

Since the 1960s, as the average age at marriage has increased and premarital sex has become more common (Ellwood & Jencks, 2004), births outside of marriage have also become more common. This increase has been seen in all education, income, and racial groups. But young women and men from lower-income families, who often don't have the academic record or money to complete college or university, are much more likely to have children before marriage. Young, single mothers are among the most economically disadvantaged groups in Canada. In 2009, approximately 27.2% of all babies were born to single (never-married) mothers: 66.7% of teenaged mothers (aged 15–18) giving birth in 2009 were single; 46.1% of mothers aged 20–25 who gave birth in 2009 were single (Statistics Canada, 2009). Minority mothers also suffer from poverty in Canada, and their numbers are increasing as well. Between 1986 and 2004, the fertility rate of Status Indian teenagers in Canada aged 15–19 was six times higher than that of other Canadian teens. In Manitoba, the fertility rate (2000 to 2004) for Status Indian women aged 15–19 was 125 births per 1,000 women, the highest of all the provinces (Big Eagle & Guimond, 2009). Having babies at a young age, without social supports and adequate income, increases the vulnerability of those mothers already disadvantaged socioeconomically and by race and gender.

The premarital sexual behaviour of those who are more disadvantaged isn't so different from that of those who are more advantaged and go to university. The key difference is that those at lower education and income levels are less consistent in using birth control; researchers are not yet sure why this is (England, McClintock, & Shafer, 2011). One factor in the increase in nonmarital births is that as premarital sex has become more common, the stigma of your pregnancy publicly revealing that you've had sex before marriage is much less than it used to be. Researchers suggest that because of this, couples do not as often marry in response to a pregnancy as previously (Akerlof, Yellen, & Katz, 1996).

Gender Inequality in Sex and Relationships

11.4.3 Discuss the role that gendered expectations play in sexual and romantic behaviour.

The availability of the birth control pill in the 1960s made it more possible to have sex as a young adult and delay marriage until after post-secondary education without fear of pregnancy before marriage. This helped women to prepare for careers by going to university or college. Thus, the availability of the pill and the advent of more premarital sex went along with increased gender equality in education and the labour market (Bailey, 2006).

Yet while women's career aspirations are now much more equal to men's than they once were, gender differences in what is expected in the romantic and sexual realm have changed surprisingly little, even at the same time that the acceptability of premarital sex was changing. In my college online survey (mentioned earlier), when asked who asked whom out on their most recent date, students reported that the man did the asking in about 90 percent of cases. When asked who initiated sexual activity on a hookup, more reported that men did than women.

Interestingly, hookups lead to orgasm much less often for women than men. Figure 11.10 shows the percentage of male versus female university students who reported having an orgasm depending on whether the event they were reporting on was a first-time hookup with this partner, the second or third hookup with this partner, the fourth or more hookup with this partner, or the most recent time in a relationship of at least six months when they did something sexual beyond just kissing. The figure shows that both men and women are much more likely to orgasm with a partner when they've hooked up several times before. This is partly because they go farther sexually. Talking to women, my research team and I learned that it is also because partners learn more about how to please each other with experience. Both men and women have an even higher chance of orgasm in relationships. This is again partly because they go farther sexually and have more practice with each other. Interviews with men and women students revealed that it is also because of the affection in relationships that makes partners care more about each other's pleasure.

The gender gap in orgasm is much larger in early hookups than in later hookups with the same partner, and the gender gap in orgasm is smallest in relationships (see Figure 11.10). Women have orgasms only one-third as frequently as men during first hookups. This gender gap in orgasm is much bigger than the gender gap in pay! Using in-depth interviews, a team of researchers I was part of found that men report really caring about the pleasure of their girlfriends in relationships but they report being much more selfish in hookups. In contrast, women seemed to feel an obligation to try to give pleasure to their male partners whether they were in casual hookups or relationships. Interpreting this finding, we argued that the sexual double standard may

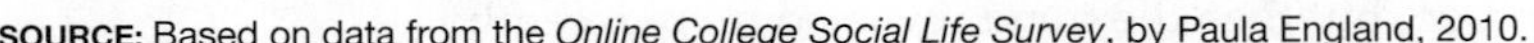

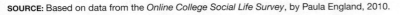

Figure 11.10 Percentage of University Men and Women Reporting Orgasm in Various Contexts

SOURCE: Based on data from the *Online College Social Life Survey*, by Paula England, 2010.

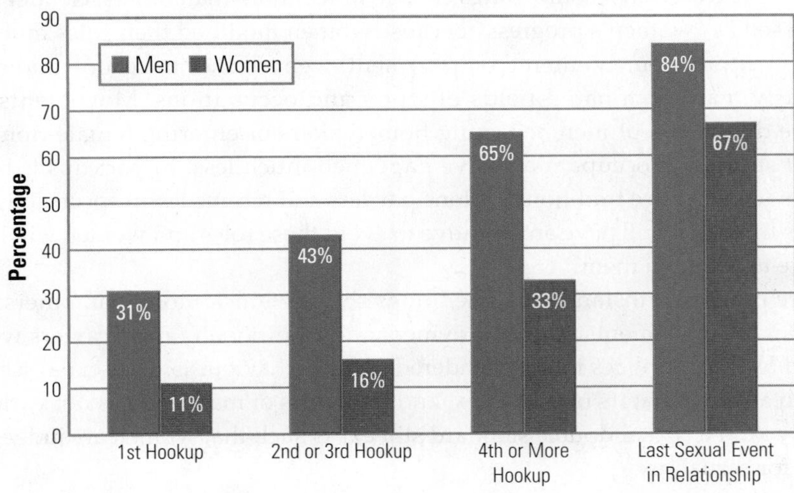

explain this. That is, perhaps men and women are more ambivalent about whether women deserve sexual pleasure in a hookup than they are about men's entitlement to pleasure in a casual context (Armstrong, England, & Fogarty, 2012).

Overall, while sex before marriage has become more acceptable, the extent to which sexual and relational behaviour follows gendered expectations has changed very little. While of course there are exceptions, the expectation that men ask women on dates, initiate sexual activity, propose marriage, and are less severely judged for casual sex still remains.

Conclusion: The Puzzle of Gender Inequality

As we've seen, gender and sexuality are linked. When people are committed to the idea that men and women are naturally and appropriately different, a bias against same-sex relationships often results because such relationships challenge the idea that roles need to be assigned based on one's sex. Gender and sexuality are also linked because our cultural beliefs about how we are supposed to act—at work, in social gatherings, or anywhere else—affect how we act when we have sex as well. Gender norms also create the sexual double standard under which peers judge women more harshly than men for casual sex.

Neither gender nor sexual practices are static. That is how we know that they are, at least in part, socially constructed, although they are undoubtedly affected by biology as well.

Many sociologists used to believe that the shifts in the system of gender and sexuality were unidirectional and continuous. In other words, for a few decades it looked like things were getting increasingly more permissive regarding sexuality and ever more equal between men and women. A person's sex came to dictate less about how the person was treated or expected to act. Many gender inequalities in job opportunities, pay, and leadership declined. Tolerance for sexual minorities increased. Premarital sex lost much of its stigma.

But recent research has made clear that these matters do not go only in the direction of more permissiveness in sexual matters and more equality between men and women. Some changes have plateaued or even reversed. We've seen that many forms of gender equalizing—declining segregation of occupations, reduction of the sex gap in pay, and egalitarian attitudes—moved most dramatically in the 1970s and 1980s, with slowdowns or reversals since 1990. In the sexual arena, intercourse among teens became more common, but then the trend reversed more recently.

We've also seen that some things change much more than others. Gender change is discussed as "women's progress" because women modified their roles much more than men. More women entered employment, went farther in school, and entered previously male-dominated fields of study and occupations. Movements in the opposite direction—of men becoming homemakers or entering female-dominated fields of study and occupation—have happened much less. In part this is because activities women have traditionally done pay less and receive less respect, and as long as that is true, men will have an incentive to avoid these roles and women will have an incentive to abandon them.

Here is another instance of some things shifting much more than others: Women's dramatic movements into employment and traditionally male careers were not matched by large changes in how gendered sexual behaviour is. The sexual script that sees men as the initiators of dates, sex, and proposals of marriage has not varied dramatically. And a sexual double standard still exists such that women are judged more harshly for casual sex.

One of the remaining puzzles for sociologists studying gender and sexuality is to understand which things change, why equalizing changes sometimes reverse, and why some things are so resistant to change.

CHAPTER SUMMARY

The Big Questions Revisited 11

11.1 **Where Do Gender Differences Come From?** Are differences between men and women all natural, or are they shaped by society as well as biology? This section explored the differences between men and women and examined where these differences come from.

Gender Differences

Sex Versus Gender: The Social Construction of Gender

Learning Objective 11.1.1: Distinguish the concepts of sex and gender and explain how gender is socially constructed.

Gender Socialization

Learning Objective 11.1.2: Describe the process of gender socialization.

Variation in Gender Differences

Learning Objective 11.1.3: Explain how gender differences vary by setting and time.

The Impact of Stereotypes

Learning Objective 11.1.4: Discuss the role of stereotypes in constructing social expectations of gender.

11.2 **How Have the Lives of Women and Men Changed in the Last 50 Years?** Women's lives have changed so much in the last 50 years that we often call the changes a gender revolution. This section explored some of these changes, as well as how they have affected men's lives.

The Gender Revolution

Rising Women's Employment and Education

Learning Objective 11.2.1: Discuss reasons for the dramatic increase in women's employment and education since 1960.

Change in Women's Jobs and in the Pay Gap

Learning Objective 11.2.2: Describe occupational sex segregation and explain the gender pay gap.

The Impact on Men

Learning Objective 11.2.3: Discuss the impact of the gender revolution on men's roles.

11.3 **How Are Our Sex Lives Shaped by Biology and Society?** There is no question that sexual attractions and behaviour are affected by biology, but as we discussed in this section, they are also strongly affected by social construction.

Sexuality

Sexual Orientation

Learning Objective 11.3.1: Discuss the relative influence of biology and society on sexual orientation.

Sexual Behaviour

Learning Objective 11.3.2: Discuss the impact of biology and society on sexual behaviour.

Sexual Minorities

Learning Objective 11.3.3: Identify the challenges that lesbian, gay, bisexual, transgendered, and questioning individuals encounter.

11.4 **How Has Sexual Behaviour Changed in the Last 50 Years?** Sexual behaviour of young married adults has changed substantially over the last several decades, but what about the extent to which sexual and relational behaviour is affected by gender norms and inequalities? This section explored sexual behaviour and gender inequalities in the sexual realm.

The Sexual Revolution and Beyond

Premarital Sex

Learning Objective 11.4.1: Discuss how attitudes toward premarital sex and the context in which it typically occurs have changed over the last 50 years.

Births Outside of Marriage

Learning Objective 11.4.2: Discuss changing rates of births outside of marriage.

Gender Inequality in Sex and Relationships

Learning Objective 11.4.3: Discuss the role that gendered expectations play in sexual and romantic behaviour.

Learn the Terms

cohabitation (p. 311)
double standard of sexuality (p. 307)
feminist movement (p. 299)
gender (p. 290)
heteronormativity (p. 308)
heterosexism (p. 308)
homophobia (p. 308)
hookup (p. 311)
intersex individual (p. 292)
occupational sex segregation (p. 300)
patriarchy (p. 293)
probability sampling (p. 310)
random-assignment experiment (p. 294)
sex (p. 292)
sexual minority (p. 307)
sexual orientation (p. 306)
social construction of gender (p. 293)
stereotypes (p. 295)
transgendered (p. 293)

Chapter 12

Families and Family Life

by Kathleen Gerson*

Blue Lantern Studio/Corbis

A "one size fits all" model cannot describe the many shapes that today's families take or the quality of the interactions among their members.

Learning Objectives

12.1.1 Identify family forms that can be found throughout human history and across diverse societies and households.

12.1.2 Explain how residence patterns and kinship systems contribute to different definitions of family.

---

*An earlier version of this chapter was coauthored with Stacy Torres.

12.2.1 Discuss the concerns of proponents of the family decline perspective regarding the nature of families today.

12.2.2 Discuss how the economic restructuring approach explains changing family arrangements.

12.2.3 Discuss the mismatch between the structure of jobs and the caretaking needs of families.

12.3.1 Explain how marriage has become deinstitutionalized in today's society.

12.3.2 Discuss how the conflict between family needs and work pressures affects family life.

12.4.1 Discuss the research on the effects of growing up in a household where both parents are employed.

12.4.2 Analyze the research on the effects of divorce and single parenthood on children.

12.4.3 Discuss the research on the impact of same-sex parenthood on children.

12.4.4 Identify the reasons why some family pathways remain stable or improve, while others face difficulty.

12.4.5 Explain the relationship between class cultures, childrearing practices, and the transmission of inequality from one generation to the next.

12.4.6 Identify the benefits and drawbacks of the extended period of early adulthood experienced by young adults in North America.

12.5.1 Compare and contrast government policies toward families around the world.

12.5.2 Discuss how U.S. social policy on family life measures up to that of comparable nations.

12.5.3 Discuss how the United States might achieve a more effective, inclusive approach to family support.

"That's a typical family." We've all heard this phrase before, but is there a typical family? And how can we really know what life is like in someone else's home? Often our perceptions as outside observers are quite different from the perceptions of those who are family members. Consider the story of 24-year-old Josh, who grew up in Oceanside Terrace, a small, working-class, suburban community on Long Island not far from the hustle and bustle of New York City. In a survey, Josh reported growing up with his biological parents and two brothers in a household where his mother stayed home during his early years. From the outside, Josh's childhood home seemed to be what we tend to think of as a typical traditional family, but his family experience was much more complex than it appeared. Josh was back for a brief visit to celebrate his parents' anniversary before moving to a new job on the West Coast when I sat down with him one morning to talk about his family life.

Josh grew up with his biological parents and two brothers in the kind of household North Americans like to call "traditional" (for an overview of this period, see Coontz, 1992). His father was a carpenter, and his mother stayed home until he started school, but Josh recounts a sequence of events that left him feeling as if he lived in three different families. The first, anchored by a breadwinning father and a home-centred mother, did indeed take a traditional form. Yet this outward appearance mattered less to him

The Big Questions

To make sense of family life, both in the North American context and beyond, this chapter will consider a variety of questions.

1. **What is a family?** To begin at the beginning, we first need to examine the meaning of the term *family*. What is a family, and what are the various ways to define it? Answering this question leads to the next one.
2. **Why are families changing?** To understand the contemporary debate over "family values," we need to map out the competing views about the current state of the North American family, as well as how we got here and what we need to do in response.
3. **What challenges do we face as we develop relationships and balance family and work?** Some pressing issues that affect North American families today include the decline of permanent marriage and the new contours of adult commitment, as well as the blurring of gender divisions and the rise of work–family conflict.
4. **What is it like to grow up in a twenty-first-century family?** The experiences of children growing up in twenty-first-century families and transitioning to adulthood are very different from what they were. How have these changes affected children and young adults?
5. **What social policies around the world best support changing families?** Finally, we will place this overview of North American family life today in a comparative perspective. By examining how other countries have experienced and tackled many of the same challenges, we will be in a better position to create the supports that families will need to thrive in the years to come.

than his parents' constant fighting over money, housework, and the drug habit his father developed in the army. "All I remember is just being real upset, not being able to look at the benefits if it would remain like that, having all the fighting and that element in the house," Josh told me.

As Josh reached school age, his home life took a major turn. His mother found a job as an administrator in a local business and, feeling more secure about her ability to support the family, asked her husband to move out and "either get straight or don't come back." Even though his father's departure was painful and unusual in this neighbourhood, where two-parent homes were the norm, Josh also felt relief. His parents' separation provided space for his mother to renew her self-esteem through her work outside the home. Josh missed his father, but he also came to accept this new situation as the better of two less-than-perfect alternatives.

Yet Josh's family changed again a year later when Josh's father "got clean" and returned home. Even more remarkable, when his parents reunited, they hardly seemed the same couple. Time away had given his father a new appreciation for his family and a deepened desire for greater involvement in his children's lives. Josh's mother displayed major changes as well, for taking a job had given her pride in knowing she could stand on her own. As Josh's father became more attentive and his mother more self-assured, the family's spirits and fortunes lifted. In Josh's words, "that changed the whole family dynamic. We got extremely close."

In the years that followed, Josh watched his parents build a new partnership quite different from the conflict-ridden one he experienced in his earliest years. He developed a new and closer relationship with his father, whom he came to see as one of his best friends. He also valued his mother's strengthening ties to work, which not only nourished her sense of self but also provided enough additional income for him to attend college.

Josh's story exemplifies several important but often hidden truths about family life in contemporary societies. First, families are not "types" but are rather a set of dynamic processes and paths that develop in unexpected ways over time. In other words, families are films, not snapshots, and family life is an unfolding, often unpredictable process. Despite the apparent stability and continuity Josh's family may have shown on a survey checklist, a closer look revealed a domestic life that actually changed in fundamental ways. Second, families can look very different depending on one's point of view. Survey and census questions may reveal a snapshot of how a family looks at one or even several points in time, but an in-depth interview that charts the ups and downs of family life is more likely to reveal how family life is a pathway where crucial events often trigger unexpected transitions and unforeseen outcomes. Third, families come in all shapes and sizes, and it is misleading to assume that one type is better than another. A "one size fits all" model cannot describe the many shapes that today's families take, nor can it capture the quality of interactions among their members.

Finally, and perhaps most crucially, Josh's story reveals how the tumultuous changes of the last several decades require us to think in new ways about family life in advanced, postindustrial societies like Canada or the United States. In a rapidly changing world, Josh's parents were neither able nor willing to maintain a static set of arrangements for organizing their marriage or providing emotional and financial support to their children. As they developed new responses to a host of unexpected events, Josh's family changed dramatically. Its shift from a breadwinner–homemaker to a single-parent to a dual-earner home exemplifies both the growing diversity of family forms and the increasingly fluid nature of family life. These changes offer today's young adults options their parents barely imagined and their grandparents could not envision. Yet they also pose new challenges for creating and sustaining intimate relationships, for bearing and rearing children, and for integrating earning a living with caring for others. In the context of twenty-first-century North America, some families may thrive and others may not, but all of today's families face uncharted territory.

12.1 What Is a Family?

StockHouse/Shutterstock

The Many Ways We Define *Family*

The family is a core institution in all societies. It provides the first and most immediate context for our physical, emotional, and social development. As we age, family issues confront us with many of life's most crucial choices—whether and whom to marry, how to shape our sexual activity, whether to bear children and how many to bear, and how to raise the children we choose to have. Families influence us in ways so deep that it is difficult to exaggerate their importance. Yet their power to shape our destiny depends on their links to other institutions. Families are shaped by the societies they inhabit, but they also have the power to transform those societies.

Most of us think we know what a family is, even if we cannot always offer a precise definition. Yet *the family* can have many meanings. In this section we will explore how we define family, starting with a global and historical perspective.

A Global and Historical Perspective

12.1.1 Identify family forms that can be found throughout human history and across diverse societies and households.

Although families are a universal social institution, their forms vary greatly across diverse social settings. We sometimes think that the phrase *traditional family* refers to an independent household anchored by a husband who concentrates on earning an income, a wife who focuses on childrearing and housekeeping, and their biological children. Yet this picture is inaccurate and misleading. From a global and long-term historical perspective, it is clear that the independent homemaker–breadwinner household is a relatively rare, modern, and short-lived arrangement.

Many other family forms can be found throughout human history and across diverse societies and cultures. Patterns such as arranged marriages, **polygamy** (when a person, typically a man, has multiple marital partners, typically wives), and multigenerational households, for example, were common prior to the rise of modernity in the West, and they continue to hold sway in many non-Western cultures. Some societies, especially those ruled by monarchies, have allowed marriages between cousins and even siblings among the ruling elite in order to keep the transfer of inherited power within an enclosed family system. And some cultures, deemed **patrilocal**, require a wife to live with her husband's parents and obey their authority.

The homemaker–breadwinner household rose to prominence as an ideal family type in North America in the mid-twentieth century, largely as a consequence of post–World War II economic prosperity and the growth of the suburbs. But while a majority of North American households took this form for much of the 1950s, many did not. Working-class and minority communities, in particular, were more likely to find the middle-class ideal of a home with the father as sole earner either out of reach or unappealing. Equally important, many husbands and wives who lived in these so-called traditional households found them unnecessarily stifling. When renowned feminist Betty Friedan spoke of middle-class women's confinement to domesticity as "the problem that has no name" (Friedan, 2001/1963, p. 57) and sociologist William Whyte (1956) referred to the conformity (and financial pressures) expected of the "organization man," they both identified a growing sense of unease about the reigning 1950s family structure.

Monkey Business/Fotolia

According to recent surveys, North Americans consider a legally married couple of one man and one woman, with one or more children, to be a "family." Sociologists often refer to this type of family as a *nuclear family*.

rSnapshotPhotos/Shutterstock

Since the peaking of the homemaker–breadwinner household in the mid-twentieth century, we have seen the rise of a diverse array of family forms, including single-parent homes.

Since that time, North American families have changed in vast and unanticipated ways, reminding us that the history of family life is a history of change. We have seen the rise of a diverse array of family forms, including dual-earner, single-parent, same-sex, and single-adult homes, which now vie with breadwinner–homemaker households for social and cultural support. Because these changes leave no one untouched, family life has become the site of both private struggles and public contention. If the 1950s produced a misleading belief in the ideal family, the twenty-first century leaves us facing instead a series of puzzles and paradoxes. Is the family declining, or is it here to stay? Do families shape people, or do people shape families? Is there one best family form, or is it better to have a variety of family forms and practices? When it comes to these (and many other) questions, there are no simple answers. Instead, we need a sociological lens that allows us to see family life from a variety of perspectives, just as a prism allows us to see light in all of its hues.

Household or Kinship System?

12.1.2 Explain how residence patterns and kinship systems contribute to different definitions of family.

For social scientists who study population issues (called *demographers*), the term *family* refers to a group of people who live together in a household and share biological and/or legal ties. Statistics Canada (2011b) defines *household* as any person or group of persons living in the same dwelling; the type of dwelling, that is, whether private or collective, does not matter, so long as all members occupying the dwelling do not have a "usual" address elsewhere. *Census family*, then, is defined by Statistics Canada as any configuration of parents (single, married, divorced, same-sex) and children living in the same dwelling. In fact, grandchildren living with grandparents are considered to be a census family. Even if this includes the "traditional" family construct, in the eyes of Statistics Canada it appears as though the notion of family is quite broad.

People seem to disagree with any strict definition, preferring instead to use more subjective measures. A recent national survey found that Americans offered a variety of criteria for deciding when a household is a family (Pew, 2010); the definitions from Statistics Canada (above) would seem to corroborate this, and agree with a more inclusive idea of what constitutes households or families. Figures 12.1 through 12.5 indicate the extent to which Americans consider various arrangements to be a "family." These definitions are also linked to differences in ethnic and class cultures. Minority subcultures and residents of poor neighbourhoods are more likely to create wide networks of caretaking and financial support that may not fit any of these definitions. The anthropologist Carol Stack famously described the broad support networks that people in poor neighbourhoods may rely on as "fictive kin"—that is, people whom we rely on, provide support for, and feel close to as if they were family members (Collins, 1991; Stack, 1974).

The rise of **same-sex marriage** provides a vivid example of how social changes in the way people live prompt major—even revolutionary—changes in the ways we define *family*. Although largely inconceivable for most of the twentieth century, legally recognized same-sex marriages became a flash point of social and political contention in the closing decades of the century, as gays, lesbians, and transsexuals began to claim family rights that were taken for granted by heterosexuals. On July 20, 2005, Canada became the fourth nation in the world and the first outside of Europe to legalize same-sex marriage nation-wide; in 2015 the U.S. Supreme Court made same-sex marriage a right nationwide. In a remarkably brief time span, a majority of public opinion had shifted from opposition to support for legally recognizing and accepting families anchored by same-sex couples, much as opposition to interracial marriage had evaporated many decades before. Such sea changes in how North Americans view families underscore the subjective process that produces definitions of *the family* and points to the likelihood that our definitions will continue to expand as new ways of living emerge.

The complexities of defining family become even greater once we consider other societies and cultures. In contrast to the view that a family is defined by a household that shares legal ties, anthropologists who study families in many different cultures call them

Figures 12.1–12.5 What Criteria Make a Household a Family?

SOURCE: Data from *The Decline of Marriage and Rise of New Families: A Social and Demographic Trends Report* (p. 94), by Pew Research Center, 2010, Washington, DC: Pew Research Center (http://www.pewsocialtrends.org/2010/11/18/the-decline-of-marriage-and-rise-of-new-families/).

Figure 12.1 A Husband and Wife With One or More Children

Figure 12.1 shows a strong consensus that a married couple with children is a family.

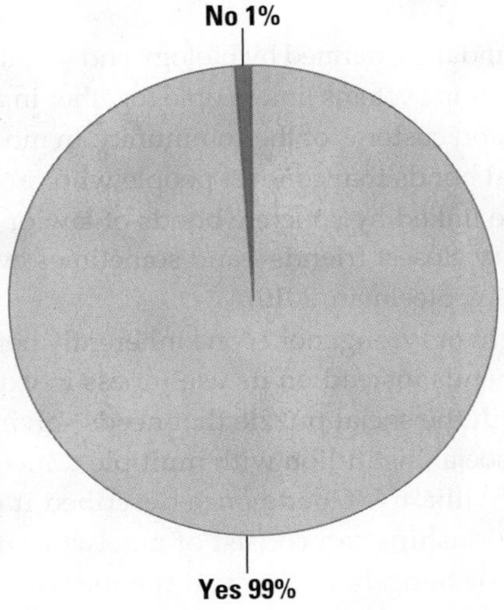

Figure 12.2 An Unmarried Man and Woman Who Live Together With One or More Children

But as Figure 12.2 shows, there is slightly more disagreement when people are asked if unmarried couples with children are a family.

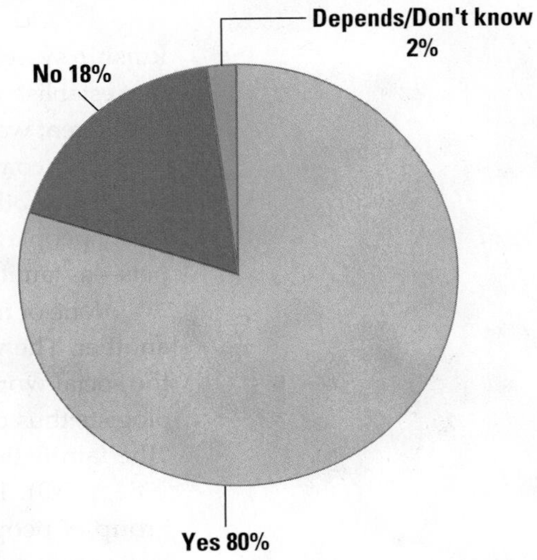

Figure 12.3 A Gay or Lesbian Couple Living Together and Raising One or More Children

In Figure 12.3, we can see that people disagree even more when they are asked whether same-sex couples with children are a family.

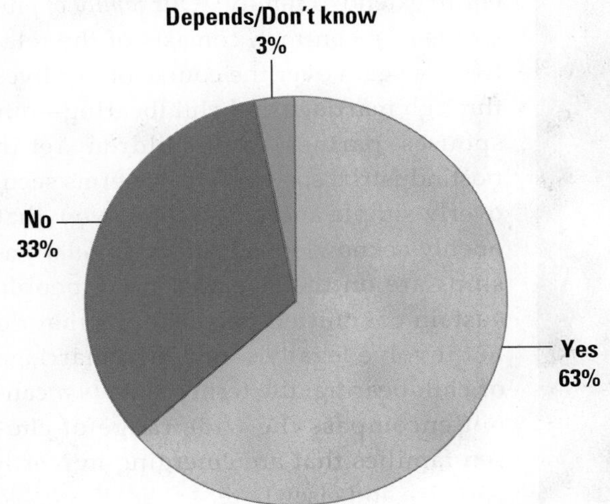

Figure 12.4 A Gay or Lesbian Couple Living Together With No Children

While 63 percent of respondents perceive same-sex couples with children to be a family, a small majority do not consider same-sex couples without children to be a family.

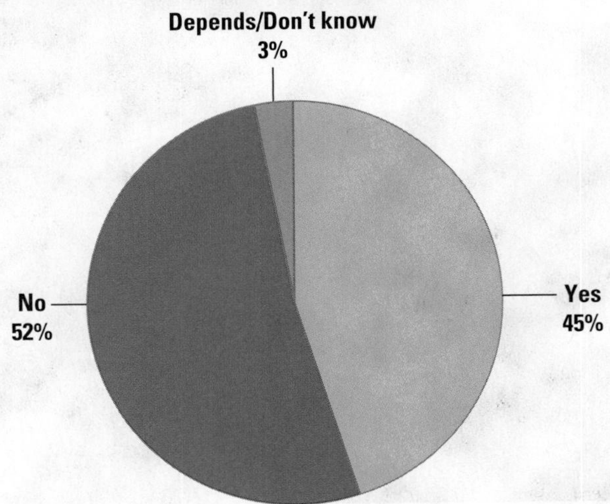

Figure 12.5 An Unmarried Man and Woman Who Live Together With No Children

Less than half of respondents believe that unmarried heterosexual couples without children are a family.

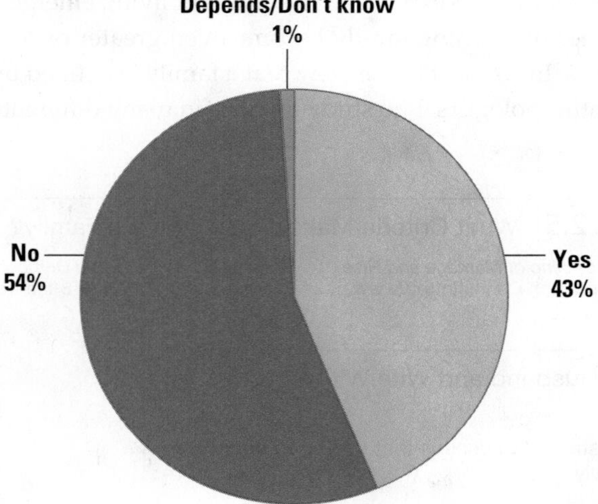

kinship systems—the social links and boundaries, defined by biology and social custom, that establish who is related to whom. Kinship systems link people together in a variety of different ways, depending on the rules and customs of the community. In modern settings, it is common to stress the emotional bonds that connect people who care deeply about each other, whether or not they are linked by concrete bonds of law or biology. Many people today thus refer to their very closest friends—and sometimes even their pets—as family (Powell, Bolzendahl, Geist, & Steelman, 2010).

None of these definitions is either right or wrong, nor is one inherently better than another. The value of any definition depends instead on its usefulness in explaining the social world, and that can change with the social puzzle that needs solving. Sociologists thus conceive of the family as a social institution with multiple dimensions—"the familistic package," as sociologist William J. Goode once described it (Goode, 1982, p. 10). This package of social relationships can consist of a network of **kin**, a group of people who share a residence or household, or even the individuals that ordinary people perceive as family members. Cultural meanings guide definitions, perceptions, and decisions about who is a member of one's family and who is not.

Sociologists also distinguish between the families we inherit and the families we create (Streuning, 2010). Our *family of orientation* consists of the people linked to us by birth—our parents, siblings, and extended kin (technically, our entire extended family). Our *family of procreation*, in contrast, consists of the relatives we gain over the course of our lives through marriage and childbearing—our spouses, partners, and children. Yet in postindustrial societies, these terms seem overly simple and out of date. Now that openly acknowledged same-sex relationships are on the rise and many people sustain committed partnerships that do not involve legally sanctioned marriage or childbearing, the term *procreation* cannot encompass the wide range of chosen families that are emerging in North America and elsewhere.

Who do you consider to be your family? Some people today refer to their close friends (or even their pets) as family.

Blend Images/Alamy Stock Photo

Our definitions also shape the questions we can pose about family life. If we define families as systems of kinship, our focus turns to questions about how kinship links and boundaries are mapped in any given society: Who counts as a member of the **nuclear family**—that is, the socially recognized parents and their dependent children—and who counts as extended kin (for example, are distant relatives you have never met usefully described as "kin")? If we turn to other kinds of societies, these distinctions get even more complicated. In premodern societies, kinship lines sometimes included a number of people who extend far beyond the nuclear unit to encompass a whole clan. In some tribal societies, the biological parents are not even recognized as the social parents. For example, the work of the pioneering anthropologist Bronislaw Malinwoski found that among a tribe known as the Trobriand Islanders, a child's uncle—that is, his or her mother's brother—performed many of the social tasks that modern Western societies associate with fatherhood, such as providing material support and enforcing discipline, while a child's biological father acted in a similar way toward his sister's children (Malinowski, 1913/1964).

Modern societies, in contrast, draw boundaries that limit kin to a much smaller number of people, rarely extending beyond cousins and second cousins (Lévi-Strauss, 1964). Because modern societies are large and complex, they have fewer concerns about intermarriage within kinship groups than do simple societies. Yet this complexity also requires more attention to creating legal standards for who is and is not considered a family member as well as for establishing the lines of responsibility and obligation among those who are deemed members of a family. The rise of divorce, remarriage, and out-of-wedlock childbearing has complicated these concerns. Equally important, the rise of reproductive technologies means that an increasing number of children may have both social parents and biological parents, including a sperm donor, an egg donor, or a surrogate mother. As the boundaries and definitions of parenthood blur and grow, kinship systems become more difficult to chart.

As we examine the many ways that family life develops—as an institution and a set of lived experiences—we first need to understand how and why families (and family life) in contemporary American society have been changing, and why those changes have frequently been the topic of social controversy and division (Risman, 2010).

12.2 Why Are Families Changing?

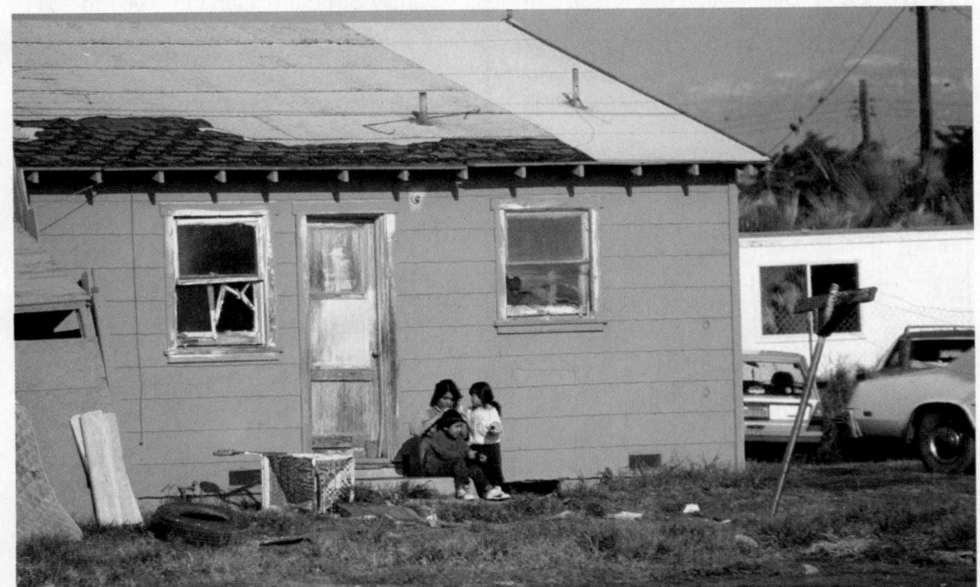

Wolfgang Spunbarg/PhotoEdit, Inc.

Changing North American Families: A Controversial Topic

Given the many ways that we can define and understand the family, it is perhaps no surprise that the study of family life lends itself to multiple interpretations and disagreements. Heated debates not only have taken place among scholars and journalists but also have played an important role in recent elections and political campaigns. This has not always been the case; at many times in North American history, the topic did not provoke nearly as much contention. In the mid-twentieth century, for example, few people objected to defining the family—or at least the ideal family—as a household with a breadwinner husband, a homemaker wife, and their dependent children. Why, then, is family life so controversial today? The most obvious reason is that, unlike the post–World War II era, one family type no longer dominates others. In 1961, married couples accounted for 91.6% of census families. By 2011, this proportion had declined to 67.0%. This decrease was mostly a result of the growth of common-law couples. A mosaic of living arrangements—including dual-earning married couples (straight and gay), nonmarried, cohabiting straight and gay couples, single-parent families, and single adults living alone or with others—coexist side by side. Figure 12.6 shows how the composition of households has changed over the past 40 years.

The rise of diverse family forms has not only transformed the residential landscape; it has also undermined an earlier consensus about what makes a group of individuals into a family. In the wake of such a vast and ongoing social shift, it is perhaps inevitable that a thorny political struggle would ensue. On one side are those who argue that the erosion of the "traditional" couple, with an earner husband and caretaker wife, endangers society; on the other are those who argue that supporting many different family forms is necessary for social justice and personal well-being. These differing perspectives suggest different causes and reach different conclusions about the consequences of family change (Giele, 1996).

The Family Values Perspective

12.2.1 Discuss the concerns of proponents of the family decline perspective regarding the nature of families today.

Some critics argue that changes in the traditional family reflect a weakening of **family values**—the orientations people have toward family responsibilities—which

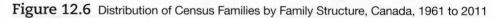

Figure 12.6 Distribution of Census Families by Family Structure, Canada, 1961 to 2011

SOURCE: From *Fifty Years of Families in Canada: 1961–2011; Families, Households, and Marital Status, 2011 Census of Population* (Figure 1), by Statistics Canada, 2012, cat. no. 98-312-X2011003, Ottawa: Statistics Canada (http://www12.statcan.gc.ca/census-recensement/2011/as-sa/98-312-x/98-312-x2011003_1-eng.pdf). Copyright 2012 by the Minister of Industry. This does not constitute an endorsement by Statistics Canada of this product.

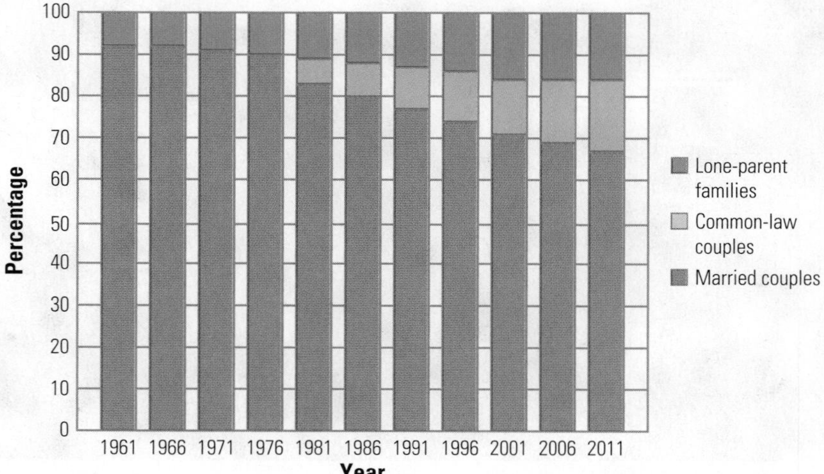

created rising selfishness and unfettered individualism. They see the growth in non-traditional living arrangements as evidence that people have become less willing to assume their proper adult obligations. Proponents of this *family decline* perspective believe lower marriage rates, along with rising rates of premarital sex, couples living together without marrying, divorce, and increasing births outside of marriage, reflect a decline in adult commitment. They worry that the increasing number of single mothers and pregnancies outside of marriage endangers children. Even in two-parent families, they are concerned about employed mothers' absence from the home, as well as the blurring of gender distinctions and the weakening of fathers' position as head of household that women's entry into the workplace appears to represent. Many of these critics see the acceptance of same-sex partnerships as a further devaluation of "traditional" heterosexual marriage. The weakening "family values" perspective suggests that all of these changes have combined to undermine the family bonds needed to raise healthy children and create a stable society. To halt this supposed family decline, they believe social policies should aim to reinvigorate "traditional marriage" and make it harder to choose other options. (Prominent proponents of the family decline perspective include Blankenhorn, 1995, 2009; Popenoe, 1988; Popenoe, Elshtain, & Blankenhorn, 1996; Whitehead, 1997. For rebuttals of the family decline perspective, see Bengston, Biblarz, & Roberts, 2002; Moore, Chalk, Scarpa, & Vandiverre, 2002; Skolnick, 2006; Stacey, 1996.)

There are two ways in which most sociologists of the family question the family values hypothesis. First, by focusing on the central role of eroding traditional values, the family decline perspective ignores many of the positive aspects of these changes, such as expansion of equality and personal choice that new family forms permit and the unshackling of women to pursue careers and independence outside the home. Second, and equally important, the cultural decline argument works more as an *evaluation* of new family forms rather than an explanation of why they have emerged. We will need to examine other theories if we are to explain *why* families have been changing.

The Economic Restructuring Perspective

12.2.2 Discuss how the economic restructuring approach explains changing family arrangements.

A second sociological perspective focuses on social structural factors as drivers of family change. In particular, what is often called the *economic restructuring* approach argues that basic social and economic forces have eroded the foundations of the breadwinner–homemaker family and required new family arrangements. Changes in men's job opportunities, such as the decline of both unionized blue-collar work and secure white-collar career paths, have left fewer men with the ability to earn enough money to support a family on their own. In a parallel development, the growth of service work has expanded the pool of jobs for women, while expanded educational opportunities have encouraged and allowed them to pursue professional careers once reserved for men. These changes, which have occurred over the past few decades (as we saw in Chapter 11), have allowed women to pursue more independent lives, but they have also made it more difficult for families to survive on only one income. Tables 12.1 and 12.2 highlight these economic changes.

From an economic restructuring perspective, blurring gender boundaries, the rise of dual-earner families, and a new emphasis on individual choice and self-reliance are all linked to the consequences of a new economic order. These changes have produced a mix of new opportunities and new insecurities. The financial stability that middle-class families once enjoyed is waning, replaced by a growing divide between the top tier of well-compensated, securely employed professionals and everyone else. If families are more vulnerable today, it is not because they have rejected good family values but rather because they cannot rely on a stable, predictable economic and social system to provide for their needs.

Table 12.1 Employment Trends of Women and Men Aged 15 and Over, Canada, 1976 to 2009

Year	Women Aged 15 Years and Over		Men Aged 15 Years and Over		Women as a Percentage of Total Employment
	Thousands	Percentage	Thousands	Percentage	Percentage
1976	3,618.2	41.9	6,129.3	72.7	37.1
1981	4,556.6	47.7	6,748.4	72.8	40.3
1986	5,138.2	50.3	6,870.3	69.6	42.8
1991	5,790.5	52.8	7,066.9	66.9	45.0
1996	6,099.0	52.1	7,322.4	65.0	45.4
2001	6,910.3	55.6	8,035.8	66.8	46.2
2006	7,757.2	58.3	8,727.1	67.7	47.1
2007	7,977.5	59.1	8,888.9	68.0	47.3
2008	8,104.5	59.3	9,021.3	68.1	47.3
2009	8,076.2	58.3	8,772.7	65.2	47.9

SOURCE: From *Women in Canada: A Gender-Based Statistical Report* (Table 5.1, p. 111), by Statistics Canada, 2011, Ottawa: Statistics Canada (http://www.statcan.gc.ca/pub/89-503-x/89-503-x2010001-eng.pdf). Copyright 2011 by Statistics Canada, Client Services Division.

Table 12.2 Percentage of the Population Who Are Employed by Highest Level of Educational Attainment, Canada, 2009

Level of Education	Women	Men	Women	Men	Women	Men	Women	Men
	15 to 24		25 to 44		45 and over		15 and over	
	Percentage							
0 to 8 years	19.4	26.0	40.8	59.1	10.8	22.7	13.7	27.1
Some high school	40.5	37.6	52.0	71.0	26.4	44.8	35.0	47.0
High school graduate	65.1	64.9	69.6	81.3	47.7	59.3	56.2	67.7
Some post-secondary	58.7	55.5	68.7	79.1	52.0	56.7	59.1	62.9
Post-secondary certificate or diploma	77.2	73.0	82.1	86.8	57.3	62.6	69.2	73.5
University degree	73.6	73.7	82.8	88.3	64.4	67.4	74.7	77.3
Total of all education levels	57.1	53.6	77.1	83.8	46.3	56.1	58.3	65.2

SOURCE: From *Women in Canada: A Gender-Based Statistical Report* (Table 5.3, p. 113), by Statistics Canada, 2011, Ottawa: Statistics Canada (http://www.statcan.gc.ca/pub/89-503-x/89-503-x2010001-eng.pdf). Copyright 2011 by Statistics Canada, Client Services Division.

By recognizing the institutional constraints over which most families have little control, the economic restructuring perspective does not assume the new family patterns reflect declining values. Instead, family shifts stem from growing constraints on the viability of more traditional options, along with expanding desires to take advantage of new opportunities. Because these shifts are irreversible, it is shortsighted and even harmful to try to turn back the clock or to blame people for their values.

The Gender Restructuring Perspective

12.2.3 Discuss the mismatch between the structure of jobs and the caretaking needs of families.

The focus on economic causes of family change is important, but it cannot provide a complete explanation. We also need to acknowledge the role played by the growing desire among many women—and men—to live in families that do not resemble the heterosexual, gender-divided household that predominated in the mid-twentieth century. A third perspective on family change focuses on *gender restructuring* and highlights the growing mismatch between the structure of jobs (and careers) and the caretaking needs of families. While the gender evolution has sent mothers into the labour force and created single-parent and dual-earner households (including straight and gay couples), complementary changes have not occurred in the structure of jobs or caregiving. To the contrary, employees who wish to move ahead or even keep their jobs are expected to place their paid work before family pursuits. Yet parents, especially mothers, are expected to shower their children with attention and are chastised for leaving them with other caretakers, even when these caretakers are devoted and competent (Hays, 1996; Moen & Roehling, 2005; Williams, 2010).

These growing conflicts can leave parents stressed and overburdened as they contend with time squeezes every bit as severe as their financial squeezes. Such work–family conflicts also create dilemmas about how to resolve a host of competing needs and values. How do adults balance the desire for personal independence with the value of lifelong commitment? How do parents trade off between the need to earn money and the need to care for their children? How do children experience growing up in diverse and changing families where new opportunities coexist with new uncertainties? How are these opportunities and uncertainties distributed across families in different classes and ethnic subcultures? And is it possible to develop social policies that reconcile the growing divide between those who wish to restore the once dominant homemaker–breadwinner household and those who support more diverse and **egalitarian relationships** (where caretaking and breadwinning tasks are shared more or less equally by both partners)?

The gender restructuring perspective acknowledges the irreversible nature of change, but it does not assume that these changes are complete. Rather, this perspective draws our attention to the dilemmas and paradoxes created by inconsistent and contradictory social arrangements that are still evolving (Lorber, 1994; Risman, 1998). To make sense of modern families, we need to understand the interplay between inescapable social forces, such as the rise of a postindustrial economy with uncertain job paths, and the efforts of individuals, families, and societies to craft innovative resolutions to the dilemmas created by incomplete change. These dilemmas take many forms, from tensions in forging adult commitments and sharing earning and caretaking tasks, to new challenges in growing up and making the transition to adulthood, to new class and ethnic inequalities. We examine each of these dilemmas in the sections that follow.

12.3 What Challenges Do We Face as We Develop Relationships and Balance Family and Work?

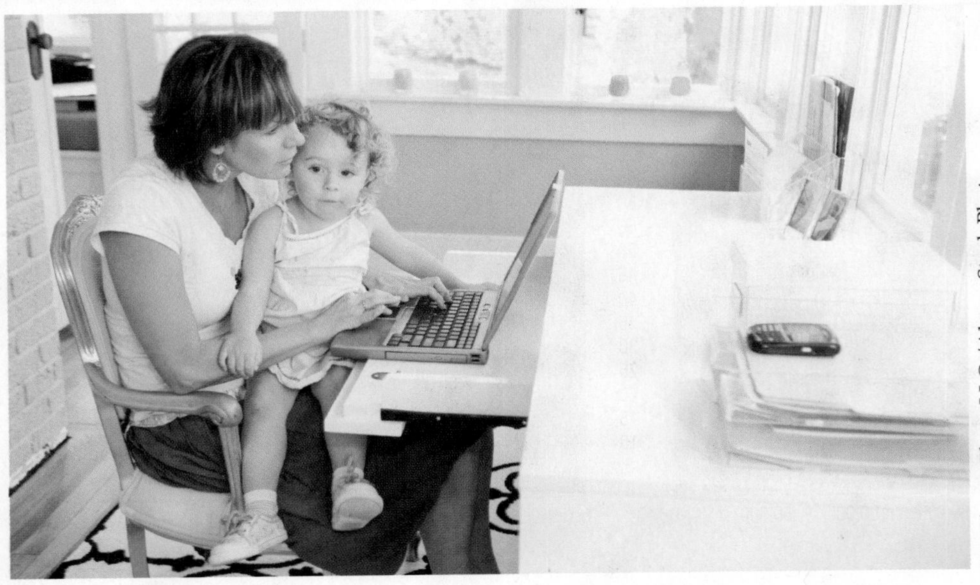

Big Cheese Photo LLC / Alamy Stock Photo

The New Contours of Adulthood Commitment

According to Statistics Canada, in 2011 46.4 percent of Canadians aged 15 and over were married (including common-law relationships); 53.6 percent were unmarried (never married, divorced, separated, or widowed). This continued a trend that had first appeared in 2001 (Milan, 2013, p. 1). Figure 12.7 demonstrates this trend.

Figure 12.7 Population Pyramids of Legal Marital Status by Single Year of Age and Sex, Canada, 1981 and 2011

SOURCE: From *Marital Status: Overview, 2011* (Figure 1, p. 2), by Anne Milan, 2013, Ottawa: Statistics Canada (http://www.statcan.gc.ca/pub/91-209-x/2013001/article/11788-eng.pdf). Copyright 2013, Minister of Industry. This does not constitute an endorsement by Statistics Canada of this product.

NOTE: In 1981, common-law partners were included with the married population. This represents about 715,700 people or 3.8% of the population aged 15 and over. Consequently, the legal married population is slightly overestimated and the single (never married), divorced or separated, and widowed populations are slightly underestimated.

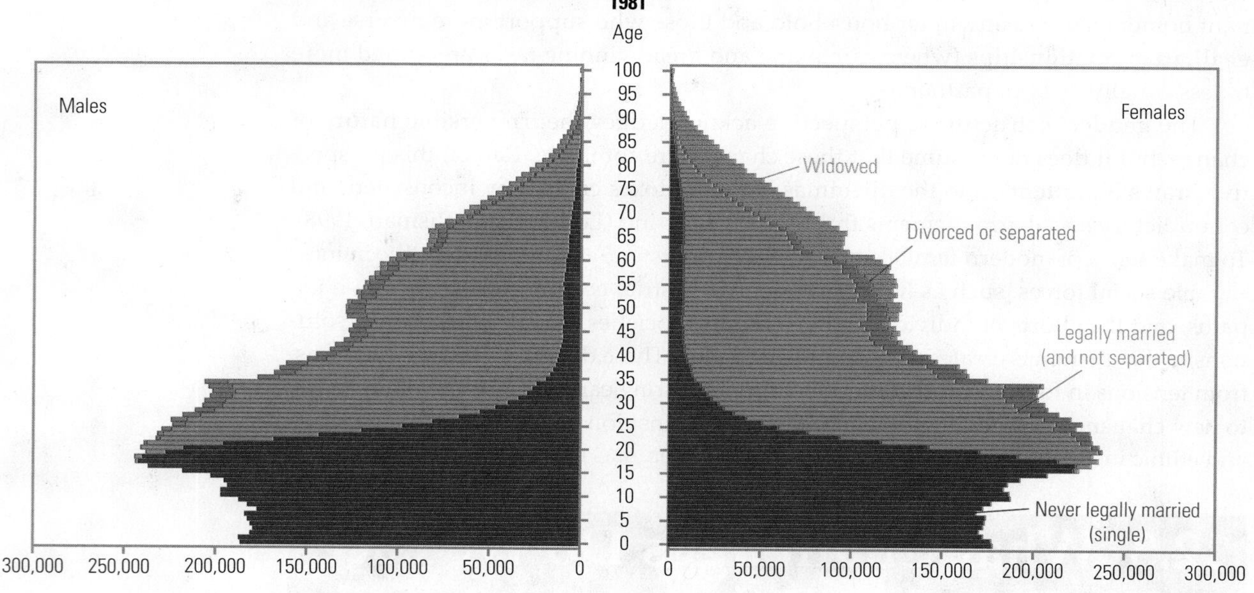

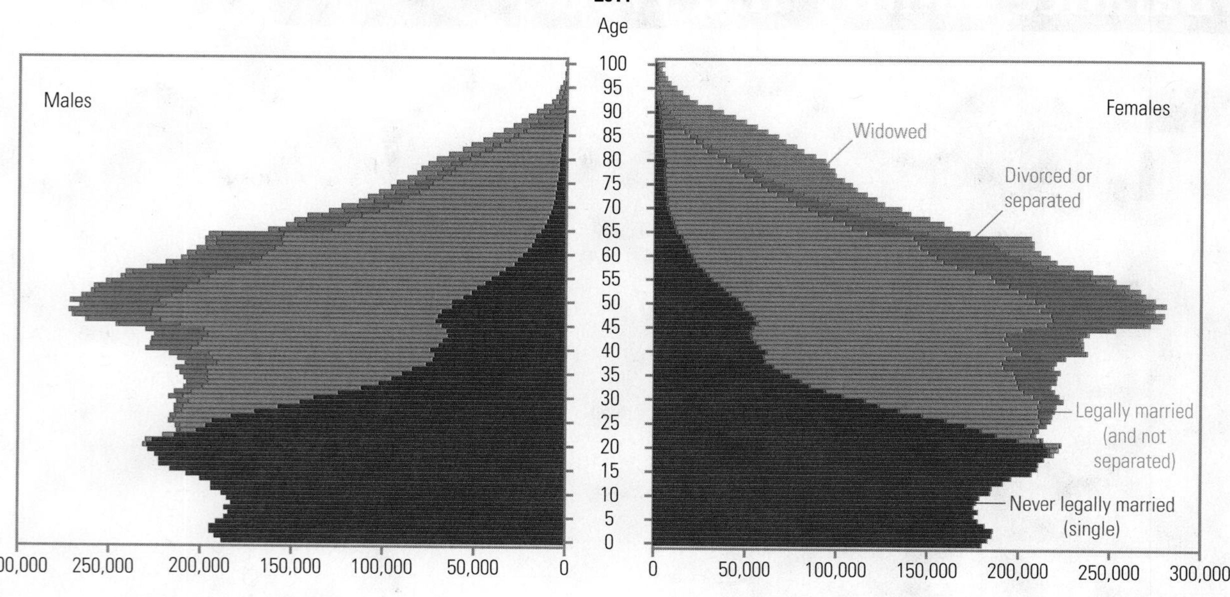

Despite these trends, rumours of the death of marriage are greatly exaggerated. The overwhelming majority of North Americans, around 90 percent, eventually marry or live in common-law partnerships, and most of those who divorce choose to remarry (Casper & Bianchi, 2002; Cherlin, 2009). Time and again, studies report that North Americans consider having a good marriage to be one of their most important life goals (Kefalas, Furstenberg, Carr, & Napolitano, 2011). Indeed, the fight for same-sex marriage rights serves as a powerful indicator of its continuing importance. Marriage to one person for life may no longer be required, but marriage remains highly valued, even though the attributes people look for in a mate have changed. Figure 12.8 illustrates how mate preferences have changed over a 70-year period.

Figure 12.8 What Women and Men Want

SOURCE: Based on data from "Measuring Mate Preferences: A Replication and an Extension," by Christie F. Boxer, Mary C. Noonan, and Christine B. Whelan, 2015, *Journal of Family Issues, 36*(2), 163–187. This does not constitute an endorsement by Statistics Canada of this product.

Qualities **Women** Want in a Mate

RANK IN 1939

RANK IN 2008

1. Mutual attraction, love
2. Dependable character
3. Emotional stability, maturity
4. Desire for home, children
5. Education, intelligence
6. Sociability
7. Pleasing disposition
8. Ambition, industriousness
9. Good health
10. Good financial prospect
11. Similar education background
12. Good looks
13. Refinement, neatness
14. Similar religious background
15. Good cook, housekeeper
16. Favourable social status
17. Similar political background
18. Chastity

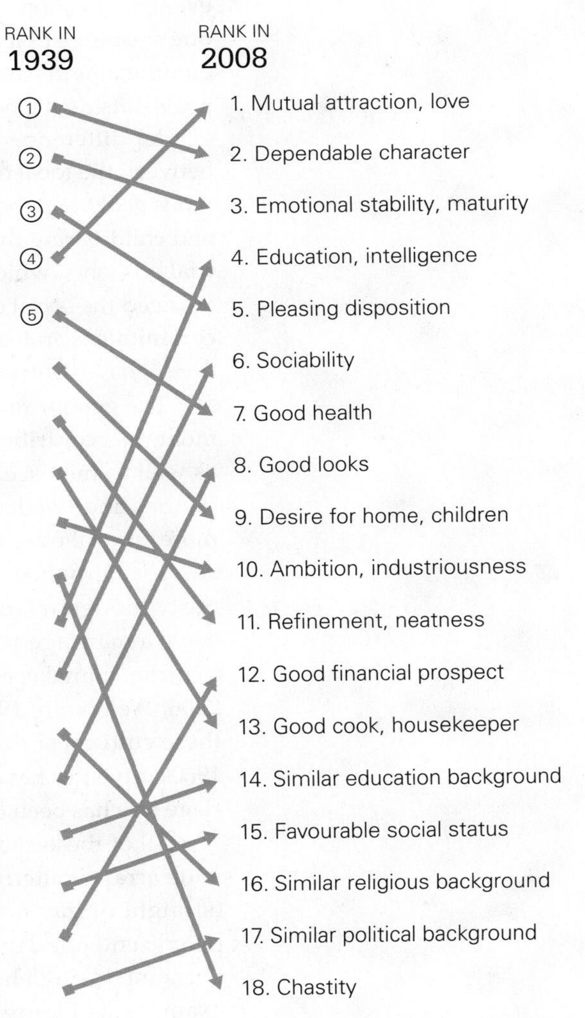

Love and Marriage

12.3.1 Explain how marriage has become deinstitutionalized in today's society.

North American culture has always seen a tension between creating lifelong commitments and retaining a measure of personal autonomy about whether and how to build intimate relationships (Swidler, 1980). Yet this tension has found different expressions as social conditions have changed. Prior to industrialization, parents exercised great control over their children's mate choices, but this control subsided when the rise of industrialization in the nineteenth century demanded a more socially and geographically mobile labour force. This new economic system fostered a new family unit, the **conjugal family**, consisting of a relatively autonomous married couple (and their children) able to seek its fortune outside the parental household (Goode, 1963). The conjugal unit not only fit well with the industrial system; it also elevated the importance of emotional considerations, such as love and companionship, over parental approval as the appropriate criteria for choosing a mate.

The industrial system also produced the physical, economic, and mental separation of the home and the workplace. As many forms of work, and especially the manufacture of goods, moved outside the home to become paid jobs, the family became the site for unpaid tasks, such as childrearing and housework. This new division between the domestic and public spheres, intertwined in earlier periods, caused a strict division—even polarization—of feminine and masculine activities and identities. In a process that one sociologist has called "the feminization of love," women became responsible for emotional and caretaking duties, while men were expected (and allowed) to pursue goals outside the home (Cancian, 1987; see also Parsons & Bales, 1954). Although these gender differences were defined as complementary, they inevitably created tensions between the ideal of individualism, which grants everyone the right to pursue autonomous goals, and the notion that women should maintain the intimate bonds of marriage and childrearing through selfless commitment to caring for others. Today's postindustrial economy, which gathered steam in the later decades of the twentieth century, has changed the social context in which family members must balance the tension between commitment and self-development. Several social shifts (often referred to as "revolutions") have contributed to altering the institution of marriage.

The gender revolution, illustrated most vividly by the rise of women's employment, has contributed to a form of economic individualism in which most women as well as men see the need to support themselves. The expansion of contraceptive options and the decriminalization of abortion have given women and their partners more control over their reproductive choices. More permissive attitudes toward sex and sexuality have destigmatized premarital sex and allowed gay and other previously hidden relationships to move out of the closet. It is also now much easier to leave a marriage without a finding of fault, and longer lifespans provide more time to make, unmake, and remake intimate bonds (Luker, 2007; Rosenfeld, 2009; Skolnick, 2006; Weitzman, 1985). The population pyramids shown in Figure 12.7 reveal how these cultural shifts have affected the divorce rate and marriage rate. Since the late 1960s, divorces have been more frequent than ever before. At the same time, the marriage rate has been declining since the 1970s.

All of these changes have combined to deinstitutionalize marriage by creating a wide array of alternatives to marriage in its traditional form, including **cohabitation** (straight or gay nonmarried couples living together), **serial relationships** (when people enter and exit a series of intimate partnerships), same-sex partnerships, and permanent singlehood (Cherlin, 1992; Smock, 2000; Smock & Manning, 2010). For example, as Figure 12.9 reveals, in 1981, 7.7 percent of 25- to 29-year-olds lived in common-law relationships; this figure nearly tripled to 22.6 percent by 2011. Individuals in their late 20s in 1981 were born between 1952 and 1956. This cohort was aged 55 to 59 in 2011, and of this group, 9.7 percent lived common-law that year.

Figure 12.9 Proportion of Population Aged 15 and Over That Lived Common-law by Age Group and Birth Cohort, Canada, 1981–2011

SOURCE: From *Marital Status: Overview, 2011* (Figure 5, p. 6), by Anne Milan, 2013, Ottawa: Statistics Canada (http://www.statcan.gc.ca/pub/91-209-x/2013001/article/11788-eng.pdf). Copyright 2013, Statistics Canada, Client Services Division. This does not constitute an endorsement by Statistics Canada of this product.

NOTE: For simplicity, not all birth cohorts are labelled.

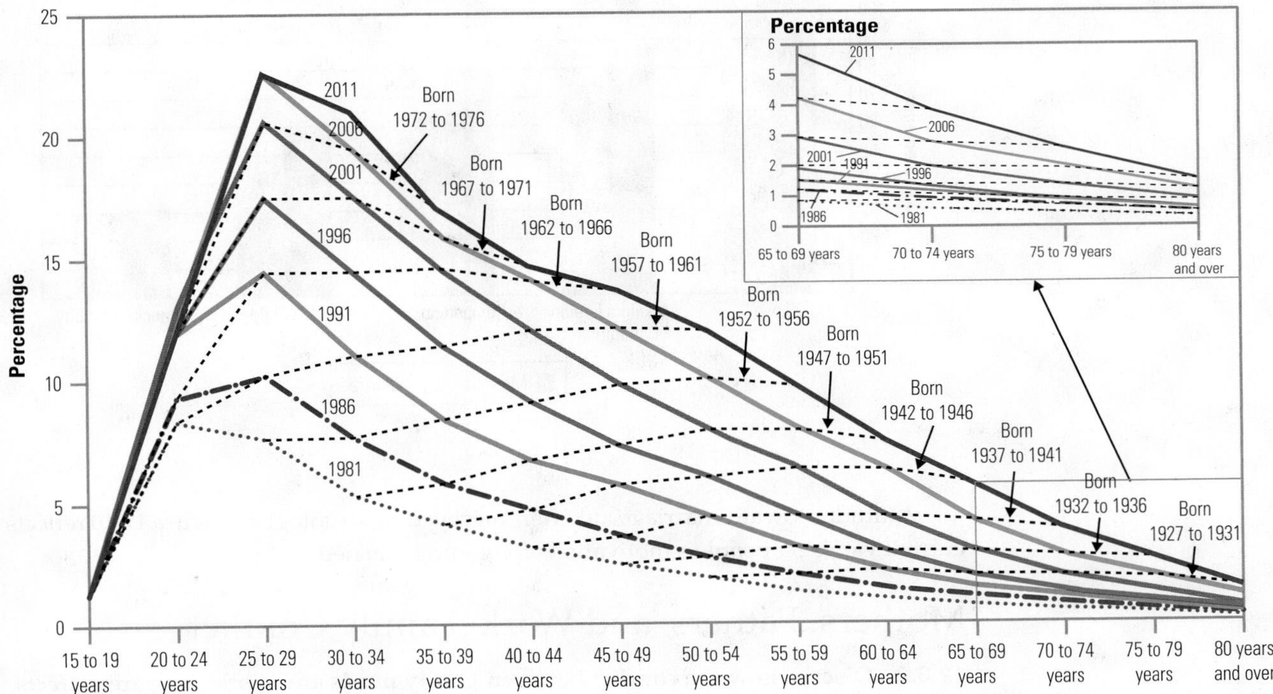

Canadians today can cohabit prior to (or instead of) marriage, engage in sexual activity and bear children without marrying, and leave a marriage if it seems unworkable. The shift from a system in which getting married was a prerequisite for forming a family to one in which it is one option among many has transformed the meaning of marriage itself. Marriage is still a highly valued, but nevertheless voluntary, bond that adults may decide whether or not to make or, indeed, unmake. As they ponder this decision, contemporary adults are more likely to stress the importance of love, respect, and mutual interests than to seek relationships built around a notion of different but complementary gender roles. One recent survey found that most married adults believe that love (95 percent) and companionship (82 percent) are very important reasons to get married, compared to only 31 percent who cite financial stability; and most singles agreed. In another survey, 62 percent said that sharing household chores is very important for a successful marriage, while 53 percent cited an adequate income (Pew Research Center, 2007a, 2010). These ways of measuring a successful marriage place more stress on sharing and less on distinct spheres linked to gender. In fact, the blurring of gender distinctions between women's and men's activities in the home or outside of it shows that these roles are no longer static or unchanging. These new ideals for marriage also mean that people apply new—and higher—standards when choosing a mate and deciding how to define a worthwhile relationship. Yet the stress on emotional rather than financial bonds also makes marital ties more fluid and voluntary. Now that marriage is both optional and reversible, the search for love has superseded the requirement to marry (Coontz, 2005).

Because of the *life course revolution*, people are living longer and both men and women are more likely to marry a second time in their lives.

Mike Watson Images/Getty Images

Figure 12.10 Why Get Married? By Marital Status, Percentage Saying This Is a "Very Important" Reason

SOURCE: Adapted from *The Decline of Marriage and Rise of New Families: A Social and Demographic Trends Report* (p. 22), by Pew Research Center, 2010, Washington, DC: Pew Research Center (http://www.pewsocialtrends.org/2010/11/18/the-decline-of-marriage-and-rise-of-new-families/).

NOTE: Asked of married and unmarried separately, n = 1,306 for married and 1,385 for unmarried.

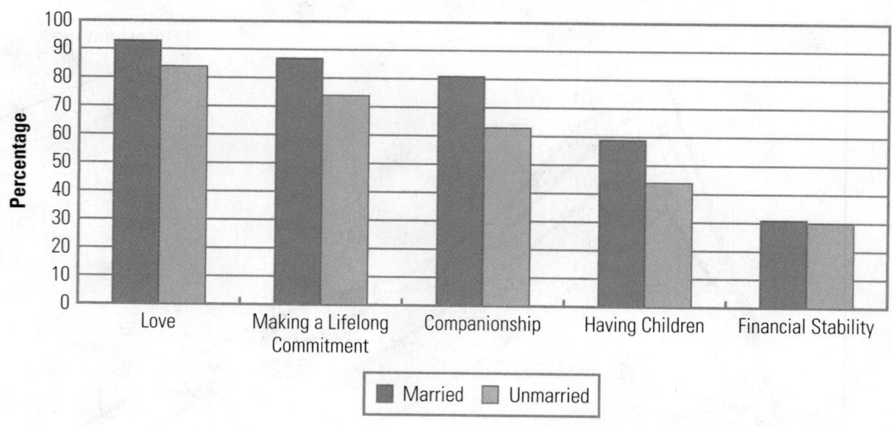

Attitudes toward marriage are often surveyed by sociologists. Figure 12.10 reflects current views on people's motivations for getting married.

Mothers, Fathers, and Work–Family Conflict

12.3.2 Discuss how the conflict between family needs and work pressures affects family life.

Once considered separate spheres, the relationship between the home and the workplace evokes a very different metaphor today. As more women, especially mothers, have joined the paid labour force and new technologies have blurred the lines between home and work, the image of family life as a distinctly private realm has given way to the image of families in conflict with the wider world, especially with the world of work. Mothers and fathers are now more likely to share breadwinning, but they also face daunting challenges about how to integrate their paid jobs with their families' caregiving needs (Hochschild, 1997; Jacobs & Gerson, 2004). In fact, although we generally use the term *work* to refer to paid jobs, unpaid work in the home is also a form of work. **Care work**, whether it is paid or unpaid, is as essential to a household's survival as is bringing in an income. Even though we often pay others outside the household to perform care work, we tend to ignore or downplay its economic value, whether it is performed by a family member without a wage or by a paid caretaker with a salary attached.

Despite the media portrayal of an "opt-out revolution," to use a term coined by journalist Lisa Belkin (2003) to portray university-educated women who leave the workplace to care for children, young women now pursue careers in unprecedented numbers (Damaske, 2011; Stone, 2007). According to one study, employment among university-educated women in professional and managerial occupations in the United States has increased across generations, with less than 8 percent of professional women out of the labour force for a year or more during their prime childbearing years (Boushey, 2008). Women's participation in the paid labour force increased for five decades in a row after World War II and today is very close to that of men. This has had important consequences for the family. For example, the difference in employment rates between mothers and childless women has declined. Most

Figure 12.11 Changes in Couples' Combined Working Time, United States, 1970 and 2000 (Married Couples Ages 18–64)

SOURCE: Based on data from *The Time Divide: Work, Family, and Gender Inequality*, by Jerry A. Jacobs and Kathleen Gerson, 2004, Cambridge, MA: Harvard University Press.

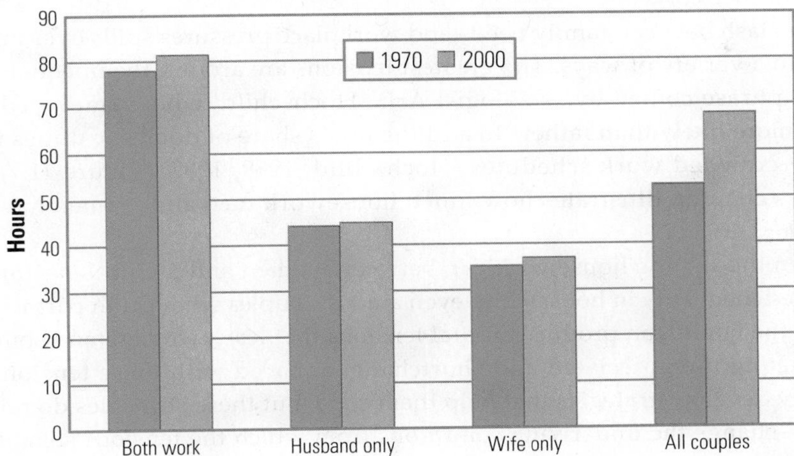

mothers now hold a paid job outside the home, even when their children are very young. Almost 55 percent of married mothers with children under the age of 1 year are employed, and that figure rises to more than 60 percent for married mothers with children under 6 years and 75 percent for those with children between 6 and 18 years (Cohany & Sok, 2007; Cotter, England, & Hermsen, 2010). Figure 12.11 shows how women have increased the combination of work and family life.

These trends make it clear that the assumption that women are likely to opt out of working at a paid job when they have children is highly misleading. Despite the persisting perception that women leave work for family reasons and men because they lose their jobs, the ups and downs of women's employment, like those of men's, much more commonly reflect the opening and closing of work opportunities as the economy shifts. Indeed, the economic recession that began in 2007 has been dubbed a "man-cession" because it was men who lost jobs at a higher rate than did women. Whether women's earnings contribute to a dual-earner partnership or provide the sole support for a household, they are often integral to the financial well-being of their families. According to one study of contemporary women's work paths, employed women now see their decision to work at paid jobs as "for the family" (Damaske, 2011).

The fact that most mothers juggle paid employment with care work has had important consequences for families.

The Washington Post/Getty Images

Despite women's movement out of the home, the organization of work remains largely based on the principle that each employee can count on someone else to take care of a family's domestic needs. Indeed, men and more than 10 percent of women workers put in more than 50 hours a week, and 60 percent of married couples work a combined total of at least 82 hours (Jacobs & Gerson, 2004). While part-time jobs are available, they often require working inconvenient schedules and rarely provide adequate income or opportunities for advancement. Indeed, many of those holding part-time jobs actually work at more than one. The best jobs remain reserved for those who work full-time, can be available for overtime if necessary, and have uninterrupted careers spanning several decades of work.

The clash between family needs and workplace pressures spills over into family life in a variety of ways. The greatest tensions are around the unequal **second shift**, a phrase coined by sociologist Arlie Hochschild, where employed mothers are more likely than fathers to add the lion's share of domestic duties to their already crowded work schedules (Hochschild, 1989, 1997). Figure 11.7, in the previous chapter, illustrates how much housework men and women have done since 1965.

Even though the housework gap between women and men has declined, the continued inequality in housework, even among couples where both partners work outside the home, can produce marital tensions that leave women (and sometimes men) feeling unappreciated and shortchanged. Faced with these tensions, couples may develop strategies that help them cope, but these strategies do not—and cannot—change the underlying conditions from which the tensions stem. Hochschild's vignettes capture many of these strategies. For example, one of the couples she studied—Nancy and Evan Holt—split tasks by their location in the house, with Evan responsible for outside duties, such as taking care of the dog and cleaning the garage, while Nancy remained responsible for the "inside" (basically everything else). While the Holts declared to Hochschild that this arrangement was designed to ease tensions in the household over who does what, allowing the couple to create a family myth of equality, it actually represents an unequal arrangement that has led to ongoing strains between them. Other couples developed different kinds of sharing myths, but most of these arrangements left the woman with the bulk of the household responsibilities.

Paradoxically, the growth of employment among mothers (in both dual-earner and single-parent families) has occurred alongside increased pressure for parents, especially mothers, to give their children more time and attention. This norm of intensive parenting conflicts with the countervailing norm that everyone should work hard and contribute financially, leaving women as well as men who wish to be involved parents to face a "damned if you do and damned if you don't" set of options (Hays, 1996). If a mother takes a job, she faces accusations of neglecting her children, but if she does not, she must defend her position as a stay-at-home mom, a social status whose symbolic value and social support have declined sharply. Research in this area reports that both employed and nonemployed mothers both expressed unease about not meeting their mothering obligations or living up to the standards expected of mothers (see Hays, 1996).

The blurred boundary between home and work produces time crunches and cultural contradictions, but it also creates new opportunities and possibilities. Women and men are both more likely to say they want to integrate earning and caring in their own lives and to establish a more flexible, egalitarian relationship with a lifelong partner. Fathers' parental involvement still lags behind that of mothers, but men are doing more domestic work than their fathers and grandfathers (Coltrane, 2004; Deutsch, 1999; Sullivan & Coltrane, 2008). The gender gap in parenting is shrinking, and couples with more equal sharing express higher levels of satisfaction and are less likely to break up (Cooke, 2006). More surprising, despite the image of the stressed, neglectful parent, parents today actually spend more time with their children than their counterparts did several decades ago. Mothers and fathers may both hold paid jobs, but they are also focusing more on their children when they are not at work (Bianchi, 2000; Bianchi, Robinson, & Milkie, 2006).

12.4 What Is It Like to Grow Up in a Twenty-First-Century Family?

Simon Rawles/Dorling Kindersley, Ltd

Growing Up in Today's Families

The increasing diversity in family structure has also transformed the experience of childhood and the transition to adulthood. An increasing percentage of children now grow up in a home with either two employed parents or a single parent or a same-sex couple (Galinsky, Aumann, & Bond, 2009; Johnson et al., 2005; U.S. Census Bureau, 2006, 2007). Children are also more likely to live in homes that change shape over time. Compared to their parents or grandparents, they are more likely to see married parents break up or single parents remarry. They are more likely to watch a stay-at-home mother join the workforce or an employed mother pull back from work when the balancing act gets too difficult. And they are more likely to see their financial fortunes rise or fall as a household's composition changes or parents encounter unexpected shifts in their job situations. Growing up in an era of fluid marriages, unpredictable finances, and mothers with new work ties shapes the contemporary world of childhood.

The transition to adulthood, like the experience of childhood, is also not what it used to be. Major events, such as graduating from school, getting a job, and getting married, now take place at later ages. In 1960, by age 30, 65 percent of men and 77 percent of women had completed all of the major life transitions that form the historic benchmarks of adulthood, including leaving home, finishing school, becoming financially independent, getting married, and having a child. By 2000, however, only 46 percent of women and 31 percent of men had completed these transitions by age 30 (Furstenberg, Kennedy, McLoyd, Rumbaut, & Settersten, 2004). These trends are not confined to the North America, as many European countries are also witnessing even greater increases in the number of 20-somethings still living with their parents (Newman, 2012). Let's explore how these changes have affected children and young adults.

Growing Up With Working Parents

12.4.1 Discuss the research on the effects of growing up in a household where both parents are employed.

Among all children in 2000, only 21 percent lived in a two-parent household with an employed father and a nonemployed mother, while 59 percent lived with an employed mother, including 41 percent who lived with two employed parents, 3 percent with an employed mother and nonworking father, and 15 percent with an employed single mother (Johnson et al., 2005).

How have these changes affected children? Fortunately, worries about the harmful effects of having two working parents are greatly overstated. Decades of research have found that, on the whole, children do not suffer when their mothers work outside the home. Instead, a mother's satisfaction with her situation, the quality of care her child receives, and the involvement of a father and other caretakers are more important than whether or not a mother holds a paid job (Galinsky, 1999; Harvey, 1999; Hoffman, Wladis, & Youngblade, 1999; Waldfogel, 2006). The children of employed mothers do just as well in their cognitive development, and among children in low-income families, they do better (Burchinal & Clarke-Stewart, 2007). Those researchers who saw a mother's employment as harmful generally pointed to thin research results showing small, temporary, and nonsignificant negative effects of being in day care for a small number of children (Crouter & McHale, 2005). In my own research, I found that almost four out of five young adults who had work-committed mothers believed this was the best option, while half of those whose mothers did not have sustained work lives wished they had (Gerson, 2011). Indeed, despite the difficulties of balancing work and family, employed mothers and two-income homes are, in the words of Rosalind Barnett and Caryl Rivers, "happier, healthier, and better off" (see Barnett & Rivers, 1996, 2004).

Growing Up With Divorced or Single Parents

12.4.2 Analyze the research on the effects of divorce and single parenthood on children.

The proportion of children born to unmarried mothers in the United States is at an all-time high of almost 37 percent, although about half of these nonmarital births are to cohabiting couples, most of whom intend to stay together and raise the child (U.S. Census Bureau, 2006, 2007). One of the most hotly debated questions in scholarly and policy circles about the future of childrearing concerns whether, or how much, children benefit from being raised by both biological parents as opposed to a single parent (either after a divorce or when one of the biological parents never lives with the child). In the case of one- versus two-parent homes, children living with both biological parents do fare better on average, but this difference declines substantially after taking into account a family's financial resources. In other words, the differences in child outcomes between single-parent and two-parent homes diminish considerably when the single parent has an income that is equal or similar to the earnings in a two-parent family. Yet, as we have seen, most two-parent families have two earning adults, while most single-parent households rely on a mother who is likely to earn less than her male counterparts, thus leaving most single-parent families to live with less income and face more economic insecurity (see Chapter 9 for more information about the effects of poverty and low income on children).

What about divorce? Most of the negative consequences of divorce for children can be traced to the high conflict and emotional estrangement preceding a breakup, along with the hostility and loss of economic support that often follows in its aftermath (Cherlin et al., 1991; Furstenberg & Cherlin, 1991; Hetherington &

Kelly, 2002; McLanahan & Sandefur, 1994). But the effects of divorce on children vary greatly, with one researcher concluding that "while certain divorces harm children, others benefit them" (Li, 2007). Children in high-conflict families whose parents divorce fare better, for example, than children raised in high-conflict families whose parents do not divorce (Amato & Booth, 1997; Rutter, 2010). While some analysts argued that all divorces are harmful in the long run, with a "sleeper effect" emerging many years later (Marquardt, 2005, p. 9; Wallerstein, Lewis, & Blakeslee, 2000), most research points instead to the large variation in divorce's consequences. One study found that over one-third of grown children felt their parents' marriage was more stressful than the divorce, which came as a relief when it reduced the long-term daily conflict between parents (Ahrons, 2006). In my own research, I found that a slight majority of those who lived in a single-parent home wished their biological parents had stayed together, but almost half believed it was better for their parents to separate than to continue to live in a conflict-ridden or silently unhappy home. In addition, a majority of children from intact homes thought this was best, but two out of five felt their parents might have been better off splitting up (Gerson, 2011). All in all, the effects of parental breakups—both negative and positive—vary with and depend on the circumstances that surround the divorce before and after it takes place.

Growing Up With Same-Sex Parents

12.4.3 Discuss the research on the impact of same-sex parenthood on children.

As same-sex relationships have become both more common and more accepted, sociologists have begun to ask if there are notable consequences for children associated with growing up in a home with same-sex parents. The rise of same-sex parenting challenges many longstanding understandings of what kinds of parents should be raising children, and it is thus not surprising that these and other changes in the way children are reared have sparked some opposition to same-sex marriage. It is understandable that those who oppose gay relationships on ideological grounds have turned to the issue of children's well-being in an effort to demonstrate the rightness of their opposition. In important respects, the unease surrounding same-sex relationships is similar to the unease some feel about the blurring gender boundaries in heterosexual relationships. Both kinds of partnerships replace a strict gender division of household tasks with a more egalitarian vision about what women and men can and should do in families.

Yet the research on the consequences of growing up in same-sex households has shown that concerns about the welfare of children, like concerns about children whose mothers work outside the home, are unfounded. While some researchers have purported to show that children reared by same-sex parents are disadvantaged, these highly controversial studies have all been found to be flawed and based on stereotypical, outdated, and unnecessarily rigid notions about how and why children thrive. Serious research has not convincingly demonstrated any consequential effects—whether the measure is cognitive, social, or sexual development—on children who are reared by a same-sex couple. Reviewing all of this research for an amicus brief filed with the Supreme Court for a recent same-sex marriage case, the American Sociological Association reported that "Children fare just as well when they are raised by same-sex parents as when they are raised by opposite sex parents. This consensus holds true across a wide range of child outcome indicators and is supported by numerous nationally representative studies" (American Sociological Association, 2012). Indeed, it is increasingly misleading to characterize heterosexual couples as "opposite sex"; to the extent that such couples do not use gender as the main criteria for assigning family tasks, their childrearing practices resemble those of same-sex couples more than they differ from them.

The Changing Face of Childhood

12.4.4 Identify the reasons why some family pathways remain stable or improve, while others face difficulty.

Most research on how a child's family structure influences his or her well-being has demonstrated that the diversity of outcomes within family types is as large as (and often larger than) the differences between them. Some researchers showed, for example, that family composition does not predict children's well-being (Acock & Demo, 1994), while others make the same case for different forms of parental employment (Parcel & Menaghan, 1994).

Children can thrive in a variety of domestic arrangements because family process is more important than family form. What matters is how well parents and other caretakers meet the challenges of providing economic and emotional support rather than the specific forms in which these challenges are met. Children care about how their families unfold, not what they look like at any one point in time. Family life is dynamic. Families are not a stable set of relationships frozen in time but rather an evolving set of situations that can change daily, monthly, and yearly as children grow. All families experience change, and even the happiest ones must adapt to these changes if they are to remain so. Family pathways can move in different directions as some homes become more supportive and others less so.

What explains why some family pathways remain stable or improve, while others stay mired in difficulty or take a downward course? My study of "the children of the gender revolution," who grew up during the recent period of family change, finds that flexibility in earning and caregiving provides a key to understanding how and why some families are able to provide for children's well-being while others are not (Gerson, 2011, p. 6). Flexible family strategies can take different forms. In two-parent homes, children fared well when couples shared breadwinning and caretaking fairly equally or when they took turns and traded places as mothers pursued committed careers or fathers encountered roadblocks at the workplace. Chris, for example, told how his family life improved dramatically when his mother's promotion at a hospital, where she worked as an intensive care nurse, allowed his father to quit a dissatisfying job as a printer and retrain for work as a machine technician, which he found much more satisfying (p. 53).

In single-parent, divorced, and remarried households, children fared better when mothers were able to find jobs that kept the family afloat and fathers remained closely involved in their children's day-to-day care. Letitia thus recounted how her home life changed for the better when her father became the primary caretaker, providing emotional support that her inattentive and often absent mother could not. In the wake of her parents' separation and her father's remarriage, she also gained a more nurturing stepmother (in her words, "my real mother") whose commitment to work also contributed to the family's financial stability.

Despite the differences in family circumstances, all of these responses involved breaking through rigidly drawn gender boundaries between women as caretakers and men as breadwinners. In a world where parents may not stay together, where men may not be able or willing to support wives, and where women may need and want to pursue sustained work ties, most families will encounter unexpected challenges, whether they take the form of financial crises or of uncertainties in parental relationships. When families are able to respond by rejecting narrow roles in favour of more expansive and flexible family practices, they are better positioned to create more financially stable and emotionally supportive homes for children. Flexible approaches to breadwinning and caretaking help families adapt, while inflexible ones leave them ill prepared to cope with the economic and marital challenges that confront today's families.

Parenting Values and Styles

12.4.5 Explain the relationship between class cultures, childrearing practices, and the transmission of inequality from one generation to the next.

Twenty-first-century families of all classes and ethnicities are changing, but not always in the same way. The causes of family inequality are complex and difficult to isolate. Does inequality reflect different family values and cultures, or does it stem from unequal access to economic and social resources? In an influential study, sociologist Annette Lareau (2003) proposed a circular link between class cultures, especially childrearing practices, and the transmission of inequality from one generation to the next. She argued that middle-class parents engage in a form of intensive parenting called "concerted cultivation," which involves a high degree of scheduled activities, a stress on the acquisition of language skills, and a sense of entitlement when interacting with social institutions such as schools. In contrast, working-class families engage in "natural growth," which involves unstructured play and leisure activities, a more informal approach in conversations, and more deference to authority figures such as teachers and doctors. While all families strive to provide their children with love and nurturance, Lareau argued that different childrearing styles leave middle-class children better equipped to succeed in high-pressure, well-compensated jobs and occupations, thus continuing the cycle of inequality.

Lareau stated that, beyond having higher incomes and more wealth, the capacity to transmit knowledge and experience to their children is an important component of the advantages enjoyed by middle-class parents. She found that concerted cultivation is easier with more resources—you can buy your children music lessons, pay to send them to summer camp, or provide the experience of travel to new places and cultures. Parents who have the skills and knowledge as well as the income to seek such options are better positioned to provide these opportunities to their children. In this way, the ability of parents to realize their values for the children often varies by class and education.

Do such childrearing practices reflect different underlying values between parents in different classes? This question continues to spark controversy, but much research suggested that this is not the case. Sharon Hays (1996, 2003), for example, has found that standards of intensive mothering, which bear a strong resemblance to Lareau's notion of concerted cultivation, exist in all classes. Sharing the same values, however, does not mean having the same resources or ability to achieve them. Consider the case of unmarried women who choose to have a child. Studies of unmarried mothers in poor neighbourhoods and middle-class single mothers by choice consistently find that all these women value motherhood highly and are not willing to forgo the experience because the right partner cannot be found (Edin & Kefalas, 2005; Hertz, 2006). Both groups rely on a support network of friends and relatives, including some men, to help rear their children. Yet there are also important differences. Poor single mothers are more likely to begin childbearing in late adolescence or early adulthood, while middle-class single mothers are more likely to postpone having a child until their late 30s or even early 40s as biological deadlines near. Older single mothers, who have the time to attain more education, income, and job experience, are better positioned to provide their children with the resources to grow and prosper than are their poorer, younger single peers.

Some parents encourage their children to try a variety of activities, filling up the child's non-school time with a steady stream of structured projects and a disciplined use of time. Other parents give children more freedom to choose their own activities, which might be unstructured play with friends, watching TV, or free time online.

bikeriderlondon/Shutterstock

Gareth Boden/Pearson Education Ltd

A great deal of evidence suggests that class culture, taken alone, does not determine family outcomes. Families vary in their ethnic and racial composition as well as their financial resources, and people who grow up in the same class can be different in other ways. Sociologist Patricia Hill Collins (2008) pointed out that class is only one of several important social identities, such as race and gender, that intersect to create different family practices. Others have shown that even siblings who grow up in the same family can be treated differently and attain different economic and social outcomes as adults (Conley, 2004). These findings point to the ways that a range of factors beyond the family environment—including supports and obstacles provided by neighbourhoods, schools, and jobs—structure children's experiences and shape their life chances. All families share the value of wanting the best for their children, but some are in a better position to provide the resources and opportunities to achieve it.

The good news is that cultivating a child's curiosity and knowledge is possible whatever a family's income. Many of the experiences most important for a child's development are not unduly costly. Reading before bed every night, visiting local museums, and taking advantage of school or community programs designed to enrich a child's experience take time, but they are activities that even parents of modest means can provide to their children.

Becoming an Adult and Forming Families

12.4.6 Identify the benefits and drawbacks of the extended period of early adulthood experienced by young adults in North America.

The markers used to decide who is—and who is not—an adult are very different today than they were several decades ago, with people much more likely to stress economic achievements over family commitments. Figure 12.12 shows General Social Survey findings related to what is considered important for adult status.

In recent years, young people have been taking longer to reach all of these markers of adulthood. For example, there has been a gradual increase in the median age at which people get married for the first time (from 21 and 23 for women and men, respectively, in 1970, to 26 and 28 in 2010). When it comes to financial and personal independence, a growing percentage of young people, even up to their mid-30s, live with (or move back in with) their parents. Almost half—43 percent—of young people between the ages of 18 and 31 were living with their parents or another relative in 2012 (Fry, 2013). This pattern, called by some the "return to the nest" or "failure to launch," has been observed in many other countries as well (Newman, 2012). In 1971, some 75 percent of Canadian 22-year-olds had left school and 50 percent of them were married; in 2001, however, half of the 22-year-olds in Canada were still in school and just a fifth of them were married (Clark, 2012, p. 20).

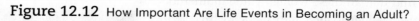

Figure 12.12 How Important Are Life Events in Becoming an Adult?

SOURCE: Based on data from General Social Survey, 2002; "Growing Up Is Harder to Do," by Frank F. Furstenberg, Sheela Kennedy, Vonnie C. McLoyd, Ruben Rumbaut, and Richard A. Settersten Jr., 2004, *Contexts, 3*, 33–41.

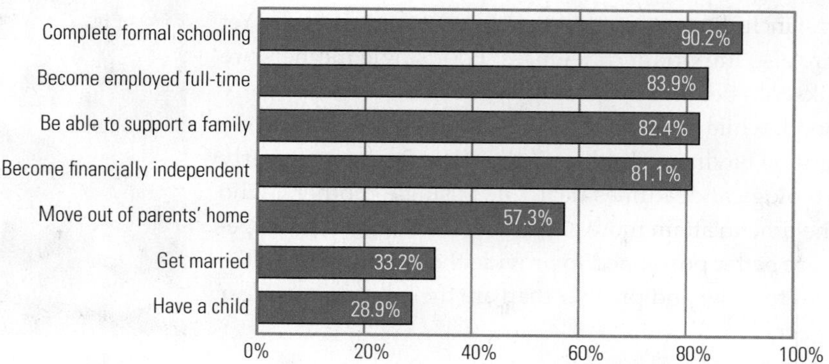

There are a number of reasons that it now takes longer to make the transition to adulthood, including the rising expectations new generations have for finding a compatible mate as well as a satisfying job and career. Another critical reason can be found in the tightening labour market, especially for those without college educations but also for those with university degrees. It has become increasingly difficult for younger workers with limited experience to find a stable, decent-paying job compared to earlier generations (Bernhardt, Morris, Handcock, & Scott, 1999). More recently, the period of slow economic growth since the recession of 2007–2009 has made it more difficult even for university graduates to find stable employment in their chosen field, with 21 percent of university graduates under age 34 reporting living at home in 2012 (Weissman, 2013). Despite the longstanding belief that children should be able to do better than their parents, recent developments in the economy have made it difficult for today's generation of young adults to find the secure jobs and predictable careers that blue- and white-collar jobs offered several decades ago.

The extended time it takes to complete the transition to adulthood has produced a new life stage that some call *delayed adulthood*, or, especially for those with university degrees, the age of independence (Rosenfeld, 2009). Is this delayed adulthood a good or bad development? Like most social changes, this expanding period of early adulthood—after adolescence but before making lifelong commitments—can have benefits and drawbacks. The research of sociologist Michael Rosenfeld (2009) found that the rise of new kinds of relationships, including interracial and same-sex couples, reflects new opportunities for young adults to forge a life that is less constrained by the preconceptions, even prejudices of earlier eras and more in tune with the realities of contemporary life. Yet some, such as sociologist Christian Smith (2011), were concerned that young adults now get "lost in transition" without a moral compass to guide them, while Michael Kimmel (2008) pointed to the emergence of a place he calls "guyland," where young men engage in potentially self-destructive pursuits, such as excessive drinking and partying, that are potentially harmful to themselves and others.

However we interpret this change, it is clear that many young adults now have more time to pursue independent goals before making major lifelong commitments and to develop ways of living that diverge from their parents' paths. This independence has also fuelled a gender revolution in young women's and men's aspirations and plans. National surveys and my own in-depth interviews have found that a majority of young people hope ultimately to create a lasting relationship but not one that is based on separate spheres for mothers and fathers. Instead, most women and men want to create a flexible, generally equal partnership where they share paid work and family caretaking while also reserving considerable room for personal autonomy (Pew, 2007b). In my interviews with young adults aged 18 to 32, I found that four-fifths of the women want an egalitarian relationship, and so do two-thirds of the men (Gerson, 2011). In addition, three-fourths of those reared in dual-earner homes report wanting to share breadwinning and caretaking fairly equally with a partner, and so do more than two-thirds of those from traditional homes and close to nine-tenths of those with single parents.

The delayed transition from childhood to adulthood has allowed younger generations to pursue personal goals before making lifelong commitments. Young adults are freed from childhood (and parental) controls and have the opportunity to develop a more independent self.

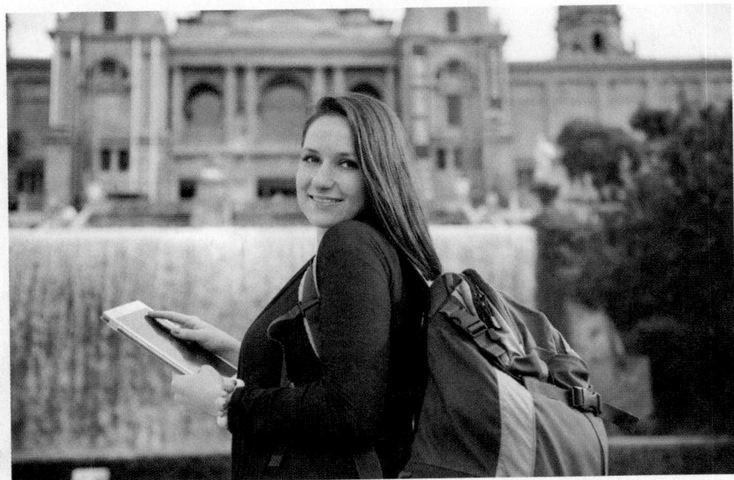
Halfpoint/Fotolia

Yet young women and men also fear their goals will be hard to achieve and may prove out of reach. Worried about finding the right partner and integrating family with work, they are pursuing what I describe as fallback strategies in young adulthood. Young women and men both emphasize the importance of work as a central source of personal identity and financial well-being, but this outlook leads them to pursue different strategies. Women are more likely

Figure 12.13 Ideals and Fallback Positions of Young Women and Men

SOURCE: From *The Unfinished Revolution: Coming of Age in a New Era of Gender, Work, and Family* (p. 320), by Kathleen Gerson, 2011, New York: Oxford University Press. Copyright Oxford University Press. Used with permission.

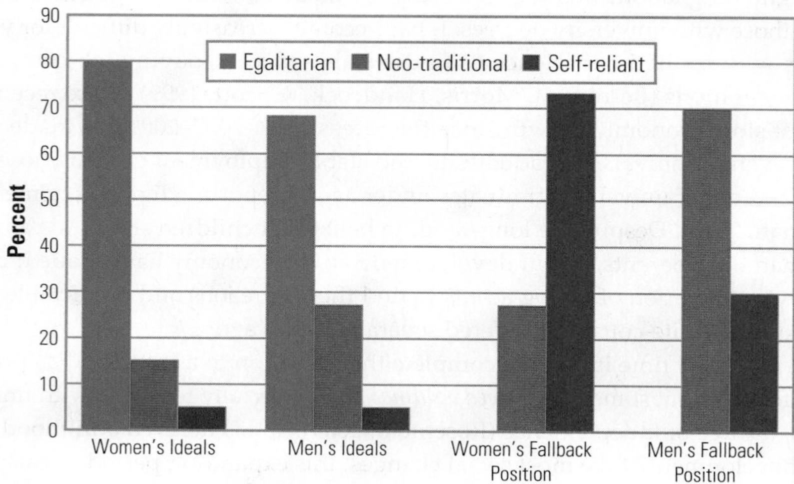

to see paid work as essential to their own and their family's survival and to prefer self-reliance over economic dependence within a traditional marriage (see Figure 12.13). Men, in contrast, are more likely to worry about the costs of equal sharing and to prefer a neo-traditional arrangement that allows them to put work first and rely on a partner for the lion's share of caregiving.

Images of young people avoiding adulthood and "failing to launch" cannot capture the complex experiences of today's young women and men. There is no evidence that young people want to create a brave new world of disconnected individuals. In the long run, they hope to balance autonomy with a satisfying, committed relationship. However, they also believe they need to take time to create a financial base, discover their own strengths and needs, prepare for an uncertain economy that demands more education and training, and find a partner whose family vision meshes with their own.

12.5 What Social Policies Around the World Best Support Changing Families?

Deborah Davis/PhotoEdit, Inc.

Families in Comparative Perspective

Families of all classes, races, and ethnicities are changing, but different groups are changing in different ways. Single-parent families, for example, are more likely to be found among African American households, where 65 percent of children live with either one parent or neither parent, compared to 34 percent of non-Hispanic white children, 24 percent of Hispanic children, and 17 percent of Asian children (Blow, 2008). And while the overwhelming majority of North Americans eventually marry, marriage rates have declined most steeply for the less educated and for members of racial minorities, where men's school and work opportunities are increasingly being squeezed (Porter & O'Donnell, 2006). Because economic inequality is linked to family differences, with a disproportionate number of poor and economically disadvantaged families found among single-parent families (most of whom are headed by women who cannot count on the economic contributions of a partner's earnings), it follows that ethnic minorities are also more likely to be overrepresented in lower income levels (see Figure 12.14).

Since the challenges facing families today are intertwined with changes taking place in other institutions, such as the economy and the workplace, individual households cannot navigate these challenges on their own. In the next section, we examine some of the ways that other countries support families, and how these examples point to ways the United States might be able to improve the way it helps families thrive.

Social Policy Around the World

12.5.1 Compare and contrast government policies toward families around the world.

From Europe to the Far East, all of the postindustrial nations have experienced similar social shifts, including a rise in women's labour force participation, the postponement of marriage and childbearing, and the proliferation of diverse family forms. Yet the policy responses to these shared demographic trends are quite distinct. The United States lags far behind many other postindustrial societies in adopting social policies that support new family forms. France, for example, allows any two people to form a civil union that bestows all the legal rights and responsibilities of a married couple.

Figure 12.14 Share of Never Married, by Race, Ethnicity, and Education (United States)

SOURCE: The Pew Research Center, http://www.pewsocialtrends.org/2010/11/18/the-decline-ofmarriage-and-rise-of-new-families/3/

NOTE: Ages 18 and older. Hispanics are of any race. Whites and blacks include only non-Hispanics.

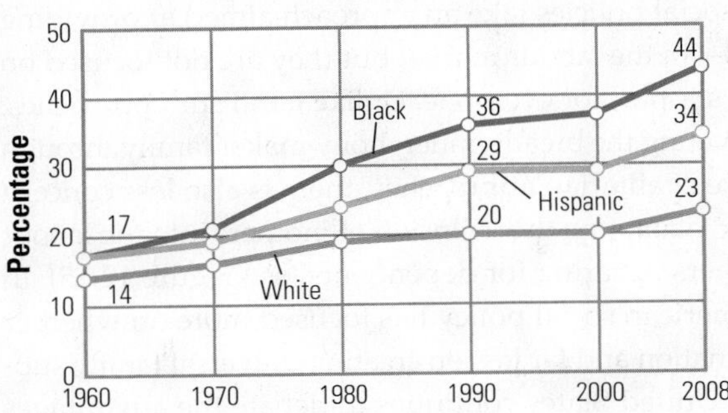

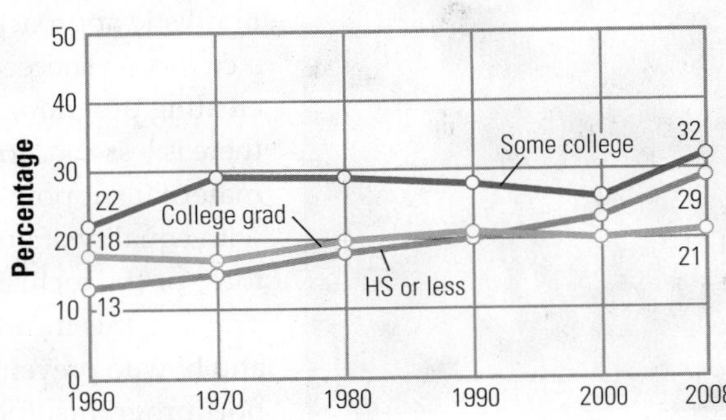

North American parents often struggle to find affordable, high-quality childcare without help from the government. Low-income families, in some cases, can find subsidized childcare if they meet certain criteria, but nonpoor families are usually not eligible for such services. In Japan, a chronic childcare shortage makes finding day-care slots a competitive process. Worried that women would choose either a career or motherhood, in 2008 Japan announced a 10-year goal of providing working parents with day care for children ages 1–5.

Tetra Images/Alamy Stock Photo

Reuters Photographer/Reuters

France, along with all the Scandinavian countries, also offers universal childcare, and Scandinavian countries guarantee paid parental leave for everyone (Gornick & Myers, 2009). In Sweden, Iceland, and Norway, these leave policies not only support employed mothers; they also encourage fathers' parental involvement by specifying that a father cannot transfer his leave time to a mother or anyone else but must instead "use it or lose it." In Canada, the parental leave may be split between the mother and father. Most Europeans can also build their families without regard to such considerations as access to health care and education, which are available to everyone whether or not they are married or employed full-time.

There are important differences across Europe in how governments try to help families. Some countries, especially in Scandinavia, have developed policies based on the principle of providing universal family supports regardless of who you are. This egalitarian approach covers a range of specific policies, including paid parental leaves, universal day care, and antidiscrimination workplace policies along with universal health care and free education. Taken together, this approach aims to reduce both gender and class inequality while providing for children's well-being regardless of the kind of family they live in.

In contrast, other countries, such as Italy, have maintained an approach that encourages maternal care but does not support women's employment or more egalitarian family forms. This familistic approach offers mothers with children, even if they are single, economic incentives for bearing children and staying home to rear them. It does not, however, stress day care, antidiscrimination at work, or other measures that would facilitate employment among mothers, encourage fathers to share in caretaking, or generally acknowledge the rise of new family and gender arrangements.

Childcare is one of the most important ways in which governments can support families, especially now that more mothers than ever before are in paid employment throughout the world. Policies toward childcare vary widely from country to country. The Scandinavian example of providing paid parental leave to fathers as well as mothers on a "use it or lose it" basis is especially instructive, since it encourages greater involvement by fathers who cannot transfer their paid leave days to a child's mother. In Sweden, parents may take up to 480 total parental leave days when a child is born or adopted, and the government subsidizes childcare after that. In France, the government provides free preschool for children from two years of age. A system of "child minders," who receive training, undergo regular inspections, and can care for up to five children at a time, supplements these day-care centres with high-quality help.

Social Policy in the United States

12.5.2 Discuss how U.S. social policy on family life measures up to that of comparable nations.

Where does the United States fit in this picture? Unlike either egalitarian or familistic approaches, U.S. social policies take an approach aimed at providing a chance to succeed—or fail—in the labour market but they are not focused on creating programs of family support for everyone. Unlike familistic approaches, there is less concern for re-creating the breadwinner–homemaker family through maternal support, but unlike egalitarian approaches, there is also less concern with equality of outcomes or facilitating the inclusion of mothers into the labour force or the inclusion of fathers in caring for dependents (see Figure 12.15). In practice, this means that American social policy has focused more on whether and how to prevent discrimination and far less on creating universal family support programs. Indeed, the United States continues to debate the advantages

Figure 12.15 Parental Leave for Two-Parent Families in 21 Countries

SOURCE: From *Parental Leave Policies in 21 Countries: Assessing Generosity and Gender Equality* (Figure 1, p. 6), by Rebecca Ray, Janet Gornick, and John Schmitt, 2009, Washington, DC: Center for Economic Policy Research (http://cepr.net/documents/publications/parental_2008_09.pdf).

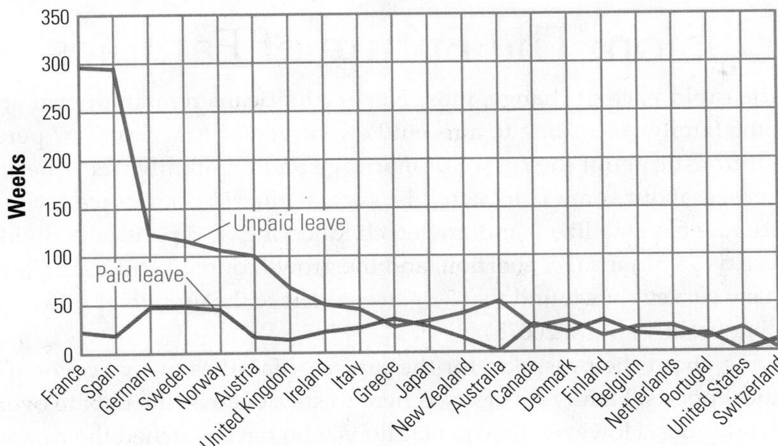

and disadvantages of the family revolution rather than accepting its irreversibility and restructuring other institutions to better fit the new realities.

Where Does the United States Go From Here?

12.5.3 Discuss how the United States might achieve a more effective, inclusive approach to family support.

What, then, would a more effective, inclusive policy approach look like? In an era of massive family change, the United States needs to think more broadly about what equal opportunity really means. Individuals live in families, and we cannot separate the fate of individuals from the well-being of their families. The nation thus needs family policies that reaffirm classic American values, such as equal opportunity, tolerance of diversity, and individual responsibility, but do so in the context of collective support for the diverse needs of the new family arrangements that are essential pieces of modern social life.

More concretely, this means a host of specific policies in diverse arenas: family support policies, workplace policies, and legislation to protect the vulnerable of all ages, family statuses, and sexual orientations. Legislative efforts need to encompass equal opportunities for all kinds of families and interpersonal relationships, including single parents, same-sex couples, dual-earner families, and single adults. At the workplace, antidiscrimination policies need to be expanded to include what Joan Williams (2000) calls family responsibility discrimination, so that those who shoulder responsibilities for caring for others will not face huge penalties for devoting time to this essential but undervalued task. Family support policies should thus aim to reduce poverty and inequality along with creating a wider institutional framework for dependent care, including the care of children, the elderly, and anyone else in need of it. Community childcare supports, in particular, will help employed parents and nurture the next generation. Jobs that offer flexible avenues for working and career building will not only help families integrate paid work and care work but also help employers attract and retain committed workers.

Antidiscrimination policies that protect the rights of all parents with caregiver responsibilities will not only even the playing field for employed mothers but also create fairer workplaces for men (of all sexual orientations and class positions) who wish to be involved as caretakers. No one policy can address all the challenges that twenty-first-century families face, but taken as a whole, these approaches will go a long way toward helping families develop their own strategies for meeting the challenges that await them in the decades to come.

Conclusion: The Future of Families

Despite the rapid pace of change, most North Americans remain upbeat about the future of the family. According to a recent Pew survey of Americans, 67 percent say they are optimistic about the future of marriage and the family. Yet Americans are also concerned about some family trends, such as the rise in divorce (even though the divorce rate has stabilized) and unwed childbearing, and politically divided over others, such as gay marriage, abortion, and the growth of paid childcare (Pew, 2010). Another Pew survey thus found that 71 percent believe the growth of unwed motherhood is a big problem (Pew, 2007b).

Thinking about the prospects for the future of families, we've covered a number of critical points. Family diversity is here to stay, even as the debate over family diversity continues. However, new generations who have watched their parents and other adults invent a mosaic of new living arrangements take for granted options that earlier generations could barely imagine. Facing their own conflicts about marriage, sexuality, work, and parenthood, young adults are increasingly weary of a divisive political rhetoric that blames families for conditions beyond their control. Most say they prefer a politics that favours a more tolerant vision that stresses similar needs rather than one that puts social groups in conflict. These aspirations point toward the possibility of a more inclusive politics that focuses on the common needs of diverse families and replaces an image of moral decline with a concern about realigning our social institutions to better fit the new circumstances of today's families.

Yet without social supports for more versatile ways of constructing families, there are good reasons for young people to be concerned about their chances of achieving these ideals. The rise of alternatives to permanent marriage means that sexual partnerships are necessarily more optional and fluid. And economic shifts, such as the rise of service-sector jobs and the decline of blue-collar ones, make women's participation in the world of paid work inevitable. These intertwined and reinforcing changes create a host of new options, but they are also on a collision course with other social institutions that remain based on a mid-twentieth-century model of static family forms. If families are films, not snapshots, then we need public discussions and social policies that see family life as an unfolding, unpredictable process in which anyone, at any time, may need some kind of help. In the context of this irreversible but unfinished family revolution, people need social supports for the diverse and changing families that exist today.

CHAPTER SUMMARY

The Big Questions Revisited 12

12.1 What Is a Family? To begin this chapter, we first needed to examine the meaning of the term *family*. What is a family, and what are the various ways to define it?

The Many Ways We Define *Family*

A Global and Historical Perspective

Learning Objective 12.1.1: Identify family forms that can be found throughout human history and across diverse societies and households.

Household or Kinship System?

Learning Objective 12.1.2: Explain how residence patterns and kinship systems contribute to different definitions of family.

12.2 **Why Are Families Changing?** To understand the contemporary debate over "family values," this section mapped out the competing views about the current state of the North American family, how we got here, and what we need to do in response.

Changing North American Familes: A Controversial Topic

The Family Values Perspective

Learning Objective 12.2.1: Discuss the concerns of proponents of the family decline perspective regarding the nature of families today.

The Economic Restructuring Perspective

Learning Objective 12.2.2: Discuss how the economic restructuring approach explains changing family arrangements.

The Gender Restructuring Perspective

Learning Objective 12.2.3: Discuss the mismatch between the structure of jobs and the caretaking needs of families.

12.3 **What Challenges Do We Face as We Develop Relationships and Balance Family and Work?** This section examined the decline of permanent marriage and the new contours of adult commitment, as well as the blurring of gender divisions and the rise of work–family conflict.

The New Contours of Adulthood Commitment

Love and Marriage

Learning Objective 12.3.1: Explain how marriage has become deinstitutionalized in today's society.

Mothers, Fathers, and Work–Family Conflict

Learning Objective 12.3.2: Discuss how the conflict between family needs and work pressures affects family life.

12.4 **What Is It Like to Grow Up in a Twenty-First-Century Family?** In this section, we discussed how the experiences of children transitioning into adulthood are very different from how they once were and what this means for today's children and young adults.

Growing Up in Today's Families

Growing Up With Working Parents

Learning Objective 12.4.1: Discuss the research on the effects of growing up in a household where both parents are employed.

Growing Up With Divorced or Single Parents

Learning Objective 12.4.2: Analyze the research on the effects of divorce and single parenthood on children.

Growing Up With Same-Sex Parents

Learning Objective 12.4.3: Discuss the research on the impact of same-sex parenthood on children.

The Changing Face of Childhood

Learning Objective 12.4.4: Identify the reasons why some family pathways remain stable or improve, while others face difficulty.

Parenting Values and Styles

Learning Objective 12.4.5: Explain the relationship between class cultures, childrearing practices, and the transmission of inequality from one generation to the next.

Becoming an Adult and Forming Families

Learning Objective 12.4.6 Identify the benefits and drawbacks of the extended period of early adulthood experienced by young adults in North America.

12.5 **What Social Policies Around the World Best Support Changing Families?** Finally, we placed American family life today in a comparative perspective. This section examined how other countries have approached social policies for families and how Americans can learn from their tactics.

Families in Comparative Perspective

Social Policy Around the World

Learning Objective 12.5.1: Compare and contrast government policies toward families around the world.

Social Policy in the United States

Learning Objective 12.5.2: Discuss how U.S. social policy on family life measures up to that of comparable nations.

Where Does the United States Go From Here?

Learning Objective 12.5.3: Discuss how the United States might achieve a more effective, inclusive approach to family support.

Learn the Terms

care work (p. 334)
cohabitation (p. 332)
conjugal family (p. 332)
egalitarian relationship (p. 329)
family values (p. 326)
kin (p. 324)
kinship system (p. 324)
nuclear family (p. 325)
patrilocal (p. 321)
polygamy (p. 321)
same-sex marriage (p. 322)
serial relationships (p. 332)
second shift (p. 336)

Chapter 13
Sociology of Religion
by Gerald Marwell*

SCPhotos/Alamy Stock Photo

It is important to almost all religious communities that their young become believers and practitioners. They incorporate children into aspects of their religion as early as they can. Here, very young Indigenous peoples participate in tribal religious practices as part of this learning process.

Learning Objectives

13.1.1 Compare and contrast the different sociological definitions of religion.

13.1.2 Identify the big five or six religions of the world and discuss the variety and diversity of contemporary religion.

13.1.3 Compare and contrast the concepts of animism and paganism.

13.1.4 Discuss the functions of religion as a social institution.

*An earlier version of this chapter was coauthored by Adam Murphree. Gerald Marwell (1937–2013) passed away after completing this chapter for the first edition of *The Sociology Project*. We believe that the revisions and updates to the chapter for the second edition would have met with Jerry's approval.

13.1.5 Describe the role that denominations and congregations play in organizing religious activity in a community.

13.2.1 Discuss the causes of segregation in American churches.

13.2.2 Discuss the relationship between class stratification and religious choice.

13.2.3 Explain who converts to what denomination or religion, and why.

13.2.4 Identify who is drawn to emerging new religions.

13.3.1 Discuss the relationship between gender and religiosity in various major religions.

13.3.2 Explain why older people tend to be more religious.

13.4.1 Explain why it is difficult to distinguish religious conflict from ethnic or class conflict.

13.4.2 Discuss the longstanding religious conflict between Hindus and Muslims in India.

13.5.1 Describe the religiosity in Europe.

13.5.2 Compare and contrast religiosity in the United States to other developed countries of the world.

13.5.3 Identify signs that religiosity in America is declining.

13.5.4 Identify possible explanations for the increase in religious persons around the world.

The late Gerald Marwell always began teaching his course on the sociology of religion at New York University by asking each student to describe his or her religious upbringing and present beliefs. Forty years ago, most of Marwell's students would have identified with one of the traditionally dominant religious traditions in North America—Catholic, Baptist, Jewish, and so forth. Today, the most common responses are very different: "I believe in God, but don't go to church"; "If following a particular religion makes someone happy, I'm not going to look down on them"; "When you get down to it, I think all religions are really about the Golden Rule—treat others the way you want to be treated."

To be sure, NYU students are not necessarily typical of other university students, much less all North American youth (in the United States almost half never enroll in college or university, whereas in Canada almost 80 percent attend some kind of post-secondary institution). Fortunately, sociologist Christian Smith and his colleagues (Smith, 2009) interviewed a representative sample of young people aged 18 to 23. Although they found many conventionally religious people in this age group, as well as a substantial number of **atheists** (who do not believe in any god) and **agnostics** (who do not believe that God's existence or nonexistence is knowable), Smith's results are surprisingly similar to what Marwell observed among his students.

Smith (2009, p. 154) calls the most common religious pattern among today's youth "moralistic therapeutic deism (MTD)," which he describes in terms of five "key beliefs":

1. A god exists who created and ordered the world and watches over human life.
2. God wants people to be good to each other, as taught in the Bible and by most religions.
3. The central goal of life is to be happy and to feel good about oneself.

The Big Questions

1. **What is religion, and what are its functions?** Sociologists have no single agreed-upon definition of religion. Nevertheless, they understand that the actual religious behaviour of people in every religion is enormously variable and fluid. In this section, we examine the incredible number of religions throughout the world and throughout history, as well as the idea that religion is a social institution and that organized religion has important social functions.
2. **How does social structure impact religious choice?** With all the religions in the world, how do people pick a religion for themselves? Here we look at the patterns of religious choice, including the impact of race, ethnicity, and social class.
3. **Why are some people more religious than others?** In this section, we discuss differences in religiosity, focusing especially on gender and age.
4. **Why do people kill each other in the name of religion?** In this section, we ask why there has been so much religious conflict historically and in the present, and discuss the difficulty of distinguishing religious conflict from ethnic or class conflict.
5. **What is the future of religion?** We save for last what has historically been the most important question for sociologists of religion: Is secularization or increased religiosity the future of religion?

4. God does not need to be particularly involved in one's life except when God is needed to solve a problem.
5. Good people go to heaven when they die.

Smith argues that MTD is moralistic because young people believe the basic job of religion is to help us be good people—to have good morals. They also tend to think that most people are intrinsically good and that all religions help people to stay good, mostly because all religions teach some version of the golden rule. MTD is therapeutic because most young people believe that religion in moderation is generally, if not always, good for people. It helps people be happier and healthier. It gets them through crises. It gives them groups to belong to and share with. It makes for closer families with shared memories and feelings.

However, MTD is a very general description of religious belief. Perhaps reflecting North America's historical idealization of religious tolerance, all religions are seen as essentially true at their core—the concept of **deism** refers to a belief in God regardless of the form he or she takes. At the same time, elaborated religious **doctrine**—the set of official beliefs and rules of particular religions—is perceived by many young people as being unrealistic and perhaps even boring. Established religions are seen as often unreasonable in their repressive rules, unscientific beliefs, and overbearing organizations. Many young people are suspicious of organized religion. They attend church rarely, if at all, except to be with their families.

Religious people, and the real religions they practise, are more complex and internally contradictory than we tend to think. For sociologists of religion, this means that we get to study the wonder of the human condition and complex cultures and the consistencies and oddities of human behaviour, all at the same time.

13.1 What Is Religion, and What Are Its Functions?

Hindustan Times/Contributor/Getty Images

A Sociological Understanding of Religion

The study of religion and society occupies a unique place in the history of sociology. The first intellectual to call himself a sociologist, Auguste Comte, thought that sociology would lead to a modern "religion of humanity," with scholars such as himself fulfilling the functions of priests. More importantly, religion was central to the classic work of two of the most-read sociologists in history, Max Weber and Émile Durkheim. Weber wrote what is perhaps the most frequently read book in sociology, *The Protestant Ethic and the Spirit of Capitalism* (Weber, 1904/1958), in which he argued that the ascetic form of Protestantism that flourished in nineteenth-century North America was critical in the development of full-blown capitalism.

Perhaps the second most-read sociological book of all time is Durkheim's *Suicide: A Study in Sociology* (Durkheim, 1898/1951), which begins with a puzzle rooted in religion: Why do areas populated mainly by Protestants have much higher suicide rates than areas populated mostly by Catholics? Later in his career Durkheim wrote perhaps the most profound and influential sociological treatise on religion ever written, *The Elementary Forms of Religious Life* (Durkheim 1912/2001), in which he examined the religion of Australian Aborigines and proposed that the idea of God basically represented the community or society.

In this chapter, we walk in the footsteps of giants as we investigate issues foundational to a sociological understanding of religion.

Defining Religion

13.1.1 Compare and contrast the different sociological definitions of religion.

Many sociologists are (and were) deeply religious people of one faith or another; today, while religion is important to many in their private lives, many would consider themselves atheists and almost all seek to study religion through a scientific, not theological, lens (Gross & Simmons, 2009). Privately, religious sociologists may hope that their work supports the argument for religion, even for their own religion. However, no sociologist today with a reasonable reputation would argue professionally and publicly that his or her beliefs are the one and only true faith and that all others are wrong. Sociologists understand their field as part of the scientific approach to human affairs, and they know that science cannot answer a question that is so certainly a matter of faith.

Furthermore, sociologists do not even agree as to what they mean when they describe "religion." There are many different and conflicting definitions in the literature. I have found it instructive to focus on two distinctive approaches: one that emphasizes sacredness, and a contrasting definition that emphasizes the supernatural. In *The Elementary Forms of Religious Life*, Durkheim (1912/2001) defines religion as the way that societies deal with things that are **sacred**—those things that are not just mundane or everyday parts of life but are worthy of awe and special treatment, such as sacred objects like the Torah, sacred behaviours like the communion ritual, sacred places like Mecca, sacred times like Easter day, and sacred people such as monks or the Dalai Lama. In other words, religion creates symbolic boundaries between certain people, objects, times, places, and other things and events in the world.

Grant Rooney/Alamy Stock Photo

There may be no god in Buddhism, but these Thai Buddhists seem to be praying to something during a religious festival.

Compare Durkheim's definition with one used by the contemporary sociologists of religion Rodney Stark and Roger Finke: "Religion is concerned with the supernatural; everything else is secondary. . . . [It] consists of very general explanations of existence, including the terms of exchange with a god or gods" (Stark & Finke, 2000, pp. 89–91). In this view, religion is a set of ideas describing the relations between the natural and the **supernatural**, including how earthly beings can obtain goods from otherworldly entities, be they healthy crops or eternal salvation.

Many interesting questions are raised by the differences between these two definitions. If supernatural beings are required for religion, where does that leave Buddhism, the "religion" of about 360 million people? Buddhist doctrine is formally atheistic—no god or gods are part of the belief system. However, many practising Buddhists act as if they believe in spirits, and many of them pray to statues of the Buddha for assistance. Furthermore, because most Buddhists believe in the transmigration of souls (i.e., reincarnation), do "souls" qualify as supernatural beings?

Alternatively, defining religion as the way people deal with the sacred means that religion has plenty of room not only for Buddhism but also for a number of phenomena not conventionally thought of as religion. For example, a good case can be made for including the revolutionary communism of early twentieth-century Europe or Chinese Marxism under Mao Zedong as a religion.

We usually call political worldviews such as communism ideologies, not religions. Interestingly, however, religion also fits the common definition of **ideology**—a set of ideas that constitutes one's goals, expectations, and actions. If sacredness turns ideology into religion, consider the fact that communism has its sacred texts, in *The Communist Manifesto* and Mao's "Little Red Book"; its sacred prophets in Lenin, Mao, and Marx; and even its mystical beliefs, such as the historical necessity of the triumph of the working class. Thus, many sociologists do consider communism the equivalent of a religion. Perhaps an even better case can be made for Nazism. For most Germans of his time in power, Adolf Hitler became a god, or at least a sacred being. Hitler's book *Mein Kampf* (1925) was a sacred text; racial purity and Aryan superiority were promoted as sacred ideas. Conquest of other countries was pursued with religious fervour.

The "sacredness" definition of religion has led sociologists to recognize a common, even necessary form of religion known as **civil religion**. Consider the way Canadians and Americans feel about their constitutions—for most, it is a sacred text. Many feel similarly

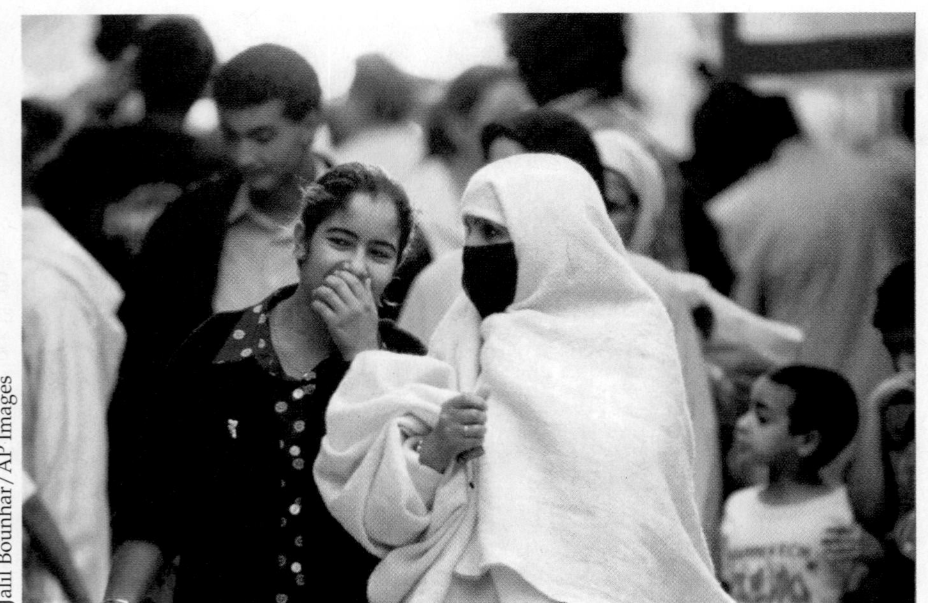
Jalil Bounhar/AP Images

In Morocco, some Muslim women are veiled, some are not. Such differences can even be found within the same family, as with this mother and daughter.

about the flag, a sacred symbol, or about the country's birthday (July 4 in the United States, and July 1 in Canada), as a day of ritual and worship at the shrine of their sacred countries. Also consider the frequently repeated claim that "Ground Zero," where the World Trade Center in New York City once stood, is "sacred ground." According to what religion is it sacred? Not Protestantism or Hinduism, or any other recognized religion. From a Durkheimian perspective, the civil religion that makes these things sacred is the same as all religions—it is the worship of the community and society, from which all good things eventually flow and on which we are completely dependent. In that sense, all religions are "civil" religions.

Regardless of which definition they use, sociologists take a rather fluid approach to understanding religion. Religion is not defined by one set of doctrines or another. Instead, it is defined by the behaviours, beliefs, and commitments of the people of a group or society. Yes, doctrine matters, because religious doctrine is also the product of people's behaviours (writings, arguments), beliefs, and commitments. But doctrine is only part of what defines a working religion.

In the real world the rigidities of doctrine are often neglected by the faithful. For example, in Catholic doctrine it is clearly wrong to use contraception, yet polling reveals that roughly 9 out of 10 Canadian Catholics approve of the practice and believe that it is acceptable for couples and teenagers to use; 98 percent of sexually active Catholic women in the United States have done just that (Guttmacher Institute, 2011; Todd, 2013), most without a moral qualm. What, then, is the correct description of the Catholic religion? As another example, most Islamic scholars agree that the Koran only asks women to dress "modestly" and does not require them to be veiled in public. Yet women in Saudi Arabia must be fully veiled or risk arrest. The Wahhabi sect that controls religious matters in Saudi Arabia insists that wearing the veil is an essential part of being a good Muslim. In other words, it is part of their Islam. In Morocco, some women who think of themselves as pious do not wear a veil, while others do. And these women, with different opinions, can be seen everywhere walking and talking together in friendship.

Even more fluid are the religious traditions and practices of most East Asian societies (Demerath, 2003). In Japan, Korea, China, much of Indonesia, and elsewhere, people seem to feel free to combine elements from different religions, almost using religion as a toolbox with applications to a variety of problems and life issues. For example, in Korea, Confucian prayers for one's ancestors may be combined with Christian prayers for God's help or grace. The Japanese often celebrate births according to Shinto (Japanese folk religion) traditions, marry in Christian rituals, bury their dead with Buddhist ceremonies—and call themselves nonreligious.

The Incredible Variety of Religions

13.1.2 Identify the big five or six religions of the world and discuss the variety and diversity of contemporary religion.

Instead of asking what the one true faith might be, sociologists from Weber and Durkheim onward have tried to understand the empirical reality before their eyes: the hundreds or thousands of different contemporary and historical religions to be found around the world and the complex overlaps, syntheses, conflicts, and differences among these faiths. What made and makes religion so fascinating is that it is everywhere, in societies remarkably different from one another, and that it is so clearly produced socially and thus requires a sociological explanation.

To begin to grasp the incredible variety of religions that exist, study the information provided in Table 13.1. Table 13.1 includes only religions that are active and involve relatively large numbers of people (1 million or more adherents) today. It does not include religions that are from the past or that are estimated to have fewer than 1 million adherents today. (The inclusion of Scientology is also

Table 13.1 Major Religions of the World

	Est. Adherents	Established	Where Originated
The Big Five/Six			
1. Christianity Includes Catholic, Orthodox, Protestant	2,200 million	30 CE	Israel
2. Islam Sunni, Shi'a	1,300 million	622 CE	Saudi Arabia
3. Hinduism	900 million	Prehistory	India
4. Chinese Syncretism	400 million	Prehistory	China
5. Buddhism Theravada, Mahayana, Vajrayana	360 million	520 BCE	India
6. Nonreligion Atheism, agnosticism	1,100 million		
Christianity-Related			
7. Judaism Orthodox, Conservative, Reform. Religion of the Hebrews, the "Chosen People." The root religion of Christian and Muslim monotheism. This-world and ethically oriented.	14 million	1300 BCE	Israel
8. Mormonism Consider themselves Christians. Believe Book of Mormon, not accepted by other Christian groups, is divinely inspired. Emphasize self-discipline and family devotion.	12 million	1830 CR	USA
9. Spiritualism Focus on understanding and communicating with disembodied entities using methods such as seances and automatic writing. Believe all people have immortal spirits.	11 million	1850 CE	Canada, USA, UK, France
10. Seventh-day Adventists Affirm Protestant beliefs. Adhere to the teachings of Ellen White, considered a prophet. Emphasize healthy living. Follow strict dietary codes and observe a day of rest on Saturday.	10 million	1863 CE	Canada, USA
11. Jehovah's Witnesses Affirm Christian God but believe the Trinity is unbiblical. Believe 144,000 chosen will go to heaven, while others live forever on a new earth. Emphasize evangelism and healthy living.	7 million	1879 CR	Canada, USA
12. Unification (Moonies) Believe founder Sun Myung Moon is the second coming of Christ. Emphasizes forming harmonious families to bring about the Kingdom of God on Earth.	1–3 million	1954 CE	South Korea
13. Aladura Mix Anglican and African rituals, focusing on healing and this-worldly salvation. Prominent role played by prophets who are believed to have extraordinary healing powers.	1 million	1918 CE	Nigeria
14. Rastafari Believe God (Jah) became incarnate in Haile Selassie. Emphasize worldly salvation, freedom from oppression, and return to Africa. Practise dietary restrictions and ritual marijuana use.	1 million	1920 CE	Jamaica
Hinduism-Related			
15. Sikhism Believe salvation consists of escaping the cycle of reincarnation and uniting with God. Emphasize moderate living and distinctive dress, including the turban, that symbolizes devotion.	23 million	1500 CE	India

(Continued)

Table 13.1 *Continued*

	Est. Adherents	Established	Where Originated
16. Jainism Believe that the soul is eternal, uncreated, and can attain divinity. Practise complete nonviolence, including toward animals, and asceticism. Meditate through chanting mantras.	4 million	550 BCE	India
Far Eastern (Chinese, Buddhist) Religion–Related			
17. Taoism Believe in living according to the Tao, the principle behind everything that exists, to achieve inner peace and longevity. Yin and yang. Cultivate detachment from worldly concerns.	20 million	550 BCE	China
18. Falun Gong Focus on regulating the body's vital energy through stretching and meditation exercises. Believe adherents can gain superhuman powers through these practices.	10 million	1992 CE	China
19. Confucianism Emphasize ethical practices. Cultivate virtues such as loyalty, honesty, and concern for others. Focus on maintaining social harmony. Not concerned with supernatural forces or beings.	5 million	500 BCE	China
20. Shinto (Japanese folk) Believe in spiritual entities called *kami*. Practise rituals focused on securing blessings and avoiding evil through calling on the kami. Kami are believed to reside in shrines.	2–4 million	<300 BCE	Japan
Composites of Major Religions			
21. Baha'i Believe god has successively revealed himself through the prophets of major religious traditions. Practise daily prayer and hold monthly communal feasts.	5–7 million	1863 CE	Iran
22. Cao Dai Emphasize the underlying similarity of all religions. Venerate a diverse array of saints including political, religious, and artistic figures. Salvation is escaping the cycle of reincarnation.	4–6 million	1926 CE	Vietnam
New Religious Movements			
23. New Age Diverse and personalized, practises using tools and techniques such as crystals, tarot cards, astrology, and yoga. Tend to see the divine as an impersonal force. Believe in reincarnation.	5 million	1900s CE	Canada, USA, Europe
24. Wicca Generally believe in coequal god and goddess as well as lesser deities. Worship and rituals occur in covens or individually. Core principle is "Do what you will as long as no one is harmed."	1–3 million	1930s CE	UK
25. Scientology Participate in special counselling sessions ("auditing") to purify mind and spirit and to unlock inner potential. Church materials and auditing sessions provided in exchange for donations.	(70,000)/2 million	1954 CE	USA

SOURCE: Based on data from *The Big Religion Chart: Comparison Chart*, 2016 (http://religionfacts.com/big_religion_chart.htm). Copyright 2016 by ReligionFacts.

problematic, in that although the movement claims more than 2 million adherents, outside estimates are as low as 70,000; but we have included it here.) And even as a picture of contemporary religion, Table 13.1 is very approximate and incomplete. A complete and nuanced listing would take at least a book. For example, to save space we have compressed Roman Catholics, Eastern Orthodox, Baptists, and other religions into a single category: Christianity. The adherents of those sects might strongly disagree with being lumped together. At the same time, we give separate space to Jehovah's Witnesses and Mormons, whose adherents consider themselves Christians but also have crucial additional beliefs and doctrines that make them very different from the rest of Christendom (and would not be considered "Christians" by most other Christians). The table also combines Sunni, Shi'ite, and Sufi Muslims into a single category, which also does not capture the very important differences among these different groups of Muslims. In fact, all of the major religions had early periods in which geographically separated areas

Figure 13.1 A Global View of Religion

Six countries are shown as split Islam/Christianity: Bosnia and Herzegovina, Côte d'Ivoire, Kazakhstan, Nigeria, Tanzania, and Eritrea.

Based on data from *CIA World Factbook*, by United States Central Intelligence Agency, 2012, New York: Skyhorse; *ReligionFacts* (http://www.religionfacts.com/); *Eurobarometer 225: Social Values, Science, and Technology*, by European Commission, 2005, Luxembourg: Office for Official Publications of the European Communities (http://ec.europa.eu/COMMFrontOffice/PublicOpinion/index.cfm/Survey/getSurveyDetail/yearFrom/1973/yearTo/2005/surveyKy/448).

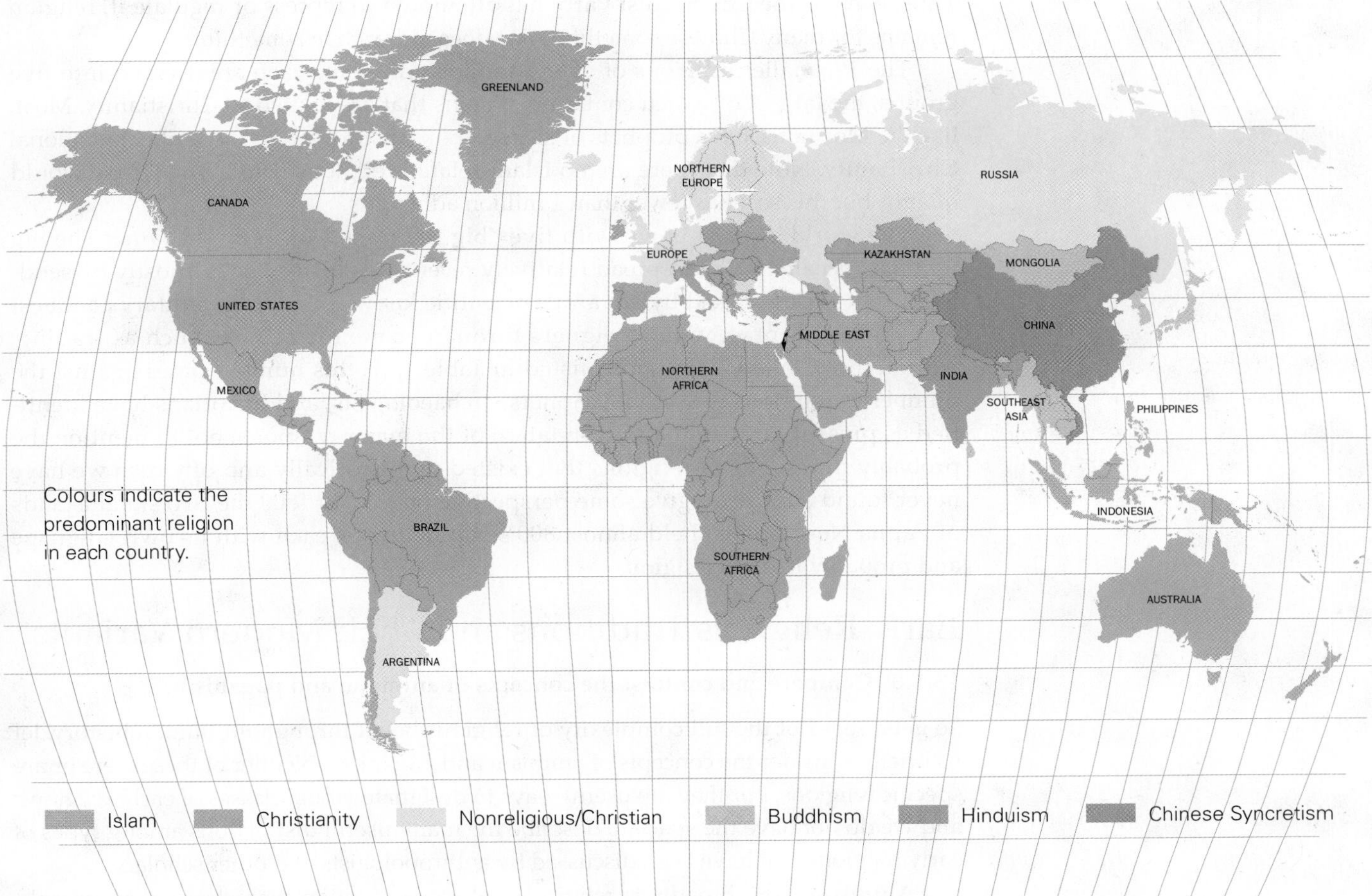

practised somewhat different versions. Only later were these forged into a relatively consistent pattern through force or compromise. Later still, perhaps, these experienced schisms produced newer and divergent versions of what was for a while considered a single religion.

To give you a sense of where the major religions of the world are practised, the map in Figure 13.1 shows where in the world the five (or six) religions with by far the most adherents dominate: Christianity, with approximately 2.2 billion adherents, is the largest; Buddhism, with 360 million, is the smallest. The sixth "religion" is **irreligion**—which refers to the absence of religion and which dominates numerically in many countries generally considered Christian, and also in many Far Eastern countries like China and Japan. The next largest religion in Table 13.1 is Sikhism. With approximately 23 million adherents, Sikhism has far fewer adherents than the "big five" (or six) religions.

Chinese syncretism is perhaps the most complicated of the major religious traditions. The Chinese have long exhibited a highly **syncretic** approach to religion, that is, one that combines elements of different religions, making their beliefs and practices difficult to classify. At one point, Chinese religious scholars articulated the "Unity of the Three Religions," which taught that Buddhism, Taoism, and Confucianism were all ultimately equivalent and complemented each other. Thus, people could mix the three traditions. The Chinese emperor typically employed Buddhist, Taoist, and Confucian religious figures in his court simultaneously. Similarly, today many Chinese turn to a diverse set of sources, including folk religion and practices we might consider superstition, to attempt to manipulate luck and secure favourable circumstances. Thus, even as the Communist Party has attempted to repress or regulate it, religion remains for many Chinese something one does rather than something one is.

The 19 smaller religions of over 1 million adherents each are divided into five groups, the largest of which contains religions that are related to Christianity. Most, like the Mormons, have prophets or sacred books in addition to those of conventional Christianity. Note that there are no Islam-related religions listed. The Druze would qualify, but this sect has fewer than 1 million adherents.

The world did not begin with five "big religions," or even with one. The big religions became so widespread relatively recently as history goes, mostly by sending missionaries backed by advanced scientific knowledge, or by military conquest or increased contact with foreigners through economic activity such as trading. Although there are 25 religions listed in Table 13.1, this number pales against the number of religions that ethnographers, archaeologists, and historians have identified as present prior to the consolidation of the major religions, not to mention the probably thousands of religions that existed prehistorically and of which we have never found a trace. To give some perspective on this, in 1800 the two small islands of Papua New Guinea held almost 800 separate tribes, each with its own language and probably its own religion.

Early Religious Traditions and Their Modern Variants

13.1.3 Compare and contrast the concepts of animism and paganism.

To get a sense of the full complexity of religious belief throughout human history, let us briefly consider the concepts of animism and paganism. Neither of these were or are specific religions, but they are useful ways to designate whole classes of early religions, and we do not have the space to describe the many useful distinctions among types of early religions that have been discussed by anthropologists and other scholars.

Animism refers broadly to religions that ascribe human characteristics to animals, plants, and inanimate objects such as rocks and mountains; see "spirits" as present and active in the world; and/or believe in some underlying force that animates everything from the weather to human activity. These kinds of religious thinking, which often lead to ritual practices to appease the spirits or harness the forces, seem to be common in tribal cultures all over the world, although in wildly varying forms. Although it no longer dominates the world, animism has not died out. What are generally called "folk" religions such as those in China or Shinto in Japan have large elements of animism, and various major religions such as Islam are combined with folk animistic elements in places like Indonesia, as is Christianity with animism in parts of South America.

Paganism is a term coined by early Christians to refer to the other, **polytheistic** religions—those characterized by the worship of multiple gods—of their times, with Roman, Greek, and Babylonian paganism being their major referents. These religions generally envision a set of gods and attendants who rule the world and can be appealed to through ritual, prayer, and sacrifice. Pagan religions often created representations of these gods in concrete forms, or idols, which were central to their rituals. Paganism generally reflected the more centralized ideas of the empires and large societies that integrated and conquered tribal societies.

It survives today in consciously neopagan religions such as Wicca, and perhaps most prominently in the large and varied collection of Hindu gods and avatars. Radical Protestants frequently disparaged Catholicism as "pagan" because of its "excessive" reverence (idolatry) for Mary, its many saints, and its omnipresent statues and religious images.

Religion as a Social Institution

13.1.4 Discuss the functions of religion as a social institution.

Modern religions of the world are so diverse, complex, and dynamic that one might argue that religion differs with every individual. Mr. Y's Catholicism, which stresses the sense of belonging and the beauty of the liturgy, might be different from his wife's, which stresses the importance of obedience to God's laws and the sacredness of the family. Neither Mr. nor Mrs. Y knows much or cares about the intricate **theology**—discussions of the interpretation of religious matters—that mesmerizes their priest.

In fact, the authors of an influential contemporary analysis of religion, *Habits of the Heart* (Bellah, Madsen, Sullivan, Swidler, & Tipton, 1985), were particularly taken with the example of a woman named Sheila, who called her religion "Sheilaism." She described Sheilaism as taking the bits and pieces from various religions that she thought were useful or convincing and combining them into her own personal religion.

Such privatization of religion is an important contemporary trend. But it is not the central sociological reality about religion. Instead, religions are first and foremost what sociologists call **institutions**—structured and enduring practices of human life built around well-established rules or norms, and centred in important organizations (like the government, courts, churches, schools, or military). From a Durkheimian perspective, the primary social function of religion as an institution is the promotion of social order. Most actual religious organizations specialize in teaching and demanding that people follow societal norms—especially those thought of as the commandments of God or the gods or, as in Buddhism and Confucianism, the lessons of revered teachers or prophets. Religion is full of "oughts" (what is right) and "ought-nots" (what isn't), and of threats of punishment or failure in this world or the next if one does not follow these rules. In other words, religion is one of society's central mechanisms for social control over the behaviour of people. It is no accident that in many older societies it was the shamans, rabbis, imams, and priests who were also the judges in the legal system.

In most places around the world and in the past, there tended to be one dominant religion, often closely aligned with political power. Because religions tend to see themselves as the truth, they have long had a tendency to fight to dominate the community or society in which they are embedded. In small, early communities there was little deviation from a single set of animistic or pagan beliefs. This was the assumptive world that everyone shared, and one lived with it much as we believe in atoms or evolution.

In the Holy Roman Empire (ca. 800–1806 CE), there were minority religions, sometimes persecuted, sometimes not. Gradually, however, everyone was expected to be Catholic. But what came together later fell apart. After the sixteenth-century Protestant Reformation, the Anglican Church became the state church of England and the Lutheran Church became the state church in Sweden and throughout all of those parts of Europe where Protestantism had won definitive victories (not, for example, in France and Germany, where Catholics and Protestants were both entrenched). This is why North America's early legal commitment to religious **pluralism**—accepting many different religions, or all religions, as legitimate, along with the separation of church and state—was so important and so unique.

Denominations and Congregations: Serving the Needs of the Community

13.1.5 Describe the role that denominations and congregations play in organizing religious activity in a community.

Separation of church and state—one of the hallmarks of the American Revolution and now true in most but not all countries around the world—has allowed many flowers to bloom in the religious garden. Canada has no formal recognition of the separation between church and state; however, the protections provided for religious freedoms in the Canadian Charter of Rights and Freedoms are similar to those in the U.S. Constitution. Most of the world's major religious traditions contain several different types of groups under their umbrella. Known as **denominations**, these are organized religious groups with at least a few distinctive doctrines or practices that distinguish them from other such groups that are also adherents of the same religious tradition. After decades of immigration in the nineteenth and early twentieth centuries, Roman Catholicism became the largest Christian denomination in the United States, but it still represents only a minority of religious Americans. Most North Americans were and are today Protestants, but there are many denominations among Protestants: the Baptists are the largest, but there are many Presbyterians, Methodists, Congregationalists, and so forth; in Canada, the Presbyterians, Methodists, and Congregationalists united to become the United Church of Canada. By one measure there are more than 200 different denominations of Christianity in North America, and many of these have been further divided into competing branches. *The Encyclopedia of American Religions* (Melton, 2009), in its eighth edition, is an attempt to identify every single religious group in the United States and Canada and includes detailed descriptions of over 2,500 distinct religious groups. Table 13.2 identifies some (not all) of the different Protestant denominations in the United States and their relative size.

Table 13.2 Large Denominations and Protestant Religious Traditions

	Total Population	All Protestants	Evangelical Protestant Churches	Mainline Protestant Churches	Historical Black Protestant Churches
	%	%	%	%	%
Baptist	**17.2**	**33.5**	**41**	**10**	**64**
Southern Baptist Convention	6.7	13.1	26	0	0
Independent Baptist in the Evangelical Tradition	2.5	4.9	10	0	0
National Baptist Convention	1.8	3.5	0	0	26
American Baptist Churches in the USA	1.2	2.4	0	7	0
Independent Baptist in the Historical Black Tradition	0.5	0.9	0	0	7
Methodist	**6.2**	**12.1**	**1**	**30**	**9**
United Methodist Church	5.1	9.9	0	28	0
African Methodist Episcopal	0.4	0.7	0	0	6
Lutheran	**4.6**	**9.0**	**7**	**16**	**0**
Evangelical Lutheran Church in America	2.0	3.8	0	11	0
Lutheran Church, Missouri Synod	1.4	2.7	5	0	0
Nondenominational	**4.5**	**8.9**	**13**	**5**	**3**
Nondenominational evangelical churches	1.2	2.3	4	0	0
Nondenominational charismatic churches	0.5	1.0	2	0	0
Nondenominational fundamentalist churches	0.3	0.5	1	0	0
Pentecostal	**4.4**	**8.5**	**13**	**0**	**14**
Assemblies of God	1.4	2.8	5	0	0
Church of God in Christ	0.6	1.1	0	0	8
Church of God, Cleveland, Tennessee	0.4	0.7	1	0	0
Presbyterian	**2.7**	**5.2**	**3**	**10**	**0**
Presbyterian Church USA	1.1	2.2	0	6	0
Presbyterian Church in America	0.4	0.8	2	0	0
Restorationist	**2.1**	**4.0**	**6**	**2**	**0**
Church of Christ	1.5	3.0	6	0	0
Disciples of Christ	0.3	0.6	0	2	0

(Continued)

	Total Population	All Protestants	Evangelical Protestant Churches	Mainline Protestant Churches	Historical Black Protestant Churches
	%	%	%	%	%
Anglican/Episcopal	**1.5**	**3.0**	**<0.5**	**8**	**0**
Episcopal Church in the USA	1.0	2.0	0	6	0
Anglican Church	0.3	0.5	0	2	0
Holiness	**1.2**	**2.2**	**4**	**0**	**2**
Church of the Nazarene	0.3	0.5	1	0	0
Free Methodist Church	0.3	0.5	1	0	0
Congregationalist	**0.8**	**1.5**	**<0.5**	**4**	**0**
United Church of Christ	0.5	1.0	0	3	0
Adventist	**0.5**	**0.9**	**2**	**0**	**0**
Seventh-day Adventist	0.4	0.8	2	0	0
Reformed	**0.3**	**0.5**	**1**	**1**	**0**
Anabaptist	**<0.3**	**0.4**	**1**	**<0.5**	**0**
Pietist	**<0.3**	**<0.3**	**<0.5**	**0**	**0**
Friends	**<0.3**	**<0.3**	**0**	**1**	**0**
Other Evangelical/Fundamentalist	**0.3**	**0.5**	**1**	**0**	**0**
Other/Protestant Nonspecific	**4.9**	**9.5**	**7**	**14**	**8**
	51.3%	**100**	**100**	**100**	**100**

SOURCE: Based on data from the U.S. Religious Landscape Survey, Pew Forum on Religion and Public Life, Pew Research Center, 2007.

It is at the level of the denomination that we find much of the organization in what we call organized religion. Denominations train and ordain priests, ministers, rabbis, and imams. They may assist individual churches or synagogues in financial trouble. They frequently, if not always, determine the "correct" doctrine (although individual priests/ministers/imams/rabbis or other local religious leaders may not always follow those doctrines in their preaching). Denominations provide model liturgies to be followed and lessons to be taught in the church sanctuary and religious education programs.

It is within as well as between denominations that the "big" religious conflicts are fought. For example, several Episcopalian congregations recently left that denomination because the national Episcopalian leadership made an openly gay priest a bishop. When the Catholic Church decided to move from the Latin mass to one in the regional language of each society in the 1960s, so that parishioners could understand what was being said, many congregations threatened to defect—although in the end few did. The Church of Jesus Christ of Latter-day Saints (the Mormons) have suffered internal wars over polygamy (where a man may have more than one wife at the same time), which the church historically approved but had to disapprove if it wanted to be accepted under American law. Later, the Mormons fought over and eventually changed their original position forbidding black people from holding leadership positions. We may expect more internal conflicts in many denominations as they deal with the changing societies in which they function and the changing views of their members.

There are a growing number of churches, some very large, that declare themselves "nondenominational." These churches are now the fastest-growing segment of the church world. The leaders of these churches do not feel that they need some denominational leaders standing above them telling them what to do, telling them how to pray, or taking a share of their collections. So they declare themselves independent. Some of these churches, those with 2,000 or more members, are called **megachurches**. In any given week, the largest of these—currently Joel Osteen's Lakewood Church in Houston, which sits 16,000—may have 45,000 people attend its three services.

According to Mark Chaves (2004) and other religious scholars, however, denominations are not the key organizational aspect of North American religion. Instead, the most important level of organization is the local **congregation**—the specific church or temple or mosque that people actually attend.

Because congregations are founded and disbanded with great frequency, and because there are many institutions that may or may not be congregations, it is difficult to get exact figures for the number of congregations in North America. Nevertheless, it has recently been estimated that there are about 335,000 religious congregations in the United States alone (Chaves, 2004). Of these, about 300,000 are Protestant and kindred churches, and 22,000 are Catholic or Orthodox churches. Non-Christian religious congregations are estimated at about 12,000.

More than half of all congregations are regularly attended by fewer than 100 individuals. In other words, there are many small churches, often with part-time or unpaid ministers, or even no minister at all. However, more than half of all church attendance is actually in the largest churches (the top 10 percent in size). Interestingly, several of these large churches, including Lakewood, are nondenominational.

The enormous supply of churches must mean that there is a tremendous demand for church among North Americans. In fact, large numbers of North Americans do go to church regularly. In surveys, 40 to 45 percent of Americans—about 118 million people—report that they went to church the past week. However, it appears that Americans overstate their attendance. Research that counted people in the pews in one county found that only about 20 percent actually attended in a specific week—half of the 40 percent who claimed they had attended in a telephone survey. It seems that people who think of themselves as regular churchgoers don't want to "mislead" the survey by admitting they didn't go last week. And half of them didn't (Chaves, Hadaway, & Marler, 1993).

A Canadian survey reveals that the decline of religion is not as steep as sociologists once predicted, due to an influx of new Catholic and Muslim immigrants. Immigrant families are more inclined to attend church together, whereas among Canadian-born families those who attend church are more likely to be older than 55—that is, only the older members of the family attend. According to an Angus Reid Institute survey conducted with sociologist Reginald Bibby, "Among those born outside Canada, almost 40 percent are inclined to embrace religion while less a quarter reject it. Compare that to the Canadian-born, where the figures are levelling out: 29 percent embrace religion, while 27 per cent reject it" (Hutchins, 2015). Over the last four decades, secularization has increased among Christians, who make up approximately two-thirds of the religious population in Canada. Since the 1970s, the number of Canadians who identify as being Catholic has decreased from 47 percent to 39 percent, while those who identify as being Protestant has decreased even more sharply from 41 percent to 27 percent (Pew Research Center, 2013a). However, the number of Canadians who identify as belonging to other faiths, such as Islam, Hinduism, Sikhism, Buddhism, Judaism, and Eastern Orthodox Christianity, has been growing. Canadian census data (1971–2001) and the 2011 National Household Survey reveal that, "collectively, these smaller religious groups account for more than one-in-ten Canadians (11%) as of 2011, up from not quite one-in-twenty (4%) in 1981" (Pew Research Center, 2013a).

Communities come together to participate in a ritual, that is, a scripted collective activity that employs certain cherished symbols.

David Grossman/Alamy Stock Photo

Organized religion will not go away soon, at least in North America. And not only religious people like to go to church. Some who are not really believers in any religious doctrine, or even in God at all, still attend some religious services and may even describe themselves as religious. As Durkheim argued so long ago, many people go to church for the shared experience—the celebration of community, family, and common identity. As the many Jews in New York and Montreal who go to Christmas services and love the music know, and the many Christians who attend Jewish Passover seders know, people often love ritual—if not all ritual, at least the rituals they learn as part of their communities. Many people attend religious services on one or two days a year—Catholics going to Christmas Eve mass, Jews attending services on the High Holiday days, and so forth—which is a very minimal but nonetheless real involvement. Common rituals can be shared by all church members and are a sign of their togetherness. *Collective effervescence* is what Durkheim called it, and the church has always been important for providing that experience.

It would be fair to say no other institution in North America (aside from the government) provides as directly and personally for community needs. *Community* here does not mean some residential community. In an urban world, every city, and almost every suburb, is home to several congregations. The community of primary interest to each congregation is the community of co-worshippers, not the city or suburb (Chaves, 2004).

In most churches, membership qualifies you for help with all kinds of problems and for a variety of other services. The large congregations, attended by more than half of all churchgoers, are much more than religious institutions. They often provide alternatives to public schools, counselling for troubled parishioners, sports and social programs for teenagers, financial counselling, help with elderly parents, nursing homes, and even graveyards. Even small churches will help members in trouble, with visits to the sick and personal support when needed. However, Chaves (2004) warns that despite their charitable rhetoric, charity is actually a minor and sporadic activity of most congregations.

13.2 How Does Social Structure Impact Religious Choice?

Fotosearch RM/Age Fotostock

Patterns of Religious Choice

With all the religions in the world, how do people pick one religion as their own? Of course, this is a trick question. Most people don't sit down, consider a list of religions, and then choose to be one or the other. Most people are born into a religion—the religion of their parents—and throughout history most parents have belonged to the religion that has long been institutionalized in their society, community, or family. Thus, if you manage to hear about religions other than the one you are born into, you might decide to change, but the odds, and social pressure, are decidedly against that. Besides, most children love and respect their parents and are very likely to want to maintain their relationships by being like their parents in their views of the world.

In today's world most, if not all, people are aware that there are other religions than their own. They are also very aware that some form of irreligion (the absence of religion) is an alternative embraced by at least some people, somewhere. So, yes, many people change religions, or at least denominations. However, even in the United States, the most religiously pluralistic of all countries, it is estimated that only one-fifth of all people formally change their religions or denominations during their lifetimes (Newport, 2006). Given the fluidity of real religions, however, individuals may change their personal religious feelings or ideas or practices but remain within the same denomination over time.

Religious Segregation: Birds of a Feather

13.2.1 Discuss the causes of segregation in North American churches.

We do know that there are definite patterns regarding the social backgrounds of people who end up in different religions, denominations, and congregations. In North America, Sunday remains the most segregated day of the week and church the most segregated place in both Canada and the United States—and not just by race. They are also segregated by class and lifestyle and various forms of preferences. Adults attend churches voluntarily, so birds of a feather are permitted to flock together, and they do so even more than they do in other institutions (which are also segregated, although not as fully).

Perhaps the most important ingredients of North American church segregation, besides religion itself, are area of residence and social status. Different kinds of people tend to live in different places. Just look at the campus churches at your college or university. They are full of students who live on or near campus. This constitutes a group of people very much alike on all kinds of characteristics, including, to begin with, age and level of education.

Few congregations serve broad areas of a city or county. With a few exceptions, congregations tend to reside in neighbourhoods and to be seen as neighbourhood institutions. A congregation in the suburbs south of Chicago rarely attracts members from a northern suburb or from the city's core. Neighbourhoods tend be collections of people who are economically or ethnically similar. Throughout history, immigrants, and hence ethnic groups, have tended to move into areas where people they know already reside, particularly relatives and friends from home towns. They get help and a sense of comfort. The already beaten path is the way to helpful information and to safety. It is also the way to relevant churches. For example, consider the fact that 44 percent of the people living in Palisades Park, New Jersey, are of Korean ancestry (United States Census Bureau, 2010). This is no accident.

Indeed, Korean Americans (and their religious practices) provide an instructive illustration. There are a set of Protestant churches that conduct services in Korean or serve a primarily Korean American membership (see Chang, 2006, for a history). Although some came to the United States earlier, particularly after the Korean War, most Korean immigrants arrived after the 1965 change in American immigration law, which repealed the previous massive discrimination against non-Europeans. There are therefore many first- and second-generation Korean Americans in the United States.

In Korea, about 25 percent of the population describe themselves as Protestant. In the United States, however, 75 percent of Korean Americans are Protestants. To some extent this difference might reflect a special attraction to America for Korean Protestants (as compared with Korean Buddhists). More interesting, however, is the fact that almost 40 percent of Korean Protestants in the United States were previously not religious, or of another religion! That is a lot of converts and is the first clue for understanding the role and attraction of the ethnic church.

For Korean immigrants, the Korean church is much more than a religious institution. It is the centre of their community: a place they can speak Korean, eat Korean food, and share community and community values with others from a common culture. The church provides a kind of safe haven where immigrants and their children can negotiate the treacherous path from culture to culture. Were it really about religion, many or most Koreans could have attended established Protestant churches. They did not. The enormous number of Korean American converts to Christianity probably does not reflect some strong response to Christian doctrine. Instead, non-Christian Koreans clearly wanted, even needed, to associate themselves with the principal institutional centre of their community, the church. Durkheim would have it no other way.

The centrality of non-English-speaking churches for immigrant communities is not new in the United States. Polish-speaking Catholic congregations in Chicago served the same function. Italian immigrants struggled to have an Italian Catholic service and community in a New York diocese whose priests were mostly Irish, but they eventually succeeded. As Germans, Swedes, Chinese, and many other ethnic groups immigrated to North America, they did not fit very well into the established churches, even churches of their own denominations. German and Swedish Lutherans needed German- and Swedish-speaking versions of Lutheranism, where they could pray in the language they knew and mix comfortably with people from their own background. Thus, immigrants established thriving ethnic churches of their own. Today, many Catholic churches have special services for Spanish-speaking parishioners or services in Vietnamese on the West Coast, featuring Hispanic and Vietnamese priests, respectively.

Throughout North American history, however, as immigrant groups have become more settled and assimilated, their once flourishing churches have tended to disappear. Consider America's largest immigrant group—the Germans. Some came to America in colonial times, but the largest wave arrived in the first half of the nineteenth century and settled mostly in the upper Midwest. German Canadians also make up one of Canada's largest ethnic group of European origin; they came to Canada during this time period, originally settling in southern Ontario and Manitoba. Ethnic Germans who came to North America were a varied group—they thought of themselves as Prussians and Bavarians (Germany was not unified until 1871), and they were Catholic and Lutheran and Amish and Mennonite. But for all of them there were immigrant churches where German was spoken and where German culture was central to daily life. In Milwaukee and Chicago, there were German counterparts to the Polish Catholic Church. The Germans practically dominated American Lutheranism. By the

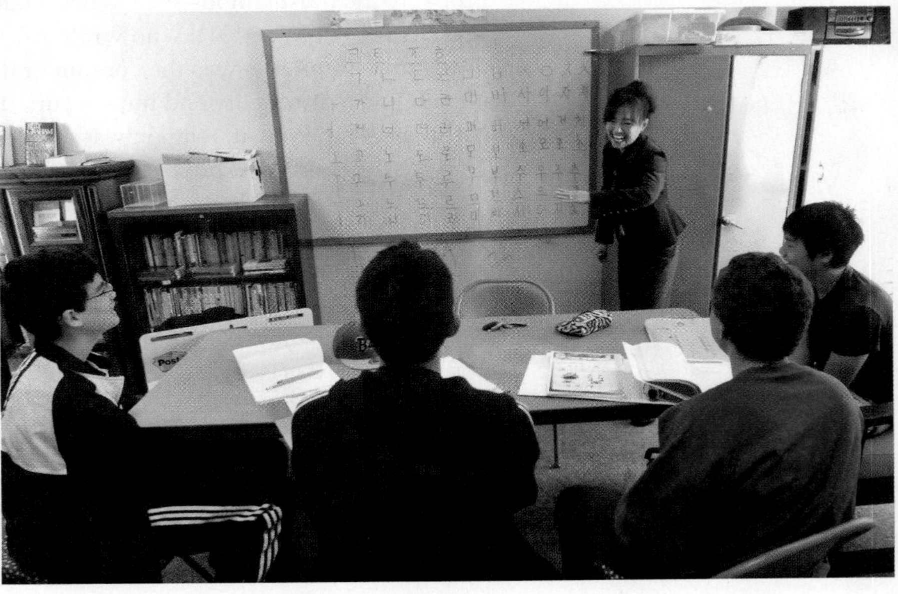

In Savannah, Georgia, young Americans in a Korean American Methodist church learn Korean, keeping their connection to the ethnic community.

Richard Burkhart/The Savannah Morning News/AP Images

mid-twentieth century German Canadian Mennonites had established churches and schools all across the country. Today, Winnipeg, Manitoba, has one of the largest urban Mennonite populations in the world, with more than 20,000 Mennonites and 45 Mennonite churches (Driedger, Epp, & Millette, 2015).

Undoubtedly, the most important—and enduringly segregated—churches in North America are the historically black churches in the United States. About 60 percent of all African Americans (more than 80 percent of African American church members) belong to traditionally black denominations, and additional African Americans belong to denominations that are integrated but attend almost completely segregated churches (Greeley & Hout, 2006). Until fairly recently (and in many churches, even now), African Americans have not been welcome in most white churches in either the North or South, and certainly not as equals.

Most black churches were established by free blacks—both in the North before the Civil War and most importantly after the Civil War. Black churches are generally religiously conservative, but because they represent a severely exploited and repressed minority, they also have emphasized a kind of **liberation theology**, a theology that emphasizes Christ's focus on helping the poor and downtrodden. For black churches this is particularly reflected in the biblical story of the Exodus—the escape of the Jews from slavery in Egypt. "Let my people go" is a favourite theme of sermons and prayers.

The importance of the black church became very clear during the civil rights struggle of the 1950s, 1960s, and 1970s in the United States. The movement leaders were mostly ministers from black churches, especially in the South. The Rev. Martin Luther King Jr. was the son of the pastor of the largest and most affluent black church in Atlanta. This gave King the backing he needed so that he could dedicate himself to the movement. No other institution in the South could provide financial support, space for meetings, and community-supported professionals like the ministers, who were not so dependent for their livelihood on the white power structure. The churches also provided sanctuary for activists—although that sanctuary was sometimes bombed or attacked. The church was also the source of the gospel songs and the liberation message that buoyed the spirits of the activists. Almost all observers agree that without the black church, the civil rights movement could not have developed as quickly and with as much strength as it did.

Social Class and Religious Preferences

13.2.2 Discuss the relationship between class stratification and religious choice.

Probably the most famous sociological statement about religion was penned by Karl Marx (1844/1977, p. 131), who wrote relatively little more about religion but once declared that religion was the "opium of the masses." Marx was provocatively linking religion to inequality and human suffering in a way that was convincing for many observers. As he saw it, religion was an illusion and a distraction that both dulled the pain of economically exploited people and offered a false substitute for the politics of class struggle necessary for their liberation.

If Marx is right, religion should appeal most to the poorest members of society—and perhaps to the rich and powerful who exploit the poor and who profit the most from their piety. The real picture, however, is much more complicated.

Pippa Norris and Ronald Inglehart (2004) recently undertook a global investigation of Marx's thesis, based on surveys they conducted around the world. They concluded, that growing up in societies that provide less personal security (physical, financial) is in fact more likely to lead people to find security through religion and prayer than is growing up in societies that provide a sense of security to more people. Those individuals who live in poverty are generally the most insecure of all. A sick child can mean the inability to go to work and a spiral into the loss of housing and other necessities. Notice, however, that Norris and Inglehart do not simply equate security with current or personal poverty. People who grow up insecure but manage to prosper may still feel very insecure. Most importantly, people who do relatively well in societies that are insecure are influenced by the collective attitudes toward religion and therefore share the **religiosity**—that is, the importance of religion in one's life—of their mostly insecure compatriots.

The poor, then, are more likely to be religious and to rely on religious institutions. In some cases their dependence on these institutions is such that they call on their religious leaders to help them deal with the real world, even in rebellious ways. As one sociologist argues, "[religion] can serve as an apology and legitimation of an unjust status quo, on the one hand, yet also as a source of resistance and protest" (Nepstad, 1995, p. 107), on the other. Two of the most-cited examples of this are the aforementioned historically black churches (and many supportive white churches, especially in the North) in the civil rights movement, and the role of many local Catholic churches in the revolutions by the poor in Latin America. The latter is often discussed under the rubric of liberation theology.

Perhaps the most striking relationship between stratification and religious choice, however, can be seen in the way that the Hindu caste system has affected the birth and growth of various religions on the Indian subcontinent. Among Hindus, the caste system provides a relatively rigid and religiously sustained ordering of people into a social hierarchy. In Hindu doctrine, people are born into different castes, which have different functions in the society. The system has sometimes been called Brahmanism because the Brahmin (or priestly) caste is at the top of this pyramid. At the bottom are the enormous number of untouchables, or Dalits, with other castes ranged in between. One cannot escape the social standing of one's caste in this lifetime. Where one is born is supposed to be ordained by one's behaviour in one's previous life. Good behaviour mostly consists of submitting to the status and conditions into which you were born.

Weber called this system one of the most logically consistent theodicies ever invented. A **theodicy** is an explanation of why bad things happen to good people. To oversimplify, in Hinduism bad things happen to you because of what you did in a previous life, not because of what you do in this life. Being good now gets you a better situation in your next life. It is a potent means of social control—probably much better than the Christian notion that God "has his reasons" for doing bad things to good people.

Not everyone is willing to accept the strictures of caste. This is one of the reasons for the popularity of so many different religions in India. Although he accepted reincarnation, the Buddha (an Indian) was strongly opposed to caste, saying that "Birth does not make one a priest or an outcaste. Behaviour makes one either a priest or an outcaste." Sikhism was partly founded in rejection of caste. Although Baha'i was developed in Persia, the largest Baha'i community in the world—2.2 million—is in India. There are an estimated 2.4 million Christians in India. All of these religions were and are particularly attractive to members of lower castes and the untouchables who sought to escape their karmic fate. For example, two-thirds of Indian Christians come from the untouchables (scheduled groups) or lower castes.

Particularly interesting is the attractiveness of Islam to the same constituencies. Islam came to India as the religion of Mughal conquerors from the sixteenth century onward, so there were other reasons for conversion if one was ambitious. But Islam also became a major way out of the caste system for many Indians and continued as an alternative for a very long time. Ironically, some scholars describe a "caste" system among Indian Muslims which divides the upper-caste Ashraf, supposedly descended from the invading Arab and Persian rulers, from the lower-caste Ajlaf, who were Indian converts. Status advantages are not easy to erase.

What about in contemporary North America? How are class and social status related to religion? Because they come from such different backgrounds—educationally, geographically, and in other important characteristics—different denominations in the United States contain surprisingly different kinds of people. Figure 13.2 shows, for

Figure 13.2 Income and Education of Various U.S. Religious Denominations

SOURCE: Pew Research Center's Forum on Religion and Public Life (2006).

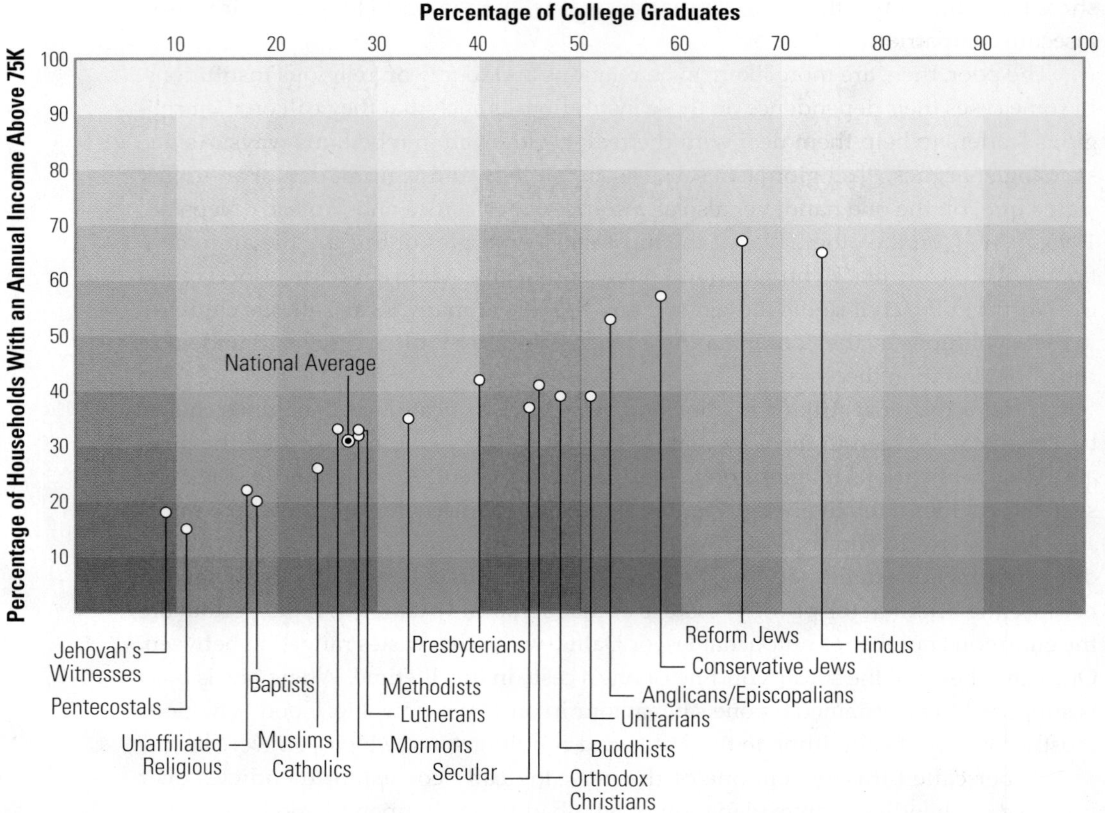

example, that Jews, Hindus, and Episcopalians in America are about three times as likely to be university graduates as Pentecostals, Jehovah's Witnesses, and Baptists. Fewer than one in five Baptists earns more than $75,000 per year, while more than half of Episcopalians make that much (Leonhardt, 2011).

In some ways Figure 13.2 underrepresents the background differences among denominations. Methodist university graduates are much more likely than Baptist university graduates to be the children of university graduates. The children of first-generation university-educated parents may be more comfortable in an urban, middle-class society than their parents and may find the appeal of conservative Christianity fading. Or perhaps it will be their grandchildren? Alternatively, they may remain most comfortable in the church in which they were raised. That church itself, however, might subtly or markedly compromise its points of difference with mainline Protestantism as its members become more like their neighbours in their lifestyles and experiences. For conservative Christians this is a time of change, as the grandchildren of the Bible Belt in the deep South accommodate the urban world of modern America.

Conversion

13.2.3 Explain who converts to what denomination or religion, and why.

Even if most do, not everyone remains in the religion they were born into. So who converts to what, and why? Leaving aside moves to giving up religion altogether (discussed in a later section), we know that in the United States people convert from one denomination or religion to another for a variety of reasons.

Among Christians, most conversions are between denominations within the same religious tradition. Conversions between Catholics and Protestants—or either and Mormons—are considered much more of a leap. For a long time, intermarriage was the dominant reason for people changing denominations (and for Jewish–Christian conversions as well). The strong notion that families should go to church together was important here. So was a simple attempt to make life less complicated or to decide "what to raise the children." There is some recent evidence that people have become more comfortable retaining their religious commitments within dual-faith or dual-denominational marriages. Perhaps this stems from older ages at marriage or from such marriages just being more common and acceptable.

Most religions seek to recruit, or proselytize, more members—as each should, if it is the true religion and cares for everyone's spiritual well-being (or for their eternal souls). In the Christian tradition, proselytizing is known as being an **evangelical**, literally someone who believes in salvation through personal conversion (or being "born again"), and evangelicals are known for their emphasis on bringing their beliefs to others. Some religions make proselytizing a strong expectation of membership; Jehovah's Witnesses often go door to door in their communities distributing literature and seeking converts, while in the Mormon Church, most members will do an extended period of missionary work, usually in early adulthood, somewhere around the world for a period of 18 months to 2 years. There are, however, a few exceptions. Hindus do not generally proselytize (although there are some aggressive gurus). Jews actually even make it difficult for people to convert, primarily because Judaism is only partly a religion. More powerfully, it is an ethnic group. In Israel, the determinant of whether one is Jewish or not is mostly whether or not one had a Jewish mother. An individual does not have to be a practising Jew; one must just have had a Jewish mother. The notion that Jews are God's "chosen people" may be the key idea in Judaism, and it obviously leads to all kinds of exclusionary assumptions about non-Jews who might wish to become members.

In turn, the idea that being Jewish is both an ethnicity and a religion has led sociologists and others to the notion of cultural Judaism, defined as claiming one's Jewishness but not accepting the doctrines of the religion. Such Jews should probably be called "ethnic Jews" because they are unwilling to give up their identification with the group despite agnostic or atheistic beliefs. Conversions between denominations within Judaism are probably as frequent as they are among Christians. For example, the children of Orthodox Jews born in the United States seem to have less than a 50 percent chance of remaining Orthodox as adults, with 29 percent becoming Conservative, 17 percent becoming Reform, and 12 percent becoming secular Jews (Amont, 2005). Figure 13.3 highlights data from a survey that asked respondents to consider whether being Jewish was more about religion or culture and ancestry.

New Religious Movements

13.2.4 Identify who is drawn to emerging new religions.

One segment of organized religion that depends almost entirely on converts are the **new religious movements**, an umbrella term for new religions and offshoots of "foreign" religions that have a foothold in Canada and the United States. Examples may be found in Table 13.1 and include such religions as Wicca, Scientology, the Moonies (the Unification Church), various Buddhist or Hindu sects. Some would include as new religious movements the Mormons, Jehovah's Witnesses, and other relatively new versions of religious doctrine, although both the Mormons and the Jehovah's Witnesses have been around since the nineteenth century.

Who is drawn to these new religions? Rodney Stark has studied a number of new religious movements and concludes that "people must have a degree of privilege to have the sophistication needed to understand new religions and to recognize

Figure 13.3 Being Jewish: Is It More About Culture and Ancestry Than Religion?

SOURCE: Pew Research Center (2013).

NOTE: "Ancestry/culture" is the net percentage saying that being Jewish is mainly a matter of ancestry, mainly a matter of culture, or volunteering that it is both ancestry and culture. "Religion, ancestry/culture" is the percentage volunteering that being Jewish is a matter of both religion and either ancestry or culture, or all three of these.

% saying being Jewish is mainly a matter of...

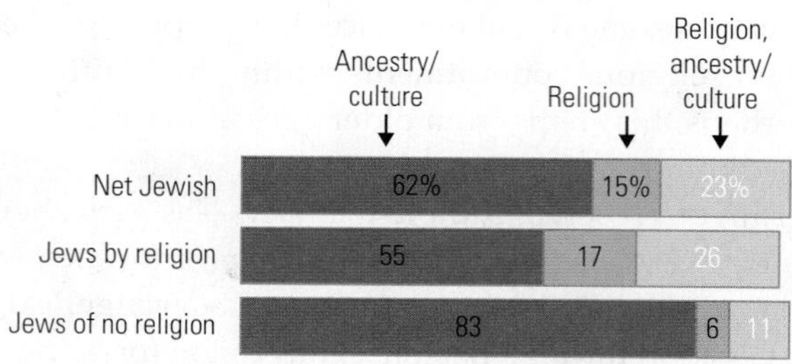

a need for them. This is not to say that the most privileged will be most prone to embrace new religious movements, but only that converts will be from the more, rather than the less, privileged classes" (Stark, 1996, p. 39). He points out that Christianity was once just such a movement—a Jewish "Jesus cult"—and its converts tended to suffer from "relative deprivation"—that is, resentment among the somewhat privileged that they actually deserved even more privilege and respect. In contrast, Stark argues, sect movements that seek to purify existing traditions, that is, to make them more like the "old-time," "true," "essential," or "authentic" version of the religion, appeal to the lower classes. Stark also asserts that irreligious people are the most likely to join new religious movements and concludes that this reflects a deep desire for some spiritual connection among those who do not accept traditional faiths.

One striking aspect of the new religious movements is that they appeal disproportionately to women. Some of these groups, like Wicca (a neopagan cult with female goddesses), are explicitly aimed at women. But many other new religions seem attractive to women. In Stark's research on early Christianity, women were more likely to convert. This was also probably true of the beginnings of Islam. In more modern and radical cults, consider the following data: 73 people were killed in the showdown between the U.S. government and the Branch Davidian cult in Waco, Texas, and 45 of them (62 percent) were female; in the 1979 mass suicide at Jonestown, Guyana, by the members of the People's Temple cult, an American religious group, 66 percent were women.

Why do more women than men take up new religions? Perhaps because they are treated so badly by the old religions. Unsurprisingly, most religious traditions support, or even mandate, traditional gender roles. They bar women from most positions of authority, restrict their dress, and sometimes blame them for the evils in the world (Eve in the major monotheistic traditions, Pandora in Greek mythology, Izanami in the Shinto creation story). Until very recently, almost all priests, ministers, rabbis, imams, monks, gurus, shamans, and other such higher functionaries of the religious establishments were male. All of Jesus's disciples were male. Women often had to sit in separate sections of the church or synagogue or mosque. They could not lead prayers, and because most were illiterate, they were not even able to read the prayers.

Some new religions seem to be better for women. As a striking example, consider the beginnings of Islam. Most Westerners seem to think of Islam as backward in its treatment of women. In fact, Mohammad prescribed a liberating revolution for women in the context of his time. In the Arab world before Islam, women were chattel, the property of their fathers and then of their husbands and then of anyone their husbands gave them to. They had no rights. Mohammad gave them rights of protection, divorce, and property, among other advances. Similarly, early Christianity gave women the right to not be killed having unsafe abortions they didn't want, not to be treated as chattel, or not to be left to die from exposure because their father wanted a son, among others. All of these were common practices in the Roman paganism of the time.

13.3 Why Are Some People More Religious Than Others?

Robert Harding Picture Library Ltd / Alamy Stock Photo

Religiosity by Gender and Age

The appeal of new religious movements to women raises an important larger question in the sociology of religion: Who practises religion? In the rest of this section, we will explore some of the ways in which religion of all types has appealed more to women and older people than men and younger people.

Women as Generally More Religious

13.3.1 Discuss the relationship between gender and religiosity in various major religions.

Despite many advances for women in North American society and elsewhere, new religions today still develop in an environment in which women are disadvantaged, in general, and second-class citizens within most of the established religions of the world, in particular. One would think such treatment would lead women to reject traditional religion to a greater extent than men. Yet most research finds just the opposite, as Figure 13.4 illustrates. One literature review argues strongly that despite their poor treatment, "the greater religiosity of women must be one of the oldest and clearest findings in the psychology of religion" (Beit-Hallahmi & Argyle, 1997, p. 142).

Figure 13.4 The Gender Gap in Religion: Are Women More Religious Than Men?
SOURCE: The Pew Forum on Religion & Public Life.

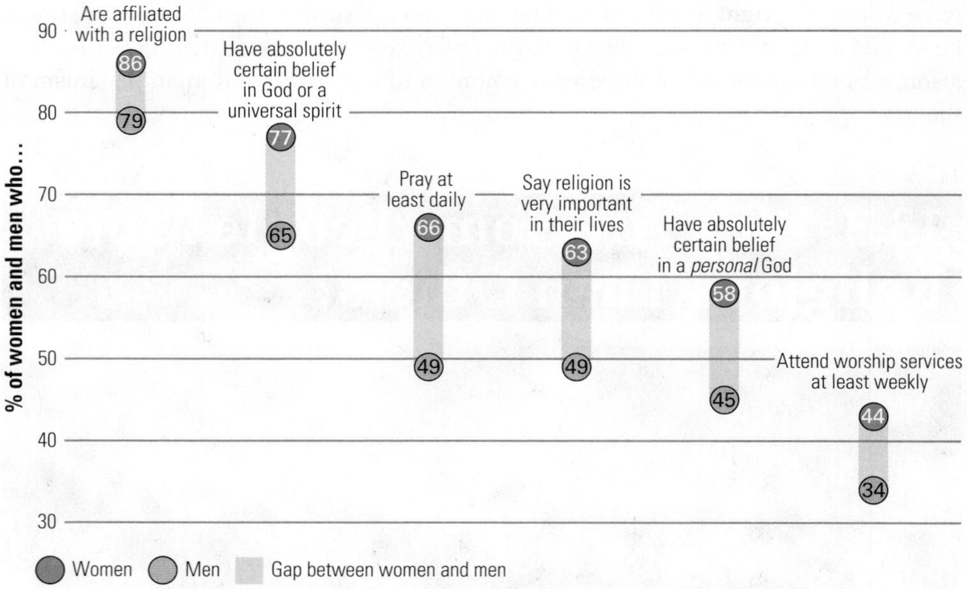

But wait a minute. One of the great things about science is that we keep reevaluating what we think we know. This is what D. Paul Sullins did in 2006, and his reanalysis of the available data across the world challenged the received wisdom in a couple of ways. Sullins concluded that (1) women were more likely to describe themselves as pious or religious across almost all societies studied, but men were more likely or equally likely to be active "organizational participants" (i.e., go to church regularly, etc.) in about 25 percent of countries; and (2) most importantly for our purposes, while the traditional pattern continues to hold among Christians, there was little difference in how devout male and female Jews (particularly Orthodox Jews) or male and female Muslims are (Sullins, 2006). Since Sullins published his analysis, more extensive data from Saudi Arabia, Egypt, Jordan, and Iran have confirmed his findings for a number of Muslim countries (Moaddel, 2007). The gender gap in religion is large in places like the United States because of the dominance of Christian and Catholic traditions, but it does not hold for all religions across the world.

Why might the relationship between gender and religiosity be different among Jews and Muslims than among Christians? This is a fascinating sociological puzzle. Consider the gender differences in the way that faith is or was lived in traditionally Muslim countries, or among Jews in some earlier, more traditional period. All male Orthodox Jews were expected to spend much of their time studying the Torah and the Talmud—in other words, in religious study. In contrast, women and girls were not allowed to participate in such activities. Women were much less likely to go to temple than men, and most did not even know how to participate in the prayers that were the major part of the service. Women performed a variety of small rituals at home, but their intellectual and perhaps emotional engagements with religion were comparatively limited.

The status of Muslim women is similar. Young Muslim boys are trained to memorize the Koran; girls are not (although some may choose to do so). The number of women who pray at the mosque is generally a fraction of the number of men. Those who do attend are shunted off to the rear or side. One of the five pillars of Muslim practise is the Hajj, or ritual visit to Mecca, which religious Muslims try to perform at least once in their lifetime. Yet males always outnumber females at the Hajj by very large margins. In general, then, Muslim men might attend services more often in some countries, while more or equal numbers of Muslim women consider themselves religious. The proposition that women are always more religious than men is really quite questionable.

Questions about Muslim and Jewish gender differences do not invalidate the consistent finding of greater female religiosity in most Christian settings. Why might this gender difference be the case among Christians? I begin by noting that in practice Christianity may be more egalitarian than Orthodox Judaism or Islam. Although all Catholic priests are male, most traditional Catholic men and women occupy similar positions toward their faith in that the priest does most of the work and the thinking for them. The men do not have to know any more than the women. They need to be obedient. In radical Protestantism, in contrast, every person, male and female, should have a personal relationship with God and read the Bible. Again, the ministers and theologians might be men, but their importance is downgraded before the individual parishioner's role in his or her own religious life.

Why Do We Become More Religious as We Age?

13.3.2 Explain why older people tend to be more religious.

One of the more interesting, if less important, reasons women are more religious than men in most places is that on average in most societies around the world women live longer than men. In most developed countries women outlive men by about five years. And, as many of us know from our own experience, older people are more religious than younger people.

For a long time, the age difference in religiosity was thought to derive from the confrontation with death becoming increasingly acute as we age. Alternatively, mature wisdom and perspective were seen to replace the rebelliousness of youth.

Today, however, most sociologists agree that the most important reason older people tend to be more religious is not aging but what is called a "cohort" difference: Older people were brought up in more religious times than younger people. Your grandparents were always more religious than you (or at least most of you). This can be clearly seen in Figure 13.5.

Figure 13.5 Attendance at Religious Services, by Generation

SOURCE: The Pew Forum on Religion & Public Life (2010).

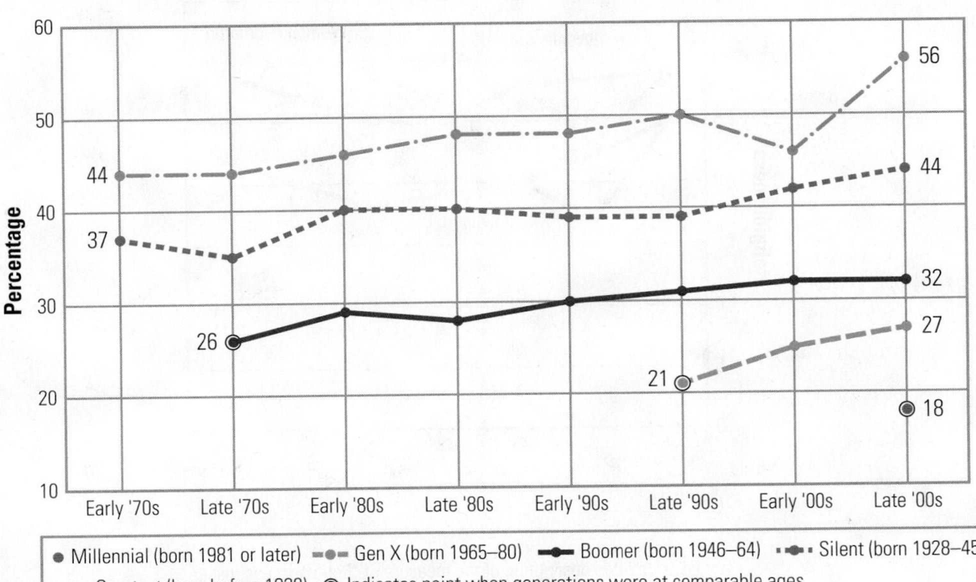

As Figure 13.5 shows, the generations (usually called *cohorts* by sociologists) born earlier are always more likely to say they go to church than the generations born later, and each generation starts at a lower level of attendance in their early 20s than the previous generation (or cohort).

The data in Figure 13.5, however, do not track the religiosity of individuals over their lifetime, which is a much more difficult job. To do so, we would have had to start the research more than 50 years ago. We have only a few such long-term studies that measured religiosity, and they are for selected, not-very-representative samples. Nevertheless, these can give us some idea of individual change. One such study follows a group of Oakland, California, students who were interviewed while in high school in the late 1920s and then interviewed several additional times, most recently in the 1990s when they were well into their 70s (Dillon & Wink, 2007). Figure 13.6 shows their religious trajectories, by gender, where the measure of religiousness is a complex combination of practices and beliefs. Note that, as expected, women in the sample were always substantially more religious than men.

The respondents were most religious when they were teenagers. The women remained at the same level in their late 30s, declined in religiosity into their 60s, and increased in their late 70s. Men simply declined rather markedly into their 60s, with some recovery in their late 70s. For both men and women, therefore, there is some evidence the ages between 60 and 80 might involve an increase in religiosity.

Unfortunately, data were not collected during this sample's university-age years. We know from other work that this stage of life, which is when most people in North America leave home, is the stage when they are most likely to reassess their religious commitments and decline in religious participation, whether they went to university or not. For example, Smith (2009, pp. 244–246) followed a representative sample from ages 13–17 to ages 20–22. He found that between 33 and 40 percent of these young people declined in religiosity, some sharply, while only 3 to 7 percent increased (the rest were "stable").

A general narrative of religiosity over the life course, at least in the United States, as reflected in the data from the Oakland study, might look something like this:

Figure 13.6 Mean Change in Religiousness Among Americans, Over Time by Gender

SOURCE: Adapted from *In the Course of a Lifetime: Tracing Religious Belief, Practice, and Change* (p. 82), by Michelle Dillon and Paul Wink, 2007, Berkeley: University of California Press. Copyright by University of California Press. Used with permission.

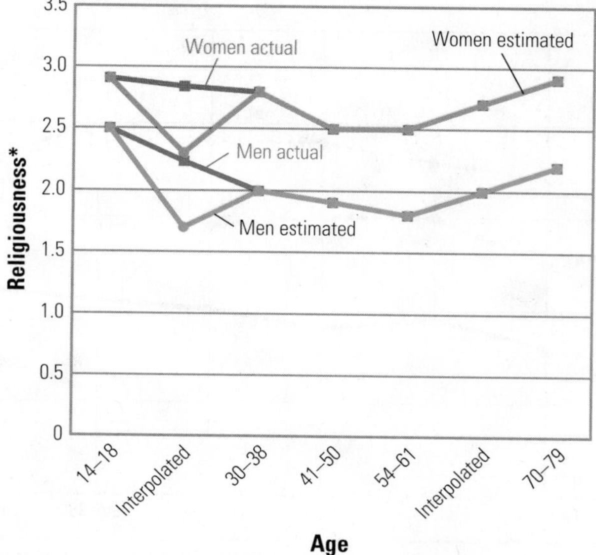

*For a detailed description of the measure of "Religiousness" used in this figure, see Dillon and Wink (2007, p. 82).

(1) Because parents, schools, and churches invest heavily in the religiosity of children, and most children accept these lessons, children's religiosity is high, if somewhat incoherent. (2) With relative independence from their parents during the post-high-school years, many of these young people lose interest in religion or in their inherited religion, or begin to be influenced by other, less religious views. (3) After people have children themselves, they tend to move to communities where churches are more important and to think that they should teach their children about religion. This is particularly important for women, who most often bear the responsibility for childrearing. Thus, there is a tendency to return to church during this life stage, which for the Oakland sample was probably ages 28 to 40. (4) After their children leave the home, some of the middle-aged return to their earlier, less religious practices and views. (5) In the oldest part of the life course, people leave their jobs and lose friends and spouses. For many, the church and the support of religion might become more important, whether they fear death or not.

13.4 Why Do People Kill Each Other in the Name of Religion?

Michel SETBOUN/Glow Images

Religious Conflict

To this point we have mostly focused on figuring out what people get out of religion and for whom religion is most important. Unfortunately, however, there is also a much darker side to the relationship between religion and society. In this day and age we have all heard of the paradox of people killing each other in the name of religion: Muslims killing Americans in New York, Jews and Muslims killing each other in Palestine, Catholics killing Protestants in Northern Ireland and vice versa; Buddhists and Hindus killing each other in Sri Lanka; Muslims and Christians killing each other in Nigeria; periodic eruptions between Hindus and Muslims in India; Sunni Iraq fighting a vicious war against Shi'a Iran in the 1980s; strict Muslims killing less religious Muslims and infidels (non-Muslims) in Syria and Iraq—all this and more in only the past few decades.

History is replete with religious wars. After all, people who are certain that their religion is the only correct one have every reason to spread that religion to other places, or defend it by force against heathens or heretics. In the first century after Mohammad's death, Islam was primarily spread by the sword. In the twelfth and thirteenth centuries, Christians launched the Crusades against Muslims. In the sixteenth century, Protestants and Catholics fought the Thirty Years' War over control of various parts of Europe. In the nineteenth and twentieth centuries, Jews were slain in pogroms by Russian Orthodox Cossacks, and faced violent attacks in many parts of Europe. In the first two decades of the twentieth century, Muslim Turks and Kurds probably killed from 1 to 1.5 million Christian Armenians. Even civil religion might be said to have its violence: During the Civil War, Northern soldiers sang "The Battle Hymn of the Republic" as they marched off to do their sacred duty to save the Union.

Distinguishing Religious Conflicts From Ethnic and Class Conflicts

13.4.1 Explain why it is difficult to distinguish religious conflict from ethnic or class conflict.

If most people are right to think that religion fosters morality, the fact that religious violence has been a repeated occurrence throughout history raises some weighty negative evidence to consider. But then, appearances can be deceiving. It is often hard to tell when a religious war is primarily a war about religion, as opposed to something else.

Consider the example of the Catholic–Protestant war in Northern Ireland in the 1970s. In a very telling sentence (supposedly a quotation from a nameless participant), Demerath (2003, p. 49) describes the war as Protestant atheists vs. Catholic atheists. He points out that with one or two prominent but really marginal exceptions, virtually all religious figures in Northern (and southern) Ireland were against the killings and confrontations. Furthermore, one could easily argue that major class and ethnic conflicts were the real sources of the war. Northern Ireland was ruled by the well-off descendents of British colonialists. Thus, ethnicity and class, as well as religion, separated the sides.

In Sri Lanka, the Buddhists are overwhelmingly ethnic Sinhalese, and the minority Hindus (18 percent of the population) are ethnic Tamils. They speak different languages, and the Tamils have long considered themselves discriminated against economically and politically. For most Tamils, the war is about the need for secession so that they can have their own country. Neither group seems to think the other should change their religion. Perhaps this too is an ethnic and economic war rather than a religious one.

We could look at many "religious" wars and find ethnic or tribal conflict more central to the problem. Serbs (who were mostly members of the Serbian Orthodox Church) killing Muslims in Bosnia called it "ethnic cleansing," not "religious cleansing." Muslims and Jews lived together fairly peacefully in British-controlled Palestine until the 1920s, when Zionists, who believed that Jews needed their own homeland so that they could defend themselves from lethal anti-Semitism around the world, particularly in Germany and other parts of Europe, began immigrating in great numbers. Threatened by the flood of Jews, Palestinian Arabs rioted and demanded the British halt the migration (Sela, 1994). Note that most of the founders of Israel were more or less irreligious, as are most Israelis today. As mentioned earlier, these secular people define Jewishness in ethnic rather than religious terms. One has the right to become an Israeli citizen if one's mother is Jewish, not if one believes in the sacredness of the Torah and that Jews are God's chosen people: ethnicity, not religion. Jews are not fighting Muslims because they believe theirs is the one true faith.

All this is not to say that there are no wars or internal mass killings that are not at least somewhat religious in basis. After the fall of the Egyptian dictator Hosni Mubarak, some Egyptian Muslims began attacking the churches of Christian Copts, who are about 10 percent of the population, calling Christians "blasphemers" for disagreeing with Islam. In recent years even inside the United States we have seen religious violence: for example, the killing of doctors who perform abortions by fundamentalist Christian vigilantes who claim to be acting on religious grounds. In the nineteenth century, Mormons were violently driven out of upstate New York and later Nauvoo, Illinois, and elsewhere because of their different religious ideas.

An Example of Religious Conflict in India

13.4.2 Discuss the longstanding religious conflict between Hindus and Muslims in India.

One of the most compelling examples of what seems to be religious violence is the long-term conflict between Hindus and Muslims in India. The partition of India into India and Pakistan (which at first included what would become Bangladesh) took place in 1947, shortly after Britain decided to end its colonial control over the subcontinent. The partition was hasty and unplanned. More than 7 million Muslims moved to Pakistan, and an approximately equal number of Hindus, Sikhs, and others moved from the territory that became Pakistan to India. From being approximately 25 percent Muslim before partition, the new India contained less than 13 percent. The new Pakistan had hardly any Hindus at all. It is estimated that between half a million and a million people died in the process as Hindus and Muslims fought over land or just over resentments in both communities.

Hindu militants in India storm the disputed mosque at Ayodhya, preparing to demolish it and clear the site for a Hindu temple.

Reuters Photographer/Reuters Pictures

After partition, communal conflict between Hindus and Muslims was common in India, although almost always local. Anything that might go wrong could begin a cycle of hostility. Muslims had conquered most of India in the sixteenth century and ruled until the eighteenth century, a fact not lost on the majority Hindus. To this day, some of them continue to write vicious screeds on the horrors of Muslim occupation, particularly in the blogosphere. For many Hindus the partition meant that India was now specifically a Hindu country, perhaps with more reason than the idea that America is a Christian country. This idea sparked the growth of a political philosophy of "Hindutva," which asserts that India should be for Hindus, and eventually led to the election of an avowedly Hindutva party to a majority in the parliament.

In the early 1990s, Hindutva politicians and a number of Hindu holy men focused on a mosque in Ayodhya that they claimed had been built on top of an important Hindu temple (what cynics have called one of the mythical birthplaces of the mythical god Rama). They demanded that the mosque be razed and the Hindu temple rebuilt. The government was opposed, envisioning the turmoil that would ensue and the hundreds of other sites that might become controversial. In December 1992, an estimated 200,000 Hindus descended on the mosque and, despite some opposition from a small number of police, razed the mosque themselves (led by Hindu "skinheads," of all things). All over India communal violence broke out, with more than 2,000 people being killed.

Yet in spite of the seemingly clear religious underpinnings of the conflict, we still need to ask: Was this really a religious conflict? Conflicts between religious groups can have elements of other things—class resentments, ethnic drives for control of land or governments, long memories of past or imagined injuries—alongside religious intolerance or fear. Religion is a potent marker of "us versus them." It speaks for the "rightness" of "our" cause. For many people in this world, security comes only from being a member of a powerful group. That group's fate is our fate—and that includes nationalism as well as ethnicity or religion. Religion provides institutional support because it has professional people to do the organizing. It works well in times of conflict.

13.5 What Is the Future of Religion?

Brian Harris/Alamy Stock Photo

Secularization Versus Increased Religiosity

If you have read this far, you might think we have surely hit all the high points in the sociology of religion. But this is emphatically not the case. I have actually saved for last what has historically been the most important question for sociologists of religion: the question of whether **secularization** or increased religiosity is the future of religion in societies around the world. For most of the twentieth century, social scientists generally argued that with modernization and the development of science, the relevance of religion to the life of society would progressively decline. In this view, the world is becoming demystified. We are abandoning superstition and becoming more and more secular. This has usually been referred to as the **secularization hypothesis** and was an important sociological theory even at the turn of the twentieth century.

More recently, however, many sociologists of religion have begun rethinking the secularization hypothesis. Stark and Finke (2000), for example, have presented data and arguments about the persisting strength of religion in highly developed countries like the United States, and claim that there is a deep-seated human need for religious commitment and practice that overrides modernization. As with many terms in the sociological arsenal, *secularization* has been used in somewhat different ways by different theorists. At its simplest level, secularization has been taken to mean that people abandon religion as unscientific or irrelevant to modern existence. Books are written about "The Death of God" and the rise of irreligion in modernized societies. But most sociologists have actually meant something more subtle by secularization. As Weber argued, sociologists do not necessarily expect people to abandon all belief in God or in their church or in religious ideas. Instead, their argument focuses on the *authority* religion has over the lives of people: Do people actually limit or suit their behaviour according to the dictates of religion? Those who argue for secularization see this authority shrinking in the modern world as life becomes more complex and modern institutions that have little to do with religion claim more and more authority over parts of people's lives.

For example, in a society dominated by agriculture, religion appears central to everything—from appeasing the weather gods to prayers for fertility or for God's support in war. In contrast, businesspeople in modern industrial societies do not pray for their production line to work. Even in religious North America today, people have to work on supposed religious days of rest so that the assembly line is not shut down. Hospitals and doctors, not priests and shamans, are experts on health. Education is delivered by professionalized schools, mostly state rather than religious. Most people have hardly any idea of the relationship between weather and food and only pray to have enough money to feed their teenage children. We can easily add many examples to this list.

It is hard to argue with the authority version of secularization in highly developed societies. Everywhere in Europe and North America, the authority of churches over the way society is run, and their ability to influence their members, has diminished over time. Stores are open on Sundays. Religious people often don't go to their church, temple, or mosque. Catholic women use birth control. Most Jews are not kosher. Evangelical Christians have high divorce rates and get abortions.

European Irreligion

13.5.1 Describe the religiosity in Europe.

Even if one asks simply whether people are religious or not, one can easily make the case that native-born people in Europe, especially Northern and Western Europe, have become very secular indeed. On any given Sunday only about 10 percent of Europeans go to church. Fewer than half of the people of Scandinavia, Holland, Germany, France, Britain, or Belgium, or of many countries that were previously part of communist Europe, say they believe in God, compared to 80 percent of Canadians and Americans (European Commission, 2005, p. 8).

Surveys tend to show that although Europeans are not opposed to religion for other people, they just want the religious to keep their beliefs private. They do not want religion in their politics (even though many European countries have large parties, usually known as Christian Democratic, which have roots in religion). Many Europeans tend to be put off by very religious people, so for example they are more suspicious of what they see as the excessive religiosity of some Muslim immigrants than they are of the fact that they are Muslims. When asked, most Europeans say that religion—of any sort—is simply is not very important in their own lives and should not be public in any way.

How can this be? Don't Western Europeans "need" traditional religion for moral order or for some vision of life after death? We don't know exactly why, but somehow they manage without. Lacking society-wide religious commitments does not seem to preclude moral and orderly behaviour. For example, Europeans have less than 25 percent of the homicide rate in the United States—for irreligious Norway it is close to 15 percent (Geneva Declaration Secretariat, 2008). The poor in Europe are given a relatively generous safety net and need neither starve nor die without medical care. If "do unto others" is the essence of Christian morality, Europeans do not seem particularly immoral.

So in many countries in Europe, the classical sociological prediction that secularization would spread seems to be confirmed. But the sharply declining rates of religious participation and religious belief in Europe are not found in most other countries around the world, and as the proportion of foreign-born people (especially Muslims) rises in many European countries, these trends may not continue.

American Exceptionalism

13.5.2 Compare and contrast religiosity in the United States to other developed countries of the world.

Among the developed countries of the world (Australia, Canada, Japan, and Israel also look a lot like Europe regarding religion), it is the United States that is considered the exception that needs to be explained. Modern as any Western European country, the United States retains a level of conventional religiosity far above almost all of the other developed countries of the world. As noted above, at least twice as many Americans as Europeans say they attend church regularly. Remarkably, two-thirds of Americans say they would not vote for an irreligious person to be president (of course, the United States has had many relatively irreligious presidents—Thomas Jefferson, Abraham Lincoln, and Franklin Roosevelt, among others; even Ronald Reagan, who often used religious language in his speeches and favoured introducing prayer into public schools, did not attend church regularly). And social issues of importance to many religious leaders (such as abortion, homosexuality, public support for religious education, whether evolutionary biology should be taught as established science or simply a theory of human evolution, and requiring prayer in public schools) are often central issues in American politics. Many non-Americans see the United States as having a very strong religious component to public life.

Where do these impressions come from, and are they accurate? Many reasons have been advanced for American religious exceptionalism. For example, Stark and Finke (2000) have argued that in most countries there has been only one established religion, while in the United States many different religions compete—a much better marketing situation. If we could buy only one cereal, those of us who do not like it might stop eating

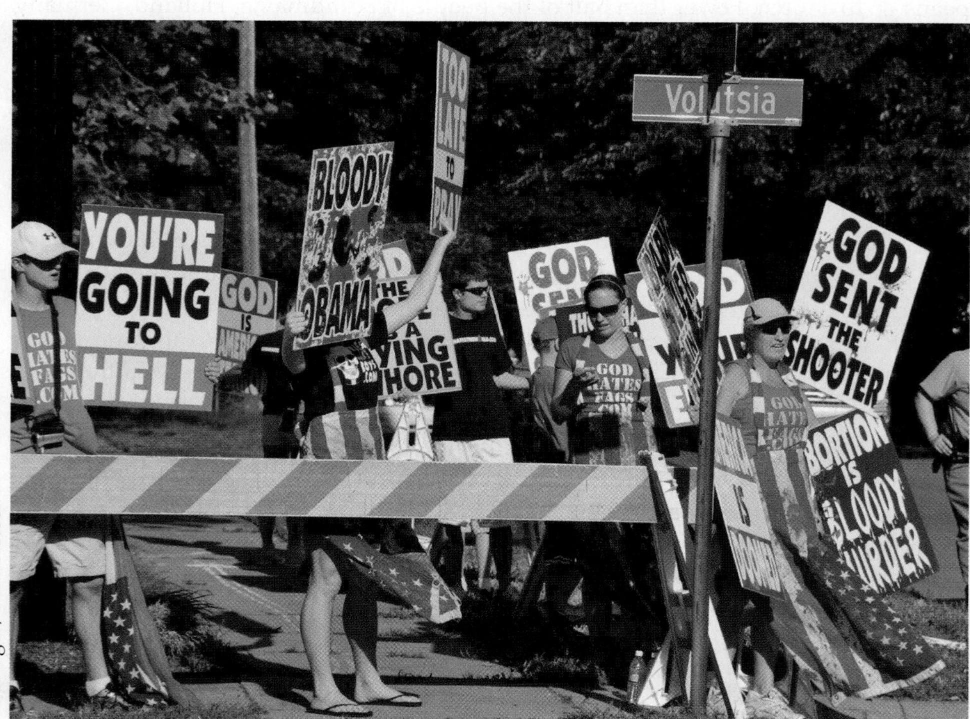

PDImages/Shutterstock

The struggle over abortion in North America is an example of how religious views are often injected into political debates. Antiabortion activists often invoke religious themes in arguments against allowing women the right to choose to have an abortion.

cereal. Of course, the advertising budgets for cereal are enormous, which no doubt supports the American addiction to these morning grains. At the same time, if one looks at religion as a commodity, one also realizes that expenditures on promoting religion are much, much higher. Consider all the TV shows and ads on TV, in newspapers, and now on the Internet. At 2 a.m. one night I found at least seven different programs promoting religion. Even more tellingly, we pay more than 300,000 clergymen to give sermons that are mostly about convincing parishioners that they should be faithful.

An alternative argument is that religion thrives in America because the nation is so ethnically, geographically, and religiously diverse. Each group clings to its religion as a means of preserving its community and culture. And, as we noted earlier, churches do continue to play an important role in providing services for people in need that the more generous welfare programs in European countries take care of. In Canada and European countries, the state does more to provide medical, social, and educational services. In the United States, public schools are underfunded; many people cannot get health insurance; the police are often ethnically alien to minorities and the poor; most jobs are not unionized and unions cannot help most people with difficulties at work; and so forth. In the absence of strong and available alternative institutions, Americans turn to their churches for hope, help, and sustenance.

But the primary evidence cited by foreigners suggesting Americans are very religious is political. Many of the social issues that have become important in recent decades have done so primarily because of the rising power and influence of evangelical, conservative, or fundamentalist Protestants. Politically conservative Protestants have consistently described themselves as highly religious, consistently report higher church attendance, and otherwise are considered more religious than adherents of "mainline" Protestant denominations. The active participation of some prominent evangelical Christian ministers in politics, notably Jerry Falwell, Pat Robertson, and others, helped further this movement.

The rise of conservative Protestantism can in many ways be seen as a reaction to the social changes brought about the movements of the 1960s and the seeming decline of "traditional" values beginning in that era. Because conservative white Protestants are disproportionately centred in the South, reaction against the civil rights revolution was also a factor. The most important of the changes in American society that began in the 1960s, however, were the changing gender roles and "sexual liberation" of women (Putnam & Campbell, 2010). Repelled by these changes and other threats to so-called family values, many conservative Americans sought to defend a more stable commitment to "traditional family values"—especially for their children—and some turned to those churches that they saw as sharing this conservative vision.

But conversion has not been the primary factor driving the growth of conservative Protestantism. Greeley and Hout (2006) have shown that about 75 percent of the growth of conservative Protestantism in American society was due to the relatively high fertility rates among conservative Protestants, which was especially striking in contrast to the sharply declining fertility of mainline Protestants during the same period. A second major factor in conservative growth was an increase in the ability of conservative Christians to retain their young people. At one time, it was not uncommon for members of evangelical Christian denominations who prospered to switch to the more socially and financially prestigious mainline churches. With increasing affluence, that became less necessary, as more successful evangelicals made for more acceptable communities for the upwardly mobile. Still, the growth of evangelical Protestants has by no means been particularly large. Indeed, the most striking trend by far is the growth of secularism, especially among young people.

Although a great deal of attention has been paid to the political mobilization of evangelical and fundamentalist Christians, looking back over the past 40 years it is clear that its impact has been modest at best. Conservative Protestants succeeded in putting a range of social issues on the political agenda for discussion, but in almost every case significant majorities of Americans did not support those positions. Whether we are talking about a return to traditional families with stay-at-home mothers, requiring prayers in public schools, banning abortion under all circumstances, or attitudes toward homosexuality, Americans have become increasingly liberal over time (Brooks, 2000). The case of same-sex marriage is an especially interesting one to note. A few decades ago, the vast majority of Americans supported the view that marriage should be between a man and a woman, and in 1996 Congress passed, and President Bill Clinton signed into law, a measure known as the Defense of Marriage Act that allowed states to refuse to recognize same-sex marriage licences granted in another state and codified heterosexual unions as the only legal marriages under all federal laws. But over time, as Chapter 11 has described, Americans have become increasingly supportive of same-sex marriage, and many states adopted measures legalizing such unions. Same-sex marriage became legal in the United States in 2015 when the Supreme Court declared civil unions (whether heterosexual or homosexual) a protected civil right.

The Future Decline of Religion in America?

13.5.3 Identify signs that religiosity in America is declining.

It is likely that no single reason uniquely accounts for American exceptionalism in religion, but that several or all factors work together to make the United States different. However, it is not clear how long that difference will be sustained. There are signs that religiosity in America may be moving in the Canadian and European direction, particularly if we just focus on native-born Americans and ignore the effects of continuing high rates of immigration.

Currently, surveys indicate that the fastest growing religion in the United States is "no religious preference." From 2.7 percent in 1960, and 8 percent a decade ago, the number of people so identifying themselves has grown to about 20 percent today (Hout, Fischer, & Chaves, 2013). Further, because young people are much more likely to think of themselves as not religious, that percentage is almost certain to increase in the near future. Explore the data in Figure 13.7 to see how the increasing percentage of Americans with no religious preference compares to the changes in Catholic and Protestant membership.

Figure 13.7 An Increasing Percentage of All Americans Have No Religion

SOURCE: Pew Research Center

NOTE: Other religious affiliations and those who did not give an answer are not shown.

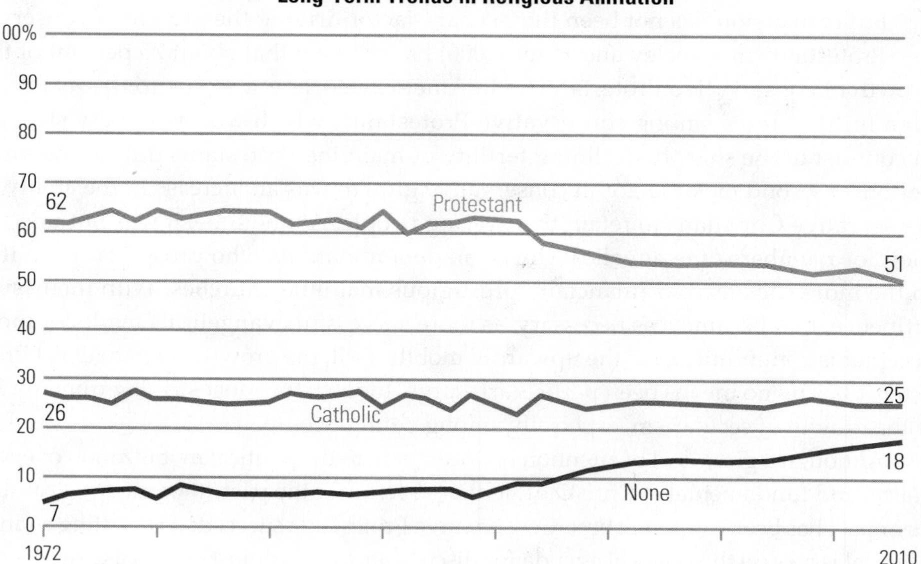

Figure 13.8 Evangelicals and "Nones" Among American Youth (Ages 18–29), 1973–2008

SOURCE: Based on data from *American Grace: How Religion Divides and Unites Us* (p. 125), by Robert Putnam and David Campbell, 2010, New York: Simon and Schuster.

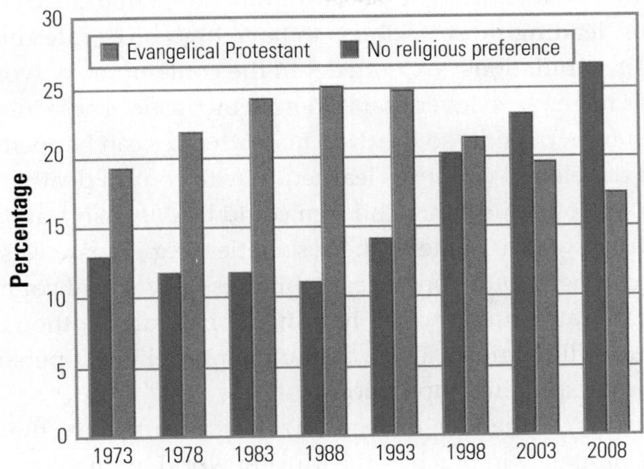

Indeed, if not for immigration from Latin America, the Catholic Church in the United States would be seen as hemorrhaging believers. Twenty years ago, Catholics made up about 22 percent of the American people. Today the percentage is about the same, despite the fact that about 80 percent of the enormous numbers of recent immigrants to America (especially from Mexico and Central America) have been Catholic. Moreover, the Catholic Church is having great difficulty finding men to take up religious vocations and become priests (although to be sure, the Catholic Church could end that particular problem if they simply allowed women to become priests or allowed priests to marry). Increasingly, priests are being imported from other countries to fill the ranks.

We can also expect the relative number of conservative Protestants to decline over the coming decades. As conservative Protestants have become more urban and educated, differences between their birth rates and those of other Americans have declined. Evangelical intellectuals are already complaining that they are losing their young to more secular orientations. Figure 13.8 is a dramatic summary of trends among youth aged 18 to 29, comparing those who declare themselves to be evangelicals with those who say that they have no religious preference ("nones"). The contrasting projections are stark and argue for continued secularization in America.

The Rise of Religion in the Rest of the World

13.5.4 Identify possible explanations for the increase in religious persons around the world.

As Norris and Inglehart (2004) conclude, a good case can be made for the secularization hypothesis in the developed modern world, and even in the United States (although more slowly than Canada or Europe). And yet, as Norris and Inglehart also say quite clearly, if we take a look at the contemporary world as a whole, we can make just the opposite argument—the world seems to be getting more, not less, religious. A higher percentage of people are probably more religious now than they were two or three decades ago, and in many countries, like Russia, Iran, and elsewhere in the Middle East, religious authority seems to have increased rather than withered.

However, on the assumption that Norris and Inglehart are right, what is the major reason for the increase in religious persons around the world? Although the causes might be complex, surely one of the most important is simple demography. Everywhere in the world, as in the United States, religious people have more children than irreligious people. The difference is even greater between societies. Religious societies have much higher birth rates than irreligious ones. In part, this simply reflects the levels of development of those societies. Before modernization all societies were mostly religious, and all societies had high birth rates and high death rates. People simply did not know how to stop having babies or how to stop death. Eventually, sanitation, medicine, and other factors brought the death rate down in industrializing and modernizing societies, leading those societies to have high birth rates but low(er) death rates, so that their populations "exploded." In the contemporary world a less-developed society does not have to invent sanitation or medicine. These ideas and materials can be brought in from outside, so the drop in death rates can happen quickly.

As the more developed countries learned how to control deaths, their birth rates also came down. People found that children could be expensive and confining in an industrial and urban world. Some of these societies (e.g., Japan, Russia, Spain) now actually have declining populations. Meanwhile, less developed countries today may have reduced death rates, but they still have high birth rates (although they are coming down) and are still religious. Thus, the number of religious persons in the world increases with these exploding populations.

Even if we return to the idea of secularization as authority, the world has seen surging religious militancy in much of the Muslim world, with relevant consequences for politics in those countries. Women are either deciding to wear veils or being forced to wear veils. Iran, once run by a secular shah and a socialist prime minister, is now controlled by its religious establishment. In Egypt, the Muslim Brotherhood won the 2011 elections in that country (only to be thrown out of office by a military coup). Other examples around the world can be found.

Reasons for this reemergence of religious political authority have complex roots but are partly a matter of the reassertion of cultural pride in a segment of the world that had been colonized and dominated by Western political, economic, and, most importantly for religion, cultural imperialism. Under these circumstances, many people found that only religion provided an alternative symbol of difference and nationalism and a legitimate basis for organization, so that it could serve as a rallying mechanism for the assertion of independence and power.

Conclusion

An old and revered saying in science is that "the more you learn, the more questions you have." And true to the saying, even after years of research and analysis, I am left with a lot of questions and ideas about the nature of religious involvements around the world. I hope you are as well. That is, after all, the hallmark of developing a sociological imagination.

I therefore want to end this chapter with a question, something to look into in the future. I will phrase the question as a proposition. It may be true, or sort of true, or not true at all. I have seen no research on the point that might provide an answer. I suspect that one of the reasons highly developed countries experience declines in religiosity is that over the long term those countries have experienced soaring life expectancies.

At the time of Christ, average life expectancy in the Roman Empire was less than 30 years. By 1870 life expectancy in England, the richest country in the world, was still only 40 years. Three of 10 babies born died by the age of one. Death was everywhere. Everyone had seen many people die. A 30-year-old had seen her mother and one or more children die, a 10-year-old her grandmother and a brother, and maybe her father. Death was even more present everywhere else in the world. No wonder people were preoccupied with death and the afterlife.

Today, life expectancy in England is about 80, in Canada 81, in the United States 78, and in Japan 82. Most young people have known no one who has died, or perhaps their aged grandparents, or a soldier in some war. But death is not an everyday event unless one lives in a retirement community. Young people don't live there. Furthermore, I suspect that many old people are not as repulsed by death as their ancestors were. With long lives behind them, their peers dying, and illnesses sapping their activity, death does not seem so cruel and forbidding. People over 70 have America's highest suicide rate, while in Canada the highest suicide rate is among those aged 50–54. Death has come gradually, in little steps. As the current cliché has it, death is a natural part of life—especially when one reaches one's 80s.

So perhaps the focus of religion on the afterlife, or next life, or on helping people to deal with death, is not as important as it used to be. And if religion is therefore less useful, it may also be less compelling. Or is it? Perhaps you would like to do some research. If you and they can bear to talk about death, talk to your grandparents. Figure out some way of getting information on this question that would be useful. Be a sociologist of religion!

CHAPTER SUMMARY

The Big Questions Revisited 13

13.1 What Is Religion, and What Are Its Functions? Sociologists have no single agreed-upon definition of religion. Nevertheless, they understand that the actual religious behaviour of people in every religion is enormously variable and fluid. This section examined the incredible number of religions throughout the world and throughout history, the concept of religion as a social institution, and the social function of organized religion.

A Sociological Understanding of Religion

Defining Religion

Learning Objective 13.1.1: Compare and contrast the different sociological definitions of religion.

The Incredible Variety of Religions

Learning Objective 13.1.2: Identify the big five or six religions of the world and discuss the variety and diversity of contemporary religion.

Early Religious Traditions and Their Modern Variants

Learning Objective 13.1.3: Compare and contrast the concepts of animism and paganism.

Religion as a Social Institution

Learning Objective 13.1.4: Discuss the functions of religion as a social institution.

Denominations and Congregations: Serving the Needs of the Community

Learning Objective 13.1.5: Describe the role that denominations and congregations play in organizing religious activity in a community.

13.2 How Does Social Structure Impact Religious Choice? With all the religions in the world, how do people choose a religion for themselves? This section explored the patterns of religious choice, including the impact of race, ethnicity, and social class on religious preferences.

Patterns of Religious Choice

Religious Segregation: Birds of a Feather

Learning Objective 13.2.1: Discuss the causes of segregation in American churches.

Social Class and Religious Preferences

Learning Objective 13.2.2: Discuss the relationship between class stratification and religious choice.

Conversion

Learning Objective 13.2.3: Explain who converts to what denomination or religion, and why.

New Religious Movements

Learning Objective 13.2.4: Identify who is drawn to emerging new religions.

13.3 Why Are Some People More Religious Than Others? In this section, we discussed differences in religiosity by age and gender.

Religiosity by Gender and Age

Women as Generally More Religious

Learning Objective 13.3.1: Discuss the relationship between gender and religiosity in various major religions.

Why Do We Become More Religious as We Age?

Learning Objective 13.3.2: Explain why older people tend to be more religious.

13.4 Why Do People Kill Each Other in the Name of Religion? This section examined why there has been so much religious conflict over history and in the present, as well as the difficulty of distinguishing religious conflict from ethnic or class conflict.

Religious Conflict

Distinguishing Religious Conflicts From Ethnic and Class Conflicts

Learning Objective 13.4.1: Explain why it is difficult to distinguish religious conflict from ethnic or class conflict.

An Example of Religious Conflict in India

Learning Objective 13.4.2: Discuss the long-standing religious conflict between Hindus and Muslims in India.

13.5 What Is the Future of Religion? We saved for last what has historically been the most important question for sociologists of religion: Is secularization or increased religiosity the future of religion?

Secularization Versus Increased Religiosity

European Irreligion

Learning Objective 13.5.1: Describe the religiosity in Europe.

American Exceptionalism

Learning Objective 13.5.2: Compare and contrast religiosity in the United States to other developed countries of the world.

The Future Decline of Religion in America?

Learning Objective 13.5.3: Identify signs that religiosity in America is declining.

The Rise of Religion in the Rest of the World

Learning Objective 13.5.4: Identify possible explanations for the increase in religious persons around the world.

Learn the Terms

agnostic (p. 352)
animism (p. 360)
atheist (p. 352)
civil religion (p. 355)
congregation (p. 364)
deism (p. 353)
denomination (p. 362)
doctrine (p. 353)
evangelical (p. 371)
ideology (p. 355)
institution (p. 361)
irreligion (p. 359)
liberation theology (p. 368)
megachurch (p. 363)
new religious movement (p. 371)
paganism (p. 360)
pluralism (in religion) (p. 361)
polytheistic (p. 360)
religiosity (p. 369)
sacred (p. 355)
secularization (p. 380)
secularization hypothesis (p. 380)
supernatural (p. 355)
syncretic (p. 359)
theodicy (p. 369)
theology (p. 361)

Chapter 14
Education

by Caroline H. Persell with Dirk Witteveen

David Duprey/AP Images

Police have begun to use sniffer dogs to search for drugs in many high schools.

Learning Objectives

14.1.1 Discuss socialization in schools.

14.1.2 Explain how credentials affect future employment opportunities.

14.1.3 Discuss how education contributes to economic growth.

14.1.4 Discuss how schools create an equal playing field for students.

14.2.1 Discuss the relationships among education, occupation, and life-course outcomes and how those affect economic success.

14.2.2 Identify the correlation between education level and health.

14.2.3 Recognize the correlation between education level and relationships or family life.

14.3.1 Discuss how social-class issues contribute to educational inequality.

14.3.2 Discuss racial and ethnic issues that contribute to educational inequality.

14.3.3 Discuss gender issues that contribute to educational inequality.

14.4.1 Explain how access to education affects academic success.

14.4.2 Explain how sources and amounts of funding affect educational opportunities.

14.4.3 Identify how public and private education varies and affects education equality.

14.4.4 Discuss the home-schooling trend.

Jake (a pseudonym for a student in a U.S. research study I conducted a number of years ago) steps out of his dorm onto a vast campus with a computer centre, multiple theatres, well-appointed seminar rooms, dining halls, art studios, tennis courts, a hockey rink, and much more. Mary (another pseudonym) enters her school through a security check and faces packed halls, large classrooms, and peeling paint. The first day of school differs dramatically for the 1 percent of young people attending elite private boarding schools like Jake's and the millions like Mary who attend crowded, decaying urban schools in North America. The differences extend far beyond the physical facilities, however, and raise provocative questions about the kinds of educational opportunities that Jake and Mary have.

Classes at elite boarding schools are often taught as seminars with no more than 15 students. Teachers know their students well and can provide extra help if needed. Students write a great deal and are carefully taught how to write well—how to make an argument and support it with evidence. Virtually everyone participates in extracurricular activities such as student government and yearbook. In contrast, in the typical U.S. public high school, less than 10 percent of students are involved in such activities.

Young people who attend elite boarding schools also benefit from university advisors who actively promote their virtues to the top universities. When we asked university advisors at such institutions to describe their jobs, one American told us, "I put the applicants' folders in the trunk of my car and drive around to [the Ivy League] universities and talk to the admissions officers about our applicants. I try to make the case for a particular student if I think the university is making a mistake." Having such advisors at one's disposal clearly makes a difference: Graduates of elite boarding schools are disproportionately represented at the most elite private universities despite the fact that most do not do as well academically as public school graduates once in university.

Mary's teachers see about four times as many students in a given day as Jake's do (160 vs. 40) and have much less time to work individually with students who need help or to help them improve their writing. Mary's larger classes (25–28 students) make seminars around an oval table impossible. Advisors at her school are responsible for anywhere from 300 to 600 students each year and find it virtually impossible to give personalized attention and advice to each one. They also lack the resources to visit university campuses and get to know university admissions officers personally. These and other differences between North American schools to be explored in this chapter suggest some of the ways schools help develop the potential of some children more than others.

The Big Questions

To understand why and how the institution of education has become so important in our lives, we need to consider the following four big questions:

1. **Why is formal education universal?** In this section, we examine the various purposes of schooling, including socialization, preparation for work, citizenship, and community life.
2. **How is education related to important life outcomes?** Here we explore education's strong relationship to many important life outcomes, including work and economic opportunities, health and life expectancy, and marital success and happiness.
3. **Is education equally available to all?** Is education the great equalizer in North American society, or does it reproduce existing inequalities? Here we examine the sociological research that investigates whether educational access, experiences, and outcomes are similar for persons of different social classes, races, and genders.
4. **How do educational systems differ?** How can there be such wide variations in the quality and types of schooling, particularly by social class and race? To address this question, we look at differences in educational systems around the world.

Most of us take it for granted that success in life requires many years of formal schooling. But the extent of education, its formal and informal purposes, and its relation to other institutions have changed dramatically over time. For most of human history, there was no formal education system separate from the family and community. Early schools taught literacy and basic arithmetic so adults could read sacred scriptures such as the Bible, Torah, or Koran; write letters; and do simple counts and tabulations. But even in Europe and North America, a classical liberal education was available only to a small, elite group of males. Today, not completing high school is uncommon: 85 percent of working-age Canadians have completed high school.

In North America, the number of schools multiplied with the rise of industrialization, the growth of cities, and the desire (and frequently the demands) of working people for opportunities for their children. Emerging occupations that placed a premium on education were also a key factor. Children could no longer learn the skills and knowledge needed for adult life simply by observing their parents or neighbours, spurring promoters of mass schooling such as Egerton Ryerson, who worked in collaboration with Jean-Baptiste Meilleur in Quebec and John Jessop in British Columbia to call for the formation of public schools that would be funded by taxes and attended by all. In most industrialized countries, a new system of universal mass education gradually took hold. In Canada today schooling is compulsory between the ages of 6 and 16. Participation in formal education increased at all levels, including post-secondary education, throughout the twentieth century. Full-time post-secondary education in Canada grew by 33 percent between 1981–82 and 1991–92 to a total of nearly 900,000 students, with 62 percent of these in university (Hale, 2013, p. 557).

Today, there are no clear paths to adult success that do not include formal education. By 2008, large numbers of countries, including Japan, the United Kingdom, and Germany, had higher rates of high school graduation than Canada and the United

Figure 14.1 Upper Secondary (High School) Graduation Rates, 2009

SOURCE: From *Education at a Glance 2011: OECD Indicators* (Chart A2.1, p. 44), by Organisation for Economic Co-operation and Development [OECD], 2011, Paris: OECD (https://www.oecd.org/education/skills-beyond-school/48631582.pdf).

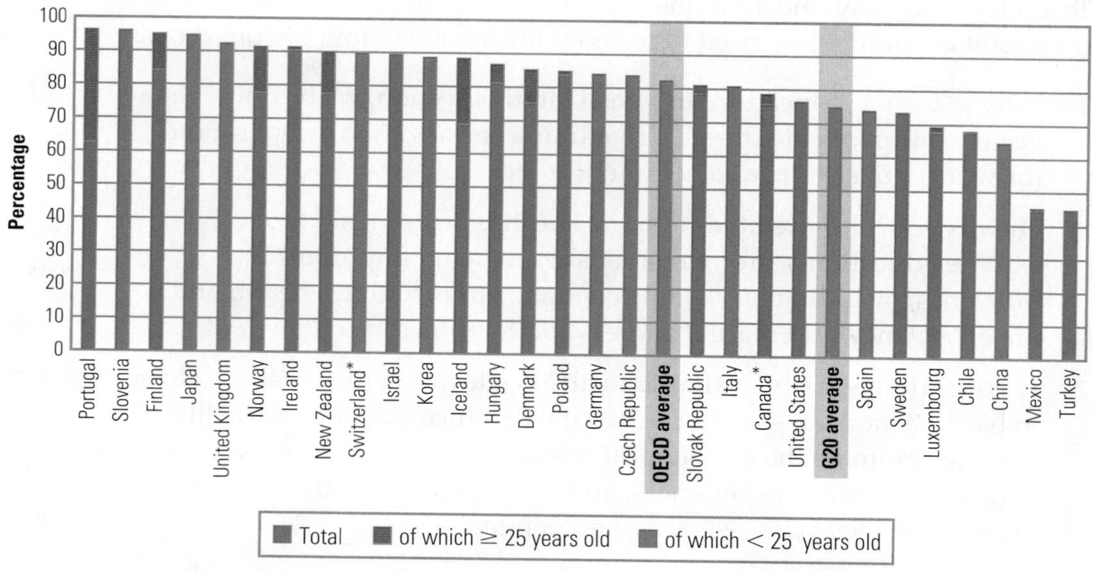

*Year of reference 2008.

Countries are ranked in descending order of the upper secondary graduation rates in 2009.

States, as we can see in data about graduation rates shown in Figure 14.1. But completion rates vary widely within Canada. In remote regions such as Nunavut, the high school completion rate is very low, at 35 percent.

14.1 Why Is Formal Education Universal?

Jeff Dunn/Getty Images

The Purposes of Education

Every country in the world today has a formal educational system and virtually all countries require all of their citizens to attend school. Why is that the case? When we think about education, the more formal purposes of schooling usually come to mind—such as learning skills and knowledge. These are obviously important both for individuals and for society. But education also serves other major societal purposes, such as socializing students, sorting people into various occupations based on their ability and performance in school, and (by increasing the average education level of everyone) the economic development of a society. Education also provides a few less formal functions that may surprise you—it is a marriage market, it may teach religion, it teaches students discipline that will be useful later in life, and it may even help prevent crime by keeping youths off of the streets. Let's examine a few of the most important societal functions of schooling.

Socialization

14.1.1 Discuss socialization in schools.

One major purpose of schooling is socializing young people into the habits, attitudes, and practices of contributing members of a community, religion, or nation. Socialization in schools takes place in both formal and informal ways. It affects students, schools, and society as a whole.

The classroom is a small society. Even though classrooms are often relatively homogeneous in terms of family background and age, it is necessary for schools to create a stable and well-functioning social environment that is suitable for learning. Starting in kindergarten, we are taught how to behave in school, including how to line up, be quiet on demand, be neat, fit into a social system, follow rules, respect authority, obey, compete, and achieve success within the boundaries of the educational system (Gracey, 2012). Together, students are unconsciously adjusting to *school discipline*: a behavioural consensus that is a reflection of society's norms and values.

The extent to which students obey the rules and regulations of teachers shapes their social skills, their attitude, and their even future educational path. This is part of what sociologists call the **hidden curriculum** of schools, referring to often unstated standards of behaviour or teachers' expectations. For example, most teachers want students to raise their hands and wait to be called on before speaking. More middle-class children may learn this at home or at preschool than do poor children. Thus the school practice may be more familiar to some than to others. Other children are taught at home to show respect for adults by being very quiet around them, so they may never speak up in class. Teachers may think they are not paying attention or not learning when they sit silently, but this is not necessarily the case. The way children conform to the hidden curriculum of a school may affect how their teachers assess them and interact with them.

Sociologists also stress the direct and indirect moral education taking place in schools. Morality can be transmitted through the formal curriculum itself. Religious schools may have the most visible and intended cultural agenda (e.g., Bible courses in Catholic schools), yet most (public) schools include ethics or social studies in their curriculum and make choices on how to teach these courses. Many other rituals and ceremonies of moral nature can be found in schools, such as the celebration of birthdays or ethnic holidays. In addition, cultural values are learned indirectly through interaction with peers and their families.

The cultural transmission taking place in schools reaches beyond the classroom and affects social solidarity at the community or national level. Virtually all schools around the world provide instruction in the history of the country. Studying the country's founders and participating in ceremonies such as singing "O Canada" are examples of the ways in which schools contribute heavily to citizenship building. Schools play a major role in

Dave Pattinson/Alamy Stock Photo

Students are first and foremost socialized through rules and regulations that apply to classroom behaviour, such as *don't speak when the teacher speaks* and *raise your hand before asking a question*. But many other social and cultural rules that are learned in school can be more subtle and indirect. For example, one of education's most important functions is to create loyal citizens for the next generation.

creating politically active and loyal citizens, mainly through civics education and history education. Western countries in particular spend quite some time and energy on teaching the fundamental elements of democracy and the encouragement of political engagement. More subtle physical references to nationalism can be found in classrooms in many parts of the world, such as the national flag or images of a monarch.

Not surprisingly, a big debate in education concerns how students are socialized. Is education largely about learning attitudes, moral values, and behaviours and producing happy, well-adjusted young people? Or is education about intellectual skills and content? Most people agree that schools should offer both social and cognitive learning experiences, but some people disagree about the relative importance of those two aspects. Others differ on whether education should be intellectual and broad in its orientation (as in a liberal arts curriculum) or more narrowly focused on specific occupations.

Future Preparation

14.1.2 Explain how credentials affect future employment opportunities.

A second major purpose of education is the training of young people for future opportunities. Sociologists and economists refer to this aspect of education as the accumulation of **human capital**: the stock of knowledge, skills, and habits that students can use to do productive labour later in life. Education provides the basis of the production of economic value; it offers the tools for individuals to increase their economic value for future employers and the social skills to adapt to the workforce.

Schooling served as a major vehicle for the preparation of the workforce even well before formal education existed. Relatively small medieval economies required the production of some goods and services, and people needed to be trained to provide them (think of shoemakers or midwives, for example). Most of these early forms of professional training took place within guilds, in which local craft organizations awarded degrees to carpenters, textile workers, and goldsmiths after an intense period of apprenticeship. The unstandardized and small-scale schooling of manual workers for economic production gradually increased until the rise of industrialization and nation-states in the late eighteenth and early nineteenth centuries. Subsequently, more standardized education rose in response to the need of increasingly specialized occupations. The changing nature of capitalism in the nineteenth and twentieth centuries led to a demand for a more educated workforce capable of staffing the growing knowledge and service-based industries.

As schools have expanded, they are increasingly used to sort and select young people for future opportunities. The educational system of today not only provides the skills and knowledge (*human capital*) that are needed in the modern workforce, but it also selects and allocates young people to various positions on the occupational ladder. It does so by testing, tracking, grading, and, eventually, awarding nationally and even internationally recognized diplomas. These credentials have become more important in the labour market than ever before. If you want to be a police officer, for example, but you only have a high school diploma, your options are limited because more cities are requiring police officers to have at least some university education, or even a university degree. Using education to screen employment applicants is called credentialism, or the allocation or sorting function of education. **Credentialism** refers to the requirement of certain specific degrees or certificates before you can be considered for a particular job. Employers may assume that applicants with more formal schooling have more knowledge and skills, including a variety of **soft skills**—knowing how to dress, act, and present oneself at work, or being able to work well with other people—that may enhance a person's job performance. Students attending schools with more frequent and intense contact with adults—think again of the elite boarding schools described at the beginning of the chapter—may learn more soft skills than public school students who have less informal contact with adults. Private schools are also less likely than public schools to engage in the practice of *social passing*. Social passing allows students to progress through the system regardless of performance. Given the dramatic increase in educational participation, people find it more challenging to find a job without having various credentials—whether that is a high school diploma or a bachelor's, graduate, or professional degree.

Some students may feel that what matters is simply the degree, not what they learned along the way. And it is certainly true that most of what you learn about whatever occupation you enter you will learn on the job, not in the classroom. However, in many fields—architecture, social work, law, computer programming, and so forth—simply having an educational credential does not ensure that you have the knowledge, problem-solving skills, creativity, and interpersonal qualities needed to perform well. Schooling, especially at the post-secondary level, is where those kinds of advanced skills and capacities are usually first acquired, but learning will continue on the job for many years to come.

As more students attend university in the North America and around the world, some sociologists have questioned the extent to which university students are studying or learning when compared to students in the past. Research on contemporary college and university students in the United States shows, for example, that college students do not study as hard as they once did, and they do not learn as much as educators claim and future employers demand (Arum & Roksa, 2010, 2014). Similarly, a study by James Côté, a sociology professor working at the Western University, analyzed a data set of 12,000 North American university students and found that study times have gone down and grades have gone up. The average grade in a Canadian university had risen from a C to a B+/A over the previous 30 years (cited in Findlay, 2010). Many students, these researchers claim, are not making the expected gains in critical thinking, complex reasoning, or the ability to communicate in writing as they move through university. Is this because they are working so much outside of school? Are these students developing their soft skills and building social networks that will be helpful in the future? Do they spend more time pestering their professors with obsessive e-mails, emotional appeals, and annoying visits to professors' offices seeking higher grades than they do studying? Are their parents intervening by calling administrators on their adult children's behalf? Can they get along in the world with social skills alone, or will their failure to enhance their cognitive skills have lifelong consequences? More research is needed to address the

Figure 14.2 Declining Hours of Homework for College Students

SOURCE: From *The Falling Time Cost of College: Evidence From Half a Century of Time Use Data* (NBER Working Paper No. 15954, Figure 1, p. 34), by Philip Babcock and Mindy Marks, 2010, Cambridge, MA: National Bureau of Economic Research (http://www.nber.org/papers/w15954.pdf).

NOTE: Average study hours per week from Project Talent (1961), National Longitudinal Survey of Youth 1979 (1981), Higher Education Research Institute (1988), National Survey of Student Engagement (2003), and Higher Education Research Institute (2004) samples are plotted as diamonds. Squares show average study time responses from these surveys adjusted for estimated framing effects, with Project Talent as the baseline. A solid line between two plotted points indicates either that the two samples were both nationally representative or that they relied on a consistent set of schools. A dotted line between points indicates that this was not the case.

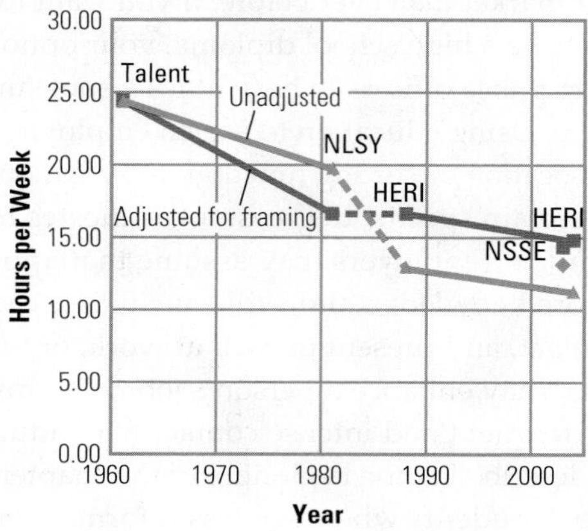

question of what current post-secondary education contributes to productive skills for the labour market, but it is an important one as social scientists and policymakers consider making changes to higher education. Figure 14.2 illustrates how hours studied by students have declined over time.

Economic Benefits of Schooling

14.1.3 Discuss how education contributes to economic growth.

Business leaders have long been interested in education because they depend on schools, colleges, and universities to prepare much of the workforce. But is education really an engine for the economic development of a society? Or is economic expansion the reason for mass education? Both of these propositions are largely true. Teaching citizens to read and do simple arithmetic fosters economic growth in developing countries. Evidence abounds that the single most effective approach to economic development is to provide elementary education to everyone, and almost all countries in the world today attempt to do that. These investments benefit both individuals in developing countries and the society as a whole. Access to primary education increases the opportunities for previously marginalized children to move up the socioeconomic ladder. And a higher literacy rate among the working population significantly boosts the human capital potential of the entire society, making it more attractive for foreign companies to invest with confidence that they will find the workers they need. Various Asian countries—including China, India, Singapore, Taiwan, and South Korea—have benefited from a strategy of focusing heavily on math, science, and engineering in secondary and higher education since the 1980s, with the goal of further developing their economies—and the remarkably rapid rates of economic growth they have achieved suggest that those efforts are paying off.

What about North America? During the nineteenth and throughout most of the twentieth century, Canada and the United States led other nations in educational attainment, providing more formal schooling to their citizens than other countries. According to some researchers, this high level of education, and the human capital it provides, played a key role in spurring economic growth in North America during this time (Goldin & Katz, 2008). Economists and sociologists widely agree that, as more people become better educated and more skilled, the workforce as a whole also becomes more productive in terms of efficiency and the potential to deliver more complicated and economically valuable work. Today, however, Canada and the United States no longer lead the world in either the amount of education received or in educational achievement (which we will discuss later in this chapter). Part of this decline may be the high cost of higher education compared to other countries; in many countries, university is either free or provided at very low cost. See Figure 14.3 for evidence of the trends in university completion for a number of different countries.

Figure 14.3 University Completion Rates Over Time

Tertiary-type A programs are designed to provide sufficient qualifications for entry to advanced research programs and professions with high skill requirements. These programs have a minimum cumulative duration (at tertiary level) of three years' full-time equivalent, although they typically last four or more years, corresponding to bachelor's degrees in North America.

SOURCE: Based on data from *Education at a Glance 2010: OECD Indicators* (Table A3.2, p. 69), by Organisation for Economic Co-operation and Development [OECD], 2010, Paris: OECD (http://www.oecd.org/education/skills-beyond-school/45926093.pdf).

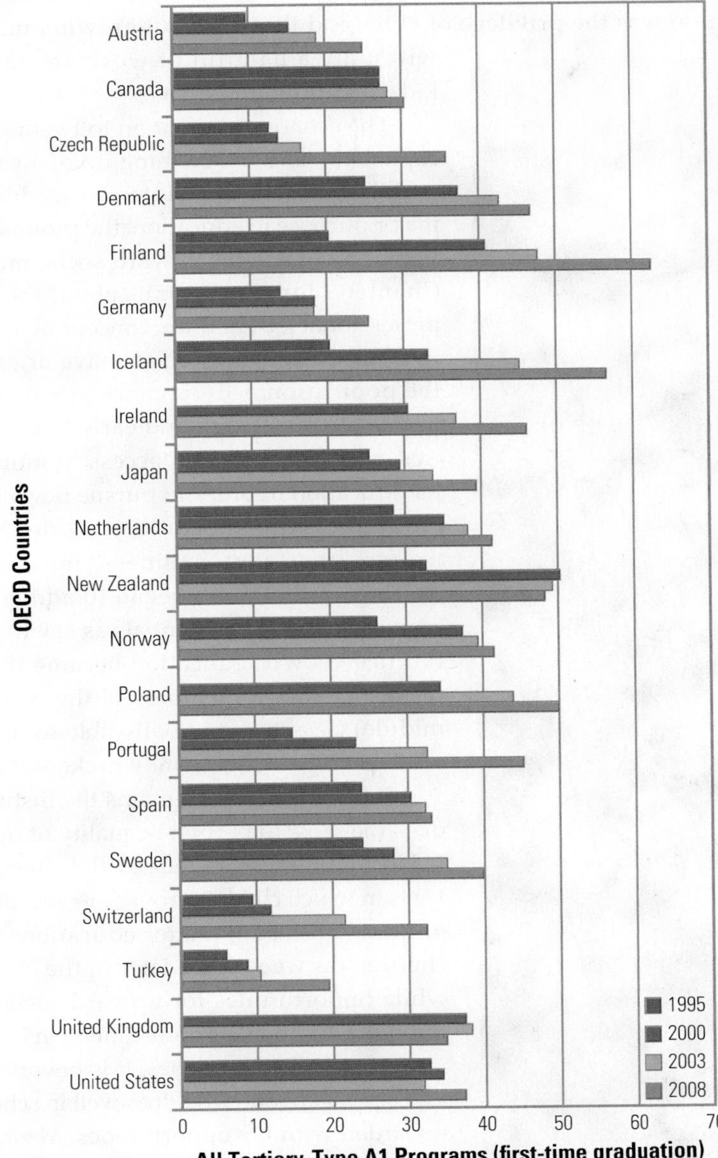

At the end of World War II, veterans were given generous grants to enroll in post-secondary education. Following the war, post-secondary education participation rates increased dramatically.

The Great Equalizer?

14.1.4 Discuss how schools create an equal playing field for students.

The meritocratic ideal of education prescribes that students are exposed to the same material and surroundings. The idea is that an equal playing field is created if students read the same books, have the same teachers, attend similarly organized schools, and are assessed on the same scale. Meritocracy theory also assumes that students from all backgrounds can compete for the most desirable outcomes (like university admission and graduation). Educational inequality, then, is a result of varying degrees of student effort instead of socioeconomic background.

Starting in elementary school, pupils are often told to do their very best in school for "their own good." Why is this idea so well known among children and adolescents in modern Western societies? In contrast, a child growing up in a working-class family in the nineteenth century may not have had that phrase drilled into his head at all, and indeed schooling may have lasted only a few years before lifetime of work began. That child probably had limited career options. Many children would work on their family farm starting at a young age. If the child's father had a skilled occupation such as carpentry, the child (if a boy) would likely become a carpenter as well (or follow a similar trade). Hence, social mobility (the ability for people to move up the socioeconomic ladder) was severely limited in the 1800s compared to today. At that time, children typically attended elementary school for a few years and only a relatively small group continued onto high school. University education was the privilege of elites and the small but growing middle class, with only a handful of working-class or farm kids attending university.

Andrew Fox/Alamy Stock Photo

The economic transition to twentieth-century capitalism, and the opening up of a vast array of middle-class jobs and professions, added a fourth major purpose to education: the promise of education as a vehicle for upward social mobility (see Chapter 9 for more details about the growth of professional jobs and the concept of social mobility). Historical sociologists have argued that as the population became more urban and literate in the late nineteenth and early twentieth centuries, people demanded access to more and better education in order to pursue new careers that modern capitalism could provide. Numerous professions—law, business, medicine, engineering, and others—began to add educational requirements and credentials as key to job opportunities. Slowly, education became the primary means by which members of the working (and middle) classes were finally able to control their work life *beyond* their family background.

Today, education remains the institution that does the most to promote equality of opportunity in North American societies. While there are many ways in which children from more privileged backgrounds can obtain better educations than poor children (as we will see later in the chapter), and while opportunities for upward social mobility through education are more limited in North America than in other countries, it is nevertheless true that almost anyone who does well in school will be rewarded with life opportunities. *Meritocracy*, the idea that competition for desirable and important positions should go to those with the best qualifications regardless of their family background, is a cherished ideal. We will see how well it works in the next section of the chapter. Explore the following information to see how this theory affects the promised equalizing function of education.

14.2 How Is Education Related to Important Life Outcomes?

Maria Janick/Alamy Stock Photo

Education and Life Outcomes

In a modern society, educational attainment has profound effects on our life outcomes. For example, consider fraternal twins Mary and Anna, who followed different life and educational pathways. Mary became pregnant at 16 and dropped out of high school. Anna graduated from high school and went on to university. At age 40, Maria is not married and is struggling to get full-time work as a sales clerk or cashier in a store. Her three children each have babies. Anna is married to an accountant, has two teenage children, and is working full-time in a hospital as a medical technician. Their stories reflect larger trends showing that the number of years of education individuals obtain is related to many important consequences in their lives, including intellectual development, occupations, earnings, working conditions, and health. Let's look more closely at these important life outcomes and consider the role education plays in them.

Career Outcomes

14.2.1 Discuss the relationships among education, occupation, and life-course outcomes and how those affect economic success.

As Anna and Mary found, people with more education are more likely to work full-time and less likely to be unemployed than people with less education, at all ages. As they enter the labour force, more educated citizens are also more likely to find jobs in higher-status occupations than those with less education. This is not surprising because occupational status and working conditions are highly related to the skills and education demanded in the most competitive professions and fields. You could not become a surgeon or a lawyer, for example, without an advanced degree and highly specialized training.

Table 14.1 Average Total Income of the Population 15 Years and Over by Highest Certificate, Diploma, or Degree, by Province and Territory: Canada, Quebec, Ontario, Manitoba, Saskatchewan

This table shows that those who have higher degrees also earn more, on average, than those with less schooling. For instance, the average yearly salary of somebody who graduated from university is considerably higher than that of a high school graduate.

	2005				
	Canada	**Que.**	**Ont.**	**Man.**	**Sask.**
			$		
Total – Highest certificate, diploma, or degree	**35,498**	**32,074**	**38,099**	**31,320**	**31,616**
Certificate or diploma below bachelor level	**30,116**	27,403	31,595	27,509	27,988
University certificate or degree	**58,767**	54,674	62,287	51,977	55,003
Bachelor's degree	**52,907**	49,030	55,982	45,804	49,148
University certificate, diploma, or degree above bachelor level	**69,230**	64,958	72,517	64,403	70,245

SOURCE: From "Average Total Income of the Population 15 Years and Over by Highest Certificate, Diploma, or Degree, by Province and Territory (2006 Census): Quebec, Ontario, Manitoba, Saskatchewan)," by Statistics Canada, 2009 (http://www.statcan.gc.ca/tables-tableaux/sum-som/l01/cst01/labor50b-eng.htm). Copyright by Statistics Canada, Client Services Division. This does not constitute an endorsement by Statistics Canada of this product.

As Table 14.1 shows, those of us with more education also earn more, on average, than those with less schooling, even when family background and academic ability are statistically controlled (Pallas, 2000).

Research on long-term labour market outcomes in Canada demonstrates that people who have a bachelor's degree or community college certificate earn more money over their working lives than those who possess only a high school diploma. The earnings premium associated with a bachelor's degree over a 20-year period between 1991 to 2010 ranges, on average, from $728,000 for men to $442,000 for women. For a community college certificate, the earnings premium is $248,000 for men and $180,000 for women (Frenette, 2014, p. 7).

Why do people with more education reap larger socioeconomic rewards? Sociologists offer two competing explanations. Human capital theory sees education as transmitting knowledge, skills, and values that persist in adulthood and that employers believe increase productivity. To the classical notion of human capital, more recent scholarship has emphasized the role of soft skills that can be imparted by the educational system. These include social skills, such as the knowledge and ability to hold a sophisticated conversation or interact well with a wide variety of people, and determination and the ability to stay on task. These soft skills, sometimes also called noncognitive traits, can be developed and enhanced in educational settings and can serve as an important complement to human capital. Critical thinking skills, also called cognitive traits, are also enhanced and developed in educational settings and can be applied universally to a wide range of tasks required across all employment settings. Many of the top-earning CEOs of Fortune 500 companies have liberal arts degrees.

In contrast, **allocation theory** sees education as channelling people into positions or institutions that offer different opportunities for continuing to think, learn, and earn. The role of the school system is to sort people out so that employers and others have a good sense of who is likely to be successful and who is not. According to this theory, an educational credential signals to employers that you have a certain set of attitudes and abilities, having advanced through the educational system to wherever you end up. This is true regardless of whether you have *actually* acquired these traits in your formal schooling (Spence, 1974). Think of it this way: Human capital sees education as changing you by making you more productive, so you are different in

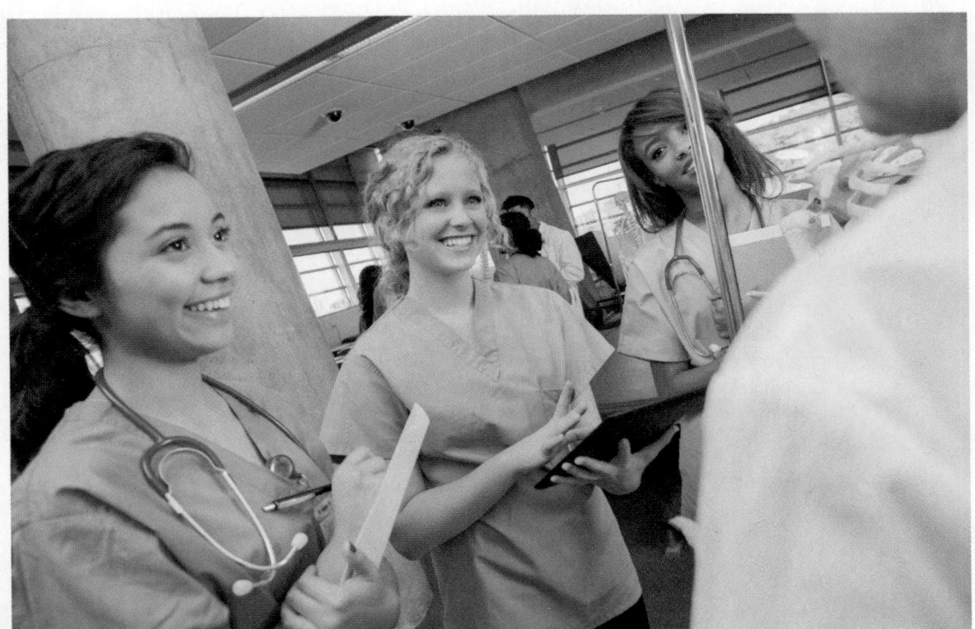

Steve Debenport/Getty Images

Credential inflation is most dramatic in fields with a high degree of social closure, like the law, but it can be found in many other less prestigious professions. For example, the nursing profession is particularly well protected by the various general degrees and specific licences, imposed by the field itself. Hence, a student who pursues a career as a nurse will need to pass many academic hurdles—more than before—in order to qualify and enter the profession. By artificially making the entrance into a profession more difficult, those who are already in are better protected against competition.

key ways that influence how much you earn. Allocation doesn't change you; rather, it moves you into different routes based on your degrees—whether a high-speed interstate highway or a two-lane winding country road, or somewhere in between—which lead to different earnings.

Another aspect of allocation theory is the role of **social closure**, an idea associated with the work of Max Weber (see Chapter 2). Closure occurs in education when it serves as a credentialing function that closes off or limits entry into some professions and thus raises the rewards of people in them. As a consequence, the value of degrees that previously secured a job in one of those professions declines. This is called *credential inflation* (R. Collins, 1979). Another implication of social closure is that, if you want to break into a certain profession, you may have to jump through a lot of educational hoops that are designed, in large measure, to hold down the number of people who can practise in a profession. One study of 488 occupations found that such closure practices affect earnings in many occupations, including those in business and finance, health, education, social services, criminal justice (Weeden, 2002). Closure practices include licensing, educational credentialing, certification, association representation, and unionization. These practices operate independently of the human capital you have.

Both human capital and allocation theories recognize that occupational positions are related to education and subsequent life-course outcomes (Pallas, 2000). In this sense, the two theories are not entirely incompatible. Schooling clearly influences the types of tasks you do at work, the amount of control you have over your work, and how much you supervise the work of others. Some (e.g., Bowles & Gintis, 1976; Ross & Van Willigen, 1997) argue that employers use educational credentials to bolster the authority of managers in the workplace, while others assume that education provides the knowledge and skills needed for direction, supervision, and planning. Regardless of what education exactly does for individual capacities, the result is that workers with higher education degrees, particularly specialized degrees (e.g., MBAs or JDs), do far less manual and routine work and more mental work. They are also more likely to supervise the work of others and to have more control over the nature and pace of their jobs. Moreover, larger national and international firms with more assets are more likely to require higher levels of education and to pay higher salaries.

One important question about the relationship between education and future life chances is whether or not people from different social-class backgrounds obtain the

Figure 14.4 Relationship of Class Background, Education, and Occupation

SOURCE: Based on data from *Understanding Society: An Introduction to Sociology* (3rd ed.), by Caroline Hodges Persell, 1990, New York: Harper and Row.

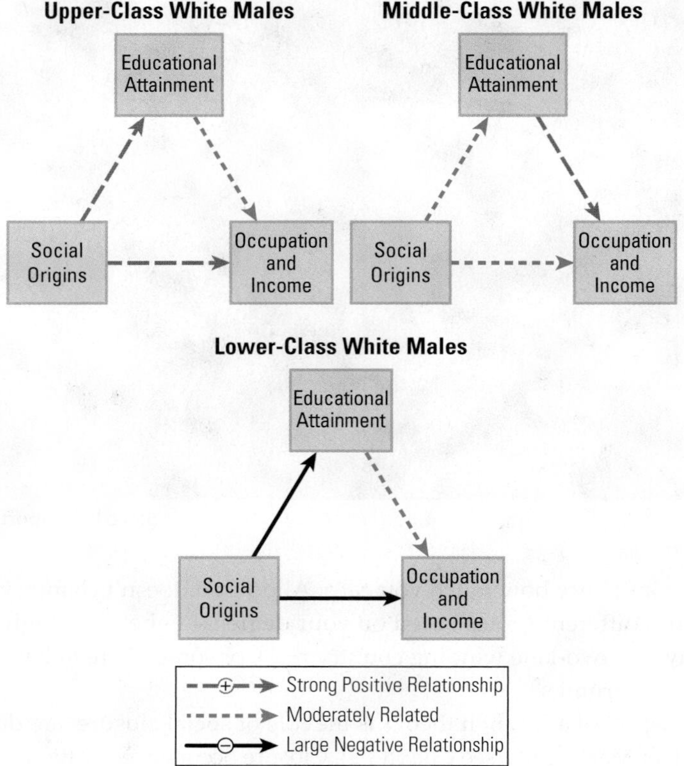

same payoff from similar levels of education. In other words, does everyone get the same benefit from a university degree, or do some people benefit more than others? Considerable research on this question over the past few decades suggests that economic outcomes for similarly educated people will indeed vary by the social class of their parents (see Figure 14.4). For members of the upper class, social background is strongly related to education level (Cookson & Persell, 1985; Espenshade & Radford, 2009). Children from wealthy families are extremely likely to graduate from university and increasingly likely to obtain graduate or professional degrees. Their occupations and income depend to some degree on their education but are also influenced by their social connections and wealth, which are a result of their family background.

For members of the middle class and those who grow up in poor families, by contrast, educational achievement may have less of a payoff. Individuals from lower-class or lower-income backgrounds are likely to obtain less education and to take longer getting it than members of other classes. Even when they do obtain a university degree, they are less likely than their upper-class peers to enter high-status and high-income occupations. Why is this so? One explanation is that people from lower-class backgrounds may have less direct knowledge of such occupations because higher-status jobs are less likely to be advertised and more likely to be obtained as a result of informal referrals. However, more educated persons from lower-class backgrounds are still more likely to be employed and earn more than people of similar social origins with less education.

In general, more educated individuals have wider and bigger social networks than their less educated peers, which helps increase their chances of job referrals and of learning about opportunities (Granovetter, 1974). People with more education are also more likely to participate in social, voluntary, civic, arts, and political events and activities than those with less education, a finding consistent across cultures and one that reinforces the strength of an individual's social network. For instance, university students often build networks of friends in their classes and meet a lot of people in their fraternities and sororities, most of whom also end up in highly skilled professions. Non-university-educated people typically lack these kinds of networks. Sociologists have also found that because more educated people have a wider array of social ties and involvement, it is not surprising that they tend to report higher levels of social support—that is, feeling that there are others on whom they "can rely for advice and encouragement" (Pallas, 2000; Ross & Mirowsky, 1989).

Health and Life Expectancy

14.2.2 Identify the correlation between education level and health.

People with more education are not only likely to find and hold better jobs, but they are also more likely to report being in better physical and mental condition, and to live healthier lives. They are less likely to smoke, for example, and, among those who do smoke, are more likely to successfully quit. Given differences like these, it is not surprising that people with more education tend to live longer, but the differences are substantial, and it is true for men and women, as well as blacks and whites. For men, the difference in life expectancy between someone with a post-secondary education and someone without is about five years, while for women it is about three years. Going to university not only pays off financially, but literally extends your life.

Why is education so positively related to health and life expectancy? One major reason is the association between education and working conditions. People with less education are more likely to be channelled into physical labour, sometimes in difficult, toxic, or dangerous conditions. For example, consider this quote from a maintenance worker who was working on a broken sewer line near my office one day in a driving rainstorm. He told me, "When I'm out here shovelling shit in the rain, I know I shoulda went to college." Such workers are also likely to have less autonomy on the job and more likely to take orders from others, which tends to be more stressful. Having extended health coverage—a key benefit of having a good job—is also positively related to better health (Finkelstein et al., 2011).

Consistent with human capital theory, there is also some evidence that more highly educated people have better access to health information, can understand it better, can better comprehend probabilities, and are in a better position to obtain the help they need (Pallas, 2000). They may also be more likely to observe good health habits such as taking medicines on a prescribed schedule, using seat belts in their vehicles, and avoiding unhealthy behaviours. Education also helps people interact more effectively with their doctors and in some cases get better care as a result.

Family Life

14.2.3 Recognize the correlation between education level and relationships or family life.

Education is also related to how likely you are to marry, your marital happiness, the type of person you select as a spouse, the age when you have children, and your likelihood of divorce. In the United States, people with higher levels of education are more likely to marry than those with less education. Among women aged 25 to 34, 59 percent of those who graduated from college or university are married, compared with 51 percent of those who did not (S. P. Martin, 2006). Among women aged 35 to 44, 75 percent of graduates compared to 62 percent of nongraduates are married, and for those 65 or older the gap is 50 percent of graduates married compared to 41 percent of nongraduates. Even more striking are the very large differences in divorce rates. University-educated couples are much less likely to divorce than non-university-educated couples. Figures 14.5a and 14.5b show marriage and divorce rates by educational level for men and women aged 45 to 52 in 2010.

Figures 14.5a and 14.5b Marriage and Divorce Rate by Education Level at Age 45–52, United States, 2010–2011

SOURCE: U.S. Bureau of Labor Statistics, 2013. Copyright by U.S. Department of Labor.

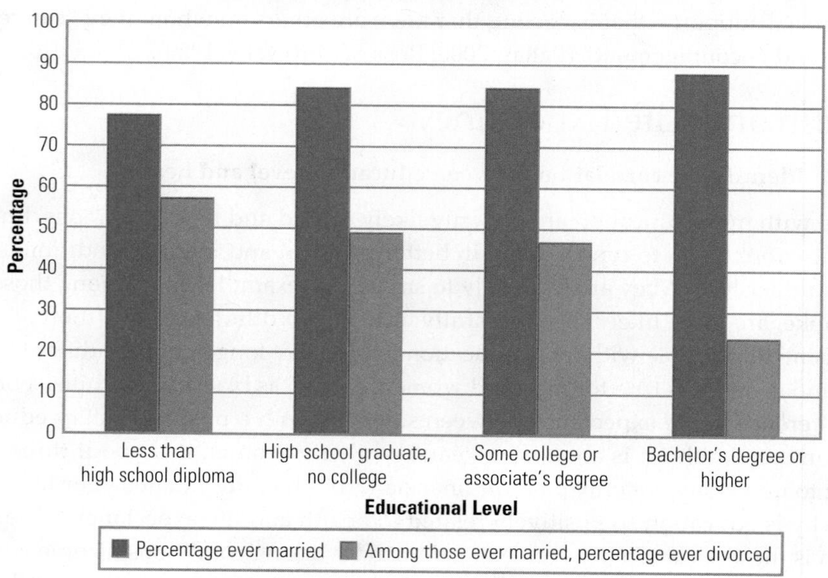

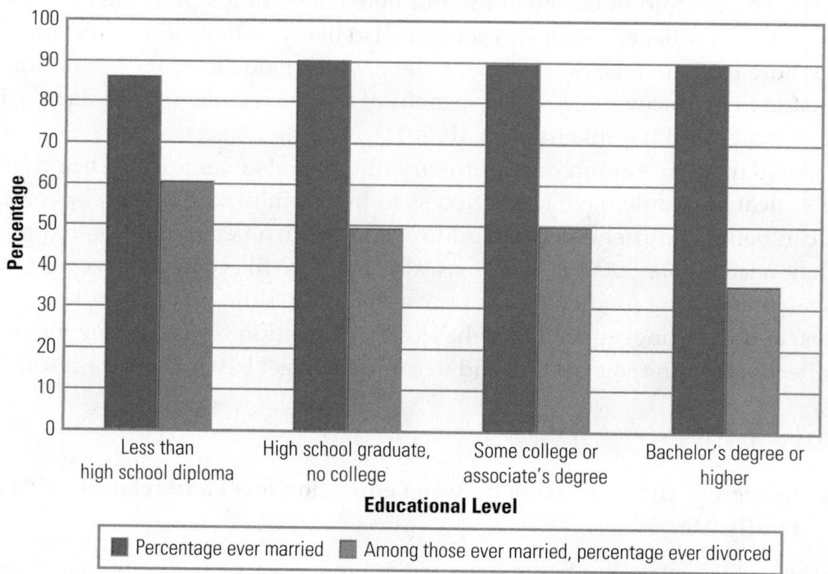

We are also increasingly likely to marry individuals with educational levels similar to our own—a practice sociologists call **educational homogamy**. The influx of women into higher education has changed the dynamics of dating. When it comes down to education, the tendency is for like to marry like. For every 100 women aged 25 to 49 with a university degree in 2006, 84 men had a comparable education. In 1981, the ratio was 157 men for every 100 women. The result is that women are now less likely than men to find a partner with the same level of education. In 2006, 64 percent of married women with a university degree had a spouse with the same level of education, a decline from 67 percent in 1981. By comparison, 67 percent of married men with a university degree in 2006 had a spouse with the same level of education, up from 38 percent in 1981. In general, university graduates today prefer to marry or form a common-law relationship with a partner who also has a university degree if they have a choice. Since education tends to increase income, this trend has widened the earnings gap between families at the low end of the income scale and those at the high end (L. Martin & Hou, 2010).

If both parents in a family have similar educational levels, there are implications for the educational and financial resources available to children in the family. As noted earlier, the pay gap between university graduates and high school graduates has increased over the past 40 years. This means that a dual-earning, highly educated family has an additional economic advantage over a single- or dual-earning lower-educated family. As a result, educational homogamy further increases the inequality between households with university graduate couples and households with high school graduate couples. A big change in recent decades is that educated people are marrying at an older age, having children later in life, and having fewer children. Women in particular are waiting longer to marry so they can spend more time pursuing education and careers. People who marry somewhat older are less likely to get divorced than people who marry younger. This might explain the "divorce divide," which shows that marital breakups are especially common among people who marry in the late teens or early 20s and do not have university degrees (S. P. Martin, 2006).

Putting these two trends together, we can now begin to understand why university-educated people are "better" at marriage than non-university-educated people. They tend to be older when they do marry, and thus are more mature and have met a greater variety of people. They know more about what is important to them, and they may be less likely to see marriage as the primary goal in life; marriage is something they choose because they want it, not because it is expected of them. They are also more likely to marry other educated people who have good incomes, and the resulting financial security that two university-educated people have also contributes to greater marital happiness and reduced likelihood of divorce.

14.3 Is Education Equally Available to All?

Radius/SuperStock

Educational Inequality

Given the importance of education in our lives, sociologists have been especially concerned with the question of whether education is equally available to all. Can education be the great equalizer as it has promised since the late nineteenth century, or does it simply reproduce existing social inequalities—or does it contribute to both patterns? Sociologists have done considerable research to investigate whether educational access, experiences, and outcomes are similar for persons of different social classes, races, and genders. In this section, we discuss some of these results and their implications.

Social-Class Differences

14.3.1 Discuss how social-class issues contribute to educational inequality.

Consider three babies born at the same time but to parents of different social-class backgrounds. The first baby is born into a wealthy, well-educated business or professional family. The second is born into a middle-class family in which both parents attended college and have middle-level managerial or social service jobs. The third is born into a poor family in which neither parent finished high school or has a steady job. Will these children receive the same education?

Education in North America is not a single, uniform system that is available to every child in the same way. Children of different social classes—like these three babies—are likely to attend different types of schools, to receive different kinds of instruction, to study different curricula, and to leave school at different rates and times. They are also likely to get very different levels of encouragement from their families and to be exposed to widely different levels of learning opportunities in their lives outside of school. As a result of all of these factors, when those babies grow up and finish their schooling, they are likely to differ far more than when they entered the world. These differences will be readily apparent to others, and may be used by other social institutions, such as employers, to select or reject them. When this happens, **social reproduction** rather than equal opportunity is occurring.

Social reproduction occurs in a variety of ways. High levels of economic inequality affect how much education people receive, as well as the quality of that education. For example, in places with more income inequality—with bigger gaps between high- and low-income families—young people who grow up in wealthier families obtain more education and children in poorer families obtain less education than in places with more income equality (Mayer, 2001). The reason seems to be that in places with greater income inequality, individuals with more education earn much more than

bikeriderlondon/Shutterstock

Will these children receive the same education? Although North American societies are based on the promise of equal opportunity for all, in reality the educational experiences of these children are likely to be quite different.

people with less education, so wealthier families may work even harder to ensure their children get more education.

The historical belief in equal opportunity for all and the reality of high and growing economic inequality creates a paradox. Some scholars call this problem the "management of ambition" (Brint & Karabel, 1989, p. 7). Many more people aspire to high-paying careers than can actually enter them. One result of this has been the growth of educational credentialism, which, as mentioned earlier in this chapter, means that more and more education is required for all jobs, especially professional and managerial occupations (R. Collins, 1979). As the required amount of education lengthens, the hurdles may be more difficult to overcome for youth from low-income backgrounds. Let's explore exactly how and why social-class backgrounds affect student achievement.

All researchers agree that the social-class backgrounds of students have been consistently related to educational success throughout history (Coleman, Campbell, Mood, Weinfeld, & York, 1966; Gamoran, 2001; Mare, 1981). Although there are a number of exceptions, students from higher-social-class backgrounds tend to get better grades and to stay in school longer than do students from lower-class backgrounds. In the United States in the last 50 years, family income has become more important than race in explaining the educational **achievement gap**. Indeed, income now is associated with more than twice the black–white achievement gap. This is a remarkable reversal of the historical trend; 50 years ago, the race gap was double the income achievement gap (Reardon, 2011). Family income is becoming much more important for children's school achievement and is now nearly as important as parental education.

Social class also has a large effect on students' attitudes and their ability to internalize the school mentality that is expected by teachers. Sociologists have pointed out that the socioeconomic origin of elementary school pupils does not necessarily affect their talent, but rather their cultural fit in the educational institution. Children growing up in middle- and upper-class families, for example, tend to be exposed to a different form of childrearing than children growing up in lower-class families. Working-class and poor children, in contrast, often have more "child-like" lives, in which their parents control most of their leisure time. More affluent parents are specifically more active in developing their children's educational interest; they stress the importance of reasoning and encourage their children to solve problems through negotiation (Lareau, 2003). Children from more middle-class backgrounds are exposed to a larger and more culturally accepted vocabulary. In consequence, children from higher socioeconomic classes are better equipped to perform well in school. They are generally better able to actively manage interactions with teachers or other educators, and they may therefore seem more eloquent than their lower-class counterparts. Teachers may also unintendedly reward these class-affected habits and attitudes, which is an additional social-class effect on student outcomes.

Although students have many reasons for dropping out of school or for failing to continue, their experiences in school may contribute to their desire to continue or to quit. Students in private schools and higher-quality public schools are much less likely to drop out than those in poorer public schools. Why? For one thing, students in private or affluent public schools are more involved in extracurricular activities than those in regular public schools; these students have made social and civic "investments" that encourage them to stay involved in their schooling. And researchers have found that on average private and high-quality public schools tend to have much stronger levels of parental involvement. Having parents who are active in a school is important for supporting student learning and strengthens the ties between children and families at the school.

Social reproduction can continue at the university level. The class background of students affects their performance in other ways besides just financial ones (although having the resources to go to university is obviously important in the first place). Class is related to the types of universities students attend, which in turn are related to university attendance. Graduates of private high schools are more likely than graduates of public high schools to attend better universities, which employers prefer when hiring for desirable jobs.

Countries like Germany, Japan, Italy, France, Switzerland, Sweden, and the Netherlands all have considerably less inequality than Canada or the United States, and all of these countries show a much weaker effect of the family's social-class background on their children's school achievement and attainment (Blossfeld & Shavit, 1993).

The negative impact of inequality can be seen in a variety of ways. At the national level, countries with higher levels of inequality tend to do worse on international tests of educational achievement than countries with lower inequality. While the most privileged students do well on standardized assessments, those from disadvantaged backgrounds do very poorly relative to their peers in other countries (Condron, 2010). For example, the United States ranked 17th in reading, which was slightly above average; 23rd in science, which was barely above average; and 32nd in math, which was below average, in the 2009 Program for International Student Assessment tests of 15-year-old students (Organisation for Economic Co-operation and Development [OECD], 2010b). But teacher quality also varies in schools around the world, so that alone may not explain differences in student learning (Montt, 2011). Another reason may be variations in how diligent students are, with young people in some parts of the world studying more. This is illustrated in the film *Two Million Minutes*, which compares six outstanding high school students in the United States, China, and India, showing how much more time U.S. students spend working at jobs and socializing compared to the Indian and Chinese students, who spend many more hours per week (and more weeks per year) on their studies.

Racial and Ethnic Gaps

14.3.2 Discuss racial and ethnic issues that contribute to educational inequality.

In addition to studying class differences, sociologists have devoted a considerable amount of research to analyzing racial and ethnic gaps in educational achievement. Despite individual exceptions, Aboriginal, immigrant, and nonwhite students tend to fare worse, on average, than those who are white or Asian Canadian, and the disparity has persisted over the last 30 years in spite of efforts to provide more equal educational opportunities. Gaps occur in standardized test scores, grade point averages, rates of placement in gifted or special education programs, dropout rates, and university attendance and graduation rates.

Young women graduate from university at higher rates than young men in the United States, Canada, Australia, New Zealand, and most countries in Europe.

EPA/Peter Foley/Newscom

The historical legacy of slavery, racial discrimination, and segregation has created severe social and economic inequalities for racial minorities that affect their education. For example, let's consider some research that has measured student performance on reading and number tests. Sociologists in the U.S. looked at a group of black and white children who shared key variables. The students were the same age and birth weight. Their parents had the same education, occupation, and income, and their mothers were the same age when they had their first child. The families had the same number of children's books in their homes, and they were equally likely to receive support from the U.S. government's Special Supplemental Nutrition Program for Women, Infants, and Children (WIC). When all of these factors were equalized, the children obtained similar scores on their reading and number tests (Fryer & Levitt, 2004a, 2004b; Yeung & Pfeiffer, 2009).

The unfortunate reality, however, is that black and white children are *not* equally likely to share these key variables that affect life chances. And the achievement gap between even those similarly matched white and black children reappears by the third grade. How can we explain this? Racial differences in educational achievement can be explained by historical and current systems of racial inequality, including neighbourhoods, families, schools, and peers, which become important for older children. Racial differences in achievement are due to social inequalities rather than to genetic differences. This is shown in research that takes into account grandparental resources, neighbourhood characteristics, and peers, as well as information on parents, students, and schools (Yeung, Persell, & Reilly, 2010). Grandparents classified as white have more education, have more wealth, and live in neighbourhoods with less poverty than black grandparents. When their children become parents, they also differ in their educational attainment, income, occupation, wealth, and neighbourhoods. White children in the third generation are much more likely than black children to live in neighbourhoods with little poverty and attend schools with many more children of average or high **socioeconomic status (SES)**—which is a broad definition of a person's class based on components such as education, income, and current occupation. These white children also have more friends who stay out of trouble. However, when grandparental resources and neighbourhoods are considered together with parental resources, neighbourhoods, parenting practices, school SES, and peers, the racial gap becomes insignificant (Yeung et al., 2010).

In Canada, educational differences among racial and ethnic groups appear to have disappeared or diminished in recent decades as a result of immigration policies that have favoured the recruitment of highly educated immigrants. These immigrant parents place a high value on educational performance and promote their children's advancement. In addition, racial diversity has demanded the increasing sensitivity to the impact of racial discrimination and prejudice in Canadian school systems (Tepperman, Albanese, & Curtis, 2012, p. 346). However, the story is quite different for Aboriginal children, particularly those who live on reserves where access to formal schooling is more limited than it is off-reserve. Aboriginal schools tend to receive less funding from the federal government than non-Aboriginal schools (which are provincially funded). In 2006, one-third (33%) of Aboriginal adults aged 25 to 54 had less than a high school education compared to nearly 13 percent of the non-Aboriginal population, a difference of 20 percentage points (Statistics Canada, 2010).

Gender Differences

14.3.3 Discuss gender issues that contribute to educational inequality.

Are there gender as well as class and racial differences in educational attainment or achievement? Throughout the world, boys and girls obtain similar amounts of education in relatively affluent and industrialized nations, and in many countries girls are now out-performing boys. In poorer nations, however, especially those with large portions of the population working in rural agriculture or countries with large Muslim populations, girls are considerably less likely than boys to obtain even an elementary school education. Gender inequality in education is an important issue in many of these countries.

When we look at gender differences in academic performance, the results vary depending on the age of the students being compared and whether grades or test scores are examined (Buchmann, DiPrete, & McDaniel, 2008). With respect to test scores, the gender gap in the United States has remained relatively stable for 30 years. Boys tend to have slightly higher test scores in math and girls in reading, but the differences *among* boys and girls are far greater than the differences *between* genders. Few gender gaps are found in the early grades, but the slight test score disparities emerge as children advance through the system (Buchmann et al., 2008).

Susan and Daniel Voyer, psychology professors at the University of New Brunswick, examined 369 studies of academic achievement of over one million boys and girl in 30 countries and found that girls earn higher grades than boys in every subject, including science (Gnaulati, 2015). In the academic achievement assessments carried out by the Programme for International Student Assessment (PISA), among a large international sample of 15-year-olds, girls out-performed boys on the reading test in all countries and in all 10 Canadian provinces. In math and science, few significant differences were found when girls' scores were compared to those of boys. Canada, France, and Germany were the only countries where gender differences in math achievement were significant—but those differences were small, certainly much smaller than those observed for reading. Overall, it appears that boys are experiencing more difficulty than girls in school across all levels. Researchers note that the reason for lower grades among boys may be because boys tend to be less conscientious than girls. Boys are more likely to fail to complete assignments or turn in homework, resulting in lower overall grades. When teachers in Ellis Middle School in Austin, Minnesota, realized that boys who aced tests were receiving overall grades of C, D, and F while students who were consistently getting A and B failed miserably, they revamped their grading policies and stopped factoring in homework completion in the students' overall grade. Homework was reframed as practice for tests, and incomplete or late assignments were noted but did not factor into the overall grade. This strategy appears to have given boys a fighting chance at receiving grades that more accurately reflect their abilities rather than their capacity for self-discipline (Gnaulati, 2015).

Young women are more likely to graduate from high school and attend university than young men, and the gap is even larger among students of colour. This represents a significant change over time. In most countries in Europe, as well as in Canada, Australia, and New Zealand, women also have higher college and university completion rates than men. We know that parents with more education and other resources have children who are more likely to be highly educated. Are these family resources equally allocated by gender? Girls and boys in the same family are arguably exposed to the same environment. Nevertheless, for children born before 1960, girls reached educational equality with boys only in the minority of families with two university-educated parents. The gender gap in university graduation rates was the largest in families where parents had a high school education or less. But for children born after the mid-1960s, one study (Buchman & DiPrete, 2006) found that a female advantage has gradually extended to all family types (Buchmann et al., 2008).

It is possible that girls' higher aspirations to attend university may partially explain their superior performance in high school and their higher rates of university graduation. The fact that girls spend more time on homework and are less likely to have disciplinary problems may also help them perform better (Buchmann et al., 2008). But the stronger performance of girls might also reflect their desire to narrow the gender pay gap through education.

The Education Policy Research Initiative (EPRI), a national research organization based at the University of Ottawa, found that eight years after graduating with university bachelor degrees in 2005, males were earning $27,300 more on average than females who graduated at the same time with the same degrees. The study looked at income tax data between 2005 and 2013 for 620,000 graduates from 14 universities and colleges. The researchers found that men who graduated from university in 2005 earned $2,800 more than women in their first year after graduation. After eight years, male graduates were earning 44 percent more on average than female graduates. This gendered pattern was repeated in all fields of study, with the largest gaps appearing in business, engineering, social sciences, and science and agriculture. One explanation may be that women take time out of the labour force to have children and then work part-time after that. The researchers noted that discrimination likely plays an important role in explaining this pay gap between men and women (Butler, 2016).

Once they go to university, do men and women study the same subjects and pursue similar degrees? As Figure 14.6 highlights, in recent decades, more women have chosen to major in traditionally male-dominated fields (computer science, natural sciences, and business, for example), but relatively few men have decided to major in nursing, early childhood education, or other traditionally female-dominated fields (England & Li, 2006; Jacobs, 1995). The gender gap in higher education favours girls compared to boys with respect to achievement and attainment but still favours males compared to females with respect to attending selective universities and choosing majors leading to higher-paying careers.

Figure 14.6 Proportion of U.S. Bachelor's Degree Recipients Who Were Women

SOURCE: Based on "Desegregation Stalled: The Changing Gender Composition of College Majors, 1971–2002," by Paula England and Su Li, 2006, *Gender and Society 20*(5), p. 666.

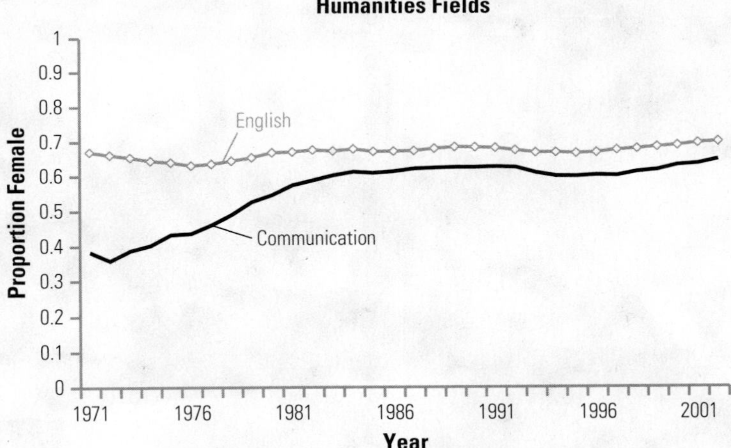

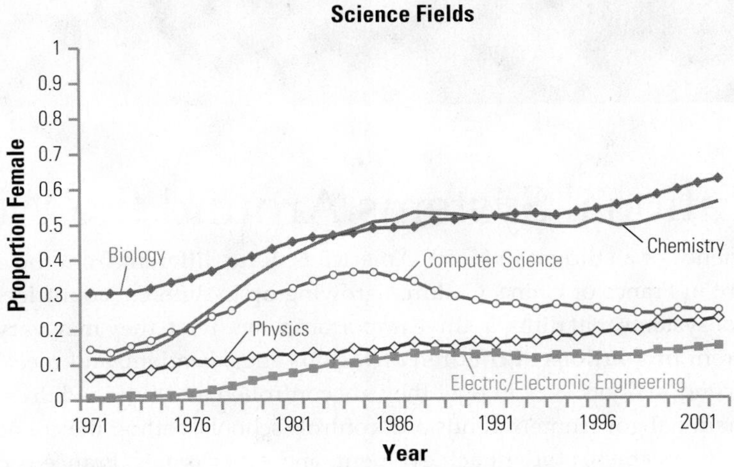

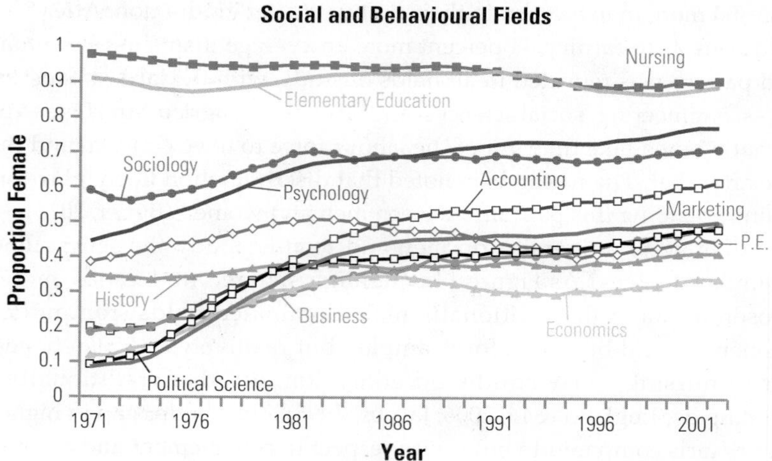

14.4 How Do Educational Systems Differ?

Sophia Paris/Handout/UN Photo/Reuters

Educational Systems Around the World

The experience of a student in North America is quite different from the experience of a student in France or China. Children growing up in different countries encounter educational systems that differ in three important ways. First, they may vary in access, with different proportions of children of various ages, genders, and races attending school. Second, schools vary in how they are controlled and financed. In some countries, the national government funds and controls schools, setting the curriculum and standards for teachers, student achievement, and other issues. France is often cited as an example of a country where the education commissioner knows what is being taught in any school on any particular day and hour. In other countries, educational institutions are controlled and funded by provinces or local governmental authorities, meaning that all pupils may not receive the same level of government funding or be exposed to the same curriculum. A third area of difference concerns the relative size of public and private education, and the degree to which public money is used to pay for private education. National differences on these three dimensions contribute greatly to variations in educational systems and their outcomes across time and place.

Access

14.4.1 Explain how access to education affects academic success.

In most countries, K–12 education is free and access to education is provided by governments. But some countries use markets to distribute access by charging school fees (e.g., South Africa for secondary school) that limit access for the poor. Some countries require children to attend school and enforce this requirement, while others forbid certain children to attend for cultural reasons. In Canada, the United States, and other affluent countries, free public schooling is available to all and children are required to attend school, usually until they are 16 or older, unless they are home-schooled, privately tutored, or otherwise educated to government standards. However, in some less wealthy countries, governments have chosen to spend some of their education money on developing universities instead of providing universal primary education. Some countries may charge school fees or have schools but no books or laboratories, and not all teachers may be trained. Consequently, around the world, access to education varies widely, with sometimes large differences by gender, class, and race.

Regarding higher education, large differences exist around the world. The costs of university education vary greatly across countries, as do the opportunities for students to receive funding. In many countries, post-secondary college or university education is free or very low cost to students. In Canada, students and their families pay tuition and other ancillary fees. Costs of higher education have soared in recent years, especially at large research institutions offering professional degrees in dentistry, law, and medicine; financial aid has been allocated less on the basis of need and more on the basis of merit; and students have been borrowing increasing amounts of money to finance their education. All of these trends make access to higher education in Canada less rather than more available to lower-income students. Participation in university education reached an all-time high in 2005–2006, rising to 24 percent of the population aged 18 to 24. The United States has the most expensive public higher education system in the world, and students and their families pay tuition and fees even in state-funded universities. Almost three-quarters of U.S. students attend public nonprofit colleges and universities, and about 1 in 10 attends each of the following: private independent nonprofit colleges or universities, private religious institutions, and private for-profit institutions. Other countries, such as Denmark and Sweden, have free public higher education and most students receive an additional loan or a scholarship. Figure 14.7 illustrates how countries compare in terms of the costs of higher education.

Some students have access to traditional printed resources and some don't, while still others have access to computers and digital media in their schools. How consequential are such resource differences?

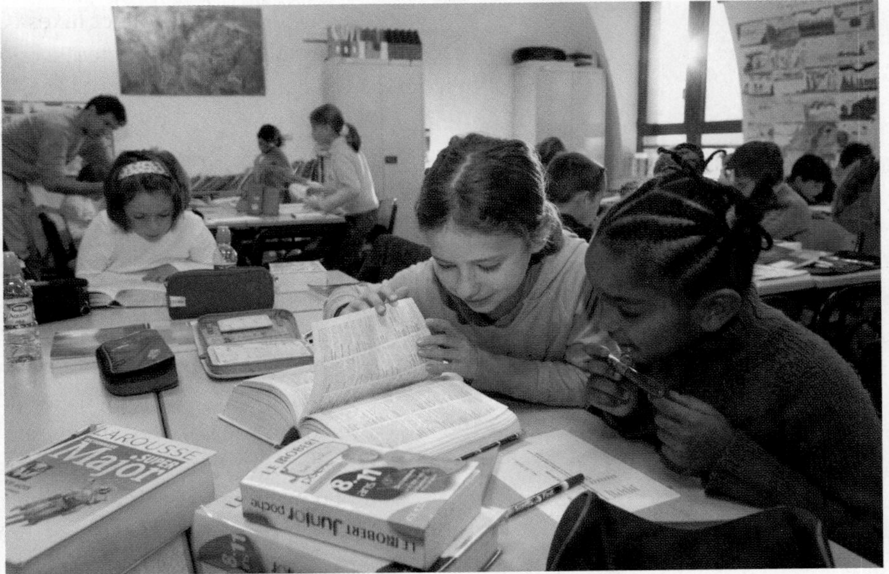

Steve Gorton/Dorling Kindersley, Ltd.

Figure 14.7 Cost of Higher Education and University Debt From an International Perspective, 2008–2009

The costs of university education vary greatly across countries, as well as the opportunities for students to receive funding. The United States has the most expensive public higher education system in the world. Other countries, such as Denmark and Sweden, have free public higher education and most students receive an additional loan or a scholarship. Think about how these institutional differences affect the access to higher education of students with various socioeconomic backgrounds.

SOURCE: From *Education at a Glance 2011: OECD Indicators* (Chart B5.1, p. 254), by Organisation for Economic Co-operation and Development [OECD], 2011, Paris: OECD (https://www.oecd.org/education/skills-beyond-school/48631582.pdf). Copyright by Organisation of Economic Co-operation and Development.

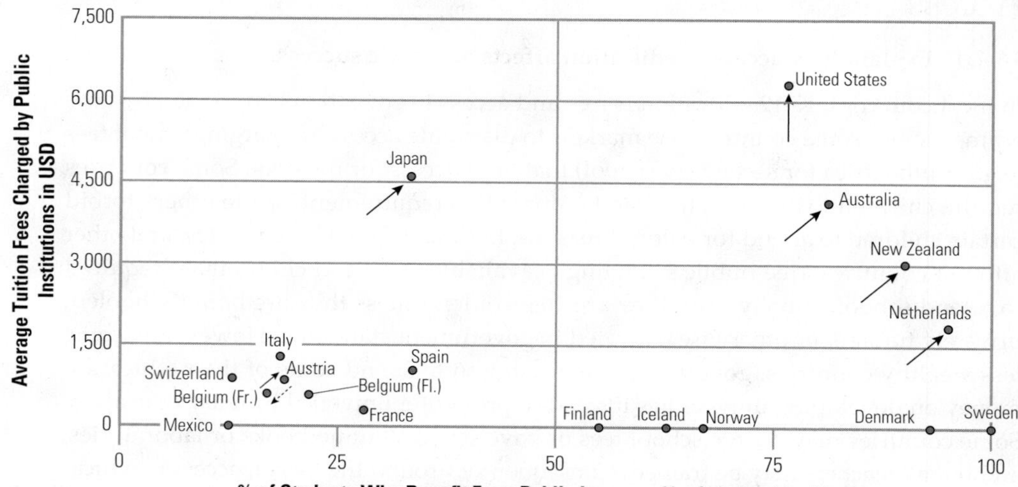

Control and Financing of Schools

14.4.2 Explain how sources and amounts of funding affect educational opportunities.

While most affluent countries have national public elementary and secondary education systems with uniform curricula, testing, and financing, some do not. The Canadian government does not oversee all of these aspects of public education. Rather, provinces and territories have their own departments of education, which set curriculum and standards for public schools. School funding comes either from provincial or territorial governments or from taxes collected by the local government or some other body able to collect taxes (Council of Ministers of Education, Canada, 2016). There are also locally elected school boards that approve school budgets and help shape educational policy.

Public Versus Private Education

14.4.3 Identify how public and private education vary and affect education equality.

Countries vary widely with respect to whether they have private schools, who attends these schools, and whether public funding pays for them. Private schools include all institutions managed by an entity other than a state or public authority.

In the United States, enrollment in public schools grew rapidly in the 1950s and 1960s as a result of the baby boom generation. After the peak in 1971, public school attendance began to decline and then rose again in the second half of the 1980s. The total public school enrollment kept breaking records each year until the mid-2000s, when it stabilized at around 55 million students. Private school enrollment in K–12 education is about 10 percent of the total enrollment in the United States. While the term *private school* denotes a wealthy, prestigious school, in fact over half of these private school students, around 3 million, are enrolled in Catholic schools, and about 75 percent of all private high school students attend a Catholic school. The second largest private school type is nonsectarian, with a total enrollment of about 1.2 million. The elite boarding schools discussed at the beginning of the chapter represent 10 percent or less of private schools in the United States and only 1 percent of all U.S. high schools.

Most countries (including the United States) do not provide direct public support for private education, although they may provide indirect support, such as tax exemption for property. In Canada, whether or not private schools receive any public funds depends on the jurisdiction (Council of Ministers of Education, Canada, 2016). Other countries, such as the Netherlands, support all forms of education with public tax monies, including religious and private schools. Almost 70 percent of schools in the Netherlands are administered by private school boards, and about 60 percent of all students there and in Belgium attend private schools. However, in most of Europe, Canada, and Israel, the vast majority of primary and secondary school students attend public schools (Torche, 2005). While some researchers have found that student achievement is higher in private schools than in public schools, others stress that variability within the public and private sectors is far greater than the variation in achievement between the sectors so it is difficult to reach firm conclusions. As discussed above, achievement differences between public and private school students are not that great when family background of the students is taken into account.

In Canada, roughly 5.6 percent of students attend a private school. Some of these are "elite" private institutions, but the vast majority of private schooling tends to have religious affiliation. Private schools, at some points, in some places in Canada, were banned in order that, in general, the quality of education received by Canadian students remain more or less equal. In Ontario, Catholic schooling is funded by the province, even though other religious groups do not receive funding; this is because explicitly Catholic education has been protected there by the Constitution of Canada. Thus, it seems as though the prime motivation for attending a private school is due to religious considerations rather than future educational opportunity or exceptional instruction, though this is sometimes a consideration (Statistics Canada, 2001).

Access, control, and financing highlight some of the ways educational systems can vary at the national level. Within countries, there are differences in the way schools are organized.

Home-Schooling

14.4.4 Discuss the home-schooling trend.

Although most people around the world are educated at public or private schools outside the home, there are a significant number who stay at home for their education. In Canada about 60,000 children are home-schooled (Van Pelt, 2015). Home-schooling advocates cite research conducted on the performance between home-schooled children and the academic average to show that more than 90 percent of home-schooled children out-perform their counterparts. Researchers note, however, that the sample sizes of the home-schooled children who take these standardized tests are not representative because the home-schooled students who take these tests are recruited or self-selecting, which may skew test scores higher. Nevertheless, in one study that examined 763 home-schooled Canadian students, grades 1 through 8, who completed the Canadian Achievement Tests, the home-schooled children whose parents reported academic motivations for home-schooling were found to have higher scores in reading, writing, and mathematics (Van Pelt, 2015, p. 11). Another study conducted in Canada found that home-schooled children who came from low-income families and whose parents had lower levels of education performed better than public school students who came from wealthier families with highly educated parents. Van Pelt concluded that her findings suggest that home-schooling may dampen some of the negative effects on school performance seen among public school children of low income and low parental educational attainment (p. 12).

In 2003, the U.S.-based National Home Education Research Institute conducted a survey of 7,300 adults who had been home-schooled. Their findings generally suggest that home-schooled people out-perform those who attended schools on standardized tests, are more involved in their communities, and are more likely to vote. This is not surprising, however, given the social-class background of the parents responsible for home-schooling. Unlike in Canada, where family income and education levels among home-schooled children tend to be lower than among those who send their children to public school, in the United States, the families who choose to home-school their children tend to have higher incomes and more education than families who send their children to public schools. Therefore, in the U.S. it is unclear what the exact effects of home-schooling itself are on students' skills and human capital. Further, socialization for students who are home-schooled works differently than for traditional students: parents and other home educators may emphasize different cultural norms and values or historical facts.

Conclusion: The Future of Education in a Global Economy

We care about education because it shapes so many important aspects of our adult lives, from intellectual development to career prospects, income level to physical health, even intimate relationships and marriage. Education also has a huge impact on the economies of entire countries and regions. In this chapter, we explored some of the major purposes of education as well as how it relates to all of these important life outcomes for individuals and societies. We also examined inequalities in education and how educational systems in North America differ from others around the world.

Educational systems are currently undergoing massive updating with the rise of new educational technologies. A number of thinkers are pondering what people need to learn to function well in the twenty-first century, and they identify some common competencies. Sociologists of education are making an important contribution to these discussions by studying how the social contexts of learning matter. For example, how can we advance *critical thinking* and *problem-solving skills*? Looking at the social context surrounding an activity or market, a defining characteristic of sociology, is part of critical thinking. It involves analyzing how parts of a whole interact to create various outcomes in complex systems; analyzing and evaluating evidence from many different sources, including its timeliness, credibility, and usefulness; assessing arguments, claims and beliefs, and alternative points of view; integrating and connecting information and arguments; drawing inferences and conclusions from information; and reflecting on what has been learned and what more needs to be learned. The rise of the Internet, with huge quantities of instantly available information of widely varying quality, makes these skills particularly important today.

Another important element in the future of education will be *communication* and *collaboration skills* across networks, including even global ones, potentially involving diverse cultures. This includes being able to lead and influence others by reasoning and persuasion rather than by trying to command obedience. Clear communication involves being able to articulate thoughts and ideas effectively orally or in writing; to listen effectively to discern meaning, knowledge, values, attitudes, and intentions; and to understand how to communicate to inform, instruct, motivate, and persuade. It might also include being multilingual. Communication is not just about grammar, punctuation, or spelling, but about the ability to think clearly and write with focus, energy, and passion (a real voice). It also entails using multiple media and technologies, being able to judge their effectiveness and weigh their impact. Effective collaboration involves working well and respectfully with diverse teams; being flexible, helpful, and willing to compromise to accomplish common goals; and sharing responsibility and credit for collaborative work.

Finally, *agility* and *adaptability* will be important, because the world and the economy are changing so quickly. People need to expect and be able to deal with disruptions, which might result from monumental events, dramatic weather patterns, or innovations, changes, and reorganization. People may need to adapt to varied roles, responsibilities, schedules, and contexts and be able to work in ambiguous situations with changing priorities. They need to be able to accept feedback on their work; deal positively with criticism, setbacks, and praise; and understand, negotiate, and balance diverse views to reach solutions.

If these are widely accepted goals of education, it is clear that applying the insights of a sociological imagination will prove vitally important. The social contexts of learning—and the challenges faced by students of varied backgrounds—are going to have to be addressed if we truly aspire to have a meritocratic educational system and society. Achieving equality of opportunity in education, as in other arenas of social life, is no easy challenge.

CHAPTER SUMMARY

The Big Questions Revisited 14

14.1 Why Is Formal Education Universal? In this section, we examined the various purposes of schooling, from socialization to preparation for work, citizenship, and community life.

The Purposes of Education

Socialization

Learning Objective 14.1.1: Discuss socialization in schools.

Future Preparation

Learning Objective 14.1.2: Explain how credentials affect future employment opportunities.

Economic Benefits of Schooling

Learning Objective 14.1.3: Discuss how education contributes to economic growth.

The Great Equalizer?

Learning Objective 14.1.4: Discuss how schools create an equal playing field for students.

14.2 How Is Education Related to Important Life Outcomes? Education is strongly related to many important life outcomes, including work and economic opportunities, health and life expectancy, and marital success and happiness.

Education and Life Outcomes

Career Outcomes

Learning Objective 14.2.1: Discuss the relationships among education, occupation, and life-course outcomes and how those affect economic success.

Health and Life Expectancy

Learning Objective 14.2.2: Identify the correlation between education level and health.

Family Life

Learning Objective 14.2.3: Recognize the correlation between education level and relationships or family life.

14.3 Is Education Equally Available to All? Is education the great equalizer in North American society, or does it reproduce existing inequalities? In this section, we examined the sociological research that investigates whether educational access, experiences, and outcomes are similar for persons of different social classes, races, and genders.

Educational Inequality

Social-Class Differences

Learning Objective 14.3.1: Discuss how social-class issues contribute to educational inequality.

Racial and Ethnic Gaps

Learning Objective 14.3.2: Discuss racial and ethnic issues that contribute to educational inequality.

Gender Differences

Learning Objective 14.3.3: Discuss gender issues that contribute to educational inequality.

14.4 **How Do Educational Systems Differ?** How can there be such wide variations in the quality and types of schooling, particularly by social class and race? To address this question in this section, we examined differences in educational systems around the world and the various ways that North American schools are organized.

Educational Systems Around the World

Access

Learning Objective 14.4.1: Explain how access to education affects academic success.

Control and Financing of Schools

Learning Objective 14.4.2: Explain how sources and amounts of funding affect educational opportunities.

Public Versus Private Education

Learning Objective 14.4.3: Identify how public and private education vary and affect education equality.

Home-Schooling

Learning Objective 14.4.4: Discuss the home-schooling trend.

Learn the Terms

achievement gap (p. 407)
allocation theory (p. 400)
credentialism (p. 395)
educational homogamy (p. 404)
hidden curriculum (p. 393)
human capital (p. 394)
social closure (p. 401)
social reproduction (p. 406)
socioeconomic status (SES) (p. 409)
soft skills (p. 395)

Chapter 15
Health and Medicine

by Ruth Horowitz and Jennifer Jennings, with Owen Whooley

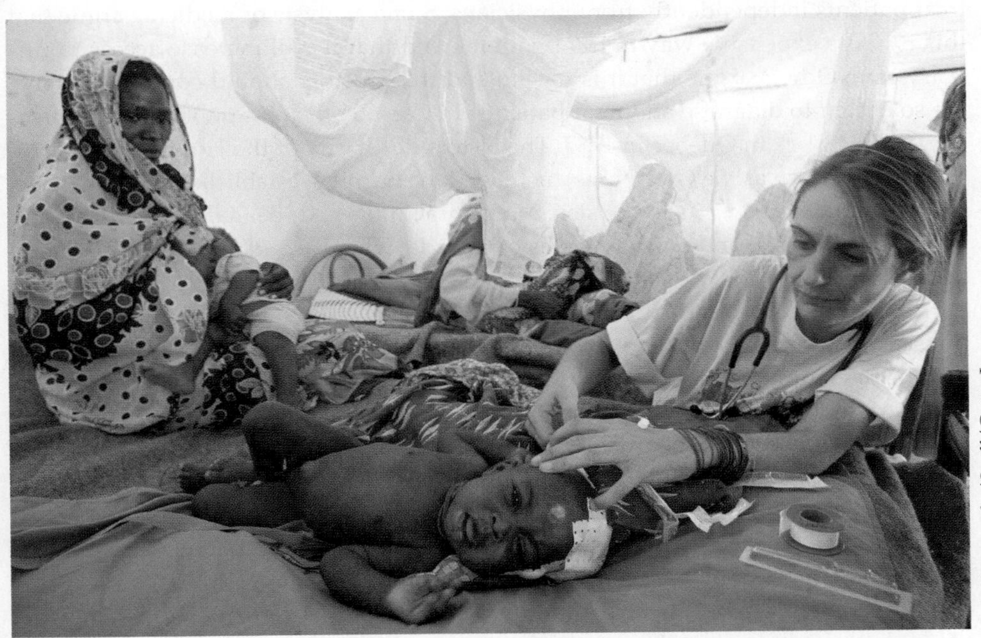

Cris Bouroncle/Staff/Getty Images

Sociologists are fascinated by questions concerning the social context of health and illness and access to healthcare.

Learning Objectives

15.1.1 Describe the population model of prevention.

15.1.2 Discuss how our social contexts and relationships help to determine the health choices we make.

15.1.3 Explain how sociologists use life-course perspectives to examine health issues.

15.1.4 Explain why where you live impacts your health.

15.2.1 Explain how socioeconomic status affects health.

15.2.2 Discuss the relationship between education and health.

15.2.3 Discuss the impact that income and wealth have on children's health.

15.2.4 Discuss sociological explanations for health disparities between races.

15.2.5 Identify explanations for gender differences in health.

15.3.1 Discuss the early days of medicine and identify the causes of public health improvements at the end of the nineteenth century.

15.3.2 Discuss the emergence of modern medicine as a powerful profession.

15.3.3 Discuss the experience of women's participation in the practice of medicine as a consequence of medical professionalization.

Nurses with advanced degrees and training—often known as **nurse practitioners (NPs)**—want to not only assist physicians and improve "care" but also diagnose and treat patients independently from physicians. Some analysts of medicine argue that this is a less expensive way to treat patients and that it will increase access to primary care. Others argue that it is unsafe and that doctors should continue to have the sole right to diagnose and treat patients. In Canada, the first public health nurses began their work in Quebec in 1737. The Sisters of Charity of the Hôpital Général, in Montreal (known as the Grey Nuns), managed the hospital, established an orphanage, and provided home visits to the sick. Nurse practitioners appeared in the 1960s, and many serve in rural and northern areas of Canada, where access to medical doctors is limited. They provide direct medical care and can prescribe certain medications and perform certain procedures. Today, nurse practitioners often work alongside family physicians, and their services are covered under the Canada Health Act.

The first author of this chapter (Ruth Horowitz) has been doing research on medical licensing and disciplinary boards across the United States. In one state she investigated, the licensing boards of nursing and physicians formed a committee that included doctors, nurses, and public (nonphysician) members to assess these issues. The arguments grew ugly at times, and, perhaps not surprisingly, different medical specialists had varying opinions. Some of the surgeons thought that nurses would do fine with diagnosis and treatment. As one surgeon put it, "that work is simple." This infuriated the family physicians and internists on the committee. These doctors expressed skepticism about the safety of patients. Some of their work would be taken over by nurse practitioners. In the end, the medical and nursing licensing boards came to an agreement about an enhanced role for the nurses. But ultimately, the change had to come before the state legislature, where the recommendations are codified into law.

Why is it so important for physicians to limit what nurses can do? Physicians traditionally have greater power than other healthcare professionals to determine what nurses, psychologists, chiropractors, and others can or cannot do. That is, physicians decide the "scope of practice" of others. Nevertheless, nurses with advanced degrees have begun to successfully challenge physicians and have gained independent practices. Conflicts over scope of practice continue, however: For example, registered nurses (RNs) often want to limit what licensed practical nurses (LPNs), who have less education, can do; and dentists work to ensure that they control who can do teeth whitening.

The Big Questions

1. **How do social contexts affect health?** We often think of health behaviours as individual choices. In this section, we explore how social contexts affect our health behaviours and how events that happen throughout our lives affect our health as adults. The relationships we have with others also play an important role in determining whether we engage in positive health behaviours.

2. **Who gets sick, and why?** Low socioeconomic status is a strong predictor of poor health. If you are highly educated, you are more likely to live a longer and healthier life than people who are not. This has been true throughout history and across many different countries. We explore why these patterns persist and the major explanations that sociologists have advanced to explain them.
3. **How did modern medicine emerge?** To understand the world of modern medicine and how healthcare is practised today, it is important to look at how it emerged. In this section we discuss the early days of medicine, the professionalization of North American medicine, the impact of medical education reform, and some important consequences on health, illness, and treatment.

15.1 How Do Social Contexts Affect Health?

Gaertner/Alamy Stock Photo

A Sociological View of Health

When you walk into a doctor's office with a few worrisome symptoms—let's say, a cough and some difficulty breathing—your doctor may ask you how you've been eating, whether you smoke, whether you've been exercising, and about your family history. Maybe you admit that you've been skipping the gym, and perhaps it's true that you have been more stressed than usual at work. You walk away with a prescription to fill and perhaps a lecture to take better care of yourself in order to calm your cough.

In treating patients, doctors are interested in the immediate causes of illness that can be remedied with medical treatments. They focus on why you got this illness at this time. The cause of your poor health could lie deep in your past—for example, perhaps you lived in a polluted city as a child—but in their offices, doctors attempt to address the immediate symptoms rather than to consider their social causes.

Sociologists usually take a decidedly different approach to the study of health. They focus on the social causes of disease within a population rather than on the immediate causes of an individual's illness. Sociologists want to know why people in some countries are much more likely to die early than those in others, or why poor people consistently die earlier than more affluent ones. Sociologists also consider how social contexts shape individual health behaviours. When confronted with an overweight person, sociologists look beyond the individual's self-control or family history and genetics to explain that outcome. People are much fatter today than in the past. It can't be solely because people have less willpower or different genes than 50 or 100 years ago. Part of the explanation for rising obesity has to reside in social factors as well. So in examining the question of why obesity rates are so high in North America today, sociologists focus on how social contexts may lead individuals to eat more, and exercise less, than is healthy. Or other social factors could be implicated, such as the rise of fast food restaurants and the increased prominence in modern grocery stores of addictive processed foods high in sugar and carbohydrates. For example, North Americans are more likely to be overweight than the Japanese. Why? One well-established finding is because of the kinds of diets that the Japanese and North Americans typically consume. The Japanese diet includes much more fish and vegetables than the meat- and processed-food-based diet of many North Americans. Instead of asking, "Why is this person overweight?" the sociological question is "Why is the North American population as a whole heavier than the Japanese population?"

In 2010, the City of Toronto proposed a ban on all soft drinks on its school properties. Other schools across the country soon followed. This was thought to help shift the distribution of risk for obesity for all school-aged children.

Dennis MacDonald/Alamy Stock Photo

The Population as Patient

15.1.1 Describe the population model of prevention.

In contemporary medical science, most approaches to studying health focus on individual genetic risk factors or individual behavioural risks. The sociological approach to improving health differs from the medical approach. Doctors focus on treating high-risk groups—for example, those most likely to have hypertension. Getting fewer people to become sick in the first place, however, might require a different strategy. We need to think not just about individuals but entire populations.

How could that be possible? Most risk factors, like blood pressure, have no clear cutoff above which high blood pressure leads to a stroke or a heart attack. Your risk increases as your blood pressure increases. The medical field necessarily establishes arbitrary cutoff points on a continuum that determine when you should receive treatment for high blood pressure (hypertension). We give people drugs for hypertension over a certain cutoff and keep an eye on those individuals right below that cutoff.

The trouble is that high-risk groups make up a small fraction of the overall population. But as the example of hypertension makes clear, health risks operate on a continuum; they are not an either/or phenomenon. Most of the cases of stroke come not from people at high risk of hypertension but from those who had much less but still elevated blood pressure. For that reason, the English epidemiologist Geoffrey Rose influentially argued in the 1980s that we could save more lives by decreasing everyone's blood pressure a little bit than by reducing the blood pressure of the most high-risk cases (**epidemiology** is the study of health in population subgroups or populations as a whole). This is often referred to as the *population model for prevention*, and it focuses on "shift[ing] the whole distribution" of risk (Rose, 1985, p. 34). Is this possible?

Shifting the distribution of risks is difficult, however, as it means changing whole societies. A number of recent public health initiatives have attempted to do that. For example, in New York City and a number of other cities, chain restaurants are now required to list the number of calories in each item. In Canada, the Ontario government proposed a similar initiative in 2015 through Bill 45, the Making Healthier Choices Act. The goal of this policy is to encourage consumers to choose healthier options and to create pressure for businesses to offer them. In theory, if they were aware that a typical muffin has over 400 calories, the average consumer could make healthier choices and eat fewer calories. Eventually, this may reduce the number of people over the line that doctors consider obese. By changing features of the social environment and treating the population as the patient, this initiative is an example of the population model of prevention. It remains an open question, of course, whether this approach will improve population health.

The Effects of Social Contexts on Individual Behaviour

15.1.2 Discuss how our social contexts and relationships help to determine the health choices we make.

So how do social forces influence our health? Suicide provides an interesting example. On its face, suicide is the most individual of acts. In the late nineteenth century, however, French sociologist Émile Durkheim sought to understand how suicide rates differed across social groups and how social change affected rates of suicide. In his book *On Suicide* (Durkheim, 1897/2006), he showed that suicide rates are affected by such things as religion, gender, being in certain organizations such as the military, or living in certain regions or countries.

One of Durkheim's most paradoxical results was that close-knit communities could be either helpful or harmful in causing suicides. In communities that were *either* very well integrated and people knew one another well *or* places where people are very disconnected from one another, more people are likely to commit suicide. Strongly integrated groups benefited from the sense of inclusion that strong social ties foster. But Durkheim also showed that *too much* integration is also associated with higher rates of suicide, as group needs take precedence over individuals' need to survive. At the same time, social ties not only integrate individuals but regulate their behaviour. Without these ties, Durkheim argued, individuals' desires could exceed their ability to fulfill them and thus lead to higher suicide rates.

Similar to Durkheim, contemporary sociologists recognize that the contexts that people inhabit and the relationships they have with others play an important role in shaping the choices that they make. Sociologists ask what features of social contexts enable or constrain particular behaviours, and they examine how norms around behaviour may affect individuals' choices. For example, norms about binge drinking appear to vary across age groups. Twenty-six percent of 18- to 24-year-olds report binge drinking (defined as more than four drinks for women and more than five drinks for men on one or more occasions in the last 30 days). For those 65 and older, that number drops to only 4 percent (Centers for Disease Control, 2011).

How might social contexts contribute to age differences in binge drinking? Social contexts shape what counts as "normal" behaviour and what behaviours are socially sanctioned or accepted. University dorms provide an example. If all of the students in a dorm binge drink on the weekends, it's more likely that if you are living in this dorm, you will, too. Social contexts also provide opportunities for engaging in binge-drinking behaviours. If you can walk down your hallway to a party where binge drinking is

Figure 15.1 Prevalence of Binge Drinking Among American Adults

SOURCE: Centers for Disease Control and Prevention, 2012.

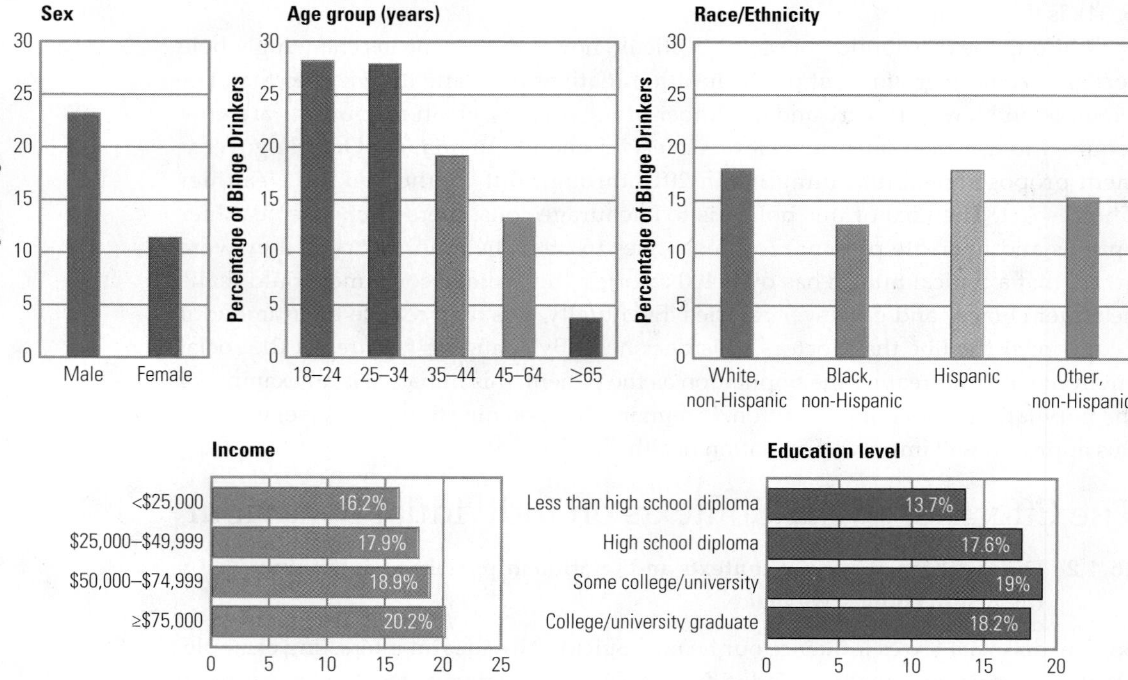

happening, it's simply easier (and tempting) to engage in that behaviour than if you have to actively seek out opportunities to do so. Some social contexts like university can also create stress that leads people to engage in health-risking behaviours to alleviate it. Binge drinking, which may alleviate stress in the short term but cause negative health outcomes in the long term, is just one example of a coping behaviour that is influenced by social context. Explore the data in Figure 15.1 to see the effects of different variables on binge-drinking prevalence.

The relationships we have with others also impact the choices we make. Our social relationships affect our health in three major ways: through social influence, person-to-person contact, and access to resources (Smith & Christakis, 2008). Obesity provides one of the best examples of the process of social influence. While obesity is often thought of as a result of choices that we privately make, most eating is social. Imagine that the person across the table from you decides to order the all-you-can-eat buffet. Because it is more convenient for your meal if you both order from the buffet, you probably follow your friend. If your friend goes back for a second and third helping, you might be less shy about doing the same. Sociologists have in fact produced empirical evidence that suggests that people who are obese are more likely to have friends who are obese (Christakis & Fowler, 2007). While it is complicated to determine what is causing obesity (as we choose our own friends and it is often said that "birds of a feather flock together"), this is nonetheless suggestive that social norms are at work.

Person-to-person contact is also important for the spread of infectious diseases. The people with whom we ride the bus or those we sit next to at work or at a concert or sporting event can have an important impact on our health. The outbreak and spread of deadly viruses, like the Ebola outbreak that originated in West Africa in the summer of 2014, provide a good example of how some forms of person-to-person contact can spread disease, and more generally how societal conditions contribute to the spread of disease. The 2014 outbreak of this acute viral illness has been the deadliest in the history of the disease. Ebola spreads within the community as the result of direct contact (through broken skin or mucous membranes) with the blood, secretions, or other bodily fluids of infected people and indirect contact with environments contaminated with such fluids. Capturing the attention of international health institutions and the global media, Ebola continues to spread throughout West Africa and has resulted in a few confirmed cases in the United States, spread across and beyond borders by healthcare workers and travellers to infected areas.

The Ebola outbreak is also an example of the connection between social status and health. Social and economic issues in West Africa have played a major role in worsening the impact of Ebola. Social indicators such as literacy, sanitation, and life expectancy reveal the vulnerability of West African communities to disease. Not only do the fragile health systems of Guinea, Liberia, Sierra Leone, and Nigeria lack human, financial, and material resources, but the communities that they serve face difficulties accessing clean water, sanitary toilets, and other basic public health measures.

The Accumulation of Health Risks Across the Life Course

15.1.3 Explain how sociologists use life-course perspectives to examine health issues.

Another way in which social contexts influence health is how what happens at one stage of our lives can impact later health. For example, babies who weigh too little when they were born are more likely to have a range of health problems as they age. Because poor early health conditions may be as important as your later health behaviours, sociologists consider how events occurring now and in the past affect your health.

An unusual natural experiment during World War II provided some of the most compelling evidence we have about the accumulation of health risks across the life course. In the winter of 1944, Germans placed a ban on food transports in the Netherlands, leading to a rapid decrease of food supplies in the country. As a result, daily adult rations decreased from 1,800 calories in December 1943 to 400 to 800 calories between December 1944 and April 1945 (Roseboom, de Rooij, & Painter, 2006).

The Dutch famine had catastrophic human consequences; by its end, more than 18,000 people had died. It had an unintended effect, however—it gave social scientists the opportunity to understand how events that happen early in our lives may affect our long-term health outcomes. Sociologists studying the Dutch famine made a fascinating observation: People born during the height of the famine were more likely to have heart disease. When we think about the causes of having heart disease as an adult, we generally think about how our behaviour during adulthood affects that outcome: how much exercise we get, how stressful our lives are, how well we manage our cholesterol levels, and so forth. But investigations of the Dutch case revealed something else: What happens *in utero* has enduring consequences. The exact timing of exposure to the famine mattered, however—those exposed during the first three months of gestation were more likely to develop heart disease, while those exposed later were less likely to have these issues.

The example of the Dutch famine illustrates a more general lesson: The social contexts we inhabit at different stages throughout our lives affect our later health outcomes. Sociologists refer to this as a **life-course perspective**. Of particular interest are the long-term impacts of adverse childhood conditions, which can have negative effects on health long after they are no longer experienced. Increasingly sociologists are thinking about health in a life-course framework. For example, rather than only examining the effects of being obese as an adult, they focus on the cumulative effects of obesity as a child, as a teenager, and as a young adult on adult health outcomes. As Table 15.1 illustrates, there are three types of life-course models that sociologists study.

Table 15.1 Life-Course Perspective on Health

Sensitive-period model (or **latency model)**	In this model, very early life exposures can affect adult outcomes but may remain latent for years. Trying to improve health in adulthood does not work if the damage is already done. The idea is that things that happen to you even before you were born—that is, while you were in your mother's womb (such as the Dutch famine)—can have long-term implications for your adult health outcomes, but their effects do not show up for a long time.
Cumulative-exposure model	Smoking may provide the best example of this model. If you are a smoker, you accumulate exposure to carcinogens over a long period of time. Each cigarette adds up, and by the time you are older, you are more likely to have emphysema and lung cancer if you have exposed yourself to these carcinogens over a longer period of time.
Social-trajectory model	According to this approach, early life experiences determine where an individual ends up in the social pecking order, which in turn influences health outcomes. For example, if you are sick as a child, you may do more poorly in school. As a result, you are less likely to go to college and thus less likely to get a higher-paying job. Because you may end up working in a job that does not provide health insurance, your health is further negatively affected.

Although these three ways in which health risks accumulate over a lifetime are different, they all strongly suggest that conditions throughout the life course contribute not only to differences among individuals but also to differences in health across countries, as we will see in the next section.

Differences in Health Across Countries

15.1.4 Explain why where you live impacts your health.

Imagine you were to enter a lottery. Unlike the lotteries most of us are familiar with, where hard cash or prizes are awarded, this lottery would determine the country in which you would be born. By sheer luck of the draw, you could be born in North America, where fewer than 1 percent of babies die in their first year of life. Or you could be born in Afghanistan or Angola, where more than 1 in 10 babies do not survive until their first birthday (World Health Organization, 2011).

These are extreme differences. Do we still see such large differences in health outcomes when we compare countries that are more similar in income and development? Let's consider the United States and Europe, which are alike in many ways. The life expectancy at birth of most Europeans is longer than that of Americans. A significant part of that difference is driven by the fact that Americans are more likely to die by age 50 because of factors such as infant mortality, murder, motor vehicle accidents, and drug-related mortality (National Research Council and Institute of Medicine, 2013). Is it that our biological differences cause this difference? That is unlikely. What are Americans doing that shortens their lives compared to Europeans? Why is their **infant mortality rate** so high when compared to other nations?

Social scientists use a range of such measures to track the health status of populations. Because health has many different facets, each of these measures provides a snapshot of a different piece of the health puzzle, and we want to look at a variety of different measures to see how well a country's healthcare system is working for its citizens. Yet, for reasons we will explore more fully later in the chapter, no matter how the numbers are cut, Americans live shorter, less healthy lives than we would expect based on the wealth of the country. For more information, examine the data in Table 15.2 for 21 different countries on several different measures.

Though many factors contribute to differences in life expectancy across countries, research shows that at least part of the blame is on the healthcare system itself. The U.S. spends about twice as much on healthcare as Canada but does not have better health outcomes. Some of the problems may be due to lack of access to the healthcare system, while other factors are public health issues such as poverty or a toxin-filled environment.

Table 15.2 World Health Measures

These recent data show that the United States had a higher rate of preventable deaths, more infant mortality, lower healthy life expectancy at age 60, and higher mortality (death) rates than almost all of the other countries in this 21-country comparison, ranking 16th out of 21 countries, worse than a number of much poorer countries (e.g., Cuba, Poland) and only better than countries much poorer than the United States. The United States spends more on healthcare than any other country in this comparison.

Country	Norway	Sweden	Switzerland	Israel	France	Australia	Republic of Korea	Netherlands	Canada	New Zealand	Germany	United Kingdom	Poland	Cuba	Estonia	United States	Turkey	Mexico	Vietnam	Indonesia	Sudan
Overall ranking excluding preventable deaths	**1**	**2**	**3**	**4**	**5**	**6**	**7**	**8**	**9**	**10**	**11**	**12**	**13**	**14**	**15**	**16**	**17**	**18**	**19**	**20**	**21**
Overall ranking including preventable deaths (based on mean of all applicable rankings)	2	1	3	6	4	5	8	7	9	11	10	12	13	14	15	16	17	18	19	20	21
Mortality amenable to healthcare (deaths per 100,000)*	**64**	**61**	*	**87.5**	**55**	**57**	**84**	**66**	**77**	**79**	**76**	**83**	*	*	**194.5**	**96**	*	*	*	*	*
Ranking	4	3	*	11	1	2	10	5	7	8	6	9	*	*	13	12	*	*	*	*	*
Infant mortality**	**2.2**	**2.3**	**3.7**	**3.3**	**3.4**	**4.1**	**3.3**	**3.4**	**4.7**	**4.7**	**3.4**	**4.1**	**4**	**4**	**2.9**	**6**	**12.2**	**13.9**	**18.4**	**43.8**	**49.3**
Ranking	1	2	9	5	6	12	4	7	14	15	8	13	10	11	3	16	17	18	19	20	21
Healthy life expectancy at age 60 (average of men and women)**	**24**	**24**	**25**	**24**	**25**	**25**	**24**	**24**	**25**	**25**	**24**	**24**	**24**	**22**	**21**	**23**	**21**	**22**	**22**	**18**	**17**
Ranking	6	7	2	9	1	3	8	10	4	5	11	13	12	15	18	14	19	16	17	20	21
Adult mortality rate**	**59**	**56**	**54**	**55**	**80**	**60**	**69**	**63**	**68**	**67**	**72**	**73**	**125**	**100**	**133**	**103**	**112**	**132**	**131**	**152**	**245**
Ranking	4	3	1	2	12	5	9	6	8	7	10	11	16	13	19	14	15	18	17	20	21
Health expenditures per capita (PPP)**	$5,391	$3,760	$5,297	$2,041	$3,997	$3,685	$2,035	$5,112	$4,443	$2,992	$4,342	$3,433	$1,377	$414	$1,294	$8,233	$1,039	$962	$216	$123	$162

* Data taken from Davis et al. (2014).

** Data taken from World Health Organization (2014).

SOURCE: Based on data from *Mirror, Mirror on the Wall: How the Performance of the U.S. Health Care System Compares Internationally* (2014 update), by K. Davis, K. Stremkis, D. Squires, and C. Schoen, 2014, New York: Commonwealth Fund (http://www.commonwealthfund.org/~/media/files/publications/fund-report/2014/jun/1755_davis_mirror_mirror_2014.pdf); *Global Health Observatory Data Repository*, World Health Organization, 2014 (http://apps.who.int/gho/data/node.main).

15.2 Who Gets Sick, and Why?

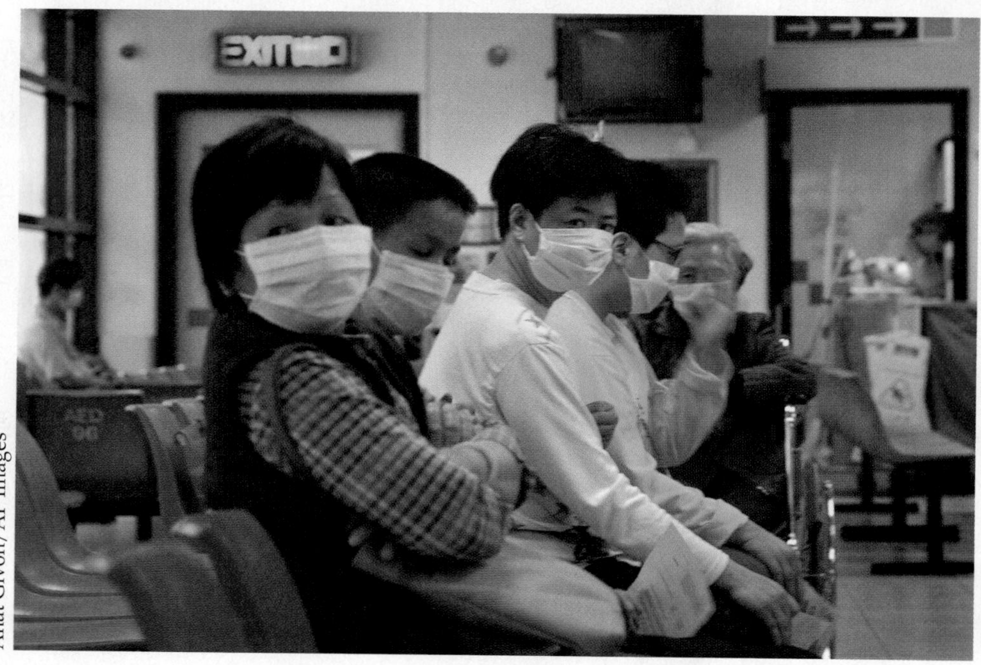
Anat Givon/AP Images

Health Outcomes Among Different Groups

In the previous section, we introduced the idea that social contexts matter for health outcomes. Now we will consider how individual factors, such as class, education, race, and gender, interact with the social contexts in which people live and influence health outcomes.

Health and Socioeconomic Status

15.2.1 Explain how socioeconomic status affects health.

What are the strongest predictors of one's health? One guess would be whether you have freely available healthcare. Or perhaps it's whether or not you smoke, what you eat, or how often you exercise. In fact, an extraordinarily strong predictor of one's health is your socioeconomic status, or SES (Adler & Ostrove, 1999). In the way social scientists define it, SES has a number of dimensions of social and economic status: education, income, and occupation. If you are highly educated, you are more likely to live a longer and healthier life than those who are not. The same is true of income and occupation. If you work in a job that has you working behind a desk all day, you are likelier to live longer than someone who performs physical labour all day. Similarly, having more income helps. When researchers talk about **health disparities**, they mean differences in health status linked to social, economic, or environmental conditions. These conditions include SES, race and ethnicity, gender, and location.

The connection between one's social status and health is one of the most consistent findings in all of the social sciences. It holds across every time period of history and place that has been studied, whether the leading causes of death are infectious diseases like tuberculosis or chronic diseases like heart disease (Marmot, 2004). Social status matters beyond being poor. There is a clear **socioeconomic gradient in health**, which means that those with lowest status are less healthy than those in the middle, who are less healthy than those at the top.

The idea of SES as a **fundamental social cause** of health attempts to explain the persistence of the association of health and SES across time and place (Link & Phelan, 1995). Over time, risk factors for poor health have changed considerably. Health information, such as the relationship between smoking and poor health, is now widely known. Technologies such as intensive care for premature infants are widely diffused. So why is it the case that higher SES people continue to enjoy better health?

Fundamental social cause theory holds that higher SES individuals have access to knowledge, money, power, and social connections that can be deployed throughout their lives to avoid disease and death. All of these resources can be deployed in a range of situations, including when it comes to health. As a result, this theory predicts that no matter what the causes of bad health, socioeconomic gradients will emerge.

The theory of fundamental causes blends the multiple dimensions of SES. However, SES is multifaceted, and each of these measures of SES has a different relationship to health. For example, the mechanisms that link education to health may not be the same as those that link occupation and health. Another concern is that the causal relationship between SES and health may differ across these measures. It could be the case that poorer health is a cause of lower occupational status. Finally, different dimensions of SES may matter differently throughout the life course. Financial resources may be particularly important at some times, but education may be more important in others.

Next we review the evidence linking each of these components of SES, and some others as well, to health outcomes.

How does education impact our health? This is a widely debated topic in medical sociology.

Dennis MacDonald / Alamy Stock Photo

Education

15.2.2 Discuss the relationship between education and health.

It is clear that those with more education live longer, healthier lives, but does having more years of education *cause* better health? On the one hand, because individuals play a strong role in choosing the amount of education they get, it could be that healthier people choose to—or are able to—attend school longer. On the other hand, those with more education use illegal drugs, alcohol, and tobacco less. Even for people with the same income, people with more education use preventative healthcare more, and they do a better job of managing existing conditions—for example, remembering to take their medications. They may also be better at managing their own care, a topic we will discuss later in the chapter.

Researchers have used a number of creative natural experiments to establish that the level of education individuals have is associated with their health. Some of the best-known studies rely on changes in compulsory education laws. Compulsory education laws determine at which age students can stop going to school. Early in the twentieth century, there were wide variations in the number of years of education students required. Over time, we began to increase the number of years students were required to attend. When these laws changed, students were required to get more years of education than their peers who were slightly ahead of them in school. But there is no reason to believe that these laws changed because health was improving, so they provide an ideal setting to determine whether getting more education *improves* health. These studies find that students who attended school for more years had higher survival rates as adults, which suggests that education does in fact have a direct effect on health (Lleras-Muney, 2005). By some estimates, the better health behaviours of the more educated can explain 40 percent of their health advantage (Cutler, Lleras-Muney, & Vogl, 2008). Scholars continue to debate why more education leads to better health behaviours.

First, it may be that education improves one's ability to understand health information, which leads to better behaviour. Second, education may improve one's ability to self-govern, which may equip those with more education to change their health behaviours when necessary. Third, family income explains some of the association between education and health (as individuals and households with more education tend to have higher incomes and can access better-quality healthcare). Finally, a central component of fundamental cause theory holds that high SES allows individuals to take advantage of new advances in medical technology. When it comes to education, the idea is that better-educated people are more aware of advances in medical science, and as a result can seek out better care.

Income and Wealth

15.2.3 Discuss the impact that income and wealth have on children's health.

People with higher incomes also have better health even after we control for their education level. Determining the relationship between income and health is even more complicated than in the case of education. Because education largely happens early in the life course, getting educated generally happens well before the onset of poor health. (To be sure, poor health in early childhood affects how much education children get.) In contrast, health can affect one's income because it affects participation in the labour force. People who are sick may work fewer hours or retire earlier, both of which reduce their income. Poor health also reduces one's wealth. When people become sick, they may have to rely on their savings when they can't work, or spend some of these savings on medications.

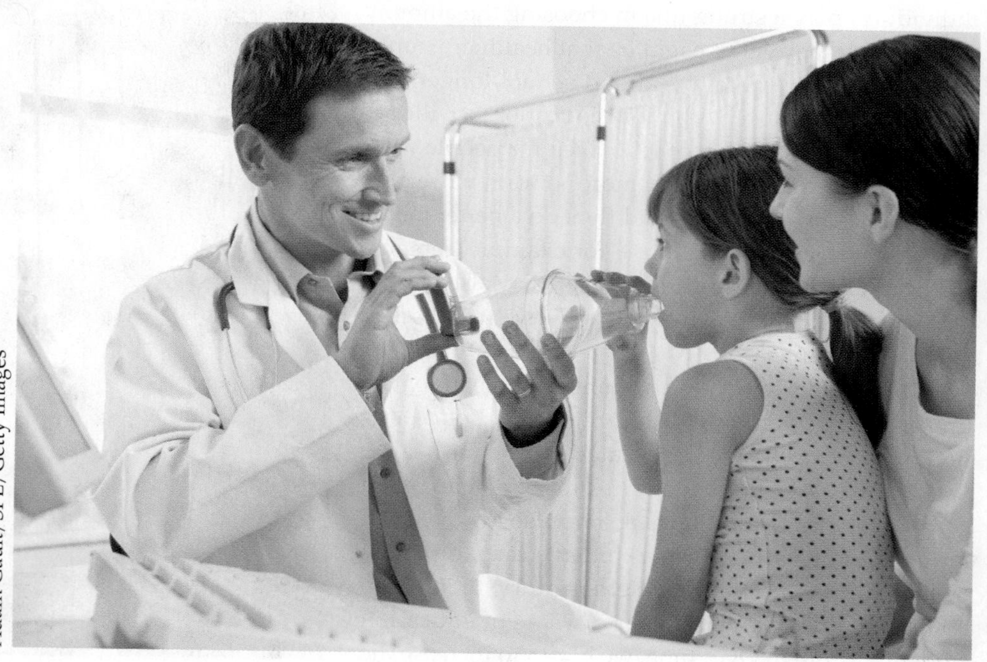

Affluent parents can ensure that their children receive prompt medical attention if health problems arise.

Adam Gault/SPL/Getty Images

Where level of education, income, and wealth clearly matter, however, is in how they affect children's health. Parents with more education and income can purchase more nutritious food and provide safer environments and better access to medical care for their children. The effects of education and family income on child health, moreover, appear to increase as a child ages (Case, Lubotsky, & Paxson, 2002). That is, the difference in the health of poorer and more affluent children is greater later in childhood. Chronic conditions, such as asthma, become more common as children age. Families with more cultural resources can use them to better control these health conditions and minimize their effects.

Race and Ethnicity

15.2.4 Discuss sociological explanations for health disparities among races.

In Canada and elsewhere, Indigenous peoples are affected by health problems at rates much higher than non-Indigenous populations, such as high rates of chronic and contagious diseases and shorter life expectancy. For example, 15 percent of new HIV and AIDS infections occur in Aboriginal people. While they made up only 3.8 percent of the population in 2006, Aboriginal people accounted for 8 percent of people living with HIV.

Other health issues for Aboriginal people include high infant and young-child mortality; high maternal morbidity and mortality; heavy infectious disease burdens; malnutrition and stunted growth; shortened life expectancy; diseases and death associated with cigarette smoking; social problems, illnesses, and deaths linked to misuse of alcohol and other drugs; accidents, poisonings, interpersonal violence, homicide, and suicide; obesity, diabetes, hypertension, cardiovascular disease, and chronic renal disease (lifestyle diseases); and diseases caused by environmental contamination (for example, heavy metals, industrial gases and effluent wastes). According to the National Collaborating Centre for Aboriginal Health (2013, 5), compared to the general Canadian population,

- Aboriginal women are 3.5 times more likely to experience violence;
- type 2 diabetes has reached epidemic levels and is four times higher among First Nations people;
- in some Indigenous communities youth suicide rates are 800 times the national average;
- the adult suicide rate among Inuit in Arctic communities is 10 times that of the general population; and
- tuberculosis infection is 26.4 times the rate in Canadian-born non-Aboriginal people.

How do we account for the poor health outcomes amongst First Nations, Inuit, and Métis people? There are three major theories in the contemporary literature:

1. *Enduring legacy of colonialism.* Indigenous peoples have worse healthcare than whites because on average they have fewer years of education, have lower incomes, and often lack access to healthcare, especially among those living on reserves (which are often isolated). Poorer health outcomes can be linked to the enduring legacy of colonialism, which puts First Nations, Inuit, and Métis people at greater risk for disease and suicide given their low SES. Basic healthcare and adequate nutrition is out of reach for many First Nations, Inuit, and Métis peoples.
2. *Exposure to discrimination and racism in everyday life that may increase stress.* When the body mobilizes its responses to stress too often, it loses its ability to regulate itself, which leaves the body at an increased risk for disease. Stress may also lead to the adoption of coping behaviours, such as overeating or abusing alcohol, that have negative effects on health.

3. *Water, sewage, crowded living conditions, and inadequate housing*. Aboriginal people often live in places without running water or sewage facilities. They often lack adequate housing and live in overcrowded homes, which can lead to higher rates of infectious diseases such as tuberculosis and high infant mortality rates.

Gender

15.2.5 Identify explanations for gender differences in health.

Gender differences in health present a challenge to the idea that more resources equal better health. Although women tend to have fewer resources than men, they live approximately four to five years longer than men, although it was as high as eight years in the 1970s (National Center for Health Statistics, 2011; Read & Gorman, 2010). According to a report by the World Health Organization the average life expectancy for women is 84 and for men it is 80.

What drives this very large difference? Men tend to engage in more risky behaviours, which make them more likely to die, but they are more reluctant than women to access healthcare services. The most important of these "risky" behaviours around the world are wars, but men also have higher rates of fatal accidents and are more likely to be the victim of a violent crime. Men are more likely to attempt suicide and be successful than women, and many more men die in work-related accidents than women do because of gender-based employment differences. Men tend to have more life-threatening chronic diseases, such as heart disease and cancer, while women tend to suffer from less deadly chronic conditions, like arthritis, anxiety, and depression, that do not lead to premature death (but do reduce quality of life).

15.3 How Did Modern Medicine Emerge?

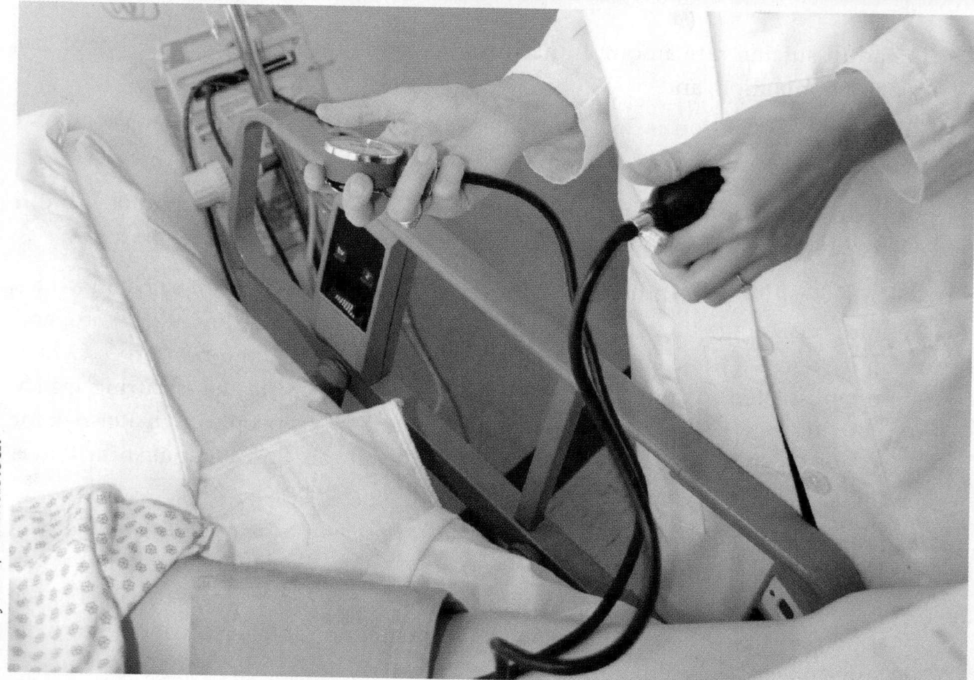

Victor Jones/Shutterstock

The History of Canadian Medicine

In various ways, up to this point, we've seen how social factors influence health outcomes. A population-based approach to medicine provides a different way of thinking about health issues than the usual individual-based approach. As individuals we do, of course, contribute to our own health when we make decisions about what we put into our bodies, whether or not we exercise, and how our parents may or may not have passed on genetic predispositions to certain diseases. But when we think about the reasons why groups vary as much as they do, or even why whole countries vary as much as they do, it raises questions about the nature and quality of the healthcare system.

To understand the world of modern medicine and how healthcare is practised today, it is important to look at how it emerged. In this section we will discuss the early days of medicine, the professionalization of medicine, and some important consequences of those reforms on health, illness, and treatment.

The Early Days of Medicine

15.3.1 Discuss the early days of medicine and identify the causes of public health improvements at the end of the nineteenth century.

In its early years, the practice of medicine was of limited value to patients, and indeed some widely used healing practices actually made people sicker. During the colonial period of the eighteenth century, most healthcare was provided by local doctors with little training, by community folk healers, or by religious leaders who took responsibility for health as well as spiritual concerns. The theory and practice of medicine has changed dramatically from when it was first practised in the seventeenth century in what was then New France. Most of the practitioners who came to Canada as settlers were not physicians but rather barber surgeons with little or no training. This custom may have been derived from the practice of bloodletting, and the application of leeches was practised for nearly every form of illness for almost 2,000 years prior to the nineteenth century. More effective yet rudimentary forms of medicine were practised by Aboriginal peoples before the French settlers arrived in North America in the mid-1600s. They were able to treat some illnesses with some effective plant remedies and physical procedures such as the sweat lodge. For instance, it was from

PHAS/Getty Images

Many groups, including homeopaths, competed to gain control over the treatment of the sick in the nineteenth century.

Aboriginal peoples that Jacques Cartier learned of a cure for the scurvy that nearly wiped out his men (Roland, 2006).

As the population in North America increased, so did our epidemics. The limits of early medicine were made especially clear during the cholera epidemic that broke out across North America in 1832. Cholera killed with astonishing speed, and the sheer intensity of its symptoms—victims assumed a bluish, ghastly appearance before dying—created widespread panic. For this reason, the cholera epidemic, which killed over 10,000, terrified people more than other diseases with higher mortality rates. The epidemic undermined confidence in the ability of physicians to heal the sick, as their treatments proved futile in arresting the course of the disease. Indeed, various "heroic" therapies (like bloodletting) and the use of mercury chloride and opium as purgatives and painkillers by orthodox physicians created additional health problems for patients.

Following the epidemic, with physicians held in low public esteem, a period of intense competition between a diverse array of medical sects and folk practitioners developed, all vying to control medicine. One prominent form of alternative medicine, known as **homeopathy**, a medical sect from Germany that used infinitesimal doses of medicine to treat disease, presented a challenge to practitioners of regular medicine. These sects were derided as "quacks" by orthodox physicians, who organized to assert their dominance in the field. Licensing bodies existed in Upper and Lower Canada from the late 1700s, but it was not until 1839 that a group of Toronto physicians attempted to incorporate as the College of Physicians and Surgeons; the incorporating act was disallowed in 1840 (Roland, 2006). The **Canadian Medical Association (CMA)**, the leading professional association of physicians in Canada, was formed in 1867. At first, the association was formed by a Quebec physician, Dr. Joseph Painchaud, as a fund to assist physicians in distress and their widows and children. Over time, the CMA devoted its efforts to maintaining professional medical standards, with the expressed goal of combating "quackery" in all its forms. In 1869, the Ontario Medical Act created a College of Physicians and Surgeons of Ontario whose aim was to examine practitioners and university graduates. Among the first medical training programs to be established was that at McGill University in Montreal under the guidance of Dr. William Osler, who assumed the chair in the mid-1870s. Medical discoveries such as anesthetic in the 1840s rendered surgery painless, and the application of antiseptics greatly reduced infection.

Medicine remained in a disorganized and primitive state—of little regulation, negligible education, folk healers, and scant research—until the end of the nineteenth century, however, when the foundation for the highly technical and scientific medicine we know today began to be established. What enabled the rise of modern medicine? A common misconception is that the health and well-being of the country improved largely because of innovations in medical science in the nineteenth and early twentieth centuries. This story holds that breakthroughs in medical discoveries led to more effective, scientifically based medical treatments, which in turn resulted in better health and declining mortality rates. For instance, Canadian medical research led to advances in anesthesiology and neuroscience, and in the treatment of diabetes, polio, malaria, heart disease, and tuberculosis (Roland, 2006). Figure 15.2 shows the dramatic changes in longevity over the past century.

The idea that science triumphed over ignorance and disease is a compelling one, but it does not tell the whole story. Historians and social scientists have shown that much of the decline in mortality prior to the 1920s resulted from the virtual disappearance of infectious diseases—like cholera, typhoid, and smallpox—that periodically created epidemics in the mid-nineteenth century. The eradication of these diseases had little to do with medical intervention but was mostly attributable to improved sanitary conditions and better **public health**—basic sanitary policies aimed at cleaning up the environment and reducing the spread of disease through measures such as street cleaning, garbage removal, and clean water supplies. The public health movement was an alliance between concerned elites, reform-minded politicians, and civic-minded

Figure 15.2 Changes in Life Expectancy From 1900 to 2010, United States

SOURCE: Based on data from "United States Life Tables, 1999," by Robert N. Anderson and Peter B. DeTurk, March 21, 2002, *National Vital Statistics Reports, 50*(6).

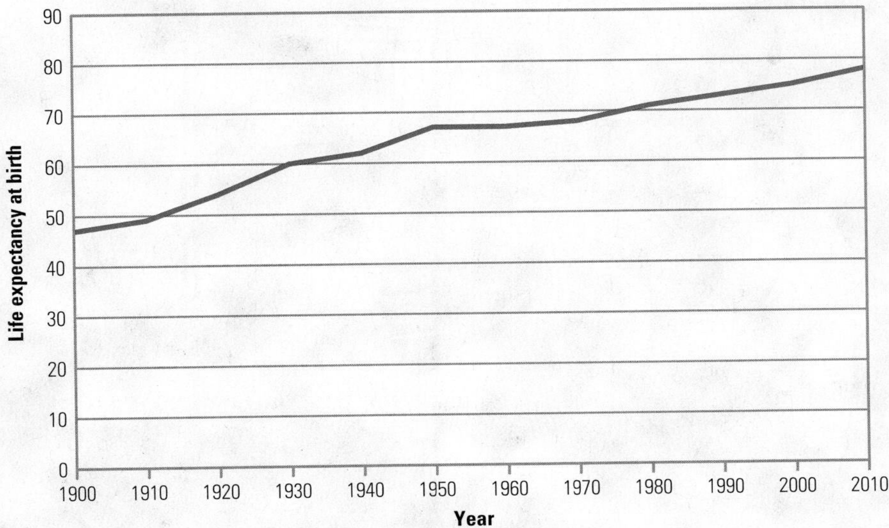

physicians (including some early women physicians). Physicians such as Sir William Osler, Norman Bethune, Robert McClure, Emily Howard Stowe, Jennie Kidd Trout, and Maude Abbott worked in Canada and across the world to promote and improve human health (Roland, 2006). Public health initiatives emerged in response to the filthy conditions of urban centres plagued by overcrowding. Public health, a field that parallels the medical profession, has contributed major advances in the treatment of population health problems in both Canada and the United States and around the world. It is the discipline that is closest to the way sociologists think about medicine, and advances policy proposals for government action to promote healthy populations.

Modern Medicine as a Profession

15.3.2 Discuss the emergence of modern medicine as a powerful profession.

If the rise of the medical profession cannot be attributed simply to advances in medical science, how did modern medicine emerge? How did physicians, a group mocked and ridiculed for much of the nineteenth century as incompetent, emerge from the early decades of the twentieth century among the most powerful professions in both Canada and the United States, commanding respect and high incomes? How did physicians, acting through the Canadian Medical Association and the local provincial associations, secure nearly complete control over the practice of medicine? Beginning in the late nineteenth century, provincial governments began to grant professional licences to physicians to practise medicine and established rules that only those who had been granted a licence could practise. The Canadian Medical Association oversaw the curriculum in universities and provided examinations to practitioners who immigrated to Canada from the United States and elsewhere. Over time, all provinces came to require that only those individuals who graduated from an approved medical school and passed an examination could call themselves physicians.

To understand this process, it is important to understand the ways in which any profession is established. The pioneering work of sociologist Eliot Freidson (2001) demonstrated that the logic of **professionalism** is that certain occupations are recognized by the public and state officials as possessing a kind of expertise that must be self-regulated and thus are granted autonomy, or a high degree of control, over their

Nineteenth-century medicine looked much different than it does today, and medical treatment took place primarily in the home.

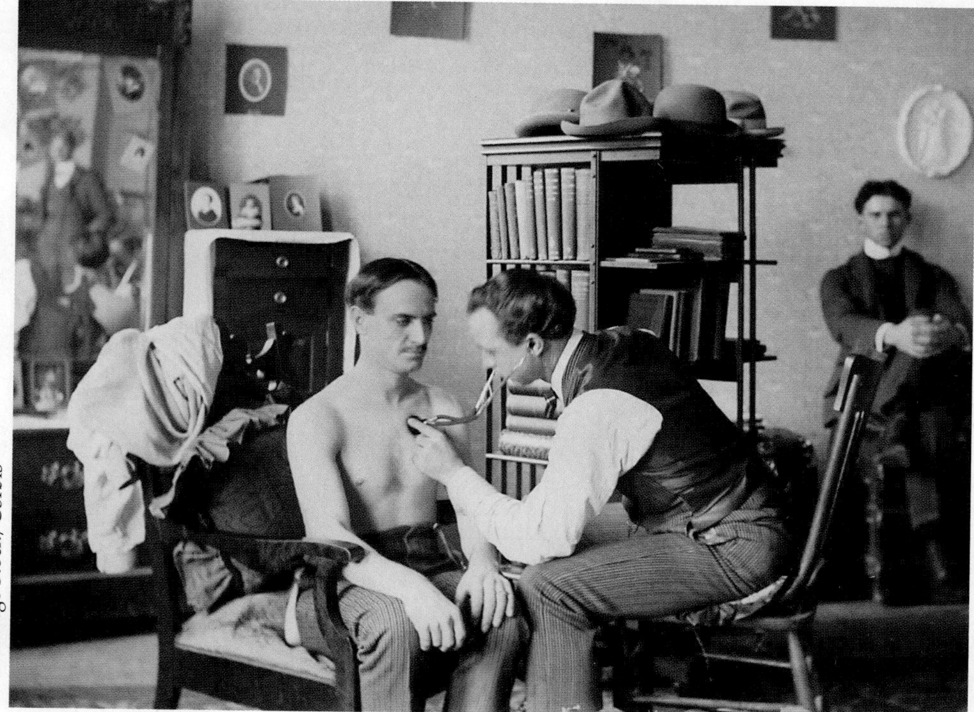

Kirn Vintage Stock/Corbis

work. Different professions—such as law, engineering, architecture, accounting, and dentistry—vary in how and to what degree they are organized and in how successful they are in obtaining control over their work. Professionals are organized into professional associations (like the CMA, or the Canadian Bar Association and provincial law societies for lawyers), which are charged with promoting their interests as specialized experts. Professional associations carry out a number of tasks aimed at solidifying authority and autonomy in the workplace; these tasks include (1) determining the standards for specialized training and education, (2) controlling membership through licensing and/or certification, and (3) establishing and maintaining professional norms through codes of ethics.

In making sense of the professionalization of medicine, it is important to understand how medicine was practised in earlier times. Nineteenth-century medicine looked different than it does today. First, doctoring took place primarily in the home, not in complex organizations like hospitals. Indeed, nineteenth-century hospitals were modest institutions focused more on charity and social welfare than on medical treatment, and they primarily served the poor. Hospitals were widely (and rightly) viewed by the middle and upper classes as bastions of illness and neglect. Therefore, for all but the very poor, medicine was conducted in patients' homes at the bedside. Second, patients retained more control over the doctor–patient interaction. Lacking sophisticated diagnostic testing and technologies, doctors depended on the external symptoms and self-report of the patient when determining both diagnosis and treatment. Third, when making their assessments, doctors eschewed complex theories and instead adopted a pragmatic and particularistic approach, catering treatment to the individual patient.

In the latter part of the nineteenth century, there were a number of key breakthroughs in medical science. In particular, new discoveries in the germ theory of disease appeared to finally provide conclusive answers to long vexing questions about the causes of disease. The bacteriological research of Robert Koch in Germany and Louis Pasteur in France were instrumental along these lines; Koch identified the bacterial agent of anthrax (1875), cholera (1884), and tuberculosis (1882), while Pasteur developed the first vaccines for anthrax (1881) and rabies (1885). Clean clothes, instruments, wounds, and hands were shown by Dr. Joseph Lister in Britain to reduce the death and infection rates in operating rooms in the 1860s. But many physicians in North America were slow to adopt these new measures.

Gender and Medical Professionalization

15.3.3 Discuss the experience of women's participation in the practice of medicine as a consequence of medical professionalization.

The successful establishment of the medical profession and the professionalization of medical education as the dominant force in medicine had a number of important consequences for the experience of health, illness, and treatment. One of the more noteworthy of these consequences was the experience of women's participation in the practice of medicine. Traditionally charged with a caretaking role in families, women were early and persistent adopters of the type of folk remedies and alternative medicine that the CMA actively sought to eliminate. Women also had a long tradition of caring for other women, exemplified in the tradition of midwifery. Early Canadian doctors were not opposed to midwifery, but opponents resented the role played by midwives as gateways to obstetrical practices. Despite the fact that for centuries midwives had control over childbirth, many physicians believed that it was only when men became involved in labour and delivery that advances were made (Mitchenson, 2002). While birthing practices differed among classes of women—lower-class women in rural and urban areas were attended primarily by midwives, while middle- and upper-class women were attended by doctors—midwifery remained a prominent option well into the early twentieth century. In 1900, 50 percent of American infants were still delivered by midwives (Ehrenreich & English, 2013, p. 103). However, as the professionalization of medicine gained steam in the early twentieth century, physicians began to view pregnancy and birth as an enticing source of income. For example, in attempting to wrest control over birthing from midwives, the American Medical Association framed its campaigns in gender stereotypes of the time that held that women were prone to irrationality and therefore could not be trusted to attend to births (Wertz & Wertz, 1989). Couching their campaign as being concerned for the health of women, physicians fought for, and won, legislation prohibiting midwifery. Obstetricians, who had a decidedly more interventionist approach than midwives, took control over birthing and in the process medicalized it. According to Kate Plummer (2000, 169) Canada also experienced the gradual curtailment of midwifery practice through professional and legal measures. The provinces of Quebec and Newfoundland sanctioned the practice of midwifery training and practice in 1788 and 1920 respectively. However, pressures from the medical profession continued to make the practice of midwifery difficult in all but the most remote areas of Canada until 1991 when the province of Ontario legalized midwifery. **Medicalization** is the process by which a human condition or circumstance, such as giving birth, comes to be understood and treated as a medical condition. Even today, as midwifery has made a comeback in many provinces, only about 4.5 percent of births in Ontario, Canada's most populated province, are attended by a midwife (Hawkins & Knox, 2003).

Women interested in the medical field until the late 1970s were encouraged to pursue the subordinate occupation of nurse. Nursing arose as a formal profession in the 1870s with the introduction of formal training and solidified its position at the end of the century with the shift of medical care from the home to the hospital. Stereotypes about the gendered notion of caring as a feminine quality and the embodiment of womanly virtue marked the nursing profession as appropriate for women, but only under the supervision of (historically male) physicians (Reverby, 1987). In Canada, nurses would become a cheap source of subordinate workers for hospitals that were essentially charitable institutions headed by doctors (Strong-Boag, 1991, p. 242). By the 1890s, public health and moral reform campaigns were spearheaded by upper-class women, nurses, and doctors to "cleanse the nation of ill-health, immorality and indolence" (p. 243). Young women who needed jobs were drawn to nursing and played a major role in those public health campaigns that sought to enhance the Canadian nation-state through the immunization of school children, elimination of venereal disease, and the reduction of infant mortality rates through hygiene and clean milk programs.

Conclusion

The importance of healthcare is obvious to everyone. As individuals, we rely on doctors, nurses, and other healthcare professionals to diagnose and treat us when we are sick. There are many ways in which a sociological model of healthcare is valuable for both understanding how healthcare systems work and trying to improve them. Sociologists have long been interested in the question of who gets sick and why, who gets the best-quality care, how and why the interactions between doctors and patients are so important, and how the organizational design of healthcare may exacerbate its problems.

To be sure, the healthcare system is under continual pressure from many different places to resist change—insurance companies, pharmaceutical and medical device companies, physicians who benefit from the current system or fear change, hospitals that seem to cut healthcare to cut costs, and even healthcare workers' own unions (who may fight changes that threaten jobs or job security). Moreover, employers are pushing more and more of the costs onto employees. Of special note are the rapidly changing technologies for healthcare, which are a source of pressure to change (for example in how patients are diagnosed and treated, as well as in permitting images to be read by specialists in other countries) but are also often very expensive and can add to the costs of treatment. Without reforming the current system of how healthcare is reimbursed, the danger of overuse is ever-present.

CHAPTER SUMMARY

The Big Questions Revisited 15

15.1 **How Do Social Contexts Affect Health?** We often think of health behaviours as individual choices. In this section, we explored how social contexts affect our health behaviours and how events that happen throughout our lives affect our health as adults.

A Sociological View of Health

The Population as Patient

Learning Objective 15.1.1: Describe the population model of prevention.

The Effects of Social Contexts on Individual Behaviour

Learning Objective 15.1.2: Discuss how our social contexts and relationships help to determine the health choices we make.

The Accumulation of Health Risks Across the Life Course

Learning Objective 15.1.3: Explain how sociologists use life-course perspectives to examine health issues.

Differences in Health Across Countries

Learning Objective 15.1.4: Explain why where you live impacts your health.

15.2 **Who Gets Sick, and Why?** Low socioeconomic status is a strong predictor of poor health. If you are highly educated, you are more likely to live a longer and healthier life than people who are not. This has been true throughout history and across many different countries. We explored why these patterns persist and the major explanations that sociologists have advanced to explain them.

Health Outcomes Among Different Groups

Health and Socioeconomic Status

Learning Objective 15.2.1: Explain how socioeconomic status affects health.

Education

Learning Objective 15.2.2: Discuss the relationship between education and health.

Income and Wealth

Learning Objective 15.2.3: Discuss the impact that income and wealth have on children's health.

Race and Ethnicity

Learning Objective 15.2.4: Discuss sociological explanations for health disparities between races.

Gender

Learning Objective 15.2.5: Identify explanations for gender differences in health.

15.3 **How Did Modern Medicine Emerge?** To understand the world of modern medicine and how healthcare is practised today, it is important to look at how it emerged. In this section we discussed the early days of medicine, the professionalization of North American medicine, the impact of medical education reform, and some important consequences on health, illness, and treatment.

The History of Canadian Medicine

The Early Days of Medicine

Learning Objective 15.3.1: Discuss the early days of medicine and identify the causes of public health improvements at the end of the nineteenth century.

Modern Medicine as a Profession

Learning Objective 15.3.2: Discuss the emergence of modern medicine as a powerful profession.

Gender and Medical Professionalization

Learning Objective 15.3.3: Discuss the experience of women's participation in the practice of medicine as a consequence of medical professionalization.

Learn the Terms

Canadian Medical Association (p. 434)
epidemiology (p. 423)
fundamental social cause (p. 429)
infant mortality rate (p. 426)
health disparities (p. 428)
homeopathy (p. 434)
life-course perspective (p. 425)
medicalization (p. 437)
nurse practitioner (NP) (p. 420)
professionalism (p. 435)
public health (p. 434)
socioeconomic gradient in health (p. 428)

Chapter 16
Crime, Deviance, and Social Control

by Troy Duster and Jeff Manza

Zuma Press/Newscom

Cyclists ride naked through London for the World Naked Bike Ride. Why is this considered deviant behaviour by many people?

Learning Objectives

16.1.1 Identify how groups distinguish themselves.

16.1.2 Discuss how statistical deviance differs from social deviance.

16.1.3 Define the term *social norm.*

16.2.1 Distinguish between interested and disinterested rule-making.

16.2.2 Analyze the history of alcohol use and how it relates to definitions of normal and deviant.

16.2.3 Analyze the history of opium use and how it relates to definitions of normal and deviant.

16.2.4 Discuss how the crusade against drug use and same-sex relationships affects the future of moral crusades.

16.3.1 Discuss how labelling theory explains deviance.

16.3.2 Determine what the 2008 U.S. financial crisis reveals about power and deviant behaviour.

16.3.3 Discuss whether violence committed during wartime is a criminal act.

16.4.1 Analyze ways in which the criminal justice system exerts social control.

16.4.2 Analyze mass incarceration.

16.4.3 Describe the changing crime rate and the trend toward mass incarceration in North America.

Why do some kinds of behaviour violate societal rules while other, similar behaviours do not? How is it that *deviant* behaviour is defined as such, and violations punished? We don't ordinarily observe the process by which deviance is defined until we notice what happens when someone tries to challenge those rules. In the fall of 1992 at the University of California, Berkeley, a tall, thin, angular 20-year-old undergraduate began coming to his classes wearing only his key chain. Known as "Naked Guy," Andrew Martinez quickly achieved local and later national and international fame. At that time, neither the campus nor the City of Berkeley had any rules or regulations requiring that someone wear clothes (Zengerle, 2006). Long known for their progressive political traditions, Berkeley citizens and elected officials grappled with the novel question of whether Martinez should have the right not to wear clothes.

For several weeks, Martinez continued to walk the streets of the city and campus and attend his classes completely in the nude. Naked Guy sightings became events, and Martinez became a local celebrity. Even when he showed up at a party fully clothed in the middle of winter, students were thrilled to see him (Richards, 2006). Defending his actions in a local newspaper and elsewhere, Martinez articulately suggested that in his view clothing was oppressive. He claimed that "when I walk around nude, I am acting how I think it is reasonable to act, not how middle-class values tell me I should act. I am refusing to hide my dissent in normalcy even though it is very easy to do so." With a local theatre troupe (the X-Plicit Players), he even helped to organize a "nude-in," which succeeded in getting two dozen sympathizers to participate.

While many people simply ignored him, some students and residents complained to campus administrators and the local police. Soon thereafter, campus officials decided enough was enough, and Martinez was suspended from the campus. He continued to appear naked in public, even attending a city council meeting unclothed to plead his case. But it was to no avail; the council passed a measure banning public nudity and shortly thereafter began arresting Martinez whenever he appeared naked in public. Eventually, Martinez disappeared from public life, and the public controversy he had created quickly disappeared from the news.

The Big Questions

1. **What is deviance?** To understand deviance, we first need to ask the question "What is normal?" We explore the origins of deviant behaviour by examining the role of groups and group boundaries in the creation of social norms. We also explore the distinction between statistical and social deviance.
2. **How is morality defined and regulated?** Societies have long tried to dictate and control individuals' behaviour and morality. We explore two moral crusades (alcohol and morphine misuse in the United States) to highlight how the process of defining normal behaviour is achieved and how certain kinds of behaviour come to be labelled deviant or even criminal. We then look at some contemporary moral crusades and consider the future of moral regulation.
3. **Who defines deviance?** Insights into deviant behaviour come from studying the social and economic positions, cultural practices, and attendant political power of dominant groups. In this section, we explore the relationship between deviance and power.
4. **How is social control imposed on society?** We examine how and where social control—the ways societies regulate and sanction behaviour in such a way that it encourages conformity and discourages deviance from the norms—comes to be formalized in the institutions of the criminal justice system. We then examine how the criminal justice system in North America has grown massively in recent decades, turning increasingly to formal punishment as a means of sanctioning deviance.

The Naked Guy of Berkeley, Andrew Martinez, attending a class at the University of California, Berkeley, in 1992.

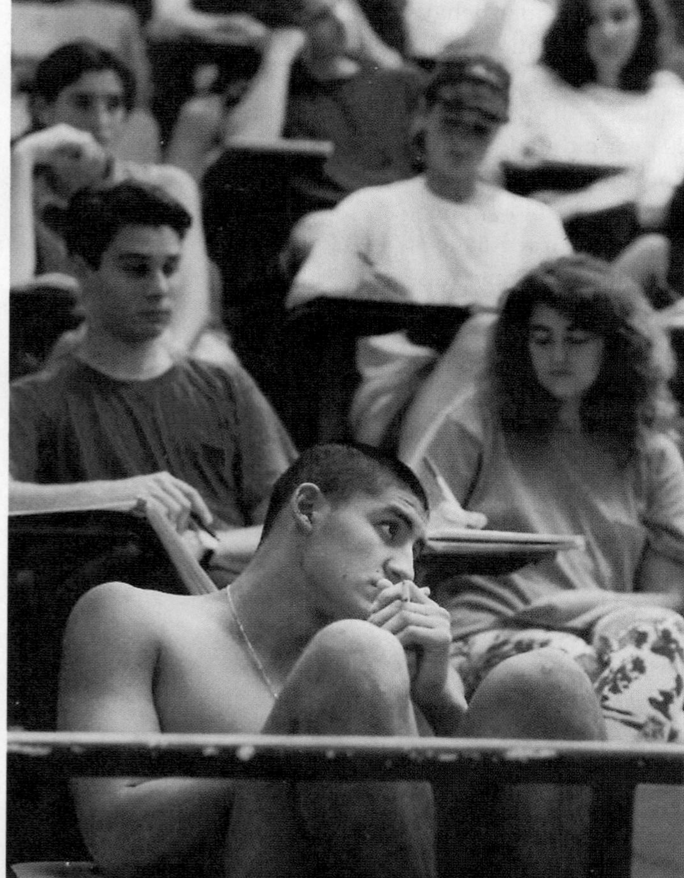

Jason M. Grow/KRT/Newscom

The story of the Naked Guy may seem like an "only in Berkeley" story, a strange and easily forgotten episode. Yet it actually raises a number of profound questions. For starters, why *do* we have to wear clothes? Who decided that clothes are a necessary part of our everyday appearance? Further, why do governments, in this case the Berkeley city government, assume the authority, in the name of the public, to arrest and punish someone simply because he or she refuses to wear clothes? It's not likely to become a leading civil rights cause anytime soon, but once we ask ourselves why covering our bodies is an obligation, we open up a whole series of questions that go right to the heart of how society exerts its force over individuals, and with what consequences. That is the subject of this chapter.

16.1 What Is Deviance?

Marko Djurica/Reuters

Deviance and the Group

Before we can consider what is deviant, we first need to ask the question, "What is normal?" And this question in turn raises a prior question: Who decides what is normal and, therefore, what is deviant? To explore these questions, we have to begin with the most fundamental of the building blocks of normality and deviance: the group.

Groups and Group Boundaries

16.1.1 Identify how groups distinguish themselves.

From small groups like families and sports teams to larger ones like neighbourhoods, organizations, and even entire nations, individuals belong to groups. Sociologists define a **social group** as a collection of people who interact with one another and who have a shared sense of belonging. Most humans across the globe are born into families that impose fundamental rules such as when and how to eat food and whom to obey. In *Civilization and Its Discontents*, Sigmund Freud (1930) pointed out that all cultures impose on their young some very strict rules about the most basic of needs (for example, at an early age, the child is told, "stop playing with your food!"), which sets up the first great conflict between individual and society. Freud saw this as one of the first lessons of dominance and social control—and, in turn, one of the first lessons about the futility of rebellion. Anyone who has reared a child understands Freud's idea as a metaphor for what happens throughout life. Just as the child ultimately gives up and accepts the behavioural rules established by others, so too must we consent to group rules and norms if we are to fit in. And here we come to the first axiom in the study of deviance and control: This early struggle is first and foremost about the *parents'* notion of normality and only secondarily about the child. Deviance and control always constitute a paired relationship, and even in this earliest of all subsequent pairings, it is the more powerful group (the parents) that determines what is normal and thus what is deviant.

Groups outside the family exert similar pressures to conform throughout an individual's life. Much of the time, our consent to these pressures is voluntary. How do groups achieve this power? One way is through *positive affirmations*—or claims—that groups use to establish boundaries. There are an infinite variety of markings, behaviours, and attributes that are possible. Examples range from cutting three lines across the forehead (as is common among the Nuer people of Sudan) to pledging fraternity or sorority X versus Y (as is common in U.S. universities). Other groups in society may wear certain kinds of clothing and body piercings or use a specific language and code of behaviour. Such positive affirmations signal who is in the group and who is out. But merely being a compliant member in good standing of a group is not the whole story; the *negative affirmations* of group membership—what we aren't allowed to do if we are to retain membership—constitute the other side of group influence. Both are important, and we need to examine them in more detail.

All groups set markers at their boundaries. Beginning with our earliest group—our family—we quickly learn who is and who is not in the group. While groups are often defined through objective criteria such as having a shared language or the same job, the identity of the group is more importantly tied to the way group members define themselves and are defined by others. In high school, students may refer to those who seem to study too hard as "nerds" and the ones who play sports as "jocks." These are not innocent labels but include value judgements. It is the symbolic ideas and values about who the group members are, what sociologists call **symbolic boundaries**, that really give a group its identity (Lamont & Molnar, 2002).

One way to think about symbolic group boundaries is to consider the role of space and how different spaces are defined. When you enter a church, for example, you are crossing not simply a physical boundary between the church doors and the outside world but also a symbolic boundary between a religious space and a secular one. The very meaning of the space is different, as is how we are supposed to behave in it. Immigration—the process of moving from one country to another—provides another good example of how physical and symbolic boundaries work to define groups. Countries often mark boundaries between themselves by establishing physical borders, perhaps most dramatically on the U.S.–Mexico border. Such borders signal to us that we are moving from a territory belonging to one group to a territory belonging to another.

However, boundaries are used to differentiate not only physical space but also symbolic space. Just because immigrants cross from the United States into Canada does not mean they have become Canadian. On the contrary, as conflicts over immigration show, people use a whole range of symbolic boundaries to differentiate those who are considered Canadian or American or German or Turkish from those who are not. These symbolic boundaries involve setting up differences between our ideas of "us" and "them," including ideas about who immigrants are and why they may be considered different.

Group boundaries are a key aspect of understanding deviance because of the role groups play in defining and setting limits of acceptable behaviour. We have powerful incentives to do as the group says we must if we want to be part of the group. Being part of a group means behaving within the boundaries of the community. As long as we abide by these rules, we can expect to enjoy the benefits of group membership, which may include status and honour, the friendship of other group members, and access to special opportunities or rewards limited to group members. Groups often police their boundaries so as to prevent outsiders (especially unwanted outsiders) from entering. Symbolic and physical boundaries are set up with the explicit purpose of keeping outsiders out, and the crossing of such boundaries by group members can be considered an act of deviance. Consider again the example of immigration: *Illegal immigration* is defined as the unauthorized crossing of a boundary. In this way deviance takes place both when someone moves outside the boundaries he or she is expected to live in and when he or she enters another group's space.

What are the benefits of maintaining and marking boundaries and restricting access to outsiders? Some groups, like political parties, gain status when they have as many members as possible. In this case, there will be few, if any, barriers to membership—anyone can decide to call him- or herself a Liberal, New Democrat, Conservative, or Green. The more the merrier. Formal membership in Canadian political parties requires you to fill out a membership card and pay a fee, although again usually almost anyone is welcome, even if there is formal process for joining. Political parties are unusual groups in that their status derives from having as many members as possible. For many other kinds of groups, however, limiting membership as a way of maintaining the status of the group is essential. If just anyone can join, membership will be devalued. Many of the most prestigious groups are very exclusive. Think of an expensive suburb—the cost of housing can be very high, in part because that suburb will typically prevent cheap apartments from being constructed. In this way, the value of houses is not diminished by having less affluent people living in their midst (and residents of expensive suburbs will often fight hard to prevent any such construction). A fancy country club, an honourary association (where only the "best" are selected to be members), or a professional sports league raise the value of membership by holding down the number of slots available to others.

Just as all groups have rules outlining what members *must do*, they also have explicit descriptions of what members *must not do*. The set of excluded behaviours, or prohibitions, is the key ingredient of deviant behaviour: It is the behaviour that violates the group consensus of what *we must not do*. Any couple that has dated or married across sharply defined group boundaries (blacks and whites, Chinese and Koreans, same-sex couples, Hindus and Muslims, and others) has likely experienced expressions of disapproval from other group members (perhaps including one's own family). The major religions of the world contain many explicit rules believers must follow. For instance, the Christian commandments forbid murder, adultery, and theft. The Koran forbids these three and adds alcohol consumption. Such prohibitions empower authorities to punish those group members who deviate, with ostracism for violators serving as one of the most important ways groups maintain boundaries.

Explicit rules banning certain kinds of behaviours are often written down. The oldest known written set of laws in human history to be placed before the public is the Code of Hammurabi. It originated in the ancient city of Babylon, around 1780 BCE. Most known for the famous retributive justice penalty of "an eye for an eye," the Hammurabi code also included a specific set of punishments that aimed to best fit specific deviant acts. Since the time of the Hammurabi code, as groups and societies began to prescribe punishments for specific acts, they have revealed in the process much about what they truly value. For example, during the early and middle parts of the nineteenth century, governing bodies in the western region of the United States sometimes imposed the death penalty for horse thieves, while a conviction for murder could be punishable by just a few years in prison. This speaks loudly to what was most valued by those with the power to decide punishment at that time.

Sentences and punishments, when they appear whimsical or irrational, raise questions about the legitimacy of the group or society making the rules. Indeed, in the late eighteenth and early nineteenth centuries, as the first prisons and criminal justice systems began to appear in Western societies, their credibility was often undermined by the arbitrary manner in which punishments for crimes were determined and given out. Some thieves were hanged for stealing cloth worth very little, while rapists and murderers often served only a few months in prison. Moreover, for the same crime, one person could get 20 years of imprisonment while another served only a few weeks. Numerous social theorists, essayists, historians, and moral philosophers observed, lamented, analyzed, and commented on how the chaotically uneven punishments undermined the legitimacy of the government's use of its punitive powers. Leading nineteenth-century philosophers argued that it was imperative to find a way to "make the punishment better fit the crime." The first major reform of the penal codes was inspired by this situation, and codification finally occurred in the mid-nineteenth century and swept through most Western societies. The most important influence on the reform movement in punishment was a book published in 1764 by an Italian social theorist, Cesare Beccaria. Simply titled *On Crimes and Punishments*, the book set forth a theory of how and why justice should be meted out to the perpetrator. His main concern was that the citizenry have a sense that the criminal justice system was fair. A key element was the open, transparent, and public nature of laws and the corresponding transparency of the punishment attached to criminal activity. This left room for the possible fluidity of the severity of punishment (attached to a specific crime) if there was a public outcry about the unfairness, an issue that remains heavily debated today in extreme cases such as that of the man sentenced to a 50-years-to-life sentence for stealing a few DVDs for his children at Christmas (one was reported to be *Snow White*); this was his "third strike" under California's three-strike criminal justice law, in which anyone receiving a third felony conviction would be sentenced to life in prison (Cannon, 2005).

Statistical Versus Social Deviance

16.1.2 Discuss how statistical deviance differs from social deviance.

As we think further about the nature of deviance, it is important to make a distinction between how frequent or rare some behaviours are, on the one hand, and whether or not those behaviours violate written or unwritten rules, on the other. Rare behaviours are "deviant" in the sense that they are uncommon but are not necessarily deviant in the sociological sense. Consider the following example: In a high school class, a small group of students may choose to wear a baseball cap, a scarf, or a beret during class. In this case, wearing head coverings could be defined as **statistically deviant** (most students do not wear head coverings during class), but it would not be defined as **socially deviant** (behaviour that violates societal rules), at least not in North America. To be sure, if one or two of those students chose to take off their clothes and get naked, it would be socially deviant, as the case of Andrew Martinez suggests. And many schools have uniforms that are required of students; those who are out of uniform are socially deviant and can expect to be sanctioned. But unless there is an explicit dress code, students usually can get away with dressing the way

In 1989, the French government banned the wearing of the hijab (scarves worn by some Muslim women) in public schools. The policy was said to be designed to prevent the display of religious symbols in public places and underscore France's secular values. The law created an international controversy, and the government soon announced that it was up to individual school administrators to decide whether to enforce it. Later, however, in 2011, the French government took a further step in the same direction by banning the wearing of full-face coverings, known as the niqab or the burqa, in any public place. In 2016, three Mediterranean towns in France—Cannes, Villeneuve-Loubet, and Sisco on the island of Corsica—banned the burkini, a garment designed for swimming that leaves only the women's hands, feet, and legs exposed. These laws transfer what might be statistical deviance (Muslims are a small minority in France) into social deviance.

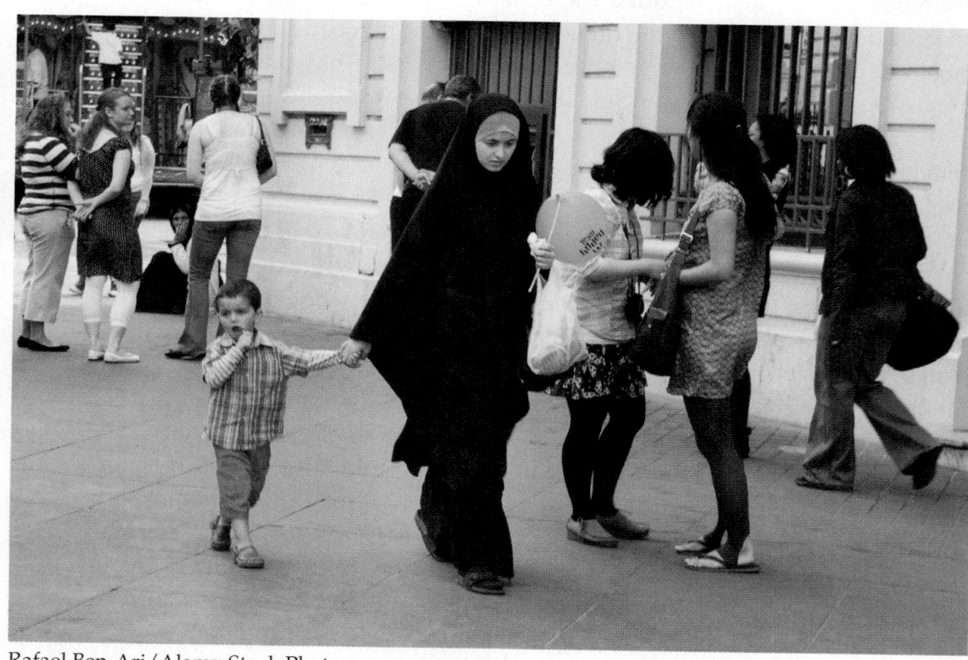

Rafael Ben-Ari/Alamy Stock Photo

they please. Those who wear unusual clothing may stand out from others, but they are not violating any rules.

The distinction between statistical deviance and social deviance is important because what is considered deviant (or even criminal) has little to do with how common it is. We might think that being socially deviant means doing something most people don't do, and likewise that acting "normal" means doing what most people do. But that is not always the case. Take smoking marijuana or committing adultery. Most adult North Americans have smoked marijuana at some point in their lives, a criminal act in many states and countries around the world. Yet most people who have smoked marijuana would probably not think of themselves as criminals (even those who regularly use the drug). Similarly, adultery is statistically very common in North America, with some estimates suggesting that between 25 and 50 percent of married people have committed adultery at some point in their lives. While adultery is no longer a criminal act, despite so many spouses cheating on each other it is still considered deviant. It violates a social norm about marriage and crosses boundaries of what is considered acceptable behaviour for a married partner.

When thinking about social deviance, it is also important to distinguish between deviant behaviour and deviant persons. Just because someone engages in some form of behaviour that others in the group or society would label deviant does not mean that the person will be so characterized. Indeed, in the normal course of life, each of us will transgress some rule, and when large numbers of people start disregarding the same rule, the typical response is to **normalize** the deviant behaviour—that is, to recast the behaviour into a frame that rescues the person as "normal" even as the behaviour is deemed deviant.

Social Norms: The Unstated Rules of Everyday Life

16.1.3 Define the term *social norm.*

Contemporary societies like Canada have vast legal systems and criminal codes that specify what is criminal or illegal activity in far greater detail than our forebears could have envisioned. When the explicit, written rules are violated, we have names for the so-called deviants—ranging from *murderer* to *thief*, from *arsonist* to *rapist* to *criminal*. Later in the chapter, we will discuss these formal rules and the ways they are administered through the criminal justice system. Yet a vital aspect of social control that is at least equally important is the enforcement of the unstated, unwritten, and nonarticulated rules—what sociologists call **norms**. Every society, even those with elaborate written rules and criminal codes, inevitably has an enormous number of *unwritten* rules of behaviour that individuals have to master in order to avoid appearing deviant. The French sociologist Émile Durkheim, writing over a century ago about such matters, called this the unstated terms of the social contract (Durkheim, 1890/1997). Durkheim was referring to the fact that rules of behaviour do not need to be written to require conformity.

For example, when you enter an auditorium and only one person is seated, "everyone knows" that unless that person is a friend, the seats on either side of him or her are off limits. If there is an alternative wide-open seat available, the norm is that strangers do not sit right next to strangers. Norms are basic rules of society that help us know what is and what is not appropriate to do in any given situation. At a very basic level, these unstated rules tell us a lot about the nature and character of our society. One of those is the "norm of engagement." Nowhere is it written, but North Americans have a near universal understanding that they must always be engaged with some object or person (Goffman, 1963). If you doubt that this is true, try the following experiment. In the presence of those who know you (family, friends, or people at work), sit for several minutes and do nothing. Have no object in your hand (no book or magazine, smartphone, iPad, or other object) and have no music or television playing to provide a possible object of your attention. Just sit there. Within a few minutes, you will experience what happens when the norm of engagement is violated: Those around you will start to become uncomfortable and wonder what is wrong with you. Should you persist long enough in this seemingly comatose state, at some point your family or friends will start to worry that perhaps some kind of mental disturbance is occurring.

It is not easy to trace where such unwritten rules of behaviour come from. In contrast to written rules and laws, which have a history that can be traced through archival research using historical records, legal case law, and other sources, the origins of norms are more obscure and often impossible to uncover. Yet we can be sure that they have their roots in societal process where the desires and preferences of powerful groups get extended throughout an entire society. The norm of engagement that sociologist Erving Goffman discusses likely has its roots in fears of idleness ("an idle mind is the devil's workshop") and is perhaps also linked to the idea that we should always use our time productively in some fashion. The norm of personal space may have its roots in larger ideas about personal privacy. But whatever the precise origin of these norms, we can be sure that they grew out of a social process of defining what is normal in light of other ideas about proper behaviour.

16.2 How Is Morality Defined and Regulated?

Will Rose/Starstock/Photoshot/Newscom

The Problem of Moral Regulation

At the centre of the societal struggle over what is and what is not deviant is a provocative question: What is morality and appropriately moral behaviour? At all times and places, societies struggle with questions of **moral behaviour**—that is, which types of behaviours will be considered good and right (or *moral*) versus those that are bad and wrong (or *immoral*). Some common examples in contemporary America would include ongoing debates over whether or not drug use or same-sex relationships are compatible with our understanding of morality. What is considered immoral behaviour is constantly at issue because in any society different groups will inevitably have different views and understandings. When societies attempt to outlaw certain kinds of previously common and widespread behaviour, it is invariably a highly controversial process. How do moral and immoral behaviour come to be defined, and how does the definition of moral behaviour change over time? How and why does society attempt to control and police the behaviour of individuals, and with what consequences?

Interested Versus Disinterested Rule-Making

16.2.1 Distinguish between interested and disinterested rule-making.

A useful place to start is to note a classical distinction between what has been called *interested punishment* versus *disinterested punishment* (Ranulf, 1938). This distinction refers to two different kinds of deviants and two different kinds of reasons for creating rules for moral behaviour and systems of punishment for their violation: (1) those that arise out of a desire to protect wealth and private property and (2) those that attempt to direct and control the behaviour of individuals. Because there is an existing distribution of wealth and power in any society, the most privileged groups and classes have a strong and direct interest in maintaining their wealth and their political domination. To be sure, we all have an interest in having our private property protected, but for holders of great wealth the stakes are much higher. Laws against theft and fraud, historically originating in the desire of the powerful to protect their wealth and privilege, eventually filtered down into ordinary criminal-law rules against theft of all kinds. Transgressors, insurgents, and rebels who threatened wealth-holders could expect firm punishment, and it was a short step from there to generalizing these types of punishment to protect everyone's property. The biblical commandment "thou shalt not steal" is entirely consistent with the interests of wealth-holders.

However, there are countless rules and laws on the books that have nothing to do with the distribution of wealth. These laws relate to innumerable behaviours, for example, tobacco use, alcohol and drug consumption, gambling, and prostitution—and can even include such behaviour as the way one dresses, engages in demonstrative behaviour in public places, or has same-sex liaisons. Because these rules, and their transgressors, have little to do with protecting wealth, these kinds of rules and laws have been described as *disinterested* punishment. These kinds of rules and the punishments for those who transgress them are designed to control the morals and social behaviour of people. Many of these laws were created by upper-class groups seeking to control and shape the lower classes. But in order for proposals for specific kinds of moral regulation to prevail, they would have to find broad popular support as well.

The two kinds of punishments are not entirely independent. Throughout North American history, right up to the present, the effort to control morality among certain lower-status groups—minorities, the poor, immigrants, and others—has been closely connected to the interests of the powerful in maintaining social order (Beisel, 1997). Moral reformers have always hoped that encouraging good behaviour on the part of the poor will make them better workers, more committed citizens, and less likely to revolt against those with more wealth and power.

An Example: The Temperance Movement as a Moral Crusade

16.2.2 Analyze the history of alcohol use and how it relates to definitions of normal and deviant.

How do moral and immoral behaviour get defined and then redefined over time? How do these behaviours relate (or not) to group interests? To help answer these questions, it is useful to study some historical examples and see how they evolved over time. One important case in North American history was the campaign against alcohol. Once upon a time, at the beginning of the nation and for its first two centuries, people drank so much alcohol that one historian suggested that Americans could appropriately be called the "Alcoholic Republic" (Rorabaugh, 1979). In the early eighteenth century, Americans drank five gallons of alcohol per capita every year. By 1830, per capita consumption had gone up even further, to seven gallons. That is the equivalent of nearly two bottles of 80-proof hard liquor per drinking adult per week—even factoring in low drinkers and nondrinkers (Okrent, 2010, p. 8). (To give a sense of the magnitude of this consumption, today Americans consume about two gallons per capita every year; in the 1830s the average person was drinking 3.5 times as much alcohol as today.) Shawn Cafferky (2003, p. 21) suggests that "there is every reason to believe that Canadian per capita consumption figures matched those of the Americans" during this period.

So how did North American societies go from being nations soaked in alcohol to the only industrialized countries to enact laws banning the consumption of alcohol, during the period known as **Prohibition** (1920–1933 in the United States; 1917–1929, depending on the province, in Canada)? The roots of this shift can be traced to the nineteenth century, during which North Americans witnessed a dramatic pendulum swing in attitudes toward alcohol. In the 1850s, while it was common for an adult male to down several swigs of hard liquor every single day, it was typically done in the home, not in taverns, saloons, or public bars, or in the streets. As more and more people moved from rural farms to cities, with industrialization and the massive influx of European immigrants in the last half of the century, all that would change.

The new immigrants were often concentrated in the poorest sections of industrializing cities. The older generation of North Americans—mainly from Northern and Western Europe—felt threatened by what they perceived as a change in values and traditions. More specifically, the movement for the prohibition of alcohol was a crusade to reestablish the traditional values that the upper middle classes believed were slipping away (Gusfield, 1963). It was, in short, the late-nineteenth-century version of "let's take our country back!"

The most prominent group calling for the prohibition of alcohol was the Women's Christian Temperance Union.

Peter Stackpole/Time Life Pictures/Getty Images

Still, it is remarkable that that both nations could go from being ones in which a pint of liquor a day was normal to a period of legally mandated prohibition. How did this happen—and more importantly, why? The story begins in a small town in Ohio in 1873, when a small group of middle-class white women entered a saloon, sank to their knees, and prayed for the souls of the owners that they might stop serving alcohol. While this is often cited as the launch of what is known as the Temperance Movement (*temperance* in this period meant moderation, not abstinence), historians note that there had been strong and insistent calls for moderation of alcohol consumption for much of the previous three decades. No single factor explains the success of the movement to rid the United States of alcohol, but there is a consensus that the new immigrants—"the infidel foreign population," as one historian has described them (Okrent, 2010, p. 26)—became the increasingly public face of alcohol excess. Eighty percent of licensed saloons were owned by first-generation Americans, and they "set at once to selling liquor ... to Italians, Greeks, Lithuanians, Poles—all the rough and hairy tribes," as one of the muckrakers of the time put it (quoted in Okrent, 2010, p. 26).

The small group of women who prayed at the Ohio saloons in December 1873 would be the initial spark that would eventually become the Women's Christian Temperance Union (WCTU). Within three months of that first pray-in, the spark ignited the closing of taverns in over 75 communities. In the next few decades, this small group would have remarkable successes in getting school boards across the United States to insert new instructional materials denouncing alcohol as an evil and then getting legislation passed at both local and state levels outlawing the sale of alcohol. Jurisdictions soon came to be known as either "dry" (no alcohol sales permitted) or "wet." A good part of the movement's effectiveness came from the fact that the most determined advocates and leaders were primarily, if not exclusively, the wives of the most successful upper-middle-class professionals; their husbands were bankers, doctors, lawyers, or very successful businessmen. During the peak of its power in the first decade of the twentieth century, the membership of the WCTU and its Canadian counterpart was overwhelmingly drawn from the ranks of the most privileged groups in North America. In 1919, Prohibition advocates succeeded in getting a constitutional amendment passed that made alcohol consumption illegal anywhere in the United States.

The main temperance organizations in Canada—the Dominion Alliance for the Total Suppression of the Liquor Traffic and the Woman's Christian Temperance Union of Canada—took their cues from their U.S. counterparts. They believed that poverty, crime, disease, and domestic abuse could be prevented through the prohibition of alcohol. Many religious groups (Baptist, Methodists, Presbyterians, and Congregationalists) strongly believed in prohibition as well and campaigned for it throughout the nineteenth century.

Yet, less than two decades later, the pendulum would swing back with ferocity. Millions of North Americans refused to stop drinking, creating a campaign of mass civil disobedience that undermined the legitimacy of the new prohibition laws. In the face of continued widespread drinking, attempts to enforce the ban on liquor would prove exceptionally difficult. The symbolic act that would break the back of Prohibition occurred when then New York governor Franklin Delano Roosevelt, shortly before he would become president, raised a glass of liquor at a public event, signalling yet another shift in the constitution of the moral centre when it came to alcohol. Prohibition would soon thereafter be repealed, and the consumption of alcohol today is permitted with relatively few restrictions (laws against driving or operating machinery while under the influence of alcohol are among the few major restrictions, although public drinking outside licensed establishments is also banned in some jurisdictions).

As Canadian temperance movements began to realize that they could not prevent people from consuming alcohol, they lobbied all provincial and territorial governments to control the sale of alcohol through liquor control boards that exist to the present day. By 1930 all provinces in Canada except for Prince Edward Island had rescinded alcohol prohibition and imposed provincial regulations on the sale of alcohol.

The Campaign Against Opium

16.2.3 Analyze the history of opium use and how it relates to definitions of normal and deviant.

While the alcohol crusade was one major example of a moral crusade that successfully, if only temporarily, turned everyday behaviour into deviant behaviour, a very different morality play of normality and deviance was being staged in relation to another mind-altering substance, opium, and its two derivates, morphine and heroin, in the same time period. The similarities and differences between these two campaigns can tell us much about what factors influence the construction of deviance.

Opium has been around for thousands of years, but morphine was not discovered and developed until the first decade of the nineteenth century. It took 50 years before it would become the most effective painkiller in medical history, in large measure owing to the invention of the hypodermic needle in 1856. This would occur just in time for the American Civil War.

The toll of human suffering during the American Civil War was monstrous, not just in terms of the huge proportion of the U.S. population that was killed but also those who suffered maiming injuries and debilitating health consequences that would last their full lifetime. In this context, morphine would be introduced, fast becoming the preferred drug for dealing with pain of all kinds. When the war ended, ex-soldiers often returned home with strong habits. While injections of morphine were legion for many sources of pain, a new pathway into the blood would come from ingesting the drug as a soothing syrup. For just a few pennies, one could purchase the product at the local pharmacy. Drug prescriptions were not part of the U.S. regulatory system until 1914, so anyone, of any age, could purchase bottles of this syrup, with a content of as high as 10 to 14 percent morphine. There was no Food and Drug Administration until the dawn of the twentieth century. Thus, there were no requirements to label ingredients, much less disclose proportionality of contents.

Here we come to the most fascinating feature of the "tale of two drugs" (alcohol vs. morphine). Between the end of the Civil War and 1904, records from pharmacies indicate that the heaviest usage of morphine was by middle-class, middle-aged white females (Terry & Pellens, 1970). This was the same four-decade period in which alcohol producers and distributors were being demonized and alcohol consumers were being characterized harshly by those opposing the use of alcohol. Yet at the same time, morphine use was characterized primarily as a medical problem. Rather than being labelled as social deviants, middle-class morphine consumers were the objects of sympathy, more pitied than despised. Morphine producers and distributors were not vilified; they were mainly ignored and did not register as a problem of any moral character, certainly not that of a transgression of the moral order.

During this period in Canada, opium was largely unregulated, until 1908, when the government passed the Opium Act. The legislation was aimed at controlling the traffic in opium while not making it an imprisonable offence. During the mid-nineteenth century, Chinese immigrants came to British Columbia as a source of cheap labour to build the railroads. The practice among Chinese labourers of smoking opium was initially a source of tax revenue, but soon became a means of criminalizing the behaviour of a group who were seen as a threat to white workers once they were no longer needed by the railroad companies. The government soon enacted the Opium and Drug Act (1911), which created harsher penalties for its consumers.

In the mid-nineteenth century, morphine was advertised as a soothing syrup to help manage the pain caused by teething in young children.

Stock Montage/Getty Images

Until the first decade of the twentieth century, anyone could walk into a pharmacy and purchase morphine or heroin for a few pennies without a prescription. New York State was the first to break with this practice, with the passage of the Boyle Act of 1904. The New York State legislation (and the federal law modelled upon it in 1914, known as the Harrison Act) was originally intended to give medical doctors control over the distribution of drugs by requiring prescriptions for the first time. However, when it came to the opiates, these laws would have the opposite effect. Physicians were suddenly confronted with scores of "patients" waiting for their prescriptions while regular patients were crowded out of waiting rooms. The response was to simply prescribe *en masse*—signing many prescriptions and having an assistant distribute them to those who had waited in the long lines (Duster, 1970). The federal government strenuously objected to this practice and took several physicians to court to stop it. In 1916, the Supreme Court sided with the government position, ruling in *Webb v. U.S.* that prescriptions must be individually prescribed based upon an individualized medical assessment. This ruling suddenly criminalized the practice of *en masse* prescriptions, sent several newly created law-violators to prison, and scared the medical profession away from the treatment of opiate users.

Within a few years, a black market in the production and distribution of the opiates was created, and opiate addicts were suddenly portrayed as morally reprehensible, not simply the victims of physiological dependency. Thus, in the short space of two decades, morphine and heroin addicts had been transformed in the public eye—no longer seen as middle-class, middle-aged, white female victims of a health and medical problem but as working-class, male, youthful criminals, and increasingly "of colour."

It is one of the least appreciated ironies of North American history that just when the pressure to end Prohibition peaked in the early 1930s, at that very same time laws were emerging to demonize what had previously been *normal* opiate use: those soothing syrups with a high morphine content consumed primarily by middle-class, middle-aged white women. These two juxtaposed stories offer a good example of the structural forces that shape who gets to be normal and who gets labelled as deviant. The important element to note in this story is that the pharmacology of the drugs did not change. Rather, it was the perception and representation of patterns of consumption that changed, and *that* changed everything about what was determined to be deviant behaviour and who could be categorized as engaging in immoral, deviant behaviour.

By the late 1930s, alcohol had shifted from being the metaphorical "demon rum" (the evil inherent in the mind-altering substance) to being a substance that some could gracefully handle (the casual social drinker) and some could not (the problem drinker). In sharp contrast, morphine, heroin, and opium had shifted from being medical analgesics that victimized unwitting middle-class citizens (in the late nineteenth century) to being a drug that drove the unfit to willful, licentious thrill-seeking. Again, nothing about the pharmaceutical product had changed—but those perceived as the primary consumers had been dramatically transformed into morally reprehensible deviants in just three decades.

Contemporary Moral Crusades

16.2.4 Discuss how the crusade against drug use and same-sex relationships affects the future of moral crusades.

The attempt to regulate morality remains very much part of contemporary North American society. One important example, which has parallels to the campaigns against alcohol and morphine, can be seen in the **war on drugs**. Launched by President Ronald Reagan in 1985 (although President Richard Nixon before him also briefly launched a "war on drugs" in the early 1970s) and widely embraced by

Figure 16.1 Rising Drug-Related Convictions for Whites and Blacks per Capita, United States

SOURCE: U.S. Bureau of Justice Statistics.

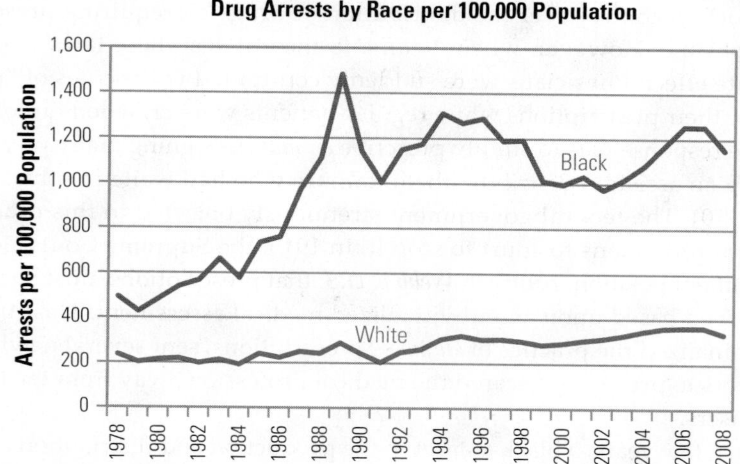

government officials across the country, the initiative involved significantly increasing surveillance of and criminal penalties for the sale, possession, and consumption of nonprescription drugs. Today, jails and prisons are filled with hundreds of thousands of drug offenders, with millions more under criminal justice supervision on probation or parole, all in the name of social order. (We will provide more details later in the chapter.) The reasons for the vast increase in the criminalization of drugs since the 1980s are complicated, but certain facts are indisputable. The groups serving time for criminal drug activity are not representative of the population actually using drugs. For example, studies show that far more poor people and far more African Americans are being arrested and convicted than white, middle-class, and affluent people (see Figure 16.1) (Tonry, 2012). Although, as Table 16.1 makes clear, whites and blacks consume illegal drugs at approximately equal rates (on average), evidence suggests these groups consume different types of drugs, and some of those are considered more socially deviant or acceptable than others. Whites are more likely to consume "popular" drugs, such as marijuana, ecstasy, OxyContin, and cocaine. African Americans consume slightly higher amounts of crack cocaine and LSD, but the difference is slim. For example, a 2011 survey from the Substance Abuse and Mental Health Services Administration showed that twice as many whites as African Americans or Latinos had used cocaine in any form (Substance Abuse and Mental Health Services Administration, 2011). Yet the white college student experimenting with illegal drugs or the suburban couple or business executive who enjoy occasionally getting high is drastically less likely to face criminal charges than are poor people or minorities.

Another important moral crusade in recent decades in North America, one that has seemingly failed to achieve its goals, has been the effort to ban or limit homosexuality and punish gays and lesbians on the basis of their sexual orientation. For centuries, homosexuality was largely practised "in the closet," although to be sure gays and lesbians were subject to arrest or harassment wherever they were discovered. Gay bars were continually subjected to police raids, but the practice of homosexuality remained sufficiently under the radar of public consciousness that few explicit campaigns or formal legal sanctions against homosexuality needed to be launched. All that would change in August 1969 when patrons of a gay bar in New York's Greenwich Village—the Stonewall Inn—fought back as police raided

Table 16.1 Percentage Aged 12 and Over Using Illicit Drugs and Alcohol by Race, 2008

Drug	White	Black
Alcohol		
Ever used	86.5	74.8
Within past year	70.4	56.9
Within past month	56.2	41.9
All Illicit Drugs*		
Ever used	50.7	46.1
Within past year	14.4	16.9
Within past month	8.2	10.1
Marijuana		
Ever used	45.1	41.1
Within past year	10.4	13.5
Within past month	6.2	8.3
Cocaine**		
Ever used	16.5	11.2
Within past year	2.2	2.0
Within past month	0.7	0.9
Crack		
Ever used	3.4	5.1
Within past year	0.4	0.9
Within past month	0.1	0.4
Hallucinogens		
Ever used	16.8	8.8
Within past year	1.6	1.3
Within past month	0.4	0.4
Inhalants		
Ever used	10.3	4.1
Within past year	0.8	0.4
Within past month	0.3	0.1

*Illicit drugs include marijuana or hashish, cocaine (including crack), heroin, hallucinogens, inhalants, or prescription-type psychotherapeutics used nonmedically.
**Includes crack cocaine.

SOURCE: Based on data from *Punishing Race: A Continuing American Dilemma*, by Michael Tonry, 2012, New York: Oxford University Press.

the bar. After three days of riots and growing protests in support of the Stonewall patrons, the movement for gay liberation and freedom was born. From that moment forward, gays have demanded and increasingly obtained full rights of citizenship, and in North America laws against homosexuality have declined or disappeared.

But this did not happen without a terrific fight, one that continues to this day. Opponents of homosexuality sought—with varying degrees of success—to follow in the footsteps of earlier moral crusades to use the legal system to repress homosexuality and/or to restrict the rights of gays and lesbians at every opportunity. In the 1970s, a number of states and local governments across the United States passed laws restricting the employment rights of gay individuals, for example, to prevent them from teaching in public schools or working at childcare centres or other public institutions. The military enforced an affirmative ban against homosexual soldiers for decades (repealed by President Barack Obama in 2009). The AIDS epidemic, beginning in 1981, provided another context for attacking homosexuals. HIV/AIDS was initially cast as a "gay disease," even though many heterosexuals were also being diagnosed as HIV-positive.

In Canada the Liberal government of Pierre Trudeau decriminalized homosexuality in 1969, but for many years gays and lesbians were discriminated against in a variety of areas of law and social policy. In 1977, Quebec included sexual orientation in its human rights code, becoming the first province in Canada to pass a gay civil rights law. The Quebec Charter of Human Rights and Freedoms made it illegal to discriminate against gays and lesbians in public employment and other areas of government. Up until the 1990s the definition of spouse in many provinces in Canada did not include a same-sex spouse, which resulted in the denial of pension benefits and refusal of adoption rights and spousal support following the breakdown of a partnership. In 1996 the federal government added sexual orientation to the Canadian Human Rights Act.

The moral crusade against homosexuality was vigorously pursued by antigay activists but ultimately did not succeed in either making same-sex unions illegal or successfully ostracizing gays. Increasing numbers of gays and lesbians in public life began to acknowledge their sexual orientation, with Svend Robinson, a member of Parliament for the BC riding of Burnaby–Douglas, openly acknowledging he was gay in 1988. Slowly, it became possible for gays to affirm their sexual orientation without fear of punishment or sanction by employers, family members, or friends. The individual ritual of "coming out of the closet," as gays and lesbians openly acknowledged their sexuality, would become so common that today virtually all North Americans have at least one gay family member or friend. In 2002, for the first time a Canadian court ruled in favour of recognizing same-sex marriages. The Ontario Superior Court found that prohibiting gay couples from marrying is unconstitutional and violates the Charter of Rights and Freedoms. In 2005, the law giving same-sex couples the right to marry was passed, making Canada the fourth country in the world to officially recognize same-sex marriage.

In the United States, a similar change has taken place. In 2003, the U.S. Supreme Court acknowledged (in *Lawrence v. Texas*, 539 U.S. 558) the shift in public attitudes and societal trends by overturning a 1985 ruling that had allowed the states to keep antigay laws on the books. While the struggle over homosexuality shifted over the following decade to a bitter campaign over the rights of gays and lesbians to marry, in 2015 the U.S. Supreme Court ruled that state-level bans on same-sex marriage are unconstitutional. It now appears that the long effort to criminalize same-sex relationships is coming to an end.

The apparent failure of the crusade against same-sex relationships portends an uncertain future for such crusades (and the effort to legislate morality). Growing numbers of younger and middle-aged North Americans, regardless of their political or religious views, favour lifestyle freedom over laws and regulations telling people what they can and cannot do (e.g., Baker, 2005). Increasingly, the line seems to be drawn at the point of behaviour that threatens to harm others; drinking is fine, but driving a car while drunk is now subject to major criminal penalties that have dramatically increased in recent years. The growing campaign to legalize marijuana—with Canada and many American states legalizing the use of medical marijuana and outright legalization having passed in Colorado and Washington and gaining ground in other U.S. states as well as Canada—exemplifies the changing dynamics of moral regulation. It is increasingly difficult for opponents of marijuana to persuade citizens that it makes sense to allow alcohol consumption (which can be at least as problematic in many ways for both individuals and society) while still outlawing marijuana. Nevertheless, the historical account we have provided in this section certainly suggests that attempts to regulate the behaviour of the poor, immigrants, and other disadvantaged groups are not likely to completely disappear.

16.3 Who Defines Deviance?

Sergey Dolzhenko/EPA/Newscom

Deviance, Crime, and Power

Much of the discussion in the chapter so far has pointed to one important conclusion: What is considered deviant, or criminal, is often completely arbitrary. We've noted that what is and is not deviant is not obvious or natural but rather the result of the conscious decisions and actions of groups and powerful individuals. But what is the connection between economic and political power, on the one hand, and the definition of deviant behaviour, on the other? Recall that our first experience with the idea of normality and its boundaries (deviance) is from the small social group into which we are born, almost universally the family or kinship unit. This small and relatively homogeneous group is our first encounter with who gets to define normality (e.g., our parents); however, as we grow up and encounter other groups, stronger and more compelling forces determine *which* group's view of normality will prevail in society as a whole. Foremost among these forces is the notion that power, whether hidden or direct, plays a role. In the historical example of how alcohol and the opiates traded places as the symbols of normal and deviant behaviour, for example, the advocates with greater access to political power had much more influence over the establishment of relevant laws. It was only when powerful groups sought to criminalize alcohol and opiates that those campaigns succeeded (and once some elites like Roosevelt and others turned against Prohibition, it was reversed). In this section, we turn our attention to other important struggles over defining deviance in which the role of economic and political power in shaping punishment becomes explicit.

Labelling Deviance and Crime

16.3.1 Discuss how labelling theory explains deviance.

In the 1960s, in an effort to understand the processes through which deviance is defined, some sociologists began doing systematic research in contexts where deviant, criminal, and abnormal behaviour were defined by individuals in positions of authority. When they did so, wherever they looked, they found plenty of evidence of arbitrariness in who was labelled deviants and how their offences were defined.

Here a few examples. One line of research involved riding around in police cars to closely observe what police officers actually do. These studies produced an important finding that cops overlook a lot of things that could be considered violations of the law, while other equally minor acts could meet with immediate arrest (Bittner, 1967; Cicourel, 1967). Other researchers studied district attorneys and public defenders, noting how often cases were dismissed and how they were dismissed. For example, lawyers on both sides would work together to get minor guilty pleas from certain suspects but not others (Sudnow, 1965). Sociologists studied intake decisions at mental institutions, where some types of mental illness are ignored and others are subjected to long stays (Goffman, 1959). This body of sociological research on how deviance gets defined has been repeatedly confirmed in later studies.

One of the more interesting of the new theories that emerged out of this research challenged the idea that there are real and objective differences in behaviour that is normal versus what is deviant. Most sociologists today argue that the *process* by which a behaviour comes to be defined as deviant is critical to understanding what actually causes it. In other words, instead of focusing on the behaviour of individuals, sociologists argue that we need to look at how the behaviour came to be defined as deviant. Deviant behaviour is "caused" by the process through which a behaviour comes to be defined, or labelled, as deviant by those in positions of political power.

These ideas are associated with what came to be known as the **labelling theory** of deviance, the idea that many kinds of behaviours are deviant solely because they are labelled as such. One of the leading labelling theory proponents, sociologist Howard Becker, argued that deviance, rather than an objective thing, is a social construction that evolves over time (Becker, 1963). An action that may be considered normal at one point comes to be defined as deviant at another point, even though the act itself may not change (recall our earlier examples of alcohol and morphine prohibition). In this way, a basic premise of labelling theory is that social control does not simply respond to deviance; it *constitutes* deviance. So, to understand deviance we need to focus on how social control actively makes certain behaviours unacceptable. Think about deviance not as a momentary act (when someone robs someone else or smokes marijuana) but as a process. In other words, look at how a behaviour *becomes* deviant. Understanding this process involves two things. First, it requires examining why and how certain behaviours and people get labelled as deviant. Second, it requires analyzing the impacts of these labels on the behaviours of the people who are labelled. Once labelled deviant (or a troublemaker or a criminal), an individual may appear to be more likely to be deviant than they actually are. For example, once labelled a troublemaker or deviant, an individual's actions are more closely scrutinized by the authorities, including teachers, police officers, employers, and others. In this way, the odds of being caught in further acts of deviance go up.

From Deviance in the Streets to Deviance in the Suites: White-Collar Crime

16.3.2 Determine what the 2008 U.S. financial crisis reveals about power and deviant behaviour.

One of the most important developments in the study of deviance and crime, and one that extended the idea of labelling theory into arenas where power is particularly important, is in the area of white-collar crime. First introduced by the famous criminologist Edwin Sutherland in 1949, the term **white-collar crime** refers to unethical business practices committed by people in the course of their work lives. Historically, white-collar crimes were handled almost solely in civil courts. This was, in Sutherland's view, often perverse: Some kinds of white-collar crime can have as much or more of a negative impact and cause injury to more people in a society than ordinary street crimes (such as burglary, robbery, vandalism, shoplifting, or assault). For example, when a corporation or business owner knowingly markets an unsafe product, far more people may suffer significantly greater harms than any thief or bank robber can cause. Sutherland concluded that when business activity damages innocent people's property or physical well-being, it is completely arbitrary to absolve the wrongdoer of criminal responsibility (Sutherland, 1949).

White-collar crime can take many forms, from those that are closer to street crimes (e.g., stealing money from your employer or using the Internet to defraud others) all the way up to those involving powerful businesses and corporate leaders who make decisions or seek profits in ways that cause injury or harm to innocent people. Perhaps not surprisingly, there has been much more agreement that lower-level white-collar crimes, such as embezzlement or fraud, are properly situated in criminal (as well as civil) courts; the treatment of higher-level white-collar crime, which is often more consequential, has remained more controversial.

We can get a better handle on the concept of white-collar crime, and the difficulties that have been raised in applying punishments to white-collar criminals, by considering a couple of recent examples: the case of Enron, a scandal-ridden energy company that went out of business in 2001, and the U.S. banking and financial crisis of 2008. Both of these cases involve a complex mixture of greed, political influence, and corruption. Let's start with Enron. Prior to its bankruptcy, Enron appeared to be one of the most successful corporations in the world. In 1996, Enron reported profits of $13.3 billion. Just three years later, in 1999, the company's reported profits had tripled, to $40.1 billion. And the very next year, in 2000, profits were reported to have soared to the $100 billion mark, making it number seven among the Fortune 500 list of companies, leap-frogging over well-known companies such as IBM, Walmart, AT&T, and Philip Morris. For an astounding six years in a row, *Fortune* magazine named Enron the "most innovative company" in America. In the fall of 2001, however, it would be revealed that these were largely fictitious profits based on enormous accounting fraud and price manipulation.

Before Enron's operations were revealed to be fraudulent, the company benefitted from its close relationship with many elected officials, including President George W. Bush (who famously and playfully nicknamed Enron CEO Kenneth Lay "Kenny Boy"). Enron executives provided enormous amounts of money to support the election campaigns of favoured politicians and as a result frequently received special treatment from government agencies. One example of the many ways in which Enron was able to take advantage of its growing political power and influence comes from the sale of electricity in California, where it won exclusive contracts to provide much of the state's energy. During the period from April 1998 to April 2000, Californians were paying on average $30 per megawatt for electricity. In June of 2000, several power plants were suddenly closed for maintenance by Enron, and prices sharply increased to $120 per megawatt—an extraordinary increase of 400 percent in just two months. Then things became worse when Enron arranged for the appearance of "congestion" (scheduling power deliveries that it never intended) so that it could charge special "congestion fees" of $750 per megawatt (Fox, 2003, p. 208). Pacific Gas and Electric, California's largest utility company, was caught in the middle and would file for bankruptcy, having run up a deficit of nearly $9 billion as a direct consequence of Enron's manipulation of the state's energy grid during this period.

Perhaps the most infamous moment in the entire Enron case involved tapes that later came to light that capture an Enron trader's derisive, scornful laugh at the plight of a California grandmother whose energy bill had just quadrupled because of his participation in an unscrupulous manipulation of the power grid. "All that money that you stole from those poor grandmothers in California? Grandma Millie. Now she wants her . . . money back for all the power you've just charged . . . !" The Enron trader replies, "F . . . Granny!" and then has a loud, sustained laugh with his buddies that should curdle the blood of any decent soul.

Enron's illegal manipulation of energy prices in California would prove to be just the tip of the iceberg of its unscrupulous practices. The company was also using a mammoth accounting fraud to create profits where none existed. The "Enron scandal," as it came to be known, involved creating false profits by reporting phony income from fictitious offshore companies created by Enron's financial officers. When the first journalists and government officials began raising questions about the company's accounting practices, senior Enron executives began selling their shares in the company while repeatedly promising shareholders that all was right with the company, and even urging others (including Enron's own employees) to buy the company's stock. In November 2001, within days after the scandal was revealed, the value of the stock would fall from its peak of $90 (in 2000) to just a few pennies. The full details of the scandal are complex, but the bottom line is that when the company filed for bankruptcy, all of the company's shareholders, its 20,000 employees (many of whom received stock bonuses that executives knew would eventually be worthless), and communities around the world where Enron was operating suffered as the company collapsed. The reputation of the huge accounting firm of Arthur Andersen, where several of the accountants who had helped Enron with their fraud were employed, was destroyed, and the company was forced to fold, costing thousands more people their jobs.

In contrast to most cases of white-collar crime, the fraud in the Enron case was so extreme and blatant that three senior executives would serve time in prison, though CEO Kenneth Lay died before he could begin his prison sentence. Still, given the depths of the fraud at Enron, it is a remarkable commentary on the shortcomings of white-collar justice that only three people were sent to prison for a fraud that had such enormous impact on so many people and communities.

Let's now look at a second, even more dramatic example of the special treatment of white-collar crime, in the banking and financial crisis that hit the United States, Europe, and ultimately the global economic system, in 2008. To understand this case more fully, and how and why many banks and other financial corporations were able to take actions that generated billions of dollars in profits while causing millions of homeowners to lose their homes, we need to briefly investigate the historical background. After the banking collapse in the United States during the Great Depression of the 1930s, new laws and regulations were put in place to prevent another collapse of the banking system. Banks were limited in the kinds of risky investments they could make. While many in the banking world objected to these constraints, for decades they served to reduce the risk of financial crisis. But beginning in the 1980s, as memories of the Great Depression faded, powerful banking interests persuaded the U.S. Congress to begin loosening the rules and allowing banks to take on more risk in the search for higher profits. For example, in 1982, Congress voted to deregulate the savings and loan (S&L) industry. Risky investments by S&Ls ensued almost immediately, and within a decade some had gotten rich while scores of these institutions failed. As a direct consequence, taxpayers were slapped with a bill of $124 billion. But that was only the beginning.

By the 1990s, the growing movement to tear down banking and financial regulations had reached a fever pitch. The U.S. Congress and President Bill Clinton, at the urging of the financial industry, undid many of the remaining restrictions on the banks. In this increasing "anything goes" environment, financial companies aggressively pursued new avenues of profit. One of these, which would ultimately trigger the development of the financial crisis, was the mass marketing of new home-mortgage products, known as *subprime loans*, to consumers who had little hope of repaying them. Playing on the desire of most Americans to own their own home, the subprime loans typically had a low initial "teaser" rate but the fine print revealed that they would eventually jump to a much higher rate. Many of the people taking out these loans did not understand the risk they were accepting, and laws that once might have protected them had been eliminated in the name of deregulation.

The story is more complicated than we can fully convey here, as the levels of fraud throughout the home-mortgage industry were breathtakingly pervasive and complicated. One key point was that the banks and loan companies making the subprime loans discovered that they were able to make handsome profits reselling the loans to other investors, who then assumed all of the risk. So they soon began giving out loans to virtually anyone they could find who would sign the paperwork. The secondary institutions (other banks, insurance companies, and investment firms) that bought up the subprime loans were continually assured they were safe. At this level, far removed from the original loan, the new loanholders could not understand, nor were they fully informed about, the risks they were accepting.

The crisis began to unfold in 2007, when the U.S. economy went into recession, unemployment started to rise, and home prices began to decline at the same time that many subprime loans were being reset to their higher rate. Large numbers of subprime borrowers began defaulting on their loans. As a result, the repackaged loans went into default, and in short order the entire financial sector would face a severe crisis that would ultimately require the federal government to provide many billions of dollars to keep the big banks from going out of business. The phrase "too big to fail" came to be applied to large banks that had taken on these risky loans. Although all other businesses in America go bankrupt when they make poor decisions, in this case the risks to all of American society if large banks were allowed to fail was too great to let happen. The federal government's bailout of the banks would keep them in business, but the full cost of the financial crisis of 2007 and 2008 is still being felt today. Unemployment rates shot up after the crisis began, and the American economy has performed very poorly by historical standards since then.

By effectively lobbying the U.S. Congress to overturn regulations of financial institutions and energy production, powerful corporate actors enabled the redefinition of what would constitute normality, deviance, and criminality. By their own admission in congressional testimony, many bank and financial executives acknowledged routinely practising deception in withholding vital information from their own clients in relation to mortgage and subprime loans (and in the sale of financial products related to those loans). Goldman Sachs, the most famous financial firm in the world, paid $50 million in fines and faced many embarrassing revelations about its executives' behaviour and treatment of their clients during the crisis. On December 4, 2011, the CBS television news journal *60 Minutes* aired a two-part segment in which two whistle-blowers testified as to just how systematic fraudulent mortgage-loan practices had indeed become "normal." These mid-level managers had explicitly warned senior management, only to be ignored, then offered monetary settlements to remain silent, then fired for not cooperating with the firm's cover-up.

The actions of Enron in the 1990s and early 2000s, and later those of many in the financial sector in the 2000s, were clearly fraudulent and in violation of federal and state laws, but the criminal justice system had great difficulty deciding whether and how to punish them. To be sure, a tiny handful of top Enron officials did receive modest prison sentences, but so far virtually no one in the mortgage

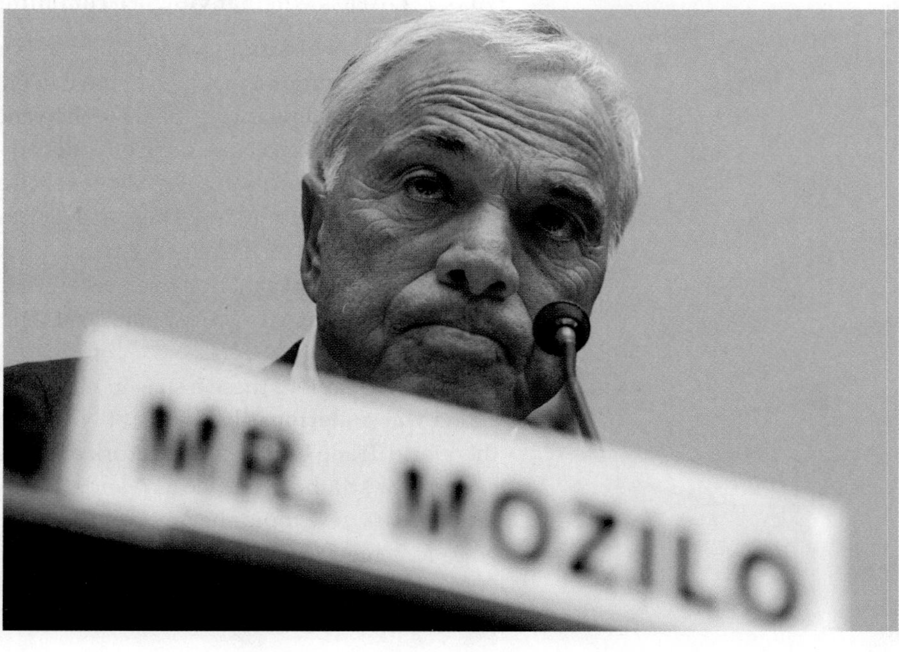

Countrywide Financial Corporation CEO Angelo Mozilo testifying before Congress about his firm's promotion of subprime mortgages.

Kevin Lamarque/Reuters

industry has served prison time. In April 2014, only one banker—a mid-level Credit Suisse executive named Kareem Serageldin—has received a prison sentence (in this case, 30 months for lying about the value of his bank's securities) (Eisinger, 2014). Fines have been imposed, but often in trivial amounts given the millions of dollars that have been lost. For example, one of the most aggressive offenders in the subprime scandal was Angelo Mozilo, president and CEO of Countrywide Financial, one of the companies that led the way in issuing and profiting from subprime loans. Despite making about $500 million while at Countrywide, Mozilo not only did not go to prison, but he ended up settling the case against him by paying a fine of $47.5 million (a fraction of the wealth he accumulated during the subprime era).

Contrast this with the rough treatment of low-level drug offenders we mentioned in the previous section. Such examples dramatically typify the frequently light treatment of white-collar crime compared to other kinds of crime, and, in doing so, they raise two critical points. First, the kinds of deviant behaviour that get punished, and the severity of the punishment, is often linked in part to who the perpetrator is. Second, we are reminded again that what counts as a punishable crime is in large part shaped by the overall distribution of power. One of the reasons so few banking executives have been held criminally liable is that the cost of pursuing cases against them is enormously expensive for the government because the accused can afford to hire expensive lawyers and fight on all fronts. The costs of pursuing these cases in court is now so high that the federal government is bringing to justice barely half as many white-collar crime cases as it did 20 years ago (Eisinger, 2014).

At the peak of the media coverage on predatory bank loans, the first author of this chapter was confronted by a provocative question from his 11-year-old nephew: "So which is worse, to rob an old lady of her purse, or to rob her of her pension?" This question captures an old idiom about the differences between blue-collar crime, or street crime, and white-collar and corporate crimes. It is hard, if not impossible, to make the case that robbing an old lady of her purse is a worse offence, but it is certainly vastly more likely to be punished by the criminal justice system. If we contrast the treatment of Enron and banking officials who engaged in fraudulent subprime activity with the rough treatment accorded drug offenders, it is hard not to be very concerned about basic fairness of that system.

State Deviance, Terrorism, and War Crimes

16.3.3 Discuss whether violence committed during wartime is a criminal act.

If powerful corporations and executives can engage in deviant behaviour without much risk of criminal penalty, so too can entire governments. In the case of what we might call **state deviance**—that is, policy and actions carried out by governments and government employees in their official capacities—criminal courts and international law rarely issue sanctions even against actions that lead to deaths or injuries of large numbers of innocent people. Just as the criminal justice system has trouble punishing corporations and corporate executives, so too are government officials often able to avoid any criminal sanction even when their actions cause significant harm or death to others. It reminds us, once again, that when it comes to determining what is deviant behaviour, power matters.

We will explore these issues in more detail in this section in the context of the so-called **war on terror**—the efforts of North American governments since the attacks on the World Trade Center in New York and the Pentagon on September 11, 2001, to find, capture, or kill those individuals and groups suspected of plotting terrorist actions. In recent years, few topics have received more attention than **terrorism**—the use of violence to achieve some political objective. No one defends terrorism. Anyone who uses force to kill innocent people violates the universal rule against murder. Extreme examples such as the beheading of journalists or innocent people shock our conscience.

But if we consider each human life equally valuable and sacred, it is sometimes hard to say who the real terrorists are. For example, in the name of fighting terrorism, both the U.S. and Canadian governments and their leading government officials have assumed the right to violate international law and widely accepted views about human rights in the modern world.

Studying deviance can help us better understand issues related to terrorism. Let's first ask the question: What is terrorism? To appreciate how the modern understanding of terrorism developed, it is important to first explore the concept of the *theatre of war*. Five hundred years ago, European armies were composed of men who designated the battlefield as the sole appropriate arena of conflict. Much like contemporary prize-fighters who are limited to the ring, boxing gloves, and rounds set off by agreed-upon parameters, these battlefields delimited the legitimate landscape for the war. While there were skirmishes that leaked off the battlefield, the arena of conflict was established by this limited notion of an agreed-upon terrain.

In the theatre of war, generals deploy troops, have their men dig trenches, and take hills to capture the high ground. But what of situations in which one army so outnumbers another, or is so much better equipped, that there is no real contest? Do generals really want to go into battle when their numbers are one-tenth that of their enemy? The answer is no, at least not in a straightforward battlefield encounter, where their inferior numbers inevitably lead to doom. Instead, strategy enters the formula, and tactics evolve. In the case of the European armies half a millennium ago, methods such as cutting armies off at passes and starving them by destroying supply lines began to enter the theatre of war as legitimate strategies. That is, before opponents ever got to some place called the field of battle, it was legitimate to intercept and harass them, to use decoys, and even send false signals, among other tactics. "All is fair in love and war" goes the saying, which made sense (at least for war) once armies began fighting their opponents using a variety of tactics not all of which were limited to the theatre of war.

It is only a matter of degree to shift away from grand strategy on or around the battlefield, to the cunning of ambush (before the "battle"), to the next major development. **Guerrilla warfare** happens when a fighting force hides from its enemy and carries out targeted raids designed to wear down its numerically superior opponent. So long as European nations were doing battle with each other, the notion of a theatre or arena of battle was more or less agreed on as to the terms of action and ultimate settlement. However, in the colonial period, European powers had to battle people who were to face them with inferior arms and employing different rules of the game. Their inferior arms meant that Europeans could slaughter thousands of natives at will. That slaughter was never called terrorism. Yet one may ask, what greater terror is there than to be enslaved on one's own land by a people who have contempt for your culture and your way of living?

More important to this line of argument, however, is that the colonized would later employ tactics that would shift the very meaning of war. Now, rather than regular soldiers conducting a battle in designated uniforms, increasingly *the people* themselves might be the enemy. In some ways, the Americans were among the first to use such tactics, during the Revolutionary War. The British redcoats, marching in formation, were fair game for the locals. The locals were usually not in uniform. They could devise clever ways of attacking an initially superior enemy. Later, other colonized people around the world would further blur this distinction. Women could and did carry muskets and fire them. Children could be used as runners. In guerrilla war, any actor in the occupied territory could be a soldier in disguise.

Seen from this angle, the emergence of terrorism in the contemporary world is a progression from the battlefield to the strategic ploys of generals to avoid the battlefield, to guerrilla warfare, and finally to terrorism. If we are to understand terrorism, we must try to penetrate the social and political situation of the perpetrators of terrorist acts. On the surface, the most powerful nations clearly dominate the weaker nations, and the United States has by far the strongest military in the world. In the theatre of war, a weak nation would no more do battle with a strong nation than a welterweight would get into the boxing ring with a heavyweight. But outside the ring, the welterweight, even the lightweight, is equal to the heavyweight, by using different rules of engagement. And, indeed, outside the theatre of war, the guerrilla warrior begins to equalize matters by finding ways to make the fight fairer.

Let's move forward in time to the post-9/11 era. North Americans have heard a great deal about the attacks on 9/11 and the continuing threat of a terrorist attack from al-Qaeda and other organizations such as the Islamic State in Iraq and Syria (ISIS) since then. The government and the media have stoked fears about the possibility of further attacks on American citizens. And several dramatic videos of the beheading of American and other citizens by terrorist groups in foreign countries have added to that fear.

Yet we hear far less frequently about aspects of the war on terror where the U.S. government has sanctioned and employed tactics such as the kidnapping and torture of suspected terrorists, using drone strikes to attack housing complexes occupied by suspected terrorists as well as children and adults not involved in any terrorist activity, and assuming the right to kill without trial people accused of membership in terrorist organizations (Brooks & Manza, 2013, Chapter 1). The question is, why is it terrorism when al-Qaeda kills innocent Americans but not terrorism when the U.S. government engages in similar actions that lead to the deaths of innocent civilians? We even have a new name for what the United States has been engaged in since 9/11: **counterterrorism**. The term is informative. America's enemies engage in terrorism, while the U.S. government practises counterterrorism.

The counterterrorist actions of the U.S. government—which claims to adhere to international standards and respect for human rights—have included the use of tactics such as drone strikes on other countries' territories, torture, the kidnapping of suspected terrorists, and in some cases their execution without trial. During this period, a single powerful metaphor dominated much of the thinking of government officials (and one that exerted considerable influence within the media and broader public as well). The metaphor was that of a "ticking time bomb," the idea that additional terrorist plots and attacks were imminent, and in order to foil them, immediate and unconditional action was necessary. Officials in the White House crafted legal memos that claimed to justify the use of a variety of tactics that were not in accord with current international or American constitutional law (and that would later be denounced by virtually all legal scholars who examined them).

The bombing of the World Trade Center, September 11, 2001, and the bodies of innocent people killed by an American drone strike in Afghanistan, which residents say claimed 150 lives. Why is one of these attacks considered terrorism and the other not?

Beth Dixson/Alamy Stock Photo

Yola Monakhov/AP Images

Using these memos as a cover for their actions, for several years the government rounded up many people suspected of being involved in terrorist activity and took them to hidden locations where they could be subjected to "enhanced interrogation" techniques, otherwise known as torture, in the hopes of gathering intelligence. We know now—as a result of many important journalistic revelations—that many of the interrogation techniques used by agents of the Central Intelligence Agency (CIA) and special military units defied the international human rights protections codified in the **Geneva Conventions**, a series of international agreements about the fair treatment of prisoners of war (for some of the most important of these accounts, see Hersh, 2005; Lichtblau, 2008; Mayer, 2008). We also know, from these same sources, that many of the people subjected to torture had little or no connection to any terrorist or terrorist activity.

The techniques of torture used in these investigations, especially in the period from 2002 to 2005, are important to learn about. They included sleep and sensory deprivation, isolation, and repeated beatings, as well as humiliation, forcible administration of drugs, and (most famously and brutally) "waterboarding," a technique that simulates the sensation of drowning. Evidence of these top-secret interrogations was uncovered and revealed over an extended period of time, and the full story of the administration's use of torture cannot yet be written. But the first unambiguous evidence of torture came with the release of photographs of inmate abuse at the Abu Ghraib prison in April 2004, reported by *New Yorker* reporter Seymour Hersh and broadcast in a special *60 Minutes* report. An official military review of treatment of inmates at Abu Ghraib rebuked the prison's commanding officers. Interviews with prison officials and military investigators, as well as evidence shown in the photos that were released (and more graphically in photos not released for public viewing), documented gross mistreatment of inmates. This included evidence that inmates had been raped and sodomized, physically and deliberately injured, urinated upon, and subjected to attacks by guard dogs. At least one inmate was killed, and many others suffered serious injuries.

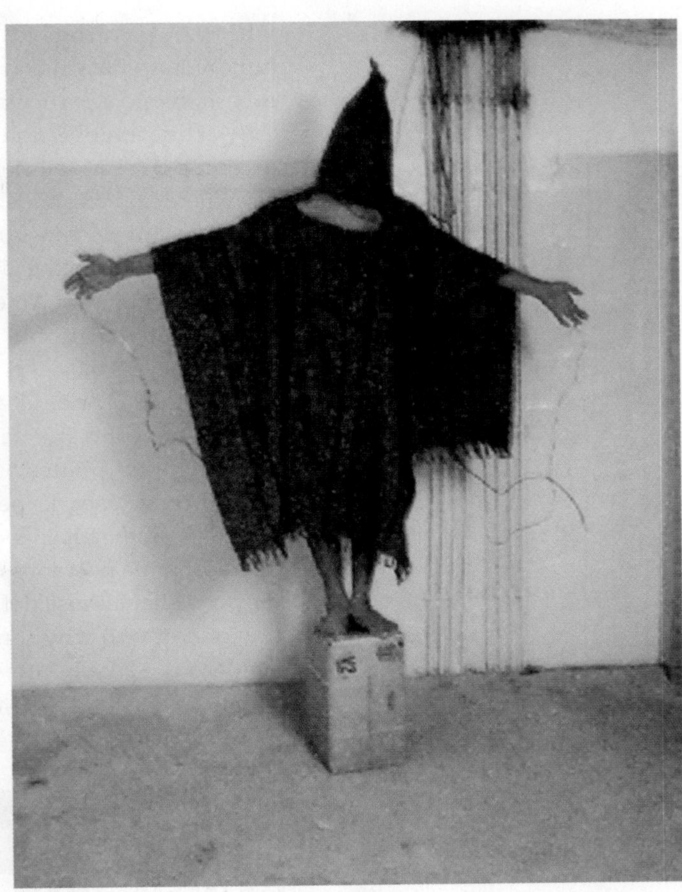

AP Images

How might institutional deviance of a military culture have supported the seemingly individual acts of deviance at Abu Ghraib?

The initial response of the U.S. military to the abuses at Abu Ghraib was to place blame on specific (and mostly lower-level) military personnel and their immediate supervisors, implying these were random, unauthorized occurrences (Hersh, 2005). Whatever the particulars of the chain of command at Abu Ghraib, later evidence suggested that the systematic use of torture was quite widespread and sanctioned by officials at the very top of the U.S. government (including then vice president Dick Cheney, who has openly and repeatedly defended the use of torture in later interviews since leaving office in 2008). Abu Ghraib was only one of a number of sites where torture was employed, but it is the one we know most about. Some of the other unknown sites were called "black sites," foreign prisons operated by the CIA or the American military (or sometimes the military or secret police of friendly nations) in which individuals accused of terrorist activities could be interrogated outside the reach of any legal authority. Secret prisons were located in countries such as Poland, Romania, and Lithuania, and other facilities have been identified in Africa and the Middle East. The existence of black sites was initially denied by the government, but in September 2006, President George W. Bush publicly acknowledged their existence. Suspects have also sometimes been turned over to foreign governments known for their use of torture and other aggressive techniques of interrogation and punishment (Mayer, 2008).

In spite of the worldwide condemnation of the American government's use of torture from 2002 to 2005, only a handful of low-level officers at the single Abu Ghraib prison have been sent to prison. Why is this the case? As the strongest military power in the world, perhaps the United States does not have to play by the same rules as everyone else; it can, and does, refuse to participate in international legal proceedings that have been brought against high government officials involved in planning and sanctioning the use of torture.

After 2005, President Bush ended the use of torture in investigations, and President Obama made that a binding legal requirement on the U.S. military by issuing an executive order banning the use of torture in 2009. But other policies in the war on terror that have continued or even increased in recent years have raised similar questions about state deviance and war crimes. For example, the American military has widely used unmanned drone planes in Afghanistan, Pakistan, and Yemen to attempt to kill suspected terrorists. These strikes—which involve sending U.S. planes into countries where the governments have repeatedly demanded they not fly—have also killed hundreds of innocent civilians (Bergen & Tiedemann, 2010; Mayer, 2008). In June 2012, in response to a particularly horrific incident in which 18 innocent people were killed, the American government agreed to reduce its use of drone strikes in Afghanistan except in cases of self-defence (Associated Press, 2012). But the drone strikes continue elsewhere (in Pakistan and Yemen, for example), and the larger issue of culpability of the powerful remains. Imagine if the Canadian or Mexican government repeatedly sent airplanes into the United States to kill people it said were involved in terrorism, and lots of innocent Americans, including children, were being killed in those bombings. Would Americans not view that as mass murder and demand that the people responsible for the attacks be held criminally liable?

It should now be clear that the central insights from the sociological study of deviance do not come from attempts to explain the personal characteristics, attributes, or pathologies of pirates or terrorists, of alcohol runners or drug cartel operatives, of predatory loan sharks peddling subprime loans or of CIA agents torturing suspected terrorists. Rather, insights into such deviant behaviour come from studying the social and economic positions of those who define and label deviance and crime, and how they can shape those definitions to suit their own purposes. The answer to the question of how and why some kinds of behaviours are punished while other, seemingly similar, ones are not comes from the explicit values articulated by those in power.

16.4 How Is Social Control Imposed on Society?

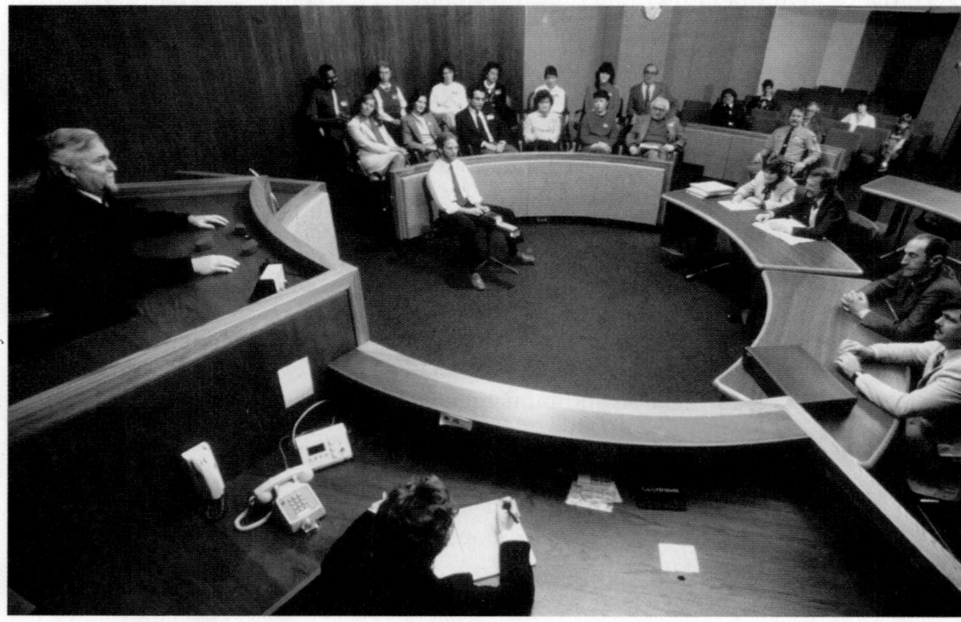

Stock Connection Blue/Alamy Stock Photo

The Institutions of Social Control

As we have seen so far, society imposes rules about normal and deviant behaviour, most definitively by establishing criminal laws and criminal codes, which deliver the final word about what is deviant behaviour when the prison door slams shut. When some kinds of deviance become crimes, they pass into the realm of the *institutions of social control*—such as the police, criminal courts, and prisons and jails—that are all around us.

In this section, we examine how and where **social control**—the various ways societies regulate and sanction behaviour to encourage conformity to and discourage deviance from the norms—comes to be formalized in the institutions of criminal justice. Before we get there, however, we must first turn to some basic features of the system of societal sanctions that lie behind the formal institutions of social control.

Sanctions and Rewards as Forms of Social Control

16.4.1 Analyze ways in which the criminal justice system exerts social control.

A key dimension of social control occurs through **sanctions**, or punishments that groups and societies establish to enforce norms. Sanctions include punishments of various kinds—at the extreme, imprisonment. But sanctions are not the only way social control is promoted. We often follow rules and norms not just because we are worried about punishment but also because we may seek rewards that good behaviour provides. Positive rewards might include things like praise, awards, and salary raises. Doing what the boss wants, no matter how irrational it may be, can be a good way of moving up in the company (whereas challenging the boss can put an employee at risk).

Sociologists also distinguish between formal and informal sanctions and rewards. *Formal sanctions* are those used to enforce the norms that are written into law and are usually carried out by a group of people who have been given the specific task and power to do so, including the police or school principals. Examples of such sanctions are fines or arrests (and possible prison sentences), while formal rewards might be getting good grades or promotions. *Informal sanctions* might include such things as insults or giving someone a dirty look, while informal rewards include things like giving people compliments.

Although social deviance usually elicits a negative response, there are actually some occasions in which acting in a deviant way, especially against the authorities, may elicit a positive response, while conformity, or simply following the rules and norms, elicits a negative response. Think of the classic example of Robin Hood. Robin Hood was a thief, and society generally believes that robbery is a deviant act. However, Robin Hood's act of stealing from the very rich and giving the money to the destitute poor is often viewed as heroic. Or consider the cases of Mahatma Gandhi or Martin Luther King Jr. Violating laws against public protests, Gandhi and King are heroic figures today for refusing to bend to the will of an oppressive authority. The model of civil disobedience they popularized is now universally acknowledged as right and proper in certain situations. Or think of the cool "bad boy" or "bad girl" at the high school you attended (every school has one or more such figures). They defy authority and the rules and often have more status for doing so.

There are also occasions in which conforming to the norms or rules will be met not with a positive response but a negative one. Consider for example people who do whatever it takes just to please others and get their approval. In school or work settings, these conformists may be ridiculed by other students (or coworkers) as the teacher's (or employer's) pet, while at the same time they may be rewarded by their teacher (or not, if their conformity is too obvious and becomes grating for the teacher). In the extreme case, simply following the orders of Adolf Hitler and the Nazi government during World War II is not regarded as an appropriate defence for murdering people in concentration camps. In fact, the deviants of Nazi Germany, who refused to go along (and in many cases lost their lives) are now considered the heroes of that period. In all of these situations, it is not so simple as saying that following rules and norms entails approval while not following social norms means disapproval. Knowing how to strike the right balance reflects a full understanding of the written and unwritten rules.

The ambiguities in the line between deviance and conformity have created pressures to expand formal sanctions. Historically, as societies have grown and become more complex, there has been a shift from emphasis on informal means of social control toward more formal means. In the contemporary world, the dominant form of social control is through the criminal justice system and its central institution of discipline, the prison.

The Criminal Justice System

16.4.2 Analyze mass incarceration.

The kinds of behaviours that come to be considered "criminal" leave no room for ambiguity, and all modern societies have developed institutions of criminal justice for sanctioning these particular types of deviant behaviour. The **criminal justice system** includes criminal law (in the United States, the federal government and each state have their own criminal codes, although in Canada and in many other countries a single national criminal code exists), the police forces that identify and apprehend offenders, the lawyers, judges, and court system that evaluate evidence of guilt and assigns sentences when a conviction is obtained, and the jails and prisons where offenders may be sentenced to serve time (as well as probation and parole officers who supervise convicted offenders not in prison). In North America, we distinguish between jails and prisons. In Canada, **jails** and detention centres generally hold people who are accused before a trial, those who have breached a condition of their release, or people convicted of lesser crimes, crimes that have a maximum sentence of less than two years of **incarceration**, or imprisonment. **Prisons**, by contrast, are where convicted persons serving a sentence of two years or more are held once they have been convicted of a serious crime.

Why do societies punish? We can identify four possible goals, or purposes, of punishment: (1) to exact *retribution* for the victims of criminal acts; (2) to *deter* offenders and others from committing crimes in the future; (3) to *incapacitate* or otherwise prevent offenders from committing further crimes; and (4) to *rehabilitate* or reform offenders. **Retribution** is a form of simple vengeance, founded on the notion that those who have committed crimes should suffer for the harm they have caused others. Modern proponents of retribution argue that the punishment should fit the crime already committed rather than future crimes that the criminal or others might commit. In contrast to retribution, which is designed to redress crimes already committed, **deterrence** endeavours to prevent future crimes by creating a disincentive to violate the law by threatening punishment.

Not all convicted offenders are sentenced to jail or prison; in fact, many will receive **probation**, a form of punishment where an offender is allowed to live in her or his community as long as no further offences are committed for the length of the sentence. The goals of retribution and deterrence do not require imprisonment. However, the other two purposes of punishment relate specifically to the use of imprisonment. Putting people in jail or prison can serve one of two purposes: It removes them from society (so that they commit no further offences, at least for some period of time); and it can also provide a context for **rehabilitation**, which involves the attempt to help offenders stop committing further crimes through therapy, education, and job training.

Analysts may differ on which of the four purposes of punishment is most important and beneficial for society. And the four purposes are not incompatible with one another: A long prison sentence could both deter others from engaging in the same behaviour *and* remove the offender from her or his community. Many criminologists agree that imprisonment functions as a very weak deterrent to crime, however, and note its high social and economic costs to society. Whatever the exact understanding of the general purposes of punishment, it has long been the case that imprisoning someone is something extraordinary, generally reserved for the most significant violations of the law. Yet, as we explore in the next section, in recent years in the United States and to a lesser extent Canada, this is no longer the case.

Crime and Mass Incarceration in North America Today

16.4.3 Describe the changing crime rate and the trend toward mass incarceration in North America.

The American criminal justice system in recent years has undergone a remarkable change. The incarcerated population in the United States has grown 700 percent over the past 40 years—in other words, there are seven times more people in prison today than in 1972, when figures are adjusted for overall population size (i.e., the figure takes into account that the entire population of America has grown in this period). For the first three-quarters of the twentieth century, except for a notable uptick during the Depression years of the late 1930s, the incarceration rate (i.e., the number of prisoners per capita) remained relatively constant. People who committed serious crimes would be sent to prison, but most offenders would receive other penalties. Beginning in the early 1970s, however, the number of people housed in prisons began to grow steadily every year and would continue to do so for the next 30 years before numbers finally levelled off around 2005. More people were being sentenced to prison, sentences became longer, and judges and parole boards had greatly reduced discretion to let people off for good behaviour. New categories of deviance—mostly having to do with drugs—became increasingly criminalized, with sellers and simple users much more likely to be sentenced to prison than before.

Canada has only recently begun to embark on a similar path. The Conservative government of Stephen Harper sought to increase the use of punishment to deter crime through the use of mandatory minimum sentences aimed at reducing the discretion of judges. The 2014–2015 Annual Report of the Correctional Investigator, Howard Sapers, revealed that Canada's prison population is now at its highest level ever, even though the crime rate has been decreasing over the past two decades. Between 2005 and 2015, the federal inmate population grew by 10 percent, but the Aboriginal inmate population grew by 50 percent and the black inmate population grew by 69 percent. Both Aboriginals and blacks are overrepresented in the federal inmate population. The federal incarceration rate of blacks is three times their representation in Canadian society. Similarly, Aboriginals make up 4.3 percent of Canadian society but represent 24.6 percent of the total inmate population in federal prisons. During this decade, the population of women behind bars increased by over 50 percent; Aboriginal women make up 35.5 percent of women in custody (Sapers, 2015, p. 2).

Despite the fact that crime rates in Canada are at an all-time low, Canada's prison population has grown in the 2000s as a result of an American-style tough-on-crime political agenda. It appears as though Canada is embarking on a costly crime control policy: It now costs approximately $108,376 a year to house a male inmate, and nearly twice that much to house a female inmate. The federal budget of Correctional Service Canada (CSC) increased 40 percent between 2008 and 2013 to $2.6 billion (Brosnahan, 2013). Planned spending for federal corrections for 2015–2016 is down slightly to $2.3 billion due to Corrections Service Canada's contribution of $300 million to the government's deficit reduction plan. The cuts resulted in federal inmates and their families bearing the costs to keep themselves clothed, fed, housed, and cared for while behind bars. Other cost-saving measures resulted in the closing of the prison farms, and cuts to funding for reintegration and release programs, as well as psychological services (Sapers, 2015, pp. 3–4).

These changes are occurring in Canada at the very moment in history when crime rates are at their lowest point and when the U.S. government is now admitting that mass incarceration was a costly mistake. Sapers pointed out in his earlier 2013 report that the United States has realized that more people in prison does not mean safer streets because if there were a relationship between public safety and incarceration, then the downtowns of big American cities would be the safest environments in the world, and they are not (Brosnahan, 2013).

Figure 16.2 Declining Crime and Rising Incarceration Rates, United States

After being particularly elevated during the 1970s and 1980s, the crime rate fell nearly 45 percent between 1990 and 2012.

SOURCE: Based on data from the Hamilton Project and Bureau of Justice Statistics, 2011.

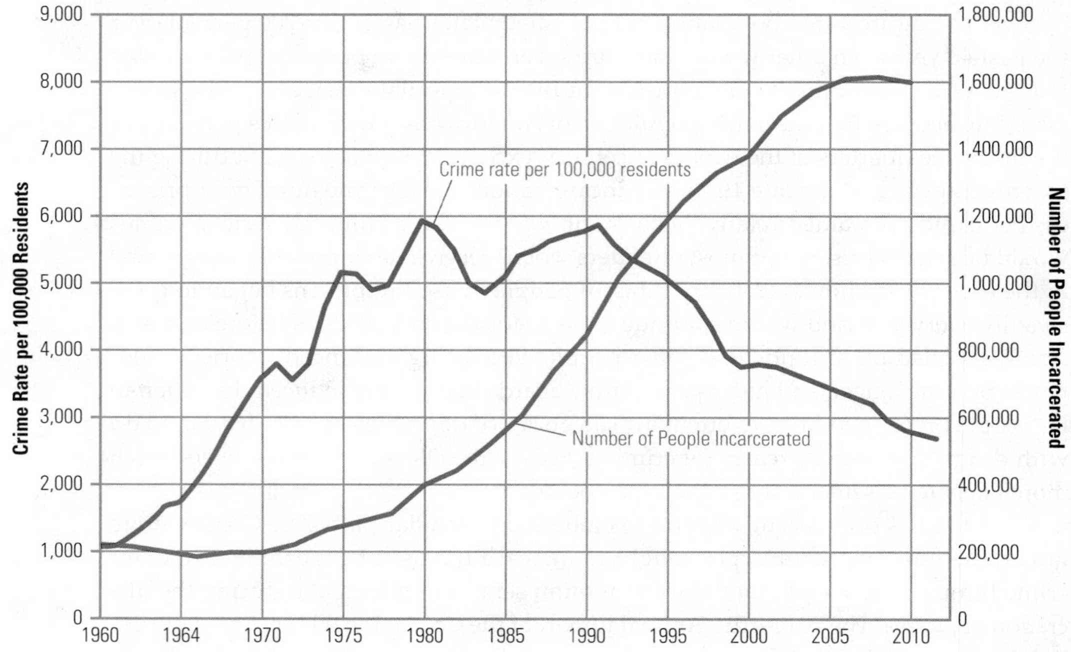

Crime rates tend to be highest in areas that are poorer, are more urban, and have higher unemployment rates, but all across North America crime rates have declined dramatically, by about one-third, since the early 1990s. To get a better view of these trends, take a look at the crime rate and the number of people in prison plotted together in Figure 16.2. In this graph, these two lines show that in spite of the dramatic decline in crime since the 1990s, the incarceration rate (shown here just for prisoners) has increased dramatically. The connection between crime and punishment, in other words, has changed dramatically in this period.

The growth of the prison population over the past 40 years is not only historically unique within the United States but unprecedented around the world as well. The United States incarcerates vastly more people per capita than almost any other country in the world today. To see this, examine the data in Figure 16.3.

Many scholars have come to describe this level of punishment as **mass incarceration**, a situation where vastly greater numbers of people are held in prisons than in earlier periods of history or in comparison to similar countries (Garland, 2001). The countries having high incarceration rates that are close to U.S. rates are Russia, Cuba, and South Africa, not the Western European countries, Canada, Australia, or Japan. The United States sends six to eight times as many people to prison as those countries, and more than 10 times as many people as Japan and countries in Northern Europe!

Presented with this information, many people would simply conclude that the United States has a much higher crime rate than these other countries. It could indeed be argued that if crime rates in America are much higher than they are in other countries, it makes sense that there should be many more people in prisons and jails than in other countries. Is this the case? The best available data come from international "victimization surveys," in which citizens in many countries are asked identical questions about whether they have been the victims of a long list of crimes, ranging from petty theft to sexual assault to aggravated assault. (The only crime that respondents

Figure 16.3 Incarceration Rates in OECD Countries

With an incarceration rate of 710 inmates per 100,000 residents, the United States stands in stark contrast to the typical incarceration rate of 115 among OECD nations.

SOURCE: Based on data from Glaze and Herberman, 2013; Walmsley, 2013.

NOTE: All incarceration rates are from 2013, with the exception of the rates for Canada, Greece, Israel, the Netherlands, Sweden, Switzerland, and the United States; of these countries, all rates are from 2012, with the exception of Canada, whose rate is from 2011–2012. The incarceration rate for the United Kingdom is a weighted average of England and Wales, Northern Ireland, and Scotland.

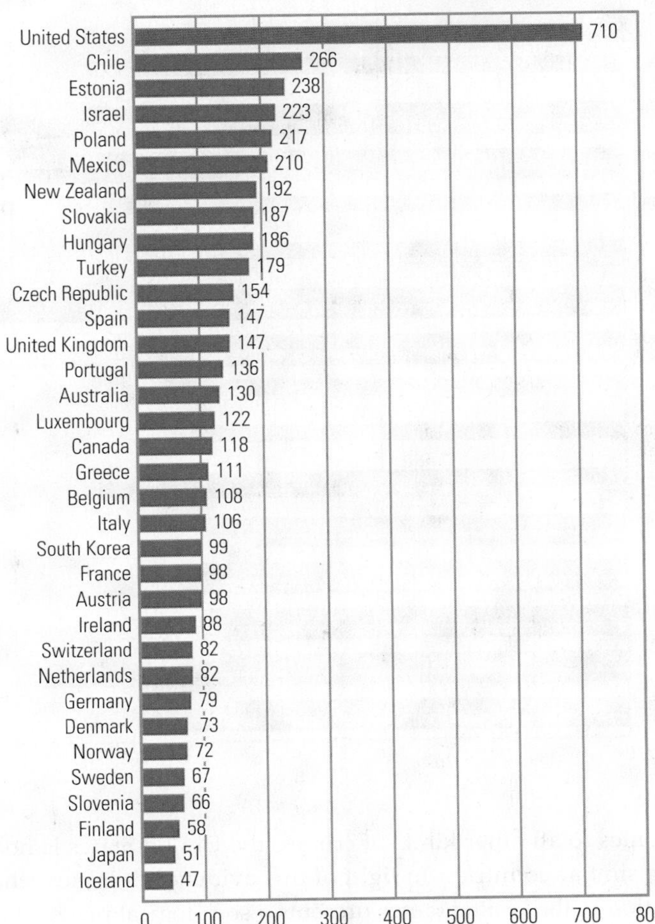

aren't asked about is murder because the victim obviously wouldn't be around to answer the survey!) Examine how the United States compares with other countries in Figure 16.4.

According to the victimization surveys, the United States has crime rates that are close to the average of similar nations, with the exception of a relatively high rate of murder, which is a rare crime in any society (see Figure 16.4). The current murder rate in the United States—about 5.5 per 100,000 population—is two to three times the comparable rate in some European countries, and this is a worrisome difference. Violent crimes cause more fear than any other type of crime. But the odds of being murdered are still exceptionally small in the United States: A city of 100,000 can expect to have five or six murders a year, and a comparable city of 100,000 in a typical European country could expect to have two or three murders. The majority of murders are committed by family or friends, not strangers, suggesting that at least some of the higher U.S. murder rate is attributable to the much easier availability of guns, which may escalate a dispute into a murderous event. So why are Americans so afraid of murder? One reason may be media coverage.

Figure 16.4 Comparative Crime Rates

Percentage of people who reported being victimized by crime in the previous year (surveys administered 2003–2004).

SOURCE: From *Criminal Victimization in International Perspective: Key Findings from the 2004–2005 ICVS and EU ICS* (Figure 3, p. 43), by Jan van Dijk, John van Kesteren, and Paul Smit, 2007, The Hague, Netherlands: Boom Juridische uitgevers (http://www.unicri.it/services/library_documentation/publications/icvs/publications/ICVS2004_05report.pdf).

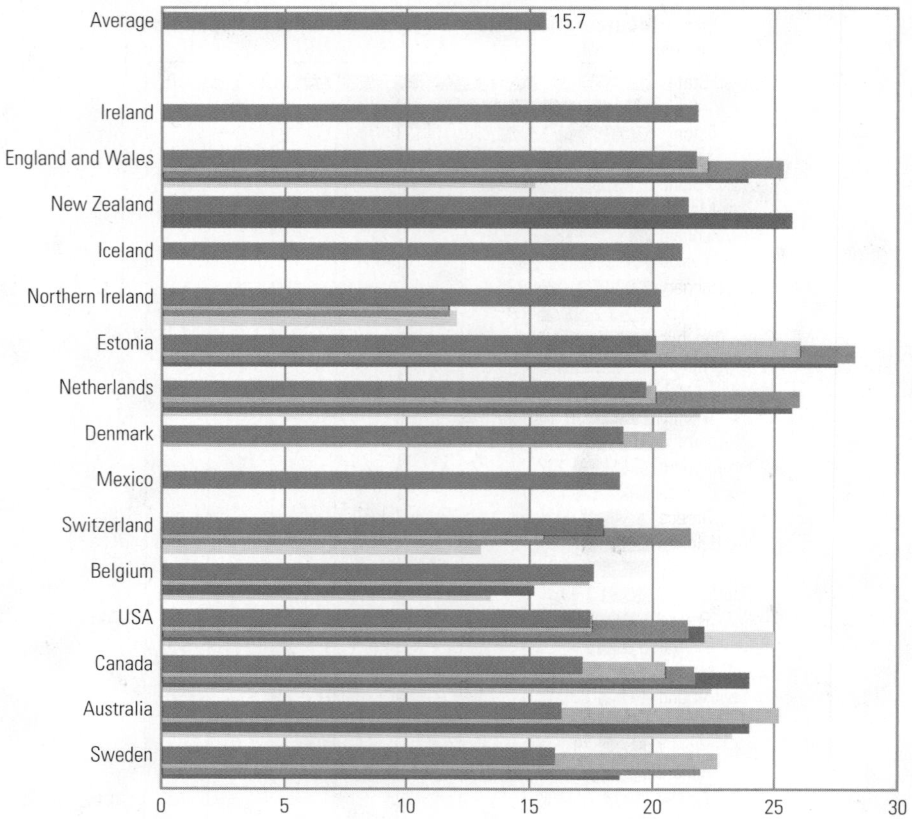

When it comes to all other kinds of crimes, the United States is not very different from other, similar countries. In light of this evidence, it is clear that the rise of mass incarceration in the United States presents a sociological puzzle. When we look at the relationship between all crimes and prisoners per capita, the United States is completely different from all similar countries in terms of how many people are sent to prison. There is nothing in this astounding development that is "natural": Other societies most like the United States with similar crime rates put far fewer people in prison. There is no rulebook for how many people have to be given felony convictions for their behaviour and no close connection to actual levels of criminal activity.

So why has the criminalization of deviant behaviour in North America increased so dramatically in recent years, and particularly in the United States? This is a question that many social scientists are now debating, and there are several competing theories about it. Two major factors behind the rise of mass incarceration have proved especially important. First, the latest moral crusade against certain kinds of individual behaviour, this time targeted against drugs (particularly certain kinds of drugs that are disproportionately consumed by poor people and minorities) had a major impact. The war on drugs launched by President Reagan in 1985 (discussed earlier) spread quickly around America and encouraged police and criminal justice officials to arrest and convict those accused of the possession or sale of drugs. State governments, as well as the federal government, passed mandatory minimum sentences for drug offenders, which had the effect of dramatically increasing the proportion of people in prison for drug-related offences. For example, in 1988, shortly after the beginning of Reagan's war, 17 percent of all people convicted of felonies were drug offenders. Just 14 years later, that figure had nearly doubled, reaching 32 percent of all inmates (Manza & Uggen, 2006, Chapter 4). More recently, the number of drug offenders receiving longer prison terms has declined, but the number receiving lesser sentences has soared (Kohler-Hausmann, 2014).

A second key factor in the steady increase in incarceration rates involves politics. Beginning in the 1960s, many politicians began to have success running for office as proponents of "tough on crime" laws. Perhaps the first major politician to make fighting crime an overtly political issue was Republican presidential candidate Barry Goldwater, in 1964. Although Goldwater would lose that election badly, other politicians followed in his footsteps in promising to reduce crime. Richard Nixon won the presidency in 1968 promising a "law and order" government, declaring war on "the criminal elements which increasingly threaten our cities, homes, and our lives" (quoted in Hagan, 2010, p. 150). Around the country, politicians promoted longer sentences and more punishment. Liberal judges—that is, judges thought to be too lenient on criminals—were increasingly targeted for removal from the bench (many American states and local jurisdictions elect judges, making this possible). Public support for harsher policies was reflected in opinion polls and surveys.

Why did North Americans want more and more people in prison? The period from the late 1960s onward saw the convergence of three important trends that would fundamentally transform the criminal justice policy environment: (1) a conservative backlash to the social movements and cultural trends of the 1960s; (2) an economic downturn in the 1970s that precipitated a search for both reasons and scapegoats for social problems after 1973; and (3) intensive media scrutiny of urban crime resulting from the lasting images of urban riots in the 1960s in many U.S. cities. The most careful research suggests that conservative politicians, where they controlled state governments, moved first and fastest on crime, with the liberals following suit later (Manza & Uggen, 2006, Chapter 4; Western, 2006, Chapter 3). Coming out of the bloody political battles of the 1960s, conservative politicians found political opportunity in platforms calling for tough penalties, but many liberal politicians increasingly came to accept the new tough-on-crime policy environment.

The role of **racism**—stereotypes based on perceived characteristics rooted in skin colour—has long been particularly important in relation to crime (and criminal justice policies). Racial stereotyping about criminality has been pervasive throughout North American history. Research on the media coverage of crime shows that racial minorities are significantly overrepresented in portrayals of criminal offenders (Entman & Rojecki, 2001). The evidence suggests that whites are at least as likely to use illegal drugs as blacks, but blacks are *three times more likely* to be sent to prison for a drug-related offence (Tonry, 2012; Western, 2006, p. 46–47). A number of analysts have reached the conclusion that the rising prison population reflects a "new Jim Crow," as Michelle Alexander (2010) has put it; in the U.S. African American men are being rounded up and sent to prison in such high numbers that prison is increasingly the dominant institution in the lives of many young black men. In Canada, both blacks and Aboriginal people are vastly overrepresented in the criminal justice system, suggesting a similarly racialized system of justice.

Conclusion: Deviance and the Sociological Imagination

The sociological study of deviance raises powerful questions for the sociological imagination, and in many ways studying what is normal and what is deviant is to take a microscope to all of a society in its full complexity. We have explored a number of these puzzles in this chapter. For example, understanding how and why certain kinds of actions come to be labelled and punished for being socially deviant in one context while other similar or worse actions in another do not is an enduring issue in all human societies. There are no obvious answers, but as we explore more deeply, we do find one important pattern that recurs no matter what the particular form of deviance: Those individuals and groups with power have a special capacity to define or impose particular definitions of deviance and to turn those definitions into written laws and forms of punishment (or avoid having those same laws applied to them). Defining deviance downward—when the powerful define ordinary behaviour of the weak as deviant—is a common pattern that the study of deviance reveals.

A particularly dramatic example of this conclusion can be seen in the war that created the United States of America. Imagine what would have happened if Britain had won the American War of Independence. There is little doubt that George Washington, John Adams, Thomas Jefferson, and scores of others that history today has anointed heroes of the American Revolution would have been hung as traitors (Paul, 2009). In fact, in 1779, at a particularly bleak moment in the war, Jefferson abandoned his Virginia home and "headed for the hills" just to escape such a likely fate (Gordon-Reed, 2008, p. 136). Had the British prevailed, those colonists who sided with the British would have been anointed heroes. Of course, because the American revolutionaries did win the war, Washington, Adams, and Jefferson are U.S. heroes; those who sided with the British were branded traitors, and some were put to death.

This lesson can be seen in an ongoing controversy over police departments' use of "stop and frisk" tactics, whereby police officers are free to detain anyone they think might be carrying a weapon or posing a threat to the police officer. Almost 700,000 people were frisked in 2011 in the U.S., and well over 80 percent of those were either African American or Latino. Although young black and Latino males between the ages of 14 and 24 make up just 4.7 percent of New York City's population, they received 42 percent of all stops. With the election of a new mayor and appointment of a new police chief in 2013, there have been some changes but the use of stop-and-frisk tactics continues. While the official purpose of the stops is to look for weapons, in the vast majority of arrest cases, the police find not a gun but rather a small amount of marijuana or other drugs (Kohler-Hausmann, 2014; New York Civil Liberties Union, 2011). For example, while police found fewer than a dozen guns in stop-and-frisk actions, over 50,000 people were arrested for simple marijuana possession in New York in 2010 and 2011, and over 45,000 in 2014, in most cases resulting from a stop-and-frisk event in which a police officer found not a gun but marijuana in someone's pocket. Because so many of the people being stopped are young minority men, it is hardly surprising to learn that most of the people being arrested for marijuana use, and thereby put into the criminal justice system, are young black and Hispanic men. A similar controversy exists in Canada over what is known as *racial profiling*, whereby visible minorities are subject to more stops and requests for identification, known as *carding*, by police officers than whites. Starting in 2017, if police in Ontario stop someone on the street, they must tell the person why, and that the person has a right not to talk to police. Refusing to talk to police when stopped on the street or walking away cannot be used as grounds to compel information.

When a group is intensively policed in the way that young minority men have been in major metropolitan cities, their deviance—even if it is minor—will be uncovered. This does not mean, of course, that it is a fair process. In fact, as we have already noted, the best data we have suggest that whites use as many drugs as nonwhites or more, yet whites are just a tiny percentage of those being convicted for drug possession. Societies often pay far more attention to the possibility of deviance from below than above. It would indeed be interesting—even if it is inconceivable that it would be undertaken—to see what would happen if carding tactics were routinely applied to residents of wealthy suburbs!

One of the challenges of the sociological imagination is the need to look beneath the surface of social life to uncover the normally hidden forms of inequality and injustice in the world around us. In no arena of social life is this more apparent than in the case of deviance and criminal justice. Once we begin to scrutinize what is "normal" and what is "deviant," a new way of looking at the world presents itself.

CHAPTER SUMMARY

The Big Questions Revisited 16

16.1 What Is Deviance? In order to understand deviance, we first need to ask the question, "What is normal?" This section explored the origins of deviant behaviour by examining the role of groups and group boundaries in the creation of social norms. We also examined the distinction between statistical and social deviance.

Deviance and the Group

Groups and Group Boundaries

Learning Objective 16.1.1: Identify how groups distinguish themselves.

Statistical Versus Social Deviance

Learning Objective 16.1.2: Discuss how statistical deviance differs from social deviance.

Social Norms: The Unstated Rules of Everyday Life

Learning Objective 16.1.3: Define the term *social norm*.

16.2 How Is Morality Defined and Regulated? Societies have long tried to dictate and control individuals' behaviour and morality. In this section, we explored two moral crusades in the United States to highlight how the process of defining normal behaviour is achieved and how certain kinds of behaviour come to be labelled deviant or even criminal. We then examined some contemporary moral crusades and considered the future of moral regulation.

The Problem of Moral Regulation

Interested Versus Disinterested Rule-Making

Learning Objective 16.2.1: Distinguish between interested and disinterested rule-making.

An Example: The Temperance Movement as a Moral Crusade

Learning Objective 16.2.2: Analyze the history of alcohol use and how it relates to definitions of normal and deviant.

The Campaign Against Opium

Learning Objective 16.2.3: Analyze the history of opium use and how it relates to definitions of normal and deviant.

Contemporary Moral Crusades

Learning Objective 16.2.4: Discuss how the crusade against drug use and same-sex relationships affects the future of moral crusades.

16.3 Who Defines Deviance? Insights into deviant behaviour come from studying the social and economic positions, cultural practices, and attendant political power of dominant groups. In this section we explored the relationship between deviance and power.

Deviance, Crime, and Power

Labelling Deviance and Crime

Learning Objective 16.3.1: Discuss how labelling theory explains deviance.

From Deviance in the Streets to Deviance in the Suites: White-Collar Crime

Learning Objective 16.3.2: Determine what the 2008 U.S. financial crisis reveals about power and deviant behaviour.

State Deviance, Terrorism, and War Crimes

Learning Objective 16.3.3: Discuss whether violence committed during wartime is a criminal act.

16.4 How Is Social Control Imposed on Society? This section examined how and where social control comes to be formalized in the institutions of the criminal justice system. We also explored how the criminal justice system in America has grown massively in recent decades, turning increasingly to formal punishment as a means of sanctioning deviance.

The Institutions of Social Control

Sanctions and Rewards as Forms of Social Control

Learning Objective 16.4.1: Analyze ways in which the criminal justice system exerts social control.

The Criminal Justice System

Learning Objective 16.4.2: Analyze mass incarceration.

Crime and Mass Incarceration in Today

Learning Objective 16.4.3: Describe the changing crime rate and the trend toward mass incarceration in North America.

Learn the Terms

counterterrorism (p. 464)
criminal justice system (p. 468)
deterrence (p. 468)
Geneva Conventions (p. 464)
guerrilla warfare (p. 463)
incarceration (p. 468)
jail (p. 468)
labelling theory (p. 458)
mass incarceration (p. 470)
moral behaviour (p. 448)
norm (p. 447)
normalize (p. 447)
prison (p. 468)
probation (p. 468)
Prohibition (p. 450)
racism (p. 473)
rehabilitation (p. 468)
retribution (p. 468)
sanction (p. 467)
social control (p. 467)
social group (p. 443)
socially deviant (p. 446)
state deviance (p. 462)
statistically deviant (p. 446)
symbolic boundary (p. 444)
terrorism (p. 462)
war on drugs (p. 453)
war on terror (p. 462)
white-collar crime (p. 458)

Chapter 17

Social Movements and Revolutions

by Jeff Goodwin

Mario Tama/Staff/Getty Images

The Occupy Wall Street movement grew in size and spread very rapidly across North America in the fall of 2011.

Learning Objectives

17.1.1 Discuss how social movements affect political and social structures.

17.1.2 Discuss how social movements contribute to a society's moral codes.

17.1.3 Define the political-process perspective and discuss how understanding social movements can vary as movements change over time.

17.2.1 Analyze the political, economic, organizational, demographic, and cultural factors that ignite and fuel social movements.

17.2.2 Explain how cultural approaches to the study of social movements differ from resource mobilization and political-process approaches.

17.2.3 Explain how individual traits, biographical availability, framing, and cultural attitudes influence participation in social movements.

17.3.1 Discuss how organizers and participants increase awareness and further the goals of movements.

17.3.2 Explain why social movements use certain tactics but not others.

17.3.3 Explain the sociopolitical reasons for the decreasing popularity of certain movements.

17.3.4 Distinguish between successful and unsuccessful outcomes.

17.3.5 Discuss the cultural consequences of movements.

17.4.1 Distinguish between political and social revolutions.

17.4.2 Describe the potential role of violence in revolutions and different types of violent and nonviolent conflicts.

17.4.3 Describe characteristics of revolutionary situations and how those situations can transform territories politically and socially.

17.4.4 Discuss the two requirements for a strong revolutionary movement to take place.

17.4.5 Describe the kind of political environments that encourage revolutionary movements.

On September 17, 2011, several hundred people marched to Wall Street in Lower Manhattan with the goal of occupying a public space in front of or near the Stock Exchange. Their ultimate objectives were unclear, but the protesters were opposed to the tremendous economic and political power of banks, financial institutions, and corporations generally. They claimed to speak for the 99 percent of the population who have no control over these institutions. Wall Street itself was blocked by police, but the protesters occupied a small park—known as Zuccotti Park—not far away. Many of the protesters began to sleep overnight in the park, which became a site for political discussions and for organizing marches and other protests. And so began the Occupy Wall Street movement.

Police evicted the protesters from Zuccotti Park just two months after they occupied it. In the meantime, however, the movement organized several demonstrations in New York City with thousands of participants, including a demonstration in Times Square on October 15 in which perhaps 20,000 people participated.

The Big Questions

Scholars and activists themselves have asked four key sets of questions about social movements and revolutions. This chapter examines how sociologists have answered these questions.

1. **What are social movements?** Social movements play a crucial role in contemporary societies. Through them we can learn about the world around us. We start the chapter by defining social movements and exploring what we can learn by studying them.

2. **Why do movements emerge, and who joins them?** The most frequently asked question about social movements is why they emerge when they do. In this section we examine how movements take shape and look at who joins or supports social movements.

3. **What do movements accomplish?** Why do movements use certain tactics and not others? Why do movements decline or disappear? In this section we look at what movements do and what changes and outcomes movements bring about, including unintended consequences.

4. **What are revolutions, and why do they occur?** Finally, we look at why some social movements are revolutionary, and what causes revolutionary situations to occur. When and why have revolutionary movements been able to take state power? We conclude the chapter by examining how democracy shapes social conflict and the prospects for revolution.

The mass media began to focus on the movement, and politicians began speaking about inequality and the economic problems of the "99 percent" and the fact that almost all of the gains from economic growth in recent years have gone to families at the very top (or the "1 percent"). Protesters unexpectedly began to occupy public parks and other public spaces in dozens of cities and towns across the United States—in Washington, Boston, Chicago, New Orleans, Portland (Oregon), Oakland—as well as many major Canadian cities such as Toronto, Montreal, and Vancouver, and beyond. Police eventually evicted protesters from virtually all the parks they had occupied, and the movement gradually disintegrated over the next several months. Activists from the movement, however, have continued to meet and organize a range of smaller protest activities against banks and corporations, although without the same level of media attention.

The rise and fall of the Occupy movement raises a number of questions that have preoccupied sociologists interested in social movements and revolutions. Why did this movement develop when it did? Who participated in it? Why did the protesters use certain tactics and not others? Sociologists also have questions about the impact of movements: What changes did the movement bring about and what caused it to decline? Was Occupy a revolutionary movement? Is a revolution possible or likely in a countries like Canada or the United States? Or are other countries, with different problems and political institutions, more likely to have revolutions in the future?

17.1 What Are Social Movements?

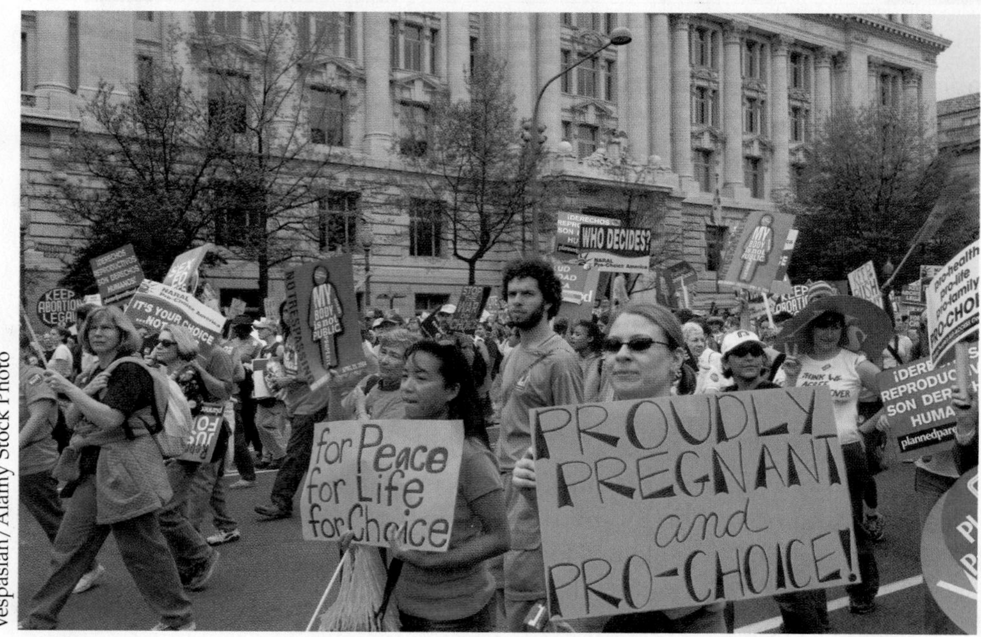

Vespasian/Alamy Stock Photo

Studying Social Movements

Throughout history, people have complained about the things they dislike. Sometimes they do more than complain; they band together with others to try to change things. In modern societies, more than ever before, people have organized themselves to pursue a dizzying array of goals, and they have used a wide variety of tactics to attain those goals. There are the strikes, pickets, and rallies of the labour movement, aimed at unionization and better wages but also (sometimes) at political goals. The women's movement has tried to change family life and gender relations through persuasion and lawmaking. Animal rights activists have broken into labs and "liberated" experimental animals. There have been many conservative and right-wing movements as well, from North Americans opposed to certain kinds of immigrants from the nineteenth century onward (and still today) to movements opposed to taxation and "big government." Some activists have picketed and even bombed abortion clinics in recent years.

Some of these movements have looked for opportunities to claim new rights while others have responded to threats or violence. Some have sought political and economic emancipation and gains, while others have fought against lifestyle choices they disliked or feared. Some have created formal organizations, others have relied on informal networks, and still others have used more spontaneous actions such as **riots**, which are unplanned collective protests, loosely organized at best, involving attacks on property and (sometimes) persons. Movements have regularly had to choose between violent and nonviolent activities, illegal and legal ones, disruption and persuasion, radical and moderate demands, reform and revolution.

Social movements are conscious, concerted, and sustained efforts by ordinary people to change (or preserve) some aspect of their society by using extra-institutional means. *Extra-institutional means* are collective actions undertaken outside existing institutions, like courts and legislatures, although movements may also work through such institutions at least part of the time. Movements are more conscious and organized than fashions or **fads** (behaviours that spread, often rapidly, among a specific population and are repeated enthusiastically for some period of time before disappearing, often rapidly). Movements last longer than a single protest or riot. There is more to them than formal organizations, although such organizations usually play a part. They are composed mainly of ordinary citizens as opposed to wealthy elites, politicians, or army officers. They need not be explicitly political, but many are. Movements protest against something, either explicitly as in antiwar movements or implicitly as in the back-to-the-land movement that is disgusted with modern urban and suburban life.

Why should we care about social movements? Examining protesters and their points of view is certainly a good way to comprehend human diversity. For example, why do some people think animals have rights? Why do others think that the United Nations is part of a sinister conspiracy? But aside from studying social movements to understand the diverse array of viewpoints in society, sociologists also study movements because they are windows onto a number of aspects of social life. These include politics, human action, social change, and the moral basis of society. Finally, social movements often bring about changes that might not otherwise occur.

Politics, Human Action, and Social Change

17.1.1 Discuss how social movements affect political and social structures.

Social movements are a main source of political conflict and change. They often articulate *new* political issues and ideas. As people become attuned to some social problem they want solved—for example, climate change—they often form some kind of movement to push for a solution. Political parties and their leaders rarely ask the most important questions or raise new issues; bureaucracy sets in, and politicians spend their time in routines. Typically, movements outside a society's political institutions force insiders to recognize new fears and desires among specific social groups. Politicians were generally not discussing growing inequality in Canada and especially the United States or the power of corporations; it took the Occupy movement to initiate a public discussion about these issues.

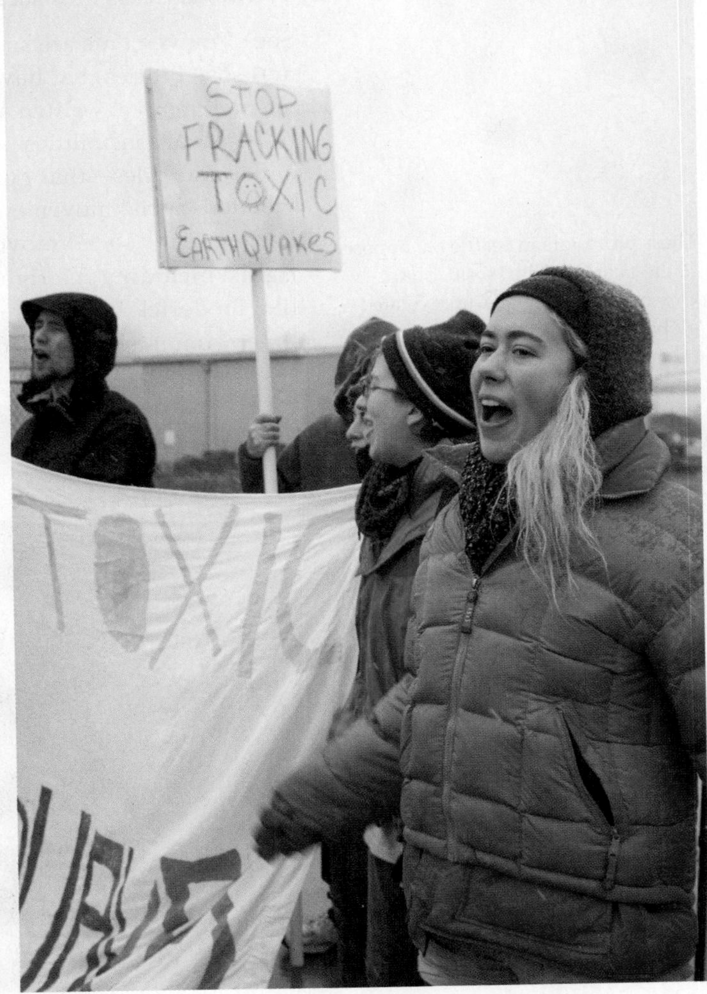

These students from Oberlin College are protesting hydraulic fracking in Ohio. One of the interesting questions in the study of social movements is why students are so often involved in movement activity.

Jim West/Age fotostock

Scholars of social movements ask why and how people do the things they do, especially why they do things *together*; this is also the question that drives sociology in general, especially sociological theory. Social movements raise the famous question asked by seventeenth-century philosopher Thomas Hobbes regarding social order: Why do people cooperate with each other when they might get as many or more benefits by acting selfishly or alone? The study of social movements makes the question more manageable: If we can see why and how people voluntarily cooperate in social movements, we can understand why and how they cooperate in general. Political action sheds light on action in other spheres of life. It gets at the heart of human motivation. For example, do people act to maximize their material interests like wealth and power? Do they act out rituals that express their beliefs about the world or simply reaffirm their place in that world? What is the balance in movements between symbolic action—which is intended to spread a message—and instrumental (i.e., goal-oriented) action—which is intended to bring about some specific change?

Social movements are also a central source of social and political change. In North America, movements are at least partly responsible for most of the progressive laws of the past century, including women's right to vote, the right to organize unions, and civil rights for African Americans and other minorities, including gay, lesbian, and transgendered people. Of course, there are other sources of social change, including corporations, which are out to make a profit: They invent new technologies that change our ways of working and interacting. Corporations are always inventing new ways of extracting profits from workers and inventing new products to market. These changes typically disrupt people's ways of life: A new machine may throw people out of work or make them work harder. Toxic wastes may be disposed of near a school. People react to these changes, and resist them, by forming social movements.

But while corporations are the main source of technological change, they are rarely a source of change in values or in social arrangements. Why? In modern societies with tightly knit political and economic systems, the big bureaucracies demand economic and political control and stability. So they try to routinize social life in order to prevent the unexpected. They resist changes in property relations, for example, which are one of the key components of capitalism.

So innovation in values and political beliefs often arises from the discussions and efforts of social movements. Why don't societies just endlessly reproduce themselves intact? It is often social movements that develop new ways of seeing society and new ways of directing it. They are a central part of what has been called *civil society* or the *public sphere*, in which groups and individuals debate their own futures (Cohen & Arato, 1992).

Moral Sensibilities

17.1.2 Discuss how social movements contribute to a society's moral codes.

Social movements are similar to art in this sense: They are efforts to express ideas and sensibilities that have not yet been well articulated, that journalists or novelists may not yet written about, and that lawmakers have not yet addressed. We all have moral sensibilities—including unspoken intuitions as well as articulated principles and rules—that guide our actions or at least make us uneasy when they are violated. Social movements are good ways to understand these moral sensibilities. For example, social movements have challenged ideas about who deserves legal rights, including the right to vote. In the nineteenth century, radical abolitionists like Frederick Douglass fought to end slavery and give rights to African Americans; women's movements have fought for the right to vote and for reproductive rights (including access to contraceptives and abortions); antiabortion activists argue that human fetuses have rights; Aboriginal groups assert entitlements to land; and many people now believe that certain animals have at least some rights, like the right not to be used in scientific experiments. It's safe to say that social movements have dramatically changed the moral sensibilities of societies over the past two centuries.

These protestors in Seattle are opposed to the politics of the World Trade Organization. Why has unregulated global trade led opponents to forge ties across the borders?

John G. Mabanglo/AFP/Newscom

Social movements play a number of crucial roles in contemporary societies. We learn about the world around us through them. They encourage us to figure out how we feel about government policies and social trends and new technologies.

In some cases they even inspire the invention of new technologies or new ways of using old technologies. Most of all, they are one means by which we work out our moral visions, transforming vague intuitions into principles and political demands. Movements have been one of the most important means by which ordinary people have limited the power of elites. Movements translate widespread feelings that individuals may share into a collective form that can express these feelings with concrete proposals or demands for change.

Understanding Social Movements Today

17.1.3 Define the political-process perspective and discuss how understanding social movements can vary as movements change over time.

Sociologists and other scholars have emphasized different aspects of social movements at different historical moments. They once largely feared movements, seeing them as dangerous mobs. Later scholars were much more sympathetic, emphasizing that movements are quite rational, carefully weighing the costs and benefits of their actions. Some scholars have stressed the political nature of movements. The **political-process perspective** on social movements, for example, emphasizes that movements are primarily concerned with politics, and that they are a normal response, under certain circumstances (such as when normal political channels are blocked), providing a way for people to become involved in political controversies. Movements emerge and may be successful if those political processes create opportunities for certain kinds of collective protest. Still other scholars emphasize the cultural side of movements, exploring the work that goes into creating powerful symbols, convincing people that they have grievances that can be remedied, and building a sense of solidarity or connectedness among certain people.

Recently sociologists have begun to recognize and study even more aspects of political controversies. For example, many movements have a global reach, tying together protest groups and networks across many countries and even forming international organizations. The environmental movement and the protest against the World Trade Organization and the unregulated globalization of trade are examples. Yet many of our theories about movements still assume they operate within the context of a single national state.

Our understanding of social movements has evolved as movements themselves have changed. Like everyone else, scholars of social movements are influenced by what they see happening around them. Much protest of the nineteenth century took the form of riots, so it was natural to focus on the nature of crowds and "mobs." Scholars who examined the labour movement, the suffragettes, and the North American civil rights movements recognized that claims of new rights necessarily involve the state, so it was natural for them to focus on the political dimensions of protest. Social scientists who came of age in the 1960s and after were often favourably disposed toward the social movements around them and so portrayed protesters as reasonable people. Many of the movements of the 1960s and after were not about rights for oppressed groups but about lifestyles and cultural meanings, so it was inevitable that scholars sooner or later would turn to this dimension of protest.

Likewise in recent years, several important social movements have become more global in scope. The so-called alter-globalization or global justice movement against the power of multinational corporations and international financial agencies is one example. Many movements are also interested in changing our emotional capacities, especially movements influenced by the women's movement, which argued that women were disadvantaged by the ways in which different emotions were thought appropriate for men and for women. Research on social movements will undoubtedly continue to evolve as social movements themselves evolve.

17.2 Why Do Movements Emerge, and Who Joins Them?

akg-images/Newscom

Movement Origins and Recruitment

The most frequently asked question about social movements is why they emerge when and where they do. Where we think a movement comes from colours the way we view its other aspects—its goals, participants, tactics, and outcomes.

How Movements Take Shape

17.2.1 Analyze the political, economic, organizational, demographic, and cultural factors that ignite and fuel social movements.

In general, theories of movement origins focus either on the characteristics of participants or on conditions in the broader environment that potential participants face. It is also possible to link these two perspectives.

Scholars have discovered a range of factors that explain why a movement emerges when and where it does:

- political factors such as divisions between authorities or lessened repression from the police and army;
- economic conditions such as increased income, especially among those sympathetic to a movement's cause, or alternatively an economic crisis that throws many people out of work;
- organizational conditions such as social network ties among or formal organizations of aggrieved populations (such as churches, schools, and athletic leagues);
- demographic conditions such as the increased population density and human connectedness that comes with industrialization (if you live a mile from your nearest neighbour, it is hard to organize collectively); and

- cultural factors such as shared moral intuitions or sensibilities that support the movement's cause—of course, potential protesters must understand such factors as real opportunities for collective protest before they can take advantage of them.

In the 1960s and 1970s, a group of researchers noticed that social movements usually consist of formal organizations, and they built their theory of social movements by analyzing when and how grievances become movements (McCarthy & Zald, 1977). Known as the **resource mobilization approach**, this theoretical perspective emphasizes the importance of resources, such as money or the availability of volunteers to work, for generating and sustaining social movements. The more resources a movement is able to employ or mobilize, the more successful it is likely to be. This school argues that there are always enough discontented people in society to fill a protest movement, but what varies over time—and so explains the emergence of movements—is the resources available to nourish it. These researchers accordingly focused on how movement leaders raise funds, sometimes by appealing to wealthy people, sometimes through direct-mail fundraising from thousands of regular citizens. As a society grows wealthier, moreover, citizens have more money to contribute to **social movement organizations (SMOs)**—the formal organizations that support and sometimes initiate movements—and so there are more movements than ever before. With this point of view, the researchers' focus shifted decisively away from the kinds of individuals who might join a movement and toward the organization and resources necessary to sustain a movement. Although movement resources are not enough by themselves to explain the rise of movements, sociologists do consider resources an important part of any explanation of movement emergence.

The theoretical paradigm that has concentrated most on movement emergence is the political-process approach, mentioned earlier in this chapter (e.g., McAdam, 1982). According to this perspective, economic and political shifts that occur (usually independently of protesters' own efforts) open up a space or create opportunities for the movement. Because this approach views movements as primarily political, making demands of the state and asking for changes in laws and policies, it regards changes in the government or state as the most important opportunity a movement needs. Most often, this consists of a slackening in the repression that organizers are otherwise assumed to face, perhaps because political authorities are divided (the movement may have found some allies within the government) or because powerful political and economic actors have divergent interests. There may be a general crisis in the government, perhaps as a result of fighting (or losing) a foreign war, which distracts leaders and may bankrupt the government. In many versions of this perspective, the same factors are seen as explaining both the rise of the movement and its relative success.

Resources, organization, and a sense of new opportunities all undoubtedly encouraged the U.S. civil rights movement, beginning in 1955 and growing rapidly thereafter, to work to abolish segregation of blacks. By the fifties, the migration of millions of African Americans out of the rural South provided them with more resources and denser social ties; black churches and colleges were organizations through which money and people could be channelled to civil rights work; and a new, more optimistic cultural outlook prevailed. These factors encouraged more extensive political mobilization, beginning with the National Association for the Advancement of Colored People (NAACP), which in turn won inspiring legal victories, especially *Brown v. Board of Education* in 1954, which held that racially segregated schools violated the U.S. Constitution. In the next year, African Americans in Montgomery, Alabama, successfully carried out a long boycott of segregated public buses, finally forcing the local government to allow anyone to sit anywhere.

Alongside resource mobilization and political-process approaches, social networks play a role in mobilizing people. **Social networks** are the webs of ties or connections that link individuals (and organizations) to one another, thereby facilitating

Fred W. McDarrah/Contributor/Getty Images

This march in New York City occurred on the first anniversary of the Stonewall rebellion, then known as "Gay Liberation Day." Many of the first wave of gay rights activists had learned about movement building as participants in other sixties movements, such as the anti–Vietnam War movement and the civil rights movement.

communication and the coordination of collective action. Although networks can explain *who* is recruited, the very existence of social ties among potential recruits can be a prerequisite for the emergence of a social movement. People who cannot communicate with one another cannot act together. If most political process theorists emphasize conditions in the external environment (especially the government) that allow a movement to emerge, network theorists look at the conditions within the community or population of those who might be recruited. In the case of the civil rights movement, for example, network ties between church members became a critical source of recruitment into the movement (Morris, 1984). Individuals with dense ties to a large number of people and/or organizations can play key roles in movements by reaching, persuading, and mobilizing other people to participate in building a movement. It was not an accident that many of the early leaders of the civil rights movement came from black churches or black colleges.

Scholars who have studied the 1969 Stonewall rebellion in New York City and the subsequent development of a militant gay and lesbian movement across Canada and the U.S. also emphasize the critical importance of social networks. The Stonewall rebellion involved violent confrontations between police and gay men and lesbians over the course of several days following the arrest of gay patrons at a bar called the Stonewall Inn in Greenwich Village. This rebellion, apparently a spontaneous eruption of gay militancy, in fact marked the public emergence of a long-repressed, covert urban subculture. The gay movement was also able to draw on preexisting networks of activists in the radical movements then current among American youth. The "gay liberation" movement recruited from the ranks of both the anti–Vietnam War movement and the women's movement. It also borrowed its confrontational tactics from these movements. Many lesbians and gay men had already been radicalized and educated in the arts of protest by the feminist and antiwar movements.

The theoretical approaches discussed thus far redefined somewhat the central question of movement emergence. Scholars began to see movements as closely linked to one another because leaders and participants shifted from one to the other or shared social networks, or because the same political conditions encouraged many movements to form at the same time. So researchers began to ask what caused entire waves or "cycles" of social movements to emerge rather than asking about the origins of single movements. One cannot fully understand any one of the movements of the 1960s cycle of protest, for example—including the civil rights movement, the women's movement, the farm workers' movement, and the anti–Vietnam War movement—without knowing something about the other movements in this cycle.

Cultural Aspects of Social Movements

17.2.2 Explain how cultural approaches to the study of social movements differ from resource mobilization and political process approaches.

In recent years, some sociologists have begun focusing on developing cultural approaches to the study of social movements, which link social movements to broad historical developments. Among these broader social changes that have influenced the kinds and types of social movements have been the shifts from an industrial or manufacturing society to a postindustrial or knowledge society in which fewer people process physical goods and more deal with words and symbols and other forms of knowledge in their jobs. Many contemporary social movements can be seen as efforts to control the direction of social change largely by controlling a society's symbols and self-understandings.

In cultural approaches, the goals and intentions of protesters are taken very seriously. For instance, the origin of the animal protection movement has been linked to broad changes in sensibilities over the last 200 years that have allowed citizens of the industrial world to recognize the suffering of nonhuman species—and to worry about it. Such concerns would simply not have been possible in a society where most people worked on farms and used animals both as living tools (horses, dogs, dairy cows) and as raw materials (food, leather, etc.). The point of this research is to observe or ask protesters themselves about their perceptions, desires, and fantasies without having a theory that predicts in advance what protesters think and feel. Perceptions are crucial in this view.

From this perspective, the work of sociologist Charles Kurzman (1996) helped change the way scholars think about shifts in political opportunities for protest. Political process theorists had insisted that these were objective changes, independent of protesters' perceptions, but Kurzman's research shows that the perceptions may matter as much as the underlying reality. Kurzman's research on the Iranian Revolution (1978–1979), in which the king (or shah) was overthrown by a popular uprising, indicates that there were no objective political changes on the eve of the revolution that suddenly weakened the monarchy or created new opportunities for protest. Indeed, despite considerable police repression and expressions of U.S. support for the monarchy, protest against the shah continued to grow, and people gradually came to believe they could topple the regime. A movement can sometimes succeed, apparently, if it thinks it can.

Protesters may fail to see (or seize) opportunities, and they may imagine opportunities for protest when none seems to exist, however. The slackening of police repression, divisions among wealthy elites and politicians, and so on (the "opportunities" of political process theorists) may only have an effect if they are perceived as such. And people may sometimes rebel (and sometimes win), even when the political environment does not at first seem promising, when the cultural context of protest is changing. In other words, cultural perceptions about the world can potentially play as important a role in motivating social movements as changes in the state or society that are emphasized by political process theorists, who had not fully appreciated cases where perceptions and objective realities diverged.

Cultural sociologists have thus reached different conclusions than those expressed by resource mobilization and political process theorists, partly because cultural sociologists have examined different kinds of social movements and look for different factors driving movements. Most political process theorists, for example, have focused on movements of groups that have been systematically excluded from political power and legal rights—in other words, groups that are demanding the full rights of citizenship. Cultural theorists have been more likely to examine movements of those who already have the formal rights of citizens—who can vote, pressure legislators, and run for office—but who nonetheless feel they must step outside normal political institutions to have a greater impact. Resource mobilization theorists assume that people know what they want and simply need the resources and organization to pursue it; cultural sociologists recognize that in many cases people only gradually figure out what they want, often because movement organizers persuade them of it (e.g., that animals can suffer like humans, that marijuana should be legal, or that the government is inherently evil).

Cultural sociologists have reasserted the importance of perceptions, ideas, emotions, and grievances, all of which resource mobilization and political process theorists once thought did not matter very much or could simply be taken for granted. But these are examined today in the context of broader social and political changes, not in isolation from them. It is not as though people first develop goals and then decide to go out and form movements to pursue them; there is an interaction among ideas, mobilization, and the broader environment. Some people get pulled into movements by friends or family and are only slowly converted to the movement's cause; their political beliefs are a consequence, not a cause, of joining the movement. Research suggests, for example, that over 40 percent of committed antiabortion activists had ambiguous views about abortion or even considered themselves "pro-choice" when they initially joined the movement; it was only after they spent some time in the movement, interacting with long-term activists, that they came to emphatically oppose abortions (Munson, 2008).

Recruitment: Joining or Supporting Movements

17.2.3 Explain how individual traits, biographical availability, framing, and cultural attitudes influence participation in social movements.

Once activists form groups or networks and begin to think of themselves as a movement (or at least a potential movement), their next step is usually to try to expand their ranks by recruiting others to their cause. Like accounts of movement origins, sociological theories of recruitment have evolved over time from an emphasis on individual traits to one on availability for activism, and finally toward a synthesis of these dimensions.

Scholars once tended to see protesters as swept up in crowds, acting in abnormal and sometimes irrational ways because of frustration with their individual circumstances. In some theories marginal, isolated, and alienated members of society were seen as most likely to join social movements; in others it was those who were insecure or dogmatic. Such claims were usually demeaning to protesters, who were thought to be compensating for some sort of personal inadequacy or psychological problem, but subsequent empirical research did not generally support the image of protesters as more angry, isolated, or alienated than others.

The economist Mancur Olson (1965) suggested that protesters are perfectly rational, arguing that they do not join groups if they think they can gain the benefits that these groups pursue without taking the time to participate. In other words, people may become *free riders* on the efforts of others, letting others protest while benefiting from their successes. You don't have to join the environmental movement to enjoy the clean air that it wins for all of us—so why join it and go to the trouble of participating in protests? Another reason to free ride is that your own participation in or contribution to a collective effort would not seem to make a noticeable difference once the group consists of more than a few dozen people. What can a group of 101 people accomplish that a group of 100 can't? So to attract participants, Olson argues, movements must provide "selective incentives" that are enjoyed only by those who actually participate, such as interesting political discussions, the possibility of making new friends, extended health insurance, or retirement benefits for trade union members.

Olson challenged scholars of social movements to show *how* organizers manage to overcome the free rider problem, helping to inspire the resource mobilization paradigm described above. The challenge Olson raised shifted attention from what kinds of *people* protest to what kinds of objective *conditions* facilitate protest. Attitudes and grievances were dismissed as insufficient to cause protest, for many people had the right attitudes and interests but did not participate. As part of this new agenda, **biographical availability** was seen as necessary for participation: People with few family or work obligations—especially young people without children—were particularly available to devote time to movement activities (McAdam, 1988). People who have major commitments on their time, by contrast, are less able to participate (although they can donate money, which is often a key resource for movements to develop).

In addition to biographical availability, a person's social connections to any particular movement can predict whether he or she will join the movement. Social networks are usually a precondition for the emergence of a movement as well as the explanation for who is subsequently recruited to it. Physically scattered or socially isolated people are the least likely to join a movement. In the extreme case of *bloc recruitment*, organizers bring a whole social network or organization virtually intact into a movement. This suggests that—contrary to Olson's view—people do not make decisions to join movements (or not) as isolated, self-regarding individuals but in concert with others in their networks. And the approval of peers in one's network may be an important selective incentive that leads individuals to join a movement.

Different kinds of social networks can be used for recruitment. They may not be political in origin or intent. Black churches and colleges were crucial to the Southern civil rights movement in the 1950s, fundamentalist churches helped fuel antiabortion protests in Canada throughout the 1980s, and mosques facilitated the Iranian Revolution. Networks developed for earlier political activities can also aid recruitment into a movement that develops later—one reason why a history of previous activism makes someone more likely to be recruited. The clustering of movements in waves or cycles makes this mutual support especially important, as one movement feeds into the next. Because of these networks, prior activism and organizational memberships help predict who will be recruited (and who will not be).

Social media like Facebook and Twitter can also be used to recruit people to political protests, as was seen during the so-called Arab Spring of 2011, where in several Middle Eastern countries longstanding dictators were overthrown by large, unprecedented protests. Social media allow multitudes of people who have never met before and who have no other connections to communicate with one another and spread the word about what is going on. They make it possible to organize huge protests in a much shorter span of time and over greater distances than was previously possible. They allow activists to direct people to assemble at specific places and at specific times before the authorities have time to react. This can be especially important where authoritarian regimes are likely to break up protests violently—it is more difficult for the authorities to respond that way when the protest group is very large. However, government authorities may also monitor social media—or attempt to shut them down altogether—in an attempt to control protest. So social media can be used to organize as well as disrupt movements.

Without denying the importance of personal contacts and communication networks, recent studies have also examined the cultural messages transmitted across these networks. For example, what have been called "suddenly imposed grievances" that are produced by dramatic and unexpected events may be important for recruitment. The partial nuclear meltdown in 1979 at the Three Mile Island power plant in Dauphin County, Pennsylvania, which led to the evacuation of nearly 200,000 people, alerted the public to the risks of nuclear energy, giving a big boost to the antinuclear movement (Walsh, 1981). Recruitment is also more likely when people feel that they have a chance of success. This sense of optimism and efficacy has been called "cognitive liberation" (McAdam, 1982). People may have lots of grievances, as well as ties to individuals in a movement seeking to redress those grievances, but they are probably less likely to join that movement if they don't think it can succeed.

Scholars view direct personal contacts as important because they allow organizers and potential participants to achieve a common definition of a social problem and a common prescription for solving it. In successful recruitment, organizers offer ways of seeing a social problem that resonate with the views and experiences of potential recruits. The Occupy movement, for example, spread very rapidly across North America in 2011 because its message about the power of banks and corporations and the plight of the "99 percent" resonated with people during a time of economic crisis and home foreclosures. But it is not as if everyone was equally likely to participate or support the goals of the movement. Networks are important *because* of the cultural meanings they transmit. Networks and meanings are not rival explanations; they work together. Explore Figures 17.1, 17.2, and 17.3 to learn more about who participated in or supported the Occupy Wall Street movement.

Figure 17.1 What Do Supporters of the Occupy Movements Look Like?

SOURCE: Based on data from "Occupy Wall Street Survey Results," by Costas Panagopoulos, October 2011, Center for Electoral Politics and Democracy, Fordham University (www.fordham.edu/download/downloads/id/2538/occupy_wall_street_survey.pdf); Fast Company, 2011; Pew Research Center, 2011.

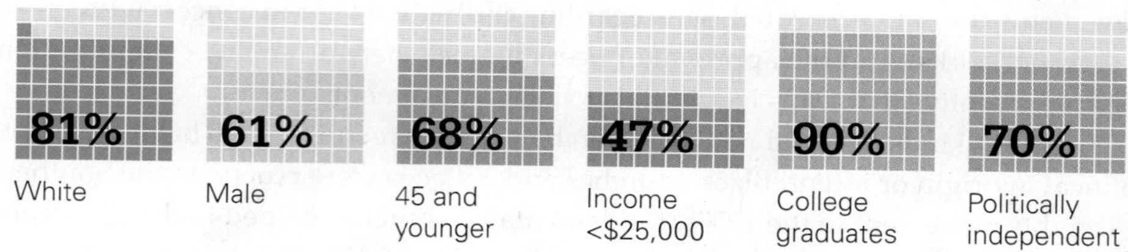

Figure 17.2 Where Do Occupy Wall Street Activists Work?

SOURCE: From *Changing the Subject: A Bottom-Up Account of Occupy Wall Street in New York City* (Figure 2, p. 12), by Ruth Milkman, Stephanie Luce, and Penny Lewis, 2013, New York: Murphy Institute, City University of New York (http://www.documentcloud.org/documents/562862-changing-the-subject-2.html).

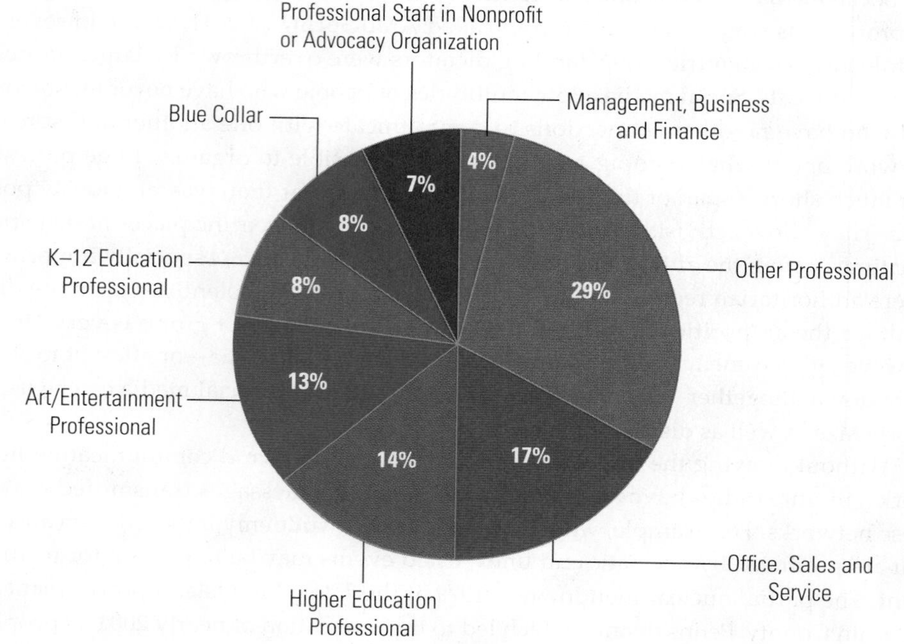

Figure 17.3 Political Views of Those Active in the Movement in New York City

SOURCE: Based on data from "Occupy Wall Street Survey Results," by Costas Panagopoulos, October 2011, Center for Electoral Politics and Democracy, Fordham University (www.fordham.edu/download/downloads/id/2538/occupy_wall_street_survey.pdf).

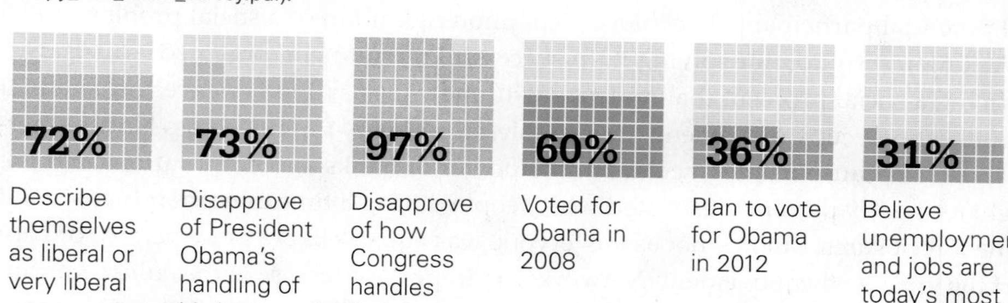

Another way that cultural factors influence the rise of social movements, and their ability to have an impact, is the way movements present their grievances to nonmembers. This process is known as **framing,** and it refers to the specific ways in which ideas and beliefs are presented to other people. Scholars of movements focus on how activists try to frame or present their ideas so that they make sense to or resonate with the beliefs of potential recruits and supporters. Scholars have distinguished three successive types of framing that are necessary for successful recruitment: *diagnostic*, in which a movement convinces potential converts that a problem needs to be addressed; *prognostic*, in which it convinces them of appropriate strategies, tactics, and targets; and *motivational*, in which it exhorts them to get involved in these activities (Snow & Benford, 1988). Frames are more likely to be accepted if they fit well with the existing beliefs of potential recruits, if they involve empirically credible claims, if they are compatible with the life experiences of the audiences, and if they fit with the stories or narratives the audiences tell about their lives. Frames, in short, must resonate with the salient beliefs of potential recruits if they are to be effective.

Collective identity is another concept used to get at the mental worlds of people and to explain how people are recruited into movements. A **collective identity** is one's belief that one belongs to a certain group (or groups) with distinctive characteristics and interests (e.g., women, the working class, feminists). In order to devote time and effort to protest, people must usually feel part of a larger group they think they can help. Not all identities come easily to people; they may have to be consciously created, which is one of the things that some movements do. The gay and lesbian movement, for example, still devotes a lot of its energy to making it possible for gays and lesbians to feel comfortable with themselves and to identify themselves publicly as gay or lesbian (i.e., to "come out of the closet"). Obviously, people who for whatever reason do feel themselves to be part of a group or who find it difficult to identify themselves publicly with a certain group are unlikely to become politically active on its behalf.

Another cultural approach emphasizes how attitudes and worldviews matter. Political scientist Ronald Inglehart (1977) has argued that new "postmaterial" values and beliefs have emerged in the advanced industrial nations since the 1960s. Through most of human history, in his view, people have been forced to worry about basic material needs such as food, shelter, and security, but since World War II the advanced industrial world has been largely spared traditional privations. Those born after World War II—at least the university-educated and affluent middle class—were "freed" to pursue "higher" goals such as control over their lives, environmental protection, and satisfying work rather than worrying primarily about their paycheques. The spread of mass communication and higher education contributed to the same trends. The result has been less emphasis on economic redistribution, class-based political organizations, or the pursuit of political power—again, at least where the affluent middle class is concerned. Instead we have seen movements critical of large bureaucracies, meaningless work, complex technologies, and many different forms of oppression. One can certainly better understand who is likely to support the environmental movement or the animal rights movement by using the concept of postmaterial politics. These movements have a primarily middle-class social base, even though they are not pursuing the narrow economic interests of this class. So the growth of a postindustrial sector of the economy helps explain not only changes in political concerns over time but also different sympathies across parts of the population at any given time.

It turns out that another contemporary movement has a primarily well-educated and middle-class social base: the followers of the late Osama bin Laden (Kurzman, 2002). Two sociologists found that engineers were significantly overrepresented in the ranks of Islamic radicals (Gambetta & Hertog, 2009). While many Westerners assume that the Islamic world is mired in religious superstition and rejects modern rationality, bin Laden's followers are much better educated than their peers and use the latest technologies and media. They are not motivated by narrow class or economic interests but by their opposition to the policies of the U.S. government in the Middle East, even as they use religious language and look nostalgically backward to a golden age of Islam. Attitudes and worldviews matter for recruitment, but they are not always what we assume them to be!

Recruitment to social movements, however, involves more than ideas about how the world works. The moral and emotional dimensions of recruitment are equally important. In fact, all the key factors that explain recruitment depend heavily on their emotional impact on people. Social networks, for example, are often grounded in the emotional bonds among their members: We pay attention to people in our networks, and what they say, because we are fond of them or trust them. The term **moral shock** is also meant to incorporate some of the moral and emotional dimensions of recruitment to movements. A moral shock is an unexpected event that surprises, distresses, and outrages people, often to the point of motivating them to join a movement to eliminate the source of their outrage. Moral shocks may be so strong that they lead people without social ties to activists to seek out or even form a group to redress their grievances (Jasper, 1997). An example of a moral shock is the impact of the *Roe v. Wade* Supreme Court decision of 1973, which legalized abortions under certain circumstances, on many religious Americans, especially Catholic women. For these women, it was as if the Supreme Court had legalized the murder of certain kinds of children. Although they had not been politically active previously and knew no political activists, these women formed the core of the early antiabortion movement (Luker, 1984).

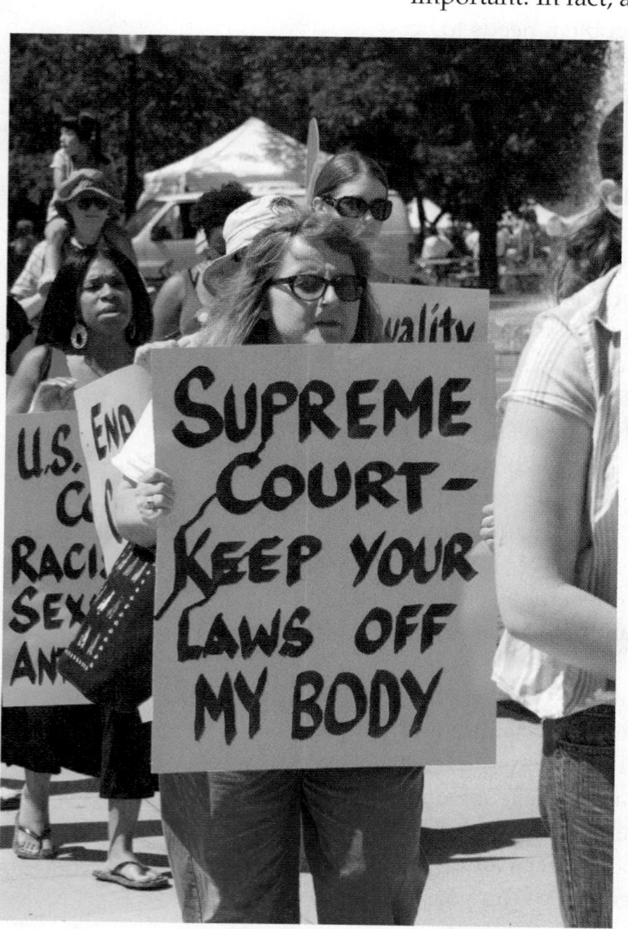

Jim West/Alamy Stock Photo

Recent scholarship on movements pays more attention to what goes on inside people's heads (and hearts) than previously. Protest is no longer seen as an attempt to compensate for some psychological problem but as part of an effort to impose meaning and morality on the world, to forge and express a collective identity, to create or reinforce emotional bonds with others, and to define and pursue collective interests. These are things that all humans desire and seek. There is today considerable

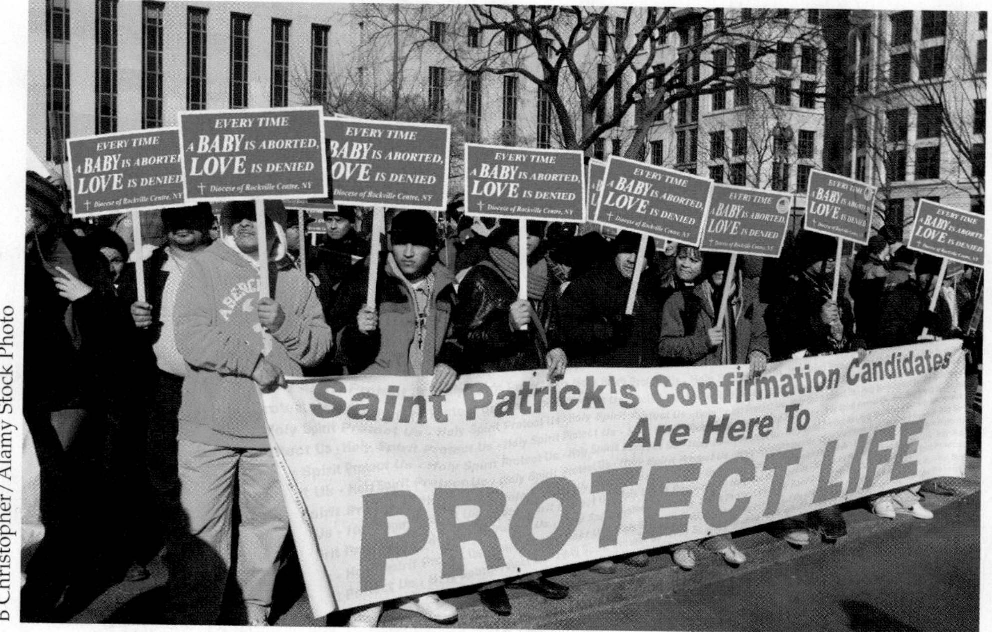

B Christopher/Alamy Stock Photo

Movements against and for a woman's right to terminate her pregnancy provide a good example of framing attempts. Those in favour of legal abortion refer to broader values such as personal freedom, bodily integrity, and women's rights to frame their campaigns. Accordingly, their label "pro-choice" suggests that their opponents are pro-coercion and against individual liberties. However, the antiabortion movement also refers to values such as bodily integrity or personal freedom, namely those of the fetus. Their self-framing as "pro-life" implies that their opponents are anti-life or even pro-death.

consensus that positions in networks and cultural orientations (cognitive, moral, and emotional) are equally important in recruitment. But there are also cases in which cultural messages can be used to recruit people in the absence of social networks, relying on moral shocks instead of personal ties. For virtually all social movements, only a small fraction of potential recruits actually join, and it takes all the factors we have considered to understand who does and does not sign up.

17.3 What Do Movements Accomplish?

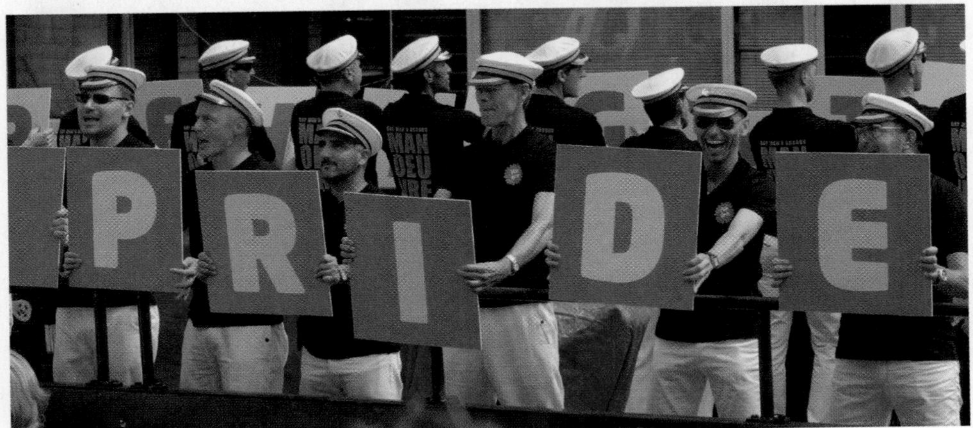

wareham.nl (Algemene Nieuws)/ Alamy Stock Photo

Movement Tactics and Outcomes

If you are in a social movement, one of the most pressing questions you will face is *What is to be done?* That is, how do you choose tactics that will help your cause? How do you recruit more people, attract the news media, put pressure on the rich and powerful, or favourably impress political decision-makers? Tactical decisions are the real "stuff" of social movements. A few sociologists have looked at how these decisions are made, how and when protesters innovate in their tactics, and what the tradeoffs are between different kinds of tactics. Practitioners as well as academics have addressed these issues.

The Strategies of Movements

17.3.1 Discuss how organizers and participants increase awareness and further the goals of movements.

The tactical choices of activists are usually made in the heat of conflict and so can be hard to explain in a rigorous fashion. These choices depend in part on the instincts of movement leaders, who themselves may not always be able to explain why they made one choice rather than another. Decisions are sometimes made quickly, and it may be difficult to reconstruct the process later—when being interviewed by a sociologist, for instance.

Tactical choices are usually made during the course of interactions with other decision-makers: with one's opponents, of course, but also with the police, the media, legislators, potential allies, and many others. To take just one example, before most rallies or marches today, leaders negotiate with the police over where they will go, what they will do, how many will be arrested (if any), and so on. Leaders must also

PATRICK DOYLE/AFP/Getty Images

Shown here, protesters participate in the 100% Possible Climate March on Parliament Hill in Ottawa. Why are some protest tactics used repeatedly over the years?

make tactical choices with regard to their own followers as well as opponents: how to placate disaffected factions, how to keep members coming back to future events, and how to increase or simply maintain the membership. As a result, any given action is probably designed for several different audiences at the same time. But an action that satisfies one audience may not please another.

Protesters hope to change their opponents' behaviour through persuasion, intimidation, or imposing costs (financial or otherwise) on them. Raising the costs of "business as usual" is generally necessary when movements confront powerful elites (especially the wealthy) who have not been elected. These elites can simply ignore protesters or try to repress them if they become threatening. Strikes and boycotts, however, hurt the wealthy economically and may lead them to make concessions to protesters so that their factories and farms can continue to make profits. If the costs caused by the disruption that movements create are greater than the costs of making concessions to the movement, elites may decide to make concessions in order to end the disruption. The costs of making some concessions are so threatening to elites, however, that they may decide to fight hard and even violently against a movement for years or even decades (Luders, 2010).

Movements also seek to undermine their opponents' credibility with the public, media, and government officials. When it comes to government, protesters hope to change laws, policies, regulatory practices, and administrative rules, and/or to stop government harassment of their activities. From the courts, protesters typically strive to have unfavourable laws struck down or at least interpreted in new ways. With both courts and police, they hope for tolerance of their protests. Social movements seek to use the news media to spread their message and sometimes to undermine their opponents. Protesters may also approach professional groups, such as engineers, to change their standards. They may seek allies in other protest groups. And from the public at large, they may hope for new recruits, sympathy, contributions, or at least a change in awareness. Finally, they even have goals for their own members: personal transformations and continued fervour for the cause. In other words, movements have a lot of goals to balance in their tactics, and striking the right balance is sometimes extremely difficult.

Tactical Repertoires of Movements

17.3.2 Explain why social movements use certain tactics but not others.

Movement leaders are usually familiar with only a limited number of tactics. The sociologist Charles Tilly (1986, p. 4) developed the phrase "repertoire of contention" to describe the range of tactics available to protesters in any given society in a particular period. Most social movements will draw upon a very similar repertoire because that is what they know, at least in the short run. There are many possible tactics that movement leaders are not familiar with or do not have the knowledge to utilize, including (hypothetically) tactics that might be extremely beneficial to the movement. Tilly was interested in explaining how repertoires of contention changed over long stretches of time, while other scholars have been concerned with explaining why particular leaders choose certain tactics and not others from the existing repertoire: Why a march rather than a letter-writing campaign? Why wait a week before responding to your opponents' actions rather than acting immediately? Why choose one cultural frame rather than another for a speech or website?

Saul Alinsky, one of the greatest community organizers and movement innovators of the twentieth century, wrote a great deal about tactics in the course of trying to improve the living conditions of poor neighbourhoods, particularly in Chicago (Alinsky, 1971). Alinsky developed tactical principles that are not unlike those of army generals: Try to take your opponents by surprise, and try to make them think you are more powerful than you are. Try to use tactics your own followers enjoy and are familiar with. The idea of keeping the pressure on your opponents is important because you never know where and when your opponent will be vulnerable or will make a blunder. The greater the pressure, the greater the chance you will trip them up. Alinsky also recognized that it is usually necessary to portray your enemy as an utter villain, a real flesh-and-blood person who can be blamed, not an abstract principle. Thus, protest movements during the Arab Spring of 2011 demonized dictators like Hosni Mubarak in Egypt. Protesters demanded that the authoritarian regime in Egypt be replaced with democracy, but they usually called simply for the overthrow of Mubarak, who symbolized all that was wrong in the country. Such demonization can lead to strong emotions and polarization. Alinsky's rules are quite general, but they can be helpful reminders to social movement leaders.

In describing civil rights sit-ins, sociologist Aldon Morris (1984) exemplified the resource mobilization approach to tactics. He is not so much concerned with the origins of the sit-in tactic or the strategic thinking behind its use. Rather, he is concerned with revealing the indigenous organizations and social networks through which the sit-ins rapidly spread, arguing against a view of the sit-ins as spontaneous eruptions. Morris (1984, Chapter 3) also touches on another important issue: the emergence of "movement centers" with resources, social ties (especially preachers and NAACP activists), and regular meetings (usually at churches). Other theorists have called these **free spaces**, places relatively free from surveillance where oppositional ideas and tactics can develop and spread. Free spaces are places like churches, schools, union meeting halls, or other places where movement participants can feel free of harassment by their opponents.

The use of violent tactics by social movements has been one area of enormous interest in recent years. To even develop careful research, it is necessary for scholars to try to dispel some of the myths surrounding the use of violent tactics. They point out that guerrilla warfare and terrorism are often rational political responses to state violence and conflicts over territory, not the handiwork of psychopaths or religious fanatics, as the media and politicians often suggest. Scholars and journalists are often hesitant to emphasize the rationality or achievements of political violence, in part because of their moral discomfort with it. In the case of the antiapartheid movement in South Africa, this has led some scholars to avoid discussing violence altogether and to portray the movement, misleadingly, as an entirely nonviolent civil rights struggle like that in the United States. But political violence, like war, is a kind of routine politics by other means that movements may choose to use in combating their enemies (and, it should be noted, the opponents of social movements often control or have influence over far more powerful tools of violence in the form of police and military forces, and the long history of violence against social movements shows a willingness on the part of the powerful to use force). That said, recent research indicates that nonviolent movements may be twice as likely to succeed as violent movements, even against very repressive regimes (Chenoweth & Stephan, 2011). This is because ordinary people usually find it much easier to participate in nonviolent movements, so they tend to be much larger than violent movements, and because government officials and soldiers are more likely to defect to nonviolent movements.

Although social movements are defined, in part, by their use of extra-institutional tactics (those that are outside existing political institutions) to pursue their political goals, protest can also take place *within* institutions. For example, gays and lesbians in the U.S. military have fought alongside allies outside the military to overturn the so-called "don't ask, don't tell" policy that prohibited them from serving as openly gay or lesbian. Thus, free spaces *outside* regular institutions are not always enough for movements to flourish; sometimes they can also thrive *within* dominant institutions.

The choice of strategies and tactics is certainly an area in which research is ongoing. One limitation of existing research has been that most scholars have thought about the movement as their unit of analysis: how each grows, operates, and affects the world around it. But tactical choices are made in close interaction with other actors in the same field of conflict, including opponents and allies, actual and potential. These interactions are like a game of chess: Each player's tactical moves are shaped as much by the moves of the other players as by one's preferred or ideal course of action. So movements often end up doing things they would rather not do but feel they must—in extreme cases, using violence even if it means killing innocent civilians. But this is not surprising. In an ideal world, after all, people would not need to make hard choices about political tactics; they would already have the things their movements are fighting for.

The Decline and Disappearance of Movements

17.3.3 Explain the sociopolitical reasons for the decreasing popularity of certain movements.

Not surprisingly, scholars have had much more to say about why social movements arise than why they decline or disappear altogether. Nonetheless, several hypotheses about movement decline have attained some prominence. Most explanations for movement decline focus on the surrounding political environment, which may constrain as well as facilitate movements. Of course, the very success of a movement in changing laws or government policies may undermine many people's motivations for participating in that movement. Movement organizations may also be legally recognized by the government, leading to their institutionalization and declining reliance on disruptive protest. Government concessions of this type, even if they do not redress all the grievances and concerns of movement participants, may nevertheless be sufficient to satisfy or placate many people, who will then drift away from the movement or from protest tactics. Social movements, in short, may become victims of their own limited successes. The labour movement is a prime example of this dynamic. After militant and sometimes deadly strikes in the 1930s led to the legal recognition of trade unions and the right to collective bargaining, unions gradually turned away from strikes and the aggressive recruitment of new members. As a result, the proportion of workers who belong to unions has been declining since the 1950s.

Movements may also decline as a result of their own internal dynamics and evolution. The women's movement, for example, has gradually lost its radical vision and militancy (Epstein, 2001). This was a result in part of intense ideological conflicts within the movement between radical feminists, who had provided much of the movement's activist core and ideological inspiration. Gradually, and partly because of its own success in opening up new professional careers for women, the women's movement as a whole took on a middle-class outlook. It became more concerned with the career opportunities and material success of individual women than with the group solidarity of women or with addressing the concerns of poor and working-class women. A number of women's organizations have now been successfully institutionalized, including the National Organization for Women (NOW) in the United States and the National Action Committee on the Status of Women (NAC) in Canada, whose aims were to lobby government to bring about gender equality in all spheres of social life.

The sociologist Joshua Gamson (1995) emphasizes yet another way in which a movement's internal dynamics may lead to break up and decline. As we have seen, movements typically require—or themselves attempt to create—clear and stable collective identities. How can we make claims and demands on others, after all, if we do not know who "we" and "they" are? Many recent movements have been centrally concerned with establishing, recasting, or defending collective identities, including previously stigmatized identities. But collective identities, sociologists argue, are not "natural" or given once and for all; they are culturally constructed and continually reconstructed. Some identities, moreover, may obscure or devalue other identities that people have. As a result, people have often attempted to blur or reconfigure certain identities. Hence Gamson's question: Must movements organized around a particular identity self-destruct?

Gamson shows how the gay and lesbian movement has been shaken in recent years by "queer" theorists and activists who have challenged fixed sexual identities like "gay," "lesbian," and "straight." Queer activists have also challenged the assimilationist goals of mainstream (and generally older) gay and lesbian activists, some of whom object to the very use of a stigmatized label like "queer." To some extent, Gamson points out, queer activism developed out of the growing organization of bisexual and transgendered people, whose very existence challenges the notion of fixed sexual and gender identities.

Ultimately, the gay and lesbian movement, and indeed all movements, face a dilemma: To be politically effective, they may feel a need to emphasize exclusive and secure collective identities, but this may paper over and effectively ignore important differences among movement participants—differences based on race and class, for example, which may later erupt in a way that weakens the movement.

John Whelihan/ZUMAPRESS/Newscom

One of the unintended consequences of the bombing of a federal building in Oklahoma City in 1995, which killed 168 people, was a decline in the activities of right-wing militia groups.

How movements handle this dilemma in order to avoid self-destruction—how they weigh and balance competing and potentially disruptive identity claims—is an important question for future research.

Movements may also decline because the political opportunities and the free spaces that have helped give rise to them begin to contract or disappear. Divisions among the wealthy and powerful may be resolved, or (perhaps because of such unity) authorities may decide to harshly repress or crack down on a movement. Both of these factors are usually invoked to explain the violent demise of the democracy movement in China in 1989. A number of scholars have also pointed to repression as a key factor in the decline of the U.S. labour movement since the 1950s, or more specifically, they have argued that union decline is largely explained by aggressive employer opposition to unions, which has been facilitated by laws and policies that favour employers over workers. One does not see the same type of employer resistance to unions in much of Europe (or Canada), mainly because laws discourage it. As a result, unions have held their own in these countries in recent years, while American unions have gotten much weaker. American unions have also been hurt by recent factory closings; many businesses have transferred their operations to parts of the country (mainly the South, where unions are much less common) or to other countries where unions are weak and wages relatively low.

Another example of how repression may be triggered (and can seriously harm a movement) can be seen in the ways that some movements may provoke such a backlash against them that they lose ground. For example, the mobilization of far-right militia groups against the U.S. government which led to the Oklahoma City bombing in 1995 inspired closer surveillance and repression of these groups than had previously existed—not to mention extremely negative media coverage. Their number and activities declined sharply after the bombing.

Many scholars point out that while repression is often effective, it does sometimes fail. Police violence sometimes demobilizes protesters and crushes insurgents, but it sometimes backfires, spurring even more people to take to the streets or to take up arms. The timing of a repression effort can matter. Research on Central America during the 1970s and 1980s (Brockett, 1993) suggests that ruthless repression was most effective when authorities used it before movements had become strong—before a cycle of protest had begun and before people were already active and organized. Organized activists redoubled their efforts, went underground, and often turned to violence, joined by others seeking protection, justice, and sometimes revenge.

Repression can also backfire if the repressors misread the movement's purpose and its participants' motivations. U.S. counterinsurgency efforts in Iraq failed because officials assumed that popular attitudes toward insurgents and the government are based on short-term cost–benefit calculations; they failed to see how insurgencies are deeply rooted in class, ethnic, or religious conflicts (Roxborough, 2007). Accordingly, attempts by the United States to win over the "hearts and minds" of the Iraqi population by providing material benefits proved insufficient. Insurgent movements are less interested in popularity or legitimacy per se than in monopolizing political control at the grassroots level; such movements constitute an alternative government. Effective counterinsurgency, then, requires establishing local political control, a project that requires a great deal of time and manpower—something that outside powers may be unwilling to commit.

Outcomes

17.3.4 Distinguish between successful and unsuccessful outcomes.

Social movements have a number of effects on their societies, some of them intended and others quite unintended. A few movements attain many or most of their goals, while others at least manage to gain recognition or longevity in the form of protest organizations, but many if not most are suppressed or ignored. While sociologists used to talk about the success or failure of movements, today they are more likely to talk about movement *outcomes* in recognition of the unintended consequences of movements. Some movements may not get what they want, but they may still bring about significant benefits for their constituents. Some movements affect the broader culture and public attitudes, perhaps paving the way for future movements. Others leave behind social networks, tactical innovations, and organizational forms that later movements can adopt and use.

When thinking about what movements can achieve, it is useful to distinguish between *acceptance* (or recognition) versus the achievement of some specific goal (such as new government policy or law) (W. Gamson, 1990). Acceptance occurs when a movement or SMO comes to be regarded as a legitimate representative of a group by its opponents. Acceptance is generally crucial for the stability and longevity of a protest group, especially when its main opponent is the state. But sometimes movements win concrete benefits for their constituencies, such as old-age pensions, voting rights, clean air, tax cuts, or new healthcare programs for the poor.

Acceptance and concrete victories don't necessarily go together; a movement can attain one but not the other (or neither). The sociologist William Gamson has described four general types of movement outcomes based on whether a movement is fully accepted or not and whether it wins many new advantages or none (see Table 17.1). Movements that win a "full response" (i.e., full acceptance and many new advantages) are the most successful; the least successful movements are those that "collapse" by failing to win acceptance or any new advantages. There are also two outcomes that fall somewhere between success and failure. A movement is "preempted" when it wins new advantages but fails to win acceptance; and a movement is "co-opted" when it is accepted by its opponents but fails to win any new advantages for its constituents.

Explaining movement outcomes is complicated by the fact that success in the short and the long term may not coincide. In some cases, these even conflict with each other, as when a movement's initial successes inspire strong countermobilization on the part of those under attack. The pro-choice movement, for example, was quite successful in liberalizing abortion laws in a number of states and then seemed to win a huge victory with the *Roe v. Wade* Supreme Court decision in 1973. But this decision, as we have seen, which legalized certain types of abortion, sparked a formidable countermobilization by the antiabortion movement. This countermobilization has succeeded in making it more difficult to obtain an abortion in many parts of the United States, especially if one is a minor. In contrast, movement efforts that are unsuccessful in the short run may turn out to have big

Table 17.1 Four Types of Movement Outcome

	Wins Acceptance	Gains New Advantages	Examples
Full Response	✓	✓	American Federation of Labor; American Federation of Teachers
Preempted Movement	x	✓	American Free Trade; Tobacco Night Riders
Co-opted Movement	✓	x	Bull Moose (Progressive) Party; American Association of University Professors
Collapsed Movement	x	x	International Workingmen's Association; National Student League

SOURCE: Based on data from *The Strategy of Social Protest* (2nd ed., p. 29, Appendix A), by William Gamson, 1990, Homewood, IL: Dorsey.

effects in the long run, as in the case of martyrs who inspire outrage and additional mobilization.

Cultural Consequences of Movements

17.3.5 Discuss the cultural consequences of movements.

Overall, researchers have shown that only a few large and enduring movements have had profound effects on their societies. The labour movement won the 40-hour workweek and the right to collective bargaining with employers. The civil rights movement eliminated laws enforcing racial segregation and won voting rights for African Americans. The women's movement won laws against sex discrimination and forever changed the way people think about gender differences. A large number of movements have met with considerable repression. Others have attained some acceptance for their own organizations without obtaining tangible benefits for those they represent (i.e., they have been co-opted). Still others have pushed the government to establish a new agency or regulator in response to their demands, only to discover later that this agency was ineffectual or taken over by the movement's opponents. Scholars of social movements would like to believe that the movements they study affect the course of history, but they have often had to assert this without much good evidence.

More recently, the cultural and personal consequences of activism—many of them unintended—have begun to receive careful attention from sociologists. Being an activist in any movement may profoundly change the activist: For example, being active in a social movement often changes people from being passive and accepting of the world around them to a more direct, engaged stance toward issues they care about, and that can change the rest of their lives. The activist identity is itself an important effect of social movements, but it is just one of many potential cultural effects of movements. For example, some movements have helped to articulate new ways of thinking and feeling about the world. Thus, animal protectionists developed widespread sympathy for nonhuman species into an explicit ideology of outrage at the harm done to animals. Other movements raise issues for public debate, forcing informed citizens to think about a topic and decide how they feel about it. The pro-choice and pro-life movements are prime examples. Today, citizens are virtually expected to have an opinion on the abortion issue. A majority may reject a movement's perspective, but it can still cause them to think more deeply about their own values and attitudes. Even those who disagree with antiabortionists still have to decide *why* they disagree. Still other social movements inspire scientific research or technological change, as the environmental movement has.

There may be even broader cultural effects of social movements. On the one hand, they give people a moral voice, helping them to articulate values and intuitions and think through issues that they do not have time to think about in their daily lives. (Should women be able to have abortions? Should lesbians and gay men be able to marry and adopt children? Should the government provide a job to everyone who wants one?) This is extremely satisfying for most movement participants as well as the general public. On the other hand, social movements can also generate extremely technical, scientific, and practical knowledge. They engage people in politics in an exciting way—rare enough in modern society. Unfortunately, some movements may go too far, when instead of trying to be artists they try to be engineers, telling others what is good for them rather than trying to persuade them. This has often happened when movements have taken state power and tried to impose their views on others, which brings us to the topic of revolutions.

17.4 What Are Revolutions, and Why Do They Occur?

Barry Iverson Photography/Newscom

Understanding Revolutions

In everyday conversation, transformations in ways of thinking, technologies, and even fashions and consumer goods are often described as revolutionary. Sociologists, however, generally define **revolution** as a type of profound political or social change. Social movements, as we have seen, are a type of sustained collective action that sometimes help bring about revolutions, but they sometimes produce only small changes or none at all.

Defining *Revolution*

17.4.1 Distinguish between political and social revolutions.

Sociologists generally define *revolution* in one of two ways. Some define revolutions as any change of government or political regime brought about, at least in part, by social movements or popular protest. Others define revolutions (or *social revolutions*) more narrowly as entailing not only a change of regime but also fundamental changes in a society's economic institutions and class structure (e.g., the French, Russian, and Chinese revolutions). (Although some government officials may sometimes support revolutions, revolutions differ from *coups d'état*, which involve the overthrow of a government by other political or military authorities with little if any popular support or active participation by ordinary people.) Social revolutions thus differ from those revolutions (sometimes called *political revolutions*) that bring about new political regimes but little if any change in economic or class structures (e.g., the English or American revolutions). Of course, what begins as a political revolution may end up being a social revolution. For example, the political revolution in Russia in February 1917, which overthrew the czar, helped pave the way for the social revolution of October 1917 when the radical Bolshevik Party (later renamed the Communist Party) seized power and oversaw a dramatic transformation of Russian society, including the dispossession of landlords and factory owners.

Table 17.2 Major Social Revolutions

Country	Year
France	1789
Mexico	1910
Russia	1917
Yugoslavia	1945
Vietnam	1945
China	1949
Bolivia	1952
Cuba	1959
Algeria	1962
Ethiopia	1974
Angola	1975
Mozambique	1975
Cambodia	1975
Laos	1975
Iran	1979
Nicaragua	1979
Eastern Europe	1989

NOTE: The listed dates are conventional markers that refer to the year in which revolutionaries initially overthrew extant political authorities. Revolutions, however, are best conceptualized not as events but as processes that typically span many years.

For some analysts, including Marxists, revolutions necessarily involve a substantial redistribution of property or the creation of a new type of economy or mode of production. Yet other analysts argue that revolutions may radically alter everyday life for millions of people without bringing about much economic change—through dramatic political and cultural changes, for example. However defined, most scholars agree that social revolutions have been relatively rare, if momentous, occurrences. By most counts, fewer than two dozen major social revolutions have taken place during the past two centuries. See Table 17.2 for more information about some of the major social revolutions since 1789.

Notice that the revolutions that occurred in the Middle East and North Africa during the so-called Arab Spring of 2011 are not included in Table 17.2. These would properly be called political rather than social revolutions. They did overthrow dictators and brought about changes in political regimes, but they did not substantially change the economic institutions, the distribution of property, or the class structures of these societies. The revolution in Egypt might even be described as a half-revolution. It overthrew the dictator Hosni Mubarak and destroyed Mubarak's powerful political party, but some elements of the old political regime—above all, the armed forces and the judiciary—survived the revolution intact and continue to wield tremendous power. An Islamic movement organization, the Muslim Brotherhood, did manage to win elections in 2012, and for a brief time the Brotherhood controlled the legislature and the office of the presidency (to which Mohamed Morsi was elected). But shortly thereafter, as popular protests against Morsi grew, the military stepped in and overthrew the newly elected government and installed one of its own leaders in the office of the Presidency. Looking at the big picture, Egypt's rich elite (which includes many military officers) has also held onto its wealth and economic power, and most Egyptians have seen little significant change in their lives.

Revolutions, Violence, and Other Forms of Conflict

17.4.2 Describe the potential role of violence in revolutions and different types of violent and nonviolent conflicts.

Many sociologists view violence as an essential characteristic of revolutions, and many, if not most, revolutions have in fact involved considerable violence between the parties contending for state power. This is especially true of social revolutions, which have threatened powerful elites. Foreign states, moreover, have often intervened militarily in revolutionary situations or attacked newly installed revolutionary governments. Some revolutionary regimes, furthermore, have employed considerable violence to reorganize society along new lines, and some have even perpetrated genocide or mass murders or have attacked neighbouring countries in order to shore up their rule. Still, the extent of violence in revolutions is quite variable, and some have occurred with comparatively little bloodshed. Some sociologists, furthermore, have detected a trend in recent decades toward relatively nonviolent revolutions (e.g., Iran in 1979, Eastern Europe in 1989, Tunisia and Egypt in 2011, and Ukraine in 2014). For these reasons, violence is best viewed as a potential component of revolution, not as one of its defining characteristics.

ZUMA Press, Inc./Alamy Stock Photo

These nonviolent protesters in Tahrir Square in Cairo, Egypt, are shouting slogans against the dictator Hosni Mubarak.

Revolutions stand apart analytically from such kindred forms of political conflict as wars (interstate or civil), popular rebellions, riots, and *coups d'état* (the overthrow of a government, usually led by the nation's military). Historically, however, these latter forms of conflict have often been closely connected with revolutions or revolutionary situations. Interstate wars, for example, sometimes help to cause revolutions by weakening armies—thereby creating political opportunities for revolutionary movements, as political process theorists would say—as well as by inflaming popular grievances, including perceived threats to one's nation; in turn, revolutions often result in interstate wars, usually because foreign powers seek to destroy those revolutionary movements or regimes they perceive as threats. France, Russia, Vietnam, Cuba, Iran—all were invaded shortly after revolutionaries took power. The revolutionary situations created by radical social movements, furthermore, often take the form of civil wars, and radical movements bring about actual revolutions, of course, if they successfully seize state power.

Similarly, social movements that initially seek reforms within the existing political system—the kind of movements this chapter has focused on thus far—become **revolutionary movements** if they ultimately attempt to overthrow the government, which often happens when the political order breaks down or when the government persistently refuses to implement the reforms desired by such movements. Spontaneous riots, furthermore, may help to precipitate revolutions, and riots have occurred frequently as a result of the breakdown of political authority that characterizes revolutionary situations. Finally, *coups d'état* may become "revolutions from above" if their leaders mobilize masses of people and implement radical political or socioeconomic changes. In sum, while revolutions, and especially social revolutions, are a distinctive and comparatively rare form of political conflict, they are often connected, whether as cause or consequence, with other and more frequently recurring types of conflict, including social movements.

Revolutionary Situations

17.4.3 Describe characteristics of revolutionary situations and how those situations can transform territories politically and socially.

Many movements and rebellions explicitly aim to depose oppressive political authorities and, often, reorganize the social order from top to bottom. When such movements obtain substantial popular support, one may speak of the existence of a **revolutionary situation**: a situation in which two or more political groups or movements claim to be the rightful or legitimate rulers of a certain territory or population.

There have been hundreds of revolutionary situations around the globe during the past two centuries. Most movements that try to bring about revolutions, however, do not succeed in overthrowing the government. If the government's armed forces remain strong and cohesive, revolutionaries are typically defeated or confined to peripheral regions within the national territory. Most revolutionary situations, in other words, do not result in actual political, let alone social, revolutions. A revolution typically requires the prior weakening or collapse of the government's "infrastructural power"—its capacity to enforce its will on the society that it claims to govern. Military might is the main source of a state's infrastructural power. While revolutionary movements sometimes muster the power to incapacitate governments (by winning over military officers, soldiers, and government officials, for example), such movements just as frequently overthrow governments that have already been fatally weakened by interstate wars, economic and fiscal crises, or divisions and conflicts among the rich and powerful. The French Revolution, for example, occurred in part because the monarchy was in a state of fiscal collapse, and the Bolsheviks were able to seize power in Russia partly because the Russian army had been decimated in what was then known as the Great War (i.e., World War I).

Revolutionary situations can be understood as moments when regimes come into sharp conflict with radical social movements that are demanding power; such situations arise when the regime can no longer manage or accommodate the competing interests and demands of the groups they are meant to govern, sometimes because elites themselves are in conflict. A revolutionary situation opens up the possibility of deep political and social change should the radicals emerge victorious.

The famous Russian revolutionary Vladimir Ilyich Lenin famously stated that revolutionary situations display "three major symptoms": (1) a crisis or split among the upper classes; (2) unusual suffering among the lower classes; and (3) "a considerable increase in the . . . independent historical action" of the lower classes (Lenin, 1915/1964, p. 213). Since Lenin's time, scholars of revolutions have developed these basic insights. The most crucial "symptom" Lenin listed—acute suffering among the masses—typically means that a population loses many of its material resources. Accordingly, some scholars of revolution understand revolutions as a product of relative deprivation—a feeling that one does not have what one deserves. More likely, Lenin meant that revolutions disrupt everyday lives and routines, which prompts people to defy economic and political authorities. In this sense, revolutionary situations require the weakening or breakdown of "the regulatory controls inherent in the structures of institutional life" (Piven & Cloward, 1977, p. 11). Economic crises, wars, and even natural disasters typically cause these dislocations. Ordinary people feel the consequences—they endure the loss of work or lowered wages, are sent into bloody and often unpopular wars, or suffer the breakdown or even collapse of institutions on which their survival depends (work, markets, transportation, policing, schools, and so forth).

For governments, furthermore, such shocks disrupt the existing balance of political forces. To preserve regime stability, political elites may seek new allies from new sectors of the population, who consequently have enhanced influence. Once new allies are secured, governments may discard old allies, exclude formerly incorporated groups, or significantly elevate the costs of their incorporation. As disturbances redefine the inclusiveness of the political regime and activate ordinary people in new ways, political alignments are redrawn and the balance of power shifts. Acute shocks typically release ordinary folk from passivity, activating their grievances through new organizational structures and institutional avenues. In sum, one precondition for revolutionary situations consists of massive disruptions that break down routinized systems of social control. Subsequently, explosions of political protest may place regimes under great duress.

Tunisians gather around a statue depicting the vegetable cart of Mohamed Bouazizi, who set himself on fire in December 2010 in an act of protest that triggered the so-called Arab Spring.

oubeir Souissi/Reuters/Landov

A highly publicized example of a revolutionary situation is the Arab Spring of 2011. At that time people very rapidly poured into the streets, demanding the removal of repressive dictators. But most of these dictators—in Tunisia, Egypt, Libya, Yemen, and Syria—had been in power for decades. What was new was the economic crisis gripping the region. People were upset with rising food and fuel prices, and young people in particular could not find the kind of work for which they had been educated—or sometimes any work at all. It is telling that the Arab Spring began with protests in Tunisia in December 2010, which were a response to the self-immolation of an educated young man, Mohamed Bouazizi, who was trying to survive by selling vegetables from a cart. But Bouazizi did not have a proper permit for his cart, and he burned himself in protest (he later died in hospital) after a municipal official (and her aides) confiscated his cart and publicly humiliated him.

Profound social dislocations like mass unemployment may be necessary for revolutionary situations to emerge, but they are clearly insufficient. Lenin identified another indispensable condition for revolutionary situations: The shock must create a crisis or division among the upper classes, which in turn fractures the foundations of the government. These divisions and the resulting political destabilization provide an opening or opportunity that magnifies pressures from below and that newly mobilized people can exploit. Such a crisis typically occurs when the usual consensus over arrangements for settling the competing claims of the upper classes collapses, often as a result of wars or state-led efforts at economic modernization that generate growing fiscal pressures on elites. As agreement over how the costs of fiscal and institutional reform should be distributed disintegrates, the institutional coherence of the regime comes under enormous strain. The state's capacity to control and enforce its will on the population within the territory it claims to govern may begin to contract and even collapse.

Upper-class disunity and state breakdown may follow two general scenarios. In the first, a crisis, such as a fiscal emergency provoked by international war, may generate instability as elites resist the tax burdens that state officials impose. The ensuing crisis in the regime (as state power and legitimacy disintegrate) then serves to facilitate and exacerbate rebellion by ordinary people who are mobilizing through existing networks and organizations. This is the story of the French, Russian, and Chinese revolutions (Skocpol, 1979). In the second scenario, the shock unleashes mounting pressure from a social movement or movements below. No longer bound by the institutions of social control, this movement generates a crisis among the upper classes, who are pulled into opposing directions by the developing movement itself. One upper-class faction might strive to repress the growing pressures from below, extracting more resources to cover fiscal gaps, clamping down on democratic rights, and generally resorting to coercion. Another faction, by contrast, might enact reforms, resigning itself to accommodating popular demands to preserve its rule. In this scenario, if the social movements did not add pressure, the upper classes might converge on a unified and stabilizing response, preventing regime collapse. This is the story of the Cuban, Iranian, and Nicaraguan revolutions, and of the Arab Spring. In either scenario, the cohesion of the police and armed forces is crucial for preventing the fall of the regime. If the costs of war, repression, or reform divide or weaken the military and undermine its ability to act in a unified and decisive manner against popular movements, then revolution becomes likely or even inevitable.

In short, elite division and institutional collapse can either result from or result in a popular movement from below. In either event, the upper classes find it impossible to coexist under the existing regime. The revolutionary crisis intensifies as disaffected upper-class groups undermine the power and legitimacy of state institutions.

Revolutionary Movements and the Seizure of State Power

17.4.4 Discuss the two requirements for a strong revolutionary movement to take place.

These two conditions—divisions among the elites and institutional collapse—when combined would seem to be sufficient to produce a revolutionary situation. If ordinary people are thrust into collective action because the regulatory capacity of key institutions has eroded and if upper-class divisions have led to the state's infrastructural power collapsing, a powerful insurrection would seem likely. However, Lenin raised a third condition: a social movement's capacity to take advantage of divisions among the elites and institutional collapse in order to place radical transformation on the national agenda. Simply stated, an existing regime is likely to be able to survive a crisis and remain stable if ordinary people prove incapable of organizing themselves into a revolutionary social movement that can effectively topple it.

Consider the case of Morocco during the Arab Spring. Morocco is one of the poorest countries in North Africa and the Middle East—poorer than Tunisia and Egypt—and the vast majority of its people are struggling economically. But while there were some protests calling for political reforms in Morocco following the revolutions in Tunisia and Egypt, they were comparatively small and intermittent. As a result, Morocco's King Mohammed VI was easily able to hold onto power after enacting a few modest reforms.

Two things are required for a revolutionary movement to create a revolutionary situation. The first requirement is that ordinary folk must possess considerable collective leverage over the rich and powerful. When ordinary people play necessary or highly valued roles in crucial institutions, their threats of withdrawing their collective contributions would be disruptive. Important industries, for example, depend on the labour of ordinary workers to function; when workers withdraw that labour during a strike, these industries shut down, and their owners cannot make profits. When rank-and-file soldiers in an army refuse orders to attack protesters, the army is useless to elites. Thus, when the lower classes enjoy structural power rooted in their essential institutional roles, their capacity for generating costly disruptions is enhanced (Schwartz, 1976). In the context of an economic crisis, elite vulnerability to such disruptions grows. The central point is that the institutional roles of the lower classes must translate into a capacity to undertake collective actions that challenge the power of the upper classes.

Most accounts of the Egyptian uprising in 2011 focus on the occupation of Tahrir Square in central Cairo by thousands of people. But the dictatorship of Hosni Mubarak may have been more deeply shaken by the strikes and work stoppages that occurred during the occupation, culminating in a general strike in the days before Mubarak's resignation (Schwartz, 2011). (A *general strike* occurs when workers in an entire city or country refuse to work, as opposed to workers in a single industry or factory.) The strikes hurt many businesses across the country—the tourism industry was already reeling from the loss of business caused by the political unrest—which may have convinced top military officers (many of whom are also businessmen) that Mubarak had become a threat to their own interests. The military refused to disperse the protesters in Tahrir Square, urged Mubarak to resign, and took power for themselves.

Image Asset Management Ltd/SuperStock

Vladimir Lenin (1870–1924), shown here in October 1917, was not only the most famous leader of the Russian Revolution but also studied and wrote about revolutions more generally. What did he consider the main causes of revolution?

The second requirement is what Lenin called "independent historical action" by the masses. In other words, activists must secure the political and ideological resources they need to convert increased political activity and leverage into decisive collective action. These resources include ideas, organization, and tactics, as well as the ability to obtain information, process it, produce it, and deploy it among followers. Clearly, ideas and ideology play an important role in the origins and outcomes of revolutions. However, they do not operate as autonomous forces that drive the contenders in a revolutionary situation. After all, radical ideologies have existed and appealed to many people in most if not all modern societies. They have seldom, however, given rise to strong revolutionary movements, much less to revolutions.

Culture, broadly understood, matters in revolutionary situations when particular ideologies are able to shift the balance of forces, weakening authorities and upper classes. When social dislocations and state crises offer openings for radical social movements, the tactical decisions and framing work of activists can be decisive. When the strategies and ideologies promoted by radical activists resonate with ordinary people—that is, when "frame alignment" occurs—and when they are not only consistent with but also promote increased popular mobilization, thereby maximizing its disruptive impact, they can be the final necessary ingredient that provides such mobilization with the capacity to overthrow a regime. In fact, Lenin ended his famous statement on revolutionary situations with an important qualification: "Not every revolutionary situation," he explained, "gives rise to a revolution; revolution arises only out of a situation in which the above-mentioned objective changes are accompanied by a subjective change, namely, the ability of the revolutionary class to take revolutionary mass action strong enough to break (or dislocate) the old government, which never, not even in a period of crisis, 'falls,' if it is not toppled over" (Lenin, 1915/1964, p. 213). Revolutions, in other words, are only possible when there are strong social movements that can topple governments in deep crisis.

Political Environments That Encourage Revolutionary Movements

17.4.5 Describe the kind of political environments that encourage revolutionary movements.

Revolutionary situations are likely to arise in authoritarian and repressive political contexts. In fact, no popular revolutionary movement has ever overthrown a long-consolidated democratic regime (however, the democratically elected government of the Ukraine, led by President Viktor Yanukovych, was removed from power by force in 2014 and replaced by an unelected interim leadership amid mass protests and sniper fire). The great social revolutions of the twentieth century toppled kings and dictators (as in Russia, China, Cuba, Iran, and Nicaragua), extremely repressive colonial regimes (as in Vietnam and Algeria), and the Soviet-imposed single-party regimes of Eastern Europe. In fact, revolutionary movements tend to prosper when governments sponsor or defend—with violence when necessary—economic and social arrangements that are widely regarded as unjust (i.e., as not simply unfortunate or inevitable). In certain societies, unless citizens see state officials sponsoring or protecting those arrangements—through legal codes, taxation, conscription, and, ultimately, force—revolutionary movements aimed at overthrowing the state are unlikely to become strong. People may blame their social "superiors" or employers for their plight, for example, or even whole classes of such elites, yet they may not challenge the government unless they widely perceive that it will stand behind and defend those elites at all costs.

Often, revolutionaries and activists gain strength from indiscriminate, but not overwhelming, violence by weak states against social movements and oppositional politicians and activists. For reasons of simple self-defence, people who are targeted by the state may join clandestine groups or even arm themselves. Those with families or friends who have been victimized by the state may also join or support revolutionary movements to seek revenge against the perpetrators. Social movements and political parties have generally turned to disruptive strategies, including armed struggle, only after their previous efforts to secure change through legal means were violently repressed. Under repressive conditions, ordinary people often view mass disruption, including armed struggle, as a legitimate and reasonable means of political contestation.

The connection between repressive authoritarianism and revolution is clearly illustrated by the Arab Spring of 2011. The six countries that experienced broad popular uprisings—Tunisia, Egypt, Libya, Bahrain, Yemen, and Syria—are dissimilar in many ways. These countries have different levels of economic development and urbanization; some are ethnically divided, others more homogenous; some have been very close allies of Western powers, others not. But what they all had in common were longstanding dictators (or a monarch, in the case of Bahrain) who would not tolerate threats to their continued rule. The rulers' violence and intransigence forced their political opponents to give up their dreams of incremental reforms and take to the streets. Only disruptive mass movements, most concluded, could bring an end to the reign of these autocrats. And of course they were right. Mass protests in Tunisia and Egypt convinced the armed forces in those countries to abandon their support for dictators. In Libya, Yemen, and Syria, mass protest led to divisions in and defections from the armed forces, resulting in much bloodier conflicts. Only the king in Bahrain has managed to retain the solid support of his military forces—supplemented by troops from neighbouring Saudi Arabia—in the face of a broad popular uprising.

In contrast to authoritarian regimes, let us now consider governments that are widely perceived to be liberal and democratic (e.g., the United States, Canada, Ireland, Colombia, Mexico, South Africa, India, and Japan). More liberal and democratic governments tend to pacify and channel, but hardly do away with, social conflict. Elections have sometimes been described as the "democratic translation of the class struggle" (Lipset 1960/1981, p. 230). Democracy channels a variety of social conflicts—including class conflicts—into party competition for votes and the lobbying of representatives by interest groups. People are not as tempted to rebel against the government because they know that, in only a few years, they have a chance to elect new leaders. In addition, democracies have generally provided a context in which social movements can win concessions from economic and political elites, although this often requires a good deal of disruption. But movements that aim at overthrowing democratic governments rarely win much popular support unless those governments (or their armies) push people into rebellion by indiscriminately repressing protesters. By and large, people prefer using the ballot box, which is why there have been few large-scale attempts to overthrow long-established democracies in Western Europe and North America.

This does not mean that radical social movements go unrewarded in democratic societies. Democracy by no means eliminates social conflict; in fact, in many ways democracy encourages a flowering of social conflict by providing the political space within which those groups outside ruling circles can make claims on political authorities and economic elites. Not just political parties, then, but a whole range of social movements, trade unions, interest groups, and professional associations can become the organizational vehicles of political life in democratic polities. Their repertoires of contention include electoral campaigns, lobbying, strikes, boycotts, demonstrations, and civil disobedience—forms of collective action that may be quite disruptive and undertaken for quite radical ends but that are not aimed at bringing down the government.

Democracy, then, dramatically reduces the likelihood of revolutionary change, but not because it brings about social justice. Formal democracy is fully compatible with widespread poverty, inequality, and popular grievances of all sorts. This is why movements for social justice so often arise in democratic contexts. But, again, these movements almost always view the state as an instrument to be pressured and influenced, not as something to be seized or smashed. Revolutionary movements, for their part, develop not simply because people are angry or aggrieved but because the government under which they live provides no other mechanisms for social change, violently repressing those who peacefully seek incremental reforms. This said, the spread of democracy will not necessarily render revolution *passé* as a form of political struggle. Radical leaders and parties have sometimes been able to amass a broad following in democratic contexts and to win elections (for example, Salvador Allende in Chile in 1970 and Hugo Chávez in Venezuela in 1998, 2000, and 2006). Perhaps during the twenty-first century we will see some democratically elected governments attempt to revolutionize economic and political institutions. As yet, however, the democratic route to revolution has never been successfully travelled.

Conclusion: The Future of Movements and Revolutions

We began this chapter by looking at the Occupy Wall Street movement. Like other social movements, the Occupy movement did not emerge spontaneously but grew out of the planned actions of preexisting networks of activists. The movement's tactics were not spontaneous either. Activists in the Occupy movement, like activists before them, chose tactics with which they were already familiar. The tactic of occupying public spaces was inspired by the occupation of Tahrir Square during the revolution in Egypt earlier in the year. And the movement spread rapidly across the country, like movements before it, because it framed its ideas about inequality and the power of banks and corporations in a way that appealed to a great many people during a time of economic crisis. There were also networks of activists in cities and towns across the country, most of whom had been active in previous movements, who could spread the movement's ideas and organize occupations of their own. None of this would surprise sociologists who have studied past movements.

The history of social movements and revolutions assures us that we will undoubtedly see many more in the years ahead. Three years after the Occupy movement, there were numerous protests in a number of U.S. cities against police brutality against African Americans. As long as ordinary people feel that the rich and powerful are oppressing them (or at least ignoring their needs and interests), and as long as people can safely connect with one another and find ways to pressure (or overthrow) the rich and powerful, movements and revolutions will remain part of the human condition.

CHAPTER SUMMARY

The Big Questions Revisited 17

17.1 What Are Social Movements? Social movements play a crucial role in contemporary societies. Through them we can learn about the world around us. We started the chapter by defining social movements and exploring what we can learn by studying them.

Studying Social Movements

Politics, Human Action, and Social Change

Learning Objective 17.1.1: Discuss how social movements affect political and social structures.

Moral Sensibilities

Learning Objective 17.1.2: Discuss how social movements contribute to a society's moral codes.

Understanding Social Movements Today

Learning Objective 17.1.3: Define the political-process perspective and discuss how understanding social movements can vary as movements change over time.

17.2 Why Do Movements Emerge, and Who Joins Them? The most frequently asked question about social movements is why they emerge when they do. In this section we examined how movements take shape and looked at who joins or supports social movements.

Movement Origins and Recruitment

How Movements Take Shape

Learning Objective 17.2.1: Analyze the political, economic, organizational, demographic, and cultural factors that ignite and fuel social movements.

Cultural Aspects of Social Movements

Learning Objective 17.2.2: Explain how cultural approaches to the study of social movements differ from resource mobilization and political-process approaches.

Recruitment: Joining or Supporting Movements

Learning Objective 17.2.3: Explain how individual traits, biographical availability, framing, and cultural attitudes influence participation in social movements.

17.3 What Do Movements Accomplish? Why do movements use certain tactics and not others? Why do movements decline or disappear? In this section we looked at what movements do and what changes and outcomes movements bring about, including unintended consequences.

Movement Tactics and Outcomes

The Strategies of Movements

Learning Objective 17.3.1: Discuss how organizers and participants increase awareness and further the goals of movements.

Tactical Repertoires of Movements

Learning Objective 17.3.2: Explain why social movements use certain tactics but not others.

The Decline and Disappearance of Movements

Learning Objective 17.3.3: Explain the socio-political reasons for the decreasing popularity of certain movements.

Outcomes

Learning Objective 17.3.4: Distinguish between successful and unsuccessful outcomes.

Cultural Consequences of Movements

Learning Objective 17.3.5: Discuss the cultural consequences of movements.

17.4 What Are Revolutions, and Why Do They Occur? Why are some social movements revolutionary, and what causes revolutionary situations to occur? When and why have revolutionary movements been able to take state power? We concluded the chapter by examining how democracy shapes social conflict and the prospects for revolution.

Understanding Revolutions

Defining **Revolution**

Learning Objective 17.4.1: Distinguish between political and social revolutions.

Revolutions, Violence, and Other Forms of Conflict

Learning Objective 17.4.2: Describe the potential role of violence in revolutions and different types of violent and nonviolent conflicts.

Revolutionary Situations

Learning Objective 17.4.3: Describe characteristics of revolutionary situations and how those situations can transform territories politically and socially.

Revolutionary Movements and the Seizure of State Power

Learning Objective 17.4.4: Discuss the two requirements for a strong revolutionary movement to take place.

Political Environments That Encourage Revolutionary Movements

Learning Objective 17.4.5: Describe the kind of political environments that encourage revolutionary movements.

Learn the Terms

biographical availability (p. 488)
collective identity (p. 491)
fad (p. 480)
framing (p. 491)
free space (p. 495)
moral shock (p. 492)
political-process perspective (p. 483)
resource mobilization approach (p. 485)
revolution (p. 501)
revolutionary movement (p. 503)
revolutionary situation (p. 504)
riot (p. 480)
social movement (p. 480)
social movement organization (SMO) (p. 485)
social network (p. 485)

Chapter 18
Environmental Sociology

by Colin Jerolmack

Gabriel Bouys/AFP/Getty Images/Newscom

The coast of northwestern Alaska is crumbling into the sea as global warming melts the frozen earth that glues the landscape together. Shown here, a home destroyed by beach erosion tips over in the Alaskan village of Shishmaref.

Learning Objectives

18.1.1 Explain how a society's environment contributes to the cultural and religious traditions it develops.

18.1.2 Discuss the ways in which modern societies gained more control over their environment and developed stratified social structures.

18.1.3 Explain determinism and social constructivism, and the ways in which environment both guides and constrains social life.

18.2.1 Identify the variety of environmental transformations caused by climate change.

18.2.2 Discuss how the rapid depletion of major natural resources—oil, coal, forests, living species, and water—affects all forms of life.

18.2.3 Discuss how attitudes toward waste and modes of waste removal threaten our health and environment.

18.2.4 Discuss the impact human consumption has on air and water supplies.

18.3.1 Identify early preservationist figures and movements that have contributed to environmental awareness.

18.3.2 Discuss environmental racism and what progress is being made to ensure equal protection for all people.

18.3.3 Explain the reasons some groups are more adversely affected by natural disasters than other groups.

18.3.4 Identify the connection between global environmental responsibility and global environmental equality.

18.4.1 Compare the advantages and disadvantages of self-regulation and political regulation of environmental resources.

18.4.2 Explain how economic systems focused on competition and expansion can contribute to serious environmental issues.

18.4.3 Discuss ways in which technology, politics, and lifestyle changes can contribute to environmental protection and sustainability.

In the remote and rugged region of northwestern Alaska, on a small island separated from the coast by five miles of choppy Arctic waters, lies the village of Shishmaref. While its nearly 600 Indigenous Inupiat inhabitants enjoy some of the conveniences of modern living, such as television and snowmobiles, they maintain a traditional lifestyle in which they obtain the necessities of life through hunting, fishing, and bartering. For centuries, the Inupiat of Shishmaref and the mainland have developed and relied on a vast stock of knowledge about animal migration patterns, ocean currents, and seasonal variations in ice thickness in order to persevere in such an unforgiving climate. However, in recent years their environment has changed in rapid and threatening ways. Since 1979, more than 20 percent of the polar ice cap has melted as a result of rising global temperatures, and scientists predict that summer Arctic sea ice could disappear entirely by 2030. The Inupiat fear that their livelihoods, their villages, and their culture will vanish along with the glaciers.

These days, the sea surrounding Shishmaref freezes later and thaws earlier than ever before. With the decrease in sea ice, which forms a protective barrier around the island, Shishmaref has become vulnerable to storm surges. Large waves eat away 10 miles of the coast every year and literally pull houses out to sea. Lacking the resources to fortify the island perimeter, villagers recently voted to abandon their homes and relocate to the mainland. Many residents worry about the loss of their community and way of life, and the state government worries about who will pay the estimated $200 million cost of building a new village and moving all the residents.

In 2009, I travelled to northwestern Alaska to study the consequences of climate change for Indigenous people. My guide was Caleb Pungowiyi, a resident of the town of Kotzebue and a senior advisor to Oceana, a nonprofit ocean conservation organization. Caleb did not need to look at the annual reports on sea ice retreat to determine that exceptional global warming is occurring—he could look to his backyard. Hunting expeditions, and travel in general, have been curtailed because snowmobiles are falling through ice that once was rock solid. Hotter, drier summers are leading to a rash of brush fires. Permafrost—the eternally frozen earth under the tundra that holds the landscape together—is melting, leading to coastal erosion, landslides, and sinkholes that are destabilizing towns and swallowing up houses. As animals such as caribou and bearded seals adjust their migration and mating habits in response to warming temperatures, hunting becomes a less reliable means of securing food.

The Big Questions

The Alaskan case touches on a number of important questions that the field of environmental sociology seeks to address.

1. **How does social life relate to the natural environment?** Environmental sociologists study the *interaction* between environmental facts and social facts and emphasize their interdependency (Freudenberg & Gramling, 1989). Every society consumes and transforms the natural environment to satisfy its needs and desires, yet every society must also adapt to its physical surroundings and confront natural limits. And while there is an objective natural world "out there," how we interpret and interact with it is always influenced by cultural, political, and economic processes.
2. **How has human activity harmed the environment?** The most pressing environmental problems of our time—such as deforestation, water pollution, and global warming—are the results of human activities. Finding solutions to these problems will require collective social action, and making those solutions equitable may prove to be the biggest challenge of all.
3. **How do environmental factors impact inequality?** Consider the devastating natural disaster Hurricane Katrina, which overwhelmed New Orleans's man-made levees in 2005, killing 2,000 people and displacing over 1 million more. As the storm menaced the Gulf Coast, wealthier residents were able to evacuate because they had automobiles and the finances to pay for hotel rooms. The poorest residents—many of whom were black—did not have the means to get out and became stranded in their homes as the water rose. As a result, they were disproportionately represented in the storm's death toll. When sociologists examine environmental catastrophes like Katrina, they ask questions such as "How does the structure of society shape the effects of these natural events?"
4. **How can we create more sustainable societies?** As the global population expands and environmental degradation worsens, it seems that there are simply not enough natural resources for every human being on Earth to use as much oil and electricity, and dispose of as much waste, as citizens of wealthy nations currently do. How can members of rich countries be convinced to adopt more sustainable lifestyles? And how can we enact international environmental regulations yet still help developing countries increase their standard of living through industry?

Given the high cost of groceries that must be flown in from southern communities to the North American North and the lack of steady jobs, Indigenous peoples of the North are caught in a double bind: their traditional lifestyle may soon cease to be viable, but there are few feasible alternatives. The future of this region likely holds many more scenarios like that of Shishmaref—impoverished and politically marginalized communities forced to abandon their ancestral homes and many of their customs in the face of global warming.

Although the evidence for climate change may not be obvious in places like New York City, in the extreme conditions of the Arctic the signs of global warming are clearly recognizable. While scientists compile records to demonstrate that the changes occurring in Alaska and elsewhere are unprecedented, the Inupiat already know this to be true because of the unprecedented challenges they face on a daily basis as they struggle to secure their existence.

The plight of Indigenous Northerners introduces us to the core concern of **environmental sociology:** understanding the ways that society simultaneously shapes and is shaped by the physical environment (Catton & Dunlap, 1980). While the Inupiat traditional lifestyle and culture were forged as adaptations to their natural world, the contemporary environmental crisis that threatens to overwhelm the Inupiat has social origins. There is now a virtual consensus in mainstream environmental science that much of the global warming we are witnessing is the result of burning fossil fuels. Environmental problems, then, have both societal causes and social consequences. There is another sense in which the predicament of the Inupiat is emblematic: Indigenous groups, minorities, and the poor have historically suffered the most from environmental degradation. The costs of environmental problems are unevenly distributed, reflecting and reproducing social inequality.

18.1 How Does Social Life Relate to the Natural Environment?

Accent Alaska.com / Alamy Stock Photo

Understanding Environment–Society Relations

Many social transformations have accompanied the transition of societies from traditional to modern forms: capitalism supplanted feudalism; people migrated from small villages to large cities, the division of labour intensified, close-knit communities gave way to mass societies characterized by impersonal and contractual ties, and so on. Yet as societies went through these dramatic social changes, their relationship to the physical environment was also rapidly transformed. In fact, many social theorists have concluded that the transition of societies from traditional to modern forms was, to a large degree, driven by the development of technology that enabled greater exploitation of natural resources. Environmental sociologists see the relationship between environment and society as dynamic and interdependent, and they seek to understand how this relationship varies over time and across social contexts.

Traditional Societies

18.1.1 Explain how a society's environment contributes to the cultural and religious traditions it develops.

The term *primitive*, though sometimes considered to have a negative meaning, can be usefully employed to think about how traditional societies have typically interacted with their environment. *Primitive* evokes the image of a preindustrial society in which people live close to the land, build simple homes out of natural materials, rely on their feet for transportation, hunt and gather, make only superficial changes to the environment, and consider nature to be sacred.

The field of anthropology was born over a century ago out of the study of preindustrial societies. As Western powers colonized far-flung regions of Africa and Latin America, they encountered people who lived much like the imaginary "primitive" society described above. Anthropologists lived among these strangers in order to understand their cultures and lifestyles. Here were people, it seemed, virtually untouched by the forces of modernization. Here were societies characterized by a lack of control over, and a dependence on, nature. These environment–society relations structured their cultural and religious systems.

The anthropologist Bronislaw Malinowski (1948) spent the years surrounding World War I observing native culture in the Trobriand Islands of the Western Pacific. He noticed that the islanders performed elaborate ceremonial rites before they set out on fishing expeditions in the ocean but that such rituals were entirely absent from their fishing trips in the lagoon. The reason for this difference was simple. Fish were plentiful in the lagoon, and the waters were calm. Thus, islanders could predict that fishing would be safe and produce a high yield. The yields from ocean fishing were far less predictable, and such trips could be treacherous. Facing a situation that was out of their control, they resorted to magic to try to bring a sense of order and predictability to the natural world. This finding explained many of the systems of magic that anthropologists found in traditional cultures, and it helped explain the relative absence of these systems in modern societies, which tame nature through the application of science.

In Papua New Guinea, Indigenous societies were traditionally organized into clans that each adopted a particular animal as the sacred symbol—or totem—of the group. We can find traces of totemism in modern societies as well, such as when sports teams use an animal as their mascot and group name.

Deco/Alamy Stock Photo

Social scientists noted another common feature of traditional societies—they often attributed spiritual significance to nature. Émile Durkheim, one of the founders of sociology, produced one of the most well-known explanations of "primitive" religion based on his study of Aboriginal tribes in Australia. He noted that these tribes were organized into clans based on spiritual rather than blood kinship, with each clan adopting a particular plant or animal—called a totem—as the symbol of the clan. Clans considered their totem plants or animals to be sacred, and so killing and consuming them was generally taboo. Clans inscribed ceremonial objects with the emblem of their totem, which made these objects sacred as well. This belief system, called **totemism**, was common among many Indigenous groups—including Aboriginal peoples of North America.

Durkheim realized that it was only once plants or animals became a symbol of the clan that they were elevated to the status of sacred. He took this as evidence that the Aborigines did not actually consider nature to be divine. Rather, the totem was sacred because it stood for the clan. Durkheim did not think that the Aborigines were as different from modern societies as they first appeared. Every society has its sacred objects and rituals that help bring together its members as a community. Americans, for instance, salute the flag, and North Americans play the national anthem before sporting events. "Primitive" people chose animals and plants as their sacred objects, Durkheim believed, simply because their lifestyles were intimately connected to nature (Durkheim, 1915).

Modern Societies

18.1.2 Discuss the ways in which modern societies gained more control over their environment and developed stratified social structures.

As natural forces came to be more understandable and predictable through the accumulation of scientific knowledge, the environment became a safer, more useful, and more urban place. Humans ceased to be the playthings of nature and were able to apply technology to exert greater control over their surroundings. The first step in this process was the agricultural revolution. Through animal and plant domestication and the invention of the plow, tangled forests gave way to manicured fields. Irrigation channels reduced humans' dependency on rainfall. Permanent settlements sprang up, trade intensified, and roads were developed.

The next great technological leap was the Industrial Revolution, ushered in by the invention of the steam engine. While the Industrial Revolution gave rise to modern capitalism, it was—as Karl Marx and Friedrich Engels (1932/1977) observed—founded on the "subjection of nature's forces to man." Entire forests were destroyed for their lumber, mountains were levelled to expose coal seams, holes were punched deep into the Earth's surface to extract oil, rivers were dammed and rerouted, fields were smothered in cement, and smokestacks blackened daylight skies. We used technology to alter our environment in seemingly miraculous ways: Projects such as the diversion of the Colorado River westward through almost 500 kilometres of tunnels, dams, and aqueducts made possible the transformation of a bone-dry desert into the expansive metropolis of Los Angeles, and the City of Chicago even succeeded in permanently reversing the directional flow of its river so that sewage and industrial toxins were carried away from the city. The Industrial Revolution hastened urbanization. Cities became the centres of industry, and the advent of trains and highways allowed people to fill in the countryside with sprawling suburbs.

Marx and Engels argued that "the whole internal structure" of a society, including the "nature of individuals," was dependent on the extent to which its members could harness technology to transform natural resources into social goods (Marx & Engels, 1932/1977, p. 161). The lack of productive technology in early hunter-gatherer societies, they believed, kept the social structure of these groups very simple. There was little division of labour—perhaps just one chief who had authority over everyone else—because almost all of the members of a tribe had to busy themselves with looking for food sources. Because everybody performed the same tasks, there was little individuality.

Once humans began to transform vast stretches of forests into fields through agriculture, a more complex social structure could develop. A division of labour emerged because it only took a fraction of a society's members to produce enough food for everyone. Other members could be enlisted to produce tools or serve as warriors. An elite class also began to take shape as those who owned the agricultural food surpluses—and the land—could translate these resources into economic power.

As societies moved from agriculture to the production of goods, made possible on a grand scale by the technological advances of the Industrial Revolution, their social structure became even more stratified. Ever more sophisticated divisions of labour emerged as peasants migrated to cities to work for wages, and factory owners maximized efficiency by dividing up the job of a single skilled craftsman into discrete tasks that could be carried out by a team of relatively unskilled workers.

Marx and Engels's thesis leaves us with a puzzle: Why did some societies develop more quickly than others? Why, for example, did the Industrial Revolution take place in Western Europe and not Southern Africa? Jared Diamond, a professor of geography, argues that global inequalities emerged in prehistoric times and are rooted in differences in people's environments—namely, geographic differences in the availability of naturally occurring food sources (Diamond, 1997).

Diamond provides a compelling illustration of his thesis in New Zealand. A thousand years ago, the favourable climate of present-day New Zealand enabled a group of Polynesian settlers known as the Maori to develop a thriving agricultural society. At one point, a group of Maori moved to the Chatham Islands. For hundreds of years, this society—which became known as the Moriori—remained isolated from the Maori on the mainland. But because the Chatham Islands did not support the tropical crops that the Moriori brought with them, they reverted back to the hunting and gathering lifestyle of their pre-agricultural ancestors. Because natural resources were so scarce, the Moriori remained a small society with little division of labour. Meanwhile, the Maori continued to improve their agricultural technology so that they could support many people. Population density and resource abundance spawned a division of labour: a stratum (or segment of society) of craft- and tool-making specialists, a group of political leaders, and a warrior class. Over time, the Maori invaded and conquered other societies and acquired new technologies from them, such as guns. Everything came around full circle in 1835, when the Maori arrived in the Chatham Islands with axes, guns, and other weapons. Finding a tiny, peaceable society with simple technology and a rudimentary political system, the Maori slaughtered and enslaved the Moriori with ease.

Though cut from the same cloth, in the intervening centuries the Maori and Moriori developed in different directions based on adaptations to their environment. Diamond contends that the societies around the globe that developed the fastest were those graced with an abundance of plants and animals that could be readily domesticated. Many parts of Europe and Asia (particularly in the region known as the Fertile Crescent) naturally possessed many of the large mammals that could be domesticated—horses, pigs, cows, and sheep—as well as many of the cereals and grains that would become the backbone of agriculture, such as wheat. As these societies flourished and modernized, they settled new places, conquered the locals, and brought their technology, animals, and crops with them. This is the modern history of the Americas, whose relatively resource-deprived and preindustrial Indigenous societies were defeated by technologically advanced invaders from Europe.

Our society is now a long way from the world of rain dances and enchanted forests. As Max Weber (1904/2008) famously observed, the cold, hard rationality of science and economics drained the natural world of magic and mysticism. Modern societies primarily view the environment as a source of natural resources. Their success at taming and exploiting it encourages cultural attitudes of humans as separate from, and superior to, the natural world—a belief called **anthropocentrism** (literally, "man in the middle").

The Environment–Society Dialogue

18.1.3 Explain determinism and social constructivism, and the ways in which environment both guides and constrains social life.

Marx, Engels, and Diamond are sometimes labelled **determinists** because their theories imply that a society's environment, or the technology that it has developed to exploit its environment, determines everything else—from its social structure to individuals' thoughts. But it is perhaps more appropriate to say that they view material conditions as the most fruitful *starting point* for understanding the development of society. Marx and Engels's conception of social change is in fact rooted in the assumption that there is a reciprocal relationship between environmental and social conditions. The transition from an agricultural to a capitalistic mode of production, for example, was realized through social revolutions that reorganized society around commodity production.

Though many scholars reject the argument that the environment is the most important determinant of social structure, the notion that the environment guides and constrains social life has become an important part of sociological thought. For example, in the early 1900s an influential group of sociologists at the University of Chicago turned to **ecology**—the branch of science that studies the relationship between organisms and their environment—to explain the physical and social organization of modern cities. They examined how natural landscape features like rivers served as both resources and barriers that dictated where industries were placed and how city streets were laid out. Further, these Chicago sociologists saw the city as the "natural habitat of civilized man," in which various sections of the city were akin to ecological niches (Park & Burgess, 1925, p. 2). Human behaviour, it was believed, could be largely understood as social adaptations to a particular urban area: Ethnic and neighbourhood conflict was rooted in competition for scarce resources, such as jobs, and deviance was largely a product of living in derelict slums, not an individual pathology. Urban sociologists continue to explore the ways that the built environment shapes behaviour and social outcomes: Important recent studies explore the effect that one's neighbourhood has on one's chances for upward mobility.

Beliefs, values, and ideas also play an important role in guiding environment–society relations. For instance, there is evidence that the Europeans who settled the Americas committed wanton environmental destruction, slaughtering wildlife and burning forests in excess of their material needs, because they viewed the untamed wilderness as alien and literally God-forsaken. They aimed to reproduce the "civilized" pastoral landscapes of their beloved European countryside (Taylor, 1998). Historian William Cronon points out that the rapid development of Chicago, which transformed from prairieland to a teeming metropolis in only a few decades, cannot be explained by environmental factors alone. Despite the fact that other emerging cities such as St. Louis arguably boasted more natural advantages and were situated closer to existing markets and settlements, "boosters" successfully sold the promise of a great city to speculators on the East Coast, who bought up prairie lots that they had never seen. These investments, in turn, actually brought the dream of the Midwestern metropolis to life (Cronon, 1992).

Why do different people interpret the environment differently? The value that a person places on the Amazon rainforest, for example, depends on his or her position in society. The multinational lumber company sees a profitable commodity to be harvested, environmentalists see a priceless natural sanctuary to be left untouched, and the few remaining Indigenous communities see a home that enables their physical and spiritual well-being. The profit-seekers' orientation encourages them to cut down the forest, while the preservationists' orientation encourages them to protect it against any human incursion. Where do these differing orientations come from? The answer, many sociologists argue, can be found by studying the social contexts in which environment–society interactions are embedded. Research shows, for example, that people's socioeconomic

Dennis Donohue/Fotolia

Environmentalists rejoiced at the reintroduction of the endangered gray wolf to Yellowstone Park, but many local farmers viewed the event as a threat to their community and lifestyle. What are other examples of how social contexts shape the way that people interpret nature?

status and political orientation strongly condition whether or not they believe scientific claims about climate change or whether they consider human-induced ecological disruptions to be a problem at all (Taylor & Buttel, 1992).

To get a handle on how social contexts shape people's interactions with the environment, sociologist Rik Scarce documented the conflict that erupted over the reintroduction of the gray wolf into Yellowstone Park. In sociological terms, he was interested in the **social construction** of the environment—the process by which the natural world was interpreted and made meaningful to people who lived in the vicinity of the park. In an era that celebrates the restoration of ecosystems to their original state, the return of once-endangered gray wolves was a feel-good story to many people. But Scarce found that local farmers had a different view. One concern was economic: Wolves would eat their livestock. But their animosity toward the wolves ran deeper. For years, farmers felt that their community was slowly being undermined by the growing presence of wealthy neighbours who valued the area only for its wilderness and did not involve themselves in local life. This feeling led farmers to interpret the reintroduction of gray wolves as a misguided effort by "outsiders" to impose their will on the local community (Scarce, 2005).

People's attitudes toward ecological restoration in Yellowstone were patterned by their social position in society, revealing how our relationships with nature reflect who we are and what we value (Greider & Garkovich, 1994). We interact with the environment, then, not just in a material sense, but also in a profoundly social sense (Bell, 1994).

18.2 How Has Human Activity Harmed the Environment?

Tyler Olson/Shutterstock

Contemporary Environmental Problems

If our relationships with nature reflect who we are, then it may be time to take a long, hard look in the mirror. In pursuit of material comfort and profit, individuals and corporations have irreparably damaged the oceans and surface of the Earth and destabilized its natural equilibrium. The end of the last ice age over 10,000 years ago ushered in an era of natural global warming known as the Holocene; but in just 200 years we have sped up the process of global warming so much, and altered the Earth's topography and chemistry so dramatically, that we seem to have pushed the Earth into a new geologic era. Fittingly, geologists propose to call this era the Anthropocene (Zalasiewicz, Williams, Steffan, & Crutzen, 2010). Given the social and economic origins of so many contemporary environmental problems, it is appropriate that sociologists are increasingly turning their attention to an area of study that was once thought to be the exclusive domain of the natural sciences.

Global Warming

18.2.1 Identify the variety of environmental transformations caused by climate change.

In 1958, the chemist Charles David Keeling began monitoring the levels of carbon dioxide (CO_2) in the atmosphere. The results were startling. Each year evidenced a greater concentration of CO_2 than the last, and the escalation corresponded with global increases in the burning of **fossil fuels**, which are energy sources such as coal, oil, and natural gas that are made of fossils that decomposed over millions of years under high pressure. Though the concentration of atmospheric CO_2 held steady for thousands of years, over the last 50 years it has increased by 20 percent. CO_2 emissions can linger in the atmosphere for a century and produce what is called the **greenhouse effect** by allowing the sun's heat to pass through to the Earth's surface while stopping it from spreading back into space. As a result, the Earth's average temperature continues to rise. This is called **global warming**. To be sure, experts debate the precise degree to which CO_2 emissions contribute to global warming, but there is now wide agreement in the mainstream scientific community that human activity is the primary culprit.

Climatologist Michael Mann and his colleagues have demonstrated that global temperatures were more or less constant over the past 1,000 years and that the spike in global temperatures over the past half century maps onto the spike in atmospheric CO_2. The Intergovernmental Panel on Climate Change estimates that Earth's global surface temperature increased about 0.8°C over the twentieth century, and it estimates an increase of 4.0°C this century. While some skeptics point to the occasional April snowstorm or an unusually harsh winter as evidence that global warming is not happening, such an argument confuses short-term weather events with long-term climate trends. The long-term warming trend is unmistakable, and it is unequal to anything human history has witnessed. Figure 18.1 illustrates how CO_2 rates have risen significantly since 1960 and how temperatures remained relatively constant until they climbed noticeably starting in 1900.

While a growing number of automobiles, planes, and factories are producing ever-greater carbon emissions, deforestation is crippling the Earth's natural ability to absorb CO_2. Sea ice in the Arctic is melting so quickly that it may only be a few decades until the Arctic Sea is devoid of ice in the summer; and the thickness of wintertime sea ice may thin from 3.5 metres to less than 1 metre (Kolbert, 2007). Because the ocean absorbs more heat than does ice (which deflects light), sea ice retreat hastens the warming of the ocean, which in turn speeds up the melting of the ice floating on its surface. As a result of melting mountaintop glaciers, and because water expands as it warms, the sea level is rising. The small island nation of the Maldives, whose highest point is only 2.4 metres above sea level, is already contending with the effects

Figure 18.1 Rising Rates of Atmospheric CO_2 and Global Temperatures

Although the level of atmospheric CO_2 concentration—measured in parts per million (PPM)—fluctuates by season, the overall trend has been upward for many decades in a row. Notice the dramatic increase in average temperature, starting around 1900.

SOURCE: A) Based on data from Scripps Institute of Oceanography, Scripps CO_2 Program, 2012. B) Based on data from Jones and Mann, 2004; Jones et al., 2005.

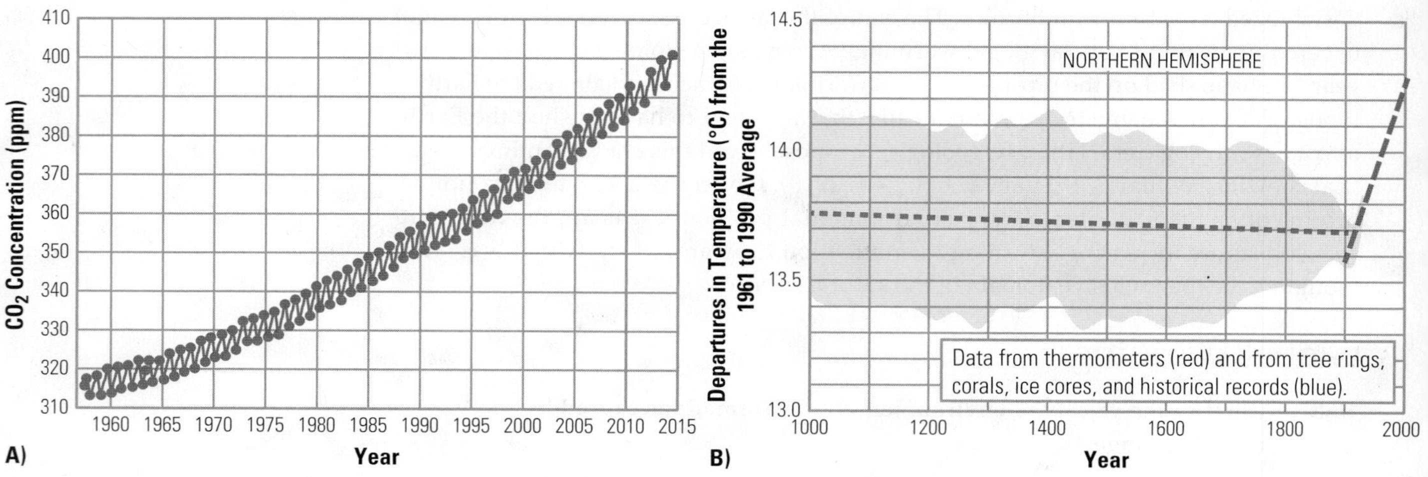

of sea level rise. The ocean is advancing over the rims of its islands and may eventually cover them entirely. The nation's president held an underwater cabinet meeting to draw attention to its plight, and he has even considered purchasing land in other countries in case the entire nation is forced to abandon its homeland.

The sea level is predicted to rise anywhere from several centimetres to 2 metres this century, depending on the extent to which nations act to limit carbon emissions. Assuming a "business-as-usual" scenario, meaning that companies and industries are allowed to continue environmentally harmful production practices in the pursuit of profit maximization, millions of people could be displaced, and some coastal cities like New Orleans might need to be abandoned, while many others would have to build massive levees. Global warming also means that millions of farmable hectares around the world may become arid and useless. While this would directly threaten critical food sources, it would also alter the Earth's ecosystems so dramatically that many plant and animal species would be unable to adapt. While the polar bear has become the poster child for animal endangerment due to global warming, scientists predict that as many as 20 to 50 percent of all animal species may become extinct over the next 100 years because of rising temperatures (Kolbert, 2007). Of course, some species would thrive in warmer weather—we can expect mosquitoes to expand their habitat, introducing malaria to new locales.

The Maldives, a small island nation, may soon be completely underwater as melting glaciers and warming ocean temperatures make the sea level rise. Some climatologists predict tens of millions of global environmental refugees in the coming decades as more coastline is swallowed by the sea.

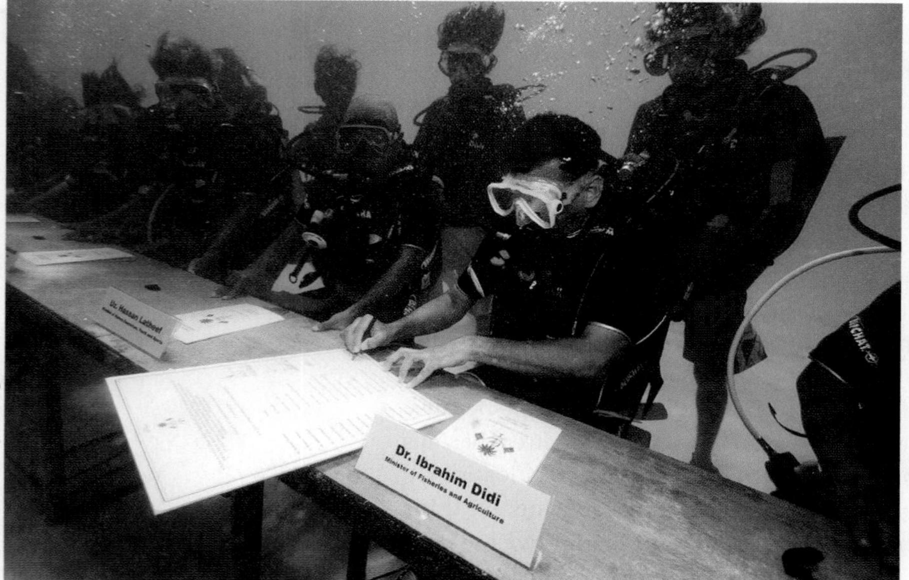

HO/AFP/Getty Images/Newscom

The notion of global warming does not fully capture the complexity of how carbon emissions impact the Earth's climate. Global warming upsets the balance of ecosystems to such a degree that they become destabilized. Some regions of the planet may even become temporarily cooler because of the disruption of oceanic and atmospheric circulation. Climatologists predict that extreme weather events, from heat waves to droughts to floods, will likely occur with greater frequency. We may see so-called hundred-year storms, like Hurricane Katrina, happening several times in a single generation as tropical storms are able to gather greater force from the additional heat and evaporation given off by warming oceans. Because of the variety of environmental changes that warming temperatures are producing, a growing number of scientists prefer to use the term **climate change** instead of *global warming*. Whatever name one chooses, the changes that corporations and consumers are producing in our environment through carbon emissions pose the single greatest hazard to both our ecosystems and humanity. Putting the brakes on global warming has been called the most important task of this century—and beyond.

Natural Resource Depletion

18.2.2 Discuss how the rapid depletion of major natural resources—oil, coal, forests, living species, and water—affects all forms of life.

On April 20, 2010, a British Petroleum offshore drilling operation known as the Deepwater Horizon exploded off the coast of Louisiana. The explosion killed 11 workers and spewed over 50,000 barrels of petroleum *per day* into the Gulf of Mexico for three months. Technology seemed unable to stem the flow, as rust-coloured crude oil burst through the underwater containment cap and crept toward the shorelines despite the use of chemical dispersants and controlled burns on the ocean's surface. The petroleum created an 200-square-kilometre "kill zone" in the ocean where virtually all sea life was destroyed. Black tar washed up on the coast, injuring wildlife and scaring off vacationers. Gulf Coast fishermen were out of work for months.

The United States is the world's leading consumer of oil, burning through almost 19 million barrels every day—one-third of which must be imported (India, whose population is about four times larger than that of the United States, consumes 3 million barrels per day). About 72 percent of the oil consumed in the United States is used to power its automobile-centred transportation system (United States Energy Information Administration, 2009). No one knows how long the world's supply of "black gold" will last, though many experts predict a timeframe of several generations, not centuries. Despite this forecast, wealthy countries have been slow to move away from their dependency on oil. In fact, most have sought to increase domestic oil production and invest in new techniques of oil extraction, such as open-pit mining of bitumen and hydraulic fracturing ("fracking"), to reduce their reliance on imports from the Middle East and Russia. Drilling rigs move farther and farther offshore and dig deeper and deeper, sometimes in dangerous ways (as we saw dramatically in the Deepwater Horizon explosion). And industry is setting its sights on protected natural areas like the Arctic National Wildlife Refuge in Alaska because of their potential caches of oil.

The explosion of the Deepwater Horizon drilling rig symbolizes the environmental and human costs of our dependency on increasingly scarce natural resources like oil. Why has North America been slow to adopt renewable energy sources such as solar and wind power?

US Coast Guard Photo/Alamy Stock Photo

Ever since the Industrial Revolution, humanity's energy requirements have escalated exponentially. The most valuable sources of energy, like petroleum, come from deep underground or within mountains. As highlighted in Table 18.1, oil, coal, and natural gas—which are nonrenewable resources, meaning that there is a limited supply that cannot be replaced—currently provide about 85 percent of the energy consumed around the world (United States Energy Information Administration, 2010).

Table 18.1 Global Energy Sources (Quadrillion BTU)

This table presents the absolute level of energy produced at a global level by each source in 2005 and 2010, as well as projections for the next decades.

Total World	2005	2010	2015	2020	2025	2030	2035
Liquids (gasoline, diesel, and kerosene)	170.8	173.2	187.2	195.8	207.0	216.6	225.2
Natural Gas	105.0	116.7	127.3	138.0	149.4	162.3	174.7
Coal	122.3	149.4	157.3	164.6	179.7	194.7	209.1
Nuclear	27.5	27.6	33.2	38.9	43.7	47.4	51.2
Other (including renewables like solar and wind)	45.4	55.2	68.5	82.2	91.7	100.6	109.5
Total	**471.0**	**522.1**	**573.5**	**619.5**	**671.5**	**721.6**	**769.7**

SOURCES: Figures for 2005 and 2010 based on data from United States Energy Information Administration, International Energy Statistics database (as of March 2011); *Balances of OECD and Non-OECD Statistics*, International Energy Agency, 2010 (www.iea.org). Projections based on *Annual Energy Outlook 2011*, by United States Energy Information Administration, 2011, Washington, DC: U.S. Department of Energy; AEO 2011 National Energy Modeling System, 2011; World Energy Projection System Plus, 2011.

The Industrial Revolution was built on coal, which released plumes of black smoke into the sky as it fired everything from steam engines to the furnaces that melted iron. Today, coal combustion still generates a third of the electricity consumed by Americans and is the world's greatest source of electricity (United States Department of Energy, 2011). Like drilling for oil, obtaining coal can be disruptive and unsafe. Massive tunnels are burrowed into the ground or the tops of mountains are sheared off with the aid of dynamite. Thousands of miners around the world are killed each year by underground explosions or corridor collapses. Cleaning and processing coal produces large amounts of toxic sludge, which is often stored behind makeshift dams next to where the coal is extracted. In one infamous incident in West Virginia, 132 million gallons of sludge breached a dam and poured down the mountainside, levelling a town and killing 125 residents (Erikson, 1976). Though coal combustion is a leading source of air pollution and global warming, it is attractive because coal reserves are widely dispersed around the globe. This means that many countries do not need to rely on imports because they can extract it domestically.

Perhaps the most environmentally harmful form of resource depletion is deforestation. Tropical rainforests provide a natural habitat for two-thirds of all species on the planet, including many plants that are used in medicine, and play a crucial role in capturing CO_2 and converting it into oxygen. Though forests are often cut down to produce paper and lumber, most deforestation is a result of farming. As the global demand for beef continues to grow, firms and individual ranchers are eager to burn down stands of trees and replace them with pastures where cattle can graze (see Figure 18.2).

A Greenpeace report attributes 80 percent of deforestation in the Brazilian Amazon to cattle ranching, and the United Nations estimates that, through the slashing and burning of CO_2-absorbing trees, meat production contributes more to global warming than either car tailpipes or industrial smokestacks (Greenpeace, 2009). Deforested areas also suffer greatly from soil erosion, sometimes degenerating into desert-like landscapes. Ecologists estimate that deforestation is causing the extinction of as many as 50,000 plant and animal species every year (137 species per day), and they predict that the rainforests, which once covered 14 percent of the Earth's land surface, may be entirely gone by the end of this century unless major restrictions are put in place and enforced (Kolbert, 2007).

Animal and plant species also face extinction because we consume them faster than they can reproduce. A dramatic example is the collapse of the cod-fishing industry. Cod were once so numerous off the eastern coast of Canada that explorers reported catching them with baskets. Over the course of the twentieth century, massive mechanized trawlers replaced small fishing boats. The sea filled up with

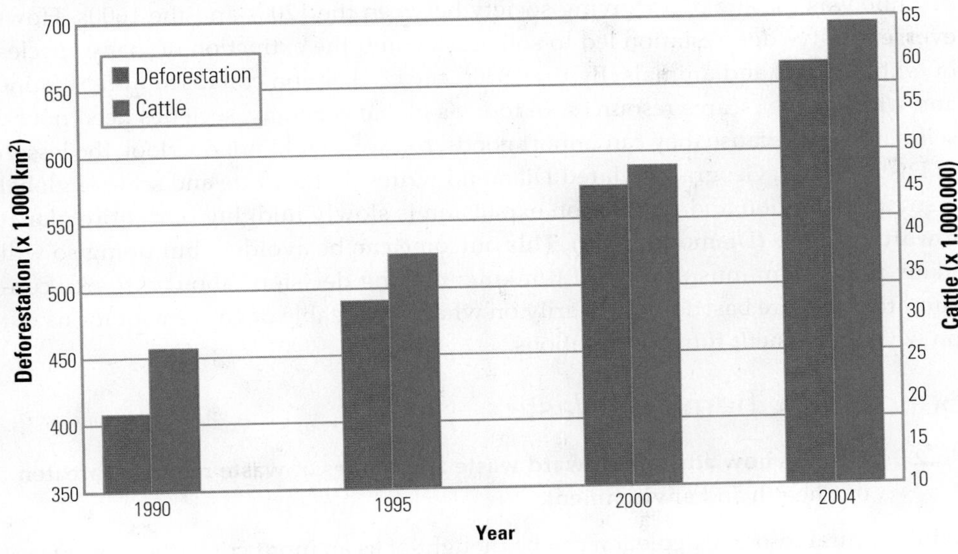

Figure 18.2 Total Cattle Herd Size and Deforestation in the Amazon

SOURCE: Based on data from *Amazon Cattle Footprint: Mato Grosso: State of Destruction*, by Greenpeace, 2009, São Paulo: Greenpeace Brazil (http://www.greenpeace.org/international/en/publications/reports/amazon-cattle-footprint-mato/).

gigantic nets that scraped the bottom of the ocean floor. Profits soared as trawlers worked around the clock, processing and freezing the fish below deck. At their peak in 1968, trawlers hauled in 800,000 tonnes of cod in a year. But by the early 1990s, cod were so overfished that their entire population was estimated to be just 1 percent of what it had been 30 years before. A complete ban on cod fishing was implemented in 1992, leading to the loss of over 40,000 jobs. To this day, however, the cod population has not rebounded. Though the fishing industry now places restrictive quotas on the amount of a given species that can be caught, the number of marine species that are threatened by "factory fishing" steadily increases ("A Run on the Banks," 2001).

Water is one of the most precious natural resources and may be the one most taken for granted in developed countries. Though global access to clean water has increased dramatically over the past several decades, many experts worry that supply will not keep pace with demand. Around the world, the amount of water held in *aquifers*—naturally occurring underground wells—is declining. The Ogallala Aquifer, which is tucked beneath parts of eight states in the American Midwest and which supplies almost a third of the groundwater used for irrigation in the United States, is currently only regenerating 10 percent of the amount of water that is taken out each year. But anticipated future water shortages may very well make water the most valuable natural resource of the next century.

Expanding populations and global development are also leading to conflict between cities, states, and nations as they vie to secure the rights to access, divert, and dam bodies of water to secure their own livelihood. The longest river in the world, the Nile, is a case in point. The Nile has nurtured Egypt for thousands of years. In order to prevent annual flooding and create a reliable water reservoir, Egypt constructed an enormous dam across the Nile in the 1960s. It is estimated that the Aswan Dam increased Egypt's irrigated land area by one-third, and the dam also became an important source of hydroelectricity. However, upstream countries such as Uganda and Tanzania complain that colonial-era agreements prevent them from building their own dams. The 10 upstream nations demand a new treaty that grants them greater rights to the Nile's precious water. As a downstream nation, Egypt worries that such a treaty would mean that the river flow is greatly diminished by the time it reaches the

Aswan Dam, and conservationists fret over whether the Nile can support such massive development without being reduced to a trickle.

Natural resource depletion is not a unique problem of the modern era. Historians point to Easter Island as evidence. It appears that the small island off the coast of Chile was the site of a thriving society between the 1200s and the 1600s. However, extensive deforestation led to soil erosion and the extinction of many species of edible plants and animals. By the 1800s, the civilization collapsed amid famine and warfare over scarce resources. In today's global economy, societies need not be self-sufficient because they can import goods, but we should not overlook the lesson of Easter Island. Geographer Jared Diamond writes that the rate and scale of global resource depletion and population expansion is slowly nudging our entire planet toward collapse (Diamond, 1995). This outcome can be avoided, but doing so will likely require an unusual way of thinking: making decisions about resource consumption that are based not primarily on what is profitable or convenient for us but on what will benefit future generations.

Solid and Chemical Waste

18.2.3 Discuss how attitudes toward waste and modes of waste removal threaten our health and environment.

While natural resource depletion can be thought of as an input crisis, the world faces an output crisis that is just as serious. Though the production of some amount of waste is unavoidable, wealthy countries like the United States create such an excess of garbage that they have been labelled "throw-away societies." Much of this is about convenience: Disposable razors, diapers, and cups mean that we do not have to sharpen blades, clean messy cloth diapers, or walk around with our own beverage containers. But all those plastic bags, Styrofoam peanuts, and wrappers add up.

Despite the mantra of "reduce, reuse, recycle," the amount of trash that each American produces in a day has nearly doubled between 1960 and 2011 (from about 1.1 kilograms to almost 2.2 kilograms). This equals 227 million tonnes of solid waste per year. To this annual figure must be added the nearly *7 billion* tonnes of industrial waste generated by American businesses and the untold amounts of hazardous waste—from paint can lids to spent nuclear fuel—that require special collection and storage methods (Environmental Protection Agency, 2011). Less than a third of plastic and glass bottles produced in the United States actually get recycled, and recycling still requires massive energy inputs (Environmental Protection Agency, 2011).

In Canada, municipal waste generation has been increasing steadily since 1990. Canada produced 777 kilograms per capita of municipal waste in 2008, twice as much as the best performer, Japan. Canada's municipal waste generated per capita has been steadily increasing since 1990. It has consistently been higher than in the U.S. over the past two decades. Figure 18.3 shows these trends: What is our garbage trying to tell us about the "throw-away society" lifestyle?

In 1960, virtually no one thought about recycling, yet today most people know about the need to recycle. Towns and cities (and most companies) encourage recycling by providing waste disposal bins on various properties, and state, provincial, and federal laws require many kinds of recycling as well. Take the increase in paper waste: North Americans increasingly prefer to read and consume digital versions of newspapers, magazines, and books rather than hard copies. In workplaces, people rely mostly on digital forms of communication, including e-mail and websites. Yet, despite the awareness and increased recycling and digital practices, we are generating more unrecycled waste than ever!

Why are North Americans producing so much more trash today than they did 50 years ago? Given that elaborate packaging helps producers sell commodities and that most consumers pay a flat fee for garbage removal regardless of how much

Figure 18.3 What Our Garbage Says About Us

Canada ranks in last place out of 17 countries and gets a "D" grade on the municipal waste generation report card.

SOURCE: Conference Board of Canada "Municipal Waste Generation" http://www.conferenceboard.ca/hcp/details/environment/municipal-waste-generation.aspx. Used with permission.

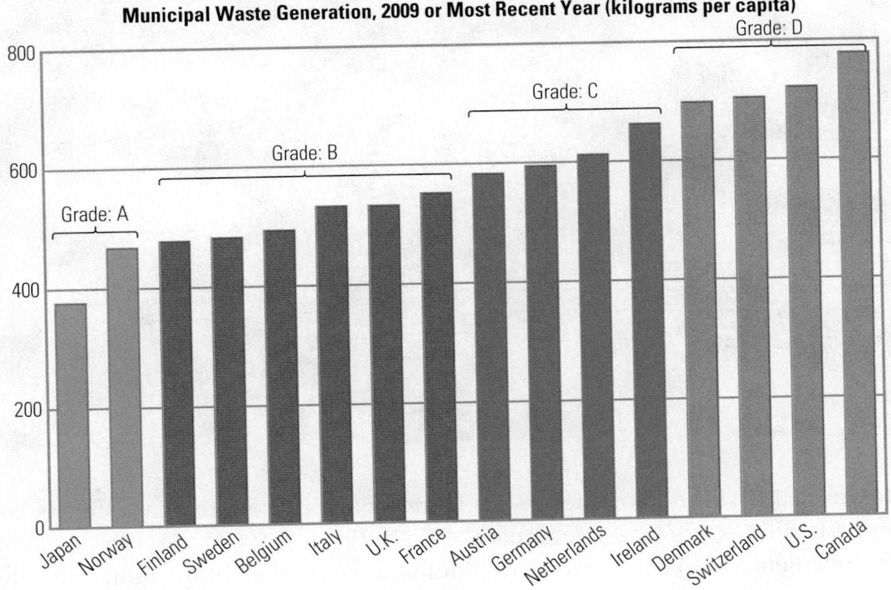

they throw out, both buyers and sellers have little incentive to be more conscientious about waste. In addition, many products—from pens to toasters to cars—are increasingly designed to provide a limited amount of use before they need to be replaced. This allows producers to make more money. Consumers generally accept it because these less durable products are cheaper, and it is easier to buy a new one than to get the old one fixed. But those old pens, toasters, and cars have to go somewhere.

Where does all of this waste go, and with what consequences? Most of our waste is simply dumped into massive holes and covered over. Though it may be out of sight and out of mind, much of our trash (like that old TV) will linger in landfills for centuries. The problem is that these landfills keep filling up, and nobody wants a trash heap in their backyard. New York City ran out of landfill space in the early 2000s and had to pay hundreds of millions of dollars per year to ship its trash to cash-strapped regions of Pennsylvania and Virginia, where poorer residents now *do* live with trash heaps in their backyard. Similarly, the city of Toronto shipped 140 truckloads of waste to a site in Michigan, until the municipality purchased a new landfill site in 2006 for $220 million (Hasham, 2013).

Landfills are also toxic stews where battery fluid mingles with mercury, and household cleaners and other industrial hazards slowly leach into the surrounding earth and groundwater. In 1953, the Hooker Chemical Company covered over a giant chemical dump known as Love Canal and sold it to the city of Niagara Falls, New York, for a dollar. Convinced that the hazardous waste was safely sealed below ground, the city built a school on the site and oversaw the construction of about 100 nearby homes. It took 25 years for residents to realize there was a problem. After a period of heavy rain in 1978, rusted metal drums filled with carcinogenic waste broke through the surface of people's backyards; puddles of oozing toxins choked trees and plants to death; and children playing outside returned home with chemical burns. The number of area miscarriages, birth defects, and cancer cases skyrocketed. While the Love Canal tragedy led to more stringent federal regulations of toxic waste disposal,

Benoit Daoust/Shutterstock

Tailpipe emissions from automobiles harm the atmosphere—and our lungs. What alternative forms of transportation do you think might be available for commuters in cities like Toronto?

there are still thousands of sites in the United States where toxic waste has been improperly disposed of (Szasz & Meuser, 1997).

Convenience has its consequences. But the full cost of all of the industrial waste and throwaway products and packaging that sustain modern lifestyles and corporate profits is not reflected in their sticker price. Though efficient waste management systems seem to make rubbish disappear, the environment pays the penalty. As Love Canal indicates, the cost may also be borne by people's bodies. This is especially true in poor countries, where erratic trash collection and the lack of proper facilities for the disposal of toxins means that waste may spread disease as it festers in the streets.

Air and Water Pollution

18.2.4 Discuss the impact human consumption has on air and water supplies.

The freeways of Los Angeles were designed to whisk commuters across the sprawling city at speeds of 55 miles per hour. These days, however, the average rush hour speed on Los Angeles freeways may be 5 or 10 miles per hour, and "rush hour" now means a time window as wide as 5:00 to 10:00 a.m. and 3:00 to 7:00 p.m. The average Los Angeles resident spends almost four days a year sitting in traffic. Yet even as those millions of cars sit idle on congested freeways, they continue to pollute the air. Los Angeles is legendary for its **smog**, a smoky haze produced when tailpipe emissions that linger in the atmosphere chemically react with the sunlight. Los Angeles continues to endure "smog alerts," where schools are closed and residents are warned to stay inside because of poor air quality. Smog can burn the lungs and irritate the eyes and nose, and it has been known to aggravate asthma, bronchitis, and other respiratory illnesses.

Toxic air pollution is as much a product of smokestacks as tailpipes. In one year, a single coal-based electrical plant pumps tens of thousands of metric tonnes of noxious gases into the atmosphere. These include nitrogen oxide and sulfur dioxide, which react with water molecules in the air to create acid that returns to earth when it rains. So-called **acid rain** has been shown to kill plant life and marine animals. Industrial pollutants have also severely depleted the atmosphere's ozone layer, which shields the Earth's surface from the sun's ultraviolet radiation. UV rays are harmful to a number of plant and animal species and have been linked to cancer and cataracts in humans. The toxins most responsible for ozone depletion are chlorofluorocarbons (CFCs), which until recently were commonly found in aerosol sprays and liquid coolants.

No one can avoid inhaling microscopic pollutants produced from the combustion of fossil fuels. Their effects can mimic those of cigarette smoke, and it is estimated that 50,000 Americans die each year from cardiopulmonary diseases linked to breathing in toxic particles (Dollemore, 2008). In October 2010, it was estimated that almost 600 residents of Hong Kong had died since the beginning of the year because of air pollution. Over the same nine-month period, experts also attributed a staggering 4.63 million doctor visits and 45,000 hospitalizations to poor air quality caused by coal-burning plants and automobiles (Bryskine, 2010). Though city air quality is improving somewhat in developed societies as a result of cleaner technologies, it is worsening in developing countries that must rely on cheaper, dirtier methods to produce energy. Mexico City's smog is so thick that the nearby mountains are often shrouded in brown haze. Clean air and healthy lungs are luxuries it can't afford.

Clean, potable water is another luxury that many people in developing countries cannot afford. Over half the world's rural population still lacks access to clean water, leading desperate people to rely on polluted sources—including sewage—to supply their cooking, bathing, and drinking needs. Exposure to contaminated water causes tens of thousands of deaths each year worldwide from preventable diseases such as dysentery and cholera—diseases that Americans have not had to worry about for many years.

North Americans, however, are hardly immune to concerns about water quality. Aside from acid rain, contamination of rivers, streams, and aquifers from agriculture and industry is common. Unlike in Canada, where farm waste is regulated under federal and provincial laws, in the United States farm waste for the most part is not regulated under federal laws. Cow manure, which is often filled with infectious agents such as *E. coli*, regularly enters waterways as runoff after a rainstorm. Agricultural runoff, which can also include chemical agents from synthetic fertilizers, is the single biggest source of water pollution in the United States. It is not, however, the only source. A *New York Times* investigation found thousands of instances where companies openly flouted the Clean Water Act but were never punished. In one case, the drinking water in a West Virginia town was contaminated with lead, manganese, and nickel because coal companies purposely injected over 2 billion gallons of toxic sludge into the ground over a period of five years. Residents who continued using the stained yellow drinking water suffered from severe rashes, rotting teeth, miscarriages, and kidney and bladder diseases. The problem of chemical wastes being discharged into drinking water goes beyond the coal industry, encompassing natural gas extraction ("fracking"), dry cleaners, gas stations, and sewage treatment plants (Duhigg, 2009). Bacterial contamination of water in the town of Walkerton, Ontario, killed at least 7 people and made over 2,300 others sick as a result of improper practices and systematic fraud by the public utility operators following the privatization of water testing in Ontario.

Pollution is cheap. Consumers want inexpensive goods and sources of energy, and producers operate in a cutthroat environment where they must keep down costs to be competitive. Unless firm, enforceable limits are placed on the amount of air and water pollutants that businesses can generate, or unless businesses are given financial incentives for adopting "greener" (or more environmentally friendly) practices, we should expect pollution to worsen. It is unlikely that most producers and consumers will voluntarily discontinue "business as usual" and pay the higher cost of sustainability.

18.3 How Do Environmental Factors Impact Inequality?

Philip Lange/Shutterstock

The Environmental Movement and Social Inequality

In response to the unfolding ecological crisis, a powerful social movement has emerged over the last half century that challenges "business as usual." The movement has made notable gains in remedying some of the damage wrought by society on the environment, but socially produced environmental problems have also led to new social problems. And not everyone suffers equally: The wealthiest people tend to reap most of the benefits and suffer few of the costs of environmental problems. One of the most vital contributions that sociologists have made to the study of environmental problems is an understanding of how they are linked to social inequality.

The Environmental Movement

18.3.1 Identify early preservationist figures and movements that have contributed to environmental awareness.

As early as the 1800s, there were those who sensed something tragic about the destruction of natural landscapes in the face of urbanization. None may be more famous than the philosopher Henry David Thoreau. His 1854 book *Walden* documented a two-year experiment in which he built and lived in a cottage on the wooded outskirts of Boston. Living simply and close to the land, he wrote, rejuvenated the spirit and reawakened the senses. A rallying cry against overcivilization and the social ills of the city, *Walden* framed the discourse for future generations of **preservationists** (Brulle, 1996)—those who believe that the environment has intrinsic value and should be maintained in as pristine a state as possible. The leading figure of early efforts to preserve the countryside and wilderness in the United States was John Muir, who successfully petitioned U.S. president Theodore Roosevelt—an avid outdoorsman—to set aside the Yosemite

Elena Elisseeva/Shutterstock

Algonquin Park is the oldest provincial park in Canada and has been protected by the Ontario government since the late 1800s. What pristine environments can you think of that are most threatened today by development?

area as a protected national park in 1906. Among Muir's many other lasting legacies was founding the Sierra Club, which to this day is the most influential environmental protection group in the United States. Firmly a believer in preserving nature in pristine form, Muir rejected the utilitarian view of **conservationists**, who argue that the point of environmental protection ought to be to responsibly manage natural resources so that they are available for commercial use by future generations.

Americans were usually ahead of Canadians in establishing conservationist goals, likely due to the smaller numbers of settlers and a pioneer mentality that saw Canada's natural resources as unlimited. Workers in the lumber industry, who became concerned about the rapid depletion of Canadian forests, championed early conservationist efforts. These lumbermen established the Canadian Forestry Association in 1900. The first Canadian national park—Banff—was established in 1885, followed by Yoho and Glacier national parks in 1886 (Hummel, 2010). The establishment of the parks initially had much to do with generating revenue for the government through tourism along the newly built Canadian National Railway line (Hummel, 2010); however, in 1911, Canada became the first nation to establish an agency devoted to preserving and managing its national parks. The Dominion Parks Branch, now Parks Canada, ensures the preservation of over 200,000 square kilometres of parks and reserves that feature a remarkable array of landscapes and wildlife (Campbell, 2011). The preservation of Canada's natural environment and cultural heritage sites is a key feature of Canadian national identity.

It took until the second half of the twentieth century for environmental problems to begin to be seen as dire threats to humanity. There may have been no greater wakeup call than Rachel Carson's bestselling 1962 book *Silent Spring*. The book's title referred to an imagined future where songbirds could no longer be heard because they had all been killed by pesticides like DDT. Carson blamed the government for allowing the use of toxins without knowing the long-term consequences, and she compared pesticides to nuclear fallout: "Can anyone believe," she asked, "it is possible to lay down such a barrage of poisons on the surface of the earth without making it unfit for all life?" (Carson, 1962, p. 8).

Silent Spring directly led to the ban on the use of DDT in the United States. A worldwide ban was later formalized under the Stockholm Convention. But, perhaps more fundamentally, the book led North Americans and others around the world to question

Anonymous/AP Images

The Cuyahoga River fire was one of the key moments that inspired the environmental movement of the late 1960s and 1970s. Can you think of any contemporary environmental problems that have resulted in popular political protest?

their faith in better living through chemistry. Carson argued that science had been hijacked by the titans of industry, who were driven by short-term profit, and that there was little reason to assume that chemical producers cared about public safety. She also challenged society's anthropocentrism, contending that humans are only one component of a fragile ecosystem that, if further degraded, could undermine the foundations of mankind's existence. Grassroots movements began to spring up across the country, advocating for stronger government regulation of the chemical industry.

Before the decade of the 1960s ended, and amid the emergence of the civil rights movement, several catastrophes brought the environmental movement to a head. In 1969, a massive oil spill off the coast of California killed thousands of marine animals and blackened the shoreline of Santa Barbara, while Cleveland's Cuyahoga River actually caught on fire because the surface of its brown, oozing, toxic water was covered in oil. These events sparked tremendous public outrage, resulting in the first Earth Day the following year and a string of significant political victories for the environmental movement. Most notably, the Nixon administration—which was generally on the side of "big business" and thus viewed environmentalism as a threat to productivity and profit—bowed to this unprecedented groundswell of popular protest by creating the Environmental Protection Agency (EPA) and signing the Clean Water Act into law. Meanwhile, bestselling books like Paul Ehrlich's *The Population Bomb* (1968) sounded alarm bells about the potential collapse of societies as an exploding global population pressed up against the limits of finite natural resources (see Chapter 19 for more details). Though new technologies demonstrated that humans could extend natural limits (for example, genetically altering plants to increase crop yields), more and more people recognized that technology was not a cure-all as the scope of environmental risks kept increasing.

Despite growing public concern about our planet's health, efforts to enact environmentally friendly policies are routinely thwarted by political alliances between private businesses and conservative lawmakers—many of whom voice skepticism about scientific claims regarding environmental problems or contend that "going green" will harm the economy (Dunlap & McCright, 2011). United States president George W. Bush, for instance, memorably refused to sign the Kyoto Protocol, an international pledge to cut carbon emissions, because, he said, it was not clear that global warming was caused by people and the pact would result in a loss of productivity and jobs. In 2011, Canadian prime minister Stephen Harper withdrew from the Kyoto Protocol, citing the accord's failure to include the world's two largest greenhouse gas emitters, China and the United States. More recently, companies engaged in fracking, a process by which oil and natural gas are extracted from shale rock by the injection of millions of gallons of water and sand laced with toxic chemicals into the ground, have been able to avoid submitting to more stringent environmental regulations and having to disclose the contents of what they pump into the earth (which they argue is a trade secret) by maintaining close ties with business-friendly governors of the American states where they drill.

Environmental Justice

18.3.2 Discuss environmental racism and what progress is being made to ensure equal protection for all people.

In the summer of 1978, a trucking company illegally dumped 31,000 gallons of used transformer oil along hundreds of miles of roads in Warren County, North Carolina. The location was no accident: This was the poorest county in the state, and 65 percent of its residents were black. Adding insult to injury, the state decided to place a hazardous waste landfill in the area that would store the used oil but also serve as a repository for toxins from other counties. Rather than accept their fate, locals fought back. As a group, they lobbied against the proposal, filed a civil lawsuit, and were arrested for staging protests. The language and strategies they employed helped shape an emerging social movement (Szasz & Meuser, 1997).

While the environmental movement of the 1960s and 1970s advocated for the preservation of natural areas and for increased federal regulations to protect air and water, many minorities and people in poverty felt that the movement did not address the problems that affected them. Their concerns were grounded in the disproportionate number of hazardous waste facilities that were placed in their communities and in the higher rates of asthma and other environment-induced illnesses that they had to endure. A 1987 report issued by the United Church of Christ found, based on a comparison of zip codes across the United States, that race was the most significant predictor of living close to a hazardous waste facility (e.g., garbage incinerator, sewage treatment plant). As shown in Figure 18.4, the higher the concentration of minorities in a particular zip code, the greater the number of hazardous waste facilities it contained (Commission for Racial Justice, 1987).

The report's findings echoed the pioneering research of sociologist Robert Bullard, who showed that 21 of Houston's 25 garbage dumps and incinerators were located

Figure 18.4 Percentages of People of Colour Living Near Hazardous Waste Facilities, United States

SOURCE: Based on data from *Toxic Wastes and Race at Twenty, 1987–2007*, by Robert D. Bullard, Paul Mohai, Robin Saha, and Beverly Wright, 2007, Cleveland: United Church of Christ Justice and Witness Ministries (http://www.ejnet.org/ej/twart.pdf).

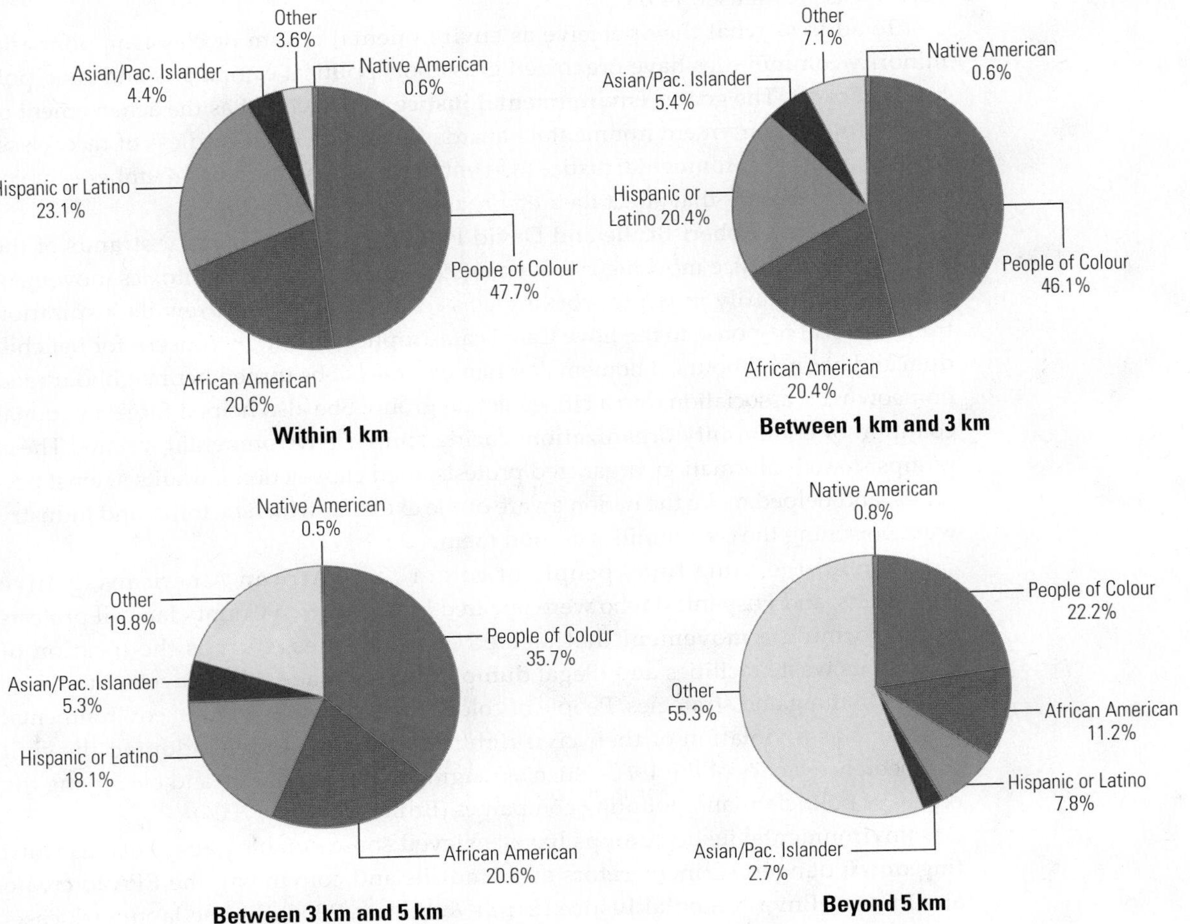

in black neighbourhoods even though blacks comprised only 25 percent of the city's population (Bullard, 1983). The disproportionate share of environmental hazards has been labelled **environmental racism** by Bullard and other sociologists (Bullard, 1990). Though the term *environmental racism* suggests conscious discrimination against minorities, it is often the case that polluting industries choose the path of least resistance, placing facilities where land is cheaper and where residents are not politically organized (Brulle & Pellow, 2006). Such decisions often seem to be based on economics rather than race, but the enduring association between poverty and nonwhites in the United States means that the areas where environmental hazards are clustered usually have the highest concentration of minorities. In the past, discriminatory housing practices forced minorities to live in undesirable neighbourhoods with greater levels of pollution; today, those with low incomes simply cannot afford to move to cleaner, healthier places.

New York University's Institute for Environmental Medicine has been looking at the link between air pollution and health in the South Bronx, historically one of the poorest neighbourhoods in the city, and in the 1970s and 1980s one of the poorest in the country. Home to many poor and working-class people of colour, the South Bronx also hosts over a dozen waste-transfer stations, a sewage-treatment plant, and miles of congested expressways. It has one of the highest hospitalization rates for asthma among children in New York. By placing air-monitoring devices in students' backpacks, the NYU researchers found that children in the South Bronx were exposed to unhealthy levels of air pollution from car exhaust on a regular basis. They also saw that the students exhibited symptoms of asthma, such as wheezing, during the times when the amount of air pollution was highest (Fernandez, 2006). This and other studies show that people in the poorest neighbourhoods, most of whom are nonwhite, often do not breathe the same air or drink the same water as their wealthier counterparts (Szasz & Meuser, 1997).

To address what they perceive as environmental racism or classism, poor and minority communities have organized grassroots political campaigns and sued polluters in court. The goal is **environmental justice**, conceived of as the achievement of equal protection from environmental hazards for all people, regardless of race, class, or geography. Environmental justice also entails giving community members a voice in shaping decisions that affect their environment and their health.

Sociologists Robert Brulle and David Pellow identify two major strands of the environmental justice movement that emerged in the 1980s. The antitoxics movement was based primarily in white working-class communities and drew its inspiration from the local response to the Love Canal catastrophe. Fuelled by concern for her children and her neighbours, a homemaker named Lois Gibbs turned her neighbourhood homeowner's association into a citizen action group. She also helped forge a national coalition of community organizations facing similar environmental threats. These groups shared information, organized protests, filed class-action lawsuits against polluters, and helped make the nation aware of the extent to which factories and industry were poisoning the communities around them.

Around the same time, people of colour (e.g., African Americans, Native Americans, and Hispanics) who were inspired by the Warren County landfill protests began forming a movement that tackled similar issues, such as the location of hazardous waste facilities and illegal dumping. What made their movement unique was its framing and strategies. People of colour explicitly defined local environmental problems as a violation of their civil rights, and many of them adopted the civil disobedience tactics of the 1960s, such as staging massive protests and occupying the offices of politicians and polluting companies (Brulle & Pellow, 2006).

Environmental justice groups have achieved some notable gains, such as shutting down dangerous incinerators and landfills and convincing the EPA to create an Office of Environmental Justice (Brulle & Pellow, 2006). In one landmark case,

Navajo in New Mexico—who were unwittingly exposed to harmful levels of radiation for decades by mining companies that extracted uranium on behalf of the U.S. military—helped propel the passage of a law in 1990 that requires the government to compensate people who have suffered from nuclear bomb testing and uranium mining. Increasingly, environmental justice movements are cropping up in developing countries, where they challenge the business-as-usual tradeoff of pollution for profit and attempt to hold wealthy countries accountable for local environmental problems caused by global warming.

The Social Dimension of Natural Disasters

18.3.3 Explain the reasons some groups are more adversely affected by natural disasters than other groups.

In July of 1995, the residents of Chicago baked in one the city's most severe heat waves. In just one week, over 500 people died as a direct result of the heat. Medical workers were so overwhelmed that they had to store the corpses in refrigerated meatpacking trucks until they could perform autopsies. Were these deaths the unavoidable consequence of natural events? While the mayor, and for the most part the media, framed them this way, NYU sociologist Eric Klinenberg argued that the massive loss of life was in fact a "structurally determined catastrophe" that could mostly have been prevented (Klinenberg, 1999, p. 240). The heat wave did not take lives at random. Rather, Klinenberg discovered that vulnerability was concentrated in "the low-income, elderly, African-American, and more violent regions of the metropolis" (p. 250). Poor neighbourhoods were underserved by municipal agencies that could have reached out to social isolates and people without air conditioners, and their local hospitals were overwhelmed and understaffed. Klinenberg also argued that the city had allowed poor neighbourhoods to become so deteriorated and dangerous that residents feared leaving their homes even as the temperatures rose to dangerous levels. As a result, they quietly and anonymously perished.

Many of the people left behind after Hurricane Katrina forced the evacuation of New Orleans were poor and black. How does the sociological concept of "environmental inequality" challenge typical understandings of natural disasters?

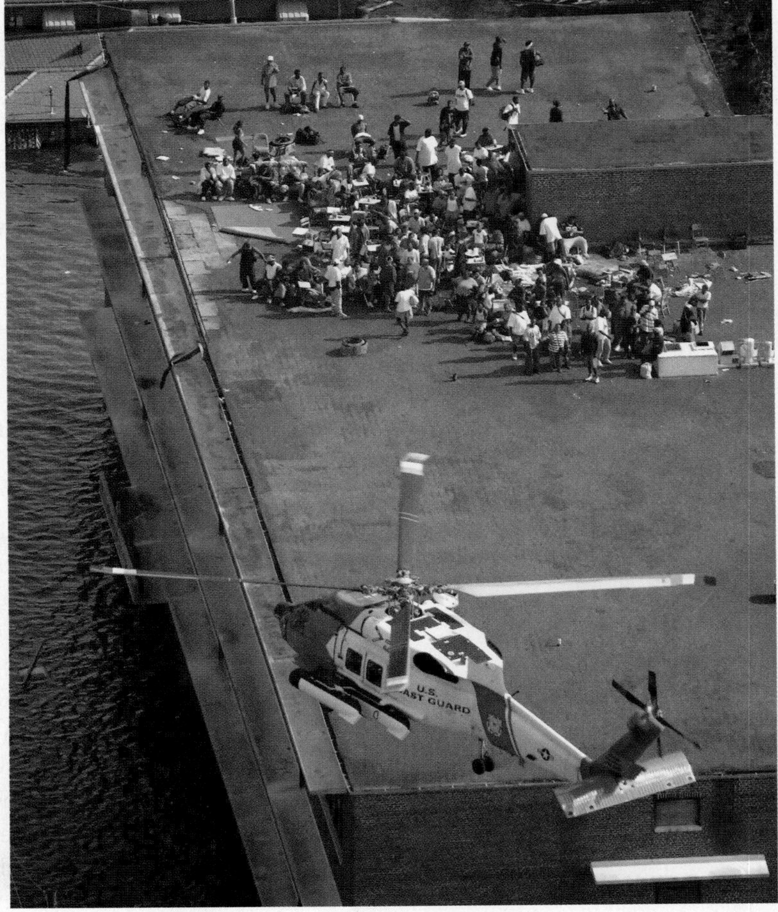

David J. Phillip/AFP/Getty Images/Newscom

While sociologists do not deny the destructive power of natural disasters such as floods, earthquakes, and heat waves, they analyze the ways in which the outcomes of such events—such as who lives and who dies, who evacuates and who remains—are patterned by social forces. In the wake of Hurricane Katrina, most of the desperate faces of those stranded on their roofs or packed into the temporary shelter of New Orleans's Convention Center were poor and black. Despite these arresting scenes, politicians and media pundits hotly debated whether or not poor people of colour disproportionately suffered from the storm. Sociologists played a key role in offering evidence of social disparities and revealing government neglect of the vulnerable.

NYU sociologist Patrick Sharkey found that blacks, along with the elderly, were much more likely to die as a result of Hurricane Katrina than would be expected given their presence in the population; and he showed that deaths were concentrated in New Orleans's black communities (Sharkey, 2007). A panel of social scientists convened by the Social Science Research Council (SSRC) showed that many of the people who stayed behind lacked the necessary means to evacuate, most notably a car and money for a hotel. The SSRC panel also documented the major role that governmental disorganization and miscommunication played in hindering assistance to vulnerable residents. The Federal Emergency Management Agency (FEMA), for instance, failed to coordinate evacuation plans with local officials and neglected to give the go-ahead to the U.S. military to begin airdrops of food and water rations (Social Science Research Council, 2006).

Socially patterned differences in vulnerability are even more pronounced on a global scale, as revealed by the earthquake that rocked poverty-stricken Haiti in 2010. Lacking the money to erect reinforced buildings, Haitians had little choice but to inhabit structures that crumbled under the force of the 7.0-magnitude quake, killing over 100,000 people and leaving over 1 million more homeless. The substandard quality of the nation's infrastructure, from roads to hospitals, also contributed to the high number of casualties.

Global Environmental Inequality

18.3.4 Identify the connection between global environmental responsibility and global environmental equality.

In 1984, over 40 tons of highly toxic gas escaped from a pesticide plant in Bhopal, India, and killed nearly 10,000 people who lived in a nearby slum. In the subsequent 20 years, as many as 20,000 premature deaths resulted from lingering bodily effects of exposure. The factory belonged to the Union Carbide Corporation, an American chemical producer that was lured to India by its lower environmental standards and lax rule enforcement. Though Union Carbide denied responsibility, the facility was operating with "safety equipment and procedures far below the standards found in its sister plant" in West Virginia (Broughton, 2005, p. 2).

In the global economy, production and consumption are usually disconnected. If we look at the labels on our clothing or the packaging of our electronics, we will likely see that they were made in China or another country where companies can pay workers cheaper wages than in North America—and where companies can pollute more. In this way, wealthy countries benefit from cheap industrial and consumer goods while developing countries bear the environmental and health risks.

More and more sociologists are reconnecting the points of production and consumption, and documenting the environmental suffering that the developing world endures to prop up Western lifestyles. In one study, ethnographers studied an impoverished shantytown in Argentina surrounded by an immense petrochemical compound (Auyero & Swistun, 2009). The village's 5,000 residents suffered from convulsions, rashes, psychological problems, bloody noses, and constant headaches—all of which are linked to ingestion of lead and other toxic industrial chemicals. The source of much of the pollution was Shell Oil, an American subsidiary of a Dutch multinational company that used the facility to carry out the dirty process of refining crude oil so that it is ready for global consumption and industrial use.

Despite overwhelming evidence, the researchers found that residents remained unsure about the causes of their illnesses and rarely mobilized against Shell. This was because Shell, as a powerful and wealthy company, was able to manipulate how residents perceived and responded to contamination. Many of the locals worked for Shell, and Shell also ran a town health clinic and performed its own environmental tests. Because residents could not afford independent doctors or consultants, their main source of information about illness and exposure came from biased Shell representatives, and locals risked losing their jobs if they protested. Their enduring suffering is one of the hidden social costs of the world's refined oil (Auyero & Swistun, 2009).

The greatest environmental problem that the world faces today—climate change—may also be the greatest source of environmental inequality. While rich nations have, by far, contributed the most to climate change, poor countries disproportionately suffer from its effects. For those who must make a living off the land, small changes can have huge impacts on their ability to subsist. A report issued by Columbia University researchers concluded that climate change is already forcing as many as 50 million people, almost all of them living in the least developed countries, to migrate to new areas in order to secure a livelihood. Given the dismal forecast of continued deforestation, melting glaciers, rising sea level, and an increase in the frequency and intensity of extreme weather events, we can expect hundreds of millions of worldwide "environmental refugees" by the year 2050 (Warner, Ehrhart, de Sherbinin, Adamo, & Chai-Onn, 2008).

18.4 How Can We Create More Sustainable Societies?

esbobeldijk/Shutterstock

Consumption, Production, and Sustainability

Many experts believe that the global population is growing so rapidly that in several generations the Earth may no longer be able to support everyone. The problem is not merely numbers, for if we were all hunter-gatherers we would consume far less resources and produce much less waste. According to biologist Paul Ehrlich (1968), the impact that a given group of people has on the environment is a function of the size of its population multiplied by its degree of affluence and its level of technology. For example, wealthy, developed countries tend to use an exponentially greater amount of natural resources *per person* than poor, less developed countries. In 2012, North Americans constituted only 6 percent of the world's population but consumed about

22 percent of the world's energy (United States Central Intelligence Agency, 2012; United States Energy Information Administration, n.d.). A single North American consumed as much energy as dozens of people in developing countries.

Where does all this energy go? The last time I went to a concert, I looked out and saw the glow of thousands of cellular phones and the flashes of countless digital cameras—devices that did not exist just a few decades ago. As the concert let out, many folks listened to their iPods on their way to the parking lot, where they got into their cars. Many likely turned on any number of appliances when they got home: microwaves, televisions, laptops, and so on. Understandably, most people in poor countries would like to enjoy the material comforts that wealthy nations take for granted. But something has to give. Even though new technologies enable us to stretch Earth's natural limits, ecologists believe that we will eventually hit the wall.

Innovations in food production are predicted to lag behind population increases, rising levels of air and water pollution are damaging our habitat's ability to sustain us, and the Earth's finite resources are being exhausted. Despite the fact that current consumption and pollution patterns are already unsustainable, the world's energy demand in 2030 is predicted to be 40 percent greater than it was in 2007. Over three-quarters of that increase will likely come from dirty, nonrenewable fossil fuels (United Nations Development Programme, 2010). As depicted in Figure 18.5, scientists predict that global carbon emissions will increase by more than 30 percent between 2007 and 2035.

Ecologists argue that, to avoid impending environmental and social crises, societies must work toward a model of **sustainability**, which refers to development and consumption that satisfy a society's current needs without imperiling the ability of future generations to do the same. Achieving long-term sustainability in the face of surging global production of waste and carbon dioxide emissions is, perhaps, the single most pressing social problem of the future.

Figure 18.5 World Energy-Related Carbon Dioxide Emissions, 2007–2035

The vertical axis indicates the carbon dioxide emissions, measured in billions of metric tonnes. The figure shows how the world's total emission of CO_2 is expected to increase steadily over the next two decades—from around 30 billion metric tonnes in 2007 to more than 40 billion tonnes in 2035. However, as indicated by the red bars, developing countries will experience a much larger increase of carbon dioxide emissions compared to the developed OECD countries.

SOURCE: From *International Energy Outlook, 2010* (Figure 10, p. 8), by United States Energy Information Administration, 2010, Washington, DC: U.S. Energy Information Administration (http://www.eia.doe.gov/oiaf/ieo/world.html).

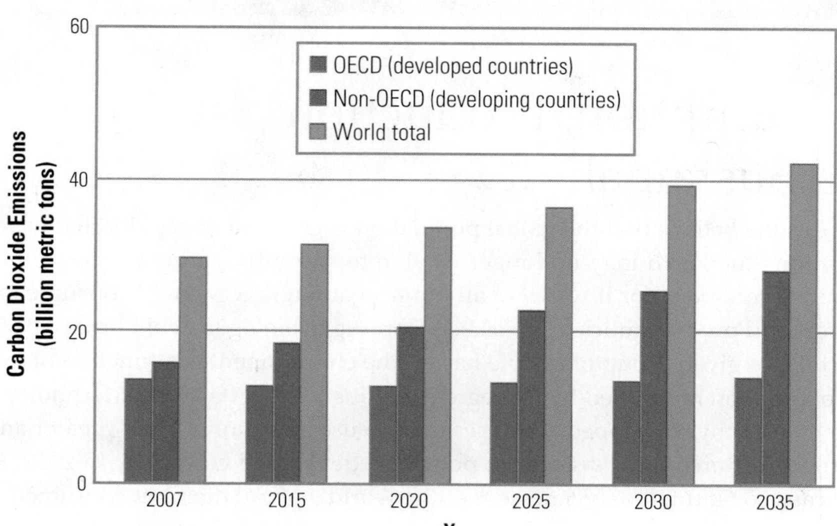

The Tragedy of the Commons

18.4.1 Compare the advantages and disadvantages of self-regulation and political regulation of environmental resources.

A key principle of economics is that competition among commodity producers trying to capture a greater share of the market leads to lower prices for consumers. Many economists point to this as evidence that a free market self-regulates and produces optimal collective outcomes. But in the influential article "The Tragedy of the Commons," ecologist Garrett Hardin (1968) contended that the opposite is often true: Each individual acting in his or her own self-interest will, in the long run, bring ruin to everyone.

Imagine a shared pasture (the "commons"), Hardin wrote, where herders graze cows. Because they earn a living from their cows, all herders have an interest in maximizing the number of cows they have grazing in the pasture. The herder who adds a cow to the pasture reaps all the benefits from that cow, but the negative impacts on the pasture created by overgrazing are distributed across all herders. Because, in the short term, he gains more than he loses, each herder concludes that he should keep adding cows to the pasture—until finally the pasture is entirely overgrazed. The freedom of each herder to pursue his interests produces collective devastation.

Hardin's analogy of the commons highlights the tension between short-term and long-term rewards, and between individual and collective interest. Economists rightly point out that businesses will adopt more sustainable practices if and when there is a market for them. But ecologists, pointing to societies that collapsed in the past, argue that preventing future environmental calamity requires making sacrifices today. As discussed earlier, the cod-fishing industry collapsed because each trawler sought to maximize its own haul of fish without regard for future generations. Global warming threatens us all because it is in the short-term economic interest of people, firms, and nations to continue business-as-usual practices rather than pay the cost of going green. The lesson is that we cannot expect the majority of people to regulate themselves as long as the negative consequences of their actions (1) will not be apparent until far in the future or (2) will fall on other people.

In order to promote environmentally friendly behaviour, Hardin argued, we need to restrict the amount of a particular resource that a single entity can use (e.g., permits or quotas), enact economic sanctions that punish polluters (e.g., taxes or fines), and create economic incentives that reward sustainable practices (e.g., tax breaks). The idea, in other words, is to replace self-regulation with political regulation. Our entire planet is our "commons." If we continue to eschew regulation and foul our own nest, future generations may find it uninhabitable.

The Treadmill of Production

18.4.2 Explain how economic systems focused on competition and expansion can contribute to serious environmental issues.

A number of sociologists agree with Hardin but go even further, arguing that uncontrolled destruction of the environment is an essential feature of the contemporary economic system. Sociologist Allan Schnaiberg forcefully advanced this perspective through his concept of the "treadmill of production" (Schnaiberg, 1980, p. 231). While one of the principles of ecology is balance and a tendency toward equilibrium, such as when a forest fire clears out the underbrush so that new trees can grow, the pursuit of profit tends toward disequilibrium. The basis of capitalism is continued economic expansion—measured in profits, market shares, gross domestic product, and so on. Producers, labourers, and governments all share an interest in growing the economy by increasing production and consumption. Doing so, of course, entails the consumption of more energy and the production of more pollution. Thus, economic expansion increases wealth, but at the expense of the environment. Schnaiberg argued that the

Havana1234/Fotolia

The toxic effects of governments who avoid environmental protections for fear that they will harm profits can be seen clearly in the smog-filled skies of Beijing.

treadmill of production helps ensure a business's profits by externalizing the environmental costs of its activities to the poor and the powerless, meaning that economic growth also increases environmental inequality (Schnaiberg, 1980).

Economic growth is driven by competition. While competition among producers leads to technological innovation and lower prices, it can also discourage sustainable business practices. Why should one producer voluntarily pay the higher cost of adopting cleaner technology if she does not have to? This would decrease her profits, and if she raised prices to reflect her higher cost of doing business, consumers would go elsewhere.

There is an important place, then, for regulations that might apply to everyone. However, businesses faced with costly environmental laws may simply move their facilities to regions that have fewer restrictions. Similarly, countries or states sometimes loosen environmental regulations to lure businesses away from other regions. These two dynamics set in motion a race to the bottom, wherein companies and governments conspire to remove or avoid environmental protections that harm profit. The toxic effects of the race to the bottom are evident from the Bhopal gas leak in India to the smog-choked skies of Beijing.

The implication of the treadmill-of-production idea is that achieving environmental sustainability will likely require a major restructuring of the economy away from a materials-intensive growth model. And the lesson of the race-to-the-bottom phenomenon is that political remedies will have to be harmonized across regions so that polluters do not pick up and move somewhere else when new regulations are put in place. These are tall orders, but some important steps have already been taken in this direction.

Toward Sustainability

18.4.3 Discuss ways in which technology, politics, and lifestyle changes can contribute to environmental protection and sustainability.

While technological innovation will most likely play a central role in helping societies reduce their impact on the environment, it is no silver bullet. Reining in pollution on the scale and timetable needed to head off an ecological crisis will also require that governments take a more active role in regulating pollution and steering the economy away from the treadmill of production. Last but not least, sustainability requires civic engagement. While the notion of the throw-away society points to the unsustainability of contemporary lifestyles, it implies that everyday citizens can vote for sustainability with their wallets by changing their patterns of consumption.

Technology will have a major role to play in making societies more sustainable. Recall that 85 percent of the world's energy comes from fossil fuels. Because fossil fuels are nonrenewable, and because their combustion is the leading source of global warming, transitioning to **renewable energy** sources that are capable of being replaced by natural ecological cycles, such as wind, sunlight, and water, would have major environmental benefits. This is already happening. Solar panels and wind turbines have started to take their place alongside hydroelectric dams as viable and important sources of green energy. Between 2007 and 2008, renewable energy consumption in the United States grew a record 10 percent. Canada has become a world leader in the production and use of energy from renewable resources. Despite this promising sign, as of 2013 over 90 percent of the energy consumed by North Americans was still derived from nonrenewable resources (United States Energy Information Administration, 2013). We can expect, however, that the decades ahead will see an enormous increase in renewable energy production. The federal government has begun actively promoting renewable energy as both good for the environment and good for the economy. Factories have sprung up to meet the growing demand for wind turbines and solar panels, providing local jobs in an era of outsourcing.

Because nuclear power does not produce greenhouse gases, it has increasingly been touted as a sustainable source of energy. Indeed, the United States, Canada, France, Germany, and Japan have included nuclear power as a key ingredient of their green energy portfolios for the coming decades. However, in addition to the fact that spent fuel rods must be securely stored for 10,000 years before they cease to be a public health risk, high-profile accidents leave people questioning whether nuclear power is environmentally friendly. On March 11, 2011, an earthquake off the coast of Japan unleashed a tsunami that flooded the Fukushima Daiichi nuclear plant and knocked out its power. As the nuclear fuel overheated, explosions tore through the reactors. Radioactive plumes forced evacuations throughout the region and contaminated crops and groundwater. Though a very rare event, the Fukushima disaster fuelled enough anxiety about nuclear energy that the German government promptly abandoned the chancellor's pro-nuclear policies and agreed to shut down all of its nuclear power plants—which provide almost a quarter of Germany's energy—by 2022.

As more people around the world pursue middle-class lifestyles, the demand for automobiles escalates. Unless we develop cars that do not rely on oil, any gains made in reducing carbon emissions through wind, solar, or nuclear power will be cancelled out by tailpipe emissions. The development of hybrid vehicles has been an important step in reducing carbon emissions, and their popularity shows that there is a market for green cars. Hybrids are powered by gasoline combustion, like traditional vehicles, yet they also draw energy from batteries. By using less gas, hybrids can produce significantly lower carbon emissions. However, hybrids still pollute. A number of manufacturers aim to create alternative fuel vehicles that do not emit any carbon.

One promising path to this objective is the electric vehicle (EV), which draws all of its energy from batteries. Rather than filling up at a gas station, the driver plugs the EV into an electrical outlet. EVs have actually been around for decades and are beginning to be mass produced. But several technological obstacles must still be overcome before they become attractive to consumers: The batteries are heavy, bulky, and expensive, and require considerable amounts of time to recharge; and many EVs can travel less than half the distance of gas-powered vehicles before they need to refuel. Tesla Motors, a California-based company that I've makes only electronic cars, has overcome some of these obstacles, but its cars currently cost $80,000 or more, a price far above the reach of all but a tiny percentage of North Americans. Given the strides made over the past decade, however, there is reason to believe that EVs will eventually be competitive

Jim West/PhotoEdit, Inc.

The mass production of plug-in electric vehicles means fewer cars on the road producing tailpipe emissions. But where the electricity comes from that powers these cars matters: If it is derived from burning fossil fuels like coal, then the decrease in tailpipe emissions might be cancelled out by increased smokestack emissions. Tesla has established a national network of battery-charging stations that use solar power, one model for the future.

with gas-powered vehicles. For EVs to truly be green, though, the electricity that powers them must come from clean and renewable resources rather than coal or oil. Tesla has taken steps in this direction by building a national network of refuelling stations, many of which are powered by large solar panels above the station.

Politics has played an important part in promoting the development of green technology; but many environmentalists are pushing governments to assume a larger role in moving societies toward sustainability. While governments offer tax rebates to businesses that adopt green technology, environmentalists seek federal legislation that would place a legal limit on carbon emissions. In the absence of federal U.S. regulations, some regions are creating climate action plans themselves. States in the northeastern United States and many Canadian provinces, for instance, have set a target to reduce the region's total carbon emissions to 10 percent below 1990 levels by the year 2020. New York City aims to reduce its citywide carbon emissions to 30 percent below 2005 levels by 2030. One way to reduce regional carbon emissions is to limit suburban sprawl. Because cities cluster people and the businesses that serve them within a self-contained area where many errands can be done on foot, bike, train, or bus, urban living is a surprisingly green lifestyle. The state of Oregon has long recognized this—since the 1970s, it has enforced land-use laws that concentrate residential and commercial growth in urban areas.

One method for achieving carbon reduction goals is through a **cap-and-trade program**. The idea is that governments set a limit on the total amount of carbon emissions that are allowable (the cap) and then sell permits to businesses that entitle them to a designated amount of emissions. If firms need to emit more than their permit allows, they must purchase pollution credits from firms that are emitting less than their permit entitles them to (the trade). Such a system ensures a reduction in the total amount of carbon emitted into the atmosphere, rewards firms that move toward clean technology, and makes dirty firms pay for their pollution. The European Union was an early adopter of a trading program for greenhouse gases.

To prevent a race to the bottom, in which firms move their operations to regions that have not implemented limits on greenhouse gas emissions, nations would need to work out an international agreement in which all countries sign on to reduce the global carbon footprint. Though achieving such a task is daunting, there is historical precedent. In 1987, countries from around the world gathered in Montreal to tackle the threat of ozone depletion. Acknowledging that the primary source of the so-called ozone hole over Antarctica came from aerosol sprays and liquid coolants containing CFCs, 196 countries eventually signed on to an agreement to phase out the production of these pollutants by 2000. Under guidance from the United Nations, wealthy nations set aside a special fund to help developing countries meet the phase-out requirements. Dubbed the Montreal Protocol, the CFC phase-out agreement is usually considered the most successful international environmental treaty of all time. Figure 18.6 shows the dramatic decline in CFC production after this landmark agreement.

Though curbing carbon emissions is more complicated, the Montreal Protocol is a useful framework. Important efforts have been made, most notably the 1997 Kyoto Protocol. Industrialized nations committed to reducing greenhouse gas emissions by an average of 5 percent below 1990 levels by 2012, set aside a fund to aid developing

Figure 18.6 Levels of CFC Production Before and After the Montreal Protocol (1987)

SOURCE: European FluoroCarbons Technical Committee, 2012.

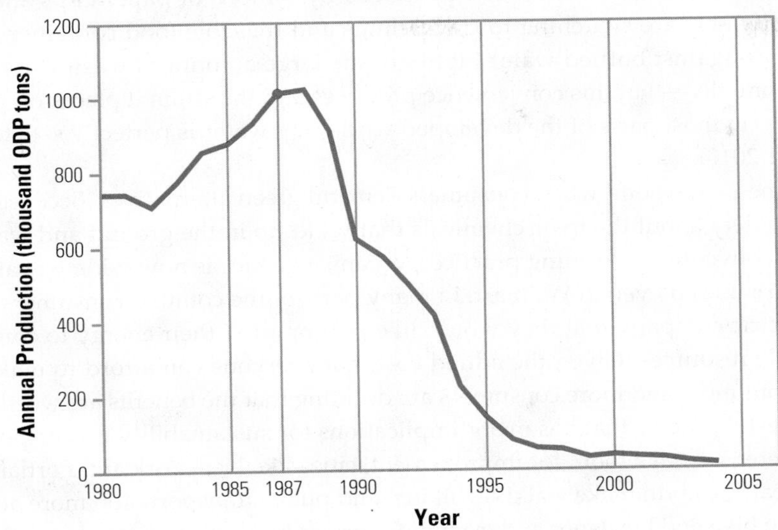

countries in adapting green technologies, and laid the foundation for an international cap-and-trade agreement. However, Kyoto highlighted the tension between environmental and business interests. The United States, at the time the world's largest polluter, refused to ratify the agreement because it would hamper economic growth. Meanwhile, environmentalists argued that the 5 percent carbon emissions goal was far too meager to prevent dangerous levels of global warming. Newly industrialized countries such as China and India were largely exempt from emissions reductions on the controversial but reasonable grounds that wealthy nations had been allowed to develop without pollution restrictions.

With the Kyoto Protocol set to expire, countries gathered again in Copenhagen in 2009 to try to hammer out the next treaty. Though the United States and China—the world's largest polluters—seemed open to committing to a reduction in carbon emissions, in the end no legally binding international agreement was produced. Developing countries remained unconvinced that their ability to modernize would not be overly constrained by the agreement, and countries disagreed over the extent to which wealthy nations ought to adopt stricter emissions targets to reflect the disproportionate role they played over the twentieth century in contributing to global warming. These conflicts make it apparent that the obstacles to solving environmental problems can be more political than technological, and finding equitable solutions is often challenging. While the world still waits for a binding international treaty on greenhouse gas emissions, Chinese president Xi Jinping and American president Barack Obama signed a landmark climate pact in November 2014: China pledged, for the first time, to cap its greenhouse gas emissions by 2030, and the United States promised to reduce its greenhouse gas emissions well below previous commitments. Given that the two countries account for 45 percent of the world's greenhouse gas emissions, the accord is widely seen as a "game changer" with the potential to re-energize international climate talks.

While economics and politics are key arenas where changes are necessary in order to move toward sustainability, environmentalists stress that small changes to one's lifestyle can also have a major impact. California alone uses 19 billion disposable plastic bags every year—600 bags every second (Californians Against Waste, 2011). These bags are made from the nonrenewable resource petroleum, and their production releases toxins into the air. Essentially nonbiodegradable, after one use plastic bags usually wind up in a landfill or become litter that fouls the land and waterways and chokes unsuspecting animals. To avoid this waste, many people are turning to reusable bags made out of durable materials like canvas. Similarly, consumers concerned about the waste produced by billions of paper cups and Styrofoam containers are switching to travel mugs and reusable food containers. Public campaigns against bottled water highlight the large amount of waste—1.4 million tonnes annually—that this convenience produces and the strain it places on precious resources (in most parts of the developed world, tap water is perfectly safe to drink) (Baskind, 2010).

Businesses respond when consumers demand green alternatives. Because of consumer anxiety about the toxic chemicals that wind up in the ground and water as a result of conventional farming practices, organic produce is now widely available in supermarkets and even in Walmart. In many parts of the country, consumers can tell their electric company that they would like part or all of their energy to come from renewable resources. Given the added cost, not everyone can afford to make these choices, but more and more consumers are deciding that the benefits are worth it.

A lifestyle choice that has major implications for sustainability is transportation. While there is always room for improvement, cities like New York and Portland have taken great strides to make walking, biking, and public transportation more attractive by adding bike and bus lanes and extending service hours and regional service.

But old habits die hard. As I look out my office window in Manhattan, a sea of cars (especially yellow cabs!) chokes the six-lane road. Large SUVs containing a single occupant idle for minutes at a time, and tailpipe exhaust fills the air above them. Meanwhile, a few cyclists zip by, regularly beating cars to the same destination, but the nearby bike lanes remain underutilized. Many of those automobile commuters will fight traffic for over an hour to get to their homes in Long Island or New Jersey, even though a commuter train does the same journey in less time.

Certainly, many North Americans seem to have no choice but to drive most of the time—particularly if they live outside of urban areas. Green transportation advocates recognize this reality. Rather than expecting people to ditch their cars, they urge people to be more selective about when and how they use them. Can they carpool? Is the train a viable option? Considering one's alternatives for a particular trip, rather than simply making one's car the default choice, could go a long way in reducing greenhouse gas emissions.

Robert Stainforth/Alamy Stock Photo

Walking and bicycling are two of the most environmentally friendly—and healthy—ways to get around. What could your city or town do to make these transportation options more attractive?

Depending on where you live and how much money you have, certain sustainable practices may not be an option for you. But everyone can take steps to learn more about the wider ecological impacts of their lifestyle and then decide what environmentally friendly changes are possible or attractive to them. One easy way to do this is to calculate your carbon footprint. A number of websites will estimate the amount of carbon emissions that you or your household are responsible for each year based on information you provide about transportation choices, electricity usage, and so on. After computing your carbon footprint and comparing it to the national and global average, the websites offer tips on how you can take steps to reduce your environmental impact (check out the Ecological Footprint calculator at the Center for Sustainable Economy's website at http://www.myfootprint.org/).

Conclusion: Linking Environmental and Social Facts

Environmental sociology opens up new vistas for social analysis. Studying the ways in which environment and society are enmeshed fosters dialogue between the natural and the social sciences. Environmental sociology encourages us to recognize that the "natural" is always linked to the social. Because the ways that we interact with our environment—whether we seek to protect or destroy it—are based on our interpretations of it, solving environmental problems will require acknowledging, and reconciling, disparate environmental worldviews.

Environmental sociologists make it clear that solving environmental problems will require significant social change, not just new technology. But is the pursuit of profit incompatible with sustainable development? Certainly, history has shown that capitalism leads to environmental degradation. However, the last several decades have witnessed the emergence of green technologies and innovative environmental policies such as cap-and-trade programs for carbon emissions. While there is still a long way to go, societies are nonetheless making strides toward sustainability without sacrificing their gross domestic product. This has led a number of scholars to argue that economic growth *can* be adapted to sustainable goals. As society's preference for environmentally friendly products and industries escalates, so goes the argument, firms will compete for market shares by producing green commodities and technologies. Can we leave it to the economy to produce sustainability? Would this alleviate environmental inequality or exacerbate it?

Sociologists agree that there is a correlation between socioeconomic status and environmental risk. But what, exactly, is the nature of this relationship? While some studies clearly show that poor people of colour are more likely to live near toxic waste facilities, this reveals a correlation but not causation. We are left wondering: Did companies discriminate by locating the facility there, or is it simply the case that both the residents and the firm settled in an area because it was affordable? Also, given that the majority of those in poverty are nonwhite, sociologists are often unable to determine whether it is race or class that plays the most important role in determining environmental risk.

How do we define and measure environmental risk? Even if we find that a poor neighbourhood has higher rates of asthma than the surrounding areas, for instance, how can we actually demonstrate that the increased rate is because of nearby smokestacks and not other factors such as diet or lack of exercise? At this point we do not have enough data, or the right instruments, to precisely map the connections among geography, socioeconomic status, and risk. Gaining the ability to do so is crucial because environmental justice will be achieved only if we can reveal the mechanisms of injustice.

CHAPTER SUMMARY

The Big Questions Revisited 18

18.1 **How Does Social Life Relate to the Natural Environment?** In this section, we explored how every society consumes and transforms the natural environment to satisfy its needs and desires while also adapting to its physical surroundings and confronting natural limits.

Understanding Environment–Society Relations

Traditional Societies

Learning Objective 18.1.1: Explain how a society's environment contributes to the cultural and religious traditions it develops.

Modern Societies

Learning Objective 18.1.2: Discuss the ways in which modern societies gained more control over their environment and developed stratified social structures.

The Environment–Society Dialogue

Learning Objective 18.1.3: Explain determinism and social constructivism, and the ways in which environment both guides and constrains social life.

18.2 **How Has Human Activity Harmed the Environment?** The most pressing environmental problems of our time—such as deforestation, water pollution, and global warming—are the result of human activities. This section described contemporary environmental problems and discussed how they are caused by industrial production and consumption.

Contemporary Environmental Problems

Global Warming

Learning Objective 18.2.1: Identify the variety of environmental transformations caused by climate change.

Natural Resource Depletion

Learning Objective 18.2.2: Discuss how the rapid depletion of major natural resources—oil, coal, forests, living species, and water—affects all forms of life.

Solid and Chemical Waste

Learning Objective 18.2.3: Discuss how attitudes toward waste and modes of waste removal threaten our health and environment.

Air and Water Pollution

Learning Objective 18.2.4: Discuss the impact human consumption has on air and water supplies.

18.3 **How Do Environmental Factors Impact Inequality?** This section explored how sociologists examine environmental catastrophes, such as Hurricane Katrina, and how the structure of society shapes the effects of these environmental hazards.

The Environmental Movement and Social Inequality

The Environmental Movement

Learning Objective 18.3.1: Identify early preservationist figures and movements that have contributed to environmental awareness.

Environmental Justice

Learning Objective 18.3.2: Discuss environmental racism and what progress is being made to ensure equal protection for all people.

The Social Dimension of Natural Disasters

Learning Objective 18.3.3: Explain the reasons some groups are more adversely affected by natural disasters than other groups.

Global Environmental Inequality

Learning Objective 18.3.4: Identify the connection between global environmental responsibility and global environmental equality.

18.4 **How Can We Create More Sustainable Societies?** In this section, we discussed the social, political, and economic obstacles to adopting sustainable lifestyles in developed and developing countries, and we explored the ways in which we might be able to overcome these obstacles.

Consumption, Production, and Sustainability

The Tragedy of the Commons

Learning Objective 18.4.1: Compare the advantages and disadvantages of self-regulation and political regulation of environmental resources.

The Treadmill of Production

Learning Objective 18.4.2: Explain how economic systems focused on competition and expansion can contribute to serious environmental issues.

Toward Sustainability

Learning Objective 18.4.3: Discuss ways in which technology, politics, and lifestyle changes can contribute to environmental protection and sustainability.

Learn the Terms

acid rain (p. 528)
anthropocentrism (p. 518)
cap-and-trade program (p. 542)
climate change (p. 523)
conservationist (p. 531)
determinist (p. 519)
ecology (p. 519)
environmental justice (p. 534)
environmental racism (p. 534)
environmental sociology (p. 515)
fossil fuel (p. 521)
global warming (p. 521)
greenhouse effect (p. 521)
preservationist (p. 530)
renewable energy (p. 541)
smog (p. 528)
social construction (of the environment) (p. 520)
sustainability (p. 538)
totemism (p. 517)

Chapter 19
Population

by Lawrence L. Wu

Antony Ratcliffe/Alamy Stock Photo

Why are sociologists so fascinated with studying population change and aging societies?

Learning Objectives

19.1.1 Discuss why it is relevant to study population trends.

19.1.2 Identify ways in which population is studied.

19.2.1 Define the first demographic transition and its role in understanding how populations change.

19.2.2 Compare fertility and mortality trends between underdeveloped and developed countries.

19.2.3 Discuss how the rate of immigration relates to the speed at which the population size changes.

19.3.1 Explain the connection between declining infant mortality and fertility decline.

19.3.2 Explain the connection between fertility and economic development.

19.3.3 Explain the connection between improved birth control, changing attitudes about bearing children, and fertility decline.

19.3.4 Explain the connection between the costs and benefits of childrearing and fertility decline.

19.3.5 Explain the connection between changing norms and values and fertility decline.

19.4.1 Discuss how the epidemiological transition explains differences in health conditions affecting those in poorer and richer countries.

19.4.2 Discuss how the aging of the generation contributes to the overall graying of societies.

19.4.3 Explain why some countries will age more quickly than others.

19.4.4 Discuss the role of health and healthcare as a population ages.

19.4.5 Discuss why population aging creates financial pressures for governments and societies.

19.4.6 Understand how countries differ in how they treat older, very sick people.

How do social scientists think about population? We can begin to understand its importance if we reflect on our own families. Let's look at holiday gatherings as an example. In my case, my parents divorced when I was a teenager, so rather than having holiday gatherings at a parent's home, the Wu family usually gets together at my sister's with her spouse and two kids. I would host at my home, but since I do not have children, and since my mother enjoys spending time with my niece and nephew, she flies from Los Angeles to stay at my sister's. Holiday gatherings mean holiday meals seated among a few generations, perhaps including in-laws, around the holiday dinner table (or tables in the case of our family). We do what many families do at holiday gatherings: We eat too much, drink too much, exchange presents, talk, and watch the kids play.

And talking, at least in my family, means recounting family history, a topic that invariably comes up during the holidays. Here's a quick sketch of my family's history. Both my parents were born in China, in Shanghai, in 1930. They came to the United States in 1949, attended college, met each other in 1956, and married in 1957. I was born a year later, and my sister was born about two years after me. (This means that both of us were born at the tail end of the baby boom, something we discuss in greater detail below.) My mother's parents had a total of four children, all of whom were born in China: my two uncles (one of whom died of AIDS in the late 1980s), my mother, and another daughter who died in childhood. My father's parents had nine children, all of whom were also born in China: Two died during childhood, and the remaining seven are my father, one uncle, and five aunts.

This pattern of large families in past generations and much smaller families in current generations turns out to be central to understanding a key demographic debate of the past few decades. For example, in the 1960s and 1970s, when I was growing up, it was taken for granted that *the* most pressing population issue was rapid population growth. *The Population Bomb*, published in 1968 by American biologist and educator Paul Ehrlich, summarized this view, noting that the world's population was growing much too rapidly and that there would soon be very dire

The Big Questions

1. **Why study population?** Between 1910 and 2012, the world's population doubled in size—not once but twice. When will the world's population next double in size? Although the field of demography began to take form in the late nineteenth century, it can be traced back much further. Concerns about population trends date back 6,000 years, when the first population census was taken. There are many reasons why governments and policymakers need to know about population trends, including the risk of overpopulation. In this section, we describe some of those reasons.
2. **How do populations change over time?** To better understand the dynamics of population change, in this section we look at how mortality and fertility have changed for different nations and what these changes might imply for the demographic futures of these nations.
3. **What factors influence fertility?** Populations change over time largely because fertility practices also have been changing (i.e., the decision to have a child). In most countries around the world, women are having fewer babies than 50 or 100 years ago. Why is this happening? In this section, we explore some of the leading explanations for declining fertility.
4. **How are trends in aging and mortality emerging as critical issues in many societies?** Some countries have many very young people but very few old people, while others have many old people now and will have even more old people in the future as life expectancy increases. What do these trends mean for employment and health conditions in countries like these? In this section, we ask about the demographic implications when populations begin to age.

consequences. Ehrlich's argument was not new; in fact, 180 years earlier, English scholar Thomas Malthus (1798) also argued that rapid increases in population would lead to widespread misery.

Today, most social scientists who study population issues agree that there are two pressing problems related to population growth. One is, as before, the problems facing nations and regions in the world in which population growth continues to be very rapid and in which it would be highly desirable for population growth to be curbed. The second, seemingly paradoxically, concerns nations and regions of the world in which populations are aging rapidly and may even experience decline, sometimes at a very rapid pace. For those nations facing rapid population aging and potential decline, it would be highly desirable for these trends to be curbed.

There is a larger demographic story that helps to resolve this apparent paradox in which the problem in some cases is too rapid population growth and other cases is the possibility of too rapid population decline in the future. As we will see, these very different patterns of population growth also have profound implications for aging. Aging societies face dramatically different challenges than younger ones. In aging countries the challenges of improving population health have shifted from reducing infectious diseases (like tuberculosis) to managing chronic diseases like heart disease and diabetes for a growing fraction of the population.

In this chapter, we discuss all of these issues and demonstrate the importance of examining population and population trends for studying broader trends in society.

19.1 Why Study Population?

demarfa/Fotolia

Population and Censuses

As noted in the introduction, the bestselling book *The Population Bomb*, written by Paul Ehrlich and published in 1968, summarized a pervasive mid-twentieth-century concern—that the world's population was growing much too quickly and that this ticking time bomb would soon have catastrophic effects (Ehrlich, 1968). How long has it taken for the world's population to double in size? We reached a landmark around 2012, when the world's population hit 7 billion. Why were Ehrlich and many others so alarmed about the world's population growth? Let's look at some global population data in Table 19.1. In 480 BCE, the world's population is estimated to have been about 110 million. It wasn't until 800 CE that the world's population reached 220 million, thus taking 1,280 years to double. In 1330, or 530 years later, the world's population had doubled again, and it doubled again in the 480 years between 1330 and 1810. (The world's population fluctuated dramatically during this latter period because of the Black Plague and the repeated epidemic outbreaks that followed.)

The crucial part of the story starts around 1810, when the world's population began growing much more rapidly than ever before. The number of human beings alive doubled in the 100 years between 1810 and 1910, doubling again during the next 57 years, and again in the next 45 years, at which point we get to the approximately 7 billion people alive today.

So the impression that Table 19.1 provides is simple but dramatic, and on the face of it looks very much like the projections of Ehrlich (and Malthus before him). While it once took 1,280 years for the world's population to double, the most recent doubling

Table 19.1 Doubling of the World's Population Through History

Date	Population (in millions)	Years to Double Population Size
480 BCE	110	
800 CE	220	1,280
1330 CE	440	530
1810 CE	875	480
1910 CE	1,750	100
1967 CE	3,500	57
2012 CE	7,000	45

SOURCE: Based on data from U.S. Census Bureau, 2012.

took only 45 years. Wouldn't these numbers imply that Ehrlich was right? To answer this, let's pose the same question, but instead of looking backward historically, let's ask it looking forward to the future. How many years will it take for the world's population to double again, from 7 to 14 billion? And will the next doubling be in about 30, 40, 50, or 60 years?

Perhaps surprisingly, the answer is "none of the above" (Lam, 2011). That is, what nearly all **demographers** (social scientists who do research on populations and population trends) who study this question would say is that, unlike what Ehrlich believed and unlike past history, the world's population is unlikely to double again to 14 billion, certainly not in the foreseeable future. Thus, most demographers would view Ehrlich's claim as either simply wrong or, at the very least, as a much too simplistic portrait of what is in reality a more complicated situation. In the next section, we'll continue exploring why most demographers believe that 7 billion people will not double any time in the foreseeable future. To see why, we need to learn more about why demographers and governments study these issues.

The Census and Population Research

19.1.1 Discuss why it is relevant to study population trends.

Although the field of **demography**—the study of population—as we know it today began to take form in the late nineteenth century, the desire for knowledge about population trends goes back thousands of years. Most scholars believe the first population **census** took place nearly 6,000 years ago in Babylonia (an area that is part of modern Iraq). A census is a count of everyone (or everything) residing in a particular location; a national census attempts to **enumerate** (or systematically count) all persons living in the country at the time the census is conducted. (Early census data rarely reflected complete population records as the census ignored slaves and sometimes women and children, but sometimes included cattle!) The Babylonians were very systematic, attempting to count not only people but also the amount of land, livestock, and basic foodstuffs held by each household. There is evidence that the ancient Egyptians conducted censuses around this time as well. In the pharaonic era, censuses were taken in 3340 BCE and in 3050 BCE, using papyrus manuscripts to record the results. It appears that the Egyptian censuses were used for some early population-planning initiatives, such as deciding how much land each family in the Nile Delta region would receive. The term *census* itself originated in ancient Rome, from the Latin word *censere*, and for a period of time the Roman Empire carried out periodic censuses every five years in order to locate people, identify recruits for its military forces, and collect taxes. An early census that is especially well regarded for accuracy for its time was conducted in China in 2 CE, identifying a population of almost 58 million people in the lands ruled by the Han Dynasty. Other early censuses were conducted in places like ancient Israel, India, and the Inca Empire in Central America. The record of these early censuses provides fascinating insight into the abilities and efforts of early governments and rulers to achieve even minimal understanding of the peoples they sought to control and rule; however, these censuses largely fell into disuse in the Middle Ages. One exception is the famous census undertaken by William the Conqueror in 1086, which attempted to identify all landowners and land holdings being brought under Norman rule, presumably in an effort to improve and enhance tax collection in England and Wales. The results were compiled into a book known as the *Domesday Book* (perhaps because, like the Biblical Day of Judgement, there was no appealing it as a record of legal title to land).

The modern census can trace its origins to beginnings of the Industrial Revolution and the settlement of national borders in the eighteenth century. Early national censuses include those conducted in Prussia (1719), Russia (1722–1723), Switzerland (1747), Sweden (1749), Spain (1768), the United States (1790), France and England (1801), and Canada (1871). Canada established that a new census would be conducted every five years, and many other nations have established and maintained regularity in their population counts as well. Today, governments all around the world, whether democratic or authoritarian, generally profess to share an interest in population trends in their country. They invest significant resources in attempting to map those trends through a national census, often supplemented by other types of population data collection.

Given how pervasive the national census has become, we might want to ask why governments think that it is so important to know how many people are living in a country, region, city, or town. Several key reasons can be identified:

- As noted above, many nations, both historically and now, want to know about the size of their population because this determines how much can be collected in taxes and how many persons (typically young males) might be available should war or other armed conflict arise.
- Population analysis is essential for estimating future social needs, such as whether to build or not build more roads, houses, schools, churches, office buildings, or any other socially important physical infrastructure. Before making those decisions, officials and policymakers need to have a good idea whether (and how fast) the population of an area might be growing.
- Population size is important for determining political boundaries. For example, seats in a national legislature (such as Parliament) are often based on population size.
- Population trends can have a huge impact on a national (or regional) economy. The composition of a nation's (or region's) population will impact how productive it will be and is a big factor in predicting whether to invest (or not) in business and jobs in the area or country. For example, a country with a large percentage of university graduates can offer businesses a more skilled and adaptable workforce than a country with a small percentage of university graduates.
- Population trends also have important consequences for government policy. If there are too many young people, jobs for those seeking to enter the labour market might be scarce and create social pressures without some effort to generate opportunities. If there are too many older people working beyond a country's widely accepted retirement age, the cost of providing them with pensions may become prohibitively expensive (as some countries around the world are now facing).

The *Domesday Book* is the surviving record of a population and land census conducted in 1086.

- Businesses are also keenly interested in the demographic characteristics of a population because many things that they sell are geared to specific segments of society. Thus, clothes, music, and other goods and services bought by young people (one "demographic") are often very different than those bought by older adults.

These are just some of the reasons why businesses, governments, and others find it important to know about populations. But the study of populations is also important because it provides valuable insight into the changing nature of societies. To say that a country or city has a population of X at one point in time, and a population of Y at another hardly exhausts what we can learn about the study of population. Here, for example, are just a few of the kinds of population-based trends that demographers study and that provide very important insights.

- *Racial and Ethnic Composition:* Many societies, including Canada, are undergoing significant changes in the racial and ethnic mix of their populations, driven especially by the movement of people across borders. The shift in the population size of various groups accumulates over time, and demographers have developed ways of seeing trends before they begin to become clear to everyone.
- *Marriage and the Family:* As divorce rates and the percentage of children being raised by a single parent have changed in recent decades, demographers have not only charted the basic trends but also explored the consequences for children growing up with a single parent, in poverty, or both.
- *Employment Issues:* Just as people and the families they grow up in change, so too do jobs—and frequently we can see mismatches in a region or even an entire country in the availability of jobs and the availability of workers with (or without) particular sets of skills.
- *Life Expectancy:* How long can the average person born in a particular country or region today expect to live (and how does that figure differ for subgroups in a population, such as men and women or ethnic majorities and minorities)? The answer to this question is interesting in its own right (rising life expectancy around the globe is one of the most important changes of the past 100 years), but it can tell us a lot about more than that. For example, it is often hard to compare the quality of life in two very different societies, or over time. But by looking at differences or changes in life expectancy, we can begin to draw some intriguing conclusions. How long people in any society can expect to live will be determined in part by the quality of food they have access to, the quality of the healthcare they receive, the quality of the water they drink and the air that they breathe, even the amount of stress that daily living imposes. When life expectancy is rising in a country or region, it is almost certain that many other things are improving as well (Deaton, 2013).

These examples highlight some of the ways in which population research can provide information even before events actually happen. Because population research is partly about documenting **stylized facts** (empirical information that we can surmise or determine with a great deal of certainty) about population and population trends, it provides the foundation for much of the rest of the social sciences. Many important debates and questions, including many of the questions we have been posing throughout this book, have a population component. Those include changes in social structure, urban/suburban/rural residence, education, religious involvements, political participation by different groups, crime rates (e.g., who commits crimes), and prison populations.

Studying Population

19.1.2 Identify ways in which population is studied.

Population dynamics, the subject of the rest of this chapter, concerns how the size of any place or group has changed in the past or how it might change in the future. That group could be a small town or the entire world population, or it could be the number of Jews in Canada or the number of Muslims across the globe. Population dynamics is a central topic of research for demographers. It involves issues that reach far beyond adding up the number of births and deaths. In particular, understanding population dynamics requires a detailed understanding of demography's "big three": **fertility** (the birth rate, typically measured by the number of live births per woman of childbearing years), **mortality** (typically measured by the number of deaths in a particular calendar year), and **migration** (how many people move into and out of a given region or country). In this chapter, our focus will be on the first two: fertility and mortality. Migration is discussed in more detail in chapters 10 and 20.

How a region's or a nation's population will change over time is determined by the "big three": how many people are born, how many people die, and how many move in or out. Thus, to know how many people will be in Canada in 2020, we need to know the size of the Canadian population in 2010 and estimate the number of births between 2010 and 2020, minus the estimated number deaths during this same period, plus the numbers who move into the country, minus the numbers who move out of the country.

This may seem like simple arithmetic; however, the less-than-simple part is at the heart of population dynamics: How is it that populations change over time? And if population size is determined by fertility, mortality, and migration, then it necessarily follows that understanding population change requires *both* describing changes in fertility, mortality, and migration *and* understanding what might be causing these changes. All of these make population issues much more interesting and much more challenging to social scientists.

Here's a basic example to illustrate how one change affects another. Let's suppose that in Society A, women and their partners suddenly decide to have fewer children; in fact, they want to have only 1 or 2 rather than 3. (Until recently, Society A couples preferred to have 2 or 3 children, but not as many as 4.) At first glance, this change might not seem like such a big deal; but the impact on the population of this society will be increasingly dramatic over time because there will be many fewer children than before. That is, if the average Society A woman has 1.5 children, in 5 years there will be fewer kindergarten students, and perhaps a few teachers and school administrators will notice (or be laid off from their jobs). In 18 years, there will be fewer children applying to colleges, which may put pressure on some schools, but there will also be fewer people of peak crime age so there may be less crime. An important consequence will also be fewer entry-level workers than before, so employers may have to increase the wages they are offering to attract the workers they need, and some may have trouble filling all of their jobs.

Demographers will be the first to notice that the number of live births each year per woman has declined, and if their research is properly noticed, government officials should begin to try to respond appropriately. But demographers want to know not just how much decline in the birth rate has occurred, but why. Decline could result from any number of factors. For example, more women may want to have careers and may feel that having fewer (or no) children is a better way to organize their lives. Perhaps improved methods of birth control are contributing to the decline. The decline could be concentrated among some groups of women but not others. Changes in marital patterns may be a factor. (If more couples choose to cohabitate but not marry, this may affect the numbers of children that are born.) While fully answering the question of why the birth rate is falling may require using many of the tools of a sociological imagination, we can glean important insights by looking at what is changing in a particular population.

19.2 How Do Populations Change Over Time?

frans lemmens/Alamy Stock Photo

Population Dynamics

To better understand the dynamics of population change, let's look at how mortality and fertility have changed for a few different nations, and what these changes might imply for the demographic futures of these nations.

The First Demographic Transition

19.2.1 Define the first demographic transition and its role in understanding how populations change.

The **first demographic transition** (see, e.g., Bulatao & Casterline, 2001; Coale, 1973; Davis, 1963; Hirschman, 1994; Notestein, 1953) is the transition by a region or country from a period of high fertility and high mortality to a period of low fertility and low mortality. To understand this part of the population story, we need to concentrate on a set of stylized facts that we know with great certainty. These stylized facts allow us to describe the characteristic features of the first demographic transition. The first demographic transition is about historical change; specifically, it is a story about change in fertility and mortality and those two elements within three historical demographic periods: pretransition, mid-transition, and posttransition.

For nearly all of human history (and thus before the first demographic transition), both mortality and fertility were very high. Fertility tended to be a bit higher than mortality, but only very slightly, and this meant that the world's population grew, but very slowly. The world as a whole was in a pretransition era. Fast-forward to today and look at a country like Canada, where there is both low mortality and low fertility. Because of this low fertility and low mortality, Canada can be said to be a posttransition society.

Now, what happens in the middle of the first demographic transition? During this phase, first mortality declines, followed later by a decline in fertility. So putting all of these pieces together, the story of the first demographic transition involves (1) an initial pretransition period characterized by high fertility and high mortality, then (2) a transitional period in which mortality first declines followed by a decline in fertility, and then (3) a posttransition period in which both fertility and mortality are low.

So, let's focus on the transitional period in the middle, where mortality begins to decline but fertility remains high. Slow population growth for nearly all of human history was the result of births and deaths more or less cancelling each other. Then we entered a period in which mortality declined, meaning fewer deaths, but fertility remained high, meaning as many births as previously. The simple arithmetic of many births but fewer deaths equals rapid population growth. This means that in this middle period, we see something very different and something very new. This is the world that Thomas Malthus and Paul Ehrlich observed and wrote about and that seemed to them to imply a population time bomb. But their story didn't take into account the other crucial part of the first demographic transition, which is that fertility does not remain high; it eventually declines, but only after mortality has begun its decline. And this is another crucial part of the story: In the middle of the first demographic transition, population growth can be very rapid when mortality falls but fertility remains high.

Sayyid Azim/AFP/Getty Images

Sudan is currently experiencing a period of rapid population growth, growing from 9 million people in 1950 to 44 million in 2010.

The final part of the story, which is perhaps the most interesting and most consequential, is that once fertility decline has begun (or in some versions of the story, once it passes a certain threshold), it does not reverse; as a result, demographers have observed that high fertility pretransition eventually declines to much lower levels posttransition. Without exception, at least to date, we have never seen nations and regions that have gone through the first demographic transition return to pretransition levels of high fertility. Fertility levels, posttransition, have been observed to fluctuate, sometimes falling a bit, sometimes rising a bit, but have never returned to the high levels of fertility that characterize pretransition. These are the stylized facts characterizing the first demographic transition.

Changes in Fertility and Mortality Around the World

19.2.2 Compare fertility and mortality trends between underdeveloped and developed countries.

We can now better understand why Malthus and Ehrlich were so alarmed, but also why the world's population of 7 billion is very unlikely to become 14 billion in the foreseeable future. In the 1950s and 1960s, a large number of countries had experienced recent and quite marked declines in mortality. But because these mortality declines were recent, they were not yet accompanied by a decline in fertility. As a result, the world's population soared in the middle of the twentieth century, increasing at an extremely rapid rate. It is not surprising that many people like Ehrlich were so alarmed about the rapid growth of the world's population. But what was less obvious was that fertility decline would also take place. And fertility decline is indeed a remarkable stylized fact—something that has been extremely well documented by demographers. Just about everywhere, fertility decline has either taken place, is well underway, or is in its initial stages.

Fertility decline is thus the key to why the 7 billion humans alive in 2012 will almost certainly not imply 14 billion humans in the foreseeable future. Although fertility remains high in many poor nations and regions of the world, fertility decline has begun in virtually all of these nations. This, then, is also the more complete story behind the numbers in Table 19.1. For most of human history, fertility and mortality were high but mostly cancelled one another out, so that population growth was slow. This implies a long time for the world's population to double in size. Then at some point, mortality begins to decline, but fertility remains high, resulting in very rapid increases in population. At a last stage, mortality decline is accompanied by fertility decline, and we see a hint of this in Table 19.1 in the slowing of the doubling time for the world's population.

We can tell the same story not only for the world as a whole but also for specific nations. In this section, we will look at this from 1950 to 2010 for one underdeveloped country, Sudan, and two rich, developed countries, Canada and Japan. Let's begin by examining what happened in Sudan between 1950 and 2010. In Figure 19.1, the first graph for Sudan tells a story of very rapid population growth, from 9 million in 1950 to 44 million in 2010—an increase of 489 percent in 60 years. Thus, in terms of doubling times, Sudan's population doubled between 1950 and 1980 (30 years) and doubled again between 1980 and 2005 (25 years).

The second graph tells the story of the first demographic transition for Sudan—why its population has been growing so rapidly—which is that Sudan is very much in the middle of its first demographic transition. This graph plots mortality (red curve, scale on the right-hand axis) and fertility (blue curve, scale on the left-hand axis), and shows how they have changed in Sudan between 1950 and 2010. The patterns we see follow exactly the storyline for what happens during a nation's first demographic transition, which is that we first see high fertility and high mortality, then mortality declines, followed at some later point by a decline in fertility. Thus for Sudan in 1950, both mortality and fertility were high. Our measure of fertility, the **total fertility rate**, was just under 7 for Sudan in 1950. (The total fertility rate is defined by both a level, 7 in this case, and a calendar year, 1950, and what it means is that were fertility in Sudan to remain at 1950 levels, the average woman would have about 7 children over her lifetime.) But mortality in Sudan was undergoing a steady but quite rapid decline during this period; by contrast, fertility did not begin declining until 1980 or so—and note that Sudanese fertility remains high, at an average of roughly 4 children per woman in 2010.

Figure 19.1 Sudan's Population, 1950–2010

SOURCE: Based on data from United Nations, Department of Economic and Social Affairs, 2011; U.S. Bureau of the Census, 2012.

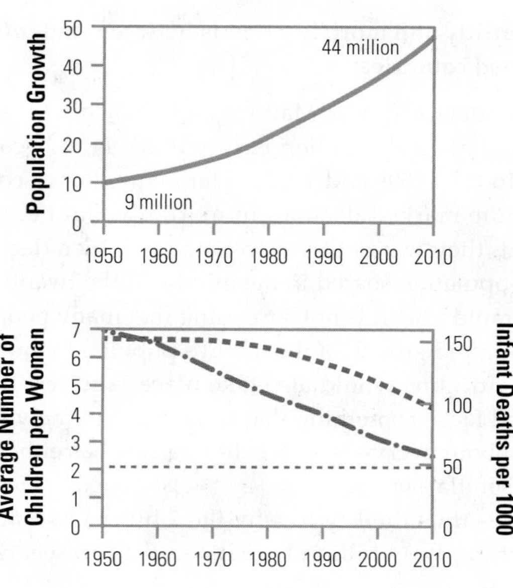

So the case of Sudan illustrates the standard first demographic transition arithmetic: rapid decreases in mortality, but much later and slower decreases in fertility, which in turn imply very rapid population growth. And this is exactly what we see in Sudan: 9 million people in 1950, 44 million in 2010.

What is the story for Canada? As the first graph for Canada in Figure 19.2 illustrates, population growth has been far slower in Canada (14 million people in 1951; 34.1 million in 2010) than in Sudan. The second graph for Canada shows part of the reason why. Canadian mortality has been fairly steady throughout this period, but the same was not true of fertility, which hit a peak of 3.8 children per woman in 1961 at the height of the baby boom but then declined, fluctuating between 1.5 and 1.8 children per woman between 1971 and 2011.

So the story of the first demographic transition is repeated in Canada as well, but we are now at the end of the story, with low mortality but moderately high fertility in 1961 and low levels of mortality and low fertility in 2011. The Canadian baby boom, which we discuss in more detail below, led to a temporary increase in fertility, but at levels far below pretransition levels of Canadian fertility. Thus, we see in Figures 19.1 and 19.2 the start of the first demographic transition in Sudan and the end of it in Canada.

Figure 19.2 Canadian Population, 1867–2012

SOURCE: Based on data from *Historical Statistics, Estimated Population and Immigrant Arrivals, Annual (persons)* (Table 075-0001), Statistics Canada, 2015, CANSIM database, (http://open.canada.ca/data/en/dataset/aa26844e-f9b6-408d-86a6-c00f933999b5); and *Estimates of Population, by Age Group and Sex for July 1, Canada, Provinces and Territories, Annual (persons unless otherwise noted)* (Table 051-0001), Statistics Canada, 2013, CANSIM database (http://www5.statcan.gc.ca/cansim/a26?lang=eng&id=510001).

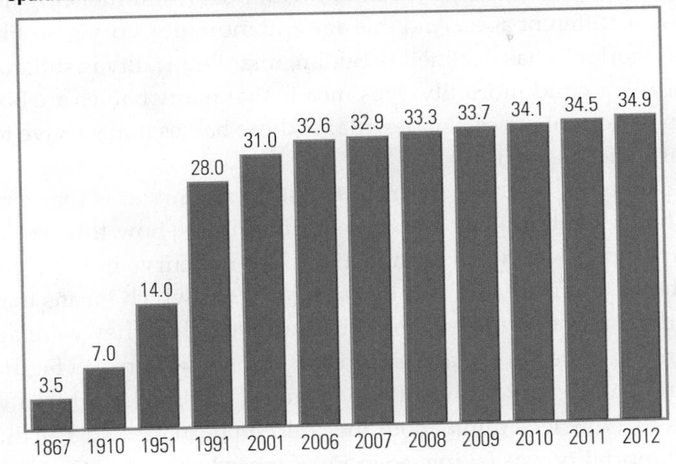

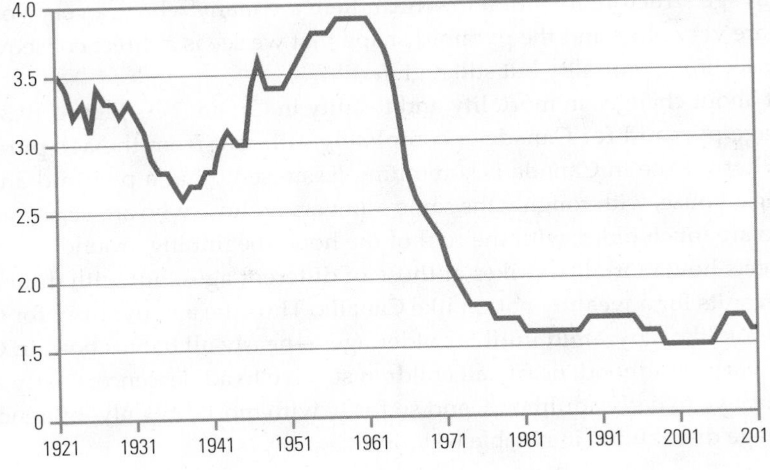

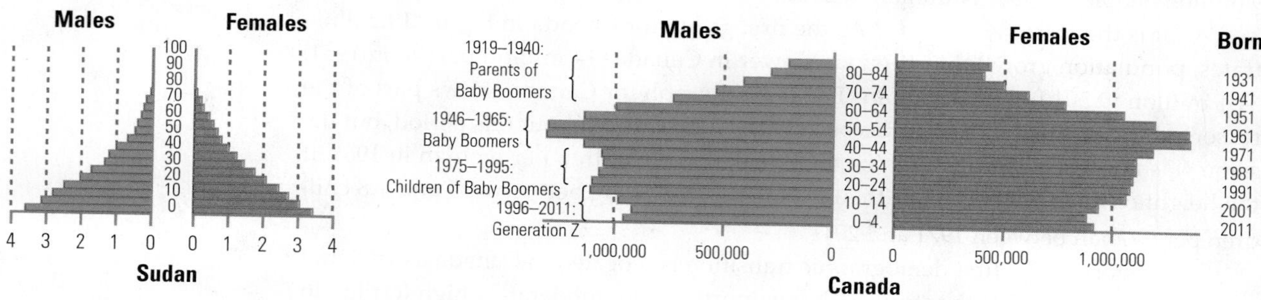

Figure 19.3 Age Pyramids for Sudan, 2010, and Canada, 2011

SOURCE: Figure for Sudan based on data from United Nations, Department of Economic and Social Affairs, 2011; figure for Canada adapted from "*Basic Demographics and Vital Statistics for Canada*," by University of Ottawa, 2015 (http://www.med.uottawa.ca/sim/data/Vital_Stats_e.htm).

That we see the start and end of the first demographic transition in Sudan and the Canada has very real consequences, which we can see when comparing the graphs for these two nations in Figure 19.3. These graphs give what demographers call **age pyramids**, in which we have plotted the age distribution for these countries in 2010, with the numbers at the youngest ages at the bottom of the graph and the numbers at the oldest ages at the top, and with males and females on the left- and right-hand sides, respectively. Compare the age pyramids for Sudan and Canada.

The age pyramid for Sudan is just that, a sharp pyramid, in which the largest numbers in the population are the very young and the fewest are the very old. This reflects the fact that Sudan is a poor nation, with poverty influencing how mortality strikes at those of different ages. And this age and mortality story goes like the following: Although mortality has declined in Sudan, infant mortality is still quite high, and the same is true for child mortality. This means that many babies are born but many more die than in rich countries like Canada; of those babies that survive to early childhood, some also die; and so forth.

But the even more important part of the story for Sudan is that fertility continues to be high but mortality has begun to decline. To see how this works, let's think about those in Sudan who were born in 1970. The red curve in the second graph in Figure 19.1 shows that mortality was declining in 1990, which means that fewer born in 1970 would die and that more were living in 1990, when they were age 20, an age when many in Sudan began to have children. But the blue curve in Figure 19.1 shows that fertility remained very high in 1990, meaning that more children were born in 1990 than before. Now let's think about the children born in 1990. Fertility continued to be high but mortality was falling, so more of those babies born in 1990 survived to have children than among previous generations. And so forth as the years passed. The result is an age structure in Sudan in which there are many who are very young but few who are very old—and the pyramid shape that we see is a direct consequence of two facts, declining mortality but still high fertility.

What about changes in mortality and fertility in Canada? As Figure 19.3 shows, the 2011 age pyramid for Canada is completely different from the age pyramid in Sudan. What we see in Canada is something less resembling a pyramid and more resembling a house, with roughly the same numbers of those who are very young and those who are much older, with the roof of the house beginning around age 60. This again reflects how mortality strikes at those of different ages, but with dramatically different results for a wealthy nation like Canada. Thus the age pyramid for Canada does not look like a pyramid until far older ages—nearly all babies born in Canada survive to early childhood, nearly all children survive to adolescence, nearly all adolescents survive to early adulthood, and so forth, with mortality only influencing the Canadian age distribution in notable ways after age 60.

Figure 19.4 Japan's Population, 1950 to 2010

SOURCE: Based on data from United Nations, Department of Economic and Social Affairs, 2011; U.S. Bureau of the Census, 2012.

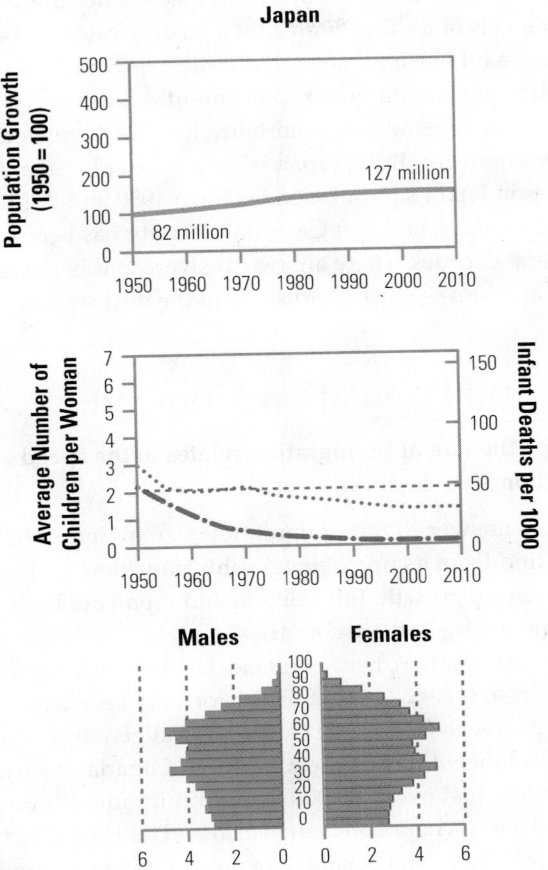

The other very important fact is that Canadian fertility has for several decades been at what demographers call **replacement fertility**. The idea is simple in that if, on average, each person in a generation had two children, this would imply a more or less unchanging size in the population—each father and mother would, on average, produce two offspring, thus replacing themselves by this number of offspring. (Demographers usually put replacement fertility at 2.1 children per woman to deal with the relatively small numbers of those who die before reaching the typical ages of childbearing.)

Figure 19.4 provides data for Japan, another rich nation. The first graph shows that the population in Japan has grown from 82 million in 1950 to 127 million in 2010. Japan experienced population growth between 1950 and 2010, as was true for Sudan and Canada, but Japan's population growth has been far slower than either of these countries. As we see in the second graph, Japan has completed its first demographic transition, with low levels of both fertility (blue line) and mortality (red line). What is particularly important to note is that Japan has had below-replacement levels of fertility for several decades, in sharp contrast to Canada, where fertility levels have been around replacement levels for several decades. The consequences of these differences—replacement levels of fertility spanning several decades in Canada but below-replacement levels of fertility spanning several decades in Japan—are very apparent when comparing the age pyramids for Canada and Japan, particularly their shapes at younger ages. As we noted earlier, the Canadian age pyramid doesn't resemble a pyramid until older ages, with roughly the same numbers of people in each five-year age group until age 60 to 64. Japan's age pyramid is very different, with sharply declining numbers at younger ages. The fact that we see sharply declining numbers in Japan's age pyramid at younger ages lines up almost exactly with trends in Japanese fertility shown in the blue curve for Japan—since the 1970s, Japan has had below-replacement levels of fertility, with a total fertility rate in Japan of 1.3 in 2010.

So stepping back a bit, we have seen that fertility in Sudan is substantially above replacement, fertility in Canada is at replacement, and fertility in Japan is below replacement. These facts, together with mortality, are clearly reflected in the age pyramids for these three countries. But if Japan is at below-replacement fertility, why is it that we see increases in Japan's population between 1950 and 2010? We could ask the same question for Canada, given that Canadian fertility has been at roughly replacement levels for several decades. There are two answers to this question—immigration and population momentum—which we discuss in the next section.

Immigration and Population Momentum

19.2.3 Discuss how the rate of immigration relates to the speed at which the population size changes.

We already know the answer to why population size in Sudan has been increasing rapidly—it is in the middle of its first demographic transition, and so is still experiencing very rapid population growth. But Canada and Japan are both posttransition, so why is population increasing in these countries?

Let's begin with immigration, because at one level it just involves the usual demographic arithmetic and so is easy. Canada has historically been a nation of immigrants. About 95 percent of people in Canada today are not Indigenous Canadians but instead arrived, or are descendants of those who arrived, in Canada at various points in history. In 2010, there were just over 280,000 legal immigrants (those who had not yet become citizens) and somewhere between 35,000 and 120,000 illegal immigrants out of the 34 million people living in Canada. By contrast, Japan's immigrant population has always been extremely small. So part of the answer for why the population of the Canada is larger in 2010 than in 1950 lies in the continuing flow of immigrants, both legal and illegal, to Canada. (The more complete answer for how migration affects change in a nation's population involves the numbers of in- and out-migrants, but in the case of Canada, in-migration vastly outnumbers out-migration.)

The other reason the populations of Japan and Canada have continued to grow over the last 60 years is **population momentum**. This refers to the tendency of a population that has been changing in size to continue to change in size even if factors such as fertility and mortality have shifted to levels that would, in the long run, imply no change in population size. Population momentum is very similar to the momentum of a physical object. Take, for example, a jet airplane that has been climbing rapidly. If the pilot were to ease off on the jet thrusters, the plane would continue climbing, at least for a while. So growth in the population of Canada or Japan is not unlike a jet that has been climbing, with the jet continuing to climb for a while even if the pilot eases up on the thrusters. This also means there is a level of fuel supplied to the jet thrusters that makes the plane eventually fly at a constant altitude—neither climbing nor descending. Anything less than this level means that the jet will eventually begin to descend, and anything above this level means that the jet will continue climbing.

The jet plane analogy for Japan is that the pilot is supplying less fuel than what is required to keep the plane at a constant altitude. Population momentum means that Japan's population did in fact continue to grow between 1950 and 2010. But as this analogy also suggests, Japan grew more rapidly during the first 30 years and less in the last 30 years of this 60-year period—Japan's population was 82 million in 1950 and 116 million in 1980, but only 127 million in 2010.

We began this chapter by noting that people like Malthus and Ehrlich thought that there was a ticking time bomb in the extremely rapid growth in the world's population. While what they worried about reflected a very simple view of population change, we now know that curbing extremely rapid population growth (in countries like Sudan) can help avoid issues that stem from overpopulation, including poverty and disease. But we also noted that demographers now worry about a second and completely different problem—that of population aging, in which some regions and countries of the world are facing rapid increases in the numbers of older people, a topic we will take up later in the chapter.

19.3 What Factors Influence Fertility?

Pathdoc/Fotolia

Theories of Fertility Decline

We have now seen that fertility decline is key to understanding population dynamics. Decades of research by demographers and other social scientists have documented in great detail when and how quickly fertility and mortality have declined, both historically and in more modern times, for countries around the world. The stylized facts emerging from this research tell us things that we know with great certainty about the first demographic transition and about fertility decline in particular. But while there is near universal agreement on what the facts concerning fertility decline are, there is anything but universal agreement on *why* fertility has declined. Social scientists strive to figure out the "why."

Several theories (or theoretical hypotheses) provide plausible answers for why fertility has declined. We'll discuss five in this section. Keep in mind the possibility that the reasons behind fertility decline may be very different before and after the first demographic transition. We should note that demographers and social scientists have yet to agree on which of these hypotheses is largely correct, whether all of them have some merit, or whether one or more of them should be abandoned. Research in this area remains very active.

Infant Mortality

19.3.1 Explain the connection between declining infant mortality and fertility decline.

A first theory argues that declines in infant mortality can cause fertility decline. Proponents of this hypothesis begin from the observation that for much of human history, both mortality and fertility were high. But one consequence of high mortality levels is that a couple cannot be certain whether an infant who is just born will survive or will die before reaching adulthood. As a result, couples will typically try to have many children to ensure that at least a few will survive. As mortality begins to decline, however, so too will the need to have many children. This explanation is attractive because it not only tells us why fertility declines but also addresses why fertility decline occurs only after mortality has begun its decline (during the first demographic transition). However, this theory is not very good at explaining why we see fertility differences between posttransition countries, such as Canada and Japan. Mortality is low in both countries, but fertility is substantially lower in Japan. For these reasons, this argument is a plausible candidate for explaining fertility decline before and during the first demographic transition but is far less plausible for explaining fertility differences among countries that have completed the first demographic transition.

Economic Development

19.3.2 Explain the connection between fertility and economic development.

Fertility rates are also related to the patterns of economic development, or more specifically, to how advanced a nation's economy is. This hypothesis argues that fertility will decline as a country undergoes economic and social development and becomes richer. An early version of this hypothesis was that economic development was necessary if the first demographic transition was to occur (Notestein, 1953). In other words, as poor countries became more prosperous economically, their mortality and then fertility rates would begin to fall. For a graphical demonstration, Figure 19.5 plots the fertility rate on the *y* axis and gross domestic product (GDP) per person on the *x* axis.

Figure 19.5 Total Fertility Rate Versus GDP per Capita

SOURCE: From *The CIA World Factbook*, by the U.S. Central Intelligence Agency, 2012, New York: Skyhorse.

NOTE: Only countries with over 5 million population are shown.

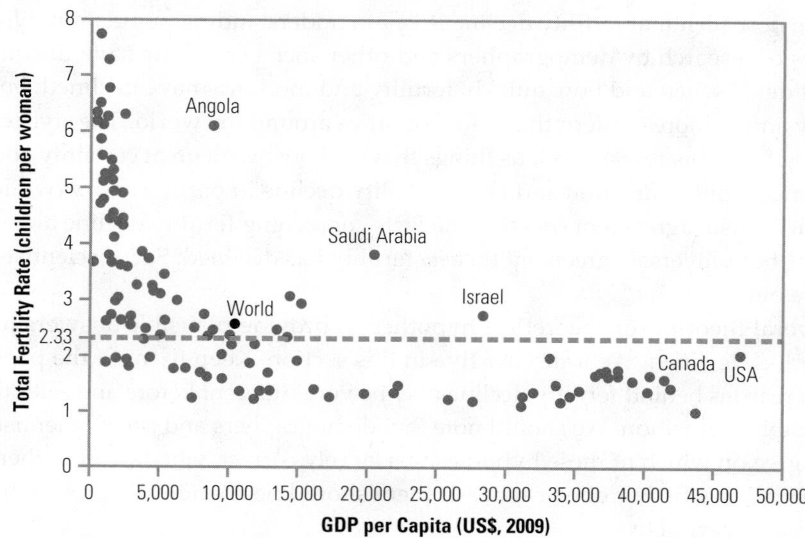

Although Figure 19.5 shows a clear relationship between economic development and fertility, there is also a lot of variation at every level of GDP per person. For example, there are rich countries, like Saudi Arabia, Israel, and even the United States, that have significantly higher fertility than would be predicted. Further, even very poor nations like Sudan can and have adopted policies that very quickly lead to improvements in infant mortality. Moreover, the same pattern of reductions in fertility found elsewhere has followed once infant mortality declines. Social scientists now know that there are a number of things that can greatly reduce infant mortality, including building systems for waste and sewage disposal, the provision of clean drinking water, access to hospitals or clinics to monitor the health of pregnant women and to help women when they give birth, and a variety of improvements in the nutrition, health, and medical care of infants, children, and their mothers. Social scientists also see education as an extremely important component of social development, particularly the education of women. The argument here is that in less developed countries, increases in literacy and education will, in turn, lead to improvements in infant health and to decreases in infant mortality, with this then followed (at some later point) by a decline in fertility.

Yet another way in which social and economic development may limit fertility is if development also carries with it the prospect of better lives for young people. If so, the prospect of upward mobility for offspring may lead parents to have higher aspirations for their children, which may in turn lead such parents to have fewer children relative to those parents who do not see such opportunities for their children (Davis, 1963). But as was the case for the infant mortality hypothesis, this hypothesis speaks most directly to why fertility declines before and during the first demographic transition but is far less plausible in explaining why we see different levels of fertility post transition.

Birth Control

19.3.3 Explain the connection between improved birth control, changing attitudes about bearing children, and fertility decline.

Another hypothesis holds that two profound changes affected fertility: (1) the growing acceptance of the view that people can (and should) exercise control over their fertility, and (2) technological advances in the means by which women and couples can control their fertility. For most of human history, a central purpose of marriage was to have children. Today, this is no longer the case. Many happily married couples with no fertility issues choose not to have children (and do not suffer any stigma as a consequence). Further, since the 1960s individuals and couples have had many ways of preventing unwanted pregnancies by using an effective method of contraception. The appearance of the birth control pill was critical to this new era of contraception. As couples could now exercise a considerable degree of control over the timing, spacing, and number of births, they were much less likely to produce an extra, unintended child.

Proponents of the hypothesis that improved birth control combined with changing norms about the necessity of having children lowered fertility had argued that fertility control is one of the great social changes that accompanied the first demographic transition. In pretransition societies, wanting to prevent or control births could well have been simply irrelevant. In the modern world (particularly in developed countries), however, factors like furthering education, pursuing career goals, and working toward financial stability affect whether and when people have children. So, one possible advantage of this hypothesis is that it provides an explanation for fertility changes before, during, and after the first demographic transition.

Childrearing

19.3.4 Explain the connection between the costs and benefits of childrearing and fertility decline.

Often cited by economists, a fourth hypothesis holds that fertility decline results from the costs and benefits of having and raising children. This theory focuses on how larger social changes might affect fertility-related behaviours at the individual level (e.g., women, men, couples, and parents). Proponents of this theory argue that before the Industrial Revolution, countries like Canada and those in Europe were *agrarian societies*, which meant that the overwhelming majority lived in rural areas and worked as farmers, sharecroppers, peasants, or other agricultural workers. In such agrarian economies, children were a net benefit to parents because they provided additional labour for tending crops or livestock. They were also a potential safety net; the surviving children could take care of their aging parents. But with industrialization, increasing numbers of workers migrated to urban areas and cities to work in factories, which lessened the economic benefit of having many children who could help work in the fields even at young ages. In the twenty-first century, how parents weigh the costs and benefits of children will also explain why we see much lower fertility in a country like Japan than in Canada.

Like the hypothesis about birth control's role, this hypothesis possibly explains changes in fertility across multiple historical periods; however, we need to take a couple of factors into consideration. First, this hypothesis supposes that individuals and couples actually weighed the costs and benefits before, during, and after the first demographic transition, whereas the birth control theory sees the idea of rational choice in fertility-related behaviours as something very new and very modern. In addition, this hypothesis places great emphasis on material conditions for a given family—the economic costs versus the benefits to parents of having another child—whereas the birth control hypothesis places less emphasis on material conditions and far more emphasis on the evolution of ideas, norms, and culture—how it is that parents might think about the issue of having another child and how this has changed over time. These are the kinds of issues social scientists keep in mind when considering different hypotheses.

Norms and Values

19.3.5 Explain the connection between changing norms and values and fertility decline.

Another hypothesis for fertility decline argues that recent fertility change is a consequence of changes in norms and values accompanying what some have called the **second demographic transition** (Lesthaeghe & van de Kaa, 1986). Proponents typically point to very substantial changes in family life in rich countries like the United States, Canada, and Japan. Some of these include historical increases in divorce (Preston & McDonald, 1979), premarital sexual activity (Joyner & Laumann, 2001), increased cohabitation where couples live together without being married (Bumpass & Lu, 2000), and out-of-wedlock childbearing (Wu, 2008). All of these changes reflect, at least in part, yet another dramatic shift that has occurred in the modern world: the evolving ideas of what we might ideally want from being in a relationship, from being married, or from being a parent. In times past, people were expected to marry and to have children, and, as a result, many did. But this also meant (so the argument goes) that if you did not, then people were likely to think that something was wrong with you. Today, people are far more likely to say that you should have children only if and when you feel that this makes sense for you and your partner. This would imply that having children is now very much a matter of choice, and this also means that there are a number of good reasons for choosing to have no children or only one child. Proponents of this hypothesis conclude that the emerging norms and values due to the second demographic transition mean that there will be lower fertility than in the past, including (in some cases) the very low levels of fertility observed in countries like Japan.

19.4 How Are Trends in Aging and Mortality Emerging as Critical Issues in Many Societies?

Gallo Images/Contributor/Getty Images

The Implications of an Aging Population

In this section, we will discuss the demographic results when populations begin to age. We will first explore what the first demographic transition implies for the health conditions of populations. We will then turn to the aging of the baby boom generation in Canada and Japan and compare how quickly aging might occur in these two countries.

The Epidemiological Transition

19.4.1 Discuss how the epidemiological transition explains differences in health conditions affecting those in poorer and richer countries.

As we saw earlier in this chapter, the first demographic transition carries with it a shift from age pyramids like that in Sudan to those that we see in Canada and Japan. How might the first demographic transition influence health when we think about overall health in a nation's population? The answer is something that social scientists now call the *epidemiological transition* (Omran, 1971). **Epidemiology** is the study of health-related events in populations, their characteristics, their causes, and their consequences. The **epidemiological transition** refers to the transition of a population from health conditions primarily involving infectious disease (often extremely deadly to infants, children, and young adults in poor and developing countries) to health conditions primarily involving chronic disease (often shaping the health conditions of individuals, and especially the elderly, in rich countries like Canada and Japan). The story behind the epidemiological transition is that the first demographic transition has very important implications for diseases and health conditions affecting countries like Sudan and countries like Canada and Japan.

Infectious diseases develop from bacteria, viruses, parasites, and other contagious agents. The common cold, the flu, and HIV are examples of viral infections, while bacterial infections develop from harmful germs and microorganisms. (For example, harmful bacteria may multiply and make you very sick if it is in something you've eaten that hasn't been cooked under sanitary conditions or at the right temperature.) Infectious diseases do not usually kill people in countries like Canada and Japan, but they are an extremely common cause of death, especially for infants and young children, in poor and developing countries like Sudan.

However, we have seen a steady decline in mortality even in very poor countries like Sudan. And at least part of the reason that mortality has declined is that many poor countries have been able to tackle at least some sources of infectious disease. For example, they have improved conditions by cleaning up and protecting water supplies and by immunizing and providing better healthcare and nutrition to infants, children, and mothers. But as should be obvious, advances in our scientific understanding of infectious disease do not in any way guarantee that mortality will decline—instead, declining mortality often requires very serious social action and social policies on the part of poor and developing countries. For evidence on the growth of life expectancy around the world, explore Figure 19.6.

The epidemiological transition also involves a transition to chronic disease. **Chronic diseases** and, more generally, chronic health conditions are diseases and health conditions that are persistent. Examples include serious heart and respiratory problems, diabetes, high blood pressure, obesity, cancer, Parkinson's disease, Alzheimer's disease, and HIV/AIDS. Many of these chronic health conditions are not the result of an infectious disease but instead involve risk factors that we can influence, at least in part, by things like eating healthy foods, getting enough exercise, avoiding tanning booths or too much sun, and being careful about sexually transmitted diseases. (HIV/AIDS is an infectious disease that caused many deaths in Canada in the 1980s and 1990s; however, it can now be treated, if diagnosed promptly, in ways that make it much more of a chronic condition.) This is why one of the first researchers who wrote about the epidemiological transition characterized it as a long-term shift in mortality and disease patterns in which infectious diseases are "gradually displaced by degenerative and *man-made* diseases" (Omran 1971, p. 516; emphasis added).

The other notable fact about chronic health conditions is that not only do they tend to strike at older ages but they typically do not kill when they first strike, and when they do kill, they often kill slowly. This is the chronic aspect of these health conditions—if you suffer from a chronic health condition, you may die of it eventually, but in countries like Canada and Japan, you most often will not die from it right away. And for many of these chronic conditions (obesity, high blood pressure, heart or lung disease, some but not all cancers, HIV/AIDS), you can live for quite a long time and lead something resembling a normal life if you know how to manage the condition and have the means to manage it.

Aging of the Baby Boomers

19.4.2 Discuss how the aging of the baby boom generation contributes to the overall graying of societies.

The **baby boom** refers to the period following World War II from 1946 to 1964, during which Canada experienced a notable, extended, but ultimately temporary spike in fertility. Those born between 1946 and 1964 are referred to as the *baby boom birth cohorts* (or the *baby boomers*). (A **birth cohort** refers to persons born during the same period of time.)

Figure 19.6 Life Expectancy at Birth Around the World

SOURCE: From *The CIA World Factbook*, by the U.S. Central Intelligence Agency, 2012, New York: Skyhorse.

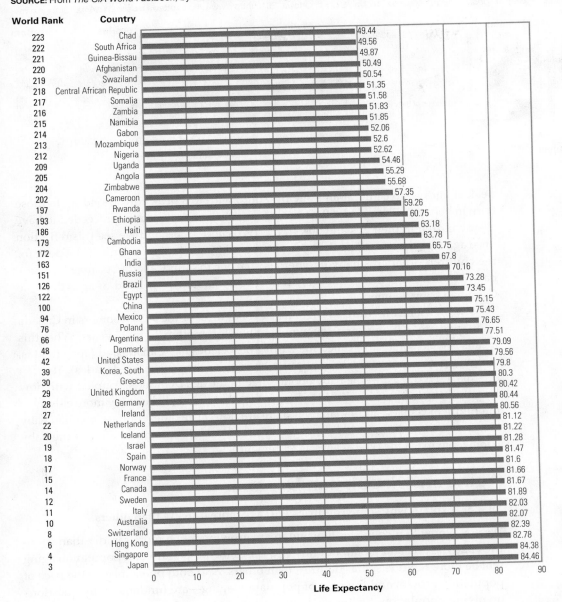

World Rank	Country	Life Expectancy
223	Chad	49.44
222	South Africa	49.56
221	Guinea-Bissau	49.87
220	Afghanistan	50.49
219	Swaziland	50.54
218	Central African Republic	51.35
217	Somalia	51.58
216	Zambia	51.83
215	Namibia	51.85
214	Gabon	52.06
213	Mozambique	52.6
212	Nigeria	52.62
209	Uganda	54.46
205	Angola	55.29
204	Zimbabwe	55.68
202	Cameroon	57.35
197	Rwanda	59.26
193	Ethiopia	60.75
186	Haiti	63.18
179	Cambodia	63.78
172	Ghana	65.75
163	India	67.8
151	Russia	70.16
126	Brazil	73.28
122	Egypt	73.45
100	China	75.15
94	Mexico	75.43
76	Poland	76.65
66	Argentina	77.51
48	Denmark	79.09
42	United States	79.56
39	Korea, South	79.8
30	Greece	80.3
29	United Kingdom	80.42
28	Germany	80.44
27	Ireland	80.56
22	Netherlands	81.12
20	Iceland	81.22
19	Israel	81.28
18	Spain	81.47
17	Norway	81.6
15	France	81.66
14	Canada	81.67
12	Sweden	81.89
11	Italy	82.03
10	Australia	82.07
8	Switzerland	82.39
6	Hong Kong	82.78
4	Singapore	84.38
3	Japan	84.46

We can see the Canadian baby boom in the second graph of Figure 19.2, which shows that the Canadian total fertility rate stood at 3.4 in 1951, rose to a peak of 3.9 in 1961, and fell in later years. The baby boom can also be seen very clearly in the age pyramid for Canada. Let's take another look at the age pyramids displayed in Figure 19.3. The Canadian peak of 3.9 in 1961 for the total fertility rate corresponds with the broad peak in the Canadian age pyramid covering those who were 50 to 54 in 2011 (the youngest of the baby boomers) to those aged 60 to 64 in 2011 (the oldest of the baby boomers). Note also that there is another broad peak in the Canadian age pyramid, one covering ages 15 to 19, 20 to 24, and 25 to 29 in 2011 and thus corresponding to those born in the years 1981 through 1985, 1986 through 1990, and 1991 through 1995. Many in these birth cohorts are the children of the baby boomers; thus, we see a *reflection* of the baby boom in the children of this period.

Something very similar shows up in Japan's age pyramid, seen in Figure 19.7. Japan also experienced a baby boom and, as in Canada, this shows up in the sharp

Figure 19.7 Age Pyramids for Japan, 2010, and Canada, 2011

SOURCE: Figure for Japan based on data from the U.S. Census Bureau, 2012; figure for Canada adapted from "Basic Demographics and Vital Statistics for Canada," *Society, the Individual, and Medicine*, by University of Ottawa, 2015 (http://www.med.uottawa.ca/sim/data/Vital_Stats_e.htm).

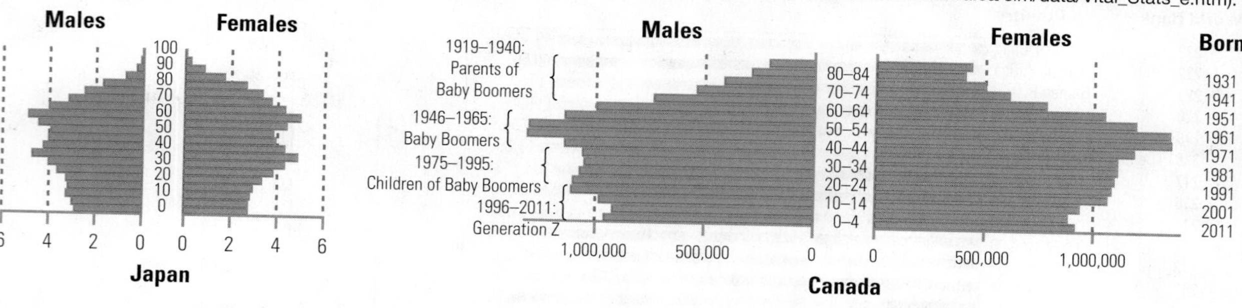

peak at ages 60 to 64 in Japan's age pyramid, with this peak corresponding to those born in between 1946 and 1950. These Japanese baby boomers then proceeded to have their children in their 20s and 30s, in the 1970s and 1980s, and we see this reflection once again as the second peak at younger ages in Japan's age pyramid. (The peak for the children of Japan's baby boomers is sharper than in Canada because Japanese baby boomers had their children, on average, in a narrower band of ages than the Canadian baby boomers.)

If we then fast-forward to 2011 and beyond, most of the baby boomers in Canada and Japan are still alive and can expect to live for another 15 to 25 years. What this means is what some have called the *graying* of societies like Canada and Japan (that is, a higher percentage of the total population is older than in earlier decades). You can see this in Figure 19.7—the baby boom bulge in the age pyramids, coupled with how long the baby boomers are likely to live, means that there will be many more elderly in the future in Canada and Japan than there are now. (The oldest of the Canadian baby boomers—those born in 1946—turned 65 in 2011 and so were the first of the baby boomers to reach the typical ages at retirement.)

Aging and Population Dynamics

19.4.3 Explain why some countries will age more quickly than others.

We now know that countries like Sudan are growing much more rapidly than countries like Canada and Japan. But this also raises the possibility that population aging will be more rapid in some countries than others. And both phenomena—the pace of population growth and the pace of population aging—are fundamentally questions involving population dynamics. A comparison between Japan and Canada, seen in Figure 19.7, tells us a lot about what we need to know (and thus can reasonably expect looking into the future) about the pace of population aging in Canada and Japan. And the answer is that we can reasonably expect that population aging will be far more rapid in Japan than in Canada.

The reason for this is easy to see, and it lies in the shapes of the Canadian and Japanese age pyramids. *Population aging* refers to the relative numbers of young and old people in a population, and the age pyramids give us very detailed information about this for Japan for one particular calendar year—in the data displayed in Figure 19.7, the calendar year 2010. Now predicting what the future will look like is speculative; it requires guesses about mortality (that is, how future mortality will strike those of different ages) plus guesses about fertility (that is, how future fertility will fill in the numbers at the bottom of future age pyramids). Looking again at Figure 19.7, you may have already guessed the answer, which is that Japan will, in all likelihood, be aging much more quickly than Canada. And the fundamental reason for this is fertility—the fact that fertility in Japan has been at subreplacement levels for many decades.

Table 19.2 Population Size and Subreplacement Fertility Level

Mean number of children per women	2.0	1.9	1.8	1.7	1.6	1.5	1.4	1.3	1.2	1.1	1.0
Years until population halving	901	279	161	112	84	66	54	45	38	33	29

SOURCE: Based on formula from "The Emergence of Lowest-Low Fertility in Europe," by Hans-Peter Kohler, Francesco C. Billari, and Antonio Ortega, 2002, *Population and Development Review 28*(4), 641–680.

Should these trends continue into the future, Japan's population can be expected to decline once mortality begins thinning the ranks of Japan's baby boom generation. How quickly might Japan's population decline? Any answer to this question again has to be speculative, but we can nevertheless give fairly precise answers under the speculative "what if" scenario of "What if a nation's fertility remains at a particular subreplacement level for a long time?" Take a look at Table 19.2 to see how long it would take for a population to halve in size—that is, decrease by a factor of two—if fertility remains at a particular subreplacement level for a very long time.

What Table 19.2 shows is that if fertility in a population were to remain just a bit below replacement, population decline would be very gradual, but that population decline can be very rapid at other subreplacement levels of fertility. So, let's use a hypothetical nation as an example. If Nation A has an average of 1.9 children per woman rather than the replacement level of 2.1 children per woman and if this were to continue for a long time, Nation A's population would indeed decline, but quite slowly, taking roughly 280 years to halve in size. However, if Nation A has an average of 1.4 children per woman and if this were to continue for a long time, its population would take only 54 years to halve in size—an extremely rapid pace of population decline. Now, let's go back to Japan. Because Japan's fertility has been between 1.2 and 1.4 for several decades, there is the distinct possibility that Japan will experience very rapid population decline. And what has been both surprising and fascinating to demographers is that many countries besides Japan have equally low levels of subreplacement fertility. (The list includes Austria, Cuba, the Czech Republic, Germany, Greece, Hong Kong, Italy, Poland, Russia, Singapore, South Korea, Spain, and Taiwan.) Thus countries like these face not only the prospect of rapid population aging but also the possibility of rapid population decline at some point in the future should fertility remain at very low subreplacement levels.

Health in an Aging Population

19.4.4 Discuss the role of health and healthcare as a population ages.

What does it mean to be healthy in old age? As defined by the World Health Organization (2011), health is "a state of complete physical, mental, and social well-being and not merely the absence of disease or infirmity." What makes health different from many social goods is that it is difficult to carry out life without it. If you are unhealthy, it is difficult to get more education, to perform well at work, or to maintain meaningful relationships.

Life expectancy is one of the most common measures used to describe the health of a population. It is defined as the average number of years a population at some age can expect to live. As we discussed earlier in this chapter, life expectancy has increased substantially in the last century in developed countries, and many poor countries as well. Canadians' life expectancy at birth in 2009, for example, was 81.1 years (World Bank, 2011). Canadians' life expectancy has increased by 10 years since 1960, but it nonetheless lags behind some other countries around the world. The Japanese, for example, can expect to live 82.9 years.

Marmaduke St. John/Alamy Stock Photo

Very few people born in the early twentieth century reach 100 years of age. However, as life expectancy increases, we face a growing social problem of adequately housing and caring for a growing number of people who are far beyond their working years. It is entirely possible that one or more of this centenarian's offspring will also have very long lives.

Life expectancy tells us how long we might expect to live, but knowing when we might die does not tell us everything we might want to know about health in later years. As we reach certain ages, many of us want to know how many "good years" we have left—years when we can anticipate good health and ability to do a normal range of activities. Because of this, social scientists also track **healthy life expectancy**, the average number of healthy years one can expect to live if current patterns of death and illness remain the same. The World Health Organization is currently tracking three measures of healthy life expectancy: expected years of life in good health, expected years of life free from limitation of activity, and expected years of life free from selected chronic diseases.

Chronic disease prevalence also provides a different portrait of Canadians' health status. In 2007, almost one-third of Canadians reported that they had a chronic disease. Together, these measures of health tell us how ill our population is and provide a framework for understanding the impact of an aging population on society as a whole. Researchers continue to debate whether increases in life expectancy will translate into increases in the number of years that we live free of disease or will simply prolong the amount of time that we spend being unwell at the end of our lives.

Financing Old Age and Healthcare in Aging Societies

19.4.5 Discuss why population aging creates financial pressures for governments and societies.

Because of declines of fertility and increases in life expectancy in developed countries, many countries are now facing significant problems financing retirement and healthcare costs for the elderly. By 2030, 1 in 8 people in the world will be 65 or older (National Institute on Aging, National Institutes of Health, U.S. Department of Health and Human Services, & U.S. Department of State, 2007). According to Statistics Canada, on July 1, 2015, for the first time, there were more people aged 65 and over than children aged 0 to 14 years. Nearly 1 in 6 Canadians was at least 65 years of age or older. Population projections suggest that the share of persons aged 65 and older will continue to grow and that 20.1 percent of the Canadian population will be aged 65 and older by July 1, 2024 (Statistics Canada, 2015). In aging societies, the number of younger working people for each person 65 and older has been shrinking so that there are fewer people who will be able to share the cost of healthcare for the elderly.

When people reach a point where they are no longer able or expected to work, virtually all societies attempt to provide for their well-being. In poorer countries, this often means that the elderly live with children who will support them. In richer countries, however, retirement increasingly comes with the expectation that an acceptable minimal level of social support for the aged will be provided by the government. Since 1928, most Canadians over the age of 65 can receive monthly **Old Age Security** payments. Since 1965, Canada has also had the **Canada Pension Plan (CPP)**, an earnings-related social insurance program. The CPP program mandates that all employed Canadians who are 18 years of age and over contribute a prescribed portion of their earnings income to a nationally administered pension plan.

Canada implemented a universal healthcare system (**medicare**) beginning in 1946 in Saskatchewan. The universal health insurance program was later adopted all across the country. Various levels of government pay for approximately 70 percent of Canadians' privately delivered healthcare needs.

So, let's recap the trends: (1) There are fewer people of working age to pay taxes to support the Canada Pension Plan, Old Age Security, and medicare. (2) There are more older people using those benefits. The result? An aging population puts significant pressures on government finance. But as difficult as these problems are for Canada, they are far more daunting in Japan. That is, even though both Canada and Japan are graying societies, what we saw in Table 19.2 raises the possibility that Japan's population will not only grow older but will also grow smaller, with fewer new workers replacing those that retire, leaving a much smaller tax base from which to draw to pay for these important health and well-being programs.

Death and Dying Around the World

19.4.6 Understand how countries differ in how they treat older, very sick people.

We often think of death as the most individual event in our lives. We may hear people lament that they will "die alone," and people have a wide variety of personal preferences about the kind of death they hope to have. These preferences are a function not just of individual idiosyncratic tastes but of the cultures, religions, and nations in which we are embedded.

The rise of chronic disease as the cause of death, rather than an acute event like a heart attack, creates new challenges in caring for people at the end of their lives. Chronic diseases generally unfold slowly, so those suffering from them can expect to experience a series of health emergencies that ultimately culminate in their death. This change may have important implications for how we choose to manage death, for example, by not only trying to prevent death but also reducing the pain and stress that can accompany the end of life, a period that now extends for much longer than ever before.

Canada tends to operate around a heroic model of medicine, where we expect doctors to do everything they can to prolong lives. A relatively small number of Canadians have defined the conditions under which they prefer to die in a legal document, called an **advance directive**. For example, an advance directive might specify that someone does not want to be placed on a ventilator if that is necessary to sustain his or her life. Others might suggest that they only want **palliative care**, which is defined by the World Health Organization (2016) as "an approach that improves the quality of life of patients and their families facing the problem[s] associated with life-threatening illness, through the prevention and relief of suffering by means of early identification and impeccable assessment and treatment of pain and other problems, physical, psychosocial and spiritual." One of the best-known types of palliative care is **hospice care**, which focuses on eliminating suffering—physical and mental—for terminally ill patients.

According to data that bring together measures about the quality, cost, and availability of end-of-life care from around the world (Economist

Chronic diseases like cancer and heart disease now kill a higher fraction of North Americans, creating the need for more end-of-life care options than we have had in the past.

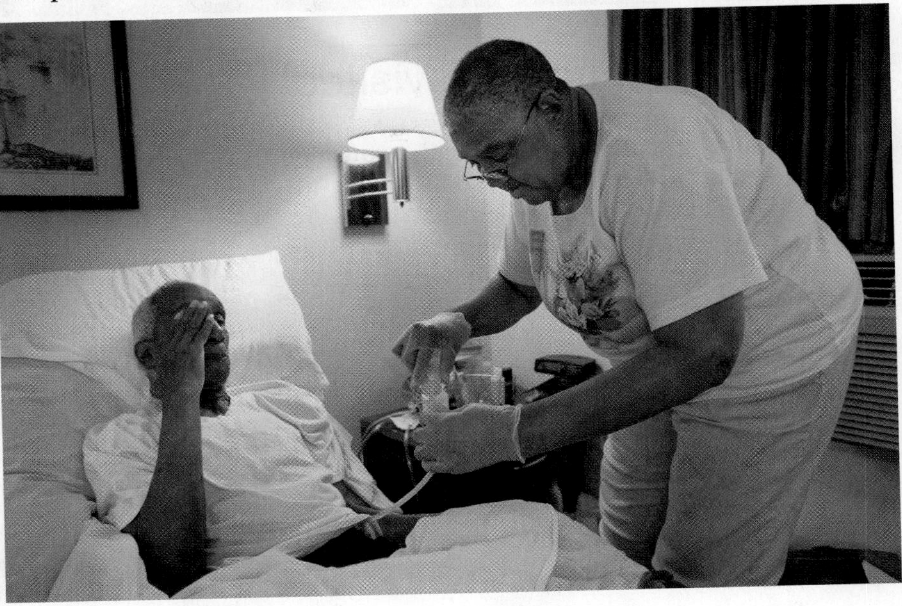

Jerry Wolford/Polaris/Newscom

Intelligence Unit, 2010), there is substantial variation between countries in end-of-life care. Developed countries like the United Kingdom and Australia are consistently rated as providing the best quality of care, while India, Uganda, Brazil, and China are rated as providing the worst.

We have seen that aging societies, and the individuals who live in them, are in many respects the victim of their own success. The multiple social challenges that they face—chronic disease, financial burdens, and issues around an extended period of end-of-life care—exist precisely because of increases in life expectancy over the last century. Aging societies also provide a clear example of a larger sociological principle: Our social institutions adapt to the changing social contexts and conditions that they face.

Conclusion

We began this chapter by noting that in the 1960s and 1970s, it was taken for granted that *the* most pressing population issue was very rapid population growth and that this ticking time bomb would spell disaster for the world. But you now know the reasons behind what might otherwise seem like a paradox—why it is that most who study these issues now point to not one but rather two problems of population change: too rapid population growth in some countries and rapid population aging (and the possibility of very rapid population decline) in others. These trends result from changes in fertility and mortality, but also migration. We have not examined migration in much detail in this chapter (as we devote Chapter 10 to that topic), but the key point is that the combination of fertility, mortality, and migration produces continual change across societies. These are the reasons why the ticking population time bomb that Malthus and Ehrlich so feared has not, in fact, come to pass. What we now worry about in the twenty-first century is another ticking time bomb, that of climate change. While most scientists agree that global warming is the result of human activity, the notion that population growth is the principal driver of climate change is inaccurate, as we discuss in great detail in Chapter 18.

On a more general note, the very earliest sociologists—Marx, Weber, and Durkheim—were fascinated by how the modern world was different from what the world was like in earlier times. Sociologists today continue to study change—and population trends are very much at the centre of that research.

CHAPTER SUMMARY

The Big Questions Revisited 19

19.1 Why Study Population? The world's population has doubled in size twice since 1910—taking first 57 and then 45 years to double. When will the world's population next double in size? This section examined reasons why governments and policymakers need to know about population trends, including the risk of overpopulation.

Population and Censuses

The Census and Population Research

Learning Objective 19.1.1: Discuss why it is relevant to study population trends.

Studying Population

Learning Objective 19.1.2: Identify ways in which population is studied.

19.2 How Do Populations Change Over Time? To better understand the dynamics of population change, in this section we looked at how mortality and fertility have changed for different nations and what these changes might imply for the demographic futures of these nations.

Population Dynamics

The First Demographic Transition

Learning Objective 19.2.1: Define the first demographic transition and its role in understanding how populations change.

Changes in Fertility and Mortality Around the World

Learning Objective 19.2.2: Compare fertility and mortality trends between underdeveloped and developed countries.

Immigration and Population Momentum

Learning Objective 19.2.3: Discuss how the rate of immigration relates to the speed at which the population size changes.

19.3 What Factors Influence Fertility? Populations change over time largely because fertility practices also have been changing (i.e., the decision to have a child). In most countries around the world, women are having fewer babies than 50 or 100 years ago. Why is this the case? In this section we explored some of the leading explanations for declining fertility.

Theories of Fertility Decline

Infant Mortality

Learning Objective 19.3.1: Explain the connection between declining infant mortality and fertility decline.

Economic Development

Learning Objective 19.3.2: Explain the connection between fertility and economic development.

Birth Control

Learning Objective 19.3.3: Explain the connection between improved birth control, changing attitudes about bearing children, and fertility decline.

Childrearing

Learning Objective 19.3.4: Explain the connection between the costs and benefits of childrearing and fertility decline.

Norms and Values

Learning Objective 19.3.5: Explain the connection between changing norms and values and fertility decline.

19.4 How are Trends in Aging and Mortality Emerging as Critical Issues in Many Societies? Some countries have many very young people but very few old people, while others have many old people currently and will have even more old people in the future as life expectancy increases. What do these trends mean for employment and health conditions in countries like these? In this section, we asked about the demographic implications when populations begin to age.

The Implications of an Aging Population

The Epidemiological Transition

Learning Objective 19.4.1: Discuss how the epidemiological transition explains differences in health conditions affecting those in poorer and richer countries.

Aging of the Baby Boomers

Learning Objective 19.4.2: Discuss how the aging of the baby boom generation contributes to the overall graying of societies.

Aging and Population Dynamics

Learning Objective 19.4.3: Explain why some countries will age more quickly than others.

Health in an Aging Population

Learning Objective 19.4.4: Discuss the role of health and healthcare as a population ages.

Financing Old Age and Healthcare in Aging Societies

Learning Objective 19.4.5: Discuss why population aging creates financial pressures for governments and societies.

Death and Dying Around the World

Learning Objective 19.4.6: Understand how countries differ in how they treat older, very sick people.

Learn the Terms

advance directive (p. 573)
age pyramid (p. 560)
baby boom (p. 568)
birth cohort (p. 568)
Canada Pension Plan (p. 572)
census (p. 552)
chronic disease (p. 568)
chronic disease prevalence (p. 572)
demographer (p. 552)
demography (p. 552)
enumerate (p. 552)
epidemiological transition (p. 567)
epidemiology (p. 567)
fertility (p. 555)
first demographic transition (p. 556)
healthy life expectancy (p. 572)
hospice care (p. 573)
infectious disease (p. 568)
life expectancy (p. 571)
medicare (p. 573)
migration (p. 555)
mortality (p. 555)
Old Age Security (p. 572)
palliative care (p. 573)
population dynamics (p. 555)
population momentum (p. 562)
replacement fertility (p. 561)
second demographic transition (p. 566)
stylized facts (p. 554)
total fertility rate (p. 558)

Chapter 20
Globalization

by Vivek Chibber

Bill Bachmann/Alamy Stock Photo

How far-reaching is globalization? What is driving it, and what are its limits? These are questions we will explore in this chapter.

Learning Objectives

20.1.1 Discuss the two key changes responsible for the development of globalization.

20.1.2 Analyze the ways in which globalization has expanded steadily since the nineteenth century.

20.2.1 Discuss the extent of international trade and investment in globalization.

20.2.2 Explain why economic integration clusters around regions.

20.3.1 Analyze the role that value chains play in globalization.

20.3.2 Outline the benefits and costs of China's export zones.

20.4.1 Discuss the benefits of globalization to economic growth.

20.4.2 Summarize the consequences of the North American Free Trade Agreement (NAFTA).

20.4.3 Discuss the impact of globalization on the economic performance of low-income countries.

We have all had this experience at some point: We pull up in our car at a fast food restaurant, place an order at the speaker, and then drive on to the window to pick up our food. The person at the window greets us with a smile; she asks us if we would like to add anything to our order and then hands us our bag of food. Usually, we peer into the bag to make sure she got everything we asked for—"Did you remember to add extra ketchup?" She assures us that she did, we smile back, and then drive away.

Sounds simple, right? Not any longer. Here is what is happening in many local fast food drive-throughs. You drive up and place your order—but the person listening to you and taking the order is not the one who greets you as you drive up to the window. Your order goes to a worker wearing a headset and sitting in front of a computer hundreds or thousands of miles away. That worker then types your order into the computer and it appears on the screen of the cashier whom you meet at the drive-through window. What used to be a simple exchange between you and an attendant a few feet away has turned into a three-part transaction between people an enormous distance away from one another but completed in the same amount of time. It is as if distance just doesn't matter anymore.

We have all heard that globalization is breaking apart assumptions about how and where goods and services are produced. Products that used to be made under one roof are now produced in separate sites thousands of kilometres apart, and assembled by workers in yet other locations before they reach us. Could that happen with services too? It used to be taken for granted that while the manufacture of goods can be broken up and dispersed across distant locations, a service has to be provided on site. It would never occur to most of us that something as personal as taking an order at a restaurant could also be outsourced, just like the manufacture of a car. Yet even that is beginning to occur.

Just how far has globalization gone? What is driving it, and what are its limits? These are the questions that we tackle in this chapter.

The Big Questions

In this chapter, we examine the basic facts about the process of globalization—what it is, when it started, what its driving forces are, and what its effects have been. Of course, we are examining a process that is still very much underway and that is constantly evolving.

1. **What is globalization?** Discussions of economic policy rarely refer to the idea of globalization in the sociological sense. What does it mean, and how can sociology make sense of it? In this section, we examine globalization and its origins.

2. **How far-reaching is globalization?** To evaluate how far-reaching the process of globalization has been, we examine two issues. First,

we need to know to what extent countries are participating in international trade and investment. Second, do countries integrate equally with different parts of the world?

3. **What drives globalization?** In this section, we explore how recent phenomena such as outsourcing, global value chains, and regional trade agreements have become important components of globalization. We also examine China's explosive economic growth and the human costs that sometimes accompany globalization.
4. **What are the benefits and drawbacks of globalization?** Has globalization lived up to its promise? Here we assess whether globalization has been good for economic growth.

20.1 What Is Globalization?

Thomas Marchessault/Alamy Stock Photo

Globalization and Its Origins

Globalization is not a carefully defined scientific concept. It has become part of sociological research, but it was adopted by social scientists because it was already in common currency in the media and popular discourse by the 1980s. Like any popular concept, it is often used in different ways by different people, and this ambiguity has even been imported into some social science discussions. But one thing most of its usages have in common is that they refer to the process through which national economies are becoming linked with one another. For this chapter, we define **globalization** as the integration of economic activities across national borders.

To get a sense of what this means, imagine a world in which every country is a self-contained economic unit. Everything that is consumed by its population is made within the country—whether it is clothing, food, electronics, homes, or other goods—and everything that is produced gets consumed within the national borders. There is no trade, and there is also no immigration. This would be a perfectly deglobalized world. By *deglobalized,* we mean a world in which every country consumes only what it produces for itself—there is no trade. But now suppose that over time, some countries began to interact with one another economically. Perhaps they began to trade some of their products, with some selling their agricultural products to their neighbours and others selling electronic goods. This would begin a process of trade in which countries would begin to **export**—that is, sell their goods to other countries—and **import**—that is, buy goods produced in other countries. Or entrepreneurs in one country could keep selling to their own home markets, but they could decide to move their production to another country, perhaps for cheap labour. This would begin a process of **foreign investment**, in which it is not goods that leave a country but investments. Or it could also turn out that some people decide that there are better jobs to be had in a neighbouring country and begin a process of **emigration**, the process of moving from their home to another economy. All of these decisions would be part of a process of globalization, of moving from a condition of economic isolation to one in which economies are linked to each other in various ways.

As the example above shows, economic integration can be carried out in a number of ways. Perhaps the most common is through international trade—a process by which people in one country sell products or services to customers in another country. But integration can also be carried out through the movement of **factors of production**—capital and labour (land is also a factor, but land can't travel across borders!). Firms in one country can invest in another one, either by moving their facilities to another country or by buying up existing plants and equipment in the target country. Finally, people can also move between countries, bringing about a flow of labour that adds to the pool of workers in one country while reducing it in another. All of these activities are dimensions of globalization.

The Beginnings of Globalization

20.1.1 Discuss the two key changes responsible for the development of globalization.

When did globalization begin? Has the world always been globalized, or is it a recent phenomenon—and if so, how recent? The answer depends on different dimensions of globalization and which dimension we focus on. For example, if we equate globalization with the spread of international trade, we get a very different answer than if we equate it with one country investing in another.

International trade has existed for centuries, even millennia. It is possible to trace it back to the most ancient societies, stretching back thousands of years. So, not surprisingly, those sociologists who equate globalization with trade have announced that the world began to globalize as far back as 5,000 years ago. If we accept this definition, there is nothing special about the last few centuries; all that has changed over the past 5,000 years is the *degree* of economic integration. But most social scientists reject this definition and also the idea that globalization has proceeded more or less evenly over millennia. Clearly, something has changed in the recent past. To most people who study the subject, the 1870s marked a turning point in global economic integration. This shows up in several indicators—the degree of trade, the flows of investment, and, most of all, the convergence of international prices. **Price convergence** is simply when the price of a good sold in different places tends toward the same level, for instance, when a car in Mexico City sells at the same price as the same car would in Atlanta. It seems safe to say that there appears to have been a dramatic uptick in globalization in the past couple of centuries, especially since the 1850s.

A mid-nineteenth-century steam engine transports goods across the United States. The American railway lines created a national market for many consumer goods and also played a crucial role in making them available for export to Europe.

Everett Collection/ Age Fotostock

Why did globalization not start earlier? Two important changes had to occur before globalization could really take off: (1) a change in infrastructure—especially in transportation and communication—and (2) transformation in society's economic systems.

The most obvious reason that globalization did not take off earlier is that the means to bring it about were still somewhat primitive. The integration of national economies requires considerable advances in communication and transportation. On this score, the really revolutionary changes in the modern era occurred after the 1850s.

In transportation, two changes around the middle of the nineteenth century were truly revolutionary. First, the expansion of railways across the giant land masses of Europe, Asia, and Latin America were critical to allowing goods produced in the interior of the country to be brought out to the coasts and made available for import. Before the advent of the railway, economic production and consumption had to be largely local, or confined to a small geographical area. The long journey from one region to another meant that perishable goods had to be consumed locally or they would rot in transit. The nineteenth and early twentieth centuries saw the mass implementation of railways in both Canada and the United States. But Canada and the United States were not alone. In Western Europe, Russia, India, and Australia, railway construction boomed, as hundreds of thousands of miles of new lines were laid to connect inland markets that had until that point been isolated.

The second great advance was in the advent of the steamship. Railways could transport goods across national borders only within the same landmass. For intercontinental trade to take off, there also had to be a revolution in oceanic travel. Steamships were available for transport in the early nineteenth century, but they were too expensive for anything but occasional use. Until the 1850s, they were mostly utilized for transporting high-cost luxury items, primarily on inland rivers. A series of technological advances made steamships more efficient and lowered their costs around the middle of the century. By the 1870s, they were becoming the major source of transoceanic transportation (O'Rourke & Williamson, 2000, pp. 33–35).

While the railroad and steamship were important in lowering transportation costs, the invention of the telegraph brought about a revolution in communication. It is hard to imagine today, but the telegraph probably had a greater impact on economic activity than either the telephone or the computer in the twentieth century. The telegraph allowed the first long-distance communication of text, beginning in the early nineteenth century and improving throughout that century with commercial applications appearing by the mid-nineteenth century and the first wireless telegraph networks operational by the 1880s. By the beginning of the twentieth century, it was possible to send messages across the Atlantic Ocean, creating the first truly global form of instantaneous communication.

While the great leaps in technology and transportation were critical for globalization to take off, their effectiveness would have been limited had it not been for another transformation. This was a change in the way that people related to markets. Until the mid-nineteenth century, markets played a relatively minor role in the lives of most people in the world. The vast majority of humanity lived in the countryside as **peasants**, or agricultural producers who predominately produced goods for their own consumption rather than to sell on the market. It was only as this class of peasants was integrated into market production that the pace of globalization could pick up speed.

Globalization is a process through which the sale of goods and services spreads across national borders, expanding across the world. But for this to happen, there has to be an expansion of the market for those goods and services—people have to want to *buy* them. But even in the nineteenth century, most people in the world mostly consumed what they produced for themselves on their farms and in their locality. This meant that they only went to markets periodically for those things they couldn't produce at home. And this, in turn, meant that the *demand* for goods and services in the market always remained limited. People living in cities were the most reliable source of demand for consumption goods because they didn't have their own land like peasants did. But cities in the nineteenth century accounted for only a small proportion of the global population. Most of humanity was still located in the countryside, and this part of the population was geared toward self-subsistence, or living off the land. The place for market-produced goods was still very limited in most areas, meaning that the economic system was predominantly a **precapitalist economy**.

For those reasons, globalization remained limited well into the nineteenth century. As long as most of the world economy was still precapitalist, consisting of peasants who toiled on their own plots of land, producing for themselves much of what they consumed, the market for goods and services remained very small. For markets to become more important in people's lives, the scope of the markets would have to expand. More specifically, the *demand* for market-produced goods would have to increase. For this to happen, peasants had to be induced or forced to become dependent on the market for their survival. How were peasants forced to become dependent on the market? Either wealthy landlords or farmers could offer to buy up their land, or they could be pushed off the land by various means—sometimes they lost the land because they fell into debt, or they had to sell bits of it off to pay taxes. Either way, peasants would find themselves suddenly without their traditional means of survival—the ability to work their own plots with their own labour. Once this happened, they had little choice but to work for a wage—either in the city in factories or small shops, or in some other kind of employment.

North Wind Picture Archives/Alamy Stock Photo

The process through which peasants lost access to land and the ability to produce their own necessities without having to buy them contributed to the rise of a capitalist economy and provided the basis for the uptick in globalization.

This process through which peasants gradually lost access to land and the ability to produce their own necessities without having to buy them is central to the rise of the modern **capitalist economy**. Capitalist economic systems are distinguished by the fact that almost everyone has to buy in the market whatever they consume. Onetime peasants now had to purchase the wheat or rice that they once grew on their own plots. They had to buy clothes that they had once produced from wool, cotton, or flax grown on their own homesteads. In other words, they became market dependent. The fact that so many people had to turn to the market for goods meant that demand for goods expanded enormously in the second half of the nineteenth century. This growing demand provided the real basis for globalization's expansion.

The growing demand for goods was one of the reasons that governments expended so much energy on expanding transportation infrastructure. As people in distant rural areas turned to the market for purchase of goods, governments felt considerable pressure to improve the transportation infrastructure, so goods produced in one part of the country could be delivered to other parts where they were in demand. Increasingly, much of the new transportation infrastructure was being used not just for internal consumption but for export markets. For example, starting in the 1880s, both Britain and France relied on Canada to exploit natural resources and promoted farming of wheat to trade with other nations such as the British West Indies. During this same period, the United States became a major source of wheat for Western Europe. This export of wheat from midwestern North America across the Atlantic was a major component of nineteenth-century globalization. It is an example of how the change in social structure combined with improvements in material infrastructure and technology to create the first real explosion in globalization.

The Course of Globalization: From the Nineteenth Century to Today

20.1.2 Analyze the ways in which globalization has expanded steadily since the nineteenth century.

Globalization had become a very powerful force by the early 1900s. So can we assume that, once the necessary preconditions were in place, it proceeded smoothly through the course of the twentieth century? For many analysts, there is a sense that globalization is something like a tidal wave, an unstoppable process against which governments are more or less helpless. We have seen that it took some very profound changes for it to take off—there was certainly nothing automatic about globalization before 1850. But once these changes had in fact taken place, once capitalism spread across Europe and much of the world, did the integration of economies become unstoppable?

In fact, it did not. As Figure 20.1 shows, after 1913 and for more than 50 years, the world actually underwent **deglobalization**—a process in which international economic integration decreases over time. Figure 20.1 shows a commonly used measure of global economic integration, which is trade as a proportion of **gross domestic product (GDP)**, or the value of all goods and services sold on a nation's market within a defined period. The idea behind this measure is that globalization cannot get very far unless countries are trading with one another. The extent to which a country is involved in trade is therefore an effective early indicator of how deeply connected it is to other economies. For many advanced economies, trade as a proportion of total economic activity actually went down between 1914 and the 1970s. This means that the economies of many countries became less integrated with the rest of the world in these years in spite of the fact that they had become more capitalist and despite the dramatic improvements in transportation and communication. These economies became more globalized from 1850 to 1914 and then deglobalized between 1914 and 1970.

The process of deglobalization began with World War I. The years of military conflict caused enormous disruption in normal patterns of trade and investment, which derailed the process of economic integration that had begun in preceding decades. Once the war ended, governments tried to put trade and investment back on track. But then, just a little more than 10 years later in 1929, the global economy

Figure 20.1 Ratio of Merchandise Trade to GDP, Current Prices (Imports and Exports Combined)

SOURCE: Based on data from *Globalization in Question* (3rd ed.), by Paul Hirst, Grahame Thompson, and Simon Bromley, 2009, London: Polity Press.

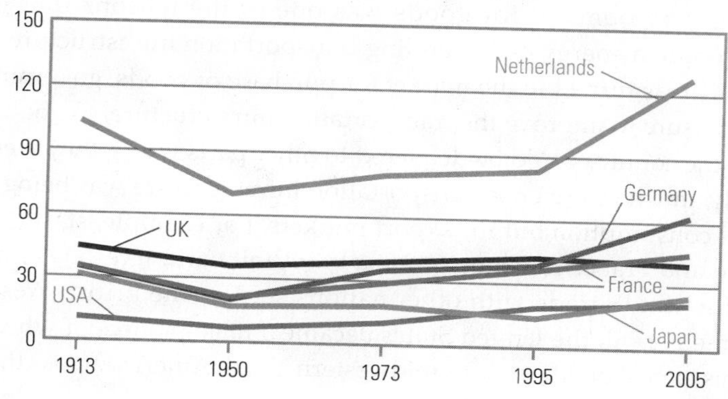

was hit by what has come to be known as the Great Depression. The Depression also caused enormous disruption to international trade and investment because as economies all over the world collapsed, exporters found that the markets for their goods disappeared almost overnight. This was another powerful shock to the whole process of globalization.

The war and the Great Depression certainly derailed the economic integration that had begun after 1850. But shocks are temporary phenomena. Economies recover, and trade and investment resumes its normal course. There had to be something more to the story in these decades if globalization didn't manage to reach the levels of 1914 until the very end of the century. Might there have been something else that created obstacles to reglobalization? In fact, there was—the power of the state. Government policies that established greater control over national economies played a major role during this period of deglobalization.

The most important factor that worked against the resumption of a globalized world was that, after the Great Depression, governments all over the world passed measures to insulate their economies from excessive vulnerability to global economic shocks and to gain more control over the flow of economic activity. After the wrenching experience of two world wars and the Great Depression, governments resolved to achieve greater control over their own national economies. They wanted to have greater influence over the goods that entered and exited their countries as well as the flow of capital into and out of national production. Toward this end, they implemented a number of measures designed to put brakes on the free flow of goods and services. Two instruments crucial for this were tariffs and capital controls.

A **tariff** is a tax that is imposed on imports or exports. It adds to the price of the traded good, thereby making it more expensive. It raises revenue for the government, but it also makes the good less attractive to customers because it is now more expensive than its rivals. This has the predictable effect of reducing the flow of this good into the market. Everything else being equal, it is a trade-depressing measure. **Capital controls** are restrictions imposed by the government on the movement of investment out of, or into, the country. An example would be a case where a shoe manufacturer wanted to sell his factory and open up a new one in another country. In order to transfer his funds to a bank in that country, he would first have to get permission from his own government. In this way, his government would exert some control over the movement of funds out of its borders. These capital controls are designed to give government greater sway over the flow of investment, allowing it to increase or decrease the quantity of investment as a response to changing economic conditions. The government can make it harder for investors to "take their money and run" out of the country; it can also make it harder for investors to enter the country if the state feels that some investors are hurting national interests. Together, tariffs and capital controls act as brakes on the free flow of capital and goods. The decades between 1930 and 1970 were marked by a very wide use of both of these measures as well as a host of other instruments designed to allow states more control over economies. This was what turned the temporary shock of 1929 into a more enduring era of deglobalization.

The fact that it was state policies that triggered a process of deglobalization helps us understand why *reglobalization* ensued in the 1970s after a decades-long hiatus. Starting in the 1970s, and then increasingly from the 1980s onward, states moved to remove many of the controls and restrictions they had placed on trade and capital flows. This was part of the turn to the more market-based policies that governments across the world have enacted since the 1970s. As states changed course and began to allow more mobility to goods and money, the process of economic integration resumed its course, much as it had in the early twentieth century. It is this second phase of globalization that we have lived through for the past quarter-century and that seems so often to be a force out of our control.

What conclusions can we draw from this past century? The big lesson is that there is nothing natural or inevitable about globalization. Even though trade and migration have been around for thousands of years, all economies remained localized and quite limited in their degree of international integration until quite recently. It took some very dramatic changes in underlying conditions for globalization to expand beyond its centuries-old limits. Just as importantly, even after capitalism spread across much of the world, globalization still did not become an unstoppable force. After the first 50 years of increasing integration of production across national borders, the world experienced 50 years of deglobalization. This was made possible by state action. It wasn't until states turned to a more market-oriented strategy that globalization resumed its course. This tells us that the ebb and flow of globalization since 1900 has been governed mainly by political factors and that globalization has depended on a suitable political environment. States may very well have the power to begin a new era of deglobalization if citizens demand it (Gindin & Panitch, 2012).

Globalization has always been politically driven—the main forces controlling the degree and the pace of globalization have been governments and their policies, not technology. Keep this important point in mind because it is common to hear in the media and in political debates that we cannot stand in the way of globalization. This makes it seem as though it is an inexorable force. But we have seen in this section that it is not. It is made possible by political decisions taken by governments, and it has been scaled back, also as a result of governmental decisions.

20.2 How Far-Reaching Is Globalization?

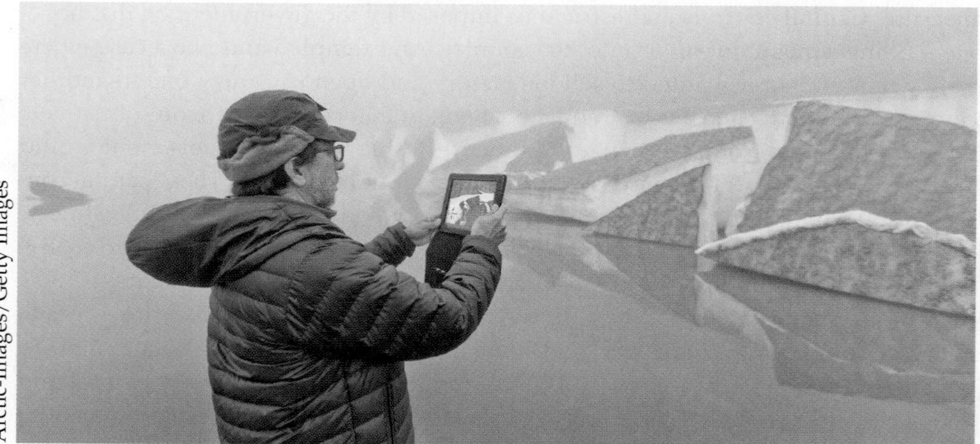

Arctic-Images/Getty Images

Globalization's Reach

We now know something about the origins of globalization. The next question is, just how far-reaching has this process been? There are two issues that we have to examine. First, how much international trade and investment is occurring? We need to know to what extent countries are participating in international economic activity. Second, do countries integrate equally with different parts of the world? Sometimes we get the impression that in today's world every corner of the globe is more or less equally connected to the others. But is this true? Or is it the case that countries tend to group together with their neighbours in what is called *regionalization?*

The Degree of Globalization

20.2.1 Discuss the extent of international trade and investment in globalization.

So far we have focused on the fact that globalization receded in the middle parts of the twentieth century before it resumed course in the 1970s. But Figure 20.1 also showed us another important fact—that even in the first decade of the twenty-first century the degree of globalization was not much more than it had been in the early twentieth century. In fact, some countries—like Japan and England—have still not caught up with their levels of globalization 100 years ago. Japan traded 31 percent of its domestic production in 1914, compared to only 24.7 percent in 2005, and England slid from just under 45 percent in 1914 to 40 percent in 2005. So even while trade and export dependence has increased in the past 30 years, it is not entirely new. How could this be so? How could trade dependence have been as great then as it is now for so many countries? One reason is that in 1914, the countries with the more advanced economies were also colonial powers. England and France were both very deeply integrated with their colonial empires. This opened up markets for their goods. Firms selling in the colonies of their home country had real advantages over their rivals from other countries because they had better knowledge of the conditions and often had better access to sales and marketing networks. This created a powerful drive for colonial exporters to expand into the markets in the lands their governments ruled. This kind of trade integration was not usually very beneficial to entrepreneurs in the colonized countries, but it did create a very globalized world, even if its benefits were weighted toward the rich West.

Now let's see if trends in international investment show a greater level of integration than simple trade. When firms from one country make investments in another, it is known as **foreign direct investment (FDI)**. So as international investment increases in size and scope, it shows up in international statistics as an increase in the flow of FDI. For international production to become more integrated, the share of FDI should be increasing over time. This means that more of what is produced across the world comes from international investment as opposed to investment by local firms. If we look at the data, the result is not what we might expect. In 2010, the gross fixed capital investment in the world economy was almost $14 trillion. Of this, total FDI, calculated as the sum of inward- and outward-oriented FDI, amounted to $2.57 trillion. This means that foreign investment never accounted for more than one-fifth of total global investment (United Nations Conference on Trade and Development [UNCTAD], 2011, p. 24, Table 1.5). Flows of FDI tend to be quite volatile, rising and falling from year to year. But since the 1990s, the range has remained around 10 to 20 percent (Sutcliffe & Glyn, 2010, pp. 87–88). In other words, more than 80 percent of global investment today is carried out within national borders, usually more. This tells us that factories and firms are not as footloose as some of the popular images might have us believe. Almost all investors stay within their own national border.

The Importance of Regions

20.2.2 Explain why economic integration clusters around regions.

Now let's explore a second question: Even if globalization is increasing, is it bringing together the parts of the world into a seamless whole? Or does economic integration cluster around small regions?

Consider how far goods actually travel. In a nonglobalized world, goods tend to stay in small geographical zones. They do not travel very far because their consumption is carried out close to the regions where they were produced. If globalization was a process by which countries transmitted goods to all corners of the world, we would expect to find that as it takes hold the distance travelled by goods also increases. However, for most countries, with the exception of Canada and the United States due to their trade relations with China, there has not been a very significant change in the average distance travelled by imports and exports in this period. There is variation in this trend in the 1965–2000 period. During this time, 77 countries experienced a decline in the distance of their exports and imports, and 39 countries had an increase in their trading distance (Carrere & Schiff, 2004).

This regional bias for trade is further confirmed by the increase in the regional share in total trade over the last few decades. The *trade intensity index*, which is the ratio of intraregional trade share relative to the region's share in global trade, is used to obtain a measure of regional bias. All regions demonstrate this bias, with Latin America (except for Mexico) showing the strongest regional bias (UNCTAD, 2007). In other words, we can see that the share of intraregional trade is increasing for a number of *regional blocs*—economic ties that are most densely woven between neighbouring countries and that get much thinner between countries located farther away, such as the European Union. Explore Figure 20.2 for a closer look at regional trade.

Another good indicator of the importance of regionalization over globalization is the role of the **transnational corporation (TNC)**. A TNC is a corporation that sells products in more than one country. Most trade and foreign investment is actually carried out by TNCs, not by small firms. In 2006, there were 77,000 TNCs in the global economy, employing 62 million workers and owning assets of over $4.5 trillion. Examining the trading activities of these giant corporations is a good window into the dynamics of globalization. Two facts stand out about TNCs. First, most of them locate their branches and affiliates in other countries. So 65 percent of TNC affiliates are located abroad. This tells us that they are in fact organizing their trading activities across national borders, as one would expect in a process of globalization. But how far do they actually go?

Here's a second interesting fact: It turns out that most of the trading and investment activity of TNCs is in neighbouring or nearby countries, not in far-flung regions. The world's largest firms are concentrated in the triad of the European Union, North America, and Japan. In a very careful analysis of 380 of the Fortune 500 companies in 2001, economist Alan Rugman has shown that, on average, sales in their home region were 71.9 percent of their total sales. As few as 2.4 percent of the 380 companies could be classified as truly global (meaning that they generated their revenue across the three largest regions of North America, Europe, and Asia and the Pacific and had headquarters in all of these regions). An example of a global firm would be IBM, which is an American company with 43.5 percent of its sales in its home region. The rest of its sales come from Asia (20 percent) and Europe, the Middle East, and Africa (28 percent). Only 6.6 percent of the 380 companies were biregional, that is, had at least 20 percent of their sales from at least two regions but less than 50 percent in their home region. For example, BP, which is a British company, received 36.3 percent of its revenues from the European market and 48.3 percent from the American market. Three percent were host-region oriented, that is, more than 50 percent of their sales came from a single region that was not their own. DaimlerChrysler was the largest in this group. This Europe-based company made 60 percent of its sales in North America. However, an overwhelming majority of the companies were home-market oriented. That is, 320 out of the 380 made a majority of their sales in their home region. For example, Walmart, which is the number-one firm on the Fortune 500, made 94 percent of its sales in North America. On average, the sales in the home regions of such firms are 80 percent. Moreover, very few of these firms have a significant presence outside of these three regions, such as in Latin America or the Indian subcontinent. Of the 500 largest TNCs, only 9 are truly global, that is, derive at least 20 percent of their business from each of the following regions: Asia, North America, and Europe. For the vast majority of the TNCs, over 80 percent of their sales are done within the geographical region in which they are located. So here, too, regionalization dominates over globalization (Rugman, 2005).

We see the same pattern in labour flows. The stock of international migrants has increased from 65 million in 1965 to 215 million in 2013 at an average rate of

Figure 20.2 Globalization or Regionalization?

SOURCE: Based on data from *The Regional Multinationals: MNEs and "Global" Strategic Management*, by Alan Rugman, 2005, Cambridge: Cambridge University Press.

NOTE: Arrows represent percentage of sales by region.

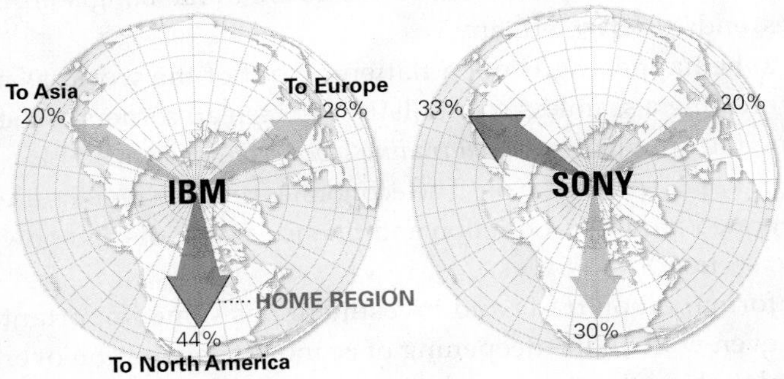

Truly global transnational corporations
As of 2001, fewer than 2 percent of the 500 largest corporations in the world fell into this category.

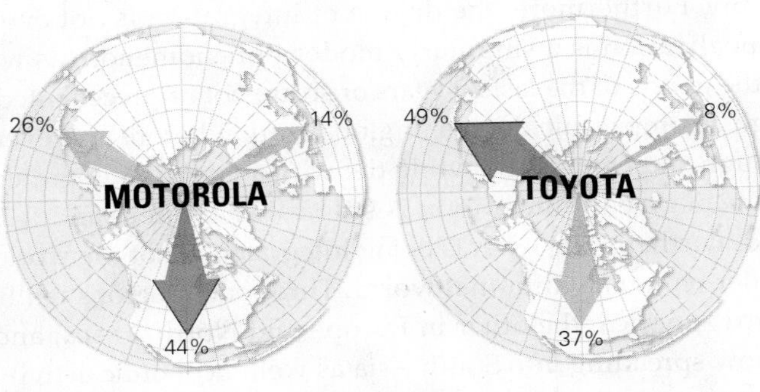

Biregional
This category represented 5 percent of the 500 largest corporations in 2001.

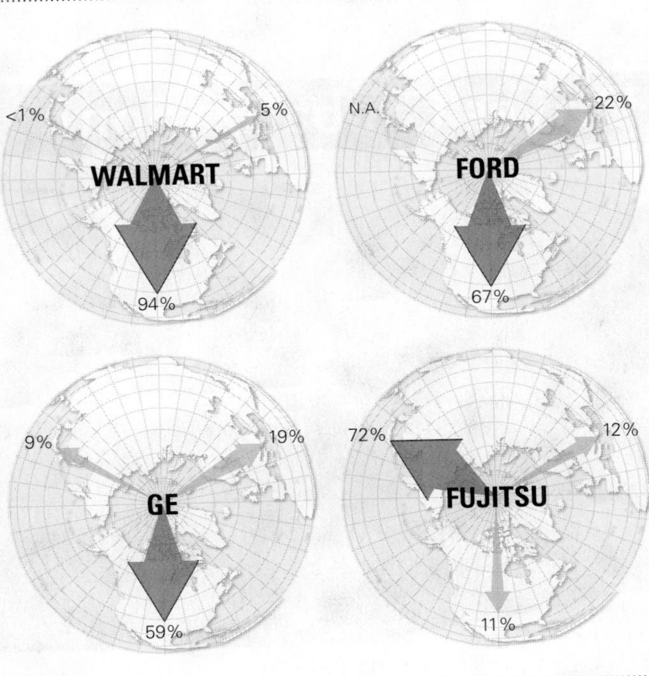

Predominately domestic
Some of the very biggest corporations in the United States and Japan still sell mostly in their home regions.

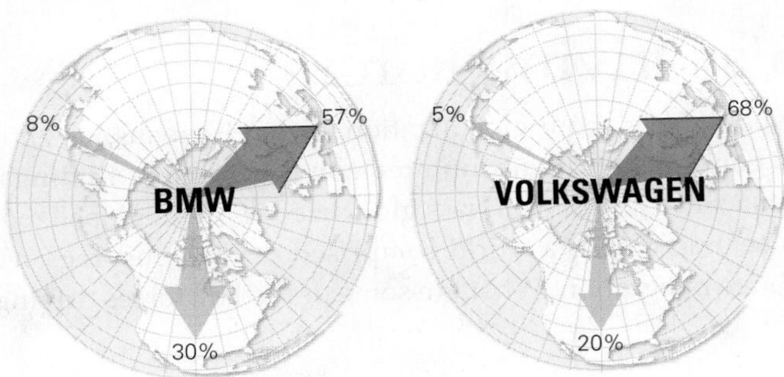

Predominantly European
Some of the most thoroughly internationalized companies in Europe still sell mostly to other European countries.

1.3 percent per year between 1990 and 2000. However, a closer look at migration statistics reveals that the top migration corridors are between neighbouring countries. As of 2010, the top migration corridor was United States–Mexico, followed by cross-border flows between Ukraine and Russia. Other prominent corridors are India–Bangladesh, India–United Arab Emirates, and Turkey–Germany.

Hence, what appears to be happening is not a flattening out of the world as a whole. Globalization is not creating a seamless web of links between all corners of the world; rather, it is promoting the growth of *regional trading blocs*. The three main blocs are around North America, Europe, and East Asia. The economies of these regions are becoming more tightly integrated around production and finance. (We'll discuss how this is happening in the next section.)

Taken together, this information on trade and investment has some important implications. It means that even with all the deepening of economic integration over the past quarter-century, global production and exchange still primarily revolve around the national economy. Furthermore, the degree of integration is not even very new. Even though globalization is a singularly modern phenomenon, as we saw earlier in this chapter, the trends of the last 20 years or so are not unprecedented. The world has been through a comparable degree of globalization before and even managed to reverse it through state action. So while the world is more integrated than it was 40 years ago, the degree of integration is still rather limited, and it is certainly not unprecedented. Furthermore, what is being integrated is not the world as a whole, but rather smaller regions within that world. Three such regions really stand out: one around North America, the other in Europe and North Africa, and the third in East Asia and now spreading into South Asia as well. Economic activity tends to flow within these regions, and less so between them.

20.3 What Drives Globalization?

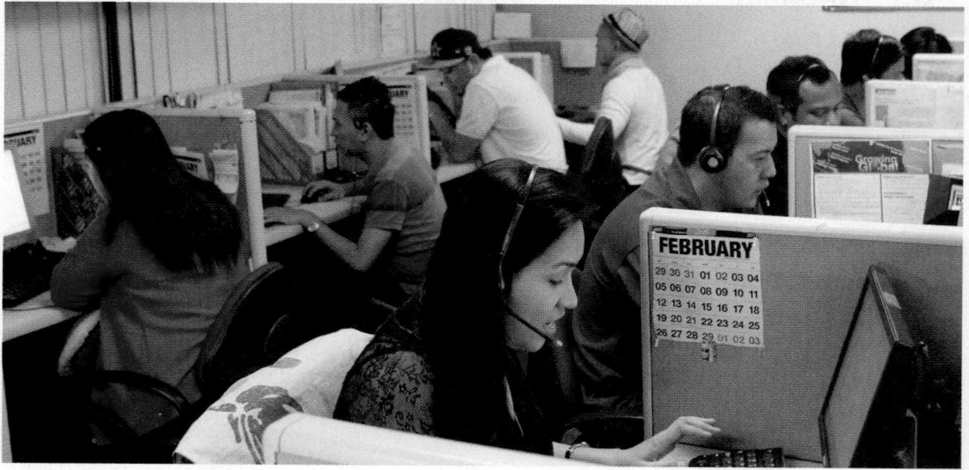

Landov

Globalization's Driving Forces

We now know some of the basic facts about globalization—what it means, when it started, and how far it has gone. We have encountered some surprising findings. The world has not moved in a steady path from less globalized to more globalized. And in fact, what seems to be emerging is a world comprised of economic regions, not a seamless web of economic integration. What are some of the key forces driving globalization?

Outsourcing and Global Value Chains

20.3.1 Analyze the role that value chains play in globalization.

Most people know that a common phenomenon in recent years has been the practice of **outsourcing**, when producers take activities that they once did in-house and farm them out to other firms in remote locations. Outsourcing is part of a larger process that is called the creation of **global value chains**, which are sets of linked operations that organize the production of any particular product. In fact, much of what we know about globalization has been driven by global value chains.

Take the production of an automobile. This involves a long set of activities, starting with the manufacture of steel and rubber, their transportation to an auto plant, the manufacture of mechanical parts, their assembly into a car frame, painting, installation of upholstery, and so forth. All these activities are linked together in a chain of operations. In the era of deglobalization, it was common for many of these processes to be carried out in-house, ensuring the value chain was compact and geographically contained. But in recent years, as transportation and communication costs have declined and as employers seek cheaper labour, companies have turned to breaking apart various components of the value chain in their operations and moving the various operations to remote locations. Activities that were once carried out under one roof now take place hundreds of miles away. But they don't typically move across the world. Instead, they tend to move to neighbouring regions.

For example, let's consider the process of producing clothing, which involves three primary steps: the spinning of thread, the weaving of fabric, and the final assembly of the clothing. These three steps have important differences. Spinning, especially of synthetic fibers, is immensely capital intensive, which means it involves high-technology machinery usually operating on a very large scale. The weaving of fibres into cloth is somewhat less capital intensive and involves a lower level of technical sophistication. The final assembly of clothing is very different: It involves a lot of manual labour, with relatively little use of automated machinery. In addition, it can be split up into many small-scale factories (Dicken, 2011, p. 308). Together, these three steps make up the value chain of clothing production.

What has happened is that these three steps, especially the final assembly step, now typically occur in different places. A lot of the spinning and weaving that goes into garments is still done in the Canada and the United States, but since the 1980s, the more labour-intensive part of the value chain has moved to Mexico and the Caribbean. Garment producers establish assembly operations in these low-wage countries in areas that are set up as *export processing zones*. These are locations where the governments give foreign manufacturers special privileges and tax breaks in return for setting up operations there. The TNCs get low-cost operations, and the host country gets more jobs for its labour force. The garment producer sets up operation and brings in cloth woven in North America. This is then further processed and assembled in the export processing zone and re-exported to North America. A chain of operations that was once located within the same plant has now been dispersed across nations. But its dispersal hasn't sent those operations all the way across the

Workers at a clothing factory in Guadalajara, Mexico, making garments for Walmart. It is very common for firms to hire mostly women, because employers believe that they are a more manageable labour force than men. Not surprisingly, sexual harassment complaints from workers in these factories are very high.

Guillermo Arias/AP Images

globe. Typically, it has been spread out over neighbouring countries, or countries that are near each other.

What has this meant for the countries that are participating in regional integration? We can ask this question from a bottom-up perspective or a top-down one. From the bottom-up perspective, we look at what the implications have been for labour—for the people actually doing the work in the export processing zones or the TNCs. From the top-down angle we look at what it has meant for overall economic growth—has it sped up development and industrialization? Has it meant faster growth for the global South (the poorer developed countries in the world)? There is no better place to look than China as a hothouse for what globalization has meant on the ground.

China's Export Zones: A Case Study

20.3.2 Outline the benefits and costs of China's export zones.

China's explosive economic growth of the past few decades has been a striking example of a country attempting to take advantage of the changing geography of global production. China has become a centre of manufacturing as part of fragmented global supply chains. A truly immense quantity of goods sold in North America is labelled "made in China"— $400 billion worth in the United States (United States Department of Commerce, 2012) and another $48.1 billion in Canada (Gauthier & Meredith, 2012, p. 2) in 2011. Yet China has established itself in a very particular position in the global value chain. Instead of designing products or producing the more sophisticated components like computer processors, Chinese factories most often *assemble* components produced elsewhere into final products, which are then reexported to consumer markets like the United States. For instance, in 2006, 80 percent of the value of consumer electronics exported from China simply represented the value of the imported components, not any work actually done in China (Koopman, Wang, & Wei, 2009). The final assembly step that is performed in China is often one of the simplest in the production process. Instead of advanced technology or highly skilled labour, this assembly step requires above all a large, willing, and *low-cost* labour force. This is what China offers to the multinational corporations that build factories or hire contractors there.

The supposed promise of this kind of manufacturing is that by hooking into the global economy, it will stimulate the growth of other, more advanced industries. Indeed, China's exports have played a central role in its astonishing economic success of the past three decades and have meant real benefits for ordinary workers in China. Wage levels and working conditions are not worse in factories producing for exports than in other jobs in China. Young people in rural China migrate in massive numbers to the coastal regions (where export manufacturing has blossomed) because work in the factories offers them an opportunity to improve their families' livelihoods that is simply not available in agriculture.

Women working in an electronics plant in Guangdong, China. These plants have become notorious for their long hours and very weak protections for their employees.

Lou Linwei/Alamy Stock Photo

Nonetheless, the benefits of economic growth do not change the fact that the life of a worker in China's export assembly factories is gruelling and difficult. Producing mass quantities in even less time is very appealing for the multinational corporations that locate manufacturing in China, but not necessarily for the workers who have to achieve these results. Consider this story, told by a former Apple executive to a reporter for the *New York Times*. A few weeks before the iPhone was to be released, Apple redesigned the screen but was intent on keeping to the original deadline. So, on the very day the redesigned screens began to arrive around midnight at the assembly factory in China, a foreman went over to the workers sleeping in the company's dormitory and roused them from their sleep. They were each given a biscuit and a cup of tea. They were then told to go to their workstations, at which point they began a 12-hour shift assembling the iPhones. The result? Within four days, the plant was producing 10,000 units a day.

In the executive's words, "The speed and flexibility is breathtaking. There's no American plant that can match that" (Duhigg & Bradsher, 2012). This speed and flexibility comes from the fact that Chinese workers have to work far longer and harder than employees in any American factory and earn less as well. On paper, workers in China—as in North America—have a 40-hour week, but in reality workers have no choice but to put in extensive overtime, even if it is sometimes labelled "voluntary"—after all, workers could "choose" to lose their jobs instead of "voluntarily" working overtime. The actual working day is 10 to 14 hours long, often with only a 10-minute break. During peak seasons of heavy output, employees in some factories work seven days a week. Including overtime, workers typically earn between $350 and $450 a month, compared to minimal living expenses of $200 to $300 a month. Because employees are often migrants, it is common for them to live in company dormitories, where they are bunked 6 to 10 people per room (China Labor Watch, 2011). In all, working at one of these factories is almost more than a job: It encompasses the entirety of the workers' lives.

In addition, Chinese workers lack the kinds of institutional protections long taken for granted in advanced economies like Canada and the United States. Chinese factories usually do have unions, but they do nothing to represent workers' interests to their employers. In interviews conducted by a human rights group, China Labor Watch, employees who went to the so-called worker care centres at every factory said they were offered only "psychological consolation" instead of real help solving problems in their jobs; in many firms, workers were unaware there was a formal union organization at all. Employers also seek to skirt what protections do exist. For instance, some try to keep their workers in the dark about provisions for compensation for work-related injuries guaranteed by labour law or their contracts. Other companies utilize external "labour dispatch agencies" that free the company of any contractual relationship with—and thus legal responsibility for—their workers at all. Lacking these basic protections and mechanisms for addressing grievances, these working conditions often are unsafe: There are many reports of workers being exposed to dangerous chemicals and of being injured or killed in workplace accidents (China Labor Watch, 2011; Duhigg & Barboza, 2012).

The Chinese example shows that while the spread of global value chains has indeed provided some benefits to labour in host countries, this has come with a cost. Firms often go to these areas not just for the cheaper labour there but also because workers have fewer protections and less recourse against employers' demands for greater flexibility and responsiveness from their employees. But there are potential costs on the other side as well, to the workers of the country from which the firms are exiting. In a careful study carried out for the U.S. Trade Deficit Review Commission, Cornell University economist Kate Bronfenbrenner found that employers in the United States used the threat of exit as a means of gaining advantage over employees, especially in union-organizing drives. Two facts stand out about this tactic. First, the threats were effective more often than not. The study found that when employers warned of the likelihood of plant shutdowns and flight to other locations, more than two-thirds of organizing drives failed. The second interesting fact is that managers actually followed through with plant closings in fewer than 3 percent of the cases where they issued the threats. In other words, in most of the cases, managers were using workers' fears about globalization against them. Even though the chance of capital flight was very low, workers believed that the threat was real (Bronfenbrenner, 2000).

How representative are these studies? It is not easy to say because teasing out the actual effects of globalization on wages and working conditions is no simple task. Workers' pay, their conditions of work, and their hours are affected by many factors, of which globalization is just one. Isolating globalization's effect is hard to do because none of the changes occur in an experimental setting. What we can say is that the increase in global capital flows and trade has not brought clear-cut benefits to labour. What the effects are, whether they are positive or negative, depends on how globalization interacts with other factors, such as the level and quality of democracy, trade union strength, and economic growth.

20.4 What Are the Benefits and Drawbacks of Globalization?

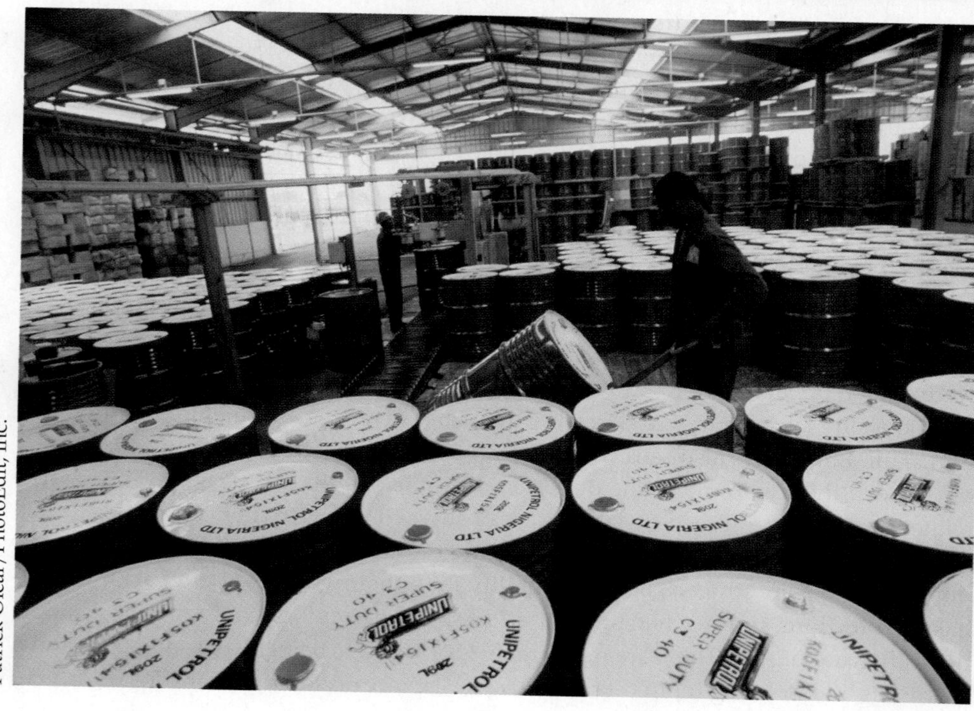

Patrick Olear/PhotoEdit, Inc.

The Effects of Globalization

The process of globalization is also occurring in the cultural domain. For example, the entertainment industry is one of the most visible examples of culture being globalized. The United States exports films and television shows to every continent, and some American films have become among the highest grossing films in many other countries. However, the flow of culture works in every direction. Mumbai, India—known as Bollywood in the entertainment industry—is also a major exporter of movies, mainly to the Middle East and Africa, but also to more Western nations as well. Cuisine is another area where the impact of globalization has been enormous. The spread of fast food restaurants—first invented in America—all over the world provides one example of how globalization is changing the way people eat. Some of the most popular restaurant chains in America now have a vast network of overseas locations. The increasing popularity of foreign cuisines has brought new tastes and

Music has always been one arena where the spread of ideas crosses borders. Today, American-style hip-hop, often reinvented in diverse locales such as Cambodia (shown here), is among the most popular music of young people around the world. But hip-hop itself has international roots, having absorbed musical influences from Africa.

Tom Vater/Alamy Stock Photo

ideas about food all over the world. Virtually all Americans today sometimes eat at restaurants serving foreign cuisines. And the influence of foreign foods and cooking ideas are growing. A serious chef anywhere in the world is likely to integrate ideas from other cuisines to create new and original dishes. It would be difficult to argue against the idea that one of the major benefits of globalization has been the increased exposure of people all over the world to the ideas, foods, and cultural products of people elsewhere.

But the main promise of globalization by its advocates has been that, by freeing up opportunities for trade and investment, it should give a boost to economic growth. Globalization is, in this sense, part of the turn to more market-based economic policies that have been promoted by governments all over the world since the 1980s. In order to understand the power of the globalization idea, we need to take a brief detour to understand what models of development were in place before the 1980s, when trade and investment flows really took off again.

In this next section, we will ask ourselves: What kinds of economic policies were practiced by developing countries in the years of deglobalization—the 1930s to the 1980s? What has changed in recent years? We will then take a look at the empirical record of these past years and compare it to the record of the earlier decades to get a sense of how the two compare. Armed with this information, we can draw some conclusions about the relative merits of globalization as a model of economic development.

Economic Policies in Developing Countries: 1930s to 1980s

20.4.1 Discuss the benefits of globalization to economic growth.

From the 1930s to the 1980s, most countries in the developing world oversaw very ambitious periods of rapid industrialization. These were years in which these nations—in Latin America, Asia, the Middle East, and Africa—tried to change their economies from agriculture to industry. To do this, they relied a great deal on the involvement of the state to regulate markets, provide protection to firms, control prices, and protect local industry from global competition. This model has come to be known as state-led development, but its more technical designation is **import-substituting industrialization (ISI)**. In economic literature, ISI has become associated with the kind of development policies poor countries used in the middle of the twentieth century. But in fact it has been used by every country that has tried to industrialize since the eighteenth century. It was used by England to ward off competition from Dutch entrepreneurs, then by the United States in the early 1800s to catch up with England, then by European countries in the middle of the nineteenth century, and then by the developing countries during the twentieth century (Chang, 2002).

At the heart of ISI was a commitment to nurture national industry in the face of international competition. When countries try to industrialize, their entrepreneurs face some considerable disadvantages. Usually, they have to produce for markets in which goods are already being sold by more experienced firms from richer countries. Take the case of textiles, where a new firm might try to enter a developing country. If a new manufacturer decides to set up a textile factory, she has to face the fact that the shirts she produces will compete against shirts being sold by other firms, usually from richer countries, but certainly by firms with more experience and more money than she has. How can she break into the market? To help her in this venture, her government might implement measures to make things easier. It could impose tariffs on shirts imported from other countries to raise their price; it could provide her with cheap credit to lower costs; it could also help her acquire the latest technology. All these measures are part of a strategy to give her some help against imported goods that she has to compete against. If successful, she will be able to push the imported shirts out of the market and become the dominant seller in the local market—she will have substituted her own goods for the imports. This is why the strategy is called import substitution.

For ISI to work, it takes extensive government intervention in markets, as we just described. During the decades stretching from the Great Depression to the 1980s, this meant that governments were enabling their national firms to succeed in local markets and push out foreign producers. So, for example, as Brazilian textile producers grew in their own experience and power, they pushed American textile producers out of the market. This is why ISI and deglobalization in some products went together. When globalization took off in the 1980s, it was part of a larger shift toward more market-friendly policies associated with neoliberalism. In the developing world, neoliberalism came in the form of a policy package known as the **Washington Consensus**. This was a term coined by economist John Williamson, and it describes the main components of a policy package that replaced ISI in the developing world during the 1980s.

The policies that were implemented under the Washington Consensus were broadly oriented to opening up the domestic economy to international finance and capital, lowering trade barriers, and liberalizing the domestic economy. This is also why they are associated with recent globalization—because they aimed to open up emerging economies to goods and capital from the advanced world and also to encourage more exports from the former to the latter. Hence, just as the middle decades of the twentieth century were a time in which state controls and deglobalization went together, so at the end of the century, liberalization and globalization went together. Keep this important point in mind when we try to assess the impact of globalization on economic growth. It is not very easy to separate the effects of economic integration from the effects of deregulation, less state intervention in the economy, and fewer controls over financial flows. The two dimensions of economic policy acted together, and separating the effects of one from the other is not always possible. Let's look at the North American Free Trade Agreement (NAFTA) as an example of integration and deregulation operating together.

NAFTA: A Case Study

20.4.2 Summarize the consequences of the North American Free Trade Agreement (NAFTA).

Passed in 1993, NAFTA has been one of the most widely studied instances of globalization in recent years, and it has also attracted its share of scholarly debate (Feller, 2008). In the debates that preceded its ratification, supporters of NAFTA, including Canadian prime ministers Brian Mulroney and Jean Chrétien and U.S. presidents George W. Bush and Bill Clinton, argued that it would result in rising incomes for everyone and lead to the creation of tens of thousands of jobs in Canada and the United States (Clinton, 1993; Hufbauer & Schott, 1993). Opponents decried the lack of effective labour and environmental protections in the treaty and worried that it would exert a downward pressure on wages and living standards, as companies would be able to move their operations in order to take advantage of lower wage and production costs abroad without losing access to domestic markets (Franklin, 1993).

Assessing NAFTA's consequences nearly two decades after it went into effect on January 1, 1994, is tricky because it is hard to disentangle the effects of the free trade agreement from other factors that shape social and economic outcomes. Notably in Mexico, NAFTA's implementation was quickly followed by a massive financial crisis in 1994 and 1995 (also known as the "Mexican peso crisis"), which may or may not have been linked to the agreement. Everyone agrees that NAFTA produced a significant increase in cross-border trade and financial flows, and its defenders, including many business groups, think tanks, and politicians, claim that this contributed to economic growth (Abramowitz, 2008; Office of the United States Trade Representative, 2008). Critics of NAFTA, however, insist its positive benefits have been largely limited to already economically advantaged groups, and they blame it for contributing to elevated levels of income inequality and stagnating wages and living standards for workers and other nonelite groups (Public Citizen, 2008). Economist Robert Scott, for instance, has found that the subsequent explosion in the United States' trade deficit with Mexico engendered a net loss of over 680,000 jobs north of the border, with more than 60 percent of such "job displacement" occurring in the manufacturing sector (Scott, 2011). Declining industrial employment had particularly harmful consequences for the job prospects of unskilled workers and weakened labour's bargaining position with employers; thus, NAFTA fed escalating pay and income disparities as well as a growing gap between median wage levels and productivity growth (Bernstein & Mishel, 2007).

One consequence of economic globalization since the 1980s has been an increase in the frequency of financial crises. In most of these instances, the result has been a cutback in social programs and an increase in unemployment. Here we see protestors in Mexico City hurling rocks at government offices in the wake of the peso crisis of 1994.

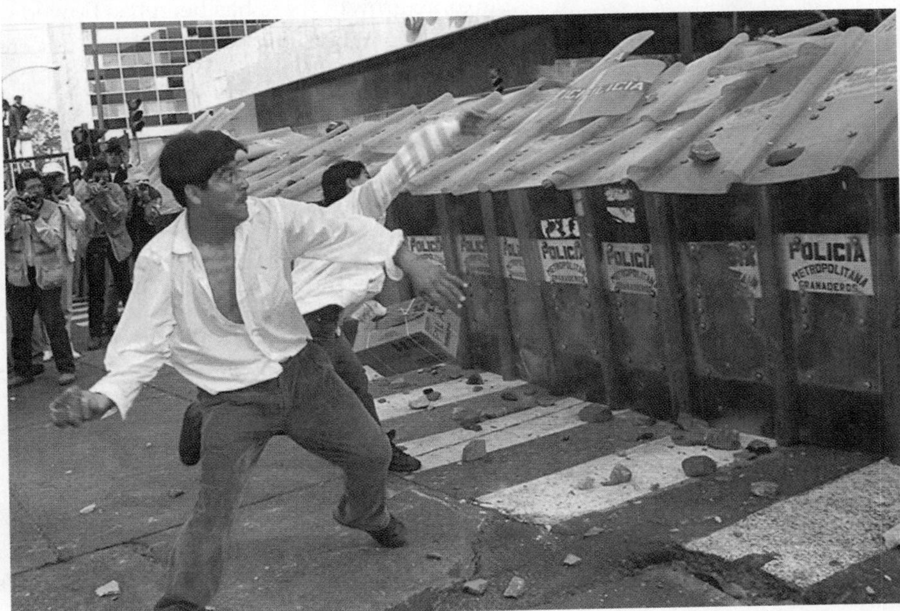

Gerardo Magllon/Staff/Getty Images

Meanwhile, the substantial rise in FDI into Mexico resulted in only minimal employment gains while intensifying various forms of inequality (Audley, Papademetriou, Polaski, & Vaughan, 2003). In part, that is because many of the jobs newly created by NAFTA were in the informal sector or did not provide standard benefits (such as paid vacations or extended health and retirement benefits). Nearly all of the growth in manufacturing employment was due to greater work opportunities in the low-wage and highly exploitative *maquiladoras*, which are mostly foreign-owned export assembly plants that constitute a significant, and rapidly growing, segment of Mexico's industrial sector. Furthermore, expanded employment in manufacturing was largely outweighed by losses suffered in Mexico's agricultural producers as a result of the influx of cheaper, sometimes heavily subsidized U.S. farm imports (Henriques & Patel, 2004). The result was a massive migration out of the Mexican countryside (Bacon, 2012). Improved access to Mexican markets benefited large U.S. agricultural producers but did not prevent the elimination of hundreds of thousands of smaller family farms during the NAFTA era. These sorts of considerations have led some onetime supporters of NAFTA to conclude that it failed to provide the boost to living standards they expected while exacerbating a wide array of socioeconomic problems (DeLong, 2006).

Has Globalization Lived Up to Its Promise?

20.4.3 Discuss the impact of globalization on the economic performance of low-income countries.

One of the most direct ways to assess whether globalization has fulfilled its promise is by looking at growth rates. And here the evidence seems pretty clear. Examine Figure 20.3, which compares the rate of growth in GDP during the ISI era—that is, 1950 to 1980—with growth rates in the decades of rapid globalization. What stands out as you look at these growth rates?

Figure 20.3 points to two facts in particular. First, economic growth was better during the ISI era throughout the developing world. We see that in all four of regions covered—East Asia, Latin America, Africa, and the Middle East—growth slowed down after the end of ISI. Second, we see that some regions did better than others. East Asia managed to sustain decent growth, even though it was lower than in the earlier years. But Latin America and the Middle East witnessed a more dramatic slowdown. This tells us that even though globalization did not deliver as promised, the disappointment with its results was greater in some regions than in others. In fact, the slowdown in growth inside the developing world was part of a global decrease in growth rates after 1980. The advanced countries witnessed a deceleration of their own. This is a bracing discovery. We have seen in other chapters that inequality within countries has increased over the past 30 years, in some cases dramatically. When we combine that with the finding that growth rates have also slowed down, we see that economic conditions for the poor and very poor have become much worse. Income growth has been very meagre in national economies, and on top of that, what little income growth there has been has flowed mainly into the bank accounts of the very rich—true in both the developed and underdeveloped worlds.

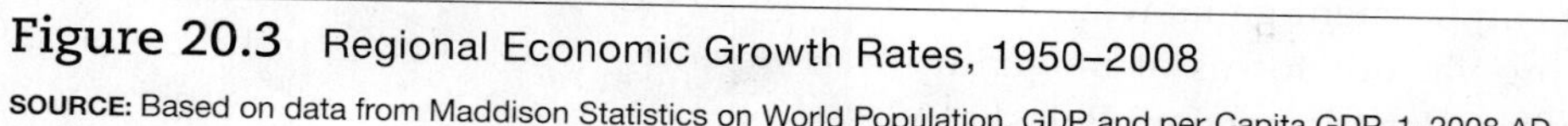

Figure 20.3 Regional Economic Growth Rates, 1950–2008

SOURCE: Based on data from Maddison Statistics on World Population, GDP and per Capita GDP, 1–2008 AD.

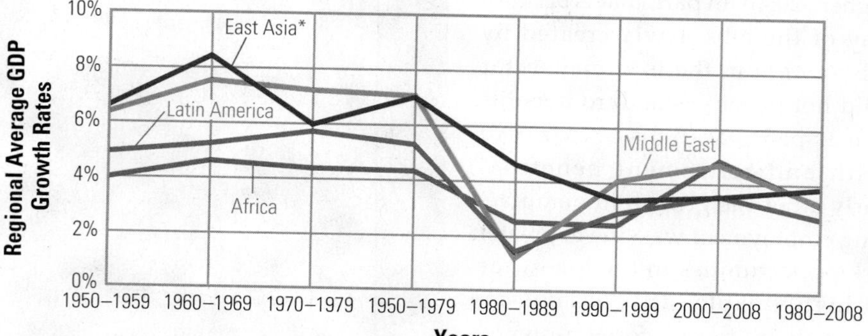

*Excludes China.

In sum, the impact of globalization on the economic performance of low-income countries has been mixed at best. To begin with, globalization has failed to reduce the gap between wealthy and poor countries. In fact, global inequality has been accentuated as Northern industrialized countries are now further ahead than they were in the post-war years, before open markets and transnational production took hold. Besides growing world inequality, globalization has not only reinforced polarization between wealthy countries and less developed countries, but has also generated sharp disparities within the global South. Whereas the few East Asian industrializers were able to sustain robust pre-1980 growth rates—and even fewer countries, namely China and India, were able to take off in the era of open world markets—most low- to middle-income countries, which benefited notably during the decades of state-led development and regulated markets, saw their growth, productivity, and investment stagnate with the turn to globalization.

Conclusion: Globalization in Retrospect and Prospect

In this chapter, we walked through three major points. First, globalization is and always has been a politically driven phenomenon. In other words, it is not the result of unavoidable economic forces sweeping away all that comes before them. We have seen that it took very specific political and social conditions to bring globalization about. One condition was the spread of capitalism as a specific economic system. Capitalism makes everyone within the economy market dependent—everyone has to fully participate in buying and selling to survive. Until this happened, there were very tight limits on how far globalization could proceed. For the change to come about, it took massive efforts by states. The turn to capitalism was not automatic. It developed through long and arduous policy directives from governments, either enticing peasants to give up their plots of land or coercing them into it. Even after the turn to capitalism, massive investments in transportation and communication technology were still needed for globalization to take off. These also required a governmental action because infrastructure investments did not promise immediate profits for private investors. Railroads, for example, were either built within the public sector or needed large subsidies to attract private investors. When globalization took off in the 1870s, it seemed like it was driven by purely economic forces, but behind it was the heavy and ever-present hand of the state.

The importance of governments and government policies is also evident in the way economic integration ebbed and flowed in the twentieth century. The onset of globalization has not been in the form of a steady growth from 1870 to now. In the early twentieth century, it probably seemed like market integration was an unstoppable force which all governments and all economies were powerless to stop. Yet by 1950 it already seemed like a thing of the past. The world during the years after World War II was one in which there was still plenty of trade and international investment, but it was subordinated to production and exchange within national borders. The re-globalization that has occurred since the 1980s has again been driven by state policies, such as the lowering of tariffs, the opening up of capital markets, and the deregulation of markets. Taken together, all these points show that globalization has been the product of social and political initiatives. And this means—crucially—that there is nothing natural about it. It can be modified, and even significantly changed, by state policy.

The second major point discussed in the chapter is that even while globalization is a reality, we should not exaggerate its extent. The media and political leaders often tell us that we are in an era of unprecedented economic integration. The *New York Times* columnist Thomas Friedman famously announced in his bestselling book that, with globalization, the world had become flat—meaning that every part of the world was becoming woven into the same seamless fabric (Friedman, 2005). But as we have seen, there are two caveats to this observation. First, in historical terms, the extent of real economic integration today is probably no more than it was in 1912. So it is not accurate to say that we are in a new world. Rather, we are now catching up to a world from a century ago. Second, whatever integration exists is more closely structured around regions than it is around the globe. Distance, culture, history—all the things that sociologists study—still matter a great deal in economic dynamics.

A third major point we discussed is that globalization is not a panacea. In fact, on most counts, the years of increased economic integration have witnessed worse economic outcomes than earlier years. This does not mean that we should push for a new era of deglobalization, as there are also benefits that come with economic integration. And as we highlighted earlier, it is not easy to disentangle the effects of globalization itself from the effects of neoliberalism and the deregulation of markets more specifically. It could very well be that globalization accompanied by a more active state, more redistribution, and more regulation of market outcomes could yield better results than would a new era of deglobalization. But while some kind of globalizing economy might be desirable, we can probably conclude that the kind we have actually *had* has not lived up to expectations. But how do we modify it if it is an unstoppable force? The point is that it is not. Knowing that globalization has always been governed by political forces, and that it has relied on state support and state indulgence, we can also have some confidence that if we are unhappy with its results, there is something that an activated citizenry can do about it.

CHAPTER SUMMARY

The Big Questions Revisited 20

20.1 What Is Globalization? Discussions of economic policy relate to globalization. What does *globalization* mean, and how can sociology make sense of it? In this section, we examined globalization and its origins.

Globalization and Its Origins

The Beginnings of Globalization

Learning Objective 20.1.1: Discuss the two key changes responsible for the development of globalization.

The Course of Globalization: From the Nineteenth Century to Today

Learning Objective 20.1.2: Analyze the ways in which globalization has expanded steadily since the nineteenth century.

20.2 How Far-Reaching Is Globalization? To evaluate how far-reaching the process of globalization has been, we examined two issues: (1) to what extent countries are participating in international trade and investment, and (2) whether countries integrate equally with different parts of the world.

Globalization's Reach

The Degree of Globalization

Learning Objective 20.2.1: Discuss the extent of international trade and investment in globalization.

The Importance of Regions

Learning Objective 20.2.2: Explain why economic integration clusters around regions.

20.3 What Drives Globalization? In this section, we explored how recent phenomena, such as outsourcing, global value chains, and regional trade agreements, have become important components of globalization. We also examined China's explosive economic growth and the human costs that sometimes accompany globalization.

Globalization's Driving Forces

Outsourcing and Global Value Chains

Learning Objective 20.3.1: Analyze the role that value chains play in globalization.

China's Export Zones: A Case Study

Learning Objective 20.3.2: Outline the benefits and costs of China's export zones.

20.4 **What Are the Benefits and Drawbacks of Globalization?** Has globalization lived up to its promise? In this section, we assessed whether globalization has been effective for economic growth.

The Effects of Globalization

Economic Policies in Developing Countries: 1930s to 1980s

Learning Objective 20.4.1: Discuss the benefits of globalization to economic growth.

NAFTA: A Case Study

Learning Objective 20.4.2: Summarize the consequences of the North American Free Trade Agreement (NAFTA).

Has Globalization Lived Up to Its Promise?

Learning Objective 20.4.3: Discuss the impact of globalization on the economic performance of low-income countries.

Learn the Terms

capital controls (p. 583)
capitalist economy (p. 581)
deglobalization (p. 582)
emigration (p. 579)
export (p. 578)
factors of production (p. 579)
foreign direct investment (FDI) (p. 585)
foreign investment (p. 578)
globalization (p. 578)
global value chains (p. 589)
gross domestic product (GDP) (p. 582)
import (p. 578)
import-substituting industrialization (ISI) (p. 594)
outsourcing (p. 589)
peasant (p. 580)
precapitalist economy (p. 581)
price convergence (p. 579)
tariff (p. 583)
transnational corporation (TNC) (p. 586)
Washington Consensus (p. 594)

Glossary

absolute poverty A measure of the minimum requirements needed for people to have basic standards of food, clothing, health, and shelter. Any individual or family falling below this fixed amount is defined as living in poverty. The official U.S. government definition of poverty is an absolute measure based on an estimate of minimum living standards first established in the 1960s and adjusted for inflation thereafter.

access The ability or right to approach, enter, exit, communicate with, or make use of research sites and materials.

achievement gap The gap in educational attainment between any two social groups (men and women, whites and nonwhites, upper and lower class, etc.).

acid rain Rain containing acid that is formed when the gaseous air pollutants nitrogen oxide and sulfur dioxide react with water molecules in the atmosphere.

advance directive Written instructions (such as a living will) that a person prepares in the event that he or she is no longer able to make decisions at the end of life.

age pyramid A diagram that plots the age distribution of a population, with the numbers of people at the youngest ages at the bottom of the graph and the numbers at the oldest ages at the top, and with males and females on the left- and righthand sides, respectively.

agenda setting The ability to decide which of the many possible topics for discussion, debate, and possible action that exist in the world will actually be considered. Agenda setting can take place in any institutional setting where decision-making occurs.

agnostic A person who believes that the existence of God or other supernatural beings is unknowable and therefore claims to neither believe or not believe in any faith.

allocation theory A theory regarding the impacts of education that focuses on how education channels people into positions or institutions that offer different opportunities for continuing to think, learn, and earn.

animism The belief that a supernatural power organizes all plants, inanimate objects, and natural phenomena and that the universe itself along with all of these objects has a soul or spiritual essence.

anthropocentrism The belief that humans are separate from and superior to the natural world.

assembly line A type of factory in which each worker performs one or a handful of small, discrete tasks, with a conveyer belt moving pieces to each workstation. A finished product results from the input of many workers across an entire factory.

assimilation The process by which immigrants come to be incorporated into their new society by taking on the cultural tastes and practices of the new society.

association The existence of a relationship between two variables, where a change in one variable is related to a change in another variable.

atheist A term used to describe anyone who actively rejects the possibility of a god or any other supernatural being.

authority The ability to compel others to do things without needing to resort to threats. For Max Weber, authority requires legitimacy; that is, individuals grant authority to those they believe have a legitimate right to rule.

baby boom The post–World War II period in North America from approximately 1946 through 1964. During this period, fertility was high. The birth cohorts born during the baby boom years produced a generation of North Americans that was the largest in history.

biographical availability An individual's freedom to participate in a movement or protest due to a (relative) lack of constraining obligations created by work, school, family, or community.

birth cohort A group of individuals in a population born within a given time period. Thus the 1995–1999 birth cohort refers to those born between 1995 and 1999.

bourgeoisie The group in a capitalist economy who own businesses and employ people to work for them. This term is used in the Marxist tradition to refer to the most powerful class in a capitalist society.

brain drain The departure of a significant number of the most educated and skilled citizens, who go to live and work in other countries.

bureaucracy A type of organization that has rules and responsibilities for each position (or job) spelled out, in which selection into those positions occurs on the basis of merit (not typically by election or inheritance). Many bureaucracies are also responsible for setting out policies and procedures that are to be adhered to by others.

Canada Pension Plan An earnings-related social insurance program that mandates that all employed Canadians who are 18 years of age and over contribute a prescribed portion of their earnings income to a nationally administered pension plan.

Canadian Medical Association The leading professional association of physicians in Canada, formed in 1867.

cap-and-trade program A system in which a limit is placed on the total amount of carbon emissions that are allowable (the cap) and in which businesses buy and sell permits that entitle them to a designated amount of emissions (the trade).

capital A resource that can be used to make investments. Economic capital refers to the possession of financial assets that can be invested in a business. Other types of capital have also been suggested, for example human capital (the skills, education, or knowledge an individual possesses, which can be used to earn higher income) and cultural capital (the cultural knowledge possessed by an individual which impacts an individual's capacity to speak and interact with others in a sophisticated way).

capital controls Government policies that limit the movement of capital (i.e., funds available for investment) into or out of a country.

capitalism An economic system organized around private property and market exchange. In a capitalist economy, goods that are produced for consumption are distributed via exchange on the market.

capitalist economy An economic system in which goods and services are exchanged through markets, in which prices are established by what buyers are willing to pay, and in which property is privately owned. Under capitalism, markets extend to the hiring of workers at wages determined by negotiations between individuals (or unions) and employers. The role of government in regulating a capitalist economy varies widely, producing different types of capitalist economies around the world today.

capitalist state The governing institutions and legal system in a capitalist society.

capitalist world system A concept invented by Immanuel Wallerstein to describe the ways in which capitalist economies are linked in a global system, in which rich, developed countries are able to exploit undeveloped countries through a global division of labour in which poor countries provide raw materials and lower-skill labour.

care work All types of caring for other people, typically in one's own family, including childcare, elder care, or taking care of a disabled or sick adult.

caste society A society in which a person's social position is determined by the family he or she is born into.

causal inference A statement about cause and effect that claims that a change in one variable is the cause of a change in another variable.

causality When change in one variable is a direct cause of change in another variable. For example, long-term smoking is established as a cause of increased risk of lung cancer.

census A count of the members of a current population.

central planning An economy in which governments plan the amount of goods to be produced and their price for consumers. In the twentieth century, central planning was commonly practised in communist countries, such as the Soviet Union, China, and countries in Eastern Europe.

charisma Derived from a Greek word meaning *gift of grace*, the idea of *charisma* was introduced into the sociological study of social change by Max Weber, who used the term to refer to unique individuals who claim special powers or gifts that their followers believe to be true.

chronic disease (or chronic health condition) A health condition that is long lasting, including heart disease, cancer, arthritis, diabetes, asthma, and chronic obstructive pulmonary disease.

chronic disease prevalence The total number of cases of a particular disease in a population, or the proportion of disease cases compared to the population as a whole.

civil inattention The act of ignoring other people to an appropriate degree even while noticing that other people are present.

civil religion The sacred beliefs, practices, and symbols associated with a particular nation-state or community, which may or may not contain elements of a traditional organized religion.

class The sociological concept that refers to a group of people who share a similar social and economic position in society.

class analysis The study of society focused on class or changes in the system of class inequality. Emphasis is placed on examining how, when, and where people's actions and beliefs are influenced by their economic position.

class reproduction The processes that cause class boundaries and distinctions to be maintained over time.

class struggle The idea that classes of people who are treated differently by the economic system are inevitably going to be in conflict with one another.

climate change The variety of changes in weather patterns produced by warming global temperatures.

code of ethics A set of guidelines that outlines what is considered moral and acceptable behaviour in some context (such as within an organization or profession).

coercive isomorphism Similarities between organizations that arise out of legal or other requirements. Organizations become similar because they have no choice.

cohabitation The act of an unmarried straight or gay couple living together.

collective identity One's belief that one belongs to a certain group (or groups) with distinctive characteristics and interests (for example, women, the working class, or socialists). Not all such identities come easily to people; they may have to be consciously created, which is one of the things that some movements do.

colonist An inhabitant of a colony, usually established by a foreign power.

comparative–historical research A method of research that examines differences across countries or in different historical periods to try to understand what factors cause some specific change to occur.

conflict theory A type of social theory that emerged out of dissatisfaction with structural functionalism and held that all societies are characterized by conflicts that arise from the uneven distribution of power and wealth between groups.

congregation A specific religious body that meets regularly.

conjugal family A family consisting of a relatively autonomous married couple (and their children) able to seek its fortune outside the parental household.

conservationist One who argues that the point of environmental protection ought to be to responsibly manage natural resources so that they are available for commercial use by future generations.

constructivist A view of society that sees social categories such as race or gender as social creations, not biological facts.

consumption The act of purchasing and using goods and services.

correlation The existence of a relationship between two variables. A correlation exists when a change in one variable is related to a change in another variable. It does not necessarily imply, however, that the change in one variable is the *cause* of the change in the other. Correlation can be contrasted with **causality**.

counterculture A group whose ideas, attitudes, and behaviours are in direct conflict with mainstream culture.

counterpublic Alternative public organizations created by disadvantaged social groups.

counterterrorism Measures undertaken to fight or combat terrorist organizations, including military strikes and surveillance of suspected terrorist groups.

credentialism A requirement that one must obtain certain specific degrees or certificates before one can be considered for a particular job.

criminal justice system The entire body of laws and institutions that regulate and punish criminal activity. This includes written laws, courts, and other organizations where guilt or innocence is determined, as well as the places (such as jails and prisons, but also probation and parole offices) where those who have been convicted of a criminal offense are supervised.

cross-national comparison Research that focuses on explaining the differences between countries, such as understanding why some outcome is observed in one country and not another.

cross-sectional Research based on data that are collected at one point in time.

cultural capital The type and level of education and cultural knowledge possessed by an individual. Having a high level of cultural capital signifies one's high status in the eyes of others.

cultural omnivore A cultural elite that demonstrates high status through a broad range of cultural consumption and knowledge, including low-status culture.

cultural relativism The idea that cultural meanings and practices must be evaluated in their own social contexts.

cultural universal A cultural trait common to all humans and societies.

culture Systems of belief and knowledge shared by members of a group or society that shape individual and group behaviour and attitudes. A society's culture includes its language, customs, symbols, rituals, and other forms of meaning that are widely shared.

culture industry The production for profit of popular music, movies, books, television, social media, and other types of mass-culture products by capitalist enterprises.

culture wars Disagreements about the proper role of family and religious values in society.

curriculum The structure of coursework and content of a sequence of courses making up a program of study in a school or school system.

data The facts and information used in research.

data analysis The scientific process by which researchers interpret the data they have collected.

data coding The organization of data based on key concepts and categories.

data display A visual projection of patterns in data, for example as tables or figures.

deglobalization Periods of history when economic trade and investment between countries declines.

deism Belief in the existence of a supernatural or supreme being, but rejection of the view that this supreme being actively intervenes in human affairs.

democracy A concept with multiple meanings, all of which concern the ability of ordinary people to exert direct control over their leaders. As form of governance in the modern world, democracy can be said to exist where leaders are chosen in free elections where anyone can run and the news media are freely allowed to discuss the issues and candidates. Broader conceptions of democracy incorporate a more direct role for citizen participation where everyone has the right to participate and equal resources to do so.

demographer One who studies population issues, particularly in relation to fertility, mortality, and migration, and how these processes vary among individuals in a population.

demography The study of population size, particularly in relation to fertility rates (the ratio of live births in a population), mortality (the ratio of deaths and the life expectancy of individuals), and migration across borders.

denomination An organized branch of a larger religious tradition.

dependent variable A variable that fluctuates in relation to other ("independent") variables. In research, the dependent variable is the object of explanation, or what the researcher is trying to explain.

deportation The act of sending immigrants back to their country of origin. Deportation can function as a mechanism of state power used to remove persons from the country when they are deemed to be undesirable.

deskilling The process of breaking down the tasks involved in the production of goods or services into parts that can be done by someone without specialized training.

determinist One who believes that a society's environment, or the technology it has developed to exploit its environment, determines everything else—from its social structure to individuals' thoughts.

deterrence Policies or laws that are designed to discourage an individual or group from engaging in some kind of behaviour.

deviant An individual whose actions or attitudes fall outside the generally accepted norms of a given group or society. What is "deviant" behaviour is subject to change, depending on which group(s) have the power to define what is "normal."

diaspora A group of people dispersed from their original homeland and settled in other areas for long periods of time who nonetheless retain cultural practices, memories, and ties to that space.

digital divide The social, economic, and cultural gap between those with effective access to information technology and those without such access.

discrimination Any behaviour, practice, or policy that harms, excludes, or disadvantages individuals on the basis of their group membership. Discrimination is often used by dominant groups to control opportunities and reduce the challenges from subordinate groups.

division of labour The specialization of individuals in any organization or group, or in society as a whole, particularly in relation to work. There is thus a division of labour in all of society (with different people working in different occupations), a division of labour in individual organizations (where different people perform different tasks), and a division of labour in individual families and communities.

doctrine The official beliefs and rules of a particular religion or social and political group. Most commonly used to refer to more rigid belief systems.

double standard of sexuality Judging women more harshly than men for having sex outside of marriage or outside of relationships.

ecology The branch of science that studies the relationship between organisms and their environment.

economic class A category of immigration under which skilled workers and business owners can apply for immigration to Canada.

economic restructuring Changes in the way the economy, firms, and employment relations are organized.

educational homogamy The practice of people marrying individuals with educational levels similar to their own.

egalitarian A society, organization, or group characterized by having little or very low levels of inequality.

egalitarian relationship A relationship where all members of the relationship share more or less equally in performing required tasks. In the case of intimate relationships, this includes sharing household chores, including child or elder care.

emigration The act of leaving one's country of birth to move to a new country.

emigration and immigration policies Government policies regulating the right of people to move into or out of a country.

empirical generalizability The application of conclusions from findings about one group or setting to the larger population. An empirical research result is generalizable when the same result can be found in another context.

entrepreneur One who invests money in a business.

enumerate Systematically count (as in counting population).

environmental justice The achievement of equal protection from environmental hazards for all people, regardless of race, class, or geography; environmental justice also means giving community members a voice in shaping decisions that affect their environment and their health.

environmental racism A concept that describes how poor people of colour disproportionately bear the burden of environmental hazards.

environmental sociology The study of how society simultaneously shapes and is shaped by the physical environment.

epidemiological transition The transition of a population from health conditions primarily involving infectious disease to health conditions primarily involving chronic disease.

epidemiology The study of health-related events in populations, their characteristics, their causes, and their consequences.

essentialism The view that members of a group share a fundamental, inherited, innate, and fixed quality or characteristic. This outlook presumes that races are natural groupings whose boundaries are determined by deep-seated and unchangeable traits that are found within each individual.

ethnicity A system for classifying people who are believed to share common descent, based on perceived cultural similarities.

ethnocentrism The inability to understand, accept, or reference patterns of behaviour or belief different from one's own.

ethnographer A sociologist who enters the everyday lives of those he or she studies in hopes of understanding how they navigate and give meaning to their worlds.

ethnography A qualitative research method for studying the way of life of a group of people by close observation of them over a relatively long period of time.

ethnomethodology A line of sociological inquiry (introduced by Harold Garfinkel) that studies the ways (tools and methods) members of a particular group construct social order and make sense of their everyday lives.

evangelical Someone who believes in salvation through personal conversion (or being "born again"). Evangelicals are also known for their emphasis on bringing their beliefs to others. The term is mostly associated with Christianity, although it can apply to someone of other faiths as well.

exclusionary immigration policy Policies that intentionally discrimination against certain categories of immigrants, ususally based on racial and/or ethnic characteristics.

export Goods or services that are sold outside the country in which they are produced.

extended case method A method of conducting ethnography that emphasizes the contribution of research to social theory. An ethnographer using the extended case method starts from a theoretical problem or puzzle.

factors of production The inputs—such as land, labour, capital, and technology—that go into the production of any good or service.

fad Any kind of behaviour that spreads (often rapidly) among a specific population and is repeated enthusiastically for some period of time before disappearing (often rapidly).

family class A category of immigration under which permanent residents can apply to sponsor family members to immigrate to Canada.

family values A term generally associated with views and ideas about the family that highlight the virtues of heterosexual marriage and childrearing in a traditional nuclear family with defined gender roles. Family values can also be applied to other kinds of nontraditional unions.

feminist movement A social movement whose members advocate equality between men and women in rights and opportunities.

feminist social theory Social theories that place gender relations and male domination at the centre of their conceptualization of societies.

fertility The process by which members of a population produce live births.

feudalism A social order in which those who own land (landlords) are entitled to receive the products of the labourers (serfs) who are legally obligated to work for the landowner.

first demographic transition The transition by a country or region from a pretransition period of high fertility and high mortality, to a mid-transition period of declining mortality followed by declining fertility, to a posttransition period in which both mortality and fertility are low.

forces of production One part of the modes of production; the technological and productive capacity of any society at a given point in time.

foreign direct investment (FDI) A type of investment by a company in one country to produce goods or services in another. This could involve the purchase of an existing business in the second country or building factories and/or offices in the second country and hiring workers.

foreign investment Investment of capital from one country into another.

fossil fuel An energy source, such as coal, oil, or natural gas, that is made of fossils that decomposed over millions of years under high pressure.

framing The specific ways in which ideas and beliefs are presented to other people. Politicians, political activists, and social movements all engage in framing efforts when they try to persuade others that their way of thinking is correct. Scholars of social movements have also focused on how activists try to frame or present their cause or ideas for change so that they make sense to or resonate with the beliefs of potential recruits and supporters.

free space Place where people gather that does not have any government or corporate surveillance, where oppositional ideas and tactics can develop and spread.

fundamental social cause A theory stating that individuals of higher socioeconomic status have access to knowledge, money, power, and social connections that are deployed throughout the life course to avoid disease and death. These resources can be deployed in a range of situations. As a result, this theory predicts that no matter what the causes of bad health, socioeconomic inequalities will inevitably emerge.

gender The ways that social forces create differences between men's and women's behaviour, preferences, treatment, and opportunities, and the characteristics of men and women that reflect these forces.

generalization Forming conclusions about broader society from research on a subgroup or sample of the broader society.

generalized other The social control exercised by commonsense understandings of what is appropriate given a specific time and place.

General Social Survey In Canada, an independent, annual, cross-sectional survey since 1985. Canada's GSS covers one topic in depth each year.

Geneva Conventions A set of international agreements between countries about how prisoners of war are to be treated.

genocide The deliberate and systematic killing of a category of people.

global value chain The full range of activities that businesses and workers provide at each stage of the production of a good or service that add to its value. While a value chain can be contained entirely within a single company, or within one country, global value chains (with production inputs from more than one country) are increasingly being found.

global warming Describes the rising of Earth's average temperature.

globalization The growing permeability of national borders and the increase in flows of goods, services, and people across national borders.

greenhouse effect The result of high levels of carbon dioxide in the atmosphere allowing the sun's heat to pass through to Earth's surface while stopping it from spreading back into space.

gross domestic product (GDP) The total value of all goods and services, plus investment and government expenditures, that a country produces.

group style The set of norms and practices that distinguishes one group from another.

guerrilla warfare A type of warfare in which an outmanned army hides from its larger opponent and engages in attacks only in situations where it thinks it can gain an advantage.

habitus A concept introduced by sociologist Pierre Bourdieu to refer to the diverse ways in which individuals develop intuitive understandings and engrained habits reflecting their class background and upbringing.

Hawthorne studies An influential series of studies at the Hawthorne plant of the Western Electric company in the 1920s. Two major findings emerged from these studies: (1) the experiment effect, which is any change interpreted by workers as management's attempt to improve conditions, especially those that provide mental stimulation and improve workers' productivity; and (2) the social group effect, in which workers who are moved to separate spaces as a group develop bonds that increase their productivity.

health disparity A difference in health status linked to social, economic, or environmental conditions, including socioeconomic status, race and ethnicity, gender, and geographic location.

healthy life expectancy The average number of healthy years one can expect to live if current patterns of death and illness remain the same.

hegemony Widely shared beliefs about what is right or wrong that legitimize and empower a society's elites.

heteronormativity A type of prejudice that claims that being heterosexual is the only normal option for an individual's sexual orientation.

heterosexism Discrimination or bias against persons because they are not heterosexual.

hidden curriculum The often unstated standards of behaviour that teachers and administrators expect from children within the education system. These often unstated expectations may reflect the middle-class biases and norms of school professionals.

homelessness An extreme form of poverty defined by lack of permanent shelter to live in.

homeopathy A medical sect, originally from Germany, that emphasized the use of small amounts of a drug known to cause a health condition in large doses to treat that very same health condition when it manifests itself in an individual.

homophobia Discrimination or bias against homosexual persons that is based in fear.

hookup Sexual behaviour (not always intercourse) that occurs in a situation that was not a prearranged date and between individuals who may or may not be interested in an exclusive romantic relationship.

hospice care The treatment of people with incurable diseases in the final stage of life. The goal of hospice care is to attempt to help patients live as pain-free as possible in their final days.

human capital An individual's stock of experience, knowledge, skills, and habits, which he or she can use to do productive labour.

hypothesis A prediction researchers make that they will test in their research.

identity The conceptions we and others have about who we are and what groups or categories we are members of.

ideology A set of ideas that constitutes one's goals, expectations, and actions.

immigration A term that describes the movement of people across borders.

immobility A situation in which individuals are unable to move from one economic or social class into another. Usually immobility means that people remain in the same social and economic situation that they are born into (in other words, in the same class or income group as their parents).

implicit prejudice or bias Prejudice based on stereotypes that can be activated without an individual's being consciously aware of holding them.

import A good or service purchased in one country but manufactured in another.

import-substituting industrialization (ISI) Government policies that attempt to replace imported goods with similar goods produced by domestic companies. Examples of such policies include putting very high taxes on certain imported goods or barring them altogether. ISI was a strategy used by many poor and moderate-income developing countries in the twentieth century in an attempt to foster domestic economic growth.

incarceration The holding of an individual in a jail or prison.

income The receipt of money or goods over a particular accounting period (such as hourly, weekly, monthly, or yearly). Income may include wages from a job, benefits from a pension or government program, or income from investments.

independent variable A factor that might help to explain some outcome of interest. An example might be the impact of educational level—in this case, the independent variable—on one's income as an adult.

in-depth interview A method of collecting data based on asking a person a set of questions and having a conversation with him or her focused on gathering information related to the research.

individual discrimination Action carried out by an individual or small group that harms, excludes, or disadvantages members of a certain group.

industrialization A process of economic change characterized by the decline of farming and the growth of factories and large-scale goods production.

Industrial Revolution The period in which mass production in factories began to develop and fostered rapid economic growth. The timing of the Industrial Revolution varied from country to country but is generally thought to have begun in the late eighteenth century and evolved throughout the nineteenth and early twentieth centuries.

inequality The unequal distribution of valued goods and opportunities in society.

inequality of opportunity The ways in which inequality shapes the opportunities for children and young adults to maximize their potential.

infant mortality rate A measure of infant mortality, defined as the number of deaths per 1,000 live births in a given calendar year, with the number of deaths referring to babies who die during their first 12 months of life.

infectious disease A disease caused by the entrance, presence, or growth of a microorganism or other foreign agent inside the body.

informed consent The voluntary participation of someone in a research project or medical treatment based on the participant/patient having a full understanding of possible risks and benefits involved.

institution A complex term used to stand for structured and enduring practices of human life that are built around well-established rules and norms or are centred in important organizations like the government, legal courts, churches, schools, or the military.

institutional (or structural) discrimination When the actions or policies of organizations or social institutions exclude, disadvantage, or harm members of particular groups. Such discrimination need not be intentional, and in practice it is often hard to discern whether or not discriminatory intentions lie behind a particular policy or practice.

institutional review board (IRB) Required at all universities that receive federal funds for research, these boards review researchers' proposals before any work can begin in order to assess the potential harm of the research for participants being studied.

institutionalization The process by which a social practice or organization begins to become an institution; the introduction of formal roles and rules in an organized form.

interdisciplinary research A method of research that integrates ideas, theories, and data from different academic fields.

interest group An organization established to promote the interests of a group or corporation, especially in Congress or at the level of state governments.

interpretative sociology The study of the meanings individuals ascribe to their actions.

intersectionality Forms of inequality that overlap and potentially reinforce one another. One's class, race, ethnicity, religion, gender, sexuality, or other characteristics may create multiple forms of disadvantage that inequality researchers should consider.

intersex individual A person who is born with a body that has some biological characteristics typically found in only male bodies, as well as other biological characteristics typically found in female bodies (for example, a penis and ovaries).

irreligion The absence of religion.

jail A place of detention where individuals are either held before trial or serve relatively minor sentences. *Prisons* generally hold offenders convicted of more serious crimes.

journalism The production and dissemination of information about contemporary affairs of general importance.

kin Other people that individuals have important social relationships with. These important others often include immediate (and sometimes extended) family members but also can include close friends and even other acquaintances who play an important (and sometimes supportive) role in one's life.

kinship system The social links and boundaries, defined by biology and social custom, that establish who is related to whom.

labeling theory A theory of deviance that stresses that many kinds of behaviours are deviant solely because they are labeled as such.

labour market The process through which employers identify and hire individuals to work under specified terms of employment.

labour process The organization of work, in terms of the relationship between workers and employers, the way specific work tasks are structured and performed, and the technologies and organizational environments in which the work is performed.

language Any comprehensive system of words or symbols representing concepts. It does not necessarily need to be spoken, as the hundreds of different sign languages in use around the world suggest.

legitimacy The acceptance of the authority of a ruler and/or system of government. Legitimacy exists when virtually all members of society accept the right of their rulers to govern their society.

liberation theology A strain of theology first associated with Latin American Catholicism that emphasizes god's concern for the poor and downtrodden and the rightness of social justice causes.

life chances An individual's long-term possibilities and potential, including future income and opportunities, given his or her current attributes such as level of education, social networks, and possession of marketable skills or assets. Members of the same class are generally said to have similar life chances.

life course The transitions individuals make as they age through their lives. A typical life course includes childhood, adolescence, the transition to adulthood and first job, perhaps becoming a parent, retiring, and death. The study of the life course by sociologists centres on the key transitions, or turning points, in individual lives and the larger social patterns they represent.

life-course perspective A model that highlights the effects that social contexts a person inhabits throughout life have on his or her health.

life expectancy (at age *x*) The average number of additional years (past age *x*) that the average person in a population can expect to live.

longitudinal research Research based on data collected over a long period of time.

looking-glass self A term coined by sociologist Charles Horton Cooley to emphasize the extent to which our own self-understandings are dependent on how others view us.

loose coupling An organizational environment in which those at the top do not have control over the activities and decisions underneath them. This often arises in complex organizations with multiple units.

low income cut-off (LICO) Statistics Canada's after-tax LICO is a level of income at which point a family spends 63.6% or more of its income on food, shelter, and clothing.

Low Income Measure (LIM) A purely relative measure of poverty used for international comparison.

lynching The killing of someone by a group, without a trial or due process, for some specified behaviour.

mainstream culture The most widely shared systems of meaning in a society. Mainstream culture includes the most widely consumed cultural products (music, literature, films), foods, and ways of speaking, as well as widely shared ideas about normal or appropriate behaviour.

market Any setting in which buyers and sellers engage in exchange.

Market Basket Measure (MBM) An absolute measure that attempts to estimate the amount of income needed by a household to meet basic needs defined as community norms.

mass communication Communication within society as a whole through the mass media (television, Internet, newspapers, radio), as opposed to between individuals.

mass incarceration A term used to describe a situation in which a very high proportion of people are held in prisons. It has been used to describe developments in the American criminal justice system over the past 30 years.

mean A statistical term that refers to the average value of a set of data. Add all values and then divide the total by the number of values used.

mechanical solidarity According to Emile Durkheim, mechanical solidarity refers to the factors that hold primitive societies together, mostly through family and kinship ties and a collective consciousness shared by all members of the community.

median A statistical term that refers to the value that lies at the middle (or midpoint) of all the data, with an equal number of cases with either higher or lower values.

medicalization The process by which some human condition comes to be defined as a medical condition, one that can be treated using medicine.

Medicare A federal government program in Canada that provides health insurance to all individuals.

megachurch Individual (and often independent) Protestant churches that average over 2,000 people in attendance at weekly services.

megacity A city with a population over 10 million.

meritocracy A system where rewards and positions are distributed by ability, not social background or personal connections.

middle class A group of people who occupy the middle positions in terms of income and status in an economic system.

migrant energy The special skills and determination brought to a country by migrants, who may be especially motivated to succeed.

migrant remittance Money sent by a migrant to family or friends in his or her home country.

migration The movement of individuals from one location, region, country, or city to another.

mimetic isomorphism The tendency of similar organizations to adopt the same kinds of rules and procedures in the belief that what works for one organization should work for others.

minimum wage Established by law, minimum wage is the lowest hourly wage a worker can be paid.

mixed-method research Research that uses evidence that is both qualitative and quantitative.

mode of production In Marxist theory, a mode of production is a concept for characterizing the dominant economic system in a society. A mode of production has two parts, the forces of production and the social relations of production.

moral behaviour Behaviour that is guided by a belief about what is right and proper to do.

moral shock An unexpected event that surprises, distresses, and outrages people, often to the point of motivating them to join or even start a movement to eliminate the source of their outrage.

mortality The process by which individuals in a population gradually die.

mover An individual who leaves a place to live in another.

multiculturalism Beliefs or policies promoting the equal accommodation of different ethnic or cultural groups within a society. It is sometimes also used to refer to the benefits of dialogue and interaction between different groups.

national culture The set of shared cultural practices and beliefs of people living within a nation-state.

nationalism A set of beliefs about the virtues of one's country. In the sociology of race and ethnicity, nationalism includes the assumption that people are inherently members of a specific nation, and that their identities are in large part defined by their national membership.

natural selection In evolutionary biology, a theory of how species evolve that emphasizes the process through which biological traits become more or less common depending on whether they enhance the survival of the species.

neo-Marxism An updated form of Marxism, neo-Marxism contends that the capitalist state could, and indeed often has, forced powerful economic classes to make "concessions" to the working class (thereby improving the living standards of all citizens).

net financial assets (NFA) The total value of savings, investments, and other convertible assets a person has, minus any debts, and excluding one's primary home (if it is owned).

network analysis A research technique that focuses on identifying the connections among individuals, groups, or organizations.

networked public An online public sphere.

new religious movement A religious group that emerges independently of existing religious traditions or makes significant revisions and additions to them.

niche A unique place or opportunity that can be profitably filled by someone or some group. Niches arise in a variety of ways, especially when existing organizations or government agencies fail to meet some underlying social need.

norm A basic rule of society that helps us know what is and is not appropriate to do in a situation. Norms evolve over time as social attitudes and expectations change, although those changes are typically very slow.

normalize To make or declare some action as normal or appropriate.

normative isomorphism The process of organizations becoming similar because of a widespread belief among their members and the members of similar organizations that they should adopt certain rules or procedures.

nuclear family A term used to describe a family consisting of a husband and wife and their children.

nurse practitioner (NP) Nurses with advanced degrees and clinical training to enable independent patient diagnoses and treatment.

occupation A job that has been formally established and has some requirements (often formalized) for training or knowledge to perform it.

occupational sex segregation When women and men are distributed differently across occupations, such that some jobs are filled mostly by men and others mostly by women.

Old Age Security The largest statutory pension program in Canada. It includes the Old Age Security pension, the Guaranteed Income Supplement, the Allowance (for those aged 60–64 who are spouses of persons eligible for the Guaranteed Income Supplement), and the Allowance for the Survivor (e.g., widows and widowers over 60).

operationalize When researchers define the methods and techniques to be used to assess and define the concepts that are being investigated.

organic solidarity According to Emile Durkheim, as societies become more advanced, they are held together through the mutual dependence of and interdependence between individuals.

organization A social group or social network that is unified by a common institutional structure, such as a government agency, a school, a business firm, the military, or a religion.

organizational isomorphism The process by which similar organizations adopt similar rules and procedures.

outsourcing Common in globalization, outsourcing refers to the contracting of parts of the production process to another party, possibly located abroad. A common example in the United States is of credit-card companies hiring people in India to handle customer service calls.

paganism Religions that generally envision a set of gods and attendants who rule the world.

palliative care All types of healthcare designed to reduce pain and suffering by improving the quality of life of patients and their families facing life-threatening illness. Hospice care is palliative care where there is no hope of curing or improving a patient.

path dependency The process by which the historical legacies and outcomes of the past impact actors and organizations in the present, making some choices or outcomes appear logical and others illogical.

patriarchy A gender system in which men have substantially more power than women in politics, the economy, and the family.

patrilocal A family relationship in which a married couple resides with the husband's parents.

peasant A person who works in agriculture but does not own the land he or she farms.

pluralism (in religion) The coexistence of individuals and religious groups with significantly different beliefs and cultures in the same society.

points system The system under which the Canadian government awards points to potential immigrants based on language skills, education, age, income and wealth, investment potential, and employment.

political-process perspective A theoretical perspective that emphasizes that movements are concerned with politics, not individual psychological states, and are a rational form of politics ("politics by other means") and a normal response, under certain circumstances, to routine institutional political processes. Movements emerge and may be successful if those political processes create political opportunities for certain kinds of collective protest.

polygamy The practice of marriage of one individual to two or more other individuals.

polytheistic Religions that worship more than one entity or god.

population dynamics The process by which a population changes in size over time.

population momentum The tendency of a population that has been changing in size to continue to change in size even if factors such as fertility and mortality have shifted to levels that would, in the long run, imply no change in population size.

poverty line Established by the government, it is the minimum income necessary to afford basic necessities. Anyone below this threshold is considered to be in poverty.

power Power has three distinct dimensions in the sociological sense: (1) the power of an individual or group to get another individual or group to do something it wants, which sometimes may involve force; (2) the power to control the agenda of issues that are to be decided; and finally (3) the power to persuade others that their interests are the same as those of a powerholder. Power can be possessed by individuals or groups.

precapitalist economy All of the different types of economies that existed before the rise of capitalism, including those based on hunting or agriculture.

prejudice Negative beliefs or attitudes held about entire groups based on subjective, selective, or inaccurate information. They lead to "prejudgment" of the individuals associated with stigmatized groups.

preservationist One who believes that the environment has intrinsic value and should be maintained in as pristine a state as possible.

price convergence When the prices of goods sold in different places tend toward the same level, adjusted for currency values.

prison A place of detention where people convicted of felonies (serious crimes requiring at least one year of detention) are held.

privilege The ability or right to have special access to opportunities or claims on rewards.

probability sampling A technique for choosing participants for a research study (i.e., a probability sample) in which each person in the population is assigned a known and likely chance of being selected. Some groups of people can be assigned different probabilities of being selected when the probability sample is stratified based on group membership.

probation A criminal conviction that does not require a prison or jail sentence. During probation, convicted offenders are subject to regular supervision but are allowed to live in their community.

professionalism An occupation that succeeds in gaining government licensing over the right to practice (and typically leaders of the occupation or professional association control the licensing process), establishes educational requirements to anyone to become eligible for license, and regulates and disciplines members of the profession when necessary.

progressive tax system A tax system in which tax rates are higher on richer people than poorer people, with the idea being that it is fair to ask those who can afford to pay more to do so. These systems can be based on a progressive income tax and can also differentially assess taxes on wealth transfers, such as inheritances.

Prohibition In Canada, depending on the province, the period from 1917 to 1929 saw the consumption or sale of alcohol barred by law.

proletariat Individuals in capitalist economies who work in exchange for pay. The term is usually reserved for people performing manual jobs and is synonymous with "working class."

proportional representation (PR) A system of elections in which seats in a legislature are divided up based on the percentage of the vote received. In many PR systems, there is a minimum threshold, such as 5 percent, for a party to cross before it receives seats.

psychoanalysis The study of the conscious and unconscious aspects of the mind and their influence on individual behaviour.

public health Public policies that aim to reduce the spread of disease and ill health among entire populations by means such as improved sanitation and garbage handling, maintaining clean water, monitoring airborne diseases, and fighting the outbreak of viruses.

public opinion The views of citizens in the aggregate on social and political topics. Public opinion is usually measured through opinion polls and surveys, where modern sampling techniques allow researchers to estimate opinions by asking a smaller representative group of citizens.

public policy All of the policies adopted or implemented by the government. A distinction between foreign policy and domestic policy is important, with the former including all policies relating to foreign governments and national security issues, while the latter refers to all of the policies and programs that aim to address social problems or issues inside the country.

public sphere A social space—physical, virtual, or theoretical—where private citizens can come together as a public body to discuss and express opinions about matters of general interest.

pull factor In the immigration context, when an individual's motivation to move to another country is based on the perceived attractions of life in the new country.

push factor When an individual decides to leave a country because of something that is making her or him unhappy (such as low pay, lack of jobs, limited opportunities, or political or religious persecution).

qualitative research Research that relies on nonnumerical data, such as words, observations, or pictures.

quantitative research Research that relies on statistical analysis of numerical or categorical data.

race A system for classifying people who are believed to share common descent, based on perceived innate physical similarities.

racialized The process of assigning a racial character to the activities of minority groups on the basis of real or imagined physical characteristics to serve racist or discriminatory ends.

racism Prejudice and/or discrimination against individuals who are members or particular racial or ethnic groups, often drawing on negative stereotypes about the group. Institutional racism refers to rules and regulations that organizations adopt that significantly harm members of a racial or ethnic group.

random-assignment experiment A study using a method of assigning participants or groups to receive different treatments that ensures that any posttreatment differences result from the different treatments they received.

random sample A technique for choosing participants for a research study in which each person in the population of interest has an equal chance of being chosen so that the sample mirrors a larger population and reflects its characteristics or dynamics.

rational-choice perspective A perspective in social and economic theory that emphasizes the centrality of individual decision making based on how individuals think about their well-being and how best to advance it. While there are a variety of different versions of the rational-choice perspective, all emphasize that individual action is the foundation of society and social order.

receiving country Host or destination countries where migrants go.

reference group A set of individuals who share similar preferences or social positions and have influence on an individual or members of a group.

refugee class In Canada, a category of immigration under which people from war-torn countries can apply for protection from persecution on humanitarian grounds.

rehabilitation The attempt to reform a convicted offender so that he or she will not commit crimes in the future. Rehabilitation often involves the use of therapies of various kinds, as well as helping an offender develop job and life skills that will help him or her desist from crime in the future.

relative poverty A term used to define people as poor not by assessing whether their resources are sufficient to obtain basic social necessities but rather by comparing their incomes relative to those of other people in society.

reliability The extent to which the same measurement technique in additional studies would end up producing similar results.

religiosity The importance of religion in an individual's life.

renewable energy Sources of energy that are capable of being replaced by natural ecological cycles, such as wind, sunlight, and water.

replacement fertility A level of fertility in which individuals in a population, on average, have a sufficient number of offspring that will imply, over the long run, no change in the size of the population.

replicated A study that has been repeated to make sure its results are correct.

representative sample A small group of people, ideally selected at random, who are similar to the entire population.

research memo An extended version of research notes, usually organized analytically, that allows researchers to work through their findings and the evidence they have to support them.

resource-mobilization approach A theoretical perspective that emphasizes the importance of resources, like labour and money, for generating and sustaining social movements. The more resources a movement is able to employ or mobilize, the more successful it is likely to be.

retribution Punishment that aims at making a criminal offender experience as much harm as he or she has caused others.

revolution A revolution consists, at minimum, of a change of government or political regime brought about, at least in part, by popular protest. Some define revolutions (or "social revolutions") more narrowly, as entailing not only a change of regime but also a fundamental change in a society's economic institutions and class structure.

revolutionary movement A social movement that seeks to overthrow a government or fundamentally change a society's economic institutions and class structure.

revolutionary situation A situation that occurs when two or more political institutions or groups claim to be the rightful or legitimate rulers of a certain territory or population. Such a situation is also called "dual power" or "multiple sovereignty."

riot A spontaneous, unplanned collective protest, loosely organized at best, involving attacks on property and (sometimes) persons.

role A position within an institution or organization that comes with specific social expectations for how to behave and be treated. Some roles may be ascribed, that is, assigned to us by birth (man, woman, white, black), and some may be achieved, that is, acquired through our actions (doctor, professor, class clown).

role conflict When two or more discordant demands are placed on individuals, rendering them unable to fulfill their own or others', expectations.

role model A specific individual who exhibits significant influence on others and acts as a reference for how to act.

sacred Holy; worthy of special reverence.

same-sex marriage A marriage between two partners of the same sex.

sample The subjects or data a researcher will include in a study.

sanction Any type of punishment, including both formal punishment (based on laws or written rules) and informal types of punishments.

scientific management A movement that arose in the late nineteenth and early twentieth centuries that attempted to improve productivity by ensuring that managers controlled all aspects of the labour process and would utilize the best practices available given existing technology and knowledge.

scientific method A step-by-step process of conducting research that begins with formulating a research hypothesis, then operationalizing variables, then collecting data, and finally drawing empirical and conceptual generalizations from the data.

second demographic transition Some scholars have argued that rich countries are now going through a new demographic transition in which fertility rates have fallen below replacement levels, a multitude of living arrangements other than marriage are emerging, and there is an increasing disconnection between marriage and procreation. Declining fertility combined with increased longevity means that populations are getting older. Finally, many societies are becoming multi-ethnic because of increased levels of immigration to stem population decline.

second generation The children of immigrants.

second shift A term created and popularized by Arlie Hochschild to refer to housework, childcare, and elder care disproportionally done by women. The first shift refers to one's paid job, whereas the second shift refers to the labour needed to keep households going.

secularization A process of declining influence or marginalization of religion in society.

secularization hypothesis A theory that as societies modernize and citizens become better educated, religion will inevitably decline.

security certificate A mechanism available under the Immigration and Refugee Protection Act that allows the Canadian Security Intelligence Service (CSIS) to collect intelligence about a foreigner living in Canada who they believe is a national security threat. A security certificate cannot be used on a Canadian citizen.

self The conscious being, personified in a human body, which is made and reformulated through social interaction.

self-fulfilling prophecy A term coined by Robert Merton to mean the process by which someone is defined in a particular way and then comes to fulfill the expectations of that definition.

self-selected When individuals have the opportunity to choose to be in some condition, those making that choice may be different than those who do not make that choice. The "selection effect" reflects the differences between those two groups.

sending country The country migrants were born in.

serf Under feudalism, a person who is legally obligated to work for the landowner.

serial relationships A pattern of having repeated, short-term intimate relationships with other adults.

sex Whether a person is classified as male or female based on anatomical or chromosomal criteria.

sex differences Differences that are assumed to exist because of anatomical or chromosomal criteria.

sexual minority A group whose sexual behaviour or attractions are unusual in a given society. Those who are homosexual, bisexual, or transgendered are sexual minorities.

sexual orientation Whether one's sexual attractions are to members of the same sex, the other sex, or both.

significant other A term coined by George Herbert Mead to mean individuals close enough to us to have a strong capacity to motivate our behaviour.

slavery A social system that denies some individuals all basic rights, allowing these individuals to be owned, controlled, and compelled to work for others.

smog A smoky air pollutant produced when tailpipe or smokestack emissions that linger in the atmosphere chemically react with the sunlight.

social capital The resources available to a particular individual through his or her connections to others.

social closure The process by which organized groups seek to establish or maintain privileged access to rewards or opportunities.

social construct An invented social phenomenon (for example a belief, discourse, or category) that is shaped by the social forces present in the time and place of its creation.

social construction (of the environment) The process by which people interpret the natural world and make it meaningful.

social construction (of race or gender) The social processes that create and sustain gender and race differences and inequality.

social context The social environments, including economic and cultural conditions, that influence people's lives.

social control The institutions, norms, and rules through which societies attempt to shape and control individuals. Behaviour that violates social rules is typically punished either formally or informally, reflecting the different ways in which social control is administered.

social distance A concept first introduced by Georg Simmel to describe how close or intimate, or apart, any two individuals or groups are with each other.

social fact According to Emile Durkheim, those regularities and rules of everyday life that exist independently and outside the control of individuals.

social forces All of the forms of social structure (hierarchies and institutions) that any individual must operate within. Social forces are related to what Emile Durkheim called "social facts."

social group A collection of individuals formed around some kind of social identity or for some specific purpose.

social hierarchy Any relationship between individuals or groups that is unequal and provides one person or group with more status and power than another.

social interaction The way people act together, including how they modify and alter their behaviour in response to the presence of others. Social interaction is governed by norms.

socialism An economic system where the government owns some or most of all productive enterprises and makes decisions about the amount and type of goods and services to be produced.

socialist society A society in which the productive forces are owned by everyone (not by individual business owners).

socialization The process by which individuals come to understand the expectations and norms of their groups as well as the various roles they transition into over the life course and how to behave in society or in particular social settings.

socially deviant Behaviour that violates the written or unwritten rules of society.

social mobility The movement of individuals from one social position into another. Intergenerational social mobility is a measure of the extent to which parents and their children have similar or different social and economic positions in adulthood. Upward mobility is said to occur when an individual's class is higher than that of his or her parents; downward mobility is the opposite.

social movement A conscious, concerted, and sustained effort by ordinary people to change (or preserve) some aspect of their society by using extrainstitutional means. "Extrainstitutional means" refers to collective actions undertaken outside existing institutions, like courts and legislatures, although movements may also work through such institutions, at least part of the time.

social movement organization (SMO) A formal organization that participates in, and may initiate or lead, a social movement. SMOs generally pool resources, like labour and money, which may be crucial for movements. Some movements encompass a number of SMOs that alternately cooperate and compete with one another.

social network The ties or connections between people, groups, and organizations.

social problem A term used to capture a wide range of individual, group, or societal behaviours or societal issues that are thought to have harmful consequences. Examples might include poverty, crime, drug abuse, homelessness, inequality, racism, sexism, and discrimination.

social relations of production One part of the modes of production; the relationships and inequalities between different kinds of people within the economy.

social reproduction The processes that transmit inequality from one generation to the next.

social solidarity The social forces that hold any society together.

social stratification A subfield of sociology that examines inequalities among individuals and groups.

social structure The external forces, most notably social hierarchies, norms, and institutions, that provide the context for individual and group action.

social theory An overarching framework that suggests certain assumptions and assertions about the way the world works. These frameworks are used for posing research questions and evaluating evidence related to those questions.

society A large group of people who live in the same area and participate in a common economy or culture.

socioeconomic gradient Reflects that those with the lowest status are less healthy than those in the middle, who are less healthy than those at the top.

socioeconomic status (SES) A broad definition of a person's social class based on components such as education, income, and occupation.

sociological imagination The capacity to think systematically about how many things we experience as personal problems—for example, debt from student loans, competing demands from divorced parents, or an inability to form a rewarding romantic relationship at college—are really social issues that are widely shared by others born in a similar time and social location as us. It involves taking into account how our individual lives are impacted by historical and social contexts.

sociology The study of societies and the social worlds that individuals inhabit within them.

soft skills Also called noncognitive traits, these are social skills—such as knowing how to dress, the ability to hold a sophisticated conversation, or interacting well with a variety of other people—that may enhance a person's job performance.

spurious relationship When two factors seem to move in the same direction but both are themselves caused by something else (i.e., a third factor), sociologists refer to the apparent relationship between the first two factors as a spurious relationship.

state All of the agencies and offices of governing institutions, including government bureaucracies, law and the legal system, and the military, constitute what sociologists call the state. It is a term that is meant to capture more than just the current government in power by incorporating the idea that the there are permanent institutions that are independent of whomever is in power.

state deviance Deviant behaviour by governments or government agencies.

statistically deviant Behaviour that is different or unusual but not necessarily in violation of social norms.

status A distinct social category that is set off from others and is associated with a set of expected behaviours and roles for individuals to assume. The category can often involve prestige, such as that accorded to individuals and to important social or economic roles (like "priest," "lawyer," "truck driver"). An individual's status may reflect some accomplishment or position attained, one's membership in a particular group, or both.

status group A term invented by Max Weber to describe any group that forms a common identity and develops ways of distinguishing insiders from outsiders.

stayer One who chooses not to leave.

stereotype A simplified generalization about a group (e.g., women or men) that is often false or exaggerated. Stereotypes are most often negative, although positive stereotypes can sometimes be found.

stratification system The full range of social hierarchies found in any society, which create inequalities between individuals and groups.

structural functionalism A theory of society in which individuals, groups, and the institutions of any society are guided by an overarching social system and can be explained by the needs of society to reproduce itself.

structural inertia The extent to which an organization's rules and routines are relatively fixed and difficult to change.

stylized facts A series of facts or empirical regularities that we think we know with great certainty.

subculture A relatively small group of people whose affiliation is based on shared beliefs, preferences, and practices that distinguish them from the mainstream or larger social group to which they also belong.

supernatural Attributed to a force or entity beyond scientific understanding and the laws of nature.

survey A type of research in which information is derived by asking people to answer standardized questions, which may collect information about any aspect of human life of interest to the investigator, including information about jobs, employment, family life, health, education, and policy or political attitudes and values.

sustainability A system of development and consumption that satisfies a society's current needs without imperiling the ability of future generations to do the same.

sweatshop A workplace that may be characterized by unsafe conditions, very low wages, and harsh working conditions.

symbol Something that communicates an idea while being distinct from the idea itself.

symbolic boundary The distinctions people make between themselves and others on the basis of taste, socioeconomic status, morality, or other differences.

symbolic capital Your reputation.

symbolic interactionism A theory of the social world that focuses on the meanings that individuals give to objects and social practices and how they use symbolic meanings in their interactions with one another.

syncretic Combining religious ideas and practices drawn from more than one distinct tradition.

tariff A tax on goods being imported into a country.

taste A person's cultural preferences.

terrorism A type of warfare in which a weaker group challenges a more powerful group by attacking civilian targets of importance to the more powerful group. State terrorism occurs when a country's military attacks civilian populations.

theodicy A justification of the goodness and rightness of god, or more generally of a particular religious system, in the face of the evils of the world.

theology Discussions and systematic reasoning about god and other religious matters.

theoretical generalizability The application of conclusions from findings based on a sample or case to larger sociological processes and theories about the world.

thick description A rich, detailed description of the ways people make sense of their lives.

tool kit In the sociology of culture, the view that culture is a set of symbolic skills, devices, or strategies that people learn throughout their lives, and can deploy strategically in different situations. The tool kit also supplies a set of ideas to justify a course of action retrospectively.

total fertility rate A measure of fertility in a given calendar year reflecting the fertility of women at different childbearing ages. A total fertility rate of 3.2 in 2010 in a given population means that the average woman would have 3.2 children during her lifetime, *if* fertility rates in this population remained the same.

totemism A belief system in which clans adopt a plant or animal as their group emblem and declare it sacred.

transfer A term used in immigration research to refer to the transfer of money from an immigrant back home, or to an immigrant from her or his family back home.

transgendered Individuals who were assigned one sex category at birth based on anatomical criteria but who come to believe they belong in the other gender category and take action to be in the other category.

transnational corporation (TNC) A company with business operations in multiple countries.

university wage premium When people with less than a university degree have seen their earnings decline or have increasing trouble finding good jobs.

urban area A geographic area with a high population density, defined by Statistics Canada as having a population of at least 1,000 and a population density of at least 400 people per square kilometre. The U.S. Census bureau defines urban areas as those with 1,000 people per square mile and with surrounding areas that have a density of at least 500 people per square mile. (A kilometre is approximately 0.62 of a mile.)

urbanization The growth of cities.

validity The extent to which the measurement a researcher uses accurately measures what it is intended to measure.

value A judgement about what is intrinsically important or meaningful. When it comes to research, values held by sociologists shape their views of and perspectives on the questions they ask.

visa A legal status specifying the terms and length under which someone may live (or visit) another country. It may range from permission to enter for a few days to being allowed to live there permanently (in the United States, the latter type of visa is known as a "green card").

war on drugs The United States' effort to reduce the sale and consumption of illegal drugs by increasing police surveillance and punishment of drug offenders.

war on terror The U.S. government's effort to combat terrorism, especially in the period since the attacks of September 11, 2001.

Washington Consensus The common prescriptions of Washington, D.C.–based organizations such as the International Monetary Fund, the World Bank, and the U.S. Treasury Department for how developing countries should respond to economic problems or crises. These prescriptions typically suggest that developing countries should engage in free trade, reduce the role and expense of government, and more generally encourage the growth of free markets.

wealth The wealth of an individual or family is the net value of all assets owned by an individual or family, including the value of their home.

weighting In a survey where there are differences between some known property of the population being studied and the completed interviews (such as the percentage of women, or minorities, or some other key population characteristic), the results can be adjusted by giving slightly more importance to the responses of each member of an undersampled group.

welfare state The bundle of programs that provide social insurance and social assistance for people falling into one or another category of attributes (such as old age, disability, or poverty). The most important types of welfare-state programs are old-age pensions (known in the United States as Social Security), health insurance programs, unemployment insurance, job training programs, and general welfare assistance for the very poor. Some analysts also include education in the mix of programs considered part of the welfare state.

white-collar crime Illegal activities undertaken by businesses or by individuals working for corporations.

white settlers A Caucasian person who arrives, especially from another countury such as Britain or France, to a new country to live on and use the land.

widening income inequality The growing gap between the rich and everyone else in society. It is often expressed as a ratio that compares the percentage of income to a percentage of a population to illustrate the extent to which income is distributed in an unequal manner.

working poor People who do not make enough income to be free from poverty, even if they work full time.

References

THE SOCIOLOGICAL IMAGINATION

Mills, C. Wright. (2000). *The sociological imagination*. Oxford: Oxford University Press.

Morning, A. (2011). *The nature of race: How scientists think and teach about human difference*. Calgary: University of Calgary Press.

PREFACE

Kuhn, T. (1962). *The structure of scientific revolutions*. Chicago: University of Chicago Press.

Mills, C. Wright. (1959). *The sociological imagination*. New York: Oxford University Press.

CHAPTER 1

Arum, R., & Roksa, J. (2011). *Academically adrift*. Chicago: University of Chicago Press.

Arum, R., & Roksa, J. (2014). *Aspiring adults: College graduates hopeful and adrift*. Chicago: University of Chicago Press.

Burley, G., & Awad, A. (2015). *The impact of student debt*. Retrieved from Canadian Federation of Students website: http://cfs-fcee.ca/wp-content/uploads/sites/2/2015/03/Report-Impact-of-Student-Debt-2015-Final.pdf

Canadian Centre for Policy Alternatives. (2014, September 10). *Infographic: An education in inflation, 2014*. Retrieved from https://www.policyalternatives.ca/publications/facts-infographics/infographic-education-inflation-2014

Civil Rights Act of 1964, US Pub. L. No. 88-352, 78 Stat. 241.

Comte, A. (1839–1853/2009). *The positive philosophy of Auguste Comte* (Harriet Martineau, Ed. & Trans.). New York: Cambridge University Press.

Mills, C. Wright. (1959). *The sociological imagination*. New York: Oxford University Press.

Robinson, J. (2011, April 29). The cost of the college bubble [article]. Retrieved from http://www.popecenter.org/2011/04/the-cost-of-the-college-bubble/

Sharkey, P. (2010). The acute effect of local homicides on children's cognitive performance. *Proceedings of the National Academy of Sciences, 107*, 11733–11738. doi:10.1073/pnas.1000690107

Statistics Canada. (2014, February 25). Survey of financial security, 2012. *The Daily*. Retrieved from http://www.statcan.gc.ca/daily-quotidien/140225/dq140225b-eng.htm

Watts, D. (2011). *Everything is obvious once you know the answer: How common sense fails*. New York: Crown Books.

CHAPTER 2

Beauvoir, S. de. (1952). *The second sex*. New York: Bantam.

Blumer, H. (1969). *Symbolic interactionism*. Englewood Cliffs, NJ: Prentice-Hall.

Bourdieu, P. (1979/1984). *Distinction: A social critique of the judgment of taste*. Cambridge, MA: Harvard University Press.

Brenner, R. (2006). *The economics of global turbulence*. New York: Verso.

Chodorow, N. (1978). *The reproduction of mothering*. Berkeley: University of California Press.

Choo, H. Y., & Ferree, M. M. (2010). Practicing intersectionality in sociological research. *Sociological Theory, 28*, 129–149. doi:10.1111/j.1467-9558.2010.01370.x

Collins, P. H. (1990). *Black feminist theory*. New York: Routledge.

Connell, R. W. (1987). *Gender and power*. Palo Alto: Stanford University Press.

Crenshaw, K. (1991). Mapping the margins: Intersectionality, identity politics, and violence against women of color. *Stanford Law Review, 43*, 1241–1299. doi:10.2307/1229039

Dahrendorf, R. (1959). *Class and class conflict in industrial society*. Stanford: Stanford University Press.

Davis, K., & Moore, W. (1945). Some principles of stratification. *American Sociological Review, 10*, 242–249. doi:10.2307/2085643

Dobbin, F. (2011). *Inventing equal opportunity*. Princeton: Princeton University Press.

Du Bois, W. E. B. (1899/1995). *The Philadelphia negro*. Philadelphia: University of Pennsylvania Press.

Du Bois, W. E. B. (1903/1997). *The souls of black folks*. New York: St. Martin's Press.

Du Bois, W. E. B. (1903/2008). The talented tenth. In *The Negro problem: A series of articles by representative negroes of today* (pp. 31–76). Amherst, NY: Humanity Books.

Du Bois, W. E. B. (1935). *Black reconstruction in America, 1860–1880*. New York: Harcourt, Brace.

Durkheim, E. (1890/1997). *The division of labor in society*. New York: The Free Press.

Durkheim, E. (1895/1982). *Rules of sociological method*. New York: The Free Press.

Durkheim, E. (1897/1997). *Suicide*. New York: The Free Press.

Foucault, M. (1977). *Discipline and punish*. New York: Pantheon.

Goffman, E. (1959). *The presentation of self in everyday life*. New York, NY: The Free Press.

Joas, H., & Knobl, W. (2009). *Social theory: Twenty introductory lectures*. New York, NY: Cambridge University Press.

Marx, K. (1859/1978). Preface to *A contribution to the critique of political economy*. In R. Tucker (Ed.), *The Marx–Engels reader* (pp. 3–6). New York, NY: Norton.

Marx, K. (1867/1976). *Capital*. London, UK: Verso.

Marx, K., & Engels, F. (1848/2011). *The communist manifesto*. New York, NY: Verso.

McCall, L. (2005). The complexity of intersectionality. *Signs, 30*, 1771–1800. doi:10.1086/426800

Mead, G. H. (1934). *Mind, self, and society*. Chicago, IL: University of Chicago Press.

Mills, C. Wright. (1956). *The power elite*. New York, NY: Oxford University Press.

O'Connor, J. (1973). *The fiscal crisis of the state*. London, UK: MacMillan.

Parsons, T. (1937/1967). *The structure of social action*. New York, NY: The Free Press.

Parsons, T. (1951). *The social system*. New York, NY: The Free Press.

Parsons, T., & Smelser, N. (1956). *Economy and society*. New York, NY: The Free Press.

Poulantzas, N. (1978). *State, power, socialism*. London, UK: Verso.

Simmel, G. (1964). *Conflict and the web of group affiliation*. New York, NY: The Free Press.

Simmel, G. (1908/1971). The stranger. In D. N. Levine (Ed.), *Georg Simmel: On individuality and social forms* (pp. 143–150). Chicago, IL: University of Chicago Press.

Smith, D. (1974). Women's perspective as a radical critique of sociology. *Sociological Inquiry, 44*, 7–13. doi:10.1111/j.1475-682X.1974.tb00718.x

Wallerstein, I. (1974). *The modern world system I: Capitalist agriculture and the origins of the European world economy in the sixteenth century*. New York, NY: Academic Press.

Wallerstein, I. (2011). *The modern world system IV: Centrist liberalism triumphant*. Berkeley: University of California Press.

Weber, M. (1904/ 2008). *The Protestant ethic and the spirit of capitalism*. New York, NY: Norton.

Weber, M. (1922/1978). *Economy and society*. Berkeley: University of California Press.

West, C., & Zimmerman, D. (1987). Doing gender. *Gender & Society, 1*(2), 125–151. doi:10.1177/0891243287001002002

Wright, E. O. (1985). *Classes*. London, UK: Verso.

Wright, E. O. (1997). *Class counts*. New York, NY: Cambridge University Press.

CHAPTER 3

Armstrong, E. A., & Hamilton, L. T. (2012). *Paying for the party: How college maintains inequality*. Cambridge, MA: Harvard University Press.

Burawoy, M. (2009). *The extended case method*. Berkeley: University of California Press.

Burawoy, M., Blum, J. A., George, S. M., Gille, Z., Thayer, M., George, S., Gowan, T., Haney, L., Klawiter, M., Lopez, S. H., & Riain, S. (2000). *Global ethnography: Forces, connections, and imaginations in a postmodern world*. Berkeley: University of California Press.

Burawoy, M., Burton, A., Ferguson, A. A., & Fox, K. J. (1991). *Ethnography unbound: Power and resistance in the modern metropolis*. Berkeley: University of California Press.

Canadian Institutes of Health Research, Natural Sciences and Engineering Research Council of Canada, Social Sciences and Humanities Research Council of Canada. (2014). *Tri-Council policy statement: Ethical conduct for research involving humans* (2nd ed.). Retrieved from Secretariat on Responsible Conduct of Research website: http://www.pre.ethics.gc.ca/pdf/eng/tcps2-2014/TCPS_2_FINAL_Web.pdf

Canadian Sociological Association. (2012). *Statement of professional ethics*. Retrieved from http://www.csa-scs.ca/files/www/csa/documents/codeofethics/2012Ethics.pdf

Civil Rights Act of 1964, US Pub. L. No. 88-352, 78 Stat. 241.

Coleman, J., Bremner, R. H., Clark, B. R., Davis, J. B., Eichorn, D. H., Griliches, Z., Kett, J. F., Ryder, N. B., Doering, Z. B., & Mays, J. M. (1966/1974). *Youth: Transition to adulthood; Report of the Panel on Youth of the President's Science Advisory Committee*. Chicago, IL: University of Chicago Press.

Coleman, J., & Hoffer, T. (1987). *Public and private high schools: The impact of communities*. New York, NY: Basic Books.

Duneier, M. (1999). *Sidewalk*. New York, NY: Farrer, Strauss, and Giroux.

Geertz, C. (1973). *The interpretation of cultures*. New York, NY: Basic Books.

Geertz, C. (1983). *Local knowledge: Further essays in interpretive anthropology*. New York, NY: Basic Books.

Gerson, K. (2011). *The unfinished revolution: Coming of age in a new era of gender, work, and family*. New York: Oxford University Press.

Haney, C., Banks, W. C., & Zimbardo, P. G. (1973). A study of prisoners and guards in a simulated prison. *Naval Research Review, 30*, 4–17.

Hochschild, A. (1989). *The second shift*. New York, NY: Viking.

Literary Digest. (1936, October 31). Landon, 1,293,669; Roosevelt, 972,897: Final returns in *The Digest*'s poll of ten million voters. *122*(18), 5–6.

Luker, K. (2010). *Salsa dancing in the social sciences*. Berkeley: University of California Press.

Luxton, M. (1980). *More than a labour of love*. Toronto: Women's Educational Press.

Milgram, S. (1963). Behavioral study of obedience. *Journal of Abnormal and Social Psychology, 67*, 371–378. doi:10.1037/h0040525

Pager, D., & Quillian, L. (2005). Walking the talk: What employers say versus what they do. *American Sociological Review, 70*, 355–380. doi:10.1177/000312240507000301

Tilly, C. (1986). *The contentious French*. Cambridge, MA: Harvard University Press.

Weber, M. (1904/1976). *The Protestant ethic and the spirit of capitalism*. New York: Scribner's.

CHAPTER 4

Asch, S. (1955). Opinions and social pressure. *Scientific American, 193*, 1–8. doi:10.1038/scientificamerican1155-31

Atkinson, M. (1984). *Our masters' voices: The language and body language of politics*. London, UK: Methuen.

Collins, R. (2008). *Violence: A micro-sociological theory*. Princeton, NJ: Princeton University Press.

Davidson, J. (1984). Subsequent versions of invitations, offers, requests, and proposals dealing with potential or actual rejection. In J. Heritage & J. Maxwell Atkinson (Eds.), *Structures of social action: Studies in conversation analysis* (pp. 102–28). New York, NY: Cambridge University Press.

Duneier, M., & Molotch, H. (1999). Talking city trouble: Interactional vandalism, social inequality, and the "urban interaction problem." *American Journal of Sociology, 104*, 1263–1295. doi:10.1086/210175

Durkheim, E. (1912/1995). *The elementary forms of religious life*. New York, NY: Free Press.

Garfinkel, H. (1967). *Studies in ethnomethodology*. Englewood Cliffs, NJ: Prentice-Hall.

Goffman, E. (1959). *The presentation of self in everyday life*. Garden City, NY: Doubleday.

Goffman, E. (1978). Response cries. *Language, 54*, 787–815. doi:10.2307/413235

Haney, C. (2003). Health issues in long-term solitary and "supermax" confinement. *Crime & Delinquency, 49*, 124–156. doi:10.1177/0011128702239239

Katz, J. (1999). *How emotions work*. Chicago, IL: University of Chicago Press.

McPherson, M., Smith-Lovin, L., & Cook, J. M. (2001). Birds of a feather: Homophily in social networks. *Annual Review of Sociology, 27*, 415–444. doi:10.1146/annurev.soc.27.1.415

Menchik, D. A., & Tian, X. (2008). Putting social context into text: The semiotics of email interaction. *American Journal of Sociology, 114*, 332–370. doi:10.1086/590650

Merton, R. K. (1968). *Social theory and social structure: Toward the codification of theory and research* (enlarged ed.). New York, NY: Free Press.

Milgram, S. (1963). Behavioral study of obedience. *Journal of Abnormal and Social Psychology, 67*, 371–378. doi:10.1037/h0040525

Nippert-Eng, C. (2010). *Islands of privacy*. Chicago, IL: University of Chicago Press.

Richardson, P. (2009). Doing things with wood: Builders, managers and Wittgenstein in an Idaho sawmill. *Critique of Anthropology, 29*, 160–182. doi:10.1177/0308275X09104084

Rosenhan, D. L. (1973). On being sane in insane places. *Science, 179*, 250–258. doi:10.1126/science.179.4070.250

Scheff, T. J. (1999). *Being mentally ill: A sociological theory*. New York, NY: Aldine de Gruyter.

Schegloff, E. A. (1996). Confirming allusions: Toward an empirical account of action. *American Journal of Sociology, 102*, 161–216. doi:10.1086/230911

Schegloff, E. A. (2000). Overlapping talk and the organization of turn-taking for conversation. *Language in Society, 29*, 1–63. doi:10.1017/S0047404500001019

Simmel, G. (1950). The metropolis and mental life. In K. Wolff (Transl.), *The Sociology of Georg Simmel* (pp. 409–424). Glencoe, IL: The Free Press.

Spitz, R. A. (1945). Hospitalism: An inquiry into the genesis of psychiatric conditions in early childhood. *Psychoanalytic Study of the Child, 1*, 53–74.

Sudnow, D. (1967). *Passing on: The social organization of dying*. Englewood Cliffs, NJ: Prentice-Hall.

West, C. (1984). When the doctor is a "lady": Power, status and gender in physician–patient encounters. *Symbolic Interaction, 7*, 87–106. doi:10.1525/si.1984.7.1.87

West, C., & Zimmerman, D. H. (1977). Women's place in everyday talk: Reflection on parent–child interaction. *Social Problems, 24*, 521–529. doi:10.2307/800122

Zimbardo, P. (2007). *The Lucifer effect: How good people turn evil*. New York: Random House.

Zimmerman, D. (1970). The practicalities of rule use. In J. D. Douglas (Ed.), *Understanding everyday life: Toward the reconstruction of sociological knowledge* (pp. 221–238). Chicago: Aldine.

CHAPTER 5

Bowlby, G. (2002). Farmers leaving the field. *Perspectives on Labour and Income* (online edition), *3*(2). Retrieved from Statistics Canada website: http://www.statcan.gc.ca/pub/75-001-x/00202/6086-eng.html

Canadian Bill of Rights, SC 1960, c 44.

Civil Rights Act of 1964, US Pub. L. No. 88-352, 78 Stat. 241.

Corsaro, W., & Eder, D. (1990). Games children play. *Annual Review of Sociology, 16*, 197–220. doi:10.1146/annurev.so.16.080190.001213

Deutschkron, I. (1989). *Outcast: A Jewish girl in wartime Berlin*. New York, NY: Fromm International.

Durkheim, E. (1895/1982). *Rules of sociological method*. New York, NY: Free Press.

Goldin, C., & Katz, L. (2008). *The race between technology and education*. Cambridge, MA: Harvard University/ Belknap Press.

Haggerty, K. D., & Doyle, A. (2015). *57 ways to screw up in graduate school*. Chicago, IL: University of Chicago Press.

Kahneman, D. (2011). *Thinking, fast and slow*. New York, NY: Farrar, Straus, and Giroux.

Marx, K. (1883). *The eighteenth brumaire of Louis Bonaparte*. New York, NY: International Publishers.

Khlevniuk, O. (2008). *Master of the house: Stalin and his inner circle*. New Haven, CT: Yale University Press.

Pierson, P. (2000). Path dependence, increasing returns, and the study of politics. *American Political Science Review, 94*, 251–67. doi:10.2307/2586011

Savage, C., & Baker, P. (2013, May 22). Obama, in a switch, to limit targets of drone strikes. *New York Times*. Retrieved from http://www.nytimes.com/2013/05/23/us/us-acknowledges-killing-4-americans-in-drone-strikes.html?hp&_r=0

Wright, E. O., & Dwyer, R. (2003). The patterns of job expansions in the USA: A comparison of the 1960s and 1990s. *Socio-Economic Review, 1*, 289–305. doi:10.1093/soceco/1.3.289

CHAPTER 6

Anderson, B. (1991). *Imagined communities: Reflections on the origin and spread of nationalism* (rev. ed.). London, UK: Verso.

Appadurai, A. (1996). *Modernity at large: Cultural dimensions of globalization*. Minneapolis: University of Minnesota Press.

Bourdieu, P. (1984). *Distinction: A social critique of the judgement of taste* (R. Nice, Trans.). Cambridge, MA: Harvard University Press.

Bourdieu, P. (1992). *The logic of practice* (R. Nice, Trans.). Cambridge, MA: Polity Press.

Boyd, D. (2008). Why youth (heart) social network sites: The role of networked publics in teenage social life. In D. Buckingham (Ed.), *MacArthur Foundation Series on digital learning: Youth, identity, and digital media* (pp. 119–142). Cambridge, MA: MIT Press.

Brooks, C., & Manza, J. (2007). *Why welfare states persist*. Chicago, IL: University of Chicago Press.

Burgess, J., & Green, J. (2009). *YouTube: Online video and participatory culture*. Cambridge, MA: Polity Press.

Canada. (1992, August 28). *Charlottetown accord (Consensus report on the Constitution)*. In *The Canadian encyclopedia*. Retrieved from http://www.thecanadianencyclopedia.ca/en/article/charlottetown-accord-document/

Canada. House of Commons. (2006). *Meech lake accord*. In *The Canadian encyclopedia*. Retrieved from http://www.thecanadianencyclopedia.ca/en/article/meech-lake-accord-document/.

Caplan, G. (2010, May 28). Deciphering sides in Canada's "culture wars." *The Globe and Mail*. Retrieved from http://www.theglobeandmail.com/news/politics/second-reading/deciphering-sides-in-canadas-culture-wars/article1314270/

Castells, M. (2009). *Communication power*. Oxford, UK: Oxford University Press.

Clarke, J., Hall, S., Jefferson, T., & Roberts, B. (1975). Subcultures, cultures and class: A theoretical overview. In S. Hall & T. Jefferson (Eds.), *Resistance through rituals: Youth subcultures in post-war Britain* (pp. 9–74). New York: Routledge.

Eliasoph, N., & Lichterman, P. (2003). Culture in interaction. *American Journal of Sociology, 108*(4), 735–794. doi:10.1086/367920

Fischer, C. S. (1975). Toward a subcultural theory of urbanism. *American Journal of Sociology, 80*(6), 1319–1341. doi:10.1086/225993

Fraser, N. (1992). Rethinking the public sphere: A contribution to the critique of actually existing democracy. In C. Calhoun (Ed.), *Habermas and the public sphere*, pp. 109–142. Cambridge, MA: MIT Press.

Freeman, S. (2014, March 20). Canada's digital divide persists: CIRA report shows. *Huffington Post Canada*. Retrieved from http://www.huffingtonpost.ca/2014/03/20/digital-divide-canada-broadband-access_n_4995560.html

Gans, H. J. (1999). *Popular culture and high culture: An analysis and evaluation of taste* (2nd ed.). New York, NY: Basic Books.

Geertz, C. (1972). Deep play: Notes on the Balinese cockfight. *Daedalus, 101*(1), 1–37.

Gitlin, T. (2007). *Media unlimited: How the torrent of images and sounds overwhelms our lives* (rev. ed.). New York, NY: Metropolitan.

Habermas, J. (1962/1989). *The structural transformation of the public sphere: An inquiry into a category of bourgeois society* (T. Burger with F. Lawrence, Trans.). Cambridge, MA: MIT Press.

Hall, S., & Jefferson, T. (Eds.). (1975). *Resistance through rituals: Youth subcultures in post-war Britain*. New York, NY: Routledge.

Hindman, M. (2008). *The myth of digital democracy*. Princeton, NJ: Princeton University Press.

Holt, D. B. (1997). Distinction in America? Recovering Bourdieu's theory of tastes from its critics. *Poetics, 25*, 93–120. doi:10.1016/S0304-422X(97)00010-7

Horkheimer, M., & Adorno, T. W. (1947/2002). *Dialectic of enlightenment: Philosophical fragments* (E. Jephcott, Trans.; G. S. Noerr, Ed.). Stanford, CT: Stanford University Press.

Hunter, J. D. (1991). *Culture wars: The struggle to define America*. New York, NY: Basic Books.

Jenkins, H. (2006). *Convergence culture: Where old and new media collide*. New York, NY: NYU Press.

Kahn, S. (2009). *Privilege*. Princeton, NJ: Princeton University Press.

Klinenberg, E. (2007). *Fighting for air: The battle to control America's media*. New York, NY: Metropolitan.

Klinenberg, E. (2012). *Going solo: The extraordinary rise and surprising appeal of living alone*. New York, NY: Penguin.

Lareau, A. (2003). *Unequal childhoods: Class, race, and family life*. Berkeley: University of California Press.

Lippmann, W. (1922). *Public opinion*. New York, NY: Harcourt, Brace.

Marx, K., & Engels, F. (1845/1972). The German ideology: Part 1. In R. C. Tucker (Ed.); S. Ryazanskaya (Ed.), *The Marx–Engels reader* (pp. 146–200). New York, NY: Norton.

McChesney, R. W. (1999). *Rich media, poor democracy*. New York, NY: New Press.

McLuhan, M. (1964). *Understanding media: The extensions of man*. Cambridge, MA: MIT Press.

Nielsen. (2011). *Television Audience Report, 2010–2011*. Retrieved from http://www.nielsen.com/us/en/insights/reports/2011/television-audience-report-2010-2011.html

Norris, P. (2001). *Digital divide: Civic engagement, information poverty, and the Internet worldwide*. Cambridge, UK: Cambridge University Press.

Palfrey, J., & Gasser, U. (2008). *Born digital: Understanding the first generation of digital natives*. New York, NY: Basic Books.

Peterson, R. A., & Kern, R. M. (1996). Changing highbrow taste: From snob to omnivore. *American Sociological Review, 61*(5), 900–907. doi:10.2307/2096460

Postman, N. (1985). *Amusing ourselves to death: Public discourse in the age of show business*. New York, NY: Penguin.

Schudson, M. (2003). *The sociology of news*. New York: Norton.

Sewell, W. H., Jr. (2005). *Logics of history: Social theory and social transformation*. Chicago, IL: University of Chicago Press.

Statistics Canada. (2010, March 9). Projections of the diversity of the Canadian population. *The Daily*. Retrieved from http://www.statcan.gc.ca/daily-quotidien/100309/dq100309a-eng.htm

Statistics Canada. (2012). *Portrait of Families and Living Arrangements in Canada: Families, households, and marital status, 2011 Census of Population*. Ottawa, ON: Minister of Industry. Retrieved from http://www12.statcan.gc.ca/census-recensement/2011/as-sa/98-312-x/98-312-x2011001-eng.pdf

Swidler, A. (1986). Culture in action: Symbols and strategies. *American Sociological Review, 51*(2), 273–286. doi:10.2307/2095521

Swidler, A. (2003). *Talk of love: How culture matters*. Chicago, IL: University of Chicago Press.

Takhteyev, Y., Gruzd, A., & Wellman, B. (2012). Geography of Twitter networks. *Social Networks, 34*(1), 73–81. doi:10.1016/j.socnet.2011.05.006

Tobin, J. J., Wu, D. Y. H., & Davidson, D. H. (1989). *Preschool in three cultures: Japan, China and the United States*. New Haven, CT: Yale University Press.

Williams, R. (1976). *Keywords: A vocabulary of culture and society.* Oxford, UK: Oxford University Press.

Willis, P. (1977). *Learning to labor: How working class kids get working class jobs.* New York, NY: Columbia University Press.

CHAPTER 7

Block, F. (1987). *State theory*. Philadelphia, PA: Temple University Press.

Broadbent Institute. (2012). *Towards a more equal Canada: A report on Canada's economic & social inequality.* Retrieved from https://d3n8a8pro7vhmx.cloudfront.net/broadbent/pages/4483/attachments/original/1438883643/towards_a_more_equal_canada.pdf?1438883643

Broadbent Institute. (2014). *The wealth gap: Perceptions and misconceptions in Canada*. Retrieved from https://d3n8a8pro7vhmx.cloudfront.net/broadbent/pages/31/attachments/original/1430002077/The_Wealth_Gap.pdf?1430002077

Buffett, W. (2011, August 14). Stop coddling the super rich. *New York Times*. Retrieved from http://www.nytimes.com/2011/08/15/opinion/stop-coddling-the-super-rich.html

Canadian Labour Congress. (2012). *What did corporate tax cuts deliver? A background report for corporate tax freedom day 2013.* Retrieved from http://canadianlabour.ca/sites/default/files/media/what-did_corporate_tax_cuts_deliver-2014-en-web.pdf

Domhoff, G. W. (2006). *Who rules America? Power, politics, and social change*. New York, NY: McGraw-Hill.

Gaventa, J. (1980). *Power and powerlessness: Quiescence and rebellion in an Appalachian Valley*. Oxford, UK: Clarendon Press.

The Globe and Mail. (2015, October 13). Who Canada's 10 most generous political donors have contributed to. Retrieved from http://www.theglobeandmail.com/report-on-business/who-canadas-ten-most-generous-political-donors-have-contributed-to/article26793752/

Goffman, E. (1971). *Relations in public*. New York: Harper.

Grant, T., & Curry, B. (2013, September 11). The wealth of the nation: A snapshot of what Canadians earn. *The Globe and Mail*. Retrieved from http://www.theglobeandmail.com/news/politics/who-are-the-1-per-cent-a-snapshot-of-what-canadians-earn/article14269972/?page=all

Hacker, J., & Pierson, P. (2010). Winner-take-all politics. New York: Simon and Shuster.

Kocieniewski, D. (2011, March 24). G.E.'s strategies let it avoid paying taxes altogether. *New York Times*, p. A1.

Lee, M., & Ivanova, I. (2013). *Fairness by design: A framework for tax reform in Canada*. Retrieved from Canadian Centre for Policy Alternatives website: https://www.policyalternatives.ca/sites/default/files/uploads/publications/National%20Office/2013/02/Fairness_By_Design_A_Framework_For_Tax_Reform_In_Canada_0.pdf

Lemert, C. (1997). *Social things*. Lanham, MD: Rowman & Littlefield.

Mackenzie, H. (2012). *Canada's CEO elite 100: The 0.01%*. Retrieved from Canadian Centre for Policy Alternatives website: http://www.policyalternatives.ca/publications/reports/canada%E2%80%99s-ceo-elite-100

McCall, L. (2013). *The undeserving rich: American beliefs about inequality, opportunity, and redistribution*. New York, NY: Cambridge University Press.

Mischel, L., Bernstein, J., & Shierholz, H. (2009). *The state of working America, 2008–2009*. Ithaca, NY: Cornell University Press.

Mischel, L., & Bivens, J. (2011, October 26). *Occupy Wall Streeters are right about skewed economic rewards in the United States* (Briefing Paper #331). Retrieved from Economic Policy Institute website: http://www.epi.org/publication/bp331-occupy-wall-street

Murphy, B., Roberts, P. & Wolfson, M. (2007). High income Canadians. *Perpectives on Labour and Income, 8*(9). Retrieved from Statistics Canada website: http://www.statcan.gc.ca/pub/75-001-x/2007109/article/10350-eng.htm

Piven, F. F, & Cloward, R. (1997). *The breaking of the American social compact*. New York, NY: The New Press.

Smeeding, T., Robson, K., Wing, C., & Gershuny, J. (2009). *Income poverty and income support for minority and immigrant children in rich countries* (Working Paper No. 527). Retrieved from Luxemburg Income Study website: http://www.lisdatacenter.org/wps/liswps/527.pdf.

Smith, A. (1776/2011). *The wealth of nations*. New York, NY: Simon & Brown.

Statistics Canada. (1999). *Survey of financial security*. Retrieved from http://www23.statcan.gc.ca/imdb/p2SV.pl?Function=getInstanceList&Id=131449

Statistics Canada. (2005). *Survey of financial security*. Retrieved from http://www23.statcan.gc.ca/imdb/p2SV.pl?Function=getInstanceList&Id=131449

Statistics Canada. (2012). *Survey of financial security*. Retrieved from http://www23.statcan.gc.ca/imdb/p2SV.pl?Function=getInstanceList&Id=131449

Winters, J. (2011). *Oligarchy*. New York, NY: Cambridge University Press.

CHAPTER 8

Arum, R., & Müeller, W. (2004). *The reemergence of self-employment: A comparative study of self-employment dynamics and social inequality*. Princeton, NJ: Princeton University Press.

Becker, G. (1976). *The economic approach to human life*. Chicago, IL: University of Chicago Press.

Braverman, H. (1974). *Labor and monopoly capital*. New York, NY: Monthly Review Press.

DiMaggio, P., & Powell, W. W. (1983). The iron cage revisited: Institutional isomorphism and collective rationality in organizational fields. *American Sociological Review, 48*, 147–160. doi:10.2307/2095101

Doleac, J., & Stein, L. (2010). *The visible hand: Race and online market outcomes*. Unpublished paper, Department of Sociology, Stanford University, Standard, CA.

Duxbury, L., & Higgins, C. (2012). *Revisiting work-life issues in Canada: The 2012 national study on balancing work and caregiving in Canada*. Retrieved from Carleton University website at: http://newsroom.carleton.ca/wp-content/files/2012-National-Work-Long-Summary.pdf

Gambetta, D., & Hamill, H. (2005). *Streetwise: How taxi drivers establish their customers trustworthiness*. New York, NY: Russell Sage Foundation.

Gertler, M., & Rogoff, K. S. (Eds.). (2006). *NBER macroeconomics annual 2005*. Cambridge: MIT Press.

Gladwell, M. (2000). *The tipping point: How little things can make a big difference*. Boston: Little, Brown.

Goldin, C., & Katz, L. (2010). *The race between education and technology*. Cambridge, MA: Harvard University Press.

Granovetter, M. S. (1973, May). The strength of weak ties. *American Journal of Sociology, 78*(6), 1360–1380. doi:10.1086/225469

Hannan, M., & Freeman, J. (1989). *Organizational ecology*. Cambridge, MA: Harvard University Press.

Hochschild, A. (2012). *The outsourced self: Intimate life in market times*. New York, NY: Metropolitan Books.

Lewis, M. (2014). *Flash boys: A Wall Street revolt*. New York, NY: Norton.

Lichtenstein, N. (2009). *The retail revolution: How Wal-Mart created a brave new world of business*. New York, NY: Metropolitan Books.

Polanyi, K. (1944/1957). *The great transformation: The political and economic origins of our time*. Boston, MA: Beacon.

Rose, D. (2003). *The march of dimes*. Charleston, SC: Arcadia.

Segal, D. (2012, June 23). A Georgia town takes the people's business private. *New York Times*. Retrieved from http://www.nytimes.com/2012/06/24/business/a-georgia-town-takes-the-peoples-business-private.html

Uzzi, B. (1999). Embeddedness in the making of financial capital: How social relations and networks benefit firms seeking finance. *American Sociological Review, 64*, 481–505. doi:10.2307/2657252

Uzzi, B., & Dunlap, S. (2005, December). How to build your network. *Harvard Business Review, 83*(12), 53–60, 151.

Vallas, S., Finlay, W., & Wharton, A. S. (Eds.). (2009). *The sociology of work: Structures and inequalities*. New York, NY: Oxford University Press.

Weber, M. (1922/1978). *Economy and society*. Berkeley: University of California Press.

Wright, E. O., & Dwyer, R. (2000–2001). The American jobs machine: Is the new economy creating good jobs? *Boston Review, 25*(6), 20–26.

Wright, E.O., & Dwyer, R. (2003). The patterns of job expansions in the USA: A comparison of the 1960s and 1990s. *Socio-Economic Review, 1*, 289–325. doi:10.1093/soceco/1.3.289

CHAPTER 9

Bakija, J., Cole, A., & Heim, B. (2012). *Jobs and income growth of top earners and the causes of changing income inequality: Evidence from U.S. tax return data*. Retrieved from Department of Economics, Williams College website: http://web.williams.edu/Economics/wp/BakijaColeHeimJobsIncomeGrowthTopEarners.pdf

Blanden, J. (2009). *How much can we learn from international comparisons of social mobility*? (CEE DP 111). Retrieved from the London School of Economics website: http://cee.lse.ac.uk/ceedps/ceedp111.pdf

Brandon, E. (2012, July 11). Retiree net worth declines. *US News*. Retrieved from http://money.usnews.com/money/retirement/articles/2012/07/23/retiree-net-worth-declines

Bricker, J., Dettling, L. J., Henriques, A., Hsu, J. W., Moore, K. B., Sabelhaus, J., Thompson, J., & Windle, R. A. (2014, September). Changes in U.S. family finances from 2010 to 2013: Evidence from the survey of consumer finances. *Federal Reserve Bulletin, 100*(4).

Brown, A. (2014, March 3). Forbes billionaires: Full list of the world's 500 richest people. *Forbes*. Retrieved from http://www.forbes.com/sites/abrambrown/2014/03/03/forbes-billionaires-full-list-of-the-worlds-500-richest-people/#2947b0446c87

Bussuk, E. L., Murphy, C., Coupe, N. T., Kenney, R. R., & Beach, C. A. (2011). *America's youngest outcasts, 2010*. Retrieved from The National Center on Family Homelessness website: http://www.homelesschildrenamerica.org/media/NCFH_AmericaOutcast2010_web.pdf

Citizens for Public Justice. (2013). *Poverty trends highlights, Canada 2013*. Retrieved from http://www.cpj.ca/files/docs/Poverty-Trends-Highlights-2013.pdf

Collin, C., & Jensen, H. (2009). *A statistical profile of poverty in Canada* (PRB 09-17E). Retrieved from the Parliament of Canada website: http://www.lop.parl.gc.ca/content/lop/researchpublications/prb0917-e.htm

Conference Board of Canada. (2013). *Income inequality*. Retrieved from http://www.conferenceboard.ca/hcp/details/society/income-inequality.aspx

Conference Board of Canada. (2014). *Income per capita*. Retrieved from http://www.conferenceboard.ca/hcp/provincial/economy/income-per-capita.aspx

Corak, M. (2012). Inequality from generation to generation: The United States in comparison. In Robert S. Rycroft (Ed.), *The economics of inequality, poverty, and discrimination in the 21st Century*. Retrieved from http://milescorak.files.wordpress.com/2012/01/inequality-from-generation-to-generation-the-united-states-in-comparison-v3.pdf

Credit Suisse. (2013). *Global wealth report, 2013*. Retrieved from https://publications.credit-suisse.com/index.cfm/publikationen-shop/research-institute/global-wealth-report-2013/?CFID=921881&CFTOKEN=1c1dec534fca81c1-8C77F60D-BC15-8246-3221C30D972ECD35

Duhigg, C., & Barboza, D. (2012, January 25). In China, human costs are built into the iPad. *New York Times*. Retrieved from http://www.nytimes.com/2012/01/26/business/ieconomy-apples-ipad-and-the-human-costs-for-workers-in-china.html

Erikson, R., & Goldthorpe, J. (1992). *The constant flux: A study of class mobility in industrial nations*. Oxford, UK: Clarendon Press.

Flannery, K., & Marcus, J. (2012). *The creation of inequality: How our prehistoric ancestors set the stage for monarchy, slavery, and empire*. Cambridge, MA: Harvard University Press.

Frank, R. (1999). *Luxury fever*. New York: The Free Press.

Friedman, T. (2012, January 28). Made in the world. *New York Times*. Retrieved from http://www.nytimes.com/2012/01/29/opinion/sunday/friedmanmade-in-the-world.html

Gaetz, S., Donaldson, J., Richter, T., & Gulliver, T. (2013). *The state of homelessness in Canada, 2013*. Toronto: Canadian Homelessness Research Network Press.

Galarneau, D., & Fecteau, E. (2014). *The ups and downs of minimum wage*. Retrieved from the Statistics Canada website: http://www.statcan.gc.ca/pub/75-006-x/2014001/article/14035-eng.pdf

Garfinkel, I., Rainwater, L., & Smeeding, T. (2010). *Wealth and welfare states: Is America laggard or leader?* Oxford, UK: Oxford University Press.

Goldin, C., & Katz, L. (2010). *The race between education and technology*. Cambridge, MA: Harvard University Press.

Maddison, A. (1995). *Monitoring the world economy, 1820–1992*. Paris: OECD.

Marx, K., & Engels, F. (1848/1983). *Manifesto of the Communist Party*. New York: International Publishers.

Mishel, L., & Davis, A. *CEO pay continues to rise as typical workers are paid less* (Research Brief #380). Retrieved from the Economic Policy Institute website: http://www.epi.org/publication/ceopay-continues-to-rise/

Neckerman, K., & Torche, F. (2007). Inequality: Causes and consequences. *Annual Review of Sociology, 33*, 335–357. doi:10.1146/annurev.soc.33.040406.131755

Oishi, K. S., & Diener, E. (2011). Income inequality and happiness. *Psychological Science, 22*, 1095–1100. doi:10.1177/0956797611417262

Oxfam. (2015). *Wealth: Having it all and wanting more*. Retrieved from the Oxfam International website: http://www.oxfam.org/en/research/wealth-having-it-all-and-wanting-more

Pew Research Center. (2014, February 11). *The rising cost of not going to college*. Retrieved from http://www.pewsocialtrends.org/2014/02/11/the-rising-cost-of-not-going-to-college/sdt-higher-education-02-11-2014-0-03/

Piketty, T. (2014). *Capital in the 21st century*. Cambridge, MA: Harvard University Press.

Piketty, T., & Saez, E. (2003). Income inequality in the United States, 1913–1998. *Quarterly Journal of Economics, 118*, 1–39. doi:10.1162/00335530360535135

Saez, E. (2012). Tables and figures: Updated to 2012. In T. Piketty and E. Saez, Income inequality in the United States, 1913–1998, *Quarterly Journal of Economics, 118*. Retrieved from http://elsa.berkeley.edu/~saez/

Smeeding, T. (2006). Poor people in rich nations: The United States in Comparative perspective. *Journal of Economic Perspectives, 20*(1), 69–90. doi:10.1257/089533006776526094

Smith, A. (1776/1976). *An inquiry into the nature and causes of the wealth of nations*. London, UK: MacMillan.

Statistics Canada. (2007). High-income Canadians. *Perspectives on Labour and Income, 8*(9).

Statistics Canada. (2010). Minimum wage. *Perspectives on Labour and Income, 11*(3). Retrieved from http://www.statcan.gc.ca/pub/75-001-x/topics-sujets/pdf/topics-sujets/minimumwage-salaireminimum-2009-eng.pdf

United States Central Intelligence Agency. (2011). *C.I.A. world factbook*. New York, NY: Skyhorse.

United States Economic Policy Institute. (2010). *State of working America preview*. Retrieved from http://www.epi.org/publication/state_of_working_america_preview_the_declining_value_of_minimum_wage/

Wilkinson, R. (2006). *The impact of inequality: How to make sick societies healthier*. New York, NY: The New Press.

Winters, J. (2011). *Oligarchy*. Cambridge, UK: Cambridge University Press.

Wolff, E. N. (2010). *Recent trends in household wealth in the United States: Rising debt and the middle-class squeeze—An update to 2007* (Working Paper no. 589). Annandale-on-Hudson, NY: Levy Economic Institute of Bard College.

Wright, E. O. (1986). What is middle about the middle class? In J. Roemer (Ed.), *Analytical Marxism* (pp. 114–140). New York: Cambridge University Press.

Yalnizyan, A. (2010). *The rise of Canada's richest 1%*. Retrieved from the Canadian Centre for Policy Alternatives website: https://www.policyalternatives.ca/publications/reports/rise-canadas-richest-1

CHAPTER 10

Barrionuevo, A. (2012, May 17). At over $90 million, sale of midtown penthouse sets a New York record. *New York Times*. Retrieved from http://www.nytimes.com/2012/05/18/realestate/midtown-penthouse-at-one57-sells-for-new-york-record.html

Boyd, M., & Vickers, M. (2000). 100 years of immigration in Canada. *Canadian Social Trends, 53*, 2–13.

Provincial Elections Amendment Act, S.B.C. 1947, c 28.

CBC (Canadian Broadcasting Corporation). (2009, August 21). Security certificates and secret evidence. *CBC News*. Retrieved from http://www.cbc.ca/news/canada/security-certificates-and-secret-evidence-1.777624

Chipman, J. (2013, October 6). Secret Supreme Court hearing focuses on security certificate. *CBC News*. Retrieved from http://www.cbc.ca/news/canada/secret-supreme-court-hearing-focuses-on-security-certificate-1.1913196

Citizenship and Immigration Canada. (2011). *Backgrounder: Facts on Canadian immigration history*. Retrieved from http://www.cic.gc.ca/english/department/media/backgrounders/2011/2011-06-27.asp

Constitution Act, 1982, being Schedule B to the Canada Act 1982 (UK), 1982, c 11.

Cornell, S., & Hartmann, D. (2007). *Ethnicity and race: Making identities in a changing world*. Thousand Oaks, CA: Pine Forge Press.

Dikötter, F. (2008). The racialization of the globe: An interactive interpretation. *Ethnic and Racial Studies, 31*(8), 1478–1496. doi:10.1080/01419870802208388

Dominion Elections Act, 1874, 37 Vic, c 9.

Evett, I., Gill, P. D., Scranage, J. K., & Weir, B. S. (1996). Establishing the robustness of short-tandem-repeat statistics for forensic applications. *American Journal of Human Genetics, 58*, 398–407.

Giddens, A., & Sutton, P.W. (2012). *Sociology* (7th ed.), Cambridge: Polity Press.

Graham, H. D. (2002). The origins of official minority designation. In J. Perlmann and M. C. Waters (Ed.), *The new race question: How the census counts multiracial individuals* (pp. 288–299). New York: Russell Sage Foundation.

Green, A. G., & Green, D. (1996). The goals of Canada's immigration policy: A historical perspective. *Canadian Journal of Urban Research, 13*(1), 102–139.

Greenwald, A. G., & Banaji, M. R. (1995). Implicit social cognition: Attitudes, self-esteem, and stereotypes. *Psychological Review, 102*, 4–27. doi:10.1037/0033-295X.102.1.4

Hale, S. M. (2013). *Contested sociology: Rethinking the Canadian experience*. Toronto: Pearson.

Hall, B. S. (2011). *A history of race in Muslim West Africa, 1600–1960*. Cambridge, UK: Cambridge University Press.

Immigration Act, 1976, SC 1976–77, c 52.

Immigration and Refugee Protection Act, SC 2001, c 27.

Jacobson, M. F. (1998). *Whiteness of a different color: European immigrants and the alchemy of race*. Cambridge, MA: Harvard University Press.

Jasso, G. (2011). Migration and stratification. *Social Science Research, 40*, 1292–1336. doi:10.1016/j.ssresearch.2011.03.007

Kim, N.Y. (2008). *Imperial citizens: Koreans and race from Seoul to LA*. Stanford, CA: Stanford University Press.

Lawrence, B. (2003). Gender, race and the regulation of Native identity. *Hypatia, 18*(2), 3–31. doi:10.1111/j.1527-2001.2003.tb00799.x

Maimbo, S. M., & Ratha, D. (2005). Remittances: An overview. In S. M. Maimbo & D. Ratha (Eds.), *Remittances: Development impact and future prospects* (pp. 1–16). Washington, DC: World Bank.

Massey, D. S., Arango, J., Hugo, G., Kuaouci, A., Pellegrino, A. & Taylor, J. E. (1993). Theories of international migration: A review and appraisal. *Population and Development Review, 19*, 431–66. doi:10.2307/2938462

Mincer, J. (1978). Family migration decisions. *Journal of Political Economy, 86*, 749–773. doi:10.1086/260710

Morning, A. (2008). Ethnic classification in global perspective: A cross-national survey of the 2000 census round. *Population Research and Policy Review, 27*(2), 239–272. doi:10.1007/s11113-007-9062-5

Nelkin, D., & Lindee, M. S. (1995). *The DNA mystique: The gene as cultural icon*. New York: Freeman.

Obasogie, O. K. (2014). *Blinded by sight: Seeing race through the eyes of the blind*. Stanford, CA: Stanford University Press.

Quillian, L. (2006). New approaches to understanding racial prejudice and discrimination. *Annual Review of Sociology, 32*, 299–328. doi:10.1146/annurev.soc.32.061604.123132

Rapoport, H., & Docquier, F. (2006). The economics of migrants' remittances. In S.-C. Kolm & J. M. Ythier (Eds.), *Handbook of the economics of giving, altruism and reciprocity: Applications* (Vol. 2, pp. 1135–1200). Amsterdam, Netherlands: North-Holland.

Statistics Canada. (2015). *Aboriginal identity of a person*. Retrieved from http://www.statcan.gc.ca/eng/concepts/definitions/aboriginal2

Tepperman, L., Albanese, P., & Curtis, J. (2012). *Principles of sociology*. Toronto, ON: Oxford University Press.

Valdés, G. (2003). *Expanding definitions of giftedness: Young interpreters of immigrant background*. New York, NY: Erlbaum.

Van Ausdale, D., & Feagin, J. R. (2001). *The first R: How children learn race and racism*. Lanham, MD: Rowman and Littlefield.

Weber, M. (1922/1978). *Economy and society*. Berkeley: University of California Press.

Wolfe, P. (2001). Land, labor, and difference: Elementary structures of race. *American Historical Review, 106*(3), 866–905. doi:10.2307/2692330

World Bank. (2011a). *Migration and remittances factbook 2011*. Washington, DC: World Bank.

World Bank. (2011b). News and broadcast: Migration and remittances. Retrieved from http://go.worldbank.org/RR8SDPEHO0

CHAPTER 11

An Act to amend the Canadian Human Rights Act, SC 1996, c 14.

Akerlof, G. A., Yellen, J. L., & Katz, M. L. (1996). An analysis of out-of-wedlock childbearing in the United States. *Quarterly Journal of Economics, 111*, 277–317. doi:10.2307/2946680

Armstrong, E. A. (2002). *Forging gay identities: Organizing sexuality in San Francisco, 1950–1994*. Chicago: University of Chicago Press.

Armstrong, E., England, P., & Fogarty, A. (2012). Accounting for women's orgasm and sexual enjoyment in college hookups and relationships. *American Sociological Review, 77*(3), 435–462. doi:10.1177/0003122412445802

Autor, D. H., Katz, L. F., & Kearney, M. (2008). Trends in U.S. wage inequality: Revising the revisionists. *Review of Economics and Statistics, 90*(2), 300–323. doi:10.1162/rest.90.2.300

Babcock, L., & Laschever, S. (2003). *Women don't ask: Negotiation and the gender divide*. Princeton, NJ: Princeton University Press.

Bailey, M. (2006). More power to the pill: The impact of contraceptive freedom on women's life cycle labor supply. *Quarterly Journal of Economics, 121*(1), 289–320. doi:10.1162/qjec.2006.121.1.289

Bailey, J. M., Dunne, M. P., Nicholas, M., & Nicholas, M. (2000). Genetic and environmental influences on sexual orientation and its correlates in an Australian twin sample. *Journal of Personality and Social Psychology, 78*(3), 524–536. doi:10.1037/0022-3514.78.3.524

Bailey, J. M., & Pillard, R. C. (1991). A genetic study of male sexual orientation. *Archives of General Psychiatry, 48*, 1089–1096. doi:10.1001/archpsyc.1991.01810360053008

Bailey, J. M., Pillard, R. C., Neale, M. C., & Agyei, Y. (1993). Heritable factors influence sexual orientation in women. *Archives of General Psychiatry, 50*, 217–223. doi:10.1001/archpsyc.1993.01820150067007

Bergmann, B. R. (1986). *The economic emergence of women*. New York: Basic Books.

Bianchi, S. M., Robinson, J. P., & Milkie, M. A. (2006). *Changing rhythms of American family life*. New York: Russell Sage Foundation.

Bianchi, S. M., Sayer, L. C., Milkie, M. A., & Robinson, J. P. (2012). Housework: Who did, does, or will do it, and how much does it matter? *Social Forces, 91*(1), 55–63. doi:10.1093/sf/sos120

Big Eagle, C., & Guimond, É. (2009). Contributions that count: First Nations women and demography. In G. G. Valaskakis, M. D. Stout, and É. Guimond (Eds.), *Restoring balance: First Nations women, community, and culture* (35–68). Winnipeg, MB: University of Manitoba Press.

Budig, M. J. (2002). Male advantage and the gender composition of jobs: Who rides the glass escalator? *Social Problems, 49*(2), 258–277. doi:10.1525/sp.2002.49.2.258

Buss, D. M. (1994). *The evolution of desire: Strategies of human mating*. New York: Basic Books.

Canadian Charter of Rights and Freedoms, Part I of the Constitution Act, 1982, being Schedule B to the Canada Act 1982 (UK), 1982, c 11.

Canadian Human Rights Act, SC 1977, c 33.

Catalyst. (2014). *Women CEOs of the Fortune 1000*. Retrieved from http://www.catalyst.org/knowledge/women-ceos-fortune-1000

Charles, M., & Bradley, K. (2009). Indulging our gendered selves? Sex segregation by field of study in 44 countries. *American Journal of Sociology, 114*(4), 924–976. doi:10.1086/595942

Cohen, P. (2013, June 7). Gender equality: Family egalitarianism follows workplace opportunity. In S. Coontz (Co-Chair and Ed.), *Equal pay symposium: 50 years since the Equal Pay Act of 1963* (pp. 8–9). Retrieved from the Council on Contemporary Families website: https://contemporaryfamilies.org/gender-equality-family-egalitarianism-follows-workplace-opportunity/

The College Board. (2012). Retrieved from http://media.collegeboard.com/digitalServices/pdf/research/Total-Group-2012.pdf

Correll, S. (2004). Constraints into preferences: Gender, status, and emerging career aspirations. *American Sociological Review, 69*(1), 93–113. doi:10.1177/000312240406900106

Correll, S., Benard, S., & Paik, I. (2007). Getting a job: Is there a motherhood penalty? *American Journal of Sociology, 112*, 1297–1338. doi:10.1086/511799

Cotter, D. A., Hermsen, J. M., & Vanneman, R. (2011). The end of the gender revolution? Gender role attitudes from 1977 to 2008. *American Journal of Sociology, 117*, 259–89. doi:10.1086/658853

Crawford, M., & Popp, D. (2003). Sexual double standards: A review and methodological critique of two decades of research. *Journal of Sex Research, 40*, 13–26. doi:10.1080/00224490309552163

Dee, T. (2007). Teachers and the gender gaps in student achievement. *Journal of Human Resources, 42*(3), 1–28. doi:10.3368/jhr.xlii.3.528

Diamond, L. M. (2008). *Sexual fluidity: Understanding women's love and desire*. Cambridge, MA: Harvard University Press.

DiPrete, T., & Buchmann, C. (2013). *The rise of women: The female advantage in education and what it means for American schools*. New York: Russell Sage Foundation.

Eckstein, Z., & Nagypal, E. (2004). The evolution of U.S. earnings inequality: 1961–2002. *Federal Reserve Bank of Minneapolis Quarterly Review, 28*(2), 10–29.

Ellwood, D. T., & Jencks, C. (2004). The spread of single-parent families in the United States since 1960. In D. P. Moynihan, T. M. Smeeding, & L. Rainwater (Eds.), *The future of the family* (pp. 25–65). New York: Russell Sage Foundation.

Employment Equity Act, SC 1986, c 31.

England, P. (1992). *Comparable worth: Theories and evidence*. New York: Aldine.

England, P. (2010a). The gender revolution: Uneven and stalled. *Gender & Society, 24*(2), 149–166. doi:10.1177/0891243210361475

England, P. (2010b). *Online college social life survey*. Retrieved from the New York University website: http://www.nyu.edu/projects/england/ocsls/

England, P. (2011). Reassessing the uneven gender revolution and its slowdown. *Gender & Society, 25*(1), 113–123. doi:10.1177/0891243210391461

England, P., McClintock, E., & Shafer, E. (2011). Birth control use and early, unintended births: Evidence for a class gradient. In M. Carlson & P. England (Eds.), *Social class and changing families in an unequal America* (pp. 21–49). Stanford, CA: Stanford University Press.

England, P., Shafer, E. F., & Fogarty, A. C. K. (2008). Hooking up and forming romantic relationships on today's college campuses. In M. Kimmel & A. Aronson (Eds.), *The gendered society reader* (3rd ed., pp. 531–547). New York: Oxford University Press.

Finer, L. B. (2007). Trends in premarital sex in the United States, 1954–2003. *Public Health Reports, 122*, 7–78.

Gagnon, J. H., & Simon, W. (1973). *Sexual conduct: The social sources of human sexuality*. Chicago: Aldine.

Gordon, R. J., & Dew-Becker, I. (2007). Selected issues in the rise of income inequality. *Brookings Papers on Economic Activity, 2*, 169–190.

Holtzman, L. (2000). *Media messages: What film, television, and popular music teach us about race, class, gender and sexual orientation*. New York: M.E. Sharpe.

Hyde, J. S. (1984). How large are gender differences in aggression? A developmental meta-analysis. *Developmental Psychology, 20*(4), 722–736. doi:10.1037/0012-1649.20.4.722

Hyde, J. S. (2005). The gender similarities hypothesis. *American Psychologist , 60*(6), 581–592. doi:10.1037/0003-066X.60.6.581

Hyde, J. S., Lindberg, S. M., Linn, M. C., Ellis, A. B., & Williams, C. C. (2008). Gender similarities characterize math performance. *Science, 321*(5888), 494–95. doi:10.1126/science.1160364

Juhn, C., & Murphy, K. M. (1997). Wage inequality and family labor supply. *Journal of Labor Economics, 15*, 72–79. doi:10.1086/209847

Kinsey, A. C., Pomeroy, W. H., & Martin, C. E. (1948/1998). *Sexual behavior in the human male*. Philadelphia: W.B. Saunders / Bloomington: Indiana U. Press.

Kinsey, A. C., Pomeroy, W. H., Martin, C. E., & Gebhard, P. H. (1953/1998). *Sexual behavior in the human female*. Philadelphia: W.B. Saunders; Bloomington: Indiana University Press.

Kreager, D. A., & Staff, J. (2009). The sexual double standard and adolescent peer acceptance. *Social Psychology Quarterly, 72*, 143–164. doi:10.1177/019027250907200205

Levanon, A., England, P., & Allison, P. (2009). Occupational feminization and pay: Assessing causal dynamics using 1950–2000 census data. *Social Forces, 88*(2), 865–892. doi:10.1353/sof.0.0264

Lightdale, J. R., & Prentice, D. A. (1994). Rethinking sex differences in aggression: Aggressive behavior in the absence of social roles. *Personality and Social Psychology Bulletin, 20*, 34–44. doi:10.1177/0146167294201003

Maccoby, E. E., & Jacklin, C. N. (1974). *The psychology of sex differences*. Stanford, CA: Stanford University Press.

Mackie, G. (1996). Ending footbinding and infibulation: A convention account. *American Sociological Review, 61*, 999–1017. doi:10.2307/2096305

Martinez, G., Copen, C. E., & Abma, J. C. (2011, October). *Teenagers in the United States: Sexual activity, contraceptive use, and childbearing, 2006–2010 National Survey of Family Growth* (Vital Health Statistics, Series 23, No. 31). Retrieved from the Centers for Disease Control and Prevention website: http://www.cdc.gov/nchs/data/series/sr_23/sr23_031.pdf

Mazur, A., & Booth, A. (1998). Testosterone and dominance in men. *Behavioral and Brain Sciences, 21*, 353–397. doi:10.1017/S0140525X98001228

McDaniel, A, DiPrete, T. A., Buchmann, C., & Shwed, U. (2011). The black gender gap in educational attainment: Historical trends and racial comparisons. *Demography, 48*, 889–914. doi:10.1007/s13524-011-0037-0

McKenna, W., & Kessler, S. (2006). Transgendering: Blurring the boundaries of gender. In M. S. Evans, K. David, and J. Lorber (Eds.), *Handbook of gender and women's studies* (pp. 342–354). Thousand Oaks, CA: Sage. doi:10.4135/9781848608023

Mishel, L., Gould, E., & Bivens, J. (2015). *Wage stagnation in nine charts*. Retrieved from the Economic Policy Institute website: http://www.epi.org/publication/charting-wage-stagnation/

Morissette, R., Picot, G., & Lu,Y. (2012). *Wage growth over the past 30 years: Changing wages by age and education*. Retrieved from the Statistics Canada website: http://www.statcan.gc.ca/pub/11-626-x/11-626-x2012008-eng.pdf

O'Brien, J. (2000). Heterosexism and homophobia. In N. J. Smelser & P. B. Baltes (Eds.), *International encyclopedia of the social and behavioral sciences* (Vol. 10, pp. 6672–6676). London: Elsevier.

Oppenheimer,V. (1970). *The female labor force in the United States: Demographic and economic factors governing its growth and changing composition*. Berkeley: University of California Press.

Ottosson, D. (2010). *State-sponsored homophobia: A world survey of laws prohibiting same sex behavior between consenting adults*. Geneva: International Lesbian, Gay, Bisexual, Trans, and Intersex Association.

Pascoe, C. J. (2007). *"Dude, you're a fag": Masculinity and sexuality in high school*. Berkeley: University of California Press.

Regnerus, M. D. (2007). *Forbidden fruit: Sex and religion in the lives of American teenagers*. Oxford, UK: Oxford University Press.

Reskin, B. (2000). The proximate causes of employment discrimination. *Contemporary Sociology, 29*, 319–328. doi:10.2307/2654387

Risman, B. J. (2004). Gender as a social structure: Theory wrestling with social change. *Gender & Society, 18*(4), 429–450. doi:10.1177/0891243204265349

Rotermann, M. (2008). Trends in teen sexual behaviour and condom use. *Health Reports, 19*(3), 1–5.

Rotermann, M. (2012). Sexual behaviour and condom use of 15- to 24-year-olds in 2003 and 2009/2010. *Health Reports, 23*(1), 1–5.

Savin-Williams, R. C. (1998). *"And then I became gay": Young men's stories*. New York: Routledge.

Sayer, L., England, P., Allison, P. & Kangas, N. (2011). She left, he left: How employment and satisfaction affect women's and men's decisions to leave marriages. *American Journal of Sociology, 116*(6), 1982–2018. doi:10.1086/658173

Schalet, A. T. (2011). *Not under my roof: Parents, teens, and the culture of sex*. Chicago: University of Chicago Press.

Schmitt, D. P. (2003). Universal sex differences in the desire for sexual variety. *Journal of Personality and Social Psychology, 85*(1), 85–104. doi:10.1037/0022-3514.85.1.85

Sell, R. L. (1997). Defining and measuring sexual orientation: A review. *Archives of Sexual Behavior, 26*(6), 643–658. doi:10.1023/A:1024528427013

Spencer, S. J., Steele, C. M., & Quinn, D. M. (1999). Stereotype threat and women's math performance. *Journal of Experimental Social Psychology, 35*, 4–28. doi:10.1006/jesp.1998.1373

Steffensmeier, D., & Allan, E. (1996). Gender and crime: Toward a gendered theory of female offending. *Annual Review of Sociology, 22*, 459–487. doi:10.1146/annurev.soc.22.1.459

Statistics Canada. (2005). *Labour force survey*. Ottawa: Statistics Canada.

Statistics Canada. (2009). *Births*. Retrieved from http://www.statcan.gc.ca/pub/84f0210x/84f0210x2009000-eng.pdf

Stein, E. (2001). Sexual orientation: Biological influences. In N. J. Smelser & P. B. Baltes (Eds.), *International encyclopedia of the social and behavioral sciences* (Vol. 21, pp. 13995–13999). London: Elsevier.

Turcotte, M. (2011). *Women in Canada: A gender-based statistical report*. Retrieved from the Statistics Canada website: http://www.statcan.gc.ca/pub/89-503-x/2010001/article/11542-eng.pdf

Udry, J. R. (1988). Biological predispositions and social control in adolescent sexual behavior. *American Sociological Review, 53*(5), 709–722. doi:10.2307/2095817

Waterlow, Lucy. (2013, July 15). Force fed to try to find a husband: Mauritanian women are fattened up "like foie gras geese" and take dangerous animal growth hormones to satisfy men's love for larger lady. *Daily Mail*. Retrieved from http://www.dailymail.co.uk/femail/article-2364060/Force-fed-husband-How-Mauretanian-women-fattened-like-foie-gras-geesedangerous-animal-growth-hormones-satisfy-mens-lovelarger-lady.html

Willer, R., Rogalin, C., Conlon, B., & Wojnowicz, M. T. (2013). Overdoing gender: A test of the masculine overcompensation thesis. *American Journal of Sociology, 118*(4), 980–1022. doi:10.1086/668417

CHAPTER 12

Acock, A. C., & Demo, D. H. (1994). *Family Diversity and Well-Being*. Thousand Oaks, CA: Sage.

Ahrons, C. (2006). Family ties after divorce: Long-term implications for children. *Family Issues, 46*, 53–65.

Amato, P. R., & Booth, A. (1997). *A generation at risk: Growing up in an era of family upheaval*. Cambridge, MA: Harvard University Press.

American Sociological Association. (2012). Amicus Curiae *brief in Hollingsworth v. Perry*. Retrieved from http://www.asanet.org/documents/ASA/pdfs/12-144_307_Amicus_%20%28C_%20Gottlieb%29_ASA_Same-Sex_Marriage.pdf

Barnett, R. C., & Rivers, C. (1996). *She works/he works: How two-income families are happier, healthier, and better-off*. San Francisco: Harper San Francisco.

Barnett, R. C., & Rivers, C. (2004). *Same difference: How gender myths are hurting our relationships, our children, and our jobs*. New York: Basic Books.

Belkin, L. (2003, October 26). The opt-out revolution. *New York Times Magazine*. Retrieved from http://www.nytimes.com/2003/10/26/magazine/the-opt-out-revolution.html?_r=0

Bengston, Vern L., Biblarz, T. J., & Roberts, R., E., L. (2002). *How families still matter: A longitudinal study of youth in two generations*. New York: Cambridge University Press.

Bernhardt, A., Morris, M., Handcock, M., & Scott, M. (1999). *Divergent paths: Economic mobility in the new American labor market*. New York, NY: Russell Sage Foundation Press.

Bianchi, S. M. (2000). Maternal employment and time with children: Dramatic change or surprising continuity? *Demography, 37*(4), 401–414. doi:10.1353/dem.2000.0001

Bianchi, S. M., Robinson, J. P., & Milkie, M. A. (2006). *Changing rhythms of American family life*. New York, NY: Russell Sage Foundation.

Blankenhorn, D. (1995). *Fatherless America: Confronting our most urgent social problem*. New York, NY: Basic Books.

Blankenhorn, D. (2009). *The future of marriage*. New York, NY: Encounter Books.

Blow, C. M. (2008, July 12). Talking down and stepping up. *New York Times*.

Boushey, H. (2008)."Opting out"? The effect of children on women's employment in the United States. *Feminist Economics, 14*(1), 1–36. doi:10.1080/13545700701716672

Boxer, C. F., Noonan, M. C., & Whelan, C. B. (2015). Measuring mate preferences: A replication and an extension. *Journal of Family Issues, 36*(2), 163–187. doi:10.1177/0192513X13490404

Burchinal, M., & Clarke-Stewart, A. (2007). Maternal employment and child cognitive outcomes: The importance of an analytic approach. *Developmental Psychology, 43*, 1140–1155. doi:10.1037/0012-1649.43.5.1140

Cancian, F. M. (1987). *Love in America: Gender and self-development*. New York: Cambridge University Press.

Casper, L. M., & Bianchi, S. (2002). *Continuity and change in the American family*. Thousand Oaks, CA: Sage.

Cherlin, A. J. (1992). *Marriage, divorce, remarriage*. Cambridge, MA: Harvard University Press.

Cherlin, A. J. (2009). *The marriage-go-round: The state of marriage and the family in America today*. New York, NY: Alfred A. Knopf.

Cherlin, A. J., Furstenberg, F. F. Jr., Chase-Lansdale, P. L., Kiernan, K. E., Robins, P. K., Morrison, D. R., & Teitler, J. O. (1991). Longitudinal studies of the effects of divorce on children in Great Britain and the United States. *Science, 252*, 1386–1389. doi:10.1126/science.2047851

Clark, Warren. (2012). Delayed transitions of young adults. *Canadian Social Trends, 84*, 13-21. Retrieved from http://www.statcan.gc.ca/pub/11-008-x/2007004/pdf/10311-eng.pdf.

Cohany, S. R., & Sok, E. (2007, February). Trends in the labor force participation of married mothers of infants. *Monthly Labor Review*, 9–16. doi:10.1037/a0017820

Collins, P. Hill. (1991). *Black feminist thought: Knowledge, consciousness, and the politics of empowerment*. London: Routledge.

Coltrane, S. (2004). Fathering: Paradoxes, contradictions and dilemmas. In M. Coleman & L. Ganong (Eds.), *Handbook of contemporary families: Considering the past, contemplating the future* (pp. 224–243). Thousand Oaks, CA: Sage.

Conley, D. (2004). *The pecking order: Which siblings succeed and why*. New York: Pantheon.

Cooke, L. P. (2006)."Doing" gender in context: Household bargaining and risk of divorce in Germany and the United States. *American Journal of Sociology, 112*(2), 442–472. doi:10.1086/506417

Coontz, S. (1992). *The way we never were: American families and the nostalgia trap*. New York: Basic Books.

Coontz, S. (2005). *Marriage, a history: From obedience to intimacy, or how love conquered marriage*. New York: Viking.

Cotter, D. A., England, P., & Hermsen, J. (2010). Moms and jobs: Trends in mothers' employment and which mothers stay home. In B. J. Risman (Ed.), *Families as they really are* (pp. 416–424). New York: W.W. Norton.

Crouter, A. C., & McHale, S. M. (2005). Work time, family time, and children's time: Implications for youth. In S. Bianchi, L. Casper, & R. B. King, *Work, family, health, and well-being* (pp. 49–66). New York: Routledge.

Damaske, S. (2011). *For the family? How class and gender shape women's work*. New York: Oxford University Press.

Deutsch, F. (1999). *Halving it all: How equally shared parenting works*. Cambridge, MA: Harvard University Press.

Edin, K., & Kefalas, M. (2005). *Promises I can keep: Why poor women put motherhood before marriage*. Berkeley: University of California Press.

Friedan, B. (2001/1963). *The feminine mystique*. New York, NY: W.W Norton.

Fry, R. (2013). *A rising share of young adults living in their parents' home*. Retrieved from the Pew Research Center website: http://www.pewsocialtrends.org/2013/08/01/a-rising-share-of-young-adults-live-in-their-parents-home/

Furstenberg, F. F., & Cherlin, A. J. (1991). *Divided families: What happens to children when parents part*. Cambridge, MA: Harvard University Press.

Furstenberg, F. F., Kennedy, S., Mcloyd, V. C., Rumbaut, R., & Settersten, R. A. Jr. (2004). Growing up is harder to do. *Contexts, 3*, 33–41.doi:10.1525/ctx.2004.3.3.33

Galinsky, E. (1999). *Ask the children: What America's children really think about working parents*. New York, NY: William Morrow.

Galinksy, E., Aumann, K., & Bond, J. T. (2009). *Gender and generation at home and at work*. New York, NY: Families and Work Institute.

Gerson, K. (2011). *The unfinished revolution: Coming of age in a new era of gender, work, and family*. New York, NY: Oxford University Press.

Giele, J. Z. (1996). Decline of the family: Conservative, liberal, and feminist views. In D. Popenoe, J. B. Elshtain, & D. Blankenhorn (Eds.), *Promises to keep: Decline and renewal of marriage in America* (pp. 89–115). Lanham, MD: Rowman & Littlefield.

Goode, W. J. (1963). *World revolution and family patterns*. New York, NY: Free Press.

Goode, W. J. (1982). *The family* (2nd ed.). Upper Saddle River, NJ: Pearson.

Gornick, Janet C., & Meyers, M. K. (2009). *Gender equality: Transforming family divisions of labor*. New York, NY: Verso Books.

Harvey, L. (1999). Short-term and long-term effects of early parental employment on children of the national longitudinal survey of youth. *Developmental Psychology, 35*(2), 445–459. doi:10.1037/0012-1649.35.2.445

Hays, S. (1996). *The cultural contradictions of motherhood*. New Haven, CT: Yale University Press.

Hays, S. (2003). *Flat broke with children: Women in the age of welfare reform*. New York, NY: Oxford University Press.

Hertz, R. (2006). *Single by chance, mothers by choice: How women are choosing parenthood without marriage and creating the new American family*. New York, NY: Oxford University Press.

Hetherington, E. M., & Kelly, J. (2002). *For better or for worse: Divorce reconsidered*. New York, NY: W.W. Norton.

Hochschild, A. R., with Machung, A. (1989). *The second shift: Working parents and the revolution at home*. New York: Viking.

Hochschild, A. R. (1997). *The time bind: When work becomes home and home becomes work*. New York, NY: Henry Holt.

Hoffman, L., Wladis, N., & Youngblade, L. M. (1999). *Mothers at work: Effects on children's well-being*. Cambridge, UK: Cambridge University Press.

Jacobs, J. A., & Gerson, K. (2004). *The time divide: Work, family, and gender inequality*. Cambridge, MA: Harvard University Press.

Kefalas, M. J., Furstenberg, F. F., Carr, P. J., & Napolitano, L. (2011). "Marriage is more than being together": The meaning of marriage for young adults. *Journal of Family Issues, 32*(7), 845–875. doi:10.1177/0192513X10397277

Kimmel, M. (2008). *Guyland: The perilous world where boys become men*. New York, NY: HarperCollins.

Lareau, A. (2003). *Unequal childhoods: Class, race, and family life*. Berkeley: University of California Press.

Levi-Strauss, C. (1964). Reciprocity, the essence of social life. In R. L. Coser, *The family: Its structure and functions* (pp. 3–14). New York, NY: St. Martin's Press.

Li, A. J. (2007). *The kids are ok: Divorce and children's behavior problems* (RAND Working Paper No. WR-489). Santa Monica, CA: RAND.

Lorber, J. (1994). *Paradoxes of gender*. New Haven, CT: Yale University Press.

Luker, K. (2007). *When sex goes to school: Warring views on sex—and sex education—since the sixties*. New York, NY: W.W. Norton.

Malinowski, B. (1913/1964). Parenthood, the basis of social structure. In R. L. Coser, *The family: Its structure and functions* (pp. 51–63). New York, NY: St. Martin's Press.

McLanahan, S., & Sandefur, G. D. (1994). *Growing up with a single parent: What hurts, what helps*. Cambridge, MA: Harvard University Press.

Milan, A. (2013). *Marital status: Overview, 2011*. Retrieved from Statistics Canada website: http://www.statcan.gc.ca/pub/91-209-x/2013001/article/11788-eng.pdf.

Marquardt, E. (2005). *Between two worlds: The inner lives of children of divorce*. New York, NY: Crown.

Moen, P., & Roehling, P. (2005). *The career mystique: Cracks in the American dream*. Lanham, MD: Rowman & Littlefield.

Moore, K. A., Chalk, R., Scarpa, J., & Vandiverre, S. (2002). *Family strengths: Often overlooked, but real*. Child Trends Research Brief. Washington, DC: Annie E. Casey Foundation.

Newman, K. (2012). *The accordion family: Boomerang kids, anxious parents, and the private toll of global competition*. Boston, MA: Beacon Press.

Parcel, T. L., & Menaghan, E. G. (1994). *Parents' jobs and children's lives*. New York, NY: Aldine de Gruyter.

Parsons, T., & Bales, R. F. (1954). *Family, socialization, and interaction process*. Glencoe, IL: Free Press.

Pew Research Center. (2007a, July 1). *Generation gap in values, behavior: As marriage and parenthood drift apart, public is concerned about social impact*. Retrieved from http://www.pewsocialtrends.org/files/2007/07/Pew-Marriage-report-6-28-for-web-display.pdf.

Pew Research Center. (2007b). *How young people view their lives, futures and politics: A portrait of the "generation next."* New York, NY: Pew Research Center.

Pew Research Center. (2010.) *The decline of marriage and rise of new families*. Retrieved from http://www.pewsocialtrends.org/2010/11/18/the-decline-of-marriage-and-rise-of-new-families/

Popenoe, D. (1988). *Disturbing the nest: Family change and decline in modern societies*. New York, NY: Aldine de Gruyter.

Popenoe, D., Elshtain, J. B., & Blankenhorn, D. 1996. *Promises to keep: Decline and renewal of marriage in America*. Lanham, MD: Rowman & Littlefield.

Porter, E., & O'Donnell, M. (2006, August 6). Facing middle age with no degree, and no wife. *New York Times*.

Powell, B., Bolzendahl, C., Geist, C., & Steelman, L. C. (2010). *Counted out: Same-sex relations and American's definitions of family*. New York, NY: Russell Sage Foundation.

Ray, R., Gornick, J., & Schmitt, J. (2009). *Parental leave policies in 21 countries: Assessing generosity and gender equality*. Retrieved from the Center for Economic and Policy Research website: http://cepr.net/publications/reports/plp

Risman, B. J. (1998). *Gender vertigo: American families in transition*. New Haven, CT: Yale University Press.

Risman, B. J. (Ed.). (2010). *Families as they really are*. New York: W.W. Norton.

Rosenfeld, M. J. (2009). *The age of independence: Interracial unions, same-sex unions, and changing American family*. Cambridge, MA: Harvard University Press.

Rutter, V. (2010). The case for divorce. In B. J. Risman (Ed.), *Families as they really are* (pp. 159–169). New York, NY: W.W. Norton.

Skolnick, A. (2006, Fall). Beyond the "m" word: The tangled web of politics and marriage. *Dissent*, 81–87. doi:10.1353/dss.2006.0054

Smith, C., with Christofferson, K., Davidson, H., & Herzog, P. (2011). *Lost in translation: The dark side of emerging adulthood*. New York, NY: Oxford University Press.

Smock, P. (2000). Cohabitation in the United States: An appraisal of research themes, findings, and implications. *Annual Review of Sociology, 26*, 1–20. doi:10.1146/annurev.soc.26.1.1

Smock, P. J., & Manning, W. (2010). New couples, new families: The cohabitation revolution in the United States. In B. J. Risman (Ed.), *Families as they really are* (pp. 131–139). New York, NY: W.W. Norton.

Stacey, J. (1996). *In the name of the family: Rethinking family values in the postmodern age*. Boston, MA: Beacon Press.

Stack, C. B. (1974). *All our kin: Strategies for survival in a black community*. New York, NY: Harper and Row.

Statistics Canada. (2011a). *Census dictionary*. Retrieved from http://www12.statcan.gc.ca/census-recensement/2011/ref/dict/index-eng.cfm

Statistics Canada. (2011b). *Women in Canada: A gender-based statistical report*. Retrieved from http://www.statcan.gc.ca/pub/89-503-x/89-503-x2010001-eng.pdf

Statistics Canada. (2012). *Fifty years of families in Canada*. Retrieved from http://www12.statcan.gc.ca/census-recensement/2011/as-sa/98-312-x/98-312-x2011003_1-eng.pdf

Stone, P. (2007). *Opting out? Why women really quit careers and head home*. Berkeley: University of California Press.

Struening, K. (2010). Families "in law" and families "in practice": Does the law recognize families as they really are? In B. J. Risman (Ed.), *Families as they really are* (pp. 75–90). New York, NY: W. W. Norton.

Sullivan, O., & Coltrane, S. (2008, April 25). *Men's changing contribution to housework and child care*. Retrieved from the Council on Contemporary Families website: https://contemporaryfamilies.org/mens-changing-contribution-to-housework-and-childcare-brief-report/

Swidler, A. (1980). Love and adulthood in American culture. In E. H. Erikson & N. J. Smelser (Eds.), *Themes of love and work in adulthood* (pp. 120–147). Cambridge, MA: Harvard University Press.

United States Census Bureau. (2006). *Current population survey annual social and economic supplement: Families and living arrangements: 2005*. Washington, DC: U.S. Census Bureau.

United States Census Bureau. (2007). *Single-parent households showed little variation since 1994*. Washington, DC: U.S. Census Bureau.

Waldfogel, J. (2006). *What children need*. Cambridge, MA: Harvard University Press.

Wallerstein, J. S., Lewis, J. M., & Blakeslee, S. (2000). *The unexpected legacy of divorce: A 25-year landmark study*. New York: Hyperion.

Weissman, J. (2013, February 26). Here is exactly how many college graduates are living at home. *The Atlantic*. Retrieved from http://www.theatlantic.com/business/archive/2013/02/heres-exactly-how-many-college-graduateslive-back-at-home/273529/

Weitzman, L. (1985). *The divorce revolution: The unexpected consequences for women and children*. New York, NY: Free Press.

Whitehead, B. D. (1997). *The divorce culture*. New York, NY: Alfred A. Knopf.

Williams, J. C. (2000). *Unbending gender: Why family and work conflict and what to do about it*. New York, NY: Oxford University Press.

Williams, J. C. (2010). *Reshaping the work–family debate: Why men and class matter*. Cambridge, MA: Harvard University Press.

Whyte, W. H., Jr. (1956). *The organization man*. New York, NY: Simon & Schuster.

CHAPTER 13

Amont, J. (2005). *American Jewish religious denominations*. United Jewish Communities Report No. 10). Retrieved from the Berman Jewish Databank website: http://www.jewishdatabank.org/studies/downloadFile.cfm?FileID=1486

Beit-Hallahmi, B., & Argyle, M. (1997). *The psychology of religious behavior, belief and experience*. London, UK: Routledge.

Bellah, R. N., Madsen, R., Sullivan, W. M., Swidler, A., & Tipton, S. M. (1985). *Habits of the heart: Individualism and commitment in America life*. Berkeley: University of California Press.

The Big Religion Chart: Comparison Chart. (2016). Retrieved from http://religionfacts.com/big_religion_chart.htm

Brooks, C. (2000). Civil rights liberalism and the suppression of a republican political realignment in the United States, 1972 to 1996. *American Sociological Review, 65*(4), 483–505.

Canadian Charter of Rights and Freedoms, Part I of the Constitution Act, 1982, being Schedule B to the Canada Act 1982 (UK), 1982, c 11.

Chang, C. T. (2006). *Korean ethnic church growth phenomenon in the United States*. American Academy of Religion, Claremont, CA. Retrieved from Duke University website: http://www.duke.edu/~myhan/kaf0603.pdf

Chaves, M. (2004). *Congregations in America*. Cambridge, MA: Harvard University Press.

Chaves, M., Hadaway, C. K., & Marler, P. L. (1993). What the polls don't show: A closer look at U.S. church attendance. *American Sociological Review, 58*, 741–752. doi:10.2307/2095948

Demerath, N. J., III. (2003). *Crossing the gods: World religions and worldly politics*. New Brunswick, NJ: Rutgers University Press.

Dillon, M., & Wink, P. (2007). *In the course of a lifetime: Tracing religious belief, practice, and change*. Berkeley: University of California Press.

Driedger, L., Epp, F. H., & Millette, D. (2015). Mennonites. In *The Canadian encyclopedia*. Retrieved from http://www.thecanadianencyclopedia.ca/en/article/mennonites/

Durkheim, E. (1898/1951). *Suicide: A Study in Sociology* (J. A. Spaulding & G. Simpson, Trans.). New York, NY: The Free Press.

Durkheim, E. (1912/2001). *The elementary forms of religious life* (C. Cosman, Trans.). New York, NY: Oxford University Press.

European Commission. (2005). *Eurobarometer 225: Social Values, Science, and Technology*. Retrieved from http://ec.europa.eu/COMMFrontOffice/PublicOpinion/index.cfm/Survey/getSurveyDetail/yearFrom/1973/yearTo/2005/surveyKy/448

Geneva Declaration Secretariat. (2008). *Global burden of armed violence report*. Retrieved from http://www.genevadeclaration.org/fileadmin/docs/Global-Burden-of-Armed-Violence-full-report.pdf

Greeley, A., & Hout, M. (2006). *The truth about conservative Christians: What they think and what they believe*. Chicago, IL: The University of Chicago Press.

Gross, N., & Simmons, S. (2009). The religiosity of American college and university professors. *Sociology of Religion, 70*(2), 101–129. doi:10.1093/socrel/srp026

Guttmacher Institute. (2011, April 13). *Contraceptive use is the norm among religious women*. Retrieved from www.guttmacher.org/media/nr/2011/04/13/index.html

Hitler, A. (1925). *Mein kampf*. Munich, Germany: Franz Eher Nachfolger.

Hout, M., Fischer, C. S., & Chaves, M. (2013). *More Americans have no religion preference: Key findings from the 2012 General Social Survey*. Unpublished ms., Institute for the Study of Societal Issues, University of California-Berkeley.

Hutchins, A. (2015, March 26). What Canadians really believe: A surprising poll. *Maclean's*. http://www.macleans.ca/society/life/what-canadians-really-believe/

Leonhardt, D. (2011, May 11). Is your religion your financial destiny? *New York Times*. Retrieved from http://www.nytimes.com/2011/05/15/magazine/isyour-religion-your-financial-destiny.html?_r=1

Marx, K. (1844/1977). A contribution to the critique of Hegel's Philosophy of Right. In Joseph O'Malley (Ed.), *Critique of Hegel's Philosophy of Right*. Cambridge, UK: Cambridge University Press.

Marx, K., & Engels, F. (1848/1998). *The communist manifesto*. London, UK: Verso.

Melton, J. G. (2009). *Encyclopedia of American religions* (8th ed.). New York, NY: Thomson.

Moaddel, M. (2007). The Saudi public speaks: Religion, gender, and politics. In M. Moaddel (Ed.), *Values and perceptions of the Islamic and Middle East publics* (pp. 209–248). New York, NY: Palgrave Macmillan.

Nepstad, S. E. (1996). Popular religion, protest, and revolt: The emergence of political insurgency in the Nicaraguan and Salvadoran churches of the 1960s–80s. In C. Smith (Ed.), *Disruptive religion: The force of faith in social movement activism* (pp. 105–124). New York, NY: Routledge.

Newport, Frank. (2006, June 23). A look at religious switching in America today. Retrieved from the Gallup website: http://www.gallup.com/poll/23467/look-religiousswitching-america-today.aspx

Norris, P., & Inglehart, R. (2004). *Sacred and secular*. New York, NY: Cambridge University Press.

Pew Research Center. (2013a). *Canada's changing religious landscape*. Retrieved from http://www.pewforum.org/2013/06/27/canadas-changing-religious-landscape/

Putnam, R., & Campbell, D. (2010). *American grace: How religion divides and unites us*. New York, NY: Simon and Schuster.

Sela, A. (1994). The "Wailing Wall" riots (1929) as a watershed in the Palestine conflict. *The Muslim World, 84*(1–2), 60–94. doi:10.1111/j.1478-1913.1994.tb03589.x

Smith, C. (2009). *Soul searching: The religious and spiritual lives of American teenagers*. New York, NY: Oxford University Press.

Stark, R. (1996). *The rise of Christianity: How the obscure, marginal jesus movement became the dominant religious force*. Princeton, NJ: Princeton University Press.

Stark, R., & Finke, R. (2000). *Acts of faith: Explaining the human side of religion*. Berkeley: University of California Press.

Sullins, D. P. (2006). Gender and religion: Deconstructing universality, constructing complexity. *American Journal of Sociology, 112*(3), 838–880. doi:10.1086/507852

Todd, D. (2013, March 9). Canadian Catholics "ahead" of Vatican on women, birth control, homosexuality [Blog post]. Retrieved from http://blogs.vancouversun.com/2013/03/09/canadian-catholics-ahead-of-vatican-on-women-birth-control-homosexuality/

United States Census Bureau. (2010). *DP-1: Profile of General Population and Housing Characteristics: 2010*. http://factfinder.census.gov/faces/tableservices/jsf/pages/productview.xhtml?src=bkmk

United States Central Intelligence Agency. (2012). *C.I.A. world factbook*. New York, NY: Skyhorse.

Weber, M. (1904/1958). *The Protestant ethic and the spirit of capitalism*. New York, NY: Charles Scribner's Sons.

CHAPTER 14

Arum, R., & Roksa, J. (2010). *Academically adrift: Limited learning on college campuses*. Chicago, IL: University of Chicago Press.

Arum, R., & Roksa, J. (2014). *Aspiring adults adrift: Tentative transitions of college graduates*. Chicago, IL: University of Chicago Press.

Babcock, P., & Marks, M. (2010). *The falling time cost of college: Evidence from half a century of time use data* (NBER Working Paper No. 15954. Retrieved from the National Bureau of Economic Research website: http://www.nber.org/papers/w15954.pdf

Blossfeld, H.-P., & Shavit, Y. (1993). Persisting barriers: Changes in educational opportunities in thirteen countries. In Y. Shavit & H.-P. Blossfeld (Eds.), *Persistent inequality: Changing educational attainment in thirteen countries* (pp. 1–23). Boulder, CO: Westview Press.

Bowles, S., & Gintis, H. (1976). *Schooling in capitalist America: Educational reform and the contradictions of economic life*. New York, NY: Basic Books.

Brint, S., & Karabel, J. (1989). *The diverted dream: Community colleges and the promise of educational opportunity in America, 1900–1980*. New York, NY: Oxford University Press.

Buchmann, C., & DiPrete, T. A. (2006). The growing female advantage in college completion: The role of family background and academic achievement. *American Sociological Review, 71*(4), 515–541. doi:10.1177/000312240607100401

Buchmann, C., DiPrete, T. A., & McDaniel, A. (2008). Gender inequalities in education. *Annual Review of Sociology, 34*, 319–337. doi:10.1146/annurev.soc.34.040507.134719

Butler, D. (2016, July 23). Study finds widening gender gap in earnings among post-secondary graduates. *The Ottawa Citizen*. Retrieved from http://ottawacitizen.com/news/local-news/study-finds-widening-gender-gap-in-wages-among-post-secondary-graduates

Coleman, J. S., Campbell, E. Q., Mood, A. M., Weinfeld, F. D., & York, R. L. (1966). *Equality of educational opportunity*. Washington, DC: U.S. Government Printing Office.

Collins, R. (1979). *The credential society: A historical sociology of education and stratification*. New York, NY: Academic Press.

Condron, D. J. (2010). *Affluence, inequality, and educational achievement: A structural snalysis of 97 jurisdictions across the globe*. Unpublished paper, Emory University, Atlanta, GA.

Council of Ministers of Education, Canada. (2016). *Education in Canada: An overview*. Retrieved from http://cmec.ca/299/Education-in-Canada-An-Overview/

England, P., & Li, S. (2006). Desegregation stalled: The changing gender composition of college majors, 1971–2002. *Gender and Society, 20*(5), 657–677. doi:10.1177/0891243206290753

Espenshade, T., & Radford, A. (2009). *No longer separate, not yet equal: Race and class in elite college admission and campus life*. Princeton, NJ: Princeton University Press.

Findlay, S. (2010, 5 September). The decline of studying: How university students are spending less time hitting the books while earning better grades than ever. *Maclean's*. http://www.macleans.ca/news/canada/the-decline-of-studying/

Finkelstein, A., Taubman, S., Wright, B., Bernstein, M., Gruber, J., Newhouse, J. P., Allen, H., & Baicker, K. (2011). *The Oregon health insurance experiment: Evidence from the first year* (NBER Working Paper No. 17190). Cambridge, MA: National Bureau of Economic Research.

Frenette, M. (2014). *An investment of a lifetime? The long-term labour market premiums associated with a postsecondary education*. Retrieved from the Statistics Canada website: http://www.statcan.gc.ca/pub/11f0019m/11f0019m2014359-eng.htm

Fryer, R. G., Jr., & Levitt, S. D. (2004a). The black–white test score gap through third grade. *American Law and Economic Review, 8*, 249–281. doi:10.1093/aler/ahl003

Fryer, R. G., Jr., & Levitt, S. D. (2004b). Understanding the black–white test score gap in the first two years of school. *Review of Economics and Statistics, 86*, 447–464. doi:10.1162/003465304323031049

Gamoran, A. (2001). American schooling and educational inequality: A forecast for the 21st century. *Sociology of Education, 74*(extra issue), 135–153. doi:10.2307/2673258

Gnaulati, E. (2015, September 18). Why girls tend to get better grades than boys. *The Atlantic*. Retrieved from http://www.theatlantic.com/education/archive/2014/09/why-girls-get-better-grades-than-boys-do/380318/

Goldin, C., & Katz, L. F. (2008). *The race between education and technology*. Cambridge, MA: Harvard University *Press*.

Gracey, H. (2012). *Learning the student role: Kindergarten as academic boot camp*. Retrieved from the University of North Carolina at Wilmington website: http://people.uncw.edu/ricej/Intro/Kindergarten%20as%20Boot%20Camp%20by%20Harry%20Gracey.pdf

Granovetter, M. S. (1974). *Getting a job: A study of contacts and careers*. Cambridge, MA: Harvard University Press.

Hale, S. (2013). *Contested sociology: Rethinking the Canadian experience*. Toronto: Pearson Educational.

Jacobs, J. (1995, April). Gender and academic specialties: Trends among recipients of college degrees in the 1980s. *Sociology of Education, 68*, 81–98. doi:10.2307/2112776

Laetitia, M., & Hou, F. (2010). Sharing their lives: Women, marital trends and education. *Canadian Social Trends, 90*, 68–72. Retrieved from the Statistics Canada website: http://www.statcan.gc.ca/pub/11-008-x/2010002/article/11335-eng.pdf

Lareau, A. (2003). *Unequal childhoods: Class, race, and family life*. Berkeley: University of California Press.

Mare, R. D. (1981). Change and stability in educational stratification. *American Sociological Review, 46*, 72–87. doi:10.2307/2095027

Martin, S. P. (2006). Trends in marital dissolution by women's education in the United States. *Demographic Research, 15*(20), 538–560. doi:10.4054/demres.2006.15.20

Mayer, S. E. (2001). How did the increase in economic inequality between 1970 and 1990 affect children's educational attainment? *American Journal of Sociology, 107*, 1–32. doi:10.1086/323149

Montt, G. (2011). Cross-national differences in educational achievement inequality." *Sociology of Education, 84*, 49–68. doi:10.1177/0038040710392717

Organisation for Economic Co-operation and Development. (2010a). *Education at a glance 2010: OECD indicators*. doi:10.1787/eag-2011-en

Organisation for Economic Co-operation and Development. (2010b). *PISA 2009 results: What students know and can do* (Vol. 1). Paris: Organisation for Economic Co-operation and Development (OECD). doi:10.1787/9789264091450-en

Organisation for Economic Co-operation and Development. (2011). *Education at a glance 2011: OECD indicators*. Paris: OECD. doi:10.1787/eag-2011-en

Pallas, A. M. (2000). The effects of schooling on individual lives. In M. T. Hallinan (Ed.), *Handbook of the sociology of education* (pp. 499–525). New York, NY: Kluwer Academic/Plenum.

Persell, C. H. (1990). *Understanding society: An introduction to sociology* (3rd ed.). New York, NY: Harper and Row.

Reardon, S. F. (2011). The widening socioeconomic status achievement gap: New evidence and possible explanations. In R. Murname & G. Duncan (Eds.), *Social inequality and economic disadvantage* (pp. 91–116). Washington, DC: Brookings Institution.

Ross, C. E., & Mirowsky, J. (1989). Explaining the social patterns of depression: Control and problem-solving or support and talking. *Journal of Health and Social Behavior, 30*, 206–219. doi:10.2307/2137014

Ross, C. E., & Van Willigen, M. M. (1997, September). Education and the subjective quality of life. *Journal of Health and Social Behavior, 38*, 275–297. doi:10.2307/2955371

Spence, A. M. (1974). *Market signaling: Informational transfer in hiring and related screening practices*. Cambridge, MA: Harvard University Press.

Statistics Canada. (2001, July 4). Trends in the use of private education. *The Daily*. Retrieved from http://www.statcan.gc.ca/daily-quotidien/010704/dq010704b-eng.htm

Statistics Canada. (2009). Average total income of the population 15 years and over by highest certificate, diploma or degree, by province and territory (2006 Census) (Quebec, Ontario, Manitoba, Saskatchewan) [table]. Retrieved from http://www.statcan.gc.ca/tables-tableaux/sum-som/l01/cst01/labor50b-eng.htm

Statistics Canada. (2010). *Aboriginal statistics at a glance*. Retrieved from http://www.statcan.gc.ca/pub/89-645-x/89-645-x2010001-eng.htm

Tepperman, L., Albaneze, P., & Curtis, J. (Eds.). (2012). *Sociology: A Canadian perspective*. Toronto, ON: Oxford University Press.

Torche, F. (2005, October). Privatization reform and inequality of educational opportunity: The case of Chile. *Sociology of Education, 78*, 316–343. doi:10.1177/003804070507800403

Van Pelt, D. N. (2015). *Home schooling in Canada: The current picture*. Retrieved from the Fraser Institute website: https://www.fraserinstitute.org/sites/default/files/home-schooling-in-canada-2015-rev2.pdf

Weeden, K. A. (2002). Why do some occupations pay more than others? Social closure and earnings inequality in the U.S. *American Journal of Sociology, 108*, 55–101. doi:10.1086/344121

Yeung, W. J., Persell, C. H., & Reilly, M. C. (2010). *Intergenerational racial stratification and the black–white achievement gap*. Paper presented at the American Sociological Association annual meeting, Atlanta, GA.

Yeung, W.-J. J., & Pfeiffer, K. M. (2009). The black–white test score gap and early home environment. *Social Science Research, 38*, 412–437. doi:10.1016/j.ssresearch.2008.11.004

CHAPTER 15

Adler, N. E., & Ostrove, J. (1999). Socioeconomic status and health: What we know and what we don't. In N. E. Adler, M. Marmot, B. S. McEwen, & J. Stewart (Eds.), *Socioeconomic status and health in industrial nations: Social, psychological, and biological pathways* (pp. 3–15). New York, NY: New York Academy of Sciences.

Anderson, R. N., & DeTurk, P. B. (2002, March 21). United States life tables, 1999. *National Vital Statistics Reports, 50*(6).

Canada Health Act, RSC 1985, c C-6.

Case, A., Lubotsky, D., & Paxson, C. (2002). Economic status and health in childhood: The origins of the gradient. *American Economic Review, 92*(5), 1308–1334.

CBC News. (2014, May 15). Life expectancy in Canada hits 80 for men, 84 for women. *CBC News*. Retrieved from: http://www.cbc.ca/news/health/life-expectancy-in-canada-hits-80-for-men-84-for-women-1.2644355

Centers for Disease Control. (2011). *CDC health disparities and inequalities report*. Atlanta, GA: Department of Health and Human Services, Centers for Disease Control and Prevention.

Christakis, N., & Fowler, J. (2007). *Connected: The surprising power of our social networks and how they shape our lives*. Boston, MA: Little, Brown.

Cutler, D. M., Lleras-Muney, A., & Vogl, T. (2008). *Socioeconomic status and health: Dimensions and mechanisms* (NBER Working Paper No. 14333). Cambridge, MA: National Bureau of Economic Research.

Davis, K., Schoen, C., & Stremikis, K. (2014, June). *Mirror, mirror on the wall: How performance of the U.S. health care system compares internationally* (Commonwealth Fund Pub. No. 1755). Retrieved from the Commonwealth Fund website: http://www.commonwealthfund.org/~/media/files/publications/fund-report/2014/jun/1755_davis_mirror_mirror_2014.pdf

Durkheim, E. (1897/2006). *On suicide*. London, UK: Penguin Classics.

Ehrenreich, B., & English, D. (2013). *For her own good: Two centuries of the experts' advice to women*. New York, NY: Knopf-Doubleday.

Freidson, E. (2001). *Professionalism: The third logic*. Chicago, IL: University of Chicago Press.

Haller, J. S. (1981). *American medicine in transition, 1840–1910*. Urbana: University of Illinois Press.

Hawkins, M., & Knox, S. (2003). *The midwifery option: A Canadian guide to the birth experience*. Toronto, ON: Harper Collins.

Link, B. G., & Phelan, J. C. (1995). Social conditions and fundamental causes of disease. *Journal of Health and Social Behavior*, 80–94. doi:10.2307/2626958

Lleras-Muney, A. (2005). The relationship between education and adult mortality in the United States. *Review of Economic Studies, 72*, 189–221. doi:10.1111/0034-6527.00329

Making Healthier Choices Act, 2015, SO 2015, c 7.

Marmot, M. (2004). *The status syndrome: How social standing affects our health and longevity*. New York, NY: Holt.

Mitchinson, W. (2002). *Giving birth in Canada: 1900–1950*. Toronto, ON: University of Toronto Press.

National Center for Health Statistics. (2011, September 2011). United States life tables, 2007. *National Vital Statistics Reports, 59*(9).

National Collaborating Centre for Aboriginal Health. (2013). *An overview of aboriginal health in Canada*. Retrieved from http://www.nccah-ccnsa.ca/Publications/Lists/Publications/Attachments/101/aberoriginal_health_web.pdf

National Research Council and Institute of Medicine. (2013). *U.S. health in international perspective: Shorter lives, poorer health* (Eds. S. H. Woolf & L. Aron). Washington, DC: The National Academies Press.

Plummer, K. (2000). From nursing outposts to contemporary midwifery in 20th century Canada. *The Journal of Midwifery & Women's Health, 45*, 169–175. doi:10.1016/S1526-9523(99)00044-6

Read, J. G., & Gorman, B. K. (2010). Gender and health inequality. *Annual Review of Sociology, 36*, 371–386. doi:10.1146/annurev.soc.012809.102535

Reverby, S. (1987). *Ordered to care: The dilemma of American nursing, 1850–1945*. Cambridge, MA: Cambridge University Press.

Roland, C. (2006). History of medicine to 1950. *The Canadian encyclopedia*. Retrieved from http://www.thecanadianencyclopedia.ca/en/article/history-of-medicine/

Rose, G. (1985). Sick individuals and sick populations. *International Journal of Epidemiology, 14*(1), 32–38. doi:10.1093/ije/14.1.32

Roseboom, T., de Rooij, S., & Painter, R. (2006). The Dutch famine and its long-term consequences for adult health. *Early Human Development, 82*, 485–491. doi:10.1016/j.earlhumdev.2006.07.001

Smith, K. P., & Christakis, N. (2008). Social networks and health. *Annual Review of Sociology, 34*, 405–429. doi:10.1146/annurev.soc.34.040507.134601

Strong-Boag, V. (1991). Making a difference: The history of Canada's nurses. *Canadian Bulletin of Medical History / Bulletin canadien d'histoire de la médecine, 8*, 231–248.

Wertz, R. W., & Wertz, D. C. (1989). *Lying-in: A history of childbirth in America*. New Haven, CT: Yale University Press.

World Health Organization. (2011). *Constitution of the World Health Organization*. Adopted by the International Health Conference, New York, June 19–July 22, 1946; signed on 22 July 1946 by the representatives of 61 states; entered into force on April 7, 1948. Retrieved from http://www.who.int/governance/eb/who_constitution_en.pdf

World Health Organization. (2014). *Global health observatory data repository*. Retrieved from http://apps.who.int/gho/data/node.main

CHAPTER 16

An Act to amend the Canadian Human Rights Act, SC 1996, c 14.

Alexander, M. (2010). *The new Jim Crow: Mass incarceration in the age of colorblindness*. New York, NY: The New Press.

Associated Press. (2012, June 11). NATO restricts air strikes on Afghan homes to troop self-defense after civilian deaths. *Washington Post*. Retrieved from http://www.washingtonpost.com/world/asia_pacific/afghan-government-roadside-bomb-kills-pregnant-woman-and-familyen-route-to-hospital/2012/06/11/gJQABtW6TV_story.html

Baker, W. (2005). *America's crisis of values: Reality and perception*. Princeton, NJ: Princeton University Press.

Beccaria, C. (1794/2016). *On crimes and punishments* (5th ed.; G. R. Newman & P. Marongiu, Trans.). New Brunswick, NJ: Transaction Publishers.

Becker, H. (1963). *Outsiders*. New York, NY: Free Press.

Beisel, N. (1997). *Imperiled innocents: Anthony Comstock and family reproduction*. Princeton, NJ: Princeton University Press.

Bergen, P., & Tiedemann, K. (2010, April 26). No secrets in the sky. *New York Times*. Retrieved from http://www.nytimes.com/2010/04/26/opinion/26bergen.html

Bittner, E. (1967). The police on skid-row: A "study of peace-keeping." *American Sociological Review, 32*, 699–715. doi:10.2307/2092019

Brooks, C., & Manza, J. (2013). *Who is us? Counterterrorism and the dark side of American public opinion*. New York, NY: Russell Sage.

Brosnahan, M. (2013, November 25). Canada's prison population at all-time high: Number of visible minority inmates increased by 75% in past decade. *CBC News*. Retrieved from http://www.cbc.ca/news/canada-s-prison-population-at-all-time-high-1.2440039

Cafferky, S. (2003). Alcohol, consumption of, per capita (Canada). In J. S. Blocker, D. M. Fahey, I. R. Tyrrell (Eds), *Alcohol and temperance in modern history: A global encyclopedia* (pp. 21–23). Santa Barbara, CA: ABC-CLIO.

Cannon, C. (2005, October). Petty crime, outrageous punishment: Why the three-strikes law doesn't work. *Reader's Digest*. Retrieved from http://www.november.org/stayinfo/breaking3/Outrageous.html

Canadian Charter of Rights and Freedoms, Part I of the Constitution Act, 1982, being Schedule B to the Canada Act 1982 (UK), 1982, c 11.

Cicourel, A. V. (1967). *The social organization of juvenile justice*. New York, NY: Wiley.

Durkheim, E. (1890/1997). *The division of labor in society*. New York, NY: The Free Press.

Duster, T. (1970). *The legislation of morality: Law, drugs, and moral judgment*. New York, NY: The Free Press.

Eisinger, J. (2014, April 30). Why only one banker went to jail for the financial crisis. *New York Times Magazine*. Retrieved from http://www.nytimes.com/2014/05/04/magazine/only-one-top-banker-jail-financial-crisis.html?_r=0

Entman, R., & Rojeki, A. (2001). *The black image in the white mind*. Chicago, IL: University of Chicago Press.

Fox, L. (2003). *Enron: The rise and fall*. Hoboken, NJ: Wiley.

Freud, S. (1929). *Civilization and its discontents* (Joan Riviere, Trans.). London, UK: Hogarth Press.

Garland, D. (2001). *Mass imprisonment: Social causes and consequences*. Newbury Park, CA: Sage.

Goffman, E. (1959). *The presentation of self in everyday life*. Glencoe, IL: The Free Press.

Goffman, E. (1963). *Behavior in public places: Notes on the social organization of gatherings*. Glencoe, IL: The Free Press.

Gordon-Reed, A. (2008). *The Hemingses of Monticello: An American family*. New York, NY: W. W. Norton.

Gusfield, J. R. (1963). *Symbolic crusade: Status politics and the American temperance movement*. Urbana, IL: University of Illinois Press.

Hagan, J. (2010). *Who are the criminals? The politics of crime policy from the age of Roosevelt to the age of Reagan*. Princeton, NJ: Princeton University Press.

Hersh, S. M. (2004, May 10). Torture at Abu Ghraib. *The New Yorker*. Retrieved from http://www.newyorker.com/magazine/2004/05/10/torture-at-abu-ghraib

Hersh, S. (2005). *Chain of command: The road from 9/11 to Abu Ghraib*. New York: Harper.

Kohler-Hausmann, I. (2014). *Misdemeanor justice* (Unpublished doctoral dissertation). New York University, New York, NY.

Lamont, M., & Molnar, V. (2002). The study of boundaries in the social sciences. *Annual Review of Sociology, 28*, 167–195.

Lichtblau, E. (2008). *Bush's law: The remaking of American justice*. New York, NY: Random House.

Manza, J., & Uggen, C. (2006). *Locked out: Felon disenfranchisement and American democracy*. New York, NY: Oxford University Press.

Mayer, J. (2008). *The dark side: The inside story of how the war on terror became a war on American ideals*. New York, NY: Doubleday.

New York Civil Liberties Union. (2011). *Stop and frisk 2011*. Retrieved from http://www.nyclu.org/files/publications/NYCLU_2011_Stop-and-Frisk_Report.pdf

Okrent, D. (2010). *Last call: The rise and fall of prohibition*. New York: Scribner.

Opium Act, SC 1908, c 50.

Opium and Drug Act, SC 1911, c 17.

Paul, J. R. (2009). *Unlikely allies: How a merchant, a playwright, and a spy saved the American revolution*. New York, NY: Riverhead Books.

Ranulf, S. (1938). *Moral indignation and middle class psychology: A sociological study*. Copenhagen, Denmark: Levin & Munksgard and Ejnar Munksgaard.

Richards, S. (2006, May 22). Remembering the "naked guy." *Salon*. Retrieved http://www.salon.com/2006/05/22/naked_guy/

Rorabaugh, W. J. (1979). *The alcoholic republic: An American tradition*. New York, NY: Oxford University Press.

Sapers, H. (2015). *Annual report*. Retrieved from the Office of the Correctional Investigator website: http://www.oci-bec.gc.ca/cnt/rpt/index-eng.aspx

Substance Abuse and Mental Health Administration. (2011). *National survey on drug use and health*. Retrieved from http://www.icpsr.umich.edu/quicktables/quickconfig.do?34481-0001_all

Sudnow, D. (1965). Normal crimes: Sociological features of the penal code in a public defender office. *Social Problems, 12*, 255–276. doi:10.2307/798932

Sutherland, E. (1949). *White collar crime*. New York, NY: Dryden Press.

Terry, C. E., & Pellens, M. (1970). *The opium problem*. Montclair, NJ: Patterson-Smith.

Tonry, M. (2012). *Punishing race: A continuing American dilemma*. New York, NY: Oxford University Press.

van Dijk, J., van Kesteren, J., & Smit, P. (2007). *Criminal victimization in international perspective: key findings from the 2004–2005 ICVS and EU ICS* (WODC Wetenschappelijk Onderzoek-en Documentatiecentrum report no. 257). The Hague, Netherlands: Boom Juridische uitgevers. Retrieved from the United Nations Interregional Crime and Justice Research Institute website: http://www.unicri.it/services/library_documentation/publications/icvs/publications/ICVS2004_05report.pdf

Western, B. (2006). *Punishment and inequality in America*. New York, NY: Russell Sage Foundation Press.

Zengerle, J. (2006, December 31). The naked guy. *New York Times Magazine*. Retrieved from http://www.nytimes.com/2006/12/31/magazine/31naked.t.html

CHAPTER 17

Alinsky, S. (1971). *Rules for radicals: A pragmatic primer for realistic radicals*. New York, NY: Vintage.

Brockett, C. (1993). A protest cycle resolution of the repression/protest paradox. *Social Science History, 17*(3), 457–484. doi:10.1017/S0145553200018666

Brown v. Board of Education of Topeka, 347 U.S. 483 (1954).

Chenoweth, E., & Stephan, M. J. (2011). *Why civil resistance works: The strategic logic of nonviolent conflict*. New York: Columbia University Press.

Cohen, J. L., & Arato, A. (1992). *Civil society and political theory*. Cambridge, MA: MIT Press.

Epstein, B. (2001). What happened to the women's movement? *Monthly Review, 53*(1), 1–13. doi:10.14452/MR-053-01-2001-05_1

Gambetta, D., & Hertog, S. (2009). Why are there so many engineers among Islamic radicals? *European Journal of Sociology, 50*, 201–30. doi:10.1017/S0003975609990129

Gamson, J. (1995). Must identity movements self-destruct? A queer dilemma. *Social Problems, 42*(3), 390–407. doi:10.2307/3096854

Gamson, W. A. (1990). *The strategy of social protest* (2nd ed.). Homewood, IL: Dorsey.

Inglehart, R. (1977). *The silent revolution: Changing values and political styles among western publics*. Princeton, NJ: Princeton University Press.

Jasper, J. M. (1997). *The art of moral protest: Culture, biography, and creativity in social movements*. Chicago, IL: University of Chicago Press.

Kurzman, C. (1996). Structural opportunity and perceived opportunity in social-movement theory: The Iranian revolution of 1979. *American Sociological Review, 61*(1), 153–170. doi:10.2307/2096411

Kurzman, C. (2002). Bin Laden and other thoroughly modern Muslims. *Contexts, 1*(4), 13–20. doi:10.1525/ctx.2002.1.4.13

Lenin, V. I. (1915/1964). The collapse of the second international. In *Lenin: Collected works* (Vol. 21, pp. 205–259). Moscow: Progress.

Lipset, S. M. (1960/1981). *Political man*. Baltimore, MD: Johns Hopkins University Press.

Luker, K. (1984). *Abortion and the politics of motherhood*. Berkeley: University of California Press.

Luders, J. E. (2010). *The civil rights movement and the logic of social change*. Cambridge, UK: Cambridge University Press.

McAdam, D. (1982). *Political process and the development of black insurgency, 1930–1970*. Chicago, IL: University of Chicago Press.

McAdam, D. (1988). *Freedom summer*. New York, NY: Oxford University Press.

McCarthy, John D., & Zald, M. N. (1977). Resource mobilization and social movements: A partial theory. *American Journal of Sociology, 82*, 1212–1241. doi:10.1086/226464

Milkman, R., Luce, S., & Lewis, P. (2013). *Changing the subject: A bottom-up Account of Occupy Wall Street in New York City*. New York, NY: Murphy Institute, City University of New York. Retrieved from http://www.documentcloud.org/documents/562862-changing-the-subject-2.html

Morris, A. D. (1984). *The origins of the civil rights movement: Black communities organizing for change*. New York, NY: Free Press.

Munson, Z. W. (2008). *The making of pro-life activists: How social movement mobilization works*. Chicago, IL: University of Chicago Press.

Olson, M. (1965). *The logic of collective action: Public goods and the theory of groups*. Cambridge, MA: Harvard University Press.

Panagopoulos, C. (2011, October). *Occupy Wall Street survey results*. Retrieved from the Fordham University Center for Electoral Politics and Democracy website: www.fordham.edu/download/downloads/id/2538/occupy_wall_street_survey.pdf

Piven, F. F., & Cloward, R. A. (1977). *Poor people's movements: Why they succeed, how they fail*. New York, NY: Vintage.

Roe v. Wade, 410 U.S. 113 (1973).

Roxborough, I. (2007). Counterinsurgency. *Contexts, 6*(2), 15–21. doi:10.1525/ctx.2007.6.2.15

Schwartz, M. (1976). *Radical protest and social structure: The southern Farmers' Alliance and cotton tenancy, 1880–1890*. Chicago: University of Chicago Press.

Schwartz, M. (2011). The Egyptian uprising: The mass strike in the time of neoliberal globalization. *New Labor Forum, 20*(3), 32–43. doi:10.4179/NLF.203.0000006

Skocpol, T. (1979). *States and social revolutions: A comparative analysis of France, Russia, and China*. Cambridge, UK: Cambridge University Press.

Snow, D. A., & Benford, R. D. (1988). Ideology, frame resonance, and participant mobilization. *International Social Movement Research, 1*, 197–217.

Tilly, C. (1986). *The contentious French*. Cambridge, MA: Harvard University Press.

Walsh, E. J. (1981). Resource mobilization and citizen protest in communities around Three Mile Island. *Social Problems, 29*, 1–21. doi:10.2307/800074

CHAPTER 18

Auyero, J., & Swistun, D. (2009). *Flammable*. Oxford, UK: Oxford University Press.

Baskind, C. (2010). 5 reasons not to drink bottled water. *Mother Nature Network*. Retrieved from http://www.mnn.com/food/healthy-eating/stories/5-reasonsnot-to-drink-bottled-water

Bell, M. M. (1994). *Childerley*. Chicago: University of Chicago Press.

Broughton, E. (2005). The Bhopal disaster and its aftermath: A review. *Environmental Health: A Global Access Science Source, 4*(6), 1–6. doi:10.1186/1476-069x-4-6

Brulle, R. J. (1996). Environmental discourse and social movement organizations: A historical perspective on the development of U.S. environmental organizations. *Sociological Inquiry, 66*(1), 58–83. doi:10.1111/j.1475-682X.1996.tb00209.x

Brulle, R. J., & Pellow, D. (2006). Environmental justice: Human health and environmental inequalities. *Annual Review of Public Health, 27*, 103–124. doi:10.1146/annurev.publhealth.27.021405.102124

Bryskine, S. (2010, October 14). HK's 2010 air pollution death toll nears 600. *Epoch Times*.

Bullard, R. D. (1983). Solid waste sites and the Houston black community. *Sociological Inquiry, 53*, 273–288. doi:10.1111/j.1475-682X.1983.tb00037.x

Bullard, R. D. (1990). *Dumping in Dixie*. Boulder, CO: Westview.

Bullard, R. D., Mohai, P., Saha, R., & Wright, B. (2007). *Toxic wastes and race at twenty, 1987–2007*. Retrieved from http://www.ejnet.org/ej/twart.pdf

Californians Against Waste. (2011). Plastic bag litter pollution. Retrieved http://www.cawrecycles.org/issues/plastic_campaign/plastic_bags

Campbell, C. (Ed.). (2011). *A century of Parks Canada, 1911–2011*. Calgary, AB: University of Calgary Press.

Carson, R. (1962). *Silent spring*. New York, NY: Houghton Mifflin.

Catton, W. R., Jr., & Riley E. Dunlap. (1980). A new ecological paradigm for a post-exuberant sociology. *American Behavioral Scientist, 24*, 15–47. doi:10.1177/000276428002400103

Clean Water Act of 1970, U.S. Pub. L. No. 92-500, 86 Stat. 816.

Commission for Racial Justice. (1987). *Toxic wastes and race in the United States*. Retrieved from the Chicago State University website: https://www.csu.edu/cerc/researchreports/documents/ToxicWasteandRace-TOXICWASTESANDRACE.pdf

Conference Board of Canada. (2014). *Municipal waste generation*. Retrieved from http://www.conferenceboard.ca/hcp/details/environment/municipal-waste-generation.aspx

Cronon, W. (1992). *Nature's metropolis*. New York, NY: W.W. Norton.

Diamond, J. (1995, August). Easter Island's end. *Discover Magazine*, 63–69.

Diamond, J. (1997). *Guns, germs, and steel*. New York, NY: W.W. Norton.

Dollemore, D. (2008). *Newly detected air pollutant mimics damaging effects of cigarette smoke*. Retrieved from the Science Daily website: http://www.sciencedaily.com/releases/2008/08/080817223432.htm

Duhigg, C. (2009, September 13). Clean waters laws are neglected, at a cost in suffering. *New York Times*.

Dunlap, R. E., & McCright, A. M. (2011). Organized climate change denial. In J. S. Dryzek, R. B. Norgaard, & D. Schlosberg (Eds.), *The Oxford handbook of climate change* (pp. 144–160). London, UK: Oxford.

Durkheim, E. (1915). *Elementary forms of religious life*. New York, NY: Macmillan.

Ehrlich, P. (1968). *The population bomb*. New York, NY: Ballantine.

Environmental Protection Agency. (2011). *Non-hazardous waste*. Retrieved from http://www.epa.gov/osw/nonhaz/index.htm

Erikson, K. (1976). *Everything in its path*. New York, NY: Simon & Schuster.

Fernandez, M. (2006, October 29). A study links trucks' exhaust to Bronx schoolchildren's asthma. *New York Times*.

Freudenberg, W. R., & Gramling, R. (1989). The emergence of environmental sociology: Contributions of Riley E. Dunlap and William R. Catton, Jr. *Sociological Inquiry, 59*(4), 439–452. doi:10.1111/j.1475-682X.1989.tb00119.x

Greenpeace. (2009). *Amazon cattle footprint: Mato Grosso: State of destruction*. Retrieved from http://www.greenpeace.org/international/en/publications/reports/amazon-cattle-footprint-mato/

Greider, T., & Garkovich, L. (1994). Landscapes: The social construction of nature and the environment. *Rural Sociology, 59*(1), 1–24. doi:10.1111/j.1549-0831.1994.tb00519.x

Hardin, G. (1968). The tragedy of the commons. *Science, 162*(3859), 1243–1248. doi:10.1126/science.162.3859.1243

Hasham, A. (2003, 12 March). Landfill or incinerator: What's the future of Toronto's trash? *Toronto Star*. Retrieved from https://www.thestar.com/news/gta/2013/03/12/landfill_or_incinerator_whats_the_future_of_torontos_trash.html

Hummel, M. R. (2010). Environmental and conservation movements. http://www.thecanadianencyclopedia.ca/en/article/environmental-and-conservation-movements/

International Energy Agency. (2010). *Balances of OECD and Non-OECD statistics*. Retrieved from www.iea.org

Klinenberg, E. (1999). Denaturalizing disaster: A social autopsy of the 1995 Chicago heat wave. *Theory and Society, 28*(2), 239–295. doi:10.1023/A:1006995507723

Kolbert, E. (2007). *Field notes from a catastrophe: Man, nature, and climate change*. New York, NY: Bloomsbury.

Malinowksi, B. (1948). *Magic, science and religion and other essays*. New York, NY: The Free Press.

Marx, K., & Engels, F. (1832/1977). The German ideology. In D. McLellan (Ed.), *Karl Marx: Selected writings* (pp. 159–191). Oxford, UK: Oxford University Press.

Park, R. E., & Burgess, E. W. (1925). *The city*. Chicago, IL: University of Chicago Press.

A run on the banks: How factory fishing decimated Newfoundland cod. (2001, March/April). *E: The Environmental Magazine*. Retrieved from http://www.emagazine.com/archive/507

Scarce, R. (2005). More than mere wolves at the door: Reconstructing community amidst a wildlife controversy. In A. Herda-Rapp & T. L. Goedeke, *Mad about wildlife* (pp. 123–146). Boston: Brill.

Schnaiberg, A. (1980). The environment: From surplus to scarcity. New York, NY: Oxford University Press.

Sharkey, P. (2007). Survival and death in New Orleans: An empirical look at the human impact of Katrina. *Journal of Black Studies, 37*(4), 482–501. doi:10.1177/0021934706296188

Social Science Research Council. (2006). Understanding Katrina: Perspectives from the social sciences. Retrieved from http://understandingkatrina.ssrc.org/

Szasz, A., & Meuser, M. (1997). Environmental inequalities: Literature review and proposals for new directions in research and theory. *Current Sociology, 45*(3), 99–120. doi:10.1177/001139297045003006

Taylor, A. (1998). "Wasty ways": Stories of American settlement. *Environmental History, 3*(3), 291–310. doi:10.2307/3985181

Taylor, P. J., & Buttel, F. H. (1992). How do we know we have environmental problems? Science and the globalization of environmental discourse. *Geoforum, 23*(3), 405–416. doi:10.1016/0016-7185(92)90051-5

Thoreau, H. D. (1854). *Walden; or, life in the woods*. Boston: Ticknor & Fields.

United Nations Development Program. (2010). *Technology needs assessment for climate change*. New York: United Nations Development Program.

United States Central Intelligence Agency. (2012). *The CIA world factbook, 2012*. New York: Skyhorse.

United States Department of Energy. (2011). *Coal*. Retrieved from http://www.energy.gov/energysources/coal.htm

United States Energy Information Administration. (2009). *Petroleum statistics*. Retrieved from http://www.eia.doe.gov/energy-explained/index.cfm?page=oil_home#tab2

United States Energy Information Administration. (2010). *International energy outlook, 2010*. Retrieved from http://www.eia.doe.gov/oiaf/ieo/world.html

United States Energy Information Administration. (2011). *Annual energy outlook, 2011*. Washington, DC: U.S. Department of Energy.

United States Energy Information Administration. (2013). *Renewable energy trends in consumption and electricity*. Retrieved http://www.eia.doe.gov/cneaf/solar.renewables/page/trends/rentrends.html

United States Energy Information Administration. (n.d.). *Total primary energy consumption*. In *International energy statistics*. Retrieved from https://www.eia.gov/cfapps/ipdbproject/IEDIndex3.cfm?tid=44&pid=44&aid=2

Warner, K., Ehrhart, C., de Sherbinin, A., Adamo, S., & Chai-Onn, T. (2008). *In search of shelter: Mapping the effects of climate change on human migration and displacement*. Retrieved from the Center for International Earth Information Network, Columbia University website: http://www.ciesin.columbia.edu/documents/ClimMigr-rpt-june09.pdf

Weber, M. (1904/2008). *The protestant ethic and the spirit of capitalism*. New York, NY: Norton.

Zalasiewicz, J., Williams, M., Steffan, W., & Crutzen, P. (2010). The new world of the anthropocene. *Environmental Science and Technology, 44*(7), 2228–2231. doi:10.1021/es903118j

CHAPTER 19

Bulatao, R. A., & Casterline, J. B. (Eds.). (2001). *Global fertility transition*. New York, NY: Population Council.

Bumpass, L. L., & Hsien-Hen Lu. (2000). Trends in cohabitation and implications for children's family contexts in the United States. *Population Studies, 54*(1), 29–41. doi:10.1080/713779060

Coale, A. J. (1973). The demographic transition reconsidered. In *Proceedings: International population conference, Liege* (Vol. 1, pp. 53–72). Liege: International Union for the Scientific Study of Populations.

Davis, K. (1963). The theory of change and response in modern demographic history. *Population Index, 29*, 145–166.

Economist Intelligence Unit. (2010). *The quality of death: Ranking end-of-life care across the world*. London: The Economist.

Ehrlich, P. (1968). *The population bomb*. New York, NY: Ballantine.

Hirschman, C. (1994). Why fertility changes. *Annual Review of Sociology, 20*, 203–233. doi:10.1146/annurev.so.20.080194.001223

Joyner, K., & Laumann, E. O. (2001). Teenage sex and the sexual revolution. In E. O. Laumann & R. T. Michael (Eds.), *Sex, love, health in America: Private choices and public policies* (pp. 41–71). Chicago, IL: University of Chicago.

Kohler, H.-P., Billari, F. C., & Ortega, A. (2002). The emergence of lowest-low fertility in Europe. *Population and Development Review, 28*(4), 641–680. doi:10.1111/j.1728-4457.2002.00641.x

Lam, D. (2011). How the world survived the population bomb: Lessons from 50 years of extraordinary demographic history. *Demography, 48*(4), 1231–1262. doi:10.1007/s13524-011-0070-z

Lesthaeghe, R., & van de Kaa, D. (1986). Two demographic transitions? In R. Lesthaeghe and D. van de Kaa (Eds.), *Population growth and decline* (pp. 9–24). Deventer: Van Loghum Slaterus.

Malthus, T. R. (1798). *An essay on the principle of population*. London: J. Johnson.

National Institute on Aging, National Institutes of Health, U.S. Department of Health and Human Services, and the U.S. Department of State. (2007). *Why population aging matters: A global perspective*. Retrieved from the National Institute on Aging website: https://www.nia.nih.gov/research/publication/why-population-aging-matters-global-perspective

Notestein, F. W. (1953). Economic problems of population change. In *Proceedings of the eighth international conference of agricultural economists*, pp. 13–31. London, UK: Oxford University Press.

Omran, A. R. (1971). The epidemiologic transition: A theory of the epidemiology of population change. *Milbank Memorial Fund Quarterly, 49*(4), 509–538. doi:10.2307/3349375

Preston, S. H., & McDonald, J. (1979). The incidence of divorce within cohorts of American marriages contracted since the civil war. *Demography, 16*(1), 1–25. doi:10.2307/2061075

Statistics Canada. (2013). *Estimates of population, by age group and sex for July 1, Canada, provinces and territories, annual* (Table 051-0001, CANSIM database). Retrieved from http://www5.statcan.gc.ca/cansim/a26?lang=eng&id=510001

Statistics Canada. (2015a, September 29). Canada's population estimates: Age and sex, July 1, 2015. *The Daily*. Retrieved from http://www.statcan.gc.ca/daily-quotidien/150929/dq150929b-eng.pdf

Statistics Canada. (2015b). *Historical statistics, estimated population and immigrant arrivals, annual* (Table 075-0001, CANSIM database). Retrieved from the Government of Canada website: http://open.canada.ca/data/en/dataset/aa26844e-f9b6-408d-86a6-c00f933999b5

United States Central Intelligence Agency. (2012). *The CIA world factbook 2012*. New York: Skyhorse.

University of Ottawa. (2015). *Basic demographics and vital statistics for Canada*. Retrieved from http://www.med.uottawa.ca/sim/data/Vital_Stats_e.htm

World Bank. (2011). World development indicators: Life expectancy at birth. Retrieved from http://data.worldbank.org/indicator/SP.DYN.LE00.IN

World Health Organization. (2011). *Constitution of the World Health Organization*. Adopted by the International Health Conference, New York, June 19–July 22, 1946; signed on 22 July 1946 and entered into force on April 7, 1948. http://apps.who.int/gb/bd/PDF/bd47/EN/constitution-en.pdf?ua=1

World Health Organization. (2016). *WHO definition of palliative care*. Retrieved from http://www.who.int/cancer/palliative/definition/en/

Wu, L. L. (2008). Cohort estimates of nonmarital fertility. *Demography, 45*(1), 193–207. doi:10.1353/dem.2008.0001

CHAPTER 20

Abramowitz, M. (2008, April 22). White House defends NAFTA as Bush meets with heads of Mexico, Canada. *Washington Post*.

Audley, J. J., Papademetriou, D. G., Polaski, S., & Vaughan, S. (2003). *NAFTA's promise and reality: Lessons from Mexico for the hemisphere*. Washington: Carnegie Endowment for International Peace.

Bacon, D. (2012, January 23). How US farm policies fuel Mexico's great migration. *The Nation*.

Bernstein, J., & Mishel, L. (2007). *Economy's gains fail to reach most workers' paychecks* (Briefing Paper No. 195). Washington, DC: Economic Policy Institute.

Bronfenbrenner, K. (2000). *Uneasy terrain: The impact of capital mobility on workers, wages and union organizing*. Retrieved from the Cornell University ILR School website: http://digitalcommons.ilr.cornell.edu/reports/3/

Carrere, C., & Schiff, M. (2004, February). *On the geography of trade: Distance is alive and well* (World Bank Policy Research Working Papers #3206). Retrieved from the World Bank website: http://documents.worldbank.org/curated/en/128881468778205018/pdf/wps3206geography.pdf

Chang, Ha-joon. (2002). *Kicking away the ladder*. London: Anthem Press.

China Labor Watch. (2011). *Tragedies of globalization: The truth behind electronics sweatshops*. Retrieved from http://www.chinalaborwatch.org/pro/proshow-149.html

Clinton, W. J. (1993). Remarks at the signing ceremony for the supplemental agreements to the North American Free Trade Agreement. In *Public Papers of the Presidents of the United States* (Vol. 2, pp. 1495–1490). Washington, DC: U.S. Government Printing Office.

DeLong, J. B. (2006, September 30). Neoliberalism has a patchy Mexican record. *Taipei Times*.

Dicken, P. (2011). *Global shift*. New York, NY. Guilford.

Duhigg, C., & Barboza, D. (2012, January 26). In China, the human costs that are built into an iPad. *New York Times*.

Duhigg, C., & Bradsher, K. (2012, January 12). How the U.S. lost out on iPhone work. *New York Times*. Retrieved from http://www.nytimes.com/2012/01/22/business/apple-america-and-a-squeezed-middle-class.html

Feller, G. (2008, April). Focus: NAFTA: A controversial treaty. *Global Finance*.

Franklin, S. (1993, February 18). Unions urge Clinton to renegotiate trade pact. *Chicago Tribune*.

Friedman, T. (2005). *The world is flat: A brief history of the twenty-first century*. New York, NY: Farrar, Straus and Giroux.

Gauthier, A., & Meredith, K. (2012). *Canada's merchandise trade with the world: 2011*. Retrieved from the Library of Parliament website: http://www.lop.parl.gc.ca/content/lop/ResearchPublications/2012-41-e.pdf

Gindin, S., & Panitch, L. (2012). *The making of global capitalism*. London: Verso.

Henriques, G., & Patel, R. (2004, February 13). *NAFTA, corn, and Mexico's agricultural trade liberalization* (Americas Program Special Report). Retrieved from http://www.cipamericas.org/archives/1009

Hirst, P., Thompson, G., & Bromley, S. (2009). *Globalization in question* (3rd ed.). London, UK: Polity Press.

Hufbauer, G. C., & Schott, J. J. (1993). *NAFTA: An assessment*. Washington, DC: Institute for International Economics.

Koopman, R., Wang, Z., & Wei, Shang-Jin. (2008, June). How much of Chinese exports is really made in China? Assessing domestic value-added when processing trade is pervasive (NBER Working Paper No. 14109). doi:10.3386/w14109

Office of the United States Trade Representative. (2008). *NAFTA: Myths versus facts*. Retrieved from https://ustr.gov/sites/default/files/NAFTA-Myth-versus-Fact.pdf

O'Rourke, K., & Williamson, J. G. (2000). *Globalization and history: The evolution of a nineteenth century Atlantic economy*. Cambridge, MA: MIT Press.

Public Citizen. (2008). *Debunking USTR claims in defense of NAFTA: The real NAFTA score 2008*. Retrieved from http://www.citizen.org/documents/NAFTA_USTR_Debunk_web.pdf

Rugman, A. (2005). *The regional multinationals: MNEs and "global" strategic management*. Cambridge, UK: Cambridge University Press.

Scott, R. E. (2011). *Heading south: US–Mexico trade and job displacement after NAFTA* (Briefing Paper No. 308). Washington, DC: Economic Policy Institute.

Sutcliffe, B., & Glyn, A. (2010). Measures of globalization and their misinterpretation. In Jonathan Michie (Ed.), *Handbook of globalization* (2nd ed., pp. 61–78). Cheltenham, UK: Edward Elgar.

United Nations Conference on Trade and Development. (2007). *Trade and development report*. New York, NY: United Nations.

United Nations Conference on Trade and Development. (2011). *World investment report*. Retrieved from http://unctad.org/en/PublicationsLibrary/wir2011_en.pdf

United States Department of Commerce, Census Bureau, Foreign Trade Division. (2012). Top U.S. trade partners. Retrieved from the International Trade Administration website: http://www.trade.gov/mas/ian/build/groups/public/@tg_ian/documents/webcontent/tg_ian_003364.pdf

Index

D

E

Q

R

S